D0926969

Haydn, Mozart and the Viennese School

Haydn, Mozart and the Viennese School

1740 – 1780

Daniel Heartz

University of California, Berkeley

W·W·Norton & Company

New York   London

Copyright © 1995 by W. W. Norton & Company, Inc.

All rights reserved

Printed in the United States of America

First Edition

The text of this book is composed in 10.5/13 Palatino,

with the display set in Stuyvesant and Snell Roundhand.

Composition and Manufacturing by The Maple-Vail Composition Services.

Library of Congress Cataloging-in-Publication Data

Heartz, Daniel.

Haydn, Mozart, and the Viennese School, 1740–1780 / Daniel Heartz.

p.   cm.

Includes index.

1. Music—Austria—Vienna—18th century—History and criticism.

2. Haydn, Joseph, 1732–1809.   3. Mozart, Wolfgang Amadeus,

1756–1791.   I. Title.

ML246.8.V6H4   1994

780'.9436'1309033—dc20   93-47001

ISBN 0-393-03712-6

W. W. Norton & Company, Inc., 500 Fifth Avenue, New York, N.Y. 10110

W. W. Norton & Company Ltd., 10 Coptic Street, London WC1A 1PU

1 2 3 4 5 6 7 8 9 0

In memory of my parents

Contents

List of Illustrations

CREDITS

Figs. 4.7, 4.8: Berlin, Staatsbibliothek-Preussischer Kulturbesitz, Musikabteilung mit Mendelssohn Archiv. Fig. 5.2: Berkeley, Music Library, University of California. Fig. 4.6: Budapest, Magyar Országos Levéltár, Esterházy files. Fig. 4.2: Darmstadt, Hessische Landes- und Hochschulbibothek. Figs. 1.5, 1.12: London, by permission of the British Library. Figs. 7.8, 7.9: Milan, Accademia di Brera. Fig. 3.9: Paris, Bibliothèque Nationale, Musée de l'Opéra. Fig. 7.4: Salzburg, Internationale Stiftung Mozarteum, Mozart Museum. Figs. 8.2, 8.6: Salzburg, Neue Ausgabe sämtliche Werke. Figs. 8.3, 9.2, 9.3: Salzburg, Museum Carolino Augusteum. Fig. 7.7: Salzburg, Stiftskirche St. Peter. Fig. 9.8: Stockholm Drottningsholms Teatermuseum. Figs. 3.5, 3.7, 7.8, 7.9: Turin, by courtesy of the Musei Civici de Torino. Figs. 1.7, 4.1: Vienna, Historisches Museum der Stadt. Fig. 2.1: Vienna, Kunsthistorisches Museum. Figs. 1.2, 2.8, 3.8: Vienna, Österreichische Nationalbibliothek, Albertina. Figs. 1.11, 9.4: Vienna, Österreichische Musiksammlung.

List of Color Plates

Preface

OME twenty years ago, on commission from W. W. Norton, I began working on *Music in the Classic Era*, a book that was supposed to take its place alongside the pathbreaking works by Reese, Bukofzer, and others in the Norton History of Music series. My progress was somewhat impeded by several other obligations, notably writing articles for *The New Grove Dictionary of Music and Musicians* and planning the 1977 International Musicological Society Congress in Berkeley, then editing its Report. Nevertheless, by 1980 I had written chapters on Naples, Venice, Paris, and Mannheim, and was forging ahead with what I thought would be a final chapter or two on "Vienna and the Austrian-Bohemian School." My strategy was to subdue the vastness of the subject by concentrating on the primary creative centers, leaving for later consideration places that imported most of their music and musicians.

During a research trip to Vienna in 1981 I came across the chronicles of Viennese concert and theatrical life ca. 1760, compiled by one Philipp Gumpenhuber, and in consequence a new approach began to seem inevitable. After a few more years of work I realized that Vienna could not be added as a finale to what I had already written, but would have to stand on its own. The time span of 1740 to 1780, corresponding to the reign of Empress Maria Theresa, gradually came to seem right to me, because she broke with the past in many cultural areas, including music. By 1780 Gluck had fallen silent, and some of the other major figures, such as Vanhal and Steffan, had done their best work. Haydn and Mozart both encountered the decisive turning points of their careers around that time, as well.

A particular advantage of focusing on Vienna during these four decades is that the generation led by Haydn emerges naturally from the previous one led by Wagenseil and Gluck. Stylistic terms and inherited ideas about periodization ultimately mattered less to me than the common denominators of geography, culture (including religion), and political history. German historians had made a fundamental error, as early as 1800, of placing eighteenth-century Viennese music in the lineage of Bach and Handel. North German and Lutheran traditions held almost no sway in Vienna, where the musical inheritance was indigenous, Catholic, and, to a considerable extent, Italian, with an admixture of French currents, especially around 1760.

As early as the IMS Congress in Ljubljana in 1967, I have been venting my frustrations with the periodizations of eighteenth-century music and the use of such reductive terms as "Baroque" and "Classic." The latter is particularly unfortunate because it was transferred from German literary *Klassik*, the stamping ground of Herder, Goethe, and Schiller. Weimar and Vienna have almost nothing in common. Yet German cultural self-agrandizement has encouraged the appropriation of what was an Austrian-Bohemian achievement in music. In his recent book on Haydn's *Farewell* Symphony, James Webster demonstrated in no uncertain terms that the traditional notions of "Classical style" and "Classical period" (which would have astonished Haydn and Mozart) are flawed beyond redemption and need to be replaced. May the present study contribute to the discussion that must inevitably follow on how to replace them.

With the completion of this book, it is my intention to return now to the chapters I wrote in the 1970s, bring them up to date and extend them, so as to form a companion volume on French, German, and Italian music, covering the period from Vinci and Pergolesi to Paisiello and Boccherini, under the tentative title *Galant Music and the Rococo Age*. The formation and spread of the galant style, a subject not addressed in the present study, will be explored there. For this book it suffices to know that a *cadence galante* is defined by the presence of IV or ii⁶/₅ before I⁶/₄–V–I and the melodic descent of the treble (as, for example, in the cadence of the minuet from the ballroom scene in Mozart's *Don Giovanni*). If the present volume and *Galant Music* manage to please and prove useful, I can foresee returning to Vienna for another volume. It would wind up the careers of Haydn and Mozart, describe Beethoven's first decade in Vienna, intertwined with the tumultuous times surrounding the French Revolution, and cover much else of interest that occurred during the *fin de siècle*.

I set out in this volume to give equal treatment to Haydn and Mozart. Yet Mozart ended up getting more space than Haydn, who was the more important historical figure, in my estimation. The extent of the literature on Mozart accounts for some of the discrepancy—its recent explosion occasioned by the bicentenary commemorations of his death still continues. Some but not all of the most recent scholarship I have been able to incorporate. The same is true of Haydn. From the huge secondary literature on Mozart the most valuable materials for the last three chapters were provided by the detailed prefaces to the individual volumes of the new Mozart edition (or *Neue Mozart Ausgabe,*) which was all but complete, conveniently for me, by the end of 1990. I wrote the three Mozart chapters last and finished them by the end of 1992; by mid-1993 additions and changes were no longer practical.

A more fundamental reason why Mozart required more space than Haydn is that the letters of the Mozart family throw more light on music and life in the eighteenth century than any other documents of the time. I have translated afresh all passages quoted from that correspondence rather than rely on Emily Anderson's deft and stylish translation into English, which is incomplete and sometimes not technical enough for my purposes. All other translations are mine as well unless specified to the contrary. I have left simple passages in French untranslated.

Any project of such long standing as this one accumulates a formidable number of debts to individuals and institutions. In over thirty years together on the faculty of the Department of Music at the University of California, Berkeley, one colleague in particular has been my friend through thick and thin: an inspiring connoisseur of eighteenth-century art and music, Alan Curtis. What draws us together, I believe, besides friendship, is a common faith in the uniqueness of every creative artist, indeed, of every single piece of music and every performance thereof. If I have met some of his needs as a scholar-performer concerned with recreating *settecento* music, I shall have discharged at least part of my debt to him.

Several scholars are thanked by name throughout the pages of the book, but I would be remiss if I did not also thank them here. Gerhard Croll of Salzburg University was particularly helpful with regard to the illustrations, as was Laurence Libin of the Metropolitan Museum of Art in New York. James Webster took the trouble to read and comment in detail on my Haydn chapters when I was visiting professor at Cornell University in 1985. For Chapter 6 on Haydn's contemporaries, I had the advice and criticism of several specialists: Allan Badley on Leopold Hofmann, Howard Picton on Steffan, and Paul Bryan on Vanhal.

Some of my former students who are now established scholars in their own right, working in the field of eighteenth-century studies, came to my aid repeatedly: Kathleen Hansell and Marita McClymonds offered counsel on the shape and scope of the book at crucial moments of decision; Thomas Bauman aided me with the section on Ditters; John Rice generously put his extensive Salieri materials at my disposal; without Bruce Alan Brown's fundamental work on Gluck, Chapter 3 could not have been written, and the same scholar provided me with material on Starzer and help with some of the illustrations.

It is a particular pleasure for me to thank my Berkeley "team" of experts working closely with me during the last few years: cartographer Cherie Semans; portrait artist Carole Peel; typist Katherine Heater; music typographer George Thomson; and above all, my tireless research and editorial assistant, Michelle Dulak, who placed the entire book on disc and suggested many emendations during the process. The final surge leading to publication was facilitated by my tenure of the Jerry and Evelyn Hemmings Chambers Chair in Music (1992–94), which allowed me a reduced teaching load and the financial resources to keep my team going.

As music editor for many years at W. W. Norton, Claire Brook displayed the patience of Job throughout all the turns I have taken. She allowed me to be true to myself by following wherever the material seemed to lead. She accepted that my authorial relationship to the visual arts made for a quite different kind of book from its predecessors in the Norton History of Music series. Not only did she accept my emphasis, she encouraged me to trace my own path. In fact, she fought for my vision of how the book should look in order to approach doing justice to its subject. Without such a vision and support I doubt that I would have persevered to the end. Her wisdom and editorial experience have contributed mightily to making the most of what I had to offer. I thank her for all this and for maintaining her relationship to this project after her official retirement as music editor.

DANIEL HEARTZ
Berkeley, California
April, 1994

Introduction

OR centuries the House of Habsburg ruled the Holy Roman Empire, a loose confederation of states that, around 1200, extended from Rome to the Baltic Sea. In theory every emperor was freely chosen by the few powerful rulers holding electoral votes (the electors). In fact the Habsburgs exercised imperial hegemony almost continuously. By the eighteenth century this unwieldy conglomeration of hundreds of principalities, small and large, had shrunk from its medieval size with the loss of Italy, Holland, and Switzerland. But what remained was still vast. (See map, p. xxii).

The empire conferred prestige on the Habsburgs, but their claim to being a major European power lay in those hereditary provinces clustering around Austria known collectively as the crown lands or, more simply, the monarchy. The western half of the monarchy fell within the empire. Bohemia was one of the electoral states (but subject to direct rule from Vienna from the 1630s), and thus its king, wearing one crown, could elect himself emperor and wear another. The Habsburg family came originally from southern Germany and possessed many territories in Swabia along the upper reaches of the Danube River (pockets of land too small to be indicated on our map except in the case of Breisgau, at the headwaters of the Danube).

Austria's resurgence in the eighteenth century followed a period of disastrous losses to the invading armies of the Ottoman Empire, which advanced all the way to the walls of Vienna in 1683. The city's siege was lifted by the combined forces of Duke Charles of Lorraine and King Jan

The Habsburg Monarchy and the Holy Roman Empire in 1740

Territories of the Monarchy ▨   Border of the Empire ◝

Sobieski of Poland. The Ottoman forces gradually withdrew after this high point of Turkish expansion. Particularly devastated in their wake was the border area between Hungary and Austria, which had to be repopulated (largely by settlers from Croatia and Swabia).

The rivalry between the Habsburgs and the Bourbon dynasty ruling France led to frequent conflicts after Austria's resurgence. Emperor Leopold I had two sons who survived infancy: Joseph, by his second wife, and Charles, by his third. When the Spanish line of the Habsburgs died out in 1700, Leopold put forward the claim of Charles to the throne of Spain; meanwhile Louis XIV, who had married the infanta Maria Theresa, claimed the same for his second grandson, Philip. Thus began the War of the Spanish Succession (1701–13). Joseph I, having succeeded his father as emperor in 1705, pursued the war along with several allies on behalf of his younger half-brother, Charles.

Joseph I died suddenly of smallpox in 1711, leaving no male heir. Charles succeeded him as Charles VI, fully intent on becoming the first emperor since Charles V to unite the crowns of Spain and Austria. But his allies, including England, Holland, and Savoy, were no more pleased by this threat to the balance of power than was France, so the war was concluded with the Peace of Utrecht. By its terms the Bourbon prince became king of Spain as Philip V, with the proviso that the French and Spanish crowns could never be united. Austria was richly compensated with several provinces formerly under Spanish rule: the southern Netherlands (henceforth the Austrian Netherlands, roughly equivalent to present-day Belgium), Lombardy, the kingdom of Naples (without Sicily), and Sardinia. In 1720 Sardinia was exchanged with the House of Savoy for Sicily. Thus Austria replaced Spain as the major power in Italy, and gained a very lucrative foothold on the North Sea.

Charles VI also failed to produce a male heir. He foresaw the dire consequences possible from this situation, and in order to avert them, he persuaded the European powers to ratify a pragmatic sanction. This guaranteed (1) the indivisibility of the various territories making up the monarchy, (2) their rule, failing the birth of a male heir, by his eldest daughter, Maria Theresa, and then by her heirs, and (3) in case of this line's extinction, the right of the daughters of Joseph I and their descendants to inherit.

In early 1736 Maria Theresa married Francis Stephan, duke of Lorraine (grandson of Vienna's liberator in 1683). She soon began bearing children. The first male was Joseph, born in 1741, destined to become her co-ruler and eventual successor as Emperor Joseph II. By the time she was finished with childbearing in 1756, she had presented her husband with sixteen sons and daughters, the last two being Marie Antoinette, future queen of France, and

Maximilian, future archbishop of Cologne and, as such, young Beethoven's principal patron.

In the War of the Polish Succession (1733–35), elector Augustus III of Saxony wrested the Polish throne from Stanislav Lescynki, the father-in-law of Louis XV. As compensation, Lescynki received the duchy of Lorraine to rule as long as he lived, after which it reverted to France. He made of his capital, Nancy, the jewel of Rococo architecture it still is. Forced to give up Lorraine, his patrimony, Francis Stephan received Tuscany as indemnification (the Tuscan throne had conveniently become vacant with the death of the last Medici in 1737). It was as grand duke and duchess of Tuscany that Francis and Maria Theresa entered Florence in 1739—a triumphal arch constructed to mark the occasion, the Porta Galla, still stands. Tuscany remained the private possession of Francis and was not technically a part of the monarchy, but in the interests of simplicity it is shaded the same as the rest of the crown lands on our map. The successful marriage and beautiful progeny of Francis and his wife marked the beginning of a new dynasty, that of Habsburg-Lorraine.

There were other changes of rule in Italy during the 1730s. Austria was routed from the kingdom of Naples by Charles, the son of Philip V of Spain. It recouped this loss by gaining control of the duchy of Parma, which provided a strategic link between Lombardy and Tuscany. Thus we arrive at the territorial situation in 1740, when Maria Theresa succeeded her father, Charles VI. The question then agitating many minds was whether all the parties to the pragmatic sanction would honor their promises.

Frederick II of Prussia, who also ascended to the throne in 1740, at once acted in bad faith by invading and occupying Silesia. Still more serious, potentially, several challengers—including Charles Albert, elector of Bavaria, Philip V of Spain, and elector Augustus III of Saxony (husband of the eldest daughter of Joseph I)—contested Maria Theresa's right to the succession.

Charles Albert of Bavaria, whose family included both Spanish and Habsburg forebears and who was married to the other surviving daughter of Joseph I, coveted both the empire and the monarchy. With the help of a French army, he invaded Austria and Bohemia in 1741. The following year he managed to get himself elected and crowned Holy Roman emperor as Charles VII at Frankfurt. Much to Maria Theresa's dismay, a majority of the Bohemian nobility supported him. She never forgave them.

The turning point for Maria Theresa came when, with her infant son in her arms, she made her legendary appeal to the Hungarian nobles at the diet of Pressburg. Although they had forever been rebelling against the hated Habsburgs, the nobles were won over in spite of themselves. Their ancient statutes allowed no provision for a female ruler, so Maria Theresa was crowned king of Hungary. She conceded much to the great nobles, including exemption from taxation. Their support in the military struggles turned the tide of war in her favor.

Habsburg armies drove Charles Albert and his allies out of Bohemia; he died in early 1745. Maria Theresa was crowned queen of Bohemia in 1743, and her consort was crowned Emperor Francis I at Frankfurt in 1745. Maximilian Joseph, son of Charles Albert, surrendered all claims to Austria and the imperial title but retained Bavaria. Throughout the century Austria's foreign policy remained focused on trying to absorb Bavaria, which was regarded as vital to the "rounding off" of Habsburg territories between Bohemia and the Tyrol. Had Bavaria succumbed, the nominally independent state of Salzburg would have soon followed.

The interests of the monarchy often clashed with those of the empire, whose rulers were sworn to protect the weak and oppressed. Increasingly evident as the empire struggled toward its demise in the last years of the eighteenth century was its lack of will or power to protect anyone. A notable example was the failure of Charles VI to prevent the ruthless expulsion of Protestants from the archdiocese of Salzburg, a member state, in spite of the protests from other states. Was the imperial title really worth fighting for? Evidently it was, because Maria Theresa in 1764 spent over 2 million florins for the election and coronation of her son Joseph as "King of Rome," a ludicrous title meaning that he would automatically become emperor at his father's death.[1]

Silesia was not the only province lost to the monarchy in the 1740s. In the western theater of war France quickly seized the Austrian Netherlands. These were restored to the Habsburgs by the peace treaty of 1748. Alliance rather than enmity with France clearly offered Austria its best chance of retaining Belgium. The famous reversal of alliances of 1756 was mainly the work of Austria's foremost statesman, Prince Anton Wenzel Kaunitz. Henceforth the Catholic powers of France and Austria were allied against the Protestant kingdoms of England and Prussia. The initial result was the Seven Years War (1756–63), during which Austria made futile attempts to regain Silesia. For its pains, France suffered the loss to England of many overseas colonies, including Canada.

What the Habsburgs failed to gain on the fields of battle they often won by marital diplomacy. Parma, lost in 1748, provides a case in point. It was so crucial to Austrian power in Italy, although but a small duchy, that

[1] Derek Beales, *Joseph II*, vol. 1, *In the Shadow of Maria Theresa 1741–1780* (Cambridge, 1987), pp. 110–16.

Joseph's first marriage was with Isabella of Parma. (His second, after her death, was with Maria Josepha, sister of Maximilian Joseph of Bavaria.) Maria Theresa could scarcely run out of marriageable offspring. She supplied a daughter, Maria Amalia, to the duke of Parma, and a son, Ferdinand, to the last descendant of the Este family of Modena, Maria Beatrice (in the interests of clarity our map combines the duchies of Modena and Parma). When Francis Stephan died in 1765, Maria Theresa's nearly grown son, Archduke Leopold, was ready to succeed him as Grand Duke Pietro Leopoldo of Tuscany (the future Emperor Leopold II). When her husband's younger brother, Charles of Lorraine, died in 1780, she had her daughter, Maria Christina, take his place as regent in Brussels. At the time of her death in late 1780, Maria Theresa counted among her greatest triumphs having supplied childbearing wives to the king of Naples (Maria Carolina) and to Louis XVI, king of France (Marie Antoinette).

The cultural ramifications of these dynastic marriages were many. Patronage of the arts came naturally to the Habsburgs. Every imperial wedding required musical as well as literary and visual celebrations. For Archduke Joseph's first marriage in 1760, the poets Frugoni, Migliavacca, and Metastasio matched their skills with Traetta, Gluck, and Hasse, respectively, and the scenic artist Servandoni was brought all the way from Paris to stage Gluck's *Tetide* in the large Redoutensaal of the Hofburg in Vienna. (See Plate IX.) At Milan, whose Archduke Ferdinand married Maria Beatrice d'Este in 1772, the specially commissioned operas were composed by Hasse and the young Mozart. Longer-term consequences often ensued. The rapprochement of Austria and France after 1750 had profound cultural effects for both countries. Had Marie Antoinette not wed the dauphin in 1770 and become queen of France (1774), it is doubtful that Gluck would have conquered Paris with his operas, or Haydn with his symphonies.

Europe in the eighteenth century was far more cosmopolitan than it has been at any time since. Nationalism of the nineteenth-century variety was uncommon. Ideas and people flowed freely across borders, even those of enemy regimes. And yet political affiliations still decided much that affected the arts. The small territory of Lucca supposedly possessed its independence as a republic and thus does not appear shaded on our map. In reality it was a protectorate of the Habsburgs, even more so than Mozart's Salzburg, and hence it is not surprising that several members of the talented Boccherini family from Lucca turned up in Vienna around 1760. At this time Haydn was working for the Bohemian count Morzin, whose shaky financial condition led him to dismiss his musical band. It was Haydn's good fortune, and ours, that he next gained employment with Prince Paul Esterházy, one of Hungary's wealthiest and most art-loving magnates. The Esterházys had

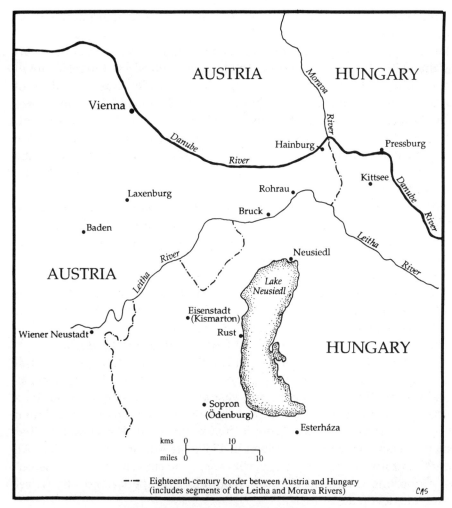

The Austrian-Hungarian Border in Haydn's Time

been pillars of support for Maria Theresa in her early struggles, and remained so.

The Esterházys owned the fertile lands bordering the shallow and marshy Lake Neusiedl south of the Danube. (See map above) They ruled this area as virtually autonomous princes from their seat in Eisenstadt (Kismarton). Other settlements of note were Kitsee north of the lake, Rust on its western shore, and the sizable commercial center of Sopron (Oedenburg) to the south. Farther to the south and east Prince Nicholas Esterházy would begin building his new palace of Esterháza in the 1760s. This palace and

Sopron are still in Hungary today, but Eisenstadt and Rust are now part of the Austrian province of Burgenland.

The eighteenth-century border between Hungary and Austria ran in part along the Leithe River, a tributary of the Danube. Bruck was the major town on the Leithe, a short distance downstream from which was the village of Rohrau, where Joseph Haydn was born in 1732. The lord of these lands was Count Harrach, in whose castle Haydn's mother had worked as a servant. A few miles to the north was the market town of Hainburg on the Danube; in the principal church here, Kapellmeister Reutter from Vienna heard the eight-year-old Haydn sing and recruited him into the service of St. Stephen's Cathedral.

North of the Danube the border between Austria and Hungary (or more specifically, Slovakia, then a province of Hungary) was formed by the Morava River, east of which the Palffys ruled from their castle at the confluence of the Morava and the Danube—these beautiful surroundings are depicted by Brand, one of the great painters among Haydn's contemporaries. (See Plate XII.) The Palffys, like the Esterházys, not only were close to Austria in the physical sense, they also were among the partisans who supported Maria Theresa most strongly at the diet of Pressburg.

The mixture of Slavs, Magyars, and Austrians in the border area provided the rich cultural setting in which Haydn was born and spent most of his life. Vienna itself was a melting pot of these and many other peoples, as befitted the multinational capital of a vast and polyglot empire. Countless musicians from all quarters, but especially from the monarchy, were drawn to this city as if to a magnet. From Bohemia came Gluck and many other Czech musicians. Haydn first arrived in 1740, the Mozarts in the 1760s. All sought their fortunes at the imperial court or in the city's many other institutions supporting music; to all these institutions, imperial and otherwise, Chapter 1 is devoted.

Haydn, Mozart
and the
Viennese School

1

Musical Life
in Vienna

The Hofburg

THE main seat of government of the Habsburg Empire was the complex of buildings in Vienna known as the Hofburg. It was the focal point of the empire's musical hierarchy as well. Here the imperial family resided during the colder part of the year. On Daniel Huber's monumental bird's-eye view of Vienna, dating from ca. 1770, their main residence can be seen at the top in the buildings surrounding "der Burg Platz" (Figure 1.1). To the left, along the perimeter, are the small imperial chapel or Hofkapelle (with its spire), the library ("K. Bibliothek"), and the Augustinian monastery and church. These edifices still stand.[1]

The imperial chapel was the predominant musical institution during the first half of the eighteenth century. Under Charles VI it acquired an opulence that was never again equaled. The Hofkapelle then numbered over a hundred members, which necessitated an enormous expenditure from the imperial treasury, although it had but meager revenues. The Habsburg lands,

[1] A 1760 street-level view of the complex exists, an anonymous drawing reproduced in Moriz Dreger, *Baugeschichte der k. und k. Hofburg in Wien bis zum 19. Jahrhundert* (Österreichische Kunsttopographie 14) (Vienna, 1914), illustration no. 252. The drawing served as a sketch for the background of the huge oil painting at Schönbrunn Palace showing the arrival of Princess Isabella of Parma in 1760 (from the atelier of Martin van Meytens).

3

though far-flung in terms of territory, were not rich in industry or commerce, and much of the wealth was held by the church, which did not pay taxes. After Maria Theresa succeeded her father in 1740, she had to fight several devastating wars in defense of her patrimony. She also had to pay pensions to many musicians no longer able to serve. It was almost inevitable that, given these circumstances, the Hofkapelle should begin its long decline. Kapellmeister Johann Joseph Fux was receiving 3,100 florins annually when he died in 1741; among his successors, Georg Reutter was appointed at 1,200 florins in 1751, the same sum that Giuseppe Bonno received in 1788.[2]

Habsburg rulers up to and including Charles VI were intent on reviving the medieval notion of the Holy Roman Empire as a divinely ordained state in which the emperor shared ecclesiastical power with the pope. They poured their scarce resources into church building and everything to do with the religious life, including music. With the accession of Charles' daughter Maria Theresa, this attitude changed. For all her piety, the empress is remembered not as a builder of churches but as the instigator of plans to insure that church lands and wealth contributed to the commonweal—plans that were carried out in a more radical fashion by her son Joseph II. Life under Charles VI was like a religious pageant, the court moving about from one church to another in constant celebration of the events of the liturgical year. By the time his grandsons came to rule, there was still religious pageantry on a few high holidays, but the traditional court stations to honor a lengthy calendar of saints were cut back. Joseph closed many monastic institutions. He also ordered that altars and statues be greatly reduced in number in public churches. His decrees of 1783 eliminated most religious processions. When Charles Burney visited Vienna in 1772, he was told by an Italian that the Austrians were extremely addicted to processions ("portatissimi alle processioni"), the implication being that they outdid even the Italians in this department. Burney approved because of the musical consequences: the common people learned to sing in parts while perambulating. An anonymous drawing of a religious parade on the feast of Corpus Christi passing along the side of the Hofburg and before the façade of the Michaelerkirche captures well this typically Viennese practice (Figure 1.2).

The Hofkapelle was a fifteenth-century Gothic chapel located near the ramparts between the imperial library and the Burg Platz. It can be found on Huber's map in Figure 1.1 by its small steeple; the public entrance is to

---

[2] Ludwig Köchel, *Die kaiserliche Hof-musikkapelle in Wien von 1543–1867* (Vienna, 1869; reprint 1976), p. 72. For an assessment of the standard of living in Vienna allowed by these salaries, see Bruce C. MacIntyre, *The Viennese Concerted Mass of the Early Classic Period* (Ann Arbor, 1986), pp. 20–26.

FIGURE 1.1. Detail from Daniel Huber's map of Vienna, c. 1770.

FIGURE 1.2. Anonymous drawing of a Corpus Christi procession passing by the Hofburg.

FIGURE 1.3. *OPPOSITE*. The Hofkapelle in 1705. Drawing by J. Ch. Sambach.

Die Frohnleichnahms Prozession, über den Michaelerplatz aõ 1780.

the right, through the middle door with the staircase leading down to ground level in two directions. Normally the court heard mass in this chapel during the winter season of residence in the Burg. Here the imperial musicians regularly performed their functions. During Lent it was customary for the court to hear German and Latin sermons in this chapel, as well as many musical performances, including oratorios, *sepulcri*, and settings of the *Stabat mater*. The Order of the Golden Fleece *(Toison d'Or)*, the highest in the realm, held many of its services in the Hofkapelle, and the *Toison-Amt* regularly on Christmas. Certain ceremonial occasions of a more political nature also took place within these walls. Here Emperor Joseph I received the allegiance of the Lower Austrian Estates with a *Te Deum* in 1705.

An engraving by Pfeffel and Engelbrecht depicting the event gives us the best idea of what the chapel looked like in the first part of the eighteenth century (Figure 1.3). The highly elaborate main altar decorated with many

Das Te Deum Laudamus in der Hoff Capellen

1. Ihre May: der Kayser. 2. Ihre May: die Kayserin 3. Ihre Durchl: Drchl: die Ertzherzoginen. 4. Bischoff zür Neüstatt. 5. Obr: Erb Caplan . 6. Obr:
Erb Marschall. 7. Obr: Erb Pannier. 8. Angesetzter Hatschiern Hauptmann. 9. Angesetzter Trabanten Hauptmann. 10. Obr: Erb Mündtschenck
11. Obr: Erb Trüchsäss. 12. Obr: Erb Cammerer. 13. Obr: Erb Vorschneider. 14. Der N: O: Heroldt 15. Obr: Erb Hoffmaister. 16. Obr: Erb Stallmaister 17. Obr:
Erb Jagermaister. 18. Obr: Erb falckhenmaister. 19. Obr: Erb Stabelmaister. 20. Der N: O: Landt Marschall. 21. Die gesambte N: O: Ständte. 22. Die Kay: Hatschiern: u: Trabanten Guardi.

J. C. Huchhofer. delin.   J. A. Pfeffel et C. Engelbrecht. sc.

statues was built in the mid-seventeenth century, along with the rest of the interior, which included the typically Baroque spiraling columns of the scarcely less elaborate side altars. An organ can be seen in the right foreground, without pedals, and topped with a statue of King David playing his harp. The emperor is seated on the Gospel side. Shoulder-length wigs bedeck most of the men; the court ladies appear only in the gallery high above. When Maria Theresa repeated this ceremony at the beginning of her reign, this engraving was revised only slightly. But in the subsequent years the chapel was gradually transformed so that it lost its Baroque aspects; remodeling was completed by 1772.[3]

The later eighteenth-century aspects of the chapel are best illustrated by an anonymous print depicting Joseph II witnessing the marriage of his nephew Francis with Elizabeth of Württemberg in 1788, before the assembled court and clergy (Figure 1.4). Gone are the frilly Gothic traceries around the arches, gone the Baroque altars, to be replaced by a single main altar with no sculpted saints, only the fourfold crucified Christ (above the tabernacle and in front of it, to the Epistle side of the altar, and in symbolic form as the Cross of Lorraine on the Gospel side). These two pictures tell more than words how the House of Habsburg-Lorraine differed from the House of Habsburg. The ladies, much more numerous on the later occasion, wear the latest Paris fashions, and the men have short wigs. An air of informality permeates the whole assembly, more characteristic of the French court than of the old Spanish etiquette. Joseph II, a tall man, stands under his baldachin in a relaxed pose. The figures in surplices at the right may include singers. One of the curious features of the rebuilt chapel is the proliferation of boxes above the ground floor, just as in a theater. The curvilinear shape of three of them correspond, in fact, to the boxes in the Burgtheater at this time (cf. Figure 1.10). Moreover, the use of mirrors behind candles for lighting comes from the theater. More light was admitted through windows too because of the way they were redesigned. The emperor must have wished to keep this marriage ceremony a relatively simple affair, or he would have selected the much larger Hofkirche (Augustinerkirche), where he was married in 1760 and where his mother and father were wed in 1736. Another engraving of the Hofkapelle was made by Hieronymus Löschenkohl to illustrate the homage paid by the Lower Austrian Estates to Leopold II on 6 April 1790.[4]

[3] Dreger, *Baugeschichte der k. und k. Hofburg*, p. 293.
[4] Illustrated in John A. Rice, "Vienna under Joseph II and Leopold II," in *Man and Music: The Classical Era*, ed. Neal Zaslaw (London, 1989), fig. 40, p. 160.

FIGURE 1.4. *OPPOSITE*. The Hofkapelle in 1788.

Churches

THE *AUGUSTINERKIRCHE*, OR *HOFKIRCHE*

THE Hofkirche was a long Gothic hall church begun in 1327. During the sixteenth century it was declared a court church and given into the charge of the Augustinians. Holy days when processions were called for were generally celebrated in the Hofkirche, as were great state occasions when large numbers of people had to be accommodated, such as weddings of the heir to the throne. Funerals for members of the ruling family and for defunct foreign princes were celebrated in the choir of this church. The imperial crypt was not located here but in the plain Kapuzinerkirche nearby, on the Neuer Markt (see Figure 1.1, bottom left). Fischer von Erlach the elder designed the elaborate *Castrum Doloris* erected in the choir of the Hofkirche after the death of Joseph I in 1713;[5] that tastes changed very little during the reign of Charles VI may be seen from the quite similar *Castrum Doloris* built at his death, designed by Fischer von Erlach *fils*.[6] When the emperor created a new member of his Order of the Golden Fleece, or when he bestowed a cardinal's hat, he sat not in his oratory but under a baldachin on a throne on the Gospel side of the altar, that is to say the place of honor allocated the pope in other circumstances, while the celebrating bishop was relegated to a throne on the Epistle side.

The marriage of Maria Theresa and Francis Stephan of Lorraine was celebrated in the Hofkirche on 12 February 1736. An engraving by Elias Böck shows the moment in the ceremony after the bride has pronounced her "Volo" in acceptance of her husband and the papal nuncio has joined their hands in wedlock.[7] It was also the moment when the imperial chapel began a *Te Deum* with trumpets and drums, which was the signal for firing the first salvos from the bastions. The artist shows three trumpeters with raised instruments alongside the timpani, behind them several string players. Was he taking liberties by placing the court musicians in such a prominent spot, just a step down from the altar on the honorific Gospel side? Probably not.

---

[5] Illustrated in Friedrich W. Riedel, *Kirchenmusik am Hofe Karls VI (1711–1740)* (Munich and Salzburg, 1977), opposite p. 33.

[6] Reproduced in Hans Sedmayr, *Johann Bernard Fischer von Erlach* (Vienna and Munich, 1956), illustration 146.

[7] Gerda and Gottfried Mraz, *Maria Theresia: Ihr Leben und ihre Zeit in Bildern und Dokumenten* (Munich, 1979), p. 33. The engraving is also reproduced in *Maria Theresia und ihre Zeit* (Catalogue of the Exhibition at Schönbrunn Palace) (Vienna, 1980), p. 32; it is joined by another engraving showing the wedding banquet in the small court theater, where instrumental musicians play from a balcony.

This was their normal place in the earlier part of the century, and they had access to it by a special door to the street.[8]

On 6 October 1760 the nineteen-year-old crown prince, who later became Joseph II, wed Princess Isabella of Bourbon-Parma in the Hofkirche, an event commemorated by a large painting from the workshop of Martin van Meytens, imperial court painter, conserved at Schönbrunn Palace. (See Plate II.) In the painting Maria Theresa and Francis occupy the canopied imperial oratory, with their numerous progeny assembled to their right. Before the high altar three bishops unite husband and wife. The altar is sparsely adorned, the only image being a Christ on the cross. Candles abound here and throughout the church; the emphasis on simplicity, elegance, and light, remarked on above in the remodeling of the Hofkapelle, is very much in evidence here already in 1760. No musicians can be identified as such among the throng of people depicted filling the choir, ladies on the left, gentlemen on the right. Several faces look around and up in the air, as if in astonishment (one figure even points upward to his neighbor). Since the moment when bride and groom join hands is the same as in the 1736 picture, we assume that it once again gave the signal for the *Te Deum*, which has just burst forth from somewhere high in the nave, to the delight and wonder of all. The general impression is of a dark and cavernous space made radiant not only by thousands of candles and the wave of optimism engendered by the great event itself, but also, and not least of all, by the musical brilliance that has just been unleashed, which can be felt even though its source is not depicted. Some special gallery may have been erected for the court musicians on this occasion. Not until 1784–85 was the still extant musicians' gallery built above the west door at the rear of the church. The position of the musicians near the altar, characteristic of earlier centuries, often gave way, during the era of sumptuous Viennese symphonic masses, to a placement in more remote parts of the church.

Descriptions of musical performances in the Hofkirche are rare. Friedrich Nicolai left fairly detailed ones after his visit in 1781. Someone had told him he could hear Gregorian chant sung there, but he was disappointed in this respect:

> The singing was accompanied by organ alone, which also played a few short movements by itself. From its nature it could have been four-voiced, as the organ accompaniment demonstrated (and this alone shows that it could not have been Gregorian chant); but I heard mostly all the voices in unison, and only occasionally two voices that proceeded in thirds and sixths. Since the highest voice was a tenor, and various good bass voices also took part, this song

[8] Riedel, *Kirchenmusik am Hofe Karls VI*, p. 39.

could have had a festive air if everything were not so forced in tempo ["gewaltig gejagt"] and split into disjunct tones, whence sprang no semblance of a serious effect.[9]

On another day Nicolai chanced on a requiem mass as he was going to visit the imperial collection of natural objects. He was later told that such requiems took place every Monday in one of the chapels of the Hofkirche.

> The performing forces and the execution could not have been worse. There were only two violins, one player to a part and badly played, one cello and one double bass, two trombones, and a positive organ. The chorus was also very weak. But the composition was remarkable. It was perhaps by Fux or his contemporary and colleague Caldara, and consequently had a simple, noble song, full of expression. A beautiful and moderately slow aria sung by a choirboy greatly touched me; he had a pure, sweet, and flexible contralto, although still untutored with respect to execution and *portamento di voce*. The aria was accompanied by a concertante tenor trombone throughout, and no other instrument. Yet there was so much in this strange and simple combination that it awakened a somber, holy, and exalted sensation. Those long-drawn-out, gentle tones, constantly following one another, constantly meeting, roused a silent astonishment. Particularly a few places, where the trombone sank down deeper and deeper and was sustained there, as the contralto, after a couple of bars' rest, softly sounded gradually louder tones of long duration in the high register— they went straight to the heart. For a long while I had heard nothing more judicious.

THE KARLSKIRCHE

THE Karlskirche, dedicated to Saint Charles Borromeo, represents a special case. It is acclaimed as the greatest architectural accomplishment of the reign of Charles VI, to be compared with the New University (1754) under Maria Theresa and the General Hospital (1784) under Joseph II, both designed by French architects. Charles vowed he would build the church to commemorate the terrible plague in 1713, and chose a plot of empty land outside the walls within sight of the Burg. Working with his great architect Johann Bernard Fischer von Erlach, Charles planned it as a symbol of the universal monarchy he claimed as king of Spain (which he was crowned in 1706) and Holy Roman Emperor. Like his sixteenth-century ancestor Charles V, the last emperor who had united both crowns in his person, he chose the two

[9]Friedrich Nicolai, *Beschreibung einer Reise durch Deutschland und die Schweiz*, 4 vols. (Berlin, 1784), vol. 4, section 10, "Von der Musik in Wien."

pillars of Hercules as his emblem, along with the same motto, "Plus oultre." The two pillars still stand guard in front of the Karlskirche today, and played a prominent symbolic role in the interior of Fischer von Erlach's other completed masterpiece for Charles VI, the imperial library. It did not matter that Charles VI lost the crown of Spain in 1711; he persisted in the dream and clung to stiff Spanish court etiquette his life long.

Building the Karlskirche filled most of Charles VI's reign and consumed enormous sums. At last, in 1737, the new church was consecrated, although still not quite finished. Salomon Kleiner made an engraving of it the same year. (See Figure 1.6, p. 29.) The emperor attended a solemn pontifical mass there the following year, and once again in 1739, his last visit. The church was given into the care of the Knights of Malta and seems to have seen little use by the court during subsequent reigns. Joseph II, of a very different mind about imperial glory from his grandfather, turned it into a parish church in 1783. Marriages of state continued to be celebrated in the Augustinerkirche, including that of Napoleon to Archduchess Marie Louise in 1810.

THE CATHEDRAL

ST. STEPHEN'S CATHEDRAL was frequented by the court more than any other church, after the Hofkapelle and the Hofkirche. Vienna's largest Gothic structure by far, it became the seat of the bishop in 1469 and was raised to the seat of an archbishop in 1723, at the insistence of Charles VI with the pope. The building underwent surprisingly little *Barockisierung*, compared with most Viennese churches. It was too large for anything but a remodeling on a colossal scale, and the diocese was in fact small and poor in revenues. Charles Burney praised the Roman-style Baroque of the Jesuit University Church as "an elegant modern building," but he had this to say about the cathedral: "The church is a dark, dirty and dismal old Gothic building, though richly ornamented; in it are hung all the trophies of war, taken from the Turks and other enemies of the house of Austria, for more than a century past, which gives it very much the appearance of an old wardrobe." Tradition dictated that the court, led by the imperial family, should attend a pontifical service in the cathedral on great feasts such as Easter, Corpus Christi, Immaculate Conception, and St. Stephen's Day (26 December). The feast of the Most Holy Name of Mary (the Sunday after 8 September, or Nativity BVM) was made an occasion of particular solemnity commemorating the lifting of the Turkish siege of Vienna in 1683, with procession, *Te Deum*, and pontifical services, the emperor participating. Burney was present for this event in 1772, and reported it in detail:

Sunday 13th [September]. There was a procession through the principal streets of this city to-day, as an anniversary commemoration of the Turks having been driven from its walls in 1683, by Sobieski king of Poland, after it had sustained a siege of two months. The Emperor came from Laxenburg to attend the celebration of this festival, and walked in the procession, which set off from the Franciscan's church, and proceeded through the principal streets of the city to the Cathedral of St. Stephen, where *Te Deum* was sung, under the direction of M. Gasman, imperial *maestro di capella*. The music was by Reüter, an old German composer, without taste or invention. As there was a very numerous band, great noise and little meaning characterized the whole performance. I hoped something better would have succeeded this dull, dry stuff; but what followed was equally uninteresting. The whole was finished by a triple discharge of all the artillery of the city, and the military instruments were little less noisy now, than the musical had been before.[10]

We may gather from this that where the emperor was present, so were the imperial chapel musicians. Joseph II's maestro di cappella, Florian Gassmann, took command of the combined musical forces of court and cathedral and presumably chose the music performed, in this case that of his just-deceased predecessor, Georg Reutter. Five days earlier Burney had visited the cathedral on the feast of the Nativity BVM. The court was not present. There was elaborate music under the direction of Leopold Hofmann, maestro di cappella of the cathedral. Burney was more pleased with this music making and with the music itself, especially the symphonies of Hofmann, but he complained that the organ "was insufferably out of tune, which contaminated the whole performance." Small organs were planted in different parts of the building, but the big organ at the back of the church was long out of commission, as Burney explained:

The first time I went to the cathedral of St. Stephen, I heard an excellent mass, in the true church style, very well performed; there were violins and violoncellos though it was not a festival. The great organ at the west end of this church has not been fit for use these forty years; there are three or four more organs of a smaller size in different parts of the church, which are used occasionally. That which I heard in the choir this morning is but a poor one, and as usual, was much out of tune; it was played, however, in a very masterly, though not a modern style. All the responses in this service, are chanted in four parts, which is much more pleasing, especially where there is so little melody, than the more naked *canto fermo* used in most other catholic churches [in other places]; the

---

[10] Charles Burney, *The Present State of Music in Germany, The Netherlands, and United Provinces*, 2nd ed. (London, 1775; reprint 1969). Burney's invaluable descriptions of Viennese music in 1772 will be referred to subsequently as Burney, *German Tour*, or simply as Burney.

treble part was sung by boys, and very well; particularly by two of them, whose voices, though not powerful, had been well cultivated.

An engraving of 1712 shows Charles VI making one of his many ceremonial visits to the cathedral.[11] The emperor kneels at an oratory under a baldachin on the left (Gospel) side of the altar. Trumpets protrude from a high balcony on the same side, near the transept. Later in the century the court orchestra and chorus were placed on bleachers erected to the right of the high altar. Carl Schütz shows this placement in his engraving of the visit of Pope Pius VI to Vienna in 1782.[12] (Joseph II did not deign to meet the pontiff on this uninvited visit.) The same placement is mentioned at the high mass on 6 April 1790 for Leopold II: "The royal chapel made music from the usual choir opposite the royal oratory."[13] The Brotherhood of Saint Cecilia, made up of leading court musicians as well as aristocrats, normally celebrated their patroness' day (22 November) with high mass and elaborate concerted music in the cathedral.

Burney was more generous to Vienna's cathedral music than some native critics writing in the following decade. Joseph Richter is remembered as an apologist for the reforms of Joseph II and as the author of the satirical *Eipeldauer Briefen*. His *Picture Gallery of Catholic Abuses*, published in 1784, ostensibly in Frankfurt and Leipzig but actually in Vienna, contains an explanation of how Viennese church music had degenerated (his term):

> The maestri di capella wished to outdo each other, and perhaps the populace itself was tired of the eternal, serious sameness. Thus there soon slipped into the church style unnoticed a trio from a menuet, then the thrum-thrum of a symphony, then again fragments of waltzing music, and finally half and whole opera arias; moreover, they thought nothing of profaning God's temple with the crowing of Italian capons. Comic opera singers of both sexes exchanged the theater for the church with regularity. The primo buffo who played the Marchese Villano in the carnival opera took over the role of Saint Peter in Lent,[14] and the prima donna who sang to us instilling love and voluptuousness in the

---

[11] Reproduced in Riedel, *Kirchenmusik am Hofe Karls VI*, facing p. 16. For evidence of a placement of the musicians near the main altar, on the Epistle side, see p. 45.

[12] Reproduced in Ignaz Schwarz, *Wiener Strassenbilder im Zeitalter des Rokoko* (Die Wiener Ansichten von Schütz, Ziegler, Janscha, 1779–1798) (Vienna, 1914), p. 21. Also reproduced in MacIntyre, *The Viennese Concerted Mass*, plate 9.

[13] Hieronymus Löschenkohl, *Beschreibung der Huldigungsfeyerlichkeiten . . . 1790 . . .* (Vienna, 1790), p. 12: "Die königliche Kapelle machte Musik auf dem gewöhnlichen Chor, dem königlichen Oratorio gegenüber."

[14] Baldassare Galuppi's setting of Chiari's *Il marchese villano* (Venice, 1762) was performed in Vienna in 1767.

theater wished now to make up for our sins, and hers, with a touching *Stabat mater*. So many repentant sinners were attracted by this penitential song that it was necessary to set guards at the doors, just as at the entry-free balls. But things became the most colorful whenever the feast of a great saint or church patron was celebrated. Then a strong orchestra was not enough; trumpets and timpani were added on the sides of the choir, which engaged in a contest with the trumpets and drums of the main orchestra.[15]

Richter concludes his argument two pages later, after saying that even the larger churches had become too small for this kind of racket. (Cf. Burney on the cathedral music of 13 September 1772.) He proposes sending all these instruments back where they came from—the trumpets and drums to the military field, the horns to the forest, the bass fiddles, flutes, and other instruments to the dance halls—and restricting church music to the sternly festal organ alone (in line with one of Joseph II's decrees of 1783).

Richter's lurid picture in words was reinforced by an actual picture, as happened regularly in his *Bildergalerie* (Figure 1.5). A Viennese artist, Johann Ernst Mansfeld, made the engraving; it depicts a large Gothic church with transept and high altar, which in a Viennese context suggests St. Stephen's. Not content to let the picture speak for itself, Richter annotated it so that the connection with his main text would not be lost. He specifies: the high altar is lit from top to bottom; the choirmaster beats the time for the orchestra on the left; an opera singer with feathered headdress sings the *Stabat mater*; a fat bass stealthily draws a bottle of wine from beneath the music stand; trumpets and drums adorn the orchestra on the other side of the choir; members of the Christian congregation turn their heads toward the female opera singer.

The secularization of church music that accelerated under Maria Theresa engendered many such responses. The empress herself forbade the use of trumpet and drums in church in 1753. The ban, probably ineffectual anyway, as seems to have been the case with many imperial decrees, was relaxed the following year with respect to baptisms in the ruling family. When Maria Theresa recovered from a serious illness in June 1767, a *Te Deum* with trumpets and drums was ordered and took place in the cathedral. Exactly contemporary with Richter's *Bildergalerie* was the publication of Friedrich Nicolai's *Reise* (1784), relating his visit to Vienna in 1781. There are more than a few textual parallels concerning church music. Nicolai writes:

> With respect to composition, Catholic church music up to a few years ago still retained a lot of individual character. But now operatic music forces itself every-

[15] Joseph Richter, *Bildergalerie katholischer Misbräuche* (Frankfurt and Leipzig [Vienna], 1784).

FIGURE 1.5. J. E. Mansfeld. Satire of Viennese church music.

where, also in church, and what is worse, the vacuous ["fade"] kind of new-fangled Italian operatic music. This I found also in Vienna, only more so. I knew not with many a Credo or Benedictus whether I was hearing music from an Italian opera buffa or not. The best kind was always when the music remained of a pleasant and lovely kind, so that it did not sink too low in character. That was at least bearable. Seldom did I hear anything moving or sublime. What was supposed to be magnificent was mostly only noisy.

Johann Pezzl, like Richter an ardent defender of the reforms instituted by Joseph II, chimed in with a denunciation of "profane vows crowed sweetly down from above—often a chorus from an opera buffa changed into a Sanctus"; his assessment of the effect of the reforms, from a series of sketches of Vienna he wrote between 1786 and 1790, will be quoted below.

OTHER CHURCHES IN CITY AND SUBURBS

THE city within the walls was crowded with churches and monastic institutions; the suburbs boasted more in addition, but these were mostly destroyed by the Turks in 1683 and had to be rebuilt. The Michaelerkirche, directly across from the Burgtheater, assumed importance as a parish church for the court and its environs. Consecrated in 1221, it was originally in the Romanesque style, and was wealthy enough over the centuries to be remodeled often in keeping with later styles. Its great organ (by David Sieber) was first sounded in public for the entrance of the emperor on 25 January 1714. Burney described the instrument in detail and praised its tone. The old Minoritenkirche, also near the palace, was the seat of a Court Brotherhood of the Holy Cross. St. Peter's occupied the location of an old church that was razed to the ground (unusual for Vienna) to make way for the domed church erected 1702–15 on plans by Angelo Montani and Johann Lukas von Hildebrandt. Admired by Burney as a miniature replica of St. Peter's in Rome, this church was annually visited by the court in solemn thanksgiving for Vienna's delivery from the plague in 1679. The court visited various other churches on the feasts of their patron saints—for example, the Franziskanerkirche on St. Francis' Day (4 October, and celebrated with particular luster when Francis Stephan reigned as Francis I and his grandson as Francis II); the Dominican Church on the feast of St. Thomas of Aquinas (7 March); the Jesuit University Church on the feast of St. Francis Xaver (3 December); the Barmherzige Brüder on the feast of the Nativity of John the Baptist (24 June).

Joseph Haydn was connected with the last-named church, located in the Leopoldstadt across the Danube north of the city. (See Figure 4.9.) After he left the choir school of the cathedral (ca. 1750), one of the ways Haydn made a meager living was to play first violin there. And he maintained his ties with the Barmherzige Brüder; it was in their church that he proposed to lead a performance of his *Stabat mater* during Lent in 1767. Performances of Haydn's *Stabat mater* in this church apparently became a tradition. Joseph Martin Kraus speaks of hearing it there on 18 April 1783 and of being disappointed by the mediocrity of the performance.[16] Another suburban church, St. Joseph's in the Laimgrube, had for its choirmaster the formidable contrapuntist Johann Georg Albrechtsberger from 1772. This church was the seat of a Confraternity of St. Joseph and often received the court on the feast of its patron (who was celebrated in Austria as a "Landespatron" on the third Sunday after Easter). The twelve-year-old Mozart provided the mass and offertory for the consecration on 7 December 1768 of the Waisenhaus

[16] Irmgard Leux-Henschen, *Joseph Martin Kraus in seinen Briefen* (Stockholm, 1978), p. 110.

(Orphanage) Church on the Rennweg, at which the emperor and his court were in attendance.

Two churches on the western side of the city merit particular attention. The Jesuit Church am Hof was a frequent destination of the court, which traditionally attended second vespers there on major Marian feast days. This church's imposing façade, in the Roman Baroque style, was designed by Carlo Carlone in 1662. Leopold Mozart says that he led a performance of his son's *Dominicus* Mass (K. 66) at this Jesuit church on 12 August 1773 to celebrate the octave of the feast of St. Ignatius of Loyola (7 August), and that it was well received (letter of 12 August 1773).[17]

Reputed for the quality of its music was the venerable old Schottenkirche on the Freyung. The church was founded for Irish monks ("Schotten") in 1155 and given over to the German Benedictines in 1418. One of the four old parish churches, it was the seat of the Brotherhood of St. Sebastian; the court visited it on the feast of St. Fabian and St. Sebastian (20 January). Johann Joseph Fux served as its organist in the early years of the century before becoming Kapellmeister at the cathedral, then at court. In the 1740s young Carl Ditters was advised by his violin teacher, Joseph Ziegler, to attend services in the Schottenkirche, "where there was a well-appointed orchestra, and the best masses, motets, vespers and litanies were sung." Ditters applied to the choirmaster, Tobias Gsur, who rebuffed him at first, but soon he was playing violin in the orchestra, under the leadership of Karl Huber. The orchestra played from the gallery in the rear of the church. As Ditters tells in his memoirs:

> It was customary for connoisseurs of music to attend the Benedictine Church in large numbers, for the music, particularly on great festivals, was of the choicest kind, and the performance first-rate. Some of Huber's admirers were sitting below when I played, and after the solo had finished they were loud in their praises, in the belief that they had been listening to Huber himself. But what was their surprise when he introduced me to them.[18]

Among the auditors, according to Ditters, was one Hubaczek, first horn in the orchestra of Prince Joseph Friedrich von Sachsen-Hildburghausen, who promptly recruited the violinist, thus making Ditters a member of Vienna's

---

[17] *Mozart: Briefe und Aufzeichnungen. Gesamtausgabe*, ed. Wilhelm A. Bauer, Otto Erich Deutsch, and Joseph Heinz Eibl, 7 vols. (Kassel, 1962–75). Letters will be identified subsequently solely by their date.

[18] *The Autobiography of Karl von Dittersdorf, Dictated to His Son*, trans. A. D. Coleridge (London, 1896; reprint 1970). I append occasional words or phrases in brackets from the original, *Karl von Dittersdorf: Lebenbeschreibung* (Leipzig, 1801).

premier concert-giving ensemble of that time. What he tells us about it will be discussed below.

The way Ditters describes the music making in the Schottenkirche puts little distance between religious services and bona fide concerts, it must be admitted. When he says that the listeners were loud in their praises, he presumably means at the conclusion of the service. And yet we cannot be sure that some sort of approbation did not follow directly after the music. Abuses of this kind were specifically reproved by an anonymous pamphlet, *Über die Kirchenmusik in Wien* (1781), in a passage that may be an attack on the Schottenkirche and its choirmaster, Tobias Gsur:

> It is especially in a [certain] monastic church of our city where things go a bit too far with respect to the music, and every Christian who does not have a wooden insensibility must be disturbed in prayer. The clerical choir director himself, in whose musical round dance ["Runde"] everything sings and whistles, composes mostly his own pieces or whatever they are called. There is hardly any opera—buffa as well as seria—which he does not know how to plunder line by line (as the experts told me) and use most cleverly. On the day of a production the top male and female singers of our stages appear in the middle of the church to be heard . . .
>
> Who, then, can really maintain that one would be able to pray fervently in the theater while listening to a Venetian marketplace, a Röschen and Kollas, [or] a love story of the working class? Why? Because the enticing song, the pleasing tones conquer our senses.
>
> I myself was present in this church when they performed such arias that had been removed from operas and metamorphosed into a Salve Regina or a Regina coeli . . . Moreover, an undertone of *Bravo, Schön,* and *chi viva* was heard from most of the listeners.[19]

Burney makes it clear that orchestral forces were common in Viennese churches not just on Sundays and feast days, but every day, and in modest as well as grand churches. For an outsider, and a Protestant to boot, Burney was remarkably equitable and clear-sighted with regard to church music. He set higher store by the formative power of good music than did, for instance, Joseph II. He even attributed to the music heard in churches the widespread musicality among ordinary people:

[19] MacIntyre, *The Viennese Concerted Mass*, p. 533. For Gsur's biography, see pp. 70–71. MacIntyre does not attempt to identify the operas referred to. The first must be Salieri's *La fiera di Venezia* (Vienna, 1772). The second is *Rose et Colas* by Monsigny, revived in Vienna in 1779–80. The third is *L'amore artigiano* by Gassmann, revived in 1779 as *Die Liebe unter den Handswerksleuten.*

There is scarce a church or convent in Vienna, which has not every morning its *mass in music:* that is, a great portion of the church service of the day, set in parts, and performed with voices, accompanied by at least three or four violins, a tenor [viola] and base [sic], besides the organ, and as the churches here are daily crowded, this music, though not of the most exquisite kind, must in some degree form the ear of the inhabitants.

Joseph II, on the other hand, took the position of a modern efficiency expert: musicians were a bothersome expense to be dispensed with, and the money saved should be spent on popular education. By decree of 25 February 1783 the emperor specified that instrumental participation in parish churches be limited to Sundays and holy days, and he even restricted music in the cathedral: "In the Cathedral of St. Stephen and in those churches that have a regular choir one Mass will be celebrated daily. This will be a chanted Mass, with or without organ accompaniment, according to the season [i.e., a cappella during Lent, as was long the practice]."[20]

Johann Georg Albrechtsberger wrote a Mass in E♭ to celebrate St. Augustine's Day (28 August) in 1784, but since the feast fell on a Saturday, he had to use only organ accompaniment, even though the style was such as had previously called for instruments. It may have been mainly a coincidence that Haydn and Mozart wrote no concerted church music from 1783 to the end of the decade. Instrumentally accompanied masses continued to be heard in Vienna, but only on Sundays (and holy days). Musical forces in even the larger churches declined greatly as a consequence of the reforms, and this helps explain why composers turned away from writing concerted masses.

Friedrich Nicolai visited Vienna nine years after Burney and took a somewhat dimmer view of its church music. We know he had read Burney in the meantime because he chides the English author about his prolixity, a complaint Nicolai was hardly in a position to make.

I heard much church music in Vienna, for there were then regularly masses with music, and since the beginning in each church was at different times, I could hear as many as three or four masses with music on every Sunday and holy day. The orchestras were not so good as in either of the theaters. There may well have been good musicians in them, but they did not play with such good ensemble. Even in St. Stephen's I found the music not so good as I imagined it would be under the direction of Leopold Hofmann. Presumably the fault does not lie

[20] Reinhard Pauly, "The Reforms of Church Music under Joseph II," *Musical Quarterly* 43 (1957): 372–82; 378. On 21 June 1783 Joseph ordered an "Index of all Music Personnel, together with their past and present paid salary" drawn up; it is reproduced in Otto Biba, "Die Wiener Kirchenmusik um 1783," in *Beiträge zur Musikgeschichte des 18. Jahrhunderts* (Eisenstadt, 1971), pp. 7–79.

with this famous man. The voices in all churches were not outstanding; even the best were only mediocre. What I said about the performance of the choir in Regensburg, namely that the choristers, especially the basses, do not shriek as powerfully as in many cities of northern Germany, is also true of Vienna.

Following this, Nicolai launches into an attack on the operatic nature of Viennese church music, which has been quoted above. But then he gets down to cases.

A few exceptions I found, e.g., in the War Church, or former Jesuit Church [the Church am Hof, the monastery of which had been turned into the Chancellery of War]; I heard on 17 June a beautiful music to a mass. It was in the modern taste, but full of noble and new thoughts. The Sanctus was accompanied only by an obbligato solo violin, which also was very well played. The Agnus Dei was accompanied throughout by an obbligato trombone that was played purely and with understanding, and made a good effect, well calculated for the church style. (The trombone has become almost entirely neglected with us in full-voiced church music, but in Austria and Bavaria the instrument is much used in church music and well played—Gluck introduced it in his opera and ballet music, often with happy consequences.)

Nicolai also mentions hearing the all-woman orchestra and chorus in the Laurentian convent, and a performance of a *Te Deum* by Johann Adolf Hasse in the Waisenhaus Church on the octave of the feast of Corpus Christi—it was taken too fast for his taste. In another passage Nicolai speaks of a procession at St. Peter's in which choral song was accompanied by cornetti, two trombones, and two bassoons.

Johann Pezzl summed up the effect of the Josephine reforms on religious institutions as follows:

In times past, the churches were cluttered beyond measure with religious pictures, ornaments, mementos, flags of the various confraternities, etc. The statues were covered with wigs, crowns, silk and woolen coats, etc. All this was supposed—in the minds of pious and simple-minded old women—to be an enhancement of the church, a contribution to the greater enflaming of Christian piety. With the holy mass there was a similar disorder. Two things were read at once so that one knew not which way to turn, or whether to kneel or stand. Here an "oremus" was sung, there an elevation tinkled, while others were beating their breasts at communion. In short it was a holy chaos, which disturbed every truly pious soul. For a few years now, more propriety, majesty, seriousness, calm, and order have reigned in Viennese churches. All the silly plunder of the confraternities has been thrown out, the statues relieved of their wigs and coats, and instead of the profane vows crowed sweetly down from above—

often a chorus from an opera buffa changed into a Sanctus—popular songs in German have been introduced.[21]

Nicolai did not agree that the German hymns represented an improvement. To him they were monotonous and overornamented, and lacked the power of Protestant hymns to raise up the hearts of the congregation. He was not the only one to complain that the texts were shallow and the tunes watery and insipid. Ultimately the hymns did not prevail. Vienna's grand tradition of concerted church music survived the cutbacks of the 1780s and emerged stronger than ever in the 1790s.

Theaters

SERIOUS OPERA IN ITALIAN

LUDOVICO BURNACINI built the wooden opera house "Auf der Cortina" in the palace gardens next to the Augustinian monastery in 1666. The building was destroyed by the besieged Viennese in 1683 for fear that its burning by the Turks would ignite the palace. Operatic performances were given to the end of the century in the Tanzsaal of 1631, occupying the wing of the palace that later housed the Redoutensaal. Francesco Galli-Bibiena completely remodeled the Tanzsaal as a court theater in 1698; it burned the following year, was rebuilt by the same architect, and opened in 1700.[22] This colossal exercise in decorative excess seems to have been the model for some of the theaters built by the succeeding generation of Galli-Bibienas.

Under Charles VI the Bibiena theater was used mainly to celebrate his name day (4 November) with a new opera, and in alternate years the birthday of his consort, Empress Elizabeth Christine (28 August). Near the imperial library was another hall in the same wing of the palace, called the smaller court theater, which was used for carnival operas and other events. The marriage banquet for Maria Theresa and Francis of Lorraine in 1736 took place here. In a description of Vienna published in 1770, the author says that

---

[21] Johann Pezzl, *Skizze von Wien: Ein Kultur- und Sittenbild aus der josefinischen Zeit* (Graz, 1923), p. 280. H. C. Robbins Landon, *Mozart and Vienna* (New York, 1991), includes an abridged translation of Pezzl.

[22] Franz Hadamowsky, "Barocktheater am Wiener Kaiserhof. Mit ein Spielplan (1625–1740)," *Jahrbuch der Gesellschaft für Wiener Theater-Forschung* (1951–52), pp. 37-39. For Pfeffel's engravings of the 1700 theater, see Franz Hadamowsky, *Die Familie Galli-Bibiena in Wien* (Leben und Werk für das Theater) (Vienna, 1962), plates 2–3.

the smaller hall was used for engagements, wedding banquets, and Italian plays during carnival.[23] Of the large theater, which he calls "das herrliche Hoftheater," he writes that "its decorations reached the highest degree of perfection; it was dedicated solely to serious Italian opera, which was given here usually only once a year, namely on St. Charles' Day, at the greatest expense, and performed with such magnificence, according to the reports of all connoisseurs, as Paris and London had never seen." It is unclear from this account whether the author had actually seen the Bibiena theater before its demolition.

Estimates vary as to how many spectators the Bibiena theater could accommodate. The point is a moot one in any case, since only the invited could attend; it was never a question of paying for entrance to see the spectacular entertainment on the emperor's name day. The aristocracy had their assigned places, bitterly fought over because of the prestige involved. Foreign ambassadors and visitors of high rank attended. Court servants were admitted to the worst seats.

Charles VI brought the best Italian librettists to work for his court opera. Pietro Pariati, a gifted lyric poet, came in 1714. Four years later Apostolo Zeno, whose strong dramatic librettos the emperor had admired in Spain, joined Pariati. Giovanni Pasquini was welcomed in Vienna a few years later. Zeno and Pariati worked often in collaboration. For composers they were given, besides Fux, Antonio Caldara, Giuseppe Porsile, and Francesco Conti. When Pietro Metastasio replaced Zeno as court poet in 1730, he worked regularly with Caldara, for whose music he could scarcely conceal his disdain. To a poet grown accustomed to the clear and simple melodies of a Leonardo Vinci, Caldara seemed like a throwback, and indeed he was for the most part, because the emperor would not have it otherwise. Caldara died in 1736, leaving the court opera in the less talented hands of Porsile and Luca Antonio Predieri. The collapse of the whole institution appeared imminent by the time Charles VI died in 1740.

An exclusively aristocratic art form, Viennese court opera had become as much of an anachronism as the extravagant Baroque curiosity in which it was displayed. Under Maria Theresa and Francis of Lorraine, the Bibiena theater was used one time only, for the wedding celebrations of 1744, when Archduchess Marianna, the empress' younger sister, wed Charles of Lorraine, the emperor's younger brother. Metastasio wrote *Ipermestra* for the occasion, and it was set to music by Hasse and Predieri, with ballets by Franz Hilverding accompanied by music of Ignaz Holzbauer. The Bibienas, in the persons of the brothers Giuseppe and Antonio, worked their stage

---

[23] Friedrich Weiskern, *Beschreibung der k. k. Haupt und Residenzstadt Wien* (Vienna, 1770), p. 153.

miracles for a final time as first and second theatrical engineers of the Habsburg court. A few years later they were allowed to leave the imperial service. An epoch had clearly ended. Giuseppe went on to design the court theater at Bayreuth, and Antonio the Teatro Comunale in Bologna, awakening criticisms confirming that the hour had struck for the Baroque style. But most devastating of all, the Bibiena court theater in Vienna, the mother church of latter-day Bibienesque invention, was dismantled in 1747–48 and replaced by the Redoutensaal.

By the time Burney visited Vienna in 1772, the old serious opera under Charles VI was only a distant memory. He was puzzled at the lack of opera seria. Had he met Joseph II and discussed the issue with him, Burney would have learned that ostentatious display was as much of an anathema to this prince as it had been an object of glory to his grandfather. As it was, Burney somehow divined a humanitarian purpose in the refusal to spend fortunes on opera seria. He chose to end the first volume of his *German Tour* with these remarks on Vienna:

> Rich as this city is at present, in musicians of genius and eminence, there is no serious opera either at the court or public theater. Lady Mary Wortley Montague mentions an opera that was performed in the open air, when she was at Vienna, the decorations and habits of which cost the emperor thirty thousand pounds sterling; and, during the reigns of the later emperors, from the first years of Leopold, to the middle of the present century, there used to be operas at the expense of the court, written, composed, and performed, by persons of the greatest abilities that could be assembled from all parts of Europe; but the frequent wars, and other calamities of this country, have so exhausted the public treasure, and impoverished individuals, that this expensive custom is now,
>
> "To my mind,
More honoured in the breach, than the observance,"
>
> For though I love music very well, yet I love humanity better.

Serious Italian opera had been performed more frequently in the Burgtheater than Burney realized, between 1748 and 1772, but it was mainly on an ad hoc basis; the singers were hired for a season or for a single opera but not taken into imperial service. Composers brought to Vienna on this basis included Hasse, Niccolò Jommelli, Andrea Bernasconi, Baldassare Galuppi, Tommaso Traetta, and Francesco de Majo—an impressive list, even by London standards. Several composers who were in imperial service on a regular basis also wrote opera seria as permitted by circumstances. They included Georg Christoph Wagenseil, Giuseppe Bonno, Christoph Gluck, Florian Gassmann, Giuseppe Scarlatti, and Antonio Salieri.

In 1753 the emperor decided at the last minute that an opera honoring Maria Theresa on her name day (15 October) should be composed. The choice fell on Metastasio's *La clemenza di Tito* (Maria Theresa's motto was "Justitia et Clementia"). The poet was horrified because, as he wrote to a friend, "from the extreme shortness of the time it will be miserably executed. The singers, who have been collected in eight days, are not equal to the enterprise for which they are called . . . They either consist of people unknown, or worse . . . [he names them] and Ottani, a painter, are the heroes and heroines of this festival. The composer is a certain Adolphati, a Venetian, settled at Genoa; all fruits wholly foreign to our climate."[24] The opera may not have been as bad as Metastasio feared, because it was repeated at Schönbrunn on 18 October, in the Burgtheater on 24 October in a gratis performance ordered by the emperor, again at Schönbrunn on 30 October, and two more times gratis in the Burgtheater on 10 and 14 November.

Important theaters for opera existed in the imperial residences outside Vienna; these included, besides Schönbrunn, theaters at Laxenburg and Schlosshof. The list of opera houses in Vienna should not omit the theater in La Favorita, the preferred residence of Charles VI. Among the more important private theaters was the one in the palace of Prince Auersperg, where Gluck's *Alceste* and Mozart's *Idomeneo* received performances during the Lenten season of 1786, as did Haydn's *Seven Last Words* a year later.

Opera seria was allowed to decline at the Viennese court beginning in the 1750s, although Maria Theresa still considered the genre indispensable for celebrating dynastic marriages and the like. After Joseph II became co-regent upon his father's death in 1765, there continued to be a few such operas given in the Burgtheater—Salieri's *Armida*, for example, in 1771. Joseph was proud enough of this successful work that he sent a copy of the score to his brother Leopold in Florence. As Maria Theresa withdrew more and more from court affairs during her last decade, it became apparent that Joseph II was unwilling to support any great expense for opera, which ruled out opera seria altogether. In any case, if we may believe what he wrote to his chancellor, Wenzel Anton Kaunitz, Joseph found the grand genre boring. This disposition did not prevent him from attending such operas when he visited his brothers in Italy (i.e., when he did not have to foot the expenses). The exchange of letters with Kaunitz on the subject occurred in 1781; their concern was how to entertain the grand duke and duchess of

---

[24] *Memoirs of the Life and Writing of the Abate Metastasio, in which are incorporated Translations of his Principal Letters by Charles Burney*, 3 vols. (London, 1796; reprint 1971), letter of 11 September 1753. In subsequent citations I sometimes add words or phrases from the original Italian, *Tutte le opere di Pietro Metastasio*, ed. Bruno Brunelli, 5 vols. (Milan, 1943–54).

Russia during their impending visit to Vienna. Kaunitz, a man of the old school, thought no expense should be spared and recommended importing a magnificent opera seria from Italy with three or four of the best voices then singing and the best ballet forces as well; Joseph answered from Versailles that perhaps something passable in ballet could be imported, but as to opera seria, not only was it too late to arrange something good, but the genre "was such a boring spectacle that he did not believe he would ever employ it."[25] It was left to the next emperor, Leopold II, to reintroduce the splendors of opera seria and full-length ballets to Vienna.

THE GERMAN THEATER AT THE KÄRNTNERTHOR

ONLY a decade younger than the Bibiena court theater was the building erected by the civic authorities in 1708–9 near the Kärntnerthor (Carinthian Gate) just to the east of the palace. Antonio Beduzzi was the architect. This theater witnessed all kinds of entertainment over its long history, but it is most notable for having housed improvised and regular plays in German; hence it was often called the German Theater. It underwent various kinds of managerial control in its time, with the court sometimes preponderant and sometimes the city fathers, but it was initially under the control of the latter. Burney called it the "public theater," as opposed to the "court theater" (Burgtheater). Ordinary citizens could pay their way in from the time of its opening; the aristocracy leased many boxes as well. An imperial decree of 1748 was deemed necessary to determine the proper place for each class.

Josef Anton Stranitzky was the principal of a troupe of comedians that performed at the German Theater in the early years. Stranitzky created the role of Hanswurst, a typical *Salzburger Gebirgsbauer*, and made it famous the world over. He played a central role in the quasi-improvised skits, derived from commedia dell'arte traditions, and he is looked upon as the founder of the *Alt-Wiener Volkskomödie*. There is evidence that he also introduced songs, along the lines of Parisian vaudeville comedies.[26] Succeeding him were Gottfried Prehauser, another famous Hanswurst, and Johann Joseph Felix von Kurz, called Kurz-Bernardon because of his most famous role. By an impe-

---

[25] *Joseph II, Leopold II, und Kaunitz: Ihr Briefwechsel*, ed. Adolf Beer (Vienna, 1873), p. 92; cited in John A. Rice, "Emperor and Impresario: Leopold II and the Transformation of Viennese Musical Theater, 1790–1792" (Ph.D. diss., University of California, Berkeley, 1987), pp. 254–55.

[26] Vladmir Helfert, "Zur Geschichte des Wiener Singspiels," *Zeitschrift für Musikwissenschaft* 5 (1922–23): 194–209; 198. Helfert reconstructs from Moravian sources a *Spielplan* for 1737–39. He quotes one source of 1736 that gives a good idea of a typical show: "The Comedy of Faust is a mixed bag of German and Italian, of prose and verse, of speaking and singing" (p. 201, n. 2).

rial decree of 1728, Italian opera was allowed in this theater only if intermingled with German comedies, "pure" Italian opera being reserved for the court theaters. Thus there was a forced marriage between the two types, and this helps to account for the frequent arias on Italian texts in surviving German plays and for the inclusion of Italian intermezzi in a work such as *Der neue krumme Teufel* (1759) by Kurz-Bernardon and Joseph Haydn.

As far as opera was concerned, the German Theater was always secondary in importance to the Burgtheater. Haydn never succeeded in staging an opera expressly written for the latter. In this respect he joined the company of Antonio Vivaldi, who may have supplied several operas to the Kärntnerthor Theater in the 1730s, and who was staying in lodgings just behind the theater when he died on 28 July 1741.[27] One opera given there in 1742, *L'oracolo in Messenia,* was certainly his, as attested by the annotation "La musica è del fù Sig. D. Antonio Vivaldi." The composer was buried in the Spitaller Gottesacker next to the Karlskirche (Figure 1.6).

The German Theater was not as large as the great opera houses of the major Italian cities, but larger than the old Théâtre Italien in Paris, which was its equivalent in many ways. Both featured improvised plays derived from the commedia dell'arte, interlarded with Italian singing, intermezzi, and ballets. A north German visitor to Vienna in 1730 described the German Theater in glowing terms and compared it favorably with what could be heard and seen in his native land:

> In Vienna throughout the year, except during Lent and Advent, German comedies are given daily in the Kärntnerthor Theater, except Fridays, which, because they are fast days, are passed more quietly and better than Sundays. The shows are given at the cost, and under the direction of Borosini, a court musician, who has put the theater on a different footing from before; the theater is not only large, broad, well lit, and well provided as to decorations and proper stage sets, but also the actors are good for the most part, and have uncommonly costly and pretty costumes, all provided by Borosini. There appear also on the stage several good dancers, male and female, who occasionally dance a ballet, but not as well as the French. The orchestra is staffed with good musicians, and all is arranged so that its like is hardly to be found in Germany.[28]

Francesco Borosini was a court singer who ran the theater under contract together with Charles Selliers, one of the court dancers.

[27] Carl F. Panagle, "Bilddokumente zu Vivaldis Tod in Wien," *Informazioni e Studi Vivaldiani* 6 (1985): 111–27.

[28] Johann Basilii Küchelbecker, *Allerneuster Nachricht vom Römisch-Kayserl. Hof* (Hannover, 1730), part I, p. 383, cited in Robert Haas, "Die Musik in der Wiener deutschen Stegreifkomödie," *Studien zur Musikwissenschaft* 12 (1925): 3–64; 21.

FIGURE 1.6. Salomon Kleiner. The Karlskirche and adjoining graveyard.

The introduction of regular spoken dramas at the Kärntnerthor Theater in 1747 has been called one of the two most important theatrical events of the century in Vienna (the other being Gluck's operatic reform in the Burgtheater).[29] Carlo Goldoni's imposition of written texts upon the improvised theater at Venice occurred at about the same time.

The court was behind the efforts to install regular German comedy in an attempt to lure the public away from its attachment to "Hanswurstiads" and "Bernardoniads." But imperial edicts and decrees seem to have had very little effect on what was a long and slow process of maturation, and very little effect either on the vulgarity of language and gesture. Maria Theresa forbade improvised comedies in 1753. She had been offended by an indecent remark Bernardon had uttered onstage in her august presence, which got him temporarily banished. Emperor Francis, on the other hand, enjoyed the free-for-all style of the quasi-improvised comedies in German, although he was also, as might be expected because of his upbringing, even more partial

[29] Gustav Zechmeister, *Die Wiener Theater nächst der Burg und nächst dem Kärntnerthor von 1747 bis 1776* (Theatergeschichte Österreichs, 2: 2) (Vienna, 1971), p. 22.

to the offerings of the French troupe. By the end of the 1750s the actor-playwright Friedrich Wilhelm Weiskern and his regular comedies, along with those of Philip Hafner, had begun to prevail over Kurz-Bernardon, who left Vienna in 1760 to tour various cities. As Johann Müller, another actor of the German Theater, explained it, "Bernardon attracted great crowds at first out of curiosity, and created as great a disappointment subsequently; he disappeared after a while, leaving the field free to actors who behaved properly."[30]

Viennese taste for the older type of comedy did not change as much or as quickly as Müller would have his readers believe. Leopold Mozart observed that the traditional fare still retained its hold in a letter from Vienna to his landlord in Salzburg, Lorenz Hagenauer, written from 30 January to 4 February 1768. "As to genres, the Viennese are not curious to see serious and rational things, of which they have little or no concept. They like nothing but foolish tricks, dancing, devils, spirits, magical spells, Hanswurst, Lipperl, Bernardon, witches, and apparitions—this is well known and their theater shows it every day." After this tirade Leopold comments on audience behavior: "A gentleman, even one decorated with the band of an order, claps his hands at the foolery of Hanswurst or simple-minded pranks, and laughs until he is out of breath. But in the serious scenes, or at touching and beautiful actions onstage, and the most sensible ways of speaking, he talks in a loud voice to his lady, so that honorable people cannot understand a word." Here Leopold is lording it over Vienna and Salzburg as an enlightened traveler who has seen the best that London and Paris had to offer in the way of theater. Like father, like son: twenty-three years later Wolfgang would echo Leopold's comments in a letter written on 9 October 1791, in which he reproves a bumptious spectator for laughing through the most solemn scenes of *Die Zauberflöte*.

The German Theater burned down on 3 November 1761, after a performance of *Don Juan* (not to be confused with Gluck's ballet on the same subject then being shown at the Burgtheater).[31] Throughout 1762 the German and French companies had to play alternately in the Burgtheater. By mid-1763 the German Theater had been completely rebuilt and somewhat enlarged; Nicolà Pacassi was the architect in charge. In its restored form it was the most modern theater in Vienna.

Burney described the Kärntnerthor Theater a decade later, after a perfor-

[30]Johann Heinrich Friedrich Müller, *Genaue Nachrichten von beyden kaiserlich-königlichen Schaubühnen und andern öffentlichen Ergötzlichkeiten in Wien* (Vienna, 1772), p. 18. Müller provides a *Spielplan* for the German troupe from the reopening of their theater (9 July 1763).
[31]For a specimen of the printed text of the songs in this German *Don Juan*, see H. C. Robbins Landon, *Haydn: Chronicle and Works* 5 vols. (Bloomington, Ind., 1976–80), 1: 244.

mance on 30 August 1772. He had mistakenly thought that he was going to the opera house: "I hoped, however, that there would be singing in this piece, but was wholly disappointed; it was a Trauerspiel, by Gotthold Ephraim Lessing, called Emilia Galotti." Burney has interesting things to say of the play and his reactions to it, even while admitting that his German was then "so young" that he could only catch the meaning now and then. His remarks on the coarseness of the language are less a result of his own perceptions than of reading Lady Mary Wortley Montague's description of the same theater in 1716, which he quotes: "I could not easily pardon the liberty the poet has taken of larding his play with not only indecent expressions, but with such gross words, as I don't think our mob would suffer from a mountebank; besides the two Sofias very fairly let down their breeches, in the direct view of the boxes, which were full of people of the first rank, who seemed well pleased with their entertainment, and assured me, this was a celebrated piece."

Burney's practiced eye for theaters took in more than his ears could of Lessing's play:

> This theatre is lofty, having five or six rows of boxes, twenty-four in each row. The height makes it seem short, yet, at the first glance it is very striking; it does not appear to have been very lately painted, and looks dark; but the scenes and decorations are splendid. The stage had the appearance of being oval, which, whether it was produced by deception or reality, had a pleasing effect, as it corresponded with the other end of the theatre, which was rounded off at the corners, and gave an elegant look to the whole.

A diagram of the theater dated 1748 confirms the accuracy of Burney's observations (Figure 1.7). Note that the orchestra, designated by the letter K, did not occupy the whole width of the stage. The large imperial box, designated B, was connected by a special passageway through the ramparts directly to the palace. Mozart referred to this box in his letter of 24 March 1781 to his father: "I would not have played a concerto but a solo on the beautiful Stein pianoforte of Countess Thun, because the emperor occupies the loge under the proscenium."

Had Burney come to Vienna four years later, he would have found the German players and singers installed in the Burgtheater, as a result of the consolidation Joseph II made in 1776, which was presented to the world under the unlikely rubric "National Theater." After this point the Kärntnerthor Theater saw only sporadic use, mainly for concerts and visiting troupes. But *Volkskomödie* of the old improvised stripe did not die out in Vienna, although banished from the imperial theaters. After wandering around a few temporary stages, Hanswurst and his companions found a

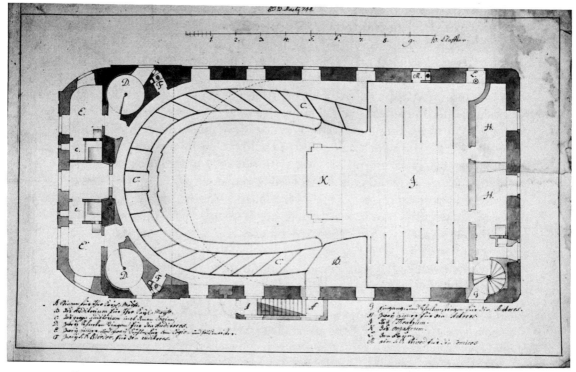

FIGURE 1.7. Floor plan of the Kärntnerthor Theater, 1748.

home in several suburban theaters constructed in the 1780s, one of the consequences of Joseph II's *Theaterfreiheit*. These included the Marinelli or Leopoldstadter Theater, built in the garden of the Czernin palace (1781), the theaters in the districts of Mariahilf (1783), Josephstadt (1788), and Landstrasse (1789), and, most famous of all, the Theater auf der Wieden (1787), which would see the first production of *Die Zauberflöte* in 1791.

Burney also describes the quality of the music heard in the German Theater on 30 August: "The orchestra has a numerous band, and the pieces which were played for the overture and the act-tunes, were very well performed, and had an admirable effect; they were composed by Haydn, Hoffman, and Vanhall." This testimony is very valuable when combined with other evidence. A personnel list of December 1775 for the "Orchestra tedesca" confirms that the band was strong: thirteen violins; three violas; two cellos; three basses; one flute; two oboes; two horns; two bassoons.[32] The parallel list for the "Orchestra francese" (Burgtheater) shows it at similar

[32] Reproduced in facsimile in Zechmeister, *Die Wiener Theater*, p. 357; on the previous page is a payment list for both orchestras from 1773.

strength. Wenzl Pichl, copyist and violinist in the German Theater from April 1774 to February 1775, copied the parts of twelve symphonies by Ditters, three by Haydn, two by Gassmann, and one each by Christian Bach and Gaetano Pugnani, as well as twelve of his own composition.[33] At the performance of Jean-François Regnard's *Le distrait* in a German translation on 6 January 1776, the audience heard between each act "a new analogous symphony which was specially written for this play by the famous Joseph Haydn." The music became Haydn's Symphony No. 60.

Two examples illustrate the use of the German Theater for opera after 1776. Nicolai describes seeing there a poor performance of Gluck's *Orphée et Euridice* given by a visiting French company on 30 June 1781. Le Petit sang Orpheus, and Mme Giorgi-Banti, Eurydice. The audience vociferated its displeasure. Four years later Joseph II wished to hear the celebrated castrato Luigi Marchesi, who was passing through Vienna. A performance of Marchesi's favorite opera seria, *Giulio Sabino* set by Giuseppi Sarti, was arranged, with the longtime Viennese favorite Catarina Cavalieri as prima donna. Since the Burgtheater was fully booked with its alternating German plays and Italian comic operas, the production was staged in the Kärntnerthor Theater. It was a success with the public and the sovereign, who gave Marchesi 600 Kremnitzer ducats and a gold ring; the total receipts of over 10,000 gulden for six performances were distributed to the other singers and orchestra members.[34]

THE FRENCH THEATER, OR BURGTHEATER

WITH the change in regime in 1740, the need was felt for an intimate playhouse near the center of the palace, a theater directly responsible to the crown, where events important to the imperial family could be celebrated. The Bibiena theater was scarcely intimate. Moreover, its overripe Baroque style did not suit the tastes of the new rulers, particularly Emperor Francis, who was the guiding force behind the efforts that led eventually to the edifice of the Burgtheater and to the theaters in the Rococo style at Schönbrunn and Laxenburg, which were also small by Baroque standards of grandeur. A tennis court in a small wooden building adjacent to the Riding School was

[33] Ibid., p. 372.

[34] This is according to Johann Müller, who was then director of the German troupe, in *J. H. F. Müllers Abschied von der k. k. Hof und National-Schaubühne* (Vienna, 1802), pp. 7–8. A rather poor engraving by J. V. Schueller, showing the two principals from this Viennese production surrounded by their weeping children, is reproduced in *Venezia e il melodrama nel settecento*, ed. Maria Teresa Muraro (Florence, 1978), fig. 8 following p. 32.

selected as the site of the new palace theater. Friedrich Weiskern prepared the plan, which was based on the imperial directive of 1741 to convert the tennis court "into an opera and playhouse . . . with a stage and orchestra space, auditorium and galleries; two royal boxes are to be installed but not others." Six years later a more thoroughgoing rebuilding was ordered so that "it would assume the proper form of a theater like others, with a proscenium decorated as beautifully as possible insofar as the space allows, as well as the necessary acoustical chambers over the frontispiece and the proscenium, and then over the orchestra, so that both the voices of the singing personnel and instrumental music may be heard more clearly."[35]

Nicolas Jadot, an architect who followed Emperor Francis from Lorraine, designed the Burgtheater. The old tennis-court space became the auditorium; an area just as large was now projected out into the Michaelerplatz for the stage house. The building became higher as well as wider. Its plain and handsome façade, with just a few slight curves matching similar ones inside the building, was finished only in 1759. Carl Schütz made an engraving in 1783 for Artaria, showing on the left the Michaelerkirche, the street leading down past the Riding School, and at right the modestly (and perfectly) proportioned Burgtheater (Figure 1.8). The old printed description accompanying this engraving says of the Burgtheater, "sa décoration est simple, mais de bon goût," whereas the Riding School is spoken of in terms of "ce goût sublime." There is an obvious conflict of generations here, Fischer von Erlach's Riding School for Charles VI being challenged like Goliath by David. For the interior of the theater many floor plans and decorative sketches survive, as well as Bellotto's detailed drawing of the orchestra and stage, showing a performance of Joseph Starzer's pantomime ballet *Le Turc généreux*, which was engraved in 1759. (See Figure 2.8.) Although it was a court theater, the Burgtheater was also open to the paying public of any class, one of Maria Theresa's major departures from the policies of her father.

The new theater became known as the French Theater, mostly because of the tenure of a troupe of French players called to Vienna in 1752 and resident until 1765.[36] A plan was afoot to install a French troupe in the court theater at least as early as Kaunitz's *Mémoire sur l'enterprise des spectacles* of

---

[35] Daniel Heartz, "Nicolas Jadot and the Building of the Burgtheater," *Musical Quarterly* 48 (1982): 1–31, sums up the extensive literature (mostly by theater historians) on the subject and is the source of these translations (pp. 4–5). Most of the illustrations in this article were ruined in the printing. They may be consulted in the plates of *Das Burgtheater und sein Publikum*, ed. Margret Dietrich (Veröffentlichungen des Instituts für Publikumsforschung, 3) (Vienna, 1976).

[36] A new wave of French influence crested at this time in Austria. See Hans Wagner, "Der Höhepunkt des französischen Kultureinflusses in Österreich in der zweiten Hälfte des 18. Jahrhunderts," *Österreich in Geschichte und Literatur* 5 (1961): 507–17, reprinted in *Salzburg und Österreich: Aufsätze und Vorträge von Hans Wagner* (Salzburg, 1982), pp. 283–96.

FIGURE 1.8. Carl Schütz. The Burgtheater (extreme right).

1750. Kaunitz was then ambassador to Paris and already planning the alliance between France and Austria that stunned the world a few years later, after he became chancellor in 1753. His cultural politics for Vienna must be understood as only one dimension of his vaster political plan. Kaunitz found the man best qualified to achieve his aims in the person of Count Giacomo Durazzo, scion of one of the most prominent families in Genoa. Maria Theresa never fully trusted Durazzo, partly because Genoa had sided against her in the War of the Austrian Succession. But she bowed to the advice of Kaunitz in this as in most matters. Durazzo improved his standing with the empress by marrying one of her favorite court ladies, a younger sister of the countess who married Nicholas II Esterházy (this helps explain how Durazzo came to serve as a kind of theatrical consultant to the Esterházys). Misunderstandings over money and quarrels with such longtime servants of the crown as Georg Reutter eventually led to Durazzo's being relieved of his post as director of the theaters (whereupon he was given an even more lucrative post as ambassador to Venice), but not before he had made his mark on music history.

Durazzo had no French playwright worthy of the name in Vienna. The spoken part of the repertory came straight from Paris, often transmitted by his correspondent, Charles-Simon Favart. For ballets and musical comedies Durazzo could call on composers of the stature of Gluck and Starzer. Gluck, after adapting many opéras-comiques from Paris to the forces available in the Burgtheater, began by the end of the 1750s to make his own settings. Out of this milieu, and with the added resources Durazzo could command as director of both theaters, Gluck and his collaborators produced such masterpieces as *L'ivrogne corrigé* (1760), the pantomime ballet *Don Juan* (1761), and his final opéra-comique, *La rencontre imprévue* (1764). The same forces, supplemented by a great singer-actor, the castrato Gaetano Guadagni, created *Orfeo ed Euridice* to celebrate the emperor's name day in 1762.

After Durazzo was dismissed as director in 1764, the French troupe continued to exist for more than a year. It was not finally dissolved until the sudden death of Emperor Francis in August 1765, when the court was visiting Innsbruck. The empress, in deep mourning for the remaining fifteen years of her life, had little to do with the theater after this point and scarcely ever attended a performance. Joseph II, now co-regent, trod an uncertain path around the eternal question of how to maintain a theatrical life worthy of a capital without exhausting the imperial revenues. Kaunitz and the nobles clamored for French plays. As a result, a second troupe of French players was duly installed in the Burgtheater in 1767.

The Mozarts ran up against the second French troupe when they were in Vienna in 1767–68. Leopold Mozart blamed the players and the expenses they required for the debacle of his son's *La finta semplice* (K. 51), composed for the Burgtheater but not performed. In a long letter of 30 July 1768 to his landlord Hagenauer, Leopold explained:

> You must wonder why Prince Kaunitz and other grandees, or even the emperor himself, does not simply order the opera to be performed. In the first place they cannot order it, because it is the business of Signor Affligio, whom some call Count Affligio. Secondly, they might order him to do it at some other time. But, since Prince Kaunitz advised Affligio, against the will of His Majesty, to import French comedians at the annual cost of over 70,000 gulden, they are now ruining him because they are not drawing the crowds hoped for. Affligio is blaming Prince Kaunitz, who is trying to move the emperor to take an interest in the French troupe and thus help defray Affligio's expenses. His Majesty has not allowed himself to be seen in the theater for many weeks . . . No one wishes to address Affligio with a sharp and commanding tone for fear he will demand his 70,000 gulden back.

If Leopold is right, his account goes some way to explain why *La finta semplice* was not performed. Mozart's first opera was composed at a time when there was an ongoing quarrel between Kaunitz and Joseph about the running of the theaters. The French players, it should be added, had many partisans besides Kaunitz. Their ballet master was no one less than Jean-Georges Noverre. Joseph von Sonnenfels, although mainly a supporter of drama in German, wrote an ecstatic review dated 8 May 1768 in praise of D'Ausfresne's acting in Voltaire's tragedy *Adelaide du Guescelin.*[37] The troupe lasted in Vienna for five years, giving its last show on 27 February 1772.

A third French troupe took up residence in 1775–76, led by Hamon, and specializing in Parisian opéra-comique. All in all, it is easy to understand why, at the time, people continued to call the Burgtheater the French Theater. In addition to everything else, its architecture and decor looked French.

Ballet was an indispensable component of the entertainment in both the French and German Theaters, but it loomed especially large in the former. As far back as the reign of Leopold I, the professional dancers in Vienna were mostly French, or French-trained. Joseph Selliers, ninth court dancer in 1734, was then theater director at the Kärntnerthor and subsequently at the Burgtheater (1741–48); he claimed credit for studying "die Ballettkomponierung" for two years in Paris under Houdé and Pécour. Franz Hilverding requested a place as court dancer in 1734 "in reward for his abilities, gained by two years study with renowned masters at Paris."[38] Hilverding was a central figure in Viennese ballet. He raised standards and created an increasingly complicated type of pantomime ballet that was not just an adjunct to operas and plays, but an art form in itself. Under these circumstances composers especially devoted to ballet began to appear in Vienna. Joseph Starzer served as "compositeur des airs pour les Ballets" for the French company from 1752 to 1758. Starzer, Ignaz Holzbauer, and Florian Deller were called to positions elsewhere on the strength of their reputations as ballet composers in the Viennese theaters. Madame Louise Bodin-Joffroi was the great strength of the first French troupe and the delight of Vienna from her appointment in 1753. She was at once dancer, singer, and actress, like Madame Favart, whose roles she successfully filled.

When Burney arrived in the late summer of 1772 after the second French troupe had been dismissed, he found in the Burgtheater an alternation of Italian operas and German plays, with ballets under the direction of Noverre:

> The second evening after my arrival, I went to the French theatre, where I saw a German comedy, or rather a farce of five acts: however, I should not have supposed the piece to be without merit, as the natives seemed much pleased with it. This theatre is not so high as that at which I had been the night before,

[37] Zechmeister, *Die Wiener Theater*, p. 68.
[38] Hadamowsky, "Barocktheater am Wiener Kaiserhof," p. 65.

but it is still better fitted up; here the best places seem to be in the pit, which is divided into two parts, and all the seats are stuffed, and covered with red baize; the scenes were seldom changed during the piece; but the principal, that is, the scene of longest continuance, was flat in front, where there were two large folding doors, as in the French theatres, for the entrance and exit of the principal characters. At each side there was an elegant projection, in the middle of which there was likewise a door, used chiefly by the servants, and inferior characters. The comedy was often too grossly farcical; but there were scenes, as well as characters, of real humor, and one or two of the *Comedie larmoyante* kind, that were truly pathetic.

We lack a repertory for the Burgtheater in September 1772 and are unable to identify this play.

Burney continues:

> The orchestra here was full as striking as that of the other theatre, and the pieces played were admirable. They were so full of invention, that it seemed to be music of some other world, insomuch, that hardly a passage in this was to be traced; and yet all was natural, and equally free from the stiffness of labour, and the pedantry of hard study. Whose music it was I could not learn; but both the composition and performance, gave me exquisite pleasure.
>
> At the end of the play, there was a very spirited and entertaining dance, planned by the celebrated ballet-master, M. Noverre, in which four principal performers displayed great abilities, in point of grace, activity, and precision.
>
> Three large boxes are taken out of the front of the first row, for the imperial family, which goes frequently to this theatre; it was built by Charles the sixth [actually Francis I]. The Empress-queen, according to imperial *Etiquette*, continues in weeds, and has appeared in no public theatre since the death of the late emperor.[39]

A drawing of the first two floors of the Burgtheater, from around 1780 (Figure 1.9), shows that there were only four loges on the left side of the ground floor; note also the passage on this side into the "Parterre noble" and into the "Orchester." One level above was the choicest spot for box holders. The "Hof Loge" to the right consisted of two boxes next to the orchestra (not three, as Burney claimed; he mistakenly included the "Director-Loge" along with the two for the imperial family). The subscribers of the boxes numbered 1, 2, and 3 on the left side of the stage and orchestra, facing the imperial

---

[39] Not true: she surprised everyone by appearing on 16 March 1768 in the imperial box at the Burgtheater to announce that a son had just been born to the rulers of Tuscany—the future emperor Francis II—and in 1770 she could not resist enjoying the bourgeois familial virtues portrayed in Diderot's first play, given in Lessing's translation as *Der Hausvater*.

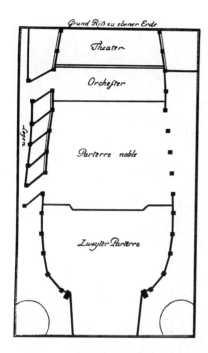
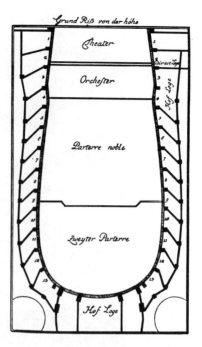

FIGURE 1.9. Floor plan of the parterre and first tier of boxes in the Burgtheater, 1780s.

boxes, for the season 1774–75 were (1) Prince Liechtenstein, (2) Prince Esterházy, and (3) Prince Kaunitz.[40] Twelve years earlier, in 1762, the situation was not much different: Prince Liechtenstein rented boxes 1 and 2; Prince Esterházy rented box 3.[41] The sizes of the two parterres were adjustable depending on the occasion. For a German comedy on 8 January 1759, the Parterre noble was shortened so that there would be more room for commoners in the second parterre. This created trouble because it was deemed less than seemly that the young archdukes who usually occupied the "Gallerie noble" behind the second parterre should look at the heads of so many commoners; the solution was to move the archdukes one floor up to the Hof Loge, usually occupied by the court ladies, and to give the latter the Parterre noble. (The Kärntnerthor Theater had a similar Gallerie noble in the same spot.)

Mansfeld's engraving of the Burgtheater in Richter's *Bildergalerie weltlicher Misbräuche* (1785) becomes more valuable when studied together with these floor plans (Figure 1.10). It is the best testimony we have about the Burgtheater's interior during the 1780s. Four side wings on the stage provide

[40] Otto G. Schindler, "Das Publikum des Burgtheaters in der josephinischen Ära," in *Das Burgtheater und sein Publikum*, p. 61; the floor plans are found on p. 37.
[41] Zechmeister, *Die Wiener Theater*, facsimile on p. 39.

FIGURE 1.10. J. E.
Mansfeld. Interior
of the Burgtheater,
1785.

a very plain and nearly unornamented setting. The straight horizontal and
vertical lines on the stage act as a foil for the slight curves decorating the
four tiers of boxes—curves similar to those ornamenting the "boxes" in the
Hofkapelle, as we have seen—and for the wide-curving *panier* of the leading
lady gesturing to the man (with such a costume and feathered headdress,
she has to be a leading lady). The audience sitting or standing in the Parterre
noble shows a wide variety of costumes and attitudes. Informality seems to

reign. One of the points of Richter's satire is the excessive informality shown by the ladies in the lowest boxes, who are talking so loudly with one another as to raise a protest from the parterre.

Haydn must have mingled often with the spectators in the parterre. We know that he witnessed Mozart's operas for the Burgtheater from the correspondence both masters had with others. Artists formed a considerable part of the Burgtheater's audience. Even the Parterre noble was not confined to the noble-born (Burney implies that he sat there). People with theater passes—poets, composers, architects, painters, leading singers, players, dancers, in short all those of importance to the theater's operations—had access to the Parterre noble.[42]

Looking back to the beginnings of the Burgtheater, we see that the opening of its doors to paying customers of whatever class, as long as they were properly clothed and properly behaved, represented a major breakthrough in the structure of Vienna's musical life. It was one thing for this to happen at the larger Kärntnerthor Theater, with its civic origins and connections, but quite another for Maria Theresa to admit the general public into the small and elegant court theater that was part of the palace itself. With this penetration of a wider public into the middle of hitherto exclusively aristocratic precincts, which could never have happened under her father, there is evident a general leveling between classes with respect to the arts. One observer of the process has gone so far as to claim that the opening of the Burgtheater to the bourgeoisie played a major factor in overcoming the artistic stagnation reached by the dynasty-glorifying operas under Charles VI.[43]

JOSEPH II'S NATIONAL THEATER

WHEN Joseph II took direct control of the theaters early in 1776, he instituted a "National Theater." For decades the two theaters offered the Viennese public a wide choice of fare: German plays (with lots of incidental music); French plays and light operas; Italian comic opera and occasionally Italian serious opera as well; large-scale ballets, as well as ballet inserts in the other genres. The variety seemed appropriate to the cosmopolitan capital of a multi-ethnic and polyglot empire. It was especially appropriate to Vienna's aspirations to be viewed as a European capital second to none. Joseph's reform of the theaters in 1776 eliminated everything but the plays in German; the result was a "national" theater in the restrictive sense (as

[42] Schindler, "Das Publikum des Burgtheaters," p. 47.
[43] Wolfgang Greisenegger, "The Italian Opera in Vienna in the XVIIIth Century," *Venezia e il melo-dramma nel settecento* (Florence, 1978), pp. 89–101.

opposed to a multinational one). From this radical surgery sprang the potential for a new kind of Viennese Singspiel. Ignaz Umlauf's *Die Bergknappen* inaugurated it in 1778. Finances had more to do with the shake-up than did any aesthetic or political notions. The paying customers were hoping that in the end they would have to pay less for what cost much less to produce; they were disappointed, and some made their complaints public.[44]

Perhaps the shocking upheaval of 1776 in Viennese theatrical life could have been predicted by the discrepancy between what the orchestra players were paid in the two theaters according to the personnel lists of 1773–74, cited above: the "Orchestra tedesca" cost 5,270 florins, while the "Orchestra francese," although playing on fewer occasions, required an annual sum of 9,470 florins. When the emperor decided to take the theater direction into his own hands, he facilitated this action by forcing the previous director into bankruptcy.[45] He dismissed the mixed company in the Burgtheater—singers, dancers, orchestral musicians, and everyone else—then installed the German company in their place. Those dismissed were promised three months' wages only, at some future time, and then on condition that the money was available to pay them. There had been talk during the theatrical crises that took place under Durazzo in the late 1750s about reducing expenses by supporting just one troupe. Somehow Maria Theresa had managed to surmount those troubled times without drastic cuts. Had she not, it is difficult to imagine her taking such draconian measures as her son did now. Her retreat from theatrical matters was not total, for she still looked into matters touching morals and kept a finger on the purse strings.[46] But it is clear from the praise and blame subsequently heaped on Joseph II that he alone was behind the massive reform of 1776.

Chaos was bound to follow in the wake of such a major shift. What to do with the no-longer-occupied Kärntnerthor Theater was a problem that admitted no easy solution. It was made available to visiting troupes as a part of Joseph's policy of *Theaterfreiheit*. Even the Burgtheater was declared open when not in use by the German company. The problems that arose from such a reckless policy can easily be imagined. Embarrassing moments must have occurred also with respect to at least some of the most talented artists who were dismissed. Take the case of Joseph Weigl, Haydn's friend and

[44] Schindler, "Das Publikum des Burgtheaters," p. 41.

[45] Franz Hadamowsky, *Die josefinische Theaterreform und das Spieljahr 1776–77: Ein Dokumentation* (Quellen zur Theatergeschichte 2) (Vienna, 1978), pp. x–xvi.

[46] Ibid., p. xxii. Maria Theresa also was responsible for appointing Count Rosenberg "Musikgraf" in 1776. As for morals, she had kept a sharp eye on the theatrical troupes long before widowhood; two *danseuses* were dismissed in 1752 for becoming too familiar with the young nobles, and another was banished in 1759 "wegen übler Conduite."

Vienna's premier cellist, who had been lured from Esterházy into imperial service to become first cello in the Burgtheater. What must Prince Nicolas have thought when Weigl was let go by the emperor? The cellist was more fortunate than most because he was taken into the surviving orchestra as of 1 January 1777, albeit at a reduced salary.

The payment records for 1776–77 reveal much else besides the names and wages of orchestra members.[47] Antonio Salieri was one of those associated with the disbanded troupe who were kept on salary, and so was Joseph Starzer (for the composition of ballet music). Franz Asplmayr was paid 51 florins 12 kreutzer for the composition of twelve symphonies. Extra musicians from the military establishment were paid for appearing in *Die drei Sultaninnen* (i.e., Favart's *Soliman Second ou Les trois sultanes* in translation). (Given the Turkish subject, this may indicate that the work featured Janissary music.) An extra harpist was also employed for the same spectacle. Intriguing are the references to city musicians:

> Eder, Jakob, Stadt Musico und comp. für 6 Köpfe beym teutschen Schauspiel: Die schöne Wienerin den 18. Julii 1776
> 3 florins 24 kreutzer

> Huber, Bangrazio, für 4 Stadt Musicos beym do do *[Die schöne Wienerin]* den 31 Julii 1776
> 4 florins

We shall meet Pancrazio Huber and the civic musicians again in connection with the carnival balls given in the Redoutensaal. Most of the payments listed to extra musicians went to those from military bands, and sometimes the instruments are named; e.g., "4 Waldhornisten" on 25 and 28 January 1777, and the same again on 11 February. For one rehearsal and two performances of *Der Fuchs in der Falle* on 23–24 November 1776, Jacob Skinner was paid the considerable sum of 21 florins for two trumpeters, one timpanist, two horn players, and two bassoonists. Trumpets and drums were still officially outlawed at this time, except in special circumstances, but the theater orchestra evidently got around this stricture. The biggest sum of all in the category of miscellaneous musical expenses went to a horn maker for three instruments "together with their crooks and tuning devices."

> Stärzer, Carl, Waldhornmacher für 3 P: Horn samt dazu gehörigen Bögen und Stöckeln zu Stimmen aller Thonen
> 114 florins 24 kreutzer

---

[47] Documentation for all the subsequent items in this and the following paragraph is given by Hadamowsky, *Die josefinische Theaterreform*.

It was typical for the time that orchestral instruments were owned by the patron, in this case the theater, not the individual. And finally, the records for 1776–77 reveal that a copyist was paid for six symphonies by the defunct Florian Gassmann, twelve by Asplmayr, and two by Johann Baptist Vanhal.

Joseph II was praised in some quarters for his National Theater as if he were a German patriot, which was probably the last thing he had in mind. He warmed to this role somewhat, but when the experiment went sour, as did so many of his reforms, the tide of opinion turned against him. In fact the German troupe did not possess an abundance of creative talent at the time. Much of what it played was mere translation or adaptation from the French. The repertory is mostly forgotten, and might be entirely so were it nor for the musical wing added in 1778, leading eventually to that most genial product of the whole movement, *Die Entführung aus dem Serail* (1782), adapted for Mozart from earlier librettos by Stephanie the Younger. Even this was not enough to keep the Viennese from wanting the return of opera buffa. By installing an excellent buffo company alongside the German troupe in 1783, the emperor was in reality admitting the limitations of the latter. Johann Pezzl, writing later in the same decade, put the matter succinctly: "The National Theater in German sufficed by itself for a while. Soon one became bored with so much sameness and the emperor, who well under- stood the restless curiosity of his Viennese subjects, restored Italian opera, or rather Italian comic opera, in 1783. It is still the reigning form."

Nicolai observed that the two companies shared the same theater, but the Italians won most of the plaudits. Archduke Leopold wrote from Vienna in July 1784 that the audience for German plays was very small. Sonnenfels complained bitterly about the emperor's lack of support for the German troupe in the same year, only months after the buffo troupe starring Fran- cesco Benucci began its epochal stint in Vienna.[48] German drama of the high- minded, literary type was not destined to bloom in Vienna under Joseph II. It might have been different had the emperor retained Lessing, who visited Vienna in 1775 and would have liked the post of theater director.[49] Similarly, during the previous reign, the greatest German literary figures, including Johann Christoph Gottsched (1749) and Friedrich Gottlieb Klopstock (1768), had come to Vienna and left empty-handed. The quasi-improvised Viennese folk comedy enjoyed a phenomenal flowering, on the other hand, thanks to Joseph's *Theaterfreiheit* of 1776, which allowed the several suburban theaters to emerge during the last decade of his reign.

[48] Preface to "Briefe über die wienerische Schaubühne" (1767–68) in *Sonnenfels gesammelte Schriften* (Vienna, 1784), vol. 5.
[49] Herbert Zeman, "Die österreichische Literatur im Aufbruch—1740 bis 1780," in *Maria Theresia und ihre Zeit* (Salzburg and Vienna, 1979), p. 371.

What the theatrical world of Vienna was like at the turn of the century is conveyed in very lively fashion by the diaries of Joseph Carl Rosenbaum, an accountant in Esterházy service who was well acquainted with Haydn. The lover and later husband of an imperial court soprano, Therese Gassmann, Rosenbaum was in privileged position with respect to the theaters. He took advantage of this fact, even hopping from one theater to another, as this entry for 1 March 1798 shows:

> To the Burgtheater where the *Bruderzwist* [play by Kotzebue] was on . . . We stayed for one act at the Burgtheater, in the stalls. Then we went to the Kärntner Thor, where *Contadina di spirito* [opera by Paisiello] and the ballet *Nina* [with music based on Dalayrac's *Nina*] were given. The audience at the Burgtheater was terribly noisy; even the actors could not understand each other. It was quieter at the Kärntner Thor.[50]

The shake-up effected by Joseph's National Theater, whereby the traditional fare offered by the two stages was reversed, is still in evidence here.

Concerts

INCIPIENT MUSICAL ACADEMIES

MUSICAL academies, or concerts, might be assumed to have taken hold in Vienna under Charles VI, if only because so much else about the court music was patterned on Italian practices. Yet, in the absence of evidence that this was the case, and in the light of hints that academies were still considered novel even in the 1750s, their beginnings may be placed under Maria Theresa. On 6 March 1745 an announcement in the official newspaper of the court, the *Wiener Diarium* (founded in 1703), alerted the public to a novelty that would take place the next day in the makeshift tennis-court theater next to the palace: "The public is hereby informed that on this coming Sunday at precisely 6:30 P.M. the Academy of various vocal and instrumental music will be held for the first time in the privileged royal theater next to the Burg."[51] Further concert dates would be announced, continued the bulletin, but they were not, at least not in the *Wiener Diarium*. The expression "for the

---

[50] *Haydn Yearbook*, vol. 5: *The Diaries of Joseph Carl Rosenbaum, 1770–1829*, ed. E. Radant (Vienna, 1968), p. 35.
[51] Helga Scholz-Michelitsch, *Georg Christoph Wagenseil* (Vienna, 1982), p. 19. See also Zechmeister, *Die Wiener Theater*, pp. 233ff.

first time" need not mean the first time in Vienna, but could mean the first time in the new theater or merely the first time during this particular Lenten season. Lenten concerts are known to have taken place in the Burgtheater in 1747.

After the remodeling in 1748, when pains were taken to make the theater as acoustically perfect as possible ("so that both voices and instruments sounded well"), the situation was ripe for Vienna to initiate a series such as Paris enjoyed with its Concert Spirituel. But specific documentation is lacking for the years close to 1750. Ditters speaks of visits of the violinist Domenico Ferrari to Vienna around this time, and in a context suggesting he was playing violin concertos in public: "He was greatly admired and handsomely treated, not only by the Imperial Court and by the managers of theatres, but also by amateurs." Ferrari made his debut at the Concert Spirituel in 1754.

Thanks to Ditters, we know something about the Friday evening concerts given by Prince Hildburghausen throughout the 1750s in the Palais Rofrano (later called the Palais Auersperg). (See Figure 6.4.) They were under the direction of Giuseppe Bonno and the leading soprano was Vittoria Tesi-Tramontini; both were imperial musicians. Other singers and orchestra players included Mlle. Heinisch, soprano; Joseph Fribert, tenor; Johann Conrad Gretsch, cellist; Johann Schmid, oboe; Tüner [Timmer], bassoon; and the two Hubaczeks on the French horn. Giuseppe Trani was first violin, and besides Ditters, the other violinists included his older brother Joseph and his younger brother Alexander. Nearly all these musicians appeared on the rolls of the Burgtheater after 1761, when the prince's orchestra disbanded. Both Schmid and Gretsch, along with Ditters, were destined to play solo concertos in the Burgtheater during the early 1760s. The prince's concerts began, following the usual Italian practice, with a symphony: "We had hardly finished tuning," says Ditters on the occasion he joined this band, "and were about to begin a symphony of Jommelli's which I knew already, when the Court composer, Bonno, stepped into the room. He had a yearly salary from the Prince for directing the grand concerts at Vienna, which were given all through the winter to the Austrian nobility." Ditters concludes, "Our Academies were acknowledged to be the best in all Vienna."

With respect to virtuosi visiting from elsewhere, the prince's concerts certainly excelled those given in the Burgtheater. Ditters lists musicians that outranked those claimed for the Burgtheater in the printed *Répertoire* of 1757, to be considered shortly.

> Whenever any *virtuoso,* singer, or player came to Vienna, and deservedly succeeded in winning the applause of the public, Bonno was ordered to arrange the terms, and to secure him for the Prince. The result was, that we had Gabrieli

[Caterina Gabrielli], Guarducci, Mansoli [Manzuoli], as singers; Pugnani and Van Maldere, on the violin; Besozzi on the oboe; Le Claire on the flute; Stamitz and Leutgeb as soloists on the horn; and other eminent players.

The natural vehicle for the instrumental soloists would have been concertos, just as the singers had their display arias. A hornist named Franz Stamitz or Steinmetz played concertos at the Parisian Concert Spirituel in 1754 and 1757. Joseph Leutgeb, recipient of Mozart's four horn concertos, played in the Burgtheater orchestra in 1762 and was also a frequent soloist, as we shall see.

Great singers constituted the mainstay of the Lenten concerts in the Burg-theater. They probably displayed nearly as many feathers and furbelows as they did when playing kings and queens on the same stage. This was only appropriate, since the singers continued to sing their favorite operatic arias, while the spiritual function of such concerts was left mainly to the chorus. (Recall Richter's satire on the opera singers performing in church during Lent.) If operatic fashions pervaded even the churches, and during the most austere liturgical seasons, they would have disturbed a Burgtheater concert even less. In sum, Lenten concerts in Vienna were neither the musical nor visual equivalent of sackcloth and ashes or a hairshirt.

An announcement in the *Wiener Diarium* on 18 February 1750 stipulated that "since all drama and comedy is suspended for the holy period of Lent, three concerts a week (Sunday, Tuesday and Thursday) will be held in the imperial Burgtheater for the enjoyment of the high nobility and the pub-lic."[52] Yet court chamberlain Khevenhüller describes a series of concerts beginning on 16 February 1755 in a way that makes them sound as if they were still regarded as a novelty:

> Today in the Burgtheater there took place the first concert, or so-called Acadé-mie de musique, which will be continued on all Sundays, Tuesdays and Thurs-days. This Lenten spectacle lasts from six to nine o'clock and an entry fee is paid. Anyone is allowed entrance. The theater was handsomely arranged and well lit. In order to attract people Count Durazzo (who heads this department now) invited foreign voices—among them a certain Signora Gabrieli, *detta la chochetta, bella voce di soprano*—and produced different varieties of choruses, ora-torios, psalms, arias and duets, which attracted a numerous audience.[53]

---

[52] Mary Sue Morrow, *Concert Life in Haydn's Vienna: Aspects of a Developing Musical and Societal Institu-tion* (Stuyvesant, N.Y., 1989), p. 39.
[53] Rudolf Graf Khevenhüller-Metsch and Hanns Schlitter, eds., *Aus der Zeit Maria Theresias: Tagebuch des Fürsten Johann Joseph Khevenhüller-Metsch, kaiserlichen Obersthofmeisters 1742–1776*, 7 vols. (Vienna, 1907–25). Entries will be cited by date only.

In years just previous to 1755 Khevenhüller did not mention any such concerts. He confirms that they took place in the Burgtheater during the Lenten seasons of 1756, 1757, and 1758, always on a thrice-weekly basis. But in 1759 the financial drain of the war caused their cancellation. Prince Trautsohn stepped into the breach by offering Lenten concerts thrice weekly at his palace. For the entrance fee of one gulden, according to Khevenhüller, patrons received illuminations as well as refreshments and a variety of musical fare. The emperor attended a few times, and the empress permitted the court ladies to attend. Prince Hildburghausen made up for the lack of oratorio by staging Metastasio's *Isaaco* (set to music by Bonno) in his palace on 18 March 1759. Both sovereigns attended this performance.

Scenic effects were an important part of the Burgtheater concerts. Metastasio reported to Prince Trivulzi in Milan, in a letter of February 1755: "The numerous orchestra and many choral singers are raised on the stage by well-placed and carefully graduated platforms ["scalini"] and surrounded by beautiful scenery." The stage was probably foreshortened by the scenic backing so as to project the sound into the auditorium with maximum effect. At a similar concert series in Milan some twenty years later, and obviously in imitation of Vienna, the stage is described as being backed so as to resemble a handsome but shallow salon, brilliantly illuminated, before which the musicians formed two rows across the length of the stage.[54] When Metastasio says "surrounded by beautiful scenery" he may mean just that. In the best depiction we have of a festive concert from the mid-century, Giovanni Pannini's painting of Jommelli directing his cantata for the marriage of the dauphin to the princess royal of Saxony in 1747, in the Teatro Argentina, Rome, puffy clouds swirl around the soloists, and the scenic effect of the whole obviously played a role as important as the words and the music.[55] Metastasio says further about the Lenten academies of 1755 in the Burgtheater, "The parterre was divided into three planes in the form of an artful cascade of water." He surely does not mean the parterre as a whole, the front section of which, the Parterre noble, included the choicest seats in the house, but the part of it next to the stage where the orchestra was located during operatic performances (the "pit," to use Burney's term, which also meant the whole ground floor). Pannini's painting helps us again here by

[54] Heartz, "Jadot and the Building of the Burgtheater," p. 25. The article speculates on orchestral placement for concerts in Vienna and elsewhere.

[55] The painting is reproduced in color in Marc Pincherle, *Histoire illustrée de la musique* (Paris, 1959), p. 123. On the occasion of its origin, see André Bourde, "Opera seria et scénographie: autour de deux toiles italiennes du XVIIIe siècle," in *L'opéra au XVIIIe siècle* (Marseilles and Aix, 1982), pp. 229–39. The painting was formerly claimed to represent Leonardo Vinci's cantata for the birth of the dauphin in 1729 (as in Heartz, "Jadot and the Building of the Burgtheater," pp. 23–24).

showing an artful decor representing the confluence of the Seine and the Elbe where the orchestra would normally be stationed.

During the Lenten season of 1755, on which Metastasio reports, the Burgtheater concerts included oratorios composed by Bernasconi, Wagenseil, and Jommelli, as well as choral Psalms by Gluck, Wagenseil, Nicola Porpora, and Giovanni Battista Sammartini. Adding Hasse and Galuppi to this list we arrive at the musical Pleiades dominating Vienna at mid-century. Andrea Bernasconi worked in Milan, Munich, and Venice; he wrote operas for Vienna in 1736, 1746, and 1749. Georg Christoph Wagenseil was altogether the most important musical figure in Vienna during the 1750s, and the most represented in Burgtheater concerts during the five years for which we have detailed records (1758–63). Jommelli's star shone particularly brightly in Vienna after his operatic successes in the Burgtheater in 1749. Gluck rivaled Wagenseil in local favor. Porpora had close ties with the Habsburgs, since they had ruled the Kingdom of the Two Sicilies under Charles VI, and he was the most fashionable singing teacher in Vienna, along with Bonno, around 1755, as well as the mentor of young Joseph Haydn. Sammartini comes as no surprise, as he was the main musician of Habsburg-ruled Milan, one whose symphonies and sacred music were well cultivated in Austria and Bohemia, to judge from surviving musical sources.

Lenten concerts in the Burgtheater were advertised by printed posters, as was the Concert Spirituel in Paris, which undoubtedly served as a model. As the carnival came to its end, with ever more frequent balls in the Redoutensaal (which may have involved the less important orchestral players of the court), preparations had to be completed for the academies, which were regularly announced a few days before Ash Wednesday. The theater was dark during the first few days of Lent, except for rehearsals. The first academy took place on the first Sunday of the new season, and every subsequent Tuesday, Thursday, and Sunday usually saw a concert until Holy Week brought all such activity to an end. Two or three oratorios furnished the bulk of the repertory during the middle part of the season, but they did not usually open it, perhaps because they required more rehearsal than time allowed during the hectic final days of carnival.

Theatrical engineers and workmen had four days only, beginning Ash Wednesday, to transform the theater from an opera house into a concert hall. Specific mention is made of this in the manuscript *Répertoire* for 1763 by Philipp Gumpenhuber, about whom more shortly: "Wednesday 16 February. We began adjusting the theater for the academies." Since there had already been several concerts on Fridays just before Lent in 1763, it becomes obvious that Lenten academies required a more elaborate setup—more platforms on the stage, for example, and more scenery. While the stage was in use nearly every night for dramatic productions throughout most of the year, there could be no question of a thorough transformation into a concert hall. Prices of entry to the concerts were the same as for regular evenings in the theater, except when there was a special seasonal reduction, as in 1763.

Concerts were accorded a few lines in the *Répertoire des Théâtres de la ville de Vienne*, printed by Johann Peter van Ghelen in 1757 for the previous five-year period, after a description of the regular offerings in the Burgtheater. The author of the *Répertoire*—someone under Durazzo, if not Durazzo himself—took pains to underscore the pious nature of the Lenten concerts, or at least the pious intentions behind their foundation, by citing oratorios first. He defined a concert as "une assemblée de Voix et d'Instrumens, qui exécutent differens morceaux de Musique, à grand Choeur, neufs et detachés des meilleurs Maîtres, comme aussi des *Oratorii, Cantates, Arie,* etc." Examples of choral pieces given are "La Traduction du Pseaulme VI (Adolphati) VIII (Gluck) CL (Wagenseil) et deux grans choeurs de Mr. Porpora, un grand choeur de Mr. San Martino [Sammartini]." No oratorios are cited by name. Individual performers come in for brief mention as an additional way of defining "concert." "When some foreign singer or instrumentalist of reputation appears, he is heard at the concert." It sounds from this as if the authorities were trying to enforce the French term *concert* (in lieu of the Italian-derived *Accademien*). There follow the names of several soloists, all instrument players, who were heard in concert up to 1757: violinists Gaetano Pugnani and Crener (Jakob Cramer?); Le Clerc (flute); Plat (oboe); Helman (pantaleon); Noel (psalterium); Kinchius (recorder); Hoffmann brothers (violin and cello); Rosetti (violin); Smith (Schmid) (oboe). Most of these are local figures who served in the orchestra of one or the other of the imperial theaters, a fact that ill supports the claim about virtuosi from foreign places. Pugnani heads the list for the obvious reason that he does fill this bill, and also because he had triumphed at the Concert Spirituel in Paris. The general purpose of the *Répertoire des Théâtres de la ville de Vienne*, as it avowed in so many words, was to put forward the claims of Vienna as a musical capital that rivaled Paris.

GUMPENHUBER'S RÉPERTOIRES (1758–63)

WE come next to the most important set of documents on Vienna's concert life that has surfaced in recent years (Figure 1.11). Philipp Gumpenhuber, "Sous-Directeur des Ballets" at the Burgtheater under Gasparo Angiolini, recorded all the theater's activities beginning where the printed *Répertoire* of 1757 left off. These manuscripts, written in a somewhat improvised French,

FIGURE 1.11. Title page
of Gumpenhuber's
Répertoire for 1761.

were meant for Durazzo and were elaborately bound with his crest. They
were without question intended as weapons to be used, as needed, to
impress the sovereigns and their highest ministers with the efficacy of Durazzo's theatrical stewardship. The manuscripts furnish a detailed record of
what the two imperial theaters offered in the way of plays, operas, ballets,
and concerts. They also note any appearances made by the theaters' personnel at functions in the imperial palaces. Long neglected by Austrian scholars
(perhaps because they are in French), they have only begun to be investi-
gated.[56] The summaries here are based on study of the originals.[57]

   Gumpenhuber's *Répertoires* give us a picture of Viennese musical life
during the crucial lustrum that spanned Gluck's opéras-comiques and

[56] Gerhardt Croll, "Neue Quellen zu Musik und Theater in Wien, 1758–1763," in *Festschrift Walter
Senn*, ed. E. Egg and E. Fässler (Munich and Salzburg, 1975), pp. 8–12. It is Croll's intention to
publish a critical edition of this rich source material.
[57] Harvard College Library, Theater Collection, MS Thr. 248–248.3; Austrian State Library, Vienna,
Musiksammlung Mus. Hs. 34580 a–c.

included his *Don Juan* and *Orfeo ed Euridice*, Tommaso Traetta's two operas for Vienna, a peak in the cultivation of the oratorio, and Wagenseil's finest instrumental works. Gumpenhuber chronicles, as does no other source, the performances of hundreds of singers and instrumentalists, visitors as well as those in local service. Moreover, he helps illuminate the arrival of a new generation of composers, one led not only by Gluck, but also by Ditters, Gassmann, Leopold Hofmann, and the brothers Joseph and Michael Haydn.

The concerts of 1758 featured choral pieces by Gluck, Porpora, and Wagenseil, as well as oratorios by Wagenseil and Baldassare Galuppi. Giuseppe Aprile was the most famous singer among the vocal soloists. The instrumental soloists were of local reputation and included Helman (pantaleon), Hirsch (flute), Jauzer (first oboe in the Burgtheater orchestra), and Woscicka (second cello in same). When Gumpenhuber writes that they played a "concert," he usually means a concerto; this becomes more clear in subsequent years when he distinguishes between "un seul" (sometimes he writes "solo" instead) and "un concert," meaning a concerto with orchestra. New symphonies abounded during the year, with Wagenseil providing most of them. The demand for symphonies in this concert series alone may have been a determining factor not only for Wagenseil's production but also for the evolution of the Viennese symphony in general. Gumpenhuber struggled to find verbal expression for a kind of symphony that was concerted with solo instruments, for example in this passage relative to an academy on 19 February 1758: "Tous les Airs ont été entremelé des Symphonies, et il y en a eu une concertée de plusieurs instrumens solo de la composition du Sr San Martino." Some early form of Sinfonia concertante was taking shape in the late 1750s, which helps explain the origins of Haydn's soloistic writing in the symphonies *Le matin*, *Le midi*, and *Le soir* of 1761. The two composers mentioned most often in connection with this kind of symphony, over the course of the *Répertoires*, are Wagenseil and Holzbauer, who returned to Vienna for a visit in the late 1750s.[58] Concertante arias employing instrumental soloists, often cited by name, constitute a related phenomenon.

Three different decors greeted those who attended the Lenten academies of 1758. At the opening concert "the theater was graced with a transparent decoration representing the protection that the august House of Austria has always accorded the arts." Perhaps this was some kind of gauze hanging

---

[58] Bruce Alan Brown, *Gluck and the French Theatre in Vienna* (Oxford, 1991), p. 139, identifies surviving scores by Sammartini, Wagenseil, and Holzbauer that qualify as early representatives of the Sinfonia concertante. Holzbauer's Sinfonia Concertante in E♭ is earlier than any of the Parisian examples of the type, argues Janet B. Winzenberger, in "The Symphonic Concertante: Mannheim and Paris" (M.A. thesis, Eastman School of Music, University of Rochester, 1967), p. 17.

suspended from the proscenium, behind which the musicians played. Or perhaps it was at the rear of the stage, its transparent quality brought out by backlighting. On 26 February the decoration was changed to a "Temple with transparent golden ornaments, in the middle of which was depicted, to the acclamations of the people, the celebrated Fame, Crown, and Name of our Sovereigns."[59] The third and last decoration appeared on 12 March, described as

> a grand new transparent picture representing Telemachus conducted by Minerva, dressed in his armor, advancing on a carpeted path toward the Temple of Immortality, from which he is shown from afar the marks of honor and glory that await him; also seen are the pitfalls of Pride, Envy and other Vices, or monsters that oppose his passage. From this well-known symbol is recalled the Idea of what one should expect of a young Hero when he is conducted by Wisdom.

The young hero was, of course, Archduke Joseph, heir to the throne.

All three decors were thus dynastic in significance and sequential in that they pertained to the past of the ruling house, the present sovereigns, and the prince who would come to reign. It would be agreeable to be able to report some link between the Telemachus legend and the musical part of the program, but such was not the case. On the day the third transparency was revealed, the main musical offering was an oratorio, *Adamo ed Eva*, set by Galuppi for four voices.

At the fourteenth and penultimate Lenten academy, on Monday 13 March 1758, the concert began at seven in the evening instead of six, we are told, because there had been that same afternoon a *service de table* in the palace, at which several new arias and several new symphonies were performed, as well as two choruses, the second "newly composed" by Wagenseil. The occasion was Archduke Joseph's seventeenth birthday. Throughout his chronicles Gumpenhuber attempts to distinguish what was new, or written for the event, from what was not. We can sense Durazzo's pride in his mission especially in this care for detail. The picture that emerges is one of intense activity in all genres, so as to provide new music worthy to stand beside that of the Galuppis and Sammartinis, obtained from elsewhere.

Gumpenhuber's *Répertoires* for the Burgtheater for the years 1759 and 1760 are missing; they may yet be found. The loss is not so great with regard to concerts as it might have been. A financial crisis in early 1759 forced the cancellation of the Lenten academies, but their place was taken to some

---

[59] Morrow, *Concert Life in Haydn's Vienna*, p. 43, garbles "Temple orné des Dorures" into "temple adorned with 'Dornres.' "

extent by public concerts offered by the Princes Trautsohn and Hildburg-hausen, as we have seen. In 1760 the festivities surrounding the wedding of Archduke Joseph and Isabella of Parma engendered reports that help to fill the gap created by the missing *Répertoire*; disputes between Durazzo and Reutter in consequence of these festivities supply further knowledge.

Under the date of 4 February 1761 Gumpenhuber listed "Les Musiciens pour les Academies," a large orchestra drawn from the Burgtheater and the German Theater. The orchestra boasted forty players, including two English horns and two trumpets. The origins of the huge orchestras for the Tonkünstler Societät concerts of the following decade are already apparent here. During the Lenten academies in 1761, revivals in concert of the wedding operas by Hasse (*Alcide al Bivio*) and Gluck (*Tetide*) plus arias from Traetta's *Armida* and Giuseppe Scarlatti's *Issipile* took place. There were also oratorios by Galuppi and Reutter (*Il ritorno di Tobia*) and Holzbauer's "newly composed" *Betulia liberata*. Caterina Gabrielli and Giovanni Manzuoli, the luminaries of the previous fall's festive operas, remained the principal vocal soloists. An Italian player of equivalent reputation, the violinist Pietro Nardini, was also attracted to Vienna by the imperial wedding, and he too remained to play in concerts during 1761, when he also served as first violinist in the Burgtheater orchestra. Vincenzo Galeotti, first cello, apparently came at the same time and for the same reason; he also made many solo appearances in concert. Other soloists in concertos included the brothers Hoffman (violin and cello), Johann Schmid (both oboe and English horn), J. B. Gumpenhuber (pantaleon), Birfriend (harp), Timmer (bassoon), Joesph Leutgeb (horn), and Ditters (violin). The last two became the most frequently represented soloists in concertos during the following two years. Composers of symphonies, besides the oft-represented Wagenseil and Holzbauer, included Franz Asplmayr (ballet composer of the German troupe), Giovanni Battista Casalli (described as an abbé), one Sciroli (of Milan?), and Joseph Ziegler (music master of the Schottenkirche and one of the early mentors of Ditters).

Gumpenhuber prefaced his *Répertoire* of 1761 for the Burgtheater with a dedication to Durazzo that, aside from the usual flowery phrases of praise, claims that his chronicle is useful and necessary in order to model the present upon the past. ("Cet Ouvrage utile et necessaire pour regler le present sur le passé.") Did he mean to say only that he was continuing what was begun with Ghelen's printed *Répertoire*? Or did he intend this record of Durazzo's accomplishments to be useful as a means by which some future age could measure itself? To enhance the beauty of the document, and hence increase its chances of surviving, a delicately drawn frame was added around the title, signed "Joseph Jehan Biderman invenit et Ex. 1762." (See the very top of Figure 1.11.) Biderman was one of the theater's engineer-designers, in which capacity he appears in the 1763 "Etat Present." Like all the volumes, this one is also enhanced by a handsome leather binding stamped in gold with Durazzo's arms. Given all the care taken in compiling and enhancing these volumes, one cannot help but think that both Gumpenhuber and Durazzo would be pleased to know that, at long last, this record of their achievements is coming to light.

An accident in late 1761 led to the Burgtheater's concert activities being increased to an unprecedented level. The Kärntnerthor Theater burned during the night of 3–4 November, after the German troupe had given its version of *Don Juan*, a customary offering following the feasts of All Saints and All Souls. Maria Theresa decreed that henceforth, concerts would be given every Friday in the Burgtheater, the proceeds going to help rebuild the old theater. Prices for these concerts were to be the same as for the comedy, both for entry and for the loges; people with subscriptions and those renting loges by the season would pay half price in addition for each event. The decree was promulgated a week after the fire (11 November). Two days later the new series of concerts began.

The year 1762 featured many of the same names and some new ones in concert. Pugnani returned to perform solos and concertos at several academies. Tenor Giuseppe Tibaldi joined the ranks of the vocal soloists. Concerts were played by Dretter (harp), the soprano soloist Rosa Bon Rovinetti (harpsichord), Johann Conrad Gretsch (cello), and Byka (cellist from the Saxon court). Johann Schmid and Timmer performed what may be the first documented instance of an oboe and bassoon concerto. Besides playing concertos of his own composition, Leutgeb played several written for him by others: Hofmann, Ditters, Michael Haydn, and probably Joseph Haydn.[60] Symphonies were provided by a certain Senft, Hofmann, Emanuele Barbella (from Naples), and Bach (Christian Bach, then in Milan). Wagenseil's serenata *Il promoteo assoluto* celebrated the birth of a daughter to Princess Isabella and Archduke Joseph. Hasse's *Alcide*, a favorite piece of the empress, was revived once again; Leutgeb played a horn concerto between the opera's two parts at one performance, and Ditters a violin concerto at another. The major musical works also included Giuseppe Scarlatti's grand cantata *I lamenti d'Orfeo*, which served as a prelude to Gluck's treatment of the subject later the same year.

The concerts of 1763 offered few departures from the norms established in the preceding years. Luigi Boccherini is the most famous name to emerge as a soloist (cello). The most frequently heard soloists were Antonio Vallotti

---

[60] Daniel Heartz, "Leutgeb and the 1762 Horn Concertos of Joseph and Johann Michael Haydn," *Mozart-Jahrbuch 1987/88* (Kassel, 1988), pp. 59–64.

(cello) and Luigi Livraghi (oboe). Ditters continued to play often, and Leut-geb continued to receive new concertos written for him as horn soloist. A rival horn player appeared (15 March) in the person of Franz Stamitz/ Steinmetz. Domenico Panzachi, tenor from the Bavarian court, made his debut on 22 April. Concertante arias contined to flourish. When the soprano Marianna Bianchi (the first Euridice in Gluck's *Orfeo*) sang in the last Lenten academy (22 March) Ditters accompanied her on the solo violin. Not to be outdone, the contralto castrato Gaetano Guadagni (for whom Gluck created the part of Orpheus) sang in the same concert an aria with cello solo played by Vallotti. Even though the Kärntnerthor Theater had opened again in mid-1762, the Friday concerts instituted to raise money for its restoration contin-ued on through 1763, which says something about the taste of the Viennese public. The concerts must have been well enough attended to justify such an expenditure.

One of the most frequent performers during the five-year period chroni-cled by Gumpenhuber was the oboist Johann Schmid, who played numer-ous concertos on the oboe, the English horn, and the flute, and who was likely the inspiration behind such unusual combinations as the oboe-bas-soon concerto of 1761, the concerto for two English horns of 29 March 1762, and Leopold Hofmann's Concerto for two oboes, played by Schmid and Livraghi on 12 November 1762. At some point in 1758, Schmid replaced Jauzer as first oboe of the Burgtheater orchestra. Another Schmid, Johann Baptist, introduced a new instrument in the spring of 1763. The description of the seventh Lenten academy (6 March) reads "concert a joué le Sr Schmid sur son nouveau instrument nommé Piano et forte." The new instrument sounded so strange to Gumpenhuber that he compared it with that Viennese favorite the pantaleon, a dulcimer-like stringed instrument, the open strings of which were plucked by metal picks. In other words, it sounded quite twangy. Schmid received special payment for his efforts, which were indeed precocious.[61] The fortepiano did not appear in public concert in London or Paris until 1768.

There was a change in the entry fee to the Lenten concerts of 1763. Prices were lowered "en faveur des amateurs de la Musique" as follows: "au Par-terre ou Gallerie Noble—1 Florin 8 X; au troisième étage—34 X; à la Gallerie au théâtre [rear of the first loges]—17 X; au quatrième étage—7 X." For the renters of boxes and those having entrée to the Gallerie noble, the price remained the ordinary one. Early in the century Lady Mary Wortley Mon-tague paid one gold ducat for a box holding four at the Kärntnerthor Theater.

[61] Eva Badura-Skoda, "Prolegomena to a History of the Viennese Fortepiano," *Israel Studies in Musi-cology* 2 (1980): 77–99; 78–79.

What is most impressive about Viennese concert life around 1760, glimpses of which Gumpenhuber has made possible, is not only its many-sidedness, but also its modernity. Notable by their absence are such famous names as Vivaldi and Giuseppe Tartini, although both composers had many Viennese connections. The public mania for solo concertos, and especially violin concertos, was gratified not by the works of these older masters but by the efforts of the younger generation of violinist-composers, resident in or visiting Vienna. Sammartini, on the other hand, could scarcely fail to be represented, given the intimate links between Milan and Vienna, plus the circumstance that this composer was continuing to evolve along the lines of up-to-date musical styles even in his sixties. In a letter addressed to Padre Martini and dated 30 June 1756, there is reference to an academy organized by Sammartini that included compositions he intended to send to Vienna.[62]

Ditters was the main violinist-composer playing concertos during the early 1760s in the Burgtheater concerts, and throws considerable light on the subject in his autobiography. When he accompanied Gluck to Bologna in 1763 for the inauguration of the Teatro Comunale, he gathered information on the musical practices he observed, some touching the violin concerto. At a vespers in the church of San Paolo, there was a chorus and band of over a hundred. Ditters was to play a concerto of his own composition there the next day.

> Between the Psalms, Spagnoletti played a concerto by Tartini, which I had prac-ticed some years before. The church was crowded with connoisseurs and ama-teurs. You could see, from the faces of the audience, that he had made his mark. "You may safely reckon on the applause of your audience to-morrow," said Gluck to me, "for your music, like your playing, is much more modern."

These remarks are in line with several others made by Ditters to the effect that the older generation—Tartini, Pietro Antonio Locatelli, and Carlo Zuc-cari he mentions by name—were considered in Vienna to be suitable only for practice, not for public performance.

FROM 1764 TO THE MOZART ERA

OPEN-AIR concerts during the warmer parts of the year helped earn Vienna its reputation as a musical city. Serenades offered in loving homage on a name day or birthday figure prominently in letters and memoirs of the

[62] Anne Schnoebelen, *Padre Martini's Collection of Letters in the Civico Museo Bibliografico in Bologna* (New York, 1979), no. 1956.

time. Even Mozart's late serenade *Eine kleine Nachtmusik* (K. 525, dated 10 August 1787) may have originated under such circumstances. A *Besetzung* of five solo instruments—two violins, viola, cello, and double bass—is what Mozart seems to have intended.[63] The work followed one of the typical patterns of the Viennese divertimento (fast, minuet, slow, minuet, fast) before the first minuet got torn out of the autograph. Nicolai makes some interesting remarks about the open-air music he heard played by Viennese bands in 1781; these are quoted below.

At the opposite pole of such public music was the private or semiprivate concert in the home. That music making in the home became more and more frequent as the century matured can be attested in various ways. Rapid growth in the music printing and instrument-making trades offers one telling indication of what was happening. The satirist Joseph Richter did not neglect this sphere of Viennese life. One of the illustrations Mansfeld created for the *Bildergalerie weltlicher Misbräuche* shows a lady at the keyboard being accompanied by strings and flute (Figure 1.12). The assembled auditors seem more interested in one another, which was the point of the satire.[64] Nicolai pointedly remarked that the Viennese liked their concerts with refreshments and amusements such as gambling, while the more enlightened public of Berlin found music by itself to be sufficient reward.

The final season of Lenten concerts under the direction of Durazzo took place in 1764. A payment record shows that Luigi Boccherini was rewarded with a gift of 66 florins 2 kreutzer, and this description was inserted in the record: "Luigi Boccherini, violoncellist, gave a great concert at which, with the assistance of his father Leopoldo, he performed, upon the violoncello, his compositions for one or two violoncellos. This concert ranks him among the virtuosi of the music academies."[65] Boccherini was the last and greatest of the Italian virtuosi promoted by Durazzo in Vienna. He and his father played together in concert again in July 1765 at Pavia and Cremona, to honor the passage of Archduke Leopold on his way to rule in Tuscany. Two years later Boccherini began appearing as a cello virtuoso at the Concert Spirituel in Paris. Whereas Pugnani gained fame at the Concert Spirituel and then came to the Burgtheater, Boccherini did the reverse.

Concerts resumed in Lent 1765, following their usual thrice-weekly pattern under the new direction of Count Wenzl Sporck, but the death of

[63] James Webster, "The Scoring of Mozart's Chamber Music for Strings," in *Music in the Classic Period: Essays in Honor of Barry S. Brook*, ed. Allan A. Atlas (New York, 1985), p. 272.

[64] Richter's text is given in Daniel Heartz, "A Keyboard Concerto by Marie Antoinette?" *Essays in Musicology: A Tribute to Alvin Johnson*, ed. Lewis Lockwood and Edward Roesner (Philadelphia, 1990), pp. 201–12.

[65] From the manuscript registers of the Theatralkasserechnung, Haus-, Hof-, und Staatsarchiv, cited by Germaine de Rothschild, *Luigi Boccherini: Sa vie, son oeuvre* (Paris, 1962) p. 16.

FIGURE 1.12. J. E. Mansfeld. Satire of a Viennese chamber concert, 1785.

Emperor Francis in August that year disrupted all routine. The Burgtheater was not even opened until the fall of 1766. Once again it seems that the nobility picked up the slack, as indicated in a report from Vienna dated August 1766 and printed by Johann Adam Hiller.[66]

Private salons played an important role in Viennese musical life. Marianne von Martínez, whom Haydn instructed in singing and keyboard playing as early as 1751 when she was seven, became a celebrated performer during the 1760s, and her apartment in the Michaelerhaus across from the

[66] See Appendix 1, last sentence of the extract.

Burg was a focal point of the city's concert life.[67] Hiller's Viennese correspondent in 1766 mentioned Mlle. Martínez first among the "ladies of both middle and high class who show great ability at the keyboard and in singing." Burney in 1772 procured an introduction to her through Metastasio, who shared the Martínez apartment. Burney heard her sing and play several times with "delight and amazement," and also had high praise for her compositions. He describes his final visit to this charmed circle as follows.

> From hence I went to Metastasio, for the last time! I found with him much company, and the St. Cecilia, Martinetz, at the harpsichord, to which she had been singing. At her desire there was a commutation of compositions between us. She had been so kind as to have transcribed for me, among other things, a song of Metastasio, set by herself, with which I had been greatly struck in a former visit.

Michael Kelly speaks of being present at the Martínez soirées when he was in Vienna during the 1780s. "When I was admitted to her *conversaziones* and musical parties, she was in the vale of years, yet still possessed the gaiety and vivacity of a girl, and was polite and affable to all. Mozart was an almost constant attendant at her parties, and I have heard him play duets on the piano-forte with her, of his own composition. She was a great favorite of his."

Even after the demise of Metastasio in 1782, the Martínez apartment remained a foyer of Italian culture in Vienna, and as such it was a necessary ancestor, in both music and poetry, to the blooming of a German-language equivalent. Privy Councillor Franz von Greiner maintained another such salon, frequented by the first composers, including Mozart and Haydn. From these concerts Viennese Lieder took wing, beginning with those by Joseph Anton Steffan that were printed in 1778, some of the texts of which were selected by Greiner himself. Leopold Hofmann and Haydn followed Steffan's example shortly afterward. Greiner's daughter Caroline Pichler was a keyboard pupil of Steffan, and she often played the concertos he wrote for her on such occasions. Central to the salon concert from this time on was the presence of a good fortepiano.

The Lenten academies in the Burgtheater in the 1770s continued as before. A new series was represented by the concerts of the Tonkünstler Societät, founded for the purpose of providing for the widows and orphans of deceased musicians by Kapellmeister Gassmann in 1771.[68] The Kärnt-

---

[67] A. Peter Brown, "Marianna Martines' Autobiography as a New Source for Haydn's Biography During the 1750s," *Haydn-Studien* 6 (1986): 68–70.
[68] The programs are given in Carl F. Pohl, *Denkschrift aus Anlass des hundertjährigen Bestehens der Tonkünstler-Societät* (Vienna, 1871).

nerthor Theater became the regular home of these concerts, which involved very large orchestral forces. An *Almanach des Theaters in Wien* for 1774 mentions that in Lent there were "6. musikalishen Akademien im Burgtheater und 3. grosse im Kärntnerthortheater" (the last referring to the Tonkünstler Societät).[69] The Friday concerts in the Burgtheater received some competition from the suburban theater in the Josephstadt, which advertised in the *Realzeitung* in 1776 that its musical academies would be "opened with trumpets and drums and garnished with arias, symphonies, concertos, Murkis, Polonoises, etc." Valuable evidence on Viennese orchestral playing and on the mammoth-sized orchestras of the benefit concerts can be gleaned from Johann Kaspar Riesbeck's *Briefe eines reisenden Franzosen über Deutschland an seinen Brüder zu Paris* (Zurich, 1783). The passages about music were printed in Cramer's *Magazin der Musik* for 1784, from which this translation was made.

> [Music] is the only thing about which the nobility shows taste. Many houses have their own band of musicians, and all the public concerts bear witness that this aspect of art is in high repute here. One can put together four or five large orchestras, all of which are incomparable. The number of real virtuosi is small; but as far as the orchestral musicians are concerned, one can hardly imagine anything in the world more beautiful. I have heard 30 or 40 instruments playing together, and they all produce one tone so correct, clean, and precise that one might think one is hearing one single string instrument. The violins are one stroke, the wind instruments one breath. An Englishman next to whom I sat thought it miraculous that throughout an entire opera there was—I won't say no mistake, but nothing of all that which generally occurs in large orchestras: a hasty entrance, dragging, or too strong a bowing or attack. He was enchanted by the purity and correctness of the harmony, and he had just come from Italy. There are upwards of 400 musicians here, who are divided into certain societies, and often work together many years. They are used to each other and have in common a severe leadership. Through constant practice, and also through the energy and cold-bloodedness which are peculiar to the Germans, they reach such a state. On a certain day of the year these 400 artists come together and give a concert for the benefit of the widows of musicians. I am assured that all 400 instruments play together just as correctly, clearly and purely as if they were 20 or 30. This concert is surely unique in the world.[70]

[69] Otto Biba, "Grundzüge des Konzertwesens in Wien zu Mozarts Zeit," *Mozart-Jahrbuch 1978/79*, pp. 132–43; 133. Biba also quotes the *Theatralkalender von Wien für das Jahr 1773*, p. 193, on the Friday academies: "Man höret darinnen die besten alten und neuen gesetzten Stücke, von hiesigen und fremden Sängern gesungen, fremde und hiesige Virtuosen auf verschiedenen Instrumenten" (One hears in them the best old and new pieces set to music, sung by local and visiting singers, and various virtuosos from here and abroad on different instruments). The emphasis on old pieces is something new.

[70] Landon, *Haydn*, 2: 214.

Compare this traveler's impressions of Viennese orchestras with those gathered by Nicolai during his visit to Vienna in 1781. Nicolai goes into some interesting details about performance practice, and how it differed in Vienna from the practice of orchestras he was used to hearing in Dresden and Berlin.

> The orchestra in the Burgtheater seems to me even superior [to the one in the Kärntnerthor Theater]. I paid close attention not only to the operas but also to the symphonies played between the acts, to which the auditors usually pay so little heed. It happened that I heard various symphonies of Haydn and Vanhal that I had often heard in Berlin and that I had partly retained in my memory. I was very attentive to their manner of performance . . . In passages calling for a short, strong bow stroke, which Haydn's works in particular require, i.e., when a series of short notes are to be touched on with a light bow, I observed the clearest difference. The Viennese play this kind of passage with an evenness and precision that up until now perhaps no large orchestra in Berlin has attained.

Nicolai goes on to say that the Viennese *Andante* had a lighter movement than he was accustomed to hearing when an *Andante* or *Adagio* of Hasse was rendered by orchestras in Dresden and Berlin, and while the Berlin orchestra's *Andante* was lighter than Dresden's, Vienna's was lighter still. To sum up the Viennese *Andante* he resorts to the French word "lestement," i.e., nimbly and freely.

In the winter of 1781–82 Philipp Jakob Martin, one of the earliest free-lance concert organizers, arranged a series of Friday concerts with an orchestra of dilettantes in the large room of the "Mehlgrube" house, built by the elder Fischer von Erlach at the top of the Neuer Markt in 1697. (See the lower left corner of Figure 1.1.) The building, owned by the city, housed a restaurant on the ground floor and a room used for concerts and balls one floor above. Mozart played his fortepiano in Martin's Mehlgrube concerts and also in his summer concerts in the Augarten. It should be added that it was Joseph II who opened the former imperial preserve of the Augarten to the public, as he did with the Prater. The most astonishing act of this kind, and a true mark of Joseph's zeal in enlightening his subjects, was his opening the imperial library to the public. Burney had less trouble working in the Prunksaal and examining its treasures than would a scholar today. This same Prunksaal was also the site of many concerts in which Mozart participated.

Another witness to the continuity of the Lenten concerts in the Burgtheater is Joseph Martin Kraus, who arrived in Vienna in April 1783 and stayed until the end of October. In his diary he noted:

> Arrived in Vienna on 1 April. The same day there was an academy in the court theater. The symphony by Rosetti in D was an imitation of one of Haydn's that

I had heard in Regensburg. Herr Umlauf directed from the harpsichord. Mme. N., Mlle. Cavalieri, and Herr —— furnished the voices. The performance was very mediocre, with the exception of the first violin and oboe. Mme. B. was heard there for the first time. The voice was strong, but unbending, and the *Manieren* always the same, which was particularly apparent as she had to repeat her first Rondo upon demand. Mlle. C. [Cavalieri] has much polish and a cool but well-sounding voice. The first bravura aria by Salieri was well composed and well sung . . . The theater has four tiers of loges.[71]

Kraus' report makes for an interesting comparison with the concert of a week earlier on which Mozart comments at length in his letter of 29 March 1783.

For the larger concerts, at least, posters or handbills were printed. One such poster, advertising the "Grand Musical Academy" given 16–17 April 1791 by the Tonkünstler Societät in the Burgtheater, gives the number of performers as more than 180 (choral as well as orchestral). The program for this concert consisted of five parts, followed by useful pieces of information:

> 1. A grand Symphony of the composition of Signor Mozart.
> 2. Excerpt from the opera *Fedra*, in which will sing in the roles
>   of Aricia .... la Signora Lang
>   of Ippolito .... il Signor Calvesi
>   of Teseo .... il Signor Nencini
> The music is by Signor Paisiello except for the aria sung by Signora Lang, which is by Mozart.
>   3. A Concerto on the Violoncello, composed by Signor Pleyel, and executed by Cajetan Gottlieb, a virtuoso newly arrived from Florence.
>   4. The well-loved chorus "Alleluja" by Signor Albrechtsberger, musician of this imperial court, and member of this society.
>   5. For the finale twenty-one wind instruments in the service of Princes Esterházy and Grassalkowich will produce a new Harmonie music composed by Signor Druschetzki, which was executed in Pressburg on the occasion of the coronation of his imperial and royal majesty [Leopold II].
>   The prices for entrance are the following: Parterre noble 1 fl. 25 kr.; *idem*, reserved seat 1 fl. 42 kr.; second Parterre 24 kr. [standing room]; third floor 40 kr.; *idem* reserved seat 50 kr.; 4th floor 20 kr.; box 4 fl. 30 kr.
>   Officers of the Garrison are asked to pay 30 kr. for entrance. Those among the nobility who do not intend to leave their boxes empty are asked to so advise the loge master in advance. Libretti with the excerpts can be procured from the loge master for 10 kr. apiece. The beginning is ca. 7 P.M.[72]

---

[71] Leux-Henschen, *Kraus in seinen Briefen*, p. 105.
[72] For a facsimile of the German-Italian original, see the article "Vienna" in *The New Grove Dictionary of Music and Musicians* (London, 1980), 19: 725.

Mozart did not belong to the society because he could not or would not furnish a birth certificate, as required by the rules for membership. He did, on the other hand, enjoy the title and salary of imperial royal chamber composer (from 1787). There may be some animus against him evident in the program's naming Albrechtsberger as an imperial court composer but not Mozart. Typical for all concerts of the time is the mixture of vocal and instrumental music, of sacred and secular, and the emphasis on novelty and virtuosity.

Haydn used the poster for the first public performance of *The Creation* in the Burgtheater on 19 March 1799 to make a plea that the audience not applaud after individual numbers. Very large choral forces participated in the performance, more than 180 according to one source, around 400 according to another.[73] The stage was set up in the form of an amphitheater to accommodate so many performers. Haydn stood on a raised platform and gave the beat. Despite the prices of entry, which were higher than usual, the theater was more crowded than ever.

The academies continued to mix vocal and instrumental music well into the nineteenth century. Other than military bands, there was no such thing as "the public concert of pure instrumental music";[74] concerts indoors always involved voices as well as instruments. Consider, for example, the occasion at which Beethoven first presented himself to the Viennese public, in a benefit concert that took place during Lent in the Burgtheater on 2 April 1800. The concert began with a symphony by Mozart and an aria from *The Creation*, continued with one of Beethoven's piano concertos, his Septet, and a duet from the same oratorio, and concluded with Beethoven's improvisations at the piano and then his Symphony No. 1.[75] The possibility for an individual to use the court theater (and orchestra) and give a concert at his own expense and risk apparently went back to the *Theaterfreiheit* edict of 1776.

When Mozart and Beethoven played their piano concertos in the Burgtheater, did they do so from the stage? An argument based on circumstantial evidence suggests that they did, and that the orchestra remained in its normal place for accompanying stage works, a few feet below.[76] But this theory does not take into consideration the special setups for Lenten concerts in the Burgtheater, in which orchestra and soloist were both onstage as part of the decor.

[73] Landon, *Haydn*, 4: 453–57.

[74] Charles Rosen, *Sonata Forms* (New York, 1980), p. 9.

[75] *Thayer's Life of Beethoven*, revised and edited by Elliot Forbes (Princeton, N.J., 1964), p. 255. Tickets for the event were to be had from the composer in his lodgings and from the box keeper at the usual prices.

[76] Richard Maunder, "Performing Mozart and Beethoven Concertos," *Early Music* 17 (1989): 139–40. Maunder did not utilize Heartz, "Jadot and the Building of the Burgtheater" for what my article has to say on this complex question.

THE REDOUTENSAAL AND OTHER BALLROOMS

THE fashion for masked balls had long been prevalent in much of Europe, and was perceived as a potential menace to sovereigns of absolute monarchies, well before the assassination of King Gustave III of Sweden in 1792. In Vienna masking was strictly forbidden at the court of Charles VI, but his successors brought with them a liberalization in this as in so many other areas. It was Emperor Francis who persuaded Maria Theresa to allow the practice, according to Khevenhüller, who was against it, and who says furthermore, "The emperor took particular delight therein since he was accustomed to such *Amusemens* from the time of his early youth in Lorraine."[77] It was also Francis who broke with the old Habsburg practice by which the sovereigns sat on special throne-like chairs in the theater, directly in front of the stage; he wanted to be in a box like his friends so that he could come and go as he pleased.

The most famous masked ball during Maria Theresa's early years was held on the occasion of her sister Marianna's marriage to Charles of Lorraine in January 1744, for which the imperial Riding School was turned into a huge ballroom: "1,000 candles provided light; the masks, among which were the ruling family, consisted of 60 couples costumed alike, and counting the unmasked onlookers, the total amounted to over 8,000 people."[78] Giuseppe Galli-Bibiena drew meticulous pictures of the event, which were then engraved very skillfully by Pfeffel—a good example of *Kunstpolitik* as it was then practiced.[79] The two large orchestras on raised platforms were placed across from each other on the long sides of the hall.

It was the practice throughout Europe, as documented by many pictures, to turn theaters into ballrooms by raising the parterre to the level of the stage (and making the latter level instead of raked). Both imperial theaters were turned into ballrooms on occasion. Khevenhüller noted (7 January 1743) that masked dancers were to be allowed, with many restrictions, first in the "Theatro im Ballhaus" (i.e., the tennis-court theater that became the Burgtheater), then in the Kärntnerthor Theater, and finally at the Mehlgrube. But the last house was open only to the high nobility; the so-called half-nobles could appear masked in the two theaters but not in the Mehlgrube. This establishment on the Neuer Markt, which we have already

---

[77] Margret Dietrich, "Theater am Hofe—zwischen Tradition und Wandel," in *Maria Theresia und ihre Zeit*, ed. Walter Koschatzky (Vienna, 1979), p. 398.

[78] Weiskern, *Beschreibung der k. k. Haupt und Residenzstadt Wien*, p. 91.

[79] One is reproduced in Ernst Wangermann, *The Austrian Achievement, 1700-1800* (London, 1973), p. 106, two in Dreger, *Baugeschichte der k. und k. Hofburg*, illustrations 234-35. The caption under the latter mentions "8000 lumi, tutti candele di Cera fina."

encountered as the seat of public concerts, enjoyed a good reputation for its balls at first, but these became somewhat disreputable in the second half of the century. Joseph Richter satirized the Viennese mania for dancing in his *Bildergalerie welticher Misbräuche* (1784) with a picture of a dance hall, engraved by Mansfeld, showing musicians on a balcony in the rear, rather disorderly dancers, and evidence aplenty of gluttonous consumption of food and drink.[80] The reference may be to the carnival balls in the salon of the Mehlgrube.

The decision to dismantle the Bibiena opera house of 1700 and replace it with the smaller and larger rooms of the Redoutensaal was carried out in 1747–48. Antonio Bibiena was paid a large sum for the work, but the court could not have been very happy with the result, since everything was remodeled in the early 1750s in line with the French style represented by Jadot. Weiskern writes: "After 1752, under the orders of the theater direction [Durazzo], the small as well as the large room was fully remodeled, both after a beautiful order of architecture, totally executed in stone, and in addition a new entrance was built, near the library."[81]

When the Redoutensaal opened for the carnival of 1748, anyone in a mask could enter by paying a fee. An engraving by Markus Weinmann shows the hall in its first state, with a masked ball in progress (Figure 1.13). The windows and pilasters with Corinthian capitals long remained but the Rococo plaster decorations on the ceiling soon began to be curtailed.[82]

Complaints from the nobility about this open-door policy persuaded Maria Theresa to restrict entrance in 1752 to the high nobility, ordinary nobility, councilors, and the military.[83] Khevenhüller speaks of a remodeling of the Redoutensaal under the date 10 November 1755, mentioning that over 60,000 florins were rumored to have been spent, and the gilding and ornaments were still not finished. In his diary for the next day he says that, against her will, the empress was persuaded by the emperor and many others to allow gambling at the balls, the profits from which went to support the theaters. The balls were so popular that they were begun in November (before Advent) in this and some other years. Another remodeling, said to have been under the direction of Ferdinand Hetzendorf von Hohenberg, took place in 1760, for the marriage of Archduke Joseph; a glimpse of the hall at that time can be seen in a painting of the wedding serenata by Migliavacca and Gluck, *Tetide*, which was performed on a provisional stage in the

---

[80] Reproduced in Daniel Heartz, *Mozart's Operas* (Berkeley, 1990), fig. 25.

[81] *Beschreibung der k. k. Haupt und Residenzstadt Wien*, p. 153.

[82] The print was published under the title "Representation de la Grande Sale [sic] des Redoutes et du Bal Masqué."

[83] Hadamowsky, "Barocktheater am Wiener Kaiserhof," p. 44, quotes the "Ballordnung" of 2 January 1752 restricting entry "auf den alleinigen Hohen Adel, Ritter-Stand, Räthe, und das Militäre."

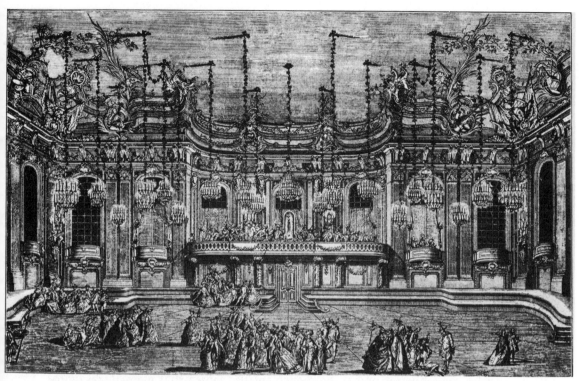

FIGURE 1.13. Markus Weinmann. A masked ball in the large Redoutensaal, 1748.

north end of the large hall.[84] (See Plate IX.) In 1788 the Redoutensaal was remodeled once more for the engagement of Archduke Francis, heir to the throne. It was partially renovated again for the wedding in 1816 of the same prince, as reigning emperor, to Karolina Augusta of Bavaria.

Pezzl gives a vivid picture of what it was like to attend a carnival ball in the Redoutensaal during his time. The balls, which stretched through the carnival season, were the chief amusement of the better public, he says.

Two large rooms in one wing of the imperial palace are devoted to Comus and Bacchus. They are open from 7 January until Ash Wednesday, at first once a week, later twice a week, and the last three days of carnival, every night. One climbs an iron staircase, passes a row of fifty bearded grenadiers, who, with their crude bearskin caps and bayonets at the ready, make the shy maiden trem-

[84]Otto Erich Deutsch, "Gluck im Redoutensaal," *Österreichische Musik Zeitschrift* 21 (1966): 521–25. The likely painter of the festival pictures is Dophonias Dederich, says Deutsch, who traces the mistaken identification of the four-year-old Mozart and his father among the onlookers to an article by Karl Schumann in the popular magazine *Epoca* for September 1963. A newly discovered drawing of the Redoutensaal ca. 1780 is reproduced in *Early Music* 20 (1992): 142.

ble when, with beating heart, she visits the famous Redoute on the arm of her beloved for the first time. Having passed through the hall of Mavors and climbed a few more steps, there suddenly opens up the great magic hall. Several thousand wax candles on great reflecting crystal lusters and pyramid-formed chandeliers in symmetric rows dazzle the eye, and the sound of trumpets and timpani, mixed with the softer tones of a hundred musical instruments, move the enchanted ear and bestir the youthful foot willy-nilly to the joyful dance . . . If only a thousand people attend, it is too empty. 1,500 makes a proper Redoute. 2,000 displaces the dancers from needed space. In the last days of carnival, when the joy seekers mount to nearly 3,000, then one is pressed. To no avail the orchestra sends down its Menuets and *Deutscher Tänze:* one can no longer execute three formal steps; everyone crowds together to the point of suffocating— a helpless human flood, which can only move in a slow wave.

From Pezzl's account it is apparent that the restrictions as to who could enter had been relaxed. But the expense of attending still exercised considerable restriction. Pezzl says that the entry fee was two gulden a head, which did not include food and drink; these were paid for extra in adjoining rooms (as was gambling). He ends his remarks by relating that "on the final night the revelers go direct from the ballroom to church in order to receive the ashes and then to bed to sleep it off."

Michael Kelly was another witness to the carnival balls in the mid-1780s, and he remembered one convenience for the ladies that even Pezzl overlooked.

The people of Vienna were in my time dancing mad; as the Carnival approached, gayety began to display itself on all sides, and when it really came, nothing could exceed its brilliancy. The ridotto rooms, where the masquerades took place, were in the palace; and spacious and commodious as they were, they were actually crammed with masqueraders. I never saw, or indeed heard of any suite of rooms, where elegance and convenience were more considered; for the propensity of the Vienna ladies for dancing and going to carnival masquerades was so determined, that nothing was permitted to interfere with their enjoyment of their favourite amusement—nay, so notorious was it, that for the sake of ladies in the family way, who could not be persuaded to stay at home, there were apartments prepared, with every convenience for their accouchment, should they be unfortunately required. And I have been gravely told, and almost believe, that there have actually been instances of the utility of the arrangement. The ladies of Vienna are particularly celebrated for their grace and movement in waltzing, of which they never tire. For my own part, I thought waltzing from ten at night until seven in the morning, a continual whirligig; most tiresome to the eye, and ear—to say nothing of any worse consequences.[85]

[85] *Reminiscences of Michael Kelly* (London, 1826; reprint 1968), pp. 201–2.

The fast, triple-metered music for waltzing that tired Kelly's ears was called "Deutsche" or "Teutsche" or even (in a dialect form) "Teich," as in the ballroom scene of *Don Giovanni*.

To relieve the crowd and press at the carnival balls, something new was tried in 1767, according to Khevenhüller, who reports under date of 11 January that balls were to be given twice weekly in the Kärntnerthor Theater, "to which all honest people were admitted, with the exception of liveried servants, also personal servants ["Leiblaquay"], but even they could come wearing their own clothes." The co-regency of Joseph II had just begun, yet Vienna was already headed for more egalitarian times, it seems. Servants could dance in an imperial theater as long as they did not look like servants. The only trouble with this second-class Redoute was that, like so many schemes tried under Joseph II, it did not work. So few people paid the entry fee, says Khevenhüller, that "we were forced to give out free passes in order to fill out the dancing in the parterre somewhat, and that despite the expenses for the music and lighting." The experiment was not repeated the following year.

Musicians on an annual salary, all musicians in imperial service for instance, including the orchestra of the Kärntnerthor Theater, would have been paid extra for playing the carnival balls; this is one way to interpret Khevenhüller's remark. But did the regular orchestra play on such occasions? Carnival was a season when both imperial theaters were operating at the maximum allowed with their regular offerings of operas, ballets, and plays with entr'acte orchestral music. There is some evidence to show that extra musicians from outside the imperial service had to be called in to meet the demands of carnival balls. Relations between the two groups were less than amicable. In 1727 city musicians were hired for the carnivals balls "Teutsche und contradäntz zu geigen"; they urgently petitioned to be taken into court service in order to spare them the impertinences inflicted upon them by the court musicians, such as tearing up their music and beating them, "although the court musicians lacked the capacity and experience" of playing the carnival balls.[86]

Vienna offered a prodigious number of taverns and the like, in which dance music and dancing were common. Weiskern in his *Beschreibung* of 1770 counted 21 cafés, 45 inns, 111 beer houses, and numerous cellars where wine was served. Many humble musicians must have earned their living in such establishments. Haydn told his biographer Griesinger an anecdote about ambling about Vienna with Ditters—an episode that likely took place in the summer of 1764, from what Ditters says in his memoirs:

[86] Hadamowsky, "Barocktheater am Wiener Kaiserhof," p. 63.

Once when Haydn was going through the streets in Vienna with Dittersdorf, they heard some Haydn minuets being very badly played in a tavern. "We ought to have some fun with these bunglers," said one to the other. They went into the tavern, ordered a glass, and listened a while. "Who wrote these minuets, anyway?" Haydn finally asked. They gave him his own name. "Ach, that's pretty miserable stuff!" he exclaimed. At this the musicians flew into such a rage that one of them would have broken his violin on Haydn's head if he had not speedily taken flight.

When Haydn told the same tale to another, Dies, he made it more lively (or Dies did):

The well-known Ditters and Haydn were young friends. Once the two were roaming the streets at night and halted outside a common beer hall in which the musicians, half drunk and half asleep, happened to be fiddling miserably away at a Haydn minuet. The dance hall pieces that Haydn of course used to compose at that time found much favor on account of their originality. "Come on, let's go in!" said Haydn. "In we go!" Ditters agreed. Into the taproom they go. Haydn places himself next to the lead violin and asks, very offhand, "Whose minuet?" The latter answers, still drier if not indeed snapping him off, "Haydn's!" Haydn moves in front of him and says, feigning anger, "That's a stinking minuet!" ["Das ist ein rechter Sau-Menuett!"] "Who says?" cried the fiddler, now angry himself, jumping out of his seat. The other players follow suit and are about to break their instruments over Haydn's head; and they would have if Ditters, a big fellow, had not shielded Haydn with his arms and shoved him to the door.

However humble and miserable these tavern fiddlers were, they obviously took some pride in their work and had enough intelligence to esteem Haydn's music. The anecdote points up how small the distance was between popular music and art music during Vienna's best period. A Haydn or a Ditters gladly took up and incorporated in their compositions traits from the manifold ethnic strains that made up the Danube monarchy. No wonder their works permeated the fabric of Viennese life in those days. Wherever one turned, there was music of quality always sounding, in the churches, the theaters, the balls, the parade grounds (from the many regimental bands), the taverns, and in the streets, where serenades were common and where even perambulations were often accompanied by instruments ("gassatim gehen"—what Khevenhüller called "Casaten" under the date of 5 June 1755). The many cassations, divertimentos, notturnos, and serenades, often for winds, from the Viennese school testify to this frequently practiced custom.

Pezzl's sketch of the carnival balls in the Redoutensaal may leave the impression that they were chaotic, from an artistic point of view. Yet we know that considerable care and invention were expended in matters of costume, choreography, and music. Khevenhüller reported on 20 January 1756 that at the court ball members of the imperial family and their company dressed up as gardeners, waiters, and menials such as would be found in a country inn, and they danced "a newly composed entrée and contredanses." Spectacles described as "Bauernfeste" or "Bauern-Hochzeit" were greatly relished by the court, particularly when marriages were celebrated (Khevenhüller, 14 June 1756, 4 August 1765, 9 April 1766). These carefully staged peasant weddings likely served as a kind of talisman to bring the bounties of fertility to the great. Dancing masters flourished in Vienna, as might be expected in a situation where all the latest fashions were on display at once in the Redoutensaal.

As to the quality of the music there, it suffices to recall that even the most famous Viennese composers did not disdain to write dances for the court balls. Haydn, Mozart, and Beethoven all wrote dances for the Redoutensaal. So did many lesser masters, renowned in their day for just this specialty. A contract of 1773 between Pancrazio Huber and the imperial court regulated the number of musicians employed (forty-three in the large room, twenty-seven in the small rooms) and the price paid them; a 1777 payment record also lists the fees for the following sets of dances: thirty-six minuets and twelve German dances by Huber; twelve minuets by Joseph Haydn; eighteen minuets and twelve German dances by Franz Asplmayr.[87] In 1780 the same three composers were paid for further new dances.

Nicolai took Burney to task for talking too much about military music and folk music, but failing to take note of the public concert given every evening just before curfew by the regimental guard outside the Burg.

> It consisted of two shawms, two clarinets, two French horns, one trumpet, two bassoons, one ordinary drum, and one bass drum. Many different kinds of pieces were played, from notation. This music is not only a pleasant entertainment, especially on a still, moonlit summer evening, but also it deserves the attention of a musician who wishes to observe his art from a variety of viewpoints. The two drums, for instance, are often used to good effect in accompanying musical ideas. One can form some ideas on the subject of rhythm here.

These thoughts lead Nicolai to dance music, the last subject he treats in "Von der Musik in Wien." It is usually good, he says, and is played in an accented and lilting manner ("markirt und hebend gespielt"). He found Austrian dances much smoother and more moderate than what passed in his homeland for "Steyerschen Tanz."

[87]Landon, *Haydn*, 2: 405.

It consisted merely of continual waltzing ["fortgehendem Walzen"] by a number
of dancing pairs. But this happens with moderate movements, and is much
more proper than the wild and violent waltzing introduced into English dances
in our country. The dance musicians have organized into a guild, called the
Spielgrafenamt. Who does not belong to this guild may not play for dancing in
public. By imperial order, this guild was abolished in 1783, but a tax on musicians still remains, as with us.

Nicolai concludes his remarks by regretting that it occurred to a lawgiver to
take measures against the innocent pleasures of his people.

Booksellers, Publishers, and Instrument Makers

VIENNA was like most Italian cities with respect to music publishing in the
early eighteenth century: the city lacked music printing almost entirely and
relied instead on copyists. During the reign of Maria Theresa this situation
began to change. Burney wrote that there were no shops devoted to selling
music in Vienna, but he was unaware of how much music was available
from the general booksellers. Nicolai, writing a decade later than Burney,
noted that printed music could be bought in Vienna from the firms of Artaria
and Toricella, that Johann Traeg dealt in manuscript copies, and that
Laurent Lausch (whom Haydn considered bringing before justice in 1787
because of his shady practices) operated a music-lending business in the
Kärntnerthorstrasse and charged 6 florins for loaning manuscript music for
six months. Franz Anton Hoffmeister joined this group as a publisher of his
own and other composers' music in the 1780s.

Advertisements in the *Wiener Diarium* offer the main means of recon-
structing what music was for sale in Vienna. Some dealers also published
catalogues that included music. Thus Johann Michael Christophori, an "Uni-
versitätsischer Buch- und Kunsthandler," published several catalogues of
books he offered for sale, among them one devoted to music in 1714.[88] His
stock consisted of practical and theoretical works in German and Latin,
mostly from the previous century, and printed mainly in Augsburg and
Leipzig.

Johann Peter van Ghelen was the leading Viennese publisher in the first
half of the century. He brought out the *Wiener Diarium* from 1722 until his
death in 1754, and in 1724 published the first edition of Fux's *Gradus ad*

[88] Hannelore Gericke, *Der Wiener Musikalienhandel von 1700 bis 1778* (Wiener Musikwissenschaftliche
Beiträge 5) (Graz and Cologne, 1960). Gericke covers the period chronologically, publisher by publisher. Her findings are the source for most of the information in the following paragraphs.

Parnassum. Other theoretical works he later advertised, published elsewhere, included Mattheson's *Der vollkommene Kapellmeister* and Emanuel Bach's *Versuch über die wahre Art das Clavier zu spielen* (both of which Haydn is said to have acquired in Vienna during the 1750s). Ghelen also offered a rich store of manuscript music, including many court operas in score. Among the many publications by the Nuremberg music publisher Johann Ulrich Haffner offered for sale in Vienna by the bookseller Johann Paul Krauss were Emanuel Bach's *Sei Sonate per Cembalo,* advertised in 1746, referring to the *Württemberg* Sonatas of 1744.

Music printing in Vienna was infrequent until the founding of the Artaria firm in the 1770s. The first publication of keyboard music by court organist Gottlieb Muffat was in Vienna in 1726. But his second collection of 1739 was published in Augsburg. When it was a question of publishing a work of particular significance for the court, the authorities were apt to turn elsewhere than Vienna. Thus Hasse's *Alcide al bivio* for the imperial wedding of 1760 was sent to Leipzig, where Breitkopf published it in a keyboard score. Gluck's *Orfeo ed Euridice* was sent by Durazzo to Paris for publication. Yet Vienna did possess at this time a music engraver in the person of Georg Nicolai, whose fine editions of instrumental works by Steffan, Wagenseil, and others were sponsored and sold by Augustin and Friedrich Bernardi.

Vienna's most prominent publisher-bookseller during the second half of the century was Johann von Trattner. He rose from a poor country background in Hungary to master the art of printing, settled in Vienna in 1739,

FIGURE 1.14. Title page of Steffan's keyboard sonatas, 1763.

and became a university printer in 1749. Named *Hofbuchhändler* in 1751, he became three years later, on the death of Ghelen, court printer. His shop was at first located in the Schottenhof; he then bought the Friesingerhof in the Graben (1773) and had it reconstructed as the Trattnerhof. Famous for his reprints of classic German authors, he was also a notable patron of music. Mozart taught Trattner's second wife, Theresia von Nagel, and wrote various keyboard works for her (e.g., the Fantasia and Sonata in c, K. 475 and K. 477). The Mozarts lived in the Trattnerhof for several months during 1784, and Mozart gave academies there. Trattner's *Catalogus Universalis Librorum* of 1765 included many musical titles he was prepared to supply in either Vienna or Prague. A great triumph for Viennese music printing and publishing was reached with Trattner's edition of Gluck's *Alceste* in 1769, a folio orchestral score that was beautifully printed from movable type, and that sold originally for 16 florins 40 kreutzer.

Joseph Lorenz von Kurzböck became a university printer in 1756 and university bookseller in 1772. He was ennobled in 1786. Kurzböck printed a pioneering Viennese song collection in 1763, Philipp Hafner's *Scherz und Ernst in Liedern*. The engraved music plates look rather clumsy, although they are legible. It was evidently enough of a task to engrave music by itself without the text, which was placed elsewhere on the page. In 1770–71 he printed Johann Daube's *Der musikalische dilettante*, using movable type for the musical examples. Then in 1774 he used type to print Haydn's *Sei Sonate da Clavi-cembalo*, dedicated to Prince Esterházy. Gerber complained that the result was awkward for the performer and printed with unimposing type-faces ("mit unansehnlichen Typen und unbequem für den Spieler"). Between 1778 and 1782 Kurzböck printed four song collections.[89] Artaria's first edition of Haydn's Sonata in E♭ (Hoboken XVI:52) was dedicated to Kurzböck's daughter Magdalena, as was Traeg's edition of the Piano Trio in e♭ (Hob. XV:31).

Jakob Bianchi came to Vienna around 1770, after a career as a physicist in Strasbourg and *Hofmechanicus* in Mannheim, and founded a business called the *Kunst- und Realzeitungs-Comptoir*. Bianchi advertised musical items for sale in 1771, as well as "Der Dilettante, eine musicalisher Wochen-schrift." His *Realzeitung* was devoted less to public affairs and more to art than the *Wiener Diarium*; it provided detailed announcements about the music offered for sale, which was never the case with the *Diarium*. Thus Steffan's keyboard sonatas prompted this rather rhapsodic outburst: "How is it possible to feel properly the powerful, strong, and tender expressions in the compositions of a Gluck or a Gassmann, without accustoming the

[89] A. Peter Brown, "Joseph Haydn and Leopold Hofmann's 'Street songs,' " *JAMS* 33 (1980): 356–57.

ear to the correct progression of harmonic and melodic tones; toward this knowledge every lover of tonal art should progress. And who can convey them there? A Steffan." The conjunction of Gluck, Gassmann, and Steffan calls attention to their common Bohemian ancestry. Perceiving Steffan's strong and diverse keyboard sonatas as a kind of cicerone to the operas of Gluck and Gassmann opens intriguing historical possibilities.

Reviews of performances also began to appear in the *Realzeitung*. Haydn's oratorio *Il ritorno di Tobia*, performed by the Tonkünstler Societät in 1775, elicited praises (see below). Giovanni Paisiello's passage through Vienna in 1776 on his way to St. Petersburg was reported in the *Realzeitung* almost like a modern-day "news item."

> A few days ago the famous maestro di cappella from Naples arrived here, and he was invited to the Burgtheater where his opera *La frascatana* was given—the favorite comedy with our public and the masterpiece in this genre. The nobility present received him with distinguished marks of great respect, and hardly did the loges and parterre lead off when a general wave of applause and vociferation expressed pleasure and gratitude for the delight this genial composer has given every sentimental soul.

Bianchi offered for sale some of the latest Parisian symphonies, including those by Jean-Baptiste Davaux and François-Joseph Gossec. He also advertised symphonies by Haydn, Ditters, and Boccherini.

The Artarias arrived in Vienna in 1766 and dealt at first mainly with art engravings. By 1775 they had a shop in the Kohlmarkt near the Michaelerkirche. A year later they were advertising "music, engraved in Paris and just arrived, of the following famous composers . . ."; their list was very long and began with Christian Bach and Carl Friedrich Abel. Most of the names were of composers active in Paris, on both this list and the subsequent one of 1777. By 1778 the firm began engraving their own scores. The Artarias operated by a subscription method whereby the customer paid one-half in advance and the rest upon delivery.

The opportune arrival of an experienced music engraver from Paris, Anton Huberty, had much to do with the beginnings of the Artarias' own music line. Huberty brought his family to Vienna in 1777, probably at the invitation of the Viennese bookseller Hermann Joseph Krüchten. Three Haydn symphonies printed by Huberty in Paris were offered by the Ghelen firm in January 1772. Huberty has been called the pioneer of music engraving in Vienna, but this claim does not allow adequate credit to Viennese predecessors like Georg Nicolai. The method used for engraving was not out of the ordinary, but the volume of music engraved by Huberty and his family in conjunction with the firms of Artaria and (from 1781) Christoph

Torricella was remarkable. The Artaria firm became Mozart's principal publisher during his final decade. With Haydn, the Artarias enjoyed friendly
relations for the most part, as is evident from their correspondence. Even
such prolific masters as Mozart and Haydn could not expect to live from
what they were paid by publishers for their music, but they could easily gain
a welcome supplement to their other earnings once a specialized industry
devoted to music publishing was fully operative in Vienna.

Before the flowering of Viennese music publishing in the 1780s, manuscript copies provided the bulk of scores and parts sold. Copies of the six
Orchestral Trios by Johann Stamitz were acquired at Vienna for Bishop Egk
in 1752. One music copyist, Simon Haschke, was especially active, judging
from the advertisements he placed in the *Wiener Diarium*. In 1767 he offered
copies of "all Wagenseil's and Steffan's keyboard concertos," as well as
works by Haydn and Hofmann.[90] The names of these four composers are
frequently found in his other advertisements. In 1769 Haschke advertised
"Trio a 4tro von denen Herren Gassman, Hofmann, Poccarini [Boccherini],
Fils, Wanhal, Haydn, Toeski, wie auch Solo, Galanterie, Concerten für die
Travers, Violin, Violoncello, desgl. Kirchensachen, Messen und Vespern
unsw." Two years later he announced that he was also able to offer music
on loan for academies. In 1774 he offered "von Hern. Stefan neue Schlag-
concerten," as well as "Eine Quantität Sinfonien, als von Hern. Ordenitz,
Hofmann, Ditters, Haydn, Vanhal, Gasmann, van Meldere, Bach, Gluck,
Toeski, Holzbauer, Ziegler, Gossec, Abbe Neumann, Canabich, Fils etc.
Concerten, Concertini, auf allerhand Instrumenten, dann a quatro, a tre,
von Hrn. Haydn 5 kleine Operetta, von andern Meistern Cantaten und
Arien." This long list concludes, "auch sind 2 Fagotti von Rokobauer, einer
links der andere rechts in Commission zu verkaufen." Another copyist,
Johann Traeg the elder, began his music-copying business in the early 1780s.
He later published printed music as well and in 1799 issued a valuable catalogue of his offerings, *Verzeichnis alter und neuer sowohl geschriebener als gesto-
chener Musikalien, welche bei Johann Traeg erschienen sind*.

The mention of bassoons for sale by a music copyist leads us to a short
consideration of Viennese instrument makers—it can only be short because
the foundations have yet to be laid in the study of the subject. Mathias Rokobauer was apparently the main maker of double reed instruments; he supplied Haydn's orchestra with instruments and reeds on many occasions
during the 1760s and 1770s. Other wind instrument makers in Vienna,
according to records of payment at Melk, included Thuhlmann and Ziegler
(flutes), Kocl, Küys, and J. Baur (oboes), Nechwalsky (clarinet), and

---

[90] Gericke, *Der Wiener Musikalienhandel*, pp. 104–5.

W. Sradka, Stehle and J. Thuhlmann (bassoons). Vienna's foremost makers of horns were Anton Kerner and Johann [Carl] Stärzer, who sold Haydn two half-step slides in 1772 (allowing C and G crooks to be converted to B and F#).[91]

The most important eighteenth-century violin makers in Vienna were the Stadlmanns. Daniel Stadlmann gained his Viennese citizenship in 1707. He may have been an apprentice in Füssen, and he is considered to be the best Austrian follower of the great Tyrolean maker Jacob Stainer.[92] He made barytons and lutes as well as violins and cellos. Johann Joseph, his son, continued the craft and became "Hof Lauten und Geigenmacher." The Reverend Gregor Mayer, with whom Nicolai and his son performed Haydn trios and quartets at Melk Abbey in 1781, owned a cello by Johann Joseph, which he willed to the abbey. A nephew of Johann Joseph, Michael Ignaz, carried the firm's business on into the nineteenth century. Other luthiers in Vienna were the Posch and Thir families. Melk obtained a viola from Anton Posch in the first decade of the eighteenth century and another from "Anton & Stephan Posch Kay[ser] hoff Lauthen Macher Wien 1740."[93] The same monastery acquired a cello inscribed "Johannes Georgius Thir fecit Viennae anno 1775." Haydn dealt with a Mathias Thier, "Lauten und Geigen Macher."[94]

Some of Melk's purchases and repair work involved makers in nearby towns such as Krems or in more distant places (Bohemia, Salzburg, Italy), but the great majority involved Viennese craftsmen. When the time came to install a new organ in the grandiose abbey church that soared above the Danube at Melk, the contract went to Gottfried Sonnholz, who styled himself "Bürgerlicher Orgelmacher zu Wien." The contract, signed in 1731, called for an instrument of two manuals, pedal, and twenty-eight stops. It took a decade to complete all the decorations, but the organ must have been usable at least in part late in 1732, when *Regens chori* Pater Colomonn Friedrich was allowed to go to Vienna in order to purchase "new instruments which conform to [the tuning of] the new organ."[95]

Fortepianos began to take their place alongside harpsichords rather early in Vienna. The Johann Baptist Schmidt who played a concert on the forte-

[91] Paul Bryan, "Haydn's Hornists," *Haydn-Studien* 3 (1973): 58. A short general survey is Gerhard Stradner, "Wiener Instrumentenbau zur Zeit Maria Theresias," in *Musik am Hof Maria Theresias*, ed. Roswitha Vera Karpf (Munich and Salzburg, 1984), pp. 168-78. See also Helga Haupt, "Wiener Instrumentenbauer von 1791 bis 1815," *Studien zur Musiwissenschaft* 24 (1960): 120-84.

[92] Walter Senn, "Stadlmann," MGG 12: 1126-27; see also Senn, *Jakob Stainer, der Geigenmacher zu Absam* (Innsbruck, 1951).

[93] Robert Norman Freeman, "The Practice of Music at Melk Monastery in the Eighteenth Century" (Ph.D. diss., University of California, Los Angeles, 1971), p. 108.

[94] Landon, *Haydn*, 2: 477.

[95] Freeman, "Music at Melk," p. 73.

piano in a Burgtheater concert in March 1763 was perhaps a brother of the Andreas Schmidt who was an organ and clavier maker.[96] Johann Andreas Stein, a key figure in the evolution of the fortepiano, probably visited Vienna twice, once as early as 1749. The best-known maker of fortepianos in Vienna, Anton Walter, figures in the correspondence of Haydn, Mozart, and Beethoven. Haydn thought Walter overrated and recommended in his stead the lighter action of Wenzel Schantz, who provided him with a new fortepiano in 1788. The Schantz brothers, Johann and Wenzel, were among the wave of immigrants from Bohemia who left during or after the troubled times of the mid-century wars. Johann returned and died in Bohemia in 1790. Schönfeld wrote in his *Jahrbuch der Tonkunst von Wien und Prag* (1796) that Johann Schantz copied English square pianos and sold them for the price of 30 ducats. Schönfeld contrasted the instruments of Walter ("for the player who loves a loud acoustical feast and an enormous sea of sound") with those of Nanette Stein-Streicher ("for performers who love not only clear, distinct, but also smooth, soft, and gentle playing").

Walter, who was also an organ builder, developed the manufacture and export of fortepianos to an unprecedented degree. In 1790 he petitioned for the title "Organ and Instrument Maker of the Imperial-Royal Court." In support of his claim, Walter stated that he had made more than 350 fortepianos; he was the first to make them as they were now universally disposed; he sold them to Poland, Saxony, Prussia, France, and Italy for 80 and 100 ducats, whereas ten years earlier keyboard instruments had to be procured abroad; furthermore, he employed fourteen workmen, more than any maker in Germany, and finally, four of his fortepianos had been purchased by the court, and the organ he built had received nothing but praise from connoisseurs.[97]

Enough evidence has been adduced to show that during at least the last part of the century, Vienna became a center of music publishing and instrument making that ranked with other European capitals. No one could have predicted as much of the industrially backward city ruled by Charles VI. Credit is due in great measure to the more enlightened policies of his successors for the unprecedented quality and quantity of music making that spread through society. As one economic historian has put it, the Austrian economy began to awaken from its long sleep during the reign of Maria Theresa.[98]

[96] Eva Badura-Skoda, "Prolegomena"; the information in this paragraph is mainly indebted to her article.

[97] Letter of 6 December 1790 from Walter to Emperor Leopold II, transcribed from the original in Rice, "Emperor and Impresario," pp. 362–64. See also John A. Rice, "Anton Walter, Instrument Maker to Leopold II," *Journal of the American Musical Instrument Society* 15 (1989): 32–49.

[98] Roman Sandgruber, *Die Anfänge der Konsumgesellschaft* (Konsumgüterverbrauch, Lebenstandard, und Alltagskultur in Österreich im 18. und 19. Jahrhundert) (Munich, 1982), p. 95.

2
Court Composers
1740-65

THE galant style made few inroads in Vienna before 1740, the year in which Maria Theresa and her consort Francis Stephan of Lorraine acceded to the throne. Her father, Charles VI, stood firm against this style, and made sure that his chief musicians, Johann Joseph Fux and Antonio Caldara, did likewise. After Francis Stephan died in 1765, Maria Theresa left most decisions in artistic matters to her son Joseph II, her co-regent for fifteen years. There was, as a result, a considerable realignment in the court music after 1765. The court composers considered in this chapter, led by Georg Christoph Wagenseil, made their decisive contributions to Viennese music during the quarter-century reign of Maria Theresa and Francis Stephan. Their pupils and successors who flourished mainly in the following quarter century, the era of Joseph II, are treated in a later chapter.

Bohemian composers and performers played a prominent role in Viennese court music during this mid-century period. The influx had begun even earlier with the arrival of Jan Dismas Zelenka, Franz Benda, and Georg Zarth, to name only the most prominent Bohemian musicians visiting the imperial capital. When Franz Tuma took up residence in Vienna, he profited from the instruction of Kapellmeister Fux. It has been claimed that Fux himself was a Bohemian, musically trained during a twenty-year residence in Prague.[1] This claim is not accepted by Fux scholars, but there may be further

---

[1] Bohumír Jan Dlabacž, *Allgemeines historisches Künstler-Lexikon für Böhmen* (Prague, 1815), s.v. "Fux."

connections between Fux and Prague, besides the famous coronation opera for Charles VI in 1723, that are still to be discovered. Similar connections pertain to Wagenseil, who served as organist under Tuma and purportedly wrote operas in the Czech language for Prague, as did Gluck, whose Czech origins are no longer disputable.

Reutter and Tuma

THE succession of both Caldara and Fux eventually passed to the single figure of Georg Reutter the younger. Reutter was born in Vienna in 1708, the son of the organist and Kapellmeister of St. Stephen's Cathedral, who had been ennobled at Rome in 1695. He was trained by his father and by Caldara, then sent as court scholar to Italy for further study in 1729 and 1730. He returned to Vienna in 1731, when, over the objections of Fux, he obtained a post of court composer, with an annual salary of 600 florins. At this time he married the daughter of a court functionary, Theresia Holz-hauer, a fine soprano who was subsequently called "La Reutter." The emperor and empress stood as godparents to their two children, named, appropriately, Charles and Elizabeth Christine. Reutter had obtained his father's position as cathedral organist at an early age, and when his father died in 1738, he also became Kapellmeister at St. Stephen's. In 1740 he was raised to the Austrian nobility by Charles VI and became Georg von Reutter. It was around this time that Reutter recruited young Joseph Haydn as a singer when passing through Hainburg.

When Caldara died in 1736, he was succeeded as vice-maestro at court by Luca Antonio Predieri, a Bolognese composer of the old school who managed to please both Fux and Charles VI. Five years later, when Fux died, Predieri became first Kapellmeister, leaving the post of second vacant. Predieri was apparently not appreciated by the new generation come to power, for he composed almost nothing for the court after 1740. Reutter assumed full control when Predieri was pensioned in 1751, but he was not given the title of primo maestro until after Predieri's death in 1767. Meanwhile he managed to garner for himself the title and remuneration of second as well as first Kapellmeister at the cathedral (by 1756). Thus in his person alone Reutter united the four most important musical posts in Vienna, an unprecedented feat, but perhaps only to be expected from someone so obsequious as to name his children after the reigning sovereigns. He remained in great favor under Maria Theresa, who had him give two music lessons a week to the young crown prince Joseph.[2]

---

[2] Derek Beales, *Joseph II*, vol. 1: *In the Shadow of Maria Theresa, 1741–1780* (Cambridge, 1987), p. 45.

FIGURE 2.1. Workshop of Martin van Meytens. Detail of the imperial wedding banquet, October 1760, showing Reutter surrounded by his musicians.

Reutter was a clever courtier, one whose noble condition and unswerving loyalty to the imperial family had much to do with his rise to power. He cut a fine figure as a man. In Figure 2.1 we see him surrounded by his musicians at the imperial wedding banquet in 1760, his right hand raised, standing in the curve of the harpsichord in a fancy embroidered coat.[3] The darker side of his favored status was apparent to many at the time as well. Repeated

---

[3]The entire painting is reproduced in color in Gerda and Gottfried Mraz, *Maria Theresia: Ihr Leben und ihr Zeit in Bildern und Dokumenten* (Munich, 1979). Reutter is depicted in a blue coat, while all the other musicians wear their red livery. There are at least two portraits of Reutter that confirm his identification here.

complaints were made about his neglect of the cathedral music. But Reutter was protected by his special relationship to the imperial family, and survived all challenges to his authority. Count Durazzo took him on directly in 1760 over the issue of the music at Joseph II's first marriage. Between theater intendant and Kapellmeister the battle was waged by way of written protocols (discussed below) that throw vivid light on the court's musical life. Reutter eventually prevailed; within a few years Durazzo was no longer intendant. This battle may have taken its toll on Reutter as well; his active years as a composer seem to have ended around 1760, twelve years before he died.

Reutter wrote some eighty masses. His *Missa S. Caroli* of 1734 honored the name day of the emperor (and, by extension, that of Reutter's newborn son). The work is archetypical of those for Habsburg festivities: its shining C-major tonality, with trumpets ("clarini") and timpani, belonged to a tradition we call the *Habsburger Prunkstil*. The Kyrie begins with a fanfare in which these military instruments, reinforced by an alto trombone, are joined by the chorus, while violins in unison rush up and down in quick notes, giving a display of the proverbial "Rauschenden Violinen à la Reutter."[4] The "Christe" is set as a trio sonata in imitative style; the concluding "Kyrie" starts as a fugue and ends with the fanfares of the opening. The writing is calculated to make a good effect in a large reverberant space, such as the cathedral. Unusual touches of instrumental color include the long concertante solo part for alto trombone in the "Gratias" of the Gloria. For the more doleful parts of the text, Reutter found appropriately somber hues. "Qui tollis peccata mundi" is set for chorus and winds, without violins; a tenor trombone joins the alto trombone and the two trumpets, and they keep up an eighth-note pulse throughout this *Adagio* in 4/4, which contains an expressive enharmonic modulation in the middle. The Credo rolls by without a single word repeated until, in an *Adagio* in c, with violins throbbing in eighth notes, the words "Et homo factus est" are repeated and intensified by the introduction of the Neapolitan-sixth chord. "Et resurrexit" brings more fanfares. Reutter chose the subdominant and a bass solo for the Benedictus (among the court singers was a much-admired basso, Christian Praun). "Dona nobis pacem" is set as a fugue into which, at the very end, military fanfares are admitted.

Works like the *Missa S. Caroli* were greatly loved throughout Austria, as evidenced by the many manuscript copies that have been discovered in different places. In 1782, when Pope Pius VI visited Vienna and presided over a pontifical mass in the cathedral, the Kyrie and Gloria chosen were by

---

[4] Edited in *DTÖ* 88 (1952) by Norbert Hofer.

Reutter. And a favorite requiem setting by the same composer was used to commemorate the tenth anniversary of Maria Theresa's death in 1790.

Reutter wrote many pieces for festive occasions of a secular nature as well, whether vocal (many on texts by Pasquini and Metastasio) or instrumental. On gala days at court, when the imperial family dined in public, the musicians were responsible for providing a *Servizio di tavolo*. Reutter's four-movement work in C, with trumpets and drums, bearing this title and a date of 1757, gives an idea of what such *Tafelmusik* was like.[5] The work lacks distinction, and Reutter does not rise above the banal in the harmonic sequences of his finale. Another *Servizio di tavolo* by him, also in C and with trumpets and drums, is dated 1745. These works belong to the Viennese tradition of the intrada symphony in C, which is thought to have originated with Caldara, who wrote two such orchestral works, called sonata, and in the forms of *Allegro, Largo, Fuga* and *Allegro, Andante, Allegro da capo*.[6] The genre had special connections with the imperial family, and was used to brighten celebrations such as birthdays. Other court composers who made contributions to the intrada symphony were Wenzel Birck and Wagenseil, from whom the legacy passed to Joseph Haydn. One of its ultimate manifestations is Mozart's *Jupiter* Symphony in C, with its blazing fugal finale in the Viennese tradition.

Reutter received extravagant praise for his church music in an anonymous article defending Austrian musicians against German critics that appeared in 1766 in the *Wiener Diarium*, "Von dem wienerischen Geschmack in der Musik" (On the Viennese Taste in Music). I argue below that the author was a young Viennese composer on the rise who very much desired a position at court, which would explain why he praised Reutter so highly—it would not have taken a sage to guess the identity of the author, and Reutter was a very clever man. Maria Theresa defended her Kapellmeister somewhat disingenuously in a letter to one of her daughters-in-law: "Put yourself in his place; his music for the church had to be very short, and performed by schoolboys, thus it was necessary to make up for this with instruments and basses."[7] The implication is that instruments made a lot of noise in his music, but only out of necessity. When Burney visited Vienna in 1772, he heard among many other compositions, most of which impressed him, a *Te Deum* by Reutter in St. Stephen's on 13 September, which he summed up as

[5] Edited in *DTÖ* 31 (1908) by Karl Horwitz and Karl Riedel.
[6] Jens Peter Larsen, "Zur Entstehung der österreichischen Symphonietradition (ca. 1750–1775)," *Haydn Yearbook* 10 (1978): 72–80; 76.
[7] Letter to Archduchess Maria Beatrice in Milan in late 1772, a few months after Reutter's death, quoted in H. C. Robbins Landon, *Haydn: Chronicle and Works*, 5 vols. (Bloomington, Ind., 1976–80), 2: 182.

"great noise and little meaning." Even so, it says something positive about Reutter that Mozart, late in his life, copied out two Psalm settings by the long-deceased master, a quiet, homophonic setting *a 4* of Psalm 131, *Memento Domine David*, and a fugal setting *a 4* of Psalm 150, *In te Domine speravi*.[8]

Franz Tuma was close to Reutter in age and alike in that he was another figure of authority in Viennese music following the demise of Fux. He was born František Tůma in Kostelec nad Orlicí, Bohemia, in 1704, and had his early musical training there. There is uncertainty about his further training, but according to Friedrich Wilhelm Marpurg he was a Vice-Kapellmeister at Vienna already by the year 1722. Tuma studied counterpoint with Fux and was employed as Kapellmeister by Count Kinsky, chancellor of Bohemia, who recommended him in 1734 as "the only [composer] capable of imitating . . . Fux and following the latter's principles."[9] He rose in the esteem of the imperial court to the point of being named to head the chapel of the dowager empress Elizabeth, widow of Charles VI, from 1741 until her death in 1750, when he was pensioned with 600 gulden per annum; he died in 1774.

Tuma's voluminous production of masses includes fourteen of the a cappella type, and dozens in the more modern style with orchestral accompaniment, resembling some of the works of Caldara. Like Reutter, he is considered a Baroque composer who only occasionally introduced hints of the galant style. His *Missa a 4* in D, dated 1746, is one of many Viennese orchestral masses to use a pair of solo trombones (and the chapel of the dowager empress employed two trombone players).[10] The mass commences with an *Adagio* that is a veritable slow introduction. The orchestra begins by stating the disjunct chords I - V^6; the chorus enters singing "Kyrie" to sustained chords in a progression that begins I - II$^{6/4/2}$ - V^6 - I. Rich harmonies with many secondary dominants and a variety of chord inversions fill out the introduction, which comes to a conclusion arrived at by an augmented sixth chord preparing V/V, then resolution on V. The rich harmonic language continues in the ensuing *Allegretto*. One of the most impressive moments in the mass comes near the end, when the opening choral progres-

[8] K^6 Anhang A 22–23. See Alan Tyson, "The Mozart Fragments," *JAMS* 34 (1981): 490–91.
[9] Milan Postolka, "Tuma," in *The New Grove Dictionary of Music and Musicians* (London, 1980). See also Camillo Schoenbaum, "Die böhmischen Musiker in der Musikgeschichte Wiens vom Barock zur Romantik," *Studien zur Musikwissenschaft* 25 (1962): 475–95.
[10] Samuel Vernon Sanders, Jr., "A Stylistic Analysis of Selected Viennese Masses, ca. 1740" (M.A. thesis, University of California, Los Angeles, 1972), p. 70. Vol. 2 contains a complete transcription of the mass. For two further examples of Tuma's writing for solo trombones, see Bruce C. MacIntyre, *The Viennese Concerted Mass of the Early Classic Period* (Ann Arbor, 1986), examples 7-19 and 10-5. On p. 90, MacIntyre says that Tuma's *Missa Sancti Stephani* (before 1747) represents a significant step in the evolution of the *missa brevis*.

sion of the Kyrie returns, once again *Adagio,* at the beginning of the Agnus Dei, lending a cyclic feeling to the whole work. On the basis of this mass, it appears that Tuma was a figure to be reckoned with in church music, a composer at least as gifted as Reutter, if not more so. The strong tradition of Viennese orchestral masses with which Haydn grew up may be one of the sources from which he later fashioned the slow symphonic introduction. Among Tuma's pupils was the noted organist and contrapuntist Joseph Seger, who in his turn taught several Czech composers.

Monn and Birck

MATTHIAS GEORG MONN, organist and composer, was born in 1717 in Vienna, where he died in 1750. Documents from 1731–32 show him to have been a chorister at the monastery of Klosterneuburg, ten miles up the Danube from Vienna. As late as August 1750, two months before his death, Monn wrote a gratulatory piece for the name day of the prior of Klosterneuburg. He was choir director and organist in the sumptuous new temple known as the Karlskirche from its consecration in 1737. Long after his death Emperor Joseph II had Monn's compositions performed and played them himself.[11]

The emperor was particularly fond of fugues, and Monn wrote many. None were printed during his short life, but over a half century later, by the year 1808, the Bureau des Arts et d'Industrie at Vienna had brought out *Six Quatuors pour deux Violons, Alto et Violoncelle, composées par Matthie George Monn. Oeuvre postume.* These are two-movement works consisting of a slow introduction and a fugue; two of them correspond to the initial movements of four-movement symphonies in *sonata da chiesa* form. Such a work is Monn's Symphony in A, which begins with a *Larghetto* of twenty-five measures in 2/4 coming to stop on V, leading to a substantial fugal *Allegro moderato* in 4/4; a short *Andante* and concluding *Presto* round out the work. A review of the *Six Quatuors* called attention to the works as musical rarities on account of their strict style ("gebundene Schreibart"). They can be compared with the posthumous publication by the same firm of quartets with fugues by Florian Gassmann (who died in 1774 and was another favorite of Emperor Joseph). Johann Georg Albrechtsberger, the famed counterpoint teacher, was probably responsible for reviving the fugal quartets of Monn, who was one of his teachers. It has been claimed that Monn was the only

---

[11] This is according to Joseph Sonnleithner in 1830, quoted by Wilhelm Fischer in his introduction to *DTÖ* 39 (1912), which is devoted to the works of Monn and his brother Johann Christoph Mann.

composer besides Albrechtsberger who consistently wrote complete fugal strettos.[12]

Monn was highly esteemed in Vienna. Abbé Maximilian Stadler, abbot of Melk from 1784 to 1786, had this to say about him in his collection of biographies:

> One of the greatest organists and composers of his time, admired by all connoisseurs among his contemporaries, he was chorus director in the Karlskirche, and wrote masterpieces in various genres, such as masses, among which those in C and in B♭ rank as classics, an *Anweisung zum Generalbass*, violin music with fugues, a requiem, keyboard pieces, concertos, symphonies, choruses, thirty divertimenti (fourteen *a 4*) . . . He also trained splendid pupils like Albrechtsberger.[13]

Monn's Mass in C is dated 1741 and scored for *ripieno* brass (trumpet and drums), strings including violas, voices with doubling instruments (sopranos by oboe, altos and tenors by trombones, and basses by bassoon et al.).[14] It is a *Missa solemnis* with large-scale fugues in the festive *Habsburger Prunkstil* represented by Reutter's *Missa S. Caroli* of 1734.

Much was made in the early twentieth century of a little work by Monn, supposedly autograph, inscribed "Spartitura di Giorgeo Mattio Monn li 24. Maggio 740," and consisting of four movements, the third a Minuet.[15] All movements are in D, which suggests, along with the modest dimensions of their binary forms, that the work belongs to the tradition of the suite or partita (sometimes called "Parthien" in Austria, and perhaps the intention behind the term "Spartitura"). The opening *Allegro*, ||: 20 :||: 21 :|| is in 4/4. The second movement is called "Aria" (unless the editors transposed this from "Air"?) and is a piece in 2/4 that is indebted for its theme to Corelli's Corelli's well-known *Giga* for violin (from Op. 5 No. 6) and followed by its *double*. The Minuet is rather leaden. A finale, an *Allegro* in 2/4, is sprightly and Pergolesian, with its three-note slides and *unisono* retorts. Monn did write true symphonies in the 1740s (in three movements without minuet), but this work does not deserve to be placed among them.

---

[12] Warren Kirkendale, *Fugue and Fugato in Rococo and Classical Chamber Music* (Durham, N. C., 1979), p. 72.

[13] *Materialen zur Geschichte der Musik unter den österreichischen Regenten*, a manuscript compiled between 1815 and 1825, edited by Karl Wagner as *Abbé Maximilian Stadler* (Schriftenreihe der Internationalen Stiftung Mozarteum 6) (Kassel, 1974), p. 94.

[14] Sanders, "A Stylistic Analysis of Selected Viennese Masses," p. 18. The entire mass is transcribed in vol. 2.

[15] Edited in *DTÖ* 31 (1908): 37–50, by Karl Horowitz and Karl Riedel. The editors transpose "Menuet" (cf. facsimile of the original in *MGG*, article "Monn") into "Menuetto" without saying so.

Monn's symphonies include one in B major, a key so rare that even Haydn used it only once in his symphonies. Its first movement uses the bifocal close to articulate the second tonal area in both parts, a very advanced formal concept for the 1740s.[16] Both outer movements begin with the progression I - V^6 - vi, which is to say, rather routinely. Novel thematic material was not one of the characteristics that made Monn so original. His Symphony in G (dated 1749) begins with an *Allegro* in 4/4 inaugurated by the violins ascending the tonic triad in even quarters, starting on the downbeat: 1 3 5 ↯. This is another commonplace, familiar from the Vivaldian concerto and from Bach's magnificent Violin Concerto in E (BWV 1042). Monn makes good use of the motif in various parts of the movement, and particularly shines in his retransition, which he begins by inverting the main motif. His minor-mode passage as secondary theme is just as modern-sounding as Wagenseil's use of the same device. But Monn achieves a sense of drama rare in Wagenseil when, just before the closure of both the prima parte and the seconda parte, he interjects a deceptive cadence, a vii^6, of V instead of an expected tonic. Bach used this same delaying device in the first movement of his *Italian Concerto*, to be sure, and the parallel is but one of many in Monn, suggesting that he was familiar with Bach's music. Haydn, who made such substitutions for the cadence a lifelong specialty, especially V$^{4/3}$ of V resolving to V^6, often as a dramatic closing gesture on a grand scale, is less likely to have been familiar with Bach's music. He grew up, on the other hand, with the music of Monn.

Monn wrote several solo concertos. One, a Concerto for Cello in g, contains a beautiful *Adagio* in 12/8 in the key of E♭ as middle movement; a hair-raising passage in ascending chromatic chords in the opening movement (which may be what attracted the attention of Arnold Schoenberg, who made an edition of the concerto in 1911–12); and outer movements that are rhythmically plodding, in the old style. An arrangement of the same concerto for harpsichord and orchestra exists in Berlin, along with several other keyboard concertos and sonatas by Monn (the provenance being the old Prussian Royal Library). The Harpsichord Concerto in D opens with one of Monn's typically short and motivic themes, this one resembling the beginning of "Rule Brittania." Its opening *Allegro* in 4/4 is clearly laid out in a ritornello structure that incorporates some elements of sonata form (a secondary area in V recurs toward the end in I). The orchestra is present in the solos as accompanist and sometimes as dialogist. Monn rounded out the work with an *Andante* (2/4) in d, a melody that threatens to turn into "A

---

[16] Robert S. Winter, "The Bifocal Close and the Evolution of the Viennese Classical Style," *JAMS* 42 (1989): 275–337. According to this usage, the bifocal close is a half cadence, the second chord of which either initiates a modulation to V or leads back to I.

Serpina penserete" from Pergolesi's *La serva padrona*, and a *Tempo di Minuetto* (3/8) in D.

That Monn was appreciated and collected in northern Germany is not surprising. With his penchant for incisive, Baroque-style themes, which he submitted to motivic development, and his contrapuntal solidity, he shared many traits with Bach and the older Bach sons. Combining these old-fashioned traits, as he does, with newer ones of a more *empfindsam* temper (such as the rising chromatics in the Cello Concerto), Monn comes close, in particular, to Emanuel Bach. Had he not died so young perhaps he would have reconciled the strict and galant streams in Viennese music.[17] Wagenseil was in a position to do so; he taught his students according to Fux, honored Bach and Handel, and was greatly respected, yet he wrote almost exclusively in the galant style after 1750 (demonstrating how far theory and practice had diverged). It was left for Haydn to fuse learned polyphony with the dramatic and homophonic sonata style in the Viennese practice.

Wenzel Birck (1718–63) was another organist-composer with strong contrapuntal skills. He was born and died in Vienna. As court scholar from 1736 to 1738, he studied counterpoint with Matteo Palotta, a Sicilian who was one of the court composers under Fux. In 1739 Birck became sixth court organist; by 1760 he was second organist after Gottlieb Muffat, who was no longer active. He figures in the Reutter-Durazzo dispute of 1760, when Reutter made claims that Birck was not only a good harpsichord player, but also one practiced in the latest musical taste.

Birck's major publication was *Trattenimenti per clavicembalo*, published by Bernardi in 1757.[18] On the title page the composer is qualified as teacher to three archdukes, that is to say, Joseph, heir to the throne, Leopold, his eventual successor, and Charles, a middle brother who died young. Joseph's well-known penchant for fugues was nurtured by Birck, according to Christoph Sonnleithner, who wrote: "The emperor was a friend in general to the strict style, in which he himself was instructed by the magnificent contrapuntist Birck."[19] Fugues figure prominently in Birck's chamber music, of which there survive seventeen *Parthien a 3*, twelve sonatas *a 3* for strings, and sixteen quartets.[20] A substantial keyboard fugue in e appears at the

[17] A similar dichotomy is evident in Monn's music for solo keyboard; see Carla Pollock, "Viennese Solo Keyboard Music, 1740–1770: A Study in the Evolution of the Classic Style," (Ph.D. diss., Brandeis University, 1984), chapter 2.

[18] Two pieces from this work can be studied in A. Peter Brown, *Joseph Haydn's Keyboard Music: Sources and Style* (Bloomington, Ind., 1986), pp. 142, 187. Brown also offers otherwise unavailable keyboard music by Monn, Schlöger, and Leopold Hofmann.

[19] Quoted by Wilhelm Fischer in the Introduction to *DTÖ* 39 (1912).

[20] Kirkendale, *Fugue and Fugato*, p. 284, lists thirty-three fugues in Birck's chamber music, and examples figure prominently throughout the book. Birck's quartets are also transmitted as symphonies *a*

beginning of the first suite in the 1757 publication, which is otherwise comprised of sonata-style pieces or dances. The second suite, in G/g, has no fugue. It seems to reflect music for a stage ballet, with titles like "La Gelosa," "Polacca," "Pierrot," "Ninfe e Pastori," and "La Zinghera." These galant trifles bear out the claim that Birck was acquainted with the latest musical styles, just as the published fugue, on a descending chromatic subject, amply justifies the claim that he was a magnificent contrapuntist.

Wagenseil

EARLY WORKS

THE leading court composer during the first two decades of Maria Theresa's reign was her music teacher, Georg Christoph Wagenseil, who was born in Vienna in 1715. He composed in all genres and left a huge oeuvre, but he was particularly admired as a keyboard composer and performer, also as a teacher. Haydn took Wagenseil as one of his models when he was emerging as a composer in the 1750s. Christian Bach adopted his light and fluid textures, his delicate *cantilena* and rhythmic verve. So did Mozart, who chose to play one of his harpsichord concertos when he first visited the Viennese court in 1762. Like his colleague Giuseppe Bonno, Wagenseil came from a family in imperial service (which boded well for his future advancement). At first destined for the study of law, he showed early promise as a keyboard performer. As a pupil of Adam Weger, organist of the Michaelerkirche, he attracted the attention of Fux, and perhaps that as well of one of the court organists, Gottlieb Muffat.

With Fux's support Wagenseil became a court scholar in 1735, and for the next three years he was trained in counterpoint and composition by Fux and Matteo Palotta. Several of his masses survive from this period, toward the end of which he applied for a position as one of the court composers, pointing out his experience in church music. A remarkable testimony by Fux accompanied his petition. Fux praised him highly and expressed his conviction (which was quite misplaced, as it later turned out) that through Wagenseil the correct style of composition would hold firm against the licentious galant style. Not only Wagenseil's sacred music but his early keyboard

4; see Larsen, "Zur Entstehung der österreichischen Symphonietradition," pp. 76–77. For the movement titles in the seventeen trio-partitas, see Jens Peter Larsen, "Wenzel Raimund Birck und Mattäus Schlöger: Zwei Hofmusiker und 'Vorklassiker' aus der Zeit Maria Theresias," in *Musik am Hof Maria Theresias*, ed. Roswitha Vera Karpf (Munich and Salzburg, 1984), pp. 108–30; 112.

suites and fugues seemed ample justification for Fux's confidence that the young composer would continue the Viennese contrapuntal tradition. He replaced Carlo Badia as *Kammercompositor* in 1739; two years later he obtained the additional position of organist in the chapel of the widowed empress Elizabeth (from 1741 until her death in 1750), the director of which was Franz Tuma.

Although only a decade younger than Tuma, Wagenseil appears to be at least a generation removed from the Bohemian master in a work such as his lovely *Missa gratias agimus tibi*, dated 1742. This is a *missa brevis* in A, which gets its name because of a little lyric phrase rising to the sixth degree with which these words from the Gloria are set (Example 2.1). The phrase appears as a motto elsewhere in the mass, starting in the Kyrie.[21] Already from this early work two traits characteristic of the mature Wagenseil are evident: he was a melodist first and foremost, and he was most comfortable working on a small scale.

EXAMPLE 2.1. *Wagenseil, Mass in A (1742), Gloria*

gra - ti - as   a - gi-mus ti - bi   pro-pter   mag-nam glo - ri-am tu - am

One of the earliest occasional works Wagenseil wrote for the court is his setting of Giovanni Pasquini's "festa di camera" *I lamenti d'Orfeo*. The occasion was St. Anne's Day, 26 July 1740, when the court honored Archduchess Marianna, Maria Theresa's much loved sister and only surviving sibling. Charles VI still reigned, but would die suddenly the following October (Fux followed him on 13 February 1741, aged eighty). Wagenseil did his best to please both strict and modern tastes in this little work. An opening Sinfonia begins with a ponderous fugal *Allegro assai* and concludes in the following movement, a blithe *Presto* in 3/8 with all the earmarks of a Menuetto galante. Similarly, in the arias there is an evident dichotomy between the older manner of continuous unfolding *(Fortspinnung)* and the newer one of building up a melody out of little symmetrical fragments, often interrupted by rests.

Pasquini's text follows the typical cantata plan for two singers: two arias apiece, led up to by recitatives. The muse Calliope (sung by La Reutter) comforts her son Orfeo (sung by the contralto castrato Giuseppe Appiani) after the loss of Euridice. The fable may seem an odd choice for a festive day, but it was so employed at the Habsburg court from Fux (1715) to Gluck

---

[21] Sanders, "A Stylistic Analysis of Selected Viennese Masses," p. 50. Vol. 2 contains a complete transcription of the mass.

EXAMPLE 2.2. *Wagenseil, operatic incipits*

a. I lamenti d'Orfeo *(1740)*

Per-sa la spe-me   dell' i - dol_ mi - o   si per-da in-sie-me va - da_ in_ ob-bli-o.

b. Ariodante *(1745)*

Dol - ce _ di - let- to   mi scher-za   in   pet - to,   mi scher-za   in   pet - to.

(1762). Orfeo's arias, both in the major mode, are distinctly more modern than those of Calliope, one of which is in minor—as if the composer were depicting a difference in generation. In Orfeo's second aria, "Persa la speme," Wagenseil writes a melody in short little matching segments, separated by rests (Example 2.2a). On the basis of this melody, he could be a fashionable Neapolitan composer, except that the reigning melodic fashion would have dictated repeating "del idol mio" as a galant redict, turning the rising conjunct third in m. 4 to a third falling to the tonic, then continuing on with the next line. A few years later, in his *Ariodante* (Venice, 1745), that is exactly what we find him doing (Example 2.2b).[22] With its ever so modish syncopations and its **a b b**′ shape, this melody could pass for one of Baldassare Galuppi's.

Ariodante did not achieve much success. The libretto was derived from an old one by Antonio Salvi. Wagenseil made the trip to Venice to become acquainted with the singers and supervise the first performances in the San Giovanni Grisostomo Theater during the fall of 1745. He received no further commissions from Venice. The beautifully preserved score in the Austrian National Library, judging by its title and contents, would seem to belong to the performance ordered to celebrate the birthday of the empress on 13 May 1746.

The opera has twenty-three numbers. Wagenseil lacked sufficient variety of invention to clothe this well-known tale of treachery and fortitude effectively. He was too reliant on the harmonic progression of descending

[22] *Ariodante,* introduction by Eric Weimer (Italian Opera Seria, 1640–1770) (New York and London, 1983). Weimer errs in claiming, in *Opera seria and the Evolution of the Classical Style, 1755–1772* (Ann Arbor, Mich., 1984), p. 33, that *Ariodante* has no **a b b** themes. In addition to "Dolce diletto," the alternate setting of "Chi a nobile imprese" has one, and so does the beginning of the overture.

EXAMPLE 2.3. *Wagenseil,* Ariodante, *opening ritornello of an aria*

6/3 chords to get pieces started (including the overture), and he seemed more at home in the lighter duple and triple meters than he was with quadruple, which was thought most appropriate for the heroics of opera seria. Of the three arias in minor, two are in 3/8 time. One of his characteristic melodies may be seen in the ritornello for strings that begins Ginevra's aria "Non m'asconda a me qual volto" (Do not hide from me that visage) (Example 2.3). The key, E written with three sharps, was one of his favorites and had already been used in his 1740 cantata. Violins in thirds high in the texture, with prominent triplet figures, suggest Galuppi, who was also partial to this phrase structure: the first phrase closes with full cadence on I; the second with a half cadence on V (i.e., an inverted period). Most unlike Galuppi is the way the bass starts moving by step in the second phrase.

Wagenseil first adopted such modern procedures as the inverted period and the **a b b'** theme in his Italian operas. He would later make good use of them in his instrumental works, which belong mostly to the 1750s. There are insights to be gained from the *Ariodante* score, particularly in regard to the substitute arias at the end (presumably for Vienna). Two of Polinesso's three arias appear recomposed for contralto instead of soprano. A comparison of the two settings of "Chi a nobile imprese" (Who undertakes noble deeds) shows that the composer made a considerable effort to achieve a broad and sweeping effect in the second, replacing the rapid bass line of the first with static and slow-moving harmonies; it was in the second setting that he wrote what was perhaps his most broadly scaled **a b b'** theme up to this time.

The success that eluded Wagenseil in Venice came to him only gradually in the operas that followed. He was commissioned by Habsburg-ruled Florence to set *Demetrio* by Metastasio for the carnival of 1746, but there were no further commissions from Florence either. Between 1746 and 1750 he wrote several full-scale operas for Vienna to celebrate the birthdays or name days of the sovereigns. Khevenhüller described how the court received them. Of *Alessandro nell'Indie* (1748), he reported that "it found no particular approbation because it was judged to be insufficiently *strepitosa* and flattering to the ear"; of *Siroe*, that "the composition did not win approval, yet it seems to please more than *Alessandro*"; finally, *Olimpiade* "met with uncommon approval, a fortune that the composer had not yet experienced."[23]

Metastasio was not exactly a silent partner with respect to Wagenseil. In a letter of 8 November 1751 he declared that the composer "wrote an opera for Venice *[Ariodante]* with which he disgraced himself; nor has he had much luck with those written here." His complaint was more precise in a letter of 16 November 1751 to the soprano castrato Farinelli in answer to a request for information about Viennese opera composers. Metastasio praised Giuseppe Bonno for his graceful, well adapted, and lively music to *Il rè pastore* and went on to say of Gluck and Wagenseil: "The first has surprising fire but is mad; the other is a portentous harpsichord player." The remark about Wagenseil is sometimes quoted without its context so that the sense of this ironic compliment is lost: as an opera composer, Wagenseil was a great cembalist.

Metastasio's opinions carried immense authority at court, especially with the empress. By saying or implying that Wagenseil was too instrumentally oriented, Metastasio was making the same charge that he had leveled against Galuppi (letter of 27 December 1749 to Farinelli), namely that he sacrificed the words to be a great composer for violins and cellos. Galuppi was not invited back to Vienna after his visit in 1749. Similarly, Wagenseil was not asked to set another operatic text of Metastasio for several years. The situation changed only in 1759–60 when he set some cantatas of the court poet for Vienna and reset *Demetrio* as the second carnival opera for Milan. Wagenseil was actually in Milan for the carnival, as we know from Metastasio's letter of 28 February 1760. There he would have met not only Sammartini but young Christian Bach, who was about to write his first opera. The youngest Bach son imbibed much of his modish galant style from Wagenseil, who was Vienna's leading practitioner of the same around 1760. Wagenseil set an older Metastasian libretto, *Gioas, rè di Giuda*, for the Lenten academies in the Burgtheater in 1755, but the new Metastasian texts of the 1750s went, with few exceptions, to Bonno and Georg Reutter for their first settings. In 1756 Wagenseil provided the music for a court ballet, Durazzo's *Le cacciatrice amante*.

[23] Helga Scholz-Michelitsch, *Georg Christoph Wagenseil, Hofkomponist und Hofklaviermeister der Kaiserin Maria Theresia* (Vienna, 1980), pp. 19–20.

EURIDICE, A PASTICCIO OF 1750

BARON LO PRESTI promised in the contract regulating his tenure as impresario of the Burgtheater (22 December 1747) to bring the best masters of Italian opera to Vienna. In fact between 1748 and 1750 he arranged for Bernasconi, Galuppi, Gluck, and Jommelli to come; and the admiration Maria Theresa and Metastasio shared for Hasse ensured that this composer's works were also well known in Vienna. Active composers located in Vienna then included Reutter, Wagenseil, and Holzbauer. To celebrate St. Anne's Day (26 July) in 1750, Wagenseil organized a pasticcio opera, *Euridice,* together with an anonymous poet, most likely Giovanni Ambrogio Miglia-vacca.[24] The celebration was in honor of Archduchess Marianna, Maria Theresa's eldest daughter, but also commemorated the empress' sister, who had died in 1744. Once again the Orpheus legend was chosen, but in this version Euridice is resurrected after her death, which was probably understood as an allegory about the younger Habsburg princess carrying on the spirit of her deceased aunt. Wagenseil restricted himself to a few arias and choruses plus the climactic scene in which Orpheus defies the Furies and wins them over with his singing. For the rest, he and his poet culled arias from five composers: Bernasconi, Galuppi, Hasse, Holzbauer, and Jommelli. Their names are indicated in the Viennese score, which appears to be a product not of haste, but rather of loving care.

   The borrowed arias may have been favorites with the court, or perhaps they were picked because their texts needed little if any alteration. Of the five additional composers, only Holzbauer could have been present in Vienna during the summer of 1750; his contribution consisted of two arias, a rather dull one in C and the beautiful *ombra* aria with English horns (a Viennese specialty) in E♭. Holzbauer may well have composed ballet music for the event in addition, for this was his responsibility at the Burgtheater from 1746 to 1750. The other composers' arias are well adapted to the purpose at hand, but Hasse's are so superior as to vocal melody and text setting that it is difficult to believe that they were not first conceived to these words. Hasse's three arias were distributed among the prima donna, La Tesi, singing Euridice, the primo uomo, Amadori, singing Orpheus, and the tenor

---

[24] Wagenseil *et al., Euridice,* introduction by Eric Weimer (Italian Opera Seria 1640–1770) (New York and London, 1983). Weimer does not attempt to identify the librettist, who is given the Arcadian name Alidauro Pentalide on the title page of the score. Migliavacca was born of a noble family in Milan in 1718. He collaborated with Metastasio on *Armida placata* for Madrid in 1747. The letters of Metastasio to Farinelli contain many details of their relationship. By 1749 Migliavacca had taken over the functions, so disagreeable to Metastasio, of adjusting librettos and acting as stage director in the Burgtheater. Following an imbroglio with the mezzo-soprano castrato Caffarelli, he left Vienna for Dresden in late 1749. But he retained many Viennese connections and returned to Vienna as librettist in the late 1750s.

singing Daphne, who was Amorevoli, of European renown and at this time
a member of Hasse's famous company at Dresden.[25] The arias occur in strategic places in the drama: Euridice's is an *aria parlante* to end the prima parte;
Daphne's, of great lyric beauty, marks her first appearance; and the third,
of a most delicate facture and instrumentation (viole d'amore, flutes, horns,
and muted violins) is the last aria of Orpheus. Recall that Galuppi and Jommelli, as well as Bernasconi, had been called to Vienna in the years just
before 1750 and that they came in person to supervise their new operas, the
scores of which were presumably left behind, in keeping with the practice
concerning commissioned works at the time. A neat piece of detective work
could perhaps unravel the mystery surrounding many of the pasticcio's
arias.

Wagenseil's contributions to *Euridice* reveal a dramatic composer of some
boldness. In the first aria he shifts back and forth between small sections in
cut time and in 3/8 in order to convey the different ideas in the text; he does
this again in a later aria for Egeria, shifting between a 6/8 *Moderato* and a 2/4
Risoluto, almost as if he were writing pantomime music. For the first appearance of Euridice, Wagenseil frames her solo in 3/4 with alternating choral
sections in 4/4; moreover, he breaks off her music in mid-phrase in order to
convey her surprise at seeing her father. Jolting musical surprises to make a
dramatic point were certain to displease Metastasio. Still less would he have
liked some of Wagenseil's text setting. In Euridice's first solo, for instance,
Tesi is given a flurry of high notes to sing on the weak last syllables of
"sospire" and "morire." The composer conveys the sense of the words and
thoughts, if he does not always observe the niceties of good declamation,
and his way of building larger musical complexes out of small contrasting
sections is quite novel. The Wagenseil who composed these pieces is easily
imaginable as the same creator praised for his operas in the Czech language
written for Prague, which are lost. The critic Laurent Garcins singled out
Wagenseil (who had some Bohemian ancestors, but no close ties with
Prague that we know about), along with Brixi and Gluck (both of whose
native tongues were indeed Czech), for their contributions to the Czech
operas, which he found superior to Italian opera because they were more
theatrical and because the songs used no da capo repetitions, but succeeded
each other rapidly so as to encourage pantomime.[26]

[25] Metastasio was in Vienna when *Euridice* was staged. He pointedly avoids mentioning it in his
letters even though he praised the singing of both Amorevoli and Amadori (letters of 18 July and 13
December 1750).
[26] *Traité du Melo-drame* (Paris, 1772), pp. 114–15. Garcins also praised Czech as a beautiful language
for music. He was an ardent defender of opéra-comique, which is the stated term of comparison to
which the Czech operas were being likened. For the original passage by Garcins, see Daniel Heartz,
"Coming of Age in Bohemia: The Musical Apprenticeships of Benda and Gluck," *Journal of Musicology* 6 (1988): 510–27; 527.

In the final scene for the two principals, Wagenseil outdid himself in this kind of naturalistic scene painting built up out of small sections, each suggestive of a characteristic motion, as in pantomime music.[27] Orpheus approaches the gates of Hades. After a few measures of simple recitative, with cadence on g, the orchestra entones a solemn E♭, *Adagio*, marked *forte e staccato*. The chord dies away in a little wavering figure that is identical with what Mozart would later write at the words "dolce morte" in the first recitative of his *Idomeneo*. Orpheus describes the horrid scene, which is painted in an obbligato recitative of such sweep and ingenuity as to recall Jommelli at his best. The passage at *Andante*, where the strings divide into three parts of slithering chromatic counterpoint, with many dynamic shadings, again suggests an uncanny parallel with Mozart thirty years later (*Idomeneo*, Act III, just before "O voto tremendo"). A cadence on B♭ ends the recitative, after which Orpheus begins to plead his case. The orchestra of strings, pizzicato, is joined by two flutes, *senza fagotti,* and plays a kind of barcarolle in a lilting 6/8 meter and in the key of g. This, of course, represents Orpheus playing his lyre.

Orpheus then sings the first stanza of his song to an expanded version of the same piece accompanied by the pizzicato strings. The Furies respond at first with an outburst in c minor, "Fuggi ormai, fuggi da questo regno!" (Flee this realm!). Dotted rhythms, whirling string figures, effective use of winds, and expressive harmonies combine to give this four-part chorus great intensity. When Orpheus sings the second verse of his song, the Furies rejoin with a short *Allegro* in E♭ that is staccato and agitated but less intense than their first outburst. After the third strophe of the song, they sing more broadly and concede him Euridice; the orchestral postlude ending in c is obviously meant as their exit music. The lovers emerge together and sing a simple little duet, mostly syllabic in setting, in E♭ and 3/8 time, like an Italian minuet. A bright madrigalistic chorus in C, expressing the surprise of those who greet Euridice's return, intertwines with strains of the duet in E♭ʼ with no transition. Such a coloristic use of tonalities distant by a third seems highly original for this date. But then, so does the whole free-flowing amalgam of recitative, song, chorus, and duet, all in the service of the drama. What a pity that Wagenseil was not given more opportunities to set scenes of this kind. As it happened, his career as a stage composer was nearly over by 1750.

---

[27] The scene is transcribed in Walther Vetter, "Georg Christoph Wagenseil, ein Vorläufer Christoph Willibald Glucks," *ZfMW* 8 (1925–26): 385–402.

OVERTURES AND SYMPHONIES

WITH the death of the dowager empress in 1750 and the disbanding of her chapel, Wagenseil was no longer obliged to serve as an organist. At the same time, he was relieved of his duties to supply church music to the court, according to a document of 31 October 1750, in which he is listed as first court composer. The growing flock of imperial children to be instructed on the keyboard claimed more and more of his time during the 1750s. Still, the composer had leisure enough to turn his abilities to instrumental genres, notably the concert symphony. His operatic overtures of the 1740s gave him experience here. The Sinfonia to *I lamenti d'Orfeo* of 1740 has been mentioned. His Venetian opera of 1745, *Ariodante*, begins with a Sinfonia in D that achieved considerable diffusion. It opens with a *Vivace* in common time based on a broad **a b b** theme (6 + 4 + 4) and containing several concerto-like features. There is no repeat sign in its middle; the seconda parte begins with the head of the main theme (**a**) on V answered immediately by the same on I. Rather old-fashioned are the stiffness of the harmonic sequences and the Sammartinian exchanges between first and second violins in order to fill up the texture. An *Andante* in d with the melody on the offbeat, a device frequently found in this composer, ends on V, leading to a very short *Allegro assai* in 3/8 that restores D and is, in everything but name, a Minuetto galante. Printed in score in both Paris and London, this symphony was chosen by Breitkopf for keyboard arrangement as late as 1761.[28]

Much superior is the overture to Wagenseil's *La clemenza di Tito* (1746).[29] The work begins with the three hammer strokes that were so common a feature of Italian arias and symphonies (the most famous example being Pergolesi's thrice-used overture). Here they give rise to a three-measure phrase in common time, ending at first on I, then upon repetition on V (i.e., an inverted period). The sequential passage with slowly changing harmonies that follows is routine, leading to a decorated pedal on V that promises a new idea. This comes in the form of the minor dominant (v) and constitutes a dialogue between *forte* octaves and soft thirds in response. The use of a momentary minor passage, another Italian trait, occurs so often in Wagenseil as to become a hallmark of his style. Also characteristic are the two clipped eighth notes that end the tutti passage in the second theme. He

---

[28] *Raccolta delle megliore Sinfonie di piu celebre compositori di nostro tempo accomodate all'clavicembalo* (Leipzig, 1761), no. 10, reproduced in facsimile in Georg Christoph Wagenseil, *Fifteen Symphonies*, ed. John Kucaba (New York and London, 1981), Appendix A. The inexpert arranger reduced the thin, three-part texture of the original to only two parts, doing away with the *Stimmtausch* and leaving nothing between the treble and the plodding bass line.

[29] It is edited in *DTÖ* 31 (1908).

had already used this energizing device to end the first theme. In the short development Wagenseil draws together these two themes, showing how they are related. The second movement is an *Andante* in b with a drooping melody in parallel thirds that prompted one critic to speak of Tartini.[30] A *Tempo di Menuetto* concludes the symphony. While other Viennese composers of his generation (Birck, for instance) varied the number of movements in their symphonies from two to four, Wagenseil decided on the three-movement format with terminal minuet and rarely diverged from it.

The companion Symphony in D by Wagenseil published in 1908 belongs to the genre of the trio symphony. Its opening *Allegro molto* in 2/4 joins tonal areas with half cadences of the modern, bifocal kind, but there is a trace of weakness in the harmonic progression with which the reprise is prepared. After two middle movements marked Menuetto and *Andante* (in b), the finale, *Allegro* in 2/4, concludes the cycle in a jaunty, comic-opera vein. Precisely this finale was singled out as demonstrating the height of inventive power among the older Viennese composers, and was praised for being "bold, saucy, rich in contrast, thoroughly new and distinct from early Haydn only because of its continuo bass line."[31] The movement opens with the same melodic-harmonic formula found in Monn's Symphony in D of 1740, and hence is hardly new in this sense. On the other hand, the **a b b** structure and clear periodization of this theme *is* modern. Perhaps it was the hiccuping octave leaps in the melody, in the manner of *La serva padrona*, that seemed "bold and saucy."

Both Wagenseil and Birck preserved one rather old-fashioned and concerto-like feature in their opening symphonic movements: the music often goes from a cadence on vi (less often iii) in the seconda parte directly into the reprise, with no retransition, or sometimes with a minimal lead-in by the bass (as is often encountered in da capo arias after the **B** section). Wagenseil's overture to *Alessandro nell'Indie* (1748) illustrates such a lead-in to the reprise in the first movement.[32] If this lead-in sounds somewhat perfunctory, what follows does not. The reprise repeats the energetic, arching main theme verbatim for four measures, then on its repetition the composer takes it higher, sweeping up to the flat seventh, whence there is a long descent into the realm of the subdominant. A subdominant substitution on this grand scale must have stunned attentive listeners in 1748. The overtures of two Viennese pasticcios of 1749, *Merope* and *Catone in Utica*, are widely attributed to Wagenseil, and a former attribution to Jommelli has been dis-

---

[30] Ernst Bücken, *Musik des Rokokos und der Klassik* (Potsdam, 1929), pp. 86–87 and Beispiel 77. More to the point is the very up-to-date way the composer used the bifocal close here.

[31] Ibid., *loc. cit.* and Beispiel 78.

[32] Edited by Kucaba, in Wagenseil, *Fifteen Symphonies*, pp. 21–48.

credited precisely because of the lack of a retransition after the cadences on vi.[33]

Wagenseil uses the minor mode in a variety of ways, some rather personal. He was very partial to the clouding of his cheerful opening movements in major with the passing clouds of minor color, which could happen at any time—a practice nicely summed up by the German word "Molltrübung." He frequently chose minor as the main mode of his middle movements, most often marked *Andante*. In the overture to *Vincislao*, written to celebrate the birthday of Emperor Francis on 8 December 1750, the C-major *Prunkstil* of the outer movements is relieved by a delicate a-minor Polonaise for strings as the middle movement (Example 2.4). Perhaps the Czech subject of the opera (King Wenceslas of Bohemia) had something to do with the choice of this Slavic dance, which, like most, begins on the downbeat. The cadential pattern ♩♫♩ ♩ , familiar from many later polonaises, is already apparent here. The gruff octaves answered by softer thirds are often found in Wagenseil, and they may be linked with this particular dance, because nearly the identical phrase occurs in the *Polonoise* for harpsichord of his Divertimento Op. 2 No. 4 (1755). Most Slavic-sounding of all is the way the D♯, prominent in m. 3, is used in a mournful descending passage in tenths with the bass in mm. 13–14. The use of exotic scales with raised fourths can be found in the folk music of various peoples of Central Europe, but a careful study of this phenomenon made in connection with Haydn has established a special connection with the Slavic lands to the north and northeast of Vienna—Moravia and western Slovakia.[34] Wagenseil's Polonaise of 1750 introduces one of the distinctive colors of Viennese music.

Wagenseil's concert symphonies achieved a diffusion in the 1750s second to no other composer. Their freshness and appeal when they were new can still be heard by ears willing to accept an order of beauty somewhat different from that of his Viennese successors, and willing to accept a few weaknesses along with many strengths. At the beginning of the Symphony in C (Kucaba C3), which begins with a wistful falling third, we can admire how the composer plays off the six-measure theme (3 + 3) against the four-measure continuations, an alternation that is sustained throughout the

[33] Heinrich Hell, *Die neapolitanische Opernsinfonie in der ersten Hälfte des 18. Jahrhunderts* (Tützing, 1971), pp. 470–83, writes (p. 479), "Such a practice recalls the old step principle, used in the earliest symphonies studied here, those by Vinci and Porpora, and entrenched in the concerto, but not met in Italian operatic symphonies after 1750, not even Venetian ones." Kucaba places them in the questionable category of his Thematic Index as Q:D3 and Q:D4. Because of certain details in the facture of the first movements, he believes they are by some Viennese hand other than Wagenseil (personal communication). Bonno is a possibility.

[34] Geoffrey Chew, "The Night-Watchman's Song Quoted by Haydn and Its Implications," *Haydn-Studien* 3 (1973): 106–24, especially 111–12.

EXAMPLE 2.4. *Wagenseil,* Vincislao *(1750), Polonaise*

i. Liotard. *Portrait of Maria Theresa*, 1762. (Vienna: Graphische Sammlung Albertina)

II. Workshop of Martin van Meytens. *The Wedding of Isabella of Parma and Archduke Joseph in the Augustinerkirche*, 1760. (Vienna: Kunsthistorisches Museum)

movement and is at its most effective when the four-measure unit is stretched to six measures just before the reprise, after an appealing retransition. Breitkopf lists this concert symphony, which must date no later than 1756, as the sixth of his first set of six, offered in 1762 (Figure 2.2, p. 102). Alongside it in the first set of six are the older operatic overtures to *Ariodante* (No. IV) and *Alessandro* (No. III).

Metric weaknesses, on the other hand, show up in the first movement of the Symphony in E♭ (Kucaba E♭2), listed as the third item in the third set of six by Breitkopf. The prima parte consists of sixteen four-measure phrases, following which the development rolls along in four-measure phrases up until the cadence on vi, when there is a two-measure lead-back by the bass, which sounds perfunctory and makes it seem, after all those four-measure phrases, as if the reprise began too soon. Moreover, there is a single extra measure around m. 139, which undermines the sense of order of the whole. The movement ends with Hasse's wedge cadence (treble descending against bass rising, both by step), which had the advantage of novelty in the 1720s and 1730s, perhaps, but was becoming a tired cliché by the 1750s.

In the opening movement of the Symphony in C (Kucaba C7, the third item of the second set in Breitkopf's list), Wagenseil resisted connecting tonal arias by sequences via the circle of fifths and used instead an effective chromatic rise in the bass line. He expanded his usual minuet finale in this work to a large-scale rondo, with the episodes in vi and i. This is the closest any Viennese composer of the 1750s came to what the Parisian symphonists were doing in their final rondeaux. Possibly Wagenseil did this in awareness of his favored status with music publishers in Paris. The Symphony in F (Kucaba F1, the fifth item in the third set of Breitkopf) also makes effective use of a long chromatic rise in the bass and features bifocal closes between key areas, but the reprise disturbs the ear by seeming to begin a measure too late.

One of the loveliest of all Wagenseil symphonies is the one in E (Kucaba E3), which contains a particularly winning *echappée* in the two-measure continuations of the six-measure main theme (3 + 3) of the first movement, put to good use in the development. Both parts of the movement conclude with the galloping figure |♫ ♩ ♫ ♫|, properly an opera buffa tag. Wagenseil was partial to E major throughout his career, and the key often inspired him to outdo himself, as is the case here. The concertante symphonies by Wagenseil listed by Philipp Gumpenhuber as having been performed in the Burgtheater around 1760 cannot be identified. At the Parisian Concert Spirituel in February 1759, a reviewer took note of a "Symphonie-concert del Signor Wagenseil."

FIGURE 2.2. Detail from Breitkopf's *Thematic Catalogue*, 1762.

102

DIVERTIMENTI FOR HARPSICHORD

WAGENSEIL was appointed a *Hofklaviermeister* in 1749. A few years later he and Birck split their responsibilities so that Birck taught the archdukes and Wagenseil the archduchesses. The Viennese *Divertimento da Cimbalo* was created for the latter. Four volumes bearing this title were handsomely engraved and published by Bernardi in Vienna between 1753 and 1763. Op. 1 was advertised in the *Wiener Diarium* for the first time in 1753, then again in 1754, 1756, 1761, and 1770, testifying to the long-standing availability as well as to the epochal success of the set.[35] The three subsequent volumes of six divertimenti each were first advertised in 1755, 1761, and 1763, respectively. Intended for the fingers of four young ladies, his august pupils, the four volumes were dedicated in turn to the archduchesses Marianna, Maria Christina, Elizabeth, and Amalia. Wagenseil wrote prefaces in Italian to each volume; the first in particular is valuable as a clue to his teaching methods. He avoided the ties used by the best composers (i.e., contrapuntal textures), he says, so as not to tire the patience of amateur players. Who would these composers be in Vienna around 1750? Wagenseil himself had composed an early set of six suites in the traditional style that were printed at Bamberg in 1740, and he was famous for improvising fugues at the keyboard. Other representatives of the fugal style in Viennese keyboard music were Gottlieb Muffat, Birck, and Monn. With his Op. 1 of 1753, Wagenseil at a single stroke pushed the latest galant styles from Italy to the forefront, and these works quickly supplanted the more old-fashioned sonatas of Monn, with their *Fortspinnung* and general bass mentality. The young generation coming along, notably Haydn and Joseph Anton Steffan, imitated Wagenseil in their divertimenti for harpsichord, not Monn.

As in his symphonies, Wagenseil preferred three movements including a minuet for his cyclic form. He was less rigid in his divertimenti about the positioning of the minuet, which is often a second movement. In Op. 1 No. 1 in D, he begins the opening *Allegro assai* in common time with two complementary three-measure phrases.[36] The polish and idiomatic quality of his style are evident from the outset. Each of the three measures brings a different texture, all beautifully suited to the harpsichord. As in his symphonic writing, the phrases end with clipped eighth notes, and in the continuation, after the three-measure phrases he switches to two-measure segments. Wagenseil begins the seconda parte with the main theme on V, but

[35] Hannelore Gericke, *Der Wiener Musikalienhandel von 1700 bis 1778* (Wiener Musikwissenschaftliche Bieträge 5) (Vienna, 1960), pp. 130–31.
[36] *6 Divertimenti für Cembalo*, ed. Helga Scholz-Michelitsch (Diletto Musicale Nr. 535 and Nr. 558). At the time of this writing, the three other sets were not available in modern edition.

ascending instead of descending, and collapsed from six to four measures (3 + 3 becomes 3 + 1). Changes such as these usually mean that there will be a double reprise, and indeed there is; whereas if he sounds the main theme on V but leaves it otherwise unchanged, it will probably not be introduced when the tonic returns. Wagenseil enhances the reprise by making his third measure introduce the subdominant; then, using the shortened form of his theme from the beginning of the development, he makes the fourth and final measure reintroduce the dominant. The span is small (only forty-five measures), but it is filled with carefully wrought and telling detail, such as the very galant raised-fifth degree pushing up to the sixth after a deceptive cadence close to the end. An *Andantino* in d follows, with a chromatic rising theme that seems to carry on the chromatic detail just noted. The *Tempo di Menuet* that concludes the work has a *minore* trio; both dances switch back and forth from triplets to duplets.

The *Allegro assai* that opens Op. 1 No. 2 in C deploys a little theme with a galant redict (2 + 2 + 2 in 2/4). Wagenseil uses the first two measures (a) as a springboard into the development, and repeats them while beginning his modulation to vi. The modulatory retransition after the cadence on vi is one of his favorites: V/ii - ii; V - I. The moment of reprise would have been a little more interesting had the composer elided it with the end of the development, but it is perfectly correct and elegant as it stands, its formality and decorum undoubtedly appreciated by the imperial family when issuing from the fingers of the eldest archduchess. Less appealing is the long harmonic sequence that follows the restatement of the main theme. Purists might find cause for complaint as well in the progression from diminished fifth to perfect fifth in the outer voices. Galuppi, who was Wagenseil's main model in keyboard as in operatic music, did not hesitate to use such progressions. The *minore* trio of the Menuet offers a good example of the minor-second appoggiature from below of which the composer was so fond. Menuet and trio serve here as second movement, following which there is a lively finale, *Allegro assai e svelto*. Its development covers the same harmonic territories as the equivalent section of the first movement, lending a subtle cyclic unity to the whole.

Op. 1 No. 4 offers a particularly blithe example of the composer's favorite key of E (here notated with three sharps, as in Examples 2.2a and 2.3). The work's opening may have introduced into Viennese keyboard music a texture of which Mozart later revealed the highest beauties in his Sonata in C (K. 330): treble melody over a two-note pendulum bass. The rising chromatic appoggiature in the middle voice of the continuation also seem to forecast Mozart. The same passage becomes a strangely dolorous-sounding general chromatic descent in the development.

The divertimenti get a little longer and more complicated in the course of the set, which is true of the other sets as well. Didactic considerations obviously played a role in ordering the sets. Op. 1 No. 5 requires the right hand to move more quickly up and down the keyboard than in any of the previous works. Op. 1 No. 6 has a fantasia-like *Largo* as a slow movement, one that is rhythmically very elaborate and poses more challenges to the performer than any other movement in the set. To end this divertimento and the set, Wagenseil had recourse to what sounds like a popular song. Something like its tune was known as "Mann und Weib," a song that had associations with the German comedians in the Kärntnerthor Theater and with Haydn.[37]

The divertimenti published in 1755 as Op. 2 are quite like the first set, but some of the *Allegro*s are even more singing. Op. 2 No. 2 in G begins with an eight-measure theme constructed as an inverted period, with the sixths inverted to become thirds (a frequent device with this composer). Op. 2 No. 4, also in G, begins with the rapid fall from the fifth down to the tonic by step, which is also a favorite beginning in Italian arias. The recipient of this set, Archduchess Maria Christina, was perhaps the most intellectually gifted of Maria Theresa's daughters, but the most musically gifted, to judge from what Wagenseil wrote for her, was the recipient of the next set, Archduchess Elizabeth. She is also known for having collected keyboard music in manuscript by many leading Viennese composers, including Haydn and Hofmann. Her playing was praised by Burney.

Op. 3 appeared in 1761 and may reflect the composer's wider horizons as a result of his trip to Milan in 1760. Note how at the opening of Op. 3 No. 2 in C he uses both an inverted period and a galant redict, but on a broader scale than before (4 + 6 + 6) (Example 2.5). From the half cadence (bifocal close) at the end, Wagenseil passes the delicate boundary from being on V to being in V, which sounds fresh because of all the emphasis on IV in the theme (an emphasis that Mozart would repeat with his similar arpeggios up to high C at the beginning of K. 330). There is a new element of spaciousness

EXAMPLE 2.5. *Wagenseil, Divertimento Op. 3, No. 2, I*

---

[37] Landon, *Haydn*, 1: 184.

apparent from the beginning of Op. 3 No. 4 as well, in which both left and right hands are required to change positions and cover a wide range. A more refined keyboard poetry is everywhere evident in these Op. 3 Sonatas (a term the composer allows himself in his preface).

The original edition of the first two pages of Op. 3 No. 3 in A allows further insight into how Wagenseil articulated his ideas (Figure 2.3). The opening theme, graced with triplet figures and trills, comes to a cadence on the third melodic degree at the beginning of m. 4; this is followed by an appendix of two measures (actually a florid example of a galant redict), bringing the melody to a close on the tonic. The theme recommences as before and comes to a half cadence in m. 10—another example of the inverted period. This bifocal close allows for the magical transformation that follows, as we accept E, the new key. A new lyric idea occurs, a descending sixth sextuplet over $I^{6/4}$, then over V of the new key, one of Galuppi's favorite ideas, used both in his operas and in his sonatas. The sequence with trills and three-note snaps that follows is well turned, a six-measure segment that gives way to four measures of alternating I and V. This is followed by a descending bass progression that further anchors the new key, a five-measure segment that is repeated in slightly varied form. Yet another segment is added and repeated, this one with a clear closing character because of the $IV^{6/4}$ harmony under the rhythmic snaps. The prima parte concludes with the descending arpeggio from high B that happens also to be the first idea we heard in the secondary key, back in m. 10. Wagenseil deserves more credit than he usually gets for spinning his short lyric ideas into motivically coherent wholes, which one critic called his "thematic mosaic style."[38]

The seconda parte after the double bar begins what sounds like a new idea, falling thirds answered by rising and falling arpeggios. There is a reference to the first theme on the way to a cadence on b, then the arpeggios assume the shape they did in the middle of the exposition. Their four-mea-

[38] Günter Hausswald, "Der Divertimento-Begriff bei Georg Christoph Wagenseil," *AfMW* 9 (1952): 49.

FIGURE 2.3. Wagenseil, Divertimento for Harpsichord, Op. 3, No. 3, I.

sure sequence leads to a return of the original sequence with the trills and snaps. Meanwhile the key has shifted from b to f♯, which is confirmed even to the point of providing the context for the descending bass passage from the exposition. There is a sense of continuity by which the reprise of the main theme seems to continue the same melodic line that descended to the cadence on vi. Note how tellingly appropriate it sounds when the composer answers the first six measures, which are unchanged, with a subdominant substitution. Many were the Viennese composers following Wagenseil who profited from this last feature after the moment of reprise. By the end of the century Heinrich Christoph Koch had codified the practice.

The last sonata in Op. 3 is in the key of E, again indicated with only three sharps. In the opening *Allegro moderato* Wagenseil deploys a modulation using long, arpeggiated chords from both modes after he gets to the dominant: I - i - $\flat$VI - vii^7 / V - V. The move to $\flat$VI lends an early nineteenth-century, almost Schubertian tinge to the harmony. The composer realized how special an effect he had created and took care to repeat it twice in the seconda parte. One of his contemporaries, the astute composer-critic who wrote "Von dem wienerischen Geschmack in der Musik" (1766)—he is, I am convinced, none other than Carl Ditters von Dittersdorf—had this to say about Wagenseil: "His delicacy, his clean passages, his strange but not unnatural modulations, with which he modulates in a way peculiar to his art through all the keys, show the discernment of a great master."[39] It could well be such borrowings from the opposite mode as found in Op. 3 No. 6 that prompted this praise for Wagenseil's modulations.

In his Op. 4 of 1763 Wagenseil reverted back to the more modest demands of Op. 1 and Op. 2. He once again used the word "Sonate" in his preface, while the title page and individual works continue to use "Divertimento." The preface refers to the works as "recently composed for your use." Archduchess Amalia evidently lacked the talent as a player of her sister Elizabeth. Consequently she did not elicit from her teacher the best of which he was capable. The last two works of the set are oddities in that they exceed the normal three movements. No. 5 commences with a prelude-like movement entitled "Ricercata," beginning in f and ending in F; it continues with an *Allegro assai* in f and a third movement with the curious designations "Menuet Imo" (in f) and "Menuet IIdo" (in F)—a usage sometimes encountered in early Haydn—and concludes with a Presto in 3/8 (in F). In No. 6 each of the four movements is in the key of A: *Vivace*, Menuet-trio, *Andante*, *Tempo di Menuet*. If "Sonata" seems an appropriate term for the demanding works attempted and achieved in Op. 3, perhaps the best corresponding term for Op. 4 would be "Sonatina."

CONCERTOS AND CONCERTED WORKS

VIENNA did not subscribe to the fashion for accompanied keyboard sonatas that was rampant in London and Paris by mid-century. Wagenseil's

---

[39] Landon, *Haydn*, 2: 129 (Landon's translation).

divertimenti for solo harpsichord acquired solo violin accompaniments when they were printed in those great capitals, but he had nothing to do with the additions. As Hummel announced in the London *Daily Advertiser* for 29 July 1761: "Wagenseil's Opera Prima having met with such general approbation by the desire of several eminent Masters, the accompaniment to it for the violin is likewise publish'd and may be had alone." The same fate befell Steffan's solo sonatas in Paris at a later date.

Wagenseil himself did write some chamber works for solo harpsichord with accompanying strings. An example is the Concertino in G for harpsichord, two violins, and bass, a manuscript of which was acquired by Göttweig Abbey ca. 1760 (Example 2.6).[40] Note that in this Viennese manuscript the Italian nomenclature for the parts of the movement is followed ("Segue la seconda parte"). The way the sections of the prima parte are joined will sound familiar. They are quoted here not for this reason but in order to test another of the statements about Wagenseil in the 1766 essay "Von dem wienerischen Geschmack in der Musik":

> His way of playing the harpsichord, and the *soli* in his concertos for that instrument, have something overpowering and captivating about them which will ensure his fame for many years to come. This instrument is little suited to singing melody, for it seems made only for accompaniment, and concertos for it are so meagre that one cannot long support them; but the art to give the harpsichord, with the help of the accompanying violins, a kind of melody was primarily reserved for Wagenseil.

When the violins first come in, they softly reinforce the harmony, the treble melody line in particular. In m. 4 they make a little link between the two halves of the phrase. When the music moves to the dominant in m. 9, the first violin softly sustains a high A, giving the illusion, perhaps, that the notes struck on the harpsichord are sustaining. Only at the cadence in mm. 24–25 do the violins go their own way against the harpsichord's reiterated chords. Even from this very modest piece, with dimensions as small as the smallest solo divertimento of Op. 1, and with demands on the keyboard soloist on a par, it is evident that Wagenseil found his own path to the Parisian type of accompanied sonata, perhaps with no awareness of doing so. The art of giving the harpsichord "a kind of melody" with the help of the violins, as demonstrated here, is little different from what Simon Simon did and said he was doing in his Op. 1, or what Charles Avison, in his Op. 7

---

[40] Michelle Fillion, "The Accompanied Keyboard Divertimenti of Haydn and His Viennese Contemporaries (c. 1750–1780)," (Ph.D. diss., Cornell University, 1982), p. 144. I have used her transcription, pp. 494ff.

EXAMPLE 2.6. *Wagenseil, Concertino in G, I*

Segue la seconda parte

(1760), said about having the violins multiply and strengthen the sound of the harpsichord.[41]

The Concertino in G is an example of accompanied keyboard music in which the harpsichord part is meant for a dilettante performer. The performer for this piece may have been one of Wagenseil's royal charges, in which case court musicians were available to play the string accompaniments. A collection of harpsichord concertos by Wagenseil that belonged to Archduchess Marianna survives in the Austrian State Library. It opens with a "Concertino" that is the same as the first divertimento of Op. 1, which is dedicated to Marianna. Most of the pieces are real concertos that begin with an orchestral ritornello, signaled by figured bass only in the surviving keyboard part. Similar to these works are the keyboard scores from the collection of Archduchess Elizabeth, comprising, besides many concertos of Wagenseil, arrangements of ballet music by Gluck and works by several other composers, notably Leopold Hofmann, Steffan, and Haydn. Paper was used very liberally, even wastefully, in these luxurious keyboard parts, as befitted the august nature of their recipients; the copyists, being paid by the page, understandably made few efforts to economize on paper.

The youngest archduchess, Maria Antonia (Marie Antoinette), figured along with her sisters as a keyboard player. In a portrait of her that was presumably painted just before she married the dauphin in 1770 at age fifteen and left for France (see Plate III), Maria Antonia is shown playing a piece with several Wagensilian features. Trouble was taken by the painter to incise a particular *Andante* in G in 3/8 time on two pages open on the music stand; the piece is marked "solo," suggesting that it also was accompanied by concerting instruments.[42] The keyboard instrument she plays is a fortepiano.[43]

Wagenseil's concertos for harpsichord carried his name and reputation all over Europe. We might expect that as a noted virtuoso of the keyboard, he would have made his concertos more intricate and demanding than his sonatas for amateurs, but many are not. The selection of earlier works offered by Walsh of London as *Six Concertos for the Harpsichord or Organ with accompaniment for Two Violins and a Bass Compos'd by Mr Wagenseil* (ca. 1765)

---

[41] Ronald R. Kidd, "The Emergence of Chamber Music with Obbligato Keyboard in England," *Acta Musicologica* 44 (1972): 122–44; 130.

[42] The painting is in the Kunsthistorisches Museum, Vienna, and is attributed to Franz Xaver Wagenschön, a Bohemian artist who was trained in Vienna. It is the subject of Daniel Heartz, "A Keyboard Concertino by Marie Antoinette?" in *Essays in Musicology: A Tribute to Alvin Johnson* (1990), pp. 201–12, which includes a transcription of the *Andante* depicted.

[43] I am indebted to Lawrence Liblin for pointing out features of the instrument depicted that indicate this.

are no more complicated than his *divertimenti*. All six concertos are in the major mode, and all are in three movements ending with a *Tempo di Minuetto* in 3/8 (or an *Allegro* having the same characteristics). The first movements are all fast and in ritornello form; the slow movements are typically in the relative or parallel minor. The keyboard part of the opening *Allegro* in common time of the first concerto fits comfortably on a double page and is only eighty-nine measures in length, allowing for an opening tutti, a solo on the same material, and a tutti on V, leading at once to the solo statement of the main theme on I with some added color by way of *Molltrübung*. Three-note slides, or *sdruccioli*, abound in these works, as they do in the composer's symphonies and sonatas. Rarely do these concerto first movements include a distinct secondary idea. Rather, some figurations around a pedal serve a closing function, as is often the case as well in Wagenseil's sonatas and symphonies. The opening movements of the third and fourth concertos are more amply proportioned than the others, but they still fall short of the parallel movements in other keyboard concertos of the time, including some of Wagenseil's. The average running time of one of the Walsh concertos could not have exceeded eight or nine minutes.

An attractive example of what might be called Wagenseil's full-scale concerto is the one in E♭ that has been published as a piano concerto.[44] The work, with a running time of eighteen or nineteen minutes, may belong to the late 1760s, after which time illnesses prevented the composer from many further creative labors. The opening *Vivace* in common time totals 218 measures. In this movement a broad periodic phraseology prevails, and most of the material falls in four-measure units. In fact, the movement is more regular in this respect than the opening movement of Mozart's first keyboard concerto, K. 175 of 1773, an *Allegro* in common time of 238 measures. The plethora of distinct ideas easily leading from one to another in Wagenseil's movement readily suggests Mozart, who would have been especially attracted by the older master's use of the well-known Credo motif 1 2 4 3 as a horn call, and also by his sensitive orchestration, including divided violas throughout. Unlike Mozart, Wagenseil gives considerable play to the dominant in the first exposition, for orchestra only. There is a distinct closing idea, heard in the tonic in the first exposition and in the dominant in the second, leading to a restatement of the same in the tonic. The movement

[44] *Concerto per Pianoforte*, ed. Alison A. Copland (Accademia Musicale 18) (Vienna, 1979). Wagenseil went out of his way to write no note for the keyboard higher than D, which suggests that the concerto was written for the harpsichord, as do many of the textures. The same is true of Mozart's K. 175. Several other "full-scale" concertos have been made available as an appendix to Patricia Sauerbrei, "The Keyboard Concertos of Georg Christoph Wagenseil (1715–1777)" (Ph.D. diss., University of Toronto, 1983); they are Scholz-Michelitsch Nos. 271 in c, 283 in E♭, 290 in F, and 297 in F.

ends with this closing idea and without any cadenza. The *Andante* middle movement is also in common time. Muted strings, without winds, project this haunting lament in c minor, which begins with a sighing fall from A♭ to G. The *Allegro molto* finale uses 3/8 time like so many finales by Wagenseil, but this one is more like a scherzo than a minuet, its playful nature evident from the contrasting three-measure and two-measure phrases at the outset. It totals 276 measures—a worthy complement to the solid pillar represented by the first movement.

Leopold Mozart took his family to Vienna for their first visit in the fall of 1762, when his son was six and his daughter eleven. Little Wolfgang, confronted with Emperor Francis and wishing for a more professional listener, had the impertinence to ask that Wagenseil be sent for: "Is Herr Wagenseil not here? He should come; he understands it." Wagenseil came and witnessed the child playing one of his concertos. Adding effrontery to effrontery, Mozart asked the court composer to turn pages for him: "Ich spiele ein Concert von Ihnen: Sie müssen mir umwenden." This anecdote stems from Nannerl and must be authentic.[45] Mozart was already composing small pieces at the time, and a few years later he was writing larger ones—symphonies and all manner of other works. He felt no need to write keyboard concertos himself until relatively late. The reason, at least in part, was that he found the concertos by Wagenseil and a few others to be perfectly suited to his needs.

THE TRAILBLAZER

WAGENSEIL was a revered teacher of composition as well as of harpsichord playing. Among his earlier pupils were Steffan, Leopold Hofmann, František Xaver Dušek, and Giovanni Antonio Matielli; among the later ones were Maximilian Ulbricht, Johann Gallus Mederitsch, and Johann Baptist Schenk, who left an account of the instruction he received:

> I began to study with him in January 1774. Wagenseil's method of teaching composition was based on the theories of Johann Fux, who had been his teacher . . . In the course of my studies I devoted some of my time to practicing the clavier. Sebastian Bach's preludes and fugues as well as the clavier suites by Handel served for my practice material . . .
> My wise teacher guided me to the art of composing in a freer style. His intentions seemed to have been to wean me from the dry movement and to

[45] As reported in the anonymous *Mozarts Leben* (Graz, 1794), taken over by Niemtschek in his biography.

direct me toward a beautifully blossoming melody. Here my paragon was Adolf Hasse for the serious compositions and Baldassare Galuppi for the comic ones. But the sublime Handel was my highest ideal as far as I was concerned. Alexander's Feast was the first work my teacher called to my attention and followed it with the oratorios Athalia and Judas Maccabaeus. Wagenseil also acquainted me with the beautiful passages which could so frequently be found in Handel's works, and in particular with his choruses, and he used these examples for his instruction. The oratorio Messiah was the last work which I studied under his guidance. Several years later, I also included the great dramatist of the tragic opera, Ritter Christof Gluck, in my studies.[46]

Schenk concludes with a touching tribute to his master:

Christof Wagenseil was a very famous composer in his days and even before the advent of Emanuel Bach he was also a well-known cembalist. The pianoforte was still unknown. This noble old man did not cease to teach me with love and patience until his death which took him away on the 1st of March 1777. For more than a decade was this poor man tortured by gout which chained him to his house. His name remains indelibly engraved on my heart.

The magnitude of the Handel revival after 1800 may have colored Schenk's recollections on the subject to some degree, but there is plenty of other evidence that Handel was indeed known and honored in Vienna during the 1770s.[47] Altogether true, in terms of the music that Wagenseil himself wrote, ring the praises of Galuppi and Hasse as paragons of "beautifully blossoming melody." Burney confirmed Wagenseil's enthusiasm for Handel and induced the ailing composer to play for him on his visit in 1772. In spite of his feeble condition, he played "in a very spirited and masterly manner."

Abbé Stadler summed up Wagenseil's historical importance with this telling observation, made from the standpoint of a man born in 1748 and writing in Vienna in the 1820s: "His keyboard works as well as his symphonies and trios for the violins and cello blazed an exemplary path by which, a short time thereafter, the current taste in music could be reached."[48] Looking at the same subject from the perspective of the mid-1770s, Carl Ludwig Junker saw a decline: "Since Haydn changed the tone of Viennese music, or gave a new direction, it is, to be sure, more characteristic than before, but

[46] Johann Baptist Schenk, "Autobiography," in *Forgotten Musicians*, ed. and trans. Paul Nettl (New York, 1951), pp. 267–68.

[47] The Handel revival in Vienna started at least as early as 1771 with *Alexander's Feast,* and even earlier in the Florence of Grand Duke Leopold. See John A. Rice, "An Early Handel Revival in Florence, " *Early Music* 18 (1990): 63–71; 69.

[48] *Materialen zur Geschichte der Musik,* p. 98.

fallen too low into trifling from the dignity ["Würde"] that Wagenseil upheld."[49] With the hindsight of the many generations that have passed since then, we can agree that Wagenseil, along with Gluck, was the most seminal figure in Viennese music during the double reign of Maria Theresa and Francis Stephan from 1740 to 1765.

Bonno

GIUSEPPE BONNO was close to Wagenseil in several respects, but he was also more limited in the sense that he specialized in vocal music. Born in Vienna in 1711, Bonno was the son of an imperial footman from Brescia. His early training was with Johann Georg Reinhardt, one of the court organists and Kapellmeister at St. Stephen's from 1727 to 1742. In 1726, when he was only fifteen, Bonno was sent by Charles VI at the emperor's own expense to study music in Naples. The Habsburgs were then masters of the Kingdom of the Two Sicilies, and were not replaced by the Spanish Bourbons until 1735. Bonno returned to Vienna in 1736. At Naples his teachers included Leonardo Leo for dramatic music and Francesco Durante for sacred music. He also studied voice and later became one of the most respected voice teachers in Vienna, his pupils numbering, among many others, the tenor Joseph Fribert, Marianne von Martínez, Catherine Starzer, and Therese Teyber. Ditters remembered him as having "an extraordinary gift for teaching singers."

Bonno applied for a post as court composer by means of a petition dated 25 February 1737. In it he mentions having studied with the best masters, both in the conservatory and privately, and having produced compositions, both sacred and secular, that met the approval of the public. A 1732 setting of court poet Giovanni Pasquini's pastorale *a 2 Nigella e Nise* is all that can be surely assigned to Bonno's Neapolitan decade. Shortly after the submission of his petition, Kapellmeister Fux was called upon to pronounce his opinion of Bonno's compositions: he found them wanting. His attestation, dated 11 March 1737, recommended that Bonno study further as a court scholar in composition because "he was inadequately trained in the ground rules of counterpoint," a deficiency that Fux promised to remedy himself. The emperor affixed his one-word assent to this proposal: "placet."

The Viennese way of teaching counterpoint can be summed up in a few words: press a copy of the *Gradus ad Parnassum* upon the pupil and tell him

---

[49] *Zwanzig Componisten: eine Skizze* (Berne, 1776), p. 28.

to come back later, after he has worked through the exercises. This is what Ditters experienced at the hands of none other than Bonno:

> At my first visit, he presented me with Fux's "Introduction to Composition," which in those days was reckoned one of the best works of its kind. It is written in Latin and consists throughout of dialogues between a teacher and his pupils . . . When Bonno handed me the volume, he said: "I assume you understand Latin?" After turning over a leaf or two, and examining a passage here and there, I answered: "Why, it is such dog-Latin that any fellow in the second class could understand it!" "Oh, indeed!" he replied, in his usual schoolmaster tone. "We don't want elegant Latinity here, but good sound theory—and that the book contains. That's what we want!" Of course he was right.

This little scene took place in the early 1750s when Bonno was at the height of his success as a composer of operas. Perhaps it reminded him of a similar scene not many years before when he was subjected to the embarrassment of having to study counterpoint under Fux, following ten years of study in Naples. The parallel with Thomas Attwood and his studies in Naples is not to be missed; when Attwood arrived in Vienna, Mozart started him over from the beginning. Salieri experienced the same fate when he came to Vienna as a young protégé of Gassmann in 1766, and his memoirs inform us in all seriousness that the *Gradus* served as his tutor not only in music but also in Latin.

Bonno persevered, and on 6 February 1739 he won a post as court composer. His early Viennese works include not only a quantity of sacred music, but also several occasional cantatas on texts by Pasquini, written to celebrate various name days and birthdays in the ruling family. Metastasio took over this function from Pasquini in the 1740s. His *Natal di Giove*, in celebration of the emperor's birthday on 1 October 1740, was set by Bonno. It was the last time that Bonno could honor his benefactor in this way because Charles VI died three weeks later.

Bonno and Metastasio collaborated infrequently during the 1740s, but shortly after 1750 they worked together on three operas that marked a high point for both of them: *Il re pastore*, *L'eroe cinese*, and *L'isola disabitata*. Ditters says that Prince Hildburghausen, Vienna's most discerning music patron at that time, commissioned Bonno, who ran the prince's concerts, to set the first two. This may well be so, but not without the complicity of Metastasio, who took an active role in deciding which of the several court composers made the first setting of his new dramas. In a letter of 16 November 1751 to Farinelli in Madrid, Metastasio reported on *Il re pastore*. Of the text he said: "It is gay, tender, amorous, short; and has indeed, all the necessary requisites for your wants. No representation here is remembered to have extorted such universal applause." Farinelli had asked for information about Viennese court composers, with a view to using their scores at the Madrid opera (his letters are lost). In the same letter the poet revealed more details about the music than was his wont: "The music is so graceful, so well adapted and so lively, that it enchants by its own merit, without injuring the passion of the personage, and pleases excessively . . . I will prevail on the composer himself to adjust it to your purpose, or new set whatever you please. The author is Sig. Giuseppe Bonno: he was born of Italian parents, and sent by Charles VI to study music under Leo, with whom he passed his first youth." There follow some uncomplimentary remarks about Gluck and Wagenseil that have been quoted above. Reutter was apparently deemed not even worthy of mention in this context.

Bonno's special qualities are apparent from the first number of *Il re pastore*, which follows the overture without a break—in a brilliant stroke the poet forewent his usual dramatic exposition in recitative and allowed the first aria to provide the setting. The third movement of the overture does not end, but comes to a stop on V, which is resolved by the ritornello opening of the aria "Intendo amico rio," sung by Amintas addressing a friendly stream. A pastoral tone is established by the lilting siciliana rhythm and the orchestration—pizzicato strings, with flutes doubling the violin thirds in the higher octave (Example 2.7). The likes of this music is not to be found in Wagenseil. It is quintessentially Neapolitan, and stems from a popular song type introduced into opera by the elder Scarlatti and then used by all the great Neapolitan masters, including Bonno's teacher Leo, who was the most mellifluous of a great school of lyric composers. Note the elegant and modish cut of Bonno's melody: **a**; **b** (ending with the upturned conjunct third); **b'** (galant

EXAMPLE 2.7. *Bonno*, Il re pastore, *(1751)*

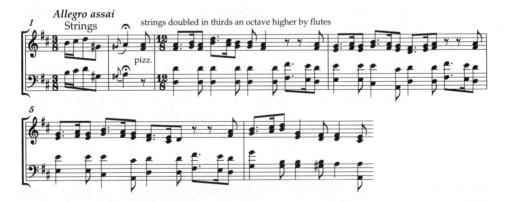

redict ending with a downturned conjunct third); **c** (to bring the phrase to a half cadence).

The harmony is no less galant, with its emphasis on IV$^{6/4}$, the vii^7 chord in **b** and **b'**, and the nicely handled cross relation between melody and bass leading to the half cadence. The doubled thirds approaching the cadence sound ever so Mozartian as well. It is not just the finesse in doubling and spacing that anticipate Mozart. This very piece, or others like it—Bonno wrote several pieces of the type—must have been lingering in Mozart's ear when he composed *Idomeneo* thirty years later. Mozart invoked these placid strains in lilting dotted rhythm in his own choral siciliana, "Placido è il mar, andiamo," near the end of Act II. Bonno's descending third in the bass, as a link between **a** and **b** and between **b** and **b'**, reappears with the same function in Mozart's bass. The vii^7 chord is one of the climactic moments of Mozart's chorus, and a similar approach to the half cadence, moreover, occurs in this very same chorus. Nearly a century ago an astute critic perceived that there was some deep-seated continuity stretching between Alessandro Scarlatti and Mozart.[50] Indeed there was, and it passed in something like a master-to-pupil relationship over several generations, by way of Leo and his Viennese disciple, Bonno.

Metastasio's enchantment with Bonno is readily comprehensible. Bonno preserved a simpler Italian style of an earlier time, and his music could not but remind the poet of the happy years he spent as a youth in Naples and Rome. When Metastasio wrote to Farinelli in early 1753 proposing that Bonno compose *L'isola disabitata* for Madrid in lieu of Porpora, who was ill, he reminded his friend that Bonno was a man "educated in Naples when it abounded in able professors, of good taste, and endowed by nature with that grace which is incompatible with extravagance: and the only one in short among those who are in this country from whom I could reasonably expect something tolerable."

Possibly Metastasio suggested to Bonno how best to set the arias. His lyric verses were never conceived, he claimed, without imagining their musical raiment. Burney preserves the poet's musical setting of "La partenza," and it is a simple minuet air in a syllabic, *parlante* style.[51] Similar traits are found in Bonno's love song of Amintas, "L'amerò, sarò costante," in *Il re pastore* (Example 2.8abc). His simple, diatonic melody projects the text with a minimum of effort (although the three-note snaps require fine vocalism so as not to sound fussy or call attention to themselves). It can be

[50] Edward J. Dent, *Alessandro Scarlatti: His Life and Works* (London, 1905), pp. 201–2.

[51] *Memoirs of the Life and Writings of the Abate Metastasio* (London, 1796), 1: 350–51, reproduced in Daniel Heartz, "Farinelli and Metastasio: Rival Twins of Public Favour," *Early Music* 12 (1984): 363, illustration 4.

EXAMPLE 2.8. *Settings of "L'amerò" from* Il rè pastore

a. Bonno (1751)

b. Gluck (1756)

c. Mozart (1775)

no coincidence that later settings of this text employed the same trochaic rhythms and similar melodic content. Gluck, in an obvious rewriting of Bonno, displays some of the extravagance that so offended Metastasio—high A is not a good choice for the harsh *i* sound of "fido." Mozart as well paid homage to Bonno in his famous setting of the song. Mozart's melody is even smoother, and the bass, by moving less, throws it into greater relief. Fux would not have approved the fifths in the penultimate measure, but they are sanctioned by a century of Italian practice. It is clear even from these three settings—and there were many others made of the poem—that Bonno created a classic with his original setting of *Il re pastore.*

Bonno brought some of the qualities that Metastasio admired in his arias to his church music. Two samples of his setting of the "Et incarnatus est" from two different Masses in C show that he preferred the subdominant for this exalted text, which inspired him to create ecstatic melodies and the most delicate orchestral effects.[52] The way he uses the raised-fifth degree in both settings proclaims the galant and *affettuoso* nature of his musical discourse.

[52] Egon Wellesz, "Giuseppe Bonno (1710–1788): Sein Leben und seine dramatischen Werke," *SIMG* 11 (1909–10): 395–442; the examples are on pp. 432–33. Wellesz made untenable claims regarding Bonno's role as a bridge from the Rococo to the *Romantik,* but he was also perspicacious enough to assert that what Riemann called Mannheim mannerisms were Neapolitan commonplaces, and very frequent in Bonno's music (see especially pp. 407–8).

Bonno wrote no masses of the largest kind (the so-called cantata mass). Like his Neapolitan teachers, he preferred to organize the Gloria and Credo of the mass into small interlocking sections, rather than into individual movements. His setting of the oratorio *Isaaco figura del redentore* by Metastasio was performed in a staged version with costumes under Gluck's direction during the Lenten season of 1759, not in the Burgtheater but in the enterprising series sponsored by Prince Hildburghausen in the Palais Rofrano. Bonno's *Isaaco* was so successful it was still performed at Vienna late in the century. For Lent 1774 the composer set Metastasio's *Il Giuseppe riconosciuto* for the Tonkünstler Societät, of which he became president in 1775. His Requiem Mass was performed at the obsequies for Maria Theresa in 1780.[53]

Honors and high positions came to Bonno late in his life, throughout most of which he was overshadowed by Reutter, Gluck, and Wagenseil. But with Gluck increasingly preoccupied with Paris in the 1770s and Wagenseil an invalid confined to his house during his last decade, Bonno was eventually thrust to the fore. When Reutter died in 1772, he was replaced as imperial court Kapellmeister not by Bonno, but by the much younger Gassmann, a favorite of Emperor Joseph II. When Gassmann died in January 1774, four musicians applied for the post: Tobias Gsur, Leopold Hofmann, Joseph Starzer, and Bonno. The post of *primo maestro* went to Bonno at the age of sixty-three, although the secret deliberations between the emperor and Count Sporck left no doubt that they considered Hofmann's qualifications superior.[54] Bonno served until what was for that period a very advanced age. He gave up his duties directing the society concerts around 1782 because of ill health. The composer finally resigned his court position in March 1788, and died the following month. Salieri was named his successor.

Ziegler and Schlöger

JOSEPH ZIEGLER was born in Vienna on 14 September 1722. Ditters, who studied violin with him around 1750, remembered Ziegler in his memoirs as "a very fine violinist and a skilful and worthy composer of chamber music; he took great pains with me." The mention of "Figler" as a soloist in the printed *Répertoire* of 1757 may refer to Ziegler. He was concertmaster in the German theater according to the records for 1756–57 and 1757–58; he was

---

[53] Sigrid Kleindienst, "Marginalien zu Giuseppe Bonnos Requiem," *Musik am Hof Maria Theresias* (Munich, 1984), pp. 131-40.

[54] MacIntyre, *The Viennese Concerted Mass*, p. 34.

also paid as a copyist there, earning a florin apiece for eighteen arias in 1753–54.[55] Abbé Stadler in his autobiographical sketch says that when he was a student in the Jesuit Seminary beginning in 1762, he became acquainted with Vienna's most famous musicians and composers, whom he lists as Reutter, Bonno, Vanhal, Haydn, Hofmann, Ziegler, Gassmann, and Mittelmeyer (organist at the cathedral).[56] The appearances of Ziegler's name at court concerts around this time suggest that he was an active and esteemed composer of symphonies. Gumpenhuber reports that for the twentieth anniversary of Archduke Joseph's birth, 13 March 1761, there was a *grande gala* and *service de table* in the palace, "lequel a commencé par une grande symphonie de la composition du Sieur Ziegler." At the academy of 29 October 1762, the composer was once again singled out: "Entre autres Simphonies on a produit une nouvelle de la Composition du Sr Josephe Ziegler." Ziegler's name appears at the head of the second violins in the "Etat du Theatre Près de la Cour depuis 4 avril jusque à la fin de l'Année 1763," and on 8 July 1763 we read about the performance at an academy in the Burgtheater of "deux Symphonies nouvelle de la composition du Sr Ziegler." None of these works is known to have survived.

In 1766 Johann Adam Hiller printed "The Present State of the Court-and Chamber-Music" in his *Wöchentliche Nachricten* (Figures 2.4–2.7).[57] Ziegler's name appears here after those of Ditters, Ordonez, and Haydn among the violinists, and he is said to be qualified "in symphonies, trios, etc." In his *Materialen zur Geschichte der Musik* Abbé Stadler includes this informative paragraph:

> Joseph Ziegler bloomed as one of the premier violin players and composers in Vienna around 1750. He was the second teacher of Herr von Dittersdorf. He composed in the new taste many sonatas and quartets for violin and transverse flute; he wrote many symphonies for the most worthy bishop of Wienerneustadt. For the church he composed many grand masses, litanies, and similar things, all of which works His Imperial Majesty the grand duke of Tuscany [Leopold] bought from Joseph Stadler, chorus director of the Jesuits and court bass, and preserved in Florence.

Ziegler was in fact a violin teacher at the Jesuit Seminary of St. Ignatius and St. Pancratius "am Stuben-Thor." When he died in 1767, his sacred music apparently passed into the hands of another musician in the employ

[55] Franz Hadamowsky, in *Jahrbuch der Gesellschaft für Wiener Theaterforschung* 11 (1959): 5–6.
[56] Gerhard Croll, "Eine zweite, fast vergessene Selbstbiographie von Abbé Stadler," *Mozart Jahrbuch 1964*, pp. 172–84; 176.
[57] For a complete translation, see Appendix 1.

Wöchentliche
Nachrichten und Anmerkungen
die Musik betreffend.

Dreyzehntes Stück.

Leipzig den 23ten Septembr. 1766.

Wien.

Von dem dermaligen Etat der kaiserl. königl. Hof- und Kammermusik, wie auch einigen andern hiesigen Virtuosen und Liebhabern einen kurzen, wiewohl zur Zeit noch unvollkommenen Abriß mitzutheilen, hat ein Freund der Musik auf Verlangen folgendes niederschreiben wollen.

1) Ist zu wissen, daß nachdem der ehemalige Director Herr Graf von Durazzo, vor zwey Jahren als Botschafter nach Venedig abgegangen, der böhmische Graf, Herr Johann Wenzel des heil. R. R. Graf von Spork, nunmehr als General = Director der Spectaculn oder als quasi Maitre des plaisirs, die Oberaufsicht über die Hof- und Kammermusik, und zu gleicher Zeit über das Theater hieselbst führet. Es ist derselbe einer der verständigsten Cavaliers so sich zu dieser Charge qualificirt gemacht, indem er ein genauer Kenner, und selbst in der Instrumentalmusik, besonders der Violin vor sehr geschickt gehalten wird.

2) Ist unser italiänischer Hof- Poet, noch der berühmte Herr Abt Pietro Metastasio, der durch seine Werke der Welt sattsam bekannt ist.

3) Finden sich, neben dem hochberühmten K. P. dermahln Chursächs. Herrn Hofcapellmeistern Johann Adolph Hassen, dessen Anwesenheit in Person allhier wir zu wissen das Glück haben, auch noch allhie der Herr Joseph Scarlatti, der mehrere sowohl ernst = als scherzhafte Opern mit Beyfall hier und in Wälschland geschrieben, wie auch der Herr Chevalier Christoph Gluck, der nebst den vorhin bekannten Opern noch neuerlich successive viele komische Opern mit Geschmack hieselbst verfertiget. Hierzu rechnet man billig einen Herrn Florian Leopold Gaßmann, so von des Kaisers Majestät auf einige Zeit nach Italien geschickt worden, und sich gegenwärtig zu Venedig aufhält. Dieser hat gegen das Ende des 1764ten Jahres die Opera Olym-

N

piade

FIGURES 2.4–7. "The Present State of the Court- and Chamber-Music, 1766."

98

piade geschrieben, und selbige ist darauf im Carneval 1765. mit Approbation hier aufgeführet worden, auch sind sonsten seine Claviersachen sehr artig.

Von der Hof=Kapelle sind dermalen zu bemerken.

Hof=Kapellmeister.

Herr Lucas Anton Bredieri, ein Mann von Verdiensten besonders in Kirchen=Sachen, so schon unter Kaiser Carl des VI. Regierung Opern geschrieben, dermalen aber als jubilatus lebt.

Herr Georg von Reuter, zugleich Musikdirector bey der Metropolitankirche zu St. Stephan, gleichfalls und hauptsächlich in Kirchenstücken, Motetten. Sonsten ist hier in dergleichen Art von Composition ein gewisser Advocat, Namens Sonnenleitner beyzuzählen, der sich hierinnen sehr geschickt erwiesen.

Kammer=Compositors.

Herr George Christoph Wagenseil, zu Wien gebohren, in omni genere notissimus.

Herr Joseph Bono, ein Italiäner.

Hof=Claviermeister.

Herr Leopold Hofmann, aus Wien, und Capellmeister bey St. Peter. Ist durch seine schönen Sinfonien und eine Menge anderer Sachen bekannt.

= Joseph Steffan, ein Böhme, in Concerten à Cembalo, Clavier Sachen, als Divertimenti und dergleichen bekannt, die meistentheils in Kupfer gestochen sind.

Cantatrici.

Frau Theresia von Reuter, Gemahlinn des Hof=Kapellmeisters, so aber nicht mehr singt.

Frau Theresia Pettmann, gebohrne Heinisch, eine Tochter von dem berühmten Hof=Trompeter gleiches Namens. Dann gehört mit hieher

Die bekannte Mademoiselle Teuberinn, so dermalen bey des Prinzen von Sachsen=Hildburghausen Durchl. Kapelle engagirt.

Sopranist.

Herr Joseph Monteriso.

Altisten.

Herr Pietro Rauzzino, und Pietro Galli.

Tenorist.

Herr Cajetan Borghi. Hierzu rechnet man den Herrn Leopold Bonscho von des Prinzen von Hildburghausen Kapelle, der zugleich ein trefflicher Violoncellist ist.

Bassi=

99

Bassisten.

Herr Christoph Braun, und Herr Carl Herrich.

Organist.

Herr Gottlieb Muffat.

Violinisten.

Herr Carl Joseph Denck, Herr Adam, und dessen Tochter, große Virtuose.

Herr Franz Thuma aus Böhmen, gewesener Kapellmeister bey Jhro kaiserl. Majestät Elisabeth, in Sinfonien, à Tre, Kirchen-Sachen.

Herr Georg Orsler, aus Schlesien, gewesener Kapellmeister von dem seel. Fürsten von Lichtenstein, in Sinfonien à 4. Kirchenstyl.

Herr Karl Ditters, in Sinfonien, Concerten u. d. g. bekannt.

Herr Leopold Hofmann, desgleichen

Herr Carl von Ordoniz, Registrant bey den Landrechten, in Sinfonien.

• • Joseph Heyden, ein Oesterreicher, Capellmeister bey dem Fürsten Esterhasi, in Sinfonien ꝛc. ꝛc.

Herr Ziegler, in Sinfonien, à Tre &c.

• • Martinus Wisdorffer.
• = Huber.
= • Hoffmann.
• • Kreibich.
• • Klemm, Schüler vom Herrn Hofmann.
• • Trani.
• = Aspelmeyer.

Herr Haßlinger dermalen zu Preßburg.

• • Anton Rosetti, Gräfl. althanischer Kammer-Musicus.
• = Johann Schnautz.
• • Cammermeyer.
• • Mannl.
• • Curara.
• • Büschelberger.

Hautboisten.

Herr Besozzi, vom Churfl. Sächsischen Hofe.

Traversisten.

Herr Schulz.

Auf der Mandora.

Herr Molli, und Herr Winter.

Harfenisten.

Herr Tretter und Herr Bierfreund.

Lautenisten.

Herr von Kohot, bey der Kais. Königl. Hof- und Staats-Canzley Secretär, so sehr in Spielen als Componiren auf diesem Instrumente berühmt.

Bassonisten.

Herr Abbe Kolofer, Herr Hofmann, Herr Himmelbauer, Herr Ledez-

ti

100

ki, ein Böhme, Herr Schloßthal, Assessor beym Stadtgericht, Herr Franciscello.

Fagottist. Herr Philipp Friedrich.

Posaunist. Herr Ferdin. Christian, einer der fürnehmsten im Kirchensatz.

Hof-Trompeter.

Herr Ernst Beyer, Herr Franz Kreibich, Herr Andreas Hübler, ingleichen Herr Neuhold, Herr Koch und Herr Hofbauer.

Auf dem Clavier und Unterweisung desselben sind sonst noch berühmt.

Herr Arbesser, Fürstl. Schwarzenberg. Hofmusicus, Viennensis.

• • Senft, ein Wiener in Partien.

• • Johann Christoph Mann, in Galanteriepartien, Concerten, Nachtmusik, Sinfonien ꝛc. ꝛc.

• • Sommer, Schüler von Herr Steffan.

• • Matthielli, Schüler vom Herrn Wagenseil.

Organisten in den Vorstädten.

Bey denen P. P. Schwarz-Spaniern, Herr Scheibpflug.

Bey denen P.P. Weiß-Spaniern, Herr Heida.

Bey denen 14. Nothelfern, Herr Martinides.

Bey St. Carolum Baromæum Herr Pircher, alle in Kirchen-Styl.

Dann verdienen noch einige von unsern Frauenzimmern, sowohl von Noblesse als mittlern Stande, die auf dem Clavier und im Singen sehr geschickt sind, mit angemerkt zu werden, als:

Die Mademoiselle Elisabeth Martinez, so unter Aufsicht des Herrn Abt Metastasio erzogen worden, componirt sehr artig.

Die Fräulein Gräfinn von Zierotni, im Singen.

Eine Fräulein, Gräfinn von Wilczec. Ein Fräulein Bar: von Gudenus.

Ein Fräulein von Collenbach.   Mademoiselle Auenbrugge.

Ein Fräulein von Hahn.   Mademoiselle Plenschütz.

Die Frau von Waldstädten, gebohrne von Schäfer.

Die Frau von Moll, Gemahl des RhR. Agenten, alle auf dem Clavier.

Die Frau Hardlin.   Die Frau Fraislin, im Singen.

Wöchentlich wird, nebst andern gestifteten Akademien, als z. E. bey dem Hrn Grafen von Collaldo, beym Herrn Landschafts-Beysitzer Herr von Rees, beym Herr von Oertel, ꝛc. wenigstens einmal, bey des Prinzen von Sachsen Hildburghausen Durchl. unter Direction des Herrn Joseph Bono musikalisches Concert gehalten.   Wien, mense Aug. 1766.

Fort-

of the Jesuits. Ziegler did not die a pauper; his wife was able to pay for his fourth-class funeral. Archduke Leopold left Vienna to assume the rule of Tuscany in 1765. Leopold's musical tastes ran to the grand and serious, as manifested in his partiality to Handel's oratorios, Gluck's tragic ballets, and opera seria, which he reintroduced from Italy to Vienna upon becoming emperor in 1790. His interest in Ziegler's orchestral church music throws further light on the formation of his tastes during his youth in Vienna. Several manuscripts of Ziegler's sacred music are preserved in the library of the Conservatory at Florence, along with many others by his contemporaries in Vienna, presumably from the collection of Leopold. In a letter of 11 August 1775 from Joseph II to Leopold, mention is made of a musical packet containing "une Grande Messe" by Gassmann, another by Bonno, and several motets by Reutter, all of which were being sent to Florence along with a harpsichord.[58]

At least six masses by Ziegler are known, and two of them prompted the author of a recent study to write: "They are fascinating works with much variety in meter (including 2/4 and 3/8), tempo and key."[59] Of Ziegler's once-imposing instrumental oeuvre all that is known to have survived at present is a Violin Concerto in A in the Gesellschaft der Musikfreunde and a Symphony in C dated 1758 in the Austrian National Library. But this has not prevented one scholar from assigning Ziegler a position of some historical importance:

> One of the most highly regarded Viennese violinists of the middle of the eighteenth century, Joseph Ziegler numbers among those worthy and able carriers of musical evolution who reduced the bravura elements of virtuosity and made it serviceable to social music making. Since his playing and his compositions were known above all by Joseph and Michael Haydn, Ditters, and Albrechtsberger, his influence on the development of classical instrumental style may be deemed considerable.[60]

Having studied both instrumental works from specially prepared scores (only parts survive), I deem otherwise.

The "Sinfonia in C" of 1758 is scored for trumpets or horns and strings. It opens with an *Allegro molto* in common time that proposes a series of short motivic phrases, moving mainly by the eighth note and often ending with the snap of two eighth notes followed by a rest. The nervous energy and lack of breadth are reminiscent of some of Wagenseil's overtures of the 1740s, particularly the first movement of the overture to *La clemenza di Tito* (1746).

---

[58] Vienna, Haus-, Hof-, und Staatsarchiv, Sammelbände Karton 7.
[59] MacIntyre, *The Viennese Concerted Mass*, p. 92.
[60] Karl Pfannhauser, article "Ziegler" in *MGG*.

From this first movement, it might be deduced that Ziegler did not follow the trend toward longer, balanced phrases and phrase parts pursued by Wagenseil in the 1750s (and also, independently, by Stamitz). But then it might also be argued that Ziegler was not aiming at a concert symphony or overture type of piece here, but more a chamber work along the lines of a "church symphony," which would explain the emphasis on contrapuntal exchange between the parts and other retrospective features such as the independent viola part (emphasized on the title page by the words "viola obbligato"). The work ends with a brief *Andante* in the tonic minor and an even briefer *Allegro assai* in 3/8 restoring the tonic major; both movements are in binary form with both halves repeated.

"Concerto Ex A à Violino Principale, Violino Primo, Violino Secondo con Basso Del Sigre Giuseppe Ziegler" is the title of the other manuscript. An opening *Allegro di giusto* in common time is pervaded by the same short-breathed motivic writing as in the symphony. In form it follows the mid-century ritornello practice described by Koch, with four tuttis and three solo entrances. Only modest demands are made on the soloist, and in this respect Ziegler was not followed by his pupil Ditters. Signs of older practice here are the fermata on V (rather than on $I^{6/4}$), indicating a solo cadenza, followed by the direction "Da Capo al Segno," indicating a repeat of the first tutti. In the second movement, an *Andante* in 2/4 and in tonic minor, the solo cadenza does occur after a stop on $I^{6/4}$, followed by a da capo indication. The finale, *Allegro* in 2/4 and in tonic major, once again uses a da capo repetition to close the work, this time without a preceding cadenza. Taken together, the concerto and the symphony do not justify the claim for Ziegler's importance to Haydn and others. Rather, they throw into relief Wagenseil's more modern and Italianate works of the 1750s as the path that opened up great possibilities.

Matthias Schlöger was born the same year as Ziegler, 1722, and died a little more than a year earlier. This information is deduced from his death notice: "30. Juni 1766. Schlöger Matthäus, k.k. Hof Klaviermeister, ist am Peter beim Auge Gotts an Lungenbrand beschaut worden, alt 44 Jahre, nachts um 10 Uhr." Ziegler also died of lung disease. There is no confirmation elsewhere that Schlöger was one of the *Hofklaviermeister*, except that Steffan was appointed to replace him in this office during the summer of 1766. Quite appropriately, then, Hiller's correspondent in Vienna, who dated his "Etat" of the court music August 1766, puts Steffan alongside Leopold Hofmann under "Hof. Claviermeister" and does not mention Schlöger, which shows that his knowledge of the court music was up-to-date.

Abbé Stadler has nothing to say about Schlöger in any of his writings. The man and his music were soon forgotten. From the "Partita a Violino

Primo, Violino Secondo e Basso Del Sgre: Matteo Schlöger," which was selected for modern edition, it is easy to understand why.[61] The work opens with an *Allegro* in 3/4 that lacks melodic profile, one of those movements so unmemorable that one has to keep glancing back to the beginning to see what the main theme was. B♭ is the key of the cycle, and for his *Largo*, common-time second movement Schlöger chooses the subdominant, E♭, evincing a modern touch in this respect. The two violins *con sordini* play in thirds and sixths quite a lot of the time, but there is some dialogue between them too. There follows a Menuetto with a quasi-canonic trio. The most interesting movement is the finale in 2/4. It begins with an inverted period such as Wagenseil might use, and closes the prima parte with an effective *Molltrübung, piano*; the minor dominant, v, is followed by a burst of major dominant, V—again very like Wagenseil. A cadence on vi follows the usual beginning of the seconda parte with the main theme on V, followed by harmonic sequences. The ensuing ten-measure retransition shows a deft touch. The first theme is not recapitulated.

Three symphonies with horns survive in the composer's own score, each signed "Matteo Schlöger." The first, in D, contains canceled four-measure phrases in the last movement indicating that Schlöger wrote out the entire first violin part before anything else. The opening *Allegro molto* in 3/4 time fills 128 measures with bustling eighth-note motion and scarcely any memorable ideas. After a cadence on vi, there is a retransition of five measures that lead to V - I in D via V/ii - ii. At this juncture the composer spares us a reprise of the characterless scale passages with which the movement opened and resorts in their stead to a previously unheard figure with chromatic alterations. His use of the raised-fifth and raised-second degrees here make Schlöger sound a little more modern than Ziegler, although the two composers are alike in their reliance on short motifs of one measure or less. Neither made much headway toward enlarging the motif to a songlike phrase of several measures, as did both Stamitz and Wagenseil by the mid-1750s. Like Wagenseil, Schlöger chose a sequence of three movements for each of these symphonies, the second movements contrasting in mode or key and the finales restoring the initial key with a fast dance movement in 3/8 time. The finale of the second symphony, in F, is a five-part rondo, **A B A C A,** with the first episode in vi and the second in tonic minor. In this regard Schlöger could have served as a model for Haydn. The third symphony is in E, a favorite key of both Haydn and Wagenseil.

A recent study gives melodic incipits for the first movements of six trio-partitas for strings and offers a transcription of the first movement of one in

---

[61] Karl Horwitz and Karl Riedel, eds., *Wiener Instrumentalmusik vor und um 1750: Vorläufer der Wiener Klassiker*, DTÖ 31 (Vienna, 1908): 89–93.

D.[62] All are in four-movement form: fast, slow, minuet, fast. The inclusion of minuets in similar partitas of Birck and Tuma is of historical importance. Haydn's symphonies were beneficiaries of this practice. As for the few surviving symphonies by Schlöger, only some contain minuets. Of nineteen incipits, nine are recoverable as complete pieces. The three autograph symphonies with horns, mentioned above, are in three movements without minuets. Among these is the Symphony in D's opening movement, described as a ritornello structure. Another group of three symphonies, in a Copenhagen manuscript, includes two four-movement works with minuets and one three-movement work without. Judging from the expositions in the first movements of the Symphonies in F and A, we can conclude that Schlöger worked on a very small scale, less ambitious than that of Haydn's Symphony No. 1 or works of Wagenseil. The exposition of the first movement of the Symphony in A, for example, devotes eight measures to the tonic and five to transition; another fifteen take us up to the double bar with repeat sign. Neither thematic invention nor continuity of musical thought is the equal of even the earliest Haydn. None of Schlöger's works can be dated.

Starzer and Asplmayr

JOSEPH STARZER was born in 1726 or 1727. Nothing is known of his early years or training. By the early 1750s he was a violinist in the orchestra of the French troupe in the Burgtheater, and he is said to have composed ballets for them in the printed *Répertoire* of 1757. Thus he was working in the field with which he is most identified before it was taken up by Asplmayr or, for that matter, by Gluck.

A happy discovery in the Turin legacy of the theater intendant, Count Durazzo, has brought to light orchestral parts for thirty-six ballets by Franz Hilverding given between 1752 and 1757;[63] payment records establish Starzer as their composer. The ballets comprise from about ten to twenty-five movements, and invariably end in the same key in which they began. Unity between movements is established by motivic relationships and by large-scale returns, among other ways. Starzer was adept at conveying peasant images when the subjects of the ballets called for them; an example is the yodeling effect that seems to capture the Austrian countryside in this

---

[62] Larsen, "Wenzel Raimund Birck und Mattäus Schlöger," pp. 108–30.
[63] Bruce Alan Brown, "Theatrical Dance in Vienna ca. 1750: New Sources on the Works of Hilverding and Starzer," paper read at the 50th Annual Meeting of the American Musicological Society, Philadelphia, 1984. I am indebted to Brown for the information and the music examples that follow.

EXAMPLE 2.9. *Starzer,* Les moissoneurs (1754), *excerpt*

excerpt from *Les moissoneurs* (The Harvesters) of 1754 (Example 2.9). Swinging back and forth between I and V as it does (note well the major ninth implied in m. 4), this dance has a freshness and local color that foreshadow some of Haydn's country scenes. It could not be mistaken for Rameau, from whom Starzer did borrow several pieces in his ballets. He also borrowed two vaudevilles from an opéra comique then being prepared by the French troupe in the Burgtheater, and used them in his ballet *Le retour des matelots* of 1755. The same year he wrote music for Hilverding's ballet *Les parties du jour* ("Le matin," "Le midi," "Le soir," "La nuit"), anticipating Haydn's symphonic trilogy on the same subject from 1761. Specifically, Starzer anticipated Haydn's borrowing of a traditional horn call (the main theme of the first movement of Symphony No. 6, *Le matin*) as well as an actual vaudeville (the main theme of the first movement of Symphony No. 8, *Le soir*). Starzer also wrote a programmatic piece for wind band called *Le matin et le soir*.

Imaginative varieties of texture help Starzer to maintain musical interest through the lengthy chain of dances required by these ballets—an accomplishment in any age. To accompany a delicate moment in the ballet *Psiché et l'amour* of 1752, the composer wrote a very soft minuet with the two violins in octaves against the bass (Example 2.10). Only at the cadences does the texture expand to three parts. Very effective are the chromatic slurs at the beginning of the second strain, and the subsequent soaring of the melody up to high D as the sequence breaks out of its pattern. A master melodist and harmonist, as this piece testifies, Starzer was one of the first, and indeed perhaps the very first, to introduce the much-disputed Viennese trait of vio-

EXAMPLE 2.10. *Starzer*, Psiché et l'amour *(1752)*, Minuet

lin octaves. In March 1758 Gumpenhuber listed among the second violins of the Burgtheater orchestra "Starzer, compose aussi les airs pour les Ballets."

Starzer's portrait figures in the telling image of Viennese court musicians and dancers drawn and engraved by Bernardo Bellotto in 1759 (Figure 2.8). The engraving records the performance in the Burgtheater of Hilverding's ballet *Le Turc généreux*, composed by Starzer and performed to honor the visit in the spring of 1758 of a Turkish emissary, come to announce the accession of a new Ottoman ruler to Maria Theresa.[64] Starzer presides over the performance at the harpsichord, according to the traditional composer's privilege. He is backed by the usual forces sustaining the continuo line, a cello and a bass, who read directly from the score on the harpsichord desk. A nearby figure, book in hand, faces the stage; he may represent Hilverding. Seventeen violin or viola players are seated across from one another at a

---

[64] Bruce Alan Brown, in another major discovery, located the score of Starzer's *Le Turc généreux* at Český Krumlov. He discusses the music with generous examples in *Gluck and the French Theatre at Vienna* (Oxford, 1991), pp. 186–93.

Le Turc Genereux.

FIGURE 2.8. Bellotto. *Le Turc généreux,* Ballet Pantomime by Hilverding and Starzer, 26 April 1758.

long music desk, in the typical Viennese fashion. Two horn players hold their bells up behind the continuo players. Normally, one would expect two oboes as well in a stage band like this. Their absence may mean only that the many string players depicted harbored some versatile wind players as well. In the right box, theater director Durazzo, to whom the print is dedicated, leans out to survey his handiwork. Durazzo actually used this magnificent print to wage battles at home and abroad, in his ongoing offensive to sustain Vienna's cultural initiative and to show how effective he was as an impresario.

In late 1758 Starzer followed Hilverding to the court of St. Petersburg, where he remained for a decade, after which time he returned to Vienna and resumed his activities as ballet composer, notably in collaboration with

III. Portrait of Marie Antoinette (1769 or 1770), attributed to Wagenschön.
(Vienna: Kunsthistorisches Museum)

IV. Painting, attributed to Lancret, of scenes from
Rameau's *Castor et Pollux* on a harpsichord lid. (Private
collection, U.S.A. courtesy of Rosenberg & Stiebel, Inc.)

Jean-Georges Noverre. Burney, who visited Vienna at the height of Noverre's success there, called Starzer "an excellent player, and as good a musician. This performer is remarkably happy in the composition of ballet and
pantomime music for the theatre." On the same occasion in 1772, Burney
heard Starzer play first violin in some Haydn quartets (probably Opus 20 of
the same year) and remarked that he "played the Adagios with uncommon
feeling and expression." Claims that Starzer himself made important contributions to the evolution of the string quartet are impossible to substantiate
in the absence of any way of dating his chamber music. It seems at least as
likely that he, like many other composers, was inspired by Haydn's chamber
music rather than the other way around. His Divertimento in C for two
violins, viola, and bass consists of four movements,[65] the second being a
Menuetto, which displays the typically Viennese octave doubling in the violins we observed in Example 2.10. Starzer writes very long and contrapuntal
developments in this divertimento, and both outer movements provide less
tonic stability in the reprise than instability in the development. Haydn, by
way of comparison, was more concerned with balancing these elements.

Starzer's ability to create free-flowing musical equivalents to pantomime
scenes without resorting to the usual dance forms endeared him to Noverre.
Experiments along these lines went so far in Noverre's *Roger et Bradamante*
of 1771 as to include scenes using the techniques of melodrama—spoken
lines (or were they acted out in dumbshow?) surrounded and overlapped by
orchestral interjections.[66] Mozart paid Starzer the compliment of notating a
whole series of his dances in the *primo ballo* of *Lucio Silla* (1773). When Joseph
II eliminated ballet as a major field of Viennese endeavor in his theatrical
reforms of 1776, Starzer's career as a stage composer was over. But he had
been active as a member of the Tonkünstler Societät since its founding in
1771, and he continued to compose for the society and lead its concerts. He
also arranged Handel's *Judas Maccabeus* for the private concerts of Baron von
Swieten, the direction of which eventually passed to Mozart. Failing health
during his last decade caused Starzer to curtail these activities as well. He
died in 1787.

A curious episode in the last part of Starzer's career was his application,
along with Bonno, Gsur, and Hofmann, for the post of Hofkapellmeister left
vacant by the death of Gassmann in January 1774.[67] The other three had
written large quantities of church music before this time, in line with their
respective posts. Would Starzer have made the application had he not writ-

[65] Edited in *DTÖ* 31 (1908): 94–104.
[66] For a music example, see Hermann Abert, "J. G. Noverre und sein Einfluss auf die dramatische
Balletkomposition," *Jahrbuch der Musikbibliothek Peters 1907*, p. 42.
[67] MacIntyre, *The Viennese Concerted Mass*, p. 34.

ten at least some church music? It seems unlikely. And yet none survives from his hand, nor do we know of any connections he had with Viennese church music, even as a performer. Schubart paid one of the most appreciative tributes to Starzer in his *Ideen*, saying that Viennese dance music reached its height in Starzer's time: "Starzer wrote such excellent ballet music that he charmed not only the Viennese public but also strangers. So much deep feeling rules in his composition it is to be regretted that we could not admire his strengths as much or more in the church style, for Starzer was created for the church."[68] An oratorio by Starzer does survive, his setting of Metastasio's *La passione di Gesù Cristo* written for the Tonkünstler Societät in 1778. Abbé Stadler reported that Starzer's last years were occupied with finishing several canons.

Franz Asplmayr was a close contemporary of Starzer and followed him into the field of ballet music. Born in Linz in 1728, Asplmayr was taught violin by his father, and was active in Vienna as a violinist by the 1750s. He served as *Secretarius* to Count Morzin from 1759 to 1761, the same time that Haydn served as the count's music director, and it may be presumed that the two composers were well acquainted. In 1761 Asplmayr took over Gluck's position as ballet composer for the German troupe. He figures as a violinist on Hiller's 1766 list of Viennese court musicians, but is not mentioned in the 1766 article on the Viennese taste in music, unlike Starzer, who was praised for his theater music. Asplmayr's greatest prominence came in connection with Noverre's ballets for Vienna (1771–75). He also figures in the history of melodrama, having made an early setting of Rousseau's *Pygmalion* in German translation. His contributions to Viennese Singspiel have been lost, as has most of his ballet music. The composer's once voluminous production of symphonies and chamber music has fared scarcely better. It speaks for the esteem in which he was held that he was paid to compose twelve symphonies for the court theater during 1776–77. The survival rate for his works is perhaps even lower than that of Ziegler, a situation that instills a cautionary reticence in any historian attempting to describe Viennese court music under Maria Theresa.

A Musical Monarch

OUR account of the court music would be remiss if it neglected to pay tribute to the musical abilities of the sovereign herself. Vienna had never seen a

[68]Christian Friedrich Daniel Schubart, *Ideen zur einer Ästhetik der Tonkunst*, ed. Ludwig Schubart (Vienna, 1806), p. 79.

woman on the throne as reigning monarch before Maria Theresa (her husband's lesser status as co-ruler was somewhat akin to that of Prince Philip as consort to Elizabeth II of England). On the other hand, the monarchy had known several very musical rulers. Charles VI delighted in accompanying his lavish court operas at the harpsichord, and he also composed, as did his three direct predecessors as emperor, many of whose compositions have been edited.[69] Other royal families could boast more than one generation of musically gifted members—Frederick II of Prussia and his cello-playing nephew and successor, Frederick William II, come to mind. But no other dynasty counted several successive generations actively engaged with music. The empress-queen saw to it that all her children received extensive instruction in music, and several turned out to be able performers.[70] Thus did the house of Habsburg-Lorraine continue one characteristic trait of the Habsburg dynasty it replaced. Archduke Rudolph, Beethoven's pupil and Maria Theresa's grandson, had plenty of precedents.

Maria Theresa learned to dance as a young child. She appeared onstage both singing and dancing as early as 1722, at the tender age of five. Her singing teacher was no one less than Johann Adolph Hasse, who shaped her musical tastes and remained her lifelong idol. Hasse first visited Vienna in early 1731, when his oratorio *Daniello*, on a text by Apostolo Zeno, was performed at court. At this time he was already the most famous composer of Italian opera, with many successes in Naples and Venice, resulting in his appointment to the lucrative post of "primo maestro di cappella di S. M. Re Augusto di Polonia ed elettore di Sassonia." He returned to Vienna for a longer stay in 1733–34, and it was at this time that he taught the sixteen-year-old Maria Theresa, as she revealed in a letter written many years later. Hasse represented the newly fashionable galant style of music and singing at its finest, but there was no question of his obtaining a commission to compose one of the court operas, because Antonio Caldara retained the exclusive favor of Charles VI in this domain. Once Maria Theresa came to reign, she invited Hasse repeatedly to compose the operas celebrating dynastic events so that in fact he became the court Kapellmeister in all but name. His last opera was one such, *Ruggiero*, composed for the marriage of Archduke Ferdinand and Maria Beatrice d'Este in Milan in 1771. The empress wrote Maria Beatrice a characteristically touching letter on 17 August 1771, sent by way of Hasse: "He is old and was my music teacher 38 years ago. I have always treasured his compositions above all others. He

[69] *Musikalische Werke der Kaiser Ferdinand III., Leopold I., und Joseph I.*, ed. Guido Adler, 2 vols. (Vienna, 1892–93).

[70] Some of their musical activities and the instruments they played are discussed in Heartz, "A Keyboard Concertino by Marie Antoinette?"

was the first one who made music more delightful and less heavy ["plus agréable, plus légère"]. He has labored long, and possibly he will not succeed so well this time, but I am grateful to him that he entered upon this work with so much vivacity and takes it himself to Milan."[71] The opera was a modest success. Young Mozart knew its arias by heart.

Ruggiero was also the last opera by Metastasio, who loomed as the major literary figure of the Viennese court, the equivalent in every way of Hasse, and also idolized by Maria Theresa her life long. Late in his life the poet answered a request from the critic Antonio Eximeno asking him to name the most successful settings of his operas (letter dated 22 August 1776): "But how would it be possible for Me to inform you of the Best Music that has been set to my operas, having scarcely heard of any but what has been performed in the theatre of the Imperial Court? and of this, the chief part has been set by the celebrated *Caldara*, an eminent contrapuntist, but extremely deficient in expression, and pleasing melody." Even after so many years Caldara's domination of the court opera in the 1730s still rankled. The master of "pleasing melody" for Burney, our translator, as well as for Metastasio and Maria Theresa was, of course, Hasse.

The vocal prowess of Maria Theresa was no myth. When in Florence in 1739, she sang in a duet with the famous castrato Senesino, "who was so enchanted by the beauty of her voice and the steadiness of her musicianship, that he had to break off in tears."[72] One of her last public appearances as a singer, if not indeed the very last, was in *Il natal di Giove*, an *azione teatrale* by Metastasio, set to music by Bonno, for the birthday of Charles VI on 1 October 1740 (he died eighteen days later). An observer wrote on this occasion, "I can truly say that in my life I have experienced nothing more beautiful, touching or perfect than Her Majesty's performance, whether in regard to song or to acting."[73] The empress' talent was such that she could have had a career as a professional singer. As to her acting abilities, they stood her in good stead for her appearance before the Diet of Pressburg, where she wooed the Hungarian nobles to her side. Once crowned as sovereign she was prevented by decorum from singing in public; yet she did not pass up the chance to sing in a private performance of Hasse's *Impermestra* for her sister's wedding in 1744.

Like her sister, Archduchess Marianna, Maria Theresa also mastered the keyboard at an early age. Before Wagenseil became their teacher, both arch-

[71] *Briefe der Kaiserin Maria Theresia und ihre Kinder und Freunde*, ed. Alfred Arneth, 4 vols. (Vienna, 1881), 3: 119.

[72] Edward Crankshaw, *Maria Theresa* (New York, 1970), p. 19. Burney is Crankshaw's source.

[73] Roswitha Vera Karpf, "Die Beziehungen Maria Theresias zur Musik," *Musik am Hof Maria Theresias* (Munich and Salzburg, 1984), pp. 93–107; 94.

duchesses were taught by the court organist Gottlieb Muffat, who on the title page of his outstanding *Componimenti Musicali per il Cembalo* (1739) proudly named himself as their "Maestro di Cembalo." This collection of suites represented quite a different stylistic pole from that of Italian opera in that Muffat was one of the first keyboard composers to exhibit specifically Austrian traits. It has been convincingly claimed that he created out of the spirit of Austrian folk music.[74] Certainly his musical invention was of a sturdy and strongly rhythmic nature, as witness the vigorous *Final* (*Allegro* in 2/4) of the first Suite in C, with a melody so attractive that Handel took it over almost immediately as the instrumental ritornello of the first number ("From Harmony . . . ") of his *Ode for St. Cecilia's Day.*

Muffat would have made an excellent composer of ballet music. He must have strengthened Maria Theresa's innate gift of rhythmic precision and ease of movement. Podewils, the Prussian ambassador to Vienna, wrote to Frederick II of her on 18 January 1747: "She dances with grace ["Anmut"] and, for her shape [she was pregnant], with considerable lightness. Although she plays the harpsichord, and that very well, and understands quite a lot about music, she does not make much of it."[75] Ostentation was not natural to Maria Theresa or to her husband, although they could scarcely avoid it completely given their positions. She made music with her children for the love of it and of them. On 5 August 1762, for example, she and several of her children sang parts in Hasse's *Laurentian* Litany in the chapel at Schönbrunn while Archduke Joseph played the organ.[76] This same year Jean-Etienne Liotard painted a beautiful pastel portrait of the empress (see Plate I). He somehow captured the warm personal qualities of the sovereign who considered herself less the ruler than the mother of her many peoples.

Crisis in 1760–61: Reutter versus Durazzo

SEVERAL disputes between Kapellmeister Georg Reutter and *cavaliere di musica* Giacomo Durazzo came to a head in 1760 at the time of the imperial wedding celebrations, which had imposed a severe strain on the court's musical and theatrical resources. The matter was so serious that it was writ-

[74] By Guido Adler in the important Foreword to his edition of Muffat's *Componimenti Musicali per il Cembalo*, DTÖ 7 (1896).
[75] Karpf, "Die Beziehungen Maria Theresias zur Musik."
[76] Otto Biba, "Die private Musikpflege in der kaiserlichen Familie," *Musik am Hof Maria Theresias*, pp. 83–92; 89. Also Karp, "Die Beziehungen Maria Theresias zur Musik," p. 103.

ten up in a report compiled by the highest authority—the court chamberlain, Johann Joseph Khevenhüller-Metsch, the same prince whose diaries constitute such an important record of daily life at the imperial court.[77] The contents of the report are paraphrased here.

In his *Pro memoria*, Durazzo claimed that upon entering his duties he tried as best he could, insofar as it was in his power, to raise the long-worsening court music to a greater state of decorum. He found that at that time there were very few skilled people among the court musicians proper, and that Reutter was hardly in a position to sustain the court chapel and fulfill his other duties as well, including the provision of chamber and table music. Having available to him only the same few skilled people, Reutter was unable to offer variety in voices or instruments, or to bring forward something special and unusual. Durazzo for his part had busied himself both before and after the wedding celebrations, for which he was allowed to hire various virtuosos, with constantly introducing not only new people but also new arias, concertos, and either selected or newly composed symphonies. He defrayed his expenses from the Festival-Academy-Redoubt budget, and also paid for all the minuets for the various *bals* without Reutter having contributed anything, although the rehearsals were very expensive; he also would have had trouble keeping the singers content had he not found someone upon whom he could rely and depend. To this end he chose Kapellmeister Gluck, who had worked for six years in court service on the composition of theatrical and concert music, according to his contract, and had attended all those musical events presented by Durazzo. Thus Gluck had been present the previous spring at Laxenburg, more recently at Belvedere, and also at the various table music concerts, when his compositions or those known to him were performed, or when singers of either sex asked to be accompanied by him, and Reutter did not have to pay anything for this.

Reutter, after complaining orally about several disputed issues to Their Majesties personally, raised the following questions in a written memorandum:

Should not the chamber and table music be primarily the responsibility of the *cavaliere di musica*? Or in the case of impediment, should the musicians be rehearsed by Reutter, as was always the case with Kapellmeisters in previous reigns? Reutter noted that his contract specified clearly that he was responsible not only for church music but also for chamber and table music. He added that Durazzo had sent him several symphonies and other pieces

[77] "Report on the misunderstanding between the *cavaliere di musica*, Count Durazzo, and Kapellmeister Reutter regarding the chamber and table music, also on the written depositions pertaining thereto, presented by both sides, Vienna, 3 January 1761," quoted in the original German by Robert Haas, *Gluck und Durazzo* (Vienna, 1925), pp. 38–51.

to perform, some of which had already been heard in the theater, and some of which had not been read through; this was a situation for which he would not stand in the first place, and in the second, it hindered him from performing his own compositions.

Has not the current Kapellmeister at all times directed the chamber and table music, and has not a court organist played the keyboard to accompany virtuoso singers? Yet it had often happened that Gluck directed, even in arias that he did not compose, and played the keyboard.

Are the court musicians, who are obligated to attend rehearsals called by the *cavaliere di musica*, or, if need be, by the Kapellmeister, also required to rehearse in the concert room ("Spielsaal") or in the singers' apartments and other private places?

Should it have happened, and often, that the church service lacked musicians because they were being used at the same time for the opera, or the French comedies, or rehearsals? This obliged Reutter to hire outsiders from his own pocket, although the court's church services should have had precedence.

And most important as a consequence, must Reutter take orders from the *cavaliere di musica* with regard to the composition and direction of the church music?

Khevenhüller began his answer to Reutter's brief by pointing out that both *cavaliere di musica* and Kapellmeister were under his jurisdiction. He reviewed the post of *cavaliere di musica* from the beginning of the century, naming as its incumbents the Marchese di Santa Cruce, Count Kufstein, Count Cavalla, Prince Pio, Count Lamberg, Count Klosy, and finally Count Durazzo. Khevenhüller continued:

> Under Charles VI no musician or singer received as much as 2000 florins officially, since that was the salary of the Kapellmeister, but in case more was needed it was paid from the privy purse or some such source. [The relevance of this piece of information is not clear with regard to Reutter's complaints, but perhaps Durazzo had arranged for some stellar performer like La Gabrielli to be paid *openly* more than the Kapellmeister.] When Predieri was named Kapellmeister in 1743 and Reutter was promoted from composer to vice-maestro, the first was responsible for the chamber and table music, and the second for the chapel music, without the one being subordinate to the other. With regard to Gluck and his six years of service as Kapellmeister, as Count Durazzo calls him in his *Pro memoria*, this office has not heard the slightest news.

More than just a jurisdictional dispute was at issue here. Gluck's very appointment and title were called into question, as were the rights of the theatrical troupes to flourish independently of the court music, as controlled by Kapellmeister Reutter. Having succeeded in blocking Gluck from entering the front door by gaining one of the posts in the imperial court music, Reutter was apparently determined to hinder him from entering any side doors as well. Khevenhüller initially sided with Reutter:

> The contract of 1751, renewed in 1757, specifies that Predieri was to be fully pensioned, and Reutter take over the church, chapel, chamber, and table music with provision of an annual sum of 20,000 florins, from which Reutter is obliged to provide able musicians in each branch, according to the numbers specified in the contract under every category, and also to hire instrumental virtuosi from time to time . . . It would naturally be difficult for Reutter, who has alone directed the court chapel music for many years, to lose the direction of the chamber and table music on account of Gluck, since he had after all the right to hire and fire musicians left fully at his disposal according to his contract, and will be expected to display them, be responsible for them, and pay the instrumental virtuosi used on gala days. It is unthinkable that Reutter should not direct the symphonies brought to him by Gluck, or that the court organist Birck should not accompany them, or that visiting artists should hesitate to have him accompany them, since both [Reutter and Birck] are practiced in the newest musical taste; or that anything should be presented to the court that had not been rehearsed.

A series of practical proposals concluded Khevenhüller's decision. Should Their Majesties find Gluck's compositions more pleasing than those of Reutter, then

1. Gluck should bring his compositions to the *cavaliere di musica* in good time so that he, Gluck, in the presence of Reutter and his musicians could rehearse them.

2. If Gluck is not taken on in the capacity of Kapellmeister, he could be given the title of composer, since the title Kapellmeister does not seem appropriate to the composition of theatrical, chamber, and table music. If he was appointed with this title already six years ago, it was only as director of the plays and musical academies, while the court musicians paid by Reutter and for whom he has responsibility cannot be placed under Gluck.

3. If Gluck is appointed composer, then he will not have misgivings about being under Reutter, as are Wagenseil and Bonno, at least when he presents his own or other compositions. About accompanying the same at the keyboard, after rehearsal under the auspices of the *cavaliere di musica*, and under the direction of Reutter, he will not demur, since it has always been the custom that composers directed their own works only in the absence of the Kapellmeister.

4. It is contrary to the dignity of a *cavaliere di musica*, especially when he is a privy counselor, to enter the chambers of a female singer in order to conduct rehearsals (a charge that may contain seeds leading to Durazzo's

eventual downfall three years later); consequently the chamber and table music rehearsals, in the case of impediments (preventing their being rehearsed where they were to be heard?), can be held at Reutter's, but in no case in said chambers, in the Spielsaal, or in other private places.

5. The *cavaliere di musica* is not to hold his theatrical and other rehearsals at times when the court musicians are liable for court service, so that Reutter will not incur any unnecessary expenses on account of having to hire extra musicians.

6. Reutter is to accept orders of Their Majesties with respect to church music if they choose to communicate them through Count Durazzo, but otherwise the direction of the church music is his sole responsibility.

The musicians under Reutter's command are shown in several of the paintings by imperial court painter Martin van Meytens and his workshop that record the imperial wedding festivities of 1760. For the *Hoftafel* held in the large antechamber of the Hofburg on 6 October 1760, the musicians were placed on the floor and surrounded by onlookers. (See Figure 2.1.) In their midst, wearing a silver wig and an elaborately embroidered blue coat, is an imposing man raising his right hand as if to give a signal; the portrait must be of Reutter and even resembles the visage captured in other likenesses of the Kapellmeister. At the harpsichord, and in livery like all the other musicians and servants, is presumably the court organist, Wenzel Birck. Behind him the continuo players look over his shoulder. Waiting to sing is a handsome soprano who just may represent La Gabrielli.

The decision of Their Majesties was that a new contract should be made with Reutter solely for the chapel, excluding other *musique* or *ball* events. From this resulted a new decree of 6 January 1761 assigning the court's chapel music to Reutter alone but excluding him from the chamber music. In another decree of the following 12 June, he was enjoined to give back some of the 20,000 florins because of the separation of chapel and chamber music (note that the situation in 1761 was the reverse at the court of France, where the chamber and chapel music were combined in an effort to save money). Reutter demurred, claiming that he did not receive enough in order to pay for the church music he was expected to provide at St. Stephen's, plus the Augustine and Jesuit churches. He stood his ground on the basis of his contracts of 1751 and 1757. But Khevenhüller found that the sum was too high for church music alone, "and since all is now sung tutti [i.e., in ensembles without elaborate solos], demanding good musicians but no virtuosi, 10,000 florins should be sufficient, indeed the fine music of the dowager empress Elizabeth cost only 8,000."

The dispute was not over. Durazzo countered with proposals to have more money assigned to the theater direction. He did not charge Reutter with fraud, but came close, saying that the payments for *Parteien* (voice and orchestra parts) should not be left to the whim of the Kapellmeister, to the extent that he was beyond reproach by the *cavaliere di musica*. Durazzo found the church music under Reutter, although satisfactory to Their Majesties, "lacking in decorum and even in propriety." Furthermore, "with respect to the chamber and table music, Kapellmeister Reutter is able to provide nothing but violins and bass, since he has neither flutes nor oboes, nor French horns and special instruments, the cost of which must be paid extra from other funds." The old practice of sharing the meager instrumental and vocal resources went on, apparently, even if Reutter was no longer responsible for the chamber and table music.

Durazzo next proposed that the moneys be reallocated to achieve efficiency so that (1) Kapellmeister Reutter would be restricted to what was spent on compositions for the chapel, as well as for supporting the boy singers and other voices, the cost for which could be reckoned at 300 florins apiece annually; this could be done if (2) the voices and instruments of the former court music were used, and in such a way that (3) the remaining sums were assigned to the *Stadtkassa* under the theater direction. Another measure proposed by Durazzo was to hire all voices for the court and theater together, for a term of one or at most two years, which would allow for changes in personnel without encumbering the treasury with pensions and other charitable gifts.

Khevenhüller lent his approval to the proposal concerning Reutter. To bolster his argument with the sovereigns, Durazzo evoked considerations of pride. Vienna's claim to being a great capital required supporting more than one theater, and Their Majesties should not imagine that two stages could be kept going without costing the court something. He called attention to the great number of places reserved to the imperial family and hence not bringing in box-office revenue; the empress alone disposed of over twenty-five loges in both theaters and had claim on others as well. The *Resolutio Caes. Regia* that came down did not resolve all the problems: "The plan of adjustment sought by Durazzo with respect to the chapel, chamber, and theater music can be granted on the basis of a firm annual amount; but it must be agreed beforehand with Reutter how he will provide by this solution the necessary instrumental music for the chapel; with respect to the theaters there will be further resolutions."

A memorandum of Durazzo's dated 19 June 1761 contains the list of both French and German theatrical troupes, reduced to the minimum ("le plus serré"): "Fewer than this would be impossible, no small provincial theater being able to do with less than twelve forces and two figurants." Out of this bleak situation there emerged, as if by miracle, the stage works that remain Durazzo's greatest achievement as impresario.

3

Gluck and the Operatic Reform

Early Works

CHRISTOPH GLUCK (he never used his middle name) was of Bohemian origin and first came to Vienna around the age of twenty, in 1734 or 1735.[1] Prince Melzi of Milan heard him sing and play there, probably in the palace of the Lobkowitz family, which Gluck's forefathers had served as foresters for generations. Melzi took Gluck into his service, and the young musician crossed the Alps for the first time when the prince returned to Milan after marrying Countess Harrach (on 3 January 1737). Once in Milan, Gluck came under Sammartini's influence, as may be judged from the style of the younger composer's trio sonatas, published by John Walsh of London in 1746. Gluck made his debut on the operatic stage in Milan in 1741 with his setting of Metastasio's *Artaserse*. Several commissions for operas ensued, from Venice, Turin, and London as well as Milan. The composer traveled to London in late 1745 to supervise rehearsals of two of his operas, which were being performed at the Haymarket Theater.

Gluck's gradual ascendancy at the Habsburg court began in 1748, when he turned his success at composing a festive opera for the wedding celebra-

---

[1] Daniel Heartz, "Coming of Age in Bohemia: The Musical Apprenticeships of Benda and Gluck," *Journal of Musicology* 6 (1988): 510–27.

tions at Dresden in 1747 into an invitation to write another festive work for Vienna. The occasion was especially grand: at once the birthday of the empress queen (13 May) and a celebration of the peace treaty of Aix-la-Chapelle, by which Maria Theresa was finally confirmed on her throne after several years of war. It was also an important date in Viennese theatrical history, marking the inauguration of the newly renovated Burgtheater, which at once became a foyer of musical excellence second to none. Gluck, now in his thirty-fourth year, rose to the occasion. His *Semiramide* is a work of astonishing power and variety. The opera did not lead to his immediate appointment, for there were no court posts available, but it led to an eventual foothold as the Burgtheater's unofficial music director.

Metastasio's *Semiramide riconosciuta* was an early work, written before the poet moved to Vienna. Leonardo Vinci first set the poem for the Roman carnival of 1729, and it was chosen to celebrate the coronation of Maria Theresa at Prague in May 1743 (possibly in a setting by her teacher Hasse). The plot made it an obvious choice. Semiramide comes close to losing her throne merely because she is a woman. The message sung by the chorus at the final turn of events could not be more clear or more topical: "Viva lieta, e sia regina" (Live happily, and be our queen). Metastasio was horrified by Gluck's impassioned music, which he was perhaps encountering for the first time. This is not too surprising, since his ideal of a musical setting for his words was attained by the Neapolitans around 1730, by the concise Vinci and the mellifluous Hasse, ideals represented at the Viennese court in Gluck's time by Leonardo Leo's pupil, the concise and mellifluous Giuseppe Bonno. Never at a loss for vivid language, Metastasio pronounced this new *Semiramide* to be "Una musica arcivandalistica insopportabile" (an arch-barbarian, unbearable music).

As for Maria Theresa, she put great faith in the judgments of her court poet. While she liked Gluck's music, she always preferred Hasse, who represented according to her lights the ultimate gracefulness of which Italian music was capable. To her daughter-in-law Maria Beatrice, wife of Archduke Ferdinand (they were installed as rulers of Lombardy), she confided in 1772, "For the theater I prefer the least of the Italians to all our composers, whether Gassmann, Salieri, Gluck, or anyone else."[2] Note that the three she mentions by name comprise two Bohemians trained in Italy and one real Italian, Salieri. Her remark testifies to the independence of the Viennese school.

[2] Letter of 12 November 1772: "Pour le Théâtre j'avoue que je préfère le moindre Italien à tous nos compositeurs, et Gaisman [sic] et Salieri et Gluck et autres. Ils peuvent faire quelquefois une ou deux bonnes pièces, mais pour le tout ensemble je préfère toujours les Italiens." (They can make one or two good pieces sometimes, but for the overall effect I always prefer the Italians.)

Necessity and tradition dictated that the overture be composed last. The idea of tying the overture to the opera so that it became a kind of dramatic argument, as the preface to Gluck's *Alceste* would later put it, was beginning to be expressed by various critics, and Rameau had already put such an idea into practice. Gluck did too. He took his cue from the last chorus, "Viva lieta," which he set to a lilting 3/8 melody falling from the fifth through the third, and made the finale of his overture similar in tune, key (G), and meter (6/8), but he made the tune even more folklike, with its 5 3, 4 2, 3 1 patterning. What a breath of fresh country air had been let in to the palace! One hesitates to say Bohemian country air because Gluck had experienced many countries by this time, and the melodic slides that lend zest to his second theme are distinctly Italianate. Gluck was pleased with this movement, as well he might have been: he used it again as late as 1775 (final ballet of *Cythère assiégée*). The overture's first movement, an *Allegro* in 2/4, is also related melodically to the final chorus, and moreover to the *Tempo di Minuetto* aria for the title role substituted at the end of Act I. This unusually simple aria is really more like a French *air*; it is a rondo, and called as such—a forerunner of many *airs en rondeau* in Gluck's later works.

The lady for whom the part of Semiramide was written was, like Gluck, very well traveled. Vittoria Tesi-Tramontini was a contralto, unusual for a prima donna, and a very fine actress who had been on the operatic stage for three decades. She sang earlier under Hasse at Dresden for many years, and created the title role in Gluck's *Ipermestra* at Venice in 1744. A Florentine, La Tesi was a favorite of Maria Theresa, and obviously a great inspiration to the composer. The high point of *Semiramide* comes in her second-act aria, also on a substitute text, "Tradita, sprezzata / Che piango! che parlo!" (Betrayed and despised, how should I complain, how speak?). The aria follows a grand and fiery obbligato recitative of the kind that Metastasio disapproved in principle, except in the smallest doses, because it put the poet too much in the shadow of the music. This aria in g minor is drawn from the melodic kernel 5 6 5, like the final chorus, but here it is the flat sixth. The soft and pathetic "tradita" uttered by the voice is punctuated by the loud and searing dissonance of an F♯ G appoggiatura in the orchestra, over an oscillating bass in thirds. For the second line, "Se pieno d'orgoglio non crede dolor" (If full of pride you doubt my grief), Gluck resorts to an imperious *unisono* passage moving in eighth notes, then slows down to quarter notes on "crede dolor." The scorn expressed in the next line brings diminished-seventh chords in the tremolo strings that point in the direction of d, the minor dominant. This key arrives with a striding figure in the bass, pushing up an octave each time we hear it, while the voice mainly declaims, using very few tones.

Gluck would use this same stalking, terror-laden bass as late as the

wrathful aria of Thoas in *Iphigénie en Tauride* (Paris, 1779), "Des noirs pres-
entimens," where it bears the text "I sense the earth opening under my feet
and the inferno ready to swallow me in its horrible pit." The master stroke
of 1748 was Gluck's compressing some of his frighteningly intense aria in g
into the *Andante* middle movement of the overture, also in g, with the theme
arching up over an octave, loud *unisoni* outbursts, poignant dissonances,
and the same harmonic structure of g to d and back.[3] In the aria, Gluck
composed only a short return to the main key after the **B** section (beginning
in E♭) and using only the second half of the **A** stanza, thus obliterating da
capo form. It is no wonder that Metastasio was overcome with surprise and
bewilderment.

Semiramide is virtually unique among Gluck's works in that he seems to
have composed it all afresh, borrowing nothing from his earlier works. In
the two operas he wrote for London in 1746, on the other hand, he made
massive borrowings from his earlier Italian works.[4] One thing this reveals is
the low estimation in which Gluck held the two librettos he was given to set
in London, *La caduta de' Giganti* and *Artamene*.

Semiramide was a success with the public and enjoyed many repetitions
after its premiere on 14 May 1748. Gluck left Vienna later the same year and
joined the Mingotti company at Hamburg, serving as orchestral leader. The
repertory included Hasse's *La clemenza di Tito* and such well-traveled intermezzi as *La serva padrona* and *Il pittore*. The troupe moved on to Copenhagen,
where Gluck set Metastasio's *La contesa de' numi* (1749) to honor the birth of
an heir to the Danish throne (the poem was originally written to honor the
birth of a dauphin in 1729, and set by Vinci in Rome). The most interesting
feature of Gluck's music in this work is the stormy one-movement overture,
during which Gluck depicts the dispute of the gods in the opening dialogue.
In 1750 Gluck joined another traveling company, that of Giovanni Battista
Locatelli (no relation to the Amsterdam-based violinist). This association
happily led to another work on the scale and of the importance of *Semiramide*. It also took Gluck back to his native land. The poem was another of
Metastasio's Roman librettos, *Ezio*, first set by Nicolò Porpora in 1728.

---

[3] Excerpts from the overture to *Semiramide* can be found in Adolph Bernhard Marx, *Gluck und die Oper*
(Berlin, 1863), 1: 164–67; the *Andante* of the overture, together with the aria "Tradita, sprezzata," is
given complete, in keyboard score, in the same work, 2 (Anhang): 29–35. Gluck does not put much
stock in the niceties of text setting, which would have been enough by itself to discredit him with
Metastasio. He even breaks up individual words, putting rests between syllables, as is common in
comic opera but infringes one of the cardinal rules of serious opera; for an example from *Semiramide*,
see Ernst Kurst, "Die Jugendopern Glucks bis *Orfeo*," *SMw* 1 (1913): 235, example 50.

[4] On the self-borrowings in Gluck's operas, see Klaus Hortschansky, *Parodie und Entlehnung im Schaffen Christoph Willibald Glucks* (Cologne, 1973) (*Analecta Musicologica* 13). The author disagrees (p. 53)
with Einstein's thesis that Gluck wanted to remain in London. *Semiramide* bears him out.

Ezio was given at Prague's Kotce Theater (1738–83), described on the title page of the printed libretto as "the new theater." From the list of actors in this libretto, we learn the names of the singers in Locatelli's company, and also that "the music is one of the most charming compositions of Signor Gluck; whoever wishes to buy separate arias, or the whole score, may find information from Signor Giacomo Calandro, the first violin of the opera." Such copies have become exceedingly rare, and perhaps they never existed in any number but could have been made on commission. *Ezio* borrows only three numbers from Gluck's previous works, all from *La contesa de' numi* of the previous year, a work that would not have been known in Prague. By Gluck's standards this is very little borrowing. *Ezio* served as a source, on the other hand, for many of the composer's future borrowings. Gluck must have been pleased with the score because he chose to revive it at the Burg-theater in 1763, a year after his *Orfeo ed Euridice* was written for the same theater; for the revival he shortened the original text considerably, eliminating both arias and recitatives (a fate increasingly meted out to the Metasta-sian warhorses), and he completely reset the recitatives, demoting one of them from obbligato to simple.[5]

The most extraordinary number in *Ezio* is the metaphor aria of the villain Massimino, on a text about a harmless brook that murmurs slowly and softly ("Se povero il ruscello / Mormora lento e basso") but can swell into a mighty stream by the time it reaches the ocean. The image of the brook explains why Gluck returned to the oboe melody of this piece when he painted the streams and brooklets bathing the Elysian fields in *Orfeo*, a borrowing for which there was an intermediate stage in Gluck's *Antigono* of 1756.[6] The *Antigono* aria is about dying and passing over the waters of the Lethe, so it too fits with the original affect, and the concept of a beautiful yet sad para-dise also suits *Orfeo*. The sustained oboe melody in all three illustrates how the composer refined this idea (Example 3.1).

Gluck's first inspiration, the *Ezio* aria, is vigorous and straightforward, a typically triadic melody such as the composer often asked singers to per-form, although it is instrumentally conceived from the beginning, and becomes obviously so when it reaches up to the high C over a minor tonic— a stunning effect of melodic climax coinciding with minor color that enables Gluck to express the dark and light sides of the situation simultaneously. In the *Antigono* aria the melody is reworked to make it more supple, less cut and dried in its first four measures. The melodic climax remains almost iden-

[5] Gabriele Buschmeier, "*Ezio* in Prag und Wien: Bemerkungen zu den beiden Fassungen von Gluck's *Ezio*," *Gluck-Studien* 1 (1987): 85–88.

[6] Full orchestral versions of the excerpts from *Ezio* and *Antigono* may be studied in Kurst, "Die Jugen-dopern Glucks," pp. 239–44.

EXAMPLE 3.1. *Gluck, related melodies in three operas*
  a. Ezio *(1750)*
  b. Antigono *(1756)*
  c. Orfeo ed Euridice *(1762)*

tical, but is followed by the introduction of a new element, wave-like triplet motions in quick notes to convey the watery image, and then by a similar concluding flourish with cadential trill.

In the last example, from *Orfeo,* Gluck truly makes the best of both preceding versions. He returns to the simpler beginning of the first, removes the falling fifth and replaces it with a softer-sounding falling second, and takes over the expressive rise to the high A (giving him a major-ninth harmonic richness) of the second version; the climax remains virtually unchanged again, and it is followed by the babbling triplet figurations. The *Orfeo* melody does not stop with the formalities of a cadence, but yields the line to other instruments, for the oboe is but one element in an intricately scored evocation of the stage setting. Hector Berlioz, who revered Gluck as a master of orchestration, praised this very scene as "a delightful descriptive symphony." That the origins of this famous example of tone painting go back to a work written for Prague is significant. Gluck could write Italian *cantilena* when he chose to, but this is not what sets him apart. At his most individual, Gluck thinks in terms of instrumental melody and instrumental tone color, in which respect he is a typical Bohemian composer, "a man made for the orchestra" according to the 1766 essayist on Viennese musical taste. Gluck acknowledged his borrowing in a sense, by dropping the aria in his 1763 revision of *Ezio*.

The composer remained in Prague after 1750, while strengthening his ties with Vienna by marrying Marianne Perger, daughter of a wealthy Viennese banker. Financial independence was one of the rewards of his marriage, and it allowed him to become increasingly demanding with respect to his craft and its deployment in the opera house. In 1751 Locatelli revived Gluck's *Ezio* in Leipzig and commissioned a new work for Prague, a setting of Metastasio's *Issipile*, staged during the carnival of 1752. Gluck tightened and simplified the libretto of the Prague *Issipile*, which survives, while the score does not, except for a few arias.

Gluck's reputation was growing steadily, as confirmed by an invitation to write a festival opera for the grandest Italian theater, the San Carlo in Naples. The impresario there, Don Diego Tuffarelli, wanted a setting of Antonio Salvi's *Arsace* to celebrate the name day of King Charles III (4 November) by "il famoso Kluk che risiede in Praga in Boemia." In a letter to a friend Tuffarelli mentioned that he expected from Gluck music of a totally different style and never heard before ("una musica di stile tutto vario e mai più inteso"), because the composer was new to Naples and extraordinarily learned at his métier ("novo qui ed oltremodo dotto nel suo mestiere"). This quest for novelty and variety, coupled with respect for the craft, helps explain why Naples remained the great musical capital that it was throughout the eighteenth century.

Gluck was perhaps the first imperial subject to be honored with a *scrittura* from the San Carlo since the Habsburgs were kicked out of Naples in 1735; he had triumphed in spite of an adverse political climate. He did not accept the libretto proposed (he had already composed the first act of *Arsace* in Milan a decade earlier). His recently acquired wealth meant that he could afford to negotiate. He made urgent requests to set in its stead Metastasio's superb *La clemenza di Tito*, even though the authorities had already assigned this libretto to Gerolamo Abos as a second opera for the same season. Gluck prevailed. He commenced the long journey together with his wife—another luxury permitted by wealth—and they arrived at Naples in late August 1752, which allowed two months to compose the opera, a long time by local standards. Even so, Gluck resorted to many borrowings from his recent operas for Prague, which would not have been known in Naples.

Legend has it that Gluck refused to call first upon Gaetano Majorano, the famous castrato known as Caffarelli, who was to sing the primo uomo part of Sesto, although custom demanded this of a composer. Instead Caffarelli called first upon Gluck, and they became fast friends. For this great singer, Gluck wrote one of his most celebrated arias.

"Se mai senti spirarti in volto" (If ever you feel breathing on your visage) in Act II of *La clemenza di Tito* eventually became "O malheureuse Iphigénie" in Gluck's overtowering *Iphigénie en Tauride*. The boldly arched phrases of the aria's melody are spanned by an oboe solo bearing some resemblance to Example 3.1; once again Gluck started with an instrumental idea (Example 3.2). A controversy arose over this very piece, concerning the dissonant

EXAMPLE 3.2. *Gluck,* La clemenza di Tito, *"Se mai senti spirarti"*

chords under a high G pedal in the voice as Sesto sings "son questi gli estremi sospiri" (these are the very last sighs) (mm. 103–5 of "O malheureuse Iphigénie"). According to an anecdote told by composer and critic Johann Friedrich Reichardt, several Neapolitan musicians took the score to the venerable Francesco Durante, pointing out the shifting orchestral dissonances against the vocal pedal; Durante refused to say whether the passage conformed entirely to the rules of composition, "but I tell you all that any one of us, beginning with myself, would count himself a great man had he conceived and written such a passage."[7] Saverio Mattei classed the aria as among the most famous of all, along with Vinci's "Vo solcando un mar crudele" and Hasse's "Se tutti i mali miei." Wilhelm Heinse called it a "heavenly song."

Prince Joseph Friedrich von Sachsen-Hildburghausen, Vienna's foremost music patron, received a copy of the sensational aria even before Gluck arrived back in Vienna in December of 1752 (Figure 3.1). The prince had it performed by Therese Heinisch and the orchestra under Giuseppe Bonno's direction—to general admiration, according to Ditters. Gluck was later presented in person to Prince Hildburghausen by Bonno, at the express wish of the prince, and Ditters recalls that Gluck subsequently led rehearsals and performances of his symphonies and arias by the prince's band by placing himself at the head with a violin ("setze sich Gluck mit der Violine à la tête"). This description has led to conjectures that he replaced Bonno as music

---

[7] Helga Lühning, *Titus-Vertonungen im 18. Jahrhundert: Untersuchungen zur Tradition der Opera Seria von Hasse bis Mozart* (Laaber, 1983), pp. 219–36 (*Analecta Musicologica* 20).

FIGURE 3.1. Christian Fritzch.
Engraved portrait of Prince Joseph
Friedrich von Hilldburghausen.

director. Not so. The place of the Kapellmeister was at the harpsichord, and
great store was set by his superior rank over the concertmaster. Vivaldi protested that he never demeaned himself by leading the violins in operatic
performances, except on the first night.[8] Mozart bridled at the very thought
of having to play violin in the archbishop's orchestra because it was a lesser
position than that of the Kapellmeister at the keyboard, and yet Mozart was
a superb violinist himself, and not above planning to snatch the violin from
the concertmaster's hands if the performance of the *Paris* Symphony looked
like it might go as badly as the rehearsal (letter of 3 July 1778).

[8] Piero Weiss, "Venetian Commedia dell'Arte 'Operas' in the Age of Vivaldi," *Musical Quarterly* 70
(1984): 213.

Gluck apparently did not feel demeaned by leading with the violin, if we may believe Ditters. There are not many pieces of evidence even to show that Gluck was a violinist, although his whole background as a Bohemian country musician whose further training was at the violinistic center that was Milan argues that he must have been. Ditters says also that Gluck became an intimate friend of the prince, because the composer was a man of the world who, aside from being a master of his craft, was very widely read. Gluck, indeed, was an intellectual compared with most musicians. In this respect, both Gluck and his disciple Ditters, with their pronounced literary bent, were unlike most Viennese musicians.

Gluck's friendship with Prince Hildburghausen led to the composition of a one-act serenata, *Le cinesi* (The Chinese Ladies), which the prince staged for Maria Theresa and Francis Stephan at his summer palace at Schlosshof, north of Vienna, in the fall of 1754. A report of the event in the *Wiener Diarium* gives Gluck the title of "Fürstl. Capellmeister," suggesting that he was drawing a salary from the prince by this time. The same occasion saw Bonno's settings of Metastasio's *L'isola disabitata* and *Il vero omaggio*. *Le cinesi* was also by Metastasio, and had been set first by Caldara in 1735, in a form calling only for three female parts representing the tragic, the pastoral, and the comic (the first was sung by the eighteen-year-old Maria Theresa herself). Metastasio modified the libretto, probably at Gluck's specific request, so as to include a male role, a brother of the first lady, who is in love with the second. To pass the time of day each of the ladies imagines herself as some non-Chinese character, giving rise to a variety of affects.

Ditters describes the performance of *Le cinesi* at Schlosshof on 24 September 1754 in some detail. Particularly valuable are his comments on the staging:

> Quaglio's decorations were quite in the Chinese taste, and transparent. Workers in lacquer, carpenters and gilders, had lavished all their resources upon them, but their chief brilliancy depended on prismatic poles of glass, which had been polished by Bohemian craftsmen, and were carefully fitted into one another in empty places, previously soaked in coloured oils. They were very effective, even in sunshine and the broad light of day, but no pen can describe the surpassing and astounding brilliancy of these prisms when lit up by innumerable lamps. The reader must imagine the reflected brilliancy of the azure-coloured meadows of lacquer, the glitter of the gilded foliage, and, lastly, the rainbow-like colors repeated by hundreds of prisms, and flashing like diamonds of the finest water. The most vivid fancy will fall short of the real magic. And then, Gluck's god-like music! It was not only the delicious playfulness of the symphony, accompanied now and again by little bells, triangles, small hand-drums, etc., sometimes singly, sometimes all together, which at the very outset, and before the raising

of the curtain, transported the audience: the music was from the first to last
an enchantment.

Ditters does not exaggerate. *Le cinesi* is Gluck's most consistent and polished work up to this date. From the outset of the overture (in D), the composer unleashes constant running sixteenth notes that, reinforced by the
percussion Ditters mentions (but not notated in the score), prefigure the
"Turkish music" so successfully projected later by Haydn, Mozart, and others. There is also a more expressive undercurrent in the first movement of
the overture, manifest in the long appoggiatura sighs of the first violins,
which prepare for the same tragic affect in the first aria.[9] The *Andante* in b
that serves as a middle movement offers pathos and a switch on its main
rising motive in the middle, resulting in appoggiaturas that cannot resolve
upward as they should. The finale, *Allegro molto* in 3/8, is far more subtle
than most Italian buffo finales, and is thematically linked with the first
movement.

Le cinesi consists of four arias and a final ensemble. Vittoria Tesi, Gluck's
Semiramide, sang the first aria. Embodying the tragic muse, she imagines
that she is Andromache after Pyrrhus has torn her son away from her—an
opportunity for an impassioned obbligato recitative followed by a grand
heroic aria in b, recalling the great aria for La Tesi in *Semiramide*, and like it
consisting largely of vocal interjections amid the orchestral torrents. The aria
lacks a contrasting middle section and da capo return, leading the astonished Silango, her brother, to exclaim as it ends, "Ah, non finir si presto,
germana amata!" (Don't stop so soon, dear sister!). Silango was sung by
tenor Joseph Fribert, who had been trained in singing by Bonno. His aria is
an enormous outpouring, which Gluck sets as a florid Minuetto galante in
A, with abundant coloratura triplets and a short middle section that goes
from vi to iii, leading to a da capo repetition; it all sounds very conventional
after the outburst of the first aria, but appropriate to the situation. Silango's
shepherdess next sings her pastoral aria in F, in common time; it also has
some brilliant coloratura writing, in order to show off the fine voice of
another pupil of Bonno, Therese Heinisch. Yet a third Bonno pupil, Catherine Starzer (sister of the ballet composer), sang the contralto role of the third
lady, who imagines she is a French coquette at her dressing table. Her recitative changes back and forth from a kind of *arioso* in 3/4 time to the more
usual kind, a preview of more Gallic things to come; she ruminates about the
Tuilleries and its young fashion plates (one of whom addresses his Phyllis as

[9] Alfred Einstein, *Gluck* (London, 1936), p. 38, fails to comment on either the Turkish or the expressive element, and confines himself to saying that the overture is "agile, mobile, weightless—a genu-
ine Italian buffo symphony."

"Charmante beauté," eliciting from Gluck a slow vocal line ornamented with grace notes and trills). The aria proper, in 3/4 and in D, includes a solo flute along with two horns and the usual strings. Gluck employs dotted rhythms constantly, hemiolas at the cadences, and other trappings of the courtly menuet, which he parodies perfectly. The abundant trills must have provoked mirth in Viennese musical circles, which were only beginning to digest the Parisian offerings of the new troupe in the Burgtheater.

To end this little entertainment, Metastasio has the three ladies assess the various theatrical modes they represent, and we hear the wise old poet, so practiced in all of them, speaking more directly on such matters than was his wont: "Tragic would doubtless be the best: it projects the warring affections of the human heart, but this voluntary weeping is a little strange. Pastoral is an innocent style, and pleasing, for a while at least, but it lacks diversity—all this talk of fields and flocks becomes boring in the long run. Comedy represents human failings and they amuse us, but it is impossible not to offend someone who sees himself pictured thereby." Silango offers a solution: "Let us stage a ballet, which everyone understands and enjoys, and which will not provoke tears or boredom, or be offensive." The ladies accept this even though it is not novel, because, as they say, "what is done well is ever new" ("quelche si fa bene è sempre nuovo"), a sentiment that could serve as a motto for Metastasio's whole career.

The finale in D, marked *Andante*, uses the vigorous rhythms of a polonaise-like dance throughout its two-hundred-odd measures in 3/4. There is a middle section in the relative minor, during which the strings play pizzicato, leading to extensive repetition of the more festive opening parts. Here, as throughout the score, Gluck delights us with his verve and his imaginative orchestral touches. The sovereigns were delighted too. Both Gluck and Bonno were rewarded with gold snuffboxes containing 100 gulden apiece. More significant still, the stage was set for Gluck's further work at the Viennese court.

When *Le cinesi* was brought to the Burgtheater in the spring of 1755, it was not as successful, in spite of Quaglio's decors, a circumstance for which Ditters blames the lack of acting skills in the Viennese cast: "The actors, except as singers (they had the great Gabrieli [i.e. Caterina Gabrielli] and others of equal merit among them), were not to be compared with ours— they had not been trained by Tesi." A great singer-actor like La Tesi could have been expected to coach fellow singers how to act. Metastasio sometimes coached singers in their roles and worked on the staging too, although he protested that these activities were beneath his dignity as *poeta caesareo*. But Metastasio was not at Schlosshof for *Le cinesi*, as his letters show. The *Wiener Diarium* praised Gluck in terms that show the composer himself took a direct hand with the actors at Schlosshof: "He has distinguished himself beyond all bounds as well in the action and representation, as in the aptness of his music, with the result that both Imperial Majesties could not praise him enough."[10] This unequivocal evidence confirms that Gluck, quite exceptionally for the practices of the time, extended the composer's authority to include the staging of his operas. The case is prophetic of what Gluck would soon achieve on the stage of the Burgtheater and later at the Paris Opéra.

Following his success with *Le cinesi*, Gluck set two other poems by Metastasio, *La danza* and *Il rè pastore*. The "Componimento drammatico pastorale," as *La danza* was called, expanded a cantata that Metastasio had originally written in 1744, when it was set to music by Bonno. As given with Gluck's music at Laxenburg in May 1755 and repeated in the Burgtheater, the work called for two singers, Caterina Gabrielli (Nice) and Joseph Fribert (Tirsi), and served as a prologue to a ballet by Joseph Starzer. Gluck must have valued his music to *La danza*, because he used all four of its arias in his last stage work, *Echo et Narcisse* (Paris, 1779). They are full da capo arias with abundant coloratura, especially the ones for Gabrielli. A long love duet concludes the work. One instrumental piece survives from the ballet music for *La danza*, and it is ascribed not to Gluck but to Starzer, who was the official composer of ballet music for both imperial theaters from 1753 until the end of 1758, when he left Vienna.[11] Gluck had no official title at the Viennese court, and he is listed only sporadically in the payment records, sometimes as composer and once (1756–57) as director of the musical academies. On Starzer's departure, he assumed the post of ballet composer.

Count Durazzo was unable at first to create a steady position for Gluck, but he called more and more on the composer's theatrical abilities. He employed the official composers as well. For his own opéra-ballet, *Le cacciatrice amanti*, given at Laxenburg in June 1755, Durazzo relied on Wagenseil. Metastasio praised the count's verses as well-adapted to music but complained about the lack of plot (which was characteristic of this Parisian genre). Georg Reutter set Metastasio's *La gara*, an occasional piece in which the three elder archduchesses, Marianna, Elizabeth, and Amalia, sang compliments to Maria Theresa on her birthday (13 May 1755) in Italian, German, and French, respectively.

For the emperor's birthday (8 December 1755), Durazzo undertook a more ambitious project with *L'innocenza giustificata*, a *festa teatrale* set by Gluck. This work, with a libretto derived from ancient Roman history (Livy),

[10] Harald Kunz, "Maria Theresia und das Wiener Theater," *Jahrbuch der Gesellschaft für Wiener Theaterforschung* (1953–54), pp. 3–71; 60.

[11] Bruce Alan Brown, "Christoph Willibald Gluck and Opéra-Comique in Vienna, 1754–1764" (Ph.D. diss., University of California, Berkeley, 1986), p. 94.

represented a move on Durazzo's part toward reforming Italian serious opera. There are three sets: the interior of the vestal virgins' house, the vestibule leading to the Senate, and the banks of the Tiber. Intrigue is lacking in this one-act drama, nor is a love interest present. Durazzo was clearly striking out in a new direction by renouncing the confidants and subplots upon which Metastasio nearly always relied in his serious operas. As in *La vestale* of Gaspare Spontini, a direct descendant of Durazzo's libretto, everything turns on the innocence of the heroine, who is at first condemned to death after letting the sacred fire go out, arousing suspicions as to her purity, then vindicated by a miracle, which she launches by her prayer. The Roman people demand her death, then proclaim her innocence, giving rise to opportunities for choral drama such as scarcely existed in Italian opera in the 1750s.

Durazzo evidently did not wish to put his skills as a lyric poet on the line against those of Metastasio, from whose works he instead borrowed the texts of eight arias and one duet. These he modified only slightly, but the recitatives and choruses were his own. Gabrielli played the leading female role of Claudia; her partner was the castrato Guarducci. Two other soloists had lesser roles. (The choice of La Gabrielli as chief vestal virgin must have raised a smile, since she was widely rumored to bestow her favors with liberality). Gluck wrote some stunning music for this prima donna: a "Cavata" in E♭, with muted strings pulsing in triplets and horns sounding ominous calls in octaves over a striding bass in quarter notes (i.e., all the trappings of an *ombra* aria) and a coloratura extravaganza near the end to rival Constanze's "Martern aller Arten" in Mozart's *Die Entführung aus dem Serail*. There are some fine overlapping effects between soloists and chorus in the final number, but in general Gluck did not yet know how to use the chorus to best dramatic effect. Even so, *L'innocenza giustificata* represents a step toward recreating antique tragedy, one that would have further consequences in Vienna. The work was revived in the Burgtheater under the title *La vestale* in 1768, a few months after the culmination of Viennese reform opera in Gluck's *Alceste*.

After writing his Roman opera with Durazzo, Gluck repaired to Rome itself, where he fulfilled a commission to set Metastasio's *Antigono* for the Teatro Argentina as the second carnival opera of 1756. Back in Vienna by March, the composer directed the Lenten academies. Later the same year he set Metastasio's *Il rè pastore*, with Gabrielli as prima donna, in order to celebrate the emperor's birthday. Why did Durazzo risk unfavorable comparisons with the original setting of Bonno, which had so pleased the poet and the public alike? The presence of La Gabrielli is probably the main reason. She was under contract to the court through the 1758–59 season, and spectacular vocalism was expected commensurate with her high salary.

Gluck set the text without changes or deletions. Several musical similarities with Bonno's classic setting of five years earlier show that he was at least trying to please in the same way Bonno had pleased, trying, indeed, to make his style more euphonious and "smiling" in keeping with the pastoral poem. But Gluck was not cut out for the task, and his score bristles with such infelicitous touches as the high A on the "i" vowel in "L'amerò." (See Example 2.8b.) Khevenhüller says that "the opera, along with two ballets that accompanied it, awakened no special applause." A sure sign that the new setting was a failure was the fact that it was not repeated. Yet the music was widely diffused. Scores and orchestral material were copied and sold; two arias appeared in print in *L'Echo* (Liège, 1758 and 1766). Gluck's strongest suit once again was his orchestral writing. The overture is particularly original, and seems to represent the turmoil in the wake of Alexander the Great's conquering armies that gives the plot its setting. It begins in C, which becomes c midway through the movement and remains in the minor, ending on V, and leading directly to the opening song for Aminta.

Metastasio wrote to Farinelli on the very day of the premiere in the Burgtheater, across from which the poet had his lodgings. His letter suggests that the opera was upstaged by the performance of the sovereign, who at age thirty-nine managed to give birth to the last of her sixteen children. It reads in part, as translated by Burney:

> I am told this instant, that my most august Patroness is happily brought to bed of a little Arch-duke. *Te Deum laudamus.* I hope that Providence, which has hitherto preserved her in similar circumstances, will protect her from all accidents. The christening will be at 7 o'clock this evening, and the new terrestial [sic] pilgrim will be named Maximilian. This is being a very obliging consort, to present to her husband with a male child on his own birth-day. But what cannot the admirable MARIA THERESA do? I write amidst the harmonious acclamations of the people, who are running in crowds towards the court. The opera which will be represented to-night in the public theatre, will certainly meet with applause: what is there that cannot please on such a day? The drama is my *Rè Pastore*, set by Gluck; a Bohemian composer, whose spirit, noise and extravagance, have supplied the place of merit in many theatres of Europe.

Metastasio goes on to praise Gabrielli for her acting and singing, but this is somewhat suspect inasmuch as he was trying to get Farinelli to hire her for Madrid. Ferdinando Mazzante (Aminta), a castrato borrowed from the Munich court for the occasion, he pronounced "a great violin player in falsetto," which was not meant as a compliment.

The Seven Years' War broke out in mid-1756 when Prussia invaded Saxony and Bohemia. It was to become one of the most costly of all wars for the imperial court. Under the circumstances, reduced expenditures for theatrical entertainments were in order. Italian serious opera was eliminated, which explains why Metastasio was making efforts to get La Gabrielli contracted elsewhere. There were no further opportunities for her to sing in Vienna until the marriage of Crown Prince Joseph and Princess Isabella of Parma in 1760. (Not by coincidence did she take the leading female roles in Traetta's operas for Parma in 1756–60). A few buffa singers and the services of the composer Giuseppe Scarlatti made it possible to put on some opere buffe between 1757 and 1759.[12] Meanwhile, Gluck's main field of operation became the musical presentations of the French troupe. Without augmenting their numbers or their expenses, this troupe, mainly offering spoken plays and ballets, began to stage the newer kinds of opéra-comique coming from Paris. Gluck's task, at first, was to adjust the imported words for the players on hand, and sometimes reset texts that had to be "cleaned up" for Vienna. It was inevitable, given Gluck's creative energies, that Durazzo should encourage him to show what he could do by making his own settings of opéras-comiques, of which he wrote no fewer than six from 1758 through 1760. As was noted in a preface to Gluck's last opéra-comique for Vienna, *La rencontre imprévue* (1764), merely retouching the operas of others was "a chore unworthy of his talents."[13]

Calzabigi and the *Lettre* of 1756

COUNT DURAZZO forged a link with Paris in furthering opéra-comique in Vienna, and he also hoped to promote Gluck's fortunes at the Paris Opéra. Durazzo's Parisian connections probably played a role in the publication of an anonymous pamphlet, long ascribed to Josse de Villeneuve, *Lettre sur le mechanisme de l'opéra italien* (Figure 3.2). The pamphlet was published at Naples in 1756 according to the title page, but in fact it was brought out in Paris by Duchesne, who is mentioned only as one of the two Parisian booksellers. The author of the *Lettre* was well versed in French opera and had experienced opera in Naples and many other cities as well. He mentions no fewer than five Tuscan theaters where he had attended opera performances.

The author purports to be a Frenchman, neutral in the ever-raging battle between the partisans of French opera and those of Italian opera. Hence the

[12] Eva Badura-Skoda, "Giuseppe Scarlatti und seine Buffa-Opern," in *Musik am Hof Maria Theresias*, ed. Roswitha Vera Karpf (Munich and Salzburg, 1984), pp. 57–75.
[13] Brown, "Gluck and Opéra-Comique in Vienna," p. 22.

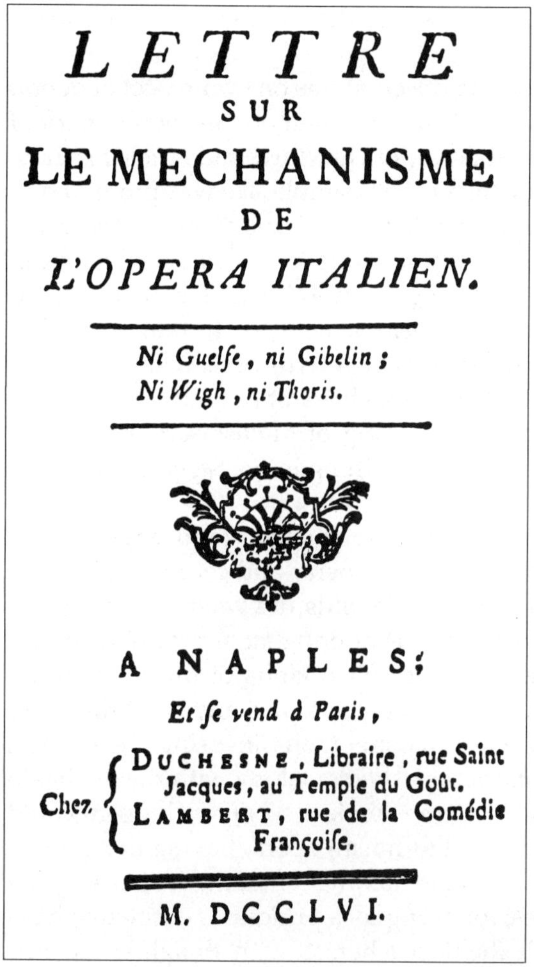

LETTRE
S U R
LE MECHANISME
D E
L'OPERA ITALIEN.

Ni Guelfe , ni Gibelin ;
Ni Wigh , ni Thoris.

A N A P L E S;

Et fe vend à Paris ,

Chez { DUCHESNE , Libraire , rue Saint Jacques , au Temple du Goût.
LAMBERT , rue de la Comédie Françoife.

M. DCCLVI.

FIGURE 3.2. Title page of the 1756 *Lettre* attributed to Calzabigi.

double inscription "Ni Guelf, ni Gibelin; ni Wigh ni Thoris." The pamphlet includes a preface by the publisher supporting the moderate position and contrasting the opera at Paris (noteworthy for decors, ballets, machines, a brilliant assembly, and public silence) with that of Naples (ravishing music, invisible beauties, and a horrendous tumult in the audience). Of the two, one could make a viable whole, he suggests, but no one until the present has thought to propose as much (which was not quite true). A parable in the form of a prophecy ends the preface. There were two African countries, one wise, *philosophe,* but lacking good fruit trees (i.e., France). A sage (Rousseau?) counsels cutting down all the trees and introducing those of the neighboring country (Italy), eliciting horror on the part of the traditionalists. An empiricist (Diderot?) says, graft the two species together and see what happens. In the end the neighboring people themselves come to borrow from the combinatory species.[14]

The *Lettre* itself is full of penetrating observations on every facet of opera. At one point the author says that he wished, without obscuring the merit of the Italians, to dissipate the marvelous vapor that surrounds their machine (Italian opera), the mechanism of which is very simple. He was prompted to undertake the task, he says, by reading Ranieri de' Calzabigi's "Dissertazione su le Poesie drammatiche del sig. Abate Pietro Metastasio," which prefaced the Paris edition of Metastasio's works in 1755, and which he read when it was reprinted (in French) in the *Journal étranger*. In that essay Calzabigi, while seeming to praise Metastasio at every turn, actually calls for a combination of the best elements of the French tradition with those of the Italian, which would mean in fact an undoing of Metastasian aria opera. Francesco Algarotti called for much the same thing in his *Saggio sopra l'opera in musica*, also published in 1755.

But the author of the *Lettre* is much more concrete (and entertaining) in his description of the workings of Italian opera, and more emphatic in recommending parts of French opera. He defends the "merveilleux" (banished by Metastasio and other Arcadians) as offering an appropriate terrain where music could work its enchantments. Two kinds of music in Italian opera are particularly successful, he says, obbligato recitative and the duet, but Italian composers were extremely parsimonious in using them. (The long and impressive duet in *L'innocenza giustificata*, along with the obbligato recitatives, show that Gluck and Durazzo were less so.) French opera could do with fewer choruses, he continues, but Italian opera, having none, must reintroduce this resource. He ridicules the domination of the Italian stage by singers and their silly prerogatives; for example, a princess is entitled to have one page to hold her train, which she busies herself with straightening during the orchestral ritornello of her aria, while a queen is allowed to have two pages and a correspondingly longer ritornello (presumably an empress would have three).

The author admires Metastasio as the "poéte du sentiment" and holds in high esteem Italian arias in the pathetic vein, which are often supported orchestrally by horns—an admirable effect that ought to be introduced at the Paris Opéra. These details apart, he dismisses Italian opera in general as an uneven pasticcio, both because the composer arrives at the last minute with his portfolio of arias and adapts them willy-nilly to whatever text is given

---

[14] Françoise Karro, "De la Querelle des Bouffons à la réforme de Gluck: Les lettres du Comte Durazzo à Charles-Simon Favart conservées à la Bibliothéque de l'Opéra," *Mitteilungen des österreichischen Staatarchivs* 38 (1985): 163–96. Karro, p. 183, poses the question of whether the preface could be by Calzabigi. The preface and the pamphlet proper are very much of a piece in style.

him, and because the prima donna and primo uomo often insist on singing what they already know and have succeeded with before. There are a few kind words for the librettos of Apostolo Zeno, Giovanni Pasquini, and Metastasio. Metastasio is praised for his "force, clarté, élégance, et finesse," but faulted because his librettos, unlike Zeno's, are most lacking in those "traits de surprise" that are the soul of operatic spectacle.

Metastasio, it is true, says this would-be French author, has learned a lot from our tragic poets. Does he not deserve as much gratitude as the Orpheus of our time (i.e. Rameau) who, in skillfully pillaging Italian productions, has changed the face of our music and prepared the revolution that must multiply our pleasures? Calzabigi wrongly seeks to minimize Metastasio's debt to Racine, continues the author. As Racine is the Euripides of France, so is Metastasio the Italian Racine. His style is "aisé, tendre, élevé, séduisant," and it is responsible for educating Italian operagoers to pay attention to the words. The best part of French opera is its management of spectacular effects. If one were to combine the best of both worlds, one should start with the librettos of Philippe Quinault (exactly where Durazzo did start when planning *Armida*). Fabulous subjects are preferable, the author says, and in a direct word to Calzabigi he denies that Metastasio has found the best way of connecting his arias, which are often no more than epilogues, to the dramatic action. The new opera to come will have a libretto on the French plan, but be Italian in its musical riches. If we succeed in naturalizing Italian riches, we can flatter ourselves in having surpassed our masters by a reasoned combination of our poems with their music, and of having above other nations of Europe the advantage of a national opera.

With this statement the pamphlet ends. It is dated from Florence, 1 March 1756, and signed by the letter "D" followed by three asterisks. Gluck was still in Italy at this date. Was Durazzo with him? More than two months later, on 23 May, Durazzo had the Austrian ambassador at Paris pay a large sum of money to the publisher Duchesne; a copy of the printed *Lettre* exists, moreover, among Durazzo's librettos and scores preserved in the National Library in Turin.[15] (This rich collection was begun in Vienna, and includes many Parisian prints sent by Charles-Simon Favart to Durazzo, plus many musical manuscripts by composers as diverse as Vivaldi, Galuppi, Francesco de Majo, Wagenseil, Starzer, Gluck, Traetta, Haydn, and others. Durazzo continued to add to his collection after becoming imperial ambassador to Venice in 1764, at which time he presumably acquired the Venetian scores [including autographs of Vivaldi's music]. Many volumes bear an *ex libris*

[15] Gentili Verona, "Le collezioni Foà e Giordano della Biblioteca Nazionale di Torino," *Vivaldiana* 1 (1969): 2–56.

consisting of his coat of arms and name, "Conte G. Durazzo A.C." [i.e., Ambasciatore Cesareo].)

The *Lettre* was formerly attributed, with insufficient proof, to Josse de Villeneuve, a finance minister in Florence; then it was attributed to Durazzo after his connections with Duchesne in Paris became known. A recent study shows why the pamphlet could not possibly have been written by Durazzo, without proposing an author who *could* have written it.[16] Was the author really French? An early reviewer found that the pamphlet's literary style proclaimed the author a foreigner. Elie Fréron, writing in 1756, the same year as the *Lettre*, said of it: "Its style is far below what we call good style, and the writer uses many bad constructions; he mixes trivial turns of phrase in great quantity with base expressions and ambiguous sentences, showing that he does not know the language that he demeans by using, nor the superior works in every genre that it has produced. He has indeed been in Florence a long time."[17] With this last quip Fréron, whether he knew it or not, hit upon the true identity of the author, who was no Frenchman visiting Florence for two years, but someone who had an intimate knowledge of what had been going on in Tuscan theaters for the past twenty years.

The author of the *Lettre*, in fact, was well acquainted with Italian opera all over the peninsula, and especially with its greatest center, the Teatro San Carlo in Naples. At the same time, this author was intimately acquainted with the latest events of the 1750s in Paris, right up through late 1755. Only one person can fill all these specifications: Calzabigi himself.

Raniero Calzabigi was born in 1714 in Leghorn (Livorno), the port city of Tuscany, all of which came under Austrian rule in 1737. From a well-off family, he was educated at Livorno and Pisa (the opera houses of both these cities are mentioned in the *Lettre*, along with those of Lucca, Siena, and Florence). In 1740 Calzabigi was admitted to membership in the Arcadian Academy (as "Liburno Drepanio") and the Accademia Etrusca of Cortona. By 1741 he was in Naples attempting, unsuccessfully, to get his librettos accepted by the San Carlo. In 1745 he won for himself a powerful patron in the Marquis d'Hospital, French ambassador to Naples, who commissioned from Calzabigi a festival opera to celebrate the wedding of the dauphin and the infanta. In 1747 he wrote *Il sogno d'Olympia* to celebrate the birth of an heir to the throne of Naples. This work brought him to the attention of Metastasio, who pronounced it "excessively natural and without enough artifice." The future literary conflict between the two poets was already forecast in these few words.

---

[16] Bruce Alan Brown, *Gluck and the French Theatre in Vienna* (Oxford, 1991), pp. 153–57.

[17] *Année littéraire* 4 (1756), lettre 10, p. 235, cited in the original French by Karro, "De la Querelle des Bouffons," p. 196.

Around 1750 Calzabigi accompanied the Marquis d'Hospital as his secretary to Paris, where he quickly met the leading figures in literary and financial circles. In 1752 he proposed his critical edition of Metastasio's works to the elder poet, and a lively correspondence was initiated between Vienna and Paris concerning this project (only Metastasio's letters survive). When the first volume appeared in 1755, it bore a dedication to the most influential person in the realm, Madame de Pompadour, *maîtresse en titre* of Louis XV. No wonder Calzabigi is so well informed in the *Lettre* about the latest royal plans for the beautification of Paris! The plans were the work of Madame de Pompadour's brother, the Marquis de Marigny. At the height of the Querelle des Bouffons in 1753–54, a battle that pitted proponents of *tragédie lyrique* against those of Italian intermezzi, Calzabigi began his wickedly satirical mock-epic poem, *La Lulliade*.[18]

Calzabigi wrote the *Lettre* to publicize his own *Dissertazione* and disseminate his ideas further by means of the French language, of which he was an ingenious practitioner (*pace* Fréron). Many authors surreptitiously reviewed or praised their own works at that time (including Charles Burney and Friedrich Schiller) if they could get away with it. In the *Lettre* Calzabigi throws would-be detectives off the scent by some mild disagreements with his *Dissertazione*. It is possible that Durazzo paid for publication of the *Lettre* not only because he agreed that the future of opera lay in combining French and Italian traditions, but because the two men were in league long before Calzabigi's move to Vienna in 1761, perhaps as early as their youth in Italy. The "D ★ ★ ★," which misled scholars into assigning the *Lettre* to Durazzo, could just possibly stand for Calzabigi's second Arcadian name, "Drepanio."

The *Lettre*, it should be noted finally, was not as original as is claimed in its preface. Its position is often close to that of the moderate faction (represented by Diderot and D'Alembert among others) of the preceding Querelle des Bouffons, of which the *Lettre* can be considered one of the last salvos. Still closer were Ami de Rochemont's *Reflexions d'un Patriote sur l'Opéra Français, et sur l'Opéra Italien* (Lausanne, 1754). This long and detailed treatise explores many of the same subjects as the *Lettre* and comes to some similar conclusions. It praises the Italians "for their warmth and imaginative genius, fecundity, and the sublimity of their ideas," when judged by the individual aria. With respect to entire operas, "they lack delicacy and the kind of merit that consists of regimenting one's strokes of imagination; their talent, marvelous as it is, puts them more in line to succeed with small things than with large." They are also charged with being too parsimonious with their

---

[18] The poem is edited and annotated, together with Calzabigi's elaborate commentary on the poem, by Gabriele Muresu, *La ragione dei Buffoni* (Rome, 1977).

obbligato recitatives. For all the praises heaped on Metastasio, the poet is still blamed for attaching his arias too loosely to the dramatic action. Rochemont claims that three weeks or a month, at most six weeks, suffice for the composition and staging of an Italian opera. The recitative, he says, gives no trouble to the composer (unlike his French counterpart). The composer writes the arias at his leisure and keeps a portfolio of them, so that he is ready to adjust them to whatever poem comes along. Here both content and language are so close to the 1756 pamphlet that it is difficult to believe that Calzabigi was unaware of Rochemont. The last part of the 1754 work is devoted to defending Lully's *Armide* against the criticism of it in Jean-Jacques Rousseau's attack on French opera, *Lettre sur la musique française* (without ever naming Rousseau).

Opéra-Comique

DURAZZO held power over the Viennese theaters such as no single person was able to exert in Paris. He was in a position to shape Viennese opéra-comique exactly as he pleased, by choosing which Parisian works would be produced and deciding how they were to be altered. Spoken dialogue, common in Paris, Durazzo banned altogether from the lyric offerings of his French troupe. The emphasis was thus all the greater on songs, dances, and pantomime. It is a fiction beloved of German and Austrian scholars that Durazzo aimed the products of the French Theater solely at the aristocracy; the truth was that he had to please the bourgeois public as well in order to fill the Burgtheater with paying customers. Durazzo himself decided Vienna's move toward the Parisian *comédie mêlée d'ariettes* and away from vaudeville comedies, doubtless with Gluck's particular gifts in mind. He led Gluck step by step to the point where Gluck was able to compete with the Parisian composers of opéra-comique, as he made clear in his request for a pension for Gluck in 1763.[19]

Up to 1758 Gluck's contribution of individual pieces to the offerings of the French troupe show him gradually adopting a style for which his many years as a master of Italian opera had not prepared him. He emerges as a master of the French style with his thirteen pieces for *La fausse esclave*, a two-act comedy by Louis Anseaume and Pierre de Marcouville, reduced to one act and first brought to the stage of the Burgtheater in a performance in January 1758, at which both sovereigns were present. By this time Gluck had become so adept at capturing a Gallic flavor that some of his tunes could easily pass for vaudevilles. One such is Lisette's "Dans un temps contraire,"

---

[19] Brown, *Gluck and the French Theatre*, pp. 437–38.

EXAMPLE 3.3. *Gluck,* La fausse esclave, *Air*

Lisette

Dans un temps con - trai - re   Faut toujours a - voir _ du _ coeur.

(Example 3.3) in which he uses the limited ambitus, repeated tones, and square cut characteristic of many popular romances, like the famous example by Pierre Gaviniès.[20] The main tune is so conjunct, simple, and naive it could easily pass unnoticed in an anthology of French folksongs.[21] Gluck treats it as a refrain that keeps coming back, as in a rondeau—another tribute to French practice. The part of Lisette was sung by Mlle Favier, a dancer with less vocal ability than Mme. Bodin, the leading lady of the troupe, who sang the part of Agathe. In Agathe's airs Gluck resorts to writing out upward-resolving appoggiaturas in the French style. The device is not unknown in Gluck's earlier music—it occurs, for instance, in the love duet of *Il rè pastore*—but from this point on it becomes frequent.

A reviewer in the *Journal encyclopédique* shortly after the premiere of *La fausse esclave* commented at length on the work and said of Gluck, prophetically: "Given the success of the work, we wish that the music of this skilled composer could be executed at Paris, in order to see whether in this first essay Gluck has been able to conserve all the verity of expression in the French words, in giving them, as he has, all the accompanimental brilliance of Italian music." First essay it may have been, but the campaign to get Gluck invited to Paris had already begun at the time of this carefully orchestrated opinion. Marrying French vocal expression with the brilliance of Italian violin writing was precisely the accomplishment claimed for and by Rousseau in *Le devin du village*. Gluck's music shows more variety than this critic's simplistic summary would suggest, and there is no doubt that Gluck was inspired to his best by the variety of shapes and lengths represented in the texts he had to set—so unlike the uniform double quatrains and verbal parsimony of Metastasio, about which Jommelli complained.[22] From the begin-

[20] Daniel Heartz, "The Beginnings of the Operatic Romance: Rousseau, Sedaine, and Monsigny," *Eighteenth-Century Studies* 15 (1981–82): 149–78; 160.

[21] Cf. the well-known nursery song "Au clair de la lune, mon ami Pierrot" for a similar structure. Also note the similarity between mm. 3–4 and the cadential phrase of the theme to the last movement of Symphonie Concertante for four winds and orchestra (K. 297^b), of disputed attribution to Mozart but of indubitable connections with Paris. "Dans un temps contraire" has been called an ancestor of Papageno's "Ein Mädchen oder Weibchen"; a closer parallel has been pointed out by Brown, *Gluck and the French Theatre*, p. 214, between Gluck's duet in F "Oui, je vous aime" in *Fausse esclave* and an anonymous duet written for Vienna's German Theater later the same year.

[22] Daniel Heartz, "Metastasio, 'Maestro dei Maestri di Cappella Drammatici,'" in *Metastasio e il mondo musicale* (Florence, 1986), pp. 315–38; 337.

ning, opéra-comique was for Gluck a liberating force, an avenue that showed one way beyond stereotyped formalism of the da capo aria.

L'isle de Merlin, ou Le monde renversé was given at Schönbrunn Palace on 3 October 1758, the eve of the emperor's name day. Social satire had always been one of the specialties of Parisian opéra-comique, and this work brought Gluck in touch with its main founding father, Alain-René Lesage, whose own *Monde renversé* of 1718 was originally provided with music by Jean-Claude Gillier. Based on one of La Fontaine's fables, *Monde renversé* enjoyed an unusual number of revivals. It was given again in Paris in 1725, 1731, and, as revised by Louis Anseaume, in 1753; it was even translated into German and brought to Hamburg in 1729 as *Die verkehrte Welt Opera comique* with added music by Georg Philipp Telemann. The work, in sum, was a classic of the genre. The *Lettre sur le mechanisme de l'opéra italien* cites it as representative of vaudeville comedy, along with *Les pèlerins de la Mecque*. Gluck composed two dozen or so numbers for his version, which is based on a textual compilation using both Lesage and Anseaume. In addition, over fourscore vaudeville tunes are named in Gluck's opera.

The overture depicts a sea storm (an agitated *Allegro* in D, in cut time), followed by a calm (*Allegretto* in 3/8, also in D); these sections were used again over twenty years later, in reverse order, as the basis for the calm and storm preceding *Iphigénie en Tauride*. The case well exemplifies how important Gluck's early works in French were for his late ones. Storms remained a French specialty after the Italians had tired of them (and before they rediscovered them). According to the initial stage direction of the Viennese libretto (taken from Lesage-D'Orneville), the audience witnessed "at stage rear an agitated sea, the remains of a shipwreck, and a sloop buffeted by the waves; Pierrot and Scapin are thrown upon the shore." In the first vaudeville the two clowns express their despair to the phrases of an incongruously cheerful tune of the old branle de Poitou type (3 x 3/4 measures), which was one of the main ancestors of the menuet.[23] Gluck intervenes with an *air nouveau* after the second, showing at once how he could adapt his new music to the homely and folklike qualities of the surrounding vaudevilles. Food and wine have appeared miraculously at the request of the men, who next wish for female companionship, which Merlin sends them in the persons of his two nieces Argentine and Diamantine.

In a *quatuor* that begins *Allegro* (3/4 in G), the pairs greet each other and exchange compliments; during a middle section (2/4 in e) the exchange becomes more lively, leading to a return of the 3/4 time and the original

[23] Daniel Heartz, "Terpsichore at the Fair: Old and New Dance Airs in Two Vaudeville Comedies by Lesage," in *Music and Context: Essays for John M. Ward*, ed. Anne D. Shapiro (Cambridge, Mass., 1985), pp. 278–304; 286.

tonic, as the ladies sing in thirds, expressing acceptance of their new beaux as husbands as long as they behave wisely. In the following brief dialogue Diamantine explains that husbands are never unfaithful on this island. "And wives?" asks Scapin. "Likewise faithful," answers Argentine. "Then the world is turned upside down here!" exclaims Scapin in the line that gives the show one of its titles ("C'est donc ici le monde renversé!"). There follows an *air nouveau* for Argentine, a *Moderato* in E♭ and in 3/4, with wind parts for one bassoon and two English horns—a favorite Viennese sonority in connection with this key, in use at least as early as Wagenseil's pasticcio *Euridice* of 1750.

Wealth is scorned on Merlin's isle, and the ladies declare that the men are eligible for their hands only if they are indigent, which the men assure them is the case. This exchange happens in a second quartet, beginning *Allegro* in F and in cut time. A middle section in 3/4, set up by a change in poetic meter, announces an impediment of some consequence: there are two ferocious rivals for the ladies' hands, eliciting a show of bravado from the men, who say they will overcome all rivals should they be a hundred thousand (the great number being conveyed by a plethora of quick notes). Reassured, the ladies begin to sing calmly in thirds about the "eternal chains" that will bind them. The men convey their economic condition by singing the smallest possible interval on "indigents," while the ladies get carried away with a chain of parallel thirds on long notes.

Gluck seized the comic possibilities like a veteran, although he had likely done nothing in this vein before (Example 3.4). He was unconstrained by any formal pattern other than what was suggested by the text. His openness to the variety of shapes suggested by his French texts already heralds the reformer to come. Bear in mind that the limitations of Vienna's French troupe were severe. If the two men in this ensemble were rarely asked to sing separate parts, it may have been because the original Pierrot and Scapin, more actors than singers, could not be trusted to do so. But even

EXAMPLE 3.4. *Gluck*, L'isle de Merlin, *Quartet*

with these limitations, Gluck achieved here an impressive bit of high comedy, quite worthy of the pitting of high voices against low in Antoine Dauvergne's *Les troqueurs* (1753), which may have served as a model, having been well received in Vienna, where it was performed by the same troupe a year earlier.

Lesage's trenchant wit ridicules philosophers, doctors, lawyers, and "petits maîtres" (men of modest birth who put on airs) in turn. The text is so entertaining that it is no wonder that more than one generation was amused by it. Along the way there is an opportunity to parody opera singers whose bad habits include improvising ornamented reprises that result in syllabic repetitions like "Près de l'ob- ob- ob- ob-jet de son a-mou- mou- mou- mou-mour toujours tendre, aimable et fi- fi- fi- fi- fi- fi- fi- fi- fi-dèle." Gluck took his cue from Jean-Claude Gillier's original score when writing his music in the form of a "Simple" and a "Double." Some of the vocal excesses Gluck would later excoriate in prose, he held up to ridicule in just as telling fashion here.

The deftness with which Gluck moved into the world of vaudevilles and Parisian wit is hardly less amazing than the topsy-turvy world of Merlin's realm. His first two essays brought him quickly to the forefront of those working in the genre. During the following year, 1759, he was involved with at least three new lyric productions by the French company: *Le diable à quatre*, *La Cythère assiégée*, and *L'arbre enchanté*.

To *Le diable à quatre* by the poet Michel-Jean Sedaine he added several new pieces, while keeping several others from the Parisian score of 1756, which was already a pastiche involving several hands. The distinction between air and *ariette* becomes lost here. Gluck's most remarkable added number, Margot's song about tobacco, is called by both names in different sources. It offers a case study of much that is fascinating about opéra-comique in Vienna: Gluck matching wits with the crafty Sedaine (after some Viennese hand, perhaps Durazzo's, had toned down the ending of the verse, which was too sexually suggestive); Gluck matching musical invention with the far from lackluster tune in the Parisian original; Gluck's new tune catching fire in Viennese society and seducing the up-and-coming young Joseph Haydn to the extent that Haydn based an entire symphonic movement upon it.[24] Besides Gluck's several vocal numbers added to *Le diable à quatre*, the Viennese scores contain lengthy ballet entries for each of the three acts. This dance music or some of it may be by Gluck too, but it should be borne in mind that the choreographer of the French troupe, Gasparo Angiolini, often composed his own ballet music, so he is a candidate as well; later in his career Angiolini staged a ballet called, in fact, *Le diable à quatre* (Milan, 1781).

La Cythère assiégée brought Gluck in touch with the most gifted lyricist among contemporary French poets, Charles-Simon Favart. Favart's light-hearted comedy about the siege of Venus' realm by Scythians, who are soon made captive themselves by the powers of love, was written as a parody of Lully's *Armide* for the Foire St. Laurent Theater in 1738. The poet revised it ten years later for Brussels, then revived it at Paris in 1754. Vienna saw a production entirely in vaudevilles in 1757. Gluck's contribution to the production of two years later consisted of twenty-six new numbers. The composer's version was also performed at Schwetzingen in 1759, and the elector there, Carl Theodore, is said by Burney to have been so pleased with the work that he rewarded the composer with a tun of the best wine from his Rhenish domains.

Favart's poem offered ample opportunity to contrast amorous with war-like sentiments. Gluck felt perfectly at home with both. His stridently masculine rhythms for the Scythians (e.g., the *Mouvement de marche* "A moi, fiers soldats") forecast the even more brutal strains of Thoas in *Iphigénie en Tauride*. The menuet in various forms and shapes carries the brunt of the amo-

---

[24] All these facets are explored in the article announcing the discovery: Daniel Heartz, "Haydn und Gluck im Burgtheater um 1760: *Der neue krumme Teufel, Le diable à quatre,* und die Sinfonie 'Le Soir,'" in *Bericht über den internationalen musikwissenschaftlichen Kongress, Bayreuth 1981*, ed. Christoph-Hellmut Mahling and Sigrid Wiesmann (Kassel, 1984), pp. 120–35. See chapter 4 for a comparison of Gluck's tune with Haydn's adaptation.

rous assaults. One air, "Avec quelle ardeur Venus et les Graces," is titled "Menuet avec Danse" and inscribed *Tempo di Minuetto*, showing that even at that time, both French and Italian variants of the dance's name were deemed necessary for purposes of communication. The sexes are differentiated tonally as well as rhythmically, as the women begin by singing in the "soft" *(molle)* flat keys and the men in the "bright" *(dur)* sharp keys.[25]

Favart's erotically suggestive verses were no doubt particularly enjoyed in Brussels in 1748, where the audience was the French army led by the libertine Maréchal de Saxe (who seduced Madame Favart among many others). Surprisingly, the verses were censored very little for Vienna, perhaps because some of the double entendres eluded Durazzo and the prim Maria Theresa; they would not have eluded the old army man of French descent who was her husband. *Cythère* was a lavish visual spectacle, as all the early critics stressed, and it may have been in connection with this visual emphasis that a greater verbal latitude than usual was allowed. Possibly the increasing reputation of Favart, soon to become Durazzo's regular Parisian liaison in theatrical matters, played a role.

Inseparably linked with Favart and with this show was the great royal painter François Boucher, who stood high in the favor of Madame de Pompadour and Louis XV. Boucher's female figures often succeeded in capturing the same titillating qualities as did Favart's words. For the two-volume edition of Favart's plays printed in Brussels in 1748, Boucher sent the playwright several drawings that were engraved as frontispieces. For *Cythère* Boucher had recourse to his stunningly beautiful painting of Armide and Renaud, which had served as his reception piece for the Royal Academy in 1734. As engraved by Cochin the drawing was reproduced again as a frontispiece to volume seven of the Paris edition of Favart (1763), whence comes our illustration (Figure 3.3).

Boucher's picture had a direct impact on the Viennese production of *Cythère*, which added a scene at the end in which, as the libretto specifies, "terraces ornamented with cascades, cradles, and many cupids holding garlands of flowers carry the eye to the distant Temple of Love, which is transparent." Carl Zinzendorf made a point of mentioning this final stage scene, which he witnessed in the revival of early 1762 and described as "a dome supported by columns, with balustrades on both sides and vases filled with fruits, everything being illuminated."[26] The Seven Years' War and the consequent theatrical economies in Vienna would have assured that the 1762

---

[25] Brown, *Gluck and the French Theatre*, p. 237.

[26] Brown, *Gluck and the French Theatre*, p. 233. Merlin's grotto in *L'isle de Merlin* had been a transparent one in Vienna in 1758. On the use of transparent decors at the Lenten academies in the Burgtheater, also in 1758, see p. 52–53 above.

FIGURE 3.3.
Boucher. *Armide
and Renaud*,
frontispiece to
Favart's *Cythère
assiegée*, 1748.

Cythère used the same sets as the original production of three years earlier. Moreover, Maria Theresa decreed that costumes be reused from show to show so that the public could see that the court was economizing. A chorus of thirty-three was used in the revival of the opera, and three months of rehearsal, mostly devoted to the chorus, which had to move with the grace of dancers, were necessary before Gluck and Gasparo Angiolini, the choreographer, were satisfied.

The importance of *Cythère* to their reform works of the 1760s is manifest. It lay in the easy blending of solos with choruses and of ballet with visual spectacle. The whole opera was in fact reduced to a pantomime version by Angiolini and was given its first performance on 15 September 1762, less than a month before the premiere of *Orfeo ed Euridice*. The last stage set of the latter showed a Temple of Love, probably the same transparency inspired by Boucher.[27] Then in 1775, Gluck transformed *Cythère* into a veritable opéra-ballet in three acts for Paris.

L'arbre enchanté followed *L'isle de Merlin* one year later to the day, to celebrate the emperor's name day in 1759. The libretto was adapted from Jean-Joseph Vadé's vaudeville comedy *Le poirier*, first produced at the Foire St. Laurent in 1752. It is a simple story derived from one of the fables of La Fontaine in which an old fool, Thomas, spies on two young lovers and is duped by them. A version using only the original vaudevilles was printed by Trattner in 1759 and is thought to have been staged in Vienna sometime earlier than Gluck's version. Ghelen printed the libretto of the version to which Gluck contributed fifteen new numbers.

L'arbre enchanté offered Gluck several piquant situations and opportunities for comic characterization. Old Thomas has a penchant for lustily accented polka melodies such as Gluck heard in abundance when he was growing up in Bohemia. In the *ariette dialoguée* "On amorce le poisson," he uses a peculiar 3/8 rhythm in which the third beat is accented by changing harmony. Most impressive of all is the slow and hymnic *ariette* "Du jeune objet que j'adore." Here it is some of the priestly music of the later operas that one hears adumbrated. The melody seems conventional at first and the harmony too, but as the piece expands both in ambitus and in terms of the length of the phrases, which pass from regular to irregular, Gluck's individual voice becomes striking. The work was a success in Vienna, so much so that Gluck chose to revive it in Paris in 1775 for a visit from Archduke Maximilian. Several numbers were transposed to higher keys to suit Parisian voices; no improvement, and particularly unfortunate in the invocation to love sung by Claudine, "Que l'objet qui m'enflamme," which was moved from the sensuous and spiritual key of E♭ to the more neutral and childlike realm of G.

In the short span of little more than two years, Gluck was called upon to match wits with some of the best comic poets the century had produced: Lesage, Anseaume, Vadé, Favart, and Sedaine. His music gained greatly in humanity from the encounter, especially his next opera, *L'ivrogne corrigé* of 1760.

In Paris another *L'ivrogne corrigé* first reached the stage of the Foire St. Laurent on 23 July 1759. Anseaume and a collaborator wrote the libretto after

---

[27] This could help explain why an early critic in the *Journal encyclopédique* (15 February 1763) described *Orfeo* as "entirely in the French taste."

a fable of La Fontaine; the tenor Jean-Louis Laruette composed the music. The printed score from Paris probably did not reach Gluck before he made his own setting.[28] Laruette's score possesses occasional melodic charms, as one might expect from a singer-composer, but it pales in comparison with Gluck's. The opening drinking song sung by Lucas depicts the peasant Mathurin, a winemaker overly fond of his product. Gluck writes a *gavotte gai* with so much Gallic *sel* that he is truly more French in inspiration than Laruette. Lurking behind his melody is the most famous contredanse of the early eighteenth century, "Cotillon" (Example 3.5ab)[29] Gluck places another lusty drinking song in G, Mathurin's "Allons morbleu! Point de chagrin," as the penultimate number of the opera; it resembles the tune of Margot's tobacco song in *Le diable à quatre*, and is made even more lusty by having a pair of horns play the entire melody as a kind of fanfare to begin and end the piece.

Between these two drinking songs there unfolds a tapestry of country manners worthy of a Greuze in his rural modes: debauchery, deceit (the characters pretend that when Mathurin awakens from his drunken stupor he is dead and has gone to hell), compassion, and reconciliation all receive their due thanks to Gluck's expanding palette of dramatic effects. The music he created for Mathurine, Mathurin's long-suffering wife, is particularly warm and appealing. She may not be a heroine, but she has the noble and generous qualities of an Alceste, to which Gluck readily responded. In "De nos tourmens—je suis confuse" she takes pity on her duped husband and

EXAMPLE 3.5.

a. Gluck, L'ivrogne corrigé, *opening Air*

b. Mouret, Contredance, "Cotillon"

[28] Brown, *Gluck and the French Theatre*, p. 255.
[29] The dance tune and its choreography can be traced back to Feuillet's *Quatrième recueil de danses de bal* (1705). See Jean-Michel Guilcher, *La contredanse et les renouvellements de la danse française* (Paris, 1969), pp. 75–76.

asks his forgiveness. The music is some of Gluck's loveliest. The demons and Furies who taunt Mathurin in hell mark the advent of an element that will assume great importance for Gluck. Vienna's French troupe did not have the resources yet to stage a full-scale infernal scene with ballet and chorus, such as the scene to come in *Orfeo*, but Gluck tried out some novel choral effects even so, using what forces he had to maximum advantage. It was by combining the resources of the French and German troupes that Durazzo would make choral opera a possibility in Vienna.

In the fall of 1760 Hasse and Gluck both composed operas with new Italian librettos in celebration of the imperial wedding.[30] Metastasio's *Alcide al bivio*, a *festa teatrale* set to music by Hasse, was sung in the Burgtheater by great voices such as Caterina Gabrielli and Giovanni Manzuoli and by a chorus of twenty-four, mostly from the German troupe; there were extensive ballet forces drawn from both troupes.[31] Gluck set the second opera, the serenata *Tetide*, by the Dresden poet Giannambrogio Migliavacca, for the same soloists. For this opera the large Redoutensaal was transformed into a theater, and the famous Servandoni was brought from Paris to work his aquatic wonders depicting the realm of Thetis. (See Plate IX.) Most of *Tetide* is in the florid Italian aria style appropriate to such stellar singers. Yet some of the score's simpler music, for example Hymen's aria (No. 12), shows the inroads upon Gluck's style made as a result of composing several shows for the modest singing talents of the French troupe.

Traetta's *Armida* (1761)

WHILE the imperial wedding operas were alternating during the fall of 1760, Durazzo was laying plans for a more imaginative operatic venture. Ever since his first visit to Paris in 1748, the count had envisaged an Italian opera that would capitalize on the beauties of Quinault's *Armide*, or so he claimed.[32] Upon his return to Genoa Durazzo sketched such an opera in prose, together with his friend the Marquis Agostino Lomellini. Many years later he employed the poet Migliavacca to write the verses for an *Armida* according to his plan, and gave the task of composing the music to Tommaso Traetta, who was in the service of the court of Parma. It was only to be

[30] Daniel Heartz, "Haydn's 'Acide e Galatea' and the Imperial Wedding Operas of 1760 by Hasse and Gluck," *Internationaler Joseph Haydn Kongress Wien 1982* (Munich, 1986), pp. 332–40.

[31] Jacques Joly, *Les fêtes théâtrales de Metastasio à la cour de Vienne, 1731-1767* (Clermont-Ferrand, 1978), pp. 506–7.

[32] Daniel Heartz, "Traetta in Vienna: *Armida* (1761) and *Ifigenia in Tauride* (1763)," *Studies in Music from the University of Western Ontario* 7 (1982): 65–88; 68–69.

expected that after the wedding between the infanta, Isabella of Parma, and Archduke Joseph, there would be some commingling of the artistic forces serving both houses. *Armida* was offered as a birthday tribute to the infanta and brought to the stage of the Burgtheater in January 1761.

It is not known if Traetta came to Vienna for the occasion, but according to the normal practice of the time he would have presided over the first performances at the harpsichord. Later, when recommending Traetta to the court of Florence, Durazzo made it clear that he had wanted to get the composer appointed to imperial service. Moreover, he linked Traetta's operatic labors at Parma with those for Vienna, but, curiously, he did not mention *Armida*:

> He [Traetta] always distinguished himself by the taste with which he wrote, both for the court of Parma and that of Vienna, the first on the occasion of the royal wedding of her highness the infanta of happy memory [*Le feste d'Imeneo*, Parma, 1760], the second for the coronation of Joseph II as King of the Romans [at Frankfurt in the spring of 1764, a reference presumably to a revival of *Ifigenia in Tauride* from the previous fall in Vienna]. So much so that Traetta would have entered the service of the imperial court had Count Durazzo remained in Vienna. Moreover, the talents and ability of Traetta being rather well-known, said Count Durazzo recommends him as the best master of music who can be found in Italy.[33]

Just what position Durazzo envisioned for Traetta in Vienna is puzzling. Recall the great difficulty the count had in creating a post for Gluck. Perhaps he was anticipating the demise of the elderly Reutter. Mortality, in the event, took its toll elsewhere. With the premature death of the infanta at the end of 1763, part of the rationale for appointing Traetta disappeared. Durazzo's dismissal as impresario came four months later, and Traetta wrote nothing further for Vienna.

Traetta had already broken with many of the conventions of Metastasian opera seria at Parma with his two operas of 1759–60, *Ippolito ed Aricia* and *I Tindaridi*, based on Carlo Innocenzo Frugoni's adaptations of the librettos of Rameau's *Hippolyte et Aricie* and *Castor et Pollux*, respectively.[34] Thus in Parma, as in Vienna, it was the French lyric stage that pointed the way to reforming Italian opera. Traetta's wedding opera, *Feste d'Imeneo*, approxi-

[33] This *Memoria*, taken from Durazzo's recommendation, is preserved in the papers of the Pergola Theater, Immobili Archives, GH vol. 14, f. 218, and was kindly relayed to me in the original Italian by Robert L. Weaver.

[34] Daniel Heartz, "Operatic Reform at Parma: *Ippolito ed Aricia*," *Atti del convegno sul settecento parmense nel 2° centenario della morte di C. I. Frugoni* (Parma, 1969), pp. 271–300; and Mary Cyr, "Rameau e Traetta," *Nuova Rivista Musicale Italiana* 12 (1978): 166–82.

mated the opéra-ballet genre of its Parisian model, Rameau's *Les fêtes d'Hébé*. *Armida* for Vienna continued the line by introducing into the opera spectacular staging, ballet, and some modest choral effects. But although elements favored in French opera were integrated into the structure, they did not predominate; recitatives leading to arias continued to be the main modus operandi.

One constant between Traetta's operas for Parma and Vienna, insuring that the elaborate aria would continue to reign supreme, was the prima donna common to all of them: Caterina Gabrielli. Her most impressive music as Armida comes in the famous scene where the sorceress is struck by the beauty of the sleeping Rinaldo just as she is about to slay him. In force of expression, the elaborate, orchestrally accompanied recitative can stand comparison with those of the finest masters in this genre, even Jommelli. Traetta blurs the point of juncture between the recitative and aria here so that we cannot tell where the one has ended and the other begun. Once the aria is fully launched, it becomes evident that Traetta exceeds all his contemporaries in sensuous beauty. But here sensuous beauty is in the service of dramatic expression, hence very much in tune with reform ideals. Traetta commands every harmonic and melodic resource of the time and marshals them so carefully that the long line sustained throughout the piece suggests the mature Mozart, even the late Mozart of Tamino's "Picture Aria."[35] The slow and regular-moving harmonies with syncopated chord tones provide support for a soaring melody, free to explore many nuances and chromatic inflections. With this aria Traetta surpassed his own best efforts to date and contributed to a deepening of expression that was not lost on Gluck and other Viennese composers.

Armida was a short *azione teatrale* for a festive occasion. Its subject, drawn from knightly romance by way of Tasso and Quinault, meant that the opera stood somewhat outside the Greek revival movement that was at the heart of the operatic reform. The same is true of Gluck's *Don Juan*, the next milestone on the way to *Orfeo ed Euridice*, in terms of subject matter. The Furies, which became so popular in the Burgtheater at this time and which figure so prominently in both *Don Juan* and *Orfeo*, made an earlier appearance in *Armida*, to which two choreographers, Gasparo Angiolini and Antoine Pitrot, contributed two ballets apiece. The emergence of Angiolini as one of the moving forces in the Burgtheater was of signal importance to the gathering reform movement.

Joseph Chamant was the scenographer of *Armida*. Apparently none of

---

[35] For a more specific comparison, see Heartz, "Traetta in Vienna," p. 79. Long excerpts from the recitative and aria in question are quoted in this article.

his work survives, for this or any other production. We at least know how the crumbling of Armida's palace looked as staged by the great designer Jean Bérain at the Opéra in Paris (Figure 3.4). This image from the libretto set the standard by which Chamant's *Armida* would have been judged. Quinault's last stage direction reads, "The demons destroy the enchanted palace and Armida leaves on a flying chariot." As depicted on her dragon car by Bérain, she seems to be in charge of the demonic demolition crew. Note that Armida's palace was no Baroque pile of twisting shapes à la Bernini, but a symmetrical, neoclassical structure in rectilinear form, like Claude Perrault's east façade of the Louvre. Its dome resembles the Pantheon in Rome.

FIGURE 3.4.
Bérain.
Frontispiece to
Quinault's
libretto for
Lully's *Armide*.

Was *Armida* the first Viennese reform opera? Durazzo wished it to be so regarded, and Calzabigi concurred, up to a point. Something about this question can be gleaned from the information Durazzo supplied the French composer-historian Jean-Benjamin La Borde, who published what he was told in his *Essai sur la musique ancienne et moderne* (Paris, 1780). La Borde visited Durazzo in Venice after the latter was installed as Austrian ambassador to the Most Serene Republic; there is no reason to doubt his sincerity in wishing to thank his host for many kindnesses by making known to the public Durazzo's accomplishments, as he says at the end of his article. La Borde mentions Durazzo's first efforts as a dramatist, the opéra-ballet *Le cacciatrici amanti* and *L'innocenza giustificata,* claiming that the latter was given a hundred performances in succession, which cannot be anything but a gross exaggeration. About *Armida* La Borde says: "His *Armida* was imitated from Quinault, and written together with his friend and fellow-citizen the Marquis Lomellini, one of the best poets of Genoa. This opera, with its choruses and ballets linked to the action, did not deceive expectation, and the Italian music, up to this point accused of flattering only the ears, was able for the first time to also charm the eyes."

A good point, certainly, this last one, in that the reform works established a new and close relationship between the sonic and the scenic. What is not said here looms even larger. There is no mention of Migliavacca's role as versifier, nor of the composer. To judge from La Borde's articles on Migliavacca and on Traetta, in neither of which *Armida* is mentioned, the French critic had little knowledge of the work aside from what he was told by Durazzo. Back in 1761, in a letter to Favart of 18 May, Durazzo had at least praised Migliavacca for *Armida,* calling him the poet who best imitated Metastasio's style; Traetta he did not mention. These failures to give Traetta his due for *Armida* must be connected somehow with the curious omission of this opera among the composer's credits when Durazzo recommended him to Florence, as noted above.

Durazzo, during his long and dreary years of exile in Venice (as he regarded them), saw a good chance to stake out his claim for fame anew as the initiator of the operatic reform. He placed his hopes in the prestige of La Borde. It has been said that history is a tale told by the successful survivors. If so, honors for a decisive breakthrough in opera go not to the soon forgotten *Armida,* but to the still robust *Orfeo ed Euridice.* Credit for being *Orfeo*'s impresario will always belong to Durazzo.

The most Italian aspect of *Armida* is easily lost from sight in discussions of its literary and historical place. As conceived for Vienna in 1761, the opera was not merely some end product of a long-germinating theory. It was written to display the vocal prowess of a particular soprano, Caterina Gabrielli.

Orfeo ed Euridice was also written as a vehicle for a great singer. Without the presence of Gaetano Guadagni in Vienna and his particular combination of acting and singing skills, there would have been no Orpheus opera such as Calzabigi and Gluck conceived in 1762. Perhaps the greatest advantage of an Orpheus opera over any other, including the wonderfully operatic *Armida*, is that its subject is the same as its main medium: the power of song.

Pantomime Ballet

ONE of the most extraordinary artistic developments of the mid-century was the flowering of a new kind of "Ballet Pantomime dans le goût des anciens." In his *La danse ancienne et moderne, ou Traité historique sur la danse* of 1754, the historian Louis de Cahusac attempted to bring together all that was known about the dance in antiquity and to make this lore useful for modern practice. Besides recommending the model of the antique pantomime dances, Cahusac proposed that dancers and choreographers should learn from the greatest paintings and sculptures of recent times, and that a dramatic action should underlie the ballet. All three ideas were taken up and pursued further by Diderot (*Entretiens sur le fils naturel*, 1757), by Noverre (*Lettres sur la danse*, 1760), and in the 1761 Viennese treatise on the subject signed by Gasparo Angiolini, which Calzabigi said he wrote. To a certain extent these men also reflected what choreographers such as Jean-Baptiste de Hesse in Paris and Franz Hilverding in Vienna were already doing.

The abandonment of Baroque conventions and dress was well along in the dance, at least in certain leading centers, by the mid-century. In London in 1734 Marie Sallé created a sensation by dancing in *Pygmalion* dressed "after the fashion of a Greek statue." She appeared in another ballet as Ariadne. It can be no coincidence that these two subjects, along with that of Medea, should later nourish the most celebrated melodramas of the century—the freedom and fantasy of pantomime ballet and melodrama alike depended on the free-flowing orchestral language of obbligato recitative. Rameau's powerful and pictorially evocative ballet music of the 1730s and 1740s also helped encourage further efforts toward making ballet dramatic. Cahusac praised an even earlier event, a "ballet en action" created after Corneille's *Les Horaces* with music by Jean-Joseph Mouret, danced at Sceaux in 1724. French tragedies often supplied the material for dramatic ballets. Esteban Arteaga claimed that Hilverding in the 1740s created dramatic ballets for the Viennese court after Racine's *Britannicus*, Crébillon's *Idomenée*, and Voltaire's *Alzire*. Molière's *Don Juan, ou Le festin de Pierre* inspired the

Angiolini-Gluck masterpiece of 1761, and 1765 saw two more pantomime ballets, *Sémiramis*, after Voltaire's tragedy (with "libretto" preceded by a "Dissertation sur les Ballets Pantomimes des Anciens"), and the even more successful *Iphigénie*, after Racine's tragedy.

Franz Hilverding (ennobled late in life with the title van Wewen) was born in Vienna to a theatrical family in 1710 and died there in 1768. He was sent by the court to perfect his dancing in Paris, where he was a student of Michel Blondy. The French plays he later transformed into ballets were classics he probably witnessed on the stage in Paris. By 1737 he had assumed a position as court dancer in Vienna. A Turkish ballet in the Kärntnerthor Theater in 1742 is credited to him. In 1744 Hilverding was responsible for the ballets that accompanied Hasse's *Ipermestra*. The ballet music for this occasion, which is lost, was the responsibility of Ignaz Holzbauer, who also collaborated with Hilverding by providing the ballet music (also lost) for Hasse's *Arminio*, given in the Burgtheater on 13 May 1747, Maria Theresa's thirtieth birthday. A year later, in the newly refurbished and extended Burgtheater, Hilverding created the ballets accompanying Gluck's *Semiramide*. An independent ballet, *Orphée et Euridice*, given in the Burgtheater in 1752, is credited to Hilverding, whose student Gasparo Angiolini would make his contribution to the same subject in the same theater, ten years later.

In 1752 Hilverding was appointed choreographer in both imperial theaters, for which he received 600 florins annually, plus increments for his pupils. At the Burgtheater his assistants included Antoine Pitrot (from Paris via the Dresden court) and Antoine Philebois; Angiolini joined the troupe from Florence as a solo dancer in the early 1750s, as did the public's favorite dancer, Louise Joffroi Bodin. At the Kärntnerthor Theater Hilverding was assisted by Pietro Lodi (the same dancer who, under the name of Pierre Sodi, worked as a choreographer at the Théâtre Italien in Paris, 1753–56 and 1758–60); the dancers also included François and Manon Bernardi and numbered thirty-one altogether, four more than at the Burgtheater.

For the Kärntnerthor Hilverding chose mainly lighter, "characteristic" ballets such as *Les jalousies du Serail* (1752), *La fabrique du cotton* (1753), and *Les bucherons tirolais* (1754). At the Burgtheater he did not eschew more ambitious subjects derived from allegory or myth, as we saw in the case of *Orphée* and evident as well in *Les quatre parties du jour en quatre ballets différens* ("Le matin," "Le midi," "Le soir," "La nuit," 1755). When Haydn inaugurated his employment in Esterházy service (1761) by composing symphonies on the times of day, he or his employer may well have remembered these ballets. Other ballets by Hilverding at the Burgtheater included *Les saisons*, *La chasse*, and *Les vendanges*, all subjects that Haydn would later paint in his own way. *Le naufrage* (1756–57), a ballet by Pitrot for the Burgtheater, has analogies in Haydn all the way from the *tempesta* finale of Symphony No. 8 (1761) to the secular cantata *The Storm* of 1792. The inroads of *le terrible* are evident in Viennese ballet well before *Don Juan, ou Le festin de pierre*.

Hilverding had a counterpart in Paris in the person of Jean-Baptiste de Hesse, a dancer born in The Hague of French actors. He was the most original choreographer of his generation (although pointedly ignored by Noverre for this very reason) and profited from the creativity of pantomime dancers such as Mlle. Sallé. He worked at the Théâtre Italien, and his ballets there inspired artists of the caliber of François Boucher and Gabriel de Saint Aubin. To critics of the time Hesse was "the most excellent composer of ballets in Europe."[36]

The *Répertoire des Théâtres de la ville de Vienne* printed in 1757 for the previous five-year period names Hilverding as the creator of no fewer than thirty-three ballets for the Kärntnerthor Theater and a staggering sixty-nine for the Burgtheater. There was some interchange in repertory between the two stages; *Orphée et Euridice* also turns up in the German Theater (1755–57). The *Répertoire* praised Hilverding as "gifted with a particular talent for these sorts of works, which, joined to an exact knowledge of his art, a continuous study of belles lettres, of fable, of painting, and of music, etc., gives his ballets an ensemble and a precision that are extraordinary." After Hilverding left Vienna in 1758, Angiolini became chief choreographer of the Burgtheater, and François Bernardi took over at the Kärntnerthor Theater. Hilverding returned to Vienna in 1764, four years before his death, but he contributed little more to the stage.

Don Juan, ou Le festin de pierre (1761)

GLUCK assumed the duties of composing ballet music for both the Burgtheater and the Kärntnerthor Theater upon the departure of Joseph Starzer in late 1758. As a composer of Italian opera, he had had no such responsibilities. His activities in adjusting and composing opéras-comiques for the French troupe brought him closer to the world of the dance. Composing in both genres, ballet and opéra-comique, was considered demeaning to a composer of Italian opera trained at the source, and Hasse in particular decried the writing of ballet music as unworthy of his calling. Gluck was

[36] Marian Hannah Winter, *The Pre-Romantic Ballet* (London, 1974), p. 87, where this quotation is assigned to "French critics such as the Parfaicts, Cahusac and Guellette." Thomas-Simon Guellette was a lawyer who left a manuscript memoir of the Théâtre Italien, portions of which have been published in modern edition.

wiser. Precisely in the simple songs and dances of opéra-comique and in the dramatic pantomime of the new-style ballets were to be found strengths that could be used to help revitalize Italian opera.

Don Juan, ou Le festin de pierre Ballet Pantomime was the title of the new work given by the French troupe in the Burgtheater on 17 October 1761. Angiolini danced Don Juan. Public judgment was favorable, and the new work remained in the repertory.

"The spectacle which I present to the public is a Ballet Pantomime in the taste of the ancients."[37] Thus begins the French preface to the ballet signed by Angiolini but actually written by Calzabigi.[38] The author defines the genre as "a kind of declamation conceived for the eyes, the message being made more apparent by means of music, which varies the sounds according to whether the mime intends to express love or hate, fury or despair." Music was more than just a helpmate; it was an indispensable means of conveying dramatic action, a point stressed at the end of the preface. Its author apologizes for having selected the Don Juan legend "with all its faults" as a subject, and for the grimness of the catastrophe: "If the public does not wish to deprive itself of the greatest beauties of our art, it will have to get used to weeping at our ballets." This has not been the case previously, claims the author, "except for our theater and the pantomimes given here by my teacher, the celebrated M. Hilverding."

The ballet comprises three scenes, the first a public street, with the commander's house on the side, the second an interior part of Don Juan's house, where he is giving a ball for his friends and mistresses, the third a crypt with the mausoleum of the commander in the middle, upon which his statue stands. This last detail does not come from Molière's play. It seems rather to be inspired by the beautiful drawing of François Boucher, engraved by L. Cars to illustrate the 1749 edition of Molière's works.[39] Boucher may have caught the visual aspect of a scene from the Parisian Fair theaters or the Théâtre Italien, where Don Juan plays were performed frequently, and whence the artist often got his ideas. The scenario concludes by describing how the Furies and specters come up from the center of the earth to torment Don Juan, who is engulfed by these monsters until at last an earthquake covers the spot with a pile of ruins. There is a more elaborate manuscript scenario in Paris, apparently connected with the original production, in

[37] The entire preface is reproduced in facsimile in Christoph Willibald Gluck, *Sämtliche Werke*, vol. 2, no. 1 (1966).
[38] Anna Laura Bellina, "I gesti parlanti ouvero il 'recitar danzando,' 'Le Festin de pierre,' e 'Sémiramis,'" in *La figura e l'opera di Ranieri de' Calzabigi*, ed. Federico Marri (Florence, 1989), pp. 107–17. The preface to *Sémiramis*, unsigned, is also by Calzabigi.
[39] Reproduced as figure 26 in Daniel Heartz, *Mozart's Operas* (Berkeley, 1990), and as plate 9 in Brown, *Gluck and the French Theatre.*

which this last and most gruesome scene is called No. 4.[40] Carl Zinzendorf's initial reaction to this *ballet de pantomimes,* as he called it, was that the subject was "extremely sad, lugubrious, and frightening."

Who was responsible for selecting the ballet's subject? Maria Theresa, well known for her strict moral code, could scarcely have been pleased with all the amorous dalliance involved, even if followed ultimately by divine retribution. The preface prudently skirts the former and concentrates on the latter. Surely so daring an enterprise as this required the authority of no one less than Durazzo, who took special pride in Viennese ballet. Durazzo boasted in his initial instruction to Favart (20 December 1759) that ballets were better produced in Vienna than in Paris, at least insofar as music and decor were concerned (a remark he was not in a position to make). One pays great attention to the matter of costumes in Vienna, Durazzo continued, and the design of the ballets is by a "bon maître" (Angiolini). "As to the subject, it is ordinarily Count Durazzo who gives or suggests it," said the count, speaking of himself in the third person. Even so, Durazzo allowed that Favart might send him ideas for ballets.

Favart was somewhat nonplussed by the count's instructions. He had been responsible for a famous pantomime ballet, *Les vendanges de tempé* (Foire St. Laurent, 1745), danced to vaudevilles, and so successful it was later revived by Jean-Baptiste de Hesse at the Théâtre Italien as *La vallé de Mont-morency* (1757), two scenes from which inspired paintings by Boucher. But in general in Paris, choreographers, not theater directors, selected the subjects for ballets. In his letter to Durazzo of 24 January 1760, Favart replied with great aplomb: "I do not doubt at all that ballets are perfectly designed and executed at Vienna; but since Noverre, Pitrot, and de Hesse have distinguished themselves in France in this art, which they have raised to the highest degree of perfection, I believe that an adept creator could still enrich himself from their ideas. Therefore I shall send their programs, and generally all the subjects for divertissements that will have had some success." The idea of printing "programs" for ballets appears to have come from Paris.

The preface does not claim any credit for Calzabigi, but having just lived a decade in Paris, the other great capital of ballet, he too may have had a hand in formulating *Don Juan.* The other collaborators are praised by name in the preface.

> The decors of this ballet have been done by Signor Quaglio with great intelligence. Monsieur Gluck composed its music. He seized perfectly the terror ["le terrible"] of the action. He tried to express the passions at work there and the

[40] Robert Haas, "Die Wiener Ballet im 18. Jahrhundert und Gluck's *Don Juan,*" *Studien zur Musikwissenschaft* 10 (1924): 1–36; Haas quotes the Paris scenario (Conservatoire MS 20) in its entirety, pp. 19–25.

dread that reigns in the catastrophe. Music is essential to pantomime. It speaks, we merely gesticulate, similar to the ancient actors of tragedies and comedies who had the verses of the play declaimed, while limiting themselves to gestures. It would be almost impossible to make ourselves understood without music, and the more it is appropriate to what we wish to express, the more we make ourselves intelligible. I shall speak of this later at greater length, on another occasion.

Gaspar Angiolini.

The promise of the last sentence was carried out in the "Dissertation sur les ballets pantomimes des Anciens," which accompanied the program to the ballet *Sémiramis* (1765) by Angiolini and Gluck. The "Dissertation," although unsigned, is also by Calzabigi, who says, moreover, that he helped Angiolini to formulate his *Lettere di G. Angiolini a Monsieur Noverre sopra i balli pantomimi* (Milan, 1773).

Gluck apparently composed *Don Juan* at first as a sequence of fifteen numbers, and these correspond to both the preface and the detailed Paris scenario. At some point Gluck added as many numbers again, mostly in the middle of the ballet, offering the choreographer the possibility of expanding the work if he so chose. The essential drama is complete in the short version.

An opening Sinfonia, *Allegro* in common time and in D major, begins with a fanfare motive deployed in two and a half measures, then repeated in sequence a tone higher over what becomes a dominant chord (the major ninth on an accented part of the beat makes this arpeggio figure sound quite Viennese). When Gluck reused this movement in the ballet music to *Iphigénie en Aulide* (1774), he regularized the components to two measures each. The Sinfonia prepares us well for the spectacle to follow by its tautness and rhythmic force—a relentless pushing forward by means of many upbeat patterns. Moreover, Gluck anticipates the ballet's eerie conclusion by turning early from D major to d minor, an unsettling *piano* commentary on the *forte* triumph of the opening. Trumpets and oboes play nearly all the time, lending a rather strident character to the whole. The stridency is enhanced by contrast with the first danced number, for strings alone, an *Andante grazioso* in D that is quite dainty in comparison, and to the symmetrical eight-measure strains of which "Don Juan and his valet arrive at the head of a band of musicians" (Paris scenario).

The following number, according to the same scenario, is "the serenade played by guitars" to the daughter of the commander, who is called Donna Elvira in the preface. It is one of the most famous and influential pieces in the score, an *Andante* in d minor, 6/8 time, in which the plucked strings of the guitars are simulated by pizzicato strings, the melody in the first violins being doubled by a solo oboe (Example 3.6). Gluck opted for flute instead of

EXAMPLE 3.6. *Gluck,* Don Juan, *Serenade*

the oboe when he reused the piece later in his *Armide* (1777), where it is called "Air sicilien." It is thus a siciliana as well as a serenade, and invites comparison with similar slow dance airs in compound meter by Neapolitan composers such as Leonardo Vinci, or Neapolitan-trained composers such as Giuseppe Bonno. Neapolitan-sixth harmonies are especially characteristic of sicilianas in the minor mode (which they typically were), and Gluck does not stint on this colorful harmonic resource. He deploys it by the third measure, and once again to harmonize the melodic peak, high B♭, in the middle of the second strain. Mozart evidently admired this piece. He placed a very similar siciliana-like piece as the last movement (a theme and variations) of his String Quartet in d (K. 421), with the telling difference that he saved the Neapolitan-sixth harmony until the end of his theme, where it becomes the true climax.

The duel between Don Juan and the commander (No. 5 of the longer version) takes the key back to D major in an *Allegro forte risoluto* for strings, which rush up and down in furious jabbing passages. After a silence there is a diminished chord built up from G♯ in the bass—this corresponds to the wounding of the commander, evidently. (Mozart in *Don Giovanni* copies both the rushing passages and the diminished chord, and they are accompanied by the specification "The Commendatore mortally wounded.") The fight resumes but only briefly before subsiding into an *Andante* in which one diminished chord gives way to another—the commander is dying. An *Allegro* like the beginning finishes the movement in D with a burst of energy as the sliding strings come to a halt—the commander is dead. As pantomime music, this is undoubtedly effective, albeit somewhat bizarre on its own terms without the action on stage. Gluck revised the duel music for use in his *Armide.*

The next scene opens in the house of Don Juan, who is giving a ball (No. 18 of the long version). This part of the ballet perhaps served as the stimulus that led Mozart and Da Ponte to extend Giovanni Bertati's original by adding a ballroom scene in Don Juan's palace to end their Act I. There can be no doubt that Mozart was well acquainted with the score of Gluck's *Don Juan.*

The A-major dance gives way to a Spanish dance in a minor, marked *Moderato* (called "Chaconne Espagnole" in the Paris scenario), that is a model for the fandango ending the third act of *Le nozze di Figaro*. A striking feature of Gluck's Spanish dance is the sustained rising line in long notes played by the second violins. The characteristic play of tonic and dominant, in unrelenting and regular alternation over a few simple rhythms in triple time, is characteristic of much Spanish dance music. Luigi Boccherini, in his Spanish period, made ample use of such traits. It is well to recall that Boccherini visited Vienna three times between 1757 and 1764 and that he too became spellbound with Gluck's *Don Juan*, as is apparent from the use he made of it later. His fascination with Spanish dance may have started in the Burgtheater.

The closest thing in the score to Gluck's recently acquired vaudevillian style is the little plucked *Allegretto* in F for strings (No. 28 of the long version; not present in the shorter version). It is a veritable "Pizzicato Polka," so comical in effect that it must have accompanied the antics of Don Juan's servants. The final phrase of the piece employs the bergamasca progression, as did the zany *philosophe* in *Le monde renversé*. There are many light pieces in the score—too many, in fact, in the long version—but this is the lightest of all. It figures among a complex of pieces, the main key of which is F, taking place just before the scene in the tombs, giving Gluck a smooth, relative major connection with the finale, and making its key of d sound inevitable.

"Finis coronat opus" (The end crowns the work), as the Mozarts, father and son, were fond of saying. In none of Gluck's works is this more true than in *Don Juan*. The Paris scenario describes the tomb scene as "ce lieu, terrible par l'horreur du silence qui y regne." Diderot explored the paradox of painting silence with music in *Le neveu de Rameau*. Gluck achieved that feat here, in the atmospheric *Larghetto* (No. 30 of the long version). Horns sustain against the gently undulating figure in the strings, *piano*, interrupted by a *forte* striding figure in even quarters in m. 4 and subsequently. An elaborate dialogue in pantomime between Don Juan and the statue of the commander is painted in these few measures, with Don Juan steadfastly refusing to repent and change his life. An alto trombone reinforces the *forte* interruptions after the first one. It would have sounded even more ghostly to Gluck's audience, for whom the trombone was a church instrument. (Gluck was the first to bring trombones into the theater.) To increase the tension, the composer introduces the *forte* passages and diminished chords at ever closer time intervals until the quiet passages have been eliminated altogether; the dynamic increases to *fortissimo*, at which point begins the bass line's descent into the finale, the famous Dance of the Furies.

An *Allegro non troppo* in 3/4, the Dance of the Furies will be familiar to some from Gluck's reuse of it in the Parisian version of *Orfeo* (1774). The dance begins *piano* with unison passages, working up by carefully marked dynamic gradation to the first *fortissimo,* when the winds, now including trombone, trumpets and oboes, enter with the first chord. The process begins again, starting in a minor and building up to a *fortissimo* statement of the first idea, but this is no ordinary reprise as in, say, a sonata form; the piece has not even reached the mid-point of its furious journey, comprising 195 measures.

The finale is laid out as a vast and irregular rondo, in which respect it resembles some of the great act-ending chaconnes of Rameau, but how unlike those gracious monuments of courtly etiquette it is in effect! Such a relentlessly grim tone painting has no precedent before Gluck. The dance is totally devoid of frills and ornaments, of anything that would soften the impact. Any sense of coming to a halt or coming to terms with a restful cadence is soon dispelled by the dissonant cries of the winds, hurled like thunderbolts by the Jove-like composer. Even without the stage picture, this piece remains a shattering experience. After its Furies are driven to a final climax, with a prolonged diminished chord (vii^7) lasting from m. 161 to m. 170, there is an awesome silence. Then the violin scales that have been running upward throughout most of the piece all bend downward, elaborating the tonic, which starts dying out, *smorzando,* and is replaced at the end by D major (just as Mozart would later close his equivalent scene in *Don Giovanni*). If the earthquake came at the very end, perhaps it coincided with this last tonal surprise.

Nothing followed this ending during the ballet's first performances; the Dance of the Furies concluded the evening's entertainment in the Burgtheater. A further glimpse of the extravagance this ballet represented (as it might have been viewed, for example, by a Metastasio) can be gained from the list of properties required onstage. Philipp Gumpenhuber specifies two swords, forty-four torches, six pairs of castanets, two lutes, two guitars, two oboes, and a great chain (presumably to make a horrid clanking noise). For this special occasion the orchestra of the French theater was strengthened by the addition of violinists from the German theater, as Gumpenhuber also specifies.

Carl Zinzendorf, we recall, described the subject of Don Juan as "extrêmement triste, lugubre, et effroyable." Yet he found great beauty in the music accompanying the catastrophe:

Le spectre s'en va et tout d'un coup l'enfer paraît, les furies dansant avec les torches allumées et tourmentent Don Juan; dans le fond on voit un beau feux d'artifice, qui représente les feux de l'enfer, on voit voler les Diables, le ballet dure trop longtemps, enfin les diables emportent Don Juan et se précipitent avec lui dans un gouffre de feu. Tout cela était très bien exécuté, la musique fort belle.[41]

Expressing the terrible so that it became a thing of beauty, so that it "gave one a good fright," as Goethe said of the painter Henry Fuseli—these are the artistic aims of a new aesthetic, one that would, some fifteen years later, come to be called *Sturm und Drang.* But who had even described such an aesthetic before 1761?

Diderot, for one, had done so, with such injunctions to artists as "Soyez sombres!" and his famous prescription in *De la Poésie dramatique* (1758), which could serve as an inscription for *Don Juan:* "La poésie veut quelque chose d'énorme, de barbare et de sauvage." Calzabigi was the most direct link between advanced aesthetic thought in Paris and the Viennese stage. His involvement with this pantomime surely went beyond putting the preface into concise, polished French.

Imagine the effect of *Don Juan,* and especially its climactic Dance of the Furies, upon the most talented young composers in Vienna in the early 1760s—Ditters, Steffan, Vanhal, the Haydn brothers, Hofmann, and Boccherini. We shall have occasion to speak of this subject again in connection with the minor-mode compositions by several of these composers of the rising generation. Suffice it to say here that Boccherini was so impressed that he made the Dance of the Furies into the finale of his d-minor symphony known as *La casa del diavolo* (Op. 12 No. 4, 1771). Let there be no doubt that musical *Sturm und Drang,* if we must use this term, began with Gluck.

Orfeo ed Euridice (1762)

T H E Orpheus legend was a favorite at the Habsburg court for celebrating festive occasions. An *Orfeo ed Euridice,* a *festa teatrale,* written by Pietro Pariati and composed by Fux celebrated the birthday of Emperor Charles VI in 1715 and was revived for the same purpose in 1728. We have observed how Wagenseil contributed a name day cantata, *I lamenti d'Orfeo,* in 1740, and how he organized a pasticcio opera, *Euridice,* for the same occasion in 1750.

[41] (The specter departs and suddenly the infernal region appears, the furies dance with illuminated torches and torment Don Juan; in the background one sees a fine fireworks display, which represents the fires of the inferno, and sees the devils; the ballet lasts too long, until the devils finally carry Don Juan away and throw him in a pit of fire. All this was very well executed, and the music very beautiful.)

Starzer wrote an Orpheus ballet that was performed in 1755. Then at the ninth Lenten academy in the Burgtheater, on 18 March 1762, Giuseppe Scarlatti's grand cantata *I lamenti d'Orfeo* was sung by two soloists and chorus, honoring the parturition of Princess Isabella. This last instance may well have given Calzabigi and Gluck the idea of writing their *Orfeo ed Euridice* to celebrate the name day of Emperor Francis later the same year.

Along with the Orphic cantata in the spring of 1762 came an opera, *Arianna*, a pasticcio put together by Giannambroglio Migliavacca and Gluck and first brought to the stage of the Burgtheater on 27 May 1762. The conjunction of Orpheus and Ariadne is intriguing. Was Durazzo or someone else familiar with Italian literature looking back to the very first operas of all, around 1600? Ottavio Rinuccini was far from forgotten during the eighteenth century; in fact, he was being paid more and more attention. Luigi Riccoboni recommended his *Euridice* and *Arianna* as model dramas in *Réflexions sur les différentes Théâtres d'Europe* (Paris, 1738). Closer to Calzabigi and Gluck still, Francesco Algarotti in his influential *Saggio sopra l'opera in musica* of 1755 paid honor to "the eldest musical dramas"—Rinuccini's *Dafne*, *Arianna*, and *Euridice*.[42] Esteban Arteaga would later praise Rinuccini's *Euridice* as the best opera poem written before Metastasio.

The moment was at hand to reinvent ancient Greek drama once again by means of the Orpheus myth. But how did it come about this time? From the musical point of view, a new Orpheus opera became possible only when the perfect singer for the main role emerged. He was Gaetano Guadagni, who came to Vienna in late 1761 or early 1762 at the peak of his long career as a contralto castrato. On 27 April 1762 he appeared in the Burgtheater as Orazio, one of the principal roles in *Il trionfo di Clelia*, a new serious opera by Hasse and Metastasio that constituted the main entertainment celebrating the royal birth. Marianna Bianchi, soprano, and Giuseppe Tibaldi, tenor, were the other main singers. All three sang in the pasticcio *Arianna*, which followed.

Much later, Calzabigi claimed all the credit for creating *Orfeo ed Euridice*. He does deserve much credit, but not our complete credence, as we shall see. Calzabigi had left Paris for Brussels in 1760, probably in ill repute, as would be the case with his departure from Vienna in 1773. In Brussels he got into the good graces of the Austrian vice-regent, Count Philipp Cobenzl, and a year later wound up in Vienna as privy councillor to the Austrian Netherlands in the finance office, which was run by the all-powerful chancellor of state, Prince Kaunitz. For the moment secure, and with influential friends in high places, he could renew his quest for literary fame. Keenly

[42] Oliver Strunk, *Source Readings in Music History* (New York, 1950), p. 658.

aware of everything to do with opera, old and new, French and Italian, Calzabigi was eager to make a name for himself in Italian letters as a librettist, which he had already tried to do in Naples. Highly ambitious, he wanted to see his name inscribed in opera history along with the Rinuccinis, the Cicogninis, and the Zenos. Most of all, he wanted to be as celebrated as Metastasio.

Returned to Italy, Calzabigi sent Gluck two librettos in 1778, an *Ipermestra* and a *Semiramide* (which is lost).[43] Gluck showed some interest in the first and had it restructured for Paris. Without informing Calzabigi, he eventually turned it over to Salieri, and the resulting work reached the Paris Opéra as *Les Danaïdes* in 1784. Understandably annoyed, Calzabigi sent an embittered letter to the *Mercure de France* the same year claiming that he was the instigator of the operatic reform in Vienna:

> I arrived in Vienna in 1761, full of these ideas [for a new kind of opera based on declamation]. A year later, Count Durazzo . . . to whom I had recited my poem *Orpheus*, persuaded me to have it performed in the theatre. I agreed on condition that the music should be written according to my ideas. He sent me M. Gluck, who, he said, would suit my taste. At this time, M. Gluck was not held to be one of our finest composers—no doubt this was an erroneous judgement. Hasse, Buranello, Jommelli, Peres and others were at the top of the tree. None of them understood what I meant by "declamatory music."[44]

Here speaks not candor, but rancor. Gluck was a very celebrated maestro long before 1762. It was as "il famoso Kluk" that he was invited to write his *Clemenza di Tito* for the San Carlo in Naples in 1752, as we saw above. Gluck's successes in Italy were many, and he was knighted by the pope in 1757. It is likely that the first part of Calzabigi's claim, that he brought a ready-made *Orfeo* to Durazzo, who then assigned Gluck to compose it, is a fabrication. The statement continues:

> And as for M. Gluck, who did not pronounce our language very well, it would have been impossible for him to declaim even a few lines as they should be spoken. I read him my poem *Orpheus*, and by reading and rereading several passages to him, I was able to show him the nuances I put into my expression, the pauses, the slowness, the quickness, the intonation, now stressed, now level and glossed over, which I desired him to incorporate in his setting.

[43] Bruno Brizi, "Uno spunto polemico Calzabigiano: 'Ipermestra, o Le Danaide,'" in *La figura e l'opera de Ranieri de' Calzabigi*, ed. Federico Marri (Florence, 1989), pp. 119–45.
[44] Cited after Patricia Howard, *C. W. von Gluck: Orfeo* (Cambridge Opera Handbooks) (Cambridge, 1981), pp. 24–25.

How Gluck pronounced Italian is quite beside the point (but a typical thing for a native speaker to complain of in a non-native). The point is that Gluck had been setting Italian texts to music with success for over twenty years before Calzabigi crossed his path. That Gluck took licenses with accepted norms of Italian text-setting, so much so as to upset Metastasio, we have already seen. But it is preposterous to claim that anyone had to teach the mature Gluck how to set *poesia per musica.*

What happened in Vienna in 1762, I propose, was the following. The elements that enabled Gluck and Calzabigi to create a truly epochal reform opera were all in place then. Of roughly equal importance were the building blocks supplied by Gluck's opéras-comiques and pantomime ballet, and Traetta's *Armida,* which showed the way in linking stage action, including chorus and ballet, to an essentially singing-oriented Italian opera. The catalyst was Guadagni, who was not only a great singer but a fine actor, a pupil of David Garrick's school of natural acting.[45] *Orfeo ed Euridice* is a show created around his great gifts; in contrast, poor Euridice (Marianna Bianchi) had to be content with a single aria in the third act. (History repeated itself a century later when Berlioz recreated the same opera around the extraordinary talents of Pauline Viardot-Garcia.) Calzabigi's experience, especially his decade in Paris, made him an ideal collaborator for Gluck, and there is no denying that, steeped as he was in both the French and Italian operatic traditions, he was in a unique position to effect a new union of the best from both. His contribution was central but not quite the *sine qua non* he made it out to be. Gluck would later show that he could create operas of the same kind without Calzabigi.

We first hear of the new work from the diaries of Carl Zinzendorf in the summer of 1762. On 8 July he was at a dinner given by Calzabigi at his residence in the Kohlmarkt, along with Durazzo, Guadagni, and Gluck; the company was regaled with the central scene, where Orpheus tries to sway the Furies, Guadagni singing his role to the keyboard accompaniment of Gluck, who rendered the part of the Furies. A month later Zinzendorf reported another dinner party at which Guadagni sang arias from the opera to Gluck's accompaniment.[46] After a long and intensive period of rehearsal, the opera was first performed on 5 October, one day late but in celebration of St. Francis, and hence his namesake, the emperor.

[45] Daniel Heartz, "From Garrick to Gluck: The Reform of Theatre and Opera in the Mid-Eighteenth Century," *Proceedings of the Royal Musical Association* 94 (1967–68): 11–27.

[46] Maria Christine Breunlich, "Gluck in den Tagebüchern des Grafen Karl von Zinzendorf," *Gluck in Wien, Gluck-Studien* 1 (1989): 62–68; 63. Howard, *Gluck: Orfeo,* p. 38, misreads these dinnertime excerpts as full performances, leading her to suggest that the opera was completed much earlier than it in fact was.

Durazzo told Jean-Benjamin La Borde that *Armida* was the first to put music in the service of the eyes as well as the ears, as we saw above. But *Orfeo* goes much further than *Armida* along these lines. It is organized on a thoroughly scenic principle, being composed of several *grands tableaux*. Tableaux are more than mere decors, because they enter in a formative sense into the music, singing, dancing, and everything else that produces the total effect. In demonstration of this, let us consider how words, music, action and stage picture are coordinated in Act I.

The printed libretto for the first production specifies for the opening act "an agreeable but solitary wood of laurels and cypresses that thin out, enclosing a little plain with the sepulchre of Euridice."[47] A famous Italian scenographer, Fabrizio Galliari, interpreted these directions in a drawing made for a subsequent production (Parma, 1769) under Gluck's direction (Figure 3.5). The inscription, presumably in Galliari's hand, follows the wording of the original printed score, only abbreviated: "Ameno Boschetto di allori e cypressi che ad arte diridato racchiude il Sepulcro d'Euridice. l. Orfeo." The four cypresses behind the tomb are shown planted farther apart than the four on either side, obeying the direction "ad arte diridato" (thinning out). Visually, the tall cypress trees guard the tomb like so many mourners. Their symmetry of 4 + 4 + 4 contrasts with the long row of laurel trees receding into the distance from the right side, so as to establish a spacious perspective. A sense of quiet orderliness pervades this scene and invades our senses even before the music and the stage movement have had a chance to work their magic.

Under the rubric "Primo Ballo," the original libretto describes what must happen onstage: "The funereal rites celebrated *by the ancients* around the tomb of the dead are represented in this ballet" (my italics). Once again, as in the preface accompanying *Don Juan*, Angiolini and Calzabigi lay claim to reviving antiquity through their pantomimes. The description continues, making clear what was required of the dancers and choral singers: "The rites consist of sacrifices, incensing, distributing flowers, draping the tomb with garlands, pouring milk and wine on it, and dancing around it with gestures of grief, while singing the praises of the departed." This vision was perhaps communicated to Gluck by poet and choreographer before he began composing the chorus of mourning in c minor. Its soft and pathetic strains should sound immediately after the fading echo of the C-major brilliance

[47] "Ameno, ma solitario boschetto di allori a di cypressi, che ad arte diridato racchiude in un piccolo plano il sepolcro d'Euridice." The directions are quoted from the critical edition of the Viennese original version of 1762, *Orfeo ed Euridice*, ed. Anna Amalie Abert and Ludwig Finscher (Kassel, 1963) (Gluck, *Sämtliche Werke*, vol. 1, no. 1). The reader is cautioned that the discussion here applies specifically to the original version of 1762, not to subsequent versions made by Gluck and others.

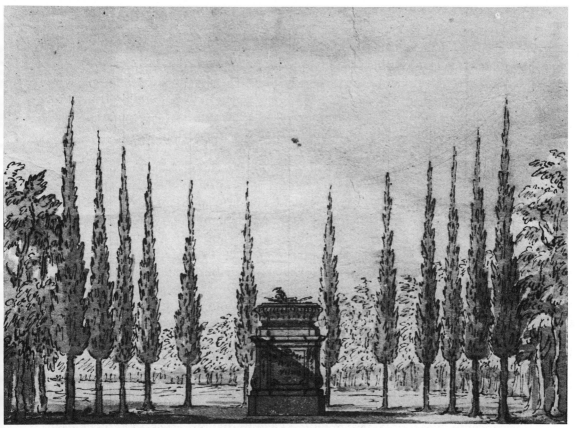

FIGURE 3.5. Fabrizio Galliari. Stage design for Act I of Gluck's *Orfeo ed Euridice*, Parma, 1769. (Museo Civico di Torino)

projected by the *Overtura*, which is nothing other than a foil to enhance the lugubrious *tombeau* by means of contrast.

The libretto goes into further detail in describing the opening *Coro*, some of it duplicating what we have just read: "At the raising of the curtain is heard the sound of a mournful instrumental ritornello ["mesta sinfonia"]." This ritornello is made all the more solemn by the use of instruments more commonly heard in church—three trombones and a cornetto (plus the usual strings). "The stage is occupied by nymphs and shepherds, followers of Orfeo, who carry chains of flowers and garlands of myrtle; some burn incense, others bedeck the marble tomb and strew flowers around it, while singing the following chorus, which is interrupted by the laments of Orfeo, stretched out on a rock in the foreground, and passionately repeating from time to time the name of Euridice." For the lead role to assume a prone position at the beginning of the opera was certainly a novelty, and must have seemed scandalous to many at the time.

Orfeo's passionate invocations of the name of his lost love (and nothing more) create an astonishing effect. Whose idea was this? It could have been that of the poet, or the composer, or indeed Guadagni/Orfeo himself, who was described by Charles Burney in his *History* in these terms: "The Music he sung was the most simple imaginable; a few notes with frequent pauses, and opportunities of being liberated from the composer and the band, were all he wanted." However the creators of the works arrived at such a novel way of introducing the voice of Orfeo, it is evident that this danced and pantomimed chorus, with solo interjections, around the tomb of Euridice called for a collaborative effort by all involved, to an extent never before seen and heard in Italian opera (unless at its very beginnings). Here is a definition of the reform that is as good as any.

The entirety of Act I is laid out on a plan, as shown in Table 3.1, that deploys recurring sections of music or recurring tonalities in a symmetry comparable to Galliari's cypress trees. Following the opening chorus in c, an orchestrally accompanied recitative for Orfeo and *Ballo* in the relative major, Eb, lead to a repetition of the opening chorus, this time ending in C so as to prepare for the Air in F, *Andante non presto*, in 3/8, sung by Orfeo to words beginning "Chiamo il mio ben così" (Thus do I call my love). The air has three slightly different strophes, interspersed with obbligato recitatives. At its conclusion Orfeo bursts into the key of D, which will return after lengthy modulations to lead into the Air for Amore in G, and return once again to conclude the act on a fiery note, *Presto*, with rushing scales and arpeggios in the strings, signaling Orfeo's heroic determination to brave the underworld and rescue Euridice.

TABLE 3.1 *ORFEO ED EURIDICE*, Act I (sung set pieces are in **boldface**)

Coro	Recit.	*Ballo*	**Coro**	**Air**	Recit.	**Air**	Recit.	**Air**	Recit.	**Air**	Recit.	Prest
c		Eb	c–C	F	f–C	F	db–F	F	D–a–D	G	G	D

Orfeo's "Chiamo il mio ben" in Act I is in fact a Romance. This genre of simply declaimed, unadorned strophic song had grown into one of the characteristic features of opéra-comique, beginning with Rousseau's *Devin du village* (1752) and reaching a first peak in Pierre-Alexandre Monsigny's setting of Sedaine's *On ne s'avise jamais de tout* (1759).[48] Monsigny's opera was produced in the Burgtheater to great acclaim in August 1762, just three

[48] Daniel Heartz, "The Beginning of the Operatic Romance: Rousseau, Sedaine, and Monsigny," *Eighteenth-Century Studies* 15 (1981–82): 149–78.

months before *Orfeo ed Euridice*. Gluck does not call "Chiamo il mio ben" a Romance, giving it only a tempo marking in Italian; similarly, in the opera's concluding ballet, he avoids the proper French labels for what are obviously a menuet, a *contredanse en rondeau*, a musette, and a chaconne, possibly at Angiolini's request. (Calzabigi in particular wished to distance himself from the French tradition. In his subsequent writings, he made it clear that it was Italian opera he was bent on reforming. He professed scorn for some features of French opera.) When François-André Philidor purloined "Chiamo il mio ben" from Gluck's score (without the recitative interjections) and used the music in *Le sorcier* (1764), he called it what it is, a Romance; in discussing this plagiarism much later, Berlioz referred to "la Romance de Gluck."[49] Amore's air in alternating slow and fast sections is also indebted to opéra-comique, and its like can be found in Gluck's own French operas for Vienna, as can parallels with "Che farò senza Euridice."[50]

In his correspondence with Charles-Simon Favart about the frontispiece for the printed score of *Orfeo*, being printed in Paris in 1763–64, Durazzo referred to the confrontation between Orfeo and the Furies as "the main locus of the drama" ("l'endroit principal de l'action"), and it was his first choice for pictorial illustration.[51] The final choice eventually fell on the scene at the end of Act II when Orfeo leads Euridice out of the other world while trying not to look at her, as he was commanded by Amore. Lacking what would have been a capital piece of visual documentation for Orfeo's great scene with the Furies, or any scenographic material at all from the first production, we have to turn elsewhere for help.

In overall scenic terms, the progression from *pompe funèbre* to the gates of hell and then to Elysium and its blessed spirits in *Orfeo ed Euridice* paralleled the sequential core of one of the greatest of all *tragédies lyriques*, Rameau's *Castor et Pollux* (see Table 3.2). This masterpiece of the Opéra's repertory was originally staged in 1737, and revived in considerably revised

TABLE 3.2 RAMEAU AND GLUCK

	Tombeau; *pompe funèbre*	Entrance to Hades; dances of the Furies	Elysium; dances of the Blessed Spirits
Castor, 1737	Act I	Act III	Act IV
Castor, 1754	Act II	Act IV, part 1	Act IV, part 2
Orfeo, 1762	Act I	Act II, part 1	Act II, part 2

[49] Bruce Alan Brown, "Durazzo, Duni, and the Frontispiece to *Orfeo ed Euridice*," *Studies in Eighteenth-Century Culture* 19 (1989): 71–97; 95, n. 41.
[50] Brown, *Gluck and the French Theatre*, p. 258.
[51] Brown, "Durazzo, Duni," p. 75.

form in 1754, during Calzabigi's sojourn in Paris. The revision got rid of the Prologue and combined the Hades/Elysium sequence in a single act, as in *Orfeo ed Euridice*, prompting a critic in the *Mercure de France* to praise what he called "a fortunate antithesis or contrast" ("une opposition heureuse").

When Gluck adapted his opera for Paris in 1774, the parallels with *Castor* did not go unnoticed. Another critic writing in the *Mercure de France* made this assessment: "The funeral scene, the depiction of hell and the Elysian fields recall—but in no way surpass—the same tableaux similarly executed in Rameau's opera, *Castor*. We believe the French composer's music to be more deeply felt, more suitable and, as it were, more apt for the localities than that of M. le chevalier Gluck."[52]

As we have seen, in a collaboration between Carlo Innocenzo Frugoni and Tommaso Traetta in Parma, Rameau's first two *tragédies lyriques* were turned into Italian operas, *Ippolito ed Aricia* (1759) and *I Tindaridi* (1760) (i.e., the two sons of Leda, Castor by Tindareus and Pollux by Zeus, hence Pollux's immortality). These two "heavenly twins," or *dioscuri*, have stolen the daughters of Leukippo, Telaira and Phoebe, in revenge for which Castor is killed. Phoebe calls for the demons to come out and bar his way to Hades, but Pollux penetrates the horrid cavern, lit by sulphurous flames, and rejoins his brother in Elysium.

From the Parma opera of 1760 there is likewise no surviving scenography, and Paris provides little help, with the exception of an anonymous painting of the tale on the inside of a harpsichord lid, an instrument once owned by the French keyboard composer Claude-Bénigne Balbastre.[53] (See Plate IV.) Burney visited Balbastre in Paris in 1770 and described the instrument in question:

> A fine Rucker harpsichord which he had had painted inside and out with as much delicacy as the finest coach or snuff-box I ever saw at Paris . . . On the outside is the birth of Venus; and on the inside of the cover the story of Rameau's most famous opera, *Castor et Pollux*; earth, hell and elysium are there represented; in elysium, sitting on a bank, with a lyre in his hand is that celebrated composer himself.

On the left we see a furious Phoebe and a demon with torches in a cavernous waste above the river Cocythus. A reddish glow pervades this eerie scene, making for its "opposition heureuse" with the cool blues and greens of Elysium, where Castor and Pollux stand together. Graceful couples lounge on

[52] Cited after Howard, *Gluck: Orfeo*, p. 73.
[53] Lawrence Libin, "A Rediscovered Portrayal of Rameau and *Castor et Pollux*," *Early Music* 2 (1983): 510–13.

the grass or dance, the whole blissful scene surveyed with great serenity by the seated Rameau at right.

The artist invoked by this *fête galante* is of course Antoine Watteau, who painted many such scenes and invented, or at least defined for all time, how Elysium should look. Albert Giraud put this superbly in two unforgettable lines of his *Pierrot Lunaire: Rondes bergamasques* (1884):

> Je revois les bleus Élysées
> Où Watteau s'est éternisé.

We have in fact two pictorial traditions involved here, one derived from Watteau's visions of Elysium and one depicting the horrors of hell that goes back all the way to the medieval mystery plays, whose creators particularly enjoyed frightening spectators with demons and monsters.

The 1764 printed score of *Orfeo* describes the setting for the first part of Act II as a "horrid and cavernous place beyond the river Cocythus, obfuscated with dark smoke illuminated by flames, which fill the entire horrible abode." By contrast, the tableau for the second part of Act II is described as a "delightful place with verdant bushes and flowers that cover the meadows, and shady nooks, plus rivers and streams that bathe them."[54] Quaglio's realization of Elysium in 1762 came in for negative comments because his foliage was not so much vernal as it was autumnal ("feuilles mortes" was the dominant impression made by his colors, according to his critics). Keep in mind the central opposition of these two tableaux as we examine next what poet and composer did to enhance them.

Calzabigi turned to one of the oldest traditions in Italian operatic verse for the Furies, and produced diction of surpassing beauty and clarity for the pleas of Orfeo. For scenes invoking Furies or specters, Italian poets had for generations used the short line of five or six syllables ending with a final dactyl, known as *quinari sdruccioli*. Here is an example from the libretto of *Giasone* by Giacinto Andrea Cicognini, set to music by Francesco Cavalli and played in Venice in 1649.[55] Medea is the singer, and she asks the infernal spirits to open the way to hell for her.

| Dell'antro magico | From the magic cave |
| Stridenti cardini | May the creaking hinges |

---

[54] The plates on opera machinery in Diderot's *Encyclopédie* show how water effects were achieved onstage at the time. See Walter E. Rex, "A Propos of the Figure of Music in the Frontispiece of the *Encyclopédie*," *Report of the Twelfth Congress Berkeley, 1977* (Kassel, 1981), p. 221. One of Watteau's paintings is even called *Les Champs Elysées* (located in the Wallace Collection, London).

[55] For the music, see Arnold Schering, *Geschichte der Musik in Beispielen* (Leipzig, 1931), no. 201.

Il varco apritemi,	Open the way to me
E frà le tenebre	And there in the darkness
Del negro ospizio	Of the black place
Lassate me!	Leave me!
Sù l'ara orribile	On the horrid altar
Del lago Stigio	Of the Stygian lake
I fochi splendino,	The flames glitter
E in sù ne mandino	And dissolve
Fumiche turbino	In smoky whirls
La luce al sol.	The sun's light.

Calzabigi follows the tradition and has his Furies declaim only in this hypnotically obsessive rhythm.

Chi mai dell'Erebo	Who dares through Erebus
Fra le caligini	Among the darknesses
Sull' orme d'Ercole	On traces of Hercules
E di Piritoo	And of Pirithoüs
Conduce il piè?	Direct his steps?

Cicognini puts "creaking hinges" on the gates to hell; Calzabigi follows suit. His Furies finally allow Orfeo passage, singing:

Le porte stridano	Let the gates creak
Su' neri cardini	Open on their black hinges
E il passo lascino	And allow passage
Sicuro e libero	Safe and free
Al vincitor!	To the victor!

Gluck had but to follow the rhythms mandated by the poetry in this case, and as a native Czech, he must have delved into all the beginning-accented verses with particular relish.[56] No one needed to tell him how to set *quinari sdruccioli*.

Calzabigi gives rhythmic flexibility and variety to Orfeo in his pleas, as opposed to the motoric sameness of the Furies. The lines are mostly of the seven-syllable variety (*settenario*), one commonly used in operatic poetry. Orfeo begins his pleading with rather general language:

---

[56] Czech is a beginning-accented language. John Tyrrel, *Czech Opera* (Cambridge, 1988), p. 260, explains: "Trochees and dactyls when set 'as they come' lead naturally to music with downbeat beginnings and (except with incomplete feet) upbeat endings. They form an exact parallel to the Czech language with its first-syllable stress and weak word-endings."

Deh! placatevi con me.	Ah! take pity on me.
Furie, larve, ombre sdegnose!	Furies, phantoms, scornful shades!
Vi renda almen pietoso	At least be merciful
Il mio barbaro dolor.	To my bitter grief.

For his second quatrain Orfeo works on the sympathy of his adversaries by comparing his lot with theirs:

Mille pene, ombre moleste,	A thousand pains, troubled shades,
Come voi sopporto anch'io!	Like you I too suffer!
Ho con me l'inferno mio,	I have my own inferno
Me lo sento in mezzo al cor.	Raging in my heart.

At his third intervention, with the Furies noticeably weakening in their opposition after his second, Orfeo pulls out all the stops, as it were, as Calzabigi turns his affective language up a notch:

Men tiranne, ah! voi sareste	Less disdaining, ah! would you be
Al mio pianto, al mio lamento,	Of my tears, and my laments,
Se provaste un sol momento	If you felt for a single moment
Cosa sia languir d'amor!	What it is to languish for love!

The last two lines in particular hint at a source by means of which Calzabigi schooled himself in such mellifluous sounds and amorous conceits. In this genre no one excelled Metastasio. One of the earliest critics of the libretto, Lablet de Morambert, wrote in an essay accompanying his translation of it into French (1764) that "M. Calsabigi marche, avec succès, dans la carrière du célèbre Métastasio."[57]

   Gluck and Angiolini had plenty to do at the beginning of Act II before even arriving at Calzabigi's text. An orchestral *Ballo* in E♭, marked *Maestoso*, modulating to V of c for the first sounding of Orfeo's lyre, was mimed throughout. The unison E♭s at the opening of the *Maestoso* connect as a kind of deceptive cadence to the strident key of D at the end of Act I. The chromatic motion upward continues, as Gluck moves the bass E♭ E♮ F F♯ G under alternating common chords and diminished sevenths. Once reached, the G becomes a pedal under a heart-wrenching descent of the upper voices, which are peppered with dissonance via suspensions, then alternating *fortes* and *pianos* as the bass supports several secondary dominants and their reso-

[57] Daniel Heartz, "*Orfeo ed Euridice*: Some Criticisms, Revisions, and Stage-Realizations during Gluck's Lifetime," *Chigiana* 29–30 (1975): 383–94; 389. The disgraceful number of typographical errors in this article bears witness to the fact that the author was never given a chance to correct proofs.

lutions: G A♭, F♯ G, E♮ F, D E♭, then down by step to B♮—the crucial tone in the whole scene-complex as it turns out.[58] A harp playing arpeggios represents Orfeo and his lyre, who makes his first appearance here, as the stage direction makes clear: "Scarcely has the curtain gone up when a horrid ritornello ["orribile Sinfonia"] begins the pantomime-dance of the Furies and specters, interrupted by the harmonies of Orfeo's lyre; Orfeo's appearance onstage unleashes the entire infernal crowd to sing the following."

The four-part chorus sings "Chi mai dell'Erebo . . ." in unison with the orchestral basses and oboes, while the higher strings provide a shuddering harmonization in sextuplets. Gluck marks the score *Andante un poco* and *Marcato*. The oboes break loose from the unisons in order to reinforce B♮, intoned as the top note of the upper strings' double-stopped G chord. A rest with fermata extends this open ending. Resolution arrives with the *Presto Ballo* in c for the Furies. It too ends up in the air, this time with an uneasy leap down to B♮ in the basses and cellos. The rushing scales sound familiar, because they are very like those at the end of Act I as Orfeo resolved to brave the inferno, as if he had an inkling of what awaited him in hell.

The Furies repeat their initial chorus and extend it by their first singing in parts. The chorus is further extended by the barking of Cerberus, imitated by five note slides in the unison strings. The chorus stops on an unresolved diminished chord built over B♮ in the bass. There is no proper resolution, only the uncanny E♭ unisons in the orchestra signaling a repeat of the opening *Ballo Maestoso*, ending on V as before. Once again the lyre-harp sounds its triplets, but this time the progression in the bass fills in the jagged diminished fourth, rising by step: B♮ C D E♭. Orfeo sings his first "Deh placatevi" at the arrival of the E♭ chord. The Furies hurl their resounding "Nò!" at him several times, first on tonic E♭ unisons, then, after modulation to V, on B♮, always reinforced by the sepulchral trombones and cornetto. The master stroke is the return to E♭, begun by the C♭ inflection in Orfeo's melody, which is then echoed by the uncanny shouts of "Nò!" on B♮. Or is it really C♭, as the basses of Orchestra I spell it (Example 3.7)? The force of this ambiguous B♮ / C♭ lies precisely in its uncertainty.[59] It is Gluck's way of painting the gruesome tableau in tones, along with all the jagged and open endings of the sections, generating an anxiety close to fear. Closed endings and recurring sections suited the air of quiet grieving in Act I, in keeping

[58] Philidor was so struck by this miraculous modulatory passage that he appropriated it in his *Tom Jones* (1765). He made further use of the *Orfeo* score in his *Ernelinde* (1767).

[59] Jean-Jacques Rousseau explains this at length in eighteenth-century terms in an essay on *Orfeo* printed posthumously in G. M. Leblond, ed., *Mémoires pour servir à l'histoire de la révolution operée dans la musique par M. Le Chevalier Gluck* (Paris, 1781; reprint 1967), pp. 21–27. Rousseau quotes the text in the original Italian, not in French, meaning that he probably used the first edition.

EXAMPLE 3.7. *Gluck,* Orfeo ed Euridice, *Act II, scene 1*

with the scenery and human movement. But the horrid scenery on the banks of the Cocythus needed a totally different kind of movement, and Gluck's language of tonal dissonance and irresolution could not be more in keeping with such a vivid scene of horror.

The enharmonic equivalence of B♮ and C♭, so unsettling in the context in which it sounds, enables Gluck to epitomize the struggle going on between Orfeo and the furies. B♮ is the leading tone to the c minor that belongs to the Furies. C♭ is the sixth above E♭ and resolves down to the dominant, B♭, preparing a return to E♭, the key that Orfeo initiates and attempts to sustain and impose. This round goes to Orfeo with the authentic cadence (the first one with any weight in the act!) on E♭ in m. 152. The Furies immediately turn this goal into e♭ minor, singing softly in parts now, at least at first, before they regain some of their old fire. Dislodged from c, they settle for a cadence in f. Orfeo accepts f and begins his second quatrain there; then he moves the music back to c, in apparent expression of the textual idea of being like the Furies in his suffering. The Furies resume in f, ending on its dominant, which Orfeo resolves by initiating his third and final strophe. Like text, like music—Gluck too pulls out all the stops. Especially poignant are the overlapping groups of three quarter notes between the voice and the strings, like groans, and the Neapolitan sixth, with fermata, for "cosa sia languir d'amor."

A diagram of the infernal scene such as was offered in Table 3.1 must necessarily be more complex, as is the scene itself. Table 3.3 shows as simply as possible how Gluck used open endings to hurry the drama along. Note that this begins to change midway through the scene at "Orfeo 1," a turning point where some of the enormous tension that has been built up begins to be released.

TABLE 3.3 *ORFEO ED EURIDICE*: Act II up to "Che puro ciel"

SCENE 1

Ballo Maestoso	Lyre + **Coro** Andante	Ballo Presto	**Coro** extended	Ballo Maestoso	Lyre + Orfeo 1 + Coro
4/4	4/4	3/4	3/4	4/4	4/4
E♭——V^6/c	c——V^3_4	c——V	c——vii^7	E♭——V/c	E♭——E♭

					SCENE 2
Coro	Orfeo 2	**Coro**	Orfeo 3	**Coro**	Ballo
3/4	4/4	3/4	4/4	3/4	3/4 [Menuet]
e♭——f	f——c	f——V/	V/c——f	f——f	F

Gluck's genial discovery of musical means to characterize the turmoil and struggle of the drama represents a great breakthrough, comparable to but on a grander scale still than the Dance of the Furies that ends *Don Juan* of a year earlier. Another way that tension is accumulated and released in this infernal scene has to do with the shattering, ambiguous B♮ / C♭, first sounded as the Furies shout their refusal repeatedly in "Orfeo 1." By the time the Furies, after a series of graduated responses, finally grant passage

("Let the gates creak open"), that unholy tone is still like a gaping wound in the tonal fabric. Gluck closes it in the final *Allegro* by insisting on its resolution, upward and downward. Resolution down to B♭ comes in the basses and then in the sopranos and altos; resolution up to C comes first in the sopranos and altos and then in the basses. Invertible counterpoint allows these lines, plunging or ascending an octave, to be switched between treble and bass. (Beethoven does something similar in the coda to the *Marcia funebre sulla morte d'un Eroe* in his Piano Sonata Op. 26.) After the final *diminuendo* from *piano* to *pianissimo* sets in, and the f-minor key is confirmed by both its dominant and its subdominant, the voice parts drop out one by one as the Furies leave the stage, the basses being the last to go. Calzabigi specified in his stage direction: "The Furies and monsters begin to retreat, dispersing behind the scene while repeating the last verse of the chorus, which continues until they have all left, finishing at last in a confused murmur. With the disappearance of the Furies, and the monsters removed, Orfeo enters the underworld."

The true goal of this vast and seamless continuum, Orfeo's goal, that is, arrives in what follows the last minor chord. F major pours forth like a vernal breath, its pastoral simplicity reinforced by two flutes, to an ever-so-gentle minuet rhythm. Instead of Furies, we see the blessed spirits dancing. The scenic change to Elysium must be instantaneous and exactly cued to the arrival of the major mode, as was easily done with the sliding sets of eighteenth-century scenography. This moment is one of the greatest in all opera—and by opera is meant not just music, but total theater. Unfortunately for Gluck, the editors of the 1963 critical edition were not thinking of total theater when they anticipated the arrival of F major by proposing a *tierce de Picardie* in the final minor chord, an anticipation that would ruin the intended effect. Eye and ear alike must be astonished with delight and surprise, at the same instant. To do otherwise is to negate Gluck's newly found way of composing scenically. This may seem like a small point, but it is not. The integration of all the elements in music drama on a new and higher plane constitutes the essence of the operatic reform. The *arioso* that comes next verifies this point once again.

"Che puro ciel" took wing from a melody in Gluck's earlier Italian operas (see Example 3.1). But nowhere before had the composer created such a vast tone poem as this painting of the atmosphere in Elysium. Calzabigi obliged by elaborating on his scenic directions, giving Gluck not only "pure sky" to work with but a whole catalogue of natural beauties: clear sun, new and serene light, sweet warblings of the birds, coursing brooks, and murmuring breezes. Gluck's stratified orchestral accompaniment supports the noble song of the solo oboe and anticipates these words before they are sung.

For those are surely birdsongs imitated by the twitterings of the solo flute, accompanied by a solo cello and the melodic turns in the second violins, and that is surely a brook being depicted by the flowing sextuplets in the first violins.

The play of light and shade is at its most intense when the solo oboe reaches its melodic peak of high C. At this moment the solo bassoon, high in its range, having entered on the E♮ above middle C, slips down a half tone to E♭, bringing a tinge of sadness and regret to all this natural beauty, also anticipating the text: Orfeo is struck by the wonder of it all, but saddened because he does not see Euridice. Note that the solo bassoon here provides the most sustained sound of all, because the string basses and cellos (other than the solo cello), sharing the same line as the bassoon, play pizzicato. The violas play mostly thirds *divisi*. The whole tableau becomes a permanently valuable lesson in orchestration, and as such it was praised by Berlioz.

If "Che puro ciel" is considered to be "only" an obbligato recitative, it must still be admired as the longest and most elaborate species of its kind up to this date. What the oboe sings certainly deserves to be considered an *arioso*, and so does much of what Orfeo sings, because it has the sustained melodiousness characteristic of his part throughout the opera. But sometimes he slips into the rapid repeated tones of recitative, and the whole rarified vision ends abruptly with a recitative cadence when the chorus announces the arrival of Euridice. She does not become visible to Orfeo so soon as this, because a chorus and ballet intervene, after which he still asks for his beloved. Only then are the two brought together. Thus ends "the most moving act in all opera."[60]

Act III begins as Orfeo seeks to lead Euridice back to the mortal world without looking at her, following the command of Amore. Euridice becomes increasingly disturbed at what she interprets as a rebuff, and Orfeo accordingly becomes more distraught. The rising arpeggio figure in dotted rhythm that begins their duet "Vieni" (*Andante* in G, in cut time) also provides Gluck with the main idea of the opera's final number, "Trionfi Amore," played at first as a ritornello by the orchestra and then sung after the ballet, in the triumphal key of D, as a kind of vaudeville finale. The suffering of both lovers in the duet finds poignant expression in a number of ways. The descending chromatic fourth of grief appears in the basses, above which the harmony consists of descending 6/3 chords. The most sustained line of all here is played by the violas, high in their range—an orchestral timbre of which Mozart would later make much use.

[60] According to Romain Rolland, cited after Howard, *Gluck: Orfeo*, p. 40.

"Che farò senza Euridice?" (What shall I do without Euridice?) is the most famous aria in the work. Actually it is not really an aria in the Italian sense, but an *air en rondeau* (**A B A C A'** coda). To those who find it insufficiently grave, sung by a man who has just lost his wife for the second time, there are several possible rejoinders. The piece really works in tandem with Euridice's despairing and frenzied air in c preceding it, and another minor-mode piece here would not have allowed for enough musical contrast. In the second episode of "Che farò," minor-mode pathos does appear, and particularly effective at this point are the repeated calls of "Euridice," harking back to the opening of Act I. The sudden dynamic accents in the piece also hint at Orfeo's perturbation, even though he is delivering a supremely melodious air. Possibly the tension between the text and the main affect of the music works to further enhance this perturbation. It is only in character for this demigod, after all, to respond to every situation with lyric outpouring, as he did even in the violent battle with the Furies.

The high point of "Che farò" comes in the third statement of the refrain, when the rising triad in the tonic is answered for the first time by a corresponding rising arpeggio over the dominant. This provides just the needed touch of surprise in such a cut-and-dried form so as to enhance our interest and sustain it to the end, which comes after the orchestra extends the new inspiration into a coda. After such a hauntingly beautiful air, followed by Orfeo's attempted suicide, Amore could only restore Euridice to life once again. Like the air itself, Euridice is destined for eternal life. Joseph Haydn paid Gluck the ultimate compliment by beginning one of his baryton trios (Hob. XI:5) for Prince Esterházy by quoting "Che farò senza Euridice?"

Orfeo ed Euridice, as originally conceived by Calzabigi and Gluck, was not a full-length opera, but an *azione teatrale* intended to fill part of an evening's entertainment celebrating the emperor's name day. Revivals of the work in other cities often accrued music by other hands, with invariably ruinous results. Gluck himself fundamentally undid the work at Paris in 1774, not so much by his additions but because of the key transpositions that had to be made to accommodate a tenor Orfeo. In no other work for the lyric stage previous to the 1762 score for Vienna had the key scheme become so crucially important. If the key of one section was changed in these vast tableaux, the whole could be seriously damaged.[61] Here is another definition of what is meant by composing scenically.

Easily overlooked by viewers and listeners today is the great challenge that this opera posed to audiences of its own time. An argument could be

[61] Frederick Sternfeld, "Expression and Revision in Gluck's *Orfeo* and *Alceste*," in *Essays Presented to Egon Wellesz*, ed. Jack Westrup (Oxford, 1966), pp. 114–29. See also John Eliot Gardiner's ardent defense of the original version, "Hands off *Orfeo*!" in Howard, *Gluck: Orfeo*, pp. 112–18.

made that *Orfeo* was so closely tailored to Guadagni's acting and singing abilities that its successful production was scarcely possible without him. But this is belied by the work's continued history right down to the present as a vehicle of choice for mezzo-sopranos in the lead role. Guadagni did carry the work to other centers of Italian opera—London, for instance, and Munich. Its production in Munich during the carnival season of 1773 was due to the efforts of the very talented composer-singer Maria Antonia Walpurgis, dowager electress of Saxony. This Bavarian princess was also a painter and poet (in both French and Italian), and hence she would naturally feel some affinity with Gluck, who on various occasions described himself not as a composer but a painter in tones, or a poet in tones. Thanks to a communiqué back to Dresden from the Saxon ambassador to the court of Munich commenting on the production, we have a valuable insight as to how the public reacted.

Munich, 7 February 1773

> Electress Maria Antonia was present at the first representation of the opera *Orfeo*, which Guadagni brought with him, and which the elector [of Bavaria, her brother] had executed for this singer. He plays his role to the hilt. There is something grand about his acting, and although his voice has begun to decline, he shines in this opera, which appears to be made expressly for him. As a spectacle it is entirely extraordinary, and I have never seen its like in this genre. The acting and the music make a great effect and arouse a sadness that penetrates the soul, to the extent that one could do entirely without the words of the poetry. It seems as if the composer, the famous Gluck, set out to make a masterpiece of a lugubrious spectacle, at which he did not fall short. Because without the conclusion, which is joyful, the spectators would go home in a very melancholy state. And besides, this spectacle is very difficult of execution. In Vienna, when it was produced, there were twenty-nine rehearsals before it could be performed, and even then it succeeded only partially. People here find that this music would be better suited to Holy Week than to a carnival opera; there were cabals in the orchestra, and the court stepped in. Her Highness the electress is strongly in favor of this opera, which meant that those who respect the wishes of this august princess took care to say no more.[62]

From this it should be clear how far Gluck pushed even an enlightened audience of the time. People did not want to hear in the opera house music so sad and lugubrious that it made them think they were in church.

The frontispiece of the first edition, printed in Paris in 1764, was the object of correspondence between Durazzo and Favart, who oversaw publi-

---

[62]Moritz Fürstenau, "Glucks Orpheus in München 1773," *Monatshefte für Musikgeschichte* 4 (1872): 216–24. The original document is in French.

FIGURE 3.6. Charles Monnet. Frontispiece to the score of Gluck's *Orfeo ed Euridice*, printed in Paris, 1764.

cation.[63] Durazzo's final recommendation for the subject of the frontispiece was the moment at the end of Act II when Orfeo takes Euridice by the hand and leads her away (Figure 3.6). The illustration's French artists, Monnet and Le Mire, have captured Elysium's verdant trees and bushes with an admirable lightness, and there is even a coursing brook. Typically French is the risqué rendering of the lovers, who are scantily clad with flowing drapery. Such seminudity could have played no role in the original production

[63] Brown, "Durazzo, Duni," pp. 71–97; 75, 81–82. Brown shows that the artists were given as a model the engraved frontispiece of Duni's *L'isle des foux*.

of two years earlier. Maria Theresa was rather prudish, and if anything of the kind had appeared on the stage of the Burgtheater, she would have been scandalized.

Durazzo specified the illustration's text, "Euridice Amor ti rende" (Love returns Euridice to you), as well as the action. Here he compounds a little problem present in the last stage direction of Act II: "A chorus of heroines leads Euridice to the vicinity of Orfeo, who, with a gesture of greatest urgency, takes her by the hand, without looking at her, and leads her quickly away." So far, so good, as long as we understand this to happen at the very end of the act. But the stage direction continues: "There follows the dance of the heros and heroines [*Ballo* in B♭, 2/4] and then a reprise of the chorus, which lasts as long as Orfeo and Euridice are still in paradise." Orfeo cannot lead Euridice quickly away if they have to observe the ballet; he could only lead her around in circles. The specification of "Euridice Amor ti rende" jibes with this stage direction; it is the second line of the penultimate chorus (*Andantino* in F, 3/8). This makes no sense because in the recitative following the *Ballo*, which follows this chorus, Orfeo is still seeking Euridice without finding her. Their meeting thus cannot take place before the reprise of the chorus in F, now marked *Allegretto*, beginning with the words "Torna, o bella, al tuo consorte." These are the words Durazzo should have indicated.

The first set for Act III offered scenographers a chance to indulge in some proto-Romantic gloom. It is described in the first edition as "a dark cave, formed as a winding labyrinth, encumbered by mossy rocks, detached from the cliffs, and overgrown with wild plants and brush." Gluck found an appropriately anguished and turbulent music in f to complement this stage picture as the curtain went up on Act III. Several scenographic sketches survive for this set, somewhat surprisingly, since there is so little material for the rest of the opera. Outstanding among them is the colored drawing executed by Giovanni Paolo Gaspari for the Munich production of 1773 (see Plate V). A nice asymmetry rules his cave, and the effect is indeed impressively massive, if not exactly overgrown.

For the princely wedding at the court of Parma in 1769, Frugoni combined three short operas by Gluck, the last being *Orfeo*, as *Le feste d'Apollo*. The Parmesan artist Pietro Antonio Martini executed several engraved plates for the elaborately illustrated libretto. His illustration for *Orfeo* shows Giuseppe Millico in the lead role, singing his final solo, his lyre at his feet (Figure 3.7). The cliffs, rocks, and plants are all in accord with the libretto. Impressively Grecian-looking is the costume, with loose-fitting tunic, cape, sandals, and leg straps. The image may correspond more with the artist's idea of how it ought to look than with how it actually looked on the stage. And yet in a center of such fastidious taste and operatic innovation as Parma, it seems

FIGURE 3.7. Pietro Antonio
Martini. Millico as Orfeo,
Parma, 1769.

unlikely that the stage showed something totally unrelated to the libretto's
illustration. Operatic costuming in the antique mode had begun.

By the nineteenth century the typical costume for Orfeo was standard-
ized so as to look quite like that in the Parma libretto of 1769. The most
famous nineteenth-century Orfeo was created by Pauline Viardot-Garcia, for
whom Berlioz made a version combining features from the original version
and the Paris version of 1774. As depicted playing the role, she resembled
Millico: bare legs, tunic gathered in the middle and billowing cape behind.[64]
Viardot, unlike any of her eighteenth-century predecessors, has left us an
account of how she projected a piece like "J'ai perdu mon Euridice." "I think
I have discovered three good ways of delivering the motif. The first time,

[64] In the *Gazette des Beaux Arts*, 1860, reproduced in "Pauline Viardot-Garcia to Julius Rietz (Letters
of Friendship)," trans. Theodore Baker, *Musical Quarterly* 2 (1916): 32–60, facing p. 44. There is also
a poor reproduction in Howard, *Gluck: Orfeo*, p. 94.

sorrowful amazement, almost motionless. The second—choked with tears (people applauded two minutes and wanted an encore!!!). The third time, outbursts of despair. My poor Euridice remarked as she arose: 'Phew! I thought it would never end!' "[65]

For the last stage set of the original production in 1762, the "Magnificent Temple dedicated to Love," there was available and probably still serviceable the last set of *Cythère assiégée*. Wartime conditions and restrictions still prevailed in Vienna, but *Orfeo ed Euridice* triumphed in spite of them.

INTERLUDE (1763–65)

CARL DITTERS charmingly recounts in his autobiography how he was able to accompany Gluck to Italy in the spring of 1763, thanks to the generosity of the empress and others. Their goal was Bologna, for which Gluck had agreed to write an opera to inaugurate the Teatro Communale, built by Antonio Galli-Bibiena. The authorities insisted that he set *Il trionfo di Clelia*, the poet's celebratory libretto of 1762. Gluck preferred *L'Olimpiade*, one of the poet's finest librettos, dating from 1733, a classic in the Metastasian canon. Perhaps Gluck agreed with those critics who maintained that the master in his sixties was not as felicitous as he had been in his thirties.

The singers for *Il trionfo di Clelia* included Giovanni Manzuoli, Antonia Maria Girelli-Aquilar, and Giuseppe Tibaldi singing the role of Porsenna, as he had in Hasse's setting for Vienna a year earlier. (All three principals would later sing in Mozart's serenata *Ascanio in Alba* for Milan in 1771.) According to Ditters, the opera, presented after seventeen rehearsals, was a great success, although the orchestra lacked the precision of ensemble he was used to in Vienna. In truth the production did not attract the public in sufficient numbers to cover its costs. Gluck presided over the first three performances from the harpsichord, as was the custom. For these the maestro di cappella, Antonio Mazzone, moved to the second harpsichord (near stage left). Gluck and Ditters returned to Vienna after visiting Parma, where they attended a performance of Christian Bach's *Catone in Utica*.

In Vienna Gluck supervised a revival of *Orfeo* in the summer of 1763. This was followed by a new opera of Traetta, *Ifigenia in Tauride*. The reform-minded libretto was by Marco Coltellini, who was born in Livorno in 1724 (not 1719, as formerly believed).[66] By 1763 Coltellini had settled in Vienna, where he was associated with his fellow Livornese Calzabigi; he left Vienna

[65] "Pauline Viardot-Garcia to Julius Rietz," pp. 46–7.
[66] Susanna Corrieri, "Marco Coltellini da stampatore a poeta di corte," *La figura e l'opera di Ranieri de' Calzabigi*, ed. Federico Marri (Florence, 1989), pp. 203–15.

in 1772 for the Russian court, where he died in 1777. Guadagni sang the main role of Orestes in Traetta's opera, and Tibaldi sang Toante. In his preface to the libretto Coltellini mentions Euripides as a model; another model was the fine *Iphigénie en Tauride* by De la Touche, a play performed in the Burgtheater in 1761. Particularly impressive in Traetta's score is the number and excellence of the choruses.[67] An aspect singled out for praise by Zinzendorf after witnessing the performance on 8 December 1763 was the natural way the Furies are introduced into the dream Orestes has about Clytemnestra, the mother he murdered in revenge for her murder of Agamemnon, his father. Gluck also admired this scene and continued to be inspired by it as late as his own *Iphigénie en Tauride* for Paris in 1779. Gluck directed a performance of Traetta's *Ifigenia* in Florence in early 1767, along with his own occasional work *Il prologo,* to celebrate the birth of a child to Grand Duke Leopold and his wife, Maria Luisa of Spain.

At the beginning of 1764 Gluck crowned his works in the opéra-comique genre with *La rencontre imprévue.*[68] Then he, Durazzo, and Coltellini traveled to Paris, at which time they may have laid plans for *Telemaco;* one of the objects of his visit was to oversee the printing of *Orfeo.* The composer next went to Frankfurt for the coronation of Archduke Joseph as King of the Romans, along with Durazzo, Guadagni, and Ditters. Durazzo's fall as impresario occurred at this time, the result of an intrigue in which Joseph played a part, prompting one critic to refer to "the first blunder in the musical politics of this doctrinaire and unperceptive monarch, who was nothing more than a crowned bureaucrat."[69] We saw in the first chapter how Joseph wreaked havoc upon Viennese opera during the following decade.

The year 1765 began with the composition of several festal works. At the insistence of his parents, Archduke, now King, Joseph married again, this time Maria Josepha of Bavaria, a princess he detested. The celebrations took place in January 1765. Angiolini and Gluck contributed a new pantomime ballet, *Sémiramis,* after the tragedy of Voltaire. The ballet can scarcely have been conceived for the occasion, since its plot was particularly gruesome: Queen Sémiramis murders her husband, Ninus, so that she can marry their son, Ninias, who then kills her. There is an impressive watercolor depicting

[67] The chorus preparatory to the sacrifice of Orestes is described in detail in Heartz, "Traetta in Vienna," pp. 81–85. For a general discussion of the whole opera, see Reinhard Strohm, *Die italienische Oper im 18. Jahrhundert* (Wilhelmshaven, 1979), pp. 305–35; the opera is treated together with Coltellini's *Telemaco,* set by Gluck (Vienna, 1765).

[68] Bruce Alan Brown, "Gluck's *Rencontre imprévue* and Its Revisions," *JAMS* 36 (1983): 498–518. Brown shows that many changes were made in the work because of the death of Isabella, Archduke Joseph's first wife, in November 1763. For a full discussion of the opera, see Brown's *Gluck and the French Theatre,* pp. 407–24.

[69] Alfred Einstein, *Gluck* (London, 1936; reprint 1964), p. 90.

FIGURE 3.8.
Jean-Louis Desprez.
The Death of
Semiramide.

the final scene from Voltaire's *Sémiramis* by Louis-Jean Desprez, who studied in Paris between 1765 and 1776 (Figure 3.8). Flames and smoke rise from the sepulcher of Ninus into an eerily moonlit sky. As mother and son emerge from the tomb, he thrusts a sword into her breast. Note the heavy framing with architectural and sculptural motifs from antiquity, which intensify the "sublime" qualities of this phantasmagoria.[70]

Of the new ballet by Angiolini and Gluck, Khevenhüller reported that "the spectacle won no applause, and in fact was entirely too pathetic and sad for a wedding." The music seems like a continuation of the end of *Don Juan*, filled with anxiety and unease, punctuated by many orchestral screams, and except for three minuets (Nos. 3, 4, and 7) almost entirely in the minor mode. Open-ended cadences are frequent, as in the Hades scene of *Orfeo*, adding to the unease. Unlike *Don Juan*, there are no discernible dance types except for the minuets, the third of which is very galant in order to paint the lust of mother for son. Gluck's musical invention is freer than ever, and even more dramatic than in *Don Juan*.

The public failure of *Sémiramis* meant that Gluck could use much of its magnificent music elsewhere, in subsequent works. A case in point is the temple march in G (Nos. 9a, 9b, and 11), the smooth-flowing half notes of which were recomposed to become the temple march in G in the first act of *Alceste* (No. 9b was reused verbatim in *Iphigénie en Tauride*). Even Gluck's failed experiments could prove suggestive for other composers. In the first number of *Sémiramis* the ghost of the murdered king exhorts his son to revenge, for which Gluck conceived a stern, almost Old Testament kind of sermon, or counterpoint lesson, with long notes climbing in the treble against an inexorable quarter-note bass figure (Example 3.8). The effect is not unlike what Haydn would do in some of his minor-mode symphonic movements a few years later.

Angiolini was duly proud of *Sémiramis*, whatever its public reception. In his *Lettere . . . a Monsieur Noverre* (Milan, 1773) he says that after 1762, "I went on to the terrible and sublime pathos of true tragedy . . . The happy success of my ballet *Don Juan* strengthened my belief in this regard. In 1765, as a consequence, I composed and produced *Sémiramis*, the most terrible subject bequeathed to us by antiquity." Angiolini says nothing about its success, but he does append a note to explain himself further. "By tragic I do not mean a mass of scenes which in various ways tend toward slaughter, but rather a simple action which gradually leads from the pathetic to the terrible, which wakens horror in me without presenting me with it, which ends with vice punished and virtue in triumph." By his own enlightened definition of tragedy, *Sémiramis* does not qualify (but *Alceste* does). He would

---

[70] Noverre praised the great tragedian Lekain for his acting in the role of the parricidal son. "In M. Voltaire's *Semiramis* he came out of the tomb of Ninus with turned-up sleeves, bloody arms, bristling hair and staring eyes. This powerful but natural picture impressed, interested and filled spectators with a sense of calamity and horror." *Letters on Dancing and Ballets*, trans. Cyril Beaumont (London, 1930; reprint New York, 1966), pp. 75–76.

EXAMPLE 3.8. *Gluck*, Sémiramis, *Pantomime*

have done better to invoke *Hamlet* and a Shakespearean conception of tragedy in defense of *Sémiramis,* with reference to which Baron Gottfried van Swieten wrote the Austrian vice-regent in Brussels, Count Cobenzl, that a group of hypochondriacs around Calzabigi wanted to install in the Burgtheater "toute la dureté des spectacles Anglais."[71]

Sémiramis joins *Don Juan* (mainly the finale) and *Orfeo* (mainly the infernal scene) in what can only be called the beginnings of a new aesthetic, in which ordinary musical beauty becomes subordinate to a greater purpose: dramatic passion. The aestheticians had an expression for this—"the musical sublime," which Friedrich Michaelis defined in an article of 1805: "Sublime notes are not a source of instant pleasure; they are often violent, even terrifying. In so far as music can depict greatness beyond the normal limits of the imagination, transfixing the listener with horror and rapture, to that extent can it express the sublime. But such music will only appeal to men of spirit and sensibility, to men of the noblest intellect."[72] And for a single note eliciting horror and rapture, we recall as our witness the famous C♭ / B♮ of the Furies in *Orfeo.*

A truly festal work for the 1765 wedding was the serenata *Il Parnasso confuso* by Metastasio, with music by Gluck, sung by four archduchesses at Schönbrunn and directed from the harpsichord by Archduke Leopold; the youngest Habsburg children took part too, as dancers. Three paintings commemorate the performance. One shows the stage from a side view capturing the four singing archduchesses, the orchestra on either side of a long bench, as in the Burgtheater, Leopold at the harpsichord, the spectators, and in the front row the imperial family; a second shows the four singers from a frontal view; a third represents the ballet.[73]

Telemaco, ossia L'isola di Circe was the main wedding opera, and it may say something about the shifting cultural politics of the court that Gluck, not Hasse, was chosen as composer this time. Or it may mean only, since the marriage was decided on in a hurry (before Joseph could once again rebel against his parents), there was only time to utilize a project that Coltellini and Gluck were already working on. The libretto was cobbled together from an old one by Sigismondo Capece (set by Alessandro Scarlatti in 1718). Col-

---

[71] Klaus Hortschansky, "Unbekannte Aufführungsberichte zu Glucks Opern der Jahre 1748–1765," *Jahrbuch des Staatlichen Instituts für Musikforschung Preussischer Kulturbesitz 1969,* pp. 19–39; 30–34.

[72] Cited after Peter le Huray, "The Role of Music in Eighteenth- and Early Nineteenth-Century Aesthetics," *PRMA* 105 (1978–79): 90–99; 98.

[73] Otto Erich Deutsch, "Höfische Theaterbilder aus Schönbrunn," *Österreichische Musikzeitschrift* 22 (1967): 577–84, reprinted in *Christoph Willibald Gluck und die Opernreform,* ed. Klaus Hortschansky (Darmstadt, 1989), pp. 98–107. All three paintings are reproduced; there is a better reproduction of the first in Derek Beales, *Joseph II,* vol. 1: *In the Shadow of Maria Theresa, 1741–1780* (Cambridge, 1987), plate 7 following p. 172.

tellini reduced it from three acts to two, but it still seems long and overly wordy. The opera was a failure with the public, yet Gluck lavished some of his most beautiful music on it. He rescued many numbers from this quickly forgotten opera and reused them elsewhere, particularly in *Armide* (Paris, 1777), which shared the theme of magical enchantment. But not everyone forgot *Telemaco*. Haydn, as we shall see, was inspired by the moving plea of the young prince in search of his father (Example 3.9). Berlioz studied *Tele-*

EXAMPLE 3.9. *Gluck*, Telemaco, *Act I, scene 6*

maco and wrote ardently in defense of parts of it—Asteria's monologue in Act I, scene 4, for instance, the same piece Berlioz sang for Mendelssohn in Rome in 1831, taunting the supercilious younger composer for not knowing his Gluck.

Far from being discouraged by the reception of *Sémiramis*, Angiolini and Gluck went on to write another pantomime ballet on a tragic subject. The court traveled to Laxenburg in May, where Khevenhüller reported on 19 May 1765 the production of "a new serious ballet, taken from the tragedy *Iphigénie*, which was better than *Sémiramis*." A letter written by Archduke Leopold the following day reports the event with some enthusiasm because the music of Gluck was beautiful and greatly pleased him: "Nous eûmes un ballet tragique représentant Iphigénie qui me plût beaucoup, la musique en étant très belle, de la composition de Gluck."[74] Leopold, a skilled musician himself, presumably would have had a copy of the score made for him. But no copy of this ballet has yet been found. Leopold's admiration for Gluck's music explains a lot: Gluck's trip to Florence in early 1767 and, two years later when *Alceste* was printed in score at Vienna, the famous preface dedicating the work to Leopold.

Maria Theresa must have been especially pleased with *Il Parnasso confuso* because she ordered from Metastasio and Gluck another work very like it for the archduchesses to sing on the emperor's name day. The work, *La corona*, was finished in the summer of 1765, but went unperformed. Emperor Francis did not live to celebrate another name day.

Alceste (1766–67)

THE court went to Innsbruck in the summer of 1765 to celebrate the marriage of Archduke Leopold with Maria Luisa of Spain. Metastasio and Hasse furnished the main festival opera, *Romolo ed Ersilia*, which was given its premiere on 6 August. Khevenhüller reported court opinion that was unusually negative—the text was "filled with tasteless and insipid love scenes," the whole was "weak and cold," and the music of the great Hasse "sad and old-fashioned." From this it sounds as if the reform operas of Traetta and Gluck were indeed changing the tastes of the court for conventional opera seria. On 18 August Emperor Francis and Joseph were in the theater, where they witnessed, according to Khevenhüller, "a serious play of Goldoni's, *Il tutore,*

---

[74] Gerhard Croll, "Ein unbekanntes tragisches Ballet von Gluck," in *Christoph Willibald Gluck und die Opernreform*, ed. Klaus Hortschansky (Darmstadt, 1989), pp. 232–35.

and the ballet of *Iphigénie*, as long as it is sad." Returning to his rooms, Francis suddenly collapsed. Joseph prevented him from falling and helped carry him to a bed, but by the time medical experts arrived, the emperor was dead.

Maria Theresa was devastated. For two years she remained in deepest mourning and she dressed in black for the rest of her life. Still, the business of ruling had to go on. On 17 September 1765 she named Joseph co-regent; she remained the ruler. Mother and son quarreled incessantly. Joseph especially disliked his mother's generosity with servants, to whom he thought she granted too many pensions. She was like a mother to legions of such people, whereas Joseph "could not match the warmth of the concern that she displayed for the state's servants as individuals."[75]

Maria Theresa was also sincerely admired by her subjects as the woman of great courage who had fought for her rights and had kept the Habsburg realms together, not least of all by her bountiful progeny. This bravery she maintained all her life, and it was Joseph who told Prince Kaunitz that when she drew her last breath in late 1780, he was astonished by "her courage, resignation, steadfastness and patience."[76]

Calzabigi or Gluck must have seen in the empress a close parallel with one of the great characters of ancient drama. In his play *Alcestis*, Euripides had Alcestis, queen of Thrace, go to her death willingly in order to save the life of her husband, Admetus. At various times in the first part of the play, she is described as the noblest, bravest, and dearest of women. But the lines that put one so much in mind of Maria Theresa are those that describe how Alcestis treated her servants. "The children clung upon their mother's dress and cried, until she gathered them into her arms, and kissed first one and then the other, as in death's farewell. And all the servants of the house were crying now in sorrow for their mistress. Then she gave her hand to each, and each took it, there was none so mean in station that she did not stop and talk with him."[77] Calzabigi probably began writing his *Alceste* soon after the period of mourning began. He made his meaning clear as to choice of subject in the dedication of the poem to Maria Theresa, with an explicit comparison between Alceste and the sovereign of the Danube monarchy: "By your virtue you show that our age cedes nothing to that of the ancients, however great was the virtue of Alceste."

Euripides gives the chorus a prominent role in *Alcestis*. Close to the beginning, after Death enters the house of Admetus, it is the chorus that takes up a vigil before the gate.

---

[75] Beales, *Joseph II*, p. 306.

[76] Ibid., p. 482.

[77] From the speech of the maid, lines 189–95, in *Alcestis*, trans. Richmond Lattimore, in *The Complete Greek Tragedies, Euripides I*, ed. David Grene and Richmond Lattimore (Chicago, 1955).

> It is quiet by the palace. What does it mean?
> Why is the house of Admetus so still?
> Is there none here of his family, none
> who can tell us whether the queen is dead
> and therefore to be mourned? Or does Pelias'
> daughter Alcestis live still, still look
> on daylight, she who in my mind appears
> noble beyond
> all women beside in a wife's duty?
> (Lines 77–85 in Richmond Lattimore's translation)

Calzabigi made this anxious waiting for news the beginning of his opera, only the vigil is not for Alceste, but for Admeto. He used other elements as well of the ancient play, to which the tone of his "tragedia per musica" is greatly indebted. That is to say, he used the first part of Euripides (up to line 475), which concerns the heroic death of the noble wife for her husband. After this Euripides veers off to another subject, the responsibilities of the bereaved Admetus as host when his friend Hercules pays him a visit, but he ties it all together in the end by having Hercules overcome Death and return Alcestis to Admetus, who is the main character in the play despite its title.

Calzabigi leaves out Hercules and concentrates on the single theme of conjugal devotion. The main character becomes Alceste. Admeto does not even appear until halfway through the opera, while Alceste is onstage throughout most of the work. In the end it is Apollo who restores Alceste to her husband. *Orfeo* was written around the talents of a particular singer. *Alceste* was not; it was inspired by the death of a ruler and the period of grief and mourning that followed. The problem with this masterpiece from the beginning was finding an actress-singer with enough stamina and dignity to do justice to the title role.

In the early months of 1767 Gluck was not in Vienna, having gone to Florence to direct a performance of Traetta's *Ifigenia* and his own *Prologo* for Grand Duke Leopold. Before leaving, or perhaps from Florence, he wrote a letter to Prince Kaunitz about what was required to stage *Alceste*, which must have been finished by the end of 1766. Gluck's letter is lost, unfortunately, and we only know about it from a covering letter by Calzabigi on the same subject. The latter is the most important verbal document that survives concerning the Viennese operatic reform, outweighing even the famous preface to *Alceste*, also by Calzabigi, although signed by Gluck. In the letter to Kaunitz it is not the polished courtier who wrote the prefaces to *Don Juan*, *Sémiramis*, and *Alceste* who appears but the real Calzabigi, witty and sarcastic. (The entire letter of 6 March 1767 may be found in a new annotated translation in Appendix 2.) The document throws considerable light on the reformers and their relationship to Prince Kaunitz.

Kaunitz was the third member, besides Maria Theresa and Joseph, of the triumvirate that ruled in Vienna during the fifteen years of the co-regency. Their governing was beset with difficulties and achieved only by dint of a continual shifting of alliances. Sometimes Kaunitz would side with the empress and sometimes with her son, and sometimes mother and son would side against him. Kaunitz had lost a round to the empress and Joseph even before the co-regency began, when Durazzo, his ally, was dismissed and replaced by Count Sporck in 1764. In 1767 the prince must have understood that *Alceste* gave him a fine chance to vindicate Durazzo and the whole reform movement. The letters to Kaunitz from Gluck and Calzabigi went over Sporck's head. Calzabigi threatened to bury *Alceste* if appropriate principal singers and choral reinforcements were not hired, which Sporck was apparently refusing to do. Who, besides Sporck, could have stood in the way of this? Maria Theresa tried to stay out of theatrical matters during her widowhood, and she rarely appeared anymore in the Burgtheater. That leaves Joseph, the "crowned bureaucrat," who was such a thorn in his mother's side despite their devotion to each other. The opera is about her, and its poem is dedicated to her, yet it nearly came to grief, it would seem, because of Joseph. No wonder the dedication of the printed score eventually went to Leopold.

The tone of Calzabigi's personal letter about *Alceste* to Kaunitz is nothing less than shocking. It is a venomous diatribe against Metastasio and all his works, especially his most recent. Although it ends with a conventional flourish of humility, there is little humility in the letter. Calzabigi was a person of violent passions and dubious morals. There was a poisoning episode in his youth, for which he was imprisoned.[78] Then there was a shady business he started in Paris with his younger brother and Giacomo Casanova. Casanova happened to be in Vienna in 1767 and painted this picture of his friend: "I went to the theater and often to dinner at the house of Calzabigi, who made a great show of his atheism ["qui faisait pompe de son athéisme"], and with impudence always spoke badly of Metastasio, who scorned him; but Calzabigi made a jest of it. A great political calculator, he was Prince Kaunitz's man."[79] Calzabigi was indeed Kaunitz's man and, if we may believe Casanova, an avowed atheist, which would have been enough by itself to scandalize the pious Metastasio, not to mention Maria Theresa.

Open warfare prevailed, then, between Metastasio and Calzabigi. Metastasio despised the younger poet, who in his turn openly ridiculed the

[78] See my review of *La figura e l'opera di Ranieri de' Calzabigi*, ed. Federico Marri (Florence, 1989), in *Music and Letters* 31 (1990): 566–69.
[79] Jacques Casanova de Seingalt, *Histoire de ma vie* (Paris-Wiesbaden, 1960), 10: 238–39.

revered master. It was one thing for Calzabigi to inveigh against the Caesar-ean poet verbally in his circle of friends. It was quite another to do so in such frank terms in writing to Kaunitz. Was there not some danger that he would overstep a certain line of familiarity with his protector? That he would, by his impertinence, elicit a negative response? For whatever reasons, this did not happen, at least not in 1767. And we must acknowledge in Kaunitz the political force that allowed the operatic reform to reach its full flowering in *Alceste*.

In his dedication of the poem to Maria Theresa on the second title page of the score, Calzabigi invoked the Latin motto "Denique sit quodvis simplex dumtaxat et unum" (Let the author be as simple as he wishes as long as he is unified) from the *Ars poetica* of Horace. This too formed part of the attack on Metastasio, whose plots were not simple, but complicated by intrigues; nor were they unitary, but multilayered, with multiple use of confidants. Calzabigi deplored confidants as a holdover from the abhorred *seicento*. He ridiculed Philippe Quinault's *Alceste*, set to music by Lully in 1674, although he did not fail to appropriate a few things from the work's third and central act, in which Alceste dies and is mourned (he was still in Paris in 1758 when Lully's *Alceste* enjoyed a triumphant revival). Gluck admitted admiration for Lully's music, and the great moment of Lully's Act III, "Alceste est morte," echoed many times by the chorus, left its mark on the dirge in the last act of the Viennese *Alceste*.

Quinault, in order to fill his five acts (preceded by a Prologue), deployed the usual amorous intrigue. Alceste has three lovers: Admète, to whom she is betrothed (not married), Lycomède, king of Scyros, and Hercules himself. The perfidious Lycomède abducts Alceste, who is rescued in battle by Her-cules and Admète, the latter being mortally wounded in the action. At this point (end of Act II) Apollon pronounces his famous oracle: Admète will die unless someone dies for him (as in Calzabigi's temple scene in Act I—this does not come from Euripides). Alceste immediately kills herself, thus elimi-nating the long agonizing process that is so important in Calzabigi's poem. In Acts IV and V Quinault has Hercules rescue Alceste on condition that she become his bride, but moved by the touching farewells of the betrothed couple, Hercules gives Alceste back to Admète amid general rejoicing. To make things more complicated still, Straton, Lycomède's confidant, and Lychas, Hercules' confidant, both love Cephise, Alceste's confidante.

Calzabigi could not do without confidants altogether. Having sup-pressed the father and mother of Admetus in Euripides, he needed Evandro and Ismene besides the central couple and their two children to stretch the action to a full-length tragedy. In fact Evandro and Ismene are not confidants in the Metastasian sense because they have no love interests. They are more like the choragus of ancient drama—people who led the chorus, or sections of it. In an opera so predominantly choral as Gluck's *Alceste*, figures were needed to direct stage traffic. Writing to one of his friends in Italy on 15 December 1768, Calzabigi commented sarcastically: "I know that according to Metastasian practice I could have Evandro in love with Alceste, and unfortunate, Ismene in love with Admeto, and unhappy, and perhaps have added a Hercules in love with Alceste, as does Quinault . . . poor Italy!"[80]

Alceste is the most unrelievedly tragic and the most monumental of Gluck's operas. As in the case with *Orfeo*, we shall deal only with the Italian version for Vienna, not the subsequent French version. Just as Calzabigi had to rely on an Evandro and Ismene to sustain the work's length, so did Gluck need to resort to simple recitative, which he did not use in *Orfeo*. Simple recitatives were often used to set up the more elaborate recitatives with orchestral accompaniment, and they gave Gluck an added color in his palette. The nineteenth century in general maligned simple recitative, calling it "dry" (*secco*). But Berlioz knew better, and praised it for the variety it added in both Gluck and Mozart.[81]

Gluck did more than any other composer could to focus on the nobility and grandeur of Alceste's self-sacrifice. Calzabigi's Admeto scarcely seems worthy of such a wife: "A sacrifice such as he accepts should not be acceptable."[82] Indeed Admeto does nothing but rage and lament during her long mortal agony. The problem for present-day listeners to the opera is undoubtedly greater than it was in the eighteenth century; today one cannot accept the premise that women's lives are worth less than men's, as was taken for granted then. And this is not the only problem the work poses. It was always questionable whether so grim and death-obsessed a work could succeed with the public. The answer to this question depends greatly on the singer of the title role.[83]

The tone of solemnity and monumental severity begins with the first notes of the *Intrada*, or overture, which leads without a break into the first scene. Three trombones color its gloomy and stentorian tones from the beginning, unlike its descendant *Don Giovanni*, where the trombones, instruments of the afterworld, are withheld from the overture and do not appear until the Commendatore speaks in the graveyard and then comes to supper. Certainly no one would expect anything but a tragic story to ensue after the

[80] Mariangela Donà, "Dagli archivi milanese: Lettere di Ranieri de' Calzabigi e di Antonia Bernasconi," *Analecta Musicologica* 14 (1974): 268–300; 281–82.

[81] Karl Geiringer, "Hector Berlioz und Glucks Wiener Opern," *Gluck-Studien* 1 (1989): 166–70; 168.

[82] Einstein, *Gluck*, p. 108.

[83] The Italian *Alceste* has not enjoyed many recordings, but an extraordinarily impressive one was made with Kirsten Flagstad in the title role in 1956.

somber strains of the *Alceste* overture, with its piercing diminished-seventh chord cries and its agitated flood of short notes, checked repeatedly by syncopation. In this sense the overture fulfills at least the first of two strictures on the subject in the *Alceste* preface: "I have felt that the overture ought to appraise the spectators of the nature of the action that is to be represented and to form, so to speak, its argument." Berlioz took issue with the second stricture.[84]

Unpredictability must have made this opera very difficult to grasp for its first audiences. Mozart's operas are easily divided into numbers; *Alceste* cannot be so divided. Alceste's first recitative and aria, "Popoli di Tessaglia," provides a case in point. The aria begins with an orchestral ritornello, giving proper weight to the entrance of Alceste. She sings only a few measures in the common time *Moderato* established by the orchestra before Gluck, in order to paint the words "Ma il mio duol consoli almeno" (But at least console my grief), switches to an *Adagio* in 3/4, during which the modulation to the dominant of this E♭ aria is made, and the voice is carried up to high B♭, Alceste's highest tone in the opera. The opening time and texture returns, now *Allegro*, in a modulatory passage, taking the music to A♭. At this juncture her two children, Eumelio and Aspasia, enter in an *Andante* in 3/4 imploring Alceste not to afflict herself. This carries the music to the key of c, where Alceste resumes singing, *Allegro* in common time, eventually working up to a climax as the music returns to E♭. A double chorus now enters directly after her last note (precluding applause, which was the last thing the creators wanted here). E♭ gives way to e♭ as the chorus on the right intones "Miseri figli!" answered by the chorus on the left, "Povera Alceste!"

There has been in this whole fluid complex of recitative, aria, duet and double chorus no verbal repetition (except on the local level of the phrase or half phrase), and no musical repetition either. It is not just that the da capo form has been banished. Even the kind of musical reprise of the initial material to be expected when Alceste returns to E♭ is not here. Calzabigi did his best to explain what Gluck was doing in the first paragraph of the preface, but his overly wordy description ends up enumerating the things Gluck was not doing. He extricates himself by having Gluck conclude: "In short, I have sought to abolish all the abuses against which good sense and reason have long cried out in vain."

Completely beyond Calzabigi's ken, to judge from the preface, was the way Gluck ensconced Alceste's first aria in a huge scene complex comprising nearly five hundred measures, and stretching over the entirety of scenes 1

---

[84] Hector Berlioz, *A travers chants* (Paris, 1927), pp. 154–56. The section on *Alceste* is excerpted in *L'Avant Scène Opéra*, no. 73 (1985), pp. 94–95.

TABLE 3.4 *ALCESTE*, Act I, Scenes 1 and 2

SCENE 1. Evandro, Ismene, populace

A	X	A	Ismene	A	Pantomime	Evandro	A	Evandro	A	Evandro
E♭	duet	E♭	c	E♭	c	B♭	E♭	B♭	E♭	B♭
mm. 29–47	47–57	57–68	69–93	93–105	106–27	128–44	145–62	162–80	180–82	183–97

SCENE 2. The above, plus Alceste and her two children

B	Recit. + Aria (Alceste)	Duet + solo	Chorus	B	Recit. (Alceste)	A	X
g	E♭	A♭——c	e♭	g		E♭	E♭
mm. 1–47	48–129	130–89	190–235	236–50		251–68	269–98

and 2 in Act I. This involved no fewer than six statements or partial statements of the opening chorus, surrounding not only the Alceste solo but also another chorus, "Misero Admeto." These two choruses appear as **A** and **B** in Table 3.4.

To be noted is the fluid way that Gluck writes himself into the reprise of **B,** raising the art of musical transition to a new height as he gradually moves from the double chorus in e♭ back into the music of "Misero Admeto." Another masterly stroke is his continual changing of the main refrain, **A.** The refrain was just beginning to be intoned again in scene 1 when Evandro choked it off with his "Tacete." This leaves in the listener a need that can be fulfilled in only one way. We simply must hear that beautiful chorus again in its entirety. And indeed we do. It becomes the closing gesture of this imposing tonal monument, the end of scene 2. What is more, we also hear an expansion of the music, labeled **X,** that closed off **A** the first time and has not been heard since. The methods of building are the same as in the first act of *Orfeo,* but the scope has been greatly enlarged.

The scene shifts to the Temple of Apollo, revealed to the strains of a solemn processional march in G. At the head of the printed score Calzabigi has placed a list of the dances, divided into "Balli Pantomimi" and "Balli Ballati." In the first category is the "Aria di Pantomimo," mm. 106–27 of scene 1, described as expressing the sadness and desolation of the populace. In the second category is the *Ballo* that opens scene 3 for the priests of Apollo. At this point another huge scene complex starts building. The chorus of supplication in c, "Dilegua il nero turbine" (Disperse the black gale), is sung three times, interspersed with other music, tying together scenes 3 and 4 in the same way that scenes 1 and 2 were laid out. The obbligato recitative of the high priest in scene 4 is initiated by a striding unison figure that projects an unease by ending on its own flat seventh, pointing forward toward the next destination (Example 3.10). Gluck is deadly serious

EXAMPLE 3.10. *Gluck, Alceste, Act I, scene 4*

in his painting of the high priest's exhortations, which grow in intensity to an almost frightening degree after the three trombones enter. The text is there to justify him: "The altar sways, the sacred tripod trembles, the earth shudders, threatening the temple." Mozart was very much in Gluck's debt for the similar music he wrote for his high priest's harangue in Act III of *Idomeneo* (1781). The same is true for the oracle's pronouncement, which follows the priest's. Gluck is more economical than even the shortest of the four successive versions of the oracle in *Idomeneo*—he accomplishes his mission in six measures (Example 3.11).

"The king will die if another does not die for him," sings the oracle. At this moment of extreme tension the orchestral basses pick up the final tone of the oracle and start throbbing in eighth notes; they are joined by the upper strings providing the rest of a triad. "Che annunzio funesto" (What a deathly announcement) is the response of the chorus, entering part by part. Against

EXAMPLE 3.11. *Gluck*, Alceste, *Act I, scene 4*

this hushed response in even half notes, a separate chorus of basses starts repeating in rapid tone, "Fuggiamo!" (Let us flee!). Flee they soon do, in an *Allegro* that ends as the parts of the chorus drop out and the *piano* becomes *pianissimo* (cf. the departure of the Furies in *Orfeo*). Left alone onstage are Alceste and her two children. She begins tentatively, questioning the truth of what she has just witnessed. But soon her resolve gains strength, and she knows what she must do. Calzabigi rises to the occasion, providing a speech that scales the heroic heights, culminating with the thought that Alceste will provide a magnanimous example of the faithful spouse to all future generations.

With this grandiose thought the recitative ends, discharging its accumulated force into the aria, which now bursts upon us. A striding bass line in B♭ against syncopated upper strings, punctuated every other measure by the *forte* blasts of the three trombones and all the other winds, conveys fortitude, struggle, and emotional ecstasy. When the words come they are "Ombre" (blast), "larve" (blast), "compagne di morte" (Shades, ghosts, companions of death). The trombones and other winds represent the infernal spirits responding to Alceste's call. This dialogue is lost in Gluck's French version of the aria, "Divinités du Styx," as Berlioz has pointed out. On the other hand, Berlioz argued vehemently against the anticlimactic scene 6 of the Viennese version, following Alceste's aria. Nothing should follow this great outburst except the end of the act, as in the Paris version, was his argument, with which it is difficult to disagree. "Ombre, larve," unlike Alceste's first aria, is in **A B A** form, with a resounding conclusion.

At the beginning of Act II Alceste is in a dark grove with rough statues to the gods of the underworld. Ismene is with her although her presence is unwanted, leading to the kind of dialogue—"Leave," "I'm leaving"—that only makes us wish she would leave and get it over with. She sings her aria, the opera's *aria di sorbetto*, to a text that begins, "Parto . . . ma senti . . . senti o Dio! Di te che mai sara!" (What will ever become of you!). This would not be so bad if Calzabigi had not used up the expression "che mai sara!" in Act I. Not surprisingly, Gluck's inspiration flags at a situation that is essentially undramatic (and therefore unnecessary). With Ismene gone, Alceste confronts the gods of the underworld, terrified but resolute, and Gluck is once again in his element. In particular, his use of the solo oboe in this scene is worthy of "Che puro ciel" in *Orfeo*, and the speech he gives to the "Numi Infernali," whose voices are heard, although they are not seen, is accompanied by the three trombones. A shuddering string orchestra, repeating an ostinato rhythm, conveys Alceste's terror at their voices, which she verbalizes. Eventually she faints at the horror of it all, but revives when an unseen chorus of the gods speaks to her in more normal tones: "Why do you wish to die so young?" A dialogue is joined, and the gods are astonished at her courage. Eventually they yield to her request that she say her final farewells to husband and children before giving herself up to death. She praises their pity in an aria in E♭ with English horns that is so poignant and beautiful it would move any powers in this or the other world. The first part of Act II finishes with a dance in c, called "Pantomimo de'Numi Infernali."

The scene shifts to an interior room of the palace. Admeto has made a miraculous recovery. A chorus celebrates this in bustling and cheerful song—the first note of cheer in the work. Celebrations continue in a *Ballo* in the same key of B♭. Evandro, Admeto's confidant, then sings an aria in F (which is no more apt or dramatic than Ismene's aria), leading to a repetition of the opening chorus and *Ballo*, in reverse order. It is clear that Evandro's aria was necessary in order to make the repetition here work, but is the repetition necessary? It seems more like padding than it does like the dramatic use of recurring choral refrains in Act I. The truth about how Admeto was allowed to recover emerges slowly, very slowly. Alceste can scarcely bring herself to reveal the truth, but her look of anguish should have told him anyway. He is not very perceptive, this husband. An agonizing duet in d between the two still fails to clear the air or bring him awareness of her sacrifice. Only after this, in a lengthy dialogue, does Alceste finally spell out the truth: "Ah husband! I am the one." General consternation spreads at this news. Admeto rages at tyrannous fate and sings an aria about how he cannot live without her. But he does nothing except leave the stage, quite in keeping with the old exit-aria convention. We wonder where he goes and what he does as Alceste begins to sink toward her death. To end Act II, there are further farewells to the children and choral laments as she slips away. Particularly moving is Alceste's last aria, with its *stringendo* ending to underscore "the greatest torment of all is parting with one's children."

Act III employs a single set, described as a "magnificent outdoor vestibule of the palace embellished with statues and trophies, and a view of the city through the columns." The act begins by restating the quandary in direct terms. Evandro says, "You yourself cannot die for her," but the very statement raises the question why he could not. Admeto answers, "The heavens would not allow it . . . Alceste has to die!" There may be a subtext here that was evident to the eighteenth century, but less so to us: as a king, Admeto was bound to preserve himself for the sake of his people. By means of an increasingly agitated recitative, Admeto works up to his big aria in c minor. Gluck takes his voice up to a sustained high A. The ending flows without a break into the following recitative. Alceste appears, supported by Ismene. She begins in a broad *arioso* in E♭, saying her final farewells, which leads eventually to a duet with Admeto in the same key. As they are advancing to embrace each other for the last time, the infernal gods make their presences known (e♭ with trombones, followed by swirling strings in chromatic descent), and a dark cloud envelops all; the gods themselves appear, and in spite of Admeto's resistance, brandishing his sword, it is all over.

The recitative cadence in c after Alceste's "son morta" is the signal for the great chorus of mourning to begin, heard first as an orchestral ritornello. Then after intervening material, the chorus proper ("Piangi o patria, o Tessagli: è morta Alceste!"), a double chorus divided between off- and onstage groups, resounds. There are three repetitions of the lugubrious refrain. Here Gluck summons up once again the high pathos and choral majesty of Act I. The effect is shattering. Tragedy and the key of c are impressed so deeply on our souls that what comes next is difficult to accept. Apollo descends in a burst of light, to the astounded comments of the survivors, and to birdlike music in G, with flutes and trills. He restores Alceste to Admeto, saying that the magnanimous act of Alceste pleased the gods. A G-major chorus of joy praising Alceste as a woman without equal ends the opera. We can accept the ending more readily by realizing that for the opera's first audiences it was Maria Theresa who was being praised as a woman without equal. Originally both the score and the text were to be dedicated to her. She allowed only the text dedication.

A great masterwork is often best understood by learning how it affected the audience for which it was created. In the case of *Alceste* we are fortunate to have an eyewitness account by a man of the theater who was unusually sensitive and probing. Joseph von Sonnenfels was professor of political science at the University of Vienna and an outspoken liberal who opposed both torture and the death penalty in the councils of the co-regency. Under the guise of a French visitor to Vienna, he admonished his fellow citizens to cultivate theater in the German language in *Briefe über die wienerischen Schaubühne* of 1767–68. His efforts in this direction culminated in the founding of the National Theater in 1776. It was Sonnenfels, a playwright of some renown among many other things, who was assigned to interrogate Caron de Beaumarchais after one of his mad escapades led him to Vienna in 1774.[85] Sonnenfels' taste tended toward the serious and the sublime. He was a friend of Lessing and a foe of the improvised Hanswurst comedy; plays and operas that were serious and independent of foreign models were most apt to please him. He was, in other words, the ideal critic for Gluck.

Sonnenfels attended several performances of *Alceste*. His review begins by extolling its composer.

> The music is in the hands of a man for whom the art of music is not just a studied series of chords and resolutions, but rather the accents of the passions . . . who knows how to discover the accents of the soul, and thus how to make song expressive and make it speaking ["redend"]; in the hands of a man who composes in the spirit of the poet and who, where the ordinary worker with notes is tied down by rules, breaks the bounds and soars over the rules, to the extent that his genial freedom becomes law-giving and a model for others; in the hands of such a man, music must work wonders.[86]

Sonnenfels does not even mention Calzabigi once by name, and one would never learn from his long review that the opera was in Italian, not German. After inveighing against Italian opera, "with its castrated singers" (bound to disgust a Sonnenfels on moral grounds) and its music "pleasing only to the ears, not to the soul" (cf. Calzabigi's letter to Prince Kaunitz in Appendix 2), he returns to Gluck. "Such a man is the creator of *Alceste*. His power of invention is enormous, and the bounds of national music are too narrow to contain him; out of Italian music, French music, and the music of all other nations, he has made a music that is his own; or, rather, he has sought all the tones of true expression in Nature, and has mastered them." Hiller, a gifted and important composer of opera in his own right, does not comment on *Alceste* and the question of national music per se, but in the index of his volume he describes it as "an Italian opera in the French manner."

Sonnenfels next takes up the relationship of the parts to the whole. Getting this relationship just right he sees as Gluck's great achievement; and remember, he was relying on his experience of the work in the theater, not on the score, which had not yet been printed. He allows the poet credit for using the "unaffected language of emotion," but it is Gluck's music to which he keeps returning.

[85] Alfred Ritter von Arneth, *Beaumarchais und Sonnenfels* (Vienna, 1868).
[86] "Über die zu Wien aufgeführte Oper Alceste, aus den Briefen über die wienerischen Schaubühne" in Johann Adam Hiller, *Wöchentliche Nachrichten und Ammerkungen die Musik betreffend*, installments 17 and 18 of October, 1768.

Alceste was for this able man a broad avenue on which he could display the fruitfulness of his ideas. It was difficult to escape uniformity and repetitiveness in this tale, which is so loaded throughout with sadness and depression. Gluck overcame this difficulty with great glory. His choruses are always substantially variegated, his recitative expressive, and the accompaniments are not a tuning up or a compulsory filler for the in-between spaces, but rather an essential part of the expression that make the whole content intelligible and make the words almost unnecessary.

The performance of *Orfeo* at Munich discussed above elicited a similar comment to the effect that the music and the stage picture were so powerful and communicative that the words were not needed. It is true that Gluck often has such a potent effect on the listener that the words are put in the shadow. Poor Calzabigi! This was just the opposite of what he intended. As he (not Gluck) wrote in the famous preface to *Alceste*, "I have striven to restrict music to its true office of serving poetry." Berlioz had the good sense to realize that his statement did not suit Gluck's music at all.

Sonnenfels goes on to praise individual scenes. He singles out the monologue of the high priest in Act I, and the way Gluck's orchestra paints the holy awe of Apollo's approaching presence. He speaks of "the great, inimitable scene following the oracle, where Gluck becomes at once poet and composer." This is an expression that Gluck used to describe himself. Moreover, André-Ernest-Modeste Grétry, who knew Gluck well, says in his memoirs that "the masterly plans of *Orfeo* and *Alceste* were suggested by Gluck himself—one is both poet and musician when operating like Gluck."

Visual metaphors also help Sonnenfels convey the greatness of what he witnessed in the Burgtheater in December 1767 and January 1768. Antonia Bernasconi, whose acting, singing, and arm gestures he describes in searching detail, was "worthy of the brush of a Raphael." Sonnenfels was especially proud of her in the title role because of her German birth. There is praise also for Giuseppe Tibaldi as Admeto. When Alceste embraces her children at the end of Act II, Sonnenfels describes Bernasconi in terms of Clytemnestra embracing her daughter as Calchas prepares the gruesome sacrifice "as painted by the French Raphael" (Poussin). This is contemporary criticism of the finest sort. The whole of it deserves detailed study.

The Mozarts returned from Moravia to Vienna in January 1768, in time to see *Alceste* in the Burgtheater. In his letter of 30 January—3 February 1768, Leopold wrote to his landlord Hagenauer in Salzburg, "There are no singers here for serious operas. Even Gluck's opera of mourning ["trauerige opera"], the *Alceste,* was performed by mere opera buffa singers." Leopold exaggerates. The tenor Tibaldi was a seria singer (and a composer as well) who had appeared in operas by Gluck, Hasse, and Traetta before *Alceste*. Bernasconi

FIGURE 3.9. François-Joseph Bélanger. Stage design for Act III of Gluck's *Alceste*, Paris, 1776.

had sung parts like Sandrina in Niccolò Piccinni's *La buona figliuola* (in which role there is in fact one pathetic aria in the minor mode) at the Burgtheater in 1766 and other comic roles. But it should not be forgotten that she made her debut in Munich in 1762 in a seria role, Aspasia, in the setting of Metastasio's *Temistocle* by her stepfather, Andrea Bernasconi.

The original *Alceste* had the advantage of being designed by Italy's greatest scenographers, the brothers Fabrizio and Bernardino Galliari of Milan.[87] Their designs have not survived, or they remain to be identified. For the

[87] Mercedes Viale Ferrero, *La scenografia del '700 e i fratelli Galliari* (Turin, 1963), p. 238, item 34, says that only Fabrizio traveled to Vienna.

Paris version of 1776, there exists an admirable design for Act III by François-Joseph Bélanger (Figure 3.9).

Theatrical records are not extant to tell us how many performances there were of the original production, but Calzabigi says that they were curtailed solely "because the delicate voice of Signora Bernasconi could dominate the entire title part with the necessary vibrancy and energy only with difficulty."[88] She was so good an actress, he might have added, that projecting the entire part must have been literally killing.

Alceste did not lack detractors in Vienna. Metastasio was silent, but one can sense his opinion in what Khevenhüller wrote: "The libretto was judged by the public once again to be pathetic and lugubrious; fortunately there was at the end a ballet by Noverre in the grotesque style, which won universal applause." The implied comparison is with *Orfeo*, and suggests that these two works were only for connoisseurs. Also implied is the notion that Noverre, the new choreographer in the Burgtheater, may not have worked with Calzabigi and Gluck as easily as did his predecessor, Angiolini.

The success of *Alceste*, despite the grumbling of one party at court, was undeniable. It raised Calzabigi's stock in Gluck's eyes to its highest point. Knowing this, we can understand more readily how Gluck allowed his librettist a free hand concerning the manifesto that would serve as a preface. As Calzabigi wrote to Count Greppi in Milan, a year after the premiere:

> The agreement between Gluck and me is that he will publish the score only subject to my approval, as I am allowing for a printed preface that explains the motive or rather the motives of the enormous change we have made in dramatic composition. This preface has not yet been written, and the title, the dedication, and, as mentioned, this most necessary preface are lacking.[89]

To be noted here especially is the use of the first person plural, "we." It contradicts Calzabigi's later claims that he alone engineered the reform of music drama.

On the strength of *Alceste*, Gluck ventured upon a third operatic collaboration with Calzabigi. *Paride ed Elena* was derived from the *Heroides* of Ovid. It reached the stage of the Burgtheater as a five-act *dramma per musica* in November of 1770, with choreography by Noverre. The new opera was a fiasco, for which Calzabigi is generally blamed. The libretto carried his vendetta against Metastasio one step further by advancing directly into the

[88] Letter of 6 April 1768 to Count Greppi in Donà, "Dagli archivi milanesi," p. 276.

[89] Letter of 12 December 1768, in Donà, "Dagli archivi milanesi," p. 280. The disputatious preface has been translated many times into English, by, among others, Einstein, *Gluck*, pp. 98–100; Strunk, *Source Readings*, pp. 673–75; and Piero Weiss and Richard Taruskin, *Music in the Western World: A History of Music in Documents* (New York, 1984), pp. 301–2.

enemy camp and attempting a galant subject, the wooing of Helen by Paris.[90] Gluck wrote much beautiful music to clothe it, but after *Alceste* his vocation was so obviously the grand and the sublime that it is a pity that Calzabigi did not have recourse again to Euripides, or to Sophocles.

The score to *Paride* was published soon after the first performance, prefaced by another manifesto written by Calzabigi and signed by Gluck. In this preface Calzabigi puts the best face possible on what can only be called a failed experiment, with a heavy dose of rationalization.

> The drama of Paris did not provide the composer's fancy with those strong passions, those majestic images, and those tragic situations that in *Alceste* shook the spectators and gave so much scope for grandiose harmonic effects. Thus the same forceful and energetic music will surely not be expected . . . There is here no question of a wife about to lose her husband, who, in order to save him, has the courage to evoke the infernal gods in a dread forest wrapped in the black shades of night; who in the extreme agonies of death still trembles for the destiny of her children, and has to tear herself from a husband she adores. Here a young lover is presented in contrast with the waywardness of a lovely and honest woman, who at last triumphs by all the wiles of an industrious passion. I had to exert myself in order to find some variety of color, seeking it in the two different nations, Phrygia and Sparta, and contrasting the rude and savage nature of the one with all that is delicate and soft in the other.

Calzabigi's idea of characteristic and contrasting national traits helped Gluck with the musical characterization up to a point, but much more would have been done to make them dramatic in a performance under Gluck. The preface goes on to emphasize the importance of carefully nuanced performance, illustrated by way of "Che farò?" in *Orfeo*. The soprano castrato Millico sang Paris, and the other roles (Helen, Cupid, and Athena) were taken by female sopranos, a limitation in vocal types that Gluck imposed on himself to see if he could triumph over it, which he did.[91] But the vocal sameness did not help to overcome a libretto that was in reality little more than a thinly veiled polemic. With this work Gluck had had enough of Calzabigi's continual badgering of Metastasio. There were no further collaborations, although Calzabigi remained in Vienna for three more years, until 1773.

Two further librettos by Marco Coltellini marked the concluding phase of the Viennese reform movement. These both followed "the new plan" (as Calzabigi put it in his letter to Kaunitz on *Alceste*) in that they blended French elements with the standard Italian stock of recitative and aria. *Amore e Psiche*

[90] Bruno Brizi, "L'impudente provocazione del Paride," in *Paride ed Elena*, ed. Cesare Galla (Program Book of the Teatro Olimpico) (Vicenza, 1988), pp. 57–90.

[91] Alan Curtis, "L'opera dei soprani," in *Paride ed Elena*, ed. Cesare Galla (Vicenza, 1988), pp. 119–24.

was set by Florian Gassmann and first performed in the Burgtheater on 5 October 1767. *Armida* may have been set as early as 1766 or 1767 by Giuseppe Scarlatti. Salieri composed it as his fifth opera for Vienna, where it reached the stage of the Burgtheater on 2 June 1771. Also worthy of mention is Coltellini's tragic intermezzo for three singers, *Piramo e Tisbe*, set by Hasse in 1768 and revised in 1770.

With Gluck's turning toward Paris for his remaining operas, and the departure of both Coltellini and Calzabigi by 1773, Vienna's direct role in the operatic reform was over. Metastasio's retirement in 1771 meant the end of opera seria as well, at least in Vienna. In a contract dated 13 April 1772, Constanza Baglioni and her sister Rosa promised to sing the parts assigned to them in Vienna "in tutte le Opere tanto serie che buffe, e nelle Accademie" (in all serious as well as comic operas, and in concerts).[92] But no more *opere serie* were performed in either of the court theaters. There were at best only a few seria roles in comic opera henceforth.

During the 1770s the focus of operatic reform shifted from Vienna to Paris, whither Gluck transferred his enormous creative energies, matching them with a whole new set of collaborators. Old-fashioned *tragédie lyrique* soon succumbed as a result. Piccinni arrived as a rival reformer with his *Roland* of 1778. French and Italian approaches to lyric tragedy fructified each other, and the gap between them, once so vast, continued to shrink. From this *rapprochement* of two great traditions the terrain was prepared for Mozart to create his *Idomeneo* in 1780–81.

[92] A facsimile of the contract is printed in Gustav Zechmeister, *Der Wiener Theater nächst der Burg und nächst dem Kärntnerthor von 1747 bis 1776* (Vienna, 1971), p. 348.

4

Haydn: Early Years
to ca. 1770

Youth in Vienna

OSEPH HAYDN was born in a farmhouse at Rohrau, Lower Austria, on 31 March 1732. Late in life he told many anecdotes about his youth to Georg August Griesinger and Albert Christoph Dies, who sometimes corroborate and sometimes contradict each other.[1] Georg Reutter, Kapellmeister of St. Stephen's cathedral, was searching the countryside for good voices around 1740 when he heard the young Haydn in Hainburg, a town on the Danube not far from Rohrau, and just upstream from Pressburg/Bratislava. According to Haydn's autobiographical letter of 1776, he was taken to Vienna and installed with the other choirboys in the Kapellmeister's house, a low building directly before the main entrance to the cathedral (Figure 4.1), where he "was taught singing, keyboard, and the violin from very good masters."[2] As long as his soprano voice held true, he sang "with great suc-

---

[1] I shall quote them from *Joseph Haydn: Eighteenth-Century Gentleman and Genius*, a translation with introduction and notes by Vernon Gotwals of the *Biographische Notizen über Joseph Haydn* by G. A. Griesinger (1810) and the *Biographische Nachrichten von Joseph Haydn* by A. C. Dies (1810) (Madison, Wis., 1963). A supplementary work of more dubious credibility is Giuseppe Carpani, *Le Haydine ovvero Lettere sulla vita e le opere del celebre maestro Giuseppe Haydn* (Milan, 1812).

[2] Haydn's letter, dated 6 July 1776, was written in answer to a request from *Das gelehrte Österreich*, in the first volume of which it was published. I use the English translation of H. C. Robbins Landon, *Haydn: Chronicle and Works*, 5 vols. (Bloomington, Ind., 1976–80), 2: 397–99. For the original German, see Joseph Haydn, *Gesammelte Briefe und Aufzeichnungen*, ed. Dénes Bartha (Kassel, 1965), pp. 76–82.

FIGURE 4.1.
Anonymous
watercolor of St.
Stephen's Cathedral,
Vienna; in the
foreground, the choir
house.

cess, not only at St. Stephen's but at court." Reutter's official positions at both institutions made for an easy exchange of musical forces between them. Joining Haydn in the choir school in 1745 was his younger brother Michael. In addition to music lessons, the boys received instruction in Latin, arithmetic, writing, and the catechism.

Reutter was too busy or too self-important to give much instruction himself. Haydn told Griesinger that he remembered only two lessons in composition from "the excellent Reutter"; on the other hand, "Reutter did encourage him to make whatever variations he liked on the motets and the Salves that he had to sing in church, and this practice early led him to ideas of his own which Reutter corrected." Griesinger quotes Haydn directly on how the fledgling composer attempted grandiose works in eight and sixteen parts: "I used to think then that it was all right if only the paper were pretty full. Reutter laughed at my immature output, at measures that no throat and no instrument could have executed, and he scolded me for composing in sixteen parts before I understood two-part setting."

Haydn's voice changed late, around 1750. There was some question of prolonging his career as a soprano, but Haydn's father, a wheelwright by trade, put a stop to this idea. Dismissed from the choir school, Haydn could expect no financial support from his family or any other source. He was on his own for the first time in his life. Eventually he moved into a garret of the Michaelerhaus, next to the Michaelerkirche. (See Figure 5.7.) With more than a tinge of romantic fancy, Griesinger describes "a wretched little attic room without a stove in which he was scarcely sheltered from the rain . . . Innocent of the comforts of life, he divided his whole time among the giving of lessons, the study of his art, and performing; he played for money in serenades and in the orchestras, and he was industrious in the practice of composition."

Haydn's life offers many examples of strokes of fortune succeeding adversity. It turned out that the Michaelerhaus, several floors lower, provided comfortable quarters for Metastasio and the Martínez family, whose daughter Marianna Haydn was instructing as early as 1751 in singing and keyboard playing, in exchange for free meals. Acquaintance with Metastasio led to Haydn's meeting Nicola Porpora, who was by this time nearly seventy but still in high repute as a teacher of singing. Porpora was "too grand and too fond of his ease to accompany on the fortepiano himself," says Griesinger, so Haydn was engaged for this task. (The instrument mentioned reflects the time of writing, not mid-eighteenth century practice; Dies relates the same incident using the term "am Flugl," meaning harpsichord.) Then, again quoting Haydn directly, Griesinger adds: "There was no lack of *Asino, Coglione, Birbante,* and pokes in the ribs, but I put up with it all, for I profited greatly with Porpora in singing, in composition, and in the Italian language." Viennese court composers like Reutter and Bonno had the advantage over Haydn of having studied in Italy with the best masters; but by a stroke of fortune Haydn, without leaving Vienna, studied with one of the last of the great Neapolitan masters.

If we reorder the gifts Haydn mentions receiving from Porpora, we arrive at a historical conjecture as to how the modern musical style was built in three stages, one reposing on the other: the Italian language, Italian singing, and the Neapolitan style of composition. Porpora came to Vienna from Dresden in 1752 or 1753. The watershed his instruction represented is stated in no uncertain terms in Haydn's autobiographical letter of 1776: "I wrote fluently and diligently [the German "fleissig" means both] but was not well grounded enough ["doch nicht genug gegrundet"] until I had the good fortune at last to learn the true fundamentals of composition from the celebrated Signor Porpora."

Through Porpora, Haydn came to the attention of other leading figures in music. One of Porpora's pupils was the mistress of the Venetian ambassador, Pietro Correr, who summered in the country near where Haydn was born. The lady of course took her singing teacher with her; he, in turn, took Haydn along. "For three months here Haydn acted as Porpora's servant, eating at Correr's servants' table and receiving six ducats a month" (Griesinger). The summer in question was probably 1754, the same during which the court visited Prince Hildburghausen's splendid residence of Schlosshof and witnessed the enchanting spectacle of Metastasio's *Le cinesi*, with Gluck's music. This was perhaps the first occasion that brought Gluck and Haydn together. Haydn told Griesinger that "he sometimes had to accompany on the clavier for Porpora at Prince von Hildburghausen's, in the presence of Gluck, Wagenseil, and other celebrated masters, and the approval of such connoisseurs served as a special encouragement to him." Both Wagenseil and Gluck proved to be important models for Haydn in his own compositions.

Haydn also studied textbooks in his quest to develop his musical skills. Later in life he remembered grappling with the exercises in Fux's *Gradus ad Parnassum* even during his earliest years as a student at the choir school. Since Haydn worked through these exercises at various stages of his long life, either by himself or with pupils, his memory may have been confused on this point. Another work that Griesinger says Haydn studied was Mattheson's *Der vollkommene Kapellmeister* of 1739. Dies sets Haydn's acquisition and study of textbooks during the time of his work with Porpora (ca. 1753–55) and mentions the texts by Fux and Mattheson and one by Carl Philipp Emanuel Bach as well, which could be nothing other than the first part of *Versuch über die wahre Art das Clavier zu spielen* (1753). Griesinger introduces Bach in a different context, as Haydn's companion in his garret when he sat at his "worm-eaten" clavier. Recent scholarship has cast doubt upon this claim, along with Haydn's supposed statements about how much he owed to Emanuel Bach.[3] There is, significantly, no mention of Bach in Haydn's crucial autobiographical letter of 1776, which is in every way more reliable than the accounts, from witnesses who were far from nonpartisan, of his musings as an old man.

Haydn's lot as a freelance artist gradually improved as a result of taking on many pupils and playing in public. By 1754 he was able to pay back a

---

[3] A. Peter Brown, *Joseph Haydn's Keyboard Music* (Bloomington, Ind., 1986), Essay VII, pp. 203–27, "Joseph Haydn and C. P. E. Bach: The Question of Influence."

loan of 150 gulden. "In the beginning Haydn received only two gulden a month for lessons, but the price gradually rose to five gulden," according to Griesinger. Sunday mornings for Haydn meant as many as three different church jobs. Evenings were often devoted to serenading. He recalled having written a quintet to such purpose in the year 1753, and as we shall see presently, it may have survived. One of these occasions led to a meeting with important consequences: Joseph Kurz-Bernardon, the actor-director, commissioned Haydn to write music for *Der krumme Teufel* after hearing the composer's serenade to Franziska, his first wife. A performance of *Der krumme Teufel* is known to have taken place at the Kärntnerthor Theater on 29 May 1753; it was banned shortly thereafter.

EARLIEST COMPOSITIONS

UPON rediscovering the *Missa brevis* in F in his old age, Haydn added the date 1749, i.e., just at the crucial juncture of his life when he had to leave the choir school. Since the work requires two solo sopranos, the temptation is strong to imagine that they were once embodied by Michael and Joseph Haydn; at the least, the two brothers must have sung music quite like this in St. Stephen's and other Viennese churches. The combination of two soprano solos with mixed choir was unusual, so much so that it strengthens the hypothesis that the two brothers were the soloists.

The music is pleasant and economical, with small melismatic solos embedded in a straightforward and mainly syllabic choral setting. The orchestra consists of two violins and bass (plus organ to realize the figured bass). This typical texture of the church trio was quite challenging for Haydn at the time. One of the most memorable moments in the work comes at the end of the Gloria, when the two soprano soloists soar unexpectedly up to high B♭ in thirds. Haydn made it even more memorable by repeating the whole ending of the Gloria to close the Credo. The beginning of the Benedictus shows particularly well how the composer was able to deploy the fashionable galant style of the mid-century (Example 4.1). Galant mannerisms include the raised-fifth degree (beginning of the solo, and repeated, *forte*, in syncopes when the violins come in at the end of the solo); the triplet-figure *sdrucciolo* on the first "venit"; trilled figures in thirds; and various kinds of expressive appoggiature.

What makes the mass more Italianate still is the phrase structure. Haydn sets the first solo as if it were a *settenario* in an Italian aria, which almost invariably produced a three-measure phrase in conjunction with triple meter. For the second phrase, he makes the two voices get through the text,

EXAMPLE 4.1. *Haydn,* Missa brevis *in F (1749)*

now slightly longer, in another three-measure segment. The third phrase completes the text and stretches out to a phrase nearly twice as long because of its melismas. Haydn allows himself more expansion here than in most of the rest of the mass, which does not last more than about twelve minutes altogether. There is no setting of "Dona nobis pacem." Rather, following an old Austrian custom, the singers were expected to reuse the music of the Kyrie as best they could to clothe the final words, as indicated in one source by the words "Dona nobis come Kyrie." The custom was evidently a precedent for the later practice of composed endings that reused Kyrie material. Haydn's joy at rediscovering so early a work of his led him to provide it with wind parts in the hope of achieving publication, which did not happen. It is noteworthy that he made no attempt to correct the often faulty part writing. What he admired in the mass, he told Dies, was "the melody and a certain youthful fire."

Other sacred works belonging to the period around or shortly after 1750 are the four motets for the feast of Corpus Christi, beginning with *Lauda Sion*. The forces are the same as the *Missa brevis* in F, except where they are expanded to include two oboes and two trumpets, in keeping with the festive nature of the texts. The fourth motet includes a two-voiced passage that presages what would later become the climax of Haydn's most famous melody of all, the "Emperor's Hymn" of 1797, using the very same tones in descending sequence from C: 8 - 7 / 7 6 5 / 6 - 5 / 5 4 3 /.[4] When Haydn tries to turn the same music into a four-part texture, he gets into trouble. He places his tenor too low to have much effect and, worse, gives him parallel unisons with the bass much of the time. The fault is covered somewhat by the exuberant decoration of the melody by the first violins—the kind of *Musikanten* decoration we can imagine Haydn improvising with Reutter's encouragement in St Stephen's. Both aspects, the faulty part writing and the florid yodeling of the violin, illustrate what Haydn meant when he said that before he studied with Porpora, he wrote fluently but not altogether correctly. What is so novel and refreshing in the Corpus Christi motets is the folklike tone that Haydn introduces.

The difference that a good and strict teacher made in Haydn's case becomes evident from the *Salve regina* in E, to which Haydn late in life assigned the date 1756.[5] This Marian antiphon often inspired extraordinary responses from composers—such is the case with Pergolesi, Leo, and

[4] The music is given in Landon, *Haydn*, 1: 154–56. Landon credits Georg Feder with calling attention to the resemblance.
[5] Excerpts are printed ibid., 1: 159–65.

Galuppi. Haydn's 1756 setting is no less extraordinary. He chose the rare key of E and began with an unusually slow tempo, *Adagio*. The violins and basses intone a unison E, *forte,* on the first beat, to which the violins answer with a falling third, 5 3, doubled at the third, softly, high above, on the second beat; the unison B *forte* on the third beat is answered similarly, 4 2. Such a beginning is so expressive it almost evokes speech. The essential Haydn is already present here. When the composer wrote *The Seven Last Words* for Cadiz Cathedral in 1786, one of his deepest and most heartfelt works, he chose for Christ's third speech on the cross, "Woman, behold thy son," not only the key of E but also a virtually identical beginning, except that the falling thirds come on the strong beats.

When the soprano solo enters singing "Salve," it is on a held B for the first measure (the falling thirds), then a held high E for the second, against which the violins sound Haydn's already familiar descending sequence from the tonic, 8 7 6 5, 6 5 4 3. An opening *messa di voce* like this was a favorite device with Hasse and, before him, with Porpora. The overlapping groups of three eighth notes between voice and accompaniment as the voice first sings "Salve regina" were made famous by Pergolesi, and can be found at the end of his *Salve regina*. The breadth of Haydn's harmonic movement, on the other hand, suggests the late *Salve regina* in F by Leo. Haydn confines the solo's melismas to the last parts of the period, and they are lavish when they come, as is the case with his teacher Porpora.

Haydn imparts a sense of cyclic unity to the work as a whole by returning to the inspired opening idea, the falling thirds above the tonic, then above the dominant, and recomposing it to form the main idea of the final part, "O clemens." The chorus enters intoning the same text in flawless four-part texture, for which Haydn surely had to thank Porpora's strictness with him. Before the piece closes, there is a dialogued duet between the two violins, in the manner of Sammartini, and a cadenza for the solo soprano. Haydn's emergence as a composer of stature in the most modern Italian styles is nowhere better studied than in this *Salve regina*. The work suggests that its composer felt a special affinity to the Blessed Virgin, who is imagined not so much in regal splendor, as Queen of Heaven, but as the personification of a radiant, blissful, and feminine grace, a brightly lit and airy vision of beauty.

Analogies are to be sought, above all, in the religious paintings of Austria's greatest artist, Franz Anton Maulbertsch, who excelled in depicting light-filled spaces. His Assumption of the Virgin, an altarpiece of 1758 for a church in Mainz, shimmers with devotional ecstasy. (See Plate VII.) Its irregular contours intensify the experience of rising to a mystical height. The renowned Assumption of the Virgin painted in 1733–34 by Sebastiano Ricci for the Karlskirche provided inspiration to Maulbertsch, who surpassed the Italian master in luminosity and expressive power.

The *Salve*'s opening provides the opportunity to mention an anonymous piece of stage music that is, in all likelihood, also by Haydn. Whereas nothing whatsoever is known to have survived from *Der krumme Teufel* (1753)—neither scenario, libretto, nor musical excerpts—the same is not true of several other German comedies of the mid-1750s. Four numbers survive from Johann Georg Heubel's *Leopoldel der teutsche Robinson* (1754), and they stand a cut above the average level of the stage music at the Kärntnerthor Theater in sophistication; one, an aria in E for Colombina, incorporates the first two measures of the *Salve* in E.[6] Because of this, and the generally high quality of the aria, attribution to anyone but Haydn is difficult. Why would a composer resort to similar music for two such different purposes, the one sacred and exalted, the other secular and commonplace? Though the situations are very different, both pieces have to do with love and the eternal feminine. Thus it is not altogether surprising that they might provoke somewhat similar musical responses in a composer like Haydn, who was very partial to women, as we know from several charming anecdotes he told about himself. One possibility that cannot be dismissed is that the musical ideas linking both pieces originated in some love song in *Der krumme Teufel*, which saw only three performances before it was banned. The normal thing to do with music once it no longer served its original purpose was to adapt it to some other use.

Concertos figure prominently among Haydn's earliest compositions. When the composer left St. Stephen's, he eked out a living with several church jobs, as he later recalled, playing first violin in the Leopoldstadt Church of the Barmherziger Brüder and organ in the chapel of Count Haugwitz as well as in the Carmelite Church in the Leopoldstadt. Organ and violin are the solo instruments called for in Haydn's earliest concertos, which he presumably wrote for himself as soloist. In 1756 Haydn's first love, Theresa Keller, took the veil (three years later he married her sister). In a letter of 1803 Griesinger mentions that "Haydn had just found a concerto for the organ and violin which he wrote fifty years ago for his sister-in-law when she took the veil."[7] To the well-known Organ Concerto in C Haydn later in

---

[6] All four anonymous pieces are edited in *Deutsche Komödienarien, 1754–58,* part 2, by Camillo Schoenbaum and Herbert Zeman, *DTÖ* 121 (1971): 17nd–41. Eva Badura-Skoda discusses the connection between the *Salve* in E and Colombina's aria, which she gives complete in a keyboard reduction, in "Teutsche Comödien-Arien und Joseph Haydn," *Der junge Haydn,* ed. Vera Schwarz (Graz, 1972), pp. 59–72. Badura-Skoda also points out the similarities between the rising melody with which the aria begins and Haydn's keyboard sonata in A (Hob. XV:5, finale).

[7] Landon, *Haydn,* 1: 81.

FIGURE 4.2. Autograph of Haydn's Organ Concerto in C, 1756.

life added the date 1756, which is perhaps a few years too early, but shows how the work, along with the *Salve* in E, was connected in his mind with the fateful year of decision that removed Theresa Keller from the secular world (Figure 4.2).[8]

Viennese concertos by which to measure Haydn's early efforts are not abundant. Those by Monn are rooted in the Baroque past, and seem to have no connection with Haydn's. The Organ Concerto in B♭ of 1753 by Gregor Joseph Werner is closer in the way it relies on chordal filigree work for the solo instrument; its *Tempo di Menuet* finale in 3/8 is quite galant. Wagenseil's very galant harpsichord concertos cannot be precisely dated, but they likely provided Haydn with his main models. Reutter contributed to the genre too, but he hardly offered a good model for a young composer; his Organ Con-

[8] Anthony van Hoboken, *Joseph Haydn: Thematisch-bibliographisches Werkverzeichnis*, 2 vols. (Mainz, 1957–71), XVIII:1.

certo in C bristles with crudities that make Vivaldi, by contrast, seem a paragon of good part writing. Nothing in earlier Viennese music quite prepares us for the polish and easy grace of Haydn's first organ concerto.

Haydn wrote his organ concertos for a solo instrument without pedals that was limited in range to C - c3 (i.e., Hob. XVIII:1, 2, 5, 6, 7, 8, and 10); works exceeding these limits at either end required the harpsichord (i.e., No. 3 in F, No. 4 in G, and the famous No. 11 in D), and it is evident that any of the organ concertos could serve as harpsichord concertos.[9] The first concerto has a gem of a *Largo* for a middle movement; near the end of the movement comes a pause on I$^{6/4}$ calling for a cadenza, the bass being approached in the modern way familiar from Mozart's concertos and found in Leo's late *Salve regina* in F (ca. 1740?), a work that Haydn's *Largo* seems close to because of its broad span and slow-moving harmonies.

The two outer movements are unusually extensive: the first is a *Moderato* in 2/4, comprising 260 measures; the third, *Allegro molto* in 3/8, with 229 measures. Each, upon reaching the beginning of the seconda parte, makes the familiar gesture of stating the main theme in V, then in I. In the first movement Haydn is not content until he has reached several cadences on vi; then he makes a leisurely move back to I for a full reprise, beginning with the main theme. Wagensilian is the way a half cadence on V is used as a springboard for an arrival in V. Also characteristic of the older master are the very galant chromatic inflections 5♯ 6 or 7♭ 5♯ 6, which occur in all three movements and help unify the cycle. It is rare to encounter Haydn in so leisurely a frame of mind as met in the concerto's outer movements, but not atypical of some of his sacred and operatic music. Time did not press Austrian churchgoers during the 1750s, when Maria Theresa was in her heyday, and Haydn was only too happy to fill up their services with cheerful, easily absorbed music. Such prolixity was the musical equivalent of long sermons. The lacy filigree of the solo part suggests nothing so much as the reluctance of the stucco workers in Rococo churches to leave any surface undecorated.

Another bright spot in Haydn's early instrumental music is represented by his cassations. The quintet that Haydn recalled composing in 1753 for one of his serenading forays may be the Cassation in G for string quintet with two violas (Hob. II:2). It has six movements, comprising the regular divertimento components of fast, minuet, slow, minuet, fast, plus an initial *Presto* in 2/4 entitled "Scherzo," which is a binary dance piece with trio and da capo. The work is attractive enough as a whole to make it plausible that Haydn should have remembered it so long. The tune of the opening movement has analo-

[9] Horst Walter, "Das Tasteninstrument beim jungen Haydn," *Der junge Haydn* (Graz, 1972), pp. 237–48.

gies with two folk tunes, one Croatian, the other German.[10] The second movement shows a rudimentary but clear sonata form. After the double bar in the middle, the seconda parte starts with the main theme on V, then on I, standard operating procedure in Italian sonatas around 1750; after modulations the reprise sets in with the main theme in the tonic minor, which mitigates the effect of several appearances of the same idea in the middle of the piece. The third movement, entitled "Menuet," expands beyond the 8 + 8-measure structure of most real minuets for dancing, to become a symmetrical structure with full reprise: ‖:A(12):‖:B(16)A′(12):‖. Its trio, in tonic minor, begins quietly, with smooth rhythms, but by the end of both periods there are offbeat accents, and *forte* contrasts erupt throughout the second strain.

The next movement, *Adagio*, is a serenade in the most specific sense. There is a two-measure "curtain," a chordal introduction played pizzicato, as if by guitars, that sweeps aside to reveal, center stage, the ardent lover pouring out his song—i.e., the first violin playing *coll'arco* (presumably Haydn himself). Haydn would repeat this device often in later works. The subordinate instruments keep up the same texture and play pizzicato throughout (except for the first viola, which plays broken chords *coll'arco*). Vocal features abound in the melody, which begins with the typically operatic *messa di voce*. Yet the melody is not really suitable for voice, but well conceived to take full advantage of the violin. The part writing is smooth and unadventurous, which probably indicates that the work postdates Haydn's tutelage under Porpora. Is this very movement not, in fact, a tribute to the Italian *cantilena* for which Porpora was so famous? Domenico Corri, who was the principal heir and transmitter of Porpora's methods of teaching, devoted the first lesson in *The Singer's Precepter* (1810) precisely to achieving the *messa di voce* on different notes of the scale. The *Adagio* ends as it began, with the two-measure curtain, which now closes, the whole tableau having taken but 24 measures (2 + 11 to a cadence on V, then 9 + 2).

Framing the *Adagio* is another Menuet, this one with more contrapuntal interaction between the bass and treble, and more chromaticism; the trio is again in tonic minor and begins with a vigorous unison passage, *forte*. The finale, *Presto* in 2/4, begins with a jocular tune in the first violin, staccato and in even eighth notes, beginning with an upbeat (Example 4.2a). The second violin and bass accompany the tune. The first viola then takes up the violin's tune, accompanied by the second viola and bass, ending on V instead of I. Haydn has pitted violins plus bass against violas plus bass throughout the work, so this movement is a summing up of one of its main textural fea-

---

[10]Landon, *Haydn*, 1: 182, quotes both.

EXAMPLE 4.2. *Haydn, Cassation in G (Hob. II:2)*

a. Main theme

b. Seconda parte

tures—a dialogue between threesomes. The work has also become a little more chromatic as it progressed, so we should not be surprised when Haydn unleashes a chromatic surge, *forte* and legato, in response to the prancing staccato eighth notes, just after the double bar in the middle (Example 4.2b). A witty exchange like this does not need words to achieve its effect, although it suggests them. Haydn has found the playful spirit that we admire so much in his instrumental music; it is amazing that he found it so early. What the composer deploys here is the same jest that would enliven the finale of the Symphony No. 97 nearly forty years later.

A delightful type of light music for entertainment by the young Haydn is the group of several divertimenti for winds, presumably written for Count Morzin's *Harmonie* band. The Divertimento in F (also called *Parthia*, Hob. II:15), dated 1760, requires pairs of oboes, horns, and bassoons. Its five movements are in the pattern familiar from Haydn's divertimenti for strings: fast, minuet, slow, minuet, fast. Only the trio of the first Minuet provides key contrast (B♭), but the movements are so short that the problem of too much tonal sameness does not arise. A similar work is the *Feld-Parthie* in F (Hob. II:16) for pairs of English horns, horns, violins, and bassoons, likewise dated 1760, which shares the same five-movement form.

THE QUARTET-DIVERTIMENTI (OP. 1 AND OP. 2)

THE *Divertimenti a quattro* that came to be published eventually as Op. 1 and Op. 2 were the first works to carry Haydn's name far beyond Vienna. For their historical importance, as well as for their intrinsic beauties, they deserve close attention. Our main concern is not with Haydn's works that remained local—the baryton trios, for example—but with the widely circulated works that gradually made Haydn the dominant figure in European music. This means in the first instance his symphonies, but second only to them his quartets. Around 1757–58 Haydn found a patron in the person of Joseph von Fürnberg. Baron Fürnberg owned an estate called Weinzierl, located in the charming countryside near Melk Abbey on the Danube, about fifty miles upstream from Vienna. Griesinger relates how the baron brought together his pastor, his manager, Haydn, and Anton Johann Albrechtsberger, who played the cello, described as the brother of the celebrated contrapuntist (Johann Georg, who was employed at this time as an organist at or near Melk). According to Griesinger, Fürnberg requested Haydn to compose something for this foursome to play. "Haydn, then eighteen years old, took up this proposal, and so originated his first quartet, which, as soon as it appeared, received such general approbation that Haydn was encouraged to write further in the same genre." Presumably Haydn played first violin in these sessions, as he is known to have done in later years. The composer's age must have been close to twenty-five, but otherwise the account is generally accepted.

Haydn had probably written string trios with two violins and bass even earlier than this; many such survive from his hand, but they cannot be dated precisely. His early trios are brief, unassuming works of a few movements, not nearly so imposing or challenging as the comparable works of Sammartini, Johann Stamitz, or Boccherini. One compositional problem Haydn had to solve in writing quartets was how to integrate the viola into a three- or four-part texture; the quartet-divertimenti show that the solution was not easy. "Basso" rather than "violoncello" is used to designate the lowest part in all the authentic sources of the quartet-divertimenti, but enough evidence exists to suggest that the works were mainly conceived with a solo cello in mind.[11]

Whether the Quartet in B♭ was in fact the first of the lot or not, it was later published as Op. 1 No. 1 many times over, perhaps leading Haydn or Griesinger to accept its temporal precedence. In the Fürnberg parts preserved in Budapest, which contain some corrections in Haydn's hand, the work occupies the fourth spot out of six.[12] Music-loving aristocrats in Vienna and Prague such as the Lobkowitz family were quick to obtain copies of the quartet-divertimenti, as were the great monasteries; the earliest manuscript to bear a date was copied by a monk at Gottweig and dated 1762.

The authentic quartet-divertimenti are in five movements, including two minuets (with their trios). (Op. 1 No. 5, in three movements, was originally a symphony.) A peculiarity in the early manuscript sources for Op. 1 No. 1 is that the trio of its first Minuet is called "Minuet secondo" (a rare but not unique usage that occurs also in the keyboard sonata in A♭, Hob. XVI:43).

The first movement of Op. 1 No. 1 opens with a *forte* unison fanfare that is succeeded by a high answer in the violins, *piano*, echoed in a modified way by the three lower strings so as to make a cadence, V - I. When the phrase is repeated, the two violins change their soft answer to the dominant, but the three lower voices rejoin with a scarcely changed V - I, as if they were paying insufficient attention to the violins' proposal—a potential source of wit and slightly unsettling. Haydn next plunges to the realm of the dominant by introducing the E♮s of its dominant. At the same time, he changes texture by having the viola double the bass. After the two violins wander in paired thirds up to high C, a new rhythmic figure in sixteenth notes, without upbeat, brings the first violin cascading down on full-textured restatements of V - I or I$^{6/4}$ in the new key of F, which is further confirmed by a *unisono* passage and more cadences. All this takes only twenty-four measures, which are followed by the usual repeat sign.

[11] James Webster, "The Scoring of Haydn's Early String Quartets," *Haydn Studies* (New York, 1981), pp. 235–38, summarizes evidence that is adduced in greater detail in his earlier studies. But see Roger Hickman, "The Nascent Viennese String Quartet," *Musical Quarterly* 67 (1981): 193–212, who argues that a string bass would suit much of this music as well as or better than a cello. Use of both together would not be without ample historical precedent.

[12] *Joseph Haydn: Werke* 21:1, *Frühe Streichquartette*, Kritischer Bericht, ed. Georg Feder (Munich, 1973), pp. 10–11.

These works were named *Quatuors dialogués* by publisher La Chevardière on their first appearance (Paris, 1764). Although the dimensions are tiny, there is already in the first movement of Op. 1 No. 1 a real sense of development and dialogue. After the double bar in the middle, the first violin proposes the descending sixteenth-note passage on V of ii, answered by the lower three instruments with their stubborn rejoinder from the beginning, which process is repeated down a tone, where the never-changing rejoinder is at least appropriate. A rising sequence and more dialogue lead to a dominant pedal, wreathed with upper and lower half steps, the kind of "tease" to which Haydn would often resort later, making us try to guess when the reprise will come. In the middle of this dominant pedal Haydn places the opening unison passage, descending instead of ascending, and in the tonic minor. The reprise then sets the theme aright, ascending and in major, but the disturbance of normality just experienced, also the seed of doubt sowed from the beginning upon the repetition of the first phrase, now becomes a surprising departure, a climb of the *forte* unison up to the subdominant instead of the tonic, to which the two violins react and the lower three voices do not, but rather restate their by now very droll answer that is always the same, V - I.

The Haydn who could "shock" like no one else, as Mozart reputedly said, is already before us in this movement. Even though he sets us up for something unusual to happen from the very beginning, and predicts what it might be by means of the added flats prior to the reprise, it still comes as a shock when we veer off to the flat side for a subdominant statement. The maneuver does not fail to interest no matter how many times we experience it. Haydn's deft manipulation of diverse metric shapes in this movement has been singled out as a decisive advance toward the "Viennese Classical style."[13]

The Minuet that follows is conventionally pretty and galant, with its raised-fifth degrees, triplets, and *cadence galante* on the dominant. Its accompanying *Minuet secondo* is in the subdominant and pits the lower voices' hornlike rises against the descending pizzicato triads of the violins (a souvenir, perhaps, of the most memorable event in the opening *Presto?*). Haydn chooses the subdominant for his *Adagio* as well. It is an Italianate aria sung by the first violin, and uses common time, the most frequently encountered meter in opera seria. The fall down by step from the fifth with the melodic turn around the tonic at the bottom was one of Mozart's favorite beginnings in the early 1770s, when he was mostly busy writing operas and other music for Italy. Presumably Haydn was responding to a type of Italian aria just as

[13] Thrasybulos Georgiades, "Zur Musiksprache der Wiener Klassiker," *Mozart-Jahrbuch 1951*, pp. 51–54.

was Mozart. Haydn renders this tribute slightly suspect by framing it with a churchly invocation in long notes with suspensions, which returns at the end as a kind of benediction (but with a tag of levity added).

Disparity verges on the comic here, or at least on incongruity, which is one source of Haydn's inexhaustible wit. It is as if the main event, a love song spun out by the soprano castrato borrowed from the opera house, were introduced into a Sunday service, with prelude and postlude provided by the local organist. Maybe this was so common a practice in Vienna as to seem less incongruous then than it does now. Haydn is very demanding of his solo singer, even bearing in mind that he is only a mock-singer impersonated by the *violino primo*. Mozart or any Italian would have given the soloist two beats' rest after the sighing fall in the middle, and then continued. Haydn plunges ahead, showing that he does not think automatically of melody in terms of human breath; in so doing, he achieves a rather unsatisfactory joint. The swoops from very high to very low that follow verge on caricature, as does the whole movement.

The second Minuet begins with a texture that Haydn made famous: violins in octaves answered by lower instruments in octaves. He was roundly attacked for this feature by critics in northern Germany, an issue we shall explore in some detail below. The finale in 2/4 is marked *Presto*, like the opening movement, with which it is comparable in length and form, even to the detail of a prominent subdominant just after the reprise. The two might even be thought exchangeable except that the first movement begins forcefully and with a four-square phrase, while the finale begins softly and with the more subtle shape of a six-measure phrase; the phrase ends with a two-note rhythmic snap, |♫ ‖|, that also appears as a phrase ending in the finales of Op. 1 No. 4 and Op. 1 No. 6. Another noteworthy feature of the finale is its motivic economy, the head motive of the main theme giving rise to both the transitional passage and to the second theme, then predominating in the development.

Haydn adheres to this five-movement scheme throughout the quartet-divertimenti. A slight rearrangement occurs in only two works. Op. 1 No. 3 in D places the *Adagio* first, and the central movement then becomes a scherzo-like *Presto* in 2/4, with a binary dance as main section, then a *minore* trio (not labeled as such) and a da capo repeat. In most of the early manuscript sources the movement is in fact entitled "Scherzo," a term Haydn often used in his early works in connection with a rapid movement in 2/4. Op. 2 No. 6 in B♭ also features a slow first movement and a Scherzo (*Presto* in 2/4 with a trio-like middle part and da capo repeat) as the central movement. Its opening movement is an *Adagio* in 2/4, with a theme in binary form of twenty measures that engenders four variations, the bass remaining the same throughout, and the last variation returning to the simple version of the theme except for the written-out repeats, which carry the subdivision of the beat to its greatest extent (thirty-second notes). Theme and variations was not a very common form in mid-century chamber music, aside from the French examples of the *air varié*. Haydn may have been starting a new Viennese practice with Op. 2 No. 6. He would follow it himself with deepening artistry in the variations on a slow theme that open Op. 9 No. 5 (also in B♭ and close to being a rewrite of the earlier theme) and Op. 17 No. 3, both of which, unlike Op. 2, offer a "cello variation."

The outer movements in Op. 1 are of roughly equal weight, but the finales tend to be more playful and exuberant even so. In Op. 1 No. 1 the finale makes the six-measure phrase the rule and the four-measure phrase the exception, the opposite of normal practice. In Op. 1 No. 2 in E♭ the outer movements show structural similarities. The seconda parte in each begins with the main theme on V, then on I, before launching into sequences touching on IV and ii, preceded by their dominants, then emphasizing vi. Op. 1 No. 6 in C begins with a *Presto assai* in 6/8 of only sixty-four measures (perhaps the lightest movement of all, explaining why La Chevardière might wish to have it close the set in his second edition of ca. 1770). The finale of Op. 1 No. 6 is an *Allegro* in 2/4 of seventy-six measures (marked *Presto* in some early sources). This finale could be perceived as slightly more weighty than the first movement, an impression furthered by the patch of minor-mode turbulence before the reprise. The minor mode does not play much of a role in the early quartet-divertimenti, being restricted mainly to the trios of minuets, where it occurs so often as to lead us to expect it; in the one piece with a slow movement in minor (Op. 2 No. 2), both trios are in major.

The works in A (Op. 2 No. 1) and E (Op. 2 No. 4) sound a little more mature than their companions, primarily because the first movements are elaborated in ways that point to Haydn's later quartets.[14] They also were entered later than the others by Haydn in his thematic catalogue. One of the composer's favorite melodic leaps, a descending seventh, enlivens the theme of the first movement of the Quartet in A, *Allegro* in 2/4. The texture is more varied here, and Haydn is able to make the viola more prominent by pairing it in duets with the second violin, as well as with the cello. There is a moment of great beauty just after the reprise when the viola plays a trill in sixths with the first violin against the descending chain of suspended dissonances between the second violin and bass (Example 4.3ab). The idea for this inserted passage clearly comes from the dissonant sevenths of the theme, occurring first chordally, then melodically, which Haydn chooses to

---

[14] On their possible date, see James Webster, "The Chronology of Haydn's String Quartets," *Musical Quarterly* 61 (1975): 43.

EXAMPLE 4.3. *Haydn, Quartet Op. 2, No. 1, I*

a. Opening

b. Reprise

replace with his inspired meditation in real four-part writing on the poignancy of dissonant sevenths. The passage looks forward to the composer's quartet writing of a decade later, and specifically to the leisurely sequential extension just at the moment of what sounds like the tonic reprise in the first movement of the Quartet in E (Op. 17 No. 1: I, mm. 63ff.).[15] Another

[15] For a totally different evaluation of the inserted passage, see Ludwig Finscher, *Studien zur Geschichte des Streichquartetts*, vol. 1: *Die Entstehung des klassischen Streichquartetts: Von den Vorformen zur Grundlegung durch Joseph Haydn* (Kassel, 1974), pp. 151–. Finscher condemns the spot as "unskilled and unorganic, with its old-fashioned sequential chain, which makes no sense here and also disturbs the symmetry of the three segments of the movement (36, 34, and 40 bars)." This is one of the rare examples where the author judges music by how it looks on paper and according to *a priori* schematic notions, instead of by how it sounds.

feature of the opening movement of Op. 2 No. 1 portends the future Haydn: motivic economy, whereby nearly everything is derived from the three upbeat eighth notes going to a downbeat in mm. 2–3. The second Minuet together with its trio takes up the melodic-harmonic content of these same measures, and the finale, *Allegro molto* in 2/4, does the same, in a different way.

Haydn showed a greater predilection for the key of E than did most of his contemporaries, one of whom, Francesco Galeazzi, pronounced it "a very piercing key, shrill, youthful, narrow, and somewhat harsh."[16] Mozart wrote no quartets in E and chose it rarely in his other instrumental music, but Wagenseil used the key often, and for some of his most beautiful instrumental works. Haydn's Op. 2 No. 2 in E opens with an *Allegro molto* in 2/4, initiated by a melodic rise in the solo violin, with a melodic turn and final falling third that we have seen the composer use before in connection with this key (Example 4.4). The answer by the other three parts to what the first violin proposes is gruff, taking only the disjunct falling third, articulated staccato, outlining a descending seventh, but then turning the legato falling third of the first violin to a rising third, also legato. After restating its plea, the first violin is answered again gruffly, but with the satisfaction of a cadence instead of a half cadence. What follows is another conjunct rise from the third up to the fifth, but stretched out in time over three measures, a case of motivic growth that also shows the composer's growth in skill and finesse. The first sounding of four-part harmony in m. 9 accounts for part of the charm and suavity of the passage (but notice that Haydn still resorts to

EXAMPLE 4.4. *Haydn, Quartet Op. 2, No. 2, I*

[16] Rita Steblin, *A History of Key Characteristics in the Eighteenth and Early Nineteenth Centuries* (Ann Arbor, Mich., 1983), pp. 110–12.

doubling the viola and bass at the cadences). Knowing what a gem he has created here, Haydn saves it in the reprise until the very end. He needed only rewrite the second phrase so as to make it close the movement. Such strategic wisdom seems beyond anything in the quartets of Op. 1. A decade later, when Haydn returned to writing string quartets, he continued on with the fashioning of weightier first movements such as distinguish Op. 2 Nos. 1 and 2.

The minuets of Op. 1 and Op. 2 have been reserved for last in this discussion because they will lead to a lengthy excursus on the matter of octave doubling and, following that, on the public reception of Haydn's early quartets. Most of the minuets that gave offense because of their octave doubling came as fourth movements; the second-movement exemplars were notably more proper and more galant (an exception being Op. 2 No. 2). Faced with providing every divertimento with two examples of this dance, each with its trio (meaning in effect four different minuets per work), Haydn cast his net rather widely over the available possibilities. The artful salon dances typically appearing as second movements were joined by a more popular and outdoor variety of dance as fourth movements. Octave doublings, as found often in the latter, were one manifestation of this popular origin. They were specifically connected, as we shall see below, with street music such as Bohemian *Musikanten* were wont to improvise.

There was more than one issue that set the critics of northern Germany at odds with Haydn's minuets. In the first place the critics denied the minuet a place in chamber music by holding fast to the old-fashioned trio sonata. To them, the minuet was an aberration of Austrian, Bohemian, and south German musicians (plus their French and Italian allies among modern composers). Haydn's adaptation of octave doublings from street music was but one of his offenses against good part writing in their eyes, the other stemming from his occasional difficulties writing an independent viola part. The second Minuet from Op. 1 No. 4 in G offers an example of both. The opening, with its two four-measure phrases, is real dance music, and close to what Haydn and many others wrote for the ballroom. Both the bass line and the melody are certainly going to penetrate in a crowded room, or even outdoors, doubled at the octave as they are (Example 4.5). The middle section, providing eight measures before the reprise, is so unaspiring that it never quits its dominant pedal, but it brings the textural contrast that is needed. On paper the viola looks independent, yet its scarcely veiled parallel octaves with the first violin insure that it will not sound independent. For this kind of part writing generations of harmony students have been faulted. When critics railed against Haydn's "voice-leading mistakes" ("Fehlern gegen den Satz"), they may have meant seeming four-part writing like this.

EXAMPLE 4.5. *Haydn, Quartet Op. 1, No. 4, IV*

In an essay on musical taste printed in the *Hamburger Unterhaltungen* of 1766, "Abhandlung vom musikalischen Geschmack," there is praise for Haydn's quartets, coupled with a reservation:

A Haydn is pleasant, witty ["scherzend"], and full of inventiveness in his Qua- tro; his symphonies and trios are the same. Whether, on the other hand, his minuets with octaves are good for everyone, I shall leave undecided. They are good for amusement; but one easily gets the impression of hearing two beggars, father and son, singing in octaves, and this is a poor subject for musical imitation.[17]

In the fall of the same year the *Wiener Diarium* published the article "On the Viennese Taste in Music," which gave Haydn a prominent place alongside Gluck, Wagenseil, and Leopold Hofmann.

> The art of writing the outer parts in parallel octaves is his invention, and one cannot deny that this is attractive, as long as it appears rarely and in a Haydn-like fashion . . . The editor of the *Hamburgischen Unterhaltungen* who was annoyed about the octave doublings of our composers must know that most of the Symphonies of Graun contain *Andanti* in which the bassoon moves in octaves with the transverse flute; and it occurred to no one to say: it is as if father and son were begging alms in one tone. One must have blunted feelings not to appreciate the gentle persuasion of octave doublings ["Monotonie"] when they cut through a full harmonic background.[18]

Johann Adam Hiller joined the fray in 1768, complaining about the "offensive octave doublings of the second violins, or another lower voice with the first violins" in Haydn's symphonies. Remote as he was in his Hungarian solitude most of the time, Haydn was not unaware of the debates raging around his octave doublings. In his autobiographical sketch of 1776 he took on his critics in no uncertain terms and also expressed the hope that some other impartial judge would come to his defense and shut them up, as had happened to them once before when they accused him of *Monotonie*. But the debate was far from finished. Heinrich Bossler, in Forkel's *Musikalischen Almanach* appendices for 1782–84, returned to the charge and attributed the practice of octave doublings to Prague's wandering *Musikanten:*

> The use of enhanced unison he [Haydn] did not invent but heard it used by *Bettelmusikanten* who go under the name of students in Prague. He only had the audacity to be the first to transplant the practice to a regularly composed piece, and his advance made other composers so bold in this matter that these doubled parts, previously privileges only of the organ and of the musical vagabonds, are now to be met in the works of almost every musical artist.[19]

That Haydn's "invention" had become a commonplace by the last quarter of the century is also evident in the article "Trio" by Johann Abraham

[17] Hubert Unverricht, *Geschichte des Streichtrios* (Tutzing, 1969), p. 156.
[18] Adapted, with revisions, from Landon, *Haydn,* 2: 130–31; for the original German, see Unverricht, *Geschichte des Streichtrios,* p. 156.
[19] Unverricht, *Geschichte des Streichtrios,* p. 157.

Schulz in Sulzer's *Allgemeine Theorie der schöne Künste* (2 vols., Leipzig, 1771 and 1774): "Trio also means, concerning two Menuets that belong together, the second one, which must be set in three parts, after which the first, *which is best set in only two parts*, is repeated" (my italics).[20]

This sounds like unconditional surrender coming from a north German. Nothing could demonstrate more concisely what a power Haydn had become in modern music. Even those who pretended to be his enemies were swept along by the Austro-Bohemian current he led. An anonymous English critic writing in 1784 summed up Haydn's battle with the German critics by saying that they accused him of "introducing a species of sounds totally unknown in that country. In the last position they were perfectly right: he had indeed introduced a new species of music: it was his own, totally unlike what they had been used to—original, masterly, and beautiful."[21]

As early as 1763 the music seller Breitkopf of Leipzig announced that he could supply manuscript copies of eight *Quadri* and six *Trii* for strings by Haydn. In Breitkopf's thematic catalogue for 1765 the eight *Quadri* appear with their incipits, and they all correspond to the early quartet-divertimenti (Figure 4.3).[22] Haydn's works stand out in his list because all the others (there are two more pages of *quadri* for 1765 besides the one reproduced here) involve both winds and strings, with the exception of the work in g by Handel, for which no instrumentation is specified. Only Haydn requires "2 violini, Viola e B." The same is true of the previous year's offerings in *quadri:* all involve winds.

Only in the later 1760s did Breitkopf begin to offer *Quattri* for two violins, viola, and bass by other Viennese composers such as Leopold Hofmann (1767), Franz Asplmayr (1768), and Florian Gassmann (1769). It is a convenience to use Breitkopf's catalogues as a gauge, but nothing can take the place of studying the Viennese manuscript tradition in depth when seeking answers to questions about dates or details of scoring. Haydn was not the only composer to write divertimentos for an all-string ensemble in mid-century Vienna. Gregor Joseph Werner published suite-like compositions for strings as early as 1748. Johann Georg Albrechtsberger left a considerable amount of early chamber music for strings, including one *Divertimento a 4* dated 1760 that follows the five-movement pattern with two minuets favored by Haydn.[23] Ignaz Holzbauer's early chamber music has yet to be assessed.

[20] Ibid., p. 96.

[21] A. Peter Brown, "The Earliest English Biography of Haydn," *Musical Quarterly* 59 (1973): 343.

[22] *Breitkopf Thematic Catalogue,* six parts and seventeen supplements, 1762–1787, edited with an introduction and index by Barry S. Brook (New York, 1966).

[23] James Webster, "Towards a History of Viennese Chamber Music in the Early Classical Period," *JAMS* 27 (1974): 212–47; see especially p. 232 and n. 87 on Albrechtsberger. For comparisons between

VIII. Quadri, del Sigr. GIVS. HAYDEN, in Vienna.

a 2 Violini, Viol. e B.

FIGURE 4.3. Detail from Breitkopf's *Thematic Catalogue,* 1765.

Haydn's temporal precedence may be difficult to establish. But once his *Divertimenti a 4* became a popular success in the years around 1760 they quickly outshone all similar works and had the effect of promoting both the medium and the five-movement cycle.[24]

By the early 1760s Haydn was known to the outside world primarily for his quartets but also for trios and symphonies. The anonymous Hamburg critic of 1766 mentions his *quatro* first, then, as an afterthought, his symphonies and trios. A similar hierarchy is apparent in the remark of Martin Schweyer, who interleaved his copy of Walther's *Musiklexikon* with additional information: "Hayden, an incomparable musician and composer, lives in Vienna and distinguishes himself in the writing of fine quartets, trios and symphonies. 1763."[25] Thanks to the composer Johann Friedrich Reichardt, we even possess a few vignettes describing early performances of the quartets. Reichardt tells two tales from the time of the Seven Years' War (1756–63), one gathered from a Prussian officer who was held captive in Austria ca. 1757–58, the other autobiographical, about how Austrian captives in Prussia were responsible for his getting to know Haydn's music toward the end of the war. The Prussian officer, one Major Weirach, told Reichardt

Haydn's and Albrechtsberger's themes, see Webster, "Remarks on Early Chamber Music," *Haydn Studies* (1981), pp. 365–67.

[24] Finscher, *Studien zur Geschichte des Streichquartetts,* 1: p. 158: "That Haydn's early quartet-divertimenti founded the short-lived southern German–Austrian–Bohemian tradition of the *divertimento a quattro* must be concluded from the dated and datable sources. This is all the more probable in light of the extraordinary diffusion enjoyed by Op. 1 and Op. 2, which in fact made a general sensation."

[25] Oliver W. Strunk, "Haydn's Divertimenti for Baryton, Viola, and Bass (after Manuscripts in the Library of Congress)," *Musical Quarterly* 18 (1932): 226.

he was quartered with the nobleman on whose estates Haydn was born [Count Harrach] and heard that artist, as modest as his genius was great, himself playing his first quartets. Haydn called them Cassatios—a word that means the same as Notturno or Serenada, altogether a "piece of music" that is at the same time suitable for performance outside. The man was modest to the point of timidity, despite the fact that everyone present was enchanted by these compositions, and he was not to be persuaded that his works were worthy of being presented to the musical world.[26]

What works can these be if not the quartet-divertimenti Haydn began writing about the same time (ca. 1757–58) for Baron Fürnberg? When the same were entered in Haydn's work catalogue, they were first called "Cassatio," an appellation only later crossed out and replaced with "Divertimento."

There are many other testimonies to the fact that Haydn by nature was shy and unassuming. Perhaps this aspect of his personality helps explain why he reacted so strongly against the bluster of self-appointed "critics." Reichardt was one of the rare north Germans to be able to transcend regional pride and recognize the original qualities even in early Haydn. In his memoirs Reichardt tells how he first became acquainted with Haydn's music, around age ten or eleven, when he was already a virtuoso violinist. He uses the third person to describe himself:

> He also played Haydn's Cassatios, which he got from the Austrians, from whom he had learned to apply a lively and piquant manner of performance, fitting to these first children of the original musical spirit of our great humorist in music. His *Paradestück* was then the very merry and spirited Cassation in B♭, of which the first movement in 6/8 still hovers about him in a very vivid way, although it has been many years since he has heard it.[27]

Reichardt goes on to recommend the use of these fresh early compositions of Haydn in teaching, even though they are too short, thin, and simple by the standards of later music. Reichardt wrote this fragmentary memoir shortly before he died in 1814. One of the earliest north German critics who welcomed Haydn's music, he had valuable things to say about the early

[26] Landon, *Haydn*, 1: 230.

[27] Hans Michael Schletterer, *Joh. Friedrich Reichardt: Sein Leben und seine musikalische Thätigkeit* (Augsburg, 1865), p. 61. The Major Weirach anecdote is given in a footnote to this one, tying them both together as bearing on Haydn's quartet-divertimenti. Otto Biba inexplicably fails to connect the two in "Nachrichten zur Musikpflege in der graflichen Familie Harrach," *Haydn Yearbook* 10 (1978): 39. Among the Austrian prisoners in east Prussia was a member of the Lobkowitz family, and it may be no coincidence that one of the best early manuscript sources for Haydn's quartet-divertimenti reposes in the Lobkowitz collection in Prague. It includes Op. 1 No. 1. See *Frühe Streichquartette, Kritischer Bericht*, ed. Georg Feder, pp. 16, 3.

v. The cave leading from the underworld. A stage design
by Gaspari for Gluck's *Orfeo ed Euridice*, 1773. (Munich:
Staatliche Graphische Sammlung)

VI. Haydn in Esterházy livery ca. 1762–63. Portrait attributed to Grundmann, repainted by Carole Peel.

quartets at a time closer to their creation. When reviewing the Quartets of Op. 33 and six recent symphonies by Haydn in 1782, he recalled:

> It is most interesting to observe Haydn's works successively with a critical eye. Even his first works, which became known among us about twenty years ago [i.e., when Reichardt got hold of Op. 1 No. 1 from the Austrian prisoners], gave signs of his benevolent spirit: there it was mostly youthful high spirits and often boisterous merriment, combined with superficial harmonic working out; more and more the spirit became manlier, the work more thoughtful, until through heightened and solidified feeling, also a riper study of the art, and above all of what makes an effect, this mature and original man and decided artist presents himself in all his works.[28]

A few words about one special imitator of Haydn are in order here. The composer of six quartets that long passed for Haydn's Op. 3 is now believed to be Roman Hoffstetter, a Benedictine monk in the monastery of Amorbach (in the Odenwald south of the Main River, the traditional dividing line between north and south Germans). These quartets continue the light divertimento style of Haydn's Op. 1 and Op. 2 Quartets in most of their outer movements. At the same time, they eliminate the second minuet, as Haydn did in his Op. 9 Quartets of ca. 1770, and they place the remaining minuet either as a second or third movement, as Haydn did in his Op. 20 Quartets of 1772. When Bailleux published the set in Paris in 1777, he may have thought the superficial resemblance to Haydn's quartets enough that he could get away with substituting a well-known name for a little-known one. Bailleux was not the most scrupulous of publishers. When Haydn's pupil Ignaz Pleyel brought out his complete edition of Haydn's quartets around 1800, he used printed sources and included Hoffstetter's quartets, which had long been circulating as Haydn's. The claim that his edition was approved by Haydn may be true, but Haydn did not pay much attention to such things in his last years. Pleyel's further claim that the works were given in the order in which they originally appeared—i.e., with Op. 3, which is his appellation, between the Quartets of Op. 2 and Op. 9—is false.

The Quartets of Op. 3 represent a clever and sometimes charming imitation of Haydn's manner, by a composer who had neither enough different ideas nor sufficient technique to sustain a set of six quartets, even if he could write some very winning single movements, such as the famous "Serenade" (Op. 3 No. 5: II). Haydn was not his only model. Mannheim orchestral clichés such as Haydn never used in quartets appear in the opening movement of Op. 3 No. 6, the Minuet of which quotes a local folksong, a practice

---

[28] Reichardt, *Musikalisches Kunstmagazin* (Berlin, 1782), 1: 205.

Haydn rarely followed.[29] Donald Francis Tovey was astute enough to be very troubled by what he perceived as foreign to Haydn in Op. 3. Yet like everyone else up to and including Tovey's generation, he was cowed by the weight of authority into accepting tradition.

Haydn composed many string trios for two violins and bass.[30] They are titled "Divertimento" without exception and are in the lighter style this term often implies, mainly in three movements. A typical movement pattern, present in several, is *Adagio, Allegro*, Menuet and trio, all in the same key. The Divertimento in D (Hob. V:15), a copy of which is dated 1762, exemplifies this pattern. Its central *Allegro* uses complementary bifocal closes and a very galant double appoggiatura in climactic position, including the raised-fifth degree. The opening *Adagio* in 3/4 exhibits the same stratified texture throughout its fifty-one measures: florid melody in the first violin, pizzicato accompaniment on the beat in the second violin, and eighth-note arpeggio figures in the bass. This movement also has an affecting use of the raised-fifth degree as long appoggiatura over IV. The work concludes with a simple Menuet with *minore* trio.

The occasional string trio shows an expansion of the first movement away from the tight motivic work of the early *divertimento a 4*, toward a looser, more florid kind of discourse, one that might be interpreted as a step in the direction of the Op. 9 Quartets. Such a piece is the *Allegro* first movement of the Trio in C (Hob. V:16), which extends to 179 measures in 2/4. Having stated the first theme in the dominant at the beginning of the seconda parte, Haydn avoids a double reprise, as he does in the scarcely less discursive *Presto* finale. The middle movement is a Menuet in C with a trio in c.

The best summary words on the importance of Haydn's *divertimenti a 4* were written by Gerber in the first volume of his *Lexicon*:

Even with his first Quatros, which became known around 1760, Haydn made a general sensation. Some took pleasure and laughed at the extraordinary naïveté and liveliness that reigned in them, while others shouted about the degradation of music into comic trifling ["Herabwürdigung der Musik zu komischen Tändelyen"] and about their unheard-of octaves. It was Haydn, namely, who intro-

---

[29] Finscher, *Studien zur Geschichte des Streichquartetts*, 1: p. 177, identifies the tune, which is set off by being played pizzicato, as "the beginning of a widespread Austrian and south German folk melody." He also identifies the tune in the first movement of the set's fourth quartet, where the composer slips into it, perhaps unconsciously, as a closing theme (mm. 74–78). The tune is, in fact, "Acht Sauschneider," used by Haydn in a Capriccio for solo keyboard (Hob. XVII:1) dated 1765. See Landon, *Haydn*, 1: 549–52.

[30] Haydn, *Streichtrios*, series 1, ed. Bruce C. MacIntyre and Barry S. Brook (Munich, 1986) (*Haydn: Werke*, XI:1).

duced in his Quatros the manner of reinforcing the melody at the octave, or allowing the first and second violins to proceed in octaves together, which makes such a great effect in expressive passages played by a large orchestra. Despite all the outcries, we quickly got used to it. Yes, and moreover, we ended up imitating it ourselves.[31]

Gerber's authority silenced most detractors. What Haydn did so daringly in his early chamber works and then in his symphonies, everyone was copying by 1790. What Gerber did not know, or wish to tell, was that the octave doublings came from Viennese dance music, and that before Haydn used them, Joseph Starzer did so in his ballet music, as we saw above in Chapter 2.

From Morzin to Esterházy Service, ca. 1759–62

HAYDN'S professional career did not advance as rapidly as that of his younger brother Michael, who was in the service of the bishop of Gross-wardein no later than 1757. According to Dies and Griesinger, Haydn's first real position was obtained only in 1759, as a result of his work for Baron Fürnberg. In Haydn's own words of 1776: "By the recommendation of the late Herr von Fürnberg (from whom I received many marks of favor), I was engaged as Directeur at Count von Morzin's." Morzin had a small orchestra, probably made up largely of domestic servants, as was common in Austria and even more so in Bohemia. Note that Haydn avoids using the title mae-stro di cappella. Griesinger says, "In the year 1759 Haydn was appointed in Vienna to be music director to Count Morzin with a salary of two hundred gulden, free room, and board at the staff table. Here he enjoyed at last the good fortune of a carefree existence; it suited him thoroughly. The winter was spent in Vienna and the summer in Bohemia, in the vicinity of Pilsen." Dies adds a few details: "The Bohemian Count von Morzin, a passionate lover of music, maintained a number of bachelor musicians. The position of chamber composer fell vacant, and this Haydn received in the year 1759."

The year 1759 was a banner year for Haydn in another respect. On 24 November the German troupe in the Kärntnerthor Theater presented a new work with Haydn's music.[32] The libretto is entitled "Der neue krumme Teu-

---

[31] Ernst Ludwig Gerber, *Historisch-biographisches Lexicon der Tonkünstler* (Leipzig, 1790).

[32] The date was first ascertained, on the basis of Gumpenhuber's chronicle, in Daniel Heartz, "Haydn und Gluck im Burgtheater um 1760: *Der neue krumme Teufel, Le diable à quatre,* und die Sinfonie 'Le Soir,' " *Bericht über den internationalen Kongress Bayreuth 1981,* pp. 120–35.

FIGURE 4.4. Libretto of Kurz-Bernardon's *Der neue krumme Teufel*, 1759. (First and last pages)

fel. Eine OPERA COMIQUE" and is further qualified as being "in two acts, with a pantomime for children entitled 'Harlequin, or The New Ram Idol in America,' the whole invented by Joseph Kurz" (Figure 4.4). At the end there is a note specifying that "Heyden composed the music of the opéra-comique as well as of the pantomime." The work probably had little to do with the earlier *Krumme Teufel* (1753) that was banned; indeed, since the same authorities watched over the theaters, actor-director Joseph Kurz-Bernardon presumably made efforts to put some distance between the new play and the old one. One scene that may have been revived involved a pantomime of swimming. Haydn made a good impression on Kurz-Bernardon at their first meeting when he fell into a lilting 6/8 rhythm at the keyboard in response to the actor's gestures mimicking a man swimming. Of the 1753 play Griesinger says, "Harlequin ran away from the waves in *Der krumme Teufel*." In the 1759 play the pantomime begins with Harlequin swimming ashore.

Kurz-Bernardon took a second wife, Teresina Morelli, in April 1758 (his first wife, the one Haydn serenaded in the early 1750s, died in 1755). Much of the new play is built around her singing and acting talents, which must have been considerable. The play was given in all six times at its initial production, four times at the Kärntnerthor and twice when the German troupe played as guests in the Burgtheater (27 November and 3 December). Can it be a coincidence that the first mention we possess of Haydn's Symphony No. 1 in D also dates from the same month of November 1759? This well-known piece, which has all the earmarks of an operatic overture, may well have functioned as the curtain raiser for *Der neue krumme Teufel*. The orchestral forces that Haydn had at his disposal in the Kärntnerthor Theater in 1759 are known, thanks to Gumpenhuber's chronicle: five first violins, five seconds, two violas, two cellos, two basses, two oboes, two horns, one bassoon, and one flute.

In *Der neue krumme Teufel*, Haydn created his most ambitious work to date. The specific citation of a composer was unique among the thirteen printed texts that survive of comedies by Kurz-Bernardon—Haydn's music and Haydn's name obviously meant something to the public. Six performances was a respectable number for a new theater piece. Perhaps there would have been more had not the season been drawing to a close, and had not Kurz-Bernardon and his wife left Vienna for several years at the end of 1759. There were more than a dozen revivals of *Der neue krumme Teufel*, including three in Vienna, between 1764 and 1783. Still, as incredible as it may seem, Haydn's music has yet to be found. Thus we lack the keystone of the Viennese operatic repertory in German. We cannot even answer the question raised by the reference to the work on the first and last page of the libretto as an opéra-comique: did Haydn cast a glance at Gluck's very successful opéras-comiques in the Burgtheater when writing his own comic opera? We know how much he admired some of Gluck's airs because he paid them the sincerest kind of flattery.

Der neue krumme Teufel was no small work. Eighteen musical numbers had to be composed—arias, duets, recitatives (although most of the dialogue was spoken), and choruses—for the main work. The pantomime, a separate drama, required ten vocal pieces and pantomime music as well. In addition came an Italian intermezzo, *Il vecchio ingannato*, in which Kurz-Bernardon and his wife also played, along with one Cattarina Meyrin. Haydn is not mentioned specifically in connection with the intermezzo, and it may have been sung to preexistent music. Galuppi's setting survives in the case of at least one aria, "M'ha detto la mia mamma."[33] We know how much Haydn

[33] From *Il conte Caramella* (1749). A series of three dialect arias in Italian in Act II, scenes 3–5, sung by Teresina Kurz-Bernardon, also can be found in settings by Galuppi, in *Le virtuose ridicole* (1752). The texts in all cases are by Carlo Goldoni.

admired the melodiousness of Galuppi's comic operas because one of his students tells us as much.[34] When *Der neue krumme Teufel* received its first production in November 1759 it stood alone on the program, except for concluding ballets (unnamed). In other words, it was a full-scale theatrical work, the first and main event of the evening's entertainment. It had to be preceded by an overture; even spoken plays received overtures in those days. And Haydn's Symphony No. 1 possessed the requisite scope to inaugurate an evening at the theater.

Haydn must have spent the summer of 1760 at Lukaveks, the Morzin country estate near Pilsen in Bohemia. Griesinger says about the composer's later sojourns in the Hungarian countryside: "Hunting and fishing were Haydn's favorite pastimes during his stay in Hungary . . . In riding Haydn developed no skill, because after he had fallen from a horse on the Morzin estates, he never trusted himself again to mount." By the month of October 1760, Count Morzin and his musicians were surely back in Vienna, for no nobleman of the Habsburg realms would have wanted to miss the festivities surrounding the marriage of Crown Prince Joseph to Princess Isabella of Parma. On 26 November 1760 in St. Stephen's Cathedral, Haydn married Maria Anna Keller, daughter of a wig maker. In the marriage document Haydn is styled "der hochgeehrte Hr. Joseph Hayden, Musik-Direktor bey titl. Hrn. Grafen v. Morzin." Frau Haydn bore no children and was eventually a source of considerable chagrin to her husband, but they never separated.

Haydn became a symphonist with the small band at his disposal under Count Morzin. Griesinger says: "As music director in the service of Count Morzin, Haydn composed his first symphony"; this statement is followed by the incipit of Symphony No. 1 in D. There is no contradiction involved in the use of this work as an opera overture as well as a concert symphony. Opera overtures made up the largest part of the repertory of the concert symphony at this time. A set of Haydn's early symphonies that belonged to the son of Baron Fürnberg are numbered—some, it has been claimed, in Haydn's hand.[35] Assuming that the numbering has at least some connection

---

[34] Landon, *Haydn*, 1: 98. Robert Kimmerling, one of Haydn's students in the 1750s and later *Regens chori* at Melk, wrote on the printed score (1758) he possessed of Galuppi's *Il mondo alla roversa*, "NB Haec operetta placuit Josepho Haydn, magistro meo. Recommendavit mihi, suo discipulo ut sapius persolvum, propter bonum Cantabile."

[35] Landon, *Haydn*, "The Fürnberg-Morzin Legacy," 1: 239–42 and 280–83. Landon identifies nineteen Morzin symphonies; No. 37 is dated 1758, but the date may be a later scribal addition. Jens Peter Larsen adds to the early group Symphonies Nos. 14 and 25, in *Haydn Yearbook* 10 (1978): 78. Georg Feder, who discovered these sources, is more cautious than Landon about identifying Haydn's hand in the numbering: *Haydn Studien* 1 (1965): 16, n. 17. See also Larsen, "Haydn's Early Symphonies: The Problem of Dating," *Music in the Classic Period: Essays in Honor of Barry S. Brook*, ed. Allan A. Atlas (New York, 1985), pp. 117–31.

with Haydn, we can regard the first three as a little group in its own right: Fürnberg No. 1 in D (= No. 1); No. 2 in C (= No. 37); and No. 3 in G (= No. 18). D, C, and G are the most frequent keys encountered in the composer's vast symphonic output, and they occur in this order of frequency. When Haydn wrote his first three symphonies for Prince Esterházy in the spring of 1761, they were again in D, C, and G respectively, and constituted the trilogy of *Le matin, Le midi,* and *Le soir.* Long-standing practice dictated the precedence of D, the most brilliant of orchestral keys, whether it was a question of inaugurating an evening in the theater or a set of symphonies. When Haydn chose to close his grand symphonic series in 1795, it was again with a work in D, the *London* Symphony.

Taken together, Symphonies 1, 37, and 18 are representative in that they illustrate three types of movement structure that were common when Haydn began his career as a symphonist: the overture type in three movements, fast, slow, fast; the four-movement work with minuet that expands the previous model; and the work with an opening slow movement, reminiscent of the old *sonata da chiesa.* That the Symphony No. 1 in D belongs to the overture type is manifest in certain features other than its movement structure and its key, which is the normal one for Italian operatic sinfonie: the opening *crescendo* with eventual sweep of the violins up to high D, an ascent that is repeated, arpeggiated, in the form of a "rocket" at the beginning of the finale; and the three hammer-stroke chords that serve to punctuate important arrivals in the opening movement, which, typically, is in common time.

In the Symphony No. 37 in C a Minuet with trio is the second movement of four. This work is more typical of Haydn than the Symphony No. 1 because of its motivic economy. The finale, in particular, exhibits a Haydn-esque playfulness such as was observed above in connection with the lighter genres; the gruff assertiveness of the diatonic tuttis is played off against the coy answers, *piano,* with chromatically inflected degrees. After the double bar the music moves through a few diminished seventh chords and their resolution, then settles on a dominant pedal with various minor seconds resolving up or down. In the reprise Haydn wittily reinforces his point by switching between descending and ascending minor seconds when he rewrites the main theme.

Symphony No. 18 in G begins with an *Andante moderato* in which the second violins first sing the theme: a falling fifth followed by little melodic segments separated by rests. It is as if Haydn were thinking of an aria, or rather a duet, for the first violins enter answering the seconds and in dialogue with them. The theme could easily be set to an Italian *settenario* line— for instance, "Parto, ma tu ben mio" (from Metastasio's *La clemenza di Tito*).

With the twenty or so symphonies of 1759–60 for Count Morzin's band, Haydn quickly advanced to the front rank of Viennese instrumental composers of the day, taking a place beside the older Wagenseil and such younger figures as Ditters, Leopold Hofmann, and Steffan. Some additional highlights of these symphonies will serve to summarize his achievement.

The Symphony No. 3 in G features a canonic Minuet. The second movement, *Allegro*, of the Symphony No. 5 in A generates great rhythmic élan by its use of dotted figures in 3/4 time, and even more excitement when the pattern overlaps itself in the reprise. The fourth and final movement of this symphony, *Presto*, is short and begins with a duet, *piano*, for the two violins (like the finale of Mozart's *Paris* Symphony), after which the tutti enters, *forte*. The first movement of the Symphony No. 15 in D is a *Presto* preceded by a thirty-three measure *Adagio* ending on V—too long to be thought of as a slow introduction, perhaps, but surprising in that it returns at the end, abbreviated by ten measures, thus framing the *Presto* (somewhat like the effect of the slow introduction's return in the first movement of the *Drumroll* Symphony). The Minuet of the Symphony in B♭ (Symphony "B"—Hob. I:108) deserves study. Here Haydn's increasing comic gift is audible from what seems like a displacement of the half phrases, in that the answer comes before the question (as well as after it). The three symphonies in C (Nos. 20, 23, and 33) are particularly festive because of their use of trumpets and timpani (in addition to horns and oboes). At this time Haydn used trumpets and timpani in no other key; only gradually did they become available to him in D and a few other keys. There are divertimenti, trios, and other compositions that can be attributed to Haydn's period of service to Count Morzin, but they pale in significance compared with this substantial corpus of symphonies.

Haydn's works for Count Morzin provided a stepping stone to a higher post, just as his work for Baron Fürnberg had recommended him to Morzin. Prince Paul Esterházy heard Haydn's first symphony and liked it, according to Griesinger, who also says that Morzin dismissed his band in 1760. Haydn was ready to accept a new appointment. In his autobiographical letter of 1776 the composer describes his passage as if it were direct: "bei Herr Grafen von Morzin als Directeur, von da aus als Capellmeister bei Sr. Durchl. den Fürsten." Haydn's full title under Esterházy was Vice-Kapellmeister, the Oberkapellmeister being Gregor Joseph Werner. Contracts signed on 1 April 1761 with other Esterházy musicians mentioned their duty to obey the Vice- as well as the Oberkapellmeister, but Haydn did not sign his contract until 1 May 1761.

Giuseppe Carpani in *Le Haydine* tells a vivid tale that also suggests that Haydn was already in princely service before this time. According to Carpani, Haydn composed a solemn symphony to celebrate the prince's birth-day (22 April 1761). During the performance, the increasingly invalid prince, seated in his large chair and surrounded by his court, interrupted the players in the middle of the first *Allegro* and asked who had written such a beautiful thing. "Haydn" was the answer. The prince promptly declared Haydn henceforth to be in his service. "But you are already in my service, how is it I have not seen you?" The timid Haydn did not know what to reply, but the prince rescued him from his embarrassment: "Go and get dressed like a Maestro."[36] Haydn parted with his own hair reluctantly, and from this point on he wore the courtier's wig. Carpani places this scene at Eisenstadt castle. But contracts signed by the prince throughout April and including 1 May give Vienna as the city, thus it is more likely to have taken place, if it took place at all, in the Esterházy palace in the Wallnerstrasse, Vienna (Figure 4.5).

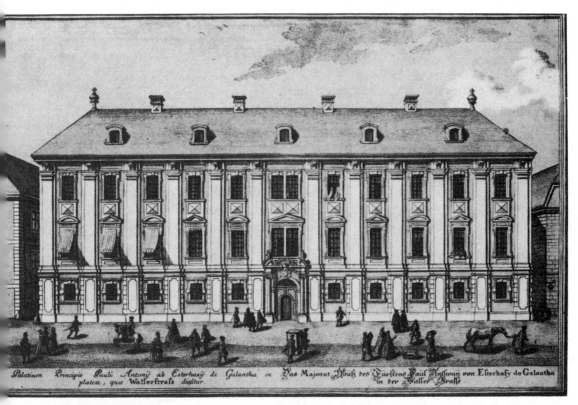

Palatium Principis Pauli Antonÿ ab Esterhazÿ de Galantha in platea, quæ Wallerstrasse dicitur.   *Das Majorat Hauß des Fürsten Paul Anthony von Esterhasÿ de Galantha in der Wallner Strasse*

FIGURE 4.5. Salomon Kleiner. Engraving of the Esterházy Palace in the Wallner-strasse, Vienna.

[36]Landon, *Haydn*, 1: 345.

The contract Haydn signed on 1 May 1761 bound him to several strict provisions. For an annual salary of 400 florins, good for three years, he agreed to take charge of all the princely music except the choir at Eisenstadt. He also agreed to compose whatever pieces the prince wished, and to keep such new compositions specifically requested by the prince from being copied for anyone else. Dies says that the prince presented Haydn with the times of day as a theme for a composition, and adds that Haydn set them to music in the form of quartets, which are very little known. It would follow from the contract that these pieces were little known because copies were discouraged. Haydn's Symphonies Nos. 6–8, called *Le matin, Le midi,* and *Le soir,* are believed to be the "quartets" referred to by Dies. *Le midi* bears this title and the date 1761 in the autograph, which Haydn kept with him all his life. Autographs for the other two do not survive, but their titles and special characteristics are enough to confirm that the three symphonies belong together.

The symphonic trilogy of 1761 represented a brilliant achievement. All three works share a zest for display, an abundance of concertante writing that betrays Haydn's eagerness to show off all the solo and ensemble abilities of his new charges, as well as his own inexhaustible mine of ideas. Yet each symphony has a distinct personality of its own, appropriate to its subject.

Symphony No. 6 in D opens with a slow introduction, *Adagio,* in which the music gradually swells from *pianissimo* to *fortissimo* while rising in pitch, commonly interpreted to represent the morning's first event, a sunrise. The ensuing *Allegro* in 3/4 begins with a fanfare motive in the solo flute, one with links to the *Tuba pastoralis* melodies used by Bohemian composers in their Christmas compositions (Example 4.6). Haydn gives the fanfare to the solo horn just before the reprise. The second movement also begins with an *Adagio* in which the slow rise from D is present in another form. The same slow passage, differently elaborated, closes this movement, thus providing a frame for its main part, marked *Andante,* which deploys for its theme one of Haydn's favorite melodic progressions, 5 3, 4 2 (as in the *Salve regina* of 1757). Even the violone (double bass) gets a solo in the *minore* trio of the Minuet. In the rapid ascending scales in D of the finale, Haydn again refers to the beginning of the symphony.

EXAMPLE 4.6. *Haydn, Symphony No. 6, Le matin (1761), I*

Symphony No. 7 in C begins with an even grander slow introduction and with energetic, pomp-laden effects in dotted rhythm, inherited from the old French *ouverture*, but the *Allegro* is one of those rushing torrents in 3/4 that seem to be a specialty with composers in the Habsburg domains. The second movement offers an operatic *scena;* the solo violin and solo cello begin with an elaborate obbligato recitative, marked "Recitativo Adagio," leading to a blissful duet that begins with a *messa di voce* in the violin. It may be that Haydn was showing his prince how much he had learned from the recent Italian operas in the Burgtheater by Hasse, Gluck, and Traetta, which continued to be revived in concert form throughout the spring of 1761. Also revived in the same season was Gluck's *Diable à quatre* of 1759.

Haydn borrowed from Gluck the popular air about taking snuff to open his Symphony No. 8 in G, *Le soir.*[37] For a finale Haydn wrote a *Presto* in 6/8 called "La tempesta." It begins softly, with *detaché* chords sounding like the first drops of rain. Lightning strikes in the form of the solo flute's jagged descending arpeggios in mm. 15–16, a device familiar from operatic storms. The whole orchestra enters *forte* unison when the flute reaches bottom—the musical equivalent of thunder. These three elemental motives suffice Haydn to draw out a convincing finale to a very witty work. The trilogy has offered not only a parade of concertante effects and symphonic master strokes, but also a kind of catalogue of styles and genres current in Vienna, from the Italian *scena* to the racy vaudeville airs of opéra-comique, from the grandly theatrical *ouverture* to the program-music effects of a Vivaldi or a Francesco Geminiani.

Haydn's use of Gluck's tobacco air invites questions. Why did Haydn choose it? What does his treatment of it tell us? If Prince Esterházy commanded these works on the times of day, did he also go a step further and tell Haydn to use Gluck's tune? He would have heard it in the Burgtheater, where he kept a regular box, like much of fashionable Vienna. Let us suppose a scenario in which the prince did suggest the tune to Haydn. Note that Haydn slips in a few "improvements," just as he would later make a few changes in "Che farò senza Euridice" from Gluck's *Orfeo* when turning it to use as the main theme of a baryton trio for Prince Nicholas Esterházy. To begin with, he leaves out Gluck's opening ritornello, choosing to commence straight away with the popular melody. In the first phrase he smoothes out the tune by conjunct melodic thirds where the original had skips (Example 4.7ab). He then emphasizes the saucy little two-measure addition, breaking the four-measure norm, on "Depuis ce moment la" by a change of dynamic and instrumentation (solo flute added an octave above

[37]Daniel Heartz, "Haydn und Gluck im Burgtheater."

EXAMPLE 4.7. *The "Tobacco Song" in Gluck and Haydn*

a. Gluck, Le Diable à quatre *(1759)*

b. Haydn, Symphony No. 8, Le soir *(1761), I*

the violins). Haydn gives this moment sharper profile also by taking the line down to the dominant on a strong beat, providing more momentum to the ensuing tonic, and by the *forte* dynamic and *unisoni* on the equivalent of the line "Mais mon mari me défend cela," the key line, which Gluck harmonizes. In the following phrase he again smooths out the skips with conjunct thirds, as he does once more in the third from last measure.

EXAMPLE 4.8. *Haydn, Symphony No. 8, II, canonic duets*

Gluck's tune provides abundant melodic material for Haydn to spin out his whole first movement. Its 5 3, 4 2 / 4 2, 3 1 middle part was a long-standing melodic favorite with both Gluck and Haydn. To make a canon out of "Mais mon mari me défend cela," as Haydn does in mm. 181–89 in the seconda parte, he must give up his "improvement" in the melody and revert to the original version (Example 4.8). This little canon involving the four-part strings prophesies the mature Haydn; to the folklike matter of the melody the composer brings the elements of learning, lightly worn. But the surprises of the movement are by no means over with this delightful moment. Haydn works up to a climax with rhythmic intensification and whirring scales that seem ready to lead to tonic G. Instead, the passage ends with a resounding E♭! This surprising arrival of the flat sixth degree is both startling and comic. It is as if the brakes to the carriage had suddenly been applied.

Haydn next makes motions as if to end, which the movement seems ready to do a few moments later. If we bring to mind again the scenario of the prince, seated in his large armchair, taking in the music he had commissioned down to its main theme, we can almost hear him beginning to remonstrate with Haydn—recall Carpani's tale about his interrupting with a question in the middle of a movement—"But where is Gluck's ritornello?" "Here it is!" answers Haydn in the final segment. The composer has the last laugh, and not only here, but also at the end of the "Tempesta" finale, where the whirring scales of the first movement combine with the bass cadence formulae of Gluck's ritornello.

Haydn's penchant for open-air pictorialism suggests comparison with Austria's foremost landscape painter, Johann Christian Brand. Brand's numerous views of the Danube valley particularly endeared him to its inhabitants. Count Nicholas Palffy, the Hungarian chancellor, commissioned Brand to paint the lofty Palffy castle of Devín, situated at the confluence of the Morava and Danube rivers. (See Plate XII.) The painting dates from 1752–53 and counts as one of the first in central Europe to celebrate a natural setting of great beauty with such telling realism. Its point of view is the west bank of the Moldava, across from which the Carpathian mountain chain rises. The Danube flows in the distance on the right, and a few miles down-stream was the Hungarian capital of Pressburg. People about to cross or having crossed by boat between Austria and Hungary are dwarfed by the magnificence of nature but they too are painted with a lively realistic touch. Brand's delight in the locale and in the qualities of light seem spiritually akin to Haydn's "Times of Day" symphonies, which were also the result of a special command.

Let us return to the "solemn symphony" Carpani claimed Haydn composed for Prince Esterházy's last birthday celebration of 22 April 1761. The notion of solemnity suggests that the symphony may have been one of those that begin with a ponderous slow introduction or with an impressive slow movement. Symphony No. 25 in C hovers between both possibilities. Its opening *Adagio* begins like a trio sonata, the subject being passed from second violins to firsts to the basses; but when it comes to rest on the dominant, it starts sounding less like a church sonata and more like a slow introduction. The opening motivic rise from C to A, which becomes suspended over a B in the bass, is turned around when the first violins propose the descent of A to D, and then A to C to B. The contrapuntal element gives way to a melodic-harmonic one. After another pause on the dominant, Haydn reinterprets his opening material another way. He collapses the two-voiced progression to a single unison *forte* in the strings, C up to A, then low B up to G.

This reduction to the kernel of the idea gives Haydn an expressive motto incorporating his favorite downward seventh leap. It also suggests the mysterious motto openings of much later slow introductions, where so much of the entire work is compressed in so few notes as to lend an air of wonder and mystery, as if the key to a puzzle were being offered. If this symphony began with m. 15, Haydn would have achieved just this effect. He would also have adumbrated the beginning of the slow introduction to Mozart's *Linz* Symphony. There is something uncannily close to Mozart too in the modal wavering between major and minor, the rise via 6/3 chords, and the ensuing descent for the third and last arrival at the dominant (the first violins arrive via A C B). Like some of Haydn's great slow introductions of later years, the *Adagio* becomes close to a matrix for what follows.

In the Symphony No. 25 Haydn seems to be discovering, step by step, the power and awe of the kind of slow introduction fraught with consequences for the whole work. The main thematic material of the *Allegro molto* is a rise through the triad up to G, answered by a rise up to A over the subdominant, as if Haydn were "composing out" the first measure of the *Adagio*. In the descent that follows, the melody touches A C B C . Even the trilled ending from F to E may be found in m. 4 of the *Adagio* and in its conclusion. All these correspondences are of the kind that the keen ear can hear. And if the listener misses the connection with the slow introduction *(Adagio)* at first, Haydn makes it clearer still in the seconda parte. At the reprise he takes up the cadential figure A C B C and moves it up via the trilled figures until the answering cadence comes with high D F E. He does it again by transforming the secondary material, a duet for the first and second violins alone, until it too becomes motivic. The Minuet that follows is not related in any obvious way to the opening movements, unlike the finale, which is. After the double bar in the finale, the contrapuntal potential of the theme is put to the test and provides more than one kind of stretto. But the movement as a whole, like the opening *Adagio*, demonstrates the eventual banishment of counterpoint by homophonic and even monophonic discourse.

This terse and impressive symphony is important in a historical sense because it shows more clearly than any other how central the church sonata was in leading Haydn to create the slow introduction of the modern symphony. The work has been assigned to both the Morzin and the early Esterházy symphonies,[38] and seems indeed to stand on the threshold between both.

One of Prince Paul Esterházy's last projects in Eisenstadt was the building of a new theater, located in a glass house behind the castle, where vast formal gardens in the French style were laid out by Louis Gervais in 1760 (Figure 4.6). Expert help came from Count Durazzo, who signed receipts to the effect that he had supervised the work on the theater in July 1761; this project went on throughout the summer and fall of 1761.[39] One of the fascinating items in these documents is a purchase of silver cloth in Vienna (17 September 1761) "in order to make wave and shell effects in the theater." The prince's worsening condition prevented him from deriving much enjoyment from his new theater. Which works were given there we do not know. Haydn would have presided at the harpsichord over musical entertainments.

The friendship of Durazzo with the Esterházys may help explain how the nearly complete offerings of both imperial theaters (which were under Durazzo's direction) found their way to the music library of Eisenstadt castle in the form of librettos and musical scores. Something else may be explained by the connection as well. Durazzo was in regular correspondence with Charles-Simon Favart in Paris; the two exchanged music among many other things. Haydn's music reached Paris very early and was printed there with regularity from 1764 on. Durazzo may have been one of the Viennese links

---

[38] Jens Peter Larsen says "before or around 1760" in *Haydn Yearbook* 10 (1978): 78. Landon, *Haydn*, 1: 552, opts for the early Esterházy years.

[39] Landon, *Haydn*, 1: 360–61.

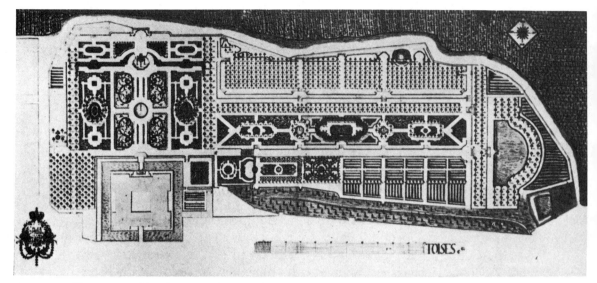

FIGURE 4.6. Plan by Louis Gervais for the formal gardens of Eisenstadt Palace, 1760.

in the chain by which Haydn, although buried, as it were, in the countryside throughout much of the year, became known so quickly in Paris. Haydn remained in touch with Durazzo as late as 1783, at which time he wrote Artaria that he valued Count Durazzo's house above all others.[40] Another tie bound Durazzo and Prince Nicholas Esterházy: both were married to members of the Weissenwolf family.

Haydn was approaching his thirtieth birthday when Prince Paul died in Vienna on 18 March 1762. On 3 March the composer wrote a letter summoning the court musicians at Eisenstadt to Vienna, signing himself "Heydn Capell-Meister." During the period of mourning nothing but sacred music was heard at the Esterházy court. The new prince, Nicholas, was ready by May to welcome to Eisenstadt a troupe of Italian comedians that included Girolamo Bon, who was also a stage designer, and his wife Rosa Ruvinetti, who had sung intermezzi with Domenico Cricchi at the Burgtheater in 1758. Haydn wrote arias for a comedy called *La Marchesa Nespola* that has been connected with the 1762 visit of Bon and his wife. Prince Nicholas must have been pleased because he raised Haydn's salary by one half to 600 florins (on 5 July 1762) in a new charter given to the court music, which now included a *Feld Musique* of six players: two oboes, two horns, and two bassoons.

One of Haydn's frequent duties in his role as Vice-Kapellmeister was to act as godfather at the baptism of children born to his musicians. On 3 July

[40] Haydn, *Gesammelte Briefe*, no. 53, p. 126.

1762 he and his wife became godparents for the child of a prominent non-Esterházy musician, his exact contemporary, the hornist Joseph Leutgeb. Haydn's wife was present for the event in Vienna, but the composer was absent, doubtless busy with the theatrical offerings at Eisenstadt. The link with Leutgeb offers clues about the relationship between Haydn and the central focus of Viennese concert life during these years, the academies in the Burgtheater.

Joseph Leutgeb was the most prominent horn soloist in Vienna in the early 1760s, and evidently one of the best received solo players on any instrument. A frequent soloist at the academies in the Burgtheater, he played no fewer than fourteen horn concertos between 27 November 1761 and 28 January 1763; for three of these Gumpenhuber cites a composer's name: (Leopold) Hofmann, 11 June 1762; Michael Haydn, 2 July 1762; and (Carl) Ditters, 5 November 1762. Gumpenhuber describes the second academy in these terms: "Concert a joué Le Sr. Leitgeb sur le Cor de Chasse de la Composition de Sr. Michel Hayde." After several years in the service of the bishop of Grosswardein in Hungary, Michael Haydn returned to Vienna. On 15 September 1762 Joseph and Michael Haydn visited Rohrau together. Unlike many siblings aspiring to excellence in the same field, the two brothers remained devoted to each other throughout their lives, which says a great deal about both of them. This year, which brought Michael Haydn back to Vienna, which provided Leutgeb with so many horn concertos, was also the year of Joseph Haydn's great Horn Concerto in D.

The Concerto for horn and orchestra in D is dated 1762 in Haydn's hand. In comparison with the other peaks among Haydn's concertos, this work ranks high. It is far removed from the superabundance of decoration in his very rococo Organ Concerto in C of 1756. For individuality of tone and consistency of inspiration, the work deserves to stand beside the beloved Cello Concerto in D of 1783, the best-known of the keyboard concertos (No. 6 in D of 1784), and the late Trumpet Concerto in E♭. Its personal stamp as well as its virtuosity fairly shout that the intended soloist was none other than Joseph Leutgeb, who later inspired Mozart to write several superb works for him. The works for solo horn and orchestra of 1762 by both Haydns must have been composed in a spirit of fraternal rivalry and affection, also in direct collusion with Leutgeb, who would eventually go to Salzburg as a colleague of Michael Haydn.[41]

Haydn's new contract of 1762 contained the same restrictive language about allowing his works to circulate as did the original contract. This could

[41] Daniel Heartz, "Leutgeb and the 1762 Horn Concertos of Joseph and Michael Haydn," *Mozart-Jahrbuch 1987/88*, pp. 59–64.

explain why his name appears not once in Gumpenhuber's chronicles of the academies in the Burgtheater. If, as seems clear, one of the many anonymous horn concertos Leutgeb played in 1762 was in fact the new one by Joseph Haydn, it is possible that some of the many anonymous symphonies reported by Gumpenhuber may also have been Haydn's.

The Symphonist Gathers Momentum

H A Y D N wrote a wedding opera, *Acide e Galatea,* to celebrate the marriage between the son of Prince Esterházy and Maria Theresa Erdödy in January 1763.[42] The poet of this *festa teatrale* was Giovanni Ambrogio Migliavacca, who had contributed the serenata *Tetide,* set by Gluck, to the imperial wedding of 1760. *Tetide,* plus *Alcide al bivio* by Metastasio and Hasse for the same occasion, provided a standard by which the poetry, music, and production of *Acide e Galatea* were judged. Haydn acquitted himself well, managing to draw inspiration from the work of his distinguished elders without copying them outright. His continuing efforts to come to terms with the vocal art of Hasse were to reach a climax a few years later with the *Stabat mater.*

Acide e Galatea was presumably composed in the fall of 1762, when Gluck's *Orfeo ed Euridice* was having its triumphant run in the Burgtheater. Haydn wrote a piece known as the "Aria di Dorina," on the text "Costretta a piangere," which has been assigned to 1762 along with other fragments thought to have belonged to his comic opera *La Marchesa Nespola.*[43] Given a verse form in *quinarii sdruccioli,* Haydn sets it in the traditional way: ♩ ♩ ♩ ♩. ♪♪ ♩. He maintains the same rhythmic pattern throughout, just as does the most famous example of *quinarii sdruccioli* from this time, the Chorus of Furies in *Orfeo,* "Chi mai dell'Erebo / Fra le calligine." Haydn apparently transferred the music of "Costretta a piangere" to Galatea's aria "Troppo felice / Troppo beato," which is in *quinarii,* but not *sdruccioli.* The result works, but it is not as happy a text setting.

Haydn's orchestra acquired two additional horns in the course of 1763 (by 1 August). Wonderful new possibilities were opened up by the rare opportunity to write for four horns. The outstanding Symphony No. 13 continues the festive air and concertante bravado of the times-of-day symphonies of two years earlier. The opening *Allegro molto* is built on a driving fanfare

---

[42] Daniel Heartz, "Haydn's *Acide e Galatea* and the Imperial Wedding Operas of 1760 by Hasse and Gluck," *International Haydn Congress 1982* (Munich, 1986), pp. 332–40. See also Günter Thomas, "Anmerkungen zum Libretto von Haydns Festa teatral 'Acide,' " *Haydn-Studien* 5 (1982): 118–24.

[43] Landon, *Haydn,* 1: 425–38; 446–49.

figure that rises through the tonic triad for three measures, then does the same on the dominant, and after three more measures on the tonic like the first segment, the violins climb up to high D. The goal is the same at the beginning of Symphony No. 1 in D, but how much more forceful this beginning is! The fourth three-measure segment leads from the high D down to a tentative sounding cadence, with the third in the treble, the second two measures then being echoed, *piano,* an octave lower. With the echo, the sway of the three-measure module is broken. Yet the transition that follows continues with six measures that could be interpreted as either 2 + 2 + 2 or 3 + 3. The dynamics from *forte* to *piano* argue for 4 + 2, but the harmony, with arrival on V a main consideration, by analogy with the beginning of the movement, argues for 3 + 3. If the former wins out, it is because the last two measures constitute a *piano* echo of the first two. The three chordal hammer strokes to conclude the prima parte also conclude the seconda parte, and what is more, they signal the end of the development, thus imposing utmost clarity of form. The hammer strokes also bespeak the proximity of the Italian sinfonia, which Haydn has surpassed in rhythmic interest, just as he has far surpassed his own Symphony No. 1.

All the winds are silent in the slow movement of Symphony No. 13, an *Adagio cantabile* in G that consists of a very tender song for Joseph Weigl, the first cellist, beginning with the galant melodic inflection 5 5♯ 6. The Minuet (called Menuet) begins with a sturdy four-measure phrase, followed by a quasi-echo of mm. 3 and 4—i.e., it continues one of the modules of the opening movement. The next phrase, of six measures, also contains a two-measure echo of its last two measures, but not an exact one. After the double bar the echoes become more capricious still, providing an object lesson in Haydn's soon-to-be-renowned wit. The trio, which offers a flute solo, again juggles two- and three-measure phrases. Haydn ends both periods with a *forte* unison that sounds like a souvenir of Bohemia, an eighth-note passage, 2 3 4 2 5 3 1, that comes close to the traditional Czech melody employed by Stamitz in his *Sinfonia pastorale.*

The finale, *Allegro molto* in 2/4, is based on the Credo theme 1 2 4 3 so dear to Mozart and used to launch the finale of his last symphony. As serious a proposition as this famous whole-note theme in the strings seems to be, the winds erupt, as if in mockery, with their two measures of jubilation, which overlap the fourth measure of the theme. Thus the four-measure Credo theme is turned into a five-measure comedy. The dialogue becomes even funnier when the strings give in and repeat the wind figures, as if to say, "All right, have it your way." Haydn juggles both aspects, comic and serious, throughout the movement, keeping them in balance successfully until the inevitable final stretto, where the contrapuntal element comes to dominate. Here one must make an effort of the will to avoid comparison with what Mozart does in the same place with the same theme. Haydn's symphony is a masterpiece too, perhaps his greatest symphonic work to date.

The Symphony No. 72, thought to date from 1763 because of its four horns and its style, is even more showy than Symphony No. 13, but not quite as satisfying. Instead of marking the phrases off with their sustained chords, as do the horns in the first movement of Symphony No. 13, the four hornists begin an extraordinary concertante display, each with his own scale passage or arpeggio. The horns remain prominent throughout the movement and conclude it with a final flourish, lending the piece the air of a full-fledged sinfonia concertante. The *Andante* in 6/8 that follows is a showcase for the flautist Franz Siegel and concertmaster Luigi Tomasini. In the Menuet Haydn again plays with multiple echoes, offering further stylistic confirmation that this work is close to Symphony No. 13. The finale is a variation movement on a perfectly symmetrical theme, 8 measures + 8 measures, each strain being repeated. After being stated by the strings, the theme serves as a scaffold upon which to exhibit in turn flute, cello, violin, violone, oboe, and horns. A concluding *Presto* in 6/8 comes as a refreshing relief from the squareness of the theme; its rollicking rhythms perhaps suggested hunting, the court's favorite pastime, to the first auditors.

If Haydn put his four *cors de chasse* in the spotlight in this symphony, it may be because he felt impelled to justify the expense an added pair of hornists represented. He lost two of the players, who died, in 1764. Not until 1765 did he have four horns again, allowing him to write the *Horn Signal* Symphony (No. 31), which ends with a theme and variations like the Symphony No. 72, and with a more interesting "hunting" *Presto* to conclude the whole. Two other symphonies are dated 1763, No. 12 in E and No. 40 in F, but they call for the normal pair of horns only. The former is especially intriguing for its unusual key and its quiet beginning, like a string quartet. Symphony No. 29 of 1765, also in E, has a quiet beginning as well.

In the spring of 1764 Prince Nicholas traveled to Germany to attend the coronation of Archduke Joseph as Roman King, a ceremony that took place on 3 April in Frankfurt am Main. Haydn welcomed him back with the cantata *Da qual gioia*, which included an elaborate harpsichord solo in its second movement, one that Haydn probably played himself. The opening movement, an *Allegro di molto* in common time and in the key of C, belongs to the *Habsburger Prunkstil* associated with Reutter, the strings rushing up and down scales in sixteenth notes against triadic, fanfare motives in the winds—apt music for filling a large hall with festive clatter.

Haydn's most memorable symphony of 1764 was No. 22 in E♭, *Le philo-*

sophe, in which he employed "corni inglesi," as he had done before in a divertimento of 1760 (Hob. II:16). English horns (tenor oboes pitched a fifth lower than the normal oboe) belong to a specifically Viennese tradition. A pair of them were used in the Burgtheater at least as early as the pasticcio *Euridice* of 1750 (in an aria by the Viennese-born Ignaz Holzbauer). Gumpenhuber's list of orchestra personnel in the Burgtheater for February 1761 includes "Les deux frères Koffer [Kapfer], corns angloises." The two brothers were lured into Esterházy service at approximately the same time as Haydn, their contracts dating from 1 April 1761. Under date of 8 April 1761 they sold to their new employer two bassoons, two oboes, and two "Englische Horn." It may be assumed that most professional oboists were skilled on at least two of these three instruments. On 25 March 1762 a new concerto for two English horns was heard in one of the Burgtheater academies, played by Schmidt and Mayer, first and second oboe players in the theater orchestra. Gluck took advantage of the same two players when calling for two English horns in the first act of his *Orfeo* later the same year.

If the Esterházy English horns saw little use before 1764, it was perhaps because they needed repair. Surviving in Haydn's hand is a document, dated 9 July 1764, acknowledging repairs on Esterházy instruments by Mathias Rockobauer, who delivered reeds for oboe, bassoon, and English horn.[44] *Le philosophe* (as it is called on the manuscript parts in the Este Library in Modena) was presumably written shortly thereafter; the autograph score bears the date 1764. Its opening *Adagio* is a kind of chorale prelude in dialogue between the horns and the English horns, accompanied by a "walking bass"—a texture that looks backward (to Bach and the Lutheran tradition) and forward (to the Chorale for the Armed Men in *Die Zauberflöte*). The English horns participate importantly in delivering thematic material in the other movements as well. The work is one of Haydn's finest in the mold of the "church symphony" (which will be considered in its own right in the next section).

Another of the same type is the more lyrical Symphony No. 21 in A for the usual scoring of strings, two oboes, and two horns. It begins with an *Adagio* that is extraordinarily poetic and free in form, like a reverie. Two other symphonies dated 1764 are in the normal four-movement sequence. The final movement of No. 23 in G fades away to a *pianissimo* for strings alone, and then further disintegrates into silence, its last sound being a pizzicato chord. No. 24 in D goes through some of the same Italian sinfonia gestures as the Symphony No. 13 in D of the previous year, but with less originality.

[44] Ibid., 1: 396.

In 1765 Haydn was able to replace the two horn players who had died and write for four horns again. The Symphony No. 31 *alla Posta* ("with the horn signal") was his inspired response. Hints that this work was a special one for Haydn are present from its very beginning. As the horns sound their fanfare, the violins intone falling thirds, *piano*, on the weak beats, following a unison tonic, *forte*, an idea that goes back to the *Salve regina* in E of 1756. At m. 9 the first horn sounds the *alla Posta* melody by itself, which means leaping back and forth between the sixteenth and eighth partials.[45] The melody occupies a second eight-measure segment. Haydn then continues on in large symmetrical units (of four, six, and eight measures), lending the movement a new sense of spaciousness and power. When the strings reach the goal of their transition by descending to low A, the solo flute answers with a rising scale, unaccompanied, not once but thrice, a simple but effective combination of timbre and idiomatic display in lieu of a "second theme." To close the prima parte, *alla Posta* returns on the dominant, against which the violins descend in thirds and sixths, sounding a cadential phrase that could not serve for anything but a closing idea.

After the double bar there is a feint toward vi, which is prepared by its dominant, only to be answered by tonic D in the guise of a dominant resolving to G, over which the solo flute sounds its rising scale, then repeats the same a degree above on A. The basses move up to A♯, then B, which is resolved to e in a flurry of activity, after which the basses move up to F♯ chromatically and stay there, quietly supporting the closing material (*alla Posta* + descending thirds in the strings). The arrival of the relative minor, b, is the big tonal event in this movement, partly because vi was threatened and withheld at the beginning of the seconda parte, partly because Haydn downplays the beginning of the reprise by withholding the opening fanfare and substituting d for D (just as in the first movement of Symphony No. 24). To make us anticipate all the more a return to the opening of the movement, Haydn resorts to the three hammer-stroke chords of V that often signal "reprise to follow." The surprise and disappointment that ensues is all the greater for this deceptive "sign." *Alla Posta* returns first, and the opening horn fanfare (with descending thirds in the violins) is not heard until the final eight measures of the movement, so that they become its high point of interest.

For the slow movement of Symphony No. 31 Haydn writes an *Adagio* in 6/8 in concertante dialogue for violin (Tomasini) and cello (Weigl), who are supported by pizzicato strings in serenade fashion. Tomasini gets the lion's

---

[45] On this melody, see Horst Walter, "Das Posthornsignal bei Haydn und anderen Komponisten des 18. Jahrhunderts," *Haydn-Studien* 4 (1976–80): 21–34.

share of the beginning, but Weigl has the last word. The idea is not new, but it is even more lovely in this treatment than in the earlier concertante dialogues. What is new, on the other hand, is the presence of the four horns and their disposition—two in the tonic, G, and two in the dominant, D, allowing them to play an important thematic role in both areas. Gluck had been a pioneer in placing the natural horns in both V and I in his quartet from *Tetide* (1760) and had demonstrated the magnificent effects of answering back and forth between his two pairs in the opening ritornello. Haydn plays his two pairs off on a larger scale, and they are so prominent as to become concertante partners with Tomasini and Weigl.

The ensuing Menuet employs the four horns but makes no great demands on them; in the trio it is the turn of the Kapfer brothers (oboes) and Siegel (flute) to shine (and also the first horn as well, at the end of each strain). The finale, *Molto moderato* in 2/4, is a theme and variations on a tune of two eight-measure strains, each repeated, and thus constitutes a revisit to the territory staked out in the finale of the Symphony No. 72. Every leading player in Haydn's small orchestra gets his turn with the theme, down to the double bass player Schwenda in the seventh and last variation. Each player having saluted the prince in his turn, the tutti launches into a *Presto* in 3/4 that has certain features associated with the act-ending theatrical chaconnes of French operas. These somewhat gruff and menacing sounds (especially the turn to the minor) give way to gaiety and revel when answered with what sounds like a folktune in the major. What could possibly top this in bringing the symphony to an end? The brilliant opening of the first movement! This return caps an altogether stunning achievement and puts the seal of unity on the whole. Haydn's command of tonal architecture reaches a new level in this work, which is at once a logical step in the chain of accomplishments represented by his heroic-theatrical symphonies in D, leading from No. 1 (1759) to No. 6 (1761) to No. 13 (1763) and No. 24 (1764), and a new beginning on a still grander scale.

Three other symphonies are known to belong to the year 1765: No. 28 in A, No. 29 in E, and No. 30 in C (*Alleluia*), the last of which will be considered in the next section. All three require the usual strings and pairs of oboes and horns. The first two begin quietly with a movement in 3/4 marked *Allegro di molto,* and continue with a slow movement in 2/4. It takes a few measures before the listener can tell whether the first movement of the Symphony No. 28 is in 6/8 or 3/4, and this ambiguity is one of its charms, along with its very tight motivic structure, in which everything is derived from the first rhythmic motive (Figure 4.7). Hiller did nothing to enhance his stature as a critic when he wrote deprecatingly of the Symphony No. 28 in 1770: "A local composer has recently put the symphony in more bearable form and elimi-

FIGURE 4.7. Autograph of Haydn's Symphony No. 28, 1765.

nated the eccentricities . . . would that the silly trio together with its minuet were suppressed." The amount of unison and octave doubling in the Menuet might be expected to annoy Hiller, but the trio is a most innocuous little dance in the minor, with the simplest kind of Ländler accompaniment.

"CHURCH SYMPHONIES" AND MINOR-MODE SYMPHONIES

HAYDN'S early symphonic examples of what has been called *sonata da chiesa* form (Nos. 5, 11, 12, 21, and 22) share several features besides an initial slow movement. The most obvious is a single tonality for all the movements. Trio sonata texture with subject-and-answer construction predominate in the slow movements. Canonic or other contrapuntal devices appear prominently in minuets and in one or both fast movements. Slow-moving chorale-like melodies appear against faster counterpoints. Sequential passages are apt to be frequent, more so than in Haydn's other symphonies. All these features taken together proclaim the retrospective character of the group. With these works Haydn looks back to the perfection of the Corellian *sonata da chiesa,* as so many other composers continued to do throughout the century. For the sake of simplicity these works will be called "church symphonies," in full awareness of the precarious nature of any hypothesis assigning them to use in church. Any kind of symphony of the time was usable in church.[46]

The *Adagio* that opens the Symphony No. 22 (*Le philosophe*) presents a melody in slow-moving tones, like a cantus firmus, played, as we have seen, by the horns and English horns in turn (the latter instruments may have been especially associated with church music). This extraordinary movement perhaps lingered in Haydn's memory decades later. Griesinger reports Haydn as saying that he "oftentimes portrayed moral characters in his symphonies. In one of the oldest, which, however, he could not identify, the dominant idea is of God speaking with an abandoned sinner, pleading with him to reform. But the sinner in his thoughtlessness pays no heed to the admonition." Dies received similar information from Haydn, and an additional clue: the movement in question was an *Adagio*:

> I had already resolved a long time ago to ask Haydn how much truth there was in the assertion (which I had several times heard and also read) that he sought in his instrumental pieces to work out some verbal problem or other selected at will? Whether, for example, he had ever thought of expressing in a symphony a coquette, a prude, and so on? "Seldom," answered Haydn. "In instrumental music, I generally allowed my purely musical fantasy free play. Only one exception occurs to me now, in which in the Adagio of a symphony, I chose as a theme a conversation between God and a heedless sinner." On a later occasion the talk turned again to this Adagio, and Haydn said he always expressed the Deity with love and goodness. I begged Haydn to designate the theme of the

[46]Neal Zaslaw, *Mozart's Symphonies: Context, Performance Practice, Reception* (Oxford, 1989), p. 58.

Adagio, because it would be sure to interest most readers, but he no longer remembered in which symphony it is to be found. (Twenty-first visit)

The symphony as sermon is not our normal concept of Haydn's aims, nor was it his either, according to his own words (as quoted by Dies). Yet the idea had occasional validity. Carpani throws a little further light on the question. After discussing Haydn's *Seven Last Words*, written originally as a set of instrumental *Adagio*s for Holy Week services at Cadiz Cathedral, Carpani continues:

> Some other symphonies by Haydn were written for the holy days. They were sounded in the chapel at Eisenstadt, in that of the imperial court, and in other churches on such occasions. They were written in G, D and c. Besides sorrow there shines through them a characteristically Haydnesque vivacity, and here there become obvious some traits of anger, with which the composer was perhaps envisioning sinners and Jews.

Note that Carpani places these special works in a context of being performed in church.

Evidence from all over Europe confirms that Haydn's symphonies and many other symphonies were indeed performed in church and during liturgical ceremonies. One of the most touching accounts is the recollection of young Fernando Sor when he was enrolled in the choir school of Montserrat Monastery ca. 1790:

> They awakened us at four o'clock in the morning when it was still dark, and we went to the chapel before five . . . Mass was accompanied by a small orchestra comprising violins, cellos, double basses, bassoons, horns, and oboes, everything being played by children, the eldest of whom could have been only fifteen or sixteen. At the Offertory we played the Introduction and Allegro of one of Haydn's Symphonies in D, at the Communion the Andante, and at the last Gospel, the Allegro.[47]

The piece in question could be the well-traveled *Imperial* Symphony (No. 53 in D), shorn of its Minuet, but with the slow introduction to the opening fast movement intact. The majesty and solemnity of Haydn's slow symphonic introductions stem ultimately from a sublimation of certain features of the opening *Adagio* movements in his early works. Assuming that the function of Haydn's early church symphonies was, at least originally or on certain occasions, to help in the celebration of the mass helps explain one of their

[47] Brian Jeffrey, *Fernando Sor: Composer and Guitarist* (London, 1977), pp. 117–30.

most salient features: a single tonality for all movements. During mass, symphonic movements were not sounded in direct succession typically, but at widely spaced intervals, separated by intervening music.

Symphony No. 30 in C of 1765 has church connections of a special sort. It is known as the *Alleluia* Symphony because Haydn incorporates from the outset in the second violin part the beginning of a liturgical melody, C D E C D C.[48] The opening *Allegro* is a fine specimen of the composer's "normal" symphonic first movements of the time, the only unusual feature of which is the length of time spent in the minor mode (see the second theme area, where the rising third motif engenders a new theme over a rocking two-note bass, first in major, then in minor, and finally in major). The development is mainly taken up with a vigorous sequence in which the basses play the first three rising tones of the chant in a circle of fifths progression. The *Andante* in 2/4 that follows as a second movement is in the dominant, not a usual choice in a "normal" symphony of this time, when the subdominant was Haydn's favorite choice except when the keynote contained four or more flats. The preponderance of concertante writing for flute could explain why Haydn chose G for this movement instead of F, G being a better key for the flute. The finale is a *Tempo di Menuet, più tosto Allegretto*, which starts as a regular Minuet with trio in F, but then goes into a second trio in a before the reprise, which Haydn writes out and to which he adds a coda. The main minuet theme is derived from the rising thirds that open the work. A hint of an "Amen" lingers in the final cadences of the third movement, with IV more stressed than V. In one of the early church symphonies, No. 18 in G, Haydn also chooses as third and concluding movement a *Tempo di Menuet*, which is a regular minuet except for the written-out reprise and added coda.

Haydn took a further step with the Symphony No. 34 in d/D, written ca. 1766. The work begins with a slow movement in minor, an *Adagio* in d, that deploys long horn pedals and plumbs many of the expressive possibilities then available, including melodic syncopations, extreme dynamic contrasts, plus chords of the diminished seventh and Neapolitan sixth. The sepulchral effects of the penultimate *Larghetto* of Gluck's *Don Juan* (1761), which is also in 3/4 and in d, with its trombone and use of alternating *fortes* and *pianos* at short range, may well have inspired Haydn to write a passage such as that in mm. 75–82 (Example 4.9). A new consciousness of minute dynamic control in Viennese music stems primarily from Gluck, whose *Don Juan* remained as shockingly modern as when it first appeared. Rapid and frequent dynamic change was one of the currents that fostered the fortepiano,

---

[48] Landon, *Haydn*, 1: 569. Neal Zaslaw, "Mozart, Haydn, and the *Sinfonia da Chiesa*," *Journal of Musicology* 1 (1982): 95–124, specifies (p. 113) that the melody "appeared in the liturgy only once during the year, at the end of the Epistle reading of Holy Saturday Mass."

EXAMPLE 4.9. *Haydn, Symphony No. 34, I*

of course, and the passage in question shows Haydn well on his way to the impressive Sonata in c (No. 20) of 1771. A gauge of just how modern such effects were at the time is provided by critics like Reichardt, who objected specifically to many dynamic changes following one another, comparing them to overspiced food—i.e., damaging to taste.[49]

The second movement of Haydn's Symphony No. 34 arrives with what sounds like a burst of light in D, a brilliant *Allegro* in common time, the winds sustaining while the first violins make great melodic leaps up a tenth

---

[49] In *Briefe eines aufmerksamen Reisenden die Musik betreffend* (Frankfurt and Leipzig, 1774), 1: 11–12.

in half-notes, D F♯, E G, against the bustle of eighth notes and sixteenth notes in the other strings. This long-note melody is of a type that a Tartini or a Sammartini might have written thirty years earlier; distinctly Sammartinian is the use of rhythmic diminution upon reiteration of the subject. The suspended D in the bass in the second measure, a ii$^{4/2}$ resolving to V$^{6/5}$ progression, is another old-fashioned trait such as can be found frequently in the early Haydn church symphonies, of which this work is one of the last stragglers as well as a bridge to the minor symphonies of the late 1760s and early 1770s. The second theme is not archaic in the least, being mainly a pedal on V over which the oboes descend in thirds while the strings alternate *fortes* and *pianos* (the oboe descent is very like that of the finale of Symphony No. 24 in D). To end the prima parte, Haydn makes his violins rush up to A in sixteenth notes, whence they descend by leaping down a seventh twice, then three times more in rhythmic diminution before reaching the cadence. Apparently pleased by this emphatic conclusion, Haydn changed it in the seconda parte only in pitch, moving it up to high D. The ensuing Menuet and trio do not offer anything out of the ordinary. The striding bass of the finale, *Presto assai* in 2/4 with triplets, seems to be generated by the suspended D in the bass that sets the *Allegro* in motion harmonically. Something faintly old-fashioned attaches to this movement too; it contains a minor trio (not designated as such) and a written-out reprise plus a short coda.

Haydn wrote another symphony in d/D not long after Symphony No. 34, the so-called *Lamentatione* Symphony (No. 26), believed to date from around 1768 and known to have been composed by 1770. It begins with an *Allegro assai con spirito* in common time in which the syncopations that appeared momentarily in the opening of the Symphony No. 34 now take over the whole treble line. The parallel is reinforced by melodic similarities. Against the stream of syncopations in the treble, the bass strides resolutely forward in even quarters on the beat. Without any transition the music moves to the relative major as the second violins and first oboe begin to quote what is labeled in the score "Chorale," a melody that has been identified as the tone used to recite the Gospel during Holy Week.[50] Note that Haydn places the chant in the next highest voice, as he did in the *Alleluia* Symphony, and when this voice moves in half notes against the eighth-note figuration of the first violins, the texture is not unlike that which commences

---

[50] By Landon, *Haydn,* 2: 291. Neal Zaslaw, "Mozart, Haydn, and the *Sinfonia da Chiesa*," says that the melody is equivalent to "the reciting tones for the Passion narratives . . . used on Palm Sunday, Holy Tuesday, Ash Wednesday [he means the Wednesday of Holy Week], and Good Friday for the Gospels according to the four Evangelists." The passage is repeated in Zaslaw, *Mozart's Symphonies,* pp. 81–82.

the *Allegro* of Symphony No. 34. The development includes one long circle of fifths harmonic sequence in which the syncopated treble against bass descends in chains while the oboes play whole notes in rising fourths—another relic of ecclesiastic polyphony. Haydn adds four measures of dominant pedal at the joint with the second key area in the reprise, otherwise he changes little; what appeared in F in the prima parte appears in d in the seconda parte.

Symphony No. 26 continues with an *Adagio* in 2/4 in F, which quotes in the middle voice the plainchant for the Lamentations of Jeremiah, sung on Maundy Thursday, Good Friday, and Holy Saturday. A striding bass with octave leaps reminds one of the finale of the Symphony No. 34 and offers another hint that these two works are in several respects twins. Toward the end of the *Adagio* Haydn veers off tonally as if to conclude in d, but he restores F in the final phrase. It is a nice touch of modal uncertainty, made possible by the many repeated tones of his quoted melody and certainly in keeping with much music heard in church. It is also a nice touch because the third and last movement, marked simply "Menuet," restores the initial key of d. The Neapolitan chord makes a prominent appearance as it did in the first movement of Symphony No. 34. There is something rather mysterious about the lengthy silences that add an extra measure to the regular phrases, and hence lessen the dance character. At the reprise the theme is treated canonically. The *maggiore* is filled with abrupt dynamic contrasts, and the symphony ends very softly, *Menuet da capo*. Concrete evidence such as the plainchant in two of its movements argues that the *Lamentatione* Symphony must be a church symphony as much as or more than any in the Haydn canon, even though it does not open with a slow movement. Its stylistic links with the other works discussed here are many and diverse. An opening slow movement is obviously only one among several criteria by which these works are set apart as a group.

Two other minor-mode symphonies fall in the late 1760s, No. 39 in g and No. 49 in f, for which Haydn's autograph is dated 1768. The first begins with an *Allegro assai* in common time, a *piano* theme with "knocking" eighth notes and to which Haydn lends an uncanny sense of perturbance by the measure of silence he places after the first half cadence. The first phrase is diatonic, the answering phrase very chromatic, beginning D E♭ and ending with an insistently repeated C♯ D. Upon repetition there is no pause but rather an unexpected plunge into the relative major. The *Andante* in 3/8 that follows is in E♭, a favorite companion of g long before Mozart's famous examples of the same. It begins innocently enough but works up to quite a climax in the middle, with paired rising minor seconds, G A♭, F♯ G. The following Menuet features a theme in which both D E♭ and C♯ D play a role. An *Allegro di molto* in common time returns to the outlines of the first movement's main theme, and also plunges into the relative major in the same way. The rising minor-second motif comes to the fore in various ways in the finale, especially in the development. It seems as if Haydn invites us to hear the whole symphony as emerging from an idea close to its opening. But if he had indeed wanted us to hear such subtle motivic connections, would he not have made them between the incipits of each movement? In the companion work, Symphony No. 49, he did just this.

Haydn opens all four movements of the Symphony No. 49 in f by using, one way or another, the motto C D♭ B♭ C. This is so close to the "hidden motif" of Symphony No. 39 as to leave little doubt about the affinity between the two. Symphony No. 49 is obviously a church symphony, and the name it acquired early, *La passione*, points again to a connection with Holy Week. Its motto may well refer to another plainchant. All of its movements are in the same key, and the *Adagio* is placed first. The subject of the second movement, *Allegro di molto* in common time, is one of those contrapuntal subjects in long notes and great leaps (like the subject of the corresponding movement in Symphony No. 34) against which runs a countersubject in eighth notes that is just as important in sustaining the thematic flow. The syncopations with which the treble continues recalls the opening of the *Lamentatione* Symphony. So stern and gloomy a vision as projected by *La passione* does not contradict the possibility that it was intended as the musical equivalent of a Lenten sermon, or at least a Lenten meditation. In some early sources it bears the ironic title "The Quaker of good humor."[51]

The date of the Symphony No. 39 has given rise to conjectures. It has been put as early as 1765 because of its four horns, or after 1 March 1767, when Haydn could again call upon a fourth horn. But there is no dated reference to the work before 1770. Its motivic ties with *La passione* (1768) suggest that it is close in date—an essay using some of the same minor materials but in a "normal" four-movement format.

Three minor-mode symphonies belong to the early 1770s. No. 44 in e, the so-called *Trauer-Symphonie*, maintains the same key throughout. Its *Menuetto Allegretto* is canonic, and there is an imitative treatment of the head motif at the end of the first movement that is like a fugal stretto. The slow

---

[51] A manuscript of probable Viennese origin bears the inscription "nel suo entusiasmo il Quakuo [quakero] di bel'umore. Questa Sinfonia serve di Compagna à quella del Philosopho Inglese dell istesso autore." The Italian word for "Quaker" is "Quacchero" or "Quaquero." The linking with another church symphony, *Le philosophe*, raises interesting possibilities. The qualification "Inglese" may stem from the *corni inglesi* of that work. But the strangeness of both works may have seemed to Viennese ears the province, temperamentally remote, of English Quakers and philosophers.

movement is an *Adagio* in E that seems to take its initial melodic descent from the trio of the preceding Minuet. In the finale (*Presto* in 2/4) Haydn resorts to suspended long-note dissonances and other contrapuntal devices; for the conclusion he invents a new ending to the main theme, which is otherwise withheld from the reprise. The sequence of movements, with Minuet second and *Adagio* third, surrounded by fast outer movements, is the same that Haydn adopted in the contemporaneous Quartets of Op. 9 and Op. 17. Of the two other minor-mode symphonies, No. 52 in c (ca. 1771) belongs here as the culmination of the whole group, while No. 45 in f♯ (*Farewell* Symphony) of 1772 shows Haydn overcoming his minor-mode preoccupations; this work will be treated elsewhere.

Rarely does Haydn use so angry a tone of voice as in the Symphony No. 52 in c. Its first movement, *Allegro assai con brio* in common time, opens with a blazing ascent, *unisoni*, that rises with ever greater leaps upward until reaching the top of the *Schreckensakkord,* sounding like the approximation of a shriek. When Haydn repeats the opening, *piano* instead of *forte*, legato instead of staccato, he achieves a smoldering sense of latent power and unease (partly owing to the prominent false interval E♭ B♮). The first arrival at the relative major in root position inaugurates a combination of whole notes, like a cantus firmus, against a moving counterpoint in eighth notes, an effect that looks back to the church symphonies and the *Allegro* of Symphony No. 34 in particular. Haydn's ire seems to reach a peak with the *fortissimo* chord of e♭—a foil for the more gentle second theme, with its *piano* dynamic, regular harmonic progression, and less jagged contours. (The falling seventh in the middle of this theme corresponds to the insistent falling sevenths in the *Allegro* of Symphony No. 34.) A kind of dialogue ensues between the violent elements and the gentle theme, a contrast of opposites that suggests Emanuel Bach, as does the *pianissimo* written-out retard at the end of the gentle theme's second statement. In the development Haydn intensifies the debate by shortening the time span between violent outbursts and gentle pleadings. The initial theme is stated in f, where it yields a higher and more climactic shriek. The reprise sets in in m. 109, after an extensive development of 45 measures.

Haydn could have mitigated the severity of the movement had he wished to, by allowing the gentle theme to be sounded in C instead of c on its second statement. Instead he remains resolutely in minor and leads the more lyric theme up to a melodic peak of high C, whence it floats down, in a lovely *pianissimo*, with a little dotted falling motif of which Mozart later became very fond (Example 4.10). Note the poignant use of dissonances, the suspended treble G resolving into an expressive melodic turn, and the succeeding B♭ appoggiatura against the B♮ of the harmony. The moment is

VII. Maulbertsch. *Assumption of the Virgin Mary*, 1758. (Oeffentliche Kunstsammlung Basel, Kunstmuseum. Donation Gottlieb Lüthy 1936. Photo: Martin Bühler, Basel)

VIII. Anonymous painting of a Turkish scene on the opera
stage at Esterháza. (Munich: Deutsches Theatermuseum)

EXAMPLE 4.10. *Haydn, Symphony No. 52, I*

Allegro assai con brio

Strings *pp*

like a last plea for mercy, but the tutti will have none of it, closing the movement instead with another angry reaffirmation of the minor keynote. This
may indeed be the Symphony in c to which Carpani refers when recalling
those played in church and mentioning the hints of anger with which
Haydn, thinking thoughts appropriate to Lent, would smite sinners and
infidels. The only other candidate, Symphony No. 78 in c/C of ten years
later, is by comparison an essay in good-natured gaiety.

A mollified Haydn emerges in the following movement, an *Andante* in C
and in 3/8. But it too unleashes powerful tutti passages (including winds)
and instant contrasts between *forte* and *piano*. Haydn saves the horns for the
moment of reprise. The *Menuetto Allegretto* is in c and offers a study in seconds, mostly minor seconds, while the Trio is in radiant tonic major but
does not lack the seconds or the offbeat *sforzato* accents of its companion.
The finale, *Presto* in 2/4, begins with a duet between the two violin sections,
which is then repeated as a duet between the violins in unison and the bass.
Duet beginnings like this were still quite original in finales at the time. (For
other examples, see Haydn's Symphony No. 47 of 1772 and Mozart's *Paris
Symphony* of 1778.) Motivically, the duet's top part is derived from the
salient intervals opening the first movement. Another reminder of the first
movement comes with the melodic climax of the finale's second and more
lyric theme, a falling figure in dotted rhythm with four repeated-tone
afterbeats as in Example 4.10. The passage ends with a soft deceptive
cadence followed by strident chords, tutti *forte,* a silence, and then a rush up
the scale to E♭ for a final and vehement sounding of E♭ B♮, filled in by step—
the false interval from the very beginning of the work. Here it is finally and
emphatically resolved to tonic C. Haydn's concerns for cyclic unity are evident in this great work. As in other works from around the same time, his
concerns focus particularly on the beginning and ending measures of the
cycle.

The church symphony prepared the way for an accomplishment like
Symphony No. 52. But in this work its elements have been so sublimated
and transformed that only a few devices, mainly in the first movement,
remain to remind us of the legacy. Since anger and severity are conveyed
with unprecedented vehemence here, it is no wonder that the literary con-

cept of *Sturm und Drang* has sometimes been invoked as an aid with which to understand Haydn's intentions. But Haydn's minor-mode works from around 1770 do not need any such extramusical explanation. At the time, the composer was immersed as never before in writing serious and large-scale choral music for the church, some of it as severe as the Symphony No. 52. His minor-mode symphonies represent a corollary activity.

Sacred Music

H A Y D N had little occasion to write church music as long as the Oberkapell-meister, Gregor Joseph Werner, was still capable of performing his duties. An early *Te Deum* in C, ascribed to both Joseph and Michael Haydn, apparently belongs to Joseph's first years in Esterházy service and was perhaps written in connection with some celebration within the princely house. Haydn was not called upon to write new festive operas after the wedding opera *Acide e Galatea* of 1762–63 until the comic intermezzo *La cantarina* of 1766. Italian cantatas filled the need for celebrating the prince's name day (6 December) in 1763 and 1764, and allowed Haydn to keep in practice writing Italian recitatives and arias in the most elaborate seria style without actually writing an opera. *La cantarina* satirized the opera seria singer, and showed how well Haydn commanded both buffa and seria styles.

By 1765 Prince Nicholas was spending most of his time at Süttor, the site south of Lake Neusiedl where the new castle of Esterháza was rising. Meanwhile musical affairs back at Eisenstadt had become rather disorganized, or so the complaints of the aged and failing Werner led the authorities to believe. There resulted a stern directive, signed at Süttor on 3 November 1765 and entitled "Regulatio Chori Kissmartoniensis," that admonished Haydn to take better care of the cappella's instruments and make sure that all members performed their regular duties. Lest his servants should succumb to idle ways, the prince specifically enjoined Haydn

> to take especial pains that all the members of the chapel appear regularly at the church services and fulfill their duty and obligations in a proper and disciplined fashion . . . ; in our absence to hold two musical academies each week in the Officers' Room at Eisenstadt, viz., on Tuesdays and Thursdays from two to four o'clock in the afternoon, which are to be given by the musicians . . . ; to assure that in future no one is absent without permission from the church services or the above-mentioned academies (as was the case hitherto), a written report will be delivered to us every fortnight, with the name of, and the reason for, any presuming to absent themselves from duty.

FIGURE 4.8. First page of Haydn's thematic catalogue.

To this Prince Nicholas appended a postscript that shows he was not satisfied with what he knew about Haydn's output as a composer. "Haydn is urgently enjoined to apply himself to composition more diligently than heretofore, and especially to write such pieces as can be played on the gamba [baryton], of which pieces we have seen very few up to now; and to be able to judge his diligence, he shall at all times send us the first copy, cleanly and carefully written, of each and every composition."[52]

Haydn's compositions for the baryton did take a spurt in the second half of the 1760s. Another consequence of the directives may have been his

[52] Landon, *Haydn,* 1: 420.

eventual decision to keep an *Entwurf-Katalog,* in which he jotted down the incipits of his works (Figure 4.8). He had been a prolific composer for many years, especially in the chamber and symphonic genres; his thematic catalogue would henceforth furnish proof, if proof were needed. The failure of Prince Nicholas to perceive the truth of the matter in the first place was apparently one of communication.

THE FIRST MISSA CELLENSIS

H A Y D N became Kapellmeister with the death of Gregor Werner on 3 March 1766; henceforth he was in charge of the church music as well. During 1766 he began composition of a huge cantata mass, a task that apparently occupied him over the next few years.[53] This work, *Missa Cellensis,* is filled with such sublime moments of inspiration it deserves to rank with the greatest choral achievements of the 1760s. Haydn's mass is not without many moments of lesser inspiration and some reliance on decidedly routine and old-fashioned traits—necessarily the case, perhaps, in a situation where the materials at hand to build such a large work were so heterogeneous and partly unrefined. But at its best, as in the setting of the Benedictus, the mass achieves a powerfully direct, unornamented speech, one that would still sound modern forty or fifty years later, and that dispenses with some of the clichés of galant music. What Haydn caught a glimpse of with this mass was the course that would lead him ultimately to compose *The Creation, The Seasons,* his late masses, and their harbinger, the second *Missa Cellensis* of 1782.

"Cellensis" refers to the pilgrimage church of Mariazell in Styria, not far distant from Vienna. This church did not have the musical forces to perform such a gigantic mass, nor did it have a tradition of performing such works. But the Styrian Confraternity in Vienna celebrated a pontifical mass in honor of Our Lady of Mariazell on 8 September, feast of the Nativity BVM, with performances taking place in the court church (Augustinerkirche),[54] and Haydn's mass was most likely written for this solemn occasion. A tradition that is difficult to trace also connects it with the Viennese Brotherhood of Saint Cecilia, hence the popular name of *Cecilia Mass.* Founded in 1725 under imperial patronage, this guild celebrated the feast of its patron saint on 22 November with a solemn high mass, at first in St. Peter's, later in St. Stephen's Cathedral. Such an event is reported as taking place in 1767 by the

[53] James Deck, "The Dating of Haydn's *Missa Cellensis in honorem Beatissimae Virginis Mariae:* An Interim Discussion," *Haydn Yearbook* 13 (1982): 97–112.
[54] Otto Biba, "Die kirchenmusikalischen Werke Haydns," *Joseph Haydn in seiner Zeit* (Eisenstadt, 1982), p. 143.

EXAMPLE 4.11. *Haydn*, Missa Cellensis *(1766), slow introduction*

Wiener Diarium, and it is not impossible that Haydn's new *Missa solemnis,* as he later called it, was used on this feast day.[55]

The mass opens softly, with seven measures of *Largo* in common time, a smooth chordal progression coming to a stop with a fermata on the dominant. As in several symphonies of the late 1760s and early 1770s, Haydn explored here the slow introduction that was pregnant with meaning for the entire cycle to follow (Example 4.11). Crucial features include the high F in the soprano, the double suspension of F D resolving to E C, then the expressive suspension of E over F, the tenor's ascent to high F in order to repeat the F E suspension, and the deceptive cadence V - vi. The return from vi involves the three lower voices in chromatic movement while the soprano holds a long suspended C. The touch of tonic minor is no less important than the emphasis on the chords I, vi, IV, and V. These five triads provide Haydn with the keys of all the movements to follow (the only exception being the "Gratias agimus" of the Gloria, which is in e when it is not in G).

The Kyrie proper follows as a resolution, an *Allegro tutti forte* in common time. Its theme deploys material from the *Largo* introduction, most prominently the F resolving to E in both octaves. Haydn expands the theme to a leisurely fifty-six measures, using ritornello structure with cadences on V and vi, then a return to I. The "Christe" is set to an *Allegretto* in 3/4 in a minor that pits tenor solo against chorus. Reminiscent of Sammartini are the sequential exchanges between the two violin parts. Here and in several other moments of the mass the oboes double the violins much of the time, even

---

[55] Landon, *Haydn,* 1: 420. In his letter of ca. 1779 to an unidentified publisher, Haydn refers to the mass as "Una Messa solene" (Haydn, *Gesammelte Briefe,* no. 25).

in florid writing, lending an old-fashioned Handelian touch to the orchestral sonority. The final "Kyrie" is fugal, in keeping with tradition. It begins with the intonation of the word "Kyrie" on C in dotted rhythm, like the opening *Largo*. The fugue that emerges relies on a kind of scalar counterpoint that is not very demanding of its composer, the result being rather diffuse and sprawling. Haydn had a way to travel still, it seems, before he would be able to produce a concentrated fugal masterpiece such as the finale of his Quartet in C from Opus 20.

Haydn may have established a record length with his setting of the Gloria—821 measures and a playing time about equal to that of all the other movements taken together. Even the Gloria from the Mass in b by Johann Sebastian Bach did not exceed 785 measures, and Mozart in his unfinished Mass in c set the Gloria to a total of 737. Haydn adopted a sevenfold division of the Gloria text, which was typical of the Neapolitan school, and found in most masses by Hasse, who may well have been one of Haydn's models.[56] The seven large sections are given in Table 4.1.

TABLE 4.1 *MISSA CELLENSIS:* Gloria

			measures
1. "Gloria"	*Allegro molto* 3/4	choral homophony	1–128
2. "Laudamus"	*Moderato* 4/4	soloists	129–188
3. "Gratias"	*Alla breve*	choral fugue	189–334
4. "Domine Deus"	*Allegro* 3/4	soloists	335–578
5. "Qui tollis"	*Adagio* 4/4	choral homophony	579–635
6. "Quoniam"	*Allegro molto* 4/4	soprano solo	636–726
("Cum Sancto"	*Largo* 4/4 [transition]	choral homophony	727–731)
7. "In Gloria"	*Allegro molto* 4/4	choral fugue	732–821

Haydn allowed himself to be especially discursive in setting section 4, "Domine Deus," in which alto, tenor, and bass each sing long solos, repeating similar musical material, and then the three sing the same material

[56] Walther Müller, *Johann Adolph Hasse als Kirchenkomponist: Ein Beitrag zur Geschichte der neapolitanischen Kirchenmusik* (Leipzig, 1910), p. 53. See also the *Missa romana* attributed to Pergolesi, in which not only is the Gloria divided into sections as in Haydn, but each section also shows similarities in the kind of texture and treatment it is accorded with Haydn's setting: Giovanni Battista Pergolesi, *Missa romana*, ed. Raimund Rügge (Zürich, 1975). Helmut Hucke says this mass is one of two attributed to Pergolesi that seem to be authentic: "Pergolesi's *Missa S. Emidia*," in *Music in the Classic Period: Essays in Honor of Barry S. Brook*, ed. Allan A. Atlas (New York, 1985), pp. 99–115.

together. For the tenor there is coloratura; for the bass, huge leaps from the top to the bottom of his range in a manner more appropriate to a bassoon (were those familiar with Haydn's music perhaps reminded of the monster Polyphemus, so brilliantly characterized in a bass aria in *Acide e Galatea?*). As the movement is about to conclude after its long journey, Haydn applies the brakes by injecting one of his favorite surprises, a loud and emphatic $V^{4/3}$ of V, resolving to $V^{6/5}$. This delaying tactic will see much more dramatic use toward the very end of the mass. It is already prepared by the $V^{4/3}$ of V in the opening *Largo*.

The "Qui tollis peccata mundi" is particularly impressive and reveals musical links with several other parts of the mass (Example 4.12). While the strings throb in sixteenth notes, the sopranos outline the false interval from E♭ down to B♮, at the arrival of which the violins make a stabbing leap up to A♭, and descend by outlining the diminished seventh chord. Sopranos and altos then sing the false interval (with no intervening tones) in imitation. The suspensions that follow produce a particularly keening dissonance between high G and the A♭ in the altos. Here Haydn deploys a *locus classicus* of musical rhetoric, denoting tragic passion. A few years later Gluck would open his overture to *Iphigénie en Aulide* (1774) with the same dialogue at the same pitches—an overture that Abbé Arnaud praised for capturing the essence of the whole tragedy. Gluck had used this passage earlier in his *Telemaco* (1765), which may have directly inspired Haydn. (See Example 3.9.)

The progression by which an augmented sixth chord leads to the dominant in Haydn is the same in Gluck too, but Gluck offers nothing so imaginative and piercing as Haydn's stabbing high C, *forte*, in the first violins. The progression closely resembles the coming to a stop with a fermata in the last three measures from the slow introduction that opens the mass. Here the A♭ in the bass makes the music even more ominous. The throbbing strings in c minor and the same false interval from E♭ to B♮ to C (sung unaccompanied as the tenor ends his recitative) will return in the Credo to clothe the most elemental Christian belief: "Et incarnatus est de Spiritu Sancto ex Maria Virgine, et homo factus est." More impressively still, Haydn will revert to c and the thematic descent from E♭ to B♮ to clothe the words "Benedictus qui venit in nomine Domini." With these musical linkages the composer stresses the central mystery of the Christian faith, emphasizing first the world's sins, then the coming of Christ to expiate them. The particular false interval used so powerfully by Haydn in this mass figures importantly as well in the string quartets and symphonies composed a few years later. It is not impossible that there was a carryover in Haydn's mind between the religious sphere and a work so permeated by the E♭ B♮ false interval as the Symphony No. 52 in c.

EXAMPLE 4.12. *Haydn*, Missa Cellensis, *Gloria*

Another impressive moment in the Gloria is the *Largo* transitional passage at "Cum Sancto Spiritu," which begins by emphasizing the triad of a minor, almost as if it were continuing the musical discourse from the middle of the *Largo* that opens the mass. The upper voices drift down, making double suspensions over the bass, and most expressively in the false interval present in A F to G E over C♯. The resemblance to the opening *Largo* becomes more distinct with the approach to the concluding dominant chord with fermata. From this springboard Haydn launches into his big fugue on the final words of the Gloria. Although the subject and its treatment are quite square, there is no denying the driving power with which Haydn pushes the movement to its final cadence.

After the extraordinary proportions of the Gloria, Haydn trimmed his sails and set the Credo to a mere 386 measures (even though its text is nearly twice as long as that of the Gloria). The traditional cantata mass division of the Credo into three large sections is observed, with "Et incarnatus est" treated as median slow movement. Haydn took care to unite the outer fast movements musically by bringing back the soprano's frequent Credo motive (which is related to the mass's slow introduction) just before the section "Confiteor unum baptisma." The jubilation of the Credo's outer movements, coming after all the festive C major of the Gloria, runs the risk of too much sameness, which makes it seem even longer than it is (lending an ironic twist to the words "cujus regni non erit finis"). Yet Haydn rouses himself to an exciting climax that caps the whole movement and somehow rescues it from being merely another colossal monument of *Habsburger* C-major *Prunkstil*. In a kind of coda, after the cadence has already been made several times, Haydn takes his sopranos up to high A, from which they fall a seventh, while the first violins and first trumpet keep pursuing the ascent up to the high tonic, giving the illusion that the sopranos do too (Example 4.13a). To achieve his goal, Haydn sacrificed the part writing, allowing parallel fifths between the tenors and the basses. He changed the doubling to rectify this at the very end of the mass, where the same expressive leap and rising of the treble line up to the high tonic, now in rhythmic augmentation, serve as a climax to the entire cycle (Example 4.13b). The expressive leap for sopranos played a part in the Gloria too, when Haydn set the words "propter *magnam*" to ever wider descents: diminished fifth–major sixth–diminished seventh, a sequence to which the final descending seventh seems a fitting end.

The Sanctus begins modestly, with a tone of understatement that is welcome after the heaven-storming conclusion of the Credo. Haydn layers the accompaniment to the choral basses as a delicate filigree, with oboes sustaining, first violins chirping little slides, and second violins providing arpeggio figures. "Che puro ciel" in Gluck's *Orfeo* had offered the model of a similarly stratified filigree accompaniment, in that case as a tone painting of babbling brooks and twittering birds in Elysium. Viennese audiences may well have connected Gluck's vision of paradise with Haydn's. The suspended high F in the sopranos from the very beginning of the mass figures with prominence in "Pleni sunt coeli."

EXAMPLE 4.13. *Haydn*, Missa Cellensis

a. End of the Credo

For the Benedictus Haydn once again adopted a huge scale, as is apparent at once from the long orchestral prelude. The violins, doubled at the octave below by a solo bassoon, begin by intoning a falling false interval; enter the chorus (Example 4.14). The overlapping groups of three quarter notes between the melody and its accompaniment have a long lineage in Italian sacred music (cf. the heart-wrenching conclusion of Pergolesi's famous setting of *Salve regina*). But the more immediate inspiration for Haydn may have been operatic. Once again we find a close parallel in Gluck's *Orfeo,* when Orpheus pleads with the furies for the final time (at the words "se provaste un sol momento cosa sia languir d'amor"). This similarity and the aforementioned link with Gluck's music strengthen claims that Gluck was the central figure in the wave of minor-mode pathos inundating Vienna during the 1760s.

The Benedictus deploys several unusual and surprising features. Haydn has the chorus enter in the middle of the orchestral phrase that follows Example 4.14, stating the same falling phrase in the relative major. This creates an impression akin to breaking into the middle of a conversation. The phrase with which the chorus enters, a unison fall from fifth to tonic, will also be the chorus' last utterance in the movement, in tonic minor. Unexpected as well is the octave G, tutti *forte,* hurled on the second beat as a syncopation, by means of which the orchestra calls the proceedings back from E♭ to C; there follows a tense silence after a diminished-seventh chord, and then the initial descending theme in inversion. When the diminished seventh chord returns, the strings fall silent on the second beat as before, but

EXAMPLE 4.14. *Haydn,* Missa Cellensis, *Benedictus*

the oboes and bassoons, *forte*, sustain throughout the measure, an uncanny anticipation of some of the eerie, sustained wind effects that Mozart would achieve in his *Idomeneo*, and predictive as well of certain orchestral effects in the funeral march of Beethoven's *Eroica* Symphony. Everything about the Benedictus, in fact, suggests a solemn procession, almost funereal, and akin to the temple scenes in Act III of Mozart's *Idomeneo*. The movement is also highly symphonic in nature.

The Agnus Dei reverts to the key of a, thus framing the end of the mass as did the "Christe" at the beginning, and carrying out the move to the relative minor signaled from the very outset in the slow introduction. Haydn sets "Dona nobis pacem" as a double fugue in a, gradually worked out so as to end by restoring the keynote, C. It would be difficult to say in what precise sense this music projects the meaning of the words, and yet it does so very effectively. The suspended sevenths of the bass subject interact with the suspended sevenths of the tenor countersubject so as to give great forward momentum to the fugue, into which Haydn must have poured a lot of effort. An impressive stretto sets in toward the end, with tenors entering on high G and sopranos ascending to a suspended F and then a suspended E. The moment sounds so satisfying and familiar because it is the same progression used in the slow introduction at the outset of the mass. The proceedings seem to be all but over at this point, but Haydn decides to enhance the excitement through one of his well-used delaying tactics. Instead of the cadence expected in m. 126, he slips in a vii^6 of V chord (which is also predicted in the slow introduction). The orchestra seizes upon this chord and prolongs it, *fortissimo*, with timpani rolling on low C and the first trumpet all the way up to high C. It is left to the chorus, singing *piano* and bringing back the entire phrase "Agnus Dei dona nobis pacem," to work out the resolution of Haydn's harmonic "surprise," which is done by lowering the bass from A to A♭, producing an augmented sixth chord and leading to the dominant and ultimate tonic. The last and climactic move of the sopranos to high A (with violins up to high C), linking the end of the mass with the end of the Credo, was shown in Example 4.13b. Using a slow introduction to predict tonal and motivic events throughout a long cyclic work and to forecast, most notably, some feature at the very end was a great achievement of this first *Missa Cellensis*. It would have profound consequences for Haydn's later works, especially his symphonies.

The probability that the great Mass in C that Haydn began during 1766 was performed in Vienna is greater because of an anecdote told to Vincent Novello by Johann Andreas Streicher. Streicher, apparently relating what Haydn had told him, said that the aged Hasse stood alongside his onetime pupil the empress, who would have been seated, at an audience of a mass described as the first by Haydn heard in public. Hasse left Vienna for good in early 1773. There is no evidence to suggest a performance of any other mass by Haydn in Vienna during Hasse's last years there.

> [At] the first Mass which Haydn produced in Public, the Empress Maria Theresa was present—Hasse stood by her and she asked his opinion of the young composer. Hasse told the Empress that Haydn possessed all the qualities that are required to form the highest style of writing, viz., beautiful and expressive melody, sound harmony, original invention, variety of effect, symmetrical design, knowledge of the power of the different instruments, correct counterpoint, scientific modulations and refined taste. Hasse also predicted that Haydn would become one of the greatest Composers of the Age. This liberal opinion so encouraged Haydn that from that time he exerted himself to the utmost to fulfil the flattering prediction, and he at the same time resolved never to give a harsh or severe opinion himself upon the production of any young Composer but always to do his utmost to encourage their first attempts, and to persevere in their studies with energy and enthusiasm.[57]

STABAT MATER

IN 1767 Haydn composed a setting of the famous medieval poem in sequence form *Stabat mater dolorosa*. As a meditation on the Passion as observed through the eyes of Mary, and in terms of our relationship to it as individuals, the poem has a curiously pietistic character, reminiscent of many of the cantata texts set by Johann Sebastian Bach. The Council of Trent had removed the *Stabat mater* from the liturgy, but Pope Benedict XIII restored it in 1727 for use on the feast of the Seven Dolours (15 September). The sequence also found a place as an Office hymn on the Friday after Passion Sunday, and had long enjoyed popularity during the Lenten season, whether approved for the liturgy or not. There were many settings made during the eighteenth century—both Alessandro and Domenico Scarlatti set it, as did Emmanuele Astorga, Boccherini, Tartini, Traetta, and nearly every Viennese court composer. But the most famous setting of all remained that made by Pergolesi in 1736, shortly before his death.

So unrelentingly lugubrious a poem as the *Stabat mater* presented a challenge to composers of any age, but particularly in an age that preferred light and cheerful music. Even Pergolesi's setting did not escape censure; Padre Martini found much of it wanting the seriousness required by the words. It

---

[57] *A Mozart Pilgrimage: The Travel Diaries of Vincent and Mary Novello in the Year 1829*, ed. Nerina Medici and Rosemary Hughes (London, 1955), p. 196.

says something about the attractiveness of Pergolesi's setting, as well as about its perceived deficiencies, that many hands attempted to improve it, among them Hiller, Abt Vogler, and Sebastian Bach. The peculiar appeal of Pergolesi's *Stabat mater* to German sensibilities may be gauged from these revisers. Haydn may have chosen to set the poem, assuming the choice was his, to prove a point: he could make a thoroughly serious and appropriate setting even of this text and thereby confound the criticism, stemming from northern Germany, that his art was one of levity and an unacceptable mixture of comic and tragic. The possibility also exists that Haydn, encouraged by Hasse's praises, set out to write something specially suited to please the elderly master he so greatly revered.

Nowhere else did Haydn come closer to the Neapolitan school than in his setting of the *Stabat mater*. One number in particular, "Vidit suum dulcem natum," approaches Pergolesi in its melodic traits, rhythmic quirks, and thin texture. Haydn, like Traetta, even adapted a feature of Pergolesi's text setting, the breaking up with rests of "dum e–mi–sit spiritum" in order to convey the last gasps of the dying Christ. The possibilities of text painting offered in general by the poem may have been a deciding factor that led Haydn to set it. He delighted in conveying "tremebat" in No. 2 with written-out trills in three parts (such as Mozart found appropriate for mirthful situations in comic opera). "Poenas mecum divide" in No. 8 prompted the composer to initiate a section in which the accompaniment features little afterbeats, divided from the main beats. The most picturesque, and most Haydnesque, moment of all is the fiery *Presto*—a welcome relief after so many slow and plodding movements—to which he sets No. 11, "Flammis orci ne succedar." The four soloists joined together against the chorus in No. 10, "Virgo virginum," produces some attractive antiphonal effects, and the piece brings back the pair of English horns in connection with the key of E♭, thus establishing a symmetry with the beginning. But this number is too long for its material, as is true of the work as a whole. The problem is the same that beset some sections of the Mass in C begun in 1766: sluggishness together with diffuseness.

Haydn took care with the tonal planning of the whole, as is evident from the third relationships between g, E♭, and c/C, established at the beginning of the work and brought back at the end, and from the long chain of tonalities related by a third in the middle (see Table 4.2).

The falling-third relationship at the outset, so important for the whole key structure, focuses on the very pitches with which the chorus utters its last "Benedictus" in the Mass in C, G G E♭ C. The great achievement of that Benedictus is not matched anywhere in the *Stabat mater*. Its ending is

TABLE 4.2 STABAT MATER

No.	1	2	3	4	5	6	7
	g	E♭	c–C	F	B♭	f	d
	solo	chorus					
	4/4	3/8	4/4				

No.	8	9	10	11	12	13	14
	B♭	g	E♭	c	C	g	G
			soloists + chorus				
		4/4	3/4	4/4	4/4		

particularly disappointing; the last sizable gesture is a quite superfluous roulade of great length for the solo soprano, Anna Sheffstoss-Weigl.

Hasse was greatly impressed with Haydn's *Stabat mater*, which must have seemed to him an added vindication of the Neapolitan style that he more than anyone else had brought to flower in central Europe. Haydn sent him the score with a request for corrections and criticism. This we know from a precious letter Haydn addressed to his superior at court, Anton Sheffstoss (father of the soprano), requesting permission to visit Vienna for a Lenten performance of the work in the Church of the Barmherzige Brüder in the Leopoldstadt (Figure 4.9). Haydn's honesty and zeal for improvement, his modesty and piety, are all apparent in his request.

Eisenstadt, 20 March, 1768

Nobly born, Highly respected Sir!

You will recall that last year I set to music with all my powers the highly esteemed Hymn called Stabat Mater, and I sent it to the great and world-celebrated Hasse, with no other intention than that in case, here and there, I had not expressed adequately words of such great importance, this lack could be rectified by a master so successful in all his works. But contrary to my merits, this exquisite tonal artist ["aus erlesene Ton: kunstler"] honored the work with inexpressible praise and wished for nothing more than to hear it performed by the strong musical forces appropriate to it ["dazu gehörig wohl besetzten Music"]. Since there is a great lack of singers *utruisque generis* in Vienna, I would therefore humbly and obediently ask His Serene and Gracious Highness through you, Sir, to allow me, Weigl and his wife, and Friberth to go to Vienna next Thursday, there on Friday at the Ffr. Miseric: to further the honor of our gracious prince by the performance of his servant; we would return to Eisenstadt on Saturday evening.

FIGURE 4.9. Ziegler. Engraving of the Church of the Barmherzigen Brüder in the Leopoldstadt.

> If His Highness so wishes, someone other than Friberth could easily be sent up. Dearest Mons. Sheffstoss, please expedite my request; I remain, with the most profound veneration
>
>
>
> Your nobly born Sir's
> most devoted servant
>
> Josephus Haydn mppria
>
>
> P.S. My compliments to all the Messieurs. The promised Divertimenti will be delivered to His Highness one of these next weeks.[58]

The implication concerning the tenor Carl Friberth is that the prince might not have been willing to part with his services even for a few days. Haydn was willing to accept a substitute in his place, but evidently indispensable were his soprano soloist and his first cellist. It is not known if permission was granted and the Viennese performance took place. If it did, would

---

[58]Landon, *Haydn,* 2: 144. I have retranslated some phrases using *Gesammelte Briefe,* no. 7. Landon says the divertimenti mentioned in the postscript refer to baryton trios.

Haydn have presided as first violin or at the keyboard? And did Hasse attend the performance? In his autobiographical letter of 1776 Haydn listed the *Stabat mater* among those compositions that had received the most approbation, and added a comment, the only one of his works mentioned that is singled out in this way: "The Stabat Mater, about which I received (through a good friend) a testimonial of our great composer Hasse, containing quite undeserved praises. I shall treasure this testimonial all my life, as if it were gold; not for its contents, but for the sake of so worthy a man."

The praises of Hasse surely smoothed the way for the *Stabat mater* to become one of Haydn's best-known vocal works. Hiller, who did not deem Haydn worthy of inclusion in his biographies of famous composers (1784), although he included his own life, saw fit to make a German parody text of the *Stabat*, which he published in keyboard score in 1781. The work was published in full score in both London and Paris, the latter edition in connection with a performance that took place at the Concert Spirituel on 9 April 1781. An anonymous critic had some interesting things to say about the music, which he pronounced a decided success.

> Its beginning is noble and touching; there is so much adroitness and intelligence in the easy transition by which the composer passes from the first strophe, set as a solo, to the second, which is set as an expressive chorus. The piece "Vidit suum dulcem" announces this composer's great resourcefulness, as does the quartet "Virgo Virginum praeclara," which is interrupted from time to time by small choruses that have the most seductive effect. The accompaniments are brilliant and sturdy, in a word worthy of this excellent master.[59]

Pergolesi's ever-admired setting was performed at the same concert. It still won partisans in this contest between musical styles of different generations, according to the same critic, who expressed his admiration for Pergolesi's uniting of great simplicity with intense expression.

In 1768 Haydn wrote an a cappella Mass in d, *Sunt bona mixta mala*, which was long known only as an incipit but lately turned up in fragmentary form.[60] The autograph fragment breaks off after the beginning of the Gloria, and it is possible that Haydn never finished the work.

In 1770 or 1771 Haydn wrote a setting of the *Salve regina* in g that constitutes a kind of pendant to his *Stabat mater*, as is evident not only from the key and the slow tempo of the opening movement, in which there is an abundance of word painting, but also from the prominence of certain expressive harmonies such as the Neapolitan chord and the augmented sixth. The

---

[59] *Mercure de France*, April 1781, pp. 127ff.
[60] H. C. Robbins Landon, "A Lost Haydn Autograph Re-discovered," *Haydn Yearbook* 14 (1983): 5–8.

four solo singers for whom Haydn wrote here must enter with the latter chord and prolong it after the orchestra drops out, a powerful effect that is related to others like it in the Benedictus of the first *Missa Cellensis*. This opening comes back in the *Largo* setting of the words "Jesum ostende nobis." The Neapolitan chord so prominent in the first number returns at a climactic moment of the last number to clothe the words "O dulcis virgo Maria." The piece dies away in a *pianissimo* as g gives way to G. (Compare the last two numbers of the *Stabat mater*.)

The Great Organ Mass

HAYDN'S masses were sung not only in his immediate circle but in monasteries throughout Austria. The letter he wrote about his Latin cantata *Applausus* (1768) to the monks of the Cistercian Abbey of Zwettl in Lower Austria tells us several things of value, as does the composition itself. Standards of performance were high in such rural monasteries. Haydn counted on a full symphonic band, one used to playing his symphonies, and he stressed the importance of the strict observance of his dynamic markings, ranging from *pianissimo* through several gradations to *fortissimo*. The composer offered some suggestions for the precise orchestral forces to be employed as well. "Use two players on the viola throughout, for the inner parts sometimes need to be heard more than the upper parts, and you will find in all my compositions that the viola rarely doubles the bass"; and further on, concerning the bass line, "I prefer a band with 3 bass instruments—'cello, bassoon, and double bass—to one with 6 double basses and 3 'celli, because certain passages stand out better that way."[61] He wanted no overlapping of voice and orchestra in the obbligato recitatives, even though the notational convention dictated such on paper. He left this matter up to the cembalist, whom all others were to follow. This suggests that a harpsichord rather than organ continuo realization was expected.

Haydn's Mass in E♭ titled *Missa in honorem Beatissimae Virginis Mariae* probably dates from the end of the 1760s. It has become known as the *Great Organ* Mass because of its elaborate concertante solos for organ and to distinguish it from the *Little Organ* Mass, a *missa brevis* in B♭ of ca. 1775 that also includes a solo part for organ. Falling between these two works is the pastoral *Nicholas* Mass in G (1772), which appears to have been written in a great hurry to celebrate the prince's name day. The key of E♭, employed in con-

---

[61] Landon, *Haydn*, 2: 146–48.

junction with two English horns, lends the *Great Organ* Mass its special atmosphere, at once tender and rarefied. We need to look for its like no further than the two movements in E♭ with English horns in another of Haydn's Marian works, "O quam tristis" and "Virgo virginum praeclara" in the *Stabat mater*. Both those movements were in triple meter with moderate to slow tempos, not particularly minuet-like and yet not avoiding galant clichés associated with the minuet, such as the falling *cadence galante* in parallel thirds of "O quam tristis." The mass begins with a Kyrie set as an *Allegro moderato* in 3/4 that also deploys chains of parallel thirds and a sweetly sensuous euphony. It offers in addition a fugal treatment of the chorus, the theme of which resembles the Kyrie of Haydn's early *Missa brevis* in F; both share a gentle descent from fifth to tonic and subsequent rise to accent the sixth degree, followed by the fifth. The organ solo, presumably played by Haydn, states this theme first, softly doubled by the two violins (there are no violas).

Haydn makes of this mass a personal tribute to Mary, and it becomes even more personal if he was the organ soloist. The work achieves a nearly miraculous blending of Austrian lightheartedness with the solemnity of choral polyphony. The fugal writing seems more assured than ever, particularly at the end of the Gloria. Just after the choral sopranos work their way up to high A♭, their melodic peak throughout the mass, Haydn does not hesitate to introduce little um-pah, um-pah figures in the organ solo, making the ending sound more like a country dance than a churchly "Amen." He dissolves solemnity and replaces it with joy. In other terms, he seems to envision a brightly lit paradise with angels dancing round the Virgin. To Haydn, the Deity inspired thoughts not of wrath and vengeance (sinners inspired those, we are told), but of love and goodness.

Polar swings between light and shade give this mass a tincture quite peculiar to it. The rather somber, imploring setting *a* 4 of "Miserere nobis" in the Gloria surrounds a bass solo setting of "Suscipe" that is given a lilting, Ländler-like accompaniment in the violins. The whole section, beginning with "Gratias," is in 3/8, and it projects a decidedly Neapolitan tone, as does so much of the *Stabat mater*. The last utterance of "Miserere" brings a resounding Neapolitan-sixth chord. "Et incarnatus est" in the Credo is set as an elaborate tenor solo (presumably for Carl Friberth). Somewhat surprising is the textual setting, allowing a long melisma on "homo fa———ctus est," but then one is constantly surprised throughout. As at the end of the Gloria, Haydn closes the Credo with a substantial fugue, then brings on the organ solo, this time with frilly scales and trills. The Sanctus opens fugally, which is unusual; homophonic writing then bursts forth to convey the fullness of "Pleni sunt coeli." Only at the last "Hosanna in excelsis" do the choral sopranos ascend to their climactic A♭.

Haydn decided upon the Benedictus as the spot for the work's main organ solo, and a veritable concerto it is (he calls the part "Organo concerto" throughout). The Agnus Dei begins in A♭, and from this subdominant moves quickly to its own subdominant, D♭. The two English horns are prominent in both passages, but they drop out when the strings and organ continuo play a little *affettuoso* passage with galant chromatic inflections like those we usually associate with Mozart, although they come from the Italian mainstream: 8 5♯ 6 , 8 4♯ 5. One of the fine points of the Agnus Dei is the way Haydn brings back his somber setting *a 4* of the entreaty "Miserere nobis" from the Gloria, somewhat transformed, to clothe the return of the same words at the end of the mass. This is one of many examples that could be adduced to show why the mass is so satisfying and unified in character. The "Dona nobis pacem" provides another by interspersing powerful chordal statements and fugal writing with lacy arabesques on the organ.

The relationship of surface ornament to the basic structure might be said to be at issue in Haydn's treatment of the solo organ as a kind of appendix, the cake frosting as it were. But if this is so, there are analogies of the most precise kind with the way stucco ornaments were used to mask and soften contours in Rococo churches (from which the image of frosting on the cake is neither visually nor psychologically remote). Having demonstrated in the Benedictus of the first *Missa Cellensis* that he could reduce ornament to a minimum, to the point of nearly doing without it, Haydn now delights in showing us how attractive the ornament can be in a popular work such as this mass. Bright indirect lighting and the love of graceful lines and abundant ornament, inspired above all by the concept of feminine grace embodied in the Blessed Virgin Mary, made the Rococo churches of Austria and southern Germany a special enclave of popular religious feeling within the Catholic faith. It should come as no surprise to find similar qualities in the church music of Haydn and Mozart, who sought to please and delight the devout in surroundings like these. One author has made a convincing case that the churches were built largely as community efforts springing from the populace.[62] The smaller the place, the more this tended to be true. Popular inspiration is evident as well in music. In a work like the *Great Organ* Mass Haydn made an effort to reach out to the people and join some of their music to the learned traditions of sacred music.

---

[62] Karstin Harries, *The Bavarian Rococo Church Between Faith and Aestheticism* (New Haven, Conn., 1983).

Keyboard Music

WORKS for solo keyboard played a subordinate role in Haydn's oeuvre. In this book they will not receive the more extensive treatment accorded his quartets and symphonies. Hiller in 1768 went so far as to say that "the clavier does not suit Haydn as well as the other instruments, which he uses in the most fiery and galant symphonies."[63] It is true that Haydn was not a keyboard virtuoso, as were Wagenseil and Steffan, with whom Hiller placed Haydn. The keyboard music of all three, being mainly for amateur performers on the harpsichord, is stylistically very similar. Amateurs evidently appreciated Haydn. Keyboard works under his name began to circulate widely in the 1760s; Breitkopf offered one as early as 1763. In addition to the early solo pieces, Haydn wrote several works for keyboard with accompaniment.[64]

The earliest authentic work to survive may well be the Divertimento in G (Hob. XVI:6). Its first three movements—*Allegro*, Minuet, *Adagio*—survive in Haydn's autograph, while the finale, *Allegro molto*, does not. The *Allegro* consists of several different ideas strung together rather loosely, mosaic-fashion, giving an impression of diffuseness not unlike that in Haydn's Symphony No. 1. Moreover, the *Allegro*'s opening theme is very close to the *Andante* of Symphony No. 1 in melody and rhythm. What Haydn does with the main theme in these two movements rewards comparison. Both begin with an inverted period and bifocal close in the manner of Wagenseil. (By inverted period I mean antecedent phrase closed, consequent phrase open.) The symphonic movement is peppered with dynamic marks, which are altogether lacking in the keyboard work. Both open the seconda parte with the main theme on V, as happens also in Haydn's early Organ Concerto in C. In the divertimento the statement on V leads quickly to the head motif of the main theme on I. This too was standard procedure.

The Minuet (Haydn's preferred spelling up to 1760) is very mannered, its melody bedecked with dotted rhythm, trills, and triplet figures against a bass moving in quarters, doubled at the octave in the concluding phrases of both strains. Its trio turns to tonic minor and a little sighing figure with trills on the top note of the sigh alternating with ascending triplet figures in conjunct thirds that come from the Minuet. This alternation is also present in the *Andante* of Symphony No. 1 (mm. 39–44), leading us to suspect even more that the two works were conceived not far apart. The prominence of

---

[63] *Wöchentliche Nachrichten* (Leipzig, 1766–70), 3: 84. For a counterargument, see Brown, *Haydn's Keyboard Music*, Essay 1, pp. 3–9.
[64] On Haydn's accompanied keyboard works, see Brown, *Haydn's Keyboard Music*, pp. 23–42.

the raised fourth in the second measure of the trio, following upon the flat sixth and fifth, sounds a mournful and peculiarly Slavic note; this sort of thing can be found in Wagenseil, but it is more prominent still in his favorite pupil, Steffan, the Bohemian emigré whose Op. 1 sonatas were first advertised in 1759 (cf. the Trio of his Op. 1 No. 2). The way Haydn ends each period, with the bass creeping up against a treble pedal, can also be found in Steffan's Op. 1 (in the trio of No. 3).

The third movement, *Adagio,* seems to spring to life from the triplet figures and trills of the Trio. It is rather old-fashioned in movement, with the bass functioning as a continuo and rarely desisting from its "iterated quavers" (to use one of Burney's favorite terms). If there is a sense in which Haydn is less idiomatic than his Viennese colleagues when writing for keyboard, it may lie in the impression the pieces sometimes give of a transcription from orchestral or chamber music. As in a concerto, the *Adagio* comes to a full stop on $I^{6/4}$, providing the opportunity for an improvised cadenza. After this somber movement in g, the finale, *Allegro molto* in 3/8, brings back the tonic major. It is close to Wagenseil's finales in many respects, including an effective *Molltrübung* toward the end. The pert, asymmetrical main theme reaches a weak cadence on I in m. 5, continues as if with a galant redict but "gets stuck" repeating V - I over a pedal D, and ends with a half cadence. An inverted period à la Wagenseil is the result, but how freely Haydn arrives at it! No less audacious is the way he collapses his ten-measure main theme into six measures at the reprise.

A work that resembles some features of the Divertimento in G is the Divertimento in D (Hob. XVI:14), first offered by Breitkopf in 1767. The rhythmic correspondence of its minuet theme with that of the earlier divertmento argues for an original date closer to 1760. The timbre of the harpsichord is particularly well suited to the tenor-range melody with which the *Allegro moderato* in 2/4 begins, and which is emphasized as well at the beginning of the following Menuet; this melody adumbrates the beginning of the very fine Divertimento in D that is dated 1767 (Hob. XVI:19), discussed below.

Once again Haydn employs the inverted period in order to get started, but here he moves with a surer hand into the transition, which proceeds to the dominant while spinning one long lyric line, pausing only on the V of V chord. The composer then introduces a rapid descending arpeggio with final tone suspended and resolving a semitone down, except for the third time, when the line moves up by semitone and into the cadence. A *Molltrübung* extends the thought and reverts to the two-part writing heard in the transition, allowing another burst of major before the double bar. The development elaborately establishes the relative minor and occupies slightly more than a third of the movement: ‖: 36 :‖ : 38 | 36 :‖. Haydn is rarely as symmetrical as this. In the reprise he banishes four measures of transition but makes up for them by repeating the closing idea an octave lower, allowing the movement to conclude in the same tenor range where it began. The trio of the Menuet has a texture (eighth notes in conjunct melodic motion against long-held tones) that is like the trio of the second Menuet in Op. 1 No. 3.

The finale *Presto* in 2/4 also suggests analogies with the quartet-divertimenti because of the concision and economy of its thematic process. The pert little theme occupies five measures, after which there is a quarter rest, as was the case with the head motif. The head motif is used not only to start the transition but also to finish it; then it serves as a second theme on V. Concluding is a rapid descending arpeggio followed by a semitone upturn that refers back to the first movement. Each movement in this work includes prominent material that is repeated verbatim at the same pitch (but not necessarily of the same timbre, since a double-manual instrument could offer variety in this respect).

Of the various keyboard works attributed to Haydn from this early period, the Divertimento in B♭ (Hob. XVI:2) deserves special attention.[65] The opening *Moderato* in 2/4 deploys an **a b b** theme (4 3 3) with cadence on I, continued by a five-measure phrase ending with half cadence that is repeated in varied form and extended to seven measures. Wagenseil never treated the inverted period as freely as this. Haydn's second idea, downward leaps that contract—octave, seventh, sixth, fifth, diminished fifth—seems to be mocked by the falling sevenths that follow. The composer's fondness for such leaps has been noted more than once. If this divertimento is not by Haydn, it would be difficult to name another likely candidate as its composer. Some of Haydn's keyboard works of the early or middle 1760s are so modest in their proportions and demands they must have been written with the needs of beginners in mind. In the new complete edition (*Joseph Haydn: Werke*) these early works are grouped under the rubric "Neun kleine frühe Sonaten."

Several works for keyboard solo belong to the late 1760s and early 1770s. The Divertimento in E♭ (Hob. XVI:45), dated 1766 in autograph, opens with a *Moderato* in common time, a frequent choice for the many baryton trios Haydn was writing at this time, and his frequent choice as well in the *Divertimenti a quattro* of Op. 9 of a few years later. The middle movement is an *Andante* in A♭ and in 3/4, a tender lyrical solo for the right hand, accompa-

[65] Philip Radcliffe, "The Piano Sonatas of Joseph Haydn," *Music Review* 7 (1946): 139–53; 141: "Of the first four sonatas, the most interesting is undoubtedly the second, in B flat; the slow movement, in particular, is remarkably emotional for its date, and the Minuet has much charm." It no longer seems advisable to lump together under "piano sonatas" works that were written for harpsichord and called divertimenti.

nied mainly by a single line in the left; it pushes as far afield as ♭VI (F♭) just before the reprise. The finale, *Allegro di molto* in 3/4, is in sonata form like the previous two movements and is quite as substantial as they are. Increasing the weight of the finales was one of Haydn's concerns in all genres during the late 1760s.

Dating from about the same time is the Divertimento in e/E (Hob. XVI:47). In this work Haydn reverts to an opening *Adagio* in e, a kind of siciliana movement in 6/8 with dotted rhythms; it ends on the dominant, with a fermata, leading to a sprightly *Allegro* in 2/4 and in tonic major. The *Allegro* begins with a theme that falls by step from the fifth to the tonic, as in the opening *Adagio*. The finale, a *Tempo di Menuet*, begins the same way, imposing a certain motivic unity that reinforces the tonal unity of the cycle. An opening *Adagio* movement that ultimately dissolves into a transition preparing the following fast movement suggests parallels with Steffan's Op. 3 Sonatas.

In his sketches for a history of Austrian music, Abbé Maximilian Stadler claimed that "Haydn listened gladly and attentively to the masterpieces of Holzbauer, Wagenseil, and Hasse, which were improving musical taste in those days," and further, that "whoever owns and studies Haydn's first keyboard sonatas and divertimenti for violin will readily conclude that many are modeled after Wagenseil and his like. But later he took foreign products in hand, such as Philip Emanuel Bach, etc., studied them, and although he remained true to his own taste, improved his ideas more and more through his study."[66] The hauntingly beautiful Divertimento in D dated 1767 in Haydn's hand (Hob. XVI:19) has drawn attention as a work in which Haydn showed that he was indeed reaching beyond Vienna for his models. It begins with another *Moderato* in common time and a tenor melody. Many harpsichords of the time were noted for their beautiful tenor registers, and the tenor sonorities of the baryton and its accompanying low stringed instruments also seem near. Certain features of the movement have been likened to Emanuel Bach—for instance, the bell-like repetition of a pedal tone in the top voice.[67] But a more recent critic dismisses this and other parallels with the German master as too superficial to be of any meaning.[68] Yet what both composers do with such a figure in their developments is more to the point: the bass is made dissonant by the treble and forced to resolve downward in

[66] *Materialen zur Geschichte der Musik unter den österreichischen Regenten,* edited by Karl Wagner as *Abbé Maximilian Stadler* (Schriftenreihe der Internationalen Stiftung Mozarteum 6) (Kassel, 1974), pp. 132–33.

[67] Hermann Abert, "Joseph Haydns Klavierwerke," *ZfMw* 2 (1919–20): 553–73; 567.

[68] Bettina Wachernagel, *Joseph Haydns frühe Klaviersonaten* (Tützing, 1975), pp. 63ff.

both cases.[69] More than just a superficial parallel is involved here. The means used and the emotional effect achieved by Bach's treatment of dissonance Haydn makes his own.

Haydn chose the key of A for the middle movement, an *Andante* in 3/4, instead of the more usual subdominant. Everything about this movement sounds novel. It is conceived as a veritable tenor aria, surrounded by ritornello passages in the treble. There is even an opportunity for an improvised cadenza after the full stop on $I^{6/4}$, as in so many slow movements by Emanuel Bach. The aria sometimes becomes a duet when the melody diverges into two voices accompanied by bass. In terms of texture and range, we are very close here to the baryton trios that so preoccupied the composer at the time. By 1767 Haydn was very experienced at their composition, having written so many works for the dusky-voiced baryton of his prince, and having triumphed over the instrument's limitations and a texture that often pitted two tenor voices (baryton and viola) as melody bearers against the bass accompaniment of the cello. (The baryton's best key, by the way, was A.) Haydn's increasing tendency to exploit the middle and low ranges as the site of important, sometimes leading thematic material, will be chronicled below in the discussion of the three sets of string quartets that culminated in Op. 20.

The finale attains the level of the first two movements. Historically it is a path breaker, being one of Haydn's earliest rondo finales. Its refrain relates to the main theme of the first movement, but the tenor register is abandoned for the treble. A *minore* episode follows. When the refrain returns, it is varied by sixteenth-note figuration, mostly chordal, in the right hand. The second episode moves to the key of A and concentrates entirely on the tenor range, as if recalling the *Andante*. There follows the rondo theme, varied by scalar sixteenth-note passages in the right hand. To conclude, Haydn returns to the theme's original configuration, but now doubled at the octave in each hand (first strain) or one hand (second strain, with the bass in sixteenth notes)—a rousing conclusion, constructed to get the maximum volume out of the instrument and to make an appropriately climactic ending to an altogether stunning cycle. This rondo finale, with variation technique applied to the returns of the refrain, anticipates by several years Haydn's use of the same in symphonic works.[70]

---

[69] Landon, *Haydn*, 2: 339–40, quotes from the *Allegro* of Bach's third *Württemberg* Sonata and the first movement of Haydn's sonata. Typically, he fails to verbalize what makes them so close.

[70] Elaine R. Sisman, "Haydn's Variations" (Ph.D. diss., Princeton University, 1978), p. 141, says of this movement: "Haydn's first datable rondo-variation is from 1767." See also Elaine R. Sisman, *Haydn and the Classical Variation* (Cambridge, Mass., 1993), pp. 150–51.

It has been claimed that Haydn's own harpsichord imposed an upper limit of high D in his keyboard works up to 1767.[71] A group of works from the late 1760s, presumably post-1767, break this limit by reaching up to high F, perhaps indicating that they were written for a different instrument. A fragmentary work in D (Hob. XIV:5) begins in common time with a descending fanfare motive on the tonic, then initiates a singing theme in the high tenor range, with the appoggiatura of the raised fifth lending a little spice. The movement bears no tempo marking but was apparently another *Moderato*. After its opening measures the remainder of the score is lost up to some point after the reprise (twenty-one measures in tonic D to end the movement). The Menuet and trio also survive (it is the *minore* trio that soars up to high F).

The Divertimento in A♭ (Hob. XVI:46) may date from about the same time. This piece too requires an extension up to high F, and in it Haydn uses a turn symbol that he had not used before in keyboard music. The first movement is an *Allegro moderato* in common time that, partly because of the unusual key and partly because of Haydn's ever greater lyrical intensity, sounds a quite personal note. There is but a single dynamic marking in the whole work, a *forte* in the first movement placed at a crucial modulatory moment just before the reprise, warning the player to be sure to use the full instrument here. Haydn does not hesitate to push one degree further to the flat side for the ensuing *Adagio* in 3/4, which is intensely poetic. The texture is mainly three parts, both hands being required at different times to render two sustained lines at once. Just before the ending Haydn strays as far afield as the Neapolitan chord, B♭♭, which leads to I⁶ᐟ⁴ and another opportunity for an improvised cadenza. The finale *Presto* in 2/4 works almost as light relief after the *Adagio*, but it too is a thoroughly contrapuntal movement. Its theme is related to the main theme of the opening movement, six measures there being condensed into four here.

A pair of slighter works in two movements, both ending with rather overgrown minuets (but not called such), are thought to date from around 1770: they are Hob. XVI:18 in B♭ and XVI:44 in g. Besides their two-movement format, these works share a highly ornamented style and certain other technical features.[72] Both are overdecorated with turns, trills, mordents, and written-out arabesques, as if Haydn were compensating for the peculiarities

---

[71] Georg Feder, Foreword to *Klaviersonaten*, 1. Folge (*Haydn: Werke* XVIII:1) (Munich, 1970).

[72] For instance, the rising chromatic passage, syncopated against the bass, in mm. 25–29 of the opening *Allegro moderato* of the work in B♭, and the passage at mm. 41–45 in the second movement, *Allegretto*, of the work in g. Note that these similar passages aim at the same harmonic goal, the subdominant, preparing a cadence on the tonic.

of a particular instrument. Could that instrument have been a fortepiano? The sprinkling of dynamic markings, both *forte* and *piano*, added with little apparent reason to the work in B♭, might suggest as much.

EXAMPLE 4.15. *Haydn, Sonata in B (lost)*

Seven divertimenti dating from ca. 1770 are known only by their incipits in Haydn's thematic catalogue, including the "Divertimento per Cembalo in H" with this blithe singing *Allegro* theme over an oscillating pendulum bass (Example 4.15). Griesinger relates an anecdote told him by Haydn that must concern this lost work: in the course of a serious illness around 1770, the composer was confined to bed, but when he was alone he surreptitiously hurried to his clavier and composed the first part of a sonata with five sharps. Two of the missing divertimenti were in minor, corroborating Haydn's increasing preoccupation with the minor mode in symphonic and chamber music at the time.

The Sonata in c (Hob. XVI:20), dated 1771, represents a milestone in Haydn's keyboard music. For the first time, Haydn abandoned the term "Divertimento." Also, the instant dynamic alterations called for in the opening movement are clearly beyond the capabilities of a normal harpsichord. Arguments have been made accordingly that the work was written for fortepiano, or even for clavichord.[73] Actually, Haydn may have had more than one instrument in mind.

Somber parallel thirds and parallel sixths accompany the melody of the main theme in the opening *Moderato*, lending it an almost Brahmsian melancholy, which is intensified when the consequent phrase moves down an octave into the tenor range. The melody quickly regains the soprano range and comes to a cadence after touching the Neapolitan, D♭. The momentary appearance of this tone suggests to Haydn where he will go next and how he will get there. D♭ is reinterpreted as the seventh of a secondary dominant seventh leading to A♭ in a three-measure passage. This passage is then repeated up a tone in sequence, leading to B♭ and the appearance of the

[73] Edwin M. Ripin, "Haydn and the Keyboard Instruments of His Time," *Haydn Studies* (New York, 1981), pp. 302–8. Ripin maintains that the harpsichord is also an appropriate instrument for this sonata. Brown, *Haydn's Keyboard Music*, pp. 24 and 120, argues that Haydn began this sonata in 1771 but finished only the exposition of the first movement and the beginning of the finale then.

much discussed dynamic spices, which did not occur the first time. Why Haydn thought this fussy detail necessary or advisable is not clear, but the desired effect of contrast from tone to tone can be achieved by articulation as well as by dynamic change. The passage is so unimportant as to be lacking in the reprise, and undeserving of all the fuss that has been made about it. More significant is the gradual coming to a halt on the $V^{9/7}$ of the second key area, marked *Adagio,* in the little free fantasy for treble where the minor ninth yields to the major ninth. Such a device fairly shouts its allegiance to Emanuel Bach.

But this was not the first time Haydn had brought movement to a stop with an *Adagio* passage and long-held dissonant chord—there is a similar passage in the first movement of the Sonata in g (Hob. XVI:44), and it reinforces the spiritual closeness of the two works, which seem to inhabit the same world of untrammeled fantasy. The Sonata in c is far the more powerful. Its opening movement becomes ever more intense in its long and wide-ranging development: ‖: 37 :‖: 31 │ 32 :‖. There is a surprising turn to B♭ in m. 52, and an even more dramatic move when the texture and dynamics reach a *fortissimo* climax in g after a chromatically rising bass line. Haydn could have spared the indication *cresc.* here (if indeed it is his), since the music is written to achieve precisely that effect. The retransition that follows makes use of the three-measure sequence from the original transition, but in a different order, leading in, almost imperceptibly, a reprise that keeps up the intensity to the end, which is in minor thirds and sixths like the beginning.

With the *Andante con moto* in A♭ we sense the continuity that stretched from Haydn to Beethoven's *Sonate pathéthique* (Op. 13) and beyond. A♭ was an appropriate choice in Haydn's case, since this key was his first destination after establishing the tonic at the beginning of the work. The melody of the *Andante* is beset by restless syncopations and comes close to achieving the subtle, yearning quality that fills the *Adagio* of Hob. XVI:46 in A♭.

For the finale, Haydn chooses an *Allegro* in 3/4. It begins with a treble statement that is then repeated down an octave, as in the first movement. The descending fifth by step in rapid tones, heard so often in the second key area and development of the first movement, now becomes the main motif from which the finale's theme is built. Further strengthening the cyclical ties between movements is the use of descending 6/3 chords in the closing areas, just as they were used to close both parts of the *Andante.* There is an unsettling silence soon after the double bar in the middle of the finale, a feature used in the same way in the *Moderato* of Hob. XVI:18 in B♭. The reprise follows a dominant pedal and, unlike the first movement, becomes the climactic event. Haydn does not repeat the theme at the lower octave, but rather he saves this for a soft and coda-like return, after another eerie silence, later in the movement (also lending the movement a suggestion of rondo form). The end of the finale is extended in a way that indicates Haydn is thinking on the scale of a leave-taking not just from this movement but from the whole cycle. The Neapolitan sixth is stretched out to four measures on the way to the final cadence, and it, of course, harks back to the beginning of the first movement. The inward unity of the whole cycle is perhaps its most impressive feature, one that also marks Haydn's quartets and symphonies of the early 1770s.

When Haydn returned to writing keyboard sonatas in 1773, it was in order to compile a rather retrospective collection suitable for dedicating to his prince.[74] The normal harpsichord idiom returns in these works, and there is no reason to believe the prince played the *Sei Sonate per Cembalo* printed by Kurzböck in Vienna in 1774 on any other instrument. Haydn did not include the Sonata in c in this set or the similar set he published in 1776. It finally appeared with five others in 1780 in a print called by the publisher, Artaria, *Sonate per il Clavicembalo o Forte Piano*. (Haydn himself used the term "Clavier Sonaten" in correspondence with the publisher.) When he sent the Sonata in c to Artaria on 31 January 1780, he designated this work to close the set, although he was still composing the fifth sonata; he was sending this sonata ahead, he wrote, because it was the longest and most difficult ("weil dieselbe die längste und schwerste ist"), and obviously he wanted this favorite of his to be treated with special care by Artaria. That a sonata several years old could be described as the "longest and most difficult" of a group including recent compositions says much about the plateau Haydn had reached in his most demanding works of the early 1770s. He did not venture beyond their intensity of expression in his later works—there was no need to do so. From this point on, he could refine his art and at the same time make it even more appealing to his ever-widening circle of admirers.

[74] Brown, *Haydn's Keyboard Music*, pp. 302–26.

5

Haydn: The 1770s

String Quartets

*I*F HAYDN had known he would one day be considered the "father of the
string quartet," perhaps he would have assumed his paternal duties with
more constancy. He sired no string quartets as far as is known between the
early *divertimenti a quattro* of the 1750s and Op. 9 of ca. 1770.[1] He wrote many
baryton trios for Prince Esterházy during the mid- and later 1760s; these
modest pieces opened some paths to Haydn that he would take when he
did return to writing quartets. Giuseppe Carpani says that the baryton trios
caused Haydn much sweat, but his labors stood him in good stead to compose for other instruments. The leisurely *Moderato* type of opening movement is fairly common in the baryton trios, three of which (Nos. 97, 101, and
114) end with fugal finales and many of which contain fugatos.[2] Both traits
represent a departure from the earliest chamber music, mostly conceived in
the typical divertimento pattern of five movements, with two minuets and
lightweight outer movements, like the majority of the works in Op. 1 and
Op. 2.

[1] Two individual quartets listed under Haydn's name in the Breitkopf thematic catalogues for 1767
and 1768 are not known elsewhere and are assumed to be false attributions.
[2] Warren Kirkendale, *Fugue and Fugato in Rococo and Classical Chamber Music* (Durham, N.C., 1979),
p. 140. Oliver Strunk wrote this caution in "Haydn's Divertimenti for Baryton, Viola, and Bass,"
Musical Quarterly 18 (1932): 243: "If the fugue in Divertimento 101 is taken as fairly representative of
the sort of counterpoint Haydn could write on the spur of the moment in 1772, it follows that the
fugues in the Quartets op. 20, which date from the same year, cannot have been written without
long, continuous, and determined effort."

Haydn's more serious approach to chamber music emerges in the three closely related quartet sets that have come to be known as Op. 9, Op. 17, and Op. 20. He continues to call all three *Divertimenti a quattro*, but the spirit as well as the form of that older type is largely left behind, to be replaced by four-movement works with one minuet and weighty opening movements balanced (at least by Op. 20) by appropriately weighty finales. The process seems so logical and inevitable that from a compositional point of view, it would seem that Haydn had to write all three sets before attaining his goals, which were to bring the string quartet up to the level of seriousness and cyclic unity he had achieved with the symphony, and to create an obbligato chamber style in which the interest was spread through all four parts. After Op. 20 there was another long hiatus until the Op. 33 Quartets of 1781.

Unlike Op. 1 and Op. 2, which were publishers' compilations, Op. 9, Op. 17, and Op. 20 were conceived by Haydn as sets of six. There is no known external reason why Haydn should suddenly write so many string quartets; the expressed wish of his prince, perhaps upon hearing some other master's quartets, would have provided reason enough. In the case of Op. 33 Haydn made arrangements with Viennese amateurs and collectors to supply a group of quartets in manuscript; but it seems unlikely that he did the same with these earlier works, since his contract expressly forbade this in a stipulation that was not dropped until 1779.[3]

As early as the 1750s Haydn was known to play one of the violin parts in his own quartets. Throughout all his years as leader of the Esterházy orchestra, he had a superior first violinist and *maestro di concerto* in the person of his good friend and perhaps pupil in composition, Luigi Tomasini. When Prince Esterházy journeyed to Paris in the fall of 1767, he was accompanied by a retinue including Tomasini, whose trios for two violins and bass were advertised for sale the following year by the Parisian Bureau d'Abonnement de Musique. The Parisian trip must have acquainted both the prince and his first violinist with much that was going on in the musical world beyond Vienna. Boccherini, for instance, was creating a sensation with his cello playing in the Parisian salons, that of Baron Bagge in particular, and his Quartets of the Op. 1 set were first published by Vénier in April of 1767. It is not unlikely that Tomasini and Boccherini knew each other from earlier times, being close in age and both employed in Vienna starting in 1757.

The Esterházy principal cellist during the 1760s was Joseph Weigl,

[3] László Somfai, "An Introduction to the Study of Haydn's String Quartet Autographs," in *The String Quartets of Haydn, Mozart, and Beethoven*, ed. Christoph Wolff (Cambridge, Mass., 1980), p. 6, speculates that "a calculated distribution of MS copies manufactured in Viennese workshops could have been the reason for the intensive composition." Clever as the idea is, it seems applicable only to a later time in Haydn's career.

another of Haydn's close friends. Both Weigl and his wife, a soprano, left Esterházy service in 1769. The loss of this excellent cellist, for whom Haydn wrote such challenging solos in his symphonies as well as his Cello Concerto in C, thus occurred at an inopportune time with respect to explaining the increasingly important cello parts in Haydn's quartets around 1770. Or did it? When the grand duke and duchess of Russia visited Vienna in 1781, one of their entertainments was the performance in their quarters of a quartet by Haydn, the composer being present; presumably the Russians heard one from the most recent set, Op. 33, which was later dedicated to the grand duke. The players at this concert were Tomasini, first violin, and three musicians in imperial service: Asplmayr, Pancrazio Huber, and Weigl, cello. A decade earlier, when Burney was in Vienna, he heard quartets by Haydn, presumably the most recently written (Op. 20), performed at the house of the British ambassador by Starzer, Karl von Ordonez, young Count Brühl, and Weigl, who may have been a conduit by which Haydn's latest works reached the salons of the capital. The Weigls remained on close terms with Haydn, who was godparent to both their sons. Everything therefore points to Weigl as the principal cello-playing advocate of Haydn's chamber music in Vienna long after he left Esterházy service.

One of the major events in Haydn's life in the late 1760s was the gradual completion of the new palace of Esterháza, which replaced Eisenstadt as the court's major residence from spring through fall. The central building was mostly finished by 1766. Two years later the first opera house opened; this is the edifice on the left side of the garden prospect in Figure 5.1.

FIGURE 5.1. Esterháza.

Opus 9

H AYD N had little if any connection with the traditional ordering of Op. 9, which is retained here for the sake of easy reference. The florid writing for first violin characteristic of this set often suggests Italian quartet writing, and Boccherini in particular. Op. 9 No. 1 in C offers a good case in point. Its opening movement, *Moderato* in common time, gives the first violin a fairly ornate melody to begin with, three measures in length, then proceeds to make it more ornate upon repetition with sextuplets in sixteenth notes (Example 5.1). Matching these rhythmic qualities are such galant chromatic shadings as rising appoggiature on the raised fifth, then on the raised fourth degree. An excursion to the minor dominant provides more chromatic tones and stretches out the exposition considerably. The movement as a whole totals seventy-two measures of what is in effect 8/8 meter, and has been timed, with both parts repeated, at nine minutes, twenty-three seconds—

EXAMPLE 5.1. *Haydn, Quartet Op. 9, No. 1, I*

far longer than any first movement in Op. 1 or Op. 2.[4] Haydn was presumably paying homage to Tomasini's fine technique when being so generous to the first violin as he is here.

A Menuet and trio follows the first movement, as is the case in all six Quartets of both Op. 9 and Op. 17. Haydn's decision to place the dance movement second is understandable given the demanding character of most first movements in these two sets, and the consideration that slow movements, like opening movements, were mainly showplaces for the first violin. In Op. 9 No. 1 the *Adagio* is a 6/8 siciliana type in F; the second violin emerges twice to become the main voice, and it uses the opportunity to reiterate the galant appoggiature from the first movement. The play between diatonic and chromatic language that permeates the whole quartet becomes a terse and witty dialogue in the finale (*Presto* in 2/4), a specialty of Haydn from very early to very late—from the jocular divertimenti of the 1750s through finales such as this one from Op. 9 No. 1 to the rondo finales of the 1770s and 1780s, to his London works.

Op. 9 No. 2 in E♭ is the finest quartet in the set. Even so, it is not free of a certain mannerism, reminiscent of arias and concertos, that Haydn overuses here in Op. 9 and in Op. 17. The first violin, very much the prima donna, works its way higher and higher on the way to a cadence, then swoops from the stratosphere down to its lowest register, returning upward to provide the trill over the dominant and tonic resolution (Example 5.2). The device recalls Tovey's amusing description of the first violin in the slow movement of Op. 1 No. 1 as "a tragedy queen singing an appeal to generations of ancestral Caesars and accompanying with superb gestures her famous display of *Treffsicherheit* in leaping from deep contralto notes to high soprano and back. The other instruments devoutly accompany, in humble throbbing chords, when her tragic majesty has paused for breath."[5] What is

EXAMPLE 5.2. *Haydn, Quartet Op. 9, No. 2, I*

[4] Ludwig Finscher, *Studien zur Geschichte des Streichquartetts* (Kassel, 1974), 1: 206. The finale of the same quartet takes three minutes, forty seconds. Finscher shows that while Haydn keeps first movements relatively the same in length throughout Op. 9, Op. 17, and Op. 20, he gradually increases the length and complexity of the finales. See also Finscher's tables on pp. 217 and 219.
[5] Donald Francis Tovey, "Haydn," in *Cobbett's Cyclopedic Survey of Chamber Music*, 2 vols. (London, 1962–3), 1: 552.

impressive in Op. 9 No. 2 is Haydn's striving to turn this cliché to his advantage.

The prominent half-step rise A♮ B♭, implanted in our ears as a powerful *unisono* climax at the end of the first movement, sneaks into the following Menuet imperceptibly. At first it is in an inner voice played by the second violin in m. 4. Emboldened by this action, the second violin starts to move by half step until finally the first violin gives in, and in the precadential measure also sounds a rising half step. The point is a subtle one—gradual chromatic takeover. The rising minor second is embedded in the trio as well. It also inaugurates the *Adagio* in c that follows, beginning with a slow introduction in common time as the first violin meditates on the implications of B♮ and C, which tones start and end this section; an aria-like *Cantabile* in 3/4 follows, with a varied reprise of the first part. This is sung entirely by the first violin, which ends the movement, appropriately, with the half-step rise to the tonic. The short finale, *Allegro molto* in common time, also makes prominent reference to the half-step motif, and Haydn ties it specifically to the first movement by repeating the same cadential formula to end both parts, taking the first violin up to high B♭ and high G, respectively, as he did in the opening movement. The composer was clearly trying to enforce cyclic unity, as he had long since done in symphonies.

The beginning of Op. 9 No. 3 in G again suggests Boccherini because of the little chromatic fioriture as melodic turns decorating the first violin's tune and the typically galant harmonic progression I - IV$^{6/4}$ - I. The cello, often doubled by the viola, must play a seemingly endless stream of "iterated quavers" (Burney's expression again). The old-fashioned dullness of the movement has something to do with this quality of trudging along without much real movement. Haydn's basses are rarely as boring as this except in his concertos, a genre in which he rarely excelled. Indeed, the Violin Concerto in C of ca. 1765 provides some help in understanding the less successful aspects of Op. 9. The concerto was the best vehicle Haydn could provide for his concertmaster to shine in; he inscribed it in his work list "fatto per il Luigi." The Quartets of Op. 9 are obviously "made for Luigi" as well, even to the extent that they might be called the "Tomasini Quartets."

Haydn's tendency to pick up a detail from the end of one movement and place it at the beginning of another emerges in the use of the flat seventh, somewhat surprisingly, at the beginning of the Menuet in Op. 9 No. 3. The *Largo* movement in 3/4 is in the expected subdominant. Its theme deploys a cliché—in melodic terms, a double *cadence galante*—that Haydn still valued enough to use in the slow movement of the Quartet in g from Op. 20. The flat seventh is used to enhance the end of this movement as well, after the first violin has been given an opportunity to improvise a cadenza. The finale revives our interest in no uncertain terms. Haydn reverts to his jocular mode, and the second of the two initial ideas, sounding very much like a folksong quotation in reply to the proposition of the first, may in fact be related to a popular song.[6] A second theme in the dominant is derived from the "folksong" but continues differently, ending abruptly after six measures when we were expecting eight. Just when the final cadence seems inevitable, Haydn delays it by one of his favorite devices, a resounding $V^{4/3}$ of V, held two measures, then resolving to V^6 and I. The progression occurs in many of Haydn's mature works, to the extent that it becomes one of the master's signatures. In the magnificent *Missa Cellensis* of 1782, for instance, Haydn uses it as a unifying device that occurs near the beginning and, harmonically transformed, near the ending. Lovers of Haydn's music will probably be more familiar with its recurrent appearances in the London symphonies.

Every set of quartets by Haydn from Op. 9 on includes at least one work in the minor (Op. 20 has two); and keys of the major quartets were chosen so as to avoid duplication. Mozart followed Haydn in both respects in his six Viennese quartets of 1773 and in the six he later dedicated to the older master, as did Beethoven in his Op. 18 Quartets. How carefully Haydn planned his sets as balanced entities! For those who were fortunate enough to secure and to be able to play the parts, a set of Haydn quartets offered an evening of tonally varied fare to the performers and any company gathered to hear them. They still do. Very unlikely, given these circumstances, is the truth of a claim made in his memoir by Ignaz Pleyel, who studied with Haydn from 1772 to 1777, that the master, "under the influence of low spirits and chagrin," wrote six quartets, subsequently lost, all in minor.[7] Even in the *Seven Last Words* of 1785 Haydn takes care to achieve a balance between major and minor so that there is not too much of the latter.

As first published, the fourth quartet in Op. 9 is in minor, as will be true of Op. 17 and, many years later, Op. 50. This Quartet in d (Op. 9 No. 4) goes through many of the motions of the passionately intense minor symphonies that Haydn was writing about the same time, including, for instance, the first movement's prominent syncopations in the first violin and the climactic Neapolitan-sixth chord (of V) before the reprise. The Menuet continues grimly in tonic minor, while the trio offers a brief respite of tonic major. (Mozart copied the theme in the Menuetto of his Quartet in d, K. 173, of 1773.) The ensuing *Adagio cantabile* in cut time is in the relative major, and features a varied reprise. It relies greatly on florid triplets for decoration, and

[6] Finscher, *Studien zur Geschichte des Streichquartetts*, 1: p. 20, and musical example 23, pp. 386–87. Among Finscher's several examples, Mozart's use of a similar tune in the finale of the Divertimento in B♭ (K. 252) is particularly worthy of note.

[7] Landon, *Haydn: Chronicle and Works*, 5 vols. (Bloomington, Ind., 1976–80), 2: 375. The "memoir" of Pleyel in question is posthumous and dates from 1832.

once again, on the galant progression I - IV$^{6/4}$ - I for the main theme. The minor-mode finale, a *Presto* in 6/8 with contrapuntal ambitions, does not dissolve finally into cheerful major, as Haydn usually does after the mid-1770s, but remains resolutely "angry" to the end, in line with the symphonies in the minor mode of this period.

Throughout his string quartets Haydn resorted to a judiciously placed theme and variations, generally once per set. This form helped achieve the variety necessary to the performers who were entertaining themselves (and any listeners) at one sitting. Op. 2 No. 6 had begun with variations, so the precedent was at hand for Op. 9 No. 5 and, following it, Op. 17 No. 3 to do likewise. Op. 9 No. 5 is in B♭ and begins with a theme of two strains, *Poco Adagio* in 2/4, followed by four pretty if conventional variations, each increasing the figuration in speed until the last restores the theme to its initial form, except for its decorated repeats. Coming after this, the Menuet sounds a note of exuberance more than of the modesty and decorum proper to this dance. The tune is played *forte* in octaves by the two violins, beginning with an upbeat on the fifth degree and repeated on the downbeat with a melodic turn for added emphasis, then a spring up to the high tonic, while the lower instruments enter *forte* on the downbeats like a percussion section. The same idea is used at the beginnings of the Minuets of the Symphonies No. 102 and No. 103, written some thirty-five years later, only with real percussion to mark the downbeats. It is a perfect "Invitation to the Dance" and makes one involuntarily move a foot on the downbeat. No matter that Haydn is bending the most aristocratic of dances toward something that sounds more like a peasant wedding.

The finale of Op. 9 No. 5, a *Presto* in 2/4, makes up for the lack of an opening movement in sonata form with a specimen of the same more elaborate than usually encountered in the finales of this set, one that is linked thematically with the first movement. The 3/4 meter of the *Largo cantabile* third movement in E♭ suggests comparison with the *Largo* in 3/4 of Op. 9 No. 3, and indeed they both invoke the identical melodic line to end the first phrase. Recurrences like this, and the theatrical high-to-low-and-back cadences mentioned above, are more common in Op. 9 than they will be later, suggesting that Haydn later tried harder to avoid such clichés recurring within a single set. How sensitive he was to recurrent material emerges from his request to Artaria with respect to the six *Auenbrugger* Sonatas published in 1780 that an *Avertissement* be published acknowledging that although he had used the same theme in two different sonatas, this was done intentionally to show how differently it could be treated.[8]

---

[8] Joseph Haydn, *Gesammelte Briefe und Aufzeichnungen*, ed. Dénes Bartha (Kassel, 1965), p. 12.

FIGURE 5.2. Title page of Haydn's String Quartets, Op. 19.

    The divertimento lightness of Op. 9 No. 6 in A has occasioned wonderment on the part of some critics, who regard the rounded binary finale of fifty-four measures as a throwback, or worse, a failure of will in Haydn's resolve to make the string quartet a serious and respectable genre. The finale is an *Allegro* 2/4 beginning with an upbeat and scalar descents down an octave. One can hear close analogies with the finale of Haydn's Harpsichord Sonata in A, the last of the set of six of 1773. Moreover, Haydn entered the

Quartet in A last in his work list, thus confirming the published order in this case. The finale of this quartet actually does seem appropriate in context. It closes a quartet begun by a *Presto* in 6/8 of only 133 measures and of a hunting character, and continued with the usual Menuet and trio and a blithely galant slow movement. If the finale were perceived as a merry "Bon soir" to the assembled company at evening's end, how could it give offense? Indeed, its vigorous and forthright strains could be heard as a reference to the charming custom by which serenading musicians marched out to their last piece. The same down-rushing scales in sixteenth notes appear as the last movement of a duet for two violins by Boccherini (Gérard No. 62), a piece bearing the subtitle "La bona notte." In sum, the Quartet in A ends the set—which represents a great stride forward in quartet writing for Haydn—with the lightest possible touch.

OPUS 17

IF Haydn's Op. 9 (Figure 5.2) could be called his "Tomasini Quartets," so could Op. 17, written in 1770 and published a year later. But this is true for the later set to a lesser degree in that the three other parts besides the first violin come in for a greater share of the musical interest in Op. 17. The two sets have much in common even so—one minor-mode quartet and one quartet with variations, for instance, but above all the general adherence to the same four-movement plan with the minuet second. As first published, Op. 17 begins with a tonality Haydn had not used as a keynote in Op. 9, the brilliant and rarefied key of E, which usually means something extraordinarily fine with this composer; Op. 17 No. 1 is no exception. The thematic material of the first movement, a *Moderato* in common time, is unusually attractive, and its motives are used to integrate the whole movement.[9] Unusual as well is the phrase structure of the first six-measure phrase and the harmonic richness deployed, including a $ii^{6/5}$ chord that becomes a $V^{6/5}$ of V with the chromatic rise of the bass. A long *Menuet Allegretto* in E and trio in e lead to an *Adagio*, 6/8 in e, a siciliana type with dotted rhythms and the characteristic arrival of the Neapolitan-sixth chord in the precadential position.

The finale, *Presto* in 2/4, begins, like the first movement, with a six-measure phrase. But here an ordinary four-measure phrase is extended by an assertive quasi-echo of the cadence and then a measure of silence. "Assertive

---

[9] The movement even attracted Mozart to attempt recomposition. See Gerhart Croll, "Remarks on a Mozart Quartet Fragment," *Haydn Studies*, ed. Jens Peter Larsen, Howard Serwer and James Webster (New York, 1981), pp. 405–7. See also the remarks of Webster on p. 411 and the general comments by Finscher and Webster on the Haydn-Mozart relationship on pp. 407–12.

echo" is a contradiction in terms, and as such a source of Haydn's humor; other instances are the unexpected harmonic turns (e.g., the protracted augmented-sixth chord that does not resolve as such) and the veiled, uneasy onset of the reprise, followed by an inversion of the scalar main figure from ascent to descent. The movement dies away in a *pianissimo*.

Op. 17 No. 2 in F (which stands first in Haydn's autograph) opens with another *Moderato* in common time, the theme of which—a regular four-measure phrase with a galant cliché ending of four notes falling rapidly down to tonic F—seems unpromising. Upon repetition, the four measures are stretched to five as the inner voices add a written-out trill in thirds to which the cello responds twice, then proposes its own version of the trill, uninvited, by substituting upper auxiliary for lower. What started routinely becomes surprising. The same is true at the $V^{4/3}$ of V delaying the cadence on the dominant, which is heard three times, the third followed by the first violin's question-like leap up to high C and then silence. The mysterious passage with soft, slow-moving harmonies and suspensions that follows has been set up as thoroughly as if the composer were present to say, "Pay attention here! This is important." Only when the passage returns at the end of the reprise does it become apparent that the main suspension, F E in the viola, is also the main point of the seemingly prosaic first theme, sung by the first violin. What is more, upon reaching the end of the quartet, the ear should be able to perceive that the entire work is based upon the initial suspension and resolution F E F.

In the *Menuet Allegretto* of Op. 17 No. 2 suspensions gradually take over the discourse. The F E F cadence is transferred to the trio to be reharmonized in the relative minor. The *Adagio* in cut time and in B♭ begins with F E♭, but the latter is prominently turned into E♮ at the onset of the dominant. There is considerable play involving upper and lower auxiliary notes in the *Adagio* as well. The finale, an *Allegro di molto* in 2/4, brings all these items together: F E F, chains of suspensions, upper versus lower auxiliary notes, and one other item that we now realize has been prominent throughout the quartet: an unexpected V of vi (E F in the viola), heard after the double bar in the middle. In the *Adagio* the reprise begins after an unresolved V of vi. The Trio likewise ends with V of vi (the viola on E), which resolves without explanation to the tonic F of the repeated Menuetto. V of vi and its nonresolution furnish the climax of the development in the first movement. With such subtle and permeating harmonic-motivic means, Haydn extends his control over the whole four-movement cycle. Op. 9 can boast no work to compare with this. It is symptomatic of the difference that Haydn chooses to give so important a motivic role to the lowly viola, heretofore the least "equal" of the participants.

Mozart paid close attention to Haydn's quartets of the early 1770s. In Mozart's Quartet in d (K. 173) of 1773, he takes account not only of Haydn's Quartet in d from Op. 9 but also the fugal finale of the Op. 20 Quartet in C. Also, three quartets from Op. 17, Nos. 2, 5, and 6, exist in manuscript copies with dynamic indications added in Mozart's hand. These copies, preserved in Augsburg's Church of the Holy Cross, are part of Leopold Mozart's legacy (reminding us that the Mozarts frequently played chamber music at home, with Leopold as first violin and Wolfgang as either second or viola, which he usually preferred).[10] It is no coincidence that the mysterious soft passages toward the end of both parts of the first movement of Haydn's Quartet in F (Op. 17 No. 2) should find a parallel especially in Mozart's quartets, up to and including those he dedicated to Haydn in 1785 (cf. the first movements of K. 458 and K. 464).

Theme and variations open Op. 17 No. 3 in E♭, all movements of which, it has been claimed, are related by their initial theme.[11] The minor-mode Quartet of the set, Op. 17 No. 4 in c, begins with another *Moderato* in common time, and toys with the listener as to when the reprise begins; the best moment comes at the end in a coda, with hints of C major that are like rays of light piercing dark clouds. The Menuetto then fulfills the promise, while the trio reverts to c minor. The *Adagio cantabile* that follows (3/4 in E♭) belongs to the first violin to such an extent that it offers little to sustain the others players' interest. The movement is curious because Haydn writes a long florid period of thirty-three measures with modulation to the dominant, then decorates it in even more florid fashion. This constitutes the prima parte—sixty-six measures and several minutes. Aware that he could not possibly carry on in so languid a fashion by decorating the entire seconda parte, he collapses the development and the reprise, overlapping some of his material, so that together they take only forty measures with no repeat. Formally the movement is unbalanced—an experiment that Haydn will improve on in the *Adagio* of the Quartet in A from Op. 20. As in the minor quartet of Op. 9, the finale of this quartet is contrapuntally inclined and remains resolutely minor to the end, which comes in a coda emphasizing the sixth degree as in the coda of the first movement.

---

[10] These parts had been considered an acquisition from the Mozarts' Viennese visit of 1773, but a study of the watermarks and paper reveals that they were copied in Salzburg in 1771 or 1772. See Cliff Eisen, "The Symphonies of Leopold Mozart and Their Relationship to the Early Symphonies of Wolfgang Amadeus Mozart: A Bibliographical and Stylistic Study" (Ph.D. diss., Cornell University, 1986), pp. 241–42.

[11] Landon, *Haydn*, 2: 323, quotes incipits of the four movements to show what he calls their "fifthy" character. He makes the fifth more prominent than did Haydn by misquoting the *Adagio* theme: the fourth note should be G, not B♭.

Best known of the Op. 17 Quartets is No. 5 in G, nicknamed *Recitative*. It is easy to hear why chamber musicians favor this work. Before ten measures have passed in the opening *Moderato* in common time, every instrument has sung the opening measure of the tune, which contains Lombard snaps and is quite memorable. Also arresting the attention is a *fortissimo* unison from half-note E to the D♯ below after the cadence in m. 12. It is too forceful to be a sigh, and sounds more like a protest—interpreted along *redende Thematik* lines it suggests something like "Mais non!" (French is the most appropriate language to use to describe the drawing-room art of the quartet, because every salon habitué of that time aspired to speak it, and many, perhaps most, did.) Haydn makes good use of this nay-saying figure throughout the movement, turning it finally into a false interval, a descending diminished fourth in the reprise. The Menuet is mock canonic between the treble and the bass, and is followed by a trio in g that ends with a transition back to the first dance. The trio also predicts the key and the mode of the slow movement, *Adagio* in 3/4, a veritable *scena* for the prima donna (first violin) in which recitative comes into play. Of all Haydn's instrumental recitatives, this one comes closest to prefiguring the actual tones with which the basses rumble their premonition of joy in the finale of Beethoven's Ninth Symphony (Example 5.3). After the theatrics of the slow movement, the spirited repartee of the finale, *Presto* in 2/4, cannot help but suggest a buffo finale, a happy end to the plot, with only a few hints of the flat side left at the end—enough to remind us of tonic minor earlier in the quartet—that resolve via an augmented-sixth chord to the final cadential drive. The movement slips away as it began, ethereally, with the main motif left "up in the air," *pianissimo*, on the weak second measure of a four-measure phrase.

EXAMPLE 5.3. *Haydn, Quartet Op. 17, No. 5, III*

Op. 17 No. 6 in D begins with a "hunting" movement, a *Presto* in 6/8 (cf. Op. 9 No. 6). There are also gigue-like aspects to the thematic material, and even a resemblance to the Gigue of Sebastian Bach's fifth *French Suite* in G (especially to Bach's inverted form of the theme in the second strain). The harmonic plan of the first movement is adventurous, with an elaborate excursion to ♭VII in the precadential areas of both first and second parts— an almost Schubertian touch. Following the Menuetto and trio is a *Largo* in G, common time, offering the customary solo to the first violin, including multiple opportunities to improvise cadenzas. The *Presto* finale, in 2/4, is on the order of the finale of Op. 17 No. 5, with which it shares some features, most notably a *pianissimo* ending up in the air. The repeated falling thirds in the short coda seem to hark back to the hunting theme of the first movement. The finale is not lacking in feats of counterpoint, and in this respect it looks ahead to Op. 20, where major as well as minor finales will bloom with contrapuntal artifices. Op. 17 as a whole shows Haydn poised on the brink of a momentous accomplishment.

OPUS 20

THE tendency to equalize the four parts and make them more contrapuntal, encountered increasingly in Op. 17 of 1771, grew to a noticeable degree in the six Quartets of Op. 20, composed in 1772 and published two years later. A decided lessening of the element of florid virtuosity in the first violin part of these quartets makes them approachable for the good but nonvirtuoso violinist, as well as for the likes of Tomasini. To this day they remain more popular with chamber music players than Op. 9 or Op. 17. By spreading the musical interest throughout the texture, Haydn inevitably reduced the role of the first violin somewhat. In addition, the works of Op. 20 offer many startlingly audacious features. They give the impression that Haydn wrote this set for himself, and in response to his increasing European fame, as much as or more than he did in response to any local circumstances.

Haydn entered the six new quartets in his work list in this order: f, A, C, g, D, E♭. La Chevardière, who would perhaps have been wary about beginning a set with a minor-mode quartet, published the first edition in this order: E♭, f, C, A, g, D. (Parisian sets with minor quartets were not unknown. In 1769 Vénier brought out Boccherini's Quartets Op. 8 in the order D, c, E♭, g, F, A.) The Amsterdam publisher Hummel reordered Op. 20 in his reprint of ca. 1779 (with a picture of a rising sun on the title page, hence the sobriquet *Sun* Quartets): E♭, C, g, D, f, A. In this order they were taken over by Pleyel in his complete edition and by Elssler in his catalogue of Haydn's works. The reordering does not end even here. Artaria published the set in installments in 1800 (E♭, A, f) and 1801 (D, C, g), claiming that the quartets had been corrected by the composer.[12]

The Quartet in f may well be the earliest composed, as the work list suggests. It is the most studiously formal of the lot and the most retrospective, its fugal finale being based not on an original theme but on an old saw from the past, one that had seen use by Bach, Handel, and many others. It has been argued that the first three quartets composed were those in g, E♭, and f, because they follow Op. 9 and Op. 17 in placing the Menuetto second, and because the lowest part in the autograph is marked "Basso"; in the Quartets in C, A, and D, on the other hand, the Menuetto is third and the lowest part is marked "Violoncello" (the ones in C and A) or not marked at all (the one in D).[13]

In the memoir of his life, Haydn's pupil Pleyel links his teacher and Gluck in connection with the Quartet in f. Pleyel recalls a time in mid-May of 1776 when Gluck hurriedly returned from Paris to Vienna. Like Johann Friedrich Reichardt, he speaks of himself in the third person:

> In 1776, when Pleyel was in his twentieth year, and had nearly completed his studies, Gluck returned to Vienna, after bringing out his opera *Alceste* in Paris. He had not been many days in the Austrian capital, before he paid a visit to Haydn, who played to him his quartet in F minor then just written. The beauties of so fine a composition could not be lost upon the great restorer of lyric tragedy, who accordingly, bestowed on the quartet warm and well-merited applause.[14]

This is a rare kind of information to have, and credible enough except that the Quartet in f was hardly "just written." With all Gluck's travels between Paris and Vienna in the 1770s and the frenetic pace of his professional life, it could well be that the piece was new to him in 1776. What Pleyel does not mention is the cause of Gluck's precipitous return to Vienna—a personal bereavement. The Glucks had no children, but there lived with them a young niece who was like their own child. Burney recounts hearing this angelic creature sing during his visit to Gluck on 2 September 1772, and he wrote prophetically about her, describing how Gluck accompanied her in his own music and that of Traetta:

---

[12] The 1800–1 revisions are not accepted as authentic by the editors of *Streichquartette "Opus 20" und "Opus 33"* in *Joseph Haydn: Werke,* ed. Georg Feder and Sonja Gerlach (Munich, 1974).

[13] László Somfai, "Vom Barock zur Klassik: Umgestaltung der Proportionen und des Gleichgewichts in zyklischen Werken Joseph Haydns," in *Joseph Haydn und seine Zeit* (Eisenstadt, 1972), pp. 68ff., and tables; Somfai upholds his position in "Haydn's String Quartet Autographs," p. 15.

[14] Landon, *Haydn,* 2: 375.

He began, upon a very bad harpsichord, by accompanying his niece, who is but thirteen years old, in two of the capital scenes of his own famous opera of *Alceste*. She has a powerful and well-toned voice, and sang with infinite taste, feeling, expression, and even execution. After these two scenes from *Alceste*, she sang several others, by different composers, in different styles, particularly by Traetta . . . Mademoiselle Gluck is thin, seems of a delicate constitution, and, as she sings so much in earnest, I should fear for her health if she were to make singing a profession, but she is not intended for a public performer.

Alceste, the most grief-laden of Gluck's operas, was an ominous choice for the young lady, who died when only seventeen in the spring of 1776. Haydn's performance of the Quartet in f for Gluck may have been intended as a kind of condolence or perhaps as an elegiac tribute. Haydn's reverence for Gluck's music emerges in the testimony of Roman Hoffstetter, who wrote that the composer "had almost all Gluck's works in his head, and played to me often, without looking at a note, whole overtures, long recitatives, choruses, etc., from his operas at the keyboard, without omitting any of the voice parts."[15]

There is one quite Gluckian moment in the first movement of the Quartet in f, an *Allegro moderato* in common time. As the reprise is coming to a close, the bass hovers around the bottom of a six-four chord, now approaching it from below, now from above, while anchoring various harmonies. The same description could be used of the choral exclamations at the beginning of Gluck's *Alceste* (Paris version). Tovey said that this quartet foreshadows "Beethovenish tragedy." A central work of veritable tragedy like *Alceste* offers a parallel closer in time and is also closer to Haydn's emotional world.

Typical of Haydn is the economy with which he makes the *serioso* opening motif of the Quartet in f engender a new theme in the relative major. (This motif also preoccupied the composer in his Symphony No. 52 of ca. 1771.) Extraordinary for Haydn at this time are the length and far-ranging modulations of the coda, which is like a second development section and in this respect does indeed foreshadow Beethoven. The long Menuet continues the vein of intense minor seriousness of the first movement, and even the trio in F lacks the levity that trios often bring. The ensuing *Adagio* in F, in lilting dotted 6/8 time, like a siciliana, displays a certain rustic charm and simplicity, which makes it a good foil for the fugal finale. Haydn directs that the finale be played "sempre sotto voce" up until the climactic canon at the half note, when he marks a *fortissimo* in the cello part. The fugue finishes

[15] Letter to Silverstolpe of 4 September 1800, quoted in Irmgard Leux-Henschen, *Joseph Martin Kraus in seiner Zeit* (Stockholm, 1978), p. 160.

forte in all the parts, with anachronistic-sounding V - I cadences. This finale, it has been argued, works not as the inevitable consequence and conclusion of the previous movements but more like an appendix.[16]

The Quartet in g is as unlike the Quartet in f as possible—it could never serve as an elegiac tribute. Its first movement is an *Allegro con spirito* in 2/4, a "light" meter and tempo. Hardly has the first theme gotten started before a tone of grotesquery sets in. The first half-phrase is ordinary enough, an antecedent of four measures with eighth-note upbeat, alternating diatonic motion with chromatic and legato with staccato, the last of which lands on the dominant by a seventh leap downward (Example 5.4). The second half-phrase consists of three measures only, and is filled with leaping sevenths, staccato, but ending with two minor seconds, legato. Who but Haydn would think of such an outrageous consequent? It is as if he has pulled the rug from under the players. By the time the relative major is secured, Haydn has allowed an unmistakably buffo spirit to take over. This is evident in the rocking bass and treble patter before the cadence in m. 24, which is followed by an "extra" two-measure tag, *piano*, that seems like a sardonic *sotto voce* comment on the bizarre proceedings. And they do not get any more serious. The definitive cadence on B♭ becomes instead an interruption by Haydn's favorite V⁴ᐟ³ of V gesture, *forte*, leading only to V. A *fortissimo* sounding of I⁶ᐟ³ seems to promise the end of the section, but it only sets the first violin on a meandering soliloquy, sparsely supported by the other instruments and threatening to turn into a recitative, when a *forte unisono* passage with trills interrupts to call the proceedings back to order. An extended appoggiatura

EXAMPLE 5.4. *Haydn, Quartet Op. 20, No. 3, I*

[16] Finscher, *Studien zur Geschichte des Streichquartetts*, 1: p. 235.

in the melody, *piano,* another deceptive cadence, and the infamous two-measure tag, *forte,* intervene before the cadence is finally reached. An unpredictable skittishness marks this movement from beginning to end.

If the f-minor Quartet was in some sense a tribute to Gluckian tragedy, the Quartet in g seems to be a tribute to another of the revered elders: Emanuel Bach. So many hesitations, plunges, swoops, sighs, and non sequiturs could in fact be heard as a humorous parody of the Hamburg Bach. Critics of the time were alert to this possibility. Reviewing the six harpsichord sonatas dedicated by Haydn to his prince in 1773, a critic in the October 1784 issue of the *European Magazine, and London Review* found them "expressly composed in order to ridicule Bach of Hamburgh . . . No one can peruse the second part of the second sonata . . . and the whole of the third sonata . . . and believe Haydn in earnest . . . On the contrary, the stile of Bach is closely copied, without the passages being stolen, in which his capricious manner, odd breaks, whimsical modulations, and very often childish manner, mixed with an affectation of profound science, are finely hit off and burlesqued."[17]

Haydn's Sonata in E, the second of the set of harpsichord sonatas, does include in its "second part" of the first movement some fairly skittish alternations of texture and tempo (from *Allegro* to *Adagio* and back), with leaps up to the top of the keyboard and sudden bursts of quick notes—all mannerisms of Emanuel Bach. And in the third sonata, in F, the rising chromatic progression in the finale comes close to being "stolen" from the finale of Bach's first *Prussian* Sonata (in F). If Haydn in this relatively tame set of harpsichord sonatas in the Viennese tradition of Wagenseil—staid enough to be dedicated to his prince, in any case—awakened suspicion of parodying Emanuel Bach, how much more suspicious is a work like the g-minor Quartet, where the composer gave free rein to his fantasy!

From the initial idea of the Quartet in g, Haydn goes on to derive the idea for the second movement, *Menuet Allegretto* (with a trio in E♭ that works its way to an ending, like the Menuet, on a G-major chord), and the finale, *Allegro molto* in common time. The latter resumes the madcap ways of the initial movement, the seventh leap downward becoming the end of a *forte unisono* passage, following a Neapolitan chord that seems to parody the protracted, opera seria–like appearance of the same in the coda of the first movement. The slow movement alone, a *Poco Adagio* in 3/4 in the "naive" key of G, seems innocent of the mordant wit prevailing elsewhere, unless Haydn is poking fun at the *cadence galante* (the identical cadential gesture

---

[17] A. Peter Brown, "Joseph Haydn and C. P. E. Bach: The Question of Influence," in *Haydn Studies,* ed. Jens Peter Larsen et al. (New York, 1981), pp. 158–64. The author does not discuss the two sonatas mentioned specifically in this passage.

occurs in two slow movements of Op. 9). One of the rare draft sketches to survive for Haydn's quartets shows that he conceived the initial melody in this movement for cello solo and later transferred it to the first violin. This is not surprising, because the cello remains featured throughout the movement in a kind of concertante duet with the first violin. Much of Haydn's sketch was occupied with getting the concertante figuration the way he wanted it. If the Quartet in f proved how serious Haydn could be in the minor mode, the Quartet in g, far more daring and novel, shows how he could make even the minor mode a vehicle for levity. Its buffoonery serves to remind us, finally, that Haydn began his career as a secular composer writing for the Viennese equivalent of the commedia dell'arte and matching wits with the antics of Harlequin, Pantaloon, and Hanswurst.

The Quartet in E♭, which belongs chronologically with the two minor quartets for the reasons given above, was copied out in its entirety by Beethoven. It opens with an *Allegro moderato* in common time with the thematic material nicely spread through all four parts—there is even a substantial duet for viola and cello. The following *Menuet Allegretto* contains another trio that begins in one key (A♭) and ends in another (V$^{6/5}$ of f). The question posed by this odd ending finds an unusual answer when the Menuet returns, insisting on E♭. The effect is a little less perplexing than this description suggests because the f at the end of the trio was established in conjunction with the return of the theme of the Menuet—obviously just a "false start" on the supertonic, rectified by recalling the right place. This feature may have intrigued young Beethoven, who also loved false starts.

The slow movement is an exercise in close intervallic part writing, an almost churchly *Affettuoso e sostenuto* in A♭ and in 3/8 time. Haydn's point was apparently to write the most seamless movement he could, using little or no rhythmic contrast to detract from the smoothly changing harmonies. Whether he succeeded in this experiment will depend on the listener's tolerance for rhythmic sameness. Mozart must have thought he did, because the A♭ *Andante* in his Quartet in E♭ dedicated to Haydn (K. 428) manages superbly under similar restrictions. Beethoven as well may have been paying tribute to this movement in the *Andante* of his Op. 59 No. 3. In Haydn's finale, *Presto* in 2/4, pert three-measure phrases, related thematically to the beginning of the first movement, serve to jolt us out of whatever degree of somnolence was induced by the prayerlike slow movement. The finale ends with a soft cadence rhythmically weak, exactly as does the first movement.

An ascending order of perfection becomes apparent upon long acquaintance with the remaining quartets of Op. 20: those in A and C and the crowning jewel of the set, the Quartet in D. The Quartet in A begins with an *Allegro di molto e scherzando* in 6/8. Its first theme is most memorable for the little cadential figure with melodic turn in the second measure, a figure that Haydn will of course exploit precisely because it is the most unforgettable part of the thematic material. The chromatic descents at the end of each part project a delicately Mozartian wistfulness. They will recur in even more pronounced fashion as the subject of the finale of the Quartet in C, which is also in 6/8. In the *Adagio cantabile* in E, cut time, Haydn reverts to the broad violin melody, floridly decorated, so often encountered in Op. 9 and Op. 17. He also tries again, with greater success, the process of writing out a complete and differently decorated version of the prima parte, then eliding and collapsing the seconda parte (as in the slow movements of Op. 9 Nos. 2 and 4 and Op. 17 No. 4). The *Menuet Allegretto* and trio reinstate the melodic turn from the first movement, and so does the fugal theme of the finale, marked "Fuga a 3 soggetti: Allegro." (Later fugal nomenclature would indicate fugue with two countersubjects.) The descending fugal subject taken together with the long-note suspensions provided by its first countersubject form a passage the substance of which was heard in the closing area of the first movement (mm. 121–24 in the tonic).

The Quartet in C sums up much of what Haydn was striving to attain throughout Op. 9, Op. 17, and Op. 20. Its first movement, a *Moderato* in common time like most of those in the two earlier sets, alternates contrapuntal and homophonic passages at short range, but the two textures are so beautifully integrated as to blend imperceptibly together. The beginning is like a trio sonata, with the cello singing the theme against two lines of counterpoint provided by the viola, acting as bass, and the second violin. But contrapuntal discourse is abandoned even in the second and third measures as the cello and second violin stop to savor the lovely sound of repeated thirds, up and down. When the violin enters, it restates the theme at the fifth, again as in a trio sonata (and as in the opening measures of the E♭ Quartet of Op. 20). The second violin then gets its turn at the theme, back in the tonic. When it is time for the dominant to establish itself, the high instruments pair off and are answered by the low ones. This lovely sonority is pursued further and at shorter range with duets in sextuplet figures answering back and forth. (There is a similar moment in a similar place during the first movement of the Quartet in D of the same set, where the composer will derive even greater auditory pleasure from such duetting.) The way Haydn opens up to the cadential six-four chord via an augmented sixth illustrates another of his almost Schubertian touches. The development begins in a rather schematic fashion with measure-long exchanges between the outer voices and harmonic filler in the middle, leading to a restatement of the theme in d by the one instrument that has yet to sing it, the viola, followed by a gradual sinking down to the tonic for the reprise, which is collapsed from three statements of the main theme to one.

There follows an *Adagio* in common time entitled "Capriccio," which begins in the tonic minor. This is another in the series of operatic *scenas,* such as the slow movements of Op. 9 No. 2 and Op. 17 No. 5. In the earlier works the first violin played the prima donna and there was no disputing her priority. Here the first solo goes to the cello, as the opening unison ritornello is softly repeated, with harmonic accompaniment from the other three instruments. It is like an obbligato recitative of the most elaborate kind up until the first violin begins to sing a cavatina-like melody in E♭; after an interruption by the full band (an opera orchestra is inevitably suggested), singing duties are assigned to the second violin, and the first must accompany. This state of affairs does not last for long before another eruption of the unison band signals a winding down to the dominant chord, G, which is accompanied by the direction "Siegue subito il Menuet."

Thus the Menuet, marked *Allegretto,* becomes the tonal resolution of the theatrical second movement, and is itself anything but theatrical. Like a *musette tendre,* its drones and weaving voices project rural delights. Unobtrusive, it never rises above *piano,* and sinks below that at the end as the deliciously naive first phrase returns *pianissimo.* The trio takes us back to the tonic minor, as the cello states a descending figure that reminds us of the opening ritornello of the slow movement; it ends on G so that the Menuet can enter demurely in resolution just as it did the first time.

The fugal movement that follows is a tour de force of compositional skill. Haydn marks it "Fuga a 4tro soggetti" and "sempre sotto voce." The main theme of this *Allegro* in 6/8 is anything but pedantic, with its tender descending chromatic idea. When Haydn doubles this descending chromatic idea in thirds and makes lower duets echo higher duets, he reverts to one of the textural discoveries of the first movement. If these passages and indeed the whole superb movement sound uncannily like Mozart, it is because he put the same motif through many similar paces in the finale of his Quartet in A dedicated to Haydn (K. 464 of 1785). Haydn's triumph is to turn the most learned genre of music into a finale so insouciant that it ranks with his greatest inspirations. He even works in some across-the-barline hemiola à la Brahms (mm. 83ff.) to increase the rhythmic interest. The movement dances from beginning to end like a scherzo and succeeds in totally beguiling us so that we forget about all its contrapuntal artifice; it is the will-o'-the wisp of Op. 20.

Something of Haydn's exaltation after this achievement (probably the result of long and laborious effort—"lunga e laboriosa fatica," as Mozart said about writing his quartets dedicated to Haydn) emerges from the unusual

inscription he placed at the end: "Laus omnip. Deo / Sic fugit amicus ami-
cum." "Praise to almighty God" is not unusual, although "laus Deo" usually
suffices Haydn at the end of a work; "thus does friend flee friend" refers to
the technique of fugue but can also pertain to the performance with friendly
chamber players, i.e., to the social aspect of the string quartet. A merry
chase it is indeed, like whippets after hares (6/8, we recall, is the hunting
meter). In a larger, historical sense, Haydn with this movement moved so
far ahead of his contemporaries in the composition of chamber music that
only his "amico carissimo," Mozart, would (eventually) be able to catch up
with him.

The first movement of the Quartet in D, *Allegro di molto* in 3/4, runs to
nearly three hundred measures, more than any other in the set and even
surpassing Haydn's symphonic first movements of the same time in length.
Yet this movement is not symphonic in the least. It remains essentially
chamber music: subtle, delicate, and of an inexhaustible inventiveness. The
first theme sounds as if it were in 9/4 because of the three-measure units,
which combine into six-measure phrases. At issue from the beginning is
whether the "tapping" first measure is to be heard as downbeat or upbeat
(Example 5.5). The melodic shape suggests that an initial upbeat measure
would be the most musical way to perceive the theme (upper brackets), but
the harmony argues against this (lower brackets). Haydn keeps up his soft
six-measure phrases, divided into 3 + 3, until a rude shock, a *forte* chord on
the unprepared relative minor, intervenes. Here two measures of *forte* yield
to a soft four-measure rejoinder, divided into 2 + 2. In the ensuing dialogue,
the grip of the six-measure module is broken and replaced by the more normal two- and four-measure phraseology, but not without further challenges
from three- and six-measure groups, which are going to recur throughout
this long movement. After the dominant is proclaimed with up-rushing unison scale, following the ubiquitous three "taps" from the very opening, the
first violin floats down in half steps, rather wistfully, a chromatic descent
such as preoccupied Haydn in all three of the quartets in this group. The
stretching out of the sonata form occurs mainly here, as the composer takes

Example 5.5. *Haydn, Quartet Op. 20, No. 6, I*

time to savor the chromatic descent and linger over it to a different accompaniment.

What follows is all cadential, but Haydn has found new and powerfully sweet ways to stretch this closing material out too, as the instruments pair off and warble little imitations of each other's duets, sometimes inverting their figures, as is characteristic of this composer. The sound is so ravishing we wonder why it took Haydn so long to discover it. But discover it he did, and Viennese chamber music was ever the richer for it: much of Mozart's chamber music is particularly indebted to passages like this, and the same is true of Beethoven and Schubert. The second part of the first movement is as exquisitely wrought and unpredictable as was the first part, including the moment of reprise after the long development.

It was a stroke of genius on Haydn's part to place the one theme and variations of the whole set after this blithely airy movement, and moreover to select the tonic minor throughout, almost as if an antidote to the whimsy of the first movement. No musical form is more predictable and therefore comfortable than a typical theme and variations of this period, of which this is one, albeit superior in every detail to its predecessors in Op. 9 and Op. 17. After three variations featuring different players in turn, the theme recurs unadorned, *sotto voce*, always effective as a device, and like a prism through which to glimpse the distance traveled. The movement could easily end here, but Haydn decided it was worthy of a long and expressive coda, with a hint of the tragic in the protracted Neapolitan chord on the way to the final cadence, which has no third. This the listener can supply by anticipating the succeeding dance, which is of course in major and is titled "Menuet alla Zingarese Allegretto."

The Menuet is short and aggressive, with conflicting "Gypsy" accents supplied by *sforzati* on each of the three beats alternately. A Ländler-like trio allows the cello to shine in passage work that anticipates such late cello solos as the one in the trio of the Symphony No. 97 in C. Once again the movement is a perfect antidote to what preceded it, the dark and gloomy variations, with which both Menuet and trio are linked thematically by their upbeat beginnings. How can Haydn tie the whole quartet together? By having his *Presto e scherzando* finale, in common time, reestablish the mood of the first movement with its jocular theme, delicate chromatic shadings, and sometimes audacious byplay—even the delicious play of high duet against low recurs to remind us how this brilliant cycle of four movements started.

Having conquered the problem of cyclic unity in the symphony, Haydn now does the same for the string quartet, not in any overt way, such as he began trying in Op. 9, but with enormous charm and subtlety. In the Quartet in D his contrapuntal learning is ever so lightly worn, but the finale is no less shot through with polyphonic motivic work than the fugal finales of Op. 20. The four partners of the quartet, for they are truly that, discuss all manner of subjects—mundane, serious, even jocular. They are never pompous or affected, but worldly wise, as befits the best salon conversation. Of all the quartets of Op. 20, the one in D most clearly shows Haydn's future path, and indeed it would not seem out of place alongside the Quartets of Op. 33.

Cyclic unity of a high order and a thoroughly obbligato texture were finally achieved for the string quartet by Haydn in his Op. 20. With the deepening of the four-movement sequence to a cyclic organization, these works stood "directly on the cresting wave of the classical string quartet."[18] As early as 1784 an anonymous English biography of Haydn in the *European Magazine* took cognizance of his obbligato style, perhaps in response to the publication of Op. 20 in London a few years earlier:

> It must not be understood, that for the sake of pleasant melody, and sweet air, our author has neglected and laid aside that part of music that constitutes the great master, namely *imitation* and *fugue*. With these strokes of art all his capital music abounds. From his hands they neither appear pedantic nor heavy, being continually relieved by pleasant touches of fancy, and luxuriant flights of endless variety.[19]

Ernst Ludwig Gerber's famous encomium on Haydn in the *Lexikon* of 1790 elaborates on this theme, and may be indebted to the particularly happy formulation of the last sentence just quoted:

> He often assigns a crucial role to parts which usually, in works by other composers, constitute merely insignificant filling. Every harmonic artifice is at his command, even those from the Gothic age of the grey contrapuntists. But instead of their former stiffness, they assume a pleasing manner as soon as he prepares them for our ears. He has a great gift for making a piece sound familiar. In this way, despite all the contrapuntal artifices therein, he achieves a popular style and is agreeable to every amateur.[20]

Burney may have heard some of Op. 20 during his visit to Vienna. He speaks of a concert after dinner at the house of the English ambassador on 4 September 1772, a dinner at which he was seated next to Gluck:

> At length the company, which was now much increased, became impatient to hear mademoiselle Gluck sing, which she did, sometimes with her uncle's

---

[18] Finscher, *Studien zur Geschichte des Streichquartetts*, 1: p. 234.
[19] A. Peter Brown, "The First English Biography of Haydn," *Musical Quarterly* 59 (1973): 346.
[20] The translation is by Warren Kirkendale, *Fugue and Fugato*, p. 150.

accompaniment, on the harpsichord only, and sometimes with more instruments, in so exquisite a manner, that I could not conceive it possible for any vocal performance to be more perfect . . . Between the vocal parts of this delightful concert, we had some exquisite quartets, by Haydn, executed in the utmost perfection; the first violin by M. Starzler [Joseph Starzer], who played the Adagios with uncommon feeling and expression; the second violin by M. Ordonetz [Karl von Ordonez]; count Brühl played the tenor [viola], and M. Weigel [Joseph Weigl], an excellent performer on the violoncello, the bass. All who had any share in this concert, finding the company attentive, and in a disposition to be pleased, were animated to that true pitch of enthusiasm, which, from the ardor of the fire within them, is communicated to others, and sets all around ablaze; so that the contention between the performers and hearers, was only who should please, and should applaud the most!

Five slow movements in Op. 20 are marked *Adagio* (only the slow movement in the Quartet in E♭ is not). It seems likely that the cellist Weigl, Haydn's trusted friend, was the source by which the quartets were procured. They would have been the very latest quartets, surely, those just composed. Typical for concerts of that time, whether at the formal academies in the Burgtheater or at a soirée such as Burney describes, was the mixing of vocal and instrumental music, the latter taking second rank.

A few months earlier, on 28 May 1772, Carl Zinzendorf reported on the musical entertainment after dinner at Esterháza, the magnificent palace and gardens that were largely complete by then. The occasion was a visit by Prince Louis de Rohan, emissary of Louis XV: "Bon diner, puis Concert, deux chanteuses chanterent fort bien. Hayden joua du violon."[21] Haydn's place as Kapellmeister was at the keyboard, whether the singers performed with orchestra or not. His playing the violin was more of a curiosity and perhaps refers to chamber music.

The mixing of professional musicians with amateurs noted by Burney is characteristic of the time. Starzer and Ordonez were among Vienna's finest composers; Count Brühl, son of the famous Saxon statesman of the same name, belonged to the high nobility. On a celebrated occasion in 1785, recorded by Leopold Mozart, the quartet players admitted a similar social mixture:

On Saturday evening Herr Joseph Haydn and the two Barons Tinti came to see us and the new quartets were performed, or rather the three new ones [K. 458, 464 and 465] Wolfgang has added to the other three that we have already. The new ones are somewhat easier, but at the same time excellent compositions.

[21] Edward Olleson, "Haydn in the Diaries of Count Karl von Zinzendorf," in *Haydn Yearbook* (1963–64), pp. 45–63.

FIGURE 5.3.
General plan
of Esterháza.

Haydn said to me: "Before God and as an honest man I tell you that your son is
the greatest composer known to me either in person or by name. He has taste
and what is more, the most profound knowledge of composition." (Letter to his
daughter, 14–16 February 1785)

A year before Haydn wrote the Op. 20 Quartets, an essay was published
in Berlin calling him to task for want of correctness and contrapuntal
acumen:

Now the works of Heiden, Toeschin, Cannabich, Filz, Pugnani, and Campioni
are getting the upper hand. One need be only a quasi-connoisseur to notice the

emptiness, the strange mixture of comic and serious, of the trifling and the moving, that reigns everywhere. Errors against good writing, especially against the rhythm, and for the most part a great ignorance of counterpoint, without which no good trio can be made, are very frequent in all these composers. The only person who praises them is one to whom a glittering melodic line is everything. The new-fangled trios are often only solos or duets, such as anyone could write. The very same applies to the quartets of these gentlemen.[22]

Haydn took this and other similar criticisms very much to heart, as we know from the response he wrote in his autobiographical sketch of 1776, in which he cut short descriptions of his life and works in order to refute such silly vilifications at length:

In the chamber-musical style I have been fortunate enough to please almost all nations except the Berliners; this is shown by the public newspapers and letters addressed to me. I only wonder that the Berlin gentlemen, who are otherwise so reasonable, preserve no medium in their criticism of my music, for in one weekly paper they praise me to the skies, while in another they dash me sixty fathoms deep into the earth, and this without explaining why; I know well why: because they are incapable of performing some of my works, and are too conceited to take the trouble to understand them properly, and for other reasons which, with God's help, I will answer in good time. *Herr Capellmeister* von Dittersdorf, in Silesia, wrote to me recently and asked me to defend myself against their hard words, but I answered that one swallow doesn't make the Summer; and that perhaps one of these days some unprejudiced person would stop their tongues, as happened to them once before when they accused me of monotony. Despite this, they try very hard to get all my works, as Herr Baron von Sviten [sic], the Imperial and Royal Ambassador at Berlin, told me only last winter, when he was in Vienna; but enough of this.[23]

It is possible that by writing the Op. 20 Quartets of 1772, Haydn was responding in a more trenchant and telling way to the critical remarks published a year earlier.

No one could claim that Haydn's quartets lacked contrapuntal solidity after Op. 20. No one with any sense would have ranked Haydn with Carl

[22] Johann Christoph Stockman, *Critischer Entwurf einer auserlesenen Bibliothek für Liebhaber der Philosophie und schönen Wissenschaften. Zum Gebrauch akademischer Vorlesungen, vierte verbesserte und viel vermehrte Auflage* (Berlin, 1771). Foreword dated Hanau, 20 September 1770. For the original German of the passage, see Hubert Unverricht, *Geschichte des Streichtrios* (Tutzing, 1969), p. 94. The six composers' names occur in the same order and spelling in the middle of a long list of composers (beginning with Corelli and Tartini) who wrote trios for the violin in Johann Georg Sulzer's *Allgemeine Theorie der schönen Künste*, 2 vols. (Leipzig, 1771–74), s.v. "Trio" (the article is by Johann Abraham Peter Schulz).
[23] Landon, *Haydn*, 2: 399.

Joseph Toeschi, Christian Cannabich, Anton Filtz, Gaetano Pugnani, and Carlo Antonio Campioni in the first place. Haydn rarely denigrated his fellow musicians. Even so, by the time he had written Op. 20, he must have realized that he did not belong in the same company with these assorted Mannheimers and Italians, no matter how talented they were at times. What Op. 20 represented to Haydn and to the history of music was well summed up by Tovey: "With op. 20 the historical development of Haydn's quartets reaches its goal; and further progress is not progress in any historical sense, but simply the difference between one masterpiece and the next . . . no later set of six quartets, not even op. 76, is, on its own plane, so uniformly weighty and so varied in substance as op. 20."[24] Haydn's contemporaries realized this as well. Gerber in his *Lexikon* of 1790 wrote that Haydn emerged "in his full greatness as a quartet composer" in the works of Op. 20. Mozart and Beethoven confirmed as much when writing their own quartets. In its own right, and as a set of quartets that was of such great importance to Mozart, Beethoven, and even Brahms (who once owned the autograph and edited a study score), Op. 20 deserves to be considered one of the central monuments of Western music.

Symphonies: Perfection of the Cyclic Principle

ATTEMPTS to set the minor-mode works Haydn composed between 1767 and 1772 apart, as a kind of gloomy *Sturm und Drang* enclave reflecting his personal trials, are doomed to failure on more than one account. During these years Haydn wrote two sparkling comedies adapted from librettos by Carlo Goldoni, *Lo speziale* (1768) and *Le pescatrici* (1769–70). In the second, Prince Lindoro receives a metaphorical "stormy seas" aria, "Varca il mar di sponda in sponda" (Crossing the sea from shore to shore), which Haydn sets as the one minor-mode piece in the work, replete with slurred pairs of eighth notes in the violas suggesting waves (as is made explicit in the marine chorus of Act III, final scene), constant sixteenth-notes in the second violins lending a churning effect, and tumultuous syncopated figures in the first violins. As this one stormy aria is to the totality of the opera, so are Haydn's so-called *Sturm und Drang* pieces to the totality of his oeuvre—numerically a barely significant fraction. The composer held a good opinion of *Le pescatrici;* he cited it in his autobiographical letter of six years later, whereas he did not see fit to mention any of his operas of the 1760s for more limited forces, nor

[24] Tovey, "Haydn," pp. 537–38.

did he mention his German stage works at all. The high spirits and cheerfulness of these comic operas are not absent from many instrumental works of the same time.

Symphony No. 35 in B♭ offers a good case in point. It stands on the threshold of Haydn's presumed "romantic crisis," the autograph being dated 1 December 1767. The work may represent Haydn's welcome to Prince Esterházy upon his return from an autumn trip to Paris in 1767; it was probably performed in celebration of his name day, the feast of St. Nicholas on 8 December. Delightful qualities inform this symphony from the first measure to the last. The opening *Allegro di molto* in 3/4 begins with a gentle falling theme sung by the strings, *piano*, interrupted by a *forte* tutti, like a comment, to which the strings respond by reiterating their quiet fall to the tonic. A galloping figure follows (Example 5.6). If this sounds familiar, it may be because of Mozart's use of the figure in the first movement of his Symphony No. 39 in E♭ (which is also in 3/4). But Boccherini had used the same galloping figure as early as the finale of his String Trio in F composed in 1760 (Gérard No. 77), and its origins are to be sought in Italian comic opera from even earlier. Haydn used a similar figure in the giddy "rustic wedding" aria of *Le pescatrici*, "Fra cetre e cembali ti sposerò" (I shall marry you to the sound of zithers and cymbals; this text is from Goldoni's *Le virtuose ridicole*). Gassmann was also fond of using the figure in his comic operas, which, when translated from Italian into German for various stages, exerted considerable impact on Viennese Singspiel. The *locus classicus* of the galloping figure was reached with Monostatos' aria in *Die Zauberflöte*.

Haydn uses the galloping figure in his symphony to propel the movement into the long transition to V, which ends only in m. 39 after an exciting unison passage in hemiola rhythms. Instead of introducing a new theme, Haydn then sounds the main theme with a new continuation, which picks up chromatic inflections (from m. 28) and the galloping figure as it goes along. The melodic line is continuous, finally pushing up to a high 5 5♯ 6 as the climax. The intense, singing quality of these chromatic surges brings to mind the first movement in another of Mozart's symphonies, No. 33 in B♭

EXAMPLE 5.6. *Haydn, Symphony No. 35, I*

(which is also in 3/4). The development is substantial, forty-five measures following an exposition of sixty measures. Haydn takes care to link the two tonic areas of the reprise with a long rising bass line that keeps the momentum going. (Beethoven was one of the principal beneficiaries of this technique for linking one section with another.) The *Andante* in 2/4 that follows begins somewhat mysteriously, sounding for a moment as if it too were in the keynote, B♭. Any ambiguity is resolved by the end of its five-measure phrase, the real mystery of which is that its beginning is an ending and will eventually close the entire movement. Chromatic inflections in line with those of the first movement are introduced very subtly in subsequent movements. The rise F F♯ G from the end of the first movement is incorporated into the second, then becomes the main point and ending of both strains of the Menuet.

In the finale, *Presto* in 2/4, two horns in B♭ *alto* come into full play, sounding a rising fanfare to get the movement under way. Violins alone offer a soft answer, the firsts playing a descending figure with turns, the seconds accompanying with a rocking eighth-note bass, anchored on the tonic pedal. (Here Haydn adumbrates the main theme of the first movement of Symphony No. 99 in E♭, which begins with violins alone, the firsts descending with melodic turns above the rocking bass of the seconds. Not only is the Symphony No. 35 a marvel of good humor, but its prophetic finale unfolds a melodic and textural idea that still appealed to the Haydn of the London symphonies.) To partner such an attractive main theme, Haydn invents a droll second idea—comic patter in a stream of eighth notes that plays with the choice between upper and lower auxiliary notes and between legato and staccato articulations. The rising three-chord fanfare makes a few appearances in the development and finally sweeps the movement away at the close with a last "fare-thee-well." Each movement of this work is original and full of interest (an exception being the trio of the Menuet, which functions merely as subdominant contrast). What is more, the movements seem to belong uniquely to the bright and cheerful world of this particular symphony. But it is the finale that takes the honors and remains in the ear. Haydn is well on the way, with the Symphony No. 35, to achieving his own personal kind of cyclical style, wherein the finale tops all other movements in interest.

The undated Symphony No. 36 in E♭ also begins with a very fast movement *(Vivace)* in 3/4 and also deploys the little galloping figure of Example 5.6, which may indicate a temporal proximity to the Symphony No. 35. But in general, No. 36 does not attain the level of finesse in No. 35.

Three symphonies in C date from the late 1760s. No. 38, written in 1769, lacks any memorable qualities. The long harmonic sequence with which the development of the first movement begins seems like a throwback. The four-measure theme of the second movement, in the first violins, has its last measure echoed by the muted second violins, unaccompanied, and this exchange provides the idea out of which Haydn spins the whole movement. Wild leaps occupy the solo oboe after the double bar in the middle of the otherwise innocuous trio; the finale is also made a showcase for the first oboe, which may have to do with a particular player in Haydn's band at the time.

Symphony No. 41 in C, composed by 1770, is another work in the festival spirit associated with this key. The rising thirds followed by falling thirds in the violins, *piano*, after the first tutti chord, *forte*, make an attractive beginning. Haydn uses hemiola in this *Allegro con spirito* in 3/4 at the same place he did in the opening movement of Symphony No. 35. Nothing in the remaining movements seems as memorable as the opening of the first movement. Another symphony in C that belongs to the same class and was written about the same time (there is a penciled date of 1769 on Elssler's copy) is the rather better-known No. 48, called *Maria Theresa*—its pomp befits the imperial condition. In all three symphonies in C the trumpet and timpani parts found in modern editions were added after the date of composition.

Two other symphonies from the late 1760s are No. 58 in F and No. 59 in A *(Fire)*. No. 58 is a work of modest dimensions, making few demands. Its opening movement is another *Allegro* in 3/4, succeeded by an *Andante* in 2/4 that is even more dominated by triplet motion than the first movement. The *Menuet alla zoppa* ("limping") forgoes triplets for dotted rhythm, while the finale, *Presto* in 3/8, concentrates on accented offbeats.

More rewarding on the whole is the *Fire* Symphony in A. In the first movement, a *Presto* in common time, an intriguing soft and sustained passage follows the loud and motion-packed opening. The second movement, *Andante o più tosto Allegretto* in 3/4, begins in tonic minor but finishes in tonic major, for which arrival the winds are saved. It sounds rather like a minuet. Haydn must not have considered this problematic, because he does nothing to set apart the real Menuet, which shares the same rising motif with the previous movement, but in major; in the *minore* trio he resorts to the chains of eighth notes slurred in pairs that were abundantly deployed in the *Andante*.

The best movement is again the last, *Allegro assai* in cut time, which sounds a rising fanfare theme in the horns like that of the finale of Symphony No. 35, but here they are unaccompanied. Similar too in both finales are the secondary ideas, chattering strings of eighth notes with play between the upper and lower auxiliary tones. Haydn saves his stunning initial idea—the horns' solo fanfare—until the end of the reprise, where it is given a new continuation, bringing the work to a close in a flurry of excitement (cf. Mozart's repeated use of the same fanfare in the finale of his Violin Concerto in B♭, K. 207, Example 8.15). As in the Symphony No. 35, a shift of interest to the end of the work is evident, so that the finale offers not just a rounding off but a new and better perspective of the whole, as if from a higher range of mountains, and is so arranged that reaching the very end of the finale becomes the equivalent of scaling the ultimate peak.

The early 1770s were for Haydn a period of still richer symphonic masterpieces, during which a deepening of the cyclic ideal went hand in hand with ever broader and more powerful musical spans. The Symphony No. 52 in c, already discussed, stands supreme of its kind, but the *Farewell* Symphony (No. 45) of 1772 is the more pivotal work. Beginning in the odd key of f♯, the work shares a few features with the other minor-mode symphonies up to this time, but it also forecasts Haydn's manner of treating the minor mode in subsequent phases of his career. The horrors of hell, as they might be depicted in a frightening Lenten sermon, received their most extreme incarnation in the sternly severe Symphony No. 52; they no longer haunt the *Farewell* Symphony, which Griesinger refers to as "an extended musical joke." When its *Allegro assai* in 3/4 bursts upon us, impetuous and beset with strong syncopations, we seem to be in for another round of composer's ire. (Did the prince wince at what started out to be another stormy work?) Haydn chooses an odd destination for the prima parte: the minor dominant instead of the relative major. And something unusual happens in the development. In a movement of nearly unrelenting agitation, the only slackening of tension comes here, with a soft lyric theme that is new. The *Adagio* that follows is in A, the relative major—Haydn hereby bids farewell to the monotonal cycle in minor, which had so occupied him. In later years the normal choice for the second movement of a work beginning in minor will be the relative major.

The *Adagio* is in a "light" meter, 3/8, and is mostly graceful and bright but does not lack a few darker colors, such as the minor and chromatic patch ending with rising chromatic appoggiature. The *Menuet Allegretto* introduces a key, F♯, that could have been expected only in its Trio, after f♯ had been properly restored. Haydn has prepared us for a later moment in the symphony when A will yield directly to F♯. At first a jaunty duet for the two violin sections, the Menuet is soon jolted by a flat sixth, *forte*, a jarring note that hints of something awry at Esterháza.

The finale *Presto* in cut time begins in f♯ as might be expected, and continues in regular sonata form, with modulation to A and repetition of the prima parte. After the development and reprise, the music seems ready to come to an end in f♯ when there is a pause on V and a moment of silence (rests with fermatas). Instead of the expected cadence, an *Adagio* in A softly steals upon the ear, with the same 3/8 movement as the previous *Adagio*. Such a return to the tempo, meter, and key of an earlier movement in the finale could have had few if any precedents. Haydn reinforces the link by bringing back not only the graceful mood of the slow movement but also the expressive rising appoggiature embedded in a descending arpeggio. As this gracious music continues, the orchestra gradually loses strength, one part leaving the group after another. The second oboe and first horn are the last winds to depart, immediately after which the music reaches the dominant of f♯. After another moment of silence the *Adagio* theme is sounded, wanly, by the few remaining strings in F♯, whereupon we relive the unusual experience of hearing this key following upon A, as the orchestra continues to dwindle in strength. From a string quartet the band shrinks to a string trio, and finally only two violins are left—Tomasini and perhaps Haydn himself. They end *pianissimo* with F♯ on top and A♯ beneath.

There are various accounts about the origin of this extraordinary work. According to Griesinger, the symphony was written with younger orchestra members in mind, for whose wives the still incomplete castle of Esterháza could not provide accommodation.

> In Prince Esterházy's orchestra were several young married men who in summer, when the Prince stayed at Esterháza castle, had to leave their wives behind in Eisenstadt. Contrary to his custom, the Prince once wished to extend his stay in Esterháza by several weeks. The fond husbands, especially dismayed at this news, turned to Haydn and pleaded with him to do something. Haydn had the notion of writing a symphony (known as the Farewell Symphony) in which one instrument after the other is silent. This symphony was performed at the first opportunity in the presence of the Prince, and each of the musicians was directed, as soon as his part was finished, to put out his candle, pack up his music and, with his instrument under his arm, to go away. [In French the work was called "Symphonie ou l'on s'en va."] The Prince and his audience understood the meaning of this pantomime at once, and the next day came the order to depart from Esterháza.

That Haydn was able to send a dramatic message with this symphony is clear. But he achieved even more in musical terms: this is a work written in three principal keys, the recurrence of which ties the whole work together in a unique way. The finale resumes, in order, the keys of the first three movements: f♯ A F♯. In cyclic terms, the finale "explains" the whole symphony.[25]

[25] This discussion of Symphony No. 45 was written in 1983 and hence is not indebted to James Webster, *Haydn's "Farewell" Symphony and the Idea of Classical Style* (Cambridge, 1991).

Symphonies Nos. 42 in D (dated 1771) and 43 in E♭ *(Mercury)* form a quartet with Symphonies Nos. 44 and 52 in that they appear consecutively in Haydn's thematic catalogue. No. 42 begins with an unusually spacious sonata form, a *Moderato e maestoso* of 224 measures in cut time, full of harmonic and rhythmic surprises. The second movement, *Andante e cantabile* in 3/8, is in A, with the lovely writing for horns this key often brings—they enter only with the reprise. Haydn cut two passages out of this movement with the remark "because it was for entirely too learned ears." The passages in question bring the music to a virtual halt, as the first violins, unaccompanied, utter little melodic sighs, surrounded by silence. He tried something similar in the first movement of the String Quartet in g of Op. 20 (1772). Possibly the composer was willing to allow himself such whimsical moments, strongly reminiscent of Emanuel Bach, in quartets and sonatas, but was more wary in symphonies, where he had a larger audience to serve, both at Esterháza and in the great world beyond. The length and nature of the opening movement may have prompted Haydn to seek something besides sonata form for the finale. In any case, he chose a multisectional *Scherzando e presto* in 2/4 that is like a French rondeau, with its *minore* and its varied repeats of the refrain. The movement represents a step in the direction of creating his own kind of rondo finale, which will eventually be less dainty than this and less fragmented into small sections.

Haydn posed no mean challenge to players and listeners alike with his Symphony No. 43 in E♭, which acquired the nickname *Mercury* in the nineteenth century, perhaps because it is such a mercurial and many-sided work. It is a twin of Symphony No. 52 in c because of certain motivic resemblances and ranks with that work in loftiness of conception. The first movement, *Allegro* in 3/4, begins with tutti *forte* chords on tonic E♭, which alternate with soft yearning passages for strings only. By the third such passage the work has already established an individual presence. Haydn calls attention here to the false interval E♭ B♮ resolving to C (cf. Symphony No. 52) and giving rise to another chromatic alteration on the way up to the third degree (Example 5.7a). The passage is made more poignant by being rendered by the violins in octaves against lower strings in unison (actually in octaves too because of the contrabasses). To get this passage perfectly in tune requires the delicacy of a fine string quartet. The first two phrases were each of four measures; the third, quoted in the example, extends to six measures. In the following phrase Haydn invents a repeated six-measure continuation combining features of the three phrases that came before, with subtle rhythmic shifts and a rich use of the IV^7 chord in place of what had been merely IV. This lyric idea, even lovelier than what preceded it, is chosen for extension in the reprise. Moreover, the IV^7 chord, sounded so nonchalantly as a prelude to the ii⁶ᐟ⁵ chord, engenders a properly old-fashioned sequence of fifths with suspensions to close both parts of the movement.

Noteworthy in the seconda parte is the false reprise only fifteen measures into the development, followed by a dramatic silence (recalling the use of dramatic pauses in Symphonies Nos. 26 and 39). In this case, coming after the first four measures of a false reprise, silence creates the effect of a pause to take stock and ask, "Can this be right?" The real reprise arrives by a surprising harmonic maneuver and extended chromatic rises in quarter notes, slurred by the measure as in Example 5.7a. With 254 measures total, this *Allegro* is one of the longest sonata forms Haydn had written up to this date.

In the second movement, an *Adagio* in A♭, Haydn introduces the false interval from near the beginning of the *Allegro* in a new guise, so that the rising appoggiatura is followed by a descending one (Example 5.7b). The

EXAMPLE 5.7. *Haydn, Symphony No. 43*

importance of this figure might not be guessed from its medial position in the prima parte but becomes apparent in the development section, where it predominates. The theme of the Menuetto begins with the repeated tonic degree, like the opening of the first movement, and shares also the emphasis on the second, fifth, and sixth degrees. Both strains of the Trio begin as if they were in the key of c but then move away toward E♭ (Example 5.7c). One reason for such an odd beginning could be Haydn's wish to keep the false interval E♭ B♮ lingering in our ears. The conjunct thirds with slur also hark back to the first movement.

The finale, *Allegro* in cut time, begins with an arpeggiated tonic, followed by falling-second melodic sighs that sound vaguely familiar; Haydn points up the A♭ G fall by a melodic turn and rhythmic augmentation (making for a five-measure phrase), helping us to recall that A♭ G was also the destination of the melody that opened the symphony. After the dominant is established, there is a mysterious soft progression moving in slow chords, by the measure, recalling the rhythmic augmentation in the main theme (Example 5.7d; the example illustrates the chords' return in the tonic during the reprise). The passage cannot help recalling as well the ascending versus descending minor second that Haydn emphasized in the *Adagio*. Could it be that Haydn was attempting to tie together the whole symphony in his finale? Another hint that he was comes in the climactic passage with flat seventh and raised fifth that becomes in the reprise E♭ D♭ B♮ C, as if in final explanation of the mysterious false interval from the symphony's beginning.

The movement could end at the double bar with repeat sign in m. 161. But Haydn is by no means finished. In a long coda of 41 measures, pushing the finale closer to the length of the opening *Allegro*, he begins over again with the main theme. A measure and a half of silence follows the sighing A♭ G, now placed in the high octave; and emphatic cadences with A♭ G on top lead to a subdominant chord (A♭ in the bass) with the first violins up on high C, from which they drift down chromatically, doubled by the second violins an octave below. It is as if the composer were saying, "Yes, I meant those chromatics in octaves at the beginning of the symphony as something special!" Perhaps the most wonderful passage of all is the *pianissimo* chordal one at the bottom of the violins' unaccompanied chromatic fall. Here Haydn presents all twelve chromatic tones in the space of a few measures, as diminished-seventh chords are protracted to two measures and even longer, followed by silence. Several emphatic cadences conclude a coda that resolves the mystery and brings the work to an end. This coda is scaled to the size of the whole symphony, not just the finale, and addresses issues raised from the work's inception. It helps the finale sum up the experience of the entire work. Not only has Haydn achieved another instance of the uniquely appropriate and conclusive finale, he has taken another step toward a uniquely coherent cycle of four movements. He would pursue this path with notable success during the years 1772–74, a period especially fertile in symphonic masterworks.

The dated symphonies of 1772 besides the *Farewell* are No. 46 in the unusual key of B and No. 47 in G. The Symphony No. 46 begins with a tutti unison figure, a leap down a sixth and then an abrupt upturning marked staccato that has the effect of a verbal question (Example 5.8a). The answer comes in the more placid descending phrase, marked *piano*, which floats down with legato slurs from the fifth to the tonic, with the barest touch of leading tone under the tonic. Haydn must have assumed that an unmarked beginning like this would be played *forte* by his band, otherwise the *piano* makes no sense. His next move is to harmonize the initial idea, which then receives a new and much longer answer. Of the two original components, the question gets the most attention in this movement, especially in the development, which opens with entrances of this motif overlapping canonically, but the answer becomes more important for the symphony as a whole. The composer brings back the canonic overlapping idea with a running counterpoint against it just after the reprise begins, an area he often chooses for thorough recomposition and more working out.

The amateur performers of Haydn symphonies, so numerous in monasteries throughout Austria, probably greeted the composer's choice of the tonic minor (b) for the second movement with some relief—the key of B, with its five sharps, posed no small challenge. At Melk Abbey there is a copy of this symphony, dated 1777, that has been transposed down a half tone to the more ordinary B♭.[26] The work, first published by the Bureau

EXAMPLE 5.8. *Haydn, Symphony No. 46*

a. I

Vivace

b. III Menuet

Allegretto

c. IV Presto scherzando

[26] *Haydn: Werke. Sinfonien, 1767–1772*, ed. C.-G. Stellan Mörner, Kritischer Bericht (Munich, 1966), p. 30. The horns are omitted from the Melk copy, and yet they play a crucial role at the very end of the work.

d'Abonnement in Paris in 1775, may represent the first printed symphony in B major.[27] Its second movement is a *Poco Adagio* in 6/8 with dotted rhythms—a kind of siciliana, but with none of the sadness often associated with this kind of Neapolitan music; on the contrary, there is a faintly comic aura in the way the cellos and basses are made to echo the little staccato theme of the first violins, for, try as hard as they will, their nature prevents them from tossing off this figure as lightly as the violins. Yet another of Haydn's echo jokes is being played out.

The *Menuet Allegretto* places the violins in octaves, playing a theme with slurred pairs of eighth notes alternating with long notes, the significance of which does not become apparent until, in the middle of the second strain, the violins play something close to a retrograde version of the same, a moment that Haydn singles out by a *subito piano*, the first soft music in the movement (Example 5.8b). A melodic fall to the tonic from the fifth degree, with pairs of slurred eighth notes, refers back to the beginning of the symphony (the answering half of the first theme). The trio takes the minor tonic, as is so often the case with Haydn when the slow movement is also in tonic minor. It revels in unexpected dynamic accents and offers in addition the oddity of a first strain that is not repeated.

Haydn begins his finale, *Presto scherzando* in cut time, with the same fall to the tonic, and with the leading tone under the tonic too, as in the first movement (Example 5.8c). He inserts one of his long pauses at the end of the prima parte, and the development does not proceed very far before mimicking the same pause. The reprise comes early, or is it a false reprise? We are left in doubt, since much is recapitulated in the tonic and yet there is more development, ending with a long dominant pedal, which seems to signal the real reprise. But to our surprise it is the soft falling phrase from the Menuet that returns, sounding very wistful in its new context. By this genial stroke Haydn has once again tied together the whole symphony in its final moments. The recall of the Menuet ends up in the air, without a cadence, upon which the *Presto* theme returns, but it does not get beyond the falling fourth and repeated note of its second measure before getting "stuck" and sounding over and over. Then there is a silence and a double-time augmentation of the same figure, followed by an even longer silence. Haydn then outdoes himself, in a feat akin to making a score during the last play of the game. The two horns intone a low B pedal, *piano*, a new sonority that could not have been anticipated, over which the violins bid farewell to the theme with a feint to the subdominant, balanced by the dominant yielding to the tonic, *pianissimo*, reenacted as two full chords, V - I, *fortissimo*.

[27] Boccherini's String Trio in E, Op. 4 No. 3, printed by Vénier in 1768, contains a Minuetto in B, but Boccherini never used B as a principal key.

The idea of bringing back a previous movement in the finale has obvious connections with the *Farewell* Symphony of the same year, and the two works are close in other ways as well. If the *Farewell* Symphony is an "extended musical joke" making itself explicit from the pantomime of the departing players, Symphony No. 46 is no less an exercise in musical wit, but relies solely on the resources of tonal art, so thoroughly mastered by Haydn at age forty that he needed no extramusical aids to produce high comedy.[28] As in the *Mercury* Symphony, thematic recurrence helps to unify the cycle as a whole. Bringing back a third-movement theme in the finale anticipates Beethoven's Fifth Symphony.[29]

Symphony No. 47 in G is one of several from which Mozart jotted down the incipit.[30] One reason why he was attracted to it is immediately apparent in the first theme, which begins with the four-note Credo motive he used so many times, and which Haydn had used earlier in the outstanding Symphony No. 13 of 1763. Horns announce the first two tones *forte* in dotted march rhythm, answered by the legato phrase of the unison strings, *piano*. The third tone is given to the second oboe, joined by the horns. This tone is protracted for five measures instead of two and extended up to high C before being resolved by the first oboe (Example 5.9). The intensity resulting from this prolonged dominant seventh chord at the beginning of the movement accurately predicts a long and powerful development, preparing a reprise that arrives with a surprise: tonic minor. This time the dominant is protracted even longer. Haydn then elides and reorders his material so that the arrival of the tone B in the treble and tonic resolution coincide with the onset of the rather dainty second theme in triplets, which serves as a perfect foil for the insistent martial rhythms of the main theme.

Burney refers to this symphony in a letter of 6 September 1782 to his friend Thomas Twining when discussing works by Haydn available in keyboard arrangement: "There are two printed by Bland for the Harpsichord, one in G—which is begun by the French Horn. I forget how. But something like this [notation]."[31] Burney was in Vienna ten years earlier, when this

---

[28] See Hartmut Krones, "Das 'Hohe Komische' bei Haydn," *Österreichische Musikzeitschrift* 38 (1983): 2–8.

[29] As pointed out by Charles Rosen, *The Classical Style: Haydn, Mozart, Beethoven* (New York, 1971), pp. 147–48.

[30] The incipits are four in number, written down by Mozart in 1782–83 on a piece of paper preserved in the Historical Society of Philadelphia. See Köchel-Einstein, *Verzeichnis*, 3rd ed. (Ann Arbor, Mich., 1947), no. 387[d.] The other three incipits are from Haydn's Symphonies No. 62 and No. 75 and an unidentified work in C that looks as if it may be by a later-generation Mannheim composer.

[31] *The Letters of Dr. Charles Burney*, vol. 1: *1751–1784*, ed. Alvaro Ribeiro (Oxford, 1991), p. 378. I have substituted full words for Burney's abbreviations.

EXAMPLE 5.9. *Haydn, Symphony No. 47, I*

symphony was new. It is a pity he did not journey to visit Haydn then. He does recount hearing admirable orchestral works as overtures and "act tunes" in the Kärntnerthor Theater that were composed by Haydn, Hofmann, and Vanhal. He was even more enthusiastic about the orchestral music he heard in the Burgtheater, though he could not discover the name of the composer. Judging from Burney's wonder at the music's originality, the composer was probably Haydn.

Haydn did not specify a tempo for the first movement of Symphony No. 47 in his autograph, presumably because the dotted rhythm in common time signaled a march tempo. The second movement, in 2/4, he marked *Un poco adagio, cantabile.* Burney says that it is "on an old organ point," a reference to the contrapuntal interaction, with imitation and suspended dissonances, between the two violins, muted and in unison, and the lower strings. The winds are used to enhance the middle part of this theme, the last part of which is like the first but with treble and bass inverted. Haydn next proceeds to write variations on his thirty-measure theme, of the figural sort that progress to ever smaller note values. The fourth and final variation restores the theme to its original condition but with wind participation throughout, to which is added a long coda (cf. the variation movement in the String Quartet in D from Op. 20 of the same year). Haydn was probably the first composer to use variation form in the slow movement of a symphony.[32]

The Menuet continues to show him in a very contrapuntal frame of mind. This is the celebrated "Menuet al Roverso" with its accompanying "Trio al Roverso," the second strains of which are produced by reading the first strains backward. Such skill went into the task that the music sounds perfectly normal either way. Haydn must have been pleased with his feat; he used it again in the Harpsichord Sonata in A (Hob. XVI:24) of the following year, a very rare occurrence with this composer, whose voluminous works show few cases of borrowing (except in the semiprivate art represented by the baryton trios). Burney, in the letter of 1782 quoted above, has nothing to say about the third movement, but he remarks of the finale, a *Presto assai* in cut time: "Mind in the last Allegro en Rondeau, how he returns to the Subject." The movement is one of those, frequent with Haydn, in which the first theme also does service as the second theme, lending a possible cause for confusion with the rondo finale. But the movement is in sonata form. It contains a full statement of the main theme in the subdominant, which also may have suggested analogies with the rondeau. The feature Burney pointed out to his correspondent occurs just before the reprise: a rhythmic augmentation of the arpeggiated dominant chord (Haydn used augmentation to good effect in all three symphonies dated 1772). An equally attractive feature is the soft and protracted diminished chord resolving to tonic 6/4 near the end of both parts.

Symphony No. 51 in B♭ also belongs in the company of Symphonies Nos. 45, 46, and 47, although it cannot be dated exactly. The first movement, *Vivace* in 3/4, begins with contrasting ideas (like No. 46 in B), the first fanfare-like and ascending to high B♭, *forte*, the second gently falling, *piano*, to which a *pianissimo* falling third is appended, doubled by one of the two horns, *piano*. Horns in B♭ (alto) play a prominent role throughout the symphony

[32] Elaine R. Sisman, "Haydn's Variations" (Ph.D. diss., Princeton University, 1978), p. 123.

and help give it a special color. The second movement, a serenade in E♭ and in 2/4, starts with a solo for first horn that contrasts high passage work with the instrument's lowest pedal tones, reminiscent of Haydn's Horn Concerto of 1762. The Menuetto offers the oddity of two Trios, in the second of which the horns frisk about from the top to the bottom of their range.

The finale of Symphony No. 51, an *Allegro* in 2/4, is divided into many small sections, each repeated, like the finale of Symphony No. 42 (dated 1771). But this finale is even closer to the French rondeau—there are episodes in both IV and vi, and the variation element is lessened. The instrumentation of the refrain is varied upon its repetitions but not the refrain itself, except for an initial variation following its first statement. In the first return Haydn lets the horns play part of the theme, then in the second return, after the episode in the relative minor, they play almost the entire theme. A short coda ensues, ending this lighthearted and mirthful work with the identical cadential chords that sounded in the fourth measure of the first movement.

Examples of Haydn's wit abound in Symphony No. 51. In the first movement the contrast between rumbling basses, *forte,* and frolicking violins, *piano,* all playing with the interval of the third, suggests a kind of "beauty and the beast" dialogue. At the outcome of this passage there are *forte* and *piano* alternations at very short range and diminished chords leading to tonic 6/4, as at the end of Symphony No. 47. But perhaps an even more characteristic feature placing this symphony in company with the symphonies of 1772 is the rhythmic augmentation from sixteenth notes to eighths, to quarters, and finally to half notes at the same spot. For sheer exuberance and brio and a sheen all its own, Symphony No. 51 deserves to stand beside another symphony in B♭, No. 35 of 1767, with which we began this discussion of Haydn's major-mode symphonies.

Only one symphony, No. 50 in C, is dated 1773 with certainty. It is not, on the whole, up to the level of the symphonies of 1771–72, being rather retrospective in several aspects and almost coarse in some of its instrumentation. It is, on the other hand, on a par with Haydn's other symphonies in C written up to this date, and thus not an anomaly. A plausible conjecture connects its old-fashioned traits and its pomp with the visit of Empress Maria Theresa to Esterháza in 1773 (Figure 5.4).

One feature of Symphony No. 50 deserves close attention: its *Adagio e Maestoso* introduction, beginning with a rise through the triad up two octaves to high C. Haydn fashions the Menuet out of this same material. The end of the slow introduction, with bass descent C B♭ A A♭ G, becomes prophetic as well. A♭ supporting an augmented-sixth chord reappears in the Menuet, and a similar descending-bass progression prepares for the sub-

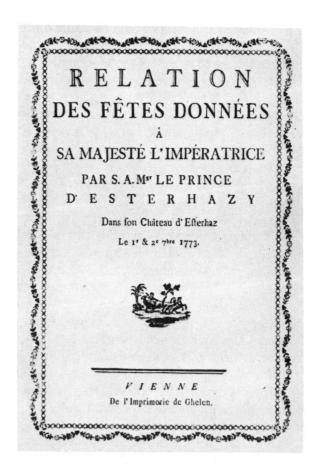

FIGURE 5.4. Festival book
for Maria Theresa's visit to
Esterháza in 1773.

dominant trio. Fourteen measures before the end of the finale, Haydn makes
a wild lunge toward the subdominant but lands instead upon a diminished
chord built up from A in the bass. In the next measure the basses descend
to A♭, generating an augmented-sixth chord, which then resolves to I⁶/⁴.³³
The augmented-sixth chord as climactic cadential progression in the key of
C forecasts some of the greatest moments in Haydn's last works (e.g., the
end of Part I of *The Creation*). The importance of this slow introduction and
its effect on the very end of the work opened up possibilities to Haydn that
he would pursue the following year, 1774, one of his greatest as a symphonist.

³³Modern editions omit the final A♭, and, following them, so do modern recordings. The editors
should go back to their sources, and if they do not find an A♭ where it must be for the sake of
musical grammar as well as musical logic, then they should supply one.

Another Empress Maria Theresa, consort to Emperor Francis II, is connected with the Symphony No. 60 in C, which was written by 1774. The empress requested a copy of the work with a view to having it performed in Vienna, prompting Haydn to refer to it in 1803 as "den alten Schmarrn," variously translated as "that old rubbish" and "the old pancake." (A *Kaiserschmarrn* today is a kind of scrambled egg pastry.) Much has been written about this "Sinfonia per la Comedia intitolato il Distratto" and its relationship to Jean-François Regnard's play *Le distrait* (1697), which was performed in German at Esterháza in 1774 by the Karl Wahr troupe. The symphony's six movements provide an entertainment akin to the old comedy itself, and a contemporary reviewer in the *Pressburger Zeitung* (6 July 1774) commented that Haydn "falls from the most affected pomposity directly into vulgarity, and Haydn and Regnard contend with one another [in] capricious absent-mindedness."[34] Musical non sequiturs such as occur in the first movement and the exotic scale in the trio of the Menuetto do indeed convey a sense of caprice and of having lost the thread of the argument. The way the *Allegro di molto* first movement gets sidetracked onto a long held subdominant chord offers another case in point. And Haydn makes use of several popular tunes, or what sound like popular tunes (one has been identified as the "Night-Watchman's Song"), which would account for the reviewer's mention of "vulgarity."

"Affected pomposity" might describe the beginning of the slow introductory *Adagio*, a reiterated C with dotted rhythm, which sweeps up an octave by scale from middle C, then proposes a rising triad in disjunct tones: C E G. The rest of the introduction is quiet and lyrical, except for an interjected *forte* vii$^{6/5}$ of V, forecasting the sudden *fortissimo* V$^{6/5}$ chord that later gets the movement back on track. When a military tattoo interrupts the *Adagio* reverie in F of the fifth movement, it recalls the initial fanfare of the slow introduction, which it extends by completing the rise through two octaves up to the high tonic. This rise predicts how the short finale *Prestissimo* will end: disjunct chords announcing the ascent C E G C. Thus is completed a cycle opened by the introductory *Adagio*. Haydn may have concocted this "omelette" (another possible translation of *Schmarrn*) in more of a hurry than usual, but even so it shows his preoccupation with tying the very end with the very beginning. For any number of reasons this symphony remains a shocker (yet another possible translation of *Schmarrn*).

The rise through the triad to the high octave appealed to Haydn as a way to begin or end a work long before Symphony No. 60. Already in the

---

[34] Robert A. Green, " 'Il distratto' of Regnard and Haydn: A Re-examination," *Haydn Yearbook* 11 (1980): 183–95. See also Elaine R. Sisman, "Haydn's Theater Symphonies," *JAMS* 43 (1990): 292–352.

Morzin-period Symphony No. 19 (1759–60) the composer begins and ends with the rise through the triad to high D, which arrives on an accented beat.[35] The fall through the triad to the tonic is equally common as a thematic generator. Of the many other works that could be cited, the Quartet in D, Op. 17 No. 6, exemplifies particularly well how Haydn took pains to establish a special bond between the opening gesture of a cyclic work and the very last thing heard.

Four symphonies bear the date 1774 in Haydn's autograph: No. 54 in G, No. 55 in E♭, No. 56 in C, and No. 57 in D. Once again the composer's main symphonic keys are represented here, almost as if he were thinking in terms of a complementary set of works. Forceful and original features abound in all four symphonies. No. 54 remains memorable for the strong emphasis it places on the tritone in the descent G F♯ D C♮, which motif figures prominently in both outer movements. Haydn added the slow introduction to the first movement apparently as an afterthought, and it too features several tritones. He also added trumpets and timpani later, making this his earliest symphony in G so orchestrated. One particular moment in the *Adagio assai* second movement stands out: the violins come to a languishing sigh on G F♯, which is answered by a resounding tutti reharmonization of the same two tones in disjunct chords—I! - V! in the key of G. It may be from this outburst that Haydn drew his idea for the beginning of the *Adagio maestoso* that prefaces the first movement.

Symphony No. 55 in E♭ is a slighter work on the whole, being more than ten minutes shorter, but it became a well-loved favorite under the nickname *Der Schulmeister* (as early as Gerber's *Lexikon* of 1812–14). The first movement is particularly distinguished, an *Allegro di molto* in 3/4 beginning with four tonic chords, *forte* |♩ ♩ ♩|♩ (and, not surprisingly, ending with them). This fast "curtain" suggests analogies with the way Beethoven chose to begin his *Eroica* Symphony, as does Haydn's soft and lyric main theme, with its alternation between trochaic rhythms and three quarter notes per measure. It is not impossible that Beethoven also learned from Haydn's stretching of four-measure phrases to six measures for climactic effect, as at the arrival on V of V. Haydn saves one nice touch for the reprise: the horns play the main theme. The ferociously dissonant chord thirty-two measures from the end makes us wonder again if Beethoven admired this movement and perhaps even remembered it at some level when writing his only symphony in E♭. The remaining movements do not match the level of the first, but the finale

[35] Jan LaRue, "Significant and Coincidental Resemblance Between Classical Themes," *JAMS* 16 (1961): 224–34, example 16, neglects to observe this parallel, presumably because his sole concern was with the incipits of both movements (their "themes"). A similar parallel, but more subtle, exists between the very beginning and ending of Haydn's Symphony No. 23 in G (LaRue's example 20).

shows Haydn experimenting with a combination of variation and rondo form (a rather questionable strategy in a symphony with a theme and variations as slow movement and also in 2/4, like the finale).

Symphony No. 56 in C brings the trumpets and drums usual to the key. Its *Allegro di molto* first movement in 3/4 resembles the identically labeled opening movement of *Der Schulmeister*. Here there is a unison plunge through two octaves from high C to middle C, which upon arrival is soft and sustained, initiating a scarcely disguised version of the old Credo motif C D F E in long notes. Loud fanfares interrupt after eight measures, this time rising and descending, a tattoo that will eventually close the movement. As in the parallel movement of *Der Schulmeister*, Haydn drops down a minor third for a surprise beginning to the development. Never before has his orchestra sounded so brilliant—the violins play up to high G to end the prima parte and high F at the end of the movement. The *Adagio* in F is at the same time nobly euphonious and filled with concertante display for solo bassoon and two oboes. A mysterious minor-mode disturbance, with the bass climbing slowly in long equal tones, contains the material out of which Haydn makes a beautiful retransition, a high point of this movement and indeed of the whole work. A whirling triplet idea in eighth notes that is only transitional in the Menuet apparently gives Haydn the main theme of his whirligig finale, *Prestissimo* in common time, with nearly constant eighth-note triplets. The tarantella pursues its course relentlessly, the composer in great good humor, and only stops finally when the violins reach the high C with which they began the work. However great the accomplishment of this finale, Haydn surpasses it in the companion symphony, No. 57 in D.

If a single symphony had to be chosen in order to represent "middle Haydn," my choice would fall upon No. 57, in which work Haydn perfected the slow introduction as a kind of guide to understanding the cycle as a whole. This *Adagio* begins with three disjunct *pianissimo* strokes on low D, preceded by its lower neighbor C♯ as appoggiatura, and answered by the piercing interval A C♯ in the first violins two octaves above, over a tutti *forte* chord of V$^{6/4/2}$. There is no resolution of the high leading tone, only the same three low Ds again, leading to V$^{6/5}$, tutti *forte*. Sustained Ds next sound in the middle and low octave in the first and second violins, harmonized only by the bass F♯. A♯ creeps in as an expressive appoggiatura over G, then on a second statement a D♯ appoggiatura over G appears; note that in combination these tones would produce the enharmonic equivalent of the Neapolitan chord G B♭ E♭. Before the introduction is over, Haydn introduces a *fortissimo* B♭, the climax of the section, on the way to pedal A.

The ensuing *Allegro* takes only six measures to make its way up to the high D that was withheld in the *Adagio*, and it does so with three staccato taps that relate unmistakably to the first measure of the work. This high D is not strong metrically, coming as it does on a weak measure. There are other resolutions to high D in the course of the symphony. The Menuetto ends with an ascent through the triad to high D, providing the theme of the trio, which begins in d but promptly moves to B♭ (what place could be more appropriate, given the slow introduction?). But none of these resolutions closes the gaping wound left by the stabbing high C♯ until, in the last measures of the finale, the first violins attend to the unfinished business at the other end of the cycle with their repeated answer in the high register: A C♯ D!

It is not just the beginning and end of the slow introduction that sows tonal seeds that will later bloom. Every element is prophetic. Take, for example, the two long appoggiature, A♯ and D♯. The first appears prominently in the main theme of the first movement and provides the leading tone in the surprising V of vi (b) at the beginning of the development (the tonal maneuver here is the same in all four symphonies dated 1774). The next nonchordal tone to appear is D♯ as the leading tone in V of ii (e). Haydn makes the reference to the slow introduction much more obvious in the finale, where the progression D A♯ B in long notes is marked *mancando pianissimo,* followed a few measures later by the same process for D D♯ E (in the bass). In the climax of the finale, just before the ascent to high D in the first violins, Haydn expunges both A♯ and D♯, almost as if they were characters in a play. In the *Minuetto Allegretto,* which has the quality of a Ländler, the composer takes cognizance of the slow introduction in its first strain by confining the dominant seventh to two inversions, V$^{6/5}$ and V$^{6/4/2}$, then bringing in the appoggiature A♯ and D♯ in combination with G. And as if this were not sufficient, the trio does not return to d minor from B♭ before sounding the full Neapolitan chord, *forte,* as its climax.

Certain rhythmic seeds are sown in the slow introduction as well. If a rhythmic diminution of the opening measures' three Ds produces the three taps on high D in the main theme of the first movement, further diminution produces the cell out of which the tarantella finale is made: three Ds in eighth-note triplets. This finale is more droll by far than the equivalent *Prestissimo* in Symphony No. 56, being invested with a sense of comic repartee from the outset, as tutti outbursts answer the first violins' insistent low Ds (again reminding us of the beginning of the slow introduction); later, impudent retorts in the lower strings answer the slides in the violins. At the same time, we are witnessing high comedy and the completion of a feat of tonal-rhythmic architecture such as Haydn would rarely surpass, even in his late works. The repeated D motif was so rich in potential Haydn could return to it and produce further glories in the finales of Symphonies No. 70 (1779) and No. 86 (1786).

EXAMPLE 5.10. *Haydn, Symphony No. 57, II*

Haydn must have felt the need to complement the high spirits of the first, third, and fourth movements with a vision of serene beauty in the *Adagio*. The symmetrical theme, ‖: 6 :‖: 6 :‖, with four variations, forswears the kind of luxuriance displayed in the slow movement of Symphony No. 56, and is instead a heartfelt, broadly arched melody, at once simple and profound. Playing *con sordini*, the strings announce the first measure pizzicato, the melody falling from the third to the tonic over I - V^7 - I (Example 5.10). This gesture returns like a motto, first in m. 3, then as a conclusion of the theme and as the last measure of every variation, ultimately the last thing in the movement.[36] There is something deeply expressive about this return to the simplest kind of beginning, reenacted over and over, leading us to ponder the identity of beginnings and endings in a broader sense. Haydn at the same time shows his utter freedom and mastery by expanding the ending of the last two variations so that they become more intensely expressive.

With a masterpiece such as the Symphony No. 57 in D, Haydn reached a new degree of cyclic unity. Its slow introduction sets up long-range tensions that require the entire four-movement span for their ultimate resolution. Few symphonists could follow him to such giddy heights. Mozart did in the 1780s, and so did Beethoven later, especially with the slow introductions to his second and fourth symphonies.

The rich harvest of Haydn's symphonies reached a high point in 1774. After this peak year there was a shift in his symphonic production. Having written such a variety of fine symphonies since 1770, it may be that Haydn's supply was adequate for some time. In any case, he wrote surprisingly few symphonies in the latter half of the decade. The prince's interest became directed more to the theater and especially Italian opera, which meant that Haydn's energies were diverted more and more into his function as *Opernkapellmeister*. Most of his music written for the marionette theater at Esterháza, belonging to the 1770s, has been lost. But several full-scale comedies on Italian librettos have survived.

The individual symphonic peaks of the late 1770s remained of very high quality. Among the most delightful is the Symphony No. 61 in D (1776). Its opening movement, *Vivace* in common time, is high comedy throughout, beginning with a first theme in buffo chatter, including a rising chromatic wail in half notes, and offering for a second theme the bergamasca progression outlined by the pizzicato strings, which does more than hint at the world of commedia dell'arte highjinks. For the lovely *Adagio* in 3/4 with muted strings Haydn, chooses A rather than the expected G as its key. The

[36] Antonio Rosetti [Rösler], a fine Bohemian-born composer, uses a similarly recurring simple progression in the slow movement of his beautiful Oboe Concerto in F of 1775.

finale is a *Prestissimo* in 6/8, which, coupled with the key of D, brings associations of the hunt—and a merry chase it is, as well as an example of Haydn's increasingly sophisticated and powerful use of the rondo form, in this case with episodes in i, IV, and ii.

The Symphony No. 66 in B♭ (ca. 1775–76?) opens with an *Allegro con brio* in common time; its reprise is ushered in by a rhythmic augmentation of the tone A, which is simultaneously changed from being a tonic (the root of V/ii) to being the third of the dominant (cf. the end of the slow introduction to Beethoven's Symphony No. 4). Most important about the Symphony No. 66 is its finale, a wonderful rondo in 2/4 marked *Scherzando e presto* in which the playful discourse is carried on for 242 measures with unflagging interest, and with new turns and colors at every episode or return of the refrain. This movement shows Haydn mastering the style that will mark his rondo finales to the end of his symphonic production twenty years later. They helped define the truly Haydnesque in music for his contemporaries, and will continue to do so for all time.

EXAMPLE 5.11. *Haydn, Symphony No. 68, I*

Symphony No. 68 in B♭, dating from about the same time as Symphony No. 66, begins with a six-measure phrase that is half buffo patter and half lyrical outburst (Example 5.11). The chromatic rise by means of the raised-fifth degree in m. 4 moving into the euphonious precadential progression of m. 5 is nicely answered by the chromatic rise into the rhythmically weak cadence of m. 6 by way of the raised-second degree. Perhaps these last two measures are mere clichés from the world of the minuet, but if so, we have not encountered them any earlier, and at the *Vivace* tempo they are bound to sound different from the minuet's ever-gracious *Moderato*. The special sounds of Mozart are also close—compare the precadential progression and rhythmically weak cadence, without chromatic alteration, in the first movement of Mozart's Symphony No. 33 in B♭ of 1779, or even closer, the same with chromatic alteration in the first movement of the Symphony No. 39 in E♭. Haydn launches into the development of his first movement with a surprising move from F major to D major as V/vi, the same *forte* surprise that greets us in the middle of the trio to the *Jupiter* Symphony. He does not make much of the oscillating staccato thirds in m. 3 in his first movement, until the E♭ *Adagio cantabile* in 2/4, his third movement, after the Menuetto. Here the figure inaugurates the movement and provides accompaniment to the melody above, as well as *forte* punctuation at the phrase endings, like a stubborn form of encouragement to the song of the first violins.

EXAMPLE 5.12. *Haydn, Symphony No. 70, I*

There is one work that epitomizes Haydn's epochal symphonic achievements up to 1780, while demonstrating anew his subtle cyclic unity: the Symphony No. 70 in D, dated on the original parts 18 December 1779, the same day that Prince Esterházy laid the cornerstone of the new opera house that would replace the one that had just burned down. For this special event Haydn returned to the key that is even more universal for the symphony than C or E♭. He wrote a taut first movement, *Vivace con brio* in 3/4, in which almost everything is derived from the initial descent through the triad (Example 5.12). The energy unleashed by this beginning is already great, and Haydn's aim was to increase it, which he did with an emphasis on ii in m. 6. Mozart, on the other hand, used the same *forte* beginning, then defused its power with gracious trills and a melody falling by step to launch his Symphony No. 28 in C of 1773. Here we have a concrete basis with which to understand what Emperor Joseph meant when he told Ditters: "I compared Mozart's compositions to a gold snuffbox, manufactured in Paris, and Haydn's to one finished off in London." Haydn speaks much more plainly and directly. The four *forte* chords on A with which he closes his exposition become four gruff-sounding C♮ unisons at the outset of his development. These repeated unisons will come into their greatest glory as one of the subjects of the finale, and they will bring the entire symphony to its final conclusion.

In the second movement, *Andante* in 2/4, Haydn turns to d minor and writes what he labels "Specie d'un canone in contrapunto doppio." Related to the minor melody is a major one, with gently falling conjunct thirds, and these two sections alternate to form the movement, as will be the case in some of Haydn's latest and greatest slow movements. The minor section has the last word, although its final chord contains no third, allowing the major to return only with the onset of the *Menuet Allegretto*.[37] This movement

---

[37] For an excellent discussion of this movement, see Gretchen A. Wheelock, *Haydn's Ingenious Jesting with Art: Contexts of Musical Wit and Humor* (New York, 1992), pp. 68–69.

begins with a four-measure phrase, the second half of which is echoed immediately, and it is answered by an equally strong assertion of the supertonic, E, before resolving back to D, *fortissimo*. The trio answers the bluster of its companion with a *pianissimo*, a gently falling conjunct third (against a rising third in the bass) that recalls the major section of the preceding movement. The trio emphasizes not only D but also the melodic progression D E A, calling the listener's attention to the last two tones, the falling fifth, by not harmonizing them. We hear the Menuet's prominent E differently on its return, as a result. Most of all, we realize soon after the finale begins that Haydn has set us up for its main fugal theme, involving the repeated Ds and the falling fifth: D D D D / E - A -. No one before Haydn had written such a lean and muscular finale, or such a totally unified symphonic cycle. The power of Haydn's pounding tonic strokes, now in major, now in minor, resounds all the way to the end of his symphonic oeuvre, and specifically in the development of the first movement of the *London* Symphony.

When Haydn's symphonies of the later 1770s were printed by Hummel of Berlin and Amsterdam soon after their composition, they met with critical success even in quarters that had hitherto been hostile to the composer. Berlin critics were impressed with their originality, learning, and charm. Carl Friedrich Cramer of Hamburg marveled at their wonderful workmanship and spoke of "this great epoch of the symphony," which he hoped Haydn would crown with still further examples. The composer did, of course, but by 1780 he had already become Europe's foremost symphonist.

Writing about Vienna as he found it in 1781, Friedrich Nicolai observed that after Fux, Austria boasted various good composers, but no outstanding geniuses of the caliber of a Sebastian or Emanuel Bach, a Telemann, a Graun, or a Hasse. He seemed, without naming him, to indict Wagenseil.

> Austrian music suited the sensuous character of the nation. Cassations, little songs ["Liederchen"], minuets, and Styrian dances passed for musical art with high- and low-born alike; serious and sublime musical thoughts aroused boredom. At length a man stood up such as Austria had not had in a long time, rich in invention, in new turns of expression, and in noble song. Joseph Haydn began, as his first works show, in the taste of the usual folk music. He knew how to make what it offered his own, and soon lifted himself far above it. His instrumental pieces, particularly his symphonies and quartets, have an unmistakable stamp of originality about them, and most of his vocal works have the spirit of simple and pleasant songs.

If Nicolai had stopped there, he would deserve to be called an astute critic. Unfortunately for his reputation, he continued, perhaps feeling bound to exert his regional sense of superiority, by trotting out the usual north

German cliché about Haydn: "He occasionally falls, presumably to please a part of his public, unexpectedly into the old low style that was so common, a complaisance that is not necessary for so great an artist." But his parting shot on the subject does manage to render justice to all that Haydn had accomplished by the 1770s: "He has transformed the musical taste of his country in large measure, and he may dare lead it further."

Opera and Oratorio

IN his autobiographical letter of 1776, Haydn singled out the following of his vocal works as having received the most approbation, in this order: *Le pescatrici* (1769–70), *L'incontro improviso* (1775), *L'infedeltà delusa* (1773), *Il ritorno di Tobia* (1775), and the *Stabat mater* (1767). We shall take his choice as our guide. The last named and earliest of these works has already been discussed. The others will be taken up in chronological order.

Construction of the new opera house at Esterháza was finished in 1768, and the building was apparently inaugurated by Haydn's *Lo speziale* in the fall of the same year (Figure 5.5). The libretto was one of Carlo Goldoni's most colorful, a *dramma giocoso* with five buffo and two seria characters that explored contemporary life in the setting of an apothecary's shop. Haydn or his poet eliminated all but the four central buffo roles: Sempronio, druggist; Mengone, his assistant; Grilletta, his ward; and her suitor Volpino. These were sung respectively by Carl Friberth, tenor; Leopold Dichtler, tenor; Maddalena Spangler, soprano; and Barbara Dichtler, soprano (in a "pants role"). Other singers were available, but they were probably not of the same caliber as these four, who formed the nucleus of Haydn's vocal ensemble.

Even in its abbreviated form, Goldoni's libretto provided a well-made farce with strongly drawn characters. Sempronio in the title role is a Pantaloon figure of a novel kind—he dotes on newspapers, maps, and geographical lore (surely a sketch from the life of some café denizen in Goldoni's Venice). He is no match for his witty young ward, whom he wishes to marry. Mengone, his assistant, does all the mortar and pestle work in the shop, although he is a peasant who can scarcely read and naturally has trouble deciphering the scrawls of prescribing physicians. Volpino ("little fox"), though clever at ruses and disguises, is eventually outfoxed by Mengone. For a short opera, the work has much to recommend it. The ensemble finales are brilliant; the ending to Act II uses capricious echoes to hilarious effect. There is a charming "Turkish" aria in Act III. With its oscillating figure between the tonic and the third degree, its Lydian fourths, and its bizarre

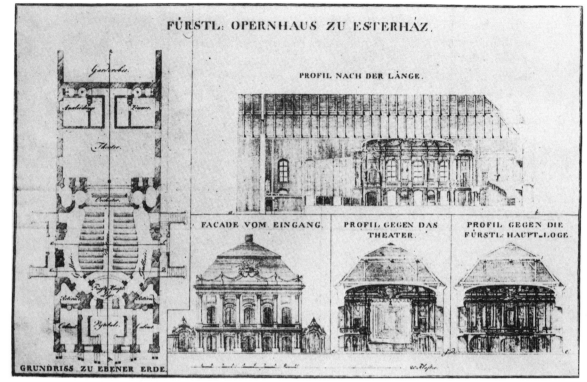

FIGURE 5.5. The opera house at Esterháza.

tonal (or rather, nontonal) progressions, this aria offers a standard with which to measure the occasional exotica in Haydn's purely instrumental music. Haydn and his prince were pleased enough with the opera to perform it in Vienna at a private residence two years later, and to revive it at Esterháza in 1774.

LE PESCATRICI (1769–70)

A YEAR after *Lo speziale* Haydn began work on another Goldoni *dramma giocoso*, *Le pescatrici* (The Fisherwomen). The arrival of some new singers strengthened his forces and allowed him to include all seven of the characters of the original libretto. Thus the work became his first full-length Italian opera, which may explain why he mentioned it but not *Lo speziale* or its predecessors in his letter of 1776. The noble pair, Prince Lindoro and Eurilda (discovered to be a princess at the end), were sung by Christian Specht, bass, and Gertruda Cellini, mezzo-soprano. In Italy and elsewhere these seria roles would have demanded high voices; Haydn's noncompliance with tradition shows how he had to make do with the voices at his disposal.[38] It also helps explain what the composer meant when he later refused a request from Prague for an opera buffa, saying his operas were too restricted by local conditions to succeed elsewhere.[39] The wise old fisherman Mastricco was played by Giacomo Lambertini, bass. Two pairs of country lovers completed the cast, played by Friberth and his new bride, Maddalena Spangler, and by the husband and wife team of Leopold and Barbara Dichtler.

Goldoni picked Taranto, on the Ionian seacoast of southern Italy, for his setting, an evocative choice that controls much of the opera. The importance of this atmospheric locale may be seen from his careful description of the unusually elaborate and numerous stage sets:

> **Act I:** seashore, then arrival of the festive bark with Lindoro; a wood; an arbor of trees shielding the sun, with turf seats placed around it.
>
> **Act II:** courtyard leading to a *giardino delizioso*; practicable hill with a fountain at its base; enclosure of thatched huts forming a square, with turf seats.
>
> **Act III:** small temple dedicated to Neptune; courtyard; the seashore illuminated at night, with a bark.

It was Goldoni's practice to point up the visual effects verbally, and he does so here, for instance with a chorus, "Bell' ombra gradita" (Beautiful, welcome shade) coming after the change to the arbor for the last part of Act I. Haydn obliges with a sextet in E♭ (the mere word "ombra" almost guaranteed this serious key) colored by pairs of horns and English horns.

The opera begins with a *Coro di pescatori* as the fishermen pull in their nets. As early as the first recitative, we learn that Nerina (Barbara Dichtler) and Lesbina (Maddalena Friberth) are interested in amorous adventure and that their "fishing" for hearts will not stop with catching those of their boyfriends. Burlotto (Leopold Dichtler) interrupts their chatter, entering with a deceptive cadence to B♭, just after they start singing in sixths and thirds (fairly rare in recitative, but indicative of the care Haydn took with this work). Burlotto's entrance in B♭ is a nice touch, adumbrating as it does the key of the first aria he sings, a very leisurely invocation (164 measures) of the storms, thunder, and lightning bravely endured by a sailor of his mettle. Long arias then follow for the other three (even though the last is called "Cavatina," it runs on for 118 measures). The most memorable of this opening set of arias is the second, Nerina's "So far la semplicetta" (I know how to play the simpleton).

---

[38] In the modern edition, *Haydn: Werke*, ed. Dénes Bartha, 25:4 (Munich, 1972), p. vii, the Vorwort offers the perverse statement that seria parts were traditionally cast with lower voices.

[39] See pp. 386–7 below for the quotation from his letter.

Approximately one third of Haydn's score for this opera has not survived. What is missing could be supplied in many cases from Gassmann's parallel setting for the Burgtheater (1771). Gassmann's setting of the first two arias in particular resembles Haydn's in rhythm and melody to such an extent there is little doubt about their dependence.[40] It is clear that Haydn's operas, even if not staged in Vienna, had a decided impact upon the capital's musical establishment.

Eurilda, presumed daughter of Mastricco, arouses animosity in the other young ladies, while the arrival of the galant Prince Lindoro seeking a lost princess quite inflames their imagination. The petty jealousies arising therefrom lead eventually to the finale of Act I, a rousing quartet for the rustic pairs, in which the men address the women with the noble titles each dreams will be hers if selected by Lindoro as his bride.

By the end of Act II Eurilda is recognized as the princess sought by Lindoro, and the second finale, once again for the quartet of rustic swains, begins with the women attempting to reinsert themselves into the good graces of the men. The singing of the ladies in thirds, as they beg forgiveness, in the *Poco Adagio* section just before the final *Presto* begins to sound like the similar scene at the end of Mozart's *Così fan tutte*.

The plot of *Le pescatrici* concludes with the general peace declared at the end of Act II, but the Italian libretto tradition in which Goldoni worked demanded a third act. The poet obliged with a scene with chorus in Neptune's temple and a serene cavatina sung by Eurilda, swearing eternal love to Lindoro. This was not quite enough, so he introduced a new plot line in which Burlotto and Friselino appear disguised as noblemen and proceed to court each other's girlfriend. The young ladies succumb without much ado, and we are now truly in the territory from which *Così fan tutte* took its departure.[41] Mastricco chastises the men after the unmasking for being so foolhardy as to tempt their girlfriends. He unites the original couples, placing hand in hand, and the opera ends happily with the embarkation of Lindoro and Eurilda.

In a comparison of Haydn's setting of *Le pescatrici* with Gassmann's, one scholar has described the first as oratorio-like, the second as "scenic."[42] The claim that Haydn's arias, unlike Gassmann's, are instrumentally conceived

[40] Georg Feder, "Bemerkungen zu Haydns Opern," *Österreichische Musikzeitschrift* 37 (1982): 154–61, examples 1–2, p. 156; and Silke Leopold, "*Le Pescatrici*-Goldoni, Haydn, Gassmann," *Proceedings of the International Joseph Haydn Congress 1982*, ed. Eve Badura-Skoda (Munich, 1986), pp. 341–51; 343.
[41] Daniel Heartz, *Mozart's Operas* (Berkeley, 1990), pp. 230–32.
[42] Leopold, "*Le Pescatrici*;" her theses raised several objections, which are also printed. For an astute analysis, see Caryl Clark's review of the Haydn Congress in *Journal of Musicology* 6 (1988): 245–57; 254–55.

sits oddly with the fact of Gassmann's borrowings of Haydn's rhythmic-melodic ideas. Perhaps Haydn's arias would be found more operatic if they were compared with those in his oratorio of this period, *Il ritorno di Tobia*.

L'INFEDELTÀ DELUSA (1773)

AN anonymous poet of lesser talent than Goldoni furnished the libretto for Haydn's next opera, which has been ascribed to Marco Coltellini. Carl Friberth may have arranged the version for Esterháza. Performed first in July 1773, the opera was repeated for the visit of Maria Theresa at the beginning of September.

Especially impressive is the opera's first vocal number, "Bella sera ed aure gente" (Beautiful evening and gentle breezes), an example of the *Introduzione*. Haydn took the opportunity to write a superb vocal quartet for soprano, two tenors, and bass, an extensive meditation on the beauties of nature in which the composer places no trammels on his inexhaustible melodic and harmonic invention.

An old peasant, Filippo (Friberth), attempts to marry his daughter Lesbina (Mme. Dichtler) to the prosperous farmer Nencio (Dichtler), but she has eyes only for the impoverished peasant Nanni (Specht), and he for her. Nanni's sister Vespina (Mme. Friberth), in love with Nencio, invents the ruses and disguises necessary to bring this plot to its only possible conclusion. The choicest and most extensive parts were those for Friberth and his wife, lending more reason to believe he was the adapter. The opera is firmly grounded in the trumpet and drums key of C major, but only Friberth, as Filippo, gets to sing an extended aria in the same key (in Act II), accompanied by high horns and timpani. Mme. Friberth as Vespina appears in Act II disguised successively as an old woman, as a German servant spouting a mishmash of Italian and German, as the Marchese di Ripafratta (a favorite Italian comic character who appears often in Goldoni's plays), and finally as the notary who comes to inscribe the (phony) wedding contract in the final scene.

The two finales are not quite as interesting and forward-looking as those in the two preceding operas. Act I ends with what is more appropriately called an ensemble of perplexity, and since there is no stage action, Haydn does not stray very far from tonic G major. In Act II the finale does not draw the maximum dramatic surprise possible in music to underline the denouement. The "infedeltà" of Sandrina's betrothal to the marchese is "delusa" (frustrated) all too quickly. The opera was revived at Esterháza in 1774.

Haydn sometimes regretted his isolation in the Hungarian countryside. He missed the stimulation of his Vienna visits, which were not as frequent as he would have liked. But in the summer of 1773 the Viennese court came to him in the person of its sovereign. With her she brought, among many others, young Archduke Maximilian, who would soon be honored in Salzburg by Mozart's *Il rè pastore*. Viennese cultural politics touched both masters even though they were not in imperial service.

Il Ritorno di Tobia (1775)

HAYDN wrote his only Italian oratorio in the winter of 1774–75 at the invitation of the Tonkünstler Societät in Vienna. The society presumably commissioned the libretto, on the biblical subject of Tobias' curing of his father's blindness by applying the entrails of a monster to his eyes. The poet was Giovanni Gastone Boccherini (one year older than his famous brother, Luigi). In 1772 Boccherini signed a three-year contract with the imperial court as theater poet, giving him wide authority over libretto revisions, costumes, decors, and staging, for which he received the annual salary of 1,200 gulden.[43] He was also obliged to supply three new librettos per year; he seems not to have done so after 1772–73, thus raising a question as to whether he served out his term, but the title page of *Tobia* leaves no doubt that he did. His contract was not renewed, for in the fall of 1775 Giovanni de Gamerra is listed as theater poet.[44] Boccherini's responsibilities would have included overseeing the publication of the oratorio's libretto. On the title page he called attention to his literary qualifications by listing his pen name as a member of the Arcadian Academy (Figure 5.6).

The performances of *Tobia* took place on 2 and 4 April 1775 under the composer's direction in the Kärntnerthor Theater. They catapulted Haydn into the middle of the imperial musical establishment, where he had not been since his *Krumme Teufel* operas of the 1750s. For the Lenten oratorios of the society, it was usual for the members of both theater orchestras as well as all the choral forces to unite, so it is likely that Haydn had most of the musicians in imperial service under his command. Yet he insisted on bringing with him his first violin, Tomasini, and his first cello, Marteau. Tomasini would have led the orchestra as concertmaster, along with Haydn at the harpsichord; Marteau, by Haydn's side, would have been a crucial accompa-

[43] Gustave Zechmeister, *Die Wiener Theater nächst der Burg und nächst dem Kärntnerthor von 1747 bis 1776* (Vienna, 1971), p. 349.
[44] Ibid., pp. 361–62.

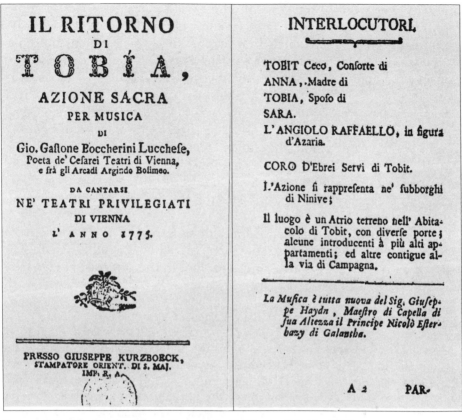

FIGURE 5.6. Libretto for Haydn's oratorio *Il Ritorno di Tobia*, 1775.

nist in the work's many recitatives. Besides these duties, Tomasini and Marteau played solo concertos between the two parts of the oratorio, the violinist on 2 April, the cellist two days later. The enmity of certain musicians in imperial service toward Haydn, notably that of the violinist Franz Kreibich, may well have been nurtured at occasions like this.

Besides his first violin and first cello, Haydn brought with him several of the vocal soloists for *Tobia:* Christian Specht, bass (Tobit); Carl Friberth, tenor (Tobia); his wife Maddalena, soprano (Sara); Margarethe Spangler, contralto (Anna); and Barbara Teyber, soprano (Raffaelle). The first three were currently in Esterházy service. Margarethe Spangler was Mme. Friberth's sister, and is not known to have had connections with the imperial court; Barbara Teyber was a sister of the more famous Therese Teyber ("Die Teuberin"). Thus Haydn was able to compose the work mainly or entirely for voices he knew and could coach even before rehearsing the work in Vienna. This helps explain why his vocal writing for the soloists is so florid, and why they were all trusted with improvised (or perhaps not so improvised) cadenzas. The specificity of Haydn's demands boded ill for further performances of this elaborately intricate (not to say overwritten) oratorio.

Haydn's poet followed the form established by the seven oratorios Metastasio wrote for the Viennese court between 1730 and 1740.[45] In these classics of the genre, there were invariably two parts, each containing a half-dozen arias preceded by recitatives; each part closed with a chorus. Boccherini expanded the model slightly, adding a chorus with soloists to begin Part I and a penultimate duet for the alto and tenor before the chorus concluding Part II. His recitative and aria texts are indebted to the Metastasian model, as is his mainly contemplative tone; nearly all direct action is excluded (although the biblical tale that provides the story is replete with action and colorful detail).

By 1775 Haydn was renowned throughout Europe. The Viennese public stood somewhat in awe of his reputation, gained by one of their own who was yet an outsider. This awe, and reverence in the presence of Haydn as music director, is projected by an anonymous reviewer of *Tobia:*

> The famous Kapellmeister Haydn awoke general applause with his oratorio . . . and his well-known skill was in evidence to greatest advantage. Expression, nature, and art are so interwoven in his work that the listener had to love the one and admire the other. His choruses, especially, glowed with a fire otherwise belonging to Handel; in short, the entire and unusually large public was enchanted, and Haydn once again was the great artist whose works are loved all over Europe, and in which foreigners recognize the original genius of a master.[46]

The critic concludes with a poem in which Haydn is placed beside not only Handel, but also Gluck and (Emanuel?) Bach. While singling out the three choruses for special praise in 1775, the critic remains oddly silent about the work's predominant ingredient, the twelve long numbers for solo singers without chorus. Nor does the new text receive mention.

The two performances were indeed well attended, and they brought a huge profit to the society. This did nothing to allay the jealousy of local composers toward Haydn. An attempted revival of *Tobia* was not made by the society until six years later, and then it foundered, ostensibly for lack of a principal who could sing the alto role of Anna. Only on 28 and 30 March 1784 was the work revived, for which occasion Haydn added two splendid new choruses and curtailed the length of the solo arias. This production,

---

[45] For an excellent study of these, as well as of Haydn's *Tobia*, see Howard E. Smither, *A History of the Oratorio*, vol. 3: *The Oratorio in the Classical Era* (Chapel Hill, N.C., 1987), pp. 51–62, 160–81.

[46] In *Realzeitung der Wissenschaften*, cited after Carl Ferdinand Pohl, *Joseph Haydn* (Leipzig, 1875–82), 2: 69.

again under the composer's direction, took place in the Burgtheater. Nancy Storace (soprano) took the role of Anna, and the other singers were also drawn from the troupe then engaged at the Burgtheater.[47] One consequence of rewriting Anna's role for soprano would have been transpositions wreaking havoc with the carefully worked out tonal scheme of the original. To date it has not been possible to reconstruct the 1784 version.

Haydn conceived *Tobia* on a grand scale, with two principal or polar keys, C and D. He began the overture with a slow introduction in c (Example 5.13). Perhaps it was this chosen key that elicited from the composer the same motif of a falling diminished fourth by step that proved so haunting in the "Benedictus" of the first *Missa Cellensis* (cf. Example 4.14). He used the same motif in E♭ to open the first vocal number. Between them is the C-major *Allegro molto* in 3/4 that constitutes the bulk of the overture, as festive and jolly as any of Haydn's symphonic first movements of the time in this key—compare, for example, the *Allegro di molto* in 3/4 opening movements

EXAMPLE 5.13. *Haydn,* Il ritorno di Tobia, *Ouverture*

[47] For the complete list of names making up the large choral-orchestral forces, see Otto Biba, "Beispiele für die Besetzungsverhältnisse bei Aufführungen von Haydns Oratorien in Wien zwischen 1784 und 1808," *Haydn-Studien* 4 (1976–80): 94–104.

of Symphonies No. 50 (1773) and No. 56 (1774). Amply proportioned, in keeping with its function of sweeping open the curtain on the evening's drama, the overture is not overly long for its material, unlike several of the arias that follow. The movement does not end but makes a transition into No. 1 in E♭. Haydn frames the end of Part II with the same keys, the duet in E♭ giving way to the final chorus in C with fugue. The latter features contrasting solo voices and tutti, like No. 1 and No. 9, the chorus concluding Part I in a blaze of D major with trumpets and drums. In 1784 Haydn strengthened the two polar keys by adding the chorus in C "Ah gran Dio!" to the middle of Part I and a great storm chorus in d/D to the middle of Part II. The way in which minor-mode turbulence is at length replaced by the serenity and calm of major-mode optimism foreshadows "Rolling in foaming billows" in *The Creation* (which is also in the key of d/D). Some of the restless, scurrying figures in sixteenth notes in the first, tempest-tossed part resemble the storm choruses in Mozart's *Idomeneo* (1781), and it is not impossible that the older master was inspired here by the younger one.

The taste of the Habsburg court for very long arias that shows up in Mozart's Milanese operas of the early 1770s is apparent as well in Haydn's *Tobia*. Mozart made a break with the *langer Geschmack* in his serenata *Il rè pastore* (also dated April 1775). Haydn did not do so until later; in *Tobia* a leisurely pace still prevailed. Haydn's enormous vocal concertos (two of which, Nos. 6 and 7, use half da capo form) are constructed, typically, around the two short stanzas Metastasio had established as the norm for arias. The amount of verbal repetition mandated by this scheme passes more agreeably when the poet is of Metastasio's caliber. Boccherini was not so blithely mellifluous as his model, and his text sometimes even emphasizes the work's *longueurs*. Just before launching into an outpouring of 263 measures (No. 12), concocted around the rather tired metaphor of the sailor seeking refuge in port from storms at sea, Tobia is made to finish the preceding recitative by declaring, "Delay can be fatal." In this case delay does become fatal, at least to any sense of dramatic continuity. We can also imagine what Metastasio must have thought when his follower introduced into another recitative (just before No. 10) so mundane an image as the unloading of backpacks from the camels. Haydn set the long recitative dialogues in all seriousness and piety, many of them to elaborate obbligato accompaniments, further slowing down the pace.

Among the great beauties of *Tobia* are the richness and variety of its orchestration. In No. 11 Sara expresses her joy at having married into the family of Tobias in an angelic concert for winds, with flutes, oboes, English horns, bassoons, and horns, supported by muted strings. But for all its individual beauties, and there are many, the oratorio was doomed to oblivion

FIGURE 5.7. Carl Schütz. View ot the Kohlmarkt; at the right, the Michaelerhaus, 1786.

by its text, one of the more motley tales from the biblical Apocrypha, treated with a naive sense of wonder but little concern for dramatic impact or continuity. The musical result has been described, along with Haydn's Turkish opera of the same year, *L'incontro improviso*, in these terms: "The total product is less than the sum of its parts, a series of effective individual movements that for the most part do not form a dramatic narrative."[48]

Perhaps Haydn might have done better to set one of the classic oratorio librettos of Metastasio, as old and familiar as these had become by the 1770s. It is a pity that he did not collaborate directly with the aged poet, who still lived in the Michaelerhaus, where the young composer had taken refuge in the early 1750s.[49] Metastasio had laid down his pen, and there was no one who could replace him. His dwelling next to the Michaelerkirche remained

[48] H. C. Robbins Landon and David Wyn Jones, *Haydn: His Life and Music* (Bloomington, Ind., 1988), p. 146.
[49] Haydn did set a libretto by Metastasio a few years later: the *azione teatrale L'isola disabitata*. The verbal beauty and ingenuity of this short opera persuaded him to give every last line of recitative the obbligato treatment. He held the result in high regard.

a focal point of Viennese culture, but mainly because of the musical soirées of Haydn's former pupil Marianne von Martínez (Figure 5.7).

L'INCONTRO IMPROVISO (1775)

A VISIT of Archduke Ferdinand and his Italian wife to Esterháza in the summer of 1775 provided the occasion for Haydn's Turkish opera. Carl Friberth translated and adapted Dancourt's *La rencontre imprévue*, set by Gluck and performed in the Burgtheater in 1763–64, an opéra-comique that Dancourt had adopted in his turn from a vaudeville comedy that went back to Lesage's *Les pèlerins de la Mecque* (1726). In line with Haydn's more limited vocal resources, Friberth reduced the number of roles from ten singing parts to eight. His libretto actually benefits from dispensing with one of the three nearly indistinguishable confidantes of the Persian princess Rezia. He also eliminated the role of the mad French painter, Vertigo, and to good effect; this role made more sense in Lesage's comedy for Paris, where it embodied a satire on the quarrel between French and Italian music, than it did for middle-European audiences. But Haydn did not give up all traces of Vertigo. Prince Ali of Balsóra, India, Rezia's lover, a role sung by Friberth himself, has a showy aria in Act III, "Ecco un splendido banchetto" (Here is a splendid banquet), in which he tries to pass himself off as a French painter in order to escape. Haydn and his poet-tenor had great fun here in depicting cannonades, exploding bombs, and other sounds of battle. Yet the aria seems dragged in for the sake of its special effects rather than inherent to the drama.

Another piece that was invented expressly to take advantage of Haydn's vocal and instrumental resources was the trio for three sopranos, "Mi sembra un sogno" (It seems to me a dream), in Act I. Rezia (Maddalena Friberth), Balkis (Barbara Dichtler), and Dardane (Elisabetta Prandtner) sing at length of their hopes of freedom from captivity. The trio is in E♭, in lilting 3/8 time, accompanied by two horns, two English horns, and strings in which the violins are muted. Haydn writes a veritable arabesque, a delicate tracery for three equal sopranos, and is so inspired in the process that he does not stop until some 240 measures plus an improvised cadenza have passed. The opening ritornello alone occupies 35 measures. The extreme care the composer took with this piece, the most glorious music in the opera, is evident in the revision he made of the transition to the dominant so that it would be simpler and more flowing.[50] Such a piece again helps us to understand Haydn's response (in 1787?) when asked by Prague for an opera buffa: "All my operas are far too closely connected with our personal circle

---

[50] *Haydn: Werke*, 25:6 (1962), gives the revision in the main text and the first version in an appendix.

(Esterháza, in Hungary), and moreover they would not produce the proper effect, which I calculated in accordance with the locality."[51] Haydn wrote long-winded arias and ensembles because for Prince Nicholas "nothing was too long," as the composer told Griesinger in 1802 apropos of making cuts in *L'isola disabitata* for its printed version.[52]

The new opera was praised in the *Pressburger Zeitung* for its comic libretto and for Haydn's magnificent music. While both reasons ring true, it cannot be said that Friberth did much to develop the principal characters, or that he planned climaxes so as to benefit the composer. His methods were very like those in the libretto for *Tobia:* too much talk and reaction to dramatic events rather than action itself.

A comparison with *La rencontre imprévue* provides a case in point. Dancourt brought the long-lost lovers together in the middle of his libretto, as Ali and Rezia meet by chance in Cairo. Gluck made this the high point of his score, a duet of amazed enchantment, "Que vois-je! o ciel! c'est l'âme de ma vie!" (No. 17). Haydn and Friberth threw away even the possibility of such a dramatic moment by relegating the meeting of the lovers to simple recitative (Act II, scene 3). It mattered not, apparently, that the opera took its very title from this unforeseen meeting. We might infer that its creators wanted to avoid direct comparison with Gluck, but this cannot be, for Haydn, in his exotic Turkish music, met Gluck head-on and bested him.

Following their meeting, Rezia sings a canzonetta in B♭, repeating the song that a bird taught her, then an *aria di bravura* in C followed by her exit. Ali sings another *bravura* aria, in D, preceding his exit. The scene complex ends with the confidante Balkis having the stage to herself for yet a third *aria di bravura* (in E♭). Even the sequence of keys rising by seconds between the numbers seems curiously inept, because Ali's metaphor aria in D with trumpets and drums should be climactic, not a prelude to the warblings of a confidante. We react more to the personalities of the singers and their individual vocal feats in such cases than to the characters they are supposed to be representing.

Following the scene complex just described, the setting passes to Calandro's room and a very funny drinking song set by Haydn in Turkish style, about the prophet's having an addled brain when he forbade wine: "Il Profetta Maometto non avea cervello netto, quando c'interdisse il vin." Ali's servant Osmin sings an aria about how they will escape by land and sea, which is accompanied by vigorous orchestral tone painting. The scene

[51] *Gesammelte Briefe*, no. 102.
[52] *"Eben komme ich von Haydn . . .": Georg August Griesingers Korrespondanz mit Joseph Haydns Verleger Breitkopf & Härtel, 1799–1819*, ed. Otto Biba (Zurich, 1987), p. 151. The letter is dated Vienna, 20 March 1802.

changes again, to a garden that will serve for the rest of Act II. Rezia and Ali converse and reminisce about a song he used to sing in praise of her eyes. "Let's sing it again," says Rezia, providing (admittedly feeble) motivation for the following love duet in the key of E (an unusual choice for this purpose in Italian opera).

The duet gives way to a four-measure transition leading directly to the second-act finale in G. The first act had ended with a trio finale for Ali, Osmin, and Balkis, a party scene with eating and drinking. The situation at the end of Act II calls forth another (lame) excuse for feasting. It begins with a leisurely celebration in 4/4 time. Rezia and Balkis are on hand, plus Ali, Osmin, and Calandro. Balkis leaves the stage after initiating the festivity. Ali and Rezia sing together "Discendi, amor di Giove, ma non volar altrove, fra noi tu dei regnar" (Descend from Jove, Cupid, but do not fly elsewhere: you should reign among us, Example 5.14). It is possible that Cupid actually did descend in a cloud here, as we shall see. Balkis and Dardane enter at the *Presto* 3/4 with the alarming news that the sultan has returned unexpectedly from the hunt and is furious with them. They urge flight, but a long stretch of ensemble music passes, portraying disbelief, then anxiety and despair, before they actually flee and the finale ends at m. 335.

One of the most charming paintings of an eighteenth-century opera in progress can be brought to bear upon the scene just described. (See Plate VIII.) It is an anonymous watercolor that was in private hands in Vienna when published in 1931.[53] Later it was acquired by the Theater Museum in Munich, where it can still be seen. The heads of the soloists are made out of ivory. The Turkish costumes point to Haydn's *Incontro*. Formerly the painting was thought to depict the sultan's clemency at the end.[54] But Friberth's libretto calls for the final scene of Act III to be played in a room lit by chandeliers. The only garden scene is in Act II. It seems likely, therefore, that the moment depicted is when Rezia, Ali, Osmin, and Calando are onstage and Cupid descends at the beginning of the Act II finale. The other figures onstage are servants, and four of them wear the same livery while making identical gestures.

More recent scholarship denies that the painting depicts Haydn's opera. The arguments made against the identification are as follows: (1) the prince's orchestra did not have red livery until 1776, a year later; (2) a list of the costumes for the opera in the Esterházy Archives does not agree with those in the picture; (3) "in the picture there are no less than six singers on the left

[53] Robert Haas, *Aufführungspraxis der Musik* (Potsdam, 1931), plate XV following p. 240. The picture was first presented in Alfred Schnerich, *Joseph Haydn und seine Sendung* (Zurich, 1926).

[54] H. C. Robbins Landon, "The Operas of Haydn," in *The Age of Enlightenment, 1745–1790*, ed. Egon Wellesz and Frederick Sternfeld (London, 1973), frontispiece and p. 178.

EXAMPLE 5.14. *Haydn,* L'incontro improviso, *second finale*

side and a group of three, in 'Turkish' costumes, on the right; it must therefore represent a big ensemble scene or finale, and we search in vain for a
scene with nine such particular figures in Haydn's *L'incontro improviso*"; (4)
"the orchestra shown does not remotely equal the lavish score of Haydn's
opera; missing in the picture are Haydn's horns, trumpets, flute, extra percussion and second bassoon (though it may have been playing out of sight
to the far left, where the corner of one of the timpani may just be seen [?])."[55]

The first objection collapses if the production depicted was a revival.[56]

[55] Landon, *Haydn*, 2: 28.
[56] Revivals were apparently frequent, although we have only sketchy knowledge of them; see ibid.,
2: 210–11.

The second needs elaboration in the form of a precise comparison. The third is obviously specious in its confusing of singers with nonsinging participants on stage. As to the fourth, Haydn's score requires no flute; the twenty or so players depicted match quite closely the number documented in payment lists of the time.[57] Versatility was expected of the eighteenth-century orchestra player, and most were able to double on at least one other instrument. The artist shows almost exclusively string players in his picture, but at the extreme right, facing the audience, there would appear to be an oboist; the second person from the right, facing the stage, may represent another.

By analogy with the orchestra in the Burgtheater depicted by Bellotto for Joseph Starzer's *Le Turc généreux*, the two horns would have been placed just behind the double basses. Both pictures show the Kapellmeister at the harpsichord with the continuo cello player at his side, reading off his score. In both, a standing bass player performs from the score on the desk of the harpsichord as well (bass notes were written especially large in manuscripts intended to accommodate this function). Trumpets and percussion as needed were brought in from outside the capelle and would not have worn its livery. Possibly they played the few numbers that required them from behind the stage or in the wings. Space was clearly at a premium in a small theater such as is depicted.

We have no idea who the artist was who depicted this scene, or to what purpose. His accuracy is high enough to suggest an insider, but even so, if he were making the picture for his own pleasure rather than for some official purpose, nothing prevented him from altering a color here, a costume there, or a face, for that matter, to suit personal whim. Such is the nature of pictorial evidence, in the absence of more controlling data.

A printed description *(Beschreibung)* of castle Esterháza dating from 1784 claims visual as well as auditory charms for the opera house there:

> It is indescribable how eye and ear are entranced. The soul is melted by the music when the whole ORCHESTRA sounds, sometimes by its touching delicacy and sometimes by its violent power—for the great composer, Herr haiden [sic], who is Kapellmeister in the service of the Prince, conducts it: but also by the excellent lighting, by the lifelike decorations, when clouds with gods are slowly lowered, or are raised from below and disappear in an instant, or when everything is transformed into a lovely garden, a magic wood, a magnificent hall.[58]

[57] Ibid., 2: 224–25.
[58] *Beschreibung des hochfürstliches Schlosses Esterháss im Königreich Ungern* (Pressburg, 1784), quoted by Landon, *Haydn*, 2: 27. Landon's "conducts" is liable to suggest the later baton-wielding method to the unsuspecting, so I prefer "directs" or "leads."

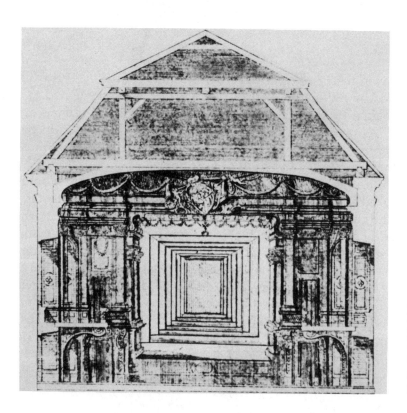

FIGURE 5.8.
Detail of the
Esterháza
opera house
(see Figure
5.5).

The speed with which the descended Cupid in the Act II finale could be made to disappear is consonant with the brief timing of the musical passage in question. As for a lovely garden, it is on hand in the atmospheric vision revealed in the watercolor. Citrus plants offer their fruits on the side. A backcloth shows a path leading down to a pond, with sheep on the banks and mountains in the distance. Garlands of roses beneath the proscenium emphasize the festive nature of what is taking place onstage and in the auditorium, for the benefit of Archduke Ferdinand. "A magnificent hall" well describes the final scene of the opera. On such a happy occasion there could be no thought of anything but a *lieto fine*.

Whoever painted the watercolor took pains with the details of both the stage situation and orchestral placement. He also paid close attention to the theater architecture. The charming Rococo scrollwork in the upper corners of the proscenium arch points to the first opera house at Esterháza, completed in 1768 and destroyed by fire in 1779. Its replacement had a higher stage but corner scrolls that are recognizably similar (Figure 5.8).[59] There is another detail of the second theater that is relevant to our quest. Describing

[59] Detail of the plate "Fürstl. Opernhaus zu Esterház" from the 1784 *Beschreibung*, reproduced in Mátyás Horányi, *The Magnificence of Esterháza* (London, 1962), p. 65.

the princely box in the *Beschreibung* of 1784, the author writes, "This main box is supported by red marble Roman pillars which are ornamented to a third of their height by gold ribs, and of which the shaft and capitals are entirely gilt."[60] As depicted in the watercolor, red and gold figure in the pillars (actually, they are pilasters) that support the proscenium, but most telling of all, they are banded to a third of their height.

Much can be learned from a comparison with the stage of Vienna's Burg-theater as it looked at the time of *Le Turc généreux* (1759, Figure 2.8). Its stage is framed by the right angles portending neoclassical severity. The opera stage at Esterháza, by way of contrast, allowed some graces from earlier and more hedonistic times. This tells us something about courtly life under Prince Nicholas and Haydn's works written to please him. In the Burg-theater Gluck's reform operas sought to challenge and overwhelm their audiences. At Esterháza Haydn in his operas was content to charm and entertain. Our artist has captured him in one of his most characteristic poses, as Kapellmeister, leading his forces from the harpsichord.

1777–1780

A VIENNESE journal devoted to theatrical matters included a detailed commentary on theater at Esterháza in 1774. The opera, as well as the German players and marionette productions, elicited the following comment:

> Each week at Esterház there is one day of opera. The following singers appear:
> 1. Herr Friberth, has a fine tenor voice, knows the theater well and writes for it well. 2. Herr Dichtler, a good comic actor. His acting is suitable and natural, so that one understands what he wants to say even if one does not speak the language. 3. Herr Specht, a good bass, has only worked for the theater for a little while but has made good progress already. 4. Madam Friberth has a clear and pleasant voice, a good education and much charm. Her timidity sometimes hampers her acting. 5. Madam Dichtler has a bright and full theatrical voice, is very vivacious and possesses an excellent memory. These are the principal singers; we have not mentioned the choral singers.[61]

Haydn had every reason to believe that with these fine singers, all of them relatively young and developed under his guidance, he would be able to create many more comic operas. Alas, his excellent little troupe was soon no more. Friberth left the princely service in May 1776 to accept the post of

---

[60] Landon, *Haydn*, 2: 27.
[61] *Historisch-kritisch Theaterchronik von Wien* (1774), translated ibid., 2: 208.

maestro di cappella in the Jesuit churches of Vienna; his wife went with him. Specht lost his voice and became a viola player in the orchestra. Barbara Dichtler dropped dead onstage in September 1776 while singing the role of Belinda in Antonio Sacchini's *L'isola d'amore*. Her husband remained, but his voice apparently declined, and he was given smaller roles from this point on. Haydn was thus obliged to start over again and build a new complement of singers.

Friberth was a great loss and scarcely replaceable. He had been the mainstay of Haydn's operatic compositions in Esterházy service ever since their beginnings, playing Acide (1763), the maestro di cappella in *La canterina* (1766), and key roles in the several works discussed above. His literary skills were invaluable. The choice of a third Goldoni libretto for Haydn, *Il mondo della luna*, may well have been made with his help. Most of the new singers were Italians. The Italian influx began even before the Friberths' departure (and may have hastened it?). Pietro Gherardi, contralto, was engaged by a contract of 7 February 1776; the hiring of this castrato indicated a turn toward more serious opera at Esterháza. Benedetto Bianchi (Buonafede in Haydn's *Mondo della luna*) was engaged on 18 April 1776. Guglielmo and Maria Jermoli arrived later, in early 1777.

Il mondo della luna was staged to celebrate the wedding of the prince's second son to Countess Maria Anna Weissenwolf in the summer of 1777. Goldoni's original libretto, written for Galuppi and staged at the S. Moisé theater in Venice in 1750, marked an early high point in the evolving genre of the *dramma giocoso*.[62] Haydn's libretto was a very recent version, adapted for Gennaro Astarita's setting in Venice in 1775, which provided a longer finale to Act II. It is probably no coincidence that Jermoli, who sang Ecclitico in Astarita's opera, sang the same role for Haydn. The seria parts were the cavaliere Ernesto, sung under Haydn by Gherardi, and Flaminia, sung by the soprano Maria Anna Puttler. For both singers Haydn wrote coloratura, as was expected of seria parts, but contrary to tradition they were not given the love duet, which went instead to Ecclitico and Clarice. Buonafede is another of Goldoni's irascible but lovable Pantaloon figures. Ecclitico dupes him into believing he has landed on the moon, and in this altered state he is eventually induced to allow the marriage of his two daughters, as well as of his maidservant Lisetta (upon whom he had his own designs, of course). The character of the opera is established from the outset by the contrast between the overture, in bright C major with trumpet and drums (ending in g), and the following chorus of Ecclitico's disciples, "O luna lucente" (O

[62] Michael Brago, "Haydn, Goldoni and *Il Mondo della Luna*," *Eighteenth-Century Studies* 17 (1983–84): 308–32.

shining moon), sung in E♭ from the terrace of Ecclitico's house in a night scene. E♭ returns for the finale to Act I, in which Ecclitico manages to persuade Buonafede that they are actually flying to the moon.

Legends woven by biographers around Haydn's next opera, *La vera costanza* (1779), have claimed more attention than the opera itself.[63] Francesco Puttini's *dramma giocoso*, set with great success by Pasquale Anfossi for Rome in early 1776, provided the text. Numerous productions of Anfossi's setting ensued, notably one at the S. Moisé theater in Venice in the fall of 1776, to which Haydn's libretto is most closely related, and one in the Kärntnerthor Theater in January 1777. Griesinger says that the emperor wished to hear Haydn's setting in order to compare it with the Italian work, but he does not specify a date. It could not have been tried on the stage as early as the 1777–78 season, even if Haydn had written the opera by then, because Vienna had no Italian company after the last remnants of the old troupe foundered with the death of the impresario Vincenzo Fanti in the spring of 1777.[64] Another possibility is that the emperor wished to try out the score in his private chamber music sessions. Dies claims that Haydn undertook the composition at the emperor's behest, submitted it, then withdrew it when the casting did not suit him, all this again without date.[65] His garbled version does not deserve credibility. Haydn composed the opera for Esterháza in 1778–79, as is abundantly documented. His original score was destroyed in a fire in 1779. From bits and pieces that survived and from his memory, he reconstructed a score for the opera's revival at Esterháza in 1785.

Puttini's libretto for *La vera costanza* belongs to the *Pamela/Buona figliuola* clan, to which *La finta giardiniera*, set by both Anfossi and Mozart, also adheres. It outdoes others of this type in the cruelty with which the principal female figure, Rosina, is treated, and the exaggerated, hence largely unbelievable pathos this engenders. She and her young son have been abandoned and disowned by the mentally deranged Count Errico (a type close to the mad Count Belfiore in *La finta giardiniera*). Driven to utter despair by the end of Act II, Rosina sings, "Dove fuggo, ove m'ascondo?" (Where shall I flee to, where hide?), which Haydn turns into a driving and powerful cry of anguish in f. The other characters are scarcely developed, but they are all

---

[63] The legends are dispelled by Horst Walter, "On the History of the Composition and the Performance of *La vera costanza*," *Haydn Studies*, ed. Jens Peter Larsen et al. (New York, 1981), pp. 154–57; see also p. 261. The points made are the same as in the German preface to his edition in *Haydn: Werke* (1976).

[64] Otto Michtner, *Das alte Burgtheater als Opernbühne von der Einführung des deutschen Singspiels (1778) bis zum Tod Kaiser Leopolds (1792)* (Vienna, 1970), p. 23.

[65] Pohl, *Haydn*, 2: 77, embroiders Dies and pushes the composition back to 1776, inventing an intrigue by which Anfossi's setting ousted Haydn's. Eva Badura-Skoda, in *International Haydn Congress 1982* (1986), pp. 248–55, tries unsuccessfully to refute Horst Walter.

hostile to Rosina at one time or another with the exception of her brother, Masino. For the two principal roles Haydn had at his disposal the soprano Barbara Ripamonte, hired on 28 April 1778, and Andrea Totti, tenor, engaged 9 June 1778. Both had sung in the Venetian production of Anfossi's version in 1776 and may have been the conduit by which the Venetian libretto reached Haydn. (Totti made something of a specialty of mad scenes, for he also performed Count Belfiore in Anfossi's *La finta giardiniera* at Esterháza in 1780.)

There is some evidence in the form of a sketch that Haydn originally composed the count's mad scene in Act II,[66] but in his 1785 reconstitution of the score he incorporated Anfossi's setting of this scene.[67] Anfossi's inspired music makes it easy to understand why. The orchestral *Andantino* for flutes, horns, and pizzicato lower strings anticipates the beginning of the aria (which sounds for all the world as if composed by Bellini) by being interjected amid snatches of the preceding recitative, beginning "Ah non m'inganno, e Orfeo che cercando Euridice suona la Tracia lira" (Ah, I am not mistaken, it is Orpheus seeking Euridice who sounds his Thracian lyre). The source of this young man's delirium is obvious—he has attended too many operas. Anfossi's brilliant *scena* has the effect of making Haydn's best efforts seem undramatic in comparison. Historically considered, it is an important step on the way to the mad scene in Paisiello's *Nina* (1789), which in its turn had consequences for Vitellia's mad scene in Mozart's last opera.[68]

Haydn kept his arias relatively short in *La vera costanza*, but does this concision reflect his practice in 1779 or that of 1785? His multisection finales to Act I (633 measures) and Act II (651 measures) begin to approach Mozart's opera buffa finales of the 1780s, at least in length. Puttini's libretto is too ineptly constructed and too lacking in motivation to allow the finales to be compared with Mozart's in dramatic effect. Even so, there are many deft touches in Haydn's music that show the great symphonist at work constructing large-scale tonal edifices. In the first finale the tonic G returns in the middle at the *Presto assai* in 3/4, and then returns again in the last *Presto* to the same five-note motto. The extent to which Haydn's orchestra carries the musical discourse can be observed in the first finale's penultimate section. Here the *Allegro* in 2/4 sung by the violins, as the voices drop in and out of the texture, could easily be mistaken for a typically pert and Haydnesque symphonic finale. The most deft touch of all is a very small one: Haydn

---

[66] *Haydn: Werke,* ed. Horst Walter (Munich, 1976), 25:8, p. 367.

[67] For his general indebtedness to some of the melodic-rhythmic ideas in Anfossi's score, see Reinhard Strohm, "Zur Metrik in Haydns und Anfossis 'La vera costanza,'" *International Haydn Congress 1982* (1986), pp. 279–95.

[68] Heartz, *Mozart's Operas,* pp. 311–16.

condenses a winningly lyric transition back to the tonic in the duet at the beginning of Act II into the most expressive moment in the *Allegretto* second movement of his overture (mm. 8–12).

A conflagration destroyed part of the palace and leveled the opera house at Esterháza on 18 November 1779. As a consequence, performance material for Haydn's music from nearly two decades in the princely service was lost. Prince Nicholas ordered the opera house rebuilt and performances of his Italian troupe to be transferred meanwhile to the marionette theater. Here Haydn directed the premiere of *L'isola disabitata* to celebrate the prince's name day on 8 December 1779. To this intensely heroic opera in miniature for four characters Haydn appended a magnificent overture that seems to depict the alternate periods of calm and storm over the "deserted island," and in this respect bears a relationship to the beginning of Gluck's *Iphigénie en Tauride*. Haydn kept the seven arias relatively short, but his decision to introduce concertante instruments into the final quartet meant that it became a rather long-winded affair; he later made cuts in the arias and recomposed the quartet.

Around the time of the fire or earlier, Haydn acquired the score of a new opera by Domenico Cimarosa, *L'infedeltà fedele*, written for the opening of the Teatro del Fondo in Naples on 20 July 1779. Perhaps he intended to include it among the many other Italian operas he was continuously directing. But circumstances demanded that the ceremonies attending the opening of the rebuilt opera house in 1780 include nothing less than a new opera of his own. After considerable revision of Cimarosa's libretto, undertaken by an unknown hand, Haydn set to work composing. The plan was to open the new house on 15 October, the name day of the empress, and perhaps it was envisaged that she herself would make another trip to Esterháza to celebrate the fortieth year of her reign. The case illustrates once again how everything in the Habsburg realms revolved around the imperial family. In the event, Maria Theresa's health deteriorated steadily in the fall of 1780 and she died on 29 November. The period of grief and mourning that followed eliminated any possibility of a festive opera opening, and besides, the new theater was not ready on schedule. A libretto for Haydn's *La fedeltà premiata* (even the title seems to point to the virtues of the empress-queen) was printed with the date "autumn 1780." The first performance took place on 25 February 1781. Its creation paralleled another and more serious opera, planned and largely composed in 1780 but delayed finally until early 1781— Mozart's *Idomeneo*.

The poet Giambattista Lorenzi called his *L'infedeltà fedele* for Cimarosa a "commedia per musica," and prefaced his poem with remarks to the effect that he sought a middle way between serious opera and popular comedy.

Could he have been so naive or credulous as to be unaware that such a means had been found by Goldoni with his epochal creation of the *dramma giocoso* thirty years earlier? For Haydn the comic roles using Neapolitan dialect were transformed, and other changes were made so as to clean up the text and make it proper for imperial eyes and ears. The libretto printed for Esterháza in 1780 bore the designation "dramma giocoso," which was modified for the 1782 revival to "dramma pastorale giocoso." This specification highlights Lorenzi's most innovative feature: the two *parti serie* are the shepherds Fileno and Fillide / Celia (sung under Haydn by the Jermolis). The nobility, on the other hand, is represented by an extravagant count, Perrucchetto ("little wig"), and the vain and haughty Amaranta ("donna vana, e boriosa") who aspires to become his countess. These are the primo buffo and prima buffa roles, and are given slightly more prominence than the third couple, Nerina and Lindoro (Amaranta's brother). The most interesting role is that of Melibeo, minister of Diana's temple, played under Haydn by the bass Antonio Pesci. Like the High Priest in *Idomeneo*, he herds young people to their death as sacrificial victims, but this being a comedy, he is corrupt and also in love, with Amaranta, as it turns out. Lorenzi's conception reflects so badly upon organized religion—the pagan times and deities fooled no one—that it could scarcely have been considered apt for presentation to Maria Theresa. No matter how much the libretto was toned down and rendered anodyne, its satire of clergy and nobility remained a biting indictment.

A recent study of the settings by Haydn and Cimarosa shows that Haydn sometimes loses sight of the limitations proper to the comic characters and gives them ennobling musical expression that fights against the text: "Cimarosa remained within the dramaturgical conventions, to the benefit of his opera. Haydn did not, which brought him some musical gains but incurred losses from the point of view of the dramaturgy . . . Haydn allowed some roles to fall out of character in their music. And his joy in the comic is not so great as that of Cimarosa, who drew out all the comic stops from wordplay to parody of the seria style."[69] Haydn is taken to task for allowing the text to become too tame (but surely Haydn did not have total freedom in this matter). One surprising conclusion is that Cimarosa often allowed the violins more independence from the voice part than did Haydn.

Haydn did model his finale to Act I (822 measures) closely on Cimarosa's (647 measures), and in several instances his invention took wing from the melodic and rhythmic shape of Cimarosa's ideas. But Haydn did more than merely copy Cimarosa. He used the ideas of his great Italian contemporary

[69] Friedrich Lippmann, "Haydns 'La fedeltà premiata' und Cimarosas 'L'infedeltà fedele,'" *Haydn-Studien* 5 (1982): 1–15; 8–9.

EXAMPLE 5.15. *Haydn*, La fedeltà premiata, *Act I, Introduzione*

as a springboard toward creating his own. The case recalls some of the uses Handel made of music by others in order to engender his own.

Haydn decisively abandoned the *langer Geschmack* of the 1770s in this 1780 score, which abounds in moderate-sized but very intense and expressive arias. If anything, the composer became so concerned with economy of expression that he challenged his listeners with irregular shapes and phrases that were "boiled down." An example is Amaranta's first solo (Example 5.15). Taking a cue from his text, which he sets syllabically, Haydn produces two three-measure phrases. His concision invalidates the noble pathos of this melodic type and renders it, if not comic, at least slightly parodistic.

Both Cimarosa and Haydn fell in with Lorenzi's traditional *quinarii sdruccioli* for the scene of horror in the second finale, as the human sacrifice nears, and set it to the obsessive repeated rhythms familiar from the infernal scene in Gluck's *Orfeo*. In Act III Fileno provokes the eventual clemency of

Diana by offering himself as a willing victim, the kind most likely to assuage divine anger—once again there is a direct parallel with *Idomeneo*. But unlike Mozart's heroic sacrifice drama of 1780–81, which concludes with amply proportioned outpourings of noble resignation and forgiveness, Haydn's mock sacrifice ends in a truce with a short dance that would seem to be more at home in a Parisian opéra-comique of a generation earlier. Here Haydn's sense of scale is sadly lacking.

Haydn's attitude toward his latest vocal works emerges in a letter to his publisher Artaria in Vienna on 27 May 1781. The composer wrote that Joseph Legros, director of the Concert Spirituel in Paris, had sent him a letter saying that his *Stabat mater* had been performed in this concert series four times to the greatest applause. Haydn continued:

> They were amazed to find me so exceptionally pleasing in vocal composition, but I am not amazed, and they have heard nothing yet; if only they could hear my Operette [meaning his short opera] *L'isola disabitata* and my most recently composed opera, *La fedeltà premiata,* for I assure you that such work has not yet been heard in Paris, and perhaps not in Vienna either. My misfortune is that I live in the country.[70]

By singling out his two last operas, Haydn may have been calling attention to their greater cogency in comparison with the earlier ones. His last remark is not the only time he expressed regret about living in the country. It implies that if he had not been so isolated, Paris and Vienna, then the world capitals of music, would have had to come to terms with his operas.

There is an inherent contradiction here between Haydn's proclaimed isolation and his seeming knowledge about what Paris had or had not heard up to 1781. Haydn probably had little idea what extraordinary force of will it took for Gluck to succeed at the Paris Opéra. The "perhaps" in his reference to the Viennese operatic scene suggests that he might not have been too well informed about that city either. But surely he did not miss the opportunity to hear Gluck's *Alceste* and *Iphigénie in Tauride,* performed in honor of the visit of the Russian crown prince and his wife in 1781. To that royal personage Haydn dedicated his latest set of quartets, Op. 33, known as the *Russian* Quartets. The anticipated visit of the Russians to Esterháza set Haydn to work on his next opera, *Orlando paladino* (1782), but the visit did not take place.

Despite his complaints, Haydn considered his isolation to be one of the factors contributing to his originality, according to Griesinger.

---

[70] *Gesammelte Briefe,* pp. 96–97.

My Prince was content with all my works, I received approval, I could, as head of an orchestra, make experiments observe what enhanced an effect, and what weakened it, thus improving, adding to, cutting away, and running risks. I was set apart from the world, there was nobody in my vicinity to confuse and annoy me in my course, and so I had to be original. [The last verb is "werden," not "sein," thus a more accurate translation would be "I had to become original."]

Haydn was already original before he entered Esterházy service. But there is no doubt that he gained enormously in technical skill and fluency under the conditions described, that he took risks and experimented until he found what worked the best. As for cutting, adding, and improving, it is particularly his operatic scores that display the marks of ongoing revision.

Was Haydn really "set apart from the world" as he (or Griesinger) claimed? The world often came to him, as we have seen, and the enormous musical holdings of the prince's library provided the equivalent of an international forum. As opera director, he enjoyed an excellent overview of what his Italian contemporaries were creating, but his encyclopedic knowledge of the field did not stop with opera. His correspondence with Artaria allows glimpses of his interest in all kinds of contemporary music and in making contact with its greatest practitioners, such as Luigi Boccherini. By 1780 the world at large did not consider Haydn anything less than the leading figure in modern music. Modest to a fault, but also proud of what he had accomplished and easy to take offense when its worth was impugned, Haydn was never preoccupied with fame or with building a myth around himself. But in the matter of his claimed isolation, he was protesting a little too much.

The Turning Point of 1780

It is well known that Mozart, in the spring of 1781, finally broke out of his service to the archbishop of Salzburg and began a career as an independent artist. Nothing quite so drastic happened to Haydn at this time, and yet he too reached a decisive turning point in his life. Although still in service to Prince Esterházy, he began to seek public patronage to a far greater extent than ever before. His new contract of 1779 removed the restrictive clause in the original agreement that forbade him to compose for anyone else without prior permission. The issue may have gradually become a dead letter over the years, but the fact remains that Haydn's intensive negotiations with publishers began only with the 1780s.

For Haydn to write a public work such as *Il ritorno di Tobia* for the Tonkünstler Societät in Vienna and direct the first performances of the work himself in the spring of 1775 was one thing. Prince Esterházy could scarcely object to what was undertaken for a charitable purpose without its reflecting badly on his house. But it was quite another matter for Haydn to send his works en masse to the Artaria firm for publication, which he began doing in 1780. The composer's new spirit of independence is prefigured by his angry letter of 4 February 1779, written just after he had signed his new contract, refusing the conditions of membership imposed on him by the Tonkünstler Societät. On 31 January 1780 Haydn sent one of his boldest compositions to date, the Piano Sonata in c (Hob. XXI:20) to Artaria as the last in a set of six (but composed ten years earlier!) for publication. No fewer than sixty letters from Haydn to this Viennese publishing firm survive from the decade of the 1780s. In 1781 the composer took it upon himself to write several noble patrons advertising his six new String Quartets (Op. 33) for sale by subscription at the price of six ducats the set and claiming that they were "written in a new and special way."

During the early 1780s Haydn seriously considered traveling abroad. Plans were laid for a visit to England, which would have been his first foray outside the Habsburg realms. They came to nothing, but in 1782 Haydn wrote three symphonies, Nos. 76–78, in anticipation of the trip. In his letter to the publisher Boyer in Paris, dated 15 July 1783, he offered the works and described them as "3 beautiful, elegant, and by no means overly lengthy Symphonies, scored for 2 violins, viola, basso, 2 horns, 2 oboes, 1 flute and 1 bassoon—but they are all very easy and without too much *concertante*."[71] The new symphonies rapidly became known in Vienna through pirated copies. It is to these works that Mozart must have been referring in his letter to his father of 15 May 1784: "I know for certain that Hofstetter double copies Haydn's work—in fact, I have his three latest symphonies." Haydn's own description of his symphonies shows that by the early 1780s he was consciously reaching out to a wide public.

Some influential critics at the same time were coming around to a new and deeper appreciation of Haydn. Charles Burney was such a critic. By 1774 he realized that the music of Carl Friedrich Abel was "sometimes tame." He asked his longtime friend and correspondent Thomas Twining, directly after this remark about Abel, "But for instrumental music, are you much acquainted with that of the Hamburgh Bach—of Haydn—Vanhall—Ditters—Hoffmann etc.?"[72] Burney had of course gotten to know the works of these masters well during his exploratory tour of two years earlier, and it is interesting that he mentions here four Viennese composers as against only

---

[71] *The Collected Correspondence and London Notebooks of Joseph Haydn*, ed. H. C. Robbins Landon (London, 1959), pp. 42–43.

[72] *Letters of Charles Burney*, 1: 165.

one German, Emanuel Bach. By 1781 he ranked Haydn, Vanhal, and Boccherini at the top for string music.[73] Two years later he carried on a fascinating debate with Twining via letters over the respective merits of Haydn and Boccherini, who, they agreed, were superior to all other composers of instrumental music. Twining argued that Boccherini was more serious than Haydn, but Burney tried to persuade him otherwise by citing several specific symphonies by Haydn. Twining replied in his letter of 22 October 1783:

> All the movements of Haydn you mention, I know very well; I allow them to be very fine—serious, & pathetic:—but I spake of general style & character only; & it still appears to me that Boccherini's genius is Tragic, & that in Haydn the graceful, the fanciful, the enjoué, the playful etc.—prevails upon the whole. — Such is my idea still—not from obstinacy, Dieu scait—but from the impression which these two charming composers make upon my ear and mind.[74]

Burney stood his ground. Of all modern composers, Haydn had become his favorite.

Haydn emerged from his semi-isolation in the years around 1780 in quite another sense. In the spring of 1781 he transmitted a portrait of himself to be engraved and sold in Vienna by Artaria (Figure 5.9). In the postscript of his letter to Artaria of 27 May 1781 he wrote, "Many people are delighted with my portrait. Return the oil portrait to me in the same case." The original oil portrait, said to have been painted by Johann Ernst Mansfeld, who executed the engraving, has been lost. Apparently it belonged to Haydn. In his next letter to the Artaria firm, Haydn began with the same topic.

> I received with the greatest pleasure the oil-portrait together with the twelve copies you enclosed of the beautifully engraved portrait. My gracious Prince, however, was even more delighted, for as soon as his attention was drawn to it, he immediately asked me to give him one. Since these 12 copies are not enough, I would ask you, good Sir, to send me another six at my expense. You can subtract the sum from my fee for the Lieder, six of which I shall send you in a few weeks . . . As soon as I come to Vienna, will you be kind enough, good Sir, to present me to the worthy Herr von Mansfeld?

If Haydn wanted to be presented to the artist, it seems likely that they had not met before, and consequently that the oil portrait was not by Mansfeld. At the bottom of the engraving, faintly visible, is the credit "J. E. Mansfeld inv[enit] et sc[ilicet]," but this might mean no more than that the pictorial

[73] Ibid., 1: 331.
[74] Ibid., 1: 376.

FIGURE 5.9.
J. E. Mansfeld.
Portrait of
Haydn, 1781.

invention of this print was Mansfeld's, not necessarily the original of the oval portrait at its center.

In his next letter to Artaria, dated 20 July 1781, Haydn returned to the subject: "You once again make me your debtor for the portraits you sent; but do they sell? I'm curious. In any event the frame-makers and gilders

FIGURE 5.10. Carl Schütz. Detail from Figure 5.7 showing the Artaria firm's office on the Kohlmarkt.

have profited by those you sent to me." From this wry comment touching on commerce, it appears that Haydn had his portrait placed in a gilt frame before giving it to his prince and others, or that the recipients were doing so. In either case Haydn's sense of his own worth could only have been enhanced. In his letter to Artaria written from Esterháza on 18 October 1781, there is mention of the six new string quartets being published as Op. 33 (Artaria's numbering), but the postscript comes back to the same old subject: "Please send me some more of my portraits." We can imagine his engraved portrait being displayed among others at Artaria's shop on the Kohlmarkt across from the Michaelerhaus, shown on the left side of Figure 5.7, with a cluster of people gathered in front (Figure 5.10).

Johann Ernst Mansfeld was one of Vienna's busiest engravers. Much of his work is mediocre in quality, perhaps a result of the rapidity required by book illustrations. With the Haydn portrait he took pains to please a more discerning clientele. The result is an outstanding work from his hand, one "beautifully engraved," as Haydn wrote. He suspends the round portrait as if it were a pendant and surrounds it with some drapery that functions almost like a stage curtain on the left side. On the right he places trees and the chastely clad figure of Euterpe, muse of music and lyric poetry, holding an aulos. Beneath, sitting on a keyboard, are a flute, trumpet, and antique lyre wreathed with a laurel crown, plus music pages bearing simulated notation. The inscription at the bottom is from Horace and is addressed to Orpheus. Complete, it should read, "Tibi, qui possis / Blandum auritas fidibus canoris / Ducere quercus / In amicitiae tessarum" (To you who are able, by caressing your melodious lyre, to lead trees into the bonds of friendship).

Haydn's features in the engraving differ markedly from the only other known depiction of him before age fifty, the oil portrait attributed to Johann Basilius Grundmann of ca. 1762–63.[75] (See Plate VI.) In the earlier portrait Haydn is quite homely, his face dominated by a long and curiously shaped nose. His livery identifies his status as a servant, and there is something not quite comfortable about the way he wears his wig and uniform. Is there perhaps the hint of a twinkle in his irregularly spaced eyes, as if he were about to break into a smile? Mansfeld depicts a more urbane Haydn, one who wears gentleman's clothes and has regular features. He manages to make his subject almost handsome (no wonder Haydn was so pleased).

The discrepancy between the two earliest portraits of Haydn to survive is not unlike the difference arrived at by Griesinger and Dies in attempting to describe Haydn's physical appearance. Griesinger paints a rather glowing picture in words: "Haydn was small in stature, but sturdy and strongly built. His forehead was broad and well modelled, his skin brown, his eyes bright and fiery, his other features full and strongly marked, and his whole physiognomy and bearing bespoke prudence and a quiet gravity." As against this Mansfeld-like *Andante commodo e sotto voce*, Dies is direct, unflattering: "Haydn had a moderately strong bone structure; the muscles were slight. His hawk's nose (he suffered much from a nasal polyp, which had doubtless enlarged this part) and other features as well were heavily pock-marked, the

---

[75] Landon, *Haydn*, 1: 355–56. The portrait was destroyed along with much of Esterháza in 1945. Carole Peel, of Berkeley, California, repainted the portrait for this book after a surviving black and white photograph.

nose even seamed so that the nostrils each had a different shape. Haydn considered himself ugly."

All portraits of Haydn beginning with Mansfeld's engraving present a more or less idealized image of the composer. Haydn's death mask shows that the earliest portrait came closer to capturing his true likeness than any of the others.[76]

[76] A photograph of the death mask is reproduced in László Somfai, *Joseph Haydn: His Life in Contemporary Pictures* (Budapest, 1969), p. 207.

6

Haydn's Contemporaries

Gassmann

FLORIAN LEOPOLD GASSMANN was born on 3 May 1729 in the town of Brüx (Most), northwest of Prague. His father was a goldsmith. A local choirmaster, Johann Woborschil, is said to have taught him singing, the violin, and the harp. (A violinist named Woborzil appeared near the top of the list of first violins in the Burgtheater orchestra after Gassmann became Hofkapellmeister at Vienna in 1772.)[1] Ernst Ludwig Gerber (1790) says that Gassmann learned the fundamentals of music in the Jesuit Seminary at Komotau (Chomutov), some twenty miles from Brüx, but the rolls there mention only a Carolus Gassmann (his brother?). By age twelve Gassmann was apprenticed to a merchant in Brüx. Not long after this he fled his parents' home and according to one tale earned enough money playing the harp in the resort town of Karlsbad that he could travel to Italy. Study with Padre Martini in Bologna is mentioned by his biographers, but there is no documentation supporting this claim.

[1] Gustav Zechmeister, *Die Wiener Theater nächst der Burg und nächst dem Kärntnerthor von 1747 bis 1776* (Vienna, 1971), p. 280 and facsimile p. 356. On the "Personal Lista von beyden Orchestra Anno 1773" Trani and Woborzil are listed as the highest-paid first violins, and next to their names an official has queried "Warum 2 Directeurs?" Gumpenhuber's *Répertoire* for 1763 lists a Wovosal among the first violins; he is probably the same as Woborzil, who in 1783 succeeded Ordonez as a violinist in the imperial court and chamber music.

A runaway Bohemian youth who earned his way by performing might be expected to become something less than a paragon of discipline and compositional craft, yet that is what Gassmann eventually became, which makes study with Padre Martini at least plausible. A normal apprenticeship for a young composer would include writing church music, followed, if he showed promise, by an opportunity to write an opera for one of the lesser theaters. In 1757 Gassmann was given the chance to set Zeno's *Merope* for the S. Moisé theater in Venice, but only the libretto, one aria, and a three-movement overture survive.[2] On the basis of the overture it would be impossible to predict a brilliant career for this composer. It shows that he knew his I - IV - V - I progression and the principle of cellular repetition, and possessed limited melodic ambitions; the rocking two-note basses in the opening *Allegro* might indicate that he knew how to profit from studying the works of Baldassare Galuppi. If there is a trace of his Bohemian ancestry still audible in this little work, it is in the alternating tonic and third at the final cadence of the last movement, and a certain rough-hewn naïveté throughout. However modest a beginning this overture represents, Gassmann succeeded in Venice, where he composed an opera annually for five years. His third opera was the first setting of Carlo Goldoni's *Gli uccelatori* (1759), a singular honor for the thirty-year-old composer. Goldoni was to remain his guiding star even after both left Venice. Count Durazzo's attempts to lure Goldoni from Paris to Vienna in 1764 may well be linked with Gassmann's engagement by the imperial court.[3]

Durazzo had not failed to notice the Venetian successes achieved by a young composer subject to the imperial crown. In the 1761–62 season at the Burgtheater, he staged Gassmann's setting of Metastasio's *Catone in Utica*, composed a few months earlier for the S. Samuele theater. After this introduction Gassmann was called to Vienna in person, as composer of ballet music succeeding Gluck. He arrived in March 1763. For an annual salary of 400 ducats he also agreed to compose operas, the first of which was another opera seria by Metastasio, *Olimpiade,* staged in the Burgtheater on 18 October 1764 with Rosa Tibaldi and Gaetano Guadagni in the leading roles. By this time Durazzo had left Vienna to take up his new post as ambassador to Venice, but there can be no doubt that Gassmann was his choice as the man who would eventually replace Maria Theresa's favorite, the aged Hasse, in continuing Vienna's grand tradition of opera seria (Figure 6.1).

[2] The work is edited by George R. Hill in *Gassmann: Seven Symphonies* (The Symphony 1720–1840, Series B, vol. 10) (New York and London, 1981), pp. 257–74. The other symphonies by Gassmann discussed here are also included in this volume.
[3] Favart's letter of 4 January 1764 congratulates Durazzo on acquiring Goldoni; possibly the whole affair was but a false rumor. In any case, Goldoni remained in France, and Durazzo, dismissed as theater director, went to Venice as ambassador in late 1764.

FIGURE 6.1. Martin van Meytens. Portrait of Count Giacomo Durazzo, 1765.

Philipp Gumpenhuber's *Répertoire* for the year 1763 allows us a few glimpses of Gassmann's first months in Vienna. Gumpenhuber noted the departure of Gluck and Ditters for Italy under date of 24 March, and five days later the arrival of Gassmann, whom he refers to straightaway as maestro di cappella: "Mardi 29 Mars. NB le même jour est arrivé le Sieur Gassmann Maitre de Chapelle." On Easter Sunday, 3 April, he noted at the palace, "Service a Table, le quel on a commencé par une Simphonie de la Composition du Sr. Gasman." This would imply that the composer had brought symphonies with him from Italy in anticipation of filling his new duties. A week later, on 10 April, Gassmann assumed his post at the harpsichord in the Burgtheater for a performance of Monsigny's *On ne s'avise jamais de tout:* "NB. c'été la 1ère fois qu'on a accompagné avec le clavecin par le Sr. Gasman." He also participated in a concert on Friday 15 April in the same theater, at which Boccherini played a cello concerto: "NB. le Sr. Gasman a acompagnié dans l'Acadmie la 1ère fois."

Gluck and Ditters returned from Italy on 6 June, and both took part in the revival of *Orfeo* at Schönbrunn on 31 July, Ditters as second chair of the first violins under Huber. In notes on a concert given at Laxenburg palace on 9 September 1763, both maestri are mentioned: "Pour accompagné avec clavecin il y avait Gluck et Gasman." The academy in the Burgtheater on Friday, 21 October, once again featured Boccherini playing a cello concerto and "une grande simphonie concertée a plusieurs instruments de la composition du Sr. Gassman." Formulations like this in Gumpenhuber usually betoken a sinfonia concertante. Finally, Gumpenhuber specifies that the ballet music for the revival of Gluck's *Ezio* on 26 December was by Gassmann.

The concert symphonies and chamber works of Gassmann were written mainly in the 1760s, after his appointment as *Hof-* and *Kammercompositor* in 1764 or 1765 and before his Italian trip of 1769–70. He wrote symphonies in sets of six each during the years 1765, 1767, 1768, and 1769. The first set achieved the most diffusion; the others were jealously guarded to prevent them from being copied. Gassmann's passion for order is apparent in the tonal sequence of the sets. In the first set the keys are related by fourths— C, G, c, F, B♭, E♭; in the last, by thirds—F, D, b, G, E♭, C. Moreover, each set begins and ends with a three-movement symphony framing four four-movement symphonies (an exception is the first set, which ends with a symphony in four movements).

In the opening *Allegro* of the Symphony in c dated 1765, Gassmann cultivated a rhythmic monotony that is typical of his outer movements. Its exposition of sixty measures never strays from the initial two-measure modules. The main idea is motivic rather than thematic, and is given a bass accompaniment in quarter notes, which are then divided into eighth notes upon repetition, to a rather schoolmasterly effect, as if demonstrating species counterpoint. The other motifs have scarcely enough profile of their own to be remembered. Gassmann scrambles these ideas in the brief reprise, the first being saved for last. It matters little in what order they come because they resemble one another and are all equally unmemorable. The composer does not try to make the reprise a dramatic event, and often it is scarcely even recognizable. Haydn's characteristic double reprise did not tempt him (perhaps because Haydn had put his stamp on this device). Gassmann often avoided the issue by choosing to recapitulate secondary material first; this he did as early as his overture to *Merope* of 1757.

Gassmann's Symphony in E♭ of 1765 is of a more modern cast, in that the composer differentiates his themes more in the first movement, but again he employs a short reprise that lacks the opening idea except for its head motif at the very end. The finale concludes with the entire initial theme, but once again the themes have so little profile that it scarcely matters in what order they occur. A monotonous rhythmic sameness pervades this finale, which operates on a two-measure module throughout. No wonder Gassmann's symphonies were admired only by the circle around Joseph II.

In the first movement of the Symphony in B♭ of 1768 Gassmann remained faithful to the short reprise with the thematic elements reshuffled. The Symphony in A of 1769 is one of his best, but its first movement resorts not only to a reverse recapitulation,[4] but also to a first idea that is more a texture than a theme, which seems like a throwback to Sammartini. The Symphony in E♭ of 1769 opens with a plodding eighth-note "walking bass" accompanying a particularly insipid 4 + 4-measure theme, in which m. 4 covers the same melodic territory as m. 3.[5] The symphony ends with an *Allegretto* in cut time that is in reality a *gavotte en rondeau*. It would not seem out of place at all in a French symphony of the time.

Gassmann's concert symphonies, in sum, are far less interesting than those of his protégé Johann Baptist Vanhal. Burney must have concurred, because he did not include either Gassmann or Wagenseil among the five Viennese composers he singled out as particularly distinguished for their instrumental music: Leopold Hofmann, Haydn, Ditters, Vanhal, and Pancrazio Huber (whose works have all but vanished). Nevertheless, Burney was emphatic in his praise of Gassmann's chamber music, which also provided some of Joseph II's favorite practice pieces. Of his first visit on 9 September 1772, Burney wrote

> to M. Gasman, *maestro di capella del corte imperiale*. He was very obliging, and did me the favour to show me all his curious books and manuscript compositions.
>
> He surprised me much by the number of fugues, and choruses which he shewed me of a very learned and singular construction, and which he had made as exercises and studies. Some of them were composed in two or three different

[4] Hill, *Gassmann*, p. xxi, argues for a subdominant recapitulation in m. 55 and for nontonic recapitulations in other symphonies, an interpretation I reject, along with the concomitant thesis of Gassmann's symphonic modernity. In his autograph Gassmann added a subdominant statement of the main theme just before the reprise, an afterthought that has the effect of weakening the impact of the reprise.

[5] This melody is quoted by Hill to illustrate "considerable melodic gift" in the article "Gassmann" in *The New Grove Dictionary of Music and Musicians* (London, 1980).

times, as well as upon two or three different *subjects;* and several of these, he said, the emperor had practiced.

From other sources we know that Joseph II held thrice-weekly chamber concerts in his apartments, in which he often played cello himself. On 13 September Gassmann paid Burney a visit, bringing a list of his works and "a great number of manuscript quartets, for various instruments." In a footnote Burney comments: "It is but justice to say, that since my return to England, I have had these pieces tried, and have found them excellent: there is pleasing melody, free from caprice and affectation; sound harmony, and the contrivances and imitations are ingenious, without the least confusion. In short, the style is sober and sedate, without dulness; and masterly, without pedantry."

Gassmann's chamber divertimenti are quite numerous, comprising seven duos, fifty-seven trios, seventy-two quartets, and thirty-four quintets; his *Divertimenti a 3* for two violins and bass are slight, two- or three-movement works ending usually with a minuet, very like Haydn's many trios of the same kind from the 1760s.[6] The finales in a set of six four-movement *Divertimenti a 4* (H. 451–56) are in fugal form. Works like these by Gassmann are credited with maintaining the models of Fux and Martini and providing a link with the next generation of Viennese composers. Their artistic success has been described in these terms: "Gassmann, like any good fugal composer, constantly varies the character and formal scheme of his fugues; much of this variety is due to the choice of diverse thematic material."[7] As an example of a theme rich with potential, one containing certain folklike qualities, the same author quotes this subject from the fourth movement of the Divertimento in G (H. 451) (Example 6.1). With its wavering between 3/4 and 6/8, the theme may offer an example of at least one sense of what Burney meant by speaking of fugues in more than one *"time."* The prime destination of Gassmann's divertimenti with fugal finales was the private chamber concert of Joseph II, in which the composer took part.[8]

EXAMPLE 6.1. *Gassmann, Divertimento in G, IV*

[6] Gassmann, *Selected Divertimenti a tre and a quattro,* ed. Eve R. Meyer (Recent Researches in the Music of the Classical Era, 16.) (Madison, 1983). The Preface provides the most up-to-date summary of this composer's life and works.

[7] Roger Charles Hickman, "Six Bohemian Masters of the String Quartet in the Late Eighteenth Century" (Ph.D. diss., University of California, Berkeley, 1979), pp. 29–30.

[8] Alexander Wheelock Thayer, *Salieri: Rival of Mozart,* ed. Theodore Albrecht (Kansas City, 1989), p. 38.

In early 1765, to celebrate the second marriage of Joseph II, Gassmann set *Il trionfo d'amore*, which Metastasio revised for the occasion; Tibaldi and Guadagni sang the principal roles. The summer months of that year were taken up with elaborate festivities in Innsbruck, where the entire court assembled to celebrate the engagement of Archduke Leopold with Maria Luisa of Spain. Gassmann's contribution was the music to a "ballo eroico," *Enea in Italia,* an allusion to Leopold's impending tour of duty as grand duke of Tuscany. Emperor Francis died suddenly on 18 August, casting a pall on the celebrations, and both Viennese theaters were closed indefinitely as a consequence. The French troupe was encouraged to seek its fortunes elsewhere, but most of the other personnel were kept on salary, free to take temporary leave. Gassmann took the opportunity to return to Venice and compose *Achille in Sciro* for the S. Giovanni Grisostomo theater.

Returning to Vienna in the spring of 1766, Gassmann found a dearth of seria singers at his disposal, but in their stead an excellent buffo ensemble. The veteran Francesco Carrattoli was available for basso buffo *caricato* parts, as were the prima buffa Clementina Baglioni and the tenor Giuseppe Pinetti, all three favorites of the public. For Baglioni and Pinetti he set Goldoni's *Il viaggiatore ridicolo,* which was given on 25 May 1766 in the Kärntnerthor Theater to much applause, according to Joseph Khevenhüller. On 11 November 1766 the opera reopened the Burgtheater. The following spring Gassmann set Goldoni's *L'amore artigiano* for the same forces (the premiere was on 26 April 1767); this work was to achieve the greatest success of all his operas, and is a key work in the evolution of Viennese opera buffa.

Goldoni wrote *L'amore artigiano* in 1761, a year before he left Venice for Paris. Gaetano Latilla made the first setting for the S. Angelo theater, and Gassmann, still in Venice at this time, surely got to know it. Like most of Latilla's music, this score has never been found. Goldoni's *dramma giocoso* capitalizes on the fad for showing various craft workers on the stage. Its main set is a little square with the house of Angiolina, a hat maker, on one side, across from the shop of Bernardo, a cobbler, who is the father of Rosina. The two young ladies are rivals for the affections of Giannino, a joiner. But Bernardo has determined that his daughter will marry the more wealthy Tita, a locksmith. Mme. Costanza, a widow of some years, provides a way out of the imbroglio by settling a dowry on Rosina, her housemaid, so that Rosina and Giannino can marry. Costanza's motives are not the purest: by getting Rosina out of the way, there will be no temptations, other than herself, for her valet Fabrizio. By Goldoni's definition a *dramma giocoso* included some seria elements, and the variety of singing styles this allowed made for the success of the genre. None of the characters can be called seria, but the romantic pair show signs of the kind of sentimental expression that made

Goldoni's *La buona figliuola,* as set by Niccolò Piccinni for Rome in 1760, such an epochal success.

Marco Coltellini is the presumed adapter of the libretto for Vienna. He replaced about half of the arias and made a major change in the cast by introducing in place of Fabrizio the French valet Giro, who speaks a mixture of French and Italian and demonstrates for Mme. Costanza the glories of the Paris Opéra. Such a character would have made less sense in Venice, but in Vienna, where French troupes in the Burgtheater were a vivid memory, he was an asset. The part was created for the tenor Pinetti (who was perhaps in reality Pinet?). Giacomo Caribaldi, another tenor, took the romantic lead, Giannino, playing opposite Baglioni as Rosina; her scolding and miserly old Pantaloon of a father was made to order for Carrattoli. The Viennese libretto listed the singers by categories; I have supplied their roles by deduction.

Prime Buffe:	La Sigra. Clementina Baglioni Poggi (Rosina)
	La Sigra. Teresa Eberardi (Angiolina)
Seconda Buffa:	La Sigra. Anna Maria Cataldi (Mme Costanza)
Primi mezzi caratteri:	Il Sigre. Giacomo Caribaldi (Giannino)
	Il Sigre. Giuseppe Pinetti (Giro)
Primo Buffo caricato:	Il Sigre. Francesco Carrattoli (Bernardo)
Secondo Buffo:	Il Sigre. Agostino Liparini (Tita)

Gassmann selected the key of B♭ for the overture, an unusual choice. It begins with the tapping sounds (repeated eighth notes *unisoni*) that are associated with Bernardo at work cobbling, as is made specific in the finale of the first act. In the reprise of the first movement the composer reverses the order of first and second themes, as was his wont in concert symphonies. After an *Allegretto* in E♭, 3/8, full of Lombard snaps and conveying perhaps the romantic aspect of the story that the audience was about to witness, there is a brusque finale restoring the keynote, surprisingly followed by an *Adagio* of several measures that prepares the first scene, as the curtain rises to reveal the piazzetta with shops boarded up on either side. It is dawn. Rosina and Angiolina, unseen, from opposite windows above, sing of their amorous hopes, first singly and then together; this *Allegretto* in B♭ and in 3/8 gives way to E♭ and 6/8 as the single object of these hopes, Giannino, appears, strumming his guitar (pizzicato strings) and singing an *aubade* intended for Rosina, but received by both young ladies with rapture.

A composite scene like this at the beginning of Act I is properly called an *introduzione,* and it contains one amazing anticipation of the greatest *Introduzione* of all, in Mozart's *Don Giovanni,* when the piece dissolves on an unresolved $V^{6/3}$ in the strings (the same $G^{6/3}$, in fact!) giving way to simple recitative. Goldoni is to be thanked for inventing the *introduzione,* just as he invented the finale, a closely parallel phenomenon. His inexhaustible wit pushed him to wring still more out of the situation at the beginning of *L'amore artigiano* by having Giannino resume his *aubade* after the dialogue in recitative, but this time the tenor's singing awakens old Bernardo, who lures him into a trap by answering in a falsetto soprano.

Gassmann's variety and careful tonal planning allowed him to sustain a high level of interest through the several arias that follow. Giro is a special case, since his music represents a different world. Gassmann chooses the key of b for his sad little minuet air "A Paris tout est beau, tout est charmant / A l'opéra, aux Tuileries / L'on s'ennuie par simpathie." After a further demonstration, this time of old-style French recitative with tortuous chromatic harmonies, Mme. Costanza expresses her doubts:

Giro:	Helas, in quello stil cromatico . . .	Alas, in this chromatic style . . .
Mme. C.:	Ohibo pare il respiro d'un asmatico.	It resembles an asthmatic's breathing.
Giro (aside):	Elle n'a pointe de goût.	She has no taste.
	Non intendete la forza d'espressione.	The force of expression escapes her.

In a Vienna where the virtues of French versus Italian opera were argued at the highest levels of state, this exchange could not have been more topical.

By the time we reach scene 18, the piazzetta has reappeared, but now the shops are open to the outside and the artisans are at work. The finale begins in G and in common time, with Bernardo tapping away and singing, "Questo Cuojo è duro, duro" (This leather is tough). Goldoni preserved the eight-syllable line for the first round of exchanges among the several characters, but he changed to five-syllable lines at the moment Tita asks for Rosina's hand: "Maestro Bernardo / A vostra figlia." Gassmann takes the cue and switches to *Allegretto,* 3/8, now in C major. Much of the time he sets the short lines to |♪♪♪|♪♪♪|, but he freely breaks the pattern with other rhythmic settings. As the young ladies warm to the fight, the modulations range more widely and land us in g minor.

Goldoni's finale ends soon after this point, with two quatrains expressing perplexity. Coltellini extended the finale by bringing in an additional character, Giro, whose E♭ with dotted rhythms coming right after the cadence on g minor makes a strong theatrical effect.[9] He reproves the quarreling girls, upon which everyone threatens him and tries to drive him away,

[9] A brief example of Giro's entrance music is quoted by Gustave Donath, "Florian Leopold Gassmann als Opernkomponist," *Studien zur Musikwissenschaft* 2 (1914): 98.

to an *Allegro* in 3/8 and in G, ending on V of D. The final section sets in, *Allegro molto*, 4/4 and in D, as blows are rained on Giro, and the finale is brought to a noisy conclusion ("O che fracasso!") in its original tonic, G. What Coltellini has provided for, perhaps at Gassmann's suggestion, is the typical *stretto* conclusion as described by Da Ponte in his memoirs.

Particularly effective is Gassmann's treatment of the male romantic lead, Giannino, sung by the tenor Caribaldi. In Act I, aside from his *aubade*, he sings an aria, No. 6, "Occhielli cari," that is one of the opera's few slow pieces (*Largo* in 3/4). Moreover, Gassmann chooses the hitherto unused key of A and enhances its sensuous qualities with muted oboes. This is only one example among many of the composer's imaginative orchestration, especially evident in his attention to distinctive wind coloring. The text of No. 6 projects another affect besides Giannino's amorous sighs for the little eyes of his beloved, namely anger at his rivals, which elicits a contrasting and buffo section in the music, after which the return to the main part is all the more moving. In Act II he sings a magnificent obbligato recitative leading up to his No. 18 aria, "D'una parte amore mi dice" (Love tells me on the one hand), the opera's grandest and most beautiful piece. It is also divided into two affects, the main one being amorous, for which Gassmann employs the most expressive tonality of all, E♭, when it is joined with a stately quality of movement, here a *Grave* in cut time (Example 6.2). The melodic-harmonic progression in mm. 3–4 is of an almost Mozartian warmth, and anticipates a progression at the beginning of the overture to *Die Zauberflöte*. Giannino fears that the beautiful Rosina will betray him, and so the music vacillates between bliss at the anticipation of love's rewards and anxiety. In the final section he embraces joy, expressed in quick 6/8 time. There is a short horn solo in this final part, which just may portray the lover's bounding heart (cf. the horns at the end of Fiordiligi's "Per pietà" in *Così fan tutte*). More about this splendid aria in E♭ will be heard in the next section on Gassmann's pupil and successor, Salieri.

A finale equivalent in span and construction to that in Act I ends Act II, a tavern scene that erupts in quarrels and in which Giannino, having passed out from overindulgence, is revived by Giro's eau de cologne. The third and last act also ends with a big finale, incorporating within it the expected love duet. Here the lovers assume *mezzo carattere* hues and are even allowed coloratura, without giving up many buffo characteristics. This finale begins in B♭ but ends in D, perhaps conveying the general surprise occasioned by the news that the lovers were already married.

The fall of 1767 saw another engagement within the large imperial family, that of Archduchess Maria Josepha to King Ferdinand IV of Naples. Metastasio and Hasse wrote the main opera, *Partenope*; Coltellini and Gassmann

EXAMPLE 6.2. *Gassmann*, L'amore artigiano, *Aria*

wrote the secondary work, *Amore e Psiche*,[10] which, with its six choruses, offered the composer scope to try something more in the vein of Gluck, whose *Alceste* was about to be performed in the Burgtheater. The castrato Venanzio Rauzzini had to be borrowed from Munich to sing the primo uomo roles in *Amore* and *Partenope*. Leopold Mozart, for one, was not particularly impressed with the singers: "Hasse's opera is very beautiful, but the singers, be it noted, are nothing out of the ordinary for such a festive occasion. Signor Tibaldi is the tenor, Signor Rauzzini from Munich, the leading castrato. The prima donna is Signora Teiber, the daughter of a violinist at the Viennese court. But the dances are excellent, the leading dancer being the famous Frenchman Vestris" (letter of 29 September 1767). A week later Leopold reported that the royal bride had contracted smallpox. Ten days later still, on 17 October, he wrote that she had died. The season came to an abrupt end.

Joseph II was responsible for the demise of opera seria in Vienna. He was unwilling to pay the high fees its singers commanded. Gassmann car-

---

[10] Gassmann, *Amore e Psiche* (Italian Opera Seria 1640–1770, 87) (New York and London, 1983). Donath, "Gassmann als Opernkomponist," quotes the ending of Act II (Appendix III) and points out (p. 71) how indebted it is to the techniques of the comic finale.

ried out the emperor's wishes in his own oeuvre, from which opera seria gradually disappeared as a result. While Leopold Mozart was scheming to get an opera buffa by Wolfgang performed in Vienna, Gassmann was successfully directing a new one in the Burgtheater (premiere on 5 January 1768), his setting of Goldoni's fine libretto *La notte critica*.

In the fall of 1768 Gassmann and Coltellini revised the composer's first comic opera, on Goldoni's *Gli uccelatori*. Then in 1769 Gassmann set Raniero de' Calzabigi's *commedia per musica* entitled *L'opera seria*, another in a long line of works parodying the serious genre.[11] Calzabigi leaves no aspect unparodied, from the nearly bankrupt impresario (Fallito), flighty poet (Delerio) and affected composer (Sospiro) to the conceited singers, their even more impossible mothers, the choreographer, and so on down to the lowly copyist and printer's boy.

Plans were laid in 1769 for an imposing imperial progress that would take Joseph II (and Gassmann as well) to Naples and Rome in early 1770. In honor of the event the Roman Teatro delle Dame commissioned a setting of Metastasio's *Ezio* from Gassmann. The fulsome preface of the printed libretto, dedicating the opera to the sovereign, mentions the origins of the poet ("our countryman") and composer ("one of your subjects who is master of his art at your imperial court"). Giovanni Manzuoli headed the cast in the title role. This time there were no complaints about opera seria from Joseph II, whose objections to the genre apparently lessened when others footed the bills.

Gassmann was still in Italy as late as mid-summer 1770. Burney encountered him in Milan on 17 July at a performance of *L'amore artigiano* in the Teatro Reggio Ducale: "The music, which had pretty things in it, was by Signor Floriano Gasman, in the service of the emperor, who played the harpsichord." Perhaps the composer was already at work on the next showpiece for Joseph II, which was to be a comic opera for Vienna's buffo troupe. The work was specially prepared to enhance imperial prestige at the meeting in early September between Joseph II and Frederick II of Prussia, which took place in Moravia. The choice of subject fell upon *La contessina*, Goldoni's old *dramma per musica* of 1743. Coltellini remade the work into a *dramma giocoso* with ensembles and action finales in line with current fashions.[12] Not much was left of Goldoni's libretto when Coltellini was finished, but it was still a tribute to the great Venetian poet that even his earliest and slightest works continued to serve as springboards.

La contessina is an empty-headed young lady, a snob of the first order,

[11] Gassmann, *L'opera seria* (Italian Opera Seria 1640-1770, 89) (London and New York, 1982).

[12] Reinhard Strohm, *Die italienische Oper im 18. Jahrhunderts* (Wilhelmshaven, 1979), pp. 278ff. The score is edited by Robert Haas in *DTÖ* 42–44.

who is indulged by her pompous father, Baccelone (formerly a peasant, now a count), and by her fawning lover, Lindoro, who lies about his social status in trying to win her hand. The servants see through the folly and pretense, as usual, and so does Lindoro's father, Pancrazio, a wealthy merchant-banker. The action is laid in Venice. Goldoni's neutral "room in the house of Pancrazio" for the first scene gives way in the new opera to a counting room where Lindoro is writing a letter, Pancrazio is standing at his ledger, pen in hand, and his apprentice Gazzetta is manipulating some counting balls—the very image of bourgeois industry and well-being.

Goldoni began with the main plot line: Lindoro confesses in a recitative that he was smitten by a young noble lady he met on the *burchiello* coming from Padua, in response to which Pancrazio admits in an aria that he too was once young and passionate. The new opera forgoes recitative at first and projects the workday activities of the three men in a *terzetto*. An ensemble for two tenors and bass was still a rather rare phenomenon around 1770, and the effect must have been all the more stunning because of its novelty. Moreover, the opening is followed, after a little recitative, by a second *terzetto* in a different key for the same three. *Così fan tutte* comes to mind inevitably, but so does *Die Zauberflöte* because of the popular and dancelike nature of the music, specifically the persistent use of an offbeat accompanimental figure in the violins associated with Papageno, |♪ ♫♫ ♩ ♪ |, found in the second *terzetto*. An aria for Pancrazio in B♭ rounds off the first scene. The tonal span actually began with the three-movement overture, which is also in B♭, and contains a subdominant slow movement, yielding a symmetrical deployment of keys that is characteristic of the composer: overture—B♭ - E♭ - B♭; Nos. 1–3—B♭ - F - B♭.

The overture begins with a little contrapuntal dialogue for its first theme, which is transformed into an imitative dialogue for the second theme (the two are reversed in the reprise). The emperor's predilections for counterpoint are easily perceived here, as they often are in Gassmann's chamber music. In terms of the drama, the contrapuntal themes of the overture predict and enhance the picture of sober industry projected by the opening scene, and pertain particularly to the wise old fox Pancrazio, who closes this segment with his aria in B♭. The link is reinforced when in the middle of his aria, at the words "Eh lasciami fare" (Let me do it), the music makes reference to the turn toward the minor mode initiating the development of the overture's opening *Allegro,* its most "serious" movement. But the Papageno rhythmic figure, mentioned above in connection with the second *terzetto* and even more prominent in Pancrazio's aria, is also planted in the first movement of the overture. This serves to warn us not to put too much stock in the overture's contrapuntal trappings, which are integrated into an overall fabric that is homophonic, extremely euphonious, buffo in tone, and more truly symphonic than the composer's own symphonies. As a testimony to Gassmann's melodic gift, be it noted that the overture's closing *Allegro molto* in 3/8 anticipates the catchy tune from Giuseppe Sarti's *Fra i due litiganti* (1782) that Mozart quoted in *Don Giovanni* ("Versa il vino").

From the banking house of Pancrazio the scene changes to the boudoir of La Contessina. The orchestra begins a sensuous Cavatina, *Andantino* in 3/4, which she will sing. To express the change of atmosphere represented by this intrusion into a feminine world, Mozart probably would have modulated up a third (*Figaro*, beginning of Act II) or down a third (*Così fan tutte*, Act I, Scene 2). Gassmann remains close to where he has been by choosing F (although it arrives after a recitative cadence on a). He colors his minuet-like music with chromatic appoggiature so that it sounds unlike most of the preceding pieces—the nearest is the *Andante* of the overture, which features the same skittish motions of the violins ascending and descending in sixteenth-note scales marked staccato. The key of A, which might have been expected here, occurs in the following *Cavatina a due* for Lindoro and his adored idol. He offers her his hand; she asks if his glove is clean, because otherwise her stomach could not stand it. This lapse into farce comes from Goldoni and is typical of his satirical portraits of *precieuses*; Gassmann's orchestra seems to laugh at the situation too by persistently reiterating the Papageno motif.

When Lindoro sings his aria, No. 8, it is a full-scale love song in A, decorated with what I refer to later as an old-fashioned "Hasse cadence" (see Example 7.14b). Perhaps it was the love interest, expressed here at its most courtly, that decided the composer to choose the same key to end the opera, when the couple are finally united, which does not happen until the final two numbers, a *Coro*, No. 28 in A (actually it is only a quartet of the two lovers and the two fathers), and the finale, No. 29 in A (which is a finale only in the French sense of the vaudeville with choral refrain and couplets for all the characters, two by two).

The first two acts end with real finales, the first in D, the second in B♭. Nowhere does the composer venture beyond three accidentals. Among the most noteworthy features of the work are its six *terzettos* distributed over the three acts, the last of which, No. 24, is so filled with action and changes of key and tempo that it becomes a quasi-finale. As in *L'amore artigiano*, Gassmann allows some numbers to dissolve into recitative instead of coming to a formal conclusion. And as in that opera, he indulges his talent for mimicry with a chanson (No. 22 for Gazzetta, masquerading as a French marquis). For all its wonderful moments the opera is too long for its material.

Gassmann wrote at least four more comic operas, including *Le pescatrici*, which bears some relationship to Haydn's setting of a year earlier, but none of them achieved the wide diffusion of *L'amore artigiano* and *La contessina*. During his few remaining years he became even more prominent in Vienna's musical life. It was mainly through his efforts that the Tonkünstler Societät, dedicated to providing for the widows and orphans of deceased musicians, was founded in 1771. Within hours of the death of Hofkapellmeister Reutter on 12 March 1772, Gassmann was appointed his successor by Joseph II. *Ex officio* he also became musical head of the Tonkünstler Societät, whose charitable concerts were inaugurated on 29 March 1772 with his setting of Metastasio's oratorio *La Betulia liberata*, in which two hundred musicians participated, according to Ditters.[13] Gassmann reversed the long decline of the Hofkapelle under Reutter by securing more financial support and raising the number of personnel from twenty to forty. He took charge of the music library with a similar spirit of efficiency, as Burney reported:

> On quitting Signor Mancini, I hastened to M. Gasman, who was waiting to carry me to the Imperial musical library. I found in it an immense collection of musical authors, but in such disorder, that their contents are, at present, almost wholly unknown. However, M. Gasman has begun a catalogue, and is promised, by the Emperor, a larger and more commodious room for these books, than the present, in which they are promiscuously piled, one on another, in the most confused manner imaginable.

Presumably the music collection was housed in the imperial library building, of which Carl Schütz made a beautiful engraving dated 1780 and dedicated to Baron van Swieten (Figure 6.2).

The intense activity of Gassmann's last years included the composition of a quantity of church music and was carried on in spite of an injury, from which he never recovered, suffered in a carriage accident during his last Italian trip in 1770. His condition worsened in 1773, and he died on 20 January 1774, a few months short of his forty-fifth birthday. He left a widow and two daughters, one born after his death. When Giuseppe Bonno succeeded him, the pension Bonno already enjoyed reverted to the imperial treasury; Joseph II assigned the pension to Gassmann's widow and her two children.

Most contemporary accounts of Gassmann's music stress its solidity and ingenuity. But these virtues had their adverse side as Burney reported: "M. Gasman is accused by some of want of fire in his theatrical compositions." Burney found an easy explanation for the "gravity of his style" in his necessary preoccupation with church music. Then, as if to make up for his earlier remark, Burney went out of his way to praise the composer's penultimate

[13] Gassmann, *La Betulia liberata* (Italian Oratorio 1650–1800, 26) (New York, 1987).

FIGURE 6.2. Carl Schütz. The Imperial Library, 1780, with the Redoutensaal on the right.

opera, *I rovinati*, the last he heard in Vienna: "There was a contrast, an apposition and dissimulation of movements and passages, by which one contributed to the advantages and effects of another, that was charming and the instrumental parts were judiciously and ingeniously worked."

It may be added that deft orchestration plus a great variety of accompanimental patterns and textures helped Gassmann sustain musical interest over long periods of time, but above all he was aided by his control of long-range goals by means of tonal contrasts. This he learned gradually in his many operas, and especially in the comic finales. His church music, which came late, for the most part, and represents a relatively small part of his output, was not a deciding force, but rather the beneficiary of techniques gained in opera. Thus in his *Missa Sanctae Caeciliae* in C we observe him arranging the six sections into which he has divided the Gloria as he might the keys of a finale: C - F - B♭ - g - G - C. Well taken is the position that "despite the overall serious tone of the work, Gassmann's prowess as an opera composer is (like Bonno's) omnipresent (e.g., in the vocal lines, key plans, and instrumentation)."[14]

[14] Bruce C. MacIntyre, *The Viennese Concerted Mass of the Early Classic Period* (Ann Arbor, 1986), p. 69; see also p. 241.

Figure 6.3. Johann Balzer.
Engraved portrait of Florian
Gassmann.

Gassmann rescued Viennese court music from the stagnation it had reached under Reutter. He preserved the contrapuntal heritage peculiar to Vienna, to which he introduced the most modern kind of orchestrally and tonally designed opera buffa. And greatly to his credit, he recognized and nurtured the talents of two younger composers, Salieri and Vanhal. Salieri became his successor and a fine opera composer in his own right, one who also deserves credit for his long-term assistance to Gassmann's widow and orphaned daughters, both of whom became important singers.

Salieri

THE professional life of Antonio Salieri spanned a half century, in the course of which he devoted himself to very different musical pursuits. Born on 18 August 1750 in the city of Legnago, he was taught by local musicians and an older brother who was a violinist. Orphaned in 1765, he was taken by a friend of his family to Venice, where he studied thorough bass with Giovanni Pescetti and singing with Ferdinando Pacini, a tenor at St. Mark's. The following year he attracted the attention of the visiting Gassmann, who took him to Vienna and saw to it that his studies were intensified. This was in June 1766, according to Salieri's memoirs of many years later. Either he errs by a few months or the date on the libretto of Gassmann's *Il viaggiatore ridicolo* (26 May 1766) is wrong. In any case, young Salieri was at his master's side during the renewal of Viennese opera buffa initiated by Gassmann after the hiatus of 1765–66, when the theaters were closed. He also came into contact with Gluck, who encouraged his earliest efforts as a composer.

Before his death in 1825, Salieri compiled some notes on his life that were subsequently translated into German by Ignaz von Mosel and published at Vienna in 1827 with additional material under the title *Über das Leben und Werke des Antonio Salieri*.[15] These memoirs, like those of Ditters, are filled with striking episodes relating to musical life in Vienna, and in almost all instances they ring true or can be corroborated from other sources.

As Salieri tells it, he was presented by Gassmann to Emperor Joseph soon after their arrival in Vienna. Joseph asked the young man to sing and play something from memory at the keyboard, which Salieri did to the monarch's satisfaction. This happened just before the emperor's private concert in his chambers, which took place daily according to one source, three times a week according to another, in the time after dinner and before the theater.

> Now began the ordinary chamber concert, of which the music that day happened to be vocal pieces from Hasse's opera *Alcide al bivio*. Salieri sang not only the alto in the choruses, but several solos with ease and correctness from the score. This pleased Joseph much and he ordered Gassmann always in the future to bring his pupil with him; this he did and so began Salieri's service at the Imperial Court, never to be interrupted so long as his powers lasted.[16]

The choice of music performed helps confirm the accuracy of Salieri's memoirs. Hasse's *Alcide* was written as part of the celebrations surrounding Joseph's first marriage in 1760, and the opera remained one of the emperor's favorite works, perhaps in part because it reminded him of his all-too-brief but happy marriage with Isabella of Parma, who died in 1763. There is also confirmation of a sort in the report of Joseph's private concerts published

---

[15] The American scholar Alexander Wheelock Thayer wrote a biography of Salieri based largely on Mosel for serialization in *Dwight's Journal of Music* (Boston, 1864). It has been published with commentary as *Salieri: Rival of Mozart*, ed. Theodore Albrecht (Kansas City, 1989).
[16] Ibid., p. 38.

shortly after his death: "The Emperor was fond of the pathetic and some-times had music by Gassmann, Ordonez, etc. placed on the stands. Gener-ally, however, favorite passages from serious operas and oratorios were played from the score."[17]

Gassmann soon began having his young Italian protégé replace him at the harpsichord in the theater, and this occupation provided Salieri with several amusing recollections. At first Salieri worked for no salary, but he received an annual monetary gift from Joseph on New Year's Day in reward for his services in chamber music and in the theater. He claims that he com-posed a quantity of vocal and instrumental music, including two symphon-ies, before writing his first full-scale opera, all of which he destroyed, and that Gassmann allowed him to write "a short Italian opera for four voices and chorus." Salieri also supplied ariettas, duets, trios, and some ballet movements for other operas that were being performed.

In late 1769 Gassmann again traveled to Italy, whence he did not return until mid-1770. In his absence Salieri, aged nineteen, was given his first chance to compose a large work for the Burgtheater's buffo troupe, the same group for which Gassmann wrote *L'amore artigiano* in 1767 and Mozart wrote *La finta semplice* in 1768. As Salieri tells it, the young poet Giovanni Gastone Boccherini, the author of the oratorio Haydn composed in 1775, was encour-aged by Calzabigi to offer Salieri a comic libretto, *Le donne letterate*, that he had written for Gassmann. Salieri's description of how he went about plan-ning his setting of the libretto is invaluable because its like can be found nowhere else. The poet went over the plot with him, and together they matched roles to singers in the company (they were not in a position to assign roles, needless to say, because only the theater direction could do that). Then Salieri read the whole libretto. "I read the poem through again, found it certainly well adapted to music, and, having read the vocal pieces for the third time, my first step was—as I had seen my master do—to deter-mine which key would suit the character of each separate piece."[18]

Salieri enlivens his account with details about how he became so fired up by the creative process that even while eating and sleeping he could think only of the opera.

---

[17] *Musikalische Correspondence* (Speyer, 28 July 1790), cited after Thayer, *Salieri*, pp. 33–36.

[18] Thayer's translation, which I continue to quote in what follows. For Moser's German original and a different English translation, see Daniel Heartz, *Mozart's Operas* (Berkeley, 1990), pp. 139, 154–55. Cf. what Carl Maria von Weber wrote about his cantata *Kampf und Sieg* (1815): "Before turning my attention to details I sketched in my mind a complete plan of the tonal canvas and determined the basic color of each section. That is to say, I wrote out clearly the sequence of keys and hence the emotional moods." Carl Maria von Weber, *Writings on Music*, trans. Martin Cooper, ed. John War-rack (Cambridge, 1981), p. 160.

As soon as I was alone, I felt an irrepressible desire to set the music of the introduction to the opera. I therefore sought to place the character and the situation of the persons of the drama vividly before my imagination, and suddenly discovered a movement of the orchestra which seemed to me fitted to bear up and give unity to the vocal music which the text necessarily made fragmentary. Now I fancied myself in the pit listening to the production of my ideas; they seemed to me characteristic; I wrote them down, put them again to proof, and as I was satisfied with them went on. So in half an hour the outline of the Introduction stood there on the music paper . . . I read the first finale, which, as to the words, began very much like the Introduction; I read it again, formed a plan of the rhythm and keys ["Plan der Tact- und Ton-Arten"] suited to the work as a whole—giving three hours to this work, but without writing a note.

Working at great speed after his carefully laid plans of the whole, Salieri finished two-thirds of the composition and orchestration in a month. He intended to wait until his master returned, he says, before completing the opera, but the failure of the current offering in the Burgtheater to please the public occasioned an immediate opportunity. He was summoned to bring his score to the theater.

According to Salieri, there was an improviso run-through of his incomplete score in the presence of Gluck, Giuseppe Scarlatti, and the theater director, Giuseppe Affligio.

I sang and played what was finished, and in the concerted pieces Gluck and Scarlatti sang with me. Gluck, who had always liked and encouraged me, showed himself at the very beginning satisfied with my work; Scarlatti, who from time to time pointed out little grammatical errors in my composition, praised also each number on the whole and, at the close, both masters said to the manager [Affligio] that if I would immediately finish the lacking numbers, they would without delay rehearse and produce the work, "in that," in Gluck's own works, "this work contains what is sufficient to give the public pleasure." . . . I promised my judges the greatest industry until the work was put upon the stage. I wrote day and night, ran to the rehearsals, went through the vocal parts with the singers, corrected the copyists, joined the poet in devising the costumes and decorations, and lived in such an unbroken strain both of mental and physical powers, that if study, drudgery and sweat did not throw me upon a sick bed, I can only think it was because my happiness acted as a protection.

The happy outcome of Salieri's encounter with the forces that ran the Burgtheater forms a curious counterpoint to the unhappy experiences of Mozart and his father with these same people the previous year. Salieri was already an insider, one who stood high in the favor of Joseph II.

Le donne letterate reached the stage of the Burgtheater in its first public performance on 10 January 1770. The general rehearsal took place on 9 January in the daytime, for the premises were otherwise occupied at night.

> That evening I went into the theater with beating heart to hear my opera announced for the performance which was done in these words: "Tomorrow the Italian operatic company will have the honor to produce a new opera entitled *Le donne letterate*, poem by Herr Gastone Boccherini, music by Herr Antonio Salieri; the first work of both." Several persons in the audience applauded which gave me sweet confidence and seemed to me a good augury. Next morning, early as I thought it possible that the bills could be posted at the street corners, I went out to see my name for the first time in print, which gave me deep gratification. But not satisfied with seeing it once—much as I feared it might have been omitted from other bills—I ran all round town to read it everywhere.

There is valuable information and insight to be gained even here. Theatrical offerings were decided on a day-to-day basis. They were announced *viva voce* in the theater itself and otherwise made known to the public by printed posters that were put up at dawn for the same evening's performance. Few posters have survived from this period. What Salieri reveals about his behavior as a nineteen-year-old, running about the streets of Vienna to read his name in print, rings altogether true because he takes no pains to cover up his naïveté. His is a typically eighteenth-century lack of self-consciousness, found as well in what Ditters says about himself.

Salieri also tells us a good deal about the singers in the Burgtheater at that time, how he humored them and managed to overcome their caprices. The tenor Giacomo Caribaldi, he says, was a servant in a Roman shop when he first appeared on the stage there, aged twenty-four. Caribaldi came to Vienna in his late twenties and appeared first in the role of Giannino in Gassmann's *L'amore artigiano*. His big aria in the second act was in E♭, as we have seen, and "had gained him immense applause, and thus the notion had become a sort of fixed idea"—the singer deduced that this key was particularly favorable to his voice. Salieri had given him no aria in his favorite key in the new opera and wondered how to get around the problem.

> At first he took to Caribaldi only an aria in the second act which leads into a trio and left him to think that the aria in the first act was not written, "which you will surely write in E♭?" said the singer. "Of course," replied the other—though it was long since finished in B♭ and there was now no time to change it. Salieri went to Domenico Poggi, another singer of the company—a good musician and friend of Caribaldi, whom he called Signor E-la-fa on account of his E♭ whim— and asked what he should do.

Caribaldi, it turns out, was not a "good musician," or at least not a complete one, because he was musically illiterate. "Poggi looked the aria through, saw it was good, and told him to tell the copyist to place three flats at the beginning of Caribaldi's vocal copy, for as he could not read music, if he only saw the three flats that would be sufficient. Poggi also promised to help carry on the deception, and hoped that here was an opportunity to cure his friend of his nonsense." Salieri spins out the tale further, and before he is finished the violinist Giuseppe Trani and basso buffo Francesco Carrattoli are drawn into the trick, which did cure Caribaldi of his obsession with E♭.

Le donne letterate enjoyed a modest success with the public, sufficient in any case to elicit further collaborations between composer and poet. In 1772 Salieri composed three comic operas, two on librettos by Boccherini, one of which, *La fiera di Venezia*, "had a splendid success." This opera, wrote Mosel in 1827, "for its excellence and for its firm hold upon the favor of the public, was the talk of old people in Vienna more than fifty years later—during which half century Mozart, Beethoven, Cherubini, and Rossini had risen upon the stage." Boccherini's imaginative libretto accounts for part of this favor. The action takes place at the Ascension Fair, and the settings alternate between intimate domestic scenes (as if painted by Pietro Longhi), canals, local landmarks such as a view of the Rialto bridge, and, for the finale of Act III (as if painted by Canaletto), the grand view of Venice across the water from the Giudecca. Boccherini made his debut as a ballet dancer in Venice in 1757, so he was well acquainted with its delights. His years as a dancer in Vienna lasted from 1759 to 1767, when he turned toward a literary career. As for Salieri, he knew Venice intimately as well.

Of *La fiera di Venezia*'s large cast of five male and three female solo singers, the two principal sopranos stand out as particularly well characterized, Marchesa Calloandra of Vicenza and the Venetian commoner Falsirena. The former is the daughter of a nobleman who is an opera impresario, and behaves with all the preciosity she can muster. The opera opens in a public square with a chorus of merchants offering their wares for sale. After six solo arias the set changes to a room in an inn with harpsichord, rented by the marchesa. Her soliloquy is a takeoff on a pastoral lament, using the clichés of the type. It begins, "Col Zeffiro, e col rio / Piango e sospir anch'io / Sfogando le mie pene" (With the breeze and the brook I also weep and sigh, venting my sorrows), and it ends "O Dio! Chi mi consola / se l'idol mio non viene?" (Egad! Who will console me if my idol tarries?). Her complaints are founded on nothing more than impatience for the arrival of her lover, the rich Duke Ostrogoto, who promptly arrives. The marchesa sings her cavatina, an *Adagio* in F, to a rustling accompaniment; there is coloratura on the last line (even though it has no "a" syllable), and the voice is carried up to high C.

The role would seem to have been created for Clementina Baglioni (the printed libretto lacks the names of the original cast).

The plot is typically complex. Ostrogoto is affianced to the marchesa but infatuated with Falsirena, who is interested in him only for his money. Falsirena enters under the pretense of being the opera singer Alamirena seeking an engagement. The marchesa sits down at her harpsichord and proposes sight reading a duet as a trial. After a few excuses the feigned *cantatrice* and her accompanist sing an Acis and Galathea duet (the piece is missing from the Viennese score), and all goes well. The trial was apparently for nought, for the marchesa next says, "My father does not do opera seria." Falsirena responds, "I also recite buffa—here is an example," which she then provides in a lengthy piece on a jargon text that incorporates both buffo patter and coloratura up to high D. The act ends with a gambling scene.

At the beginning of Act II Falsirena disguises herself as a French merchant and speaks only in French to the noble couple, who answer her back in Italian. To end this scene she sings an air in d and in 6/8, "L'Amour est un Dieux cauteleux" (cunning), a totally syllabic little piece, like a vaudeville. The marchesa comments, "Che insipida canzone." (Recall Costanza's disdain for Giro's French song in the minor mode in Gassmann's *L'amore artigiano.*) Moreover, Salieri includes a *terzetto* for three men as the second number of Act II and a duet in the minor mode for two men in Act III. These would be unusual in Italy but not in Vienna, especially after the *terzetto*s for male voices in Gassmann's *La contessina* of 1770. With his parodies of French music as well as his ensembles, Salieri has become typically Viennese.

Falsirena's most amusing disguise comes in scene 7 of Act II, where she enters as a German baroness who has just had a rough ride in a gondola: "Was verfluchte henkermässige Lehnwagen / Sind doch die Gondeln!" (What devilishly damnable vehicles these gondolas are!) She initiates a trio with the two noble lovers, in which she compares what she has just experienced with the delirium of dancing the *Teutsche:*

So wie bey den deutschen Tänzen	As in the German dances
Bey uns öfters pflegt zu gehn,	That we often perform,
Wo in Zirkelrunden Gränzen	Where, in circular patterns,
Jünglinge die Mädchen drehn:	Youths lead maidens,
So gehn Wände, Bett und Stüble	And walls, bed, and room
Alles mit mir um und um;	Spin round and round
Das ich nichts mehr seh, noch fühle	So that I neither see nor feel anything
Ach zur Hilf . . . Ich bin ganz dumm.	Ah, help me . . . I am confounded.

Salieri sets this as a lusty contredanse in 2/4 (Example 6.3). Typical of the contredanse in 2/4 is the stamping rhythm of three eighth notes at the

EXAMPLE 6.3. *Salieri*, La fiera di Venezia, *Lied*

cadence (here shown at the half cadence). Haydn and Mozart did not disdain to write sets of such dances for the balls in the Redoutensaal, and Beethoven wrote the most famous contredanse of all, used as the theme of the finale of his *Eroica* Symphony. Ditters was particularly fond of using the stamping rhythm of the contredanse in both vocal and instrumental compositions. In fact, Salieri's German song of 1772 would sound quite at home in a Singspiel such as Ditters' *Doktor und Apotheker* of fourteen years later.

After Falsirena as German baroness sings her eight lines to a contredanse melody, the action accelerates. According to the stage direction, she embraces Ostrogoto and makes him gyrate around the room with her, for which Salieri provides a *Presto* in 3/8, a veritable *Teutsche*, to which the madly whirling couple must sing while waltzing. The marchesa offers interjections of protest as well, so that the music is a kind of *terzetto*, but it is only the orchestral dance that holds the piece together (an example of the technique the composer described in connection with his first full-scale opera).[19]

The finale of Act II takes place in a brilliantly lit ballroom, with orchestra onstage. After the opening *Coro* in D, Salieri introduces a minuet in A to which the characters dance, and which evolves through several changes of key and mode, providing the framework for the action. At one point Falsirena addresses Ostrogoto as Adonis, and he replies by addressing her as Venus (Example 6.4). The first strain of this particular minuet concludes with a *cadence galante* on V, and the second strain with another on I. In this respect it anticipates the famous minuet in G danced and sung in the ballroom of Don Giovanni's palace in the first-act finale of Mozart's opera. There is no question that Mozart well knew the earlier ballroom scene. He wrote six keyboard variations on "Mio caro Adone" (K. 180) when he and Leopold were in Vienna in 1773.

Unlike the minuet in *Don Giovanni*, the dancing does not come to a halt with an attempted rape and a scream for help. But things do go wrong, to

---

[19] The origins of the waltz on the stages of Vienna go back at least a generation before *La fiera di Venezia*. Fast music in triple meter described by the sung verb "walzen" occurs as early as the 1750s. See the *Arie* "O du armer Welt" in *Deutsche Comödien-Arien*, DTÖ 64, vol. 1, p. 18.

EXAMPLE 6.4. *Salieri,* La fiera di Venezia, *Minuet*

the extent that Falsirena slaps her greedy father, Grifagno, a Pantaloon figure, then lapses into Venetian dialect, saying she wants to dance the forlana:
"Questo xe un spasso / Che il cuor m'alletta / La Furlanetta / Voggio ballar"
(This caper so delights my heart, I want to dance the forlana). The stage
direction then reads, "Ballano la Furlana." Salieri likewise lapses into Venetian dialect in his music, by replacing the minuet with a dance in 12/8 meter,
marked *forte* and *sempre staccato* (Example 6.5). Into the stream of eighth
notes in a fast tempo Salieri introduces the special melodic cadence that had
been characteristic of the forlana for generations.[20] From the visual point of
view, the forlana was a vigorous couple dance in which the woman pulled
her skirts up to her knees and mimicked the fast footwork of her partner. It
was, in other words, as far removed as possible from the modesty and dignity of the minuet.

Salieri was evidently proud of the passage from sedate minuet to vulgar
Venetian folk dance in the second-act finale. He took these two dances and
made them into the middle movements of the overture, a Sinfonia that
begins and ends with a rousing D-major *Allegro Presto* in common time. In
his own way he signaled to the audience that the setting of the opera was

EXAMPLE 6.5. *Salieri,* La fiera di Venezia, *Forlana*

[20] The cadence occurs in "La Forlana" of André Campra's *L'Europe galante* of 1697 and is probably
even older than that.

Venice, even before the curtain went up on the first scene; thus he conformed to the strictures about the function of the overture in the preface of Gluck's *Alceste*. There are many moments of musical brilliance in *La fiera di Venezia*, but none does its young composer greater credit than his genial idea of moving the minuet-to-forlana sequence to the heart of the overture.

La fiera di Venezia established Salieri's reputation. It was played in several northern European cities where opera buffa was cultivated. Salieri himself was invited to take a position in Stockholm, according to his memoirs, but Joseph II dissuaded him from leaving. At Gassmann's death in 1774, Salieri replaced his master in the chamber music, an appointment that brought him 100 ducats annually, and at about the same time he was appointed director of music in the court theaters at a salary of 300 ducats per annum. Thus he assumed some but not all of Gassmann's functions as Kapellmeister; Bonno, the new Kapellmeister, took over the rest.

There were many revivals of *La fiera di Venezia* in Vienna. Salieri's revisions of and additions to his score pose quite a problem to any prospective editor. In reaction to a production of the opera being prepared in Munich in the fall of 1785, Leopold Mozart wrote his daughter in typically caustic terms that he found it "full of worn-out commonplace ideas, old-fashioned, forced, and very empty as to harmony; only the finales are still tolerable; as for the plot, it is, as usual, stupid Italian childishness, contrary to all sound human ken" (letter of 28 November 1785).

Leopold Mozart does an injustice to the libretto of *La fiera di Venezia*—its poet possessed a considerable comic gift. Perhaps it was inevitable that he found the score's harmony thin when compared with the works his son had composed in the meantime. With *Idomeneo* and *Die Entführung aus dem Serail* as his standards of measurement, he could hardly conclude otherwise. But Salieri advanced with the times as well. He retained his innate skill for pregnant musical declamation and for matching rhythmic motion to stage action while enriching his harmonic palette.

After Joseph made the mistake of dismissing his Italian troupe, hoping that the Viennese would be satisfied with the less costly offerings of the German troupe, Salieri enjoyed frequent leaves from his post. For the Venetian carnival of 1778–79 he composed *La scuola de' gelosi* on a libretto by Mazzolà. This opera enjoyed success all over Europe in the following decade, and in 1783, modified for Vienna, it proved a triumph as the debut work of a new Italian opera buffa troupe in the Burgtheater. This was the troupe, led by Nancy Storace and Francesco Benucci, for whom Mozart and Da Ponte would soon collaborate. When *La scuola de' gelosi* was produced in London in 1786, the *Morning Post and Daily Advertiser* proclaimed, "The whole together is a masterly composition, and does great honor to Salieri, whose reputation as a composer must rise infinitely in the musical world, from this very pleasing specimen of his abilities."[21]

With the death of Gassmann in 1774, Gluck's concentration on his works for the Opéra in Paris, and the near retirement from composition of the aged Bonno, Salieri became the principal musician of the imperial court. To him, in 1778, fell the honor of composing *L'Europa riconosciuta* on a libretto by Verazi, the opera that opened the new Teatro alla Scala in Habsburg-ruled Milan.

Ditters

CARL DITTERS was born in Vienna on 2 November 1739. His father, who came from Danzig, was a costumer to the court and court theater, a métier that required as a matter of course command of the French language, and this skill he passed on to his son. Family backgrounds in imperial service often provided opportunities for talented youths to make their way through the ranks to a top court position—witness the case of Bonno. Schooled early by Jesuits, Ditters profited as well from the best music teachers, Joseph Ziegler and Giuseppe Trani in violin playing and Bonno in theory and composition. His elder brother Joseph and younger brother Alexander were also trained as violinists. From 1751 to 1761 all three held posts in the orchestra of Prince Hildburghausen, who resided in the Palais Rofrano (later Auersperg) outside the walls in the Josefstadt (Figure 6.4).

By the mid-1750s Trani noticed in Ditters "a natural turn for composition" evident in his improvised cadenzas and proposed study with Bonno. After only a few weeks' instructions with Bonno in Fuxian counterpoint, his teacher asked him to compose a sonata, according to the memoirs Ditters dictated at the end of his life.

> I wrote it, and brought it to him. After improving some notes in the bass, he asked me to try my hand at a concerto. This I accomplished in a fortnight's time. The scoring of a number of parts, however, was a sore difficulty, for not only did I come to grief often over the laws of the thorough-bass, but I violated the golden rule, that the voice should not be smothered nor drowned by the accompaniment. My teacher pointed out every fault to me, explaining his reasons, and suggesting a method for improvement, after my many blunders. Four lessons were required before I got it right.

[21] John A. Rice, "Scuola de' gelosi, La" in *The New Grove Dictionary of Opera*, ed. Stanley Sadie (London, 1992).

Prospectus Palatii MARCHIONIS de ROFRANO et PRINCIPIS de COPICIO ante Portam aulicam ad Suburbium Josephinum. a. pars Palatii Principis de Trautsohn.

Prospect des Gebäues Ihro Excell. Tit: Herrn Herrn Marquis de Rofrano Prinß von Copece vor dem Burg Thor an der Joseph Stadt. a. Ein Stück des Fürst Trautsohnischen Pallast.

FIGURE 6.4. The Auersperg Palace in the Josefstadt.

A description of how Ditters performed his violin concerto for the prince glows with pride. For every folly or sin of pride that Ditters recounts about himself there is an immediate and disarming contrition. His success with the concerto made him realize how much he still needed to study pure counterpoint, to which he returned "with all possible earnestness and zeal." He also resolved to study every new piece he heard in order "to find out why a beautiful thought is beautiful." His conclusion is astute: "How often I discovered that it was beautiful simply because it was in the right place, so that, if it had occurred elsewhere, it would either not have been remarked at all, or have spoiled the whole work."

Prince Hildburghausen commanded the imperial armies at the outset of the Seven Years' War (1756–63). During the winter of 1757–58, fourteen members of his orchestra, including the three Ditters brothers, accompanied the prince on campaign. At the ducal seat of Hildburghausen they met young Anton Schweizer, instigator of the quartet party at which the four of them played six new quartets by Richter. Returned to Vienna in 1758, the brothers resumed their normal lives and Ditters fell into "bad company." Gambling debts and poor judgment led him to run away to Prague.

In his memoirs Ditters tells how he was tempted to desert his master by a Bohemian nobleman who was impressed with six symphonies he had written, "which made a stir both in Vienna and in Prague." The nobleman, called Count N.[ostitz?], ordered six more symphonies for the fee of 24 ducats, 12 of which were paid in advance, and offered the composer a larger salary if he would defect. Once arrived in Prague, Ditters found that the count in question had left for Paris, but he was taken in by a Count Breda, who requested six symphonies and two concertos for his oboe player, paying 12 ducats in advance for them. Within a month three symphonies and one concerto were finished, and Ditters was paid another 12 ducats. But then the police caught up with the composer and accused Count Breda of making him run away. Ditters absolved the count and was taken into custody, promising to send the remaining three symphonies and oboe concerto from Vienna, but the count "did not accept the offer, and this wounded me more than anything else." The year of this escapade was 1759, suggesting that by age twenty Ditters was much appreciated as a composer of instrumental music.

In 1761 most of the musicians of Prince Hildburghausen were dismissed when the prince left Vienna again, but he provided for them by making an agreement with Durazzo that they be taken into the Burgtheater orchestra at the same salary. Ditters, who signed a contract for three years, found his duties increased manyfold. "No one suffered more than I did by this arrangement, for I had to play almost daily from 10 A.M. to 2 P.M. at operatic and ballet rehearsals, not to mention theatrical performances from 6:30 to 10:30 of an evening, as well as accompanying at the theatrical concerts, and playing solos every fortnight. I had also bound myself to appear before the Emperor and the Court on *fête* and gala days." Thanks to Gumpenhuber's *Répertoires* for the Burgtheater, we can verify that there were indeed nearly daily rehearsals requiring the orchestra, we can learn night by night what repertory was being performed, and moreover we can put to the test Ditters' claim that he was required to play solos in the academies and special *services de table* in the palace.

The names of the three Ditters brothers first appear on Gumpenhuber's list of March 1762, which means that the brothers had joined the orchestra since his previous list of March 1761. Ditters himself appears as the last of the first violins, headed by Giuseppe Trani, while his brothers are named at the bottom of the list of second violins. Other players from the Hildburghausen orchestra, besides Trani, included Timmer, second bassoon, Johann

Schmidt, first oboe, and possibly Joseph Leutgeb, first horn. All three wind players contributed greatly to the concerto repertory at the Burgtheater's academies from 1761, but no one contributed more than Ditters. The four of them appeared as solo players within a week of each other at the end of 1761: on 4 December a "Concert ont joué Monsr Leitgeb sur le Cor de Chasse, Charles Ditters sur le violon"; on 9 December a "Concert ont joué Monsr Schmidt sur le Cor Anglois, Timme sur le Basson."

Pietro Nardini, concertmaster for the Lenten academies of 1761, apparently left Vienna after their completion. He had played concertos frequently since his arrival in Vienna for the festivities surrounding the imperial wedding in the fall of 1760, the last noted by Gumpenhuber being at the academy of 9 March 1761. Ditters seems to have been hired to replace him, not as concertmaster, for which he was still too young and inexperienced, but as violin soloist. Ditters followed Nardini in a deeper sense by imitating his lyrical violin concertos, a genre in which Ditters surpassed Haydn.[22]

The reappearance of violinist Gaetano Pugnani in Vienna during the spring of 1762 meant fewer performances by Ditters than might otherwise have been exacted of him during this period.[23] But his solo performances did not cease. Ditters began 1762 with a New Year's Day *service de table* in the palace, at which he played a concerto, followed by an evening academy in the Burgtheater at which he also played a concerto, according to Gumpenhuber. He played another concerto in the academy of 29 January 1762, then again on 19 February. This is close to the rhythm of the "every fortnight" he claimed in his memoirs. But then Pugnani's appearances, beginning on 28 February, meant a respite for Ditters.

Ditters' name appears next in a different context, as a symphony composer at the academy on 30 March 1762: "La 1re symphonie a été de la composition du Sr [Leopold] Hoffmann et la dernière du Sr Ditters." At the academy on 28 May he was heard playing a violin concerto, and this was followed by appearances as a soloist on 25 June, 27 August, 24 September, and 5 November. Gumpenhuber provides this further information about compositions by Ditters that were performed: on 20 August "une grande symphonie"; on 24 September all the symphonies; on 8 October a new oboe concerto for Schmidt; on 5 November, in addition to the concerto for himself, a horn concerto for Leutgeb. Within a year Ditters had replaced Wagenseil as the most frequent contributor of new compositions to the Burgtheater concerts. According to his memoirs, Ditters, with the help of Gluck, got Durazzo to release him from some of his orchestral duties so that he

---

[22] Hans Engel, *Das Instrumentkonzert* (Leipzig, 1932), pp. 182–83.
[23] Daniel Heartz, "Portrait of a Court Musician: Gaetano Pugnani of Turin," *Imago Musicae* 1 (1984): 103–19; 108–9.

could add to his income from private teaching and concerts, a relief that evidently allowed him to compose as well.

The following year, 1763, was marked by an equal intensity of performance and composition. Gumpenhuber indicates solo concertos played by Ditters on 4 February ("de sa composition"), 20 and 22 February, and 3 and 17 March, all at academies in the theater; a *service de table* took place in the palace on 19 March. At the academy on 20 March Ditters played "un seule sur le violon" (meaning a solo sonata). On 22 March he accompanied Mlle. Bianchi in a concertante aria. Several orchestral violinists were paid more than Ditters, but only he was playing solos and concertos, according to Gumpenhuber. On 24 March Gumpenhuber noted the departure of Gluck and Ditters for Italy. In his absence, and perhaps because of his absence, another Viennese violinist tried his luck with a concerto on 4 April: Leopold Hofmann.

Gluck and Ditters hoped to spend several months in Italy, but Durazzo summoned them back quickly because they were needed for festivities attending the coronation of Archduke Joseph as King of the Romans (postponed eventually to the following spring). Gumpenhuber remarked on Ditters' return from Italy when listing a violin concerto he played at the academy of 10 June. Then he noted that Ditters performed additional concertos at the academies of 2 July and 5 August (both of these were described as "new") and at the academies of 14 October and 18 November. The revival of Gluck's *Orfeo* in July 1763 elicited two separate descriptions of the orchestra personnel from Gumpenhuber. In the first the musicians are arranged as a double orchestra (for the first act), and Ditters is listed as third of the first violins in the first orchestra (under date of 14 July); in another arrangement, under date of 31 July, the opening, Ditters has climbed all the way to second of the first violins. Vanhal, whom Ditters claimed as one of his students, is listed several places below him, at the end of the first violin section.

Ditters' rise to prominence as both a violinist and composer marked him as one of the most esteemed musicians of Vienna. His early eminence is necessary to our understanding of his subsequent career, and it helps explain why so genial a figure as Vanhal, his exact contemporary, may have chosen to study with him. This is the time, we are told in Ditters' memoirs, when he bested the virtuoso Antonio Lolli, who had conquered Vienna while Ditters was in Italy (but there is no record of Lolli playing in the Burgtheater—could Ditters have substituted "Lolli" for "Pugnani"?). His elder brother Joseph reported the sensation aroused by Lolli's playing the evening of Ditters' arrival back in Vienna. The next day Ditters went with Gluck to Count Durazzo, to announce our return. I asked him to dispense with my solo playing for one month, because, whilst I was away from Vienna, I had sketched out some new concertos, and I should have to finish them up, and learn them thoroughly, before I could exhibit my new ideas in public.

"Bravo, my son!" said the Count. "You shall have six weeks, for you have a difficult task before you. Lolli has made a great hit, no doubt, but I will stake my faith on you!"

It is not impossible to reconcile this version with the facts as related by Gumpenhuber, allowing that Ditters forgot about playing a concerto on 10 June, because the concertos that mattered were the new ones on 2 July and 5 August; when Gumpenhuber adds the annotation "un nouveau de sa composition," we should take note, but many times when he does not include such a remark, the pieces may well have been new too.

In March 1764 Ditters and an orchestra of twenty accompanied the emperor and Archduke Joseph to Frankfurt for Joseph's coronation. There he played a violin concerto at a public banquet in the Römer and another in the imperial quarters. For this he was so poorly remunerated that Durazzo paid him 50 ducats out of his own pocket. At the same time, Ditters and Durazzo reached a verbal agreement whereby the composer would receive 1,000 gulden for leading the violins in the Burgtheater and continuing to play solos; little did Ditters know that Durazzo had already been dismissed from his post as director of the theaters.

Durazzo's replacement, Count Wenzel Sporck, treated Ditters rudely and refused to honor the agreement. Even though Sporck came around by degrees to meeting his terms, Ditters, out of pride, refused to renew his contract. Instead, he exiled himself to one of the more remote corners of the empire, a two weeks' journey from Vienna—Grosswardein, then in Hungary, today Oradea in Romania. There he entered the service of the prince-bishop Adam Patachich, for an official annual wage of 400 gulden, 100 more than his predecessor, Michael Haydn.[24] The move took place in the first part of 1765, marking a major hiatus in the composer's creative life.

It is generally assumed that a group of six symphonies and six concertos first advertised by Breitkopf in 1766 belongs to the fertile period of his Burgtheater service, 1761–64. The Symphony in C, No. 4 in its group, shows the young composer at a high level of inspiration and cogency (Example 6.6).[25]

[24] Romeo Ghircoiasiu, "Das Musikleben in Grosswardein (Oradea) im 18. Jahrhundert," *Haydn Yearbook* 10 (1978): 45–55; 48–49. Ditters claims in his memoirs a salary of 1,200 gulden; the difference could have been made up from private funds of the bishop.

[25] Ditters, *Drei Sinfonien, eine Serenata*, ed. Victor Luithlen (Vienna, 1936); DTÖ 81. Not up to the level of the Symphony in C are the three early symphonies chosen for edition by Eva Badura-Skoda, *Six Symphonies* (New York and London, 1985).

EXAMPLE 6.6. *Ditters, Symphony in C, I*

Scored for the usual strings with pairs of oboes and horns, the work begins quietly, with an *Allegro moderato* in 3/4, the violins singing a lyric melody built of two-measure segments, accompanied only by the pulsing eighth notes of the second violins and cellos. The second violins join the firsts in parallel thirds in m. 7, leading to the poignant double appoggiatura sigh with trill over a deceptive cadence in m. 8, followed by a repetition of the second phrase but ending with an authentic cadence. The overall shape of the main theme is thus **a b b′**, each segment lasting four measures. Tutti reinforcement arrives only with the cadence in m. 12.

Haydn was fond of beginning a symphony softly and then bringing in the tutti, as in his Symphony No. 12 in E of 1763, or the Symphony No. 16 in B♭ (ca. 1760–63). He was also partial to *Allegro* in 3/4 for opening movements, and in the Symphony No. 23 in G of 1764 he chose the same **a b b'** phrase structure (albeit with the added piquancy of three-measure phrases). But the symphony by Haydn that opens with a movement having the closest parallels with Ditters' opening movement is No. 35 in B♭, dated 1 December 1767. In texture, rhythm, and melodic traits the two openings are very close, and other similarities follow.

After reinforcing the cadence on C with a few V - I resolutions, Ditters begins his move to V as the first violins introduce a new scurrying figure in sixteenth notes, | ♫♫ ♫♫ ♪ ₇ |, against the syncopations of the second violins. The transition gathers momentum toward a miniclimax as the first violins, now syncopated, push up to high E, the third above the high tonic of IV in the new key of G. A soft rising eighth-note idea in the violins, unaccompanied at first, serves to confirm the new key; it too rises to E, then falls down a seventh to make the cadence F♯ G (the falling seventh was a prominent feature of the main theme). The scurrying motif in the first violins returns, *forte*, to confirm the key further, and the push up to high E is restated twice before the violins cadence with a little galloping motif: | ♫♫♫♫♫♫ | ♩ ₇ ₇ |. This same rhythmic motif plays a large role in the opening movement of Haydn's Symphony No. 37, as does the push up to the high third over IV at the cadences. Ditters begins his development with the main theme on V, but fragmented eventually from two measures to one while modulating; so does Haydn, who goes on to write one of his exciting contrapuntal developments. Ditters resolves the climax on iii by a descending bass movement, after which the reprise soon sets in.[26]

The engaging *Andante* in 2/4 and in the relative minor, a, follows Ditters' opening movement. Slurred pairs of eighth notes evoke the main theme of the first movement, as does the choice of the key of a minor, the destination of the poignant resolution in m. 8 of Example 6.6. The Menuet begins with an ascent of the treble up to high C, a motion that seems to give Ditters the idea for the *Presto* finale, with its repeated scales sweeping up an octave (a gesture used by Haydn in the finale of his Symphony No. 6, *Le matin*). Ditters begins and ends the Menuet with the violins in octaves, in the much criticized Viennese manner. Although he makes effective use of suspended bass harmonies in all four movements, lending a subtle unity to the cycle,

---

[26] The development takes only twenty-one measures as compared with forty-six for the exposition and fifty-one for the reprise. Margaret G. Grave, "First-Movement Form as a Measure of Dittersdorf's Symphonic Development" (Ph. D. diss., New York University, 1977), table III-b, pp. 75–78, shows that this brevity is typical of Ditters' early symphonies.

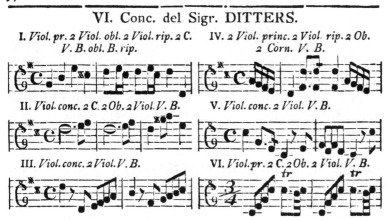

FIGURE 6.5. Detail from Brietkopf's *Thematic Catalogue,* Supplement of 1766.

his contrapuntal instincts are somewhat rudimentary and scholastic, at least in comparison with those of Haydn.

Concertos by Ditters were once numerous, as we know from his memoirs and the chronicles of Gumpenhuber. Relatively few have survived. It was in the nature of the concerto, as a showpiece for a soloist or soloists, to be jealously guarded by its recipients, hence less apt to be copied and printed. Ditters tried to keep his to himself. Nevertheless, Breitkopf was able to offer his clients a large store of violin concertos by Ditters, and at least one of the six advertised in 1766 (No. V) survives (Figure 6.5). The initial Concerto in G (lost) has an intriguing main theme, combining an arching melodic beginning, the raised fourth, and the galloping rhythm noted above. This theme may sound familiar—it begins note for note like the finale of Mozart's Quartet in G (K. 387), the first of six dedicated to Haydn.

The Violin Concerto in C proves that Ditters was a virtuoso of the first rank.[27] The pyrotechnics demanded of the soloist place the composer alongside the most brilliant of the Italian virtuosi. From this specimen it appears that Ditters' favorite *passagi* were rapid triplet arpeggios up into the stratosphere, in this case up to high C, three octaves above middle C. Great demands are placed on the performer not only with regard to fingering but also in the use of the bow. The many difficult string crossings would seem to be beyond any but the most technically advanced. Musically, the work is somewhat disappointing until the finale. The first movement is an *Allegro moderato* in common time that plods along with repeated eighth notes in the bass for much of its course. The opening (see Concerto V in Figure 6.5)

[27] *Konzert C-dur für Violine und Streichorchester,* ed. Walter Lebermann (Wilhelmshaven, 1963).

constitutes the same descent through the triad in dotted rhythm that Nardini used to launch his Violin Concerto in E♭, which may date from his stay in Vienna during 1760–61. Possibly Ditters wanted to show the Viennese public how much more he could make out of the same humdrum beginning. He uses several distinct thematic ideas in the opening orchestral ritornello (or first exposition), but none is particularly memorable.

For the first movement Ditters adopted the three solo / four tutti plan described by Heinrich Koch.[28] Ritornello 3 serves as a brief retransition after the development and cadence on vi of solo 2. There is a written-out cadenza after the pause on $I^{6/4}$, followed by only a few measures of tutti (the vestigial remains of ritornello 4). The middle movement is a *Grave* in 2/4 and in F with a main idea that is close to the beginning of the first movement. With the finale, *Presto non troppo* in 2/4, Ditters seems to come alive, using a perky and folklike antecedent-consequent theme that has a little chromatic twist to it. Humorous, and very like Haydn, is the way this chromatic piquancy is turned into a chromatic scalar motion, both rising and falling, an example of the witty repartee often found in the works of both composers.

Ditters turned to composing masses in the mid-1760s. He wrote a Mass in C for the coronation of Joseph II at Frankfurt in 1764, with abundant solo opportunity for himself as first violinist.[29] Number 7 of the *Wiener Diarium* of 1765 praised his mass for the feast of the Styrian *Landes-patron*: "The music was by the famous Herr Carl Ditters who joined the charming with the artistic according to the Church style and won the approval deserved from all experts."[30]

His new duties in the service of Bishop Patachich did not require church music, as the cathedral of Grosswardein had its own musical establishment. What Ditters says in his memoirs cannot be reconciled with the evidence of the masses composed while in imperial service. Speaking of an elaborate, two-hour choral cantata (lost) for the bishop's name day in December 1765, he reports: "Though the music of this cantata was my first unpretentious effort at a vocal work on a large scale, it was a success."

Ditters remained in touch with Vienna even while serving at a frontier post of the empire. When Count Sporck gave up trying to retain him as

[28] Heinrich Christoph Koch, *Versuch eine Anleitung zur Composition* (Rudolstadt and Leipzig, 1782–93; reprint 1969), as interpreted by Jane Stevens, "An 18th-Century Description of Concerto First-Movement Form," *JAMS* 24 (1971): 85–95.

[29] Hubert Unverricht, "Das bekannte und zugleich unbekannte Werk des Carl Ditters von Dittersdorf," *Carl Ditters von Dittersdorf, 1739–1799: Mozarts Rivale in der Oper*, ed. H. Unverricht and W. Bein (Würzburg, 1989), pp. 27–34; 30.

[30] MacIntyre, *The Viennese Concerted Mass*, pp. 64–65, citing Wilfried Schieb, "Die Entwicklung der Musikberichterstattung im *Wienerischen Diarium* von 1703 bis 1780" (Ph.D. diss., University of Vienna, 1985), p. 215.

concertmaster in the Burgtheater, he commissioned the composer to write ballet music. Ditters relates the count's words:

> If Hungary does not suit you, you can always depend upon taking up your salary of a thousand gulden here again. Meantime, as you have shown some talent for ballet writing in the *Pas des deux* which you composed for the Turchi and Paganina, you shall write four such ballets every year, and this will increase your pay by another hundred ducats. I am very sorry to be forced to lose you, but my hands are tied at Court, and I have to adapt myself to circumstances. For the same reason, I have been forced to dismiss every member of the Hildburghausen orchestra who demanded an increase of salary, or leave to quit the service.

In the summer Ditters and his musicians were less busy at Grosswardein than during the winter (when the bishop's name day and birthday both occurred) and spring. In 1767 Ditters was given three months' leave of absence to visit Vienna during the summer, and he mentions in his autobiography that while in the city he became impressed with the new Italian buffo troupe in the Burgtheater, and particularly with *L'amore in musica*, for which he bought the printed libretto with thoughts of translating it into German and setting it for Grosswardein. He did this upon his return. There is some confustion here, because the opera in question was performed in the Burgtheater in 1764, not 1767. (Dating from 1767 is Gassmann's *L'amore artigiano*, which may in fact be the libretto to which Ditters refers.)

Ditters often mistakes the exact date or chronology of events, but the events themselves are mostly verifiable. The summer of 1766 was presumably when Ditters first read an article by Schiebler and Eschenburg lauding the Berlin taste in music at the expense of the Viennese taste, "Abhandlung vom musikalischen Geschmack," published in the *Hamburger Unterhaltungen* earlier the same year.[31] The article, which questioned his friend Haydn's octave doublings and excoriated his own work as vulgar claptrap, provoked him to action.

That action took the form of a pamphlet entitled "Von dem wienerischen Geschmack in der Musik," which appeared in the supplementary series "Gelehrte Nachrichten" of number 84 of the *Wiener Diarium*, dated 18 October 1766.[32] The article was framed by aesthetic-historical remarks that could hardly have been written by any Viennese composer. But it assesses the merits of several leading composers using technical details available only to

[31] Robert Haas, "Von dem wienerischen Geschmack in der Musik," *Festschrift Johannes Biehle* (Leipzig, 1930), pp. 59–65. Haas also cites from the Hamburg article.
[32] For an English translation, see H. C. Robbins Landon, *Haydn: Chronicle and Works*, 5 vols. (Bloomington, Ind., 1976–80), 2: 128–31.

an insider and a professional. Hofkapellmeister Reutter is "unquestionably the strongest composer to sing the praise of God"; Leopold Hofmann, another court composer, "is the only one to approach the church style of Herr Reutter"; Wagenseil, *Hofkomponist*, excels in both composition and keyboard playing; his "worthiest follower," Joseph Anton Steffan, who had been named *Hofklaviermeister* in July 1766, emulates his master, yet is original.[33] The technical descriptions and references to precise examples are found in this book's discussions of the individual masters.

After Wagenseil and Steffan comes Haydn, a sequence not so surprising when we consider that Hiller also takes the composers up in this order. Haydn, "the darling of our nation," is followed by Ditters, then Gluck, who receives a veritable paean of praise for four works given their premieres in the Burgtheater between 1761 and 1764, exactly corresponding with Ditters' tenure as a violinist in the opera orchestra. Honorable mention goes to Johann Georg Zechner for his sacred works, Karl von Ordonez for his symphonies, cassations, and quartets, and Joseph Starzer and Gassmann for their theater music. This is slight praise indeed for the last two, especially Gassmann, who by 1766 was already heir apparent to Reutter. Yet it is quite in line with the animosity Ditters shows toward Gassmann in his memoirs. Surprising by their absence are Giuseppe Bonno (because his music was more Italianate than Viennese?) and Johann Baptist Vanhal. On the basis of the data cited, we can conclude that the only professional composer with an inside knowledge of the imperial musical establishment and sufficient literary acumen to have written such a polemic was Ditters.

In his memoirs Ditters tells an amusing story about himself relative to a time when he was still in the service of Prince Hildburghausen, who was showing off his musicians upon a visit to the Venetian ambassador, a reputed musical expert and self-styled *professore di violino*. Ditters was embarrassed because he had forgotten to bring a concerto or a sonata with him, but he covered up his lapse by pretending to play from some music lying on a table. He told his younger brother Alexander to improvise an accompaniment in G while he faked a sonata. The ambassador came up to the table as he was playing, much to the mortification of Ditters, and pointed to the music knowingly—it happened to be a symphony in the key of E♭—and when he thought he saw a flurry of notes coming, he exclaimed, "Adesso viene un passagio!" (Here comes a *passagio!*). Fortunately Ditters was both adept enough and rascal enough to give him satisfaction with scales and

[33] I first argued the case for Ditters' authorship of this pamphlet in a paper on Steffan given in Prague in May 1984, "Wagenseils würdigster Nachfolger." The argument is published in Daniel Heartz, "Ditters, Gluck und der Artikel 'Von dem wienerischen Geschmack in der Musik,'" *Gluck Studien* 1 (1989): 78–80.

flourishes. This is the sense of the "Passagen" with which the description of Ditters in the 1766 essay begins: "Herr Carl Ditters, seine Passagen sind meistens feurig, heftig, kühn, die aber immer eine herrschende Melodie angenehm und reizend bindet" (A pleasant and charming leading melody always ties together his mostly fiery, passionate and bold *passagi*).

Ditters on Ditters deserves complete citation in the original:

> So oft er auftritt, ist er neu; und man merkt dass in ihm ein Genie liegt, welches sich durchzuarbeiten sucht, um den höchsten Grad der Volkommenheit zu erlangen. Auch da, wo er nicht will, gefällt er, weil er den Nationalgeschmack mit der Kunst gefällig zu verbinden weiss. Bis nunzu hat ein Ditters der Nation am meisten Ehre gemacht, indem er sowohl ein guter Compositor, als grosser Violinist ist. Seine letzten Arbeiten, besonders die Messen, haben Fugen, welche die strengsten Kritiken aushalten. In seinen Concerten herrscht mehrenteils eine brillante Melodie, die mit Ordnung und Wahl so angebracht scheint, dass sie alle Vollkommenheit erreichet, deren diess Instrument fähig ist. Sollte oder könnte uns die Zeit nicht an ihm an einen Bach schenken?
>
> (However often he appears, he is new, and one notices that a genius resides in him that seeks to work its way through until attaining the highest degree of perfection. Even when he does not seek to please, he pleases, because he knows how to unite the national taste with the musical art in a pleasant fashion. Up to the present a Ditters has done most honor to the nation because he is a good composer as well as a great violinist. His latest works, especially the masses, have fugues that can stand the severest criticisms. A brilliant melody reigns in his [violin] concertos, for the most part, a melody that appears to be arranged with such order and choice that it attains the highest perfection of which the instrument is capable. Should not, or could not time give us in him another Bach?)

The emphasis Ditters placed upon fugues makes his intention clear: to repudiate his north German critics and prove that he was as learned as they. His remark about order and choice of musical materials parallels his remark in the memoirs about a musical thought being beautiful because it is in the right place. In the context of the whole parade of composers he mentions, beginning with Reutter and ending with a feeble acknowledgment of Gassmann, one could deduce that in 1766 Ditters was aiming at nothing less than becoming imperial Hofkapellmeister. Joseph II, in power slightly over a year at this time, enjoyed playing quartets with fugues, like those of Gassmann and Ordonez. A Ditters who cultivated fugues was surely on the way to becoming even more pleasing to his sovereign.

In a recent study of the *Wiener Diarium*'s music articles for the year 1766, several reasons were given why the main author of the October essay must be Ditters, but so drastic a conclusion was eschewed: "The polemical tone does not seem to correspond to the nature of the composer."[34] Ditters was not the average Viennese composer in this respect. He was closer to being a man of letters, after all, than any other composer of the Viennese school. As for polemics, who was it who urged Haydn to lash out and smite his critics? In his autobiographical letter of 6 July 1776 Haydn says that his friend Ditters wrote him from Silesia "asking me to defend myself against their hard words." Haydn remained silent, but Ditters was not loath to defend himself or Viennese music. At the end of his life, in the first volume of Rochlitz's *Allgemeine musikalische Zeitung* (1798), Ditters took up the same issues as in 1766, offering a passionate defense of Gluck and a denunciation of Kapellmeister Graun, along with the north German critics who honored him.

What seems unlikely in the 1766 essay, even for a Ditters, is the rambling preface touching on aesthetics, with a bow to Batteux and Aristotle, and a few corresponding remarks at the end, where Diderot is cited. It is difficult to imagine these scholarly trappings emerging unassisted from the pen of the fiery young violinist. Some literary type may have helped him here, perhaps one of the editors of the *Wiener Diarium*. A certain amount of artful dodging was in order after all, because it would not do to have Ditters found out. The high praise of a Ditters mass in the *Diarium* a year earlier (1765) must be seen as related to this complex question.

Ditters' employment at Grosswardein came to an end in 1769 when an enemy denounced the bishop to Maria Theresa for permitting masks and comic operas during Lent. In a rash moment of contrition the bishop dismissed his whole orchestra. Ditters tried to get him to refute the charges. Not opera but staged oratorio was what they had given in Lent (Ditters' *Isacco*), and the same thing was done at the imperial court when Bonno's setting of *Isacco* was staged. As for the other charge, no one wore a mask on his face, but merely costumes, as at Redoutensaal balls: "I myself have been present at a redoute in Vienna, sometimes as a Spanish cavalier, sometimes as a Venetian noble, sometimes as a Flemish boor."

Back in Vienna once again, Ditters says that he refused Count Sporck's renewed offer of the post of first violin in the Burgtheater because he wished to undertake a European concert tour. He made a trip to Venice and had an affair with a beautiful ballerina, aged eighteen, who was bound for Vienna as *première danseuse*. Ditters followed her there, but a friend persuaded him of the folly of such an attachment and the damage it could do his career (as it happened, the young lady's morals came to the attention of Maria Theresa, who promptly sent her packing).

[34]Norbert Tschulik, "Musikartikel aus dem *Wienerischen Diarium* von 1766," *Studien zur Musikwissenschaft* 30 (1979), pp. 91–106.

Ditters accepted an invitation to visit Troppau in Austrian Silesia from Count Lamberg, who was also visited at the time by the prince-bishop of Breslau, Count Schafgotsch, to whom Ditters bound himself for six months' service, from 1 November 1769 to the end of May 1770. Count Schafgotsch used his influence in Rome to have Ditters named a Knight of the Golden Spur, like Gluck, and presented the Cross of the Order to him as a surprise on New Year's Day 1770.

Next Ditters accepted an invitation from Count Hoditz to visit Rosswald and prepare musical entertainments for the impending stay there of the king of Prussia, Frederick II, and his nephew, the crown prince. The king used Rosswald as a stopover on his way to and from his meeting with Emperor Joseph II at nearby Neustadt in Moravia during the first week of September 1770. The entire Burgtheater forces were on hand in Neustadt, where they gave the premiere of *La contessina* by Gassmann, the greatest triumph of his career. Not one word does Ditters say about this event, but his silence speaks eloquently of his rivalry with the older composer.

Ditters returned to Count Schafgotsch in tiny Johannisberg (the count was not allowed by the Prussians to occupy his episcopal seat in Breslau). He still intended to depart on his grand concert tour, but Schafgotsch bound him to his service, using financial rewards and titles as lures. The titles culminated with a patent of nobility, secured from Vienna. From June 1773 on, the composer became known as Ditters von Dittersdorf (a nonexistent village).

Ditters had a close ally within the imperial establishment in the person of Wenzl Pichl, who was a chorister in the Burgtheater as early as 1760.[35] Ditters met him in Prague during the winter of 1764–65 and recruited him as a violinist, along with several other Czech musicians, for service in Grosswardein. The two returned together to Vienna in 1769, where Ditters arranged for his friend to take several pupils. In 1770 Pichl became first violin at the Kärntnerthor Theater at the recommendation of Ditters, who says:

> By good luck there was a vacancy for the post of first violin at the German Theatre, and Pichl got it. The pay was not more than four hundred and fifty florins a year, but he accepted it eagerly. His services were only required of an evening, so he had the whole day to himself, and could devote it to his pupils. I was happy knowing that my best friend was comfortably provided with a steady income of one thousand and fifty gulden a year.

[35] Jacques Joly, *Les fêtes théâtrales de Métastase à la cour de Vienne* (Clarmont-Ferrand, 1978), p. 506, gives a list of the chorus for *Alcide al bivio* that includes "Venceslao Pischl." For an insightful discussion of Pichl's violin concertos, see Chapell White, *From Vivaldi to Viotti: A History of the Early Classical Violin Concerto* (New York, 1992), pp. 302–05.

Pichl was also paid as a copyist by the German Theater. In 1774–75 he copied twelve symphonies by Ditters, three by Haydn, two by Gassmann, and one each by Christian Bach and Pugnani, as well as twelve of his own.

Ditters also mentions that Pichl warned him not to trust Gassmann, who commissioned an oratorio from Ditters for the Tonkünstler Societät in 1773: "But how do you know he does not mean to act fairly with me?" Ditters quotes himself asking Pichl. "Because," replied Pichl, "I have shown him several of your scores that you composed at Grosswardein, and he rejected them all." Nevertheless Ditters composed his *Esther* for Vienna,[36] and it was performed with success in December 1773, proving that their fears about Gassmann were unfounded. Ditters says that Joseph II came to every rehearsal and that he much preferred *Esther* to the oratorios of Hasse and Gassmann, a claim that is implausible in the light of Joseph's known indulgence toward his favorites.

Returned to Johannisberg, Ditters received a letter from Pichl, announcing that Gassmann had died (January 1774) and that the emperor was postponing the appointment of his successor until he knew whether Ditters would apply. Ditters describes his reaction:

> I wrote back to say that I should not apply for the post, as I was making more money in Johannisberg, and I might hope to add to it, but should the emperor expressly desire me to stand, His Majesty might command me. I really do not know whether Pichl was secretly commissioned to sound me, but I learnt afterwards that, when my answer was made known to the Emperor, he received it ungraciously.

This is perhaps the most unbelievable tale in all his memoirs—"eine höchst unglaubliche Geschichte," as one expert called it.[37] Ditters shaped his life in hopes of becoming imperial Hofkapellmeister and achieving the pinnacle of success in Vienna. Had he actually received an offer to succeed Gassmann, whom he envied beyond measure, not all his Silesian titles and emoluments would have kept him in the provinces.

Ditters' long years in exile were destined to continue, but not without artistic profit. With the meager forces at his disposal at Grosswardein and Johannisberg, he could experiment to his heart's content with comic operas on a small scale. His old friend Haydn profited from the result and produced four of his operas at Esterháza in 1776–77.

In the early 1780s Ditters began composing symphonies after the *Metamorphoses* of Ovid, and offered five of a planned set of fifteen to Artaria in

---

[36] Ditters von Dittersdorf, *Esther* (Italian Oratorio 1650–1800, 24) (New York, 1987).
[37] Robert Haas, in a footnote added to Donath, "Gassmann als Opernkomponist," p. 47, n. 3.

Vienna by letter of 18 August 1781. He finished twelve, of which six are preserved as orchestral parts. The first three he published with a dedication to the new king of Prussia in 1786, hoping to further his chances to become Kapellmeister of the Prussian court. The works occupy a modest rung in the annals of symphonic program music and attracted early criticism of a negative kind.

EXAMPLE 6.7. *Ditters*, Metamorphosis *Symphony No. 3, I*

The first movement of the *Metamorphosis* Symphony No. 3 (*Acteon*) portrays a hunt, using the customary 6/8 meter (Example 6.7ab). The tutti passage, which pushes up by step to the dominant seventh, then repeats the four tones of the V^7 chord for emphasis, resembles the stirring conclusion of the development in Haydn's overture to *La fedeltà premiata* (1780).

Ditters made a late entry into the field of the string quartet; until 1787 he refused the entreaties of friends to publish any. Then in August 1788 he submitted six quartets to Artaria, accompanied by a letter informing the firm that he had worked at composing them for thirteen or fourteen months. In this same letter he quoted an anonymous theorist as saying that with this set Ditters had bested not only Pleyel, but even Haydn. In a further effort to sell his works he referred to his great respect for Mozart's quartets published by Artaria (the six dedicated to Haydn) but said they were too consistently artful to be bought by everyone. His letter shows once again what a clever publicist Ditters was, especially of his own works. Artaria published his quartets.

The great opportunity of Ditters' composing career came in 1786, when he was commissioned to write a German opera for the Burgtheater, *Der Apotheker und der Doctor*, on a libretto by Stephanie the younger. An anonymous pamphlet of the time claimed that this work brought opera in German up to the level of Mozart's *Le nozze di Figaro*.[38] The assessment comes close to being

---

[38] *Über das deutsche Singspiel den Apotheker des Herrn von Dittersdorf* (Vienna, 1786). I am indebted to Cliff Eisen for calling my attention to this pamphlet.

FIGURE 6.6. Hieronymus Löschenkohl. Engraved portrait of Ditters von Dittersdorf, 1786.

true even if Ditters himself wrote it, which he probably did. His music at its best works some of the same dramatic miracles as Mozart's. But the libretto does not stand comparison: Stephanie adapting a wretched French model was no match for Da Ponte adapting Beaumarchais. This did not stop the public from preferring *Doktor und Apotheker* (its modern title) to Mozart's masterpiece. During 1786, the pinnacle of Ditters' career, his portrait was the subject of a fine engraving (Figure 6.6).

What Ditters offered the Viennese public to an even greater degree than Mozart's *Figaro* were catchy melodies of a folklike simplicity and directness. An example from the first act of *Doktor und Apotheker* is the duet begun by the tenor Sichel (Example 6.8a). With its fast tempo and downbeat beginning, like a polka, this tune is one of many by Ditters that sounds Bohemian

EXAMPLE 6.8.

a.Ditters, Doktor und Apotheker, *Duet*

b. Ditters, Keyboard Concerto in A, III

in its inspiration. And yet it takes only a rebarring, with upbeat beginning, for a very similar tune from the finale of an earlier keyboard concerto by Ditters to project the character of a courtly gavotte (Example 6.8b).

Doktor und Apotheker occupies an important place in the history of opera. Ditters, with all his experience writing Italian comic operas, was in an ideal position to bring comic opera in German up to a level that was internationally viable, something that had not been accomplished by Johann Adam Hiller at Leipzig or Ignaz Umlauf and his successors at Vienna. Some credit should go to Stephanie too, for making possible the first full-scale action finales in German-language opera.[39] Ditters followed up this huge success with other comedies for Vienna, and during his last decade he made several contributions to the genre in Germany as well.[40]

Ditters the critic spelled out some of the secrets of his success in an article that appeared in the first *Allgemeine musikalische Zeitung* in 1798:

> The composer, of serious as well as comic opera, must write truthfully. The poem that he sets becomes his world, which he must represent. It follows that he must study his poet's characters exactly and think his way, feel his way inside them, so to speak . . . He must learn to distinguish between the many fine nuances adherent in a single passion. These poetic directions the composer must follow rigorously, and as the poet characterizes and individualizes his personalities by various expressions and turns of phrase, so must the composer do the same with his means, through various modulations.

A year after this essay appeared, the composer breathed his last. He died on 24 October 1799, two days after dictating the final pages of his autobiography to his son—all in all a happy life devoted to music, and happily for posterity one that is recorded, warts and all, as is the life of no other eighteenth-century musician.

Several of Ditters' aspirations remained unfulfilled. He did not make a grand tour of Europe as a virtuoso. He did not become imperial Hofkapellmeister, nor was he granted a post by Friedrich Wilhelm II of Prussia when he applied to Berlin in 1786. It must have been a source of great satisfaction to him, then, to triumph at last in German comic opera.

That Ditters, the virtuoso violinist, should succeed especially in concertos and comic operas cannot be unrelated to the emergence of Mozart's most towering accomplishments in exactly these genres. Perhaps it was the suspense and *coquetterie* of when and how the soloist would enter and depart the concerto texture, and the sense of repartee with the orchestra, that gave both composers such an infallible sense of timing when it came to stage situations. Ditters' musical wit and the many traces of folksong and folkdance inspiration in his works have often led to comparisons with his friend Haydn, but the more apt comparison is with Mozart. Like Mozart, Ditters was a born man of the theater, where he did his best work. His musical career was devoted largely to showmanship, to stunning his audience with improvised *passagi* as well as melting their hearts with his solo playing.

---

[39] Paul J. Horsley, "Dittersdorf and the Finale in Late Eighteenth-Century German Comic Opera" (Ph.D. diss., Cornell University, 1988), p. 64.
[40] Thomas Baumann, *North German Opera in the Age of Goethe* (Cambridge, 1985), pp. 296–313.

Vanhal

JOHANN BAPTIST VANHAL was born in bondage on 12 May 1739 in the village of Nové Nechanice, to the northeast of Prague. Bohumír Jan Dlabač wrote an unusually detailed account of Vanhal in his *Allgemeines historisches Künstler-Lexikon für Böhmen* (Prague, 1815), based mainly on interviews he had with the composer in Vienna in 1795.[41] Vanhal's teacher was a local organist by the name of Anton Erban, he told Dlabač, who wrote: "Because of the unusual talent for music he displayed in his early youth, and also so that he could learn the German language, his father sent him to Marscherdorf [Maršov in Moravia]. There he received instruction from a certain Kozak in both music and other necessary fields of knowledge." The implication is that German was a necessity for anyone who wished to become a free man. By the end of the 1750s Vanhal had acquired the post of organist in one town, then choirmaster in another, while perfecting his skills as a violinist. He wrote several concertos and solos for violin, according to Dlabač, who continues: "The rapid progress of our young artist impressed the rulers of the town [Hněvčeves]. As a result the countess Schaffgotsch summoned him to Vienna in 1760 [1761?]. Here she arranged for instruction with Schleger. However, Vanhal was not at all satisfied and on his own began to study the scores of the greatest masters." (Schleger must be Mathäus Schlöger, *Hofklaviermeister* until his death in 1766.)

An aside in the autobiography of Ditters, who was exactly the same age as Vanhal, claims that the latter studied with him—not violin, as we might imagine, but composition. "As Pleyel learned from Haydn, so did Vanhal learn from me." Ditters returned to Vienna only sporadically after 1764, so the instruction must have taken place before then (if it took place at all—Dlabač does not mention Ditters). "Wanhal" is listed by Gumpenhuber among the first violins in the revival of Gluck's *Orfeo* at Schönbrunn on 31 July 1763, five chairs below Ditters. Vanhal's name is conspicuously absent from the composers described in the 1766 pamphlet "Von dem wienerischen Geschmack in der Musik," attributed above to Ditters. The omission is all the more strange because Vanhal's early symphonies rank close to Haydn's in their melodic appeal. In 1768 the *Wiener Diarium* made up for the slight by naming Vanhal one of the best masters in Vienna.

Dlabač continues his account as follows: "In a short time, because of his

---

[41] Jan Krtitel Vanhal, *Five Symphonies*, ed. Paul Bryan (New York and London, 1981). Bryan's Introduction includes the Vanhal entry from Dlabač in English translation, which is used throughout this section, and the work list in facsimile, pp. xlii–xlv. I am indebted to Paul Bryan furthermore for personal communications that helped me formulate this section on Vanhal.

skill in composition, he developed such a good reputation in the most imposing circles that he was asked to give lessons in keyboard, singing, and violin to members of the upper nobility. In this manner he acquired sufficient means to purchase his freedom from the bondage that was still customary at that time." We do not know who these members of the high nobility were. Young Ignaz Pleyel is said to have studied with Vanhal before he became Haydn's student around 1772. Dlabač continues:

> He realized . . . that in order to perfect himself in his profession he needed to master the Italian language as well as to further develop his aesthetic understanding of the Italian masters. Therefore, with the financial support of one of his most generous patrons, the baron Riesch, he traveled to Italy. Thus, he visited Venice, Bologna, Ferrara, Florence, Naples, Rome and other cities of this land, so interesting for the musical art. There he studied composition after the best models and also wrote a number of musical works.

The number of early symphonies by Vanhal preserved in manuscripts in Venetian libraries suggests that his works were appreciated there. Gerber says that Vanhal profited from Gluck's help in the composition of vocal pieces that won him applause, which is not impossible because Gluck was in Italy during 1769 to supervise a festival performance in Parma. There are occasional signs in Vanhal's music that he was well acquainted with Gluck's masterpieces. But of which Viennese composer could this not be said?

When Vanhal reached Rome, he came into contact with another Bohemian composer whom he knew from the Burgtheater orchestra at least as early as 1763, Gassmann. The latter was in Rome to compose the carnival opera, Metastasio's *Ezio* (winter of 1769–70). Dlabač says, "In Rome he met Florian Gassmann, musical director of the Viennese court, for whose operas Vanhal wrote some arias and with whom he returned to Vienna after the completion of two years." Actually the Italian trip lasted slightly more than one year if Vanhal returned with Gassmann, who was called back to Vienna in the summer of 1770 to finish *La contessina* in a hurry for performance in early September—it may be to this work that Vanhal contributed. Dlabač lists two operas by Vanhal on Metastasian texts, *Demofoonte* and *Il trionfo di Clelia*. Gerber says that he wrote these in Rome with Gassmann's help and that he helped Gassmann in return. The lack of printed librettos for these operas indicates that they were not performed, at least not in public. The lost operas, if they were indeed written, may have been essays in which the composer tried his hand at an unfamiliar genre. Or did he have hopes of reaching performance in Rome or some other center where opera seria was given?

Dlabač next reveals the cloud that shadowed Vanhal, perhaps for the rest of his life: "But scarcely had he arrived back in Vienna when he was overcome by a mental disturbance which hindered his musical work not a little." Gerber mentions that Vanhal met Emperor Joseph II in expectations of a good post, but his hopes were disappointed by his mental crisis. Later sources say that Riesch, his patron, secured for him the offer of a post as Kapellmeister at Dresden, but his mental illness prevented him from accepting it. Vanhal held no official position subsequently, but managed to live with the support of patrons and what income he derived from teaching and publications. In this sense he was one of the earliest independent artists.

The dogged Burney tracked Vanhal down with difficulty in 1772, when the composer was living in a garret in an obscure corner of Vienna. He had no French and little Italian, reports Burney—dashed hopes here as well, for Gerber says he went to Venice with the intention of mastering both languages, without which a Kapellmeister could not function. Burney and Vanhal struck a bargain whereby Burney would get copies of some of his symphonies. Next, says Burney, "I got him to sit down to a little clavichord, and play me six lessons which he just made for that instrument: but I found them neither so pleasing, masterly, or new, as his compositions for violins." This prompted a disquisition by Burney on how the really striking and original pieces for keyboard were by great keyboard performers, namely Handel, Scarlatti, Bach, Johann Schobert, Wagenseil, Johann Gottfried Müthel, and Domenico Alberti. Vanhal, he implies, did not belong in such company, and moreover he pillaged the music of others. Then he attacks the issue of the composer's mental state.

> A little perturbation of the faculties is a promising circumstance in a young musician, and M. V. began his career very auspiciously, by being somewhat flighty. Enthusiasm seems absolutely necessary in all the arts, but particularly in music, which so much depends upon fancy and imagination. A cold, sedate, and wary disposition, but ill suits the professor of such an art; however, when enthusiasm is ungovernable, and impels too frequent and violent efforts, the intellects are endangered. But as insanity in an artist is sometimes nothing more than an ebullition of genius, when that is the case, he may cry out to the physicians that cure him, ". . . Pol me occidistis, amici, Non servastis." M. V. is now so far recovered, and possesses a mind so calm and tranquil, that his last pieces appear to me rather insipid and common, and his former agreeable extravagance seems changed into too great economy of thought.

In this passage Burney got carried away by his own rhetoric. And unfortunately for Vanhal, other critics picked up Burney's negative remarks and repeated them, which may ultimately have had the effect of discouraging the composer himself. What struck Burney as "too great economy of thought" strikes us as an admirable ability in adapting Haydn's thematic economy to his own purposes.

Gerber claims that he also went through a process of disenchantment with Vanhal. He was a young law student at Leipzig University, and very active in local music making, when the first symphonies of Vanhal became known in that part of Germany during the late 1760s. What he says in the earlier version of his lexicon (1790) reflects his direct experience, and probably Burney's dicta as well. "Vanhal seems to live from his compositions. His first symphonies became known around 1767 and at once won general applause. One admired in them principally their fire and liveliness, combined with beautiful singing melodies. But since that time there became noticeable a certain coldness and common tone in his compositions." (Note that Burney also uses both "cold" and "common" above.) Are we to accept this theory of Vanhal's decline as a symphonist?

Vanhal's symphonies, according to Dlabač, numbered one hundred, as did his string quartets. These are round figures, but they are not far off the mark.[42] The six symphonies offered by Breitkopf under Vanhal's name in 1770 must predate the composer's departure for Italy. Four of the six bear the date 1769 in early copies, so it seems likely that they were among his last and most mature compositions before leaving Vienna; there are two impressive minor-mode symphonies in the set, in the keys of e and c.[43] It cannot be a coincidence that Haydn also turned to writing minor-mode symphonies in the late 1760s.

Vanhal's Symphony in c (ca. 1768) contains fiery first and last movements that one can well imagine kindling the enthusiasm of a Burney or a Gerber (and perhaps a Haydn as well). The Symphony in e impresses more by its lyrical and inward qualities, also by the way Vanhal has sought to unify the cycle by subtle motivic recurrences from movement to movement. Common to each movement is a descent to the tonic followed in some fashion by the leading tone—as with Haydn's symphonies in the minor mode from the late 1760s, not always at the beginning of the movement (cf. Haydn's Symphony No. 39 in g). In the finale of the Symphony in e a passage close to the end, repeated *piano*, seems to sum up this motif and yield a clue as to how the entire work hangs together. There are other features

---

[42] The Vanhal expert Paul Bryan has authenticated seventy-six symphonies, stretching from ca. 1763, when he believes the earliest were composed (as stated in a personal communication), until the early 1780s, when Vanhal stopped writing in this genre.

[43] Bryan, in Vanhal, *Five Symphonies*, includes these data in his thematic catalogue, and he also includes the relevant page from the Breitkopf list, p. xlix. The Symphonies in e and c are reproduced in modern score.

that Vanhal uses to tie his outer movements together: both plunge into the second key, G, from unresolved dominants of e; the developments of both start softly in G, after fiery climaxes confirming the same key; and both movements make use of dramatic pauses. Vanhal's Symphony in B♭ from the same set (B♭ 3) has an impressive retransition in the first movement that is paralleled by a similar progression at the same spot in the finale.[44]

The Symphony in B♭ (B♭ 1) that Breitkopf advertised along with five others by Vanhal in 1772 was claimed as Haydn's until 1934, touching off a well-known musicological dispute. A copy was found in the Esterházy collection, meaning that Haydn probably esteemed or performed it. Vanhal is even more lyrically oriented than before in this symphony, which might be interpreted as a result of his *Italienreise*. At the same time he remains close to Haydn, whether in his thematic economy or the use of a similar thematic contour in all four movements.[45] The main theme of the first movement is a singing *Allegro* laid out in a broad, twelve-measure **a b b'** design, played *piano* by strings alone, after which the initial segment, **a,** returns immediately, *forte*, with oboes and horns to begin the transition. Instead of a new second theme, **a** recurs with a new accompaniment; **b** provides material for a closing theme. The development begins with the new accompaniment to the second theme. Thus every element has been derived from the first theme, as Haydn often liked to do.

The symphony is unusually euphonious and smooth, filled with more sighing chromatic appoggiature than Haydn usually allowed, and perhaps a little lacking in virility for this reason. Is this feminine grace and sweetness some residue of the Italian experience? In any case, Vanhal has become more galant, it seems, instead of less, which was Haydn's direction around 1772. The proliferation of *cadences galantes*, occurring in all four of Vanhal's movements, is indicative of this. The symphony ends with this melodic-harmonic cliché, onto which Vanhal tacks another familiar device, the contredanse stamping rhythm in third-tonic alternation often found in Bohemian music. One composer-critic of the time, Johann Friedrich Reichardt, claimed in his autobiography that the best pieces heard in concerts in Berlin in 1771 were Haydn's symphonies "and those in imitation of them by Vanhal."

More impressive even than the Symphony in B♭ that was mistaken for Haydn's is the Symphony in a (a 2) from the same Breitkopf set of 1772. It

---

[44] Illustrated in *The New Oxford History of Music*, vol. 7, example 186.

[45] The symphony is edited by Bryan in Vanhal, *Five Symphonies*. In his Introduction, p. 50, he isolates the motif F D E♭ F B♭ as "the contour underlying the melodic material that opens each of the movements of the symphony." On the Italian question Bryan offers this, concerning the opening movement: "Its quiet cantabile style probably reflects Vanhal's response to the attractions of Italian lyricism."

begins, characteristically, with an upbeat, and there is a sense in which the whole twelve-measure theme is anacrustic, reaching a firm downbeat only with the tonic arrival at the end (Example 6.9).[46] Lurking behind the theme is the same **a b b'** shape that is used overtly to launch the companion Symphony in B♭. But here Vanhal blurs the distinction between **a** and **b** by the continuity of the rising half notes into m. 5. He greatly transforms **b** in the **b'** section by taking the high tonic in a leap, which he then fills in by step. The gentle ending of **b** in a deceptive cadence, rhythmically weak, is replaced by vigorous precadential motion and a strong cadence in **b'**.

Vanhal used similar tactics to begin the Symphonies e 1 and C 2. Here he was more original because of his free handling of the thematic mold, and more melodious. His contemporaries did not fail to recognize his melodic charm or fine rhythmic control. The *Deutsche Chronik* (Ulm, 1774) reported, "Er [Vanhal] besitzt die lieblichste Melodie, leicht, fliessend, voll Grazie ist sein Satz" (He possesses the loveliest melody, and his movement is light, flowing and graceful). *Satz* can also mean musical grammar (i.e., harmony and counterpoint). Christian Schubart praised Vanhal's ability "to combine solid harmony and lovely melody with so much skill and insight that it was no wonder that he is eagerly taken up by Germans and Italians alike."[47] Instances of what Schubart was talking about abound in the symphony in question. The lovely second theme of the opening movement, sung by the first violins and violas in octaves, seems to emerge out of the six eighth notes phrased 2 + 4 in m. 10 of the first theme. For harmonic skill and richness there is the exciting use of measure-long diminished-seventh chords to enhance the successive arrivals of pre-cadential ii^6 and I$^{6/4}$. Astute indeed is the way Vanhal uses the motif from the beginning and end of his second theme to prepare the moment of reprise.

An *Andante cantabile* movement in 3/8 continues the symphony in the tonic major, A. The memorable five-measure phrases of its main theme form an inverted period. Horns and oboes accompany only the second phrase, *forte*, ending on V. After the double bar in the middle, this same inverted

[46]Paul Bryan, "The Symphonies of Johann Vanhal" (Ph.D. diss., University of Michigan, 1955), includes an edition of movements I, II, and IV of the symphony, which are also available in an edition of Fritz Kneusslin (Zurich, 1947). Bryan, p. 203, relates the opinion, expressed to him personally by the late Paul Nettl, that the themes of this symphony display the influence of Bohemian folksong; in the case of the opening theme of the first movement, this influence is said to be apparent from the way the phrasing and the melodic construction throw the accent on the second beat, as in a particular Czech dance, the dupak.

[47]"Da er solide Harmonie, und liebliche Melodien mit so viel Klugheit und Einsicht zu vermischen wusste, so ist's kein Wunder dass er von Deutschen und Welschen gleich günstig aufgenommen wurde." Bryan translates this too freely as "It is no wonder that he is equally favorably received by foreigners," which spoils Schubart's dichotomy of melody (Italian) and harmony (German).

EXAMPLE 6.9. *Vanhal, Symphony in a, I*

period returns, with the difference that the first phrase is in V, the second in I, again with winds. After a short transition the reprise begins exactly like the first time, with the winds reinforcing only the second phrase. The movement bears a hint of rondo character because of this threefold occurrence of the second half of the main theme. In some versions the symphony includes a Menuetto I^mo and 2^ndo.

Many Vanhal symphonies exist in both three- and four-movement versions. The finale of this symphony, *Allegro* in common time, begins softly in a minor with a theme that contains clear echoes of the beginning of the first movement, including the leap to the high tonic. The full measure of diminished harmony leading to ii^6 in the second key of C also sounds a note familiar from the opening movement, as do the flurries of sixteenth notes in the first violins that follow. An impressive development makes further good use of the diminished seventh harmonies, leading to a complete restatement of the second theme in the key of e, which eventually turns to E. The listener is led to think that this is a reverse recapitulation (not rare in Vanhal) and that all that remains to come is the main theme and conclusion in a. But like Haydn, Vanhal knows how to build suspense and keep up momentum to the end of the cycle, and also how to use long pauses to dramatic effect. The dominant preparation on E leads not to the tonic minor but to a complete reprise in the tonic major, A, in the normal order, with second theme following first. A sizable coda with flourishes for the winds extends the movement further, until it dies away in several measures of *pianissimo*. Both the wind flourishes and *pianissimo* ending suggest a proximity to some of Haydn's final codas of the time. Another composer who paired a gentle and lyrical content with the key of a minor was, of course, Mozart.

Vanhal's early symphonies throw some light on the mysterious remark by Dlabač that the composer was not satisfied with the teacher he was given (Schlöger) but struck out on his own to find the best models. There is scarcely a hint in these symphonies of the contrapuntal penchant that beset the official court composers, who had no choice in the matter if they wanted to please Joseph II. A good measure of this is the artistic distance that Vanhal kept from the symphonies and quartets of Gassmann, in spite of the cordial personal relations between the two. If Vanhal told Dlabač in 1795 that he "began to study the scores of the greatest masters on his own," we have no difficulty in believing, on the basis of his own works, that these included the scores of Joseph Haydn.

The question of Vanhal's compositional decline was raised in 1776 by Carl Ludwig Junker, who treated Vanhal as the last of his "twenty composers."[48] Junker began his sketch of the composer with the words "naïveté," "flux," "melody," and "lightness" for the early works, with which he contrasted the latest works, characterized by the terms "constriction," "stiffness," and "lack of melody." On the basis of the two symphonies available from Vanhal's later output, C 11 (Breitkopf, 1775) and d 2 (Breitkopf, 1778), we must, reluctantly, agree that the composer did suffer a falling off in inspiration. These symphonies are less original in their melodic ideas and more

---

[48] *Zwanzig Komponisten: eine Skizze* (Berne, 1776). It is clear that Junker based his main impression upon what Burney said in his travel diary of 1772, some of which Junker was so indiscreet as to plagiarize.

mechanical in spinning them out. The *filo* has been stretched thin and seems in danger of breaking. Junker concluded his remarks by saying, "In his latest symphonies he seems to have taken great trouble to deny the original feeling ["Empfindung"] of the earlier ones." Perhaps it was a case more of being unable, rather than unwilling, to recapture the spontaneity and élan of his earlier years.

As late as 1783, reviewing three symphonies advertised by Hummel as Op. X in 1781 (D 17, E 5, and A 7), Carl Friedrich Cramer sent this message to Vanhal, in what seems like an attempt to spur him on:

> These three symphonies are distinguished above all others of the hitherto engraved symphonies of this well-known and celebrated man, and are full of good ideas and choice accompaniment. They are almost like the newest Haydn symphonies; they are more difficult than easy, and it would not be advisable to perform them without having played through first with all the instruments at least once. New and very pleasing are the solos for flute in the *Adagio* of the first and *Andante* of the second, and for violin in the *Adagio* of the third, whereby the other parts play pizzicato. May Mr. Vanhal not be prevented by a lessening of his faculties as a result of approaching old age from presenting other such symphonies, which will be the more welcome, however spoiled we have become by the charming ones of Haydn.[49]

Cramer's opening statement may be in direct reaction to Junker more than to Vanhal's music. As for slow movements consisting of solos with pizzicato accompaniment, Vanhal offered a long and meandering one for oboe in his Symphony in d (d 2), advertised by Breitkopf in 1778. The reference to approaching old age seems hardly appropriate to a composer aged forty-three, seven years younger than Haydn, unless it is a reference to some debilitating condition of which we are unaware. Vanhal still had many years to live (until 1813), but no more new symphonies of his appeared in print. During the long twilight of his career he wrote mainly teaching pieces and trifles for keyboard, plus church music.

Vanhal's string quartets reveal the same story as his symphonies: an immensely rewarding and prolific period followed by silence. Six sets of string quartets were published in Paris between 1769 and 1773. The earliest two, published as Op. 1 and Op. 2 in 1769, have been denied the status of "true" string quartets because they are orchestral in nature.[50] The six quartets published in 1771 as Op. 7, on the other hand, are soloistic and charac-

---

[49] *Magazin der Musik* (Hamburg, 1783), 1: 92. Bryan, "The Symphonies of Johann Vanhal," p. 28, comments: "Cramer's remarks may have been calculated as an attempt to forestall the decline in Vanhal's symphonic production."

[50] Hickman, "Six Bohemian Masters," Chapter II.

terized by motivic and thematic unity, with some fine contrapuntal touches here and there. They seem to have been composed before the Italian journey of 1769–70. Op. 6, published in 1772, resembles the divertimento-like works of Op. 1 and Op. 2. Both this set and Op. 9 (1772) may stem from the Italian sojourn. Op. 13 shows more Viennese features again, but is tempered by a greater interest in lyricism than the works before the Italian trip, quite in line with what we have observed in connection with the symphonies. Vanhal's final sets of quartets appeared in the late 1770s and early 1780s. Junker wrote that Vanhal obviously took Haydn for his model in string quartets and imitated him, not slavishly but with happy results.

Vanhal's contemporaries considered him an outstanding composer of vocal as well as instrumental music. Modern sources list as many as sixty masses by him. Dlabač lists "25 grosse und kleinere Messen" and "2 Messen de Requiem für seine Eltern" among many other church pieces. A visit by the composer to Bohemia is documented in 1784; it may have been in connection with the death of one or the other of his parents. He also wrote a "Trauergesang bei dem Tode Josephs des II." An anonymous critic singled out his vocal music for praise in the *Wiener Schriftsteller- und Künstlerlexikon* of 1793:

> Mr. Vanhal, a composer of much taste. Everything that he has delivered for many years in sacred and other music is masterful and shows a man of knowledge and practice. His Masses and his Church music are especially outstanding and please the ear and heart. It is a shame that this artist does not deliver further proof of his talents, for it has been a very long time since something new from him has appeared.[51]

Works of substance from Vanhal's last period number few indeed, although he is said to have continued composing until his final days.

Vanhal contributed to the typically Bohemian tradition of the Christmas mass, or *missa pastoralis*. His *Missa pastorell* in G exists in parts in Vienna and in Brno, the latter bearing the date 1782.[52] In the Kyrie, after the modulation to the dominant, Vanhal incorporates a long drone on d over which the soprano sounds the cadence from the carol "Nesem vám noviny," familiar from its repeated occurrences in the *Sinfonia pastorale* in D by Johann Stamitz (Example 6.10). Still more evocative is the way the first violins imitate the "Tuba pastoralis" and its typical fanfares (Example 6.11). To this same tradi-

---

[51] Ibid., p. 54.
[52] MacIntyre, *The Viennese Concerted Mass*, p. 669. MacIntyre's generous musical example in score from this previously unscored mass, pp. 73–85, provides the source for our musical examples.

EXAMPLE 6.10. *Vanhal,* Christmas *Mass in G, Kyrie*

EXAMPLE 6.11. *Vanhal,* Christmas *Mass in G, "Tuba pastoralis"*

tional call belongs the shepherd's piping that opens Haydn's Symphony No. 6, *Le matin* (*Allegro* of the first movement) and the last movement of Beethoven's *Pastoral* Symphony.[53]

The Prague publisher Schönfeld included a sad commentary on Vanhal in his *Jahrbuch der Tonkunst von Wien und Prag* (1796). The artist, he wrote, has consigned himself to oblivion, an unnecessarily harsh verdict on a composer who rose from the humblest beginnings to provide delight to music lovers everywhere. Vanhal's decline is a source of disappointment, but will not cause his many works of great distinction to be forgotten.

Just as Ditters at his best approaches Mozart the showman and prestidigitator, Vanhal at his best approaches Mozart the intimate and sometimes melancholy poet of pure beauty. Like Mozart, he combined a rich vein of Italianate melody with a fine feeling for thematic contrast. Also like Mozart, he often treated the viola as a special favorite, giving it more sustained lines. Their artistic kinship helps explain why Mozart performed Vanhal's Violin Concerto in B♭ in Augsburg in 1777. Both masters shared an undeniable Bohemian accent from time to time, in both melody and rhythm.

---

[53] More instances like this of specifically Bohemian materials in Vanhal will help underpin the claim, made by Postolka in *The New Grove,* that "elements of Czech folk melodies and rhythms played a far more prominent role in Vanhal's music than in that of his Czech contemporaries outside Bohemia."

Hofmann

LEOPOLD HOFMANN was born in Vienna on 14 August 1738, the son of a chamber servant at the imperial court. Showing a talent for music at an early age, he was taken into the chapel of Dowager Empress Elizabeth Christine as a boy soprano in 1745. Here he served under Franz Tuma and came into contact with Georg Christoph Wagenseil, the chapel's organist, who taught him keyboard playing and composition. It is possible that he studied violin with Giuseppe Trani, who also served in the chapel and was the teacher of Ditters, Hofmann's close contemporary. After the dissolution of the chapel on the death of Elizabeth Christine in 1750, Hofmann had to support himself as best he could by taking pupils and church jobs, which would have brought him into early rivalry with Joseph Haydn. He did well enough so that by the time he was twenty he could get married (Haydn waited until age twenty-seven). In the marriage register his occupation is given as "Musicus" (presumably violinist), at the Michaelerkirche.

Abbé Maximilian Stadler claims that Hofmann was organist at the Jesuit Church am Hof around 1762–63. About 1764 Hofmann succeeded Johann Nepomuk Boog as Kapellmeister of St. Peter's, one of the best positions in Viennese church music (Figure 6.7). In 1766 Johann Adam Hiller confirmed this position and also listed Hofmann as *Hofklaviermeister*, but there is no official record of the latter post until 1769, when he succeeded Wagenseil. When Georg Reutter died in 1772, Hofmann gained the two Kapellmeister posts in the cathedral, while retaining his post at St. Peter's. Two years later he applied for the post of Hofkapellmeister on the death of Gassmann. Although highly recommended and regarded as the best qualified of the candidates, he was not selected. Instead the court economized by appointing Giuseppe Bonno, who already enjoyed a pension. Joseph II resolved that the director of the court music should not also be in charge at the cathedral (as had been the case for many years with Reutter).

The deliberations of the court in 1774 reveal general concern that if Hofmann gave up the cathedral, unsuitable candidates would apply for the position.[54] He did not, in fact, leave the cathedral, but he gave his duties there less attention than the authorities deemed appropriate. A commission set up by the city council of Vienna (which was responsible for music in the cathedral) warned Hofmann about his laxness in 1784, with specific complaints that he was rarely present in person on Sundays and feast days, and that he spent most of his time at his suburban house in Döbling. Ill health

---

[54] MacIntyre, *The Viennese Concerted Mass*, p. 34 and n. 38, p. 687.

FIGURE 6.7. Carl Schütz. The Peterskirche.

may be partly responsible for his retreat from active duty and may also explain why he requested of the emperor that he be allowed to take his meals in the Kapellhaus, a request that was denied. He was so ill in early 1791 that Mozart considered applying to the city for his job, as this letter testifies.

Vienna, beginning of May, 1791

Most Praiseworthy and Most Learned
City Councillors.
Gracious Gentlemen!
When Kapellmeister Hofmann lay ill, I wished to take the liberty of applying for his post, since my musical talents, my works, and my skill in composition are well known in foreign countries, my name is treated everywhere with some respect, and I myself was appointed several years ago composer to the most eminent court here; I hoped therefore that I was not unworthy of this post and that I had earned the goodwill of the most learned city council.

But Kapellmeister Hofmann has recovered his health and in the circumstances—for I wish him from my heart the enjoyment of a long life—it has occurred to me that it might perhaps be of service to the cathedral and, most gracious gentlemen, to your advantage, if I were to be attached for the time being as unpaid assistant to this already aged Kapellmeister and were to have the opportunity of helping this worthy man in his office, thus gaining the approbation of our learned municipal council by the actual performance of services which I may justly consider myself peculiarly fitted to render on account of my thorough knowledge of the ecclesiastical style.

Your most humble servant,

WOLFGANG AMADÉ MOZART

Royal and Imperial Court Composer

The request was granted, but Mozart, who counted on outliving the "aged Kapellmeister," did not do so. Hofmann died on 17 March 1793, some fifteen months after Mozart.

Hofmann's fame as a composer came early, before Haydn's. By 1760 six of Hofmann's symphonies were published in Paris, and the Esterházy court chapel possessed three of his flute concertos, which are listed in the inventory of ca. 1759–60 under "Musique instrumentale Italienne." His symphonies and concertos figured in the Academies given in the Burgtheater during the early 1760s, and it appears that he himself took part in them. A "Hoffmann" is listed by Gumpenhuber among the first violins for the Lenten academies in 1761. Then at the academy of 12 February 1762 we read about a double concerto for violin and cello: "Concert ont joué les deux frères Hoffmann sur le Violon et Violoncelle concertés." Johann Nicolas Hofmann was a cellist in the court orchestra in 1772. Were he and Leopold brothers? A surviving concerto for violin, cello, and orchestra by Leopold suggests that they were, and that the concerto in question was the one heard in early 1762.[55] On 30 March 1762 we read, "Le Ire Symphonie a été de la composition du Sr Hoffman, et la dernière du Sr Ditters." Then on 11 June: "Concert a joué Le Sr Leitgeb sur le cor de chasse, un nouveau de la composition du Sr Hoffmann." Later in 1762 Hofmann exercised his formidable instrumental imagination on behalf of the first oboe of the Burgtheater, the multitalented Schmidt, and the sometime accessory oboist Livraghi for a concert on 12 November: "Un Concert ont joué ensemble le Sr Schmid, et le Sr Livraghi sur le Hautbois de la composition du Sr Leop. Hoffman." As his contract stipulated, Ditters was the main provider of and soloist in violin concertos at the Burgtheater during this time, but soon after Ditters left for Italy with Gluck in March 1763, a *service de table* took place at the palace on 4 April: "Concert a joué le Sr Hoffman sur le violon."

The early compositions that brought Hofmann to international attention were instrumental works, mainly symphonies and concertos. Most of them

[55] Allan Donald Jeffryes Badley, "The Concertos of Leopold Hofmann (1738–1793)," 3 vols. (Ph.D. diss., University of Auckland, 1986), 1: 23–25.

are lost. No copy of the six symphonies printed in Paris in 1760 has surfaced, and the early flute concertos once in the Esterházy library have yet to be located. We are reduced largely to repeating what critics of the 1760s had to say. They were remarkably well-disposed towards his music, which probably means that it was more bland than original. In the summary article published by Hiller on Viennese musicians in 1766, we read that Hofmann's "beautiful symphonies and a multitude of other things are known." Compared with the scorn heaped on Ditters by Schiebler and Eschenburg in the Hamburg article "Abhandlung vom musikalischen Geschmacke" (1766), Hofmann emerges very well: "A Hofmann unites the pleasing with the serious, correctness with good melody." In his response to this article, "Von dem wienerischen Geschmack in der Musik" (October 1766), Ditters used the very same words at the beginning of his paragraph on Hofmann, and underscored them with boldface type (here rendered as italics):

> *Herr Leopold Hoffmann*, his path soars ever upwards. The *serious* with the *pleasant*, *melody* with *correctness*, characterize his pieces above all others. He is the only one to approach the church style of *Hrn von Reuttern*. His Masses are full of majestic and grand thoughts, which elevate and inflame the praise of God and the prayer in the temple. His *musical Oratorio*, which was performed in honour of Saint John Nepomuk, shows us a genius who was born for lyrical poetry. Who does not feel everything that one can feel about a bloodthirsty tyrant, when the horrid words of the Hoffmann movement sound: "ut irrita consilia in vanum abeant"? The menacing pride which lurks in these words flashes from every note, every bar awakens terror in the breast, as the listener hears of the innocent's death. But serious though this style is, as pleasant and attractive is he in his symphonies, concertos, quartets and trios; one may say that *Hoffmann*, after *Stamitz*, is the only one to give to the transverse flute the proper lightness and melody.[56]

As with other Viennese composers, Ditters was keen to show his detailed knowledge of the music in question by naming a specific work and specific genres after throwing back at his detractors their generalities, the implication being that they were too ignorant to cite chapter and verse. Hofmann's writing for flute, an instrument he used in many genres, is indeed very skillful and idiomatic; one of his flute concertos in D passed for many years as Haydn's. Hofmann wrote two oratorios on John of Nepomuk, the national saint of Bohemia, and the printed libretto of 1765 for one of them contains the angry aria sung by Crudelitas that is mentioned by Ditters.[57]

Note that Ditters does not praise Hofmann as a great violinist, which he

---

[56] Landon, *Haydn*, 2: 129.
[57] Information kindly communicated to me by Allan Badley.

was. There was room for only one of those in Vienna, at least in Ditters'
mind. (This may also be the reason why Joseph Ziegler was not mentioned
at all.) Is there a tinge of envy between the lines concerning Hofmann's ever-
upward-soaring path? Like Reutter, Hofmann learned early how to feather
his nest, and died a wealthy man, whereas Ditters, as hard as he strived for
material success, was to live most of his life in the provinces and die in
poverty. Hofmann's artistic path did not continue to soar upward after a
certain point. His reputation as a composer was not only established early,
it departed early as well. Ditters does not even mention him in his autobiography.

Hiller set himself up as a kind of arbiter in the war of words between
Vienna and the north German critics. His periodical gave him a perfect
opportunity to do so, and this comparison of Ditters, Hofmann, and Haydn
appeared in its pages during 1768:

> Herr *Ditters'* . . . taste is very much for the comic, or rather it is a constant
> mixture of comic and serious elements that often do not coalesce properly. The
> [violin] concertos of Herr *Hofmann* in Vienna are better put together, are well
> conceived and with pleasant melodies; also his harmonic structure is better than
> that of other newer composers. The same applies to his trios and quartets, that
> is if one can accept the planning and style with which these gentlemen fashion
> their quartets. Herr *Hayden* has composed many quartets, quintets and concer-
> tini along these lines . . . In recent times there have been many pieces which
> because of their new clothing and different style, often lapsing into the comic
> and trifling, have threatened almost to wipe out [the earlier school of symphonic
> writers]. One perhaps guesses that we speak of the symphonies of Herren *Hof-
> mann, Hayden, Ditters, Fils* etc.[58]

The mention of Anton Filtz, the most impressive of the Mannheim symphonists after Stamitz, in the same breath with Vienna's leading symphonists at the time of writing comes as a surprise. It was one thing for the north
German critics to lump Mannheim and Vienna together, denouncing the
errors of their musical ways, but it was something else again for Hiller, a
skilled composer (albeit a rambling writer of prose), to do the same. Hiller
goes on to grant these composers some "well-written, magnificent and
affecting movements" and to praise the way their wind writing helped clar-
ify the harmony, but he returns to the charge, so dear to northern critics,
that the mixture of the noble and the common, the serious and the comic,
within the same movement was questionable. He denounces "the repellent
octaves in the second violin," which, as we have seen, Starzer had been
using with fine effect since the early 1750s. And he criticizes Hofmann's

[58] Landon, *Haydn,* 2: 154.

symphonies for being too long: "*Hayde* knows how to express himself more succinctly, and everything with him has such a pleasing exterior, that he will always have the majority of amateurs on his side, though the former [Hofmann] enjoys the approbation of most of the connoisseurs." Today we are apt to think that Hiller got it exactly wrong, that the music with the pleasing exterior but too little substance to retain the interest of connoisseurs is a piece like Hofmann's Flute Concerto in D, long attributed to Haydn.

A notable connoisseur arrived in Vienna four years after Hiller wrote these lines in the person of Charles Burney, and he heard something in Hofmann's music that particularly pleased him. Of a visit to St. Stephen's on 8 September 1772 (feast of the Nativity BVM), Burney remarked:

> There were likewise several symphonies for instruments only, composed by M. Hofman, *maestro di capella* of this church, which were well written and well executed . . . In the music composed by M. Hofman, though there was great art and contrivance, yet the modulation was natural and the melody smooth and elegant. "As much art as you please in your music, gentlemen," said I, frequently to the Germans, "providing it be united with nature; and even in a marriage between art and nature, I should always wish the lady to wear the breeches."

Thus Hiller and Burney agreed about Hofmann's mastery of the craft of composition, and Burney awarded him high praise for the elusive quality of the "natural."

Hofmann's Symphony in D advertised in Breitkopf's Supplement VII of 1773 probably dates from close to the time of Burney's visit, and may provide a few clues to what Burney was talking about.[59] It is in three movements and scored for large orchestra—pairs of flutes, oboes, horns, trumpets, and timpani, plus the usual four-part strings. The opening *Allegro molto* in 3/4 begins with a *unisono* passage for the strings alternating with the massive homophonic answer of the tutti. On its return the *unisono* ends *on* the dominant, A, whereupon the oboes enunciate a second theme in thirds *in* the dominant. Hofmann was very partial to this easy kind of join, a bifocal close that would enable him to reuse the same passage in the reprise, merely switching the oboes' second theme to tonic D. This may have struck Burney as "natural modulation." Complementary bifocal closes do help simplify composition. Perhaps the deployment of the augmented-sixth chord as a climactic moment toward the end of both the prima parte and the seconda

---

[59] I am indebted to Allan Badley for sending me a score of this symphony, which he prepared in connection with his master of music thesis, "A Study and Critical Edition of Three Symphonies by Leopold Hofmann (1738–1793)" (University of Auckland, 1981).

parte struck Burney as well. As for "art and contrivance," there is scarcely anything that can even be called counterpoint, aside from occasional canonic writing between the violins and the basses.

In the *Andante* in 2/4 that follows, Hofmann chooses the dominant for his key. The two flutes playing in thirds carry the second theme by themselves, showing once again the composer's predilection for solo flute writing. As in the first movement, the bifocal close is used for the main joints, and the same is true of the finale, an *Allegro* in 2/4 that is also in rudimentary sonata form. The contrasts in texture in this symphony are so obvious and regular as to lend it the kind of heightened chiaroscuro that would be effective in a big, echoing interior like that of St. Stephen's.

Hofmann's concertos are of particular interest, and they constitute a part of his enormous oeuvre that has survived relatively well. The majority of the keyboard concertos (of which some two dozen survive) were written for amateur performers in the solo part, as was the case with Hofmann's mentor and particular model in this genre, Wagenseil.[60] But Hofmann ventured a little beyond his teacher in some respects, by bringing the first-movement ritornello form more in line with symphonic norms, for example, and also by resorting less to the *Tempo di Menuet* finale. The thirteen surviving flute concertos, preserved mostly at Regensburg, appear to have been written for the court orchestra there, which boasted a virtuoso flautist by the name of Florante Agostinelli. Nine violin concertos are known to have existed, of which five are extant, one as a solo part only. Breitkopf advertised several in 1767 (Figure 6.8). These are technically demanding pieces, presumably written for the composer himself, but they are not so full of pyrotechnical display as some of the violin concertos by Ditters.

Of the eight cello concertos known, six survive, two of which, Nos. 1 and 7, exploit the high tessitura of the instrument in a way that suggests a highly trained soloist. The repertory of galant concertos for solo cello and orchestra is not enormous, in spite of Boccherini; Hofmann's deserve to be explored. The same is true of such rarities as his double concerto for violin and cello, the double concerto for flute and harpsichord, and the two double concertos for oboe and harpsichord, one of which is said to be the finest of all Hofmann's works in this form. The genre was an ideal medium for Hofmann because it required little thematic development, which was never one of his strong points.[61]

[60] Badley, "The Concertos of Leopold Hofmann," is the source of all the information on this genre here.

[61] Michelle Fillion, "The Accompanied Keyboard Divertimenti of Haydn and His Viennese Contemporaries (c. 1750–1780)," (Ph.D. diss., Cornell University, 1982), pp. 181–82, has this to say of the sonata form without development: "Its rudimentary middle section makes it the ideal form for the composer who is weak in developing material; symptomatically, most of the examples of this form in this repertory are found in the works of Leopold Hofmann."

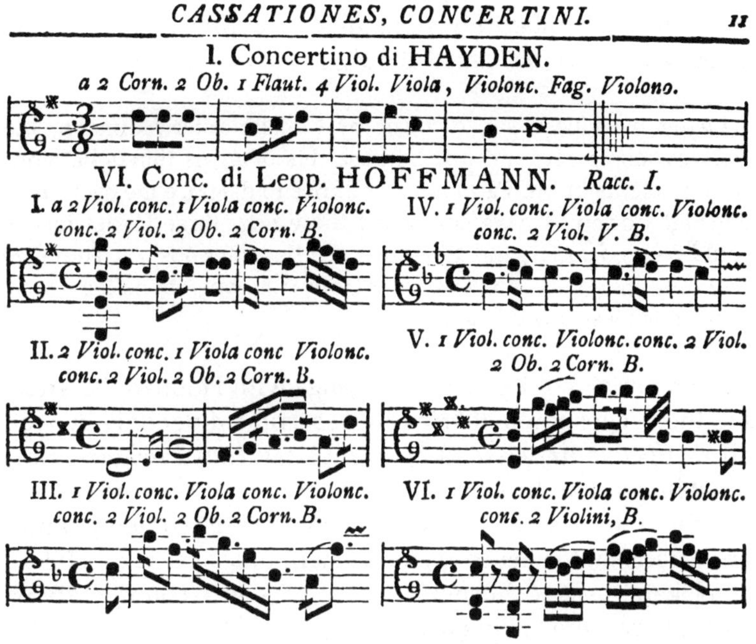

CASSATIONES, CONCERTINI.   11

1. Concertino di HAYDEN.

a 2 Corn. 2 Ob. 1 Flaut. 4 Viol. Viola, Violonc. Fag. Violono.

VI. Conc. di Leop. HOFFMANN.   Racc. I.

I. a 2 Viol. conc. 1 Viola conc. Violonc. conc. 2 Viol. 2 Ob. 2 Corn. B.

IV. 1 Viol. conc. Viola conc. Violonc. conc. 2 Viol. V. B.

II. 2 Viol. conc. 1 Viola conc Violonc. conc. 2 Viol. 2 Ob. 2 Corn. B.

V. 1 Viol. conc. Violonc. conc. 2 Viol. 2 Ob. 2 Corn. B.

III. 1 Viol. conc. Viola conc. Violonc. conc. 2 Viol. 2 Ob. 2 Corn. B.

VI. 1 Viol. conc. Viola conc. Violonc. conc. 2 Violini, B.

FIGURE 6.8.
Detail from
Breitkopf's
*Thematic
Catalogue,*
Supplement
of 1767.

After the death of Reutter, Hofmann was the most highly esteemed church musician in Vienna. As Kapellmeister of St. Peter's he earned considerably more than did, for example, Tobias Gsur as *Regens chori* of the Schottenkirche. There is a degree of superiority even in the title Kapellmeister, which was allowed only to the court, the cathedral, and St. Peter's. Hofmann composed over thirty masses, most of them with orchestra, and they bristle with obbligato writing for various instruments, as we might expect from his other music. They have not been judged very favorably by posterity: "Despite all their interesting, orchestral features and harmonic variety, Hofmann's masses often seem somewhat stiff and old-fashioned because of fussy rococo rhythms in the accompaniment and a Baroque-like unity of *affekt.*"[62] At least one contemporary of Hofmann noted an adverse reaction relative to a 1780 performance of the *Missa in honorem Sanctae Theresiae* in C: "Post Centenar Repetitionem productem ultimo ad nauseum."[63]

It was around 1780 too that the high-flying Hofmann incurred the wrath of Joseph Haydn, who was not, unlike Mozart, given to making uncomplimentary remarks about other composers. The antagonism arose when word reached Haydn that Hofmann had attempted to supplant him and his music at one of the Viennese salons, probably that of Hofrat von Greiner, at which

[62] MacIntyre, *The Viennese Concerted Mass,* p. 74.
[63] Ibid., p. 619, from the copy at Lambach monastery.

Hofmann, Steffan, and Carl Friberth were regulars. Haydn conveyed his ire in a letter to the publisher Artaria, dated 20 July 1780:

> These three Lieder have been set to music by Capellmeister Hofmann, but between ourselves, miserably; and just because this braggart thinks he alone has ascended the heights of Mt. Parnassus, and tries to disgrace me every time with a certain high society, I have composed these very three Lieder just to show this would-be high society the difference: sed hoc inter nos . . . These are only songs, but they are not the street songs of Hofmann, wherein neither ideas, expression, nor, much less, melody appear.

A piece-by-piece comparison of Haydn's arts songs with Hofmann's "street songs" has led to the suggestion that "Haydn was irritated not only by Hofmann's stiff and ineffective understanding of musical/textual relationships, but also by his inability to handle voice-leading, texture and secondary harmonies convincingly in these songs."[64] And yet some of his contemporaries praised Hofmann precisely for his correctness, harmonic structure (Hiller), and smooth and elegant melody (Burney)! It behooves us to continue trying to understand what they were talking about.

Ordonez

KARL VON ORDONEZ was born in Vienna in 1734 and baptized at St. Stephen's on 16 August.[65] His family belonged to the lower nobility and owned property in Moravia. In Hiller's 1766 "Etat" of Viennese court music, Ordonez figures among the violinists and is qualified as *Registrant*, an office he held in the Lower Austria administration, and his compositional specialty is given as symphonies. Ordonez's placement in this list shows that he also played violin with the court musicians. But he was not appointed to a salaried position in the chamber music until 1779, when he replaced Karl Huber. He was pensioned from this position in 1783 and replaced by Thomas Woborzil. In 1784 he led the second violins at the revival of Haydn's *Tobia* by the Tonkünstler Societät.[66]

[64] A. Peter Brown, "Joseph Haydn and Leopold Hofmann's 'Street Songs,' " *JAMS* 33 (1980): 356–83; 369. The claim (p. 359) that "Hofmann together with Giuseppe Bonno, Joseph Starzer and T. Gsur, assumed the position of Hofkapellmeister" is based on a misreading of *MGG*, s.v. "Hofmann."

[65] David Young, "Karl von Ordonez (1734–1786): A Biographical Study," *Research Chronicle* 19 (1983–85): 31–56.

[66] Otto Biba, "Beispiele für die Besetzungsverhältnisse bei Aufführungen von Haydns Oratorien in Wien zwischen 1784 und 1808," *Haydn-Studien* 4 (1976–80): 94–104.

Abbé Stadler says that Ordonez wrote many pieces for the church and still more for violins and instruments, that six of his quartets were published at Lyons in 1788 (actually 1777), and that many more are preserved in manuscripts (he mentions twelve in the imperial archive). "His symphonies received great applause," concludes Stadler, and he composed *Diesmal hat der Mann den willen* (1778). The opera was the second for Joseph II's National Theater, following Ignaz Umlauf's *Die Bergknappen*, and was a failure. None of the composer's sacred music has survived, yet he is praised for writing such music in the *Wiener Theater Almanach* of 1794.[67] In the 1766 article on Viennese taste in music, Ordonez is singled out for his beautiful contributions in symphonies, cassations, and quartets.

Nothing is known about the musical training of Ordonez, but some of his earliest surviving works were acquired by Göttweig Abbey in the 1750s, suggesting a possible liaison there. His early Symphony in C (C 1), for instance, entered the Göttweig collection by 1756. This work furnishes an example of a "church symphony," in that it begins with an *Adagio* of seventeen measures, ending on the tonic, followed by an *Allegro* of sixty-four measures without repeat signs (less than professionally competent is the way the harmony moves upward in parallel triads in the middle).[68] An *Andante* in a minor and a *Tempo di Menuet* finale round out the work, which by itself offers little basis for predicting a future symphonist of merit.

The Symphony in A (A 8, dating before 1766), on the other hand, is such a skilled and attractive piece it was attributed to Joseph Haydn, who also used a soft beginning for two violins alone like the one in this symphony in several works of the 1760s. Very effective in the first movement is the retransition, leading to a *forte* reprise that is doubled by the oboes and supported by the horns. In the Symphony in C with trumpets, timpani, oboes, and horns (C 9, dating from before ca. 1775), the opening *Allegro* is preceded by a short *Adagio* ending on V, the fanfares of which return in the quick tempo to end the movement (unless an *Adagio* tempo indication here was inadvertently omitted). The third and final movement is in the style and form of a *gavotte en rondeau*. Fanfares return in its coda, forging a link with the beginning of the work. This symphony was one of several by the composer published in France (by Guera in Lyons). Judging by its finale, one

---

[67] A. Peter Brown suggests that these compositions were in reality "church symphonies": Carlo d'Ordonez, *Seven Symphonies*, ed. Brown (New York and London, 1979), p. xii. All symphonies discussed here are found in this edition. See also Brown, "The Symphonies of Carlo d'Ordonez: A Contribution to the History of Viennese Instrumental Music During the Second Half of the Eighteenth Century," *Haydn Yearbook* 11 (1981): 5–121.

[68] On the composer's deficient modulatory technique, see the exchange between David Young and A. Peter Brown in *Haydn Yearbook* 16 (1985): 253, 257.

might guess that he wrote it for a French audience or in the knowledge of certain French works.

Ordonez concludes the first movement of his Symphony in F (F 11, dating before 1768) by citing the motto at the end of Monsigny's *On ne s'avise jamais de tout* (1761), one of the most successful Parisian opéras-comiques produced in the Burgtheater. There is no contradiction between this worldly connection and the favorable reception accorded Ordonez's symphonies in churches throughout Austria. Indications on some preserved parts confirm that his symphonies were actually played at liturgical services.

EXAMPLE 6.12. *Ordonez, Symphony in C, I*

Even the grand tradition of Austrian church symphonies in C with trumpets and drums admitted some works with lighter subjects, such as Ordonez's Symphony (C 8) that begins with a theme that might be from a buffa aria (Example 6.12). Ordonez uses trumpets and timpani in two of his symphonies in the key of D, as well as most of those in C, but in no other key within his seventy-odd works in this genre. His minor-mode symphonies include one in c, one in f, three in g, and one in b, representing a proportion of the whole corpus roughly equivalent to that in Haydn's symphonies up to 1780, about which time Ordonez seems to have stopped composing. He died in 1786.

Twenty-seven quartets by Ordonez have been authenticated, of which a set of six were widely diffused in manuscripts and published by Guera in Lyons in 1777.[69] These six quartets derive, like many of the composer's symphonies, from the *sonata da chiesa* tradition. They commence with a slow movement, typically using loose imitative counterpoint in the manner of a trio sonata, and they end up with an open or weak cadence that serves to prepare for the ensuing fast movement. A Menuet and Trio and another fast movement close the cycle. Fugue or fugal procedures often appear in the second or fourth movements, and the composer is at some pains to unify his cycles by thematic means. His quartets thus belong to the Austrian type represented by Matthias Georg Monn, Johann Georg Albrechtsberger, and Gassmann—in other words to the official genre promulgated by Joseph II in his own chamber concerts.

---

[69] Carlo d'Ordonez, *String Quartets, Op. 1*, ed. A. Peter Brown (Recent Researches in the Music of the Classic Era 10) (Madison, 1980).

Haydn and Ordonez were connected in various ways. The latter's *Alceste* was performed by the marionette theater at Esterháza in 1775. A parody of Gluck's masterpiece, this work also enjoyed success in Vienna, where it was performed many times in the suburban theater in the Leopoldstadt. The Haydn-Ordonez connection will be recalled as well from the memorable string quartet performance Burney heard in Vienna during his visit in 1772. (See pp. 346–7.)

Two other nonprofessional composers won special acclaim from their Viennese contemporaries during this period. Marianne von Martínez was raised under the tutelage of Metastasio, who shared lodgings in the Michaelerhaus with the Martínez family. Young Joseph Haydn taught her singing and keyboard as early as 1751.[70] Burney heard her sing and play her own compositions when he was in Vienna in 1772 and could scarcely find adequate words of praise for her skills. The following year Martínez became an honorary member of the Accademia Filarmonica in Bologna. In a letter she wrote to Padre Martini on this occasion, she said that Bonno instructed her in counterpoint and that her models in composition were Hasse, Jommelli, and Galuppi, and for the older style, Handel, Lotti, and Caldara. She composed in many genres, from keyboard miniatures and songs to grand masses and oratorios.[71] Burney praised her vocal works as "neither common, nor unnaturally new," and Metastasio said of her style that it was "a beautiful combination of ancient and modern." Hiller's Viennese correspondent in 1766 provided a list of twelve women performers, at the head of which stood Mlle. Martínez.

Christoph Sonnleithner was born in Hungary of Viennese parents. Orphaned at an early age, he was taught voice and violin by his uncle Leopold Sonnleithner, choirmaster of St. Joseph's in the Leopoldstadt. Later he studied composition with Wenzel Birck, court organist and teacher of Joseph II. He also studied law and made it his profession. Hiller's correspondent in Vienna in 1766, right after mentioning Reutter's church music, interjects the observation that Sonnenleitner was among those who have shown themselves very skillful in this kind of composition. As many as fourteen masses are attributed to Sonnleithner, and those recently studied have been judged favorably.[72] He also wrote many fugal quartets for the private concerts of Joseph II, four of which were published in 1802. His legal work for Prince Esterházy brought him into contact with Haydn.

---

[70] A. Peter Brown, "Marianna Martines' Autobiography as a New Source for Haydn's Biography During the 1750s," *Haydn-Studien* 6 (1986): 68–72.
[71] On her masses, see MacIntyre, *The Viennese Concerted Mass*, pp. 80–83.
[72] Ibid., pp. 87–88.

Albrechtsberger

JOHANN GEORG ALBRECHTSBERGER was born on 3 February 1736 in Klosterneuburg near Vienna, where he began his musical career as a boy soprano and, according to Abbé Stadler, was taught organ by Monn. Melk Abbey was his next place of study (1749–54), followed by the Jesuit Seminary in Vienna, where he was a rival with Michael Haydn for organ duties; we have this from Stadler, who was close to Albrechtsberger and is an excellent source of information about him. After a tour of duty as organist and choirmaster in Hungary (1755–57), he returned to Melk and environs, at which time the celebrated performances of Haydn's *divertimenti a 4* took place in nearby Weinzierl. Stadler tells it somewhat differently from the way the elderly Haydn remembered:

> Joseph Haydn, who composed his first divertimenti about this time at Baron von Fürnberg's not far from Melk, in which Albrechtsberger played the cello, admired Albrechtsberger's art and insisted that he had never heard anything so perfect on the organ. And in fact Albrechtsberger knew how to handle this instrument so that the pleasant could be united to the correct, wherein his playing differed from his written compositions, which often seemed too dry. Many who heard him play the organ often, and later heard the beautiful Haydn quartets with fugues [Op. 20], remember their ideas and performance from Albrechtsberger's organ playing.

Albrechtsberger succeeded officially to the post of organist at Melk on the death of his teacher Weiss in 1759. He gave up the post voluntarily in 1765, and at the insistence of Joseph and Michael Haydn, according to Stadler, he returned to Vienna. But he did not remain long before traveling through Moravia and Bohemia to Silesia in order to join his brother Anton in the service of a Baron Neissen. Anton also played cello, and there are two string trios with cello extant at Melk attributed to him.[73]

The printed sources of 1766 having to do with Viennese music and musicians fail to mention Albrechtsberger for the obvious reason that he was not in Vienna and not yet associated with the court. He returned to the environs of Melk in 1767, and settled in Vienna for good the following year, during which he married. The wedding contract names him "organ fabricator." He played the organ in various churches, and before the death of Reutter in

---

[73] Robert N. Freeman, "The Practice of Music at Melk Monastery in the Eighteenth Century" (Ph.D. diss., University of California, Los Angeles, 1971), p. 260. Perhaps the earliest piece extant by Johann Georg is a Melk manuscript of a B-A-C-H organ fugue dated 1753.

1772, he assisted the elderly Kapellmeister at a Mass in G that required him to play everything in G♯ at sight, because the organ was tuned a half step lower; Stadler says that he did it without a single mistake. From 1772 Albrechtsberger served as choirmaster at St. Joseph's in the Leopoldstadt. Also that year he became second court organist, a position promised him by Joseph II on an earlier visit to Melk. (Gottlieb Muffat became second organist in 1729, first organist in 1741, and was pensioned in 1763; he died in 1770.) Ferdinand Arbesser became first court organist in 1772, and when he was pensioned on 1 December 1791, Albrechtsberger succeeded him.[74] He then succeeded Mozart as assistant Kapellmeister to Leopold Hofmann at St. Stephen's Cathedral and, on Hofmann's death in 1793, became full Kapellmeister, a post he retained until his death in 1809.

Albrechtsberger played a role in preserving the contrapuntal heritage of Fux and adapting it to the newer musical styles of his generation. He himself wrote *divertimenti a 4* in the modern, homophonic style as early as his sojourn in Hungary in 1755–57, that is to say, as early as or earlier than Joseph Haydn. But being primarily an organist, he was bound to take a path different from Haydn's. "The so-called galant style could never be his own," wrote his pupil Ignaz von Seyfried. Albrechtsberger's most widely diffused string quartets were pieces he called *sonate* that consisted of two movements, a prelude and a fugue; their natural homes were in church, but this did not prevent them from being played elsewhere.[75] He also wrote pieces called *quartetto*, which were more in the style of a normal quartet, constructed with three or four movements, one being a minuet. These distinctions of terminology, carefully observed in his autographs, went by the boards in subsequent copies, where everything became a *quartetto*. If his fugues are compared with the quartet fugues of Gassmann, they seem wanting in original themes and in lyrical impulse, or, as Stadler says, somewhat "dry."[76] Perhaps this helps explain why Joseph II, as much as he appreciated the playing of his court organist, gave the preference to Gassmann when it came to chamber fugues.

Albrechtsberger composed over thirty masses, ranging in style from a cappella through those with minimal accompaniment of two violins and organ continuo (over one-third of his output) to the fully symphonic Mass for the Coronation of Francis II as king of Hungary; he also wrote three requiems, several vesper services, and a great quantity of shorter liturgical

[74] On Arbesser, see MacIntyre, *The Viennese Concerted Mass*, pp. 58–59.

[75] Richard William Harpster, "The String Quartets of Johann Georg Albrechstberger: An Historical and Formal Study" (Ph.D. diss., University of Southern California, 1976), pp. 45–49.

[76] The comparison is made in great detail by Warren Kirkendale, *Fugue and Fugato in Rococo and Classical Chamber Music* (Durham, N. C., 1979); see especially the summary on pp. 129–34.

pieces. A recent study of five of his masses concluded: "He used a variety of textures, energetic syllabic choruses, movements which juxtapose chorus and soloists in *concertato* fashion as well as masterful fugues in the expected places."[77]

As a pedagogue, Albrechtsberger had no equal. He was, as Haydn said, "the best teacher of composition among all present-day Viennese masters." His students were legion, and Beethoven was only one of many who profited from his instruction. In his influential *Gründliche Anweisung zur Composition* (Leipzig, 1790) he brought together the traditions of vocal counterpoint (Palestrina to Fux) with those of instrumental counterpoint (J. S. Bach to Kirnberger) and formulated his synthesis in a way that was useful to the needs of contemporary music in the late eighteenth and early nineteenth centuries. The treatise was of especial importance to Beethoven, who put some of its precepts to use directly in his *Grosse Fuge*.[78]

Steffan

JOSEPH ANTON STEFFAN, baptized Josef Antonín Štĕpán on 14 March 1726, came from the village of Kopidlno in eastern Bohemia, where his father was organist and schoolmaster. When the Prussian army invaded Bohemia in 1741, Steffan fled, eventually reaching Vienna, where he joined the household of Count František Šlik, hereditary lord of the Kopidlno estate. He studied violin with Hammel, the count's music director, whom he later succeeded. It is thought that his earliest non-keyboard works, which include church music, pieces for wind band, and sinfonias, were written for the musical forces of Count Šlik. At some time when he was still young, Steffan studied with Wagenseil. He profited greatly from the latter's manner of playing and composing for the harpsichord. It was as a virtuoso and teacher of the keyboard and as a composer for his instrument that Steffan contributed most to Viennese musical life.[79]

Steffan's Op. 1, *VI. Divertimenti da Cimbalo*, advertised in 1759 and dedicated to his students, bears strong resemblance to Wagenseil's similar sets, but actually outshines Wagenseil in textural variety and inventiveness. His Op. 2, *VI. Sonate da Cimbalo* (1760), dedicated to Archduke Joseph, ends with a set of variations on a *Tempo di Menuet* of eight measures. The set is novel for being written on a popular song (which Friedrich Wilhelm Marpurg iden-

---

[77] MacIntyre, *The Viennese Concerted Mass*, pp. 57–58.
[78] Kirkendale, *Fugue and Fugato*, pp. 261–63.
[79] I am indebted to Steffan expert Howard Picton for his detailed commentary on this section, with suggestions for its improvement.

tifies in his critique), for alternating major and minor variations, and, in the realm of keyboard technique, for deploying a variety of rapid figures in both left and right hands.

Steffan's Slavic heritage comes to the fore most notably in some of his *minore* trios, such as that in Op. 1 No. 2, in which the raised fourth degree lends a rather mournful character (particularly in the way it is used descending in mm. 6 and 8) (Example 6.13). Correspondences between Steffan's Op. 1 and Haydn's early keyboard Divertimento in G (Hob. XVI:6) are noted in our earlier discussion of Haydn.

EXAMPLE 6.13. *Steffan, Sonata Op. 1, No. 2, III*

Engraved sets of keyboard works by Steffan were being published about one a year around 1760, which means they must have been successful with amateur players. In 1762 the *Wiener Diarium* first advertised *40 Preludi per diversi tuoni scritti e dedicati alle illustrissime Signore sue scolare da Giuseppe Steffan*, then in 1763, *Parte prima del'Opera terza continente III Sonate da Cembalo*; all these publications were sold by Agostino Bernardi. The opening sonata of Op. 3 begins with an *Adagio* in g that ends with a transition preparing for the following *Allegro* in G. The *Adagio* features many melodic sighs and rich chromatic harmonies. Its intense melancholy acts as a perfect foil for the jolly *Allegro*.

This particular sonata was the probable Steffan work described (by Ditters) in the 1766 article "Von dem wienerischen Geschmack in der Musik." "Wagenseil's most worthy follower is his pupil Herr Joseph Steffan," begins the critique. "No matter how much he imitated his master, one can never deny him the newness of beautiful and unsearched-for expression ["Wendungen"], in which art and nature seem to be bound together." Next comes a list of his pieces for keyboard that had earned him the general applause of connoisseurs: concertos, divertimenti, galanteries, variations, and preludes. The claim that follows is somewhat puzzling: "Although this great harpsichord player is beset with the sickness of the learned, his work betrays a spirit, even so, that can attain to the delightful, if only he wishes to. His *Allegro* movements are mostly merry, delightful, full of dalliance and sound ideas, however melancholic the preceding *Adagio* may have sighed." The "learned sickness" might refer to Steffan's skill at improvising fugues at the keyboard, for which Wagenseil was famous, a skill that presumably passed to his pupil. More likely, the last two sentences are to be read together as pertaining to the opening of Op. 3 Parte prima No. 1. The meaning may be that Ditters found the chromatic harmonies of the *Adagio* too extreme and the texture too complex, and in this sense beset with learned sickness, in which case "sighing melancholic *Adagio*" was not meant as a compliment.

On 14 July 1766, a few months before the appearance of the article on Viennese taste, Steffan was appointed as one of the *Hofklaviermeister* (in succession to the deceased Schlöger). His special charges were Archduchess Maria Carolina (future queen of the Kingdom of the Two Sicilies) and Archduchess Maria Antonia, aged ten, and four years away from becoming the bride of the dauphin. Steffan's links with the imperial family are further confirmed by the inclusion of a keyboard piece bearing his name, otherwise unknown, in a painting that depicts Archduchess Maria Christina and her husband Albert along with Archduke Ferdinand and his wife Maria Beatrice.[80]

In terms of artistic development, Steffan had advanced considerably beyond Wagenseil in the depth and scope of his sonatas by the first part of his Op. 3. In the second part, also containing three sonatas, which was first advertised in 1771, and in three separate sonatas published between 1771 and 1776, he became still more adventurous.[81]

The Sonata that opens the Parte seconda of Op. 3 also begins with an *Adagio*, in c, a movement that is more expansive than the *Adagio* in the Parte prima, and that also adds a transition to its ending, preparing for the ensuing *Allegro e vivace* in 3/4 in C. There are two sharply profiled thematic elements in this fast movement, distinctive by their downbeat beginning (main theme) and upbeat beginning (secondary theme in mm. 26ff.). Steffan generates considerable excitement after the double bar in the middle by bringing these two elements into short-range alternation in a masterly development. He continues the interaction of the two at short range into the reprise, the sort of thing a Haydn might surprise us by doing, and indeed the rhythmic

[80] The painting is in the Ministerzimmer of the Hofburg, Innsbruck, reproduced in Gerda and Gottfried Mraz, *Maria Theresia: Ihr Leben und ihre Zeit in Bildern und Dokumenten* (Munich, 1979), p. 322. The keyboard piece is transcribed from the painting by Otto Biba, "Die private Musikpflege in der kaiserlichen Familie," *Musik am Hof Maria Theresias*, ed. Roswitha Vera Karpf (Munich and Salzburg, 1984), pp. 83–92; 92. It is an unimpressive little 2/4 air in G, with da capo repetition after a long dominant pedal.
[81] Op. 1, Op. 3, and the three separate sonatas are edited by Dana Šetková in Josef Antonín Štěpán, *Composizioni per piano*, vol. I (Musica Antiqua Bohemica 64) (Prague, 1964).

EXAMPLE 6.14. *Steffan, Sonata Op. 3, No. 4, II*

excitement and well-ordered tonal planning of the movement are closer to Haydn than to Wagenseil. The following *Andante non molto* in F is one of Steffan's loveliest movements (Example 6.14). Its main idea is an octave leap to the top of a melodic sigh, a favorite of its composer, and used previously in the Trio of the second sonata of Op. 3 Parte prima. Steffan rounds out the sonata with a Minuetto and Trio, then a final *Allegro con brio* in 3/8.

The second sonata of the set is in G and begins with an *Allegro molto* in common time that goes along its way in the usual manner until a surprise eruption of ♭VI of D is proclaimed with martial dotted rhythm. This is much bolder than Wagenseil; the surprise is also a matter of texture, an expansion to a widely spaced four-note chord. In the following movement, an *Andante cantabile* that is sung largely over an Alberti bass, there are similar textural explosions. Steffan's use of dynamic markings, including rapid alternations of *f* and *p* within the phrase, already in Op. 3, Parte prima, suggests that these early keyboard sonatas, unlike Wagenseil's, were composed for the piano rather than the harpsichord.[82]

Keyboard concertos by Steffan began appearing in Breitkopf's thematic catalogues as early as 1763. Some two dozen concertos for keyboard are preserved from the composer's early period (to ca. 1765), but only about six each from his middle (to ca. 1775) and late periods. Steffan's early works in the genre were for harpsichord, like those of Wagenseil. He found his own voice in the concertos during the 1770s, slightly later than for his sonatas. His orchestral ritornellos tended to neglect the thematic clichés of contemporary concertos, just as he avoided popular forms such as the rondo finale. His most characteristic thematic invention, featuring striking motifs, angular melodic profiles, and rhythmic variety, gradually emerged from his idiom-

---

[82] On Steffan as a pioneer of the fortepiano, see A. Peter Brown, *Joseph Haydn's Keyboard Music* (Bloomington, Ind., 1986), pp. 141–143, 189–191.

atic keyboard writing, in which he increasingly exploited the expressive capabilities of the piano.

Steffan suffered from cataracts, and by 1775 the affliction was so grave he had virtually lost his sight. He was retired from his post as *Hofklaviermeister*, and in recognition of his services Maria Theresa granted him his salary of 500 florins annually as a pension. After a fairly successful operation, he continued to teach, perform, and compose. One of his foremost pupils was Caroline Pichler, daughter of Privy Councillor Franz von Greiner, whose musical salons were among the most fashionable in Vienna around 1780. These are the circumstances that led Steffan into composing German songs with piano accompaniment, some of the texts of which were selected for him by Greiner. The first volume of *Sammlung deutscher Lieder* was printed in 1778 by Joseph von Kurzböck, whose daughter Madeleine was also a pupil of Steffan. A second volume followed in 1779 and another in 1782. All told, the *Sammlung* contained seventy-three of his seventy-six extant Lieder. For the first time, the piano was exploited in ways that opened up the future and glorious course of the Viennese Lied with independent piano accompaniment.

By the end of the 1770s Steffan was no longer considered a follower of Wagenseil. In *Das gelehrte Österreich* (1778) Ignaz de Luca praised his originality: "He studied composition with Wagenseil but did not follow this instruction, rather he introduced an individual manner into his works, with the happiest results."[83] Two decades later the Prague publisher Schönfeld took a different view, calling Steffan "a master who has outlived the taste of our epoch."

The most successful pianist and teacher of piano active in Vienna after Steffan was another Bohemian composer, Leopold Kozeluch. He was so well established as an independent musician in Vienna by 1781 that he could afford to turn down an offer to succeed Mozart as court organist in Salzburg. Kozeluch's use of slow introductions for his piano sonatas from 1780 suggests Steffan's influence. Friedrich Nicolai, toward the end of his "Von der Musik in Wien" (1784), wrote of the popularity of Kozeluch and Steffan, rather than north German masters, among the amateur musicians in Vienna:

> I myself have heard many otherwise ardent and skilled music lovers in Vienna speak of [Emanuel] Bach not only with indifference, but also with inner hostility. Kozeluch and Steffan were everything to them, as far as the clavier was concerned. I do not wish to belittle the accomplishments of those composers, but I believe that . . . whoever has come further in the knowledge of music will be pleased more by Bach's compositions.

---

[83] Dana Šetková, *Klavírní dílo Josefa Antonína Štepána* (Prague, 1965), p. 14.

FIGURE 6.9. Carl Schütz. The Graben, looking toward the Kohlmarkt, 1781.

Kozeluch was one of the first of a new kind of pianist-publisher, soon to become widespread. It seems particularly appropriate that as a fellow countryman of Steffan, he became the poorly-sighted composer's publisher by issuing, sometime between 1785 and 1792, Steffan's valedictory variations for piano on the Czech folksong "Můj milý Janku" (My dear Johnny). Many Bohemian composers who left their homeland seldom made reference to its music. But Steffan did. Moreover, he thought of his native village to the extent of bequeathing to the school there the greater part of his estate in trust. On 12 April 1797, two years after making his will, he died in Vienna.

Steffan's late-period piano music includes a dozen sonatas, five capriccios, five further sets of variations, and a small quantity of chamber music, all preserved only in manuscript copies.[84] His final style period prompted this description:

[84] Eight late-period piano sonatas are published in Josef Antonín Štěpán, *Composizioni per piano*, ed. Dana Šetková, vol. 2 (Musica Antiqua Bohemica, 70) (Prague, 1968); the capriccios are in Joseph Anton Steffan, *Capricce*, ed. Alexander Weinmann (Henle Urtext 227) (Munich-Duisberg, 1971).

The late keyboard works, solo and accompanied alike, are a strange fusion of mid-century *Empfindsamkeit* and high Classical traits, with a strong taste of early romanticism in their rhapsodic and colorful treatment of the fortepiano . . . The late works are far removed from the ordered galant world of Wagenseil. They are characterized by Classical phrase and period structures alternating with asymmetrical groupings, chromatic harmony, thick, sometimes contrapuntal textures, extremes of rhythmic variety, sudden shifts of mood, tempo, and dynamic levels, long, wandering melodies, or short tunes influenced by Bohemian and Slavic folk music,[*] and virtuoso keyboard style, all combined in restless, somewhat diffuse forms that often fail to hold together the multiplicity of effects.[85]

In Steffan's mature piano concertos, he tried formal innovations such as transferring from his sonata style the use of slow introductions in minor (in eight concertos altogether) and omitting the orchestral exposition from the first *Allegro* movement. In five mostly late-period works, he combined these two experimental techniques. The Concerto in B♭ represents the last phase of this evolution: its somber *Adagio non molto* introduction, beginning uniquely in the mediant minor, d, is a fully fledged movement for piano and orchestra, leading directly into the solo exposition of the sonata-form *Allegro* in B♭, which is dominated completely by the piano with Steffan's typically capricious writing for his instrument.[86]

Steffan is the last of Haydn's Viennese contemporaries to be discussed here because there is a sense in which he was the most advanced. Not only did he center his musical world around the piano, but his works for this instrument are full of subjective elements of expression, and his solo pieces show an attraction for programmatic depiction. From a follower of Wagenseil's crisply disciplined harpsichord idiom, he evolved into an early Romantic pianist with a distinctive and attractive musical personality.

---

[85] Fillion, "Keyboard Divertimenti of Haydn and His Viennese Contemporaries," p. 153. Her footnote (asterisk) refers to Šetková, *Klavírní dílo Josefa Antonína Štěpána*, p. 157.

[86] Joseph Anton Steffan, *Piano Concerto in B♭*, ed. Howard Picton (Recent Researches in the Music of the Classical Era 11) (Madison, 1980). The Preface provides an excellent summary of the composer's life and works. For a full study, including a thematic catalogue, see Howard Picton, *The Life and Works of Joseph Anton Steffan (1726-1797), with Special Reference to His Keyboard Concertos* (Ph.D. diss., University of Hull, 1981), published in facsimile in its entirety by Garland (New York, 1989).

7

$\mathscr{M}$ozart, $\mathscr{A}$pprentice

Salzburg and the Archepiscopal Court Music

$\mathscr{T}$HE history of Salzburg as an independent state was very largely a struggle to balance Austrian against Bavarian political power. A glance at the map on p. xxii will show why this was nearly inevitable. With Bavaria, its larger neighbor to the northeast, Salzburg shared ecclesiastical jurisdiction and economic dependence. By treaties that were often in dispute, Bavaria had rights to some of the salt *(Salz)* that gave Salzburg its name. To the west, south, and east Salzburg was surrounded by the Habsburg royal provinces of Tyrol, Carinthia, Styria, and Upper Austria, all ruled from Vienna. As a member state of the Holy Roman Empire, Salzburg owed allegiance to the emperor and the imperial diet. Since the emperor was always a Habsburg ruler, with one short exception in the 1740s, Salzburg was tied to the Hofburg in Vienna by indissoluble bonds, however much these were protested by the rulers in Munich, who kept insisting that Salzburg was a part of Bavaria.[1] Besides its salt mines, Salzburg's mineral wealth included gold.[2]

---

[1] A monastery and bishopric were founded in Salzburg during the eighth century at the invitation of its rulers, the dukes of Bavaria. By 816 the see was raised to an archbishopric, and the temporal power of its ecclesiastical ruler was recognized when he was made an imperial prince by Rudolph of Habsburg in 1278. Salzburg's independence came to an end in 1806.

[2] A good short history of Salzburg is Hans Wagner, "Salzburgs Geschichte im Überblick," *Österreich in Geschichte und Literatur* 7 (1963): 204–16, reprinted in Hans Wagner, *Salzburg und Österreich* (Salzburg, 1982), pp. 3–19.

The prince-archbishop of Salzburg was also the Metropolitan (i.e., ranking bishop) whose authority extended over all of Bavaria and far into the Austrian crown lands. From the year 1026 on, the bishop had the right to wear the cross of a papal legate, which gave him authority to convene synods. In the seventeenth century *primus Germaniae* was added to his titles.

Political power in Salzburg rested in the hands of the canons of the cathedral chapter, whose privilege it was to elect the prince archbishop. In the Middle Ages the canons were divided equally between Austrians and Bavarians, but in the last two centuries of the independent state the Austrians became ever more predominant in number. There were powerful rulers in Salzburg's history, such as Archbishops Wolf Dietrich and Paris Lodron, who dominated the canons and managed to play off the Bavarian rulers of the Wittelsbach dynasty against the Austrian Habsburgs. But after their reigns (ending with the death of Lodron in 1653) lesser men were chosen to rule, and the preponderance of canons from the Austrian crown lands led to Salzburg's gradual submission to the will of Vienna. The archbishops chosen bore names such as Thun (a noble Bohemian family), Firmian (from Tyrol), and Harrach (from Burgenland). During the reign of Archbishop Schrattenbach (1753–71), who came from the Styrian nobility, no fewer than twenty-seven of the thirty-seven canons were Habsburg subjects by birth.

As a part of the Holy Roman Empire, Salzburg was obliged to send a contingent of troops to the emperor's defense in wartime. When Elector Charles Albert of Bavaria challenged Habsburg supremacy and got himself elected as Emperor Charles VII in 1742, Salzburg entered a time of troubles. Unwilling to concede Salzburg to the Austrian sphere of influence, Charles Albert insisted that his brother be elected prince-archbishop. The canons, foreseeing the downfall of Bavarian ambitions, elected a Liechtenstein instead. Salzburg attempted to remain neutral between the warring Austrians and Bavarians, but its neutrality tilted so obviously in favor of the former that many grave threats were received from Munich. The see could not avoid becoming a battleground between the opposing forces, which led to impoverishment and a decline in population. Salzburg had already lost as much as 15 percent of its population during the disastrous forced emigration of Protestant peasants and miners under Archbishop Firmian in 1731–32—the darkest moment of Salzburg's history until the Nazis took over in 1938.

A historian recently painted this rather bleak picture of Salzburg in the eighteenth century.

> The greatness of eighteenth-century Austria that emerged in unprecedented strength after the defeat of the Turks, the wonderful time of the Rococo in neighboring Bavaria, where an overwhelming fullness of art works originated— exactly this epoch saw the gradual decline of the see of Salzburg. Culturally

overshadowed, economically dependent, politically consigned to impotence, and financially strapped, above all by the expulsion of the Protestants and the War of the Austrian Succession, Salzburg first regained some of its former intellectual and cultural bloom only at the end of its existence, under Archbishop Colloredo, when it became for a time a leading center of the late German Enlightenment.[3]

How different is his picture from the received opinions of music historians! They present Salzburg, if at all, as a mere stage, albeit a pretty one, for the appearance of Mozart. The hero is pious and kindly old Archbishop Schrattenbach, who rewarded the Mozarts liberally in spite of their flagrant behavior in remaining absent from his court. His successor, tight-fisted and mean Archbishop Colloredo, is the villain. In truth, Schrattenbach at his death in December 1771 left the see with enormous debts and an empty treasury. His successor had no choice but to economize and to reform the financial chaos he inherited.

Maria Theresa did not exert pressure on the cathedral chapter for any individual candidate during the elections of 1745, 1747, and 1753. She was content as long as one of her subjects became archbishop. On the other hand, in 1772, Joseph II brought massive pressure to bear for the election of Hieronymous Colloredo, son of the vice-chancellor of the imperial court. A festival decoration for Colloredo's entry exists in the form of a wash drawing attributed to Matthäus Siller, showing Fortuna on a globe atop a representation of Salzburg, all of it resting on a triumphal arch; Fortuna is shown linked by chains to two figures identified by their arms as Austria and Bavaria.[4] This was an ill omen, surely, with which to mark the beginning of a new regime. Yet Archbishop Colloredo surprised everyone by maneuvering between the two powers with greater skill than any of his recent predecessors, and he restored some of the independence Salzburg had enjoyed during its greatest period.

Economic dependence on Bavaria remained a threat, and fears in Salzburg increased when in 1778 Carl Theodore, the palatine elector, replaced Elector Maximilian III Joseph. As capital of *Pfalzbayern*, Munich became more powerful than ever. But relations between Carl Theodore and Salzburg, initially cool, began warming in 1779 after the Peace of Teschen, which settled the War of the Bavarian Succession. Mozart's 1780 invitation to Munich to compose the carnival opera, *Idomeneo*, can be seen as one consequence of this warming trend.

---

[3] Gerhard Ammerer, "Von Franz Anton von Harrach bis Siegmund Christoph von Schrattenbach— eine Zeit des Niedergangs," *Geschichte Salzburgs Stadt und Land*, ed. H. Dopsch and H. Spatzenegger (Salzburg, 1988), 2: 245–320; 245–46.
[4] Reproduced in *Geschichte Salzburgs Stadt und Land* (1988), 2: 455.

FIGURE 7.1. Franz Müller. Engraving of Cathedral Square, Salzburg.

The basis for Salzburg's musical eminence was laid in the seventeenth century. Under Archbishop Lodron the Benedictine University was founded in 1622 and the new cathedral was consecrated in 1628. This vast church, designed by Italian architects, was henceforth the main center of Salzburg's musical life, and was linked by a connecting structure to the palace of the archbishop (Figure 7.1). The vocal forces of the cathedral included choral deacons, choristers, and some fifteen choirboys who were instructed by the court musicians. Instrumental forces included wind and string players, organists, and, under a separate administrative department, the court and field trumpeters along with timpanists.

Heading all these forces was the Hofkapellmeister. The Bohemian master Heinrich Biber joined the Salzburg court in 1670, became Vice-Kapellmeister in 1679, and Kapellmeister in 1684. Serving under him for a time as organist and chamber musician was the well-traveled Georg Muffat. Between 1716 and 1727 the Vice-Kapellmeister of the Viennese court, Antonio Caldara, came regularly to Salzburg to oversee performances of his operas and oratorios, many for the first time.

Vienna's cultural sway in Salzburg prevailed in the visual arts as well.

Johann Rottmayr, Johann Lukas von Hildebrandt, and Raphael Donner, respectively, were called from Vienna to execute the ceiling paintings in the Residenz (1710–11), the grand staircase in Mirabell Palace (1722), and its statues (1725–28).

Leopold Mozart is the best witness we have regarding the operation of the court and cathedral music, not only in his "Report" of 1757,[5] but also in his abundant correspondence. Born in Augsburg in 1719, the son of a bookbinder, Leopold moved to Salzburg in 1737 to attend the university. There he studied philosophy and jurisprudence, taking the bachelor of philosophy degree the following year. According to the report, in which he devotes an inordinate amount of space to himself, "he entered the archepiscopal service in the year 1743 soon after completing his studies in philosophy and law." The wording suggests that he completed higher degrees, but in fact he was expelled from the university for poor attendance in September 1739. He next became a valet and musician to one of the Salzburg canons (to whom he dedicated *Sonate sei a tre per chiesa e da camera*, which he engraved himself in 1740) before entering the court music ranks in 1743 as fourth violinist in the orchestra.

In July 1756 Leopold Mozart published his most important work, *Versuch einer gründlichen Violinschule*, which made him famous. The following year he was appointed one of the three court composers. When Kapellmeister Johann Ernst Eberlin died, Giuseppe Lolli became Kapellmeister and Leopold was promoted to Vice-Kapellmeister, which post he occupied until his death in 1787.

Leopold was a prolific composer in his earlier years, to judge from the works he lists in his report. Of particular interest are "thirty grand serenades, in which solos for various instruments are introduced," a genre connected with university functions in Salzburg, which will be discussed in the next chapter under "*Finalmusik* and the Popular Element." The existence of such pieces, which are now lost, is corroborated in the correspondence Leopold carried on with his Augsburg friend Johann Jacob Lotter, publisher of the *Violinschule*.[6]

Ernst Eberlin, as Kapellmeister, heads the list of musicians in Leopold's report. The praises he sings are not without a hint of self-serving interest on Leopold's part.

[5] "Nachricht von dem gegenwärtigen Zustande der Musik Sr. Hochfürstl. Gnaden des Erzbischoffs zu Salzburg im Jahr 1757," in Friedrich Wilhelm Marpurg, ed., *Historisch-Kritische Beiträge zur Aufnahme der Musik*, 5 vols. (Berlin, 1754–78; reprint: New York, 1970), 3: 183–98. Translated in Neal Zaslaw, *Mozart's Symphonies: Context, Performance Practice, Reception* (Oxford, 1989), Appendix C, pp. 550–57. Citations from the "Report" below are in Zaslaw's translation.
[6] See Leopold's letter of 10 April 1755 in *Mozart: Briefe und Aufzeichnungen. Gesamtausgabe*, ed. Wilhelm A. Bauer, Otto Erich Deutsch, and Joseph Heinz Eibl, 7 vols. (Kassel, 1962–75).

If anyone deserves to be called a thorough and accomplished master of composition, it is indeed this man. He is entirely in command of the notes, and he composes with such quickness that many people would take for a fairy tale the manner in which this profound composer brings this or that important composition to the music-stand. As far as the number of musical compositions that he has composed is concerned, one can compare him to the two very industrious and famous composers, [Alessandro] Scarlatti and Telemann. There has appeared in print only the [IX] *Toccate [e Fughe]* for organ [Augsburg, 1747].

This printed collection figures later in the correspondence between Leopold and his son. After settling in Vienna, Wolfgang entered the circle of Baron van Swieten, who was noted for his cultivation of fugal compositions. Reaching back into his memory in an attempt to come up with some contrapuntal products of Salzburg, Mozart recalled, dimly as it turned out, Eberlin's *Toccate e Fughe*, which he requested his father to have copied for him (letter of 10 April 1782). Before long he ran across a copy of the print in question (or a manuscript source?), and in a letter to his sister of 20 April 1782 he wrote:

> Baron van Swieten, to whom I go every Sunday, has given me the works of Handel and Sebastian Bach to take home, after I played them for him . . . If Papa has not had the works of Eberlin copied yet, that is all right with me, for I have got hold of them meanwhile and perceive that (for I could no longer remember them) they are too slight ["geringe"] and really do not deserve a place between Handel and Bach.

In a wider context, the "profound composer" Leopold praised in 1757 appeared merely provincial.

Another composer Leopold singles out in his report for more than the most cursory mention is the organist Anton Cajetan Adlgasser.

> Adelgasser, from Inzell in Bavaria, plays logically, beautifully, and generally cantabile. He is not only a good organist, but also a good accompanist on the harpsichord. He owes both these skills to Capellmeister Eberlin, from whom he also learned the rules of composition. He composes acceptably as well, but he is still very markedly attached to imitating others, especially his teacher.

Adlgasser came up through the choir school of the cathedral and became court organist in 1750. In 1752 he married Eberlin's daughter. Archbishop Schrattenbach sent him to Italy for a year of study in 1764–65.

Leopold also describes the placement of six organs in Salzburg Cathedral. In the rear over the entrance was the great organ. Each of the four musicians' galleries surrounding the transept housed an organ, as can be

FIGURE 7.2. Melchior Küsell. Detail from an engraving of the Salzburg Cathedral interior.

seen from the engraving by Melchior Küsell, c. 1675, showing the interior of the church during a solemn high mass (Figure 7.2). A small organ with its bellows is visible below in the choir "next to the hymn singers."

The musicians depicted in the galleries play trumpets and trombones among other instruments, and two in the forward galleries signal across the space to each other with raised music scrolls. The interaction of these forces is described with welcome detail in the report:

> In large-scale concerted music the great organ is used only to improvise pre-ludes; during the concerted music itself, however, one of the four side-organs is

constantly played, namely, the one next the altar on the right-hand side, where the solo singers and the bass instruments are. Opposite by the left-side organ are the violinists, etc., and by both the other side-organs are the two choirs of trumpets and kettledrums. The lower choir-organ and double-bass play along only in the tutti passages. The oboe and transverse flute are heard in the cathedral seldom and the horn never. Accordingly, in church these gentlemen [i.e., the wind players] play the violin.

All four galleries *(Emporen)* were used on festive occasions. The organs in the two trumpet galleries had a single manual and pedal. The other two gallery organs were more elaborate, with two manuals and pedals. Of these the *Hoforgel* proper was the one on the right, looking toward the altar, described in 1757 as occupied by the solo singers and bass instruments. Küsel's engraving shows trombones (i.e., bass instruments) in the left gallery, which housed the "Holy Spirit organ." (Is this famous print possibly reversed with respect to the *Hoforgel* and *Heilig-geist Orgel?*) The four galleries with their organs were removed in 1859; in recent years they have been restored.[7]

Adlgasser played the *Hoforgel* for the last time at a Sunday afternoon vespers on 21 December 1777. That Sunday morning Mozart's recent Mass in B♭, K. 275 (272ᵇ), was performed in the cathedral, and as Leopold Mozart wrote his wife and son in Mannheim the following day, "the castrato [Ceccarelli] sang incomparably." Then at the vesper service

the Dixit went well, but as Adlgasser broke in after the first psalm he groped around the keyboard horribly and could come to no end. After the second psalm it went even worse, as he sustained a pedal a tone too low and pawed the keys with both hands as if a dog were running over them. Everyone thought he was drunk. At the third psalm he could play no more with the fingers of his left hand and laid his clenched fist on the keys. Only at length could I persuade him to leave the organ and let Spizeder play. Meanwhile I removed his left hand and Spizeder did the best he could to make a bass under what Adlgasser's right hand was playing. Finally we brought him, almost carried him, away and sat him on the bench where the trombones play.

Adlgasser had suffered a stroke. He died the next day. His eventual successor as court organist was none other than young Mozart himself.

Versatility was the rule among the players Leopold Mozart describes in his report. Two of the four bassoonists could also play oboe. The two horn players from Bohemia also played violin and cello, respectively. In fact, most

[7] Gerhard Walterskirchen, "Zur Wiedererrichtung der Musikemporen und Orgel in Salzburger Dom: Geschichte—Funktion—Rekonstruktion," *Mozartwoche* (1991), pp. 305–9; Ernst Hintermaier, ed., *Die Innenansicht des Salzburger Domes: Kupferradierung von Melchior Küsell (um 1675)* (Salzburg, 1992).

of the wind players are said to double as string players. All the trumpeters and the two timpanists "play the violin well." Of the ten violinists listed, five played other instruments as well. The three trombonists who belonged to the choir singers were there "to play the alto-, tenor-, and bass-trombone, which must be taken care of by the master of the town waits with two of his subordinates, for a yearly stipend." The grand total of "those who belong to the musical establishment, or who are connected to the court music in any way, amounts to ninety-nine persons." This total was exact before Leopold added "three music-servants or so called organ blowers" at the very end. The correct total is 102. The last persons he names are Johann Rochus Ege-dacher, "princely court organ-maker, born in Salzburg," and Andreas Ferdi-nand Meyer, "princely court lute- and violin-maker, born in Vienna. Both of them must be present at all times and keep the instruments in good con-dition."

From the Mozart residence in the Getreidegasse to the cathedral or the palace was but a short walk, perhaps no more than five minutes. This was just as well, because Leopold's manifold duties at court called him there often. Besides performing and directing, he gave instruction in both violin and keyboard to the choirboys of the cathedral. He was very active as a composer until around 1760, when, as his daughter Nannerl later reported, he "gave up both violin instruction and composition entirely in order to spend time not required in princely service on the education of his two chil-dren."[8] She exaggerates, but there is no doubt that after 1760 Leopold saw his mission in life differently. Not just the education of his young son and daughter, the only two of seven children to survive, preoccupied him. Their presentation to the world as child prodigies became of paramount concern.

The Child Prodigies on Tour, 1762–66

LEOPOLD MOZART was returning proofs of his *Violinschule* to Lotter in Augsburg throughout the winter of 1755–56. He began his letter of 26 Janu-ary 1756 to Lotter, "I write in haste partly because of the operas at court, partly because of my pupils, and partly because of other matters that hinder me." On the next day, the feast of St. John Chrysostom, at eight in the evening, a son was born to his wife. The baby was christened in the cathe-dral Joannes Chrysostomos Wolfgangus Theophilus. The birth took place on the premises of the house in the Getreidegasse rented from Lorenz Hage-

[8]"Data zur Biographie des verstorbenen Ton-Künstlers Wolfgang Mozart" (1792), in *Mozart: Die Dokumente seines Lebens*, ed. Otto Erich Deutsch (Kassel, 1961), p. 398.

nauer. Maria Anna Mozart, "Nannerl," had been born four and a half years earlier, on 30 or 31 July 1751.

Under Leopold's tutelage both children made rapid strides in music. By the end of the 1750s Nannerl was given her own book of harpsichord pieces, entitled "Pour le clavecin. ce Livre appartient à Mademoiselle Marie Anne Mozart. 1759." Individual minuets in the collection Leopold further inscribed with the dates Wolfgang learned to play them. Beginning in early 1761, pieces were added that the young prodigy composed himself. All the writing in Nannerl's book is in the hand of Leopold. In September 1761 young Mozart, aged five, took part in a theatrical performance with music by Ernst Eberlin at Salzburg University. His public career was launched.

Munich was the first place Leopold took his two children on exhibit. They visited the Bavarian capital during the carnival of 1762 for about three weeks beginning on 12 January. While there, they were presented at court, and the children played the harpsichord for the elector, Maximilian III Joseph. The Munich carnival opera that season was Metastasio's *Temistocle* set by Kapellmeister Andrea Bernasconi, in which his stepdaughter, Antonia Bernasconi, made her debut. The Mozarts would encounter her later in Milan and Vienna.

Vienna was the goal of the next trip. All four family members set out on 18 September 1762 and went by way of Passau, then down the Danube by boat, stopping at Linz. On the trip from Linz to Vienna little Mozart astonished the passengers by his organ playing. The family arrived in Vienna on Wednesday, 6 October. In his letter to Hagenauer of 16 October Leopold relates how they passed the customs outside the capital.

> We got quickly through the customs at the fortifications and were given a total dispensation from the main customs. For this our little Wolferl can again take the blame, for he immediately became friends with the customs officer, showed him his clavier, made him an invitation, and then played for him a menuet on his little violin ["geigerl"], and thus we were dispatched through customs. The customs officer begged permission to visit us with the greatest courtliness and to this purpose wrote down the quarter in which we are staying.

This passage contradicts the letter written by Johann Andreas Schachtner, Mozart family friend and court trumpeter at Salzburg, after Mozart's death, on the point of the little violin and Mozart's ability to play it even before reaching Vienna.

> Soon after they came back from Vienna, Wolfgang brought with him a little violin ["eine kleine Geige"] that he received as a present in Vienna. Our former good violinist, the late Herr Wenzl, brought with him six trios that he, as a

beginner in composition, wanted evaluated by Papa Mozart. We played the trios, Papa doing the bass on the viola, Wenzl the first violin, and I was to do the second violin. Wolfgangerl asked that he be allowed to play the second violin, but Papa rejected his foolish request because he had not had the slightest instruction in violin and was not capable of the task.[9]

Schachtner strings out his story at some length, finally revealing that Mozart, to their astonishment, was indeed capable of playing the part on his violin. The contradiction with Leopold's letter throws suspicion on the whole anecdote.

In the fall of 1762 the French and German troupes were alternating in the Burgtheater because of the fire that had destroyed the Kärntnerthor Theater the previous fall. A great new work was causing a sensation, Gluck's *Orfeo ed Euridice*, first performed by the French troupe at Schönbrunn on 5 October 1762. In his letter of 16 October Leopold says that he attended the opera alone on the 10th. We know what he heard in the Burgtheater that night, thanks to Gumpenhuber's *Répertoire:* a comedy by Marivaux and Gluck's new opera. Under "Dimanche 10 Octobre" Gumpenhuber entered, "Comedie française La Surprise de l'Amour suivie d'Orphée et Euridice avec son spectacle et 4 Ballets." Presumably Leopold bought a ticket at the door. In November Countess Theresa von Lodron offered the Mozarts her box in the theater so that the whole family could go. Leopold relates this in his letter of 24 November, mentioning specifically that "Dr. Bernard [their physician] took us to a box at the opera" on the previous evening. On 23 November Gumpenhuber listed, "L + + + + Boissy [a play] suivie de la 15ᵉ Representation d'Orphée et Euridice avec tout son Spectacle et 4 ballets." Thus it is certain that the child-genius who was going to become the greatest of opera composers witnessed the most advanced operatic production Vienna had to offer during its first run.

When Leopold was at the opera on 10 October, he heard Archduke Leopold say to someone in another box that "a boy is in Vienna who plays the clavier superbly, etc. etc." Archduke Joseph had also heard the news and passed it on to his mother, with the result that the Mozarts were invited to present themselves at Schönbrunn on the 12th, but this was changed to the 13th because the 12th was the name day of the youngest archduke, Maximilian. According to Nannerl's memoir of 1792 there were present not only the emperor and empress but also their grown children. Leopold's letter to Hagenauer of 16 October contains a brief description of this visit.

We were received by Their Majesties with such extraordinary graciousness that when I narrate what happened people will take it for a fable. Enough! Wolferl

[9] Letter to Nannerl of 24 April 1792, in *Dokumente*, pp. 395–98.

leaped up into the lap of the empress, put his arms around her neck, and kissed her heartily. In short, we were there from three until six o'clock, and the emperor himself came from the adjoining room to fetch me, so that I could hear the infanta [Princess Isabella of Parma, wife of Archduke Joseph] play the violin.

Two days later the empress sent the Mozarts court costumes for the children (hers from a young princess, his from the identically aged Archduke Maximilian), and the visitors were put on notice to expect further orders to appear at court.

How were those three hours filled? Nannerl and Wolfgang both played sonatas and concertos, and he improvised. According to Nannerl's memoir of 1792 Emperor Francis played games with the boy, asking him to play with only one finger, which he did perfectly, then asking him to play with the keys covered, which he did as if he had practiced doing so. From another source, also indebted to Nannerl, comes the story of Wolfgang's asking for Wagenseil and reading his harpsichord concertos, for which the court musician turned the pages.

The Mozarts' days in Vienna were filled with carriage rides to visit the houses of the high nobility. "We had to drive from Schönbrunn straight to Prince von Hildburghausen," says Leopold in the same letter of 16 October. The prince lived in the Palais Rofrano (later Palais Auersperg; see Figure 6.4). Prince Kaunitz, the Austrian chancellor, and Count Palffy, the Hungarian chancellor, vied for the chance to be entertained by the visiting prodigies; the list of others of the nobility is long. Leopold expressed concern that his children would become exhausted, and indeed they did. A sinister turn of events began on 21 October, just after another visit to the empress. Wolfgang came down with scarlet fever. Luckily, he was in bed for only ten days. Presiding over his recovery was Dr. Johann Anton von Bernhard, who received daily enquiries from many nobles about the boy's condition. Leopold assessed the setback in his letter of 30 October: "This affair has cost me at least fifty ducats, but I am infinitely grateful to God that it has turned out so well."

On 4 November, the feast of St. Charles, Leopold took Wolfgang on a drive to the Karlskirche. The social round gradually resumed. On 19 November, the Mozarts were back at court to observe the gala table, from which the empress called out to ask about the boy's welfare. On 22 November, St. Cecilia's Day, the Mozarts were invited to lunch by Kapellmeister Reutter. In December they visited Pressburg at the urgent invitation of the Hungarian nobles, returning to Vienna on Christmas Eve. After further visits the family left for home and reached Salzburg by 5 January 1763. As a postscript to his last letter to Hagenauer on 29 December, Leopold added that Maria Theresa had just lost (to typhus) another child, Archduchess Johanna, "who, when we visited at court, took my Wolferl by the hand and led him through her rooms."

From Vienna Leopold asked Hagenauer more than once to put in a good word at the Salzburg court, where Eberlin's death had left a vacancy. Upon the appointment of Giuseppe Lolli a festive concert was held at which Wolfgang and Nannerl were heard at the keyboard, and Wolfgang on the violin as well. A report in an Augsburg newspaper of 19 May 1763 confirms that Mozart played solo and in concert with others on his specially made *violino piccolo* on this occasion.[10] This same report also covers the appearances of the children at the Viennese court, where Nannerl is said to have "played the most difficult sonatas and concertos of the greatest masters on the harpsichord with a scarcely believable lightness and in the best taste." Wolfgang did the same and more. He is described as improvising "now *cantabile,* now chordally, for hours at a time." Besides this, the boy could identify the pitch of any tone sounded in whatever way, and add a bass to a theme given him. A few more feats would be added to this list on the grand tour soon to follow, but the basic repertory is already here and was first demonstrated in Vienna.

The promotion of Leopold did nothing to hold him in Salzburg. Plans were already under way in Vienna with the French ambassador and others for a major tour that would take the family to Paris, London, and Holland. The trip began with a return visit to Munich, where both children played again for the elector. Their route took them by way of Augsburg and Ulm to Ludwigsburg, where they met Niccolò Jommelli and heard Pietro Nardini play; then to Mannheim, where Elector Carl Theodore heard the children on 18 July. After visiting several other German cities, the Mozarts entered the Austrian Netherlands, then spent six weeks in Brussels. On 18 November they reached Paris, where they remained for five months, including two weeks at Versailles, where they were all presented to Louis XV and the royal family at a gala dinner on 1 January 1764. On this same occasion Wolfgang played the organ in the court chapel.

The Mozarts quickly made a great impression in Paris. In his dispatch for the *Correspondance littéraire* dated 1 December 1763, Melchior von Grimm, secretary to the Duc d'Orléans and the Mozarts' main sponsor and friend in the French capital, described the children's musical feats, which consisted of all those displayed in Vienna a year earlier. He added in the case of Wolfgang: "He writes and composes with a great facility, without need of approaching the harpsichord or trying out chords."[11] (We know from later

[10] *Dokumente,* pp. 22–23.
[11] Ibid., pp. 27–28.

evidence that Mozart preferred to compose with a keyboard instrument at hand even if he did not require one.) Grimm continued: "I wrote a minuet for him in my hand and asked him to put a bass under it. The child took his pen and without going over to the harpsichord, put a bass to it." Then a lady sang to Mozart an Italian cavatina she knew by heart and asked him to accompany her at the harpsichord. Not only did he do this, he asked her to keep repeating her solo so that he could vary the accompaniment each time—i.e., a theme and variations *all'improviso*. Grimm's account was taken up in countless other journals of the day and translated into other languages. He ended it by remarking, "It is a pity that the French understand so little about music. Father Mozart proposes to go from here to England, and then to southern Germany."

During the winter of 1763–64 in Paris, Mozart was busy, with the ever-present help of his father, composing some harpsichord sonatas for publication. The reigning keyboard player locally was Johann Gottfried Eckard, who had been brought to Paris in 1758 by Johann Andreas Stein, the instrument builder. Eckard's *Six Sonates pour le Clavecin* were engraved in 1763, with a preface saying that they could also be played on the fortepiano and clavichord, to which purpose numerous dynamic shadings were added.[12] Eckard's collection is very much of its time, which is to say taken up largely with melodies over mechanical bass patterns (of which the Alberti bass was only one). His Op. 1 No. 5 in C begins with a melody falling by step from the fifth degree, to which Mozart was partial (Example 7.1). Had the composer omitted mm. 3–4, this melody would be a regular **a b b'** in four-bar units.

Eckard's main rival was Johann Schobert, who published far more than Eckard. In his letter of 1 February 1764 to Hagenauer, Leopold Mozart refers to both.

> My son frequently accompanies in the public concerts, and when doing so he can easily transpose an aria *a prima vista*; everywhere French or Italian works are put before him, and he reads them at sight. My daughter plays the most difficult pieces that we have by Schobert, Eckard, and others, Eckard's being the most difficult, with incredible clarity, and so well that the mean-spirited Schobert cannot conceal his envy and jealousy, and so is making a fool of himself to Eckard, who is an honest man, and to others.

Earlier in the same letter Leopold wrote that Schobert, Eckard, Jean-Pierre Le Grand, and Christian Hochbrucker had brought their engraved sonatas as presents for the children, leading up to what seemed inevitable: "Now four of Wolfgang's sonatas are being engraved. Imagine the sensation when

[12]Johann Gottfried Eckard, *Oeuvres complètes pour le Clavecin ou le Pianoforte*, ed. Eduard Reeser (Amsterdam, 1956).

EXAMPLE 7.1. *Eckhard, Sonata Op. 1, No. 5, I*

the title page reveals that they were composed by a child of seven years!"

In later years Leopold had reason to regret pushing his son (and himself) into the production and publication of these juvenile works. Their diffusion, he later suspected, had something to do with the disinterest shown by music publishers in Mozart's truly fine works of the 1770s (see his letter of 12 February 1781 to Breitkopf in Leipzig). But we should not judge Leopold too harshly on this account. He lived from day to day, never certain when God would call any or all of his family home to Himself (as Leopold was fond of putting it). Strike while the iron is hot! A similar proverb exists in every language. The sonatas in question were beautifully engraved in Paris by the elderly Madame Vendome (Figure 7.3). As may be seen from the title page of the first two, they offered an additional, optional part for violin, very much the fashion in Paris and London at that time, and were dedicated to none less than a princess of the blood, Madame Victoire, second daughter of Louis XV. A second set of two sonatas was published slightly later, dedicated to Madame la Contesse de Tessé. The expected presents for such dedications, monetary and otherwise, were forthcoming and were appropriately generous.

FIGURE 7.3. Title page of the Sonates, Op. 1, Paris, 1765.

The harpsichord sonatas themselves are respectable, according to the lights of the Parisian works of Eckard, Schobert, et al. They are not as interesting as those by Eckard, but they are not indebted to borrowings from Eckard either, contrary to what has been claimed.[13] Perhaps the best that can be said about the first four sonatas, K. 6–9, is that the fourth, K. 9, shows signs of increasing depth and originality. Its opening *Allegro spiritoso* in cut time contains a rising chromatic progression as confirmation of the second key that is akin to a favorite passage of Emanuel Bach (as in the finale of the first *Prussian* sonata). This movement's development also deploys a rising chromatic passage. The *Andante,* in 3/4 and in the key of C, effectively exploits dolce parallel thirds and sixths against strident octave rejoinders in dotted rhythm. The third and final movement consists of a Menuet I and a Menuet II in the minor, after which the first is repeated.

The melody of the first Menuet of K. 9 strikes us as recognizably Mozartian. Its gentle rise and fall, its use of triplets and trills, belie, or perhaps enhance, a basic melodic shape that is folklike in its simplicity: 3 4 5, 2 3 4, 1 2 3 (Example 7.2). The accompanying violin adds nothing by sawing back and forth from D above middle C to D above in eighth notes because this D

---

[13] Eduard Reeser, in the Preface to his edition of Eckard, claims that the closing melodic formula of the *Allegro* in K. 6 is indebted to the same in the opening movement of Eckard's first sonata, but the resemblance is unconvincing.

EXAMPLE 7.2. *Mozart, Sonata K. 9, III*

pedal is already present, played by the thumb of the left hand on the harpsi-chord. Mozart reinforced the impression that there is something personal about this melody by returning to it some seven years later in the *Andante* of the Symphony in D, K. 95 (73^n), which is traditionally dated Rome, April 1770 (Example 7.3).[14] In the symphony movement the melody is given to the violins in octaves, a peculiarly Viennese sonority, and the pedal D provided by the violas is essential to complete the harmony (sustained viola parts were ever a favorite with Mozart). Cellos and basses sound both at pitch

EXAMPLE 7.3. *Mozart, Symphony in D, K. 95, II*

[14] Paul Nettl, "Mozart and the Czechs," *Musical Quarterly* 27 (1941): 329–42, was aware of the corre-spondence between the Menuet in K. 9 and the *Andante* in K. 95. He argued for a Czech connection on the basis of a movement in a symphony (undated) by Mysliveček, in which the melody moves 3 4 5, 2 3 4.

and an octave lower (basses). Instead of the mechanical reappearance of the triplets in mm. 2 and 4 of the harpsichord Menuet, there is a turning figure in dotted rhythm articulated with a slur and a staccato over the last eighth note. The triplets are saved for m. 5, and then, in the nicest touch of all, they give way to straight eighth notes that rise to a melodic peak of E that the earlier version lacked. Mozart has learned, before our very ears, how to shape a melody as an entity. It is the difference between the beginner and the advancing apprentice.

The Mozarts gave two very profitable public concerts in Paris with the help of Melchior von Grimm, who overcame all local obstacles, as Leopold informed Hagenauer in his letter of 1 April 1764. In the same letter he mentions the portrait of the Mozarts, also arranged by Grimm: "Carmontelle, an amateur, painted it very well; Wolfgang is playing the clavier, I am standing behind his chair playing the violin, while Nannerl is leaning with an arm on the clavecin, and in the other hand she holds some music, as if she were singing." (See Plate X.) Singing was not a regular part of Nannerl's act, but the artist created a beautiful interaction among the three by framing the propped-up young master between the upright figures of his father and sister. He contrasts a rust color (Leopold's coat, the chair upholstery, and the inside of the harpsichord) with the blue of Wolfgang's coat that also prevails in the sky at the top of the picture, which manages to suggest a natural setting and a painted backdrop at the same time. The two-manual harpsichord is an imposing yet graceful presence, with its gold and black case and its cabriolet legs. Dark lozenges on the floor add a pattern of their own. The Mozarts were fortunate to be served by so skilled an artist. Carmontelle's painting was engraved, and the prints subsequently figured in Leopold's commercial dealings, as did the engraved sonatas. Copies of both were later sent off on consignment to be sold by Lotter in Augsburg and Hafner in Nuremberg. They were also on sale in Paris, where Leopold had both Grimm and a banker attend to his affairs after the family departed for England.

The Mozarts quit Paris on 10 April 1764, leaving behind many belongings because they did not intend to stay long in England. They left their carriage at Calais, crossed the channel, and were in London by 23 April. Only four days later they were presented to King George III and Queen Sophie Charlotte, when the usual rituals displaying the children's skills were observed. In his letter of 28 May concerning their second visit to court on 19 May, Leopold wrote: "The king placed in front of Wolfgang not only pieces by Wagenseil that he had to read *a prima vista*, but also pieces by [Christian] Bach, Abel, and Handel." (There could have been little music by Wagenseil in circulation that Mozart had not already read through.) Next he played the organ. "Then he accompanied the queen in an aria she sang with a flute solo, and finally he took the violone part of some Handel arias that were lying around and over this plain bass ["über den glatten Bass"] he played the most beautiful melody, so that everyone was in the greatest astonishment." The boy's growing improvisatory and compositional skills astounded even Leopold, it seems, who wrote further, "What he knew when we left Salzburg is only a shadow of what he knows now. It exceeds anything one can imagine." The children also gave well-publicized public concerts in London.

The Mozarts might have returned to the Continent in the late summer of 1765 had not Leopold become seriously ill in July. By his letter of 13 September 1765 he let Hagenauer know that he had resolved to spend the coming winter in London. He was determined to earn the guineas lost to them through his illness, regardless of how insalubrious the English climate. During Leopold's forced inactivity Wolfgang kept busy composing. By November he had completed a set of six accompanied harpsichord sonatas, which Leopold paid to have engraved under the title *Six sonates pour le clavecin qui peuvent se jouer avec l'accompagnement de violon ou flaute traversière* (K. 10–15). Another copy has added to the title *traversière et d'un violoncelle*. In Paris Mozart used the terms "Menuet I" and "Menuet II" in K. 6–9. In his London sonatas the movements are called "Menuetto I" and "Menuetto II."

Mozart played these sonatas to the queen, who, according to one report, forthwith ordered that they be printed and dedicated to her.[15] Their added treble parts are violinistic and ill-suited to the flute, the inclusion of which by mention on the title page can be laid to hopes for more sales, as can the *ad libitum* cello part. (Also, Christian Bach used the identical formula in his *Six Sonates*, Op. 2 [1763].) The textures do show more variety and ingenuity in this set than in the Parisian sonatas. A couple of movements may testify to Wolfgang's interest in English dance music. The *Allegro* in 2/4 of K. 11 in G and the *Allegro* in 3/8 of K. 12 in A are relatively plain and straightforward,

[15] Article in Dutch in a Haarlem journal, dated 16 February 1765, quoted in *Dokumente*, pp. 41–42.

like many English country dances. In his letter of 27 November 1764 Leopold wrote, "Contredanses, although at home in England, are not beautifully figured or beautifully danced here, but the airs are in part good, and I shall be bringing home a whole book of these." Menuetto I of K. 13 in F gives the violin more to do than usual, in that it answers a chromatic descent with the same in canon, but in inversion. The opening *Andante maestoso* of K. 15 in B♭ takes full advantage of the possibilities offered by a double-manual harpsichord, by contrasting heavy-textured fortes with lighter-textured pianos. The second and concluding movement, an *Allegro grazioso* in 2/4, is buffo in spirit and even suggests Pergolesi at times.

The dedication of the sonatas, fulsome and in French, is dated 18 January 1765. They were published on 20 March. Between these dates Mozart had made his public debut as a composer of symphonies, at a concert on 21 February. According to Nannerl, writing some years after Mozart's death, his first symphony was composed in Chelsea during Leopold's illness in 1764, and may in fact be identical with Symphony No. 1 in E♭, K. 16.[16]

Mozart seems rather unsure of himself in this Symphony in E♭. A bizarre combination of a long-note chorale with other music marks the first and second movements. The best is the third and final movement, a *Presto* in 3/8 in the form of a simple rondo, **A B A C A,** with a surprising chromatic outburst in the longish **B** section and a **C** section that is too short. There are similar chromatic patches in the *Allegro* of K. 12.

The Symphony in D, K. 19, is dated London, 1765. It sounds more assured than K. 16 mainly because it is anchored by some of the traditional clichés of the Italian overture, known to Mozart at this time mainly through the just-published Op. 3 Symphonies of Christian Bach. The opening *Allegro* in common time begins with a gruff tutti *unisono* swinging around the tonic in dotted rhythm, contrasted with a softer response in thirds. A threefold hammer stroke is used to punctuate the end of the first group, the end of the "development," and the end of the movement. There are no repeat signs. The seconda parte begins with a lurch upward from A to an accented A♯, this too being a typical feature of the Italian overture, where a chromatic jolt was often used to connect one movement to another. Mozart shows his inexperience by never returning to the triadic opening theme at any point in the seconda parte. The *Andante* in 2/4 and in G features triplet accompanimental figures against the *cantabile* melody in the violins, who bring their song to a climax by the rising figure 5 5♯ 6, with subdominant harmony for the last. This figure is also frequent in the early sonatas, and will long remain with Mozart. The finale is a *Presto* in 3/8 as in K. 16.

---

[16] Zaslaw, *Mozart's Symphonies*, pp. 17–22, goes into detail on the ambiguous evidence and suggests other possibilities.

The Symphony in F, K. 19ª, was known only by its incipit until a set of parts in Leopold's hand was discovered in 1981. It is the superior work among this trio of early symphonies. The opening *Allegro assai* in common time offers a fine example of a "singing *Allegro*." A broad theme sung by the first violins is supported by quick-note pulsations in the other strings and sustained harmonies in the oboes and horns. There is a clear second theme after punctuating hammer strokes. Repeat signs divide the movement in half; the seconda parte is begun by the first violins adapting their broad initial theme to a statement in V. A thrust toward ii is followed by the arrival of I, as at the same spot in the first movement of K. 19. But then Mozart lingers far too long in ii before finally slipping down to I and the restatement of the second theme in tonic F.

The *Andante* is the jewel of K. 19ª. As in K. 19, the movement is in 2/4 and in the subdominant. The texture is similarly stratified, with the violins singing the melody above viola arpeggios at first, then the first violins continuing on above the undulating thirds of the seconds and violas. Christian Bach provided models for this serenade type, as for example in the *Andantino* from Symphony No. 4 of his Op. 3. Mozart's suavity and control of detail could easily suggest a much later date. In the seconda parte, just before the reprise, there is a passage with staggered, overlapping three-note groups between upper and lower strings (Example 7.4). Italian style is evoked here too, but in this case it is one of the traditional settings of the *senario* line that divides equally into 3 + 3 syllables. A famous example is the aria "Se cerca, se dice" in Metastasio's *Olimpiade*, first set to music by Antonio Caldara at Vienna in 1733 (Example 7.5). Whether Caldara was the first to use these staggered, overlapping groups of three matters little. More important is that his setting of this most acclaimed aria in one of Metastasio's best librettos set

EXAMPLE 7.4. *Mozart, Symphony in F, K. 19ª, II*

EXAMPLE 7.5. *Caldara*, Olimpiade, *Aria*

a pattern that was followed by several other composers.[17] In the case of Mozart, overlapping groups of three continued to exert their fascination all the way to the very last works, such as Tamino's "Picture Aria" in *Die Zauberflöte* and the final number of *La clemenza di Tito*. For the finale of this early Symphony in F, Mozart wrote another exuberant *Presto* in 3/8; it sounds like dance music.

The final months in London during the spring and summer of 1765 saw the Mozarts involved in a few more money-making schemes. Advertisements (beginning on 1 March) offered the public not only concert tickets for sale at their residence in Thrift Street, Soho, but also an opportunity to buy engraved sonatas and portraits, plus the chance to hear and test the children on the spot at specified hours. The advertisement of 30 May requests a fee of five shillings for this experience. Business could not have met Leopold's expectations, because the fee was cut in half in the advertisement of 8 July. In the final advertisement a day later, he added that "the Two Children will play also together with four Hands upon the same Harpsichord, and put upon it a Handkerchief, without seeing the Keys."[18] Before this, in the advertisement of 13 May for a public concert on the same day, there is mention of a "Concerto on the Harpsichord by the little Composer and his Sister, each single and both together."

The four-hand Sonata in C, K. 19[d], has been linked to these activities. It consists of an initial fast movement in cut time, a Menuetto (with trio), and a *Rondo Allegretto* in 2/4, all in the same key. The last movement features the stamping rhythm of the contredanse at cadences and an *Adagio* 3/4 section before the final return of the rondo refrain, marked *Allegro*. Naive and simple as is this rondo, it sounds a little richer and more advanced than Mozart's other London compositions. There are no manuscript sources for the sonata,

[17] See Silke Leopold, "Die Metastasianische Oper," in *Neues Handbuch der Musikwissenschaft*, ed. C. Dahlhaus (Laaber, 1985), 5: 73–84; on Galuppi's setting of "Se cerca, se dice," see Daniel Heartz, "Hasse, Galuppi, and Metastasio," in *Venezia e il melodramma nel settecento*, ed. Maria Teresa Muraro (Florence, 1978), pp. 309–39; especially 334–37 and illustration 3.
[18] All these advertisements are collected in *Dokumente*, pp. 43–45.

and the first editions did not appear until ca. 1789 in London and Paris, independently of each other. If the composer was other than Mozart, Christian Bach comes to mind on stylistic grounds (cf. the *Rondeau Allegretto* in 2/4 finale of his four-hand Sonata in C).

The return journey began in late July 1765. Leopold was persuaded by the Dutch envoy in England to head north after crossing the channel on the first of August and pay a visit to the court of Holland. Nannerl's serious illness in the fall of 1765 immobilized the family at The Hague. As soon as she began recovering, Wolfgang fell ill. The liberality with which the court and other patrons supported the young prodigies persuaded Leopold to remain in Holland through March 1766, when the eighteen-year-old prince of Orange, Willem V, was to be installed as regent of the Netherlands. In early 1766 Wolfgang produced his first symphony in the key of B♭, K. 22, a fine three-movement work quite like the previous ones. He also produced another set of harpsichord sonatas with violin accompaniment, K. 26–31, requested by the sister of the prince of Orange, Princess Nassau-Weilburg, and duly engraved and dedicated to her.

In K. 29 Mozart uses the terms "Menuetto" and "Trio." He ends K. 31 in B♭ with a set of variations on a *Tempo di Menuetto*. Thus the early sonatas with accompaniment explore all four of the main formal procedures then in use: binary dance form, sonata form, theme and variations, and rondo. The rondos are not always identified as such, but in K. 26 and K. 30 Mozart uses the French plural "Rondeaux." Throughout these sonatas the violin acquires more and more importance, by means of canonic entries and other kinds of dialogue with the keyboard, so that they can be heard as a step in the direction of the true duet sonatas, created by Mozart a decade later.

The most novel composition for the Dutch court was the *Gallimathius musicum*, K. 32, for orchestra and obbligato harpsichord, written to be performed during the celebrations surrounding the prince's installation as regent. The work is a quodlibet, a suite of short pieces based in part on popular dance tunes, which are juxtaposed so as to achieve comic effect. In an autograph sketch for the work, which shows the hands of both Wolfgang and Leopold, the Christmas song "Resonat in laudibus," alias "Joseph, lieber Joseph mein," appears in the drone movement in G, No. 4, but it was replaced in the final version with another melody, one that also sounds like a popular song. Other tunes among those that have been identified include No. 9, "Acht Sauschneider," also used by Haydn; No. 14, a minuet from Nannerl's notebook of 1759; and the Dutch national anthem, "Wilhelmus van Nassouwe," used as the subject of the fugue that ends the work, No. 17 (in which Wolfgang needed help from Leopold).

The travelers returned at last to Paris on 10 May 1766 and stayed two months. They also revisited Versailles. It was during this stay in Paris that

Michel Ollivier painted his *Thé à l'anglaise* picture of the salon at the Prince de Conti's mansion in the rue du Temple, showing in one corner Wolfgang at the harpsichord preparing to accompany the tenor Pierre de Jélyotte, who is tuning his guitar. Little is known about this Parisian visit, and what little there is comes from Grimm, who placed another encomium in the *Correspondance littéraire* dated 15 July 1766. It confirms what we know from the later report of Daines Barrington to the Royal Society in London about Mozart singing Italian arias.

> The children were dangerously ill at The Hague, but eventually their lucky star delivered them from the malady and from the doctors . . . The boy has scarcely grown at all, but he has made prodigious progress in music . . . He has composed symphonies for full orchestra, which were performed and generally applauded here. He has even written several Italian arias, and I do not doubt that before attaining the age of twelve he will have had performed an opera in some theater in Italy. Having heard Manzuoli for a whole winter in London, he profited so well therefrom that he sings, although with a very feeble voice, with as much charm as spirit. But what is most incomprehensible is that profound science of harmony, and the most hidden passages that he possesses to a supreme degree . . . At London, Bach took him between his knees and they played thus out of their heads alternately on the same harpsichord for two hours at a time in the presence of the king and queen . . . If these children live, they will not remain at Salzburg. Soon sovereigns will be fighting about who will have them. The father is not only a competent musician but a man of good sense and good spirit, and I have never seen a man of his profession unite so much talent and merit.

The father was also the obvious source of Grimm's information about London and the Mozarts' aspirations for the future: Italian opera and a royal court! Leopold originally planned to return home via Milan. In the event, their journey took them via Dijon, Lyons, Geneva, Lausanne, Berne, Zürich, and some south German courts. The last stop was Munich, where Wolfgang created a piece from a melody of a few bars given him by the elector. The trip had lasted three and a half years by the time the Mozarts reached Salzburg at the end of November 1766.

Grimm was not the only critic to praise Leopold Mozart in connection with the tour and the children's upbringing. An anonymous Swiss critic in Lausanne (probably Dr. Tissot, an eminent physician) published an article in a local journal that must have warmed the cool exterior of Leopold that we see in the anonymous portrait of him of ca. 1765 (Figure 7.4).

> We cannot see without emotion all the marks of his [Wolfgang's] affection for a father who seems worthy of it, who has given still more care to the formation of his character than to the cultivation of his talents and who speaks of education

FIGURE 7.4. Detail from an anonymous oil portrait of Leopold Mozart, c. 1765.

as wisely as of music. How well he is rewarded by success: how delightful it is for him to see his two amiable children more flattered by a look of approbation in his eyes which they seek with tender anxiety than by the applause of a whole audience . . . parents whose children have outstanding talents should imitate M. Mozart, who, far from forcing his son, has always been careful to moderate his ardour and so prevent him from abandoning himself to it. Every day the opposite attitude stifles the most promising genius and may nullify the most superior talents.[19]

The insight of this eyewitness account and that of the astute Grimm help temper the mostly negative latter-day analyses of Leopold's character on the basis of his letters.

Before returning to Salzburg Leopold had performed obeisance of a sort to his prince by presenting him with the engraved family portrait from Paris, as well as bound copies of Wolfgang's accompanied keyboard sonatas. He had also arranged for these to be performed at court. Public newspaper accounts and Hagenauer kept Salzburg informed of the triumphs and near tragedies of the Mozart family. Beda Hübner's diary entry for 29 November 1766 reads, "The world-famous Leopold Mozart, our Vice-Kapellmeister,

[19] A. Hyatt King, "A Swiss Account of Mozart in 1766," chapter 8 in King's *Mozart in Retrospect* (Studies in Criticism and Biography) (London, 1955), pp. 131–40.

arrived today with his wife and two children, a boy of ten and a daughter of thirteen years, to the relief and joy of the whole city . . . Wolfgang has not grown much on this trip, but Nannerl is rather large and almost marriage-able already."[20] Nannerl's status as a child prodigy was obviously coming to an end (but she did not marry until the then late age of thirty-three). Hence-forth attention was focused even more on Wolfgang, and primarily as a com-poser.

On the feast of the Immaculate Conception, 8 December 1766, a sym-phony by Mozart was performed in the cathedral according to the diary of Hübner, who also informs us under this date that neither of the court's most active composers, Michael Haydn or Anton Adlgasser, was willing to engage in a keyboard duel with Wolfgang. To celebrate the ordination day of the archbishop on 21 December, a visiting troupe of Italian players per-formed one of Goldoni's comedies along with a musical intermezzo, to which Mozart appended a recitative and aria as a *licenza* or farewell, K. 36 (33^i). And he composed another *licenza* aria (K. 70?) for the performances of Giuseppe Sarti's *Vologeso* at court during the carnival season of early 1767.

More ambitious vocal-orchestral works soon followed, showing that Mozart was assuming an equal place alongside the official court composers. In March 1767 he set the first part of the sacred drama *Die Schuldigkeit des ersten Gebots*, K. 35 (Michael Haydn and Adlgasser set the second and third parts). This first part consists of a one-movement sinfonia, seven arias, some elaborate obbligato recitatives as well as simple ones, and a concluding *ter-zetto* for all three characters. In May of 1767 Mozart wrote *Apollo et Hyacinthus* a musical *intermedio* set to a Latin school drama, K. 38; it consisted of a one-movement overture, called Intrada, and nine vocal numbers. A telling fea-ture of the orchestration is the frequency of divided violas, a Salzburg spe-cialty.

Vienna, 1767–68

THE most important change in Salzburg's court music that the Mozarts found when they returned home in late 1766 was the addition of a major Viennese composer, Michael Haydn, to complement more local talents. But Haydn's main impact on Mozart did not come until after the family's trip to Vienna, which began on 11 September 1767. Their sojourn in the imperial capital was originally to last only three months, Leopold intending to be back by 21 December. As with the earlier trips, illnesses, the need to make

---

[20] *Dokumente*, pp. 63–65.

money, and Leopold's boundless ambition for his son all played a part in prolonging their excursion. They would not return to Salzburg until January 1769.

Planning for the return to Vienna is in evidence as early as the first of four pasticcio concertos for solo harpsichord and orchestra, K. 37, dated April 1767 in Leopold's hand. Father and son worked on these together, as the autographs show, and their purpose was obvious. The many works by Wagenseil acquired in Vienna in 1762 had provided the Mozarts with enough harpsichord concertos to get them through the previous five years. Wagenseil, Vienna's favorite, still ranked highly with them. Leopold sent a copy of a concerto for two harpsichords by Wagenseil along with Mozart's printed sonatas as a favor to the poet Salomon Gesner in Zürich, implying strongly that Wolfgang and Nannerl had played the work when in Zürich a year earlier (letters of 14 October and 10 November 1767). The children could scarcely play old concertos by Wagenseil in Vienna. Thus Leopold decided to assemble some new ones, taking advantage of the printed music by other composers that the Mozarts had brought back from Paris. The composers represented were four German emigrés residing there, Johann Gottfried Eckard, Leontzi Honauer, Hermann Friedrich Raupach, and Johann Schobert, plus Emanuel Bach. K. 39 is dated June 1767 and the last two, K. 40–41, are dated July 1767.

What drew the Mozarts back to Vienna at this particular time were the festivities planned to celebrate the marriage of Archduchess Maria Josepha with King Ferdinand of Naples. Imperial weddings were sure to draw the wealthy and titled from all corners to the capital, and money was very much on Leopold's mind. In his second letter back to Hagenauer, dated 29 September 1767, Leopold reported that the main opera, *Partenope* by Metastasio and Hasse, was beautiful and was graced with excellent dances, but he pronounced the singers (Giuseppe Tibaldi, tenor; Venanzio Rauzzini, primo uomo; and Elizabeth Teiber, prima donna) nothing out of the ordinary for so great an occasion. His letter of 7 October introduced an ominous note: the princess-bride had contracted smallpox. This was an ill omen for the Mozarts, as it turned out.

In his letter of 14 October Leopold explained in more detail. The princess had become ill after a three-hour prayer vigil with her mother and siblings in the imperial crypt on the name day of their late father, Emperor Francis. Leopold began his next letter, dated 17 October, with a dramatic flourish: "The princess-bride has become the bride of the heavenly bridegroom. What an astounding transformation!" She died on 15 October, her mother's name day (feast of St. Theresa). Leopold noted further that she was the second Habsburg princess betrothed to the king of Naples to die, the first having been Archduchess Johanna, and next it would be the turn of Archduchess Carolina, aged fifteen. But first, of course, there had to be a period of mourning. The theaters were to be closed for six weeks. Leopold found it odd that the second opera, Gassmann's *Amore e Psiche*, involved a Greek fable in which the heroine dies and is raised to a divinity by Venus. Death was everywhere in Vienna as the smallpox epidemic spread. Leopold recognized the danger and with his family fled to the relative safety of Olomouc (Olmütz), the capital of Moravia, some ninety miles north of Vienna.

At Olomouc the Mozarts had the good fortune to be taken in by Count Podstatsky. Wolfgang came down with smallpox on 26 October and did not recover until 10 November; Nannerl then contracted the same disease, and did not recover until the end of November. Once again life-threatening illness beset both children while on their travels and was survived. By Christmas they were able to travel and so spent two weeks in Brno (Brünn), where Count Schrattenbach (brother of the archbishop) and the rest of the high nobility vied to entertain them.

Mozart's compositional work was slowed but not stopped in the fall of 1767. The Symphony No. 6 in F, K. 43, was begun in Vienna and finished in Olomouc, according to inscriptions on the first page. It may be Mozart's first symphony in four movements, and its *Andante* is derived from the duet in *Apollo et Hyacinthus*, K. 38. Symphony No. 7 in D, K. 45, followed shortly thereafter. Written on coarse paper probably acquired in Moravia, it is dated 16 January 1768, a few days after the Mozarts arrived back in Vienna. This symphony became, minus its Minuet, the overture to *La finta semplice*, K. 51 (46ª).

In his letter of 23 January 1768 Leopold informs Hagenauer that his family was received by Maria Theresa for two hours on the afternoon of the 19th. Joseph II in person escorted them to the empress, who stroked the face and pressed the hands of Frau Mozart while listening to the stories of the children's most recent illness and the trip to Paris. Wolfgang talked to the emperor about music, but there is no mention of music being made. The next letter, written between 30 January and 3 February, explains that the empress no longer welcomed music in her apartments, and referred all musical matters to her son Joseph, described by Leopold as a penny-pincher. The situation did not look promising, especially as the high nobility followed the emperor's lead in attempting to cut costs. Moreover, Leopold believed that all the professionals but one were against him. "All the keyboard players and composers in Vienna were opposed to our advancement, I learned, with the sole exception of Wagenseil, but he is confined to his house by illness and thus cannot help us or contribute much to our cause."

Leopold's scheme to have his son write an opera, already in evidence as early as the meetings with Melchior von Grimm in Paris in 1766, became obvious in this letter, which was meant not just for Hagenauer alone but for all of Salzburg.

> In order to convince the public of what is really at stake, I decided to do something extraordinary, and that is to have the boy write an opera for the theater, and what sort of an uproar do you suppose among the composers here has secretly arisen? "What? Today it is Gluck and tomorrow a boy of twelve who is seen seated at the harpsichord directing his own opera?" Yes, despite all their envy! I have even won Gluck over to our side, and although he is not quite whole-hearted about it, he will not let it show, because his patrons are our patrons, and in order to secure our position with regard to the *acteurs*, who usually cause the composer the greatest annoyance, I have taken up the matter with them myself, and one of them has given me all the suggestions for the work.

That would be Francesco Carrattoli, a basso buffo famous for decades on the stages of northern Italy and now a leader of the buffo troupe in the Burgtheater. Carrattoli presumably suggested the libretto, Goldoni's sparkling comedy *La finta semplice*, first set by Salvador Perillo in Venice in 1764. It is typical of Leopold's manipulative ways that he went behind the back of the impresario, Giuseppe Affligio, who ran the theater at his own financial risk. Gluck, a big-hearted person if ever there was one, had reason to be half-hearted about Leopold's seemingly crazy scheme to have an opera buffa written for the imperial court theater by a boy who had never been in Italy and had not written an opera before (the same was true of Leopold, who guided the planning and execution of the work). Gluck's main patron was Chancellor Kaunitz, who did indeed support the Mozarts. Leopold probably did not realize that Kaunitz represented only a third of the power structure then governing, but the crucial third in this case was in the hands of Joseph, since his mother had withdrawn from theatrical matters. The more Leopold pushed, the more the emperor resisted, until in the end the whole project fell through.

Mendacity came easily to Leopold Mozart, and it is no wonder that his son later displayed the same trait, especially when dealing with his father. In the same letter, immediately after the passage just quoted, Leopold wrote: "To tell the truth, the first idea to let little Wolfgang write an opera was given to me by the emperor himself when he twice asked the boy if he wanted to compose an opera and direct it himself." This must have sounded good when it made the rounds in Salzburg, where it could be regarded as little less than a command that the Mozarts remain in Vienna long beyond Leopold's leave. But it is false on more than one count. Winning fame by getting the boy to write an opera had long been on Leopold's mind. Further, had Joseph actually suggested the project, Leopold would have trumpeted the fact in the written complaint he later made to the emperor on 21 September 1768. There he made no mention of an imperial suggestion. Two other persons are said to have proposed the idea, one of them Carrattoli, the other the Durch ambassador. The emperor may very well have twice asked, in some astonishment, if the boy really wanted to do it, but this is not the same as initiating the idea and smacks more of a jest than it does of a proposal. Leopold wrote next that "the boy answered yes, surely, but the emperor could say no more because opera was the province of Affligio."

Leopold ended his long letter on 3 February 1768 by describing the kind of opera he intended and enumerating the singers available. "It is no opera seria, because there is no longer an opera seria here, and people dislike that genre anyway." Joseph certainly did dislike the expense required to obtain the best seria singers. "It will be an opera buffa, but one two and a half or three hours long." This tends to confirm that the libretto had already been picked. Leopold next names the excellent personnel in Vienna's buffo troupe: Giacomo Caribaldi, Carrattoli, Domenico Poggi, Filippo Laschi, and a certain Polini were the males, Antonia Bernasconi, Teresa Eberardi, and Clementina Baglioni the females. His final sentence reveals a little more of his long-term plan to conquer Italy through the medium of opera: "Is not the fame of having written an opera for the Viennese theater the best means of receiving credit not only in Germany, but also in Italy?"

Leopold was putting himself and his son in a difficult situation. It would not be the last time that he did so. At first all seemed to go well. On 30 March he wrote, "Our enemies are beaten! Nota bene here in Vienna." His enemies in Salzburg he would attack later. "The opera is going well but probably will not be performed until the emperor returns from Hungary." On 20 April he reported, "His Majesty the emperor has left for Hungary, or rather the Turkish frontiers, hence the opera will be performed in June after his return." Leopold sought and received permission to remain longer in Vienna, which was achieved at the expense of having his salary stopped in Salzburg. Meanwhile he was laying preparations for Italy. "I have received from the emperor himself all the necessary introductions for Florence, the imperial states, and Naples," he wrote on 11 May. As a further preparation he commissioned an Italian translation of his *Violinschule* to be made (which did not happen). Italy must pay its respects to Wolfgang before he grows out of childhood (he turned twelve on 27 January 1768), "or should I sit in Salzburg with the empty hope of some better fortune and allow myself and my children to be led around by the nose until I reach the age that prevents me from traveling and until the boy attains the age and the growth that prevents astonishment for his merits?"

In his letter of 29 June 1768 Leopold complained of deeply laid intrigues and malicious persecutions, of envy that assaulted the Mozarts from all sides, but he did not explain further. All was revealed in his next and very long letter of 30 July. Wolfgang's opera was supposed to have been performed at Easter. Marco Coltellini, theater poet, was the first to cause delays "on the pretext of making certain necessary changes in the libretto here and there, which he kept procrastinating so that by Easter we had received from him only two of the amended arias." The opera was next scheduled for Pentecost, and then for the emperor's return from Hungary, "but at this point the mask fell from the face, for all the composers here, with Gluck at their head, undermined everything in order to prevent the opera from being produced." There is no shred of evidence to back up this claim about Gluck's malevolence.

Next to be blamed by Leopold were the singers. "They hardly know their notes, and one or two of them have to learn everything entirely by ear;[21] they were now said to claim that they could not sing their arias, which they had nevertheless previously heard in our room and which they had approved of, applauded, and described as quite suitable for them." And the orchestra too now let its displeasure at being directed by a boy be known. Other complaints were that "the music is worthless, did not fit the words, went against their meter, showing that the boy had insufficient command of the Italian language, etc." To put a stop to all this, Leopold said that he enlisted Hasse, whom he called "the father of music," and the great Metastasio himself to contradict the slanderers by asserting that "thirty operas had been performed in Vienna which in no way can touch this boy's opera, which they both admire to the very highest degree." Even this hyperbole, probably a figment of Leopold's increasingly febrile imagination, did not stem the tide. "If this opera had been an opera seria, I should have left immediately . . . and laid it at the feet of His Grace, the archbishop. But as it is an opera buffa and, what is more, an opera that requires certain types of *persone buffe*, I must persist here in Vienna, cost what it may."

After working himself up to a frenzy in his indignation, Leopold penned the words that are probably best known from this letter. He was doing what he considered his duty in honor of the prince and his country, i.e., "announcing to the world the miracle that God had allowed to be born in Salzburg." If this sounds vaguely biblical, like the "voice crying out in the wilderness," it is intended to sound so. Leopold's mania about enemies and persecutors never more nearly approached pure paranoia than at this time.

---

[21] Caribaldi was musically illiterate, as emerges from an amusing anecdote in the memoirs of Salieri (narrated in Chapter 6). He was the tenor for whom the part of Polidoro is thought to have been intended.

In spite of all warning signs, he persisted. "It is still going to be performed, and if some fresh obstacle is raised against it, I shall lay my complaint before Their Majesties the emperor and empress and demand satisfaction such as will save our honor before all Vienna and the whole of the honest world." New obstacles were not necessary. The old ones sufficed to stop the project, when combined with Leopold's truculence. Leopold took the extreme step of lodging a formal complaint, entitled "Species facti," translated in its entirety as Appendix 3. Written in part in bluntly direct language, it was not the sort of petition that sovereigns were used to receiving. From this point on, Maria Theresa was polite to the Mozarts in public, but in letters to her children she cautioned against hiring them.

In his letter of 24 September Leopold wrote not only that he had handed over his petition to the emperor three days earlier, but also that Joseph had assigned Count Spork the task of investigating the affair, and that Affligio was ordered to answer for himself. Whether this is true or another figment of Leopold's imagination will never be known. There is no surviving response from Affligio. Had Leopold actually received any or all of the 260 ducats requested in the petition, he surely would have done some crowing about it, but he said nothing in subsequent letters.

The long sojourn in Vienna was not without its rewards, even if the main project for the Burgtheater was aborted. Mozart wrote a charming little stage work in German, the scope of which was more manageable for a twelve-year-old than the opera buffa. In his catalogue of his son's work to date, compiled late in 1768, Leopold lists the two works one after the other: "Die operetta Bastien und Bastienne, im Teutschen, hat er kürzlich hier in die Musik gesetzt. Und nun die opera Buffa La Finta Semplice, die in der Original Spart 558 seiten beträgt." The operetta may have been performed by amateurs in the country house of Dr. Anton Mesmer (but not in his garden theater, as legend has it, for that had not been built by 1768).

Following *La finta semplice* on Leopold's list was "eine grosse Messe mit 4. Singstimmen 2 Violinen 2 Hautb. 2 Violen 4 Clarinis Tymp etc." This mass was for the consecration of the Waisenhaus (Orphanage) Church in the Rennweg, an occasion to which Mozart also contributed an offertory and trumpet concerto, both lost (letter of 12 November 1768). The consecration took place on 7 December, the eve of the feast of the Immaculate Conception, according to Leopold's last letter from Vienna during this visit (14 December 1768): "Wolfgang himself beat the tactus [measure] and made good on what his enemies, by thwarting his opera, sought to deny. In the presence of the court and the public, which was present in astounding numbers, he convinced all of the evil of our adversaries. The empress sent us a beautiful present."

IX. Workshop of Martin van Meytens. Interior of the Redoutensaal during performance of Gluck's *Tetide*, 1760. (Vienna: Kunsthistorisches Museum)

x. Carmontelle. *Portrait of the Mozart Family,* 1763. (Copyright British Museum)

Mozart père & ses deux enfans.

A few days after the consecration Mozart dated his Symphony No. 8 in D, K. 48, "Vienna 13 December 1768." Like K. 43 and K. 45, this work is in four movements with Minuet, as was the norm in Vienna but scarcely anywhere else. Leopold began his letter of the following day with another apology. "As much as I wished and hoped to be in Salzburg on the ordination day of His Grace the prince, it was impossible, for we could not bring our affairs here to an end, as strenuously as I attempted to do so." What was holding the Mozarts back this time was apparently some concert for which K. 48 was intended. They left Vienna late in December and arrived back in Salzburg on 5 January 1769.

La finta semplice and *Bastien und Bastienne*

M OZART at age twelve was not without operatic experience. In addition to seeing works on the stage in Salzburg and on tour, he had, in both London and Paris, improvised recitatives and arias in the seria style, accompanying himself at the keyboard and mimicking the great singer Giovanni Manzuoli. Grimm also mentions that he had composed several arias. In his catalogue of 1768 Leopold lists "15 Italian arias composed partly in London, partly at The Hague." Only four survive, K. 21 (19^c), K. 23, K. 78 (73^h), and K. 79 (73^d), all seria arias on texts by Metastasio. Leopold was obviously aiming toward his son's setting to music one of the classic librettos of the aged court poet. Mozart gained more experience composing arias in the seria style on returning to Salzburg, as we have seen. And once in Vienna again, one of the strategies Leopold used to convince people that his son, unaided, could compose arias was to have someone pick at random a poem from the works of Metastasio: "Wolfgang took up his pen and, with the most amazing rapidity, wrote without hesitation the music for this aria for several instruments. He did this at the houses of Kapellmeister Bonno, the abbé Metastasio, Hasse, the Duke of Braganza, and Prince Kaunitz" (letter of 30 July 1768). What Mozart had never written, as far as is known, were arias or ensembles in the buffo style.

Faced with a comic libretto, *La finta semplice*, of twenty-six set pieces, mostly exit arias, the Mozarts first had to decide how to order the tonal succession. Their choices were made according to a simple but effective plan: maneuver among the common keys (those with one, two, or no accidentals), avoiding the same key in adjacent numbers, and save the special keys like A and E♭ for affective moments and for the title role, Rosina, the "feigned simpleton." Niccolò Piccinni's epochal setting of Goldoni's *La buona figliuola*

(1760), revered in Vienna as everywhere else, could have served them as a model in this respect.

Goldoni's *dramma giocoso* of 1764 is finely balanced between pure farce and romantic comedy, turning upon the advantages and disadvantages of marital union. The scene is laid in a country house outside Cremona in Lombardy, which was then one of the imperial states, making it only natural that a Hungarian military man, Captain Fracasso, should be stationed there. He is being visited by his beautiful sister, the baroness Rosina. They have attached themselves to a family consisting of Don Cassandro plus his younger brother and sister, Don Polidoro and Donna Giacinta, both of whom Cassandro tyrannizes. Simone serves the captain; Ninetta is a chambermaid in Cassandro's house.

The first set shows a garden, with an avenue of trees leading up to the front of a country house situated at the top of a hill. Four of the characters sing the opening ensemble, set as an *Allegro* in 3/4 that continues the key of D established by the three-movement Sinfonia. "Bella cosa è far l'amore! / Bello è assai degl'anni il fiori! / Bella è più la libertà!" In three short lines Goldoni announces the theme of the drama: making love may be beautiful, especially in the flower of one's age, but preserving one's liberty is even more so. As if in a vaudeville, each character next steps forward with a solo gloss. Giacinta wonders if such a moment will return. Fracasso warns anyone who would constrain him. Ninetta refuses to consider marriage. Her not-so-willing suitor, Simone, is put off by her giddiness. *Carpe diem* meets *caveat emptor*. The four sing the refrain again to conclude No. 1, which epitomizes the whole opera.

The arias that follow for three of these characters are less successful in musical terms. Nos. 2 and 3 for Simone and Giacinta are in two tempos and reveal dubious part writing here and there, betraying the haste with which the work was composed. No. 4 for Cassandro (Carrattoli's part) sounds a little more assured (but would a more mature Mozart allow some of the parallel octaves between the voice and the bass?). It is an *Allegro non molto* in 6/8 that brings back the keynote for the first time. The alternating bluster and quiet of the music have little to do with the misogynist ideas expressed by the text. Fracasso follows with an aria, No. 5 in G, that had to be written over completely, presumably because the tenor for whom it was intended, thought to be Filippo Laschi, was not satisfied with the first, multi-tempo version.[22]

---

[22] Hermann Abert deduced the likely identities of the intended singers from the descriptions of individual vocal and acting abilities given by Joseph von Sonnenfels, *Briefe über die wienerische Schaubühne* (Vienna, 1768). The *Neue Ausgabe* of Mozart's works (NMA) has turned Abert's reasoned conjectures into "facts."

The scene changes to a room in Cassandro's house for the appearance alone onstage of Rosina, the feigned simpleton herself. Without ado, the music of her orchestral introduction slips down a third with respect to the previous recitative cadence on C. Flutes accompany the strings for the first time since the overture in her aria in A (No. 6). (The tonal move anticipates the arrival of A directly after C as the two sisters begin the second scene of *Così fan tutte*.) The violins in thirds, doubled an octave below by divided violas, intone a rising melody with chromatically raised fifth degree: 3 4 5 5♯ 6, the arrival of the sixth degree bringing with it subdominant harmony in 6/4 position. The sensuous and capricious Rosina is thus captured in a musical portrait even before she begins to sing. She is allowed coloratura, in an opera that has almost no melismatic writing, lending her a more seria tone than the other characters. Aside from her long melismas, the vocal line is chopped into too many small, repeated fragments. Even so, the singer for whom the part of Rosina was probably intended, Clementina Baglioni, inspired the composer to a greater degree than the others. The Mozarts had heard her in the role of Venere in Gassmann's *Amore e Psiche*, where she was also given coloratura. (In Piccinni's *La buona figliuola* she sang the seria role of La Marchesa.)

Next, for Polidoro's aria in B♭ (No. 7), Mozart reused a piece from K. 35 of a year earlier, betraying another sign of haste. Cassandro follows with his second aria, No. 8 in F, then Rosina with her second, No. 9 in E♭. His (by Coltellini) provides opportunities for tone painting, e.g., barking dogs (for which Cerberus in Gluck's *Orfeo* provided a model). Hers is an echo piece. Its very key holds out the promise of something special, and the promise is fulfilled. It begins with a noble melody for solo oboe, an *Andante un poco adagio* in cut time, and its long-breathed melody against murmuring sixteenth-note accompaniment suggests an *ombra* aria. Ordinary horns are joined by English horns. Once again Rosina is given coloratura to decorate the last word of the first five-line stanza ("ragionar"; not by chance does the poet place the "ah" syllable last). The lengthy second stanza of eight lines prompts a different tempo and meter, *Allegro grazioso* in 3/4, also a conjunct rise of a sixth that occurs elsewhere in Rosina's music.

Everyone has had at least one aria by this point except Ninetta, the soubrette. Goldoni gave her a typically mundane response to the high-flown poetry for Rosina: "Chi mi vuol bene / Presto mel dica" (Who wants me should say so at once). Mozart set it as a *Tempo di Minuetto* in B♭ (No. 10), with galant flourishes such as triplets, trills, and three-note slides, surely a misreading of the poet's intention. The piece takes only sixty-two measures, rather short shrift considering that the singer was probably La Bernasconi, fresh from her triumphs as Gluck's Alceste. Mozart's treatment of this aria presumably intended for her can be explained by what Sonnenfels wrote: "[Bernasconi] also appeared gladly in comic roles, especially naive *mezzo carattere* ones, but not in low comic ones."

The finale of Act I, Mozart's first, is carefully laid out with a variety of line lengths to match the dramatic action by Goldoni, who invented this type of ensemble finale.[23] All seven characters take part, and the result is a little masterpiece in its own right, self-contained, and turning around a love letter and Cassandro's ring, wheedled out of him by Rosina. The buffoonery is mostly at the expense of the dim-witted Polidoro, who likewise is smitten, of course, by the lovely Rosina. The final section of rejoicing, beginning in m. 270, uses the same progression in modulating to the dominant as does the opening *Coro*, lending some sense of musical unity to the act. Both are in D. The last line of the finale, "viva amore e la beltà," resembles the end of No. 1, "bella è più la libertà." Obviously "amore" is beginning to win out over "libertà."

Act II begins on a veranda of Cassandro's house. Ninetta, Simone, and Giacinta sing arias in turn, Nos. 12–14, all in the lighter meters of 2/4, 3/8, or 6/8 (No. 14 combines 2/4 and 6/8). Giacinta, a contralto part probably created for Teresa Eberardi, sings her "Se a maritarmi arrivo" (If I succeed in marrying) in the key of A, with flutes joining the strings as in Rosina's No. 6, but the music, following the text in this case, does not approach the seria sphere—it is at most *mezzo carattere*. She exits, leaving Ninetta and Polidoro, who exit to a recitative cadence in C.

The scene changes to a lighted room with chairs; dusk has fallen. Rosina is alone onstage after a scene change once again. And once again there is a tonal disjunction. Before it was A after C; this time the move is to a third above C. No. 15 introduces the magical sound of E, with a gorgeous melody in the first violins, fluttering upward in triplets, accompanied by two bassoons in thirds, imitated by divided violas an octave higher, over the pizzicato bass and under the high dominant pedal of the second violins (Example 7.6). When this music begins again in m. 9, Rosina holds the dominant pedal, a *messa di voce* on the first word, "Amoretti," little Cupids. Their fluttering wings inspired the initial melody, as is made clear by the outbreak of many triplet figures on the word "volando" (flying). Rosina asks the Cupids not to wound her heart: "Questo cor non venite a piagar." Mozart loses momentum by putting too many stops and starts in his setting of the last two lines. But the Cupids win out in that the orchestral beginning of the piece returns at its end.

[23] For a description matching musical sections to the shape of the poem, see Daniel Heartz, "The Creation of the Buffo Finale in Italian Opera," *PRMA* 104 (1977–78): 67–78; the article errs, p. 76, by stating that Giacinta did not take part in the first act finale; she is absent from the Act II finale.

EXAMPLE 7.6. *Mozart*, La finta semplice, *Aria*

Rosina's refinement, which obviously appealed mightily to Mozart, is thrown into the starkest contrast possible by the arrival of Cassandro, drunken and loutish in his behavior, following a recitative between Rosina and the impossible Polidoro. It is all very funny, and Mozart no doubt had a good laugh in finding the right swagger for Cassandro's aria "Ubriaco non son io" (I am not drunk), No. 16 in C. Polidoro addresses the next aria, No. 17 in G, partly to his brother and partly to Rosina, whom he calls "mia moglie" (my wife). They get rid of Polidoro and play a pantomime wooing scene with each other, an obbligato recitative with constant accompanimental triplets, at the end of which Cassandro falls asleep, allowing Rosina to slip the disputed ring back on his finger. In her next aria, No. 18 in F, she begins with a lilting siciliana, *Allegro grazioso*, 6/8, in dotted rhythm, to accompany her warning to an awakened Cassandro that a woman should not be content with a single suitor. She switches to *Allegretto* in 2/4 when insisting on her freedom to have more than one lover, while her rising conjunct sixth resembles what Polidoro sang in addressing her as his wife in No. 17, and also what she sang herself in the *Allegro grazioso* of No. 9.

Coltellini intervened in the next scene, changing a solo aria for Cassandro into the dueling duet, No. 19 in D, between Fracasso and Cassandro. Cassandro is no match for a military man and, after a great deal of braggadocio, saves his skin by fleeing. Rosina enters at this point. The Hungarians have won the day, and the opera could end quickly, with Cassandro terrified of doing anything less than allowing Giacinta to wed Fracasso. Rosina says she will marry Cassandro, but first she wants to make him more jealous of his brother. After Fracasso sings an aria about scheming women (No. 20 in Bb), the second finale begins in G. It is even more farcical than the first and about as long. Cassandro threatens Polidoro with a stick. Rosina pretends to faint. Giacinta, not present, is reported to have absconded with the family fortune. Ninetta runs off to join her, and confusion reigns supreme.

Goldoni did his best to wring a third act from his slender material. Coltellini thought he could improve on that by writing substitute arias for Simone, No. 22, and Giacinta, No. 24. But his recitative following No. 22 ill prepares Ninetta's No. 23 in C, a piece Mozart completely recomposed. Coltellini's No. 24, "Che scompiglia, che flagello" (What confusion, what calamity), elicited a furious minor-mode piece from Mozart, the only one in the work. An *Allegro* in c and in common time, the aria anticipates in uncanny fashion Electra's obbligato recitative and aria in Act I of *Idomeneo*, by slipping down a whole tone to the key of bb after the initial statement in c, ending on its dominant. There follows another bellicose piece for Fracasso, No. 25 in D, and though it is his finest aria, it adds nothing we did not already know about him. Mozart probably composed both Nos. 24 and 25 for Salzburg in 1769, because rehearsals in Vienna never went beyond the second act. Among the revealing features first visible in the *Neue Mozart Ausgabe* are several original endings in the Appendix that Mozart had to strengthen, probably at the request of the singers involved (Nos. 2, 5, 8, 11, 16, 17, and 22 fall into this category). Coltellini made an important contribution by greatly expanding the third act finale.[24] The best music in this long finale comes when, after Giacinta and Ninetta ask pardon from Cassandro, Rosina admits, "I was the one who arranged it all, Cassandro has only to

---

[24] Contrary to what is claimed in Heartz, "The Creation of the Buffo Finale," p. 76.

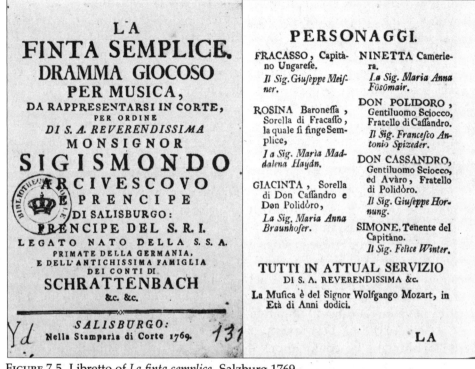

FIGURE 7.5. Libretto of *La finta semplice*, Salzburg 1769.

pardon me." She no longer feigns being a simpleton. The moment is touching partly because it anticipates that of another Rosina, asking pardon at the end of *Le nozze di Figaro*.

When the Mozarts arrived back in Salzburg, Leopold did lay *La finta semplice* at the feet of the archbishop (as he phrased it in his letter of 30 July 1768). Although Salzburg had no buffa singers per se, plans were made to perform the work, which went so far as the printing of a libretto, showing the intended distribution of the cast (Figure 7.5). The part of Rosina was assigned to Maria Magdalena Lipp, the wife of Michael Haydn, who, with her training in Venice, should have been well equipped to sing it. Although no performing score or parts have yet turned up in Salzburg, the opera was probably performed there in 1769. Leopold thought highly enough of it to take the autograph with him on the first trip to Italy the following year, hoping perhaps to obtain a hearing in the birthplace of opera buffa.

By chance or by design, the choice of Goldoni's libretto brought Mozart in touch with the dramatist who boldly transformed Italian comic opera of the mid-century. The choice of text for the other stage work Mozart composed at this time brought him into the circle of Jean-Jacques Rousseau, whose pastoral opera of 1752, *Le devin du village*, was of enormous consequence in shaping French opéra-comique. In this *intermède*, as Rousseau called it, he introduced some Italian features, such as the three-movement sinfonia, rapid and regularly pulsed simple recitative (as opposed to French recitative, often irregular and slow), and brilliant violin writing, with double stops and other devices to achieve a penetrating, sonorous effect. In other respects the work was very French in its reliance on simple strophic airs or rondo structures, dances, and pantomime. The poem, also by Rousseau, portrays rustic virtue triumphing over corrupting civilization, a type of drama perfected earlier by Charles-Simon Favart in his vaudeville comedies.[25]

Le devin du village was first performed before the court at Fontainebleau in October 1752, an occasion touchingly recounted by Rousseau in his *Confessions*. The principal singers were the best then at Paris, Marie Fel and the tenor Pierre de Jélyotte, who brought the work to the stage of the Opéra for the first time on 1 March 1753. Several hundred performances followed until finally, according to Berlioz, it was hooted off the stage in 1829. Any work this successful would engender parodies. On 4 August 1753 the Comédie Italienne offered a parody entitled *Les amours de Bastien et Bastienne*, the printed text of which was signed by Madame Favart and Harny de Guerville. In this version the rustic swains spoke a more peasant-like language, and most verses were fashioned so that they could be sung to popular vaudevilles. Madame Favart herself, a famous actress, singer, and dancer, played the role of Bastienne. The parody was nearly as successful as the original and was given by the Théâtre Italien until 1790—the Mozarts could have seen the revival on 28 March 1764, just before they left Paris for London.[26]

The French troupe in Vienna under the directorship of Count Durazzo performed *Bastien et Bastienne* often. The work figured among their offerings in 1755, 1757, 1761, and 1763, with Louise Bodin-Joffroi taking the role of Bastienne. In 1761 it was given only three days after *Le devin du village*, with the lovers played by the same actors in each.[27] Durazzo also directed the German troupe in the Kärntnerthor Theater, and in 1764 he commissioned a German translation of *Bastien* from Friedrich Wilhelm Weiskern, a regular contributor to Vienna's German theater. The translation entered the repertory of Felix Berner's children's troupe as well, and they may have played it on their visit to the Salzburg court in the winter of 1766–67, when the Mozarts were just returned from their grand tour.

[25] Daniel Heartz, "*Les Lumières:* Voltaire and Metastasio; Goldoni, Favart, and Diderot," *Report of the Twelfth Congress, Berkeley 1977* (Kassel, 1981), pp. 233–38.

[26] Clarence D. Brenner, *The Théâtre Italien: Its Repertory, 1716–1793* (University of California Publications in Modern Philology 63) (Berkeley, 1961), p. 276.

[27] Bruce Alan Brown, *Gluck and the French Theatre in Vienna* (Oxford, 1991), p. 104.

EXAMPLE 7.7. *Mozart*, Bastien und Bastienne, *Intrada*

Mozart set Weiskern's *Bastien und Bastienne* in Vienna in 1768 but exactly when is not known. The intrada that serves as an overture is appropriately pastoral in tone and modest in scope. Its opening has achieved a certain notoriety because of the comical anticipation of the beginning of Beethoven's *Eroica* Symphony in the first two bars (Example 7.7). The third and fourth bars are just as noteworthy, for they convey rusticity via a yodeling figure akin to the cow-calling motif that opens the first-movement *Allegro* of Haydn's Symphony No. 6, *Le matin*. After the briefest of tonal excursions Mozart returns to the opening theme, dismisses the yodeling figure in eighth notes, and anticipates the first four bars of Beethoven's theme. Another excursion leads to the subdominant, where the theme is stated in its full twelve-bar length, **a b b.** The short conclusion is not enough to rees-tablish G as tonic, but this is a clever way of transforming G into a dominant projecting forward into the first vocal piece, Bastienne's "Mein liebster Freund hat mich verlassen" (My dearest friend has left me), *Andante un poco Adagio* in 3/4 and in C. The piece is labeled Aria, but Lied or Air would be more appropriate. Mozart relied on short, through-composed settings of the solo texts in *Bastien*, rather than upon the longer binary and ternary forms of the arias in *La finta semplice*. In this respect he remained closer to the Viennese popular theater, as evidenced in the square-cut and very plain *teutsche Komödienarien* from the 1750s.[28]

Weiskern translated the French texts for the solo pieces quite literally. (A collaborator, Johann Müller, was responsible for the texts of Nos. 11–13.) He often retained the same syllable count, so that the German text could be sung to the French airs. His text, as a result, frequently differed from the norms of German poetry for music.[29] Take, for example, Bastienne's No. 6, which he parodies as "Würd ich auch, wie manche Buhlerinnen," after "Si j'voulions être un tantet coquette" (If I wished to flirt a little). Mozart in his setting adjusted this long line by speeding up the declamation in the third measure so as to arrive at a cadence in bar four (Example 7.8). There are similarities between this rising melody and the beginnings of No. 8 and No.

[28] Linda Tyler, "*Bastien und Bastienne:* The Libretto, Its Derivation, and Mozart's Text-Setting," *Journal of Musicology* 8 (1990): 520–52; 537–38. Tyler covers the same territory in condensed form in "*Bastien und Bastienne* and the Viennese Volkskomödie," *Mozart-Jahrbuch 1991*, pp. 576–79.
[29] Tyler, "*Bastien und Bastienne:* The Libretto, Its Derivation," p. 528.

EXAMPLE 7.8. *Mozart*, Bastien und Bastienne, *Air*

14 in *La finta semplice*—not surprisingly, given the closeness of their composition.

At some time after Mozart set the text by Weiskern and Müller, probably in 1769, verbal revisions were made by Johann Andreas Schachtner, who enjoyed a reputation as Salzburg's best poet in the German language.[30] Schachtner rewrote in its entirety the hocus-pocus text sung by the conjuring Colas in No. 10, a highlight in all versions of the work. He also reworked the prose interludes into verse, but Mozart set only the first four as recitatives, which probably indicates that a planned performance at Salzburg never took place.

Mozart's *Bastien und Bastienne* invites musical comparison with Rousseau's *Le devin du village*. They are the most similar when the same dance type is involved. Rousseau made a beautiful setting of "Je vais revoir ma charmante maitresse," to a minuet-air in g, with very high tenor part. Mozart wrote a smoothly flowing and mostly conjunct minuet-air in A (No. 11) for its equivalent, and reinforced its suavity with two flutes doubling the violins an octave above much of the time. Mozart's *Bastien* ends with a love duet in B♭ with transition at the end into a *terzetto* in D that takes the place of the extended *divertissements* of its French forebears.

Early Sacred Music

NEAR the end of his life Mozart wrote to the municipal council of Vienna offering his services in aid of cathedral Kapellmeister Hofmann, and stressing his fitness for the task because of his "thorough knowledge of the ecclesiastical style," as we saw. One year earlier he had drafted a letter to Archduke Francis, son and soon-to-be successor of Emperor Leopold, applying for the post of second court Kapellmeister, "especially since Salieri, that very skillful Kapellmeister, has never devoted himself to the church style, while I have

---

[30] Ibid., p. 532: "Most of his changes consist of softening harsh rhymes, eliminating Viennese idioms, and bringing his own brand of poetic polish to the texts."

made this style my very own since I was a youth." Mozart made a study of church music wherever he found himself, throughout his short life, but almost all his voluminous output in this genre falls in the period before his move to Vienna in 1781.

Even Mozart's very first sacred compositions show his ability to adapt different national and local styles to his own purposes. The short anthem "God Is Our Refuge," K. 20, written in London in July 1765, betrays his response to earlier English polyphony, which he could have heard only in Britain. The *Kyrie* in F, K. 33, dated Paris, 12 June 1766, reveals a richness in harmony that comes from writing many appoggiaturas and double appoggiaturas, which, coupled with the simple syllabic declamation, suggest the inspiration of the French choral music the boy heard at the royal chapel in Versailles. The Offertory *Scandi coeli limini* for the feast of St. Benedict, K. 34, is said to have been written for a Benedictine abbey in Bavaria on, or soon after, the return trip to Salzburg in 1766. Its first part is a surprisingly mature solo for soprano, accompanied by two violins and bass, in which questions in the text are set to Phrygian cadences with augmented-sixth chords, leading to a chorus for SATB, strings, trumpets in C, and timpani. A rudimentary and free fugal style in this final section indicates that the piece was in fact very early.

In Salzburg for Holy Week in the spring of 1767, Mozart wrote a sacred cantata, K. 42 (35ª), which Leopold described in his catalogue of the following year as "Eine Cantata zum hl: Grab Christi, von 2 singenden Personen. mit 2 Arien, Recitat: und Duetto." It begins with a recitative and aria in D for the Soul (bass), followed by a recitative and aria in g for the Angel (soprano), a duet for both in E♭, and a concluding chorus in C with a middle section in c. Particularly arresting here is the direct pairing of g with E♭, which can be found in the first chorus of another work for Holy Saturday, Niccolò Jommelli's setting of Metastasio's *La passione di Gesù Cristo* for Rome in 1749, and earlier in the late *Salve regina* of Jommelli's teacher Leonardo Leo. This tonal pairing can also be identified as a favorite combination practiced by Viennese composers such as Wagenseil and both Haydn brothers. Mozart ends the aria in g with a melodic cadence that long remained a favorite of his, a move by step up to the sixth degree, then a fall to the tonic and the leading tone beneath it: 5 6 1 7 1 (Example 7.9). The move from g to E♭ for the following obbligato recitative is repeated from the end of the recitative into the duet.

Mozart's first extended sacred compositions were written in Vienna in 1768 when he was twelve. Just before listing *Bastien* in his catalogue of late 1768, Leopold inscribed, "Ein Veni Sancte Spiritus à 4 Voci 2 Violini 2 Hautb: 2 Corni Clarini Tympani Viola e Basso etc." The entry refers to K. 47 in C,

EXAMPLE 7.9. *Mozart, Sacred Cantata, K. 42*

on a text appropriate to Pentecost. An opening *Allegro* in 3/4 possesses dancelike features, including precadential hemiolas in which the harmony moves in 3/2 time, with appropriately churchly 4 3 suspensions. The concluding section is a boisterous *Presto* in 2/4 on the single word "Alleluja," in which the sopranos are taken up to high G.

Directly after inscribing "eine grosse Messe" in the 1768 list of his son's compositions, Leopold added "Eine kleinere Messe à 4 Vocibus 2 Violinen etc.," and then concluded with "Ein Grosses Offertorium à 4 Vocibus etc.: 2 Violins etc. Clarini etc." The last entry refers to the lost offertory belonging with the "Great Mass" in c, and the "smaller mass" must be the *Missa brevis* in G, K. 49 (47^d). For reasons of its more limited musical technique, K. 49 is placed before the Mass in c chronologically, and thus becomes Mozart's earliest extant setting of the Ordinary of the mass. For all its brevity and imperfections, K. 49 anticipates many of his later choices as to how to set the five segments of the Ordinary.

The Kyrie of K. 49 begins with an *Adagio* of five bars in common time, serving as a kind of slow introduction in that the harmonic progression is from I to V. The choral parts commence with no instrumental prelude, but enter in pairs with a quasi-imitative texture that soon gives way to homophony. The ensuing section is *Andante* in 3/4 in the middle of which a few "Christe eleison"s are heard. There are contretemps in the part writing (e.g., the clash between the two upper voices producing parallel seconds close to the end). The same is true in the Gloria, an *Allegro* in common time, which ends with a rise to the third in the treble. The Credo begins with an *Allegro* in 3/4, one of Mozart's favorite choices for this section. He sets "Et incarnatus est" as a contrasting section, *Poco Adagio* in cut time, beginning in choral homophony without the basses, who enter at "Crucifixus." "Passus et sepultus est" brings a descending chromatic fourth in the bass. This traditional musical symbol of suffering and death would not govern all of Mozart's subsequent interpretations of the passage, but he would always introduce a heightened chromaticism here.

"Et resurrexit" follows in tonic major, *Allegro* in cut time, leaving the previous cadence on V/vi unresolved. A momentary *Adagio* stops the proceedings at "vivos et mortuos." They are resumed with an *Andante* in 3/4 at "Et in Spiritum Sanctum," the choice of triple meter apparently being made in honor of the third member of the Holy Trinity. An *Allegro* in common time at "Et unam sanctam catholicam" is interrupted by another stop for "mortuorum" and concludes with a fugue on "Et vitam venturi." The Credo ends like the Gloria, with the treble rising by step to the third degree over I - V - I. Common endings like this represent one way of building cyclic unity into the mass.

The Sanctus of K. 49 brings an *Andante* in 3/4, with an energy-generating rhythmic figure in the violins that will see much use in the next two masses as well: |♫♫ ♫ ♫ |. The "Pleni sunt caeli" Mozart sets as an *Allegro* in 3/4, the sopranos outlining the degrees 3 4 6 5, as they did in the Sanctus (and less clearly at the beginnings of the previous movements), probably a reference to some chant that has yet to be identified. "Hosanna," in cut time, brings what may be a fuller reference to the same chant model: 1 2 3 4 5 6 5 4 3. For the Benedictus Mozart repairs to the subdominant, as he would so often in subsequent masses. The movement ambles along in *Andante*, 3/4 (an interpretation of the verb in "qui venit" and a reminder that "andante" is the present participle of "andare," to walk). Here the soloists emerge for the first and only time—in longer settings they would ordinarily make a showing in the middle of the Credo and at its fugal ending. Agnus Dei begins in the relative minor, e, *Adagio* in cut time, for full chorus singing chordally, and ending with V/vi, like the "passus et sepultus est." A joyous and dancelike *Allegro* in 3/8 provides the resolution in tonic major, somewhat incongruous to the final words, "Dona nobis pacem." The work ends with a plagal cadence, with the degrees 6 5 in the treble.

The *Missa solemnis* in c/C, K. 139 (K³—114ᵃ; K⁶—47ᵃ), betrays by the huge discrepancy of its Köchel numbers the arguments that have long been waged about its date. Scholars were unwilling, initially, to allow that Mozart could have conceived such a huge and powerful work at age twelve in Vienna, and hence placed it later, in Salzburg. Now there is general agreement that this was indeed his mass for the consecration of the Waisenhaus Church in Vienna on 7 December 1768. The presence of four trumpets and two violas in the score and in Leopold's description of late 1768 helped tip the balance.

That the consecration mass was a success at its first performance we know from a source other than Leopold Mozart. The issue of the *Wiener Diarium* dated 7 December 1768 gave the following report: "The entire music was composed anew for the high office of the orphanage choir by Wolfgang Mozart, the twelve-year-old little son of Herr Leopold Mozart (Kapellmeister [sic] in Salzburg service) who is celebrated for his unusual talents. He directed it himself with great precision along with some sung motets, to the general approbation and admiration of everyone."[31]

The Mass in c/C begins on a grand scale, with chorus intoning "Kyrie," *Adagio* in common time, supported by the strings playing double stops, trombones, and oboes. This first bar of tonic minor, *forte*, is answered by the strings and trombones alone with figuration in the second bar, beginning *piano*. The process is repeated with chords that are rich, if not entirely consequential—the chromatically rising soprano line, not the bass, determines the harmonic progression, which reaches remote e♭ before settling on V of c

---

[31] Karl Pfannhauser, "Zu Mozarts Kirchenwerken von 1768," *Mozart-Jahrbuch 1954*, pp. 150–68.

(Example 7.10). The scope of this slow introduction is so vast and imperious (a quality furthered by the dotted rhythm in the chorus) that its contemporary equivalent is not easily located, not even in Joseph Haydn's masses before 1770. What models, if any, could Mozart have had for this extraordinary beginning? His pitting of choral and orchestral sonorities against each other on this scale suggests the cathedral music of an older generation of Viennese composers, namely Fux, Franz Tuma, and Reutter.

Only rarely during the rest of the mass does Mozart achieve the visionary sweep of its opening. The Kyrie continues with a bustling *Allegro* in 3/4, introduced by the orchestra alone and energized by the same rhythmic cell observed in the previous mass. The chorus enters singing in block harmonies, effectively deployed, with sopranos reaching up to high G. Arrival at the dominant takes only eight bars, after which the soloists sing a sweetly consonant second theme there, followed by choral, and then orchestral, confirmation of the new key. There is the equivalent of a development section, centering on a, where the second theme is introduced by the soloists. This second theme is eliminated from the reprise. The chorus already included "Christe eleison" in the Kyrie *Allegro*, but now comes a complete little movement in 2/4, an *Andante* in the key of the subdominant, in which the soloists sing only "Christe eleison"; it foreshadows similar discrete passages in F in the Gloria, Credo, and finally the Benedictus. Following this movement the directions read, "Kyrie Allegro da capo." With the da capo repetition the entire Kyrie extends to 232 measures. The Gloria, at 340 measures, continues on the same scale, with solo sections at "Laudamus," "Domine Deus," and "Quoniam tu solus." There is a curious choral fugue for "Cum Sancto Spirito," begun C F♯ G in the basses (answered in the tenors by G B C, and so on up to the altos and sopranos). The tritone motif C F♯ G has been heard before, and in a prominently exposed spot, sung by the choral sopranos in the Kyrie. After the Kyrie Mozart, surprisingly, takes the choral sopranos no higher than F.

The Credo is roughly equivalent in length to the Gloria at 336 measures, and is divided into sections at the usual places. It ends with a double fugue on "Et vitam venturi." The Sanctus brings an *Adagio* with dotted rhythms, like the beginning of the mass. "Hosanna" elicits overlapping groups of three quarter notes between upper and lower choral voices. The Benedictus is set as an *Andante* in common time, its gentle quality and key of F making audible a link back to the "Christe eleison" and related moments in the Gloria and Credo. Tonic minor returns for the Agnus Dei, *Andante* in cut time, introduced by three trombones, accompanied by bassi and organ. Then solemnity dissolves into tutti shouts of joy in tonic major, *Allegro* in 3/4, for "Dona nobis pacem." The mass in its totality marked a great accomplish-

EXAMPLE 7.10. *Mozart, Mass in c (1768)*

ment for Mozart. Not just its scope but also its improved part writing represent a significant advance beyond K. 49.

The *Missa brevis* in d, K. 65, was finished upon Mozart's return from Vienna to Salzburg and is dated 14 January 1769. Brief though it is, there is room for a rousing fugato at the end of the Gloria and another at the end of the Credo. The Benedictus is unusual in that it is set to a descending chromatic line, like a lament, an *Andante* for soprano and alto solos. The Agnus Dei begins and ends in d.

The *Dominicus* Mass in C, K. 66, dated October 1769, was written for a son of the Mozart family's landlord Lorenz Hagenauer, Cajetan, when he celebrated his first high mass at St. Peter's as the newly ordained Pater Dominicus. Mozart's autograph is scored for strings, including violas, two trumpets, timpani, and organ, to which he added oboes, horns, and two more trumpets in original parts for the first performance. The proportions are similar to those in the Mass in c/C, and many of the same traits apply. The Kyrie is first set as a slow introduction, *Adagio* in common time, then as an *Allegro* in 3/4 (with the whiplash fury of sixteenth notes on the first beat observed above). The division of the Gloria and Credo into sections and types of movement correspond in the main to K. 139, but the Benedictus for solo voices is set in G, rather than F. "Hosanna" receives the same treatment of overlapping groups of three notes observed in K. 139. The Agnus Dei is an *Allegro moderato* in common time that yields to an *Allegro* in 3/8 for "Dona nobis pacem."

Written on the eve of the first trip to Italy, the *Dominicus* Mass shows a strengthening of Mozart's contrapuntal acumen and an enrichment of his harmonic language. In the latter category is the deft use of the I - ii$^{6/4/2}$ - V$^{6/5}$ - I progression in the Kyrie *Adagio* as an introduction to the same in the Kyrie *Allegro*. The Credo is unified by a return to its initial music at "Et unam sanctam catholicam." Perhaps most impressive of all is the superior melodic inspiration in some of the subsidiary sections for the soloists. An example is provided by two of Mozart's favorite devices that appear in closing position

EXAMPLE 7.11. *Mozart*, Dominicus *Mass, "Laudamus te"*

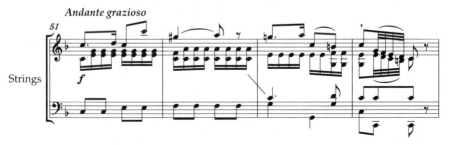

in the "Laudamus te" (Example 7.11). One is the raised-fifth degree after the high tonic over subdominant harmony, which echoes through all his works down to Tamino's ineffable "Ich fühl es." No less characteristic is the cadential figure in the treble of 5 6 1 7 1, a melodic turn with which Mozart is so delighted that he states it three times in the final cadences.

Michael Haydn

JOHANN MICHAEL HAYDN was born in Rohrau in September 1737. Around age eight he followed in the footsteps of his older brother Joseph by becoming a choirboy at St. Stephen's Cathedral in Vienna; he was reputed to have an even more beautiful soprano voice than his brother. Under the tutelage of Georg Reutter, he presumably studied counterpoint in the usual way, using the *Gradus ad Parnassum* of Fux. Michael Haydn's earliest extant composition is a *Missa in honorem Sanctissimae Trinitatis*, which is signed and dated 1754 in his hand. Also in his hand, dated 1757, is a copy of Fux's *Missa canonica*.[32] No later than 1757 he became a member of the orchestra of the bishop of Grosswardein in Hungary, who spent his time between Vienna and this remote post of the Habsburg Empire. By 1760, at the relatively young age of twenty-three, he had become Kapellmeister to the bishop. In mid-1762 he returned to Vienna.

Joseph and Michael Haydn remained devoted to each other as long as they lived. They were musical rivals in a friendly sense. On 2 July 1762 Joseph Leutgeb played a concerto for solo horn and orchestra by Michael Haydn in a concert at the Burgtheater in Vienna. The next day Leutgeb's daughter was baptized in the parish church of St. Ullrich, with Joseph Haydn and his wife as godparents. I argue elsewhere that Joseph's beautiful Horn Concerto in D, dated 1762, was also written for Leutgeb.[33] On 15 September 1762 both brothers repaired to the village of their birth in order to settle the inheritance from their late mother. Michael remained in the area through the fall of 1762, a time when the Mozarts were in Vienna, but there is no evidence that they met at this time. His Partita in F for winds is dated 22 December 1762 at Pressburg, then the seat of the Hungarian Estates General, which probably indicates that he was still in the service of the bishop of Grosswardein.

[32] For facsimile copies showing Haydn's signature on both compositions, see Gerhard Croll and Kurt Vössing, *Johann Michael Haydn: Sein Leben—sein Schaffen—seine Zeit* (Vienna, 1987), p. 25. This beautifully illustrated volume has served as my main biographical source.
[33] Daniel Heartz, "Leutgeb and the 1762 Horn Concertos of Joseph and Johann Michael Haydn," *Mozart-Jahrbuch 1987/88*, pp. 59–64.

Michael Haydn's Horn Concerto of 1762 has never been found, like most of Leutgeb's repertory of solo concertos. But several concertos by the younger Haydn do survive from around 1760, when he was already a prolific composer of both sacred and secular music. One is a Trumpet Concerto in C, dated 1762, with an orchestra of strings and two flutes. The first movement in this two-movement work is a *Moderato* in common time, in a very galant style, with multiple trills for the flutes; a bifocal close is used at the join between being *on* V and *in* V. The second movement is a robust *Allegro* in 2/4 that is monothematic and uses an ample transition to achieve the dominant. Though the concerto is quite slight, it is enough to establish its composer as a representative of the most modern Viennese style before he set foot in Salzburg.

Michael Haydn is believed to have come to Salzburg no later than June 1763, the same month the Mozart family left on their great journey. An entry in the Salzburg court diary for 24 July 1763 specifies, "The princely table was held today in the salon of Mirabell Palace on account of the rainy weather. It consisted of 24 ordinary members and eight guests. *Tafelmusique* was presented by an outside composer from Vienna by the name of Michael Heiden."[34] The location of this event was presumably the palace's garden pavilion (which was demolished in 1818; Figure 7.6). Vice-Kapellmeister Mozart's absence and the uncertainty about when he would return probably helped to insure that Michael Haydn would not long remain an outsider. After petitioning the court for a post in a document of excessive humility, he was granted by decree on 14 August 1763 the titles of "Hofmusicus und Concert-Meister" with an annual salary of 300 gulden, the same as Leopold Mozart, and with the added privilege of being admitted to the Officers' Table, which neither of the Mozarts, father or son, ever enjoyed.

Michael Haydn's first years in Salzburg were rich in compositional activity. Masses, litanies, vespers, and other genres of sacred music poured forth from his pen, as did symphonies, divertimentos, and other instrumental works. He also composed a successful Singspiel, *Rebekka als Braut* (10 April 1766), and made many other contributions to Salzburg's theatrical life.[35] The Mozarts probably did not meet Haydn until their return in late 1766. The following fall he visited them in Vienna, along with Leutgeb, who had joined the Salzburg court orchestra in 1764. In his letter of 29 November 1767 to Hagenauer, Leopold describes how Haydn had become enamored of a certain maid by the name of Theresa ("Tresel"), daughter of a Viennese hosier, but was too inhibited and laconic to woo her successfully. Yet by the

---

[34] Croll and Vössing, *Johann Michael Haydn*, p. 37.

[35] Johanna Siegel, "Johann Michael Haydn: Kompositionen für Salzburger Bühnen," *Mozart-Jahrbuch 1987/88*, pp. 85–89.

FIGURE 7.6. The Sala terrena of Mirabell Palace, Salzburg.

next year he had managed to overcome his shyness and win the hand of Maria Magdalena Lipp, daughter of court organist Franz Ignaz Lipp and a salaried court singer, whom he married in Salzburg on 17 August 1768. (The Mozarts were still in Vienna). She had spent three years studying music in Venice, 1761 to 1764, at the expense of Archbishop Schrattenbach.

Interaction between Wolfgang Mozart and Michael Haydn remained minimal before the late 1760s.[36] A turning point in Haydn's life came at the beginning of the following decade. The daughter born to his wife in January 1770 died a year later; there were no more children. Then on 16 December 1771 Haydn's patron and protector, Archbishop Schrattenbach, died after a short illness. Naturally rather reserved and taciturn, Michael Haydn became even more so in consequence of these losses. He composed one of his most important works, the *Missa pro defuncto Archepiscopo*, or Requiem, in a very short time—it was finished on 31 December 1771. Three copyists worked rapidly to prepare the parts of this very large work so that it could be performed by the entire court music, the Mozarts included, at the funeral masses in the cathedral on 2, 3, and 4 January 1772.[37] The experience was

[36] Manfred Hermann Schmid, *Mozart und die Salzburger Tradition* (Tützing, 1976), pp. 46–52, shows that Mozart's first choral fugues in 1768–69 are not indebted to Michael Haydn.

[37] Croll and Vössing, *Johann Michael Haydn*, p. 63, with facsimile of the Requiem's first page in score, from the autograph.

one that Mozart did not forget. Even twenty years later as he was working on his own Requiem, the impression of Haydn's masterwork still lingered, manifest in certain details of K. 626.

Archbishop Colloredo came to value the work of Michael Haydn as much as or more than his predecessor had done. One of the best educated and most clever rulers in Salzburg's history, he was also an absolute ruler who insisted that his commands be obeyed quickly and in full. It did not take him long to assess the modest Haydn vis-à-vis the ambitious Mozarts and their international aspirations.

By the time the Mozarts returned from Vienna in early 1769, Wolfgang showed signs of being increasingly receptive to the music of Michael Haydn. Mozart's *Te Deum laudamus* in C, K. 141 (66^b), believed to date from this year, shows some signs of inspiration from Haydn's *Te Deum* in C composed in 1760, although the styles are quite different.[38] Mozart was particularly interested in his elder colleague's dance music. From his correspondence with his sister during 1770, we know that they exchanged several of Haydn's latest minuets. In his letter of 24 March 1770 from Bologna, Mozart inquired about typical Lenten and pre-Lenten matters: "Write me who sang in the oratorio, also what its title was. Write me too about how Haydn's minuets pleased you. Were they better than the first ones?" Nannerl did more than write about them—she sent twelve minuets. To at least one melody (taken down by ear at the carnival balls?) she added a bass. In his letter from Naples of 19 May 1770, Wolfgang responded, "The twelfth minuet by Haydn that you sent me pleases me very much, and you have composed the bass to it incomparably well, without the slightest error; please try such things more often." Then in his postscript to his father's letter from Rome of 7 July 1770, he wrote her: "I am amazed that you can compose so beautifully. The song is, in a word, beautiful, and you should try this more often. You will have received the minuets by Haydn; I beg you to send me the other six soon." On 22 September 1770 from Bologna, he wrote, "Haydn's six minuets please me more than the first twelve."

Two of Michael Haydn's most successful smaller sacred pieces for chorus and orchestra fall at the beginning of Colloredo's reign: the Offertory *Tres sunt* for the feast of the Holy Trinity in 1772, and the Sequence *Lauda Sion salvatorum* for the feast of Corpus Christi in 1775. Mozart copied out the first in score; moreover, after he settled in Vienna, he asked Nannerl to send him copies of both pieces (letter of 12 March 1783). The pieces were personal favorites of their composer too, who had each work copied into one or the

---

[38] Schmid devotes a chapter to "Das Te Deum von Michael Haydn (1760) und von Mozart (um 1769)," in *Mozart und die Salzburger Tradition*, pp. 33–45.

FIGURE 7.7. Anonymous oil
portrait of Michael Haydn
holding the music of his
Lauda sion.

other of the several similar portraits painted of him in Salzburg.[39] He is
shown holding the notated incipit in such a way that the viewer can identify
it (Figure 7.7). Thus they became his "signature" compositions. A compara-
tive study of *Tres sunt* with Mozart's *Regina coeli* for soprano and orchestra,
K. 127, written a month earlier and sung at court by Haydn's wife, leads to
some fundamental conclusions about how the two composers differed:
Mozart thought in metric units from the smallest to the largest levels; his
older colleague did not, but rather composed by allowing the declamation
of the text to give shape to the music.[40]

Leopold Mozart viewed Michael Haydn with suspicion, considering him
a rival for the post of Kapellmeister at Salzburg. But his son, as we have
seen, had a high regard for the Viennese master, and the episode of their
respective string quintets with two violas from 1773 demonstrates this anew.
Haydn's Notturno in C for this combination is dated 17 February 1773. The

[39] Reproduced in Croll and Vössing, *Johann Michael Haydn*, pp. 98–103.
[40] Schmid, *Mozart und die Salzburger Tradition*, pp. 13–28.

EXAMPLE 7.12. *Michael Haydn, Notturno in G, II*

next month Mozart and his father returned from their third and last Italian tour, and soon afterward Mozart began writing his Quintet in B♭ with two violas, K. 174. Haydn then wrote another, the Notturno in G with two violas dated 1 December 1773—one of his most inspired and polished instrumental works. A precadential excerpt from the slow movement could easily pass for Mozart (Example 7.12). The *piano* three-note groups in the first violin are echoed *pianissimo* by the other strings in three-note groups that overlap those of the violin. Then the violin climbs up to high D by means of two-note sighing figures. The harmony becomes tonic 6/4 in m. 26 as the lower instruments imitate the sighs in sixths and thirds, after which the first violin makes a soft chromatic descent from its perch to the trilled A that announces the cadence.

We now leap way ahead in our story, to Mozart's Serenade in E♭ for winds, K. 375, of October 1781. Its first movement contains a precadential passage that duplicates Haydn's gesture for gesture (Example 7.13).[41] Of course, Haydn may have learned this kind of affective discourse from young Mozart. The point is their closeness.

The instrumental imagination and contrapuntal acumen shown in a work Michael Haydn wrote for Salzburg cathedral, the *Missa Sancti Hiero-*

[41] Marius Flothuis points out the correspondence of these two passages in his article "Quintette für Streichinstrumente von Michael Haydn," *Mozart-Jahrbuch 1987/88*, pp. 49–57, examples 1 and 2.

EXAMPLE 7.13. *Mozart, Serenade for winds, K. 375, I*

nymi for four-part chorus, oboes, bassoons, trombones, and organ, without strings, stirred even Leopold Mozart to sing its praises. The mass was composed for the feast of All Saints in 1777. Leopold wrote his son immediately and at length about its rehearsal and performance (he even began the letter with this description) on 1–3 November 1777, revealing information about personnel and manner of performance.

> This moment I am come from the service in the cathedral, where Haydn's Oboe Mass was performed; he led it himself ["er Tacktierte sie selbst"]. There was also an offertory, and instead of the sonata, the words of the gradual, which the priest speaks, also composed to go with the rest . . . Everything pleased me exceptionally well, because six oboists, three contrabasses, two bassoons, and the castrato [Ceccarelli], who has a six-month contract at 100 florins a month, took part. Ferlendis and Sandmayr had the solo oboe parts. The oboist at Lodron's, a certain student, the chief watchman, and Obkirchner were the ripieno oboes. Cassl and Choirmaster Knozenbry were the contrabasses beside the organ and near the trombones. Estlinger was with the bassoon, Hofer and Perwein were beside the oboes in the violin gallery. What especially pleased me was that, since the oboes and bassoons come very close to the human voice, the tutti seemed to be a pure and strongly supported vocal ensemble, as the soprano and contralto voices, strengthened by the six oboes and alto trombones, well balanced the number of tenor and bass voices. The full body ["piano"] was so magisterial that I would have gladly forgone the oboe solos. The whole thing

lasted an hour and a quarter, and for me it was too short, for the music was truly well composed. Everything flowed naturally, and the fugues, particularly the "Et vitam" etc. in the Credo and the "Dona nobis" and then the "Alleluja" in the offertory, are worked out in masterly fashion, with natural themes and no overdone modulations or too sudden transitions. The gradual, sung instead of the sonata, is a shapely contrapuntal piece for full voices throughout. Especially here the voice of the castrato did good service. Should I get hold of this mass sooner or later, I shall certainly send it to you. Note that Brunetti stood before Ferlendis, Wenzl Sadlo stood behind the bassoons, and Hafender stood behind the other oboists, and all three kept their eyes on Haydn and beat the tactus [measure] on the shoulders in front of them. Otherwise it would have gone badly, especially in fugues and in running obbligato basses. Now, finally, maybe a post of cathedral Kapellmeister or Vice-Kapellmeister will materialize [for Haydn] after so many years of work. But there will be obstacles. The latest news is that [Kapellmeister] Rust is in poor health.

As shown in Küsell's engraving of a century earlier, concerted music in Salzburg Cathedral continued to rely on hand signals given out by a principal time beater (in this case Michael Haydn) and relay signalmen who kept him in view.

The musical structure of the court was in flux around this time. At the retirement of Giuseppe Lolli, Giacomo Rust, a Roman-born opera composer, was appointed at the high salary (for Salzburg) of 1,000 gulden annually, by decree of 12 June 1777. But he complained that the bad weather in Salzburg was responsible for his declining health and returned to Italy for good in February 1778. Leopold's praises for Haydn's "Oboe Mass" make it sound as if he were resigned to the advancement of his rival, but other letters show that such was not the case. Even this letter reveals the distance between the two men in that Leopold did not have access to Haydn's new score. Years later, in reply to a request by the publisher Artaria for a copy of this score, Leopold wrote on 21 March 1786 that he would gladly oblige by sending this mass, but it had been performed only once (meaning there were very few copies), and Haydn would not let the original out of his hands.

Anton Adlgasser's death in December 1777 left vacant the post of organist at Holy Trinity Church as well as that of principal organist of the cathedral. The first vacancy was soon filled. In his letter of 29 December 1777, Leopold, with some malice, relayed the news to his son: "Who do you suppose has become organist at Holy Trinity? Herr Haydn! Everyone laughs about it. He will be an expensive organist, for after every Litany he gulps a Viertel of wine, and to other services he sends as his replacement Herr Lipp, who also drinks." There is more in this vein in Leopold's letter of 29 June 1778 to his wife and son in Paris, concerning the service on Holy Trinity Sunday in the same church: "In the afternoon Haydn played the organ for the Litany and the *Te Deum laudamus*, the archbishop being present, but so frightfully that we all were scared and thought he was going the way of the late Adlgasser. But it was only a slight tipsiness that made it difficult to get both hands and his head together. I have not heard the like since Adlgasser's mishap." Most of this letter is devoted to Leopold's behind-the-scenes machinations to insure his son's return to the Salzburg court in a higher position, and one wonders whether he has exaggerated Haydn's performance toward this same purpose.

In his reply, Mozart, eager to humor his father just after the death of his mother in Paris, makes light of the matter at first but then waxes unusually moral:

> I had to laugh heartily at Haydn's tipsiness. If I had been there I should certainly have whispered in his ear: "Adlgasser." It is really a shame when so skilled a man through his own fault renders himself incapable of performing his duties— at a function in God's honor, and in the presence of the archbishop, the whole court, and with the church full of people. That is disgusting! This is also one of the chief reasons that make me hate Salzburg—those coarse, slovenly, and dissolute court musicians. (Letter of 9 July 1778.)

The platitudes here ring false. Leopold had gone so far as to predict that Haydn would drink himself into dropsy in a few years, "or at any rate, as he is too lazy for anything, would go on getting lazier and lazier as he grows older" (same letter of 29 June 1778). But this smacks of both spite and self-delusion. Haydn remained active as a composer (unlike Leopold). In his main specialty, sacred music, much of his best work still lay ahead of him at this time.

The evidence of Mozart's respect and liking for Michael Haydn outweighs the negative views orchestrated by Leopold. In 1783, when Mozart returned to Salzburg from Vienna for a few months, he helped Haydn, who was ill, to fulfill a commission from the archbishop for six duets for violin and viola by composing K. 423 in G and K. 424 in B♭. At some time after this visit, probably in early 1784, Mozart appended a slow introduction to Haydn's Symphony in G, written for the installation of a new abbot at Michaelbeuren in May 1783. The entire work long passed as Mozart's Symphony No. 37. He took back with him to Vienna the score of Haydn's Symphony No. 17 in E♭ as well as that of the Symphony in G. As long as Leopold lived, Mozart held back something in his friendship for Michael Haydn. But soon after his father's death on 28 May 1787, Mozart invited Haydn to visit him in Vienna. Haydn did not answer the letter of invitation (now lost). We know this from Mozart's letter to his sister of 2 August 1788, in which he asks her to persuade Haydn to lend him the original scores of two tutti masses and the graduals. "Invite him to your house in St. Gilgen and play him some of my latest compositions. I am sure he will like the Trio and the Quartet" (probably the Piano Trio in E, K. 542, and the Piano Quartet in E♭, K. 493).

Nannerl was not on friendly terms with the Haydns. In her letter to her brother of 23 October 1777, she reported a rumor that was without foundation: "I wish it were true what Herr Cassel has just come to congratulate us about, namely that you and Papa were appointed to the Munich court with a salary of 1,600 gulden. I believe it is Haydn's wife and her slovenly set ["ihr geschlamp"] who spread such lies, because they wish Papa out of here, in order to be sure that her husband becomes Kapellmeister." This passage has been misread as indicating that Leopold was being considered for promotion to Kapellmeister at Salzburg, which was never the case.[42] The root of the problematic relations between Leopold and Michael Haydn was not just professional jealousy but social antipathy. Leopold was better educated and belonged to a higher class of society, or so he thought, and he did not let his children forget it.

Three Operas for Habsburg Milan

MILAN had been the main seat of Austrian power in Italy ever since Lombardy was awarded to the Habsburg Empire in 1714. A regent appointed in Vienna governed the province and decided the prestigious matter of who would compose the operas for Milan's Reggio Ducal Teatro. In 1770 the regent was Count Karl Joseph von Firmian, in whose Milanese house three arias by Mozart were performed on 12 March 1770, the composer and his father being present. As a result of this performance Firmian awarded the coveted *scrittura* or contract for the first opera of the following carnival season to Mozart, who was to receive a fee of 100 *gigliati* (gold gulden) and free dwelling in Milan during his residence there. In late July the court decided that the libretto would be *Mitridate, rè di Ponto*, an opera seria in three acts by Amadeo Cigna-Santi, and Mozart then began writing the simple recitatives, which were due in Milan by October. This meant he had to make a tonal plan for the twenty-five numbers that made up K. 87 (74ª), since the recitatives provided connective tissue between them. The experience of having composed *La finta semplice*, with its twenty-six numbers, most of them exit arias as in *Mitridate*, stood him in good stead for the task. He and Leopold arrived back in Milan on 18 October 1770.

[42] Cliff Eisen, "The Symphonies of Leopold Mozart and Their Relationship to the Early Symphonies of Wolfgang Amadeus Mozart: A Bibliographical and Stylistic Study" (Ph.D. diss., Cornell University, 1986), p. 185.

Mozart's first attempts to please the main singers cast for the opera did not succeed. The prima donna, Antonia Bernasconi, made him recompose his first efforts for her, and so did the tenor playing the title role, Giuseppe d'Ettore. The first aria, sung by the heroine, Aspasia, was originally written as a piece in G with oboes, horns, and strings, a natural choice following the three-movement overture in D (and predicted by the cadence of D G in the opening moment of the first recitative). Bernasconi had other ideas, and they resulted in Mozart's composing a grander and more heroic aria on the same text in the key of C, with the concomitant trumpets (as well as oboes and horns) (Example 7.14a). Its opening gesture over a I - IV$^{6/4}$ - I progression is one that Mozart continued to use for heroic pieces in C in several later operas, including *Il rè pastore* (No. 13) and *La clemenza di Tito*, where it inaugurates the final number. As the aria reaches the point of an expansive cadence on the dominant, Mozart deploys what I call the "Hasse cadence," which consists of the bass rising into the I$^{6/4}$ chord, against the treble descending (Example 7.14b). He would gradually abandon this time-worn cliché in the early 1770s.

Trumpets, as well as extensive coloratura, also appear in Mitridate's big aria in D that closes Act I. If the primo uomo, Pietro Benedetti, failed to receive the same treatment as the prima donna, it was because none of his aria texts was quite heroic enough to warrant such. Perhaps Mozart did not

EXAMPLE 7.14. *Mozart*, Mitridate, *Aria*

fully realize the hierarchical niceties regulating the use of trumpets when he began to compose his first opera seria. He soon found out. In early versions of the pieces he placed trumpets in B♭ in No. 9 and trumpets in D in No. 16, both for secondary characters. They were removed in the final versions.

    Mitridate was a great success even at its premiere on 26 December 1770

(St. Stephen's Day, the traditional beginning of opera's carnival season). One of Bernasconi's arias was encored at the first performance, which was unheard of, according to Leopold's letter of 29 December, and two were encored the next evening. Giuseppe Parini, reviewing the opera in the *Gazzetta di Milano* of 2 January 1771, confirmed the public's judgment: "Some arias sung by Signora Antonia Bernasconi expressed the passions in a lively manner and touched the heart." Presumably he meant not her opening *aria di bravura* but her beautiful lament "Nel sen mi palpita il core dolente" (A grieving heart beats within my breast), No. 4, set by Mozart in the key of g, for which he retained a special affinity all his life. Particularly heart-wrenching is the dissonant minor ninth above the dominant at "non so resistere" (I know not how to resist), and quite remarkable is the concision he achieves in this through-composed *Allegro agitato* of ninety-nine measures. Melodic sighs, sobs, chromatic ascents, and words broken in the middle all add to the pathetic affect.

Bernasconi was not the recipient of the title role in Gluck's *Alceste* for nothing: she was clearly a great tragedian, and as such inspired Mozart to write as moving a piece as he had ever composed up to this point. The urgency of his musical language suggests another aria in g, written exactly ten years later, that of Ilia at the beginning of *Idomeneo*. There is a similarity even in the way the transition flows out of the recitative into the aria without a break. Concision is a matter that has to be measured in historical terms. The ninety-nine measures of this aria in g should be considered by the standards of 1771, when arias were still extremely long-winded, not those of twenty years later (i.e., the forty-one measures of Pamina's "Ach, ich fühl's").

Aspasia's aria in the second act (No. 14) is one of those expressing conflict between love and duty. Mozart sets it in F as a two-tempo piece alternating between *Adagio* and *Allegro*, a type well represented in this opera. He colors it with pairs of flutes, as well as pairs of oboes and horns. Bernasconi was able to show both her impassioned declamatory style and her coloratura here, and the audience may have encored this aria on the second night. More likely, the audience awarded this honor to No. 21, her *ombra* aria in Act III (it is actually a cavatina of one strophe surrounded by extremely expressive obbligato recitatives). Mozart did not have to be told that this kind of piece demanded E♭—he had models for how to set an *ombra* aria in the greatest Neapolitan composers, from Jommelli on down. There is no coloratura in this piece; all is *parlante*, requiring the passionate declamation for which Bernasconi was famous.

Sifare, the primo uomo, comes off only slightly less well than his counterpart. He follows her heroic opening aria with a sentimental one in B♭, No. 2; then after her lament (No. 4 in g) he sings a "Parto" aria in A, with the first word set to a descending-fifth leap, as was usual with this type. His big showpiece aria is No. 13 in D, "Lungi da te" (Far from thee), with obbligato solo horn, as well as orchestral horns and oboes. At the words "se vuoi ch'io porti il piede" (If you wish that I go), Mozart uncannily anticipates the rising chromatic melody Don Ottavio sings to "pena avra de tuoi martir" (Your torment would make him suffer) in the great sextet of *Don Giovanni*. Sifare's final aria of desperation, following Aspasia's *ombra* scene in E♭, is an *Allegro agitato* in common time and in the somber tonal realm of c—an answer worthy of both the previous scene and of Aspasia's No. 4 in g. The libretto is structured so that Sifare mainly reacts to what Aspasia has said or done, putting him in a weaker position, but in his last aria in c, with its driving, syncopated rhythms and powerful dissonances, he is made her equal by dramatically compelling music.

Mozart took some hints as to how to set this libretto from its first setting by Quirino Gasparini for Turin in 1767. But one looks in vain for Mozart's profound expression of the passions in the older composer's score. The traditional view that Mozart was too young and inexperienced to do justice to *Mitridate* is no longer tenable. To mark the two hundredth anniversary of Mozart's death on 5 December 1991, the Royal Opera at Covent Garden gave a highly acclaimed production of the opera.[43]

Mitridate was a test case promulgated by the Viennese court to see if Mozart was worthy of a more sensitive task. He passed it brilliantly, and the result was his selection to compose the second of two festive operas for a marriage of great importance to Maria Theresa and her family. Long-standing plans for Archduke Ferdinand to wed Princess Maria Beatrice of Modena, the last descendant of the Este family, came to fruition in 1771. The ceremony was to take place in Milan Cathedral in mid-October, followed by the installation of the young pair as rulers of Lombardy. The main opera was *Il Ruggiero*, for which Metastasio was reclaimed from retirement for one last effort, along with his favorite composer, the great Hasse, who was also Maria Theresa's favorite. Just as in 1760, when Archduke Joseph was first wed, there was to be a second opera, a serenata, *Ascanio in Alba* (K. 111).

Giuseppe Parini, a celebrated Milanese poet who was also the critic who had reviewed *Mitridate* so favorably, wrote the libretto, a pastoral allegory about the newly wedded royal couple, in the persons of the shepherd Ascanio, descended from Venus (i.e., Maria Theresa), who weds the nymph Sylvia. Parini had to submit the poem to Vienna for approval, which must have been somewhat galling for a writer of his distinction. The approval was

---

[43] Writing in the *Times Literary Supplement* of 27 December 1991, Peter Porter says that *Mitridate* "shows that Mozart was mature enough to respond to a fine libretto, however young he was in years . . . it vindicated *opera seria* as a form."

XI. Della Rosa. *Portrait of Mozart at Verona*, 1770. (Private collection. Courtesy of the Internationale Stiftlung Mozarteum, Salzburg)

XII. Brand. Landscape of the Danube Valley at the Confluence of the Morava and the Danube Rivers, 1752–53.
(Prague: National Gallery)

given, and Mozart, in Milan again, received the poem by 28 August. He composed the three-movement overture first, contrary to the usual custom. It was an unusual case, however, because the action already began with the danced middle movement and the danced and sung finale of the overture.

On 13 September 1771 Leopold wrote that "Wolfgang will have completely finished the serenata in twelve days' time, with God's help; it is really more of an *azione teatrale* in two parts." There was in fact little distinction between these two genres, so Leopold's point is unclear. A serenata was a short festive opera in honor of some occasion or some person or persons, with an emphasis on spectacle, scenery, dancing, and choral singing, as well as solo singing. Metastasio called several of his shorter librettos for specific occasions by the term *azione teatrale*, which he seems to have invented. The most famous *azione teatrale* of all was Gluck's *Orfeo*, which had several French as well as Italian ancestors, as we saw in Chapter 3. The genre Mozart was asked to compose was quite similar to *Orfeo* in its reliance on abundant spectacle, dancing, and choruses, but considerably less dramatic in the sense of any conflict that is developed and resolved. Mozart acquitted himself beautifully as far as the many choruses and ballets were concerned. But he was at something of a disadvantage in trying to enliven Parini's pallid individual characters, and all in all, the arias do not come up to the passionate level of the best in *Mitridate*. He was also under greater constraints in the time available for composition. A bad case of parallel fifths mars the trio (No. 31).

The lessons of *Mitridate* as to the individual singers' prerogatives stood Mozart in good stead in *Ascanio*. He indulged the prima donna, Silvia, sung by Antonia Aguilar, with an ample aria in C with trumpets, No. 14, and did the same for the primo uomo, Giovanni Manzuoli, who sang the title role (No. 16 in D with trumpets). These two received four arias apiece, while the three secondary characters had to be content with two each. Even so, the young composer, showing a characteristic generosity of spirit, made No. 21 in B♭ for Fauno much longer than a secondo uomo had a right to expect. In this same year of 1771 Carlo Goldoni wrote about his encounter with the "rules" of Italian serious opera, stating that the secondary singers also pretended to claim grand pathetic arias, but that the primary singers would not stand for this and allowed them at best only *mezzo carattere* arias.[44] The *Andante ma Adagio* middle section in E♭ of Fauno's aria certainly sounds a pathetic note. It was cut (along with the da capo reprise), and probably for the reason that Manzuoli would not allow it. There does remain a splendid *aria d'affetto* in E♭ in the work, Silvia's No. 23, "Infelici affetti miei." A study of this piece will convince any keen ear how Mozart was growing in the sureness of every musical gesture, opera by opera.

---

[44] *Tutti le opere di Carlo Goldoni,* ed. Giuseppe Ortalani (Milan, 1935), 1: 687ff.

The success of Mozart's first Milanese opera, *Mitridate*, resulted in a commission for his third, *Lucio Silla*, K. 135, on a libretto by Giovanni de Gamerra. The commission arrived in the spring of 1771, and is not to be confused with the orders to compose *Ascanio*. *Lucio Silla* became the first carnival work of the 1772–73 season. (Giovanni Paisiello's setting of Gamerra's *Sismano nel Mogol* was the second.)[45] The contract, dated 4 March 1771, survives. Mozart obligated himself to supply the recitatives by October 1772, and to show up in person by 1 November in order to compose the arias and to attend the rehearsals. He was also expected to lead the first three performances in public from the harpsichord. Gamerra was relatively new to opera, having become theater poet in Milan only in 1771. From 1765 to 1770 he served at Milan in the Austrian army. He argued in the printed libretto of his *Armida* (1768) for a return to spectacle in the form of machinery, ballet, and choruses, for which the typical *dramma per musica* by Metastasio made little or no provision. He succeeded in providing an important role for the chorus in *Lucio Silla*, but the ballet remained confined to entr'actes, as was customary in opera seria, and machinery played no role onstage. The sets, on the other hand, designed by the greatest Italian scenographer of the time, Fabrizio Galliari, were magnificent. The libretto calls for this setting at the beginning of Act I: "A solitary enclosure strewn with trees and ruins of crumbling edifices. Bank of the Tiber. In the distance a view of the Monte Quirinale, with a little temple on its crest" (Figure 7.8). Galliari captured all this with a feathery lightness of touch, creating a subtle, nonsymmetrical stage picture.

Mozart and his father left Salzburg on 24 October 1772 and arrived in Milan on 4 November. According to Leopold's letter of 14 November, the main singers had not yet arrived, and Mozart was occupied composing the three choruses, altering the few recitatives he had brought from Salzburg and partly recomposing them, because Gamerra, having sent his poem to Metastasio for approval, received back a considerable list of revisions.[46] That Gamerra sought the blessing of the master in Vienna is not in doubt. He claimed in the *Argomento* of the printed libretto that he received from Metastasio a "most full approval." Leopold's letter of 14 November also says that Mozart had composed the *Overtura* as well as all the recitatives. The tardiness of the three principal singers in arriving apparently allowed Mozart time to compose the three-movement overture, the opening *Molto allegro* of which greatly outstrips the parallel movements in *Mitridate* and *Ascanio* in symphonic brilliance and élan.

[45] Friedrich Lippmann shows how close Mozart's seria style was to Paisiello's at this time in "Mozart und Paisiello: Zur stilistischen Position des *Lucio Silla*," *Mozart-Jahrbuch 1991*, pp. 580–93.
[46] Kathleen Hansell, editor of *Lucio Silla* in the NMA, was unable to document this last claim from the correspondence of Metastasio and is skeptical about it.

FIGURE 7.8. Fabrizio Galliari. Stage design for *Lucio Silla*, Act I, scene 1.

Many decisions about the tonal plan had to be altered after the singers did arrive, as can be surmised from changed recitative endings. Because of illness, the tenor engaged for the title role had to be replaced by a less experienced church tenor, with the result that the four arias planned for Silla shrank to two. With his prima donna, Anna de Amicis, and primo uomo, Venanzio Rauzzini, Mozart had to make many adjustments in what he originally planned. Rivalry between the two principals somewhat marred the premiere, but ultimately they both triumphed. As to the secondary parts, Mozart made a few misjudgments, beginning with the first number, for Cinna, the secondo uomo, sung by Signora Felicita Suardi, who was on hand when Leopold wrote his letter of 14 November 1772. Her initial aria is twice too long (281 measures!) for a secondary character, and more like the first movement of a concerto than an aria. To make amends to the primo uomo, who follows this extravaganza with a first aria of only 233 measures, Mozart gave him a beautiful obbligato recitative preceding his aria, but this of course stretches out his monologue unduly.

The opera does not really take wing until the prima donna, Giunia, sings an aria in E♭, No. 4, invoking the shade of her dead father (i.e., an *ombra* aria). The piece alternates between *Andante ma Adagio* for her mourning and

Allegro in common time for her defiance of the emperor, the unfortunate Silla, culminating in an *Allegro* in cut time. Like the Pasha in *Die Entführung*, Silla's amorous fire is stoked by resistance, and he sings an aria, No. 5, originally planned to be in C but later moved up to D and given trumpets and timpani, which at least suit his high estate, if not the text.

Mozart had to recompose not only the recitative ending before No. 5, but also what followed this aria, which was to have begun with a brooding orchestral passage in the key of a minor, very Gluck-like in its striding bass in quarter notes against violin syncopations and sustained tones in the winds and violas (Example 7.15). The passage accompanies the scene change to the subterranean tomb with the monuments to Rome's heroes (Figure 7.9). To mediate between this passage and an aria that no longer ended in C but in D, Mozart added a nine-measure transition, *Andante*, that prepares the arrival of a minor by starting on its Neapolitan, B♭. Just before the primo uomo, Cecilio, begins to sing about this lugubrious locale ("Morte, morte fatal"), the orchestra wrenches the harmony in one measure from V of a to $V^{4/3}$ of C or c. Cecilio enters in c. As he ends his musing on all-conquering death, the expected cadence on g is withheld and replaced with a deceptive cadence to E♭, and the tempo changes from *Andante* to *Allegro assai*. Abrupt modulations signal Cecilio's distress and fear at the arrival of another person. When this turns out to be his wife Giunia, who believes him dead, the music becomes meltingly consonant and noble, moving once again at *Andante*. Little rising motifs in the first violins are imitated by the violas, to

EXAMPLE 7.15. *Mozart, Lucio Silla, Act I, scene 7*

FIGURE 7.9. Fabrizio Galliari. Stage design for the tomb scene of *Lucio Silla*.

match the verbal questions, accompanied by a steady stream of sixteenth notes in the second violins. This music is so pictorial it would tell the same tale even without words.

When Cecilio realizes Giunia is not alone, he becomes fearful once again and the orchestra vacillates between *Presto* and *Andante* to paint his indecision. He hides behind an urn. An *Adagio* in C of seven measures leads, with appropriate modulation, to the ensuing choral lament in E♭, *Adagio* in cut time. Following the greatest obbligato recitative he had ever written, Mozart now proceeds to outdo anything he had previously done along choral lines, with a piece that is alternately grieving and exultant of Roman heroism.

After the great obbligato recitative for the primo uomo, it was the turn of the prima donna to shine. The chorus is followed by a seven-measure transition leading not to c, as might be expected, but to a *Molto adagio* in g; here her voice is better placed for the soaring lament Mozart gives her. A syncopated high A♭ interrupts the gentle descent into her cadence, and when her voice does finally come to rest on the tonic, G, it turns out to be not the tonic but the third of E♭, as the chorus enters with the concluding *Allegro*, a shortened statement of its opening dirge.

Lucio Silla reaches an overwhelming climax with the choral scene in the tombs. Act I might well have ended here, but there was an operatic obligation that had to be fulfilled first: the love duet. The plot did not allow it to be placed anywhere else. In Mozart's preferred love duet key of A, it is a masterpiece in its own right, expressing bliss and despair at close range. Giunia believes at first that what she beholds is only the ghost of her husband, Cecilio, hence the dark orchestral interjection before "ombra dell'idol mio."

Nothing in the rest of the opera quite matches the level of the great scene in the tombs, although there are other lovely moments, especially in the arias of the two principals. There are also some signs of haste or fatigue. Mozart gives Cecilio another obbligato recitative of stunning power before his big heroic aria, No. 9, which was originally to have been in B♭. The second choice of key, D, with trumpets and timpani, seems more appropriate to his status and to the violence of the text. Particularly effective is the cello's outlining of the dominant-seventh chord, to which the voice responds, "paventi il traditor" (Fear the traitor), a passage that made Galuppi famous in the 1740s.[47] Not so effective is the wrenching of the tonality from g to V of D at the *Presto* just before the aria begins. Cecilio, like Giunia, receives four solo arias; the best is the simplest, a *Tempo di Menuetto* in A and in 3/8, No. 21, to the text "Pupille amate non lagrimate" (Do not weep, beloved eyes). Here Cecilio bids Giunia farewell and goes to his death (he thinks). Strings alone accompany him. The melodic structure is 4 + 4 + 4, a classic example of a dancelike period with galant redict, **a b b'**. Rauzzini surely ornamented this plain melody upon its return after a contrasting section, and then on its final return as a coda. The effectiveness of simple, heartfelt melodic beauty uncovered in a tiny minuet can be compared with several small dance airs in Gluck's *Iphigénie en Aulide* (already composed in Vienna by 1773 but awaiting its premiere in Paris the following year).

The arias of the secondary characters are noticeably inferior to those of the principals. An exception is Celia's fine piece in B♭, No. 19, at the beginning of Act III (with trumpets in B♭, as in Cinna's first aria, No. 1, and in Giunia's *aria di bravura*, No. 11). Signs of Mozart's flagging inspiration show in such details as his use of the old-fashioned "Hasse cadence" in No. 15 (Celia) and No. 20 (Cinna). Most strange is Mozart's liberal use of trumpets in the opera, lending it a strident tone that is quite foreign to the composer otherwise. There are trumpets in twelve of the twenty-three numbers. Every character has an aria with trumpets, even so minor a character as Aufidio,

---

[47] Heartz, "Hasse, Galuppi and Metastasio"; see especially pp. 334–37 and fig. 3 concerning Abt Vogler's assessment of Galuppi's "Se cerca, se dice."

who sings the *aria di sorbetto* that begins the second act to a bellicose text, with coloratura for the word "lampo" (lightning). Gamerra's inexperience shows in the number of strong or martial expressions he allows the secondary characters.[48]

Lucio Silla was apparently a great success in Milan. Leopold Mozart claimed in a letter to his wife of 23 January 1773 that it had been given twenty-six times to astonishingly full houses. The number must be an exaggeration; no one could have sung either of the very demanding principal roles so many times. And besides, the theater was closed on Sundays and Fridays. Since its premiere was on 27 December, there can have been at most about fifteen performances. Also to be weighed in the balance, when judging the opera's success, is the uncomfortable fact that Mozart was never asked back to Milan.

The opera evidently remained vivid in Mozart's memory. In Mannheim in 1778 he gave Aloysia Weber Giunia's arias to sing. He referred to No. 11, "Se il crudel periglio" (If the grievous peril), in his letter of 17 January 1778 as "my aria for de Amicis with the dreadfully difficult passages" ("mit dem entsetzlichen Pasagen").[49] Ten years after *Lucio Silla* he was still reviving arias from it (letter of 29 March 1783). Not surprisingly, there was some musical carryover from *Lucio Silla* to his next opera, *La finta giardiniera*, begun in the fall of 1774.

The experiences of bringing three operas to the stage of Milan's Reggio Ducal Teatro insured that Mozart, although still only a boy, was no longer an apprentice in the vastly complicated business of operatic production. Henceforth he knew how to navigate between the shoals of professional pride represented by poets, singers, designers, and all the other collaborators necessary to such a joint effort. These trials by fire in a large professional theater endowed him with a command of the operatic craft that, for lack of similar experiences, was never afforded many other composers, including Michael Haydn and Beethoven. Joseph Haydn worked for the German Theater in Vienna during the 1750s (albeit with singers inferior to those in the Burgtheater), so he cannot be said to have lacked professional experience. But his subsequent work for the limited forces and small palace theaters of the Esterházys cannot be compared with Mozart's early experiences in Milan.

[48] Hansell in her preface to the NMA edition calls attention to Gamerra's penchant for the lugubrious, which scarcely could have pleased Metastasio, any more than could the extravagance and violence of Gamerra's language.

[49] For an analysis of this aria and its analogies with Mozart's ritornello procedures in subsequent instrumental concertos, see Martha Feldman, "Staging the Virtuoso: Ritornello Procedure in Mozart, from Aria to Concerto," in *Mozart's Piano Concertos: Text, Context, Interpretation*, ed. Neal Zaslaw (Ann Arbor, forthcoming).

Symphonies and Chamber Music
from 1770 to Early 1773

MOZART, unlike Haydn, had the good fortune to visit Italy. The experience strengthened a penchant for opera that was present from his earliest works; it also brought him into extensive contact with the *sinfonia avanti l'opera*. From about 1720 on, this genre took the form of a three-movement piece. The first movement was all bustle and fanfares—a summoning to order in a large theater required no less. The second provided contrast in mode or key, timbre, dynamics, and melodic type, allowing the third to reassert the outgoing nature of the first, often in the form of a minuet or other social dance. Mozart wrote several such works during his first visit to Italy in 1770. Specialists in the matter still argue whether Leopold had a hand in their composition, as he certainly did in their copying. They are among Mozart's slightest works.

A good representative of the style is the Symphony No. 10 in G (K. 74), now believed to have been composed in Rome in April 1770. Scored for pairs of oboes and horns with the usual strings, the work opens with a fast movement in common time (without tempo marking). The opening fanfares give way to an invigorating transition as the two violins perform three-note upward slides together in sixths, then thirds. A particularly Mozartian sonority emerges in the second theme as the basses drop out and violas sustain a line in half notes under more rapidly moving violins. There is no repeat sign at the end of the prima parte, which is signaled by three hammer-stroke chords in double stops for the violins. Rather than development, there is merely an eight-bar dominant pedal, leading, with *crescendo*, to the reprise. This movement makes transition without pause into the second movement in 3/8 and in C, with a smooth-flowing melody by step that resembles the middle sections of many Italian arias of the time. The finale is a rondo in 2/4.[50]

As important for Mozart as the composers whose works he heard in Italy was the sound of good voices and well-staffed orchestras in the large opera houses up and down the peninsula. He and Leopold heard the premiere of Jommelli's *Armida abbandonata* at the Teatro San Carlo in Naples on 29 May 1770. Mozart wrote his sister the day before that they had attended the rehearsal of Jommelli's opera, "which is well written, and really pleased me" ("che è ben scritta, e che mi piace veramente"). But on 9 June he changed

---

[50] Zaslaw, *Mozart's Symphonies*, p. 179, claims the movement is titled "Rondeaux," but this is not present in the NMA edition.

his tune in writing to his sister about the opera: "Sie ist schön, aber viel zu gescheid, und zu altvätterisch fürs theatro." Beautiful but far too sensible? And too old-fashioned for the theater? The first comment may have been ironically intended. His change of mind may reflect the less than warm reception of the Neapolitan public, who were not to be easily convinced that Jommelli had remained his old self after so many years north of the Alps. In any case, the beginning of the overture to *Armida* appears to have made its mark on the opening of the Symphony in D, K. 84 (73^q). The several symphonies in D ascribed to Mozart from this time are so much alike we wonder why they were written. As exercises in chiaroscuro, perhaps, in achieving just the right mixture of Italian brio and Italian grace, they might be said to justify themselves.

In a letter from Bologna to his sister of 4 August 1770, Mozart answered a question put by his mother as to whether he was still playing the violin: "Certainly I am. I have had the honor of going alone to churches and magnificent functions more than six times. Moreover I have composed four Italian symphonies, as well as arias, of which I have composed five or six, and one motet." The reference to the symphonies as Italian leaves no doubt that he considered the genre to exist independently of others.

The Mozarts arrived back in Salzburg on 28 March 1771 and remained there until 13 August, when they returned to Milan for *Ascanio*. The Symphony in F, K. 75 (of dubious authenticity), may have been written in Salzburg during this period. Symphony No. 12 in G, K. 110 (75^b), is securely dated Salzburg, July 1771. Its first movement, an *Allegro* in 3/4, makes a very good case for itself. The Italian brio is still present, but here Mozart writes repeat signs for both the prima and seconda parti, and the connecting passage to the reprise is more than just a V pedal. The *Andante* in C in cut time shares the same form. Italian grace of melody prevails, but there are some stern minor-second blasts that suggest a dialogue between beauty and the beast. The Menuetto is a pseudo-canon, a type that has affinities with the Haydn brothers. A little connecting passage with the melody 5 3 6 / 4 2 5 / 3 1 4 / 3 - 2 speaks the language of Mozart's serenades (the popular ramifications of melodies like this will occupy us below). The trio is in e and sternly contrapuntal, a little study in using as many minor and major seconds as possible. The finale, an *Allegro* in 2/4, is a vigorous dance (*contredanse en rondeau*) of ebullient high spirits. A year later, this type of lightweight finale will give way to more serious symphonic finales that match the opening movements.

The Mozarts returned from Milan on 15 December 1771. During the carnival in Salzburg Mozart composed two symphonies, No. 14 in A (K. 114), dated 30 December 1771, and No. 15 in G (K. 124), dated 21 February. Both

are four-movement works with Menuetto and trio. The opening *Allegro* of
K. 124 is in 3/4 but veers into what sounds like 6/8 after only twelve measures, for the second theme. It is highly unusual for Mozart to make the
modulation so quickly, but then there is something else unusual about this
second theme besides its metrical quirks. It resembles in several particulars
the opening of Joseph Haydn's brilliant Symphony No. 28 in A, dated 1765.
(See Figure 4.7.) Haydn makes so bold as to begin by confusing the listener
about the meter. His joke must have appealed to Mozart. The passages are
too close to be explained by coincidence or fortuity. Perhaps Michael Haydn
was a conduit by which his brother's music reached Salzburg.

Leopold Mozart was quite aware of the possible commercial value of
chamber music and symphonies (the difference between them was still
small). He tried to interest Breitkopf in Leipzig in commissioning works from
his son by letter of 7 February 1772. He specified that the best time to place
an order would be well before father and son were scheduled to return to
Milan in late September. The genres proposed turn out to be an approximate
plan of work for the months ahead. "You need only name what you find
most suitable. It could be keyboard compositions, or *Trio* with two violins
and a cello, or *quartetten* with two violins, a viola, and cello, or *Sinfonien* with
2 violins, viola, 2 horns, 2 oboes or flutes, and bass. In short, he will do all,
whichever kind of composition you think will be most profitable, if you let
us know soon." Although Breitkopf did not respond, Leopold clung to the
idea.

Mozart's burst of symphonic composition in Salzburg from May through
August 1772 came at a time when he was relatively free of court duties. In
the set of six symphonies he wrote at this time, the key choices are those he
already favored for symphonies: C, D, E♭, F, G, and A (only B♭ is lacking,
and Mozart had written but one symphony in that key, K. 22).

The symphonies are organized in pairs. Symphonies No. 16 in C (K.
128) and No. 17 in G (K. 129) are in three movements, with *Andante* middle
movements in 2/4 and 6/8 *Allegro* finales. Symphonies No. 18 in F (K. 130)
and No. 19 in E♭ are four-movement works with Menuetto-trio, and both
require four horns (not specified in Leopold 's letter but represented in Breitkopf's published catalogues).

Symphonies Nos. 20 in D (K. 133) and 21 in A (K. 134) are Mozart's most
ambitious works in the genre up to this date, as may be seen from the
increased lengths of their first movements. They are both in four movements
with Menuetto-trio. No. 20 requires trumpets as well as horns. It opens with
the three hammer strokes characteristic of the *sinfonia avanti l'opera* but continues after this "curtain" with a soft main theme in dotted rhythm with
trills, gently rising and falling (an idea indebted to Christian Bach—cf. the

first movement of K. 107, No. 3). As in many opening movements by Johann Stamitz, the themes are recapitulated in reverse order, the first being saved for last, where it sounds at first in its original guise, *piano*, then *forte* as conclusion. In the opening *Allegro* of K. 134 the reprise also begins with the second theme, perhaps because the first theme saw so much use in the development. A generous coda, labeled as such, concludes the movement.

The high point of the 1772 symphonies is K. 130 in F, every movement of which exhibits memorable qualities. The opening *Allegro* in common time begins with a five-bar phrase, *piano*, involving only violins and violas, which is repeated tutti *forte*. The two violins also state the second theme, the firsts with little trills and triplet figures over the rocking eighth-note bass of the seconds. Then upon repetition the violas take over the rocking bass, the basses play pizzicato, and the second violins imitate the trills of the firsts, sounding like two songbirds at play. There are also moments of power amid all the graceful exchanges—for instance, in the use of precadential diminished-seventh chords. In the *Andantino grazioso*, in 3/8 and in B♭, the violins are muted over the pizzicati of the basses and cellos. Their delicate three-bar phrases betray the *settenario* of Italian verse. Eventually these three-bar phrases will yield to four-bar ones. In the coda, labeled as such, the mutes come off, and the main theme sounds forth *unisono*, transformed so as to fall to the tonic in its second phrase. In the third movement it is the trio that astonishes by its modal harmonies. Mozart is making fun of either sanctimoniousness or compositional incompetence, perhaps both at once. The *Molto Allegro* finale in common time recalls the beginning of the first movement with the leap 8 5, then a fall by step. The closing theme, which begins with a secondary dominant, anticipates much later Mozart. Its intimate, string quartet nature, resembling a passage in the four-hand Piano Sonata in F, K. 497 of 1786, is dispelled by rude *forte* interruptions. The protracted diminished chords of the first movement return, in the cadential areas, but as a parting shot there is a pert little three-bar phrase, recalling the *Andantino*. This finale in sonata form is in fact a weighty summary of the entire symphony. Mozart wrote no more symphonies in the key of F.

Mozart had written relatively little chamber music without keyboard before the Italian journeys. In the list of his son's works from late 1768, Leopold includes "6 Trio à 2 Violini e Violoncello," but these have not survived. At their first major Italian stop, the city of Verona in January 1770, a string trio by Boccherini was set in front of the boy to read at sight. (Boccherini's first set of string trios was composed in 1760 and published in Paris by Bailleux in 1767.) Two months later Mozart wrote the String Quartet in G, K. 80 (73^f), dated "Lodi, 15 March 1770, at 7 o'clock in the evening," consisting of an *Adagio*, *Allegro*, and Minuetto-trio, to which he later added a

Rondeau Allegro. This unprepossessing little work, with all movements in the same key, had sentimental value for its composer, probably because it was his very first attempt to write a string quartet. He took it with him on the trip to Paris and wrote his father on 24 March 1778: "Before I left Mannheim, I had Herr von Gemmingen copy the quartet I wrote that evening at the tavern in Lodi, the quintet [K. 174], and the *Fischer* Variations [K. 179]."

The quartet begins with a four-bar phrase destined to become one of his favorites, a melodic type best known from Donna Elvira's entrance aria, "Ah chi mi dice mai," in *Don Giovanni* (Example 7.16b). Mozart did not necessarily hit upon this beautiful *Adagio* of his own accord—it duplicates nearly note for note the second idea in the initial slow movement of Boccherini's String Trio in C, Op. 1 No. 6 (Example 7.16a).[51] The likelihood is not remote that this very trio was the one Mozart had read from parts in Verona two months earlier.

In Salzburg in early 1772 Mozart composed the three Divertimenti for two violins, viola, and basso, K. 136–38, works in three movements that may have been intended for small orchestra as well as quartet. The first, K. 136 in D, begins with the treble melody of a fifth falling by step to the tonic,

EXAMPLE 7.16.

a. Boccherini, String Trio Op. 1, No. 6, I

b. Mozart, String Quartet K. 80, I

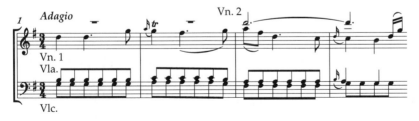

[51] Bathia Churgin pointed out the correspondence in her article "Did Sammartini Influence Mozart's Earliest String Quartets?" *Mozart-Jahrbuch 1991*, pp. 529–39.

which was one of Mozart's favorites during the early 1770s; it recurs at the beginning of the concluding *Presto* and at the beginning of K. 137. Boccherini was also fond of this beginning; we encountered it above in Example 7.1 as used by Eckard.

Mozart began composing a set of six quartets in late October and early November 1772, with the Quartet in D, inscribed "Quartetto I," K. 155 (134ª). The other five follow a symmetrical plan of keys according to the circle of fifths: D, G, C, F, B♭, E♭. The works are all in three movements, with middle movements in the minor mode in Nos. 2–5. The finales are light in weight, mostly minuets or rondos. Leopold's hand in the proceedings is quite literally discernible in that he added almost all the tempo markings.

The first quartet begins with a rather pompous movement in common time that comes to a full stop on the tonic in m. 12, a gesture common in Italian music but very unusual for Mozart (the keyboard piece in the Verona portrait of 1770 has this same feature).[52] The exchanges between the two violins are reminiscent of Sammartini. Quartet No. 2 in G shows more charm, beginning with a *Presto* in 3/8 that has the first violin yodeling over a Ländler accompaniment. After the double bar with repeat signs in the middle, Mozart introduces a new idea over a rhythmic ostinato that he impishly assigns to one instrument or another for thirty-four measures. The concluding *Tempo di Menuetto* (so inscribed by Leopold) has canonic pretensions. Quartet No. 3 in C opens with a texture Mozart loved: sustained viola against moving parts. Quartets Nos. 4 and 5 contain fewer remarkable features, which may possibly be a sign of strain upon the young composer from the task imposed.

The last Quartet, No. 6 in E♭, K. 160 (159ª), makes a fine conclusion to the set. Mozart begins it once again with the fifth-falling-by-step-to-the-tonic gesture, heard here at its most ingratiating, and followed by a IV$^{6/4}$ chord that makes a lovely continuation. The same idea is recast in triple meter for the middle movement of the keyboard Sonata for four hands in B♭, K. 358 (186ᶜ), composed in Salzburg in later 1773 or early 1774 for Mozart and his sister to play—a veritable *souvenir d'Italie*. K. 160's first movement continues with a second theme in chains of thirds, played in low position without the first violins, then repeated an octave higher by both violins against the sustaining viola. The passage that follows deserves attention.

The first violin's chromatic inflection 8 5♯ 6 / 8 4♯ 5 announces a melodic idea that will continue to intrigue Mozart for its highly emotional content through Ilia's aria in E♭, No. 11 in *Idomeneo*, all the way to Tamino's "Ich fühl es" in the Picture Aria, No. 3 of *Die Zauberflöte* (also in E♭!). Moreover, the

---

[52] D. Heartz, "The Verona Portrait of Mozart and the *Molto Allegro* in G (KV 72ª)" (forthcoming).

Picture Aria will deploy the same groups of three eighth notes overlapping one another between treble and accompaniment. Unusual for the first movements in the set, there is no double bar with repeat signs in the middle. Possibly the *Allegro* tempo (probably in Leopold's hand) should be *Moderato* or even slower. The second movement begins with harmonic uncertainty (what turns out to be a secondary dominant and its resolution) that only gradually clarifies as the key is revealed to be A♭, a stunning beginning to a winning piece. Leopold marked the movement *Un poco Adagio.* Unusual for this set is the choice of sonata form for the finale, a *Presto* in 2/4 filled with high spirits and variety of texture, including pairings between second violin and viola, and between viola and cello. Mozart had advanced greatly beyond the stiffness still apparent in the first quartet of the set.

Leopold Mozart remained fixed on the idea of selling music to the press. At least this offers one explanation why Mozart composed a set of six string quartets in addition to the arduous task of completing *Lucio Silla* and seeing it through the performances at Milan in late 1772 and early 1773. The quartets failed to attract a publisher.

8

Mozart, Journeyman

Symphonic and Chamber Music, 1773–74

N o F I R M boundary marks the end of Mozart's apprentice period. For lack of a better demarcation, the third and last return from Italy will serve. Father and son reached Salzburg once again on 13 March 1773. A month earlier Michael Haydn had composed a piece of chamber music in a new medium, his first string quintet with two violas. Mozart took immediate notice and began writing his own equivalent, the superb Quintet in B♭, K. 174. Its opening movement, *Allegro moderato* in cut time, is both brilliant in a concertante way and filled with intimate detail. The broad main theme, sung by the first violin and then by the first viola, falls by step, after a long-held first tone, from fifth to first degree. The continuation is over subdominant harmony, here by a syncopated rise through the triad that foreshadows the beginning of the *terzetto* in *Idomeneo*. The first hint of chromatic inflection arrives when the first violin begins after its initial statement with a little eighth-note figure, 8 5♯ 6, over IV. The slow movement is in E♭, an *Adagio* in common time played with mutes. There is much to admire throughout the piece until its last moments in a coda, designated as such, wherein the main motif undergoes a subtle change as a parting shot. Mozart at his most playful animates the understated Minuet, with its charming melody made from inverting 3 1 7 2 into 1 3 4 2. His original trio he replaced in December 1773 with a more chromatic one with echoes, purportedly in response to Michael Haydn's second string quintet, which had been composed in the meantime. The same is true with his original finale, a rather dense piece of writing in *Allegro* 2/4. The replacement *Allegro* is more airy and also longer, extending to no fewer than 315 measures not counting the repetitions. Much of the movement is duet answering duet. Mozart is known to have relished playing this piece (as first viola, presumably) as well as the two quintets by Michael Haydn.

THE VIENNESE QUARTETS OF 1773

WHEN the hopes of father and son of winning a post at the courts of the Habsburg princes ruling in Florence and Milan came to nothing, the Mozarts turned again to the imperial capital itself. They left Salzburg on 14 July 1773 in the archbishop's entourage and postponed their return from what was supposed to be a short stay in Vienna until 26 September. They resided in the middle of the city at No. 18 Tiefer Graben (Figure 8.1). Mozart's fixation on the string quartet continued. Prince Esterházy's maestro di cappella, Joseph Haydn, had covered himself with new glory by having sets of string quartets published in 1771 (Op. 9) and 1772 (Op. 17). Mozart, in turn, produced a set of quartets along Viennese lines in two months' time. Like Haydn's, Mozart's set consisted of six quartets, in different keys, all in four movements with minuets and trios, one in minor, and one beginning with a theme and variations. Moreover, Mozart showed his knowledge of Haydn's most recent set of quartets, composed in 1772 and published two years later as Op. 20, by writing fugal finales for the first and last quartets of his series.

Leopold now pinned his hopes on an appointment for his son at the imperial court. In his letter of 12 August 1773 he wrote his wife, "Her Majesty the empress was very gracious to us, but that is all." Nor were any other princely houses interested. And the quartets did not achieve either publication or renown for their composer.

Leopold's gamble with the new quartets, if that is what it was, put Mozart in the risky position of trying to keep up with Haydn while remaining original. It was a nearly impossible task, and he did not altogether succeed. The first Quartet, K. 168 in F, begins with a pleasing movement in sonata form, quite on a par with the last of the Milanese quartets. The work continues with an *Andante* in f, which gives notice of the composer's intentions by taking the old-fashioned theme of the fugue that closes Haydn's Quartet in f from Op. 20, putting it in triple meter, and treating it in canon.[1]

---

[1] A. Peter Brown, "Haydn and Mozart's 1773 Stay in Vienna: Weeding a Musicological Garden," *Journal of Musicology* 10 (1992): 192–230, argues against Mozart's indebtedness to Haydn and pro-

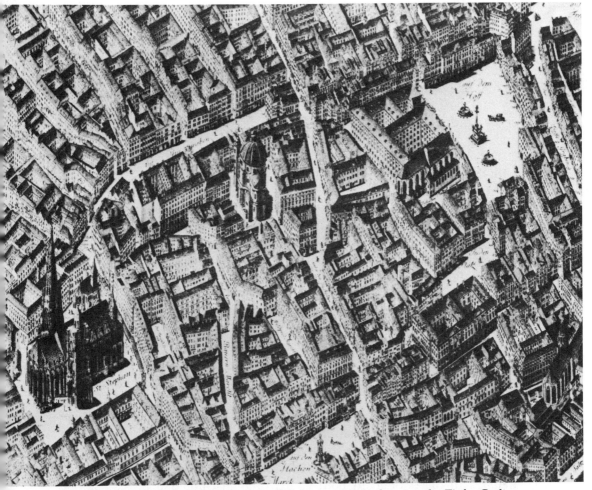

FIGURE 8.1. Detail from Huber's map of Vienna, c. 1770, showing the Tiefer Graben (upper right edge), where the Mozarts lived in the summer of 1773.

The result is a boring movement without rhythmic interest or much life. The Minuet and trio are in galant style but are not among the most interesting Mozart wrote. The finale is a bustling fugue in F, the theme of which is close to that in the finale fugue of the Quartet in A from Haydn's Op. 20. Mozart puts the theme through all the academic paces, such as *stretto* and inversion, and ends with a rushing *unisono* capped by a rousing and chordal V - I. So did Haydn. Even so, upon further hearing, the nearly constant sixteenth-note activity of Mozart's finale and its learned aspirations resemble not so much Haydn as the young Mendelssohn.

This set of quartets is laid out symmetrically, but not with such rigor as

poses as a closer parallel an *Andante* by Ordonez treating the same theme in triple meter (p. 209). Perhaps all these contrapuntal exercises sprang from a common desire to please Joseph II.

the Milanese quartets: F, A, C, E♭, B♭, d. The *Molto Allegro* opening movement of K. 169 is in 3/4 and begins with another switch on the descent from
fifth to first degree by step; it comes to a full stop on the tonic in m. 11, like
the first movement of the first Milanese quartet. The exposition seems a little
short-winded at thirty-six measures. The development is the same length
and the reprise longer, with more time spent in the second theme area:
‖: 36:‖: 36 | 45:‖. Haydn preferred to keep the seconda parte more in balance
with the prima parte by shortening the reprise. The *Andante* in 2/4 and in D
is almost entirely given to the first violin as soloist against chordal accompaniment in sixteenth-note triplets. The tonal disjunctions are the most interesting feature of this movement. An unfortunate resemblance to "God save
the Queen" will mar the Menuetto for many listeners. Mozart marked the
last movement, in 2/4, *Rondeaux Allegro*. This curious use of "rondeau" in
the plural occurs as early as K. 26 and K. 30, composed at The Hague in 1766.

K. 170 in C is the quartet that opens with a theme and variations. The
theme rather resembles Haydn's in Op. 9 No. 5, and is saved from total
squareness by a measure of silence in the second half, stretching eight bars
to nine. Like Haydn, Mozart brings back the theme in simple form at the
end. The Minuet is the second movement here, as in Haydn's Op. 9 and
Op. 17. Peeping out of Mozart's third movement, *Un poco Adagio* in cut time
and in G, as the second idea is the beginning of the *Adagio cantabile* from
Haydn's Quartet in d, Op. 9.

As in the Milanese quartets, the key of E♭ summons the best from
Mozart. K. 171 begins with a three-note motif, *Adagio,* that is ambiguous, E♭
B♮ C. It could portend the key of c, in which case it would duplicate a theme
that Haydn used often in both church and instrumental music—among
other places, as the beginning of the finale of his Quartet in c, Op. 17 No. 3.
But Mozart's second measure points to E♭ as the key, E♭ A♮ B♭. The *forte*
unison opening is thus another celebration of 8 5♯ 6, 8 4♯ 5, to be compared
with that in the Milanese Quartet in E♭. Its soft continuation outlining the
chord of the supertonic shares resonances with the beginning of a famous
Quartet in E♭ from ten summers later, K. 428, the fourth of the six quartets
Mozart dedicated to Haydn. The *Adagio* beginning of K. 171 subsides into a
dominant seventh, followed by a rest with fermata. An *Allegro assai* in 3/4
follows, beginning with a point of imitation and then outlining the supertonic. This unusual *Allegro* is in short sonata form without repeats and without development, to which Mozart appends the point of imitation and its
continuation as a coda, then brings back the *Adagio* opening, slightly
extended and made to end in E♭. Nothing in the rest of the quartet quite
rises to the level of this movement. But the third movement, *Andante* in
common time and in the key of c, with mutes, does work up to a passionate

conclusion in which the opening motif of the *Adagio* appears in c. The finale, *Allegro assai* in 3/8, begins with a typically Haydnesque play between loud outbursts and soft retorts.

The music of the last two quartets neither falls below nor rises above the level of the first four. The slow movement of K. 172 in B♭ is a fine *Adagio* in E♭, a solo for the first violin under which the second violin and viola weave a continuous chain of sixteenth notes in accompaniment, grouped in overlapping threes. The main theme of the finale, *Allegro assai* in 2/4, consists of thirds in descent in the violins overlapped by the same in the two lower instruments. Once again Mozart resorts to the descent from fifth to first degree by step, and when he repeats this immediately in a different form, with appoggiatura quick notes, questions arise. Is this creative economy? Or a sign of fatigue? (We saw above how Haydn apologized for reusing a theme in a different piece.) The Quartet in d, K. 173, begins with the same descent, written the same way, with appoggiatura quick notes. The Menuetto is also in minor and begins with the same tones in descent, now as a half note followed by four sixteenth notes. This beginning is identical with the Menuetto in Haydn's Quartet in d from Op. 9. Mozart's fugal finale is on a theme featuring a long chromatic descent. The fugal finale of Haydn's Quartet in C from Op. 20 showed how delightfully a chromatic theme could work; Mozart's effort is learned and plodding.

Leopold Mozart remained intent on selling his son's quartets and other pieces even as late as the time of *Idomeneo*. He wrote Breitkopf from Munich on 12 February 1781 in rather hurt tones proffering "Synfonien, Clavier Sonaten, quarteten, Trios etc." Breitkopf sketched a reply on the back of the same letter saying he would be interested in unpublished keyboard sonatas,[2] but nothing came of this either. While still in Vienna, Leopold must have consigned K. 168–173 to a copyist's shop, because they appear in the famous thematic catalogue known as the *Quartbuch*.[3]

SYMPHONIES

LINGERING in Mozart's ears when he returned from Italy in early 1773 were the brilliant and sonorous strains of his *Lucio Silla* and the main carnival opera for Milan, Paisiello's *Sisman nel Mogul*. Italian overture character colors to a greater or lesser degree all four of the symphonies Mozart wrote in Salzburg from March to May during that spring of 1773. They are all in three

[2] Richard Schaal, "Ein angeblich verschollener Brief von Leopold Mozart," *Acta Mozartiana* 26 (1979): 50–51.
[3] Brown, "Haydn and Mozart's 1773 Stay in Vienna," p. 222.

movements, and all but one show the typically Italian use of transitions from movement to movement. The symphonies in C and D in this group (Nos. 22 and 23) are particularly showy and lacking in much original content. The Italian overture relied mostly on stock figures and harmonic-rhythmic clichés, in keeping with the speed of composition that was usually imposed, rather than on novel ideas and their working out. We can assume that Mozart at home wrote under no such time constraints; he simply preferred the Italian style for the time being. In this light can be seen his appropriation of an entire *Andantino,* the middle movement of Paisiello's Sinfonia in D (1772), as the *Andante grazioso* of his Divertimento in E♭ for winds, K. 166 (159ᵈ), dated Salzburg, 24 March 1773.[4]

Symphony No. 22 in C (K. 162), written in early 1773, could be called the "rising-triad sinfonia." Its full sonority of oboes, horns, and trumpets, plus the usual strings, clothes a perfunctory quality of invention quite rare with Mozart. All three movements do without repeat signs. The first two employ complementary bifocal closes, a time-saving device, to be sure. As in most Italian overtures, the first movement contains minimal development; a brief excursion via secondary dominants and their resolution suffices, followed by a reprise. The original head motif of rising triad in the bass returns last of all. The third and last movement, *Presto assai* in 6/8, sounds even more banal. Perhaps nowhere else in his works, early or late, does the composer risk the possibly raucous consequences of asking oboes, horns, and trumpets to join the strings in a unison fanfare, swinging up and down the tonic triad in fast jig tempo. Very Italianate is the replacement of development in the middle of this movement by a short passage mostly in thirds and tenths over a dominant pedal.

The Symphony No. 26 in E♭, K. 184 (166ᵃ), completed on 30 March 1773, is close in spirit and time of composition to K. 162. It is another three-movement operatic sinfonia. As in many Italian specimens of the genre, the first movement ends with a transition preparing for the second, and this passage is a high point of the work. The bold opening statement, repeated chords in dotted rhythm on the tonic and then on the supertonic, is taken up a further step to the third degree, G, sounded in unisons and octaves. G then becomes a pedal preparing the *Andante* in c, but not before a very dark passage with bass motion and mostly static trebles is heard—an echo, as it were, from the transition to the tomb scene in Act I of *Lucio Silla* (cf. Example 7.15). The middle movement itself ambles along in 2/4 over a kind of walking bass. It foreshadows the tragic *Andante* of the Piano Concerto in E♭, K. 271, not

---

[4] Paisiello's movement is printed entire in the Kritische Berichte of NMA VII/17/1. Particularly interesting is Mozart's interpolation before, and little extension of the ending.

just in mode and key but in the way the second violins imitate the plaint of the first violins, and also in the manifold sighs of the strings, which derive from the sighs in the opening melody. The finale, a jolly jig, *Allegro* in 3/8, restores E♭ and is directly connected to the previous movement by a short transition in the winds. The effectiveness of the work as an overture is borne out by its use as an actual overture to a tragedy, *Lanassa,* as played by the Böhm theatrical troupe in the 1780s (with incidental music from Mozart's original incidental music to *König Thamos*).

Symphony No. 23 in D, K. 181 (162ᵇ), dated 19 May 1773, begins with the kind of orchestral brilliance needed and expected in a piece inaugurating an evening in the theater. An opening *Allegro spiritoso* in common time raises an orchestral clatter that outdoes even its close relative, Symphony No. 22 in C. The massive chords of the first two measures give way to a run by all the violins from low D up to high D two octaves above. In the *piano* that follows, the basses rise up the triad to the first three quarter-note beats under the tremolo violins and violas. After the cadence on A, there is a dominant pedal of only eight bars before the reprise sets in. This same transition occurs at the end of the movement to lead in the *Andante grazioso* in 3/8 and in G, which finally proceeds without a pause into the *Presto assai* finale in 2/4.

The charmer among this quartet of three-movement works is the Symphony No. 27 in G, K. 199 (162ᵃ), dated April 1773. It begins with the hammer-stroke chords common in overtures but then launches into a singing *Allegro* in 3/4. Mozart's symphonic first movements that are in triple time are often very lyric in character, a quality capped in the Salzburg works by the glorious Symphony No. 33 in B♭, K. 319 of 1779 (which is itself topped in this respect only by the late Symphony No. 39 in E♭, K. 543). K. 199 is in the more normal pattern for Mozart in that there are no linking transitions between its three movements. Repeat signs occur in each movement, as do real developments. The sweetness of the *Andantino grazioso* in 2/4 and in D, not C, resides in the constant parallel thirds, sung at first by the muted violins, then joined an octave above by the flutes (helping to explain the choice of key). This movement too exudes the air of Italy, never again to be breathed by its composer. It suggests summer serenades under open balconies accompanied by plucked strings (translated here into the pizzicati of the lower strings). The fugato that begins the finale, *Presto* in 3/8, is on a four-note theme, G C F♯ G, that refers back to the beginning of the singing *Allegro* in the first movement. The contrapuntal prowess shown here hints at a more serious tone in finales to come.

Symphony No. 24 in B♭, K. 182 (166ᶜ), is dated 3 October 1773 and is the first to be completed after Mozart's return from the summer visit to Vienna.

At first hearing, the work sounds like a reversion to his overture-symphonies of the previous spring. Like the Symphony in G, it contains a serenade-like middle movement, *Andantino grazioso* in 2/4 and in E♭, in which the violins are muted and are joined by two flutes, over bass pizzicati. The third and last movement is an *Allegro* in 3/8 that attempts much less than the fugal finale of K. 199. Rather rudimentary in character, it achieves a burst of orchestral brilliance, then is quickly over, like the symphonic finales of Wagenseil. The first movement, *Allegro spiritoso* in common time, also reveals affinities with Wagenseil, e.g., the inversion of sixths into thirds or thirds into sixths, and the abundance of trills in the opening statement. Wonderfully Mozartean on the other hand are the partially chromatic surges in the violins up to high D.

The veritable symphonic harvest from Mozart's visit to Vienna in the summer of 1773 was gathered in the next four symphonies, which constitute his leave-taking of the genre until the *Paris* Symphony of June 1778. Symphony No. 25 in g, K. 183, is dated 5 October 1773. Symphony No. 28 in C, K. 200 (173ᵉ), is dated the following month (the year was crossed out and replaced by 1774 on the autograph, but the work's stylistic proximity to K. 182 makes 1773 more likely). To the spring of 1774 belong Symphony No. 29 in A, K. 201 (186ᵃ), dated 6 April, and Symphony No. 30 in D, K. 202 (186ᵇ), dated 5 May. All these symphonies are in four movements with minuet as third movement. They share a sense of spaciousness and a depth of expression beyond that in the earlier symphonies. Whether or not Mozart had Joseph Haydn to thank for widening his horizons as a symphonist, it was as Haydn's near equal that he now entered the field.

Mozart's first symphony in the minor mode was written after the flurry of several masterpieces by Haydn that are in the minor mode nearly throughout, quartets as well as symphonies. The case for Mozart's acquaintance with Haydn's quartets has been put. But in addressing the question of Haydn's influence, we should not lose sight of Mozart's own previous creations in minor, particularly in his choral music. For example, in *Betulia liberata*, K. 118 (74ᶜ), a setting of an oratorio by Metastasio commissioned by a prince in Padua and composed in Salzburg in the summer of 1771, Mozart included arias and choruses in minor, to which he fittingly joined an *Overtura* in three movements, all of which are in d. The rocking motion between tonic and third degree and then between second and fourth degrees in the overture's first movement, *Allegro* in common time, anticipates in an uncanny way the final *Allegro* section of the second act finale to *Don Giovanni*, when flames begin to engulf the stage. In the overture to *Betulia* Mozart recasts this motif as the main theme of the concluding *Presto* in 2/4, the fury of which sounds akin to the final orgy of Gluck's *Don Juan*, also in d. Another thing about this overture that anticipates K. 183 is its employment of four horns, two in the tonic and two in the relative major.

The Symphony in g begins with an *Allegro con brio* in common time, the oboes announcing a four-note subject in whole notes, G D E♭ F♯which the upper strings also play in syncopations against the four even quarters of the bass. The use of this kind of "pound-note" subject is certainly central to Haydn's minor-mode works of the late 1760s and early 1770s. Mozart continues with an arpeggio up the tonic triad in the violins at the top of which is a rapid turning figure in which the rest of the orchestra (except the horns) joins. The temper of violence that the composer extracts from repeating this figure is not to be denied; the figure itself occurs twice as a climactic shudder at the very end of Haydn's Symphony No. 52 in c. Mozart ends his first group with V of g, then plunges without further ado into the relative major for the second. So does Haydn in both outer movements of his Symphony No. 39 in g (which uses four horns, similarly disposed).

Confirmation of the second key involves a canonic imitation by the second violins of the firsts at a distance of two measures. This dialogue gives way to a canonic exchange at the distance of one measure between treble and bass. Heard in terms of a chase, the passage sounds as if the pursuers are catching up with the pursued (the stuff of nightmares, this). Canonic dialogue between treble and bass becomes the main event of the development, and the figure Mozart now deploys swings from the tonic down to the fifth below and then up to the third above, 1 5 3. When it occurs in tonic g, we notice a relationship to the main themes of both Minuet and finale. No one can deny that Haydn throughout his long career liked to employ canonic dialogue in development sections. To build up the moment of reprise, Mozart precedes it with an impressive two-measure *crescendo* on a full V⁷ chord sounded by oboes and horns alone. To end the first movement, he repeats the seconda parte, then writes a substantial coda bringing back the first theme. This is hardly new for Mozart, nor is his adding the label "Coda."

Mozart outdid himself in K. 183's lovely *Andante* second movement in 2/4. Its key of E♭ (instead of the relative major, B♭) was a frequent choice for pairing with the key of g in the Viennese school, and not just by Haydn. In the first theme three-note groups of descending thirds in the muted violins overlap with three-note groups in the bassoons an octave below. Overlapping groups of three are as persistent an idea with Mozart as is his favorite contrapuntal motif, 1 2 4 3. It is noteworthy that Mozart's first beginning of the *Andante* in the autograph, which he crossed out, had a different continuation (Figure 8.2). Mozart persisted with the Italian practice of placing the two violins at the top of the score.

FIGURE 8.2. Autograph of the *Andante* from Symphony No. 25 by Mozart.

A Viennese minuet in the minor mode was virtually nonexistent in the mid-eighteenth century, but Haydn opted to include such in his spate of minor-mode works around 1770 and to follow them with finales also in minor, even ending in minor (unlike in his later works). He did allow a few rays of the major mode to shine through in the trios to minuets. Mozart followed his example with his Menuetto in K. 183, a rather gruff piece with powerful *unisoni*, relieved by the major-mode trio for winds only. The finale of K. 183 is an *Allegro* in cut time that, like the first movement, is in sonata form with both parts repeated; to this is appended a short coda, again labeled as such. The movement is of a breathless urgency, ending with a flurry of whirring strings and an emphatic cadence, V - i. Would Mozart have created such a serious work in the minor mode were it not for Haydn's similar works? Probably not.

Symphony No. 28 in C represents the antipode of K. 183. It is as galant as can be. The first measure is the same as Symphony No. 16 in C. Haydn also began a symphony (No. 70 dated 1779) with the same descent through the tonic triad in fast triple meter, |8 5 ⁊ |3 1 ⁊ |. His continuation is powerful and motivic; Mozart's is graceful and frilly, the trills and sixths inverted into tenths that sound quite Wagenseilian. At the same time, there is bone and sinew beneath the trills and other galant mannerisms. The climactic tutti passage after the clear second theme rushes toward a cadence, only to be thwarted by a deceptive resolution to vi and a return to the emphatic open- ing rhythm in the following measure. The development works over the descending figure with trills from the opening, pushing toward and finally arriving at the subdominant, which may explain the absence of the usual subdominant substitution after the beginning of the reprise. Both parts are repeated, followed by a short coda (not so labeled).

The F-major *Andante* in 2/4 is also a sonata form with both parts repeated, again followed by a short coda. The *Menuetto Allegretto* is memorable for its echoes of the violin theme by the horns, stretching four bars to six. Its trio, for strings alone, is in the subdominant and includes a wild outburst of chro- matics, *forte*, after the double bar in the middle, a foreshadowing of the simi- lar outburst at the same spot in Mozart's *Jupiter* Symphony.

The finale is a *Presto* in cut time that has for a theme a conjunct descent from the fifth degree to the tonic, each note ornamented with a trill—an audible revisiting of the first movement's main theme. Against the descent in the first violins the seconds keep up a steady stream of eighth notes. The tutti outburst after this quiet beginning stretches a four-bar phrase to five bars. This too is a big sonata form with both parts repeated, the second part plunging toward the subdominant as in the first movement. At the end Mozart brings back the first theme in a sizable coda, labeled as such. The symphony ends with a frenzy of eighth-note motion, *fortissimo* in the *unisoni* strings, *forte* in the fanfare-playing winds. Here it is Osmin's final exit in *Die Entführung* to a raging orchestral tumult that is foreshadowed.

Symphony No. 29 in A has been justly acclaimed a masterpiece of lyric inspiration. As with its companions, three of its four movements are in sonata form with both parts repeated and with codas then added. The open- ing *Allegro moderato* in cut time begins softly as the first violins offer an octave drop from A, then an upbeat figure of three eighth notes leading to the further elaboration of the tonic note with minor-second appoggiaturas from below. This passage is then repeated in a rising sequence on the second, third, and fourth degrees, whence the melody falls back by step to the tonic. Meanwhile, against these two-measure segments, actually the equivalent of a cantus firmus in double whole notes, the lower strings provide a rich and subtly changing harmonic underpinning moving in half notes. After a linking passage both violins reiterate the theme, *forte,* imitated in canon at the half note by the violas and basses, while the oboes and horns hold a long pedal. Besides the distinctive second theme for strings alone, there are soaring tutti passages and other moments so intensely lyrical as to be unforgettable. This is a good example of the richness in melodic ideas that some of Mozart's contemporaries (including Ditters) found overly generous. The development heads at once for the subdominant, D, and begins elaborating it with rising versus descending scales that will play a role in the finale. In the coda Mozart unveils a third way of treating the main theme, as a triple canon.

The *Andante* in 2/4 begins with the first violins, muted, singing a theme in dotted rhythm, which then passes to the second violins, also muted, to which the firsts add a counterpoint above in more rapid note values. This movement's coda is named as such, unlike the first movement's. In this coda the main theme is begun by the winds alone for two bars, allowing time for the violins to take off their mutes and state the theme *forte,* the firsts in the upper octave, the seconds playing the countersubject below them. The Menuetto begins softly as a little repartee between the two violin sections, sounding a figure in dotted rhythm that will dominate the movement so completely that its near absence in the trio comes as a relief.

The finale is an *Allegro con spirito* in 6/8 that derives its main theme from that of the first movement. The octave drop from A is followed by the same from D—the outer frame of the earlier theme—in between, there is a little run in sixteenth notes of which Mozart will make humorous use. Before the cadences on V he gives the violins a scalar burst downward, then before the double bar with repeat sign he inverts the scale as the violins in unison run up from E to B. To end the symphony Mozart has the violins ascend from A to E, followed by the answering cadence in the bass of E A.

Unlike its predecessor, Symphony No. 30 in D is rarely performed. Its opening *Molto Allegro* in 3/4 begins with a descent down the tonic triad, tutti *forte* in dotted rhythm, with rests on the third beat, like a chaconne, as at the beginning of the Symphony No. 28 in C; but here the second half of the descent is by step with a skip to the leading tone, decorated innocently enough with a trill (Example 8.1). The transition is notable for its overlapping groups of three eighth notes that threaten to disrupt the 3/4 meter and that are repeated to the point of obsessiveness. Preparation for the second

EXAMPLE 8.1. *Mozart, Symphony No. 30, I*

theme ends with a trill on the leading tone to E, sounded by all the strings plus the two oboes, and prolonged from one beat to two. The same trill, at once menacing and amusing, erupts on G♯ and A between the two statements of the second theme. When Mozart protracts the second statement by extending the ending from two to seven measures, we sense he is in a very jocular mood (Haydn was charged with imitating the whimsies of Emanuel Bach for less than this). The cadence with trill for the extended second theme now becomes the signal for the whole orchestra to start emitting trills, one section after another. This veritable contagion has a wonderfully ludicrous effect. Only the horns desist, as do the first violins, who try to impose order and eventually do. The development begins with a new idea, the basses marching up against the descent in the violins. A wind echo after four measures of this is not really an echo but an anticipation of what happens next in the strings. The situation takes a more serious turn with the *forte*, where the basses keep marching up and the violins imitate each other in descents. The reprise follows after a calm passage. To end the movement, Mozart brings back the passage with which the violins, in octaves, began the development. This coda, unlike others in the 1773–74 symphonies, is not preceded by a repeat sign.

As in the previous three symphonies Mozart chooses 2/4 time for the second movement, here an *Andantino con moto* in A for strings alone. It begins with canonic imitations, but after the very galant cadence with triplets in mm. 9–10 the first violins take sole possession of the melody. The movement's gait is suggestive of Haydn.[5] Two elements from the first movement make a prominent comeback in the Minuet: the shortened echo and trills. The trumpets and horns help make this a very formal piece, and we think Mozart's jocularity will not erupt here. But it does. After the double bar in the middle, he lurches into the minor mode with syncopations, and the first violins career wildly from one extreme of their range to the other over diminished-seventh harmonies and their resolution, which are worth quoting (Example 8.2). Was this intended as a parody of the *Sturm und Drang* manner? Perhaps. The trio begins softly and smoothly, a little idyll in G for strings alone, but after the double bar the same convulsions as occurred in the *Minuet* take over, *forte*; the descending progression in the example is outlined by the *unisoni* strings, with the addition of dotted rhythm.

The finale, *Presto* in 2/4, returns to the dotted rhythm combined with the descent through the tonic triad that began the work, but here beginning on the upbeat. This tutti outburst is contrasted with a little connecting passage, *piano*, for the first and second violins alone, in tenths. The continuation

[5] Théodore de Wyzewa and Georges de Saint-Foix, *Wolfgang Amadée Mozart: Sa vie musicale et son oeuvre. Essai de biographie*, 3rd ed., 5 vols. (Bruges, 1958), 2: 141–44. The authors heard Haydn in the Menuetto as well as in this *Andantino*.

EXAMPLE 8.2. *Mozart, Symphony No. 30, III*

involves trills and an ascent by step to D, the high tonic, before the modulation to the dominant begins. The second theme and closing material follow as expected. After the double bar with repeat signs, Mozart pounces on a diminished chord, tutti *fortissimo,* and repeats it for four measures in the same dotted rhythm. The resolution dwells for more than twice as long on the chord of ii, the first violins leading with a little winding figure, *piano.* Next comes the second diminished chord for four measures, *fortissimo,* the progression being the same as that exemplified above from the Minuet. Unlike the Minuet, its resolution is not to I/i but to vi. What occupied five measures in the Minuet is stretched to thirty measures here. After a short modulation we are ready for the reprise, but Mozart makes us wait while he sounds the tone A in dotted rhythm from high to low (the kind of tease for which Haydn was famous). The final joke comes in the coda, after repetition of the seconda parte. It begins with the opening fanfare *fortissimo,* followed by a rest with fermata, and it ends with the soft little winding figure over a tonic pedal, *piano,* a "throwaway" ending that is meaningless unless we perceive that it comes from the beginning of the development.

In these four symphonies of 1773–74, Mozart explored a wide spectrum of emotions from pathos to comedy. He also employed ever more subtle means of connecting the movements within a single work. This skill too may betray his indebtedness to Haydn.

Finalmusik and the Popular Element

THERE were several terms in Austrian-Bohemian use for music performed out-of-doors in celebration of some particular occasion. One of the most frequent was "cassation," derived from "gassatim gehen," meaning to perform while perambulating the streets. As early as the 1619 *Syntagma musicum* of Praetorius the words "Grassaten" and "Gassaten" are found in connection with the idea of serenading. "Serenade," "divertimento," and "notturno" are other terms frequently used interchangeably to describe the same practice. In the generation before Mozart the term "cassation" was used by both Haydns, Ditters, Leopold Hofmann, and Johann Baptist Vanhal.

In Salzburg, by long tradition, the annual event that called for particular celebration was the end of final examinations at the university, which took place during the month of August. Each class organized an evening *Finalmusik* consisting of a march across the Salzach River to the garden of the Mirabell Palace, summer residence of the prince-archbishop, who was then serenaded by various pieces, followed by a return to serenade the professors in the college building. Three early cassations from Mozart's hand survive from the summer of 1769, when the university protocol records under date of 6 August 1769: "Ad noctem musica Ex D. P. Prof. Logices ab adolescentulo lectissimo Wolfg. Mozart" (At night, music from the Herrn Logikern for the professors from the learned adolescent Wolfgang Mozart).[6] The protocol for 8 August reads, "Musica D. D. Physicorum ab eodem adolescente facta." The two pieces in question are thought to be the closely related Cassations in G, K. 63, and in B♭, K. 99 (63ª).

Mozart identified these two pieces and a third, K. 100, as Salzburg cassations by their incipits in a letter to his sister from Bologna of 4 August 1770. Nannerl elicited his response by saying that she believed his serenades were being performed under someone else's name. K. 63 is called in various sources "Divertimento" (autograph, but the title is not in the hand of either Leopold or Wolfgang), "Cassatio" (Lambach Monastery), and "Serenata" (Kremsmünster Monastery)—music of the "learned adolescent" was avidly collected in these Austrian monasteries from early on.

In this type of festive music the performers had to memorize the opening (and closing) March and actually march to it. In his letter of 10–11 June 1778 Leopold paints a picture of an unsuccessful serenade.

> The day after tomorrow is the feast of St. Anthony, and who, in your absence, will make a *Nachtmusik* for the Countess [Antonia Lodron]? Who? La Compagnie des Amateurs, that is who. Count Czernin and Kolb are the two principal violins, playing astounding solos; the composition of the *Allegro* and the *Adagio* is by Hafeneder, the Minuet with three Trios by Czernin, NB all newly composed, the March by Hafeneder, but everything is also bad and stolen—mincemeat to the highest degree ["Hickle Hackle bis in Himmel"] and out of tune—like the

[6] "Logikern" and "Physicis" constituted the advanced or graduating class; the intermediate class included "Rhetor," "Poet," and "Syntaxist," and the beginning class "Grammatiker."

world. NB Cussetti is the hornist; nobles and court councillors alike all participated in the march, but not I, because I am so miserable and have lost my ability
to play from memory. The pitiable rehearsal was held in our house yesterday.

Leopold names some of the main ingredients of this kind of music; the
March, the *Allegro*, the *Adagio*, the Minuet and trio(s), and the concertante
elements, in this case provided by solo violins. Violin solos are frequent in
Wolfgang's serenades, as are minuets with multiple trios, e.g., the Divertimento in D, K. 131, and the *Haffner* Serenade, K. 250 (242^b).

In the Cassation in G, K. 63, Mozart's first surviving piece of this type,
the movements are *Marche* (2/4), *Allegro* (4/4), *Andante* (2/4), Menuet (3/4) and
trio, *Adagio* (4/4), Menuet and trio, and *Finale Allegro assai* (6/8) (all movement
titles are in Leopold's hand). The *Marche* that begins the work is quite
unmarchlike. Its soft beginning and immediate threat of modulation betray
the hand of inexperience. The two Menuets are the most memorable movements. The first is canonic, and the leading part switches from the treble to
the bass in its second part. The *Adagio* in D surrounded by the Menuets is a
florid violin solo accompanied by muted orchestral violins, *divisi* violas, and
lightly supporting bass instruments. A simple rondo scheme, **A B A C A,**
suffices for the finale, after which the opening March would have returned.
In the paired work, the Cassation in B♭, K. 99 (63^a), there is a three-measure
transition at the end of the finale and the indication *Marche da capo*.

Mozart would gradually perfect this type of open-air summer music until
it reached the towering status of his last *Finalmusik* written in Salzburg, the
so-called *Posthorn* Serenade of August 1779 (K. 320). But this was not his last
serenade. The type lived on in *Eine kleine Nachtmusik*, K. 525, dated 10
August 1787, which originally included a Minuet movement before as well
as after its central *Romance* (not *Romanze* as German-language commentators
insist), before this movement was torn out of the autograph. We do not
know who was the honoree in August of 1787, or whether this work too was
meant for Salzburg.

Serenades and serenade-like works during Mozart's Salzburg years were
particularly prone to musical citations of popular songs or dances. The *Posthorn* Serenade itself provides an example, inasmuch as the second trio of its
second Minuet quotes the *alla Posta* melody, familiar from its use in Haydn's
Symphony No. 31 (*Horn Signal*) of 1765. Already in the *Gallimathias musicum*
(K. 32) of 1766, as we have seen, Mozart juxtaposed various melodies or
musical sections with an aim to achieving a comic effect.

Mozart cultivated folklike themes and dances particularly in the finales
of his divertimenti for Salzburg—they often depended on the rousingly popular type of fast contredanse in 2/4 time. A good example is the finale of the

EXAMPLE 8.3. *Mozart, Divertimento for winds, K. 213, IV*

Divertimento in F (K. 213) for two oboes, two horns and two bassoons, dated July 1775 and entitled *Contredanse en Rondeau* (Example 8.3). Slowed down, the melody anticipates Papageno's "Ein Mädchen oder Weibchen" in *Die Zauberflöte*, and not just its beginning but also its ending, with 4 2 5 3 (heard here in mm. 2–4 when interpreted in the key of C, the temporary destination in m. 4). Even without this parallel, the finale of K. 213 is obviously *in Volks-ton*, because of its repeated notes, suggestive of a texted tune, and its limited melodic aspirations beyond the immediate area of the tonic. It matters that Mozart chose a French title for both the refrain and the form of his simple rondo, whereas for the first three movements the usual Italian designations sufficed: *Allegro spiritoso, Andante*, Menuetto and Trio. Joseph Haydn popularized the contredanse finale somewhat later in his symphonies, but Mozart was in this case a pioneer.

In a number of works written in Salzburg during the 1770s, Mozart explored the effect of introducing popular-sounding material near the end of his final movement. In the Divertimento in D, K. 131, from June 1772, he brings the *Molto Allegro* in common time to a properly rounded conclusion, then launches a new idea, an *Allegro assai* in 3/8. This particular work features four horns, and when these instruments get to play the new theme last of all, we realize the work is a tribute to the hunt and to the *cor de chasse*. A parallel is to be observed with Haydn's Symphony No. 31, which also features four horns; they introduce a new tune during the *Presto*, in 3/4, mm. 152–62, just before the return of the fanfare that opened the symphony.

Mozart's predilection for juggling sections in different meters and different tempos in his finales comes to the fore strikingly in the Serenade in D, K. 204 (213ᵃ), written in Salzburg in August 1775 and hence a *Finalmusik*. A contredanse *Andantino* in 2/4 and in **a a' b a'** form begins the last movement. In this scheme **b** is mainly a dominant pedal, with minor-mode inflections. This initial dance is followed by an *Allegro* in 3/8 that presents a proper sonata-form exposition, ending on V, which is resolved by the 2/4 dance on I, like a rondo refrain. The development in *Allegro* 3/8 that follows could also be considered an episode. It is succeeded by the dance, but pared down to **a a' b** with fermata. Withheld is the final **a'**; in its stead is the recapitulation of the *Allegro* in 3/8, shorn of its first eight measures. In a coda the dance is represented in further reduction to only **b a'**. The way the two sections jostle and impinge on each other produces an effect of give and take like that of two characters arguing in a spoken comedy.

The finale with alternating sections in different meters and tempos reaches a high point of finesse in Mozart's last three violin concertos, K. 216, 218, and 219 of 1775. K. 216 in G, the "Concerto with the Strassburger" throws a different light on the whole question of introducing "new" themes in unexpected places in several of Mozart's Salzburg finales. If the tunes were known to his audience, as the "Strassburger" undoubtedly was, the practice points to a special kind of repartee between composer and audience.

EXAMPLE 8.4. *Mozart, Symphony No. 16, IV*

In the coda to the finale of the Symphony No. 16 in C, K. 128, dated Salzburg, May 1772, there is a jolly tune that has not been heard before, played by two horns as well as strings (Example 8.4). One commentator writes of this moment: "When the end of the Finale is nearly reached and Mozart seems already to have shown his hand, he kicks up his heels with a series of hunting-horn calls."[7] This may be so, but the new theme matches no known calls, and the cadential repeated notes could well hint that it was texted. The analogy with card playing ("shown his hand") is apt. In this game the final trump corresponds to *trompes* of the *cor de chasse* kind.

The more usual locus for a quotation in the finale was not the symphony but the divertimentos and serenades written in Salzburg. The Quartet-Divertimento in F, K. 138 (125ᶜ) of 1772, has a simple rondo for a finale, which sounds complete after a neatly symmetrical **A B A C A** form, with **B** being an episode in V and **C** an episode in vi. But along comes a new idea in the guise of a coda (Example 8.5). No theorist of this or later times allowed for the possibility of new material so late in the game, nor does normal practice embrace such a possibility, so calling this a coda goes against the grain. Note the role of repeated notes in this little ditty, which has something of a nursery rhyme naïveté about it. Mozart writes another eight-measure phrase

EXAMPLE 8.5. *Mozart, Quartet Divertimento in F, IV*

[7] Neal Zaslaw, *Mozart's Symphonies: Context, Performance Practice, Reception* (Oxford, 1989), p. 223.

extending the one above, but he ends it with the same repeated note cadence, 3 3 2 2 1, enhancing, if anything, its silliness. After this, **A** returns to end the work. Whether Example 8.5 is a citation of a popular tune or not, its effect is comic. It sounds like something we have heard even the first time we hear it.

EXAMPLE 8.6. *Mozart*, Haffner *Serenade, finale*

The finale of the *Haffner* Serenade, K. 250 (248^b), dated Salzburg, 20 July 1776, contains another example of the familiar-sounding tune in the suspiciously folklike second theme (Example 8.6). Comic it certainly is, with its staccato articulation and ludicrous trills. And Mozart increased the comic effect by doubling the melody of the first violins an octave lower in the first bassoon. Whether this is a quotation or not, the effect is once again a surprising piece of buffoonery saved for the end (in this case the end of the exposition and of the reprise). The occasion for this particular serenade was the wedding-eve celebrations of a Salzburger, Anton Spaeth, and Elizabeth Haffner, the daughter of a former burgomaster. If the tune quoted was local to Salzburg, it would have made the wedding party react with glee. Christian Friedrich Daniel Schubart in his *Ideen* offers an interesting remark on the sense of humor he found in music peculiar to the locality: "The spirit of the Salzburger is attuned to the utmost to low comedy. Their folksongs are so droll and burlesque that one cannot hear them without being reduced to heartbreaking laughter. Commedia dell'arte clowning ["Der Hanswurstgeist"] shines through all, and the melodies are mostly magnificent and inimitably beautiful." He describes in another passage, which we shall quote below, the peculiar manner in which the Salzburgers and Bavarians sang their folksongs.

Another suspiciously folklike tune adorns the finale of the *Serenata notturna*, K. 239, written in Salzburg in January 1776. This is another work in D, and Mozart called its finale a Rondeau. In keeping with this French spelling is the main theme, a very courtly *gavotte gai* in 2/4, marked *Allegretto*. Note the fussy dynamics and galant chromatic inflection of the second degree in m. 2 (Example 8.7ab). Eventually Mozart switches to a more down-to-earth melody in G, *Allegro*. The subdominant is of course a typical choice for an episode in a rondo (or a rondeau, for that matter). But this is no

EXAMPLE 8.7. *Mozart,* Serenata notturno, *finale*

typical rondo episode. It is comic relief after the high-flown rhetoric of the transitional *Adagio* that precedes it and prepares for its key, an *Adagio* replete with dotted rhythms (another French element), minor inflections, and chromaticism. We are prepared for the arrival of a grand seigneur, then in comes a country bumpkin! The *gavotte gai* returns, of course, but so does the blithe country air, in tonic D, preceded this time by a preparatory passage for pizzicato strings, which greatly enhances the *coll'arco* of the country air. The gavotte has the final word in this merry cast of characters, and is followed only by the rousing cadential repetitions with trumpets and drums appropriate to so festive a piece and so festive an occasion. Who was the recipient of this wonderful homage? We know not, but should be looking for someone whose birthday or name day fell in January.

Mozart wrote another Rondeau finale in the orchestral Divertimento in D, K. 251, dated Salzburg, July 1776. This *Allegro assai* in cut time begins with a rather dainty refrain of a Gallic flavor—not a gavotte, because it begins and ends on the downbeat, but related in character. The movement is laid out symmetrically as **A B A C A,** with the dominant being expostulated by **B** and tonic minor by **C.** The last refrain needs only a tonic conclusion to reach its blustery ending. Instead there is a measure of silence, prolonged by a fermata. And then, softly, a new theme enters (Example 8.8). A solo oboe doubles this melody of the first violins an octave higher. On repetition of the second strain, the violins take the higher octave, *forte,* as the oboe partly

EXAMPLE 8.8. *Mozart,* Divertimento, K. 251, *finale*

doubles and partly holds a pedal tone. The movement is concluded by **B,** now in the tonic, and a coda repeating the new theme and the refrain, **A.** There is, following this Rondeau, an added *Marcia alla Francese* (which abounds in dotted rhythm).

Mozart composed two serenades in honor of the name day of Countess Antonia Lodron in June 1776 and June 1777. The first is the Divertimento in F, K. 248 (with its March, K. 247). The second is the Divertimento in B♭, K. 287 (271^b; K^6—271^h). He refers to them in his letter of 2 October 1777 as "die 2 Casationen für die gräfin." K. 287 lacks an opening march, which is unfortunate because the first movement, *Allegro* in 3/4, starts with an immediate lunge to IV that seems to take for granted that the tonic has already been established. An *Andante grazioso con Variazioni* in F and in 2/4 follows, then a Menuetto and Trio in B♭, an *Adagio* in E♭, common time, and another Menuetto and Trio in B♭. What will become the finale begins with an *Andante* in common time, a pleading recitative sung by the first violins to the obbligato accompaniment of the rest. Its pathetic ending in g, followed by the stuttering, repeated-note beginning of the *Allegro molto* in 3/8, makes for the kind of incongruity that would make any listener smile. But the auditors of Mozart's time had further reason to break into laughter. This stuttering tune, prepared with such pathos, was accompanied by a patois text about the farmer's wife having lost her cat: "D'Bäurin hat d'Katz verlorn, weiss nit, wo's is'." The rapidity and vocal agility required to sing this at an *Allegro* tempo brings us back to Schubart, who remarked, "Bavarian singing is distinguished by the unusually rapid use of the tongue, which is equipped to apply a syllable to every note of the fastest run; the droll, burlesque, and low comic is expressed better by no people than by the Bavarians and Salzburgers." After the sonata-rondo form of K. 287's finale has been completed, Mozart brings back the *Andante* and a shortened form of the pathetic recitative, which this time seems to end with a question, a little on the order of Beethoven's "Muss es sein?" The answer, marked *Allegro molto* and leading to a quick and brilliant conclusion, is "D'Bäurin hat d'Katz verlorn."

Haydn also used "D'Bäurin," in a keyboard Fantasia of 1789 (Hob. XVII:4), just as he had used "Acht Sauschneider" in a keyboard Capriccio in 1765 (Hob. XVII:1).[8] There are also citations of theater music in his orchestral music, such as that of Gluck's tobacco song in the first movement of Symphony No. 8. But the practice of quoting folk material is nowhere so widespread in Haydn as it is in Mozart's Salzburg finales.[9]

There is a visual parallel to the savoring of Salzburg's local color in Mozart's music. The album of costume drawings known as the Kuenburg

[8] A. Peter Brown, *Joseph Haydn's Keyboard Music* (Bloomington, Ind., 1986), pp. 221–27.
[9] I argue in "Mozart's Sense for Nature," *19th Century Music* 15 (1991): 107–15, that Einstein erred in claiming that Mozart, unlike Haydn, had little use for the *Volkstümliche*.

FIGURE 8.3. Dancing couple in Salzburg peasant dress from the Kuenberg Collection.

Collection, now in the Museum Carolino Augusteum, Salzburg, preserves nearly a hundred depictions of Salzburgers from every walk of life, dating from between 1782 and 1790.[10] Our illustration shows a couple in *Trachten* dancing a lively folk dance, the woman with her arm around her partner's waist. (Figure 8.3.)

The Keyboard

T H E main keyboard instrument in the Mozart household was a two-manual harpsichord built by Christian Ernst Friederici of Gera in Saxony. Leopold Mozart acquired it at some time around 1760. Of this instrument the young

---

[10] Fredericke Prodinger, "Die Geschichte der Kuenburg-Sammlung," in Fredericke Prodinger and Reinhard R. Heinisch, *Gewand und Stand. Kostüm- und Trachtenbilder der Kuenburg-Sammlung* (Salzburg and Vienna, 1983), pp. 19–22. I am indebted to the kindness of Professor Gerhard Croll of Salzburg University for responding to my request for help by sending both picture and article.

Mozart was particularly fond. In his letter of 10 November 1762 Leopold wrote his landlord, Lorenz Hagenauer: "Wolferl wants me to ask you: how is the clavier doing? He remembers it often, for we have found none such here." Leopold next reports that he is having twenty-two concertos by Wagenseil copied, implying strongly that the concertos were for harpsichord. The instrument remained in Leopold's possession until his death in 1787, after which it was auctioned: "A harpsichord ["Flügl"] by the famous Friederici of Gera. Two keyboards of ebony and ivory, full five-octave compass, with special lute and buff stops ["Kornet und Lautenzug""]."[11] When Burney's correspondent Louis de Visme visited the Mozarts in November 1772, he heard Mozart "and his sister play duets on the same harpsichord."

The instrument was presumably Friederici's, and the date corresponds with the four-hand Sonata in D, K. 381 (123ᵃ), which resembles Mozart's stunning Italianate symphonies of the same year. The sonata is in three movements: an *Allegro* that begins with a massive chord, then continues with a running passage in unisons and octaves; a tender *Andante* in G and in 3/4; and a fiery *Allegro molto* in D that also begins chordally, alternating with sixths and thirds in triplets. There are dynamic markings here and there, but nothing that could not be carried out by the strategic use of a two-manual harpsichord.

Mozart wrote an even finer four-hand Sonata in B♭ for the same instrument in late 1773 or early 1774, K. 358 (186ᶜ). It begins with an *Allegro* in common time. After a four-octave unison opening, there are soft descending 6/3 chords interspersed with *forte* outbursts, but again nothing unmanageable on the harpsichord. The *Adagio* in E♭ and in 3/4 incorporates the opening of the last Milanese string quartet, K. 160 in E♭ of early 1773, but treats it differently, as might be expected from the change to *Adagio* from *Allegro*. The *Molto Presto* finale in 2/4 is as Italianate as the *Adagio*, beginning with a melody in parallel thirds, doubled an octave below and accompanied by oom-pa-pa-pa. This theme returns, harmonized by a secondary dominant (V/c), to begin the development. The movement ends with a coda, so labeled, as did the *Adagio*.

Mozart composed no more four-hand pieces specifically for himself and Nannerl to play, or at least none survives. But they may well have been able to improvise pseudo-symphonies of the kind at the keyboard. Certainly Mozart could (as the case of K. 309 will demonstrate). Their playing together at the harpsichord remained a special treat in local circles. The Salzburg official and Mozart family friend Johann Baptist Schiedenhofen recorded in his diary a gala concert in the "Tanzmeister-Saal" on the feast of the Assumption

[11] Richard Maunder, "Mozart's Keyboard Instruments," *Early Music* 20 (1992): 207–19; 210.

BVM, 15 August 1777. Josepha Duschek sang, Herr Colb played a violin concerto, and "Mr et Mselle Mozart spielten mitsam auf einen Clavecin."[12]

Leopold Mozart possessed a large clavichord, which may also have been built by Friederici. In addition to this he bought a small traveling clavichord from Stein when the family passed through Augsburg in 1763. In his letter of 3 October 1778 Mozart requested that a clavichord be placed in his room next to his writing table.

Keyboard pieces, probably sonatas, figured in Leopold's plan to get his son's work published, proposed to Breitkopf in Leipzig by letter of 7 February 1772 (see p. 558). In fact the first genre mentioned in the letter is "Klaviersachen." Perhaps Mozart had written a set of pieces by this time, or was about to do so. In his letter of 21 December 1774 from Munich to his wife, Leopold wrote, "Nannerl can bring the sonatas and variations written by Wolfgang and other sonatas, for sonatas do not take much space." It has been argued that the passage refers to a lost earlier set of sonatas, and that the first surviving sonatas, a set of six, K. 279–284, were written in Munich in early 1775.[13] K. 284, the *Dürnitz* Sonata, at least, is known to have been written in Munich while the Mozarts were there through early March 1775. Mozart inscribed the six sonatas with numerals from I to VI, and they appear from his autograph to have been written out at one time. They could well have been composed earlier, of course. They formed a set obviously compiled with an eye toward publication. But in Paris in the summer of 1778 Mozart was still looking for a publisher. He wrote in his letter of 11 September 1778 that he wished to sell three concertos to the man who had engraved his Duo Sonatas, K. 301–306, "and, if possible, also my six difficult sonatas," by which he meant K. 279–284.

The liberal sprinkling of dynamic markings in the autograph of the Munich sonatas indicates that they were written for fortepiano. Pertinent here is the information that Mozart made an impression on the fortepiano when in Munich. Schubart reports in his *Deutsche Chronik* of April 1775, "Last winter in Munich I heard two of the great keyboard players, Mr. Mozart and Capt. von Beecke; my host, Mr. Albert . . . has an excellent Fortepiano in his house. There I heard these two giants wrestle at the Klavier."[14] This is the first documentary evidence we have of Mozart playing the fortepiano. The instrument was still relatively unknown in Salzburg, and would remain so until near the end of the decade. But we saw above in connection with the portrait of Marie Antoinette at the fortepiano (Plate III), dating from 1769 or early 1770, that the instrument was not so rare in Vienna as had previously been assumed.

[12] *Mozart: Die Dokumente seines Lebens,* ed. Otto Erich Deutsch, 15 August 1777.
[13] Wolfgang Plath, "Zur Datierung der Klaviersonaten KV 279–284," *Acta Mozartiana* 21 (1974): 26–30.
[14] Maunder, "Mozart's Keyboard Instruments," p. 214.

THE SONATAS OF 1774–75

REFERENCES by the Mozarts in their correspondence to K. 279–284 as "the difficult sonatas" ("Die Schweren Sonaten") might be used to strengthen the case for the existence of an earlier set that was not so "difficult." In terms of keyboard technique, these sonatas, with the exception of the quite demanding set of variations that closes the *Dürnitz* Sonata, are only slightly more demanding than Haydn's keyboard sonatas of 1773, and this is because Mozart often calls for rapid hand displacements and rapid dynamic changes. The set is organized somewhat like the Viennese string quartets in 1773, as a series of tonalities related intervalically, up to a point: C, F, B♭, E♭, G, D.

The first Sonata, K. 279 in C, is the least interesting. It is filled with minute changes of articulation and dynamics that seem to belie the opening movement *Allegro* in common time with mostly sixteenth-note motion. These dynamic changes better suit the second movement, *Andante* in 3/4 and in F. Not all of them are readily explicable, and the music would be almost as viable without them. Also odd is Mozart's occasional disregard of the sustaining power of the instrument. Not even a modern piano can sustain the long D in the middle voice at m. 9 of the *Andante.* The harpsichord, with its greater clarity, has the best chance of projecting such part writing. In the course of the *Andante* all twelve tones are used. The finale, an *Allegro* in 2/4, has a first theme in common with the opening of Joseph Steffan's Op. 1 No. 2 Sonata. This movement is in sonata form with both parts repeated, like the other two.

The second Sonata, K. 280 in F, opens with an *Allegro assai* in 3/4 that is of the singing *Allegro* type, which almost guarantees a more inspired Mozart than the sixteenth-note filigree cum Alberti bass of K. 279's first movement. The chord of F struck four times, with which the movement begins, also ends the finale. A simple construction, the complementary bifocal close, serves this movement well, and particularly deft is the three-bar retransition into the reprise. Haydn, in the Sonata in F of his 1773 set (Hob. XVI:23), kept all three movements on the same tonic, offering an *Adagio* in f and in 6/8 as his middle movement. Mozart does the same here, which can hardly be coincidental. Haydn's *Adagio,* moreover, begins with the same siciliana idea, with an ornamented fifth degree moving to the sixth and back (Example 8.9ab). This is likely a case of Mozart's acknowledging, with admiration, Haydn's sonata of a year or so earlier, then showing how different an *Adagio* he could make out of the same beginning.

Haydn liked sextuplet accompaniments, and it must be admitted that they suit the left hand admirably well. In the example below, his phrase takes up a standard four bars. No dynamic markings appear anywhere in

EXAMPLE 8.9.

a. Haydn, Sonata in F (Hob. XVI:23), II

b. Mozart, Sonata in F, K. 280, II

Haydn's set of sonatas, and none are needed because he uses texture to swell or diminish the sound; for example, the thinning out to a single line and finally a single tone at the end of the example. Mozart begins his *Adagio* movement with a thinner sound, then introduces an enriching middle-voice imitation in the second measure. Beginnings were always *forte* unless otherwise marked in the eighteenth century, and the rule, formulated for ensemble music, also applies here. The *piano* of the third measure, which brings an imitation in the bass, serves a dramatic purpose: it enhances the *forte* outburst of the following deceptive cadence, which brings the main rhythmic motif in both halves of the measure. To drive the message home, Mozart repeats the *forte* move to VI, then sinks into the cadence, but not gently, because he marks the last eighth-note chord and its resolution *forte*. After the pause he continues, without transition, in A♭, as does Haydn. The finales of both composers' sonatas are delightful *Presto*s, Mozart's in 3/8, Haydn's in

2/4; at the beginning of the seconda parte after the repeat sign, both resort to V of g and its resolution.

The Sonata in B♭, K. 281, begins with a trill and a winding sextuplet figure that approaches the kind of melodic figure for right hand Haydn liked to use in his keyboard writing. Following the opening *Allegro* in common time is a tender *Andante amoroso* in E♭ and in 3/8, whose theme drifts down in thirds in the right hand, with a *crescendo,* reaching *forte* when the bass joins in with octaves and then expanding outward to the cadence while making a *decrescendo.* Some of the dynamic effects in these sonatas can be managed to an extent on a two-manual harpsichord, or faked on a single-manual one, but this passage is guaranteed to defeat all attempts on anything but a hammer-type instrument, upon which it is indeed "difficult." For the finale Mozart writes a Rondeau (in cut time), the only one in the set.

The fourth Sonata, K. 282 in E♭, begins with an *Adagio* in common time.[15] A Menuetto I and Menuetto II follow, terms used in the early accompanied sonatas written in London, K. 10–15. The old-fashioned nomenclature for the second minuet may confirm the retrospective cast, or the term may just be used instead of "Trio" because of the dance's length and independence. An *Allegro* in 2/4 and in sonata form concludes the sonata.

The gem of the set is the Sonata in G, K. 283, which opens with another singing *Allegro* in 3/4. The transition passage after the cadence has a "Turkish" character, with running sixteenth notes in the right hand supported by octave eighth notes in the bass. A very similar connecting passage will figure in the first of the duo sonatas with violin, K. 301 in G. The *Andante* in C and in common time is simplicity itself, with a regular antecedent and consequent as main theme, a transition of equal length, and a second theme likewise. Breaking the symmetry, Mozart chooses to repeat and extend its second half, beginning with an elision. After a statement of the main theme on ii, there is a masterly and very brief retransition to the reprise. The way Mozart changes the moving voice in the texture from one part to another (from the tenor in m. 17 to the alto in m. 18) is Haydn-like. The *Andante* ends with a beautiful coda in which the main theme is reharmonized, beginning with a secondary dominant. The *Presto* finale in 3/8 begins with thirds in the right hand over repeated bass notes, sounding like an Italian overture, but the soft second theme features winding parts over a pedal that turn into four parts sounding like a string quartet.

Mozart made the Sonata in D, K. 284, written for Baron Dürnitz, the most grandiose of the set. The first movement, *Allegro* in common time,

---

[15] See Malcolm Bilson, "Execution and Expression in the Sonata in E flat, K. 282," *Early Music* 20 (1992): 237–43.

begins with an arpeggiated tonic chord followed by a unison passage that would serve equally well for launching a symphony. The simulation of violin tremolo passages in sixteenth notes over a striding bass in quarters is also orchestral. In the original, less extended, and less brilliant version of the movement, which Mozart broke off writing in m. 71, there was only a single bar of this texture, leading to the cadence on the dominant.[16] A *Rondeau en polonaise* in 3/4 and in A (with the typical cadential rhythm of the dance) furnishes the middle movement. Twelve variations on a *Thema Andante* in cut time constitute the long finale.

In August 1776 Mozart wrote the Divertimento in B♭ for Klavier, violin, and cello, K. 254. The autograph is lost, but abundant dynamic markings in the early Parisian print by Mme. Heina indicate that the intended instrument was the fortepiano. The work is in three movements: *Allegro assai* in 3/4; *Adagio* in E♭ and in common time; and Rondeau, *Tempo di Menuetto*. Much of the writing is conceived in terms of a duet between violin and piano, and in this sense K. 254 is a forerunner of the duo sonatas with violin of 1778. Occasionally the cello gets to do more than just double the left hand of the keyboard part, so that the work is also a forerunner of the great piano trios of the 1780s. By the mid-1770s Mozart had explored most of the chamber music genres of his last decade: string quartets, string quintets, piano trios, and duo and solo sonatas.

THREE SOLO SONATAS FROM 1777–78

IN HIS letter of 17 October 1777 from Augsburg, Mozart wrote: "I must begin at once with Stein's fortepianos. Before I saw something of Stein's work, my favorite clavier was Späth's. Now I give the preference to Stein's because they damp much better than the Regensburg instruments." Franz Jacob Späth was a famous builder of organs, harpsichords, fortepianos, and tangent pianos in Regensburg (in partnership with his son-in-law C. F. Schmahl after 1774). The question has been raised as to whether Mozart's statement might concern the tangent piano, but it is clear from the context that he was comparing fortepianos.

In his letter of 23–25 October 1777 Mozart reported on a concert in which he played the *Dürnitz* Sonata, and then "a magnificent Sonata in C that popped into my head all of a sudden, followed by a concluding Rondeau."

---

[16] For an analysis of Mozart's revision of the movement, with facsimiles of the autograph and transcriptions, see László Somfai, "Mozart's First Thoughts: The Two Versions of the Sonata in D, K. 284," *Early Music* 19 (1991): 601–13.

This improvised sonata is thought to represent the origins of the Sonata in C, K. 309 (284ᵇ), written in Mannheim the following month. The opening *Allegro con spirito* in common time begins with a broad triadic gesture in half notes, *forte* in octaves, answered by soft, flowing eighth and quarter notes. The passage sounds orchestrally inspired, and offers a foretaste of the magnificent *forte* and *piano* dialogue that will begin the *Jupiter* Symphony. Another orchestral work in C by Mozart forms an even closer parallel to this sonata—the overture to the comedy *Der Schauspieldirektor*, K. 486 of early 1786. Mozart begins his *Ouverture*, marked *Presto*, with the same triadic motif in long notes, from the tonic down to the fifth and then up to the third, with a fall by step to the tonic. The parallel nature of these two movements is most obvious in their mighty development sections, which begin by putting the main motif through its paces in the minor dominant, g, followed by the same on d, then on a, and then descending to g (the overture continues the descent to F). In terms of compositional strategy, the sonata's *Allegro con spirito* offers nothing less than a sketch for the orchestral *Presto*.

The lovely *Andante un poco adagio* of K. 309, in F and in 3/4, contains elaborate dynamic markings. There is quite a lot about this movement in the correspondence. On 14 November 1778 Mozart wrote that he was teaching the sonata to Rosa Cannabich, daughter of the famed leader of the Mannheim orchestra, for whom he wrote it: "We finished with the first *Allegro* today; the *Andante* will give us the most trouble because it is full of expression and must be played accurately, with the right taste, *forte* and *piano*, as it is written." Furthermore he considered the *Andante* to be a portrait of the young lady: "I made it entirely after the *Caractère* of Mlle. Cannabich" (letter of 6 December 1777). The main idea of the *Andante* returns several times, in ever more elaborately varied guises; there is a contrasting section in the dominant, which also returns in varied form, and a short coda. Nannerl particularly appreciated this movement, of which she wrote, "It requires full attention and neatness, and one can sense that you wrote it in Mannheim" (letter of 8 December).

Nannerl's remark presumably bears upon the dynamic nuances. But this raises an interesting question. On which instrument did she play it? The clavichord? In his letter of 26 January 1778 Leopold reported that Nannerl was attracting the widest notice in Salzburg by playing the sonata, which would seem to exclude so private an instrument as the clavichord. This comment could be seen as evidence that the Mozarts were using a fortepiano before 1780, when Nannerl and Wolfgang were painted by Johann Nepomuk della Croce seated with hands crossed at the same fortepiano. By 1778 the keyboard situation was changing even in Salzburg. In his letter of 2 November 1777 Leopold wrote that Countess Schönborn, sister of Archbishop Colloredo, had ordered a fortepiano from Stein at a cost of 700 gulden.

How common the fortepiano was in Salzburg and Vienna during the 1770s has been a subject of much debate. But a comment made by Mozart's mother in her letter of 28 December 1777 from Mannheim indicates that the instrument was rare in Salzburg: "Wolfgang is highly treasured everywhere, and indeed he plays very differently from when he was in Salzburg, because here fortepianos are found everywhere, and he treats this instrument so incomparably, that people have never heard the like" ("er spillet aber vill anderst als zu Salsburg dan hier sind überall piano forte").[17]

The Sonata in D, K. 311 (284ᶜ), also written in Mannheim in the fall of 1777, is even more brilliant and more beholden to its place of composition, as may be heard in the reverse recapitulation of the first movement, *Allegro con spirito* in common time. Among the charming things about this movement are the soft lyrical passages that make up the quite chromatic second theme and the closing theme, which by contrast is diatonic. The little sighing figure in eighth notes slurred in pairs with which Mozart closes the first part is given a primordial role in the development, although it seemed the least prominent candidate of all. In one passage the figure appears in the left hand against the right hand's simulation of string tremolo in sixteenth notes, a link with K. 309. Tonic D first returns with the second theme, followed by the closing theme and only then by the proudly ostentatious first theme, with its runs up to high D (for which the Mannheim orchestra was so famous). A big deceptive cadence to vi allows Mozart to close the movement softly, with the sighing figure in sixths.

The *Andante con espressione* that follows is less mannered and delicate than the *Andante* of K. 309 but no less effective. In 2/4 and in G, it is nearly a constant song for the treble from beginning to end, the exception being the passage where the treble takes to trilling on the fifth and the left hand plays the main motif. Mozart opts for a sonata form without development here and then appends the entire main theme, slightly varied. K. 309 ended with a *Rondeau Allegretto grazioso* in 2/4; K. 311 ends with a *Rondeau Allegro* in 6/8. The movement begins *piano,* and the *forte* retort, rising up to the decorated fifth, 3 4 5, recalls the opening of the first movement. The key of D in conjunction with 6/8 suggests the hunt and the repertory of hunting calls that went with it. Before the second return of the rondo theme, Mozart includes an *Eingang* with three tempos, *Andante, Presto,* and *Adagio.* The entire movement stretches to an imposing 269 measures.

---

[17] Emily Anderson changes the thrust of this statement somewhat by translating, "he plays quite differently from what he used to do in Salzburg—for there are pianofortes here."

At first acquaintance the Sonata in a, K. 310 (300^d), composed in Paris in the late spring or summer of 1778, sounds quite different from the two showy sonatas written in Mannheim. (The three were published together at Paris by Mme. Heina.) K. 310 was Mozart's first solo sonata in the minor mode. The fact that it is in minor should hardly surprise us, since he had used the minor mode frequently in his operas and church music, had already written a quartet and symphony in minor, and was in the process of elevating the solo sonata to a genre no less serious and substantial. The first movement is not just *Allegro* but *Allegro maestoso*, in common time. Its beginning in the dotted rhythms of a march engenders everything that follows: the stream of unbroken sixteenth notes (avoiding the dotted rhythm) that constitutes the second theme and the closing section in which the dotted figure returns, led off by the trilled figure in imitation between the two trebles.[18] Mozart lays the development out in large symmetrical blocks, beginning with the main theme in C. A circle of fifths progression allots four bars each to the chords on B, E, and A, and when D arrives to complete the sequence, there begins a gradual descent in the bass, down to a pedal E. After the reprise has begun, Mozart repeats the main theme not in the treble but in the bass, with tremolo sixteenth notes forming a chain of resolving suspensions in the right hand, exactly as in the development of the first movement of K. 311.

The next movement is marked *Andante cantabile con espressione.* It is in 3/4 and its key is not the relative major, C, but F. In retrospect, F was the first tonal destination of the first movement. The relationship between a and F is the same Mozart would choose to depict Osmin's rage in *Die Entführung,* and the steady stream of sixteenth notes in the secondary and closing theme areas of the *Allegro maestoso*, especially when in the key of a, do sound rather "Turkish." The *Andante*'s development section reaches a climax in a descending sequence with trilled dotted figures reminiscent of the first movement in the left hand, against tremolo triplet sixteenth notes in a chain of suspensions in the right hand, also reminiscent of the *Allegro*.[19] The precadential chromatic surge with *crescendo* close to the end is the direct ancestor to the orchestral surges Mozart would soon write before Nos. 4 and 24 in *Idomeneo*.

Like the first movement, the finale is above all a study in rhythm, a *perpetuum mobile, Presto* in 2/4, in which the constant eighth-note motion

[18] Saint-Foix heard the piece as a kind of concerto without orchestra, and his point is reinforced by the way this passage anticipates the development in the first movement of the Piano Concerto in A, K. 488.

[19] There is a close parallel to this passage in the movement by Johann Schobert that Mozart arranged as the *Andante* of K. 39, mm. 62–66.

(equivalent in actual speed to the sixteenth notes in the *Allegro maestoso*) stops only for the cadences, and not for all of those. The main theme is beset by a dotted-quarter-note-plus-eighth-note rhythm that prevails throughout, even in the trio-like episode in A over a pedal in the middle of the piece, which is the work's most French-sounding moment. Unusual for Mozart, the movement comes close to being monothematic, with the main theme being pressed into service for all the usual functions and some highly unusual ones as well, such as its appearance in the relative, but in c rather than C, and played *pianissimo,* increasing its eerie quality. The essential unity of this sonata, which every listener can sense, has a lot to do with rhythm and with the dissonance created by combining tonic and dominant harmony in the second measure of the opening movement. Mozart transforms the melodic movement down to A and the G♯ below it into the main idea of the *Presto.*

THE DUO SONATAS WITH VIOLIN

MOZART'S determination to publish a set of six sonatas at last bore fruit with the six duo sonatas with violin he began composing in Mannheim in February in 1778 and finished in Paris the following summer. Sieber engraved them in Paris under the title *Six Sonates Pour Clavecin Ou Forté Piano Avec Accompagnement D'un Violon Dediés A Son Altesse Serenissime Electorale Madame L'Electrisse Palatine par Wolfgang Amadeo Mozart fils.* Mozart presented a copy in person to the dedicatee on his return trip home, when stopping in Munich. It was in Munich in the fall of 1777 on the way to Mannheim and Paris that he became acquainted with the six duets by Joseph Schuster that served as a stimulation. In his letter of 6 October 1777 he wrote: "I am sending my sister 6 Duetti à Clavicembalo e Violino by Schuster, which I have played often here. They are not bad. If I remain here I will also write 6 in this taste, as they please very much here. I am sending them so you can amuse yourselves together." The duets by Schuster did reach Salzburg, and Leopold and Nannerl did amuse themselves and others by playing them.

Although Mozart (or Sieber) retained the older formulation "with the accompaniment of a violin" in the title (which accurately described his first sonatas printed in Paris over a decade earlier), the point of the 1778 set is a nearly equal partnership between the keyboard and the indispensable violin. The popularity of Schuster's duets may have jogged Mozart into action, but it should be recalled that a year earlier he had written the pathbreaking

Divertimento in B♭, K. 254, which is really a duo sonata with violin masquer-ading as a trio. The inclusion of the harpsichord in first place on the title page was more than just a selling point; Mozart was less demanding of dynamic nuance from the keyboard in the duets than he was in the two solo sonatas written in Mannheim. He aimed to please a wide public, and this can be seen as well from the two-movement format he adopted, reminiscent of many symphonies concertantes. The keys of the six sonatas are G, E♭, C, e, A, and D. Only in the last does Mozart expand to three movements, with a middle slow movement in the subdominant.

The Sonata in G, K. 301 (293ª), which opens the set, well exemplifies it. The *Allegro con spirito* in common time offers an excellent specimen of a sing-ing *Allegro,* and the violin sings first. After this beautiful eight-bar theme, there is a *forte* ritornello in unison, the upbeat pattern of which generates many further passages. The violin and the left hand of the keyboard player sound the ritornello in eighth notes, while the right hand adds sixteenth notes, exactly as in the similar connecting passage in the first movement of the solo Sonata in G, K. 283. That passage led to the dominant, but here Mozart is more expansive. He repeats the first theme, this time giving it to the right hand of the keyboard player, then he deploys another idea in tonic G, a chromatic rising figure over a pedal, before the formal transition begins with an expansion on the upbeat figure from the ritornello. After the second theme proper, there are several closing ideas, the first a long descent in the violin against which the keyboard shows off feats of hand-crossing derring-do, followed by a passage with scalar burst and *crescendos.* When the pedal arrives to signal the end of the prima parte, Mozart reminds us again of the upbeat figure from the ritornello. Just as well, because he launches the development with an inversion of the same, and proceeds to draw every-thing that follows out of this as a consequence. To end the development the ritornello figure marches up the scale from D to its flat seventh, ushering in the reprise, in which the keyboard sings the theme first, followed directly, without connecting ritornello, by the violin doing the same. The rest of the material follows in order, and both parts are to be repeated. The concluding *Allegro* in 3/8 is like a Ländler or yodeling song, with a *minore* trio for the violin to sing in the middle. Even the grimly serious Sonata in e, K. 304 (300ᶜ), ends with a *Tempo di Minuetto.*

With this set of six duets Mozart created the modern violin and piano sonata. Schuster can take credit for stimulating him to do so, but Schuster's duets would be entirely forgotten had Mozart not mentioned them. Besides his six duet sonatas published in 1778, Mozart further enriched the genre with K. 296 in C, dated Mannheim, 11 March 1778, and K. 378 (317ᵈ) in B♭, probably composed just after his return to Salzburg in 1779.

La finta giardiniera and *Il rè pastore*

WOMAN as suffering victim had stirred Mozart to create great music for the part of Giunia in *Lucio Silla*. Not long after, he was given another opportunity to show his empathy with female victims in a libretto of a different kind, the *dramma giocoso La finta giardiniera,* offered him by the Bavarian court. The opera was to be the second of the Munich carnival season of 1775, the main opera being a setting of *Orfeo ed Euridice* (Calzabigi's libretto adapted by Coltellini) composed by Antonio Tozzi, maestro di cappella of the Munich court. Pasquale Anfossi had made the first setting of *La finta giardiniera* for the Roman carnival of 1774. Its success was reported back to Munich by the Bavarian envoy to the papal court, who may have sent a printed libretto along with his dispatch. The anonymous Roman libretto, attributed to Petrosellini, reached Mozart along with the commission, probably in September 1774. Anfossi's setting met with success in several theaters, including the Burgtheater in Vienna. It is an index of the good relations between Archbishop Colloredo and the Bavarian elector, Maximilian III Joseph, that Mozart was selected to compose the libretto afresh. The theater director in charge in Munich was Joseph Anton Graf von Seeau, whose good will toward the Mozarts was essential to the project. On 9 December 1774, soon after arriving in Munich, Mozart and his father paid their respects to Count Seeau.

Giardiniera, as I shall call it, was a *dramma giocoso* in the special sense of this general term, in that its roles were divided into *parti serie, parti buffe,* and *parti di mezzo carattere.* The two protagonists, Il Contino Belfiore and La Marchesa Violante, his betrothed whom he has wounded in a fit of jealous anger and left for dead, belong in the last category. Disguised as Sandrina, a gardener's assistant, Violante has with her a servant, Roberto, disguised as Nardo, a gardener pretending to be her cousin. His is a *parte buffa,* as is that of Don Anchise, Podestà di Lagonero, and his servant, the soubrette Serpetta. The *parti serie* are Arminda, gentildonna Milanese, and her lover, Il Cavalier Ramiro, who is also a soprano, a part sung in Munich by the excellent castrato Tommaso Consoli. No libretto was printed in Munich, and the identity of some singers is conjectural. The principal female role of Sandrina was sung by Rosa Manservisi, Serpetta by Teresa Manservisi (her sister?), and Belfiore by tenor Johann Baptist Walleshauser.[20] The Podestà's role was allotted to the tenor Augustin Prosper Sutor, although a Pantaloon

---

[20] Walleshauser will reappear as Giovanni Valesi when singing the role of the High Priest in Mozart's *Idomeneo* in Munich six years later.

type like this would normally require a bass. Nardo was sung by a bass, either Giovanni Rossi or Giovanni Paris. From their names it can be seen that the cast mixed German and Italian singers.

The story is set in northern Italy, in the fictional town of Lagonero. In the later version as a German Singspiel the town becomes Schwarzsee (there actually is a place with this name high above Zermatt in the Swiss Alps). "Black lake" or "Dark water" (Schwarzsee) well suits the temper of violence that runs through the plot, reaching a climax at the end of the second act when Sandrina is abducted and set down in "a deserted alpine spot with partly ruined aqueducts containing a dark practicable cave" ("Luogo deserto ed alpestra di antichi acquedotti in parte rovinate, fra quali vi è una grotta oscura praticabile"). What an opportunity for the stage designer! Possibly he was the veteran Munich artist Giovanni Paolo Gaspari. His impressive grotto for *Orfeo ed Euridice,* 1773 and 1775 (see Plate V) was in use in the Cuvilliés-theater during the run of Mozart's opera, and perhaps inspired the design of this scene.

Multiple amorous entanglements in *Giardiniera* make its plot rather hard to follow. Serpetta has set her cap for her *padrone,* and has succeeded in attracting the unwanted attentions of Nardo. Belfiore has apparently recovered from the trauma of killing Violante (as he believes). He courts Arminda, with the approval of her uncle, the Podestà, who has eyes only for Sandrina, to the despair of Arminda's faithful Ramiro. The climax of Act I comes as Sandrina recognizes Belfiore and promptly faints, initiating the long buffo finale, by the end of which we and the characters are no wiser than before.

Mozart begins the dramatic exposition in the *Introduzione* with little character sketches for five of the seven characters, set as solos between a chaconne-like refrain, *Allegro moderato* in 3/4. The refrain itself clearly derives its initial treble melody from the concluding *Finale col Coro* of *Lucio Silla*; the composer literally picks up where he left off in the operatic domain. The *Introduzione* also serves in lieu of a fast concluding movement to the *Overtura,* which up to this point has consisted of a bustling *Allegro molto* in common time, in D, and an *Andantino grazioso* in 2/4 and in A. To turn the first two movements into a symphony, Mozart added a finale, K. 121 (207a).

Irony has a strong part to play from the beginning. Together the characters sing "Che lieto giorno" (What a happy day) and other cheerful sentiments. As individuals they express their dismay at their situations, except for the Podestà, whose hopes of making Sandrina his wife are doomed from the start, so he should be dismayed as well. After hearing all their reasons for disquiet, we can only recoil at the falsity of their communal "Che lieto giorno" on its return. The case is a signal demonstration of the insincerity and falsehood so rampant in this libretto. However inept and unpalatable the text, Mozart's music brings each character to life. Even the Podestà, a panjandrum naively wrapped in his own inflated ego, becomes not just risible but sympathetic.

Relative to the great lengths of the arias for the principal singers in *Lucio Silla* (with few exceptions), Mozart scaled the arias in *Giardiniera* back to fairly modest proportions, which was appropriate to the difference in genre, but was also probably due to the abilities of the singers and the great length of the libretto. A comparison between the settings by Anfossi and Mozart with respect to aria forms is instructive.[21] Both gave the *parti serie* arias in ternary form. To the *parti buffe* Anfossi assigned simple binary arias, while Mozart preferred binary arias to which he added a closing section in a different, usually faster tempo, a combination he also gave to the two protagonists, Belfiore and Sandrina. The result is that there are no significant differences overall in length of arias between the three types of role in Mozart's setting.

Few of the aria texts are well situated or have the effect of moving the action forward. Ramiro (No. 2) sings about birds, and the Podestà (No. 3) sings about musical instruments, mentioning flutes, oboes, violas, trumpets, timpani, bassoons, and contrabasses, all of which duly make their mark in this overly long piece. When Nardo sings his first aria (No. 5), it is about beating hammers, one of the clichés specifically ridiculed by Da Ponte in his 1786 poem "The State of the Theater Poet."[22]

Mozart treated the role of Sandrina with special care. She has the most expressive music in the *Introduzione*, where she is characterized by a device that will recur throughout her part: a precadential descent to the tonic interrupted by a leap into the upper octave. The figure sounds again with very poignant affect on the word "tormentar" in her first aria, No. 4. Here she is playing the simpleton, and the aria is correspondingly plain. Even so, the subtlety of the shifting legato articulations in the opening melody hint at an identity more complex (Example 8.10ab). Anfossi used a similar melody.[23]

Belfiore's entrance, No. 6, is another high point in the first act. The key is E♭, which will have associations with him throughout the opera. Here an *Andante maestoso* in 3/4, with dotted rhythms in the strings answered by equal eighths in the winds, projects noble seriousness. But when a staccato sixteenth-note run in the violins skitters down an octave, it is as if mockery

---

[21] Volker Mattern, *Das Dramma giocoso 'La finta giardiniera': Ein Vergleich der Vertonungen von Pasquale Anfossi und Wolfgang Amadeus Mozart* (Laaber, 1989), pp. 531–33.

[22] Daniel Heartz, *Mozart's Operas* (Berkeley, 1990), pp. 99–101 ("Or il batter de'martelli").

[23] Hermann Abert contends that Mozart must have known Anfossi's score because of several similarities to his own: *W. A. Mozart*, 7th ed., 2 vols. (Leipzig, 1956), 1: 386. He does not cite this melody as one of the instances, but if it is one, it demonstrates how much more Mozart did with the same incipit. Volker Mattern does not subscribe to Abert's claims.

EXAMPLE 8.10.

a. Anfossi, La finta giardiniera, *Aria*

Allegro comodo

b. Mozart, La finta giardiniera, *Aria*

Grazioso

were being made of the pompous beginning (cf. the entrance aria of Elvira in *Don Giovanni*, also in E♭, and also with skittering descents in the violins). Belfiore enters in m. 13 singing the praises of Arminda's beauty to a melody that actually anticipates Elvira's "Ah chi mi dice mai." (Cf. also Example 7.16b.) Arminda does not take Belfiore seriously, discerning fickleness and frivolity in his protestations, his extravagant language. But she is nevertheless swayed by the thought of improving her status by becoming a countess. Her ambiguity leads to a not very decisive musical portrait in her aria, No. 7. This is followed by Belfiore's completely comic aria boasting his pedigree to the Podestà, No. 8.[24] Vacillation between the comic and serious defines Belfiore as *mezzo carattere:* he is all emotion and yearning when contemplating the lovely Arminda for the first time; when boasting to the Podestà, he descends to the latter's level.[25]

Before the finale can get under way, we must hear from Serpetta and Nardo. She sings a cavatina about wanting a husband (No. 9a), which he answers to the same music (No. 9b) by proposing himself. Then she sings a very buffa aria about her never-failing success in seducing men (No. 10). Both depart, leaving Sandrina onstage alone. Her soliloquy aria, or rather cavatina, No. 11, about the turtledove ranks, in spite of the textual cliché, as one of the most exquisite and memorable moments in the score, wherein she subtly responds to the melody proposed by the muted first violins over murmuring triplet figures.

There are nine solo vocal numbers before the first finale. Their number might not seem excessive if they were all of such musical interest as the last.

[24] Abert saw the mood swings evident here as a weakness of the libretto, and consequently of Mozart's setting. He did not realize that the incorporation of both the serious and comic was a defining concept behind this type of *dramma giocoso*.

[25] In the Singspiel version No. 8 was switched from Belfiore to the Podestà, an argument supporting Abert's view that he did not use.

But as it is, there are too many, and cuts become necessary.[26] That several cuts are feasible says much about this libretto, in which many arias are poorly motivated. Another dramatic defect pertains to how the stage traffic is handled—there are too many exits and entrances for the individual characters.

The first finale, No. 12, is filled with pathetic expressions, allowing Mozart to deploy devices such as chromatically rising or descending bass lines to good effect. In a span of some 530 measures he traverses several keys in a progression roughly summarized as follows: C - G - e - E♭ - g - D - G - C - G - D - A. His initial movement of tonic to dominant might lead us to expect (because we cannot abjure our knowledge of later Mozart) that there will be a balancing sequence of dominant to tonic concluding the finale. Such is not the case. Once the initial key of C is reached again in the middle, he continues by moving upward by fifths (or downward by fourths). The antepenultimate section in G concludes with a full-blooded and warmly lyrical passage that anticipates the penultimate choral-ensemble section of *Figaro* (Example 8.11ab). This beautiful music for full vocal ensemble has little to do with its anxiety-ridden text. It is followed by a short transition to the next key, D, the bass moving down by thirds as in *Figaro*. That Mozart remembered a particularly felicitous moment in *Giardiniera* over a decade later is a dubious proposition, even though its similar placement close to the end of a multisection finale might be used to argue that, at least in some deeper, nonconscious way, he did. The musical elements making up this moment are simple—a rise of the treble from fifth to sixth degree via half tone, then an ascent two more degrees over the tonic and subdominant chords, descending over the resolution, $I^{6/4}$ - V^7- I. Yet they take on more

EXAMPLE 8.11.

a. Mozart, La finta giardiniera, *finale, Act I*

b. Mozart, Le nozze di Figaro, *finale, Act IV*

[26] The Drottningholm videotape performance from the 1980s suppresses four arias in Act I, Nos. 2, 4, 5, and 8, and four in Act II, Nos. 15, 16, 17, and 18. It restores Ramiro's No. 2 as a substitute for his No. 18 in Act II and transposes Arminda's No. 7 from A down to G.

intense expression here than ever before, and provide considerable musical impetus for the opera immediately following, *Il rè pastore*.

The transitions are among the most genial strokes in this, Mozart's first large-scale buffo finale. To get from e to distant E♭ in the middle, he needs only two bars of *Adagio ma non molto* and a modulation via the pivotal chord on c, briefly touched. The following slow music with syncopations in E♭ provides a background for the astonishment of the Podestà at the refusal of the other characters to explain what is going on. (There is a resonance with later Mozart here too, namely with the first *Adagio* in the Serenade for winds in B♭, K. 361 [370ᵃ].) Most impressive of all, perhaps, is the transition passage leading to the final section in A. Count Belfiore is the last to sing, and he shows how weak he is as a character by being unable to choose between his betrothed, Arminda, and his ex-betrothed, now recognized as Violante/ Sandrina. The harmony underscores his indecision, unable to reach a cadence on A and thwarted in two attempts to do so by deceptive cadences to vi. On the third try A arrives, tutti *forte*, providing at least a tonal resolution. The words speak only of confusion. The key of A is not the expected terminus of this finale, which began in C, at least not by the logic taught us by Mozart's later finales. But it has its own musical logic. Mozart connects it to the beginning of the act, the *Introduzione*, by slipping back into the same pattern of overlapping statements by the orchestra and rejoinders by the vocal ensemble, here *Allegro* in 3/4, there *Allegro moderato* in 3/4. Clever staging could help reinforce the connection. Although the drama has not advanced much beyond the perplexities exposed in the *Introduzione*, at least the false façade of happiness expressed there verbally is shattered and revealed for what it was. The music is cheerfully neutral in both cases.

Act II begins with Arminda's dismissal of Ramiro and then her scornful aria in g sung to Belfiore, an *Allegro agitato* in common time with four horns. Restless eighth-note syncopations in the first violins intensify her fury. The agitated tone of this opening aria will return in the last numbers of the act, after a string of lighter or more galant arias. In No. 14, Nardo, asked by Serpetta to court her, obliges with a wooing aria in A (a key already used often). Belfiore's "Care pupille," No. 15 in F, musically close to Ramiro's aria No. 2 in F, is another wooing aria, sung to his former fiancée, and one of the rare arias in this libretto that has some action built in: she asks him to leave (we learn from what he sings); he agrees to do so if only she will let him kiss her hand, and when he does, it turns out to be the hand of the Podestà, who has been spying on them. Sandrina, still playing the simpleton, tries to placate the Podestà by singing an *aria d'affetto* in A (the same key once again!), No. 16, which ends with his leaving and her asking sympathy from the young ladies in the audience. The Podestà then sings a rather banal patter song in G, *Allegro* in 6/8, expressing bewilderment about the three women who beset him.

Great contrast is achieved by the noble cantilena of the following No. 18, a *Larghetto* in 3/4 and in B♭ for Ramiro, who expresses his undying hope of winning Arminda in an appropriately stylized and old-fashioned minuet. In the recitative that follows, Sandrina admits that she is Violante in order to save Belfiore from a murder charge, but to him she remains cold and duplicitous, setting up a big solo scene for him. Alone onstage, he receives the full treatment of obbligato recitative, the most elaborate in the score up to this point, and what amounts to an *ombra* aria in E♭, an *Adagio* in common time painting a confused mind that is about to snap, giving way to a *Tempo di Menuetto* final section. In the following recitative we learn that Arminda in her fury, with the connivance of Serpetta, is transporting Sandrina to a wild, mountainous spot in the neighborhood and leaving her prey to wild beasts there. Serpetta's aria, No. 20 in G and in 2/4, is a cynical self-defense, one of the low points of the libretto in verbal expression and, not surprisingly, in Mozart, who resorts to an incipit very like No. 16. But his inspiration comes alive at the end of this buffa aria, which is directly linked to the scene of horror that follows, as the stage darkens and G is turned into the dominant of c minor, a magnificent example of an *attacca* transition.

There is no stopping between Sandrina's outburst, "Crudeli, fermate," *Allegro agitato* in common time, No. 21, and the end of the act. She implores her tormentors not to abandon her in this veritable Gehenna. The orchestra underscores her terror with an obsessive ostinato one bar in length, with an accented and dissonant last beat. Just as she seems to free herself from the rhythmic yoke of this terror-stricken ostinato at the cadence in m. 76, it returns to initiate a passage marked *Recitativo*. It will not go away. And her final words in the recitative section explain what part the scenery has to play: "Dovunque il guardo giro, altro non vedo che immagini d'orrore" (Wherever my glance strays, I see nothing but images of horror). Sandrina's cavatina in a, an *Allegro agitato* in 6/8 with muted violins and violas, follows directly. She is all tears, sobbing, and broken words. This too dissolves into obbligato recitative, leading via an *attacca* transition into the finale, No. 23.

The second finale begins with a rising motif in E♭, *forte*: 1 2 3/ 2 3 4 / 6 7 8. The passage recalls the entrance of Belfiore in Act I, aptly so, as he is the first to sing here. This finale is shorter than the one ending Act I and hence more effective. Confusion reigns in the semidarkness onstage, as the characters try to identify one another. Confusion intensifies in the minds of the protagonists as they sing of their increasing delirium, Belfiore imagining that he hears the lyre of Orpheus (eliciting pizzicato strings). "I am Medusa," sings Sandrina, answered by Belfiore's "I am Hercules." The finale ends in c/C, a minor third away from where it began, a move that is not entirely without some tonal strategy on Mozart's part, since he began the first finale in C and ended it in A. Thus the predominating keys have been, to this point, A, c/C, and E♭, forming a tritone that sets up a resolution in Act III of penultimate B♭ and the ultimate overall tonic of D.

Mozart retains the emphasis on c/C and E♭ in Act III, which has only five numbers (he eliminated one aria). In a curious aria and duet, No. 24 in E♭, Nardo fends off the by now completely deluded lovers—Belfiore, who addresses him as Venus, and Sandrina, who proposes marriage to him. He does this by directing their attention to the skies, then escaping; in the duet part they think they see calamitous portents in the sky. The Podestà sings a noisy aria in C with trumpets, *Allegro* in common time (No. 25), in which he tries to placate Arminda and Ramiro, making little sense in the effort. Their quarrel degenerates into another rupture in the following scene, leading to Ramiro's soliloquy and rage aria, an *Allegro agitato* in c, with four horns (No. 26). This is the fourth agitated aria in the minor mode, a heavy dose of stormy and gloomy music that may well have disturbed Munich's quite timid musical establishment, especially when coming from a carnival opera buffa. In his setting Anfossi included no minor-mode pieces at all.

Just as in the third act of *Idomeneo*, E♭ finally gives way to B♭ on the way to D. It happens in the superb obbligato recitative for the lovers in E♭, leading to the love duet in B♭ (No. 27). The scene has changed from a courtyard in the Podestà's palace to a lovely meadow, depicted by the muted upper strings and pizzicato cellos and basses in music that seems to have inspired the *Andante grazioso* of the overture. Sandrina awakens from a sleep and reacts to the beauty of nature painted by the orchestra and literally by the scenery. Some distance from her Belfiore also awakens. At the moment they first catch sight of each other in m. 27, the cellos and basses momentarily abandon their pizzicati and play *coll'arco*. She still resists him and tries to flee (mutes off the strings and a sinister turn in the harmony). The duet proper, *Adagio* in B♭, brings a gradual coming together of the two. By its third tempo, *Allegro*, they are warbling together in gavotte rhythm, singing chains of sixths and tenths and deploying all the other devices familiar from the duet in *Lucio Silla*.

The few remaining loose ends are tied together in the following recitative. Arminda, bowing to the inevitable, accepts Ramiro and begs Sandrina's forgiveness, which is granted. Serpetta agrees to accept Nardo, and the Podestà says he will wait for another Sandrina to come along, whereupon they can all sing happily the short final *Coro* in D, "Viva pur la giardiniera." The chorus seems too short, in fact, to accomplish its mission of closing the long tonal span begun by the overture and *Introduzione*. But this judgment is swayed by hearing how Mozart closes the similar tonal trajectory at the end of *Idomeneo*.

FIGURE 8.4.
The elector's
loge in the
Salvator Theater,
Munich.

Did *Giardiniera* win the success that the Mozarts claimed with the singers and with the public? There are some indications that it did not. Misfor-
tune bedeviled the production, which was first given in the old Salvator
Theater on Friday, 13 January 1775 (Figure 8.4). Because of the crowded
court calendar during carnival, Fridays were the only days allowed for performances of the new opera buffa in January. But the Friday following the
premiere, the 20th, was not possible because it was the anniversary of the
death of the reigning elector's father. Teresa Manservisi became severely ill
and was unable to sing, so there was no performance on 27 January. A sec-

ond, shortened performance was given without her on Thursday, 2 February, not in the Salvator Theater but in the Redoutensaal on the Prannerstrasse. The change of venue must have raised havoc with the scenery, perhaps eliminating some or most of it, and making the complicated story even more difficult to follow. The third and last performance took place on Thursday, 2 March, and on the following Tuesday the Mozarts left Munich for Salzburg. Leopold Mozart, in his irritatingly smug manner, claimed that the opera buffa demolished the serious opera (letter of 30 December 1774) but in fact Tozzi's *Orfeo* was given seven performances.

On 14 December 1774 Leopold wrote that the premiere of the new opera would take place on 29 December. On the 28th he wrote his wife: "The first rehearsal pleased so much that the premiere is postponed to 5 January so that the singers can better learn the music, and when they know it by heart, can act it out better, thus not spoiling the opera, which would have been too hurriedly produced on the 29th." Reading between these lines, we can discern that the singers had not mastered their parts and were perhaps dragging their feet. On 30 December he wrote again confirming the January 5 date and saying that Nannerl should plan to arrive the day before. He was wrong again. On 5 January he wrote that the premiere would take place on 13 January. On 11 January Mozart wrote his mother that the dress rehearsal would take place the next day. The repeated postponements could have come about for a variety of reasons, but the most probable one is that the new opera gave the Munich forces all they could handle, and more.

There is a hint of resistance to the music in the letter Mozart wrote his mother the day after the premiere, at which he claimed that every number had been applauded: "I must of necessity remain here for the next performance, otherwise one would scarcely recognize my opera, for it is very curious here." This may mean that he had difficulty imposing his music on the singers. Perhaps they even tried to substitute some of Anfossi's setting. At the least it indicates that discipline was a problem. Leopold, always inclined to boasting and false hopes in connection with his son, wrote his wife on 11 January: "There is every likelihood that Wolfgang will compose the grand opera here this time next year." Quite the contrary, Mozart received no more invitations from Munich as long as the elector lived. Only after the elector died and was replaced by Carl Theodore, who had witnessed the second performance of *Giardiniera*, did Mozart get another chance in Munich. In his letter of 12 November 1778 from Mannheim to his father, Mozart wrote: "That damned rascal Seeau has been saying here that my opera buffa for Munich was hissed off the stage." The truth probably lies somewhere between the extravagant claims of success made by the Mozarts and the negative statement attributed by Mozart to Seeau.

Il rè pastore belongs together with *La finta giardiniera* not only because Mozart wrote one right after the other. The modest dimensions and restrained virtuosity of most arias in his opera buffa for Munich carried over to his serenata for Salzburg. There was a large seria element in the former, from which the latter could profit. Originally, Metastasio conceived *Il rè pastore* as a regular *dramma per musica* in three acts, albeit of less ambitious scope than his grandest librettos (it has only five characters). Like *Olimpiade* it featured an Arcadian pastoral setting and dealt with the pangs and bliss of young love. These elements bequeathed by the venerable poet could not have come at a more perfect time for Mozart, who was so taken with the poem that he rose to new heights of lyrical inspiration when setting it.

Imperial magnanimity forms the real subject of *Il rè pastore,* which Metastasio wrote at the direct command of Maria Theresa in 1751; Giuseppe Bonno made the first setting. Five years later the empress bore her sixteenth and last child, Archduke Maximilian, on 8 December 1756, a day when the Burgtheater resounded to the strains of Gluck's setting of the libretto. It was clever of Archbishop Colloredo or his advisers to realize that a new setting of the same poem by Mozart would be a perfect choice to enhance the visit of Archduke Maximilian to Salzburg in April 1775. So clever, indeed, that we may suspect Mozart's role in planting enough information with his superiors so that they could take credit for choosing the subject. Another libretto by Metastasio, *Gli orti esperidi* (*azione teatrale* in two acts) was chosen for the maestro di cappella of the Salzburg court, Domenico Fischietti. It was performed for the distinguished guest at court on 21 April, followed a day later by Mozart's opera.

The legacy of Munich in Mozart's new opera is not confined to its music. From Munich came the version of the libretto used, which corresponded to the two-act book set by Pietro Guglielmi for the Bavarian court in 1774, in which Tommaso Consoli sang the prima donna role of Elisa. Consoli was imported from Munich a year later to sing the primo uomo role of Aminta, and it is easy to imagine composer and castrato (he sang Ramiro in *Giardiniera*) conspiring while in Munich to make sure the archbishop "chose" *Il rè pastore.* In his letter of 7 August 1778 Mozart jests about getting Metastasio to write a libretto in which the castrato sings both prima donna and primo uomo, who never meet. The joke is all the more savory because Consoli did just this in successive years in Munich and Salzburg. He must have greatly pleased Mozart, as the music for Ramiro and Aminta suggests. Also imported from Munich was the flautist Johann Baptist Becke, who became a close friend of the Mozarts. The two flutes play an important role in the very first number, "Intendo, amico rio." In the aria No. 9 Mozart wrote concertante parts for them, especially elaborate in the case of the first flute (Becke).

All the roles except Aminta were presumably taken by Salzburg singers. There were three leading candidates for the two female soprano parts: Mme Adlgasser, Maria Anna Braunhofer, and Maria Magdalena Lipp (wife of Michael Haydn), all of whom were aged around thirty at this time. For the tenor parts of Alessandro and Agenore, Franz Anton Spitzeder and Felix Hofstädter stood available.

The story of *Il rè pastore* is relatively simple, which cannot be said of many opera librettos, even those by Metastasio, who took a long while to renounce all Baroque convolutions in plot, if not in language and diction. As the poet himself puts it in the *Argomento:* "Among the most enlightened actions of Alexander of Macedonia was to have liberated the kingdom of Sidon from the tyrant, and then instead of adding it to his dominions, restored to the throne the only son of the legitimate royal family, who, unknown to himself, led a poor and rustic life in the neighboring country-side." Just as Sandrina is discovered eventually to be the noble Violante, so Aminta, the rustic swain, is discovered to be the shepherd king of the opera's title.

From the beginning of the overture (presumably written last, but not necessarily conceived last), Mozart explores new territory. He calls it *Ouvertura,* mixing French and Italian, as in *Ascanio* and *Lucio Silla* (in *Mitridate* it is called *Ouverture*). These earlier overtures all correspond to the three-movement *sinfonia avanti l'opera* and are in the key of D. For *Il rè pastore* Mozart chose C instead of D and broke with precedent also by having only one movement (the little one-movement *Intrada* preceding *Bastien und Bastienne* does not count as an overture). More important still, he announced the tonal *coloris* of the opera by certain traits in its overture, as will be the case with all his operas from here on.

The overture begins with a rise through the tonic triad over three chordal hammer strokes (nothing untraditional here). There follows a long Mannheim *crescendo* that takes the first violins from middle C to high C two octaves above in the course of ten bars, by means of a little slurred figure pairing eighth notes and alternating lower and upper auxiliary tones. After the peak of the *crescendo* has been reached, there is a full bar of subdominant harmony followed by a broadly laid out cadence. Then the same motif returns in the guise of a four-measure phrase, with soft and ever so galant chromatic rises answering the urgent unisons. This can be regarded as the main theme, although it proceeds almost immediately to a transition preparing the dominant, with a flurry of sixteenth-note motion, the second violins answering the first violins an octave below. There is a clear second theme, with prominent dotted rhythm and inverted dotted rhythm, followed eventually by a chromatic rise in both bass (main motif) and treble, the latter pushing up to E above high C over subdominant harmony. Passages like this can be found repeatedly in the vocal numbers of the opera and thus seem to sum up the tone of impassioned *galanterie* that is its essence. Mozart's economy in using the same motif for different purposes could be heard as another of the lessons learned from the recent encounter with Joseph Haydn's music.

The overture ends with the *crescendo* from its beginning. But the final *crescendo* does not reach its goal of high C. Rather, Mozart cuts it off midway by a transition into the first number, giving the exciting impression that there was not a moment to be wasted on something so prosaic as a literal repetition. The opera is full of such surprises.

Aminta projects pastoral simplicity by singing a hauntingly beautiful and seemingly naive little piece in 6/8 as he addresses his friend the babbling brook. More cavatina than aria, it has only one stanza:

Intendo, amico rio,	I hear, friendly stream,
Qual basso mormorio;	That soft murmuring;
Tu chiedi in tua favella,	You are asking in your own way,
Il nostro ben dov'è?	Where is our dear one?
Intendo, amico rio . . .	I hear, friendly stream . . .

The little chromatic rises in paired eighth notes at "Tu chiedi" sound familiar from the overture. Mozart keeps the orchestral introduction to only seven bars, but he manages to include the melodic climax that clothes the last line, a conjunct rise up to the sixth degree, A, with a fall by skip down to the tonic. With this cadence the piece will end, or almost end, because Mozart then brings back the first line with disarming effect (as suggested by Metastasio's text layout). What we thought was a beginning turns out, to our surprise and delight, to be also an ending (another trait that could have been learned from Haydn). Such a perfect wedding of melody and poetry is enough to soften even the most hardened critic.

Elisa appears at once at the beginning of the following recitative, which is of the simple variety, like most all the dialogue (as the poet wished). She calms Aminta's fears about possible dangers to her from marauding soldiers from Alexander's army. Her aria, the first real aria, "Alla selva, al prato, al fonte" (To the wood, the meadow and fountain), treats these pastoral clichés partly in coloratura, lending her a rather flighty character. It is in G and begins with an orchestral introduction of eighteen measures that includes all the main material of the aria. A rise through the tonic triad, in unison, *forte*, inaugurates the aria, a typical seria gesture that parallels the beginning of the overture. The soft answer of the violins in thirds and in gavotte rhythm emphasizes the rise from the fifth to the sixth degree followed by falling motion, proclaiming Elisa's intimate tonal symbiosis with Aminta. There is a chromatic rise already in m. 7, up to high A from G, but the climactic chromatic rise is in the violins toward the end of the ritornello, as they push up to high E over subdominant harmony, exactly as at the similarly climactic rise in the overture. Also similar to the overture is the secondary theme (cf. the overture's closing theme) and the onset of sixteenth-note motion just as the transition to the second key begins. Before the reprise Mozart slows down the motion by giving the voice a recitative-like passage, punctuated by orchestral interjections. A very similar passage occurs just before the reprise of the first movement of the Violin Concerto in G, K. 216.

Aminta's aria in B♭, an *Allegro aperto* in common time, is laid out on a grander scale, with an air of confidence and relaxation that befits the text, "Aer tranquillo e dì sereni" (Tranquil sky and serene days). Its second idea is in gavotte rhythm, inverting sixths into thirds, and recalls the motet *Exultate, jubilate* (K. 158ª). The aria has a contrasting middle section, *Grazioso* in 3/8, for which the text ("if the Fates should change my state") was obviously responsible. Mozart is very much at home in this dignified and Hasse-like minuet movement, which he embellishes with one of his favorite sonorities, a lingering half-diminished-seventh chord, with echo in the oboes prolonged by a fermata. This aria too has several links with the violin concertos Mozart began writing the same spring.

After only minimal recitative, the principal tenor, singing the role of the conqueror, launches into his first aria, one of Metastasio's typical metaphor constructions:

Si spande al sole in faccia	Storm clouds spread over the sun
Nube talor così,	Making dark its face,
E folgora e minaccia	And lightning flashes and threatens
Sul' arido terren,	The arid earth,
Ma poi che in quella foggia	But then in this manner
Assai d'umori unì	Enough humors gather so
Tutti si scioglie in pioggia	That all dissolves in rain
E gli feconda il sen.	And fertilizes the soil.

The aria is in the key of D and includes two trumpets, in keeping with the high estate of Alexander. Mozart delights in painting the fulminations with unison runs in the orchestra. "Minaccia" provides a good excuse for coloratura, which he uses. He just may be painting raindrops as well with his detached sixteenth-note accompanimental figures for the violins in the middle section, which is a modest-sized transition, not an independent movement as in the previous aria.

Alexander having left the stage, the secondary pair of lovers come to the fore. Tamiri, disguised as a shepherdess, is the daughter of the last ruler of

Sidon, who was driven out by Alexander and who killed himself in consequence. She needs the reassurance of her lover, Alexander's companion in
arms Agenore, who provides it in a *Grazioso* in 3/8 time and in the key of G,
accompanied by strings only. Appeased, Tamiri sings of finding peace and
calm in an *Allegro aperto* in common time and in the more warmly expressive
key (especially for Mozart) of E♭, with oboes and horns added to the strings.
These two arias may sound rather ordinary, but they are perfectly suited to
their texts. Mozart bestows upon Tamiri the same chromatic rise up to the
third above the high tonic over subdominant harmony, leading to a I$^{6/4}$ chord
arrived at by chromatic ascent in the bass. Her music tells us that Tamiri as
well as Elisa is a sensitive and passionate lover, and so she will prove to be.

Aminta and Elisa next initiate a long dialogue in simple recitative,
changed by Mozart into obbligato recitative as they come to a new understanding: Aminta will go to Alexander and be recognized as king, but never
at the price of losing her. In the act-ending duet that ensues, Elisa sings first,
urging him to become king, while remaining faithful to her. He overlaps the
end of her solo, taking the music to the dominant with his protestations of
fidelity but quickly and surprisingly returning to the tonic, A. Then they
begin singing together. With this, the *Andante* in 3/4 first section ends, and
an *Allegretto* gavotte theme is proposed by the orchestra. The lovers respond
with a long-held "Ah" over subdominant harmony. Aminta initiates a
phrase that Elisa imitates in canon at the unison, one measure later; then
she in turn initiates triplet coloratura, which he imitates. The exchanges continue, there is another move to the dominant, then a return to the gavotte
theme and the earlier exchanges. As often in his love duets, Mozart saves
until close to the end the delightful procedure of having one voice hold a
pedal while the other embroiders, then reversing the roles. All Mozart's love
duets for two sopranos do this (except in *Mitridate*), and most are in the
same key of A (including the glorious pseudo-love duet for Fiordiligi and
Dorabella in *Così fan tutte*).

The miracle of *Rè pastore* continues to grow in the second act, which
surpasses the first in musical interest and originality. The breakthrough to a
new level of personal warmth and intensity of expression has a lot to do
with the libretto. Arias Nos. 8 and 9 come from Metastasio's second act, set
in Alexander's vast tent. The rest come from the original Act III, which
opened in a cave that finally gave way to the magnificent Temple of Hercules
at Sidon.[27]

Metastasio inspired visual artists as well as musicians, as Figure 8.5
shows. The elegant Paris edition of the poet's works in twelve volumes—a

---

[27] NMA II/5/9, ed. Pierluigi Petrobelli and Wolfgang Rehm (Kassel, 1985), p. ix, argues that the opera
was not staged. I believe it was.

E a te, degno di te, rendo me stesso.

Martini inv.l.Sc.17?

ADRIANO *Atto III. Scena XI.*

FIGURE 8.5. Pietro Antonio Martini. Engraved frontispiece for Metastasio's *Adriano in Siria*, Paris, 1773.

list of subscribers in the last volume includes Archbishop Colloredo—featured the work of several graphic artists of distinction. Pietro Antonio Martini of Parma contributed particularly striking frontispieces. Our example, dated 1773, for *Adriano in Siria*, combines antique costumes with appropriate architectural elements in a way that illuminates the neoclassical ideals of the time.

A greater depth of character is immediately apparent in Elisa's aria opening Act II. She has followed Aminta to the tent of Alexander only to be turned back by Agenore. She bursts forth, after only two bars of orchestral preparation: "Barbaro, oh Dio, mi vedi / Divisi dal mio ben" (Cruel man, oh God, that I should see myself separated from my love). Mozart repeats the second line but eschews the usual galant redict, **a b b'**. Instead he invents a continuous line, woven together from three unequal segments. Joining the first and second segments is a chromatic rise in the oboes, mounting up to the third above the subdominant as in Elisa's first aria, which this piece far surpasses in the subtlety of its thematic construction. The *Andante* part of the aria ends with a return to "Barbaro!" now uttered over an augmented sixth chord, the harmony and dotted rhythm of which is imitated in an orchestral outburst. During the following *Allegro* in common time she pleads for pity from Agenore. Between her lines the violins twitter, and the winds sob on the offbeat. These effects, and the impassioned vocal leaps with which Elisa continues, foreshadow Electra's first aria in *Idomeneo*.

Metastasio's Titus and Alexander are very similar in their unfailing gestures of magnanimity. In his second aria Alexander sings that the day of his true triumph will come when the vanquished are made happy and he leaves behind no enemies, a sentiment that could easily have escaped Titus. Mozart chooses *Allegro moderato* in common time and the key of F to clothe these elevated thoughts. The piece begins with a syncopated idea similar to "Aer tranquillo." Its main attraction is the lovely concertante writing for the two flutes.

"L'amerò, sarò costante," Aminta's declaration of eternal fidelity to Elisa, is also a concertante, and the jewel of the opera. We saw in Chapter 2 how Mozart profited from and triumphed over the Viennese tradition of setting this text (besting his friends Bonno and Gluck—cf. Example 2.8). There is another sense in which this aria is Viennese, and it lies in the combination of English horns with the key of E♭, which have been noted above in connection with both Haydn and Wagenseil.

The aria begins with an eight-bar orchestral introduction. Muted first violins play the theme, doubled an octave above first by the flutes and then by the unmuted *violino principale*, which also bridges over the two halves of the introduction and will join in loving dialogue with the solo voice. Whose solo violin, we may ask, was so tenderly consoling and cajoling in duet with the Aminta of Consoli? Surely it was no one but Mozart himself, whose violin playing reached its peak in 1775–76. If so, the theory of a conspiracy hatched in Munich between the composer and castrato gains in appeal.[28]

[28] For partisans of gender studies, there is the possibility here of what amounts to a same-sex love duet. Notable in the Salzburg videotape of the opera made in 1989 is the spectacle of a pretty young

Mozart designated "L'amerò" with the curious term "Rondeaux" (returns), which was the marking for several finales of his instrumental works as well. The aria is an ample five-part rondo in one tempo, an *Andantino* in 3/4, and would seem to have little in common with the show-stopping two-tempo rondos of his later operas, unless in its crucial placement just before the final series of events leading to the denouement. Mozart lavished such care on this piece as to write out lead-ins for the voice preceding each return of the refrain. Then in m. 115 there is an opportunity for a cadenza, signaled by a fermata and the final cadence, which the voice and solo violin share (ergo, a double cadenza, but it does not survive or was never written out). The final words here are "sarò costante." Mozart sets them by repeating the rise from fifth to sixth degree and fall to the tonic with which he set "sospirerò." This figure is also a reference back to Aminta's first solo in Act I, and demonstrates in a purely musical sense what it means to remain faithful. The orchestra pronounces its blessing on the couple after their cadenza in a murmuring *piano* that dwindles to *pianissimo*, similar to the orchestra's first four-bar phrase, but different in its dynamics, orchestration, and ending.

Tamiri next sings "Se tu di me fai dono" (If you bestow me) to Agenore, conveying her bewilderment that he would resign himself to the will of Alexander and allow her to become the wife of Aminta. Her music is an *Andantino* in 3/4 and in the key of A, with strings alone. It conveys soothing rather than irate qualities and yields nothing to the preceding piece for Aminta in melodic beauty. Every detail is polished and exquisite. Perhaps the most telling comment on Mozart's new sense of maturity here is to be found in the later borrowings he made from this rondo. For example, he used the phrase at the words "perchè la colpa è mia?" (Why is the fault mine?) verbatim in the second love duet for *Idomeneo*, K. 489 of March 1786. And the scalar sweeping of the violins up to the third above the high tonic, to end the rondo, recurs in still later Mozart, the duet in A in *Clemenza di Tito*, with identical function.

Tamiri's gentle reproaches to her lover set up the next aria. After only a few measures of recitative Agenore, alone onstage, bursts into an aria about the torments he suffers at losing her. His aria in c is the work's only minor-mode piece, an *Allegro* in common time. With its driving rhythms and dark sonorities the aria fractures the world of tonal beauty created by Mozart's music up to this point. The syncopated outbursts in the strings after Agenore's first two lines hark back to Sandrina's "Crudeli!" in *Giardiniera*, especially in the use of the dissonant minor-second neighboring tone in the bass

lady playing Aminta looking lovingly at the equally pretty young lady in costume onstage playing the violin solo.

line (this is prominent as well in the main motif of the overture to *Rè pastore*).
The first section ends with an unresolved dominant of c, from which Mozart
plunges to the dominant of the secondary key, E♭. Mozart creates a big middle section out of the second stanza, ending in f, followed by a chromatic
rise in unison leading to the reprise. He greatly abbreviates the reprise by
dropping most of the material from the first key area and recapitulating the
second group in tonic minor. Although this is a big ternary aria that gives
the impression of vast expanse, Mozart keeps it to a mere 126 measures in
length by his careful surgery.

To measure this new concision against the *langer Geschmack* of Salzburg
in earlier days, it suffices to glance at the enormously long arias in Mozart's
setting of Metastasio's *azione teatrale Il sogno di Scipione*, composed in mid-
1771 to celebrate an anniversary of Archbishop Schrattenbach. The work was
shelved upon the archbishop's unexpected demise on 16 December 1771,
and although it was modified so as to celebrate the installation of his successor, Archbishop Colloredo, no performance ensued.

Having shattered the bright world of tonal euphony and major-mode
contentedness with Agenore's aria, Mozart begins to rebuild it directly.
Without any break the key of C steals softly on our ears with the onset of
the following *Allegretto* in common time. Precisely here the stage picture
changes from cave to temple. This is no ritornello to the aria Alexander is
about to sing. Rather, it is scenic music, beginning placidly then building to
a climax, with a melodic trajectory up to high C, as at the beginning of the
overture. The dotted rhythms and fanfares as the climax is reached proclaim
not only the magnificent new stage setting but also accompany the arrival of
Alexander and his retinue onstage.

As Alexander asks the friendly gods who add new shoots to his crown
of laurels to grant wishes dear to his heart, Mozart reverts to a language of
majesty and heroism reminiscent of the first aria for Bernasconi/Aspasia in
Mitridate, which shares the same opening. (Cf. Example 7.14a.) Given the
number of resonances between Mozart's last opera and the second act of *Rè
pastore*, it is hardly surprising that he uses the same imposing gesture to
launch the final number in *Tito*. Alexander's third and last aria contains a
wealth of melodic ideas, and yet it is not long—Mozart brings it to a sonorous and satisfying conclusion in only 113 measures. Its music tells us
already that Alexander will create a new throne, at which news the others
join their voices together acclaiming his greatness and wisdom (chordal singing in recitative is another first for Mozart here).

Alexander then proclaims Aminta shepherd king: "è il rè pastore." For
this final recitative cadence Mozart chooses not C (a key amply represented
and taken leave of in the preceding piece) but D, which gives a tonal lift to

the end of the opera. He also may also have intended the pun on "rè" (= *re* = D). The concluding *Coro* celebrates the choice, hailing both Alexander and the gods above for so happy an outcome (the text is not by Metastasio). Mozart builds here a big rondo structure with recurring tutti refrains surrounding episodes with fewer voices, a technique he had already employed in the concluding five-part rondo *Ciaccona* of *Lucio Silla*, and will use again in the vast *Ciaccona* to end Act I of *Idomeneo*. He also used short chaconnelike ensembles to end *Giardiniera* and *Mitridate*. The final *Coro* of *Rè pastore* is a *Molto Allegro* in common time, and thus not a chaconne. But its key of D is the same as in every other concluding number just mentioned, and represents one of remarkably few bows to Italian tradition in an opera that, throughout, is highly original and personal.

Mozart reached maturity as an operatic composer in *Rè pastore*. Not by coincidence did this artistic leap have immediate consequences in the related genre of the concerto. The five violin concertos of 1775–76 continue the impassioned lyric impulse released by *Rè pastore* and provide an indispensable prelude to the first great keyboard concerto, K. 271 of 1777.

Concerto and Concertante

MOZART began writing concertos in earnest only in 1773, a third of the way through his creative life as a composer. In the early 1760s he was occupied with the harpsichord concertos of Wagenseil, as we saw in Chapter 2. Then after his experiences in the mid-1760s with the Parisian school of expatriate German keyboard players, namely Hermann Friedrich Raupach, Johann Schobert, Johann Gottfried Eckhard, and Leontzi Honauer, he and his father arranged four concertos for harpsichord and orchestra (K. 37, 39, 40, 41) out of several of these composers' accompanied keyboard sonatas. They made the sonata-form or binary movements of the originals into real concerto movements on the tutti-ritornello principle, with double expositions like those in the later concertos.[29]

In Vienna in 1768 Mozart may have tried his hand at writing an original keyboard concerto.[30] For certain he wrote a trumpet concerto at this time,

[29] Edwin J. Simon, "Sonatas into Concertos: A Study of Mozart's First Seven Concertos," *Acta Musicologica* 31 (1959): 170–85.

[30] E. H. Müller von Asow, "Ein ungedrucktes Skizzenblatt Mozarts," *Neues Mozart Jahrbuch* 1 (1941): 174–80. Einstein in K³ suggested that this sketch, forty-six measures in 3/4 and in the key of D, was intended as the slow movement of an unfinished keyboard concerto in G (K. 43ᶜ), but it may well be just another arrangement on young Mozart's part, as its rather tepid north German style suggests.

FIGURE 8.6. Drawing attributed to Johann Zoffany of an orchestra surrounding a harpsichord, 1770s.

but it is lost, and known about only from a mention in Leopold's letter of 12 November 1768. The occasion was the consecration of the Waisenhaus (Orphanage) Church on the Rennweg, for which Mozart wrote the Mass in c/C, K. 139, and an offertory, also lost. Among the boys of this orphanage, who provided the choir and the instrumental forces as well, there was, it seems, a skilled trumpet player who stood out from all the other players. The choice fell upon him as soloist. For models Mozart could have used Michael Haydn's fine two-movement Trumpet Concerto in C of 1762, or Leopold's Trumpet Concerto in D of the same year.

Back in Salzburg after more than a year in Vienna, Mozart showed no further inclinations to write concertos that we know of, although 1769 was a fertile year otherwise. The first Italian trip with Leopold began in December 1769. In Verona on 5 January 1770 he exhibited his phenomenal skills by playing at first sight "un concerto di cembalo." But he was apparently not yet ready to write a harpsichord concerto of his own. Around 1772 he once again became involved with the genre, producing three keyboard concertos with the accompaniment of two violins and bass, arranged from the Op. 5 solo keyboard sonatas by Johann Christian Bach. These three arranged concertos (K. 107, Nos. 1–3) share the same mini-orchestration as his earliest organ sonatas, written about this time for performance during mass in Salzburg Cathedral. The similarity may point to the use of these concertos for the same purpose, although the keyboard writing seems less appropriate to the organ than to the harpsichord.

The intriguing idea of Mozart performing harpsichord concertos during his Italian tours is a subject with possible links to the fine drawing attributed to Johann Zoffany, an artist of Bohemian descent who made his mark in London, then spent most of the 1770s in Italy (Figure 8.6). We can identify the instrument in the middle played by a young man as a harpsichord because of the small curve on the sounding board, indicating a four-foot bridge. In the accompanying orchestra are some twenty players. The care with which the artist has depicted the instruments and the way they are played, also the physiognomies of the players and observers (surely meant to portray real people), do indeed point to Zoffany, who was famous for his lifelike portraits of individuals within large groups.[31]

1773–1777

THE attempts that have been made to place Mozart's first Violin Concerto (K. 207) in the spring of 1773 on the basis of handwriting and paper studies fail to convince on stylistic grounds and for lack of documentary evidence. Mozart's first concerto to survive intact is probably the Harpsichord Concerto in D, K. 175, written after his return from Vienna to Salzburg, in late 1773. The piece is often referred to as a piano concerto, and undoubtedly it later became one, but it was probably conceived for a harpsichord that had a top note of D. Its many affinities with the keyboard style in the accompanied harpsichord sonatas Mozart composed in the 1760s cannot be ignored.

---

[31] When this large drawing was exhibited in the show *Mozart: Bilder und Klänge* (Salzburg, 1991), Gerhard Croll entitled the picture, which belongs to a private collection in Italy, *Konzert mit Wolfgang Amadeus Mozart*. His identification is wishful thinking, of course, but not beyond the realm of the possible.

The problems classical composers encountered in writing concertos may have loomed larger than has previously been recognized. Joseph Haydn seemed to slip backward at least a decade stylistically in his Violin Concertos in C and G of the late 1760s. Even Ditters von Dittersdorf, so assured when writing violin concertos for himself as soloist, concocted a Flute Concerto in e that sounds at times like Vivaldi. Mozart's many concerto arrangements and his reluctance to enter the field in his own right can be seen in the light of the stylistic backwardness the concerto seemed to carry, like heavy baggage. This tendancy could also help explain why K. 175 is inferior to the symphonic marvels Mozart wrought in 1773–74.

The massive orchestration of K. 175—two oboes, two horns, two trumpets, timpani, and strings—makes it unlikely that the piece was written mainly for domestic entertainment.[32] The pomp of the two outer movements, and the sheer noise of Mozart's orchestra in them, lend the hypothesis that the concerto was intended for the organ a glimmer of credibility, but the extremely busy quality of the keyboard writing argues against this theory.

The opening tutti of the first *Allegro* in K. 175 comprises thirty-two measures. It begins with a climb through the triad to high D, elaborated with much sound and fury. The second violins and violas churn away in sixteenth notes, using Alberti bass figures that will later pass to the soloist. This beginning, in common time, as might be expected for so serious and pompous an utterance, seems to promise that the hero of an opera seria is about to launch on a great metaphor aria involving stormy seas and shipwreck. As in an aria, there are threefold hammer strokes on V and on I, the latter being the conventional operatic signal for the soloist to begin. Unusual for Mozart, and perhaps for anyone else at the time, are the asymmetries of this tutti, which arrives at the even number of 32 measures by uneven phrase lengths (measured mainly by the split-level dynamics of *forte* and *piano*): 4 + 2 + 3 + 6 + 5 + 3 + 2 + 7. The most memorable melodic idea is the *piano* group of 5 measures over a dominant pedal, mm. 16–20, but this idea only stands out because the rest is so routine. Rarely has Mozart sounded so impoverished for memorable ideas as here.

When the soloist enters with the first idea, Mozart has the violins double its treble (at pitch in the first violins, then down an octave in the second violins), as if he did not quite trust the timbre of his solo instrument to penetrate. He never does this in subsequent keyboard concertos. Toward the end of the solo's exposition Mozart reverts to a closing passage very similar to one in the first aria of *Lucio Silla*, K. 135 (Example 8.12a). In K. 175

---

[32] Marius Flothuis, the editor of the work in the NMA, citing parallels with Michael and Joseph Haydn, refused to discount the possibility that the original keyboard instrument for which K. 175 was written was the organ.

EXAMPLE 8.12.

a. Mozart, Lucio Silla, *No. 1*

b. Mozart, Concerto in D, K. 175, I

c. Mozart, Sonata in C, K. 6, I

the passage forgoes the expected I⁶ᐟ⁴ by eliding directly to V⁷, a boldness Mozart must have liked, although it is difficult to understand why (Example 8.12b). The treble A in m. 78 is left as an unresolved dissonant fourth, a solecism not mitigated by the rising parallel fifths of the Alberti bass. To find their equal, we have to go back to the Parisian sonatas of 1764 (Example 8.12c). The preparation for the cadenza at the end of the first movement seems a little too abrupt; instead of a I⁶ᐟ⁴ chord with fermata, the orchestra sounds the single tone A.

The *Andante ma un poco adagio* in 3/4 and in G calls for a reduced wind complement and comes as a pleasant relief from the heroics of the first movement. It begins with an *affettuoso* melody in thirds that Mozart will use later for the aria "Non sò donde viene," K. 294, a three-measure phrase that seems to cry out for words even in this earlier instrumental form. Although the *Andante* contains a beautiful transition back to the reprise, it sounds overly long for its material, with too many repetitions of the cadential figure that first appears in mm. 17–19. But it is the finale, *Allegro* in cut time, that is repetitious in the extreme, relying on the descent through the triad from high tonic to low, in canon, for much subsequent material. Mozart infuses this theme with rhythmic energy by snapping off the last two tones as quarter notes. This too has an operatic cast, and the affect it conveys is that of rage or anger (cf. the aria "Va, dal furor portata," K. 21).

K. 175 was a great success with audiences in spite of its clatter and repetitiveness, or perhaps partly because of these traits. It seems to have been a particular favorite of Nannerl as a solo vehicle for her talents. Leopold's letter from Munich to his wife dated 21 December 1774 states that Nannerl "need not bring many concertos, for we have Wolfgang's concerto here [K. 175], and if she brings a few others, that will be quite sufficient, for who knows whether she will use them at all." Perhaps Nannerl liked K. 175 in particular because it suited Countess Lodron's "good harpsichord" (cf. Leopold's letter to Wolfgang of 12 April 1778).

Mozart was not averse to playing K. 175 himself. In 1778, writing from Mannheim on 14 February, he told Leopold: "I played my old Concerto in D, because it pleases so much here." Is there a hint of apology in this statement? K. 175 was then a little more than five years old, and Mozart had meanwhile written better works in the genre, namely K. 248 in B♭ of January 1776, not to mention K. 271 in E♭ of January 1777. However Mozart regarded K. 175, he continued to revive it even in the early 1780s. To give the concerto a new lease on life, he replaced its antiquated finale in February 1782 with a rondo cum theme and variations on a simple contredanse tune, K. 382. This new *Allegretto grazioso* movement belongs among his most popular works by intention and in audience reception. Moreover, to please his sister, Mozart sent her three cadenzas for K. 175 by letter of 15 February 1783. If played with its rondo finale, the concerto is certainly one of the most heterogeneous works Mozart left, and in fact it is little played at present, with or without its popular finale.

Close in some ways to the spirit of K. 175 is the Concertone in C, K. 190, dated Salzburg, 31 May 1774,[33] which includes concertante solo parts for two solo violins (Wolfgang and Leopold?) as well as for oboe, viola, and cello. The outer movements require both trumpets and horns but no timpani, and the opening marchlike movement, *Allegro spirituoso* in common time, shares some of the bellicose quality of K. 175's outer movements. When the solo violins enter, they sound a descending triad in canon at the distance of a measure, a clear resemblance to the original finale of K. 175. But here the descent dissolves into flowing triplets in eighth notes. There is an abundance of decorative *rosalias* throughout the Concertone. In the opening movement mechanical sequences with exchanges between the solo vio-

---

[33] The term "concertone" was used mainly by Italian or Italianate composers. In his letter of 15 April 1778 Leopold Mozart states that Myslivicek rewrote his six concertones at the behest of Archbishop Colloredo. The reference would seem to be to this composer's Sinfonie Concertanti Op. 2, published in Paris in 1768.

lins are carried out for far too long. When it is finally time for the cadenza proper (which is written out for oboe and the two solo violins), the orchestra sounds a single tone, not a $I^{6/4}$ chord.

The second movement, *Andantino* in F and in 3/4, is the work's finest, a long-breathed outpouring of amorous sighs such as can be found, typically, in Mozart's serenades. The finale is a courtly minuet, with a trio mainly for the concertante instruments, bearing the seemingly contradictory indications of *Tempo di Menuetto* and *Vivace*. There are some lovely touches, such as the *dolce* transition passage beginning in m. 37, but all in all this movement is too extended (235 measures). Mozart played the work on the keyboard in Mannheim for his friend Johann Baptist Wendling, who responded, "That is right for Paris" (letter of 14 December 1777 to Leopold).

The Bassoon Concerto in B♭, K. 191, dated Salzburg, 4 June 1774, provides a superior companion to the Concertone. Its broad opening theme with syncopations shows similarities with the openings of other works in B♭ from the mid-1770s (Example 8.13abc). The work is a milestone of sorts in the extent to which Mozart allows the peculiar timbre and technical possibilities of the solo instrument to inspire what he writes. Like the Concertone, K. 191 ends with a *Tempo di Minuetto*, this one treated *en rondeau*, with an admixture of variation.

The first Violin Concerto, K. 207 in B♭, traditionally dated 14 April 1775, ushers us into a new world, broad and expansive and far beyond the crabbed metrics of K. 175, with virtuoso display better integrated thematically than in the Concertone or even the Bassoon Concerto. Its redating to 1773 seems impossible on stylistic as well as other grounds. If the work had been

EXAMPLE 8.13.

a. Mozart, Bassoon Concerto, I

b. Mozart, Violin Concerto in B♭, I

c. Mozart, Il rè pastore, No. 3

written as early as April 1773, would Mozart have neglected to take so fine a showpiece with him to Vienna in the summer of that year? Yet we know from Leopold's letter of 12 August 1773 that once in the city, he had to borrow a violin concerto and a fiddle in order to regale his hosts after Mass and a meal on the feast of St. Cajetan.

Mozart's cultivation of the violin as a soloist was in keeping with his appointment as a *Konzertmeister* (at first without salary) to the Salzburg court. There is an extended solo for concertante violin in the Cassation in G, K. 63, of 1769—presumably Mozart himself was the violin soloist in this *Finalmusik*, as he probably was in the solo violin parts that become increasingly frequent in the Salzburg serenades of the 1770s. There are three movements with violin solo in the Serenade in D, K. 185, of 1773. The following summer of 1774 saw even more ambitious solos in the Serenade in D, K. 203, so that the three movements in question become like a miniature violin concerto in B♭, clearly on the way to the real violin concertos. Notable is the way Mozart has the solo violin in the *Andante* from K. 203 enter with a *messa di voce*, as if it were beginning to sing an aria.

The lyrical impetus that led to the violin solos and violin concertos of the mid-1770s is related to Mozart's two operas of the time, *La finta giardiniera* and especially *Il rè pastore*. Of all the solo instruments of the time, the violin was deemed to be the closest to the human voice in expressive power. The outpouring of violin concertos in 1775 can be considered as a further bonus from the compositional fervor that surrounded the creation of *Il rè pastore*. This stimulation actually worked in both directions. When Mozart painted Aminta's happiness with his pastoral life and his love for Elisa before aria No. 3 in *Il rè pastore*, he reverted to an *Andante* passage quite similar to the Andante with violin solo in K. 203 (Example 8.14ab).

K. 207 is scored for pairs of oboes and horns plus the usual strings, the normal complement for all the violin concertos. Its opening *Allegro moderato* in common time is generated by a main theme that descends through the

EXAMPLE 8.14.

a. Mozart, Serenade, K. 203, II

b. Mozart, Il rè pastore, *passage before No. 3*

triad with prominent second-beat agogic accents. The syncopated beginning of Aminta's "Aer tranquillo" in *Il rè pastore*, also in B♭ with pairs of horns and oboes, is quite close, a parallel usually overlooked (perhaps because the Violin Concerto in G, K. 216, begins identically with the aria). There is a retrospective moment in the first movement of K. 207 when a passage similar to those in K. 135 and K. 175 arrives in mm. 11–15 (cf. Example 8.12ab). Mozart untypically fails to repeat this clichéd gesture anywhere else in the movement, which suggests that he was breaking loose from ingrained habits. An impressive development section commences with a turn toward minor in m. 75 and works to a climax with a big deceptive cadence on the subdominant, E♭, *forte*, in m. 99. This prolonged chord begins the retransition to the reprise. It sounds again in m. 169, prepared by its dominant, just before the cadenza; the I$^{6/4}$ chord is arrived at from below in the bass: D E♭ F. "Aer tranquillo" goes through a nearly identical progression reaching its I$^{6/4}$ for the cadenza in m. 177. The prominent arrivals of the subdominant in the first movement of K. 207 help prepare the lyric reverie of the slow movement in E♭, an *Adagio* in 3/4, also in sonata form, with its own place for a cadenza. The initial theme, sung by the first violins over the murmuring sixteenth notes of the seconds, is like a serenade, but deeper and finer than anything of this kind before 1775.

The finale of K. 207, a *Presto* in 2/4, begins with a formal surprise. Its first period, the first sixteen measures, is less important thematically than the second (mm. 1–4 constitute a "curtain" and will not recur at all). The second period presents a horn call in four symmetrical segments (Example 8.15ab). Haydn used a nearly identical call as the main theme in the finale of his *Fire Symphony*, dating from ca.1769. Very like Haydn also is the magisterial way Mozart introduces the reprise, postponing the first idea and writing over the expected cadence on vi by eliding the beginning of the horn call with the end of the retransition. The stylistic proximity of K. 207 to *Il rè pastore* confirms that it was not likely written before the spring of 1775, as one more

EXAMPLE 8.15.

a. Mozart, Violin Concerto in B♭, III

Hns. in B♭ alto

b. Haydn, Fire *Symphony, No. 59, IV*

Hns. in A

EXAMPLE 8.16.

a. Mozart, Il rè pastore, *No. 3*

b. Mozart, Violin Concerto in B♭, *III*

comparison shows: the finale's tutti-*forte* unison figure and following *piano* in thirds has a close parallel in "Aer tranquillo" (Example 8.16ab).

Violin Concerto No. 2 in D, K. 211, is dated Salzburg, 14 June 1775. Its opening *Allegro moderato* demonstrates that this key need not be heroic and majestic. It can be playful and full of coquetterie, like the little exchanges between first and second violins, which will later become exchanges between the first violins and the soloist. And the same could be said of Alexander's first aria from *Il rè pastore,* which, while including the trumpets that go with its key of D, sounds more amusing than threatening as Mozart illustrates flashes of lightning. He approaches the cadenza in this aria and in the first movement of K. 211 via a similar harmonic route. The concerto's *Andante* in G and in 3/4 begins very simply, as if dedicated to the proposition that no instrument can outsing the violin, and yet continues with many chromatic shadings. This chromatic bent permeates the last movement, marked *Rondeau Allegro,* as well. The rondo theme plays on the expressive possibilities of moving from the fifth to the sixth degrees and back, as happens in both earlier movements, giving the work an overall cohesion that is immediately perceived by the sensitive listener. This finale, actually a very galant *menuet en rondeau,* makes a perfect conclusion to the cycle. From this moment on, some kind of rondo form will become Mozart's standard choice for concerto finales.

The flirtation between "Aer tranquillo" and the first Violin Concerto in B♭, K. 207, blooms into a consummated union in the Violin Concerto in G, K. 216, dated Salzburg, 12 September 1775, and referred to by Leopold Mozart as "the Concerto with the Strassburger" (letter of 6 October 1777). If in his second concerto for violin and orchestra Mozart was content to explore a fairly circumscribed sphere of expression, one that is delicate, *cantabile,* and galant, he opens up to much wider possibilities and greater contrasts in this, his third violin concerto. K. 216 spans a world that extends from the nobility of the seria aria of Aminta that generates its first movement to the outspokenly popular contredanse "Strassburger," introduced with great comic effect in the rondo finale.[34] To Mozart, the key of G embraced both colors or tints—ineffable lyricism on the one hand, and on the other, the homely virtues of rustic simplicity. The progress from one to the other in K. 216 is similar to that informing the outer movements of the Piano Concerto in G, K. 453, of 1784. Whereas he would choose C for the slow movement of K. 453, here he selects the more unusual key of the dominant, D. This *Adagio* in common time is scored for two flutes and horns, as well as strings, and the choice of key certainly has to do with the flutes but also with the broad, hymnic nature of the main theme, sung in a full-throated *forte* from the beginning, and which would have sounded less passionate, more neutral, if it were in C. The dialogue with Joseph Haydn is rejoined with this movement, but in this case it is the older composer who paid Mozart the compliment of writing a *Largo* in D of similar hymnic beginning, in his great Symphony No. 88 in G of 1787.

In the first movement of K. 216, *Allegro* in common time, the richness of invention is astonishing, as one memorable idea tumbles over another; there is a true sense of development, until, just before the reprise, the solo instrument becomes operatic in yet another sense, by mimicking serious recitative, punctuated obbligato fashion by the chords in the orchestra. The solo violin's recitative duplicates note for note a real recitative in Elisa's first aria in *Il rè pastore*, and the dramatic function of both is identical: heightened tension just before the reprise. The *Adagio* is another leap forward toward Mozart's full maturity, and particular attention in this regard should be paid to the progression V^7/V - V^7 in the third measure and recurring throughout the movement. Mozart saves the main melody, with its throbbing accompaniment in triplets, for the high register of the principal violin—upon its first appearance, then at the reprise, and one more time to end the movement.

Mozart's first important multitempo finale was in the Serenade in D, K. 204 of August 1775, where a jig competes with a contredanse, anticipating the finale of K. 216. The latter begins with an *Allegro* in 3/8, its fast patter in staccato repeated notes lending it a buffo character. A proper rondo ensues out of this material, **A B A C A,** but before the last refrain is able to conclude, there is an interruption. The tempo and meter switch to *Andante* in cut time.

---

[34] Dénes Bartha, "Zur Identifikation des 'Strassburger Konzerts' bei Mozart," *Festschrift Friedrich Blume,* ed. Anna Amalia Abert and Wilhelm Pfannkuch (Kassel, 1963), pp. 30–33. A French source for this same dance tune is identified in Sarah Bennet Reichart, "The Influence of Eighteenth-Century Social Dance on the Viennese Classical Style" (Ph.D. diss., City University of New York, 1984), pp. 317–20. Christoph-Helmut Mahling cited Bartha's discovery in his edition of the violin concertos for the NMA but declined to accept its consequence, leaving the identity of the concerto in question. Robert L. Marshall, *Mozart Speaks* (New York, 1991), p. 17, wrongly identifies the work as K. 218 as a result.

To the accompaniment of pizzicato strings, the solo violin begins a dainty gavotte in g, replete with trills and dotted rhythms. It sounds as if a French dandy, with handkerchief to nose, had stepped in to reprove the boisterous dance of the *Allegro*. We can almost hear the solo violin asking, "Comment faire?" to the tones G C♯ D, the same that had interrupted the first movement before the reprise. The answer is provided by the lusty repeated tones of the Strassburger, an *Allegretto* in G. Orchestra and soloist gleefully proclaim the new tune and decorate it with garlands of triplets. But the movement is not over. *Tempo primo* returns, bringing a transition heard before, the rondo theme (**A**), then **B,** previously heard in the dominant, now in the tonic. Thus this movement, which Mozart entitles "Rondeau," has a clear sonata-form component. It all ends with a soft fanfare in the winds.

The "Concerto with the Strassburger" was understandably one of Mozart's favorite pieces. He mentions playing it with himself as soloist, in a letter of 23–25 October from Augsburg that is also notable for disclosing that violin concertos by other composers were part of his repertory, in this case Johann Baptist Vanhal's Violin Concerto in B♭. He wrote his father: "Ich machte ein sinfonie, und spiellte auf der violin das Concert ex B von Vanhall, mit algemeinen applauso . . . auf die Nacht beym soupée spiellte ich das strasbourger-Concert, es gieng wie öhl. alles lobte den schönen, reinen Ton" (. . . at supper during the evening I played the Strasbourger-Concerto. It went like oil, and everyone praised my beautiful, pure tone).

These impromptu concerts in Augsburg took place in the Monastery of the Holy Cross. They were followed in the evening by a more formal concert elsewhere, for which admission was charged: "Sunday I attended mass in the Church of the Holy Cross, and at ten in the morning I went to Herr Stein's . . . We rehearsed a few symphonies for the concert. Afterward I lunched with my uncle at the Holy Cross Monastery. During the meal we had some music. In spite of their poor fiddling, I prefer the monastery players to the Augsburg orchestra." In his next letter, dated Augsburg, 25 October 1777, Mozart begins: "The concert, before expenses were deducted, brought in ninety gulden. Adding the two ducats I was given in the *Stube*, we have now taken in one hundred gulden. The expenses of the concert came to no more than sixteen gulden, thirty kreutzer. I had the hall for nothing, and many of the performers, I believe, will have given their services gratis." Details like these flesh out the struggle for survival that was overcoming the Mozarts.

The fourth Violin Concerto, K. 218 in D, composed in October 1775, begins with an *Allegro* in common time and a memorable triadic tune, marchlike because of its dotted rhythm on the second beat. The *piano* answer is a descent in tenths from high D; the third component of the opening tutti is cadential. Then the orchestra introduces a second idea, all smooth and legato eighth notes, except for a *forte* outburst in the middle. The solo violin makes a spectacular high entrance with the martial first theme, two octaves above where the orchestra played it, followed by the descending rejoinder in tenths. Still in the tonic, the solo proposes a more triadic and diatonic version of the orchestra's second theme, identifiable by its long accent on G in the middle. Only after the dominant has been established does the solo sound the orchestra's original second theme. There is a lot of virtuoso passage work that is not thematic, more by far than in the first movement of K. 216, which may explain why, at the end of the development and the regaining of the tonic, Mozart dispenses with the main theme and its soft answer in descending tenths. He begins the reprise with the solo's diatonic version of the second theme, following it with the third, cadential segment of the tutti. Perhaps the triads up and down in the bass of this passage made him reluctant to repeat the triadic opening theme per se, but we miss hearing it again, especially in its stratospheric solo rendition. The solo plays the orchestra's original second theme in the tonic, a welcome return, and with an added novelty, but it does not make up for the missing first theme. The expected cadenza finally arrives, but after so much virtuoso passage work in the course of the movement, it could sound redundant.

The A-major *Andante cantabile* in 3/4 relies for its principal theme on a subsidiary idea in the finale of the Concertone in C, a descending passage in thirds with multiple chromatic inflections. The finale of K. 218 is a rondo with an interruption in the middle, i.e., a pendant to the finale of K. 216. Its main theme begins as an *Andante grazioso* in 2/4, sung by the solo violin, then continues as an *Allegro ma non troppo* in 6/8 that includes a parody version of the *Andante*'s main theme. The following episode in the dominant is also inaugurated by the solo violin, leading to the return of the main theme, followed by an episode in the relative minor. Up to this point then the form has been somewhat predictable. The surprise arrival of another dance melody, *Andante grazioso* in cut time, takes the finale to the subdominant. This *gavotte gracieuse*, later included by Mozart in a group of contredanses (K. 269[b]) for Count Czernin, sounds like a quotation from a preexisting dance. Mozart treats it in leisurely fashion, eventually using it to round out the section in the tonic. With this intruder gone, the finale resumes with the business of removing the key contrast between the first theme (shortened) and the second.

The fifth and last Violin Concerto, K. 219 in A, dated Salzburg, 20 December 1775, outshines all the others in scale and invention. *Allegro aperto* in common time is Mozart's choice for the opening movement, which is full of boisterous high spirits and at least one touch of opera buffa in the galloping unison figure. This figure will return only once, but at a crucial moment, just before the reprise. Of supreme beauty is the first entrance of the soloist to an *Adagio* of six bars in which the violin slowly climbs the tonic triad in its highest register. When it reaches high E, the orchestral violins begin a murmuring accompaniment in thirty-second notes, an effect Mozart perfected in some of the slow movements of his serenades. The real main theme that follows also climbs the tonic triad, so that in retrospect the *Adagio* comes to seem like an ethereal, written-out *Eingang*. In addition to the surprising *Adagio*, there is the revelation that what the orchestra played to begin the concerto was not the main theme, but only the accompaniment to what is sung by the solo violin. The secondary theme has nothing duplicitous about it. Before the soloist repeats the theme in the dominant, the violin gets a new secondary theme of its own, and this act of generosity on Mozart's part foretells much in his later concertos.

For the *Adagio* in 2/4 Mozart chooses the dominant, E, a key of special radiance and tenderness, often associated in his operas with zephyrs and amorous messages. The little two-note sighs that conclude the first exposition and remain prominent throughout the rest of the movement are specifically operatic. The finale bears two designations: Rondeau and *Tempo di Menuetto*. As in the two previous concertos, there is a contrasting dance in the middle, in this case a tonic-minor *Allegro* in 2/4 that provides the concerto with its nickname—"Turkish." The *Allegro* is a complete piece in its own right. Its first section concentrates on the running sixteenth-note figures that characterize Viennese Turkish color, along with the minor mode and certain cadential rhythms. The second idea, in leaping eighth notes (accompanied by the cellos and basses *col legno* to achieve a proper percussive effect), comes from Joseph Starzer's ballet *Le gelosie del seraglio*, which had accompanied Mozart's *Lucio Silla* in Milan in 1773. Mozart's delight in creating his own harem scene here emerges especially in the ludicrous rising chromatic passage with *crescendo*, followed by the same in inversion, almost a travesty of the cry of passion this figure evokes in his later operas, most notably in *Don Giovanni*. The menuet's dainty propriety wins out, of course, and banishes the exotic minor mode with its triumphant return. Every movement of the concerto is conceived on a larger scale than those of any of the previous violin concertos. Mozart's heightened sense for dramatic chiaroscuro in the finale makes possible a grand canvas in which one entire world of expression is pitted against another.

One of the principal solo players in Mozart's violin concertos was Antonio Brunetti, after he was appointed music director to the court of Salzburg on 1 March 1776. The following year, when Mozart left on his long tour, Brunetti succeeded him as *Konzertmeister*. K. 219 was apparently too challenging for Brunetti, so Mozart, although he did not like the fellow and said so, obligingly composed a substitute for the original slow movement: K. 261, dated 1776. It is an *Adagio* in E and in common time, with two flutes and muted orchestral violins, very serenade-like in effect, and from Brunetti's point of view probably preferable to the original because it is much shorter. Leopold Mozart refers to the new slow movement in his letter of 9 October 1777 as "the *Adagio* you wrote specifically for Brunetti because he found the other one too *studiert*." One trace left by the earlier *Adagio* in E upon its replacement is the occurrence of the little sighing figures of two notes on the offbeat. Whatever Mozart thought of Brunetti, the Italian violinist was fervent in his praises of the composer, and specifically as a violin soloist. In his same letter of 9 October Leopold wrote his son, "You will I suppose not have practiced the violin at all since you have been in Munich? That would make me very sorry. Brunetti now praises you to the skies! And I said recently to him that yes, you played the violin passably well, and he cried, 'Cosa? Cazo? se suonava tutto! questo era del Principe un puntiglio mal inteso, col suo proprio danno' " (What? Fool? He can play everything! This point is poorly understood by the prince, to his own loss).

Mozart also replaced the finale of his first violin concerto with a movement entitled *Rondeau Allegro*, K. 269 (261ᵃ) of 1776. Brunetti was the recipient here as well, and presumably he found this rondo finale in 6/8 less "studied" than the original sonata-form finale of K. 207. And finally, Mozart composed a Rondo in C for him—an *Allegretto grazioso* in 2/4, K. 373, dated Vienna, 2 April 1781—also brief and modest in scope, at least in comparison with the rondo finales of his last three violin concertos.

Mozart's concertos of the mid-1770s represent in their totality a shift as decisive as any other in his career. Up through 1774 his main instrumental genre had been the symphony. After this point it becomes the concerto. Possibly the intense encounter with Joseph Haydn's latest works in Vienna during the 1773 visit decided Mozart to begin exploring an avenue other than the symphony. He may have realized that the concerto was a form of theater, and in the theater he was always more at home than Haydn. The big breakthrough came with the five violin concertos of 1775. These works are theatrical even in their genesis, for it took all five of them to release the creative surge built up by *Il rè pastore*.

There is a corollary to be observed concerning Haydn, who quit writing solo concertos after he became acquainted with Mozart's works in the 1780s. His last keyboard concerto was that in D of 1784, written one year after his last cello concerto. The late exception is his Trumpet Concerto of 1796. It is perhaps no coincidence that Mozart left no surviving solo concertos for cello or trumpet.

In January 1776 Mozart wrote the keyboard Concerto in B♭, K. 238, his first since K. 175 of late 1773. Its range extends to high F. Although dynamic markings are lacking in the first two movements in the solo part (except when the solo doubles the orchestral bass), they are present in a few spots of the finale. These few may well be later additions. They probably do not indicate fortepiano, because Salzburg had no such instrument of concert size until later. Mozart encountered the fortepiano elsewhere. As we saw above, he favored those made by Späth of Regensburg, before he became acquainted with the fortepianos of Stein in Augsburg in October 1777.

All three movements of K. 238 deploy luxuriantly chromatic passages. Mozart quickly introduces all twelve chromatic tones in a passage beginning in m. 12 of the first movement, an *Allegro aperto* in 4/4. This choice chromatic passage occurs only once again, at the *forte* entrance of the orchestra after the soloist's cadenza. Pairs of oboes and horns join the usual strings in this concerto, lending it a sonority close to that of the five violin concertos, which it resembles in its proportions and style. In the *Andante un poco Adagio* in 3/4 two flutes take the place of the two oboes, as in the *Adagio* of the Violin Concerto in G (K. 216), and with the same ethereal effect. The descending tenths of the opening recall a similar descent in the *Andante amoroso* in 3/8 of the third Munich sonata (K. 281); both slow movements are in E♭. The finale is a *Rondeau Allegro* in cut time and begins with a gavotte-like theme. Before leaving the tonic, the solo introduces a theme in parallel thirds, doubled in the left hand an octave below and lightly accompanied by the orchestra. This sounds like something out of an Italian overture. A quite similar passage in doubled thirds begins the finale of the four-hand Sonata in B♭, K. 358 (186°), dating from after the final return from Italy in 1773.

A month after K. 238 Mozart wrote the first of two concertos for noble dilettante players in Salzburg, the Concerto for three harpsichords and orchestra, K. 242 in F. Countess Lodron and her elder daughter, Aloisia, played the first and second solo parts, and the younger daughter, Josepha, the markedly easier third part. The work is spaciously laid out, leisurely, and very indulgent to the soloists, mostly at the expense of the orchestra. Polyphonic instruments such as the keyboard can provide both melody and accompaniment, of course, and if there are two or three of them, they can accompany each other, which they do frequently in K. 242. In all three movements the first and second solo parts nearly always echo each other, lending a certain monotony and predictability to the work. Mozart must have planned from the first to reduce the three soloists to two, which he did at some unspecified time in or before 1780, when, under date of 3 September, Nannerl mentioned in her diary that she and her brother played the solo parts.

Also undatable exactly is the finer and more grandiose Concerto for two pianos and orchestra, K. 365 (316ª) in E♭, which is of a melodic abundance and harmonic richness that suggest a date of composition around 1780 and a proximity to *Idomeneo*. Mozart and his sister were probably the primary performers of this double concerto, the difficulties of which exceed those of K. 242. It may be the work they played together to applause at Augsburg in March 1781.

Related quite closely to K. 242 is the *Lützow* Concerto in C, K. 246, written in April 1776 for the modest keyboard talents of Countess Lützow, wife of the commander of the garrison of Fort Hohensalzburg.[35] She is thought to have been a pupil of Leopold's. Mozart took the concerto with him on his grand tour in 1777–78, but mostly for his pupils, and not for himself, to play. The finales of K. 242 and K. 246 show these works at their most similar. Both are called Rondeau, *Tempo di Minuetto,* and they have an identical formal scheme, with episodes in vi and IV surrounding a central return of the rondo refrain, led in by the soloist. Both lack cadenzas, but include elaborately written-out examples of the *Eingang.* Judged by the composer's own standards, K. 246 sounds rather routine. Perhaps he needed some new stimulation beyond that provided by his Salzburg lady dilettantes.

At some time before 1778 the Mozarts met a lady keyboard player whom they called variously "jenomè," "genomai," and "jenomy." Legend has it that she was a Mlle. Jeunehomme, a French pianist who visited Salzburg on tour in late 1776. But no document has ever been produced to show the existence of a Mlle. Jeunehomme, much less her concert tour. Mozart's Concerto in E♭, K. 271, dated January 1777, is ostensibly the first work referred to in a passage from Mozart's letter of 11 September 1778: "I will give 3 concertos to the engraver [Sieber], the ones for jenomy and litzau and the one in B♭." "Litzau" refers to K. 246 for Countess Lützow, and the third must be K. 238 in B♭. Only two other solo keyboard concertos were written before 1778: K. 175 and K. 271. Köchel thought the work for "jenomy" was K. 175, and he may have been right. In his letter of 5 April 1778, soon after arriving in Paris, Mozart wrote his father that "Madame jenomè is also here," but he did not say whether they met. Leopold replied by sending his and Nannerl's compliments to various people in Paris, including "Madame genomai" (letter of 20 April 1778). From this meager evidence a visit to Salzburg by a French lady pianist was invented. She could as well have been a

---

[35] Maunder, "Mozart's Keyboard Instruments," raises doubts about the dynamic markings in the NMA (ed. Christoph Wolff). He says that the *cresc.* in the solo part, mm. 90 and 186 of the first movement, are found neither in the autograph score nor in the original performing parts (note 67, p. 219).

harpsichordist for all we know. And the Mozarts could have met her some-where other than Salzburg.[36]

K. 271 contains dynamic markings that indicate fortepiano. This work begins with a surprise and continues to astonish and amaze up to the very end of its three movements. Scarcely has the orchestra commenced the opening *Allegro* in common time with a rising horn fanfare, doubled by the other instruments, when the soloist enters with a response, providing a cadence. It is as if Mozart decided to move the sharing of the initial material characteristic of the reprise back to the very beginning. Or, to look at it another way, he reverted to the greater freedom of interchange in opening a concerto that had obtained a couple generations earlier. The exceptional richness of the first exposition emerges from the presence of two full-scale themes, presented by the orchestra.[37] (In the first movement of K. 365, it is the two soloists who overwhelm us with one new theme after another, in the second exposition.) An accented diminished chord, hurled by the orchestra *fortissimo* on the second beat of m. 45, then in V at m. 139, lends a note of anguish and, if interpreted in operatic terms, of anger. The quiet response to this outburst begins the closing gestures, of which there are no fewer than three.

The piano enters with a long trill on B♭, as the orchestra repeats its last closing idea (which is an inversion and diminution of the rising triad that begins the movement). This moment returns only at the end, after the cadenza. When the reprise sets in after a rich modulatory section, it is the piano that announces the opening fanfare in octaves, to which the orchestra softly responds. Then piano and orchestra switch back to their original roles. The movement takes 307 measures plus an appropriately scaled cadenza (Mozart wrote out two). It is the most amply proportioned first movement conceived by the composer up to this time. The closest to it in scope and grandeur is the opening movement of the last Violin Concerto, K. 219 in A.

Only an extraordinary slow movement could sustain the level of the highly original and monumental first movement. The challenge is similar to what Beethoven faced after the opening movement of his *Eroica* Symphony. Mozart rose to the occasion with a tragic movement in the relative minor, as would be the case later with Beethoven, partly after Mozart's example. The role of the flat sixth, A♭, in both slow movements hints at Beethoven's

[36] An intriguing speculation about the origins of K. 271 was made recently by Richard Maunder (Ibid., p. 218): "It is, perhaps, just possible that the work was written during an otherwise unre-corded visit to Munich." The Mozarts attended the carnival in Munich as often as they could. Possi-bly carnival time in early 1777 found Mozart briefly in Munich.

[37] On the interconnections between the many themes, see the full discussion of K. 271 in Charles Rosen, *The Classical Style: Haydn, Mozart, Beethoven* (New York, 1971), pp. 198–214.

indebtedness. Once again, as so often in the violin concertos, Mozart's inspiration is operatic in nature. The sorrowful melody begins in the lowest range of the muted violins, which imitate each other. A *fp* placed on A♭ at the beginning stresses this tone. The violins sustain A♭ in the middle register in m. 4, then the *crescendo* in the soaring melody leads to a first A♭ in the high register. The climax comes with the half-note A♭ in the first violins, *forte* and harmonized by N⁶, followed by a descent down to B♮. After outlining this diminished seventh, the first violins can only manage a few notes at a time, interrupted by rests and punctuated by the other strings. This sobbing effect, suggesting recitative, becomes a true recitative with the falling fourth cadence, ending with the orchestra's post-recitative cadence, 5 1, *forte* and in unison.

The soloist enters with a new melody over the orchestra's restatement of the initial theme (cf. the first movement of K. 219). To close the soloist's big section in the relative major, the piano, with single tones in the treble, softly enunciates the recitative conclusion. As in the first movement, the soloist begins the reprise, and this time it emphasizes the A♭ in the middle register not only by the *fp* dynamic but also by a trill (the instrument's most effective means of emphasizing any single tone).

An escape from c minor back to E♭ is attempted by the soloist in m. 84, prepared in the orchestra by a one-measure modulation, but soon the descending phrases press back inexorably to the minor tonic (the turning point is the high A♭ in m. 89). Hopes raised, then extinguished, only deepen the sense of tragedy. Once again the recitative passage sounds, the soloist now enunciating its tones (for the first time in tonic minor). This time the treble solo singer has an accompaniment in sixteenth notes in the left hand, is given little echoes by the violins (like the movement's opening), and does reach a cadence on c after a measure-long trill on D. This could be the end of the movement but is not. There is still a cadenza to come, and a coda.

Mozart offered alternative cadenzas once again. Cadenza A makes a big point of landing on N⁶ *forte*, with high A♭ on top, after a rising passage, *Adagio*, with trills. Cadenza B is longer and also multitempo. It concludes by singling out the two accented diminished chords from the first movement, prolonged by fermatas, and for good measure throws in the third possible diminished chord in still higher position, before sinking into an *Adagio* with trills. At the *Tempo primo* it is not the orchestra that resumes normal discourse but the soloist—another departure from precedent. The piano decorates the cadential progression with little two-note sighs in the treble, alternating with single tones in the bass, a very spare texture in this lush context, but it is merely the foil that sets up the tutti *forte* outburst of N⁶; here for the first time the violins play *senza sordino*. To conclude these tragic strains, the soloist once more declaims the recitative, slightly ornamented. Where the penultimate falling fourth should end the verbal part of the recitative, Mozart substitutes A♭ (marked *fp*) G. The answering cadence, sounded by all, including the soloist, is not 5 1, as before, but V⁷ - I.

What kind of finale could possibly close this cycle? Mozart writes a Rondeau in cut time marked *Presto*. The piano begins with a nearly unstoppable torrent of eighth-note motion. A *perpetuum mobile* at this fast tempo is far removed from the courtly dance rhythms of previous rondo finales, none of which has this kind of motoric drive. When a final return to the rondo refrain seems imminent after a long pause of V of vi, Mozart deflects the harmonic motion toward V of IV. When the subdominant arrives, after a written-out *Eingang*, it is a *Menuetto Cantabile* in 3/4. The finales of the violin concertos prepared Mozart well for this moment, with their variety of different dances incorporated within the rondo structure. But this concerto, and no other, prepares us to accept A♭, a source of painful anguish before, now as a place of elegant repose (relative, that is, to the bustle and bluster of the *Presto*). It could be argued even that this gracious minuet in A♭ is needed in order to discharge the accumulated pathos of the *Andantino*. Its strains are beautifully varied upon repetition.

Even more beautiful than the varied strains of the minuet, if possible, is the ineffable chromatic transition that leads gently back to the realm of E♭. Here is a leave-taking of the utmost *politesse*. The *Presto* does not return immediately but is prepared by another long *Eingang*, for which Mozart offers alternatives, as he did for the first *Eingang*, leading to the return of the rondo refrain. When the high B♭ trill, familiar from the first movement, appears in the solo part against a new pizzicato version of the rondo refrain, we sense that the end is near. It comes with a *decrescendo* to *pianissimo* beginning in m. 460. Meanwhile, Mozart is still transforming the main theme by repeating its head motif in a kind of *stretto* (Example 8.17). This brings us to the realization that the theme, all along, was very like the chattering of an opera buffa clown. Monostatos is already before us!

EXAMPLE 8.17. *Mozart, Piano Concerto in E♭, K. 271, III*

Mannheim and Paris, 1777–78

THE oboist Giuseppe Ferlendis from Bergamo joined the Salzburg court orchestra on 1 April 1777. Sometime before leaving Salzburg on 23 September of the same year, Mozart wrote the Oboe Concerto, K. 314 (285^d) in C for him. This is a slight work compared with K. 271. The first two movements feature only short transitions over V or V^7 in the middle instead of modulatory passages or development. Yet this concerto is so beautifully written for the oboe that, like the bassoon concerto before it, it constitutes one of the treasures in the repertory. When Mozart reached Mannheim, he presented a copy of the concerto to Friedrich Ramm, the virtuoso oboe player there, who played it repeatedly and made it his *cheval de bataille,* as Mozart wrote in his letter of 14 February 1778. The cheerful spirit of the work emerges especially in the rondo finale, the refrain of which Mozart would later use in *Die Entführung* for Blonde's lusty "Welch' Wonne, welch' Lust / Regt sich nun in meiner Brust!"

Close to the Oboe Concerto in time and in style is the Flute Concerto in G, K. 313 (285^c), written in Mannheim in early 1778 for a wealthy amateur, Ferdinand Dejean. Its first movement is slightly more expansive (219 measures with development, as opposed to 188 measures without). For its *Adagio ma non troppo* in common time Mozart picked the key of D, as he had done earlier for the slow movement of the Violin Concerto in G, with which this piece has musical affinities. Like the whole concerto, the finale, a sprightly rondo, *Tempo di Menuetto,* indicates that Dejean, although an amateur, must have been a very good flautist. Mozart's lingering in Mannheim (he was captivated by Aloysia Weber) finally enraged Leopold to the point of sending his famous ultimatum of 12 February 1778: "Off with you to Paris! and that quickly. Take your place beside great men—*aut Caesar aut nihil.* The mere thought of seeing Paris should have protected you from all flighty brainstorms" (such as touring Italy together with Aloysia).

Accompanied by his mother, Mozart arrived in Paris on 23 March 1778. She became seriously ill in June. Mozart's letters to his father about his mother's decline deserve to be compared with his music for the mastery shown in the art of transition. She died on 3 July 1778. He composed little, understandably. The main work, the *Paris* Symphony, K. 297 (300^a), completed by 12 June, pleased the public with its grandiose gestures but sounds strangely empty compared with his symphonic best. Unusual for Mozart is the proliferation of small-scale repeats.[38] Paris offered opportunities to wit-

[38] Robert Münster, in the article "Toeschi" in *The New Grove Dictionary of Music and Musicians* (London, 1980), says that the *Paris* Symphony resembles in several striking ways the symphonies that the Mannheim composer Carl Joseph Toeschi wrote for Paris in the 1770s.

ness the latest tragedies of Gluck and Piccinni at the Opéra, and Mozart did not fail to profit from them. More to the point here, he became interested in the symphonie concertante, the reigning type of concerto with multiple soloists in the French capital.

When his friend Johann Baptist Wendling advised Mozart that the Concertone of 1774 would please in Paris, he knew whereof he spoke, for it is close to being a symphonie concertante by French standards, although written probably without knowledge of the Parisian fad. Haydn had anticipated the genre with his three concertante symphonies on the times of day (1761), but these were true four-movement symphonies with minuets, displaying all the learning and knowledge of various musical styles of which young Haydn was capable. The Parisian genre was much more popular in nature; it included two or three movements and offered the public an easy blending of the melodious with the idiomatic and showy side of solo playing. François-Joseph Gossec, Jean-Baptiste Davaux, and Joseph Boulogne Saint-Georges were the principal practitioners of the symphonie concertante during the 1770s. These composers' preferred soloists were two violins (they were all violinists themselves). While showy, their solo parts did not demand the pyrotechnics of most solo concertos—good performers could shine in them without being a Ditters or a Pugnani. Besides stringed instruments, all manner of wind instruments were also fashionable as soloists in this delightful new genre, which was especially in vogue at the Concert Spirituel (Figure 8.7).[39]

Mozart saw an opportunity to capture the Parisian public with a symphonie concertante for four wind players at the Concert Spirituel. Three of the players were Mannheim friends visiting in Paris: Johann Baptist Wendling (flute), Friedrich Ramm (oboe), and Georg Wenzel Ritter (bassoon); the fourth was the renowned hornist Giovanni Punto, alias Jan Václav Stich. When Mozart went with Baron Melchior von Grimm to the Concert Spirituel on 4 April 1778, the program included Punto playing a horn concerto of his own composition and Ramm playing a new oboe concerto (not by Mozart, casting doubt on Mozart's boast that his oboe concerto was Ramm's favorite). All four of these fine solo players were heard in a new symphonie concertante by Giuseppe Maria Cambini at the concerts of 12 April and 19 April. If Mozart was telling his father the truth in his letter of 1 May 1778, he composed the work for them but the director, Jean Le Gros, did not have it copied or performed, to the consternation of the soloists. In his letter of 3 October, Mozart says he sold his score to Le Gros before leaving Paris; it does not survive.

[39] Daniel Heartz, "The Concert Spirituel in the Tuileries Palace," *Early Music* 21 (1993): 240–48.

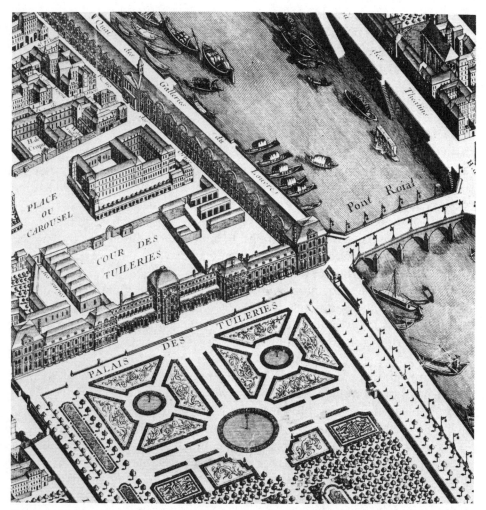

FIGURE 8.7. The Tuileries Palace, Paris, locale of the Concert Spirituel; detail from the Plan Turgot, 1739.

A symphonie concertante in E♭ for oboe, clarinet, horn, and bassoon that surfaced in the nineteenth century passed for a time for Mozart's lost work, but is now generally regarded as spurious (K. 297ᵇ).[40] If Mozart did write such a work (and at the least he must have wanted to), he would have presumably picked a key that was good for the flute, such as C, G, or D,

[40] Robert D. Levin, *Who Wrote the Mozart Four-Wind Concertante?* (Stuyvesant, N.Y., 1988). Richard Maunder, in his review of Levin in *Journal of the Royal Musical Association* 116 (1991): 136–39, concludes, "I fear that the answer to the question posed in the title of Levin's book must be: we don't know, but the evidence suggests it wasn't Mozart."

because Wendling was the senior musician among the Mannheimers and the one to whom he owed the most for hospitality in Mannheim.

A symphonie concertante that Mozart surely wrote during his mostly unhappy stay in Paris was the Concerto in C for flute and harp, K. 299. The recipients were the Comte de Guines and his daughter, but they were no ordinary dilettante players. Not one to bestow compliments lightly, Mozart in his letter of 14 May 1778 wrote that the father played the flute incomparably and that his daughter played the harp *magnifique*. This could be deduced as well from what he composed for them, a work that is richly melodious and easy on the listener, if quite demanding of the soloists—the very essence of the symphonie concertante, which is what an early hand (not Mozart's) designates the work on the autograph score: "Concertante a La Harpe e Flauto." Besides the two soloists, Mozart singles out the oboes in both outer movements for concertante treatment. Even the horns get to play the gavotte melody that is the refrain of the finale, a *Rondeau Allegro* in cut time. Strings alone accompany the sublime *Andantino* in 3/4, which features two viola parts, lending it a particularly warm and rich sonority; Viola I is sometimes the most sustained part of all, as in the opening.

In his last letter written to his father from Paris, dated 11 September 1778, Mozart, in spite of several reverses, assessed his stay in positive terms: "I assure you that this journey has not been unuseful to me—I mean from the compositional standpoint—for as to the clavier, I play as well as ever . . . I have made quite a name for myself here by my two overtures [i.e., symphonies], the second of which was performed on the 8th." The second symphony is thought to have been a work composed earlier in Salzburg.[41] Later in the same letter Mozart admits that much of his earlier music did not meet his present purposes. "As for the symphonies, most of them are not in the local taste. If I have time, I shall rearrange some of my violin concertos and shorten them. In Germany there is the taste for length ["lange geschmack"], but in fact it is better to be short and good." Leopold answered on 24 September with instructions about how to wind up his affairs in Paris that contain a surprising view on the subject. "That you ought to leave nothing behind is not my opinion, and even if it were, you should sell some music at once if you can. But music that does you no honor is better left unknown. For this reason I have not given out your symphonies because I foresee that with more maturity, which brings greater insight, you will be happy that no one has them, even though back then, at the time you composed them, you were satisfied. One gradually becomes more critical." Leopold was of course attempting to regain parental control when he wrote this.

---

[41] Zaslaw, *Mozart's Symphonies*, p. 333.

SALZBURG, 1779–80

ON THE RETURN trip to Salzburg in the fall of 1778, Mozart tarried in Nancy, Strasbourg, Mannheim, and Munich, much to his father's distress. In Nancy he admired the beautiful Rococo architecture. In Strasbourg he gave concerts. In Mannheim in November he began writing a Double Concerto in D for violin and keyboard, K. 315^f but he did not complete more than fifteen pages. Back in Salzburg after New Year 1779, Mozart resumed what was for him a normal productivity as a composer. One more attempted multiple concerto belongs to the summer or fall of this year, a "Sinfonia concertante a tre Stromenti: Violino, Viola, Violoncello" in A, K. 320^{e,} which he broke off after 134 measures of opening *Allegro*.

About this same time, Mozart wrote the masterpiece that is the greatest of all in this genre, the Sinfonia Concertante for violin and viola in E♭, K. 364. In this work the musical experiences of Mannheim and Paris reach their richest instrumental harvest. The uncompleted work for three solo string players required the viola to be tuned a whole tone higher than usual. In K. 364 the viola also uses *scordatura*, by tuning a semitone higher; i.e., its part is written in D, where it will have open strings and utmost brilliance, but will sound in E♭. Mozart's love for this instrument was intense. He preferred to play it himself in chamber music, rather than the violin. The viola's triumph in K. 364 is to match the more brilliant violin solo for solo, *passagi* included, and not be outshone. Indeed, the viola sometimes leads the procession. As in the flute and harp concerto, the solo treatment also extends to the oboes and even the horns. It is true that Mozart began this practice in the violin concertos, but it is even more prominent in these two concertantes.

The Sinfonia Concertante in E♭ begins like a solemn and grand overture, with repeated tonic chords and dotted rhythm, *Allegro maestoso* in common time. The orchestral violas are in two parts. After a prominent secondary theme for the horns, answered by the oboes, accompanied by pizzicato violins and basses (the violas alone play *arco*), a magnificent and long *crescendo* begins, as the violins ascend step by step, with trills, from low E♭ two octaves to high E♭. The *fortissimo* arrives on the final rise, 6 7 8. Mozart then sustains the climax by keeping the violins high in syncopated E♭ triads, as the lower strings begin trilling and moving the harmony to vi, and then to IV, which arrives with a *subito piano* that calls special attention to this A♭ sonority. There are parallels with the majestic first movement of the *Posthorn Serenade* in D, dated 3 August 1779, in both the syncopations and the *crescendo*. Long *crescendo*s with dramatic ascents throughout two octaves are the legacy of Stamitz and the Mannheim orchestra (but they occurred earlier in

Italian opera overtures). Mozart paid the ultimate compliment to the Mannheimers in the whopping *crescendo* at the end of Act I in *Idomeneo*, a seventeen-measure journey from *pp* to *ff*, from low D to high D, and directly parallel with the *crescendo* in the first movement of K. 364, in that the *fortissimo* arrives on the final ascent, 6 7 8.

Solo violin and viola emerge unobtrusively with a long-held E♭ as the orchestra is bringing the first exposition to a close. A formal transition to V begins with the orchestral strings intoning a mysterious unison passage in even half notes, E♭ B♮ C G, introducing a note of foreboding and a momentary stay in c that seem to forecast the pathos of the second movement. The development starts with a sudden lurch (another *subito piano*) from B♭ to g. After the reprise the mysterious soft passage is modified to straight chromatic descent, E♭ D D♭ C, after which the solo viola takes charge of leading the transition. Mozart provided written-out cadenzas both here and in the second movement. The trouble he took to get every detail of this noble work exactly the way he wanted it may be read from his elaborate sketch for the first-movement cadenza. He also sketched the very end of the movement, even though it amounts to little more than a tonic pedal.

The *Andante* in 3/4 revisits the somber world projected in the tragic slow movement in c of K. 271. As in that earlier movement, the minor-second fall from A♭ to G assumes paramount importance, but this movement does not dissolve into recitative. The opening melody climbs to high A♭ for its initial climax. Here, as in the first movement, the solo viola maintains absolute parity with the violin and with the third force represented by the orchestra. If anything, the somber tone of the viola seems more apt for singing doleful plaints than does the violin.

The finale is a sonata-rondo *Presto* in 2/4, restoring the (mainly) cheerful spirits of the opening movement, along with tonic E♭. The second episode prepares for the arrival of the relative minor, c, interspersed with measures of silence that introduce a note of hesitancy. A great moment in this work arrives when the solo viola takes charge and shepherds the music into IV instead of vi, playing the main theme in A♭. This moment sounds so right and perfect partly because the viola, being tenor to the violin's soprano, is quite at home singing a theme transposed down a fifth. There is an unmistakable parallel in Mozart's late string trio, the Divertimento in E♭, K. 563 of 1788, with its two Trios to the second Minuet, one sung by the viola in A♭, the next sung by the violin in B♭. A closer parallel still obtains in the divertimento's finale, as the harmony swerves toward vi, only to have the viola insist on playing the rondo theme in A♭.[42]

---

[42] I am grateful to Michelle Dulak for bringing this parallel to my attention.

Let us return to the subject of the wind concertante Mozart says he wrote for Paris. He was embarrassed to return to Salzburg with so little new music and wrote his father from Nancy on 3 October 1778 that "Le Gros bought the two ouvertures and sinfonie concertante from me; he thinks that he alone has them, but he errs, for they are still fresh in my memory, and, as soon as I get home, I shall write them down again." Whether Mozart had actually written down the concertante work or was deceiving his father on this point cannot be ascertained. But there does survive a wind concertante by Mozart—it forms the third and fourth movements of the *Posthorn* Serenade, K. 320. The seven movements of this last and grandest of Salzburg serenades are (exclusive of the initial March) (1) *Adagio maestoso / Allegro* in D; (2) *Menuetto Allegretto* and Trio in D and A, respectively; (3) Concertante, *Andante grazioso* in G; (4) Rondeau [Concertante], *Allegro ma non troppo* in G; (5) *Andantino* in d; (6) Menuetto in D, with two Trios, in D and A; and (7) Finale, *Presto* in D.[43]

The distinct oddities in the *Posthorn* Serenade are the two wind concertante movements in G, during which the first flute and first oboe are the main soloists, but solo duty is also required of Flauto II, Oboe II, and the two bassoons. Similarity of the timbres here to the concertante for four winds supposedly conceived for Paris should have raised suspicions long before now. This two-movement work led an existence in its own right. Old performing parts for it exist in the Stadt- und Universitätsbibliothek in Frankfurt (perhaps connected with the orchestral concert Mozart gave in Strasbourg in late October 1778?). Moreover, Mozart himself extracted the two movements for performance in Vienna in 1783. In his letter to his father of 29 March 1783, he refers to "die kleine Concertant-Simphonie [note the quasi-French spelling] von meiner letzen final Musique."[44]

When, indeed, did Mozart ever include two movements in the subdominant in the middle of a multimovement work, except in K. 320? Yet works with two movements in the same key, the latter a rondeau, represent one of the most frequent types within the vast repertory of the Parisian symphonie concertante. The G-major wind concertante in K. 320 is, I propose, an adaptation of what he envisaged writing, or actually did write, for Wendling, Ramm, et al. a year earlier in Paris. It is extremely delicate in facture, and at the same time of great popular appeal, like the flute and harp concerto.[45] Is

[43] On the surviving original performance parts for K. 320, see Cliff Eisen, "Mozart's Salzburg Orchestras," *Early Music* 20 (1992), 89–100; 95.

[44] Walter Senn, editor of K. 320 in the NMA, remarked on the "isolated character" of the two concertante movements from the rest of the work.

[45] In the *Rondeau Allegro* finale of the flute and harp concerto Mozart marks the oboes and horns "soli" as they first enter, carrying the melody. Similarly, he marks each flute and oboe part "solo" as it enters in the Concertante *Andante grazioso* of K. 320.

Perspectivischer Aufzug des Theatri in dem Hoch-Fürstl.
Lüst-Garten zu Mirabell in Salzburg.

Vue du Theatre dans le Jardin de Mirabell
à Salsbourg.

FIGURE 8.8. F. A. Dannreiter. View of the garden theater at Mirabell Palace, Salzburg.

it not, indeed, closer in style to the flute and harp concerto than any other Mozart work? One way or another, the wind concertante is the product of Mozart's experiences in Paris. Along with the more robust and profound violin and viola concertante, it crowns Mozart's contributions to the genre.

If the violin and viola concertante was completed by the summer of 1779 it likely had its first performance before the court in Mirabell Palace or Gardens (Figure 8.8). Antonio Brunetti may have played the solo violin, and Mozart the viola.

9

Mozart, Master Craftsman

Sacred Music

DURING the eight years between Mozart's final return from Italy in early 1773 and his departure for Vienna in March 1781, he composed the vast majority of his works for the church. In terms of quality as well as quantity, this repertory reigns supreme among the genres he cultivated up until *Idomeneo*. In his settings of the mass, specifically, he outstripped every other living composer, even Joseph and Michael Haydn. Our focus consequently will be on his mass settings. The glimpses we take of other forms of church music— vespers, motets, litanies, and that especially delightful local practice known as the Epistle sonata—will be mainly for the purpose of illuminating some point in connection with the masses. Only the masses include representations of every emotional state painted in the other sacred works, from the most tender miniature to the grandest visions of paradise.

MASS SETTINGS FROM 1773–74

MOZART was not called upon to write masses in Italy, nor did he make use there of his existing settings as far as we know. But the three trips to Italy (1769–73) separated by two returns to Salzburg, which lasted little more than a year, did not fail to produce other kinds of sacred compositions. Two of the most attractive are the settings of the Marian antiphon *Regina coeli,* one in C, which he composed in Salzburg in May 1772, K. 108, the other a year later, dated Salzburg, May 1772, K. 127 in B♭. The outer movements of the first display first-movement concerto form. Both antiphons require a virtuoso solo soprano who sings up to high B and high B♭, respectively, and from a later remark of Leopold Mozart we know that this soloist was Maria Magdalena Lipp (letter of 12 April 1778). More operatic even than the two Marian antiphons is the well-known motet *Exsultate jubilate,* written in Milan in January 1773 as a vehicle for the castrato Venanzio Rauzzini, the primo uomo in *Lucio Silla.* Other church works written for Salzburg between the Italian tours include two litanies, the short *Litaniae Lauretenae BVM,* K. 109, composed in May 1771, and the much longer *Litaniae de venerabili altaris sacramento,* K. 125, composed in March 1772. Both are in B♭, and the second requires trumpets in B♭, an instrument Mozart rarely used (except in *Lucio Silla*).

The little pastoral Mass in G, K. 140, of disputed authenticity, resembles nothing else by Mozart in this genre. It incorporates dance tunes by Joseph Starzer that figured in the ballet *Le gelosie del seraglio,* given with *Lucio Silla* in Milan in 1772–73. Mozart touched up the parts, we are told, and this is supposed to convince us that the music is his. Like both Haydn brothers and most composers in service, Mozart performed many works by other composers. It was only normal practice to revise whatever came to hand, as time and circumstances allowed and the music demanded.

An authentic mass setting from 1773 is the *Missa in honorem SS: mae Trinitatis,* K. 167 in C, dated June 1773. It was probably written for the Church of the Holy Trinity built between 1694 and 1702 by Fischer von Erlach (Figure 9.1). This splendid edifice was but a few steps away from the Mozarts' new dwelling across the Salzach River in the "Tanzmeisterhaus." Unlike the masses Mozart wrote for Salzburg Cathedral, this work requires no vocal soloists, but is elaborately scored for orchestra—two oboes, two *clarini,* two *trombe,* and timpani, plus the usual strings. The festive character of the work points to a celebration such as the feast of the Trinity, which fell on 5 June in 1773.

There are some glimmers of an overall unity in this mass setting. After a brief orchestral introduction the chorus begins in choral homophony, the sopranos outlining the degrees 1 2 3 4 3, in their upper octave, a motif that may be chant-related. The phrases are short, and as soon as the dominant is reached, Mozart lapses into sequential progressions over a circle of fifths progression. The choice is hardly inspired or inspiring, and gives the impression that he could think of nothing better. The same rise from first to

FIGURE 9.1. Remshard. Engraving of Trinity Church, Salzburg.

fourth degree provides the main idea of the Gloria, *Allegro* in 3/4, with effective precadential hemiola extensions. The concluding choral fugue sounds forced and depends on the orchestra to explain some of its harmonies.

The Credo is of more musical interest. In its big outer sections, *Allegro* in common time, Mozart extends the same rising motif up to the fifth. This occurs first on G at "Et in unum Dominum," treated as a canon at one measure's distance. When he does the same thing on C at "Genitum non factum," there is a sense of satisfaction as the sopranos now reach up to an accented and held high G, a tone with which Mozart is very sparing throughout the mass. The most memorable feature of the work is the ambling minuet in G (110 measures!) with ample orchestral introduction for the setting of "Et in Spiritum Sanctum." Surely Mozart is thinking of paying special homage to the third member of the Trinity with this beautiful movement. He positions the violins an octave apart at the unison and gives them ever so galant two-note snaps (Example 9.1). This manner of writing for the strings is Viennese and connected with Starzer at its inception around the middle of the century, as illustrated above in Chapter 2. Mozart's audience in Salzburg would have been perceptive enough to know at least that a ballroom dance had invaded the sanctuary, and to have smiled at the thought.

EXAMPLE 9.1. *Mozart, Mass in C, K. 167, Credo*

The melodic idea 5 3 6, 4 2 5 occurs in Salzburg divertimenti and may refer to a popular song, in which case the smiles would have been even broader.

The Sanctus begins as the sopranos rearrange the conjunct rising motif into 1 4 2 5, before restating it in close to original form in the quicker "Hosanna." The Benedictus is in F and begins with a trio sonata for the strings, onto which choral homophony is eventually layered. Even more apparent here than before is the extent to which the work is orchestrally conceived. It could not be performed as an unaccompanied choral work. There is a curious moment when the orchestra gives out three chords on the dominant C, as if this were an operatic aria and the soloist had to be given the signal to begin. The next measure starts off with a unison D—an awkward join.

The Agnus Dei reverts to C, *Adagio* in 3/4, once again with orchestral introduction. What the orchestra proposes would make a nice slow movement to a symphony, with oboes reinforcing the delicate chromatic shading an octave above the violins. The chorus enters in a low range and softly, reaching a *forte* in four measures. There are many stops and starts, as is true for the mass as a whole. Church style and galant style were not easily fused into a true symbiosis, not even by Mozart in 1773. Perhaps the most cut-and-dried fugue Mozart ever wrote (aside from the one in *The Musical Joke*) was the concluding "Dona nobis pacem," which features the tritone in even half notes: 1 8 7 4. To make this poor subject yield a stretto at the end, he had to change it to 1 8 6 3.

BREAKTHROUGH IN 1774

MOZART'S three trips to Italy did not make him any better a contrapuntist than he showed himself to be in the masses of 1769. It was a different matter with the visit to Vienna in the late summer of 1773, which brought him into extensive contact with the music of Joseph Haydn. In the mass written the following June, Mozart achieved an ideal blend of dramatic cogency, contrapuntal learning, and popular appeal. He also profited from hard study of Salzburg masters, mainly Michael Haydn.

The relationship of Mozart to Padre Martini is often mentioned in any discussion of Mozart's gradual arrival at contrapuntal mastery. In 1770 Mozart underwent an examination in counterpoint in order to become a member of the Accademia Filarmonica in Bologna. He did not fail, as has been claimed, but he was shown some better solutions by Martini.[1] A desire to become a better contrapuntist was instilled in Mozart by Martini, yet the deep study necessary thereto was not undertaken before 1773, when the Italian tours were over.

Mozart's only mass setting in the key of F is K. 192 (186^f), dated 24 June 1774 (the day celebrating the birth of St. John the Baptist). It is a *missa brevis* for the usual church trio of two violins and basses, plus the three trombones doubling the three lower choral parts that were standard at Salzburg Cathedral but not written into the score, to which were added at some later time two trumpets in C—trumpets in F were not then in use. The Kyrie opens with a brief orchestral prelude stating the material for the opening choral fugato, which also serves as the first subject in a clear sonata form. The second subject is distinct from the first mainly by its new texture of sixteenth-note accompaniment in the second violins against a pedal G in the bass. The sopranos lead the music to two firm cadences in C. After a brief orchestral ritornello they initiate a modulatory section on "Christe eleison" that is like a development, leading to the reprise. The advantages of the key of F to a composer reluctant to ask his boy sopranos for anything beyond high G are obvious in this movement: the high tonic is not shunned, and held G, the high fifth above the dominant, provides a nice climax to the exposition.

The next movement is a dancelike *Allegro* in 3/4 time, in which important cadences are marked by preparatory hemiolas (harmonies move in 3/2) like a *corrente*. The intonation of "Gloria in excelsis Deo" is left to the celebrant, after which the sopranos begin in measure-long tones, as if continuing a plainchant for "Et in terra pax hominibus." The other three sections of the chorus join them for "bonae voluntatis," the altos and tenors imitating the little figure in the sopranos, over a bass pedal. This leads to the first precadential hemiola, in which the sopranos encapsulate the beginning and end of its long-note opening melody, the restatement of which ends the movement.

The Credo, *Allegro* in common time, is unified even more obviously than the first two movements by its use of Mozart's favorite 1 2 4 3 melodic motif

[1] Manfred Hermann Schmid, *Mozart und die Salzburger Tradition* (Münchener Veröffentlichung zur Musikgeschichte 24) (Tutzing, 1976), pp. 179–83. For a comparison of Mozart's and Martini's solutions, see also Alfred Mann, *Theory and Practice: The Great Composers as Students and Teachers* (New York, 1987), p. 50.

throughout, and with the ever-recurring words "Credo, credo," which has led to the designation of the whole as *Little Credo* Mass. Noteworthy upon the first statement is the harmonization, I - V - IV^6 - V$^{6/5}$ - I, and the rhythm. The eighth-note upbeat figure (for "in unum Deum") will also mark the finale of the *Jupiter* Symphony fourteen summers later. Here Mozart puts the subject through its contrapuntal paces on various degrees in fugal sections, including strettos. For the ending he saves a special and new harmonization of the motif, I - ii$^{6/5}$ - V^7 - I, appropriate to a codetta. Ending on a weak beat like this, with the third in the soprano, softly, and *senza organo*, is a way of bidding a blithe farewell to Mozart's favorite motif.

The Sanctus, *Andante* in 3/4, begins with the basses descending in measure-long tones through the scale from F down to G. Mozart was apparently reluctant to write a low F for them here, but he does so at their final "Hosanna in excelsis." He sets the Benedictus to the same tempo and meter, but in B♭, like the trio of a minuet. Agnus Dei begins as an *Adagio* in common time in the key of d. There is a beautiful transition of four measures preparing for the final section in F, "Dona nobis pacem," set to an *Allegro moderato* in 3/8, which is like an Italian menuetto. The mass ends with a long-note plagal cadence on "pacem." The accomplishment represented by this mass in terms of contrapuntal refinement, the unity of its individual movements, and its overall unity has long made it a favorite with critics and performers alike.

The *Missa brevis* in D, K. 194 (186^h), dated 8 August 1774, provides a companion work of still smaller size to the Mass in F. It also features an Agnus Dei in the relative minor leading to a "Dona nobis pacem" in tonic major, the theme of which resembles the beginning of the previous mass. Mozart took both of these masses to Munich with him at the end of the year, or so we believe from a letter of Leopold Mozart dated 15 February 1775: "A little mass by Wolfgang was performed in the court chapel last Sunday, and I led it ["ich habe Tactiert"]; another will be performed next Sunday."

Drawings from the Kuenburg collection illustrate the figures of a *Domchoralist* and Kapellmeister of Salzburg Cathedral (Figures 9.2–3). A hierarchy is reflected not only in their dress but also in their movement. The choir singer raises a finger in order to confirm the beat. The Kapellmeister raises an arm, his hand clutching a music scroll, in order to establish the beat and guide his widely scattered forces.[2]

A curious feature of the Mass in D is the low tessitura of the voices. Mozart never takes the sopranos or the soprano solo above G in the upper

---

[2] Robert L. Marshall, *Mozart Speaks* (New York, 1991), p. 18, errs when saying that Mozart conducted in church with a baton, which became common only in the nineteenth century.

FIGURES 9.2.–3. Drawings of a choral singer and Kapellmeister in the Salzburg Cathedral (from the Kuenberg Costume Book).

octave, and rarely do they attain this pitch, being placed most of the time in the lower octave. Deprived of the dominant tone, A, in the higher octave, Mozart manages to make a virtue out of necessity. Yet one need only look to his several Masses in C to realize how important the high dominant tone is to harmonic and melodic gestation for him. If the Mass in D gives a somewhat lackluster impression, blame must be laid partly on the upper limit Mozart has imposed on himself. His naturally soaring melodic vein suffers in consequence. That the solo soprano is also curbed in this manner suggests that even the best choirboy or castrato Salzburg Cathedral could muster was not very trustworthy. Yet Mozart wrote up to high B♮ for Maria Magdalena

Lipp, as we saw, in his *Regina coeli* settings of 1771–72. Mozart lends the Mass in D a measure of cyclic unity by making the music for "Dona nobis pacem" begin similarly to the Gloria. His insistence on setting "dona" *piano* and "pacem" *forte* at the end is oddly playful.

THE MASSES OF 1775–77

THE upper level of G for sopranos that Mozart set himself must have had quite a lot to do with his self-imposed restriction to the key of C for his next several masses—no fewer than five between his return from Munich in the spring of 1775 and his departure from Salzburg in the fall of 1777. The most impressive in conventional ways is the *Missa longa* in C, K. 262 (246ª), scored for oboes, horns, trumpets, timpani, trombones, violins, basses, and organ. Paper studies place its date in mid-1775.[3] Its length of about thirty-one minutes is partly due to leisurely orchestral introductions, such as the one announcing the Kyrie, set as a double fugue that serves as the first subject of a sonata form scheme. "Et in Spiritum Sanctum" in the Credo, set, as usual, in triple meter, benefits from another orchestral introduction of ample proportions. The fugues ending the Gloria and Credo are magnificent specimens of the genre, the latter extending to 122 measures. The subject of the Credo's fugue places an emphasis on the sixth degree by beginning 5 6 5. Several climaxes conclude the fugue, but they do not include giving this head motif to the sopranos in their upper register, an impossibility because of Mozart's upper vocal limit. The violins supply what the sopranos cannot. This mass is among those of Mozart most oriented toward counterpoint; even the "Hosanna" is set, initially, to a fugato. When the word "Hosanna" returns as choral commentary on the tenor solo in F that begins the Benedictus, Mozart sets it to staggered and overlapping three-note groups. We have already observed this rhythm and texture in his instrumental music. In vocal music he often chooses it for words of three syllables. The phenomenon occurs in setting the word "Hosanna" also in the masses K. 220, K. 257, and K. 258, and in setting the first word of the Offertory *Venite populi*, K. 260.

For the sake of convenience the Mozarts sometimes designated a work by the name of the person it was written for or with whom it was connected: thus, *Lützow* Concerto, *Dominicus* Mass, *Spaur* Mass. The last may refer to the *Missa longa*, K. 262. Count Spaur, a family friend of the Mozarts, was ordained a titular bishop in ceremonies at Salzburg Cathedral on 17 November 1776, and the festive occasion would have been well suited by K. 262.

---

[3] Alan Tyson, *Mozart: Studies of the Autograph Scores* (Cambridge, Mass., 1987), p. 167.

Quite of a different order are the titles that became attached by the populace to some of its favorites among Mozart's masses. An example is the *Missa brevis* K. 220 (196[b]), dubbed *Spatzenmesse* or *Sparrow* Mass on account of the chirping figure in the violins (a short appoggiatura of the minor second below the main note) in the Sanctus and the Benedictus. The origin of this label is old and impossible to trace, but calls attention to the status of the work itself as one adopted as a favorite by the public. It still may be heard of a Sunday in even quite small churches in Austria and Bavaria, as may other favorite masses by Mozart, Haydn, and Schubert.[4]

The *Sparrow* Mass is popular in more senses than just its reception history. Mozart aimed at popularity with audiences by introducing songlike music not just in the lyrical episodes for soloists, where it was expected, but also in places where it was not expected. Such a place is the opening of the Kyrie. After only a five-measure orchestral introduction the chorus sings "Kyrie" to a three-chord progression in which the bass descends by step from I to vi, above which the treble sings 3 5 1. Mozart was partial to this idea all his life, and even at the end used it to begin the exquisite duet between the two women in *Tito*, "Ah perdona al primo affetto," and still later to begin the March of the Priests, added to *Die Zauberflöte* at the last moment. With the latter the Kyrie beginning of K. 220 shares even the continuation: a rise of the treble over parallel 6/3 chords.

The Kyrie of K. 220 deserves study for its extreme economy as well as its songful and euphonious character. In only eight measures after the chorus enters, the dominant is reached, and "Christe" is then sung to a second theme consisting of falling thirds in the sopranos and altos, onto which Mozart grafts the rising 6/3 chords that form the second half of the first theme. A statement of the second theme complex up a step serves as development leading to a reprise. He allows an extra measure so that the subdominant can sound where it did not before, but there are no other expansions. Everything is so short and yet so resonant, full and perfectly proportioned. There is room to restate the beginning as a coda in the last four measures. This too seems aimed at the popular in the best sense. Even an uninitiated listener cannot fail to perceive the formal perfection and musical fulfillment this coda brings.

Echoes of the musical material presented in the Kyrie are certainly audible in the Gloria and Credo, but it is in the Sanctus where they begin to assume the feeling of an imminent return. In the middle of a succinct seven-measure choral outburst on "Sanctus," serving as antecedent, Mozart intro-

[4]In his NMA Kritische Berichte on K. 220 Walter Senn exhausts the alphabet in listing manuscript copies of this mass; besides the great Austrian monasteries there are several parish churches holding copies in places like Laufen, Eisenstadt, Krems, and Neumarkt.

duces rising 6/3 chords. Then the chirping starts, answered by a choral consequent sung to "Pleni sunt caeli et terra" in which the main tones are reordered by another tuneful treble: 3 4 2 1. (Intimations of an even more popular mass, K. 317, called *Coronation* Mass from early on, are evident here.) The Benedictus, in G, postpones the inevitable (but note how Mozart introduces E G C over subdominant harmony, close to the end, before the chirping announces the return of C and "Hosanna"). Agnus Dei begins as an *Adagio* in 3/4 and in tonic major, a choral movement interlaced by solo presentations of "miserere." After a long dominant preparation familiar music returns for "Dona nobis pacem." First comes the second theme of the Kyrie, followed by its first theme, after a teasing wait of four measures over a G pedal (Example 9.2). Note the extension of the treble from 2 3 4 2 (recalling the falling third in "Pleni sunt caeli") upward to 3 4 5 3, then upon repetition the condensation to only the falling third 4 2, 5 3, 4 2. The violins then lead in the Kyrie's first theme, its characteristic rising third being made to sound like an inversion of all those falling thirds. This is Mozart at his most playful, and a heavenly level of play it is.

Mozart's decision to give the *Sparrow* Mass a lyrical beginning surely was bound up from the initial moments of conception with the idea of using this same lyrical music to end the cycle. For the first time he uses the beginning of a mass as its ending. The liturgy does not demand such a return or even suggest it, but there was good precedent in the music of Joseph Haydn (cf. especially the *St. Nicolai* Mass of 1772). The ears of Mozart's worshipers (and of audiences ever since) surely welcomed this rounding off, this sense of completion that brings peace and fulfillment, an achievement that is possible, desirable, and even sublime, attained by purely musical means.

By writing five masses in the same key successively within the span of two years Mozart gives the impression that he was confronting some compositional challenge of his own making. His position as second concertmaster at the cathedral did not require such activity even if it was welcomed by those in power. By the spring of 1775, with no operatic commissions in sight, and with the surge of creative energies released by *Il rè pastore* still active— evident most obviously in the five violin concertos but also in these masses— Mozart shifted his attentions away from the symphony and chamber music. It is no exaggeration to view concerto and mass, two closely related genres with respect to their main ingredient of solo versus tutti dialogue, as his main compositional focus between 1775 and 1777.

Suppose we accept the thesis that Mozart challenged himself by writing five masses in C in quick succession. Let us then put the question as follows: how much variety can the same tonality and the same vocal and instrumental forces yield from a single text? With Mozart, the answer is: a limitless

EXAMPLE 9.2. *Mozart*, Sparrow *Mass, K. 220, Agnus Dei*

amount. The smallest of the set, K. 259, known as the *Organ Solo* Mass, has a personality quite unlike any other. It is even more concise than K. 220. The Kyrie, for example, after an introduction of four measures, allots the same time and no more to the first theme and then to the second begun by the soloists in the dominant. This brings us to the six quarter-note beats of orchestral ritornello confirming the key of G. The soloists start out again, quickly introducing F♮, to which the chorus responds by introducing hints of tonic minor, just enough contrast to prepare the reprise. The soloists introduce their second theme over subdominant harmony and with the inflection of the fifth degree, 8 5♯ 6. This galant figure is not new here because the violins have already introduced it in the last measure of their prelude. The movement ends shortly thereafter.

The Gloria of K. 259 is equally terse. There is no time for tonal detours or subsections. A brief move to the subdominant suffices to set apart "Qui tollis peccata mundi." "Cum Sancto Spirito" brings not a fugue or even fugato but a return to the I -vi - IV - I progression with which the movement began. The Credo stops and changes meter only for "Et incarnatus est," given to the soloists. When the *Allegro* in common time resumes at "Et resurrexit," it is with the music from the beginning of the movement. "Et in Spiritum Sanctum" is set as an episode in the subdominant for the soloists. At the end there is not a hint of imitative counterpoint. Having dispatched the wordy Credo in a near-record (for him) eighty-eight measures, Mozart seems to change gears. He lends the Sanctus a serious mien, *Adagio maestoso* in 3/4 with dotted rhythm, but after only seven measures of this, "Pleni sunt caeli" brings an *Allegro* in cut time deploying harmonies that fill in the descending bass of the Gloria: I - V⁶ - vi - iii⁶ - IV. Both these sections are replacements for less interesting music Mozart originally wrote and crossed out in the autograph.[5] The replacement "Pleni" ties in not only with the Gloria but with the 8 5♯ 6 in the Kyrie, now led by the violins, 5 8 7♭ 6 5♯ 6, joined by the chorus singing "Hosanna" for the last three tones, and repeating the descent chromatically so as to end up inflecting the fourth degree: 8 7 7♭ 6 5 4♯ 5.

The Benedictus, *Allegro vivace* in 3/4, introduces the key of G, a welcome tonal contrast but with music that sounds rather bland after the heady chromatic patch just heard. Precisely at this moment, and perhaps because of this blandness, Mozart introduces the unexpected timbre of the organ as solo player. When "Hosanna" returns, Mozart retains the triple meter, adapting to it the chromatic passage that ties the whole mass together. Agnus Dei begins with the solo of the first violins over the pizzicato accompaniment of the seconds, *Adagio* in common time. The texture and the melody falling by step from tonic to fifth remind us of the very beginning of the mass. At "Dona nobis pacem," *Allegro* in 3/4, Mozart mediates between the diatonic falling fourth of Agnus Dei and the chromatic "Hosanna" motif, by assigning 8 7♭ 6, 8 6 5 to the soprano solo. The choral tutti at first responds

---

[5] The original versions are printed in Anhang II of NMA.

indifferently, *forte,* over the progression I - vi - ii$^{6/5}$ - V^7 - I, but to end the mass, the chorus accepts the soloist's melody, singing it *piano,* after which there are two V - I cadences, *forte,* on "dona" and "pacem." The effect produced is that of an individual having tamed the multitude.

K. 258 has been called a *Missa brevis et solemnis*. It is concise, but not as much as K. 220 and K. 259, and is, at the same time, quite showy. To its trumpets and timpani (also present in K. 220 and K. 259) were later added oboes (also true of K. 259). The duration is about eighteen minutes. Less intimate than K. 259, K. 258 occupies a middle ground between the shortest masses and the exuberant *Credo* Mass, K. 257. The Kyrie has no orchestral introduction but enjoys the relative expansiveness of a transition between the first and second themes, lacking in both K. 220 and K. 259. Economy is served by eliding some of the first group material in the reprise. What could be called the closing theme, coming right after the duetting soloists singing the second theme, is a choral rejoinder in close imitation, an unusual feature and one of the few contrapuntal passages in the whole mass.

The Gloria is concise but festive, the violins running on in sixteenth notes almost continually, stopping only for the fugato on "Cum Sancto Spirito." The Credo is an *Allegro* in 3/4 except for the *Adagio* in common time for "Et incarnatus est," a tenor solo in the relative minor with many chromatic inflections. The other soloists join in for "Crucifixus" except that the chromatically rising bass line, which controls the modulation, is sung by tutti— a typical example of Mozart's almost analytical use of dynamics and scoring. All parts become tutti at "passus," led in by the sopranos with a false interval and a modulation that prefigures the latest Mozart of all.[6] "Et resurrexit" is powerfully stated, tutti *unisoni*, as was "descendit de caelis." Compared with the two masses just discussed, the effect here is of an almost theatrical aggressiveness. As in K. 259, "Et in Spiritum Sanctum" is an episode beginning in the subdominant, announced here by three "punching" chords with double stops in the violins, an effect one might sooner expect in an instrumental rondo. Music from the beginning of the Credo returns at "Et unam sanctam." There is no fugue or fugato.

Mozart lends majesty to the Sanctus, an *Andante maestoso* in common time, by means of dotted rhythms and by spreading out his choral and orchestral resources from bottom to top, where the first trumpet holds a protracted high C. "Pleni sunt caeli" he sets imitatively, *Allegro* in cut time. "Hosanna" begins with a fugato, continuing with staggered three-note groupings and then choral homophony. Unusual for Mozart, the Benedictus continues on in tonic major, *Allegro* in cut time. The main idea is the triadic

[6] In the "Hostias" of the Requiem, K. 626, at mm. 36–38.

motif in the bass, the other parts of the chorus scarcely moving against it. By transferring this motif to the dominant and other degrees, Mozart builds up considerable momentum for the return to C. He pits the soloists against the chorus at the moment of reprise, as he had been doing from the beginning, leading to the return of the "Hosanna." Also unusual is the final section in that he does not separate "Dona nobis pacem" from the rest of the Agnus Dei. Rather, he treats it as a kind of coda, emphasizing the subdominant and finally subsiding in a protracted plagal cadence.

K. 257, the *Credo* Mass, stands out as the boldest of the group. Whether its innovations and departures from Mozart's own norms mean that it is the latest of the group remains an open question. Artistic maturity cannot be measured by statistical means, like so many rings on a tree. An artist can move backward as well as forward, or not at all. The least that can be said is that those who knew Mozart's masses for Salzburg Cathedral well were in for a shock if they listened attentively to this one. Instead of beginning with a statement in the tonic, Mozart begins with an orchestral transition from C to G, the bass moving down by thirds to F♯, which is held as the chorus and then the soloists sing a recitative-like passage, mostly in repeated notes. The analogy with recitative and opera hits the mark all the more comically if we compare this beginning (or nonbeginning, since it presumes something previous) with a well-known passage in *Figaro*, the transition to Figaro's monologue in Act I, scene 1 (Example 9.3ab). The Kyrie proper begins after this theatrical introduction, its *Allegro* in common time sounding like many another of Mozart's Kyrie settings. Something untoward happens soon enough, or better put, what should happen (because it does so in all other cases) fails to happen here: there is no modulation.[7] We expect it at the half cadence, or at the latest the second half cadence. In both cases the soloists persist in retaining the key of C for their singing of "Christe" (a tenuous pun on Mozart's part?). The effect of so much undisturbed tonic major is of breadth and nonchalance.

The Gloria lingers in tonic major for a while, through the touchingly murmured "Et in terra pax" low in the choral voice ranges, but then takes the opportunity provided by the half cadence to plunge into G. Chains of descending tenths in the violins sound very Italianate and mark the end of the section in G, followed by modulation. The approaching return to C can be guessed, and the reprise begins at "Quoniam." The low chordal murmuring now clothes "amen, amen." This movement too has a greater breadth than usual, attributable in part to its broad harmonic rhythms.

[7] It is often said that without modulation (or, specifically, sonata form), the Viennese Classical style is impossible. This movement suggests that it takes only the threat of modulation, or its expectation on our part, for the style to work.

EXAMPLE 9.3.

a. Mozart, Credo Mass, *K. 257, beginning*

b. Mozart, Le nozze di Figaro, *Act I, scene 2*

The popular appellation *Credo* Mass is made on good grounds. Mozart departed from all known precedent in this movement by returning over and over again to the words and music of a motto, "Credo, credo," which mark all important structural joints. He extracted the motto from the most common chant for the beginning of the Credo (Example 9.4ab), and he uses only

EXAMPLE 9.4.

a. Plainchant

Cre- do   in   un - um De - um

b. Mozart, Credo *Mass*

the first and last two tones, the latter inverted from G A to A G. In terms of the chant, his quotation reads "Cre–do . . . um–De," perhaps another example of an intended impertinence from the composer who could not stop inverting the letters of his own name and indulging in many other verbal pranks.

No less impressive than the whole structural concept are the different purposes to which Mozart bends his "Credo" motto. It serves as transition to G; expanded by sequence, 5 3 6 5 / 4 2 5 4, it serves as closing gesture and as modulation to the middle section, *Andante* in 6/8, for "Et incarnatus est." This pastoral meditation on Christ's birth in the relative minor produces the same response of awe and humility as the much longer pastoral at the same place in the unfinished Mass in c, K. 427 of 1783. Noteworthy is the orchestral progression confirming the turn toward C, V/ii - ii, V - I. Expanded, this progression will later provide the beginning of the Agnus Dei. "Crucifixus" Mozart sets to a descending chromatic fourth in the choral sopranos, with a stabbing *fp* marking at the beginning of each measure in chorus and orchestra alike, which the trumpets and timpani reinforce by three single tones. After this *Andante* dies away, swooning with several "dying falls," the *Molto allegro* in 3/4 strikes up again, a reprise of the movement's beginning. The motto continues to see diverse uses, preparing an episode in F (second theme material) and then in e (this remotest key touched provides the special treatment Mozart always accords to "Et in Spiritum Sanctum"), and still other destinations. There is a slight imitative flurry where we might expect a fugue, at "Et vitam venturi," but it soon gives way to the motto's insistent "Credo, credo" as coda, climbing up from altos and tenors to the sopranos, and then sounding in the basses. A unison statement of the motto, *forte* then *piano*, like the very beginning, signals the end: the sopranos ascend to their high G and begin to intone the motto to "Amen," but it is heard as four even quarters without rests, 5 3 2 1, stated three times.

The Sanctus begins in even half notes, *Allegretto* in common time, as the sopranos intone Mozart's all-time favorite chant motif, 1 2 4 3. Is the emphasis upon D, E, and F intended to atone for his having left out the three middle tones of the Credo chant ? (The very end of the mass suggests a positive answer to this question.) The continuation for "Dominus Deus Sabaoth" is soft and mitigated by a galant chromatic inflection, 5♮ 6 over subdominant harmony, a reminder of the gentle chromatic rises in the Kyrie. "Pleni sunt caeli" is forceful by comparison, working up to a rare *fortissimo* (outer choral voices and strings.) At "Hosanna" the tempo quickens to *Molto allegro*, bringing another *fortissimo* climax with sopranos falling by step from their high G over V/ii - ii. The Benedictus, an *Allegro* in F, is once again placid and built on the same harmonic progression as "Domine Deus Sabaoth." It belongs entirely to the soloists, who stretch it out to an ample seventy-three measures in common time. The reprise of "Hosanna" leaves the V/ii - ii, V - I progressions ringing in our ears—just as well, for Mozart is about to transform this material, first heard as an instrumental interlude in the Credo.

The Agnus Dei opens majestically, *Andante maestoso* in 3/4, with rising orchestral unisons outlining tonic major in no uncertain terms. The chorus, doubled by the orchestra, answers in even more forceful terms with V^7/ii - ii, as if questioning the supremacy of the tonic, or at the least delaying its lordly return. (The Church Sonata in C, K. 263, also emphasizes V^7/ii.) When the same antiphonal exchange is repeated down a step, the eighth measure of this large phrase brings not I but vi, requiring another four measures of preparation until the arrival of I in accented metric position. At this point the orchestra takes the lead again; against the soft staccato triplets of the second violins, the first violins propose a more pliant version of the tonic triad, softly, ending with the accented notes E F. The chorus responds to I - V with the corresponding melody for V - I (Example 9.5). The accented tones in the response are an appoggiatura D rising to E, sung to "miserere." (Note that rising appoggiature had marked the "Dei" in mm. 4 and 8.)

From this point the violins take charge of the rising triadic melody and use it for various purposes. It inaugurates the final section, *Allegro vivace* in common time, inducing the chorus to follow along and sing "Dona nobis pacem" to the same music. When at last the violins sing their melody alone, *piano*, the chorus follows them for the third and last time. They sing the final cadence not as a rising appoggiatura but a falling one. With this soft, "feminine" cadence we reach the conclusion of an epic that began with comedy, confronted the tragic in the "Crucifixus," and resolved all issues by drawing sublime musical consequences from a few tones. For sheer inspiration and cogency K. 257 is Mozart's greatest mass if not, indeed, his greatest composition in any genre up to this date.

EXAMPLE 9.5. *Mozart,* Credo *Mass,* Agnus Dei

Mozart's outpouring of sacred music in 1776 also included his grandest Litany, K. 243 in E♭, in which music from the beginning returns at the end. His mood when composing these works can be read to a certain extent from a letter to Padre Martini, written by Leopold Mozart over his son's name and dated Salzburg, 4 September 1776. With the letter was sent the motet *Misericordias Domini*, K. 222 (205ª), composed at Munich in 1775 in answer to a wish from the Bavarian elector to hear "Qualche Musica mia in contrapunto." This severe work in the key of d is in fact one of Mozart's most elaborate contrapuntal exercises, and it was bound to please the learned Italian prelate.[8] Its plea for mercy is also the essential point of Leopold's letter, describing the situation in Salzburg in terms that were meant to invoke pity and also to provoke Padre Martini into doing what he could to get Mozart recalled to Italy. "I live in a place where music makes very little fortune, although indeed apart from those who have left us [a reference to castrati?], we still have excellent teachers and especially composers of solid techniques, knowledge, and taste"; as examples, Michael Haydn and Adlgasser are mentioned by name, while Leopold Mozart is said to be able to put his whole heart into his composing no longer because he has been denied advancement. "As for the theater, we are in a bad way for lack of *Recitanti*. We have no *Musici* [i.e., castrati] and will not have them so easily because they want to be well paid, and generosity is not one of our defects."

[8] Martini answered Mozart's request for suggested improvements in the motet by saying that it had "everything that modern music requires, good harmony, mature modulation, moderate movement of the violins, change of key by means of the natural steps, and good conduct of the voices." This latter-day Beckmesser adds that it also has a bad case of parallel fifths between m. 92 and m. 93.

Reading between these lines, we sense the Mozarts' envy of Martini, who at least lived in a city (Bologna) with a thriving opera house. "Meanwhile I amuse myself by writing for the chamber and for the church . . . my father is maestro at the cathedral [he was vice-maestro], which gives me the occasion to write for the church as much as I want." In sum, Leopold's letter suggests that Wolfgang wrote so much sacred music in order to please himself, and in order to take advantage of the one regular venue for large-scale works open to him.

The letter continues with the oft-cited description of Salzburg masses. "Our church music is very different from that of Italy, since a mass with the whole Kyrie, Gloria, Credo, the Epistle sonata, the Offertory or Motet, Sanctus, and Agnus Dei must not exceed three-quarters of an hour at the longest, even at the most solemn mass when the prince himself officiates. This sort of composition demands special study, for even such a mass must have all the instruments—the war trumpets, timpani, etc." This is a credible definition of the short yet festive mass that was Salzburg's specialty under Archbishop Colloredo. Not many of Mozart's own masses were shorter than forty-five minutes, factoring in the time for a motet, an Epistle sonata, and the parts spoken and sung by the celebrant. Only the briefest of all from 1775–76, K. 220 and K. 259, surely qualify; perhaps K. 258 does. Mozart did indeed devote "special study" to the *missa brevis et solemnis*. Its limitations served to challenge his creative forces to the maximum. And as in the face of every other challenge encountered, he triumphed.

Mozart composed one more mass before leaving on his grand tour to Paris in September 1777, K. 275 in B♭, his first and only use of this key for a mass, although he had used it in other sacred works (e.g. the two litanies of 1771–72 and the *Salve regina* of the latter year). K. 275 is a *missa brevis* on the smallest scale, comparable to K. 220 and K. 259, with which it shares a folk-like simplicity of expression. Its most memorable feature is a veritable gavotte for the final section, "Dona nobis pacem," an *Allegro* in cut time. The movement could easily be a rondo finale in one of his instrumental works, and the insistence with which Mozart keeps returning to the refrain (more than ten times!) approaches effrontery. Not surprisingly, the work came under attack from later reformers of church music; it upset even local church musicians. On the envelope of a set of parts in the parish church of Wasserburg am Inn, dating from ca.1810, there is a telling inscription: "The Latin Mass that begins thus [incipit of Kyrie] supposedly by Joseph Haydn [sic] may not be performed again in this church, as the composition is an open mockery of the holy text."[9] The final gavotte is like a vaudeville and has been compared with the specimen of this genre at the end of *Die Entführung*.

[9] NMA I/1/4, ed. Monika Holl (1989), p. xi.

If the tune were an actual vaudeville, with the type of scabrous text so often associated with this Parisian genre, then Mozart was guilty of a truly scandalous offense. In any case, he seems to have transported himself ahead of time to the French capital on the wings of his song.

ZENITH IN 1779–80

MOZART'S post as court organist at Salzburg in succession to the deceased Anton Adlgasser was confirmed by decree of 17 January 1779. The salary was 450 gulden annually, three times what he earned as second concertmaster from 1772 to 1777. The contract specified that he was to compose new pieces for court and church as far as possible ("auch den Hof, und die Kirche nach möglichkeit mit neüen von Ihme verfertigten Kompositionen bedienen"). In this atmosphere of renewal Mozart wrote his Mass in C, K. 317, dated 23 March 1779, which probably sounded at one or the other of the many Easter celebrations the following week, along with the Epistle Sonata in C, K. 329 (317ª). With these two works Mozart fulfilled his obligations in stunning fashion. The brilliance of his new Mass in C outshone all his previous sacred works for Salzburg, even though it was only a *missa brevis*. At some time quite early, probably the coronation of Leopold II at Prague in 1791, the mass was pressed into imperial service, eventually becoming known as the *Coronation* Mass. A year later it was certainly used at the coronation of Leopold's son Francis as king of Bohemia.

The *Coronation* Mass begins with one of Mozart's grandest slow introductions, six and a half measures of *Andante maestoso* in common time, the chorus chanting "Kyrie" in a dotted rhythm that is imitated by a rising triad fanfare in the violins. Oboes and horns (added on a separate sheet to the score) sustain while the trumpets and timpani punctuate. The progression is guided by the chromatic descent of the bass from C down to F♯ (skipping only A♮), then coming to a stop on G. At *più andante* the solo soprano announces the main theme, a melodic turn around the third: 3 4 2 1. Modulation to V occurs as this figure is taken up by the solo tenor, but the soprano brings it back to tonic major, whence the two of them then explore the same figure in tonic minor, alternating with major. The cadence, marked *Maestoso come prima*, brings back both the chorus and a complete reprise of the introduction, suggesting a complete reprise of the main theme to follow. But this does not happen, for Mozart allows only a short coda of five measures emphasizing IV, *piano*, with a final echo of the main theme in the oboes and then the violins. This rich but obviously abbreviated opening has taken place in only thirty-one measures.

EXAMPLE 9.6.

a. Mozart, Coronation *Mass,* Gloria

b. *Mozart,* Idomeneo, *Chorus*

The Gloria is an *Allegro con spirito* in 3/4 that bears certain marks of a *ciaccona* (in which respect it shares traits with the original Credo of Mozart's next mass, K. 337 of 1780, marked *Tempo di Ciaccona*). It also employs a turning melodic figure in sixteenth notes on the third beat, in common with the beginning of the great orchestral-choral *Ciaccona* that ends the first act of *Idomeneo* (1780–81) (Example 9.6ab). Since this very same figure can be found in act-ending chaconnes by Rameau and other French composers, it follows that Mozart profited from his recent Paris trip even when writing sacred music for Salzburg. Many words and phrases in the Gloria (as well as the Credo) naturally suggest chaconne rhythms comparable to "Nettuno s'onori," and Mozart did not fail to take advantage of them. The Gloria as a whole is cast as a sonata form with two themes and a central section that is modulatory and mostly in the minor mode, with a coda for "amen"—a total of 198 measures.

The Credo is of roughly equivalent length, its main section being an *Allegro molto* in common time with rushing violins that keep up their sixteenth-note busywork incessantly, and that stop only in the middle for twelve measures of *Adagio* at "Et incarnatus est . . . passus, et sepultus est." The main section occurs four times, like a rondo refrain. "Et in Spiritum Sanctum" becomes an episode in the subdominant, as in the masses of 1775–76. "Amen" is set to the music of "Descendit de coelis," after which there is a short coda returning to the words and music of "Credo in unum Deum."

The Sanctus is set to an *Andante maestoso* in 3/4 with dotted rhythms, with the choral and orchestral forces at maximum strength in order to convey "*pleni* sunt caeli et terra." At these words the bass starts descending chromatically from C down to F♯, supporting the same music that began (and ended) the Kyrie. The summing up has begun. "Hosanna" reverts to fast triple meter like that in the Gloria, with which it shares the same dance-like mood and choral sonority of sopranos up to their high G for the "in excelsis" common to both. "Benedictus" brings an amiable, light *Allegretto* in 2/4 with constant sixteenth-note motion, a walking kind of piece appropriate to the verb of motion "venit." Its like is to be found in certain *Andantino* movements among Mozart's Salzburg serenades and divertimenti. The soloists have this movement to themselves, with the alto taking the melody (if it were written in the soprano's higher octave, it would require the high A that Mozart refuses to write). Obviously pleased with this lovely vocal quartet, the composer brings it back for a brief reprise after the return of the "Hosanna," necessitating a second return of its jubilant strains.

Agnus Dei is an *Andante sostenuto* in 3/4 in F, like the slow movement in a symphony, with muted violins over pizzicato basses and constant eighth-note motion. The soprano solo (presumably sung by Ceccarelli) offers a simple rising phrase, the two halves of which are bridged over by the instruments exactly as in the closely equivalent melody the Countess will later sing to the words "Dove sono" in *Figaro*. There is a brief reprise after a contrast in which Mozart writes out an ornamented version of the main theme, the violins pizzicato along with the basses. Then the violins, now *arco*, take time to mimic the ornamented version, after which there is a little transition to the key of C, the solo rising up to a held F, poised suspensefully, during which fermata the violins remove their mutes.

Resolution brings the first "Dona nobis pacem," sung by the solo soprano and tenor to the main theme of the Kyrie, *Andante con moto*. Solo bass and alto join them at the turn to minor that is equivalent to the "Christe." When the soloists have finished, the chorus takes up the same musical material, *Allegro con spirito*, turning it into a proclamation of triumph that ends like "Hosanna in excelsis," with sopranos and violins alike sweeping up to high G. What follows is coda. From the little melodic turning-down figure of the Kyrie melody, Mozart makes a figure that turns up: 3 4 2 1 becomes 2 3 1 4, and so on. And if this were not enough, he spins out another figure, *forte*, 3 2 3 4, 4 3 4 5. He did something quite similar at the end of the *Sparrow* Mass, K. 220, as we saw above. Here he is even more inspired and inventive. It is enough to provoke "tears of joy and delight" (the flautist Johann Baptist Becke's reaction on first hearing *Idomeneo* in rehearsal). The ending is postponed twice by powerful deceptive cadences to IV^6. When the end does come, it is with an exultant "pacem," the sopranos falling from their high G to E. Ending on the third like this (a favorite device with Joseph Haydn) seems much more in keeping with human optimism than ending on the tonic, which sounds more like divine might and the finality of all that is earthly.

The *Coronation* Mass is the summa of Mozart's sacred music up to this date. It profits in many ways from the several masses in C from 1775–76, yet outstrips them by far in the grandeur of its conception and the perfection of its every detail. The impeccable architecture of the whole is mainly a matter of perfect timing, that indispensable virtue of the opera composer. Mozart could hardly top the dramatic force of K. 317 in another setting of the same text, and he did not attempt to do so. In his next mass, K. 337 in C, written a year later in the spring of 1780, he went out of his way to create a work very different from K. 317. The first is boisterous to a nearly Beethovenian degree, the second so tender and rarified as to foretell Schubert. The pair of horns in the first is replaced in the second by a pair of obbligato bassoons.

Whereas the *Coronation* Mass opens with a thunderbolt from heaven and continues with portentous rhetorical gestures, its successor begins quietly. The first violins propose a little rising figure with chromatic appoggiatura, followed by the same in the second violins, with the firsts a third above—a very galant opening this, the tender, *empfindsamer* nature of which is heightened in the continuation, emphasizing the subdominant, with melody constantly in parallel thirds, bedecked with melodic turns and sighs. Subtleties abound, such as the harmonic reinterpretation of C♯ early on. The chorus then enters *forte*, singing the same material. Mozart flirts with a move to V after the one half cadence but immediately returns to I. A sudden *forte* on a $V^{4/3}/V$ chord jolts the placid proceedings three times, suggesting but not effecting modulation. (This device is a favorite delaying tactic of Joseph

Haydn.) The raised tonic, C♯, appears in yet a third context, as leading tone of $V^{6/4/2}$/ii on the way to the cadence, which arrives quietly after one more interruption. The instruments then add another cadence, fading to a *pianissimo*.

The Gloria, an *Allegro molto* in common time, begins with the burst of power denied the Kyrie, as the chorus rises in parallel 6/3 chords to the sopranos' high G for "excelsis." The same rise is then sung to "in terra pax," which suggests that Mozart will be less concerned here than usual with literal tone painting of the text. The modulation to V takes place quickly and is confirmed by the recurrence of the rising 6/3 chords in the new key. What sounds like a distinct second theme is given out by solo soprano and solo tenor at "Domine Deus," followed by modulation further afield, to the keys of F, B♭, E♭, c, and even A♭, which then becomes an augmented-sixth chord on the way back to tonic major. The harmonies are colorful, and the structure is rather loose in comparison with the tautness of the Gloria in the preceding mass. The reprise begins with "Cum Sancto Spiritu," followed by an abbreviated drive to the cadence, which arrives with a resounding "amen." The soloists then take over. Mozart expands this coda to considerable proportions, extending the rising 6/3 chords so that each one takes a full measure, a segment then repeated by the chorus. The way the composer finally places the two syllables of "a-men" on offbeats, divided by rests, is novel and another indication perhaps of his concern to make this work different from its predecessors.

The Credo was originally written by Mozart as a *Tempo di Ciaccona*. Chaconne-like features had often graced Mozart's Credos in 3/4 time, but he had never gone so far as this. His original Credo begins in the orchestra with eight measures sounding like a sketch for the Chaconne that inaugurates the ballet following *Idomeneo* (Figure 9.4). Both are indebted to the great opera-ending chaconnes by Gluck and others he had witnessed in Paris. The conflicting rhythms and second-beat accents of the genre lend Mozart's Credo a muscularity that is very attractive. He continued composing and fully scoring it in the autograph through the *Adagio* "Et incarnatus est" and the return of *Tempo primo* up to "Non erit finis," where he broke off. It is unusual for Mozart to abandon a fully scored composition so close to the end. His second Credo was shorter, offering one reason for the change, but probably not the only one.

We know very little about Mozart's activities or state of mind during the spring of 1780, but what this large-scale replacement suggests is that he was under no great pressure to finish K. 337, as he was so often with other works. The number of works dated 1780 with certainty is very small. One is the last Church Sonata, K. 336 in C, dated "nel Marzo 1780," as is K. 337. The sonata's initial melodic rise from tonic to third degree agrees with a

FIGURE 9.4. Autograph of the original Credo from the Mass in C, K. 337.

main idea in the mass, present at the beginning of the Kyrie and at the end in the "Dona nobis pacem."

The replacement Credo, *Allegro vivace* in 3/4, does not forgo all chaconne-like features; it too glories in second-beat accents. What apparently decided Mozart to rewrite, aside from the need for greater brevity, was the possibility of creating a movement more in harmony with the Gloria. Like the Gloria, the new piece relies on long successions of parallel 6/3 chords. In its overall structure this Credo, like that of K. 317, is a large-scale rondo, with several statements of the main music. "Et incarnatus" now becomes an *Andante* instead of an *Adagio*. It begins in F but moves to g for "Crucifixus," whence a long chromatic descent in the bass takes over. The section seems about to end with a cadence in d at "passus" when Mozart undercuts it with a sudden modulation to e (suggesting transfiguration?). The E gives him a common tone with tonic major as the *Allegro vivace* resumes, the violins leading the charge. Once again there is a separate episode in the subdominant for "Et in

EXAMPLE 9.7. *Mozart, Mass in C, K. 337, Sanctus*

Spiritum Sanctum." The chaconne-like refrain returns at "Et vitam venturi," assuming the form it took at "descendit."

Sanctus is an *Adagio* in common time sharing features with the Kyrie. The orchestra emphasizes chromatic rises in thirds, while the chorus sings octave leaps on C, then on G, paralleling the bass at the opening of the Kyrie. At "Pleni sunt caeli" the Kyrie is also recalled by the protracted $V^{4/3}/V$ chord, at which the violins insist on a descending tritone in dotted rhythm, inverted against itself, not once but three times, the second time with staccato afterbeats (Example 9.7). A few months later Mozart would make this violin figure the main motif of *Idomeneo*. The falling figure was already sounded by the violins in unison at the first protracted V/V in the Kyrie. The melody of "Hosanna" for solo soprano that follows, with its rising sixth and offbeat accompaniment, *Allegro non troppo*, is once again unusual, at least for Mozart. It sounds an almost Schubertian tone (as in, for example, "Guten Morgen, schöne Müllerin!"). The chorus takes up this material and makes it increasingly more dramatic and less lyrical, especially at the unexpected silence; after the silence there is a succession of descending 6/3 chords.

Benedictus offers a still greater surprise. Mozart forsakes all his usual responses to the text and sets it to a *stile antico* fugue for chorus in the austere key of a. The orchestra does nothing but double the choral voices. After only the briefest of transitions at the end, the solo soprano's Lied-like "Hosanna" resembles a voice from another world.

The lyrical tendency in this mass reaches rhapsodic proportions in the Agnus Dei, an *Andante sostenuto* in common time that Mozart chooses to set in his most emotion-laden major key, E♭. Three concertante solo instruments—oboe, bassoon, and organ—enhance the moment, as the solo soprano pours forth a melody replete with lovelorn sighs (a model, in fact, for the Countess' "Porgi amor" in *Figaro*). It takes a more substantial transition, the chorus participating, to dissolve this romantic idyll (bass rising chromatically from E♭ to G) and prepare for what comes next. The violins take off their mutes and the basses stop playing pizzicato as they intone a perky *Allegro assai* in 3/4, bringing back tonic major, but very softly, *pianissimo*. This rise of the melody, 1 2, then 2 3, sounds vaguely familiar, as do the chains of *alla Turca* sixteenth notes in the figuration (they are present from the beginning of the Credo). The chorus enters singing "dona" *forte* to the falling fourth, C G. The sopranos and basses will finally sing its fugal answer, G down to C, but not before some extraordinary happenings that make sense only in the context of the entire mass—long-held chords searching for a resolution such as the three measures of $V^{4/3,}$ then $V^{4/2,}$ but most of all the protracted A♭ accompanied this time by its own dominant chords. The soloists have the last word, the soprano softening the leap from G down to C by filling it in by step. And thus the work ends softly, as it began. The fade-out at the end is as unlike the ending of K. 317 as possible. It is rather like the ending of one of Joseph Haydn's loveliest works, the *Missa St. Joannis de Deo* of ca. 1775.

Mozart's last complete mass may sound quite unlike its predecessors, and intentionally so, if the assessment above is correct, but it is not without a close companion in date as in style. The falling by step from fifth degree to third, then to tonic, with which the solo soprano ends the mass corresponds with the main theme of the *Allegro* in the Magnificat that constitutes the last section of *Vesperae solennes de Confessore* in C, K. 339, dated 1780. (This theme may sound familiar because Mozart used it at the end of his life as the second idea in his overture to *Tito*.) The last three sections of both mass and vespers are in fact parallel in affect, as Table 9.1 shows:

TABLE 9.1. Final sections in two 1780 works

	Mass, K. 337	Vespers, K. 339
Choral fugue in *stile antico*	Benedictus in a	"Laudate pueri" in d
Lyric reverie for soprano	Agnus Dei in E♭	"Laudate Dominum" in F (solo and chorus)
Paean to joy and choral celebration	"Dona nobis" in C	Magnificat in C

Since it was traditional to set "Laudate pueri" to an old-style fugue, which Mozart had done as well in his Vespers of 1779, K. 321, it stands to reason that his choice of this procedure for the antepenultimate musical piece in K. 337, a seemingly mad one, was more borrowing from another genre than caprice.

Only four completed works date from 1780, and all were composed, presumably, before Mozart became engrossed with the commission from Munich for *Idomeneo* in the late summer or early fall. They would make a wonderfully integrated and mutually illuminating concert if heard together: Symphony No. 34 in C, K. 338 (with prominent flat sixth passage in the middle of the first movement), the Mass in C, K. 337, with the interpolation of the related Organ Sonata, K. 336, and the Vespers in C, K. 339.

K. 337 never enjoyed the same public favor as the *Coronation* Mass, K. 317, and still does not (as indicated by the number of modern recordings). But the difference between them in this regard should not be exaggerated. K. 337 was also used at the imperial coronation ceremonies of the early 1790s. In fact it figures as the first mass by Mozart in the catalogue of music held by the Burgkapelle, while K. 317 is second. Also, Johann Traeg offered parts for hire to both masses in this order during 1792. Ten years later Joseph Haydn finished his noble series of six late masses with the great *Harmoniemesse* in B♭, a work so full of youthful fire and audacity as to belie the composer's seventy years. It is just possible that Haydn was acknowledging Mozart's last complete mass by beginning the Sanctus and "Hosanna" of his last mass with a chromatic rise from the tonic. The flat-sixth degree and chord play a special role in the *Harmoniemesse* from the very beginning, but the striking point of coincidence with K. 337 is their explosive intrusion close to the end of both masses in the "Dona nobis pacem."

THE MUNICH KYRIE

WHEN Mozart went to Munich in November 1780 to complete *Idomeneo* for the court theater there, he took with him the performing materials for two masses. Surely these were his two most recent masses, K. 317 and K. 337. In his letter of 13 November 1780 to his father in Salzburg, he wrote: "Be so good as to send me the 2 scores ["2 sparten"] of the masses I have with me, and also the Mass in B♭ [K. 275], for Count Seeau will be telling the elector shortly something about them. I should like people to get to know some of my compositions in this style also. I just heard a mass by Grua—masses of this kind one could easily compose a half dozen a day." Franz Paul Grua was the prolific Vice-Kapellmeister of the Munich court, and the work

Mozart heard was at a service in the Hofkapelle on Sunday, the day before he wrote his letter. Shortly thereafter, on 15 November, he reported: "I almost forgot to tell you the best news. Count Seeau last Sunday after mass presented me en passant to the elector, who was very gracious with me. He said: 'It pleases me to see you here again,' and I said I would do my best to win his approval. He clapped me on the shoulder and said, 'On that account I have no doubt at all that everything will be very good—a Piano piano, si và lontano.' "

Carl Theodore, the elector, heard the second performance of *Giardiniera* as a guest in Munich in 1775 and presumably met Mozart then. Did they also meet during Mozart's visit of 25 December 1778 to 12 January 1779? Not according to Mozart's three letters written to his father. In the first, dated 29 December 1778, he wrote: "Just between us, and in the greatest secrecy, I am going to write a mass here. All good friends advise me to do so. I cannot describe to you what good friends Cannabich and Raaff have been to me." Mozart's plans to win a post at the Munich court thus included writing or directing his sacred music in 1775, in late 1778, and again in 1780–81.

Count Seeau was central to any such plan. He figures in the correspondence between father and son in a way that suggests there was some mistrust between him and the Mozarts lingering from the 1775 visit. In his letter of 31 December 1778 Leopold scolded his son for thinking of writing a mass for Munich: "Now it is too late, what with composing, copying, etc. God help us! and then at the end waiting for a payment, of which Count Seeau would keep half." Mozart presented a bound copy of his Duo Sonatas (K. 301–306) just printed in Paris and dedicated to the wife of Carl Theodore, Elizabeth Auguste, to the electress herself on 7 January 1779. He went with his dear friend Christian Cannabich to her rooms in the Residenz in order to do so, he wrote his father the next day. "We were with her for over half an hour, and she was very gracious. So that I may be rewarded soon I made it known that I would be leaving in a few days. About Count Seeau you need not worry, for I don't believe the matter will go through him, and if it does, he dare not grumble" (letter of 8 January 1779).

Mozart's Kyrie in d, K. 341 (368^a), has long been assigned to the period right after the premiere of *Idomeneo* in Munich, and with good reason. The autograph has been lost, but everything about this magnificent piece of music points to its having been composed for the Mannheim-Munich band, which inspired Mozart's most challenging orchestral writing in his opera. The Kyrie's orchestration alone almost excludes any other destination, and certainly eliminates Salzburg. There are no trombones, unlike the Salzburg works, but a full complement of winds in pairs, including clarinets in A, horns in F, horns in D, trumpets in D, and timpani. Two numbers in the key of d in *Idomeneo* also require two horns in F and two in D—Electra's first aria and the fleeing chorus at the end of Act II.

The overture to *Idomeneo* was Mozart's last writing task before the premiere on 29 January 1781. It ends with a jagged descending line that is actually sung at one point in the opera to the word "duol," and so we may label it the "duol" motif. Mozart begins the Kyrie in d with a similar motif, almost as if he had scarcely put down his pen after finishing the end of the overture (Example 9.8ab). The importance of dynamics in both examples should not be missed. They were one of the main features that made the Mannheim players famous. The chorus enters chanting "Kyrie" to a dotted rhythm, homophonically. Here and throughout much of the piece the orchestra is

EXAMPLE 9.8.

a. Mozart, Idomeneo, *Overture*

b. Mozart, Kyrie in d, K. 341

independent and complete in its own right as a carrier of the musical discourse. At the transition to the second section in the relative major Mozart calls on the violins to play passage work in octaves that resembles a similar challenge put to the violins in the overture to *Idomeneo.* Before writing out the opera's overture, one of the other last tasks facing Mozart was finishing the extensive ballet music that concluded the score. The big and powerful section of the ballet that is in d, labeled "La Chaconne, qui reprend," has special affinities with the Kyrie in d, which would only need to be accelerated from *Andante* to *Allegro* in order to sound like a dance in its own right. Specifically, the Kyrie exhibits many typical chaconne patterns in rhythmic terms, such as declamation on the first of the two quarter-note beats followed by a rest, as in the first entrance of the chorus and also throughout the work. Attention should also be paid to the expressive chromatic descent further along in the Kyrie. If similarities in content and musical style count for anything, it follows that the Kyrie in d was indeed written for Munich in early 1781.

At this point I call on the testimony of an author whose knowledge of Mozart's sacred music was second to none:

> The Kyrie was written in Munich in 1781 for large orchestra [the players are listed]. The depth of expression Mozart realized in his dramatic works with *Idomeneo* was achieved anew in his church music with this work. Already the key of d, which he chose only in the early mass K. 65 (61ª) of 1769, raises this Kyrie above the other mass compositions. Unity of form does not preclude an intensely colorful statement. The three-part movement flows in a serious expressive vein without sharp thematic contrasts. Harmony, chromaticism, melody, and dynamics all betray a passionate interpretation of the Kyrie cry, borne by a lively and independent orchestral web that is in contrast with the homophonic chorus.[10]

This expert's confidence in the traditional assignment of the Kyrie in d to Munich in 1781 deserves consideration.

Mozart returned to church music in Vienna in 1788, probably with a view to securing a position at the cathedral or some other church in order to help overcome his financial distress. He wrote his sister on 2 August 1788 asking her to lend him the scores of two "tutti masses" and some graduals by Michael Haydn. The possibility has been raised that the Kyrie in d might be shaken loose from Munich and the time of *Idomeneo* and redated to the end of the decade.[11] In making his case, the main proponent of this hypothesis

[10] Karl Gustav Fellerer, *Die Kirchenmusik W. A. Mozarts* (Laaber, 1985), p. 15.
[11] Alan Tyson, "Redating Mozart: Some Stylistic and Biographical Implications." This talk, first given at the American Musicological Society's annual meeting in Louisville, Kentucky, on 28 October 1983, is printed as Chapter 2 of Tyson's *Mozart: Studies of the Autograph Scores*; see pp. 27–28.

pushes the evidence and the reader rather hard: "It is possible that the powerful D-minor Kyrie, K. 341 (368ᵃ), also belongs to this period [ca.1788], but
the autograph is lost. All the editions of Köchel have followed Otto Jahn in
assigning it to Mozart's stay in Munich from November 1780 to March 1781,
but there is little to be said in favor of this."[12] The readers of this book can
judge for themselves the truth of his last remark.[13]

Thamos, Zaide, and the Approaches to *Idomeneo*

MOZART complained when he was in Paris in the summer of 1778 that
Salzburg was no place for an artist of his talents because professional musicians were not held in much consideration there, and because "one hears
nothing, there is no theater, no opera," (letter of 7 August 1778). The last
part of his complaint was only partially valid. There was no regular opera, it
is true, but plays and operettas, some quite advanced, were brought by itin-
erant troupes visiting Salzburg in the second half of the 1770s. After hard
negotiations between Archbishop Colloredo and the burgomaster, an old
dance hall near the Mirabell Palace was converted into a court theater, open
to the paying public and in operation by late 1775. Its proportions were tiny,
fifty feet long by twenty feet wide, containing at most some 600 or 700 spectators, but for a small provincial capital it was almost adequate.[14] The archbishop allotted the non-princely sum of 500 gulden annually for the purpose
of attracting any theater company that would spend the winter season in
Salzburg, and applications were received in the fall for the privilege. The
players, once installed, apparently could charge what the traffic would bear
in ticket prices in order to supplement their meager court stipend and
attempt to make ends meet. According to Johann Kaspar Riesbeck's travel
diary of 1783: "Theater madness is as strong here in Salzburg as in Munich,
and one smiles upon the arrival of a traveling acting company as in remotest
Siberia upon the return of spring."[15]

The Mozarts' dwelling since 1773 in the Tanzmeisterhaus was scarcely
more than a stone's throw across the Hannibal-Platz (now Makart-Platz) to
the new court theater (situated on the same plot as the present-day

[12] Tyson, *Mozart: Studies of the Autograph Scores*, p. 342, note 34.
[13] Monika Holl, editor of the Kyrie in NMA, follows Tyson's hypothesis and labels it "presumably
written at Vienna, 1787–1791."
[14] Ernst Hintermaier, "Das Fürsterzbischöflich Hoftheater zu Salzburg (1775–1803)," *Österreichische
Musikzeitschrift* 30 (1975): 351–65.
[15] Cited ibid., p. 360.

Landestheater). From Nannerl's diaries we know that the Mozarts were as avid theatergoers as the rest of Salzburg.

The first troupe to play in the new theater was that of Karl Wahr, whom we have already encountered in connection with Haydn and Esterháza. They gave fifty-six performances between 16 November 1775 and 20 February 1776, including Jean-François Regnard's comedy *Der Zerstreute*, for which Haydn had supplied incidental music (this subsequently became his Symphony No. 60), and the tragedy *Thamos, König in Egypten*, for which parts of Mozart's incidental music were probably used. The author of *Thamos*, Baron Tobias Philip von Gebler, as well as being a literary figure admired in his day, was a statesman—he was privy councillor to Maria Theresa and vice-chancellor of the Imperial Bohemian Court Chancery. His *Thamos*, based on Abbé Terasson's novel *Sethos* and subtitled "Ein heroisches Drama," was printed in Prague and Dresden in 1773—Leopold Mozart owned a copy, now preserved in the Mozarteum (Figure 9.5). Dissatisfied with the incidental music provided to him by Johann Tobias Statler, Gebler apparently asked Mozart to supplement or replace it, which he did by writing two grand choruses (Nos. 1 and 6) for Acts I and IV. These were performed, perhaps with some of Statler's music, at the Kärntnerthor Theater in Vienna during April 1774.[16]

Karl Wahr's choice of *Thamos* for Salzburg may have been a tribute to the young composer, and an inducement to write more incidental music. The purely orchestral entr'actes, Nos. 2, 3, and 5, are said to have been composed by Mozart for Wahr's performance of the play in Salzburg on 3 January 1775. But analysis of the handwriting in the copies that survive suggests that they were written a few years later.[17] What seems certain is that Mozart would not have remained uninvolved in a Salzburg performance of a play for which he had already written incidental music.

On his return trip from Paris to Salzburg in the fall of 1778, Mozart made costly stops in several places, to the increasing distress of his father. Mannheim was once again the music center in which he hoped for employment. To Leopold, Mannheim was no longer even a good prospect, since the palatine elector, Carl Theodore, had moved his entire court and theatrical establishment to Munich by the end of 1778. Mozart was happy enough just to be with some of his old Mannheim friends again, without worrying too much about money. He began his letter of 12 November 1778, "God be praised and thanked that I am once again in my beloved Mannheim! . . . as

---

[16] On the choral and orchestral forces for these performances, see Dexter Edge, "Mozart's Viennese Orchestras," *Early Music* 20 (1992), 64–88; 68–71.

[17] Tyson, *Mozart: Studies of the Autograph Scores*, p. 132: "The entr'actes are in a handwriting that dates from about 1777."

FIGURE 9.5. Title page and beginning of the preface from Gebler's play *Thamos*, 1773.

I love Mannheim, so does Mannheim love me. I'm not sure, but I still think I will be offered a position here." No position materialized, for Leopold was right. But Mannheim offered Mozart something even so. His own words best tell the story.

> I can *perhaps* make forty louis d'or here! To be sure, I should have to stay six weeks or at most two months in Mannheim. The Seyler company are here, whom you no doubt already know by reputation; Herr von Dahlberg is their director. He is pressing me to compose a duodrama for him; and indeed I hesitated little before agreeing, for this is a kind of drama I have always wanted to write. I don't know if I told you something about this kind of play when I was last here? Then I saw with the greatest pleasure two performances of such a work. Indeed, nothing has ever surprised me more! For I always imagined that this kind of piece would make no effect! You surely know that it is declaimed

rather than sung, and the music is like an obbligato recitative; sometimes words are spoken over the music, which makes the most magnificent effect.

Mozart continues in this same letter by naming names.

What I saw was *Medea* by [Georg] Benda. He has composed another, *Ariadne auf Naxos*—both are truly outstanding. You know that among the Lutheran Kapell-meisters Benda has always been my favorite. I love these two works so much that I carry them about with me. [Presumably he had obtained copies of the two keyboard scores printed in 1778.] Imagine my joy at having to compose just the kind of work that I have so much desired! Do you know what my opinion is? That most operatic recitative should be treated in this way, and only occasionally sung, when the words *can be well expressed by the music.*

Leopold did not know what his son was talking about. He filled page after page with recriminations about their mounting debts before finally coming around to this subject in his letter of 10 December.

I don't know and cannot really imagine what a *declaimed duodrama* might be. I suppose that in this type of opera a great deal more depends on declamation and action than on fine singing, or rather than on an outstanding voice. If so, Herr Heigl and his wife would certainly do it to perfection, as both of them also sing in the operettas and act so well that one forgets about their voices. Thus they could perform it this coming carnival. If not, you should know that the whole company will split up after carnival, with Heigl and his wife, the princi-pals, leaving the troupe and going to the Munich theater.

In his letter of 3 December Mozart had claimed, as a way of explaining his lingering in Mannheim, that he was busy composing the first act of his duo-drama *Semiramis.* His letter of 24 November to Dahlberg speaks instead of a monodrama that he would undertake to compose and see through perfor-mance for 25 louis d'or. An agreement was apparently not reached with Dahlberg, for in the letter of 3 December he speaks of composing the work without any remuneration. "To please Herr von Gemmingen and myself I am now composing the first act of the declaimed opera (that I was supposed to write) *for nothing.* I shall bring it with me and finish it at home. You see how strong my liking is for this kind of composition. Herr von Gemmingen is the poet, it goes without saying, and the duodrama is called *Semiramide.*"

Nothing survives from this work. Yet Mozart carefully preserved other fragments begun in Mannheim. Probably he did not get so far as committing music to paper, in spite of the excuses made to Leopold. This is a pity. The subject, a horror story of grisly proportions, suited his own vicissitudes in 1778. Gluck demonstrated its potential in his pantomime ballet of 1765.

A final, noncommittal reference to the subject is included in Mozart's chatty letter from Kaysersheim on 18 December, in response to Leopold's perplexed comments of 10 December.

> Concerning the monodrama or duodrama, a singing voice is unnecessary, as not a note of it is sung; there is only speaking. In a word, it is a recitative with instruments, only the actor speaks the words instead of singing them. If you could but hear it once, even with only keyboard, it could not fail to please you, and if you could hear it fully realized, you would be quite swept away, I guarantee you this.

Here Mozart again explains the genre but without a hint of any contribution of his own to it. Had he actually created his first melodrama, the response would have been different. His wavering between calling it a monodrama and a duodrama may mean that even the text had failed to reach him.

In spite of his reluctance to return to Salzburg, Mozart was curious to know about the theatrical company performing there. He questioned his father about their reception in his letter of 3 December: "Does Herr Feiner play the English horn as well? Ah, if only we had clarinets too! You cannot imagine the glorious effect of a symphony with flutes, oboes, and clarinets." In his letter of 10 December Leopold held out hope for the future.

> A certain Böhm has sent two dancers here in order to collect subscriptions for the season following Easter. This Böhm has recently had a large company of actors, singers, and dancers, supported for many years by the Moravian nobility at Brünn. Since he is reputed a good violinist and especially an effective orchestra leader, he was offered this post at the German Theater in Vienna. But he had his heart more set on directing a troupe, and since he had both financial resources and costumes, he is assembling a company for Salzburg . . . as many as twenty people may be engaged . . . *something can be made of this.* Otherwise— Herr Feiner also plays English horn, and perhaps clarinets can be found?

Johann Heinrich Böhm was born in Moravia or perhaps in Upper Austria during the 1740s. He excelled as an actor-singer as well as a violinist and orchestra leader.

Mozart's incidental music for *Thamos*, K. 345 (316ª), is thought to have been brought into its final form in connection with the visits of the Böhm troupe to Salzburg in 1779–80. The troupe played the court theater from April until early June, then repaired to Augsburg, whence the players returned to Salzburg in September and remained until March 1780. Mozart revised the two big choruses, Nos. 1 and 6, adding flutes and making very extensive changes to the latter while nearly tripling its length.

The closeness in style of the *Thamos* music to *Die Zauberflöte* is hardly surprising. An Egyptian setting and the darkness-into-light metaphor are common to both play and opera. In fact, the *Thamos* music anticipates some of that late masterpiece. "Erhöre die Wünsche, die Wünsche erhöre" at the beginning of No. 1 in *Thamos* prefigures "Es lebe Sarastro! Sarastro lebe!" in the opera's first finale not only in declamatory rhythm and verbal inversion, but also tone for tone. Three measures later in the *Thamos* chorus, a sudden lurch from G as V of C to the chord of E exactly foretells the same shift in the duet for the two men, No. 11 in the opera, just before "Tod und Ver-zweiflung war sein Lohn" (Death and despair were his reward), words (and music) so significant to Mozart that he quoted them without any context in a letter of 11 June 1791 to his wife. Mozart added a chorus to *Thamos*, on a text not in Gebler's play and thought to be by Johann Andreas Schachtner: No. 7 in d/D, replacing a purely orchestral piece in d. In its final major sec-tion, "Höchste Gottheit, milde Sonne," Mozart anticipates the beginning of *Zauberflöte*'s final chorus, "Heil sei euch Geweihten!"

The entr'actes for orchestra in the *Thamos* music are also richly inventive. No. 2 is in c, an *Allegro* in common time that is an amply proportioned sonata form of 125 measures preceded by three measures of *Maestoso* in 3/4 as "cur-tain," with the treble rising through the triad (cf. the beginning of the over-ture to *Die Zauberflöte*). No. 3 is a charming *Andante* in 3/4 and in E♭, much of it devoted to an oboe solo over muted violins. Perhaps the most impres-sive is No. 5, an *Allegro vivace assai* in common time, which begins in the key of d with furious fourth-beat *forte* accents, tutti, a passage that will recur only at the very end, closing a coda in which d becomes D. The second theme is constructed of two three-measure phrases, repeated many times but always different in the harmonization of accompanimental figures. In the long coda this theme undergoes a curious dissection when its fourth measure is excerpted and repeated over and over.

No. 4 of the *Thamos* music is in a class by itself. It begins as an *Allegro* in 3/4 and in g with strong second-beat accents, like a chaconne. This agitated beginning gives way to a placid *Andantino* in B♭. From its nature we should have been able to suspect that it was the accompaniment to a melodrama. Leopold Mozart made sure that we did not mistake it by writing verbal cues on the score that correspond to parts of the speech by Sais at the beginning of Act IV. This may be Mozart's first melodrama, which might help explain its rather tentative quality. An alternative suggestion is current to the effect that Mozart merely described the speech in music blow by blow, which would be a unique kind of piece if so. It is true that Mozart does not provide pauses for the speaker as in *Zaide*, but the piece can be performed as a melo-drama with good effect.

EXAMPLE 9.9. *Mozart,* Thamos, *sketch*

Internal musical features as well as external evidence suggest that No. 4 of the *Thamos* music was written in 1779 or 1780. Mozart began the *Andantino* section, subsequently replaced, with a slurred conjunct melodic figure in dotted rhythm, falling a fifth, with *fp* marking the first note and two staccato eighth notes at the bottom of the fall (Example 9.9). Such an innocent, gavotte-like figure! Yet it happens to be the main melodic and rhythmic motif of *Idomeneo,* begun in the fall of 1780. Mozart replaced this music with a less placid *Allegretto* in B♭, but he returned to the falling figure with *fp* marking in the agitated *Più Andante* section, the figure now becoming a falling tritone in the first violins, mirrored by a rising tritone in the second violins (Example 9.10). This version of the motif, a falling tritone in inversion against itself, anticipates elements in the second love duet in *Idomeneo,* No. 20b, and the sacrifice scene, No. 27; it also occurs in the "Pleni sunt caeli et terra" of the Mass in C, K. 337, dated March 1780 (cf. Example 9.7). In all these cases the interaction between first and second violins is the same.

EXAMPLE 9.10. *Mozart,* Thamos, *No. 4*

When at Mannheim in early 1778, Mozart heard rumors, unfounded as it turned out, that Joseph II planned to hire a composer for his new German opera company. On 11 January 1778 he wrote his father:

> I know for certain that the emperor has in mind founding a new German opera in Vienna, and that he seeks in all seriousness a young Kapellmeister who understands the German language, possesses genius, and is in a condition to bring something new into the world. [Georg] Benda of Gotha is applying, and [Anton] Schweitzer is determined to prevail. I believe it would be a good thing for me, but only if well paid, that is understood. If the emperor were to give me a thousand gulden I would write him a German opera, and if he did not wish to retain me, it would not matter. Please write to all our good friends in Vienna you can think of and tell them that I am in a position to do honor to the emperor. If he does not want to hire me, he should try me out with an opera. What he does thereafter I care not. Adieu. I beg you to act at once, otherwise someone else might forestall me.

Neither Benda nor Schweitzer could be called "young" in 1778, and the emperor was not looking for outside talent in any case, because he did not want further expense. Leopold went immediately into his campaign mode, relating the contents of his son's letter to those he thought might help, among whom were Dr. Anton Mesmer and the playwright Franz von Heufeld. His lost letter of 16 January 1778 to the latter elicited a careful response dated 24 January that allows us to reconstruct the situation in Vienna. After seconding Leopold's plan to send his son to Paris "because Salzburg is too narrow for his genius," Heufeld minced no words about the possibilities in Vienna.

> In these days we are having the rehearsals of the first opera *[Die Bergknappen]*, with text by Herr Weidmann and music composed by the theater violist, Herr Umlauf, and the premiere will soon follow. All this is only a trial, to see if the Germans can start something of the kind. But it is certain that no composer will be hired as long as Gluck and Salieri are in imperial service. To recommend someone is exactly the way of insuring that the person recommended will not be chosen, and there is no middle man who can achieve what you want either.

Heufeld's direct statement helps throw light on the failure of Leopold's plan of attack ten years earlier, at the time of *La finta semplice*. The more one of his subjects or an outsider (in the case of Leopold) pushed Joseph II, the less likely was the emperor to accede. Heufeld continued:

> I could cite you instances where people applied directly to His Majesty and were turned down. The path you propose I cannot find good, and that is the reason

why a petition would make no headway, because I am assured in advance that it would avail nothing and, in fact, work to the detriment of the petitioner. There is, on the other hand, a surer and more laudable way open to good talent, by which it could secure the emperor's favor, namely composing a work, which anyone is allowed to do. If your son will take the trouble to set some good German comic opera to music, send it in, submit it to the approval of His Majesty, and then await his decision, it could well succeed if it pleased. But in this case it would surely be necessary to be present in person. With regard to Benda and Schweitzer, your son need have no worry. I can assure you that neither will prevail—they lack the reputation here that they have elsewhere.

Benda did go to Vienna in 1778. His *Medea* and other works were performed in the Burgtheater, but he came away empty-handed after giving an academy in the spring of 1779.

Leopold sent Heufeld's original letter to his son in Mannheim on 29 January. On 4 February Mozart responded. He wanted to write an opera in the worst way, he said, "but seria, not buffa, and Italian rather than German." An Italian seria opera would have suited the talents of Aloysia Weber, with whom he was infatuated at the time. "You should not have sent me the letter from Heufeld, which gave me more pain than pleasure. The fool thinks I will write a comic opera and write one on chance, at my own expense. I believe he would have done his noble status no damage had he written 'Mr.' instead of 'your son' ["der H: sohn, und nicht ihr sohn"]. He truly is a Viennese ass. Or does he believe that people always remain twelve years old?"

In Vienna, meanwhile, Ignaz Umlauf was promoted to the post of Kapellmeister of the German theater. By 1780 Mozart was again desperate enough to escape Salzburg that he took Heufeld's advice and did what he said he would not do. He wrote a Singspiel on the chance that it would be performed in Vienna, a work that later came to be called *Zaide*. It was not primarily comic, but serious, too serious, indeed, to meet favor in Vienna, or so it was later claimed.

There are reasons to believe that *Zaide* was written very close to the time of *Idomeneo*. It may have been begun as late as August or September 1780, when Mozart had not much else to do except dream of staging an "Operette" (as he called it) with the German troupe in Vienna's Burgtheater. Gluck's "Turkish" opera of 1764, written on Dancourt's *La rencontre imprévue*, was revived in German translation as *Die Pilgrime von Mekka* in the Burgtheater on 26 July 1780, with Aloysia Weber in the female leading role. The production was a great success, with the result, I believe, that Mozart was spurred to obtain a rival text from his friend Schachtner.

Some commentators have tried to link *Zaide* with the visits of the Böhm troupe to Salzburg in 1779–80. Their arguments ignore the explicit testimony in the letters. Another argument against such a link is Böhm's subsequent failure to exploit *Zaide*. He did reuse the *Thamos* music by attaching it to another play, *Lanassa*, Karl Martin Plümicke's translation of Lemierre's tragedy *La veuve du Malibar*. Gebler's *Thamos* was a failed play, and Mozart held his incidental music in high enough esteem to lament the fact. He wrote Leopold from Vienna on 15 February 1783, "It saddens me greatly that I will not be able to use the music to *Thamos*—the play, which did not please here, is now among the works rejected for performance. For the sake of the music alone, it might possibly be given again, but this is not likely. It certainly is a shame!" *Lanassa*, on the other hand, was a success, and Mozart had the pleasure of witnessing the Böhm troupe perform it with his *Thamos* music in Frankfurt in September 1790. Mozart wrote an aria, or promised to write one, for Böhm after the troupe left Salzburg for Augsburg in March 1780, as we know from Mozart's letter to his cousin Bäsle of 24 April 1780: "It is two weeks now since I answered Herr Böhm . . . I await only a sign from him, and his aria will be ready."

The German translation of Mozart's *Giardiniera* originated with the Böhm troupe in 1779 or 1780, with the composer's collusion. But there is no way to link Böhm, who obviously appreciated Mozart and his music, with *Zaide*. Likely connected with the Böhm troupe at Salzburg in the spring of 1779, on the other hand, is the brilliant Overture-Symphony in G, K. 318, dated Salzburg, 26 April 1779. One can easily imagine this work opening an evening's entertainment in the little court theater crowded with Mozart's fellow citizens. Nannerl's diary mentions attending twenty-one performances there between Easter Monday, 5 April, and 2 June, including one on 26 April 1779.

Salzburg was not unacquainted with "Turkish" theatricals. According to a local diary entry for 30 September 1777, "The French Tragedy *Alzire* [*Zaire* by Voltaire] was performed with applause; between the acts there was performed an entirely new music by Herr Haydn that was magnificent, and which agreed entirely with the play as to its Turkish style."[18] Mozart had already departed with his mother on the trip to Mannheim and Paris, otherwise he might well have been asked to compose the incidental music. No one could doubt his familiarity with the style after the so-called "Turkish" Violin Concerto in A of 1775. Leopold wrote him about the event more than once; even he, who rarely had anything good to say about Michael Haydn, liked the music. "Haydn is said to have received only 6 Bavarian Thaler from the archbishop for his beautiful music (Che generosità!)" (letter of 9 October 1777).

[18] Otto Erich Deutsch, "Aus Schiedenhofens Tagebuch," *Mozart-Jahrbuch 1957*, pp. 15–24.

Voltaire's *Zaire* of 1732 is the ancestor of many theater pieces that end by showing the magnanimous Turkish potentate turning the other cheek (and teaching a lesson to Western rulers by comparison). One of the humblest of its offspring, Franz Josef Sebastiani's two-act Singspiel *Das Serail,* set to music by Joseph Friebert, ends with the customary magnanimity, and in its last speech the sultan points the moral: "You see now, you and your children, that not only Europe, but also Asia, can boast virtuous souls." (Kapellmeister to the prince-bishop of Passau on the Danube, Friebert was a brother of the Esterházy tenor Carl Friberth, who by coincidence was the librettist of Haydn's "Turkish" opera, *L'incontro improviso.*) The Mozarts may have run across *Das Serail* at some point, perhaps when it was performed in 1777 at Wels (between Salzburg and Linz), perhaps from the libretto printed at Bozen in the Tirol in 1779. It became one source from which Schachtner wrested the text for *Zaide.*[19] Schachtner's libretto was not printed, and a manuscript copy of it has yet to be found.

Johann Andreas Schachtner was a court trumpeter at Salzburg; he was also a poet and writer who had a certain reputation, having published his work as early as 1758. A close friend to the Mozart family, Schachtner was the source of many stories about the infant Mozart. Nannerl's diary mentions him frequently as a guest in the Tanzmeisterhaus in 1779–80. On 17 August 1780 her diary entry (in Mozart's hand!) reads in part: "My brother with Schachtner, and afterward Papa also joined them." Perhaps they were conferring about how to deal with *Das Serail.* A month later Salzburg welcomed Emanuel Schikaneder, whose troupe opened in the court theater on 17 September.

The beginning of *Zaide* departs from *Das Serail* in two particulars that are certainly Mozart's doing. One is an initial vaudeville for tenor and unison chorus of slaves, directly indebted to Gluck's opéras-comiques for its style. This leads to a prose soliloquy for the hero, Gomatz, which is broken into small verbal segments because it was meant to be set as a melodrama, and was so set by Mozart. Schachtner made his monologue, mainly about the repose sought by Gomatz as a balm for his troubles as an enslaved captive, out of the descriptive speech that begins *Das Serail:*

(Zaide observes Gomatz sleeping under a tree and speaks to him.)

> Here lies that attractive slave
> who has charmed my heart. Not until now

[19] Einstein discovered the printed libretto and reports wittily on its transformation by Schachtner in "Die Text-Vorlage zu Mozarts 'Zaide,' " *Acta Musicologica* 8 (1936): 30–37. For a complete facsimile of *Das Serail,* see the NMA Kritischer Bericht to *Zaide* by F.-H. Neumann and Gerhard Croll, pp. 75–91. For a number-by-number comparison between *Das Serail* and *Zaide,* see Linda L. Tyler, "*Zaide* in the Development of Mozart's Operatic Language," *Music and Letters* 72 (1991): 214–35; 218–20.

have I been so fortunate as to observe him closely.
What a pity that cruel fate
has thrown him in chains.
According to the color of his
face and the delicacy of his hands,
he must be a European. Oh! If only
kind Heaven would grant that he were
the one who tells me news of my
beloved parents! How gladly would I
wake him but—he sleeps too sweetly.

Mozart sets up the delicacy of Gomatz far more effectively by contrasting him with the group of crass slaves who sing the opening tune, merely repeating in unison the words and melody of the lead singer (*Vorsinger*).

Brüder, lasst uns lustig sein,	Brothers, let's be happy,
Trotzet wakker den Beschwerden;	Bravely bear your burdens;
Denkt, es ist der Fluch der Erden:	Remember, it is the curse of earth:
Jeder Mensch hat seine Pein.	Every man has his pain.
Lasst uns singen, lasst uns lachen,	Let us sing, let us laugh,
Kann man's doch nicht anders machen!	Since one can do nothing else!
Welt und Not sind einerlei,	World and need are all the same,
Keiner bleibt von Plagen frei.	No one remains free of worry.

Schachtner's doggerel effectively underlines the contradictory sentiments of the words. For all their naïveté, they say something about what it was like to live under absolutist rule, whether in Salzburg or Vienna. And they were surely written to the tune that Mozart made up (Example 9.11). The model for this four-square and blatantly popular type of vaudeville, with strong downbeats like a polka, was the well-known tune sung by Calendar near the beginning of Gluck's *Die Pilgrime von Mekka*, "Unser dummer Pöbel meint." The tune later furnished the subject to one of Mozart's finest sets of keyboard variations, K. 455 of 1784. The wit of Gluck's song lies in a sardonic contradiction between simplicity and opulence. The Calendar monk whom the public thinks is fasting is actually feasting on wine and good food. There

EXAMPLE 9.11. *Mozart, Zaide, No. 1*

is irony in Mozart's slaves too, as they complain about what cannot be changed. Those rocking fourths at the beginning of Mozart's tune foretell another labor complaint that will begin an opera, Leporello's "Notte giorno fatticar."

Gomatz separates himself from the other slaves and laments that he must associate with them, although he is guilty of no misdeed. This must have sounded a very personal cry to the Mozart who lamented his bondage to Colloredo ("The archbishop can scarcely pay me enough for the slavery in Salzburg!" he wrote on 12 November 1778) and who frequently denounced the conditions that forced him to associate with the loutish people serving the archbishop. He responded with a musical cry from the heart, the opening in d of his finest melodrama, an *Adagio* melody that sighs its way down from high to low tonic and dies out in a whisper. Only then does Gomatz speak. Among the high points of this very expressive music is a move to the still darker realms of c and f, where the violins sound a falling figure that anticipates the crux of the tragedy in Act III of *Idomeneo* when Idamante is named the victim (Example 9.12ab). To reinforce this descent, Mozart follows a cadence on d (after spoken words) with the initial *Adagio*, but in c. The sinking down from d to c occurs also in Electra's aria in Act I of *Idomeneo*, the nearness of which can be heard ever more clearly here.

EXAMPLE 9.12.

a. Mozart, Zaide, No. 2

b. Mozart, Idomeneo, No. 23

EXAMPLE 9.13.

a. *Mozart, Zaide, No. 2*

b. *Mozart, Zaide, No. 3*

c. *Christian Bach, Sonata arranged in K. 107/3, III*

Shortly after the cadence the violins rise chromatically and then descend in a jagged, minor-second-laden arpeggio that also occurs at the end of the overture to *Idomeneo*. Soon after this, there is relief for a brief moment in sleep, painted in the orchestra by a beautiful melody for solo oboe. Gomatz's oboe melody is transformed into the minuet-lullaby sung by Zaide, No. 3, which is recognizably similar not just from its rhythm but also from the way a melodic leap in the second measure becomes a wider, more expressive leap in the fourth measure (Example 9.13ab). This melodic type goes back to Christian Bach, whose keyboard Sonata Op. 5 No. 4 in E♭ Mozart arranged as his keyboard Concerto in E♭, K. 107, No. 3 (Example 9.13c).

Act I runs smoothly, with just enough tonal sense to convince our ears that Mozart planned it this way (Table 9.2). The lack of recitative connecting the numbers does not preclude dramatic or musical continuity.

TABLE 9.2   Act I, *Zaide*

No.:	1	2	3	4	5	6	7	8
	Coro	*Melologo*	Aria	Aria	*Duetto*	Aria	Aria	*Terzetto*
	D	d–c–B♭–G	G	B♭	E♭	C	F	E
	——	Gomatz	Zaide	Gomatz	Both	Gomatz	Allazim	All three

The symbiosis between Zaide and Gomatz is made clear tonally, as she sings her lullaby aria in G, the key prepared in his "melologo" (a curious term that seems to be confined to Mozart). She leaves her portrait. He revives to sing a "picture" aria in the key of his sweet dreams to the oboe melody in No. 2.[20] Their duet No. 5 in E♭ comes as tonal resolution to the previous piece as in a V - I cadence. It is scarcely a *duetto* in the Italian operatic sense, but rather a lightweight *Allegretto ma moderato* in 6/8, appropriate to the naive text, "Meine Seele hupft für Freuden" (My soul hops for joy). Its style (vocally not very demanding) and scope (only sixty-seven measures) would make it quite at home in an opéra-comique. Allazim, the slave master, agrees to help Zaide and Gomatz escape (in the missing spoken dialogue), giving Gomatz the opportunity to sing his aria of gratitude in C, which is one of the most impressive numbers in the score, and filled with musical details that anticipate *Die Zauberflöte*. A long melodic sketch survives for this aria, showing the trouble Mozart took with it. C was the key of the main episode in Zaide's rondo, No. 3, sung to the words "Ihr süssen Träume wiegt ihn ein" (Your sweet dreams rock him to sleep), and thus familiar in a sense, and right in feeling for an expression of their mutual thanks. Allazim's aria, No. 7 in F, comes as a response (and a tonal resolution). The key of E for the *terzetto* ending the act seems to be a response to the natural imagery of the text, and thus in line with Mozart's "zephyr" idylls in this key.

Act II flows less smoothly. Schachtner departed altogether from *Das Serail* here and presented Mozart with some dramaturgical problems (Table 9.3). Gomatz does not reappear until the last number. Soliman, another tenor, dominates the beginning of the act with two long arias sharing the same angry affect, surrounding the work's most comical aria, sung by Osmin.

TABLE 9.3   Act II, *Zaide*

No.:	9	10	11	12	13	14	15	[16]
	Melologo ed Aria	Aria	Aria	Aria	Aria	Aria	*Quartetto*	[Coro]
	D	F	E♭	A	g	B♭	B♭	[D]
	Soliman	Osmin	Soliman	Zaide	Zaide	Allazim	All but Osmin	

Soliman is truly magnificent in his fury at the pair's escape in his *melologo*. Mozart unleashes his trumpets and timpani and lets the orchestra rage around him (this too anticipates the next opera, and specifically the great obbligato recitative for Idomeneo between the choruses at the end of Act II). As for the attached aria, *Allegro maestoso*, its initial eight-measure phrase is weak and oddly stiff for Mozart. The "iterated quavers" in the bass eventu-

---

[20] Cf. the very similar use of an oboe melody in F to represent the dream vision of Florestan in the dungeon at the beginning of Act II in Beethoven's *Fidelio*.

ally become tiresome, and there is too much repetition. A petulant potentate is not someone for whom Mozart can summon much empathy. Osmin's laughing aria is funny but also very repetitive. In form it approaches strophic variations.

Zaide and Gomatz are recaptured, prompting Soliman to rant on further to the rather silly text of "Ich bin so bös' als gut," No. 11. Mozart does his best, but when the old-fashioned Hasse cadences appear, we sense that he has begun regressing to the time of the Milanese operas. This aria in E♭ is nevertheless crucial to his tonal organization of the act. Without any intervening spoken dialogue, the orchestra begins an *Andantino* in the key of A, to which Zaide will sing tenderly about the hopeless nightingale shut up in her cage, sobbing for her lost freedom. Here Mozart is once again in his element, but the music is not as lovely or ingenious as Sandrina's turtledove aria. Having created a tritone between Nos. 11 and 12, he proceeds to resolve it, first with a passionate aria in g/B♭ for Zaide, then with two numbers in B♭ itself. As an ultimate resolution Mozart must have intended a post-magnanimity chorus of praise in D, but he did not include one in the autograph. Act III of *Idomeneo* is also organized around an A - E♭ tritone conflict that is resolved eventually to B♭, then D.

The finest moments in *Zaide* come at the end in the two pieces in B♭. Allazim's powerful multi-tempo aria enjoins the mighty of this world to take pity on their slaves. His sentiment has no effect on Soliman, who continues to threaten death, leading to the quartet, No. 15. It is preceded by the words "lass uns miteinander sterben" (let us die together), spoken by either Gomatz or Zaide. Mozart trusts the winds alone to begin with a passage that would be very much at home in *Idomeneo* (Example 9.14a). The oboe theme of sleep in No. 2 generates the quartet's first measure (cf. Example 9.13a); here it portends the sleep of death. Compare this wind writing with the second theme in Ilia's aria No. 11 in *Idomeneo*, also for winds alone, involving the same inversion between the outer parts and a similar pattern of repeated-note afterbeats (Example 9.14b). Mozart was coming very close to *Idomeneo* by the end of *Zaide*. Masterly in the ensemble No. 15 is the way Mozart expresses conflicting emotions at close range and even simultaneously. The noble resignation of the lovers, rigor of Soliman, and pity of Allazim could be told from the music even if there were no words. Soliman spits out "sterben" as the first two quarter-note beats, followed by a half-measure rest.

Zaide deserves to be considered in its own right and not just as a preparation for the two operas that followed. That said, there is no denying that *Zaide* should also be studied in connection with *Idomeneo* and *Die Entführung*, to see how Mozart experimented with the binary aria form and unconven-

EXAMPLE 9.14.

a. Mozart, Zaide, *No. 15*

b. Mozart, Idomeneo, *No. 11*

tional text placement such as is found in the very first aria of *Idomeneo*, Ilia's "Padre, germani."[21]

Various attempts have been made to salvage *Zaide* for modern performance. No. 6 in C, Gomatz's aria of gratitude, has sometimes been moved to the end, so that his thanks are sung not to Allazim but to Soliman after the pardon. This gives the hero more to do in Act II. In terms of tonal balance, there is still need for a celebration of D to end the opera. One recording added the March in D, K. 335, as an ending, and it does make a good one. Another attempted to solve the problem by bringing back the chorus of slaves, No. 1 in D. At the least, their text would have to be rewritten to reflect Soliman's largesse. But since vapidity is built in to the music as well as the text of No. 1, the tone is not right for the ending. A better solution would be to adopt the short but jubilant chorus in D that ends *Giardiniera*, with suitable textual adjustment. With a good singing translation and a pithy spoken text between the numbers, *Zaide* could captivate English-speaking audiences. The project is worthy of an Andrew Porter.[22]

Mozart considered *Zaide* to be viable even if he did not quite finish it. This may be gathered from the comments he and Leopold made on the work. We first hear about it from Leopold, who makes it clear that *Zaide* was intended for Vienna, where it was actually being put forward, perhaps by the poet, around the time Maria Theresa died on 29 November 1780. Even in death the empress-queen exerted a commanding effect upon the arts.

> The actors in Vienna have seven weeks off and permission to travel where they will . . . With regard to Schachtner's drama there is at the moment nothing to be done, as the theaters are closed, and from the emperor, who supervises everything to do with the stage, there is no help to be expected. It is also better this way as the music is not quite finished, and who knows, besides, what kind of opportunity it might bring later of getting to Vienna. (Letter of 11 December, 1780)

Mozart replied from Munich on 13 December with a characteristically unsentimental thought regarding the great monarch upon whose lap he had sat as a child. "In Vienna and all the imperial crown lands, spectacles will recommence six weeks from now, and this seems sensible, for prolonged mourning does less good for the dead lord or lady than it does harm to so many others. Will Herr Schikaneder remain in Salzburg? If so he may still

[21] For more on formal and textual matters, see Tyler, "*Zaide* in the Development of Mozart's Operatic Language." She calls Zaide's "Ruhe sanft" (No. 3) a "simple ternary aria" (pp. 224–25), but it is a rondo, with a return of the refrain after contrasting music in the dominant, mm. 23–34, which constitutes the first of two episodes.
[22] This eminent critic has also made many excellent English singing translations.

see and hear my opera." The work in question was of course *Idomeneo*, then about two-thirds complete, but Mozart had not forgotten his little opera entirely in the heady days of putting together his grand opera. On 18 January 1781 he wrote his father, who was about to depart for the premiere in Munich: "I also wish you to bring the score of Schachtner's operetta—the Cannabich house attracts people who might hear such a work to some good purpose."

Zaide requires two tenors of uncommon acting and singing abilities. The Burgtheater boasted two such in the fall of 1780. Valentine Adamberger, Mozart's future Belmonte, made his Viennese debut on 21 August 1780. Already with the troupe in the Burgtheater was Ernst Dauer, the future Pedrillo, who sang Ali, the leading male role in *Die Pilgrime von Mekka*. Dauer was what is called in German a *Spieltenor*, an actor-singer—just what the roles of Gomatz and Soliman required. The bass Karl Ludwig Fischer, Mozart's future Osmin, joined the Burgtheater troupe in the summer of 1780. He would have made an excellent Allazim. As for sopranos, there were several on hand: Aloysia Weber and Antonia Bernasconi, both of whom Mozart knew well; Catarina Cavalieri (Mozart's future Constanze); and Therese Teyber (his future Blonde). A closer study of the technical demands in Zaide's part might reveal a "vocal portrait" that particularly suited one of these ladies.

Even after *Idomeneo* and while courting dismissal from the archbishop's service in Vienna in the spring of 1781, Mozart still remembered *Zaide*. On 18 April he wrote his father the last words we have on the subject.

> There is nothing to be done about Schachtner's operetta for the same reason that I have mentioned so often. Stephanie the younger is going to give me a new libretto, and a good one he says, and if I am no longer here, he will send it to me. I was not in a position to contradict Stephanie. I said only that the operetta was very good, except for the long dialogues, which could easily be cut, but it was not for Vienna, where people prefer to see comic pieces.

These words are undoubtedly couched so as to allow Leopold to placate Schachtner, and yet they still reveal the prickly relations between Mozart and his librettist—relations were never otherwise with any of his librettists. It appears that Mozart had complained about the text repeatedly, and specifically he decried the lengths of the spoken dialogues. Even so, he pronounced the piece very good. But there was too little comic relief for the Viennese. *Die Entführung aus dem Serail* would soon offer them much more.

Idomeneo

MOZART completed the score of *Idomeneo* in Munich between the beginning of November 1780 and the end of January 1781. A court copyist or copyists quickly turned his autograph into what is known as the Munich performing score, from which the parts were copied. Mozart retained his autograph and used it as his own rehearsal and performing copy. He gave no generic designation to the opera on it, but on the Munich performing score he inscribed, "L'Idomeneo / Drama per Musica / Di / Amadeo Wolfgango / Mozart. / 1781." He never called the work an opera seria, a term he avoided. In later years he referred to it as his Munich opera, or his grand opera ("meine grosse oper").

Idomeneo has in common with French grand opera a concept of tragedy that transcends the individual: the fates of entire peoples typically hang in the balance. In this respect it resembles Rossini's *Guillaume Tell* and Verdi's *Don Carlos*, both written for Paris. Like those epic works based on Friedrich von Schiller, Mozart's *dramma eroico* (as the first edition of *Idomeneo* in score was designated) is a very long opera and rich in choruses and ballets. All three works emphasize the same key word or concept: "liberté / libertà." Had Mozart lived but another decade, perhaps he might have collaborated with Schiller himself.

Mozart was twenty when the Revolutionary War in America broke out in 1776. Hostilities did not cease until he had completed his grand opera and seen it through its first production. Its French source spurs us to ponder the political situation in Paris for a moment. French intervention on behalf of England's rebelling colonies in North America was absolutely crucial in winning their independence. As envoy to Paris, Benjamin Franklin succeeded in persuading a reluctant French government to back the insurgents. The Treaty of Friendship was signed at Paris in February 1778, just before Mozart's arrival. Caron de Beaumarchais, the creator of Figaro, did his utmost to bring this about by firing off a barrage of letters to Count Charles de Vergennes, the French foreign minister, throughout the winter of 1777–78.[23] In the end the American army under the command of George Washington combined with the French army under the command of Lafayette and Rochambeau to force the surrender of Cornwallis and his redcoats at Yorktown, Virginia, on 19 October 1781. A new nation was born under fire, and the ideal of liberty soon proved contagious. Many historians now believe

[23] Reproduced for the first time by Gunnar and Mavis von Proschwitz, *Beaumarchais et le "Courier de l'Europe": Documents inédits ou peu connus* (Oxford, 1991), these letters make fascinating reading.

that the tumultuous sequence of events that began on 4 July 1776 led inevitably to 14 July 1789.

When Mozart was in Paris in 1778, the revolutionary ferment had already taken hold of many imaginations, including those of his friends (and at one point hosts) Baron Melchior von Grimm and Mme. D'Epinay. He could not have escaped it, but his mind was probably, as usual, preoccupied more with opera than with anything else. He was witness to the latest kind of heroic tragedy on the stage of the Opéra, where Gluckistes were battling with Piccinnistes. *Tragédie lyrique* had always been a great visual spectacle, among many other things, ever since its beginnings a century earlier with Philippe Quinault, Jean Bérain, and Jean-Baptiste Lully. Mozart was looking for a good libretto of this type when in Paris so that he too could join the fray. He came away, we now believe, with the libretto of Antoine Danchet's somber and storm-tossed *Idomenée,* which had been set to music by André Campra in 1712 (Figure 9.6).[24]

The commission to write *Idomeneo* was the result of years of "lobbying" on the part of Mozart's many friends in Mannheim and Munich, especially Christian Cannabich and Anton Raaff. Leopold made it an international campaign by enlisting Padre Martini of Bologna to petition the elector, Carl Theodore, on Mozart's behalf (see his letters of 22 December 1777 and 2 August 1778). It is to the great credit of all these friends and to the elector himself that the mission succeeded.

Joseph Anton Graf von Seeau was in charge of the theaters in Munich in 1780, just as he had been five years earlier at the time of *Giardiniera.* The change of regime did not affect him. He was confirmed by Carl Theodore in his post of "Chambellan et Intendent de la Musique et du Festin." If there was any animosity toward the Mozarts on his part left from the experiences in 1775, he did not reveal it. A drawing of Seeau by an anonymous artist ca. 1780 shows him in a jovial mood, with very prominent nose and chin.[25] Unfortunately, his papers are lost—destroyed by his own direction, it seems, at his death. Thus we lack the Munich side of the negotiations that took place in order to settle the choice of subject, librettist, and fees to be paid. That there was a detailed plan from Munich as to how to treat the old French libretto emerges from the correspondence between Mozart and his father that stretched from 8 November to 18 January 1781 and revealed many

[24] Daniel Heartz, "Mozart, His Father, and 'Idomeneo,' " *Musical Times* 119 (1978): 228-31.

[25] The drawing is reproduced in *Wolfgang Amadeus Mozart: Idomeneo 1781–1981,* ed. Rudolf Angermüller and Robert Münster (Munich, 1981), p. 75. This exhibition catalogue from the Bayerische Staatsbibliothek gathers all the visual and documentary evidence available. It contains several illuminating essays and a perversely obtuse one by Wolfgang Hildesheimer. The catalogue is cited subsequently as *Idomeneo 1781–1981.*

FIGURE 9.6. Title page of Danchet's libretto for *Idomenée*.

details about how the opera was created. This amazingly detailed and illuminating exchange remains the best exposition of operatic dramaturgy we possess from the time.[26]

The Munich carnival was as famous as any other. By long tradition, its musical high point was a serious opera in Italian. Tozzi's *Orfeo ed Euridice* occupied the spot of honor in 1775, as we saw above in connection with *Giardiniera*, the secondary opera. In 1776 it was Metastasio's *Il trionfo di Clelio*,

---

[26] The correspondence furnished the main object of Daniel Heartz, "The Genesis of Mozart's 'Idomeneo,' " *Mozart-Jahrbuch 1967*, pp. 150–64, reprinted with illustrations in *Musical Quarterly* 59 (1969): 1–19, and reprinted again with different illustrations as Chapter 2 in Heartz, *Mozart's Operas* (Berkeley, 1990). For another article on the same subject, with many new details about events at the Bavarian court, see Robert Münster, "Mozarts Münchener Aufenthalt 1780/81 und die Uraufführung des 'Idomeneo,' " *Idomeneo 1781–1981*, pp. 71–105.

set by the court chamber composer Joseph Michl; in 1776, the same poet's *Ezio*, set by Josef Mysliveček. In 1778 there was no carnival opera because of the death of Maximilian III Joseph. A break with tradition came the following year when, under Carl Theodore, Wieland's *Alkestis* in German as set by Schweitzer several years earlier was chosen, a holdover from Mannheim repertory. Perhaps in order to please the Bavarians and respect their customs, the elector did not continue to attempt the imposition of serious opera in German. (But this is not to say that the genre left Mozart unaffected; Holzbauer's *Günther von Schwarzburg* of 1777, a heroic opera built around Raaff with ample use of the Mannheim winds, particularly impressed him.)

In 1780 the carnival opera at Munich was *Telemaco*, set for the occasion by Vice-Kapellmeister Franz Paul Grua, a Mannheim-born composer of Italian descent. The first Kapellmeister to the court was Andrea Bernasconi, whom Grua succeeded in 1784. Until 1787 the Munich court remained committed to the traditional carnival opera in Italian. Yet most of the librettos were based on French models, meaning there was an essential role for spectacle, ballet, and chorus—all those seventeenth-century "excesses" that Metastasio had limited or done away with. *Idomeneo* fits a general picture, then, of Munich's typical carnival opera of 1780–87: a tragedy in Italian mixing Parisian-type spectacle with Metastasian-type arias for the solo singers.

How and when the commission for the Munich carnival opera of 1781 reached Mozart we do not know. It is not impossible that he made a short trip to Munich, which was, after all, only a long day's journey (or a day and a half). Our knowledge is limited to Nannerl's diary for the late summer of 1780, and it tells us little except that Mozart was in Salzburg between 12 August and 30 September. Many of the entries tell of attending the comedies in the court theater across the square, where Emanuel Schikaneder's troupe was performing. (Schikaneder is also reported visiting the Mozart house and participating in the family's shooting games.) But the entry on 22 August may offer a clue: "Nachmittag der Abt varesco bey uns" (An afternoon visit from Abbé Varesco). Abbé Gianbattista Varesco, a chaplain in the cathedral, was very well educated and perhaps the best poet in the Italian language that Salzburg could muster.[27] The Mozarts were not close to him, not in a social sense, at least. It seems obvious that they brought him into the picture as librettist in the new venture for Munich, where it is probable that no one had even heard of him. Noteworthy in this regard is that Varesco did not travel to Munich to witness *Idomeneo*, as far as we know.

---

[27] Varesco was well versed in the Latin and Italian classics, also in theology. See Kurt Kramer, "Das Libretto zu Mozarts 'Idomeneo': Quellen und Umgestaltung der Fabel," *Idomeneo 1781–1981*, pp. 7–43.

The advantages of choosing Varesco were clear. Poet and composer could work together hammering out the libretto. As a result, when Mozart left Salzburg for Munich in early November, he took a substantial amount of music already composed with him, perhaps most of the first act. This was possible because he already knew from Mannheim the voices that would sing Ilia (Dorothea Wendling), Electra (Elizabeth Wendling), and Idomeneo (Anton Raaff). Only in the case of the young hero, Idamante, to be sung by the twenty-four-year-old castrato Vincenzo dal Prato, was the voice unknown to him. A translation into German for the first printed libretto also originated in Salzburg (Figure 9.7), the work of Johann Andreas Schachtner, the librettist of *Zaide.*

Mozart arrived in Munich on Monday, 6 November 1780, and went straight away to find Count Seeau. He did not find the count until the next

FIGURE 9.7. Title page of Varesco's libretto for *Idomeneo.*

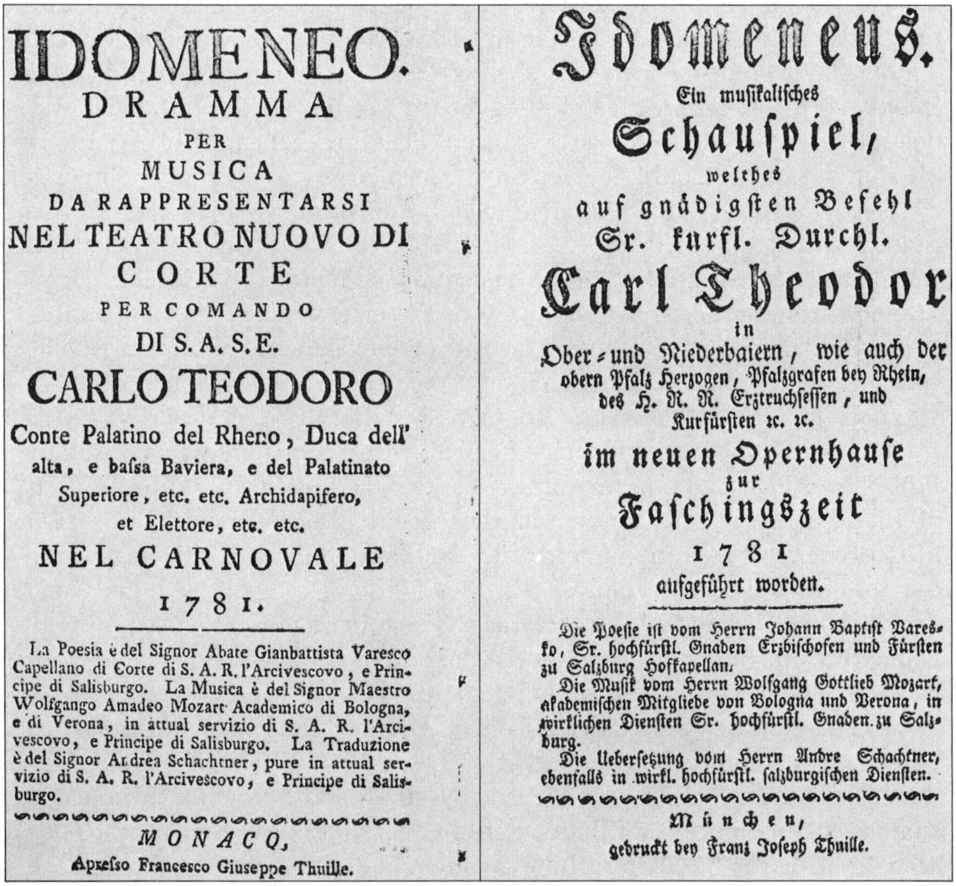
IDOMENEO.
DRAMMA
PER
MUSICA
DA RAPPRESENTARSI
NEL TEATRO NUOVO DI
CORTE
PER COMANDO
DI S. A. S. E.
CARLO TEODORO
Conte Palatino del Rheno, Duca dell' alta, e bassa Baviera, e del Palatinato Superiore, etc. etc. Archidapifero, et Elettore, etc. etc.
NEL CARNOVALE
1781.

La Poesia è del Signor Abate Gianbattista Varesco Capellano di Corte di S. A. R. l'Arcivescovo, e Principe di Salisburgo. La Musica è del Signor Maestro Wolfgango Amadeo Mozart Academico di Bologna, e di Verona, in attual servizio di S. A. R. l'Arcivescovo, e Principe di Salisburgo. La Traduzione è del Signor Andrea Schachtner, pure in attual servizio di S. A. R. l'Arcivescovo, e Principe di Salisburgo.

MONACO,
Appresso Francesco Giuseppe Thuille.

Idomeneus.
Ein musikalisches
Schauspiel,
welches
auf gnädigsten Befehl
Sr. kurfl. Durchl.
Carl Theodor
in
Ober- und Niederbaiern, wie auch der obern Pfalz Herzogen, Pfalzgrafen bey Rhein, des H. R. R. Erztruchsessen, und Kurfürsten rc. rc.
im neuen Opernhause
zur
Faschingszeit
1781
aufgeführt worden.

Die Poesie ist vom Herrn Johann Baptist Varesko, Sr. hochfürstl. Gnaden Erzbischofen und Fürsten zu Salzburg Hofkapellan.
Die Musik vom Herrn Wolfgang Gottlieb Mozart, akademischen Mitgliede von Bologna und Verona, in wirklichen Diensten Sr. hochfürstl. Gnaden zu Salzburg.
Die Uebersetzung vom Herrn Andre Schachtner, ebenfalls in wirkl. hochfürstl. salzburgischen Diensten.

München,
gedruckt bey Franz Joseph Thuille.

day, when the two men held the first of many meetings about the opera. On Tuesday Archduke Maximilian arrived from Vienna and was warmly welcomed by the elector, Carl Theodore. The following Sunday Seeau presented Mozart to the elector as he was coming from mass in the Hofkapelle. On the same day Christian Cannabich, the orchestra leader, took Mozart to lunch at the home of Countess Baumgarten, about which Mozart reported to Leopold the next day: "My friend is everything in this house, and now I am too—this is the best and most useful house here for me, and through it passed everything to do with my affair and will continue to pass, God willing." Then Mozart made up a nonsensical passage with certain initial letters that spelled "Favoriten" in allusion to the alleged position of Countess Baumgarten as the elector's *maîtresse en titre*. She was a young lady of eighteen, a born Lerchenfeld, as Mozart remarked, who was a good singer in her own right and a collector of music. After the performances of the opera were over, Mozart wrote for her the aria "Misera, dove son," K. 369, dated Augsburg, 9 March 1791. If Mozart was right, hers was the final weight that tipped the balance with the elector and decided him to commission Mozart.

By 30 November Mozart was playing "Fuor del mar," Idomeneo's *aria di bravura* in the second act, at the keyboard for the aged Raaff, who was delighted with it (or so Mozart reported). The first rehearsal of Act I took place in a room at Count Seeau's on 1 December, with only six violins but all the winds. On 16 December, again at Count Seeau's, Act II was rehearsed, this time with twelve violins. Then on 22 December Acts I and II were rehearsed with full orchestra in a large room at court, with the elector listening from an adjoining room. Since the elector was pressed for time, two scenes already established as favorites were taken out of sequence so he could hear them: Ilia's concertante aria, No. 11, and the choruses of terror and fleeing at the end of Act II, Nos. 17–18.

After the Christmas holidays rehearsals resumed. There was a "recitativ Probe" on 28 December at Dorothea Wendling's, and several run-throughs of what has come to be known as the "Great Quartet," which prompted Mozart to report disappointment with Dal Prato, and also with Raaff, who did not like to sing in ensembles. Eventually the piece went well, and Raaff declared himself satisfied. Mozart was still negotiating with Varesco through Leopold about the text of Idomeneo's last aria, the original of which Raaff had rejected, and about shortening the speech of Neptune's oracle.

The magnitude of the tasks still ahead weighed heavily on Mozart when he wrote his father on 3 January 1781, "My head and hands are so full of the third act that it were no wonder if I myself should become a third act. It alone is costing more labor than an entire opera, because there is scarcely a scene in it that is not extremely interesting." All three acts were rehearsed at court ten days later on 13 January, and the "third act was found to greatly outdo the first two." It was also found far too long, and the process of cutting began. There was probably another rehearsal on 20 January, after Mozart's last letter to his father of two days earlier. Leopold and Nannerl left Salzburg on 25 January and were present for the dress rehearsal on the stage of the Residenz theater on 27 January 1781, Mozart's twenty-fifth birthday. The premiere took place two days later.

Mozart, according to his usual procedure, wrote the overture last, but this does not mean that he conceived it last. He often composed in his mind, which ran ahead of the mechanical task of writing out the notes. This great overture is a microcosm of the opera and sets forth some of its main musical ideas. It is at once majestic and sinister, as in the upward creeping chromatic lines at the beginning and the many minor-mode borrowings. Like the overture to *Il rè pastore,* it is in one movement and makes a transition at the end directly into the first scene. In its final moments the long descents of the treble instruments over a pedal A, then a pedal D, are enriched by seventh and ninth chords formed by slowly resolving suspended dissonances, an expressive device that Mozart had already perfected in the Credo of the *Coronation* Mass. These descents are also peppered with the four- or five-tone Idamante motif, sometimes with two afterbeats (as at the beginning of the overture), sometimes with four, but at the end with only one, a fall by step down to a D we have begun to suspect is not I but V. The two final falls are interlaced with the rising minor second in jagged descent that I have called the duol motif (also prominent in the violins of the "Crucifixus" of the *Coronation* Mass and in the Munich Kyrie). Mozart may have been most stimulated by the appearance of this motif at the end of the overture to Gluck's *Iphigénie en Aulide* (1774), but we have seen that it goes back a decade earlier to a Viennese work, Gluck's *Telemaco* (cf. Example 3.9). Even Mozart's little cadence figure with grace note has thematic significance (cf. Example 9.8a). It occurs among other places at the beginning of Act III and in Idomeneo's last and summary recitative.

Musical continuity is one of Mozart's first concerns in *Idomeneo.* Just as the overture glides imperceptibly into the opening scene, so do most numbers achieve connections with what came before and after so that their beginnings and endings are blurred, making the numbers merely a part of the total fabric to an extent that the composer had never before attempted. Ilia's first statement resolves the D left as V at the end of the overture ever so gently to g. As is almost always the case with Mozart, the first tonal move in a recitative is also the last. The aria will be in g. Every detail of Ilia's long recitative, mixing simple and obbligato accompaniment, serves the purpose of dramatic exposition and deserves study. She is the captive daughter of the Trojan king Priam, rescued from the storms off Crete by Prince Ida-mante, son of King Idomeneo. She loves Idamante in spite of their lineages, but believes that he loves Electra, a refugee on Crete from the horrors that decimated the House of Atreus after the Trojan War. Ilia's terse but lyrical aria sums up her conflicts as an aria should, and as only Mozart could.

No applause was allowed to the veteran Dorothea Wendling at the end of her first aria, which concludes with the words "Ecco Idamante!" after an orchestral gesture that brooks no pause. Thus she focuses not only her atten-tion away from herself and toward him, but also ours.

Idamante enters in B♭ and will sing his first aria in the same key, made quite sensual by the presence of clarinets. Of course he will, we think. Yet Mozart rarely thought so globally in tonal terms before *Idomeneo*. The second section of Ilia's aria in g was naturally in B♭, and her thoughts of Idamante there were reinforced by the persistent recurrence of his motif in the cellos and basses. We must keep this sonority in our minds in order to enjoy Ida-mante's aria to the fullest. It is expansive, in three tempos, and conveys the impression of an exuberant young prince who, however depressed he is at the thought of the possible loss of his father, is ever more confident at the thought of a future with Ilia. Mozart allowed him a cadenza but it was cut in the course of the first performances, according to the Munich performing score.[28] Unlike the arias of the three other, experienced soloists in Act I, Idamante's reaches a real conclusion, albeit softly. By not cutting off its end-ing, Mozart may have been trying to encourage his young singer. The lei-sureliness of his aria and its lack of formal complication may also have to do with the castrato's more limited experience, whereas Ilia's aria has a breath-less quality and formal challenges, such as the anticipation of the reprise when the tonality is still in transition.

The famed winds of the Mannheim-Munich orchestra come to the fore in the following chorus, No. 3 in G, in which Trojans and Cretans together celebrate the liberation of the former at the command of Idamante. Also in evidence is Mozart's ingenuity at getting a maximum of sonority out of the chorus and bustling violins—skills honed most particularly in his Salzburg masses of the previous lustrum. All this brightness sets up the bad news, relayed by Arbace, that Idomeneo has perished attempting to land—or rather, Idamante, impetuous as he is, snatches the news from Arbace's mouth before he can utter it. Idamante turns to Ilia but then sees it is his duty to run to the shore. Majestic orchestral sounds return along with the keynote of D, as they always do in this opera when heroism is involved.

Mozart and Varesco make good use of the moment to contrast Ilia, who

[28] Robert Münster, "Neues zum Münchner *Idomeneo* 1781," *Acta Mozartiana* 29 (1982): 10–20.

is filled with pity for Idomeneo in spite of herself, and Electra, who is filled with pity for herself. Electra's solo scene gets the full obbligato treatment. Its tonal disjunctions, beginning with an unexplained fall down a whole step from b to a, tell us more about her state of mind than her words, initially. Her wildness and despair culminate in a hair-raising chromatic progression with *crescendo,* before her recitative cadence. In her aria, No. 4 in d, she sings about the Furies taking possession of her heart. The orchestra paints this with the sounds of storm: a flute arpeggio to suggest lightning, rumblings in the basses, and eerie twitters, like affrighted birds, in the violins. The master stroke comes when her reprise begins a whole tone down, in the still darker realm of c. (At the pivotal diminished-seventh chord a roll of thunder makes a good effect.) Falling down a whole tone like this astounds us, and yet the beginning of her recitative predicted it. Her dementia seems all the greater here because an aria is a more serious matter than a preparatory recitative. The aria rights itself and returns to d but does not conclude. Rather, an *attacca* transition carries us directly into the storm chorus in c. The transition accompanies the change of scene from the interior of the royal palace (probably played on a short stage) to what the libretto describes as the "shores of the sea, still agitated, surrounded by cliffs and littered with wrecked ships."

Metastasio was the model Varesco aspired to imitate in his verses, but Metastasio's dramaturgical rhythm of recitative building to aria, building to exit (with applause, the singer hoped), is only rarely observed in this opera. Its dramaturgical rhythm is more typically French, and dictated by the model: recitative builds (often from simple to obbligato) to aria, which builds to choral or balletic spectacle (sometimes both together). Electra's interior storm (and prophetic use of the key of c) gives way to a fully depicted scenic storm in c, to which the chorus of tenors and basses, divided into onshore and offshore (*Coro vicino* and *Coro lontano*), react and call out to the gods for pity.

The next scene, scene 8 of the libretto, begins, according to Mozart's autograph, just as the climax is reached. Neptune appears above the waves and in a pantomime bids the winds return to their caves. The seas gradually calm. Idomeneo appears to serene music in E♭, its cadence including the Idamante motif. The king dismisses his retinue, upon which the music moves to a cadence on C, where he will eventually sing his aria, No. 6 in C/ c. Mozart leads into it with a Phrygian cadence on E, the traditional setting for a question (here, "Which of the gods will give me aid?"). Idomeneo envisions already the sorrowful shade of the victim he must slay in order to keep his bargain with Neptune for having allowed the remains of his army a safe landing. The sad and slow first part gives way to a faster section expressing his torment. Mozart cuts off the ending by pushing ahead with a tutti *forte* passage into the following recitative. Originally he made a full stop here and gave Raaff a chance to earn whatever applause he could.[29]

Mozart made cuts in Idomeneo's first recitative because Raaff was such a poor actor, and the same is true of the scene between father and son, where he had two wooden actors to deal with. Only at its height, the very moment of recognition, does Mozart bring in the orchestra, the violins and violas rocketing up to high D, *Presto*. Any listener can learn to recognize the return to the opera's keynote here, if only from the unique timbre of string arpeggios in D. Idamante is joyous for an instant, then despairing. He cannot comprehend why his father flees him and forbids him to follow. The duol motif plays its role here, and probably originated here as far as this opera goes, because this was one of the earliest scenes Mozart sketched. More important for what is to come next is the scurrying motif in sixteenth notes that depicts Idomeneo's fleeing from him. These scurrying sixteenth notes will dominate Idamante's second aria, No. 7 in F, in which he mulls over his sudden discovery and painful loss. There is a lot of minor mode in this aria too, as appropriate to the text. At this point the libretto reads, "Fine dell'Atto primo."

What follows is labeled "Intermezzo." "The sea is totally calm. The Cretan troops disembark; the women of Crete run to meet them and express their joy in a general dance." Mozart's stirring Marcia in D accompanies the disembarcation, leading to the chorus and dance in praise of Neptune, "Ciaccona," No. 9, in D. This is a much bigger chorus than No. 5, but structured the same way as a threefold choral refrain around two different episodes for soloists. At the third refrain Mozart interrupts the conclusion by introducing a long orchestral *crescendo*—a touching homage to his players and their famous past at Mannheim. There is another surprise. After the concluding section is rejoined following the *crescendo*, Mozart interjects an unexpected diminished seventh chord, mimicking the emphatically stated chaconne accent on the second beat of the previous bar, and followed by a rest with fermata. The harmonic broadening that follows is needed after such a jolt. After this coda there can be no doubt that the Intermezzo has ended, curtain or no curtain. The act is tightly organized around the keynote.

---

[29] The original ending was not known until the autographs of the first two acts became available for study in the 1980s. For a transcription, see Daniel Heartz, "Attacca subito: Lessons from the Autograph Score of *Idomeneo*, Acts I and II," *Festschrift Wolfgang Rehm zum 60. Geburtstag am 3. September 1989*, ed. Dietrich Berke and Harald Heckmann (Kassel, 1989), pp. 88–92. The original ending of No. 13 and the original recitative cadence before No. 15 are also included in this article.

TABLE 9.4   Act I, *Idomeneo*

Overture	Act I										Intermezzo
———	No.:	1	2	3	4	//	5	6	7	8	9
D		g	B♭	G	d–c–d		c–E♭	c/C	F	D	D

(// indicates change of scene)

Act II gets off to a slow start with a scene between Idomeneo and his faithful confidant, Arbace. Apprised of the awful truth, Arbace counsels Idomeneo to send Idamante away from Crete, which the king resolves to do, commanding that Idamante escort Electra back to Greece in the hopes that some other god will look after them. This sets up the entire act and is followed by Arbace's aria, No. 10a in C. Munich in 1781 had a good actor-singer in the role of Arbace, Domenico de Panzacchi, and he had to be served. Mozart did what he could, given the minimal dramatic interest of Arbace's sentiments; he even rescored the violin parts in the autograph so as to increase the musical interest. The aria is the first in the score in the older ternary form, characterized by a separate section for the second verse after the full cadence on the dominant and before the reprise. There was even provision for a cadenza and appropriate tonal maneuvers leading up to it. Underscoring the old-fashioned nature of the piece is the torrent in the bass of "iterated quavers." Eighteenth-century operagoers coined an apt expression for the piece sung by a secondary character to open the second act: "aria di sorbetto." For the performance of the opera in Vienna in March 1786, Mozart made a major change here, substituting a new act-beginning in the key of C, with an obbligato recitative between Idamante (a tenor) and Ilia, who has heard of the plan involving Electra and is angry, followed by a pacifying concertante rondo for Idamante, No. 10b in B♭.[30]

Scene 2 of Act II brings Ilia and Idomeneo together for the first time. She is almost serene now, in comparison with her mood at the beginning of Act I. Her words and those of Idomeneo convey this, but the music conveys it ever so much more. Her aria, No. 11 in E♭, begins with the strings in low position, the violins and violas with mutes, singing a phrase with gentle rising chromatic inflections (8 5♯ 6, 8 4♯ 5) that confess amorous emotion. Ilia will sing the same to words concerning Idomeneo (whereas they really, of course, concern Idamante), but before she enters, her four concertante wind

[30] Mozart's revisions of *Idomeneo* for the performance at the Auersperg Palace theater in Vienna, under his direction, which may or may not have been staged, constitute the main subject of Daniel Heartz, "Mozart's Tragic Muse," *Studies in Music from the University of Western Ontario* 7 (1982), 183–96, revised and expanded as Chapter 3 in *Mozart's Operas*.

partners announce their presence. The players were Johann Baptist Wendling, flute; Friedrich Ramm, oboe; Georg Wenzel Ritter, bassoon; and perhaps Martin Lang, horn, all from Mannheim, as was Dorothea Wendling (who was literally the partner in the sense of being wife to the flautist). Mozart conceived this concertante aria as a whole in terms of music without regard to Varesco's verses, with the result that the poet had to change all but the beginning of his text. The aria's second subject is announced by the solo winds alone and assumes the rhythmic shape of the Idamante motif (and comes close to the main idea of the quartet, No. 15, in *Zaide*; cf. Example 9.14a). After the aria, when this very same subject is sounded by the strings in B♭, down an octave, with minor-mode inflections but "in tempo dell'Aria," we realize that Idomeneo, now alone, is pondering what Ilia meant by her words about Crete becoming an amorous sojourn. With further prompting from snippets repeated from the aria, he comes to awareness. Probably no obbligato recitative before this had used material from a preceding aria to show the mind of a protagonist at work. He realizes there will be not one victim, but three: Idamante, Ilia, and the king himself. She, like him, will die of grief. The motivation is in place for the great heroic aria that follows.

The shipwreck that Idomeneo escaped at great price now becomes the metaphorical focus of his monologue, "Fuor del mar, ho un mar in seno" (Far from the sea, I have a raging sea in my breast), No. 12a in D. It is an *Allegro maestoso* in common time, with trumpets and drums helping to emphasize the return of the keynote. Its form is ternary, and an improvised cadenza is provided for. Some rumblings of discontent with the piece, probably from Anton Raaff, reached the ears of the flautist Johann Baptist Becke, Mozart's Munich friend, who wrote to Leopold saying he was told that the music of "Fuor del mar" did not suit the words. Mozart was furious: "Whoever said such a thing knows very little Italian," he told Becke, and continued in his letter to his father of 27 December 1780 by insisting, "The aria is very well adapted to the words. You hear the *mare* and the *mare funesto*, and the musical passages suit *minacciar*." The long series of written-out trills that begin in the third measure Mozart evidently intended as a pictorial-auditory equivalent of "Rolling in foaming billows" in Haydn's *The Creation*. He continued in the same letter, "On the whole it is the most superb aria in the opera and has also won universal approval." It was undoubtedly planned from the beginning to be the centerpiece of the opera, but this conception went awry when the third act grew to be twice as long as either of the first two. Mozart's battles with Raaff and his old-fashioned habits come to the fore in the same letter. The aged tenor, nearing seventy, actually sang the whole of No. 12a, coloratura, cadenza, and all, according to the Munich performing score. It follows that the version with reduced coloratura, No. 12b, without cadenza and with its ending cut off by a transition into the following recitative, belongs to the revisions for Vienna.

Electra is a changed woman in the next scene. She receives an obbligato recitative in which the strings exude contentment in the smooth and melodious interjections that prefigure the second subject of her following aria, No. 13 in G, accompanied only by strings. Particularly beautiful in her aria are the passages for sustained violas in their high register. Into her sinewy vocal line Mozart has weaved so many written-out appoggiaturas as to border upon preciosity, hinting to us that this is not the real Electra. The autograph shows that Mozart originally brought her aria to a full stop. Only then did he rewrite the aria's ending by introducing the strains of the embarcation march, No. 14 in C (the march in the distance is first heard *in medias res*, like the march at the end of the third act of *Figaro*). Electra comments on its harmonious sounds, providing a further link between numbers. As the march gradually swells in the course of repetition, the scene changes to the port of Sidon, with fortifications along the shore; the ship awaits. This decor won special praise.

A very brief, simple recitative for Electra prepares the embarcation chorus, "Placido è il mar, andiamo" (The sea is calm, let us depart), which Mozart at first intended for the key of C, like the preceding march, as the autograph shows. Then, by a brilliant stroke, he perceived that the situation and text would be much better suited by the more rarified key of E, as yet unheard in this opera. He altered the recitative ending accordingly. Possibly he decided that the oft-repeated march provided quite enough of C and that tonal contrast was desirable here, even though it meant breaking the succession of V-to-I patterning that began with No. 12. It was only a momentary break, to be sure, because the circle of fifths was resumed with the arrival of F for the *terzetto* of farewells, No. 16.

TABLE 9.5 Act II, *Idomeneo*

No.:	10a	11	12	13	14	//	15	16	17	18
	C	E♭	D	G	C		E	F	c	d

The *terzetto* winds its way to a conclusive cadence for the voices, and the orchestra attempts the same as Idamante and Electra move toward the waiting ship. This time the cadence reached is not F, but f, signaling the beginning of a new storm, to which the chorus reacts with terror while describing the roaring tempest (besides the orchestra, enhanced by the *flauto piccolo*, there were stage effects involved such as the thunder drum—Mozart referred to the whole scene complex as "Der Donner"). Three times the people cry out, demanding to know the culprit who has offended Neptune. The bass descends by step, B♭/A♯ G♯ F♯, supporting their chordal outcries, which are echoed by the massed winds. Then there are renewed and quickened cries of "il reo, qual'è?" (Who is the culprit?) over F♮ in the bass. Idomeneo names himself, "Eccoti in me, barbaro Nume!" (the basses descend to E), "il reo!" At the revelation of his last word the keynote arrives full force with the entire orchestra, the violins rushing up and down the scale of D, then G as in the overture. This magnificent moment was originally planned to have been a cavatina for the king. But as early as his letter of 15 November 1780, Mozart wrote that an obbligato recitative with use of the full orchestra would make a far better effect because of all the noise and confusion onstage, "and besides, is the thunderstorm likely to subside so that Raaff can sing an aria?"

Idomeneo defies Neptune and says that he is an unjust god if he would sacrifice an innocent victim. At this blasphemy the people of Crete, understanding nothing and further terrorized by the appearance of a sea monster, begin to flee, singing the final number of the act, the precipitous chorus No. 18 in d, an *Allegro assai* in 12/8 (an unusual meter for Mozart). As they straggle off the stage, the voice parts drop out of the texture one by one (an effect parallel to the end of the fleeing chorus in the first act of Gluck's *Alceste*). The act ends *pianissimo*, with a solo oboe (Ramm) sustaining high D over low strings and horns.

Act III begins with the strings sustaining the chord of A. Ilia is alone in the royal garden. She confides her laments to the amorous breezes, plants, and flowers, the first of which become the subject of her aria "Zeffiretti lusinghieri," No. 19 in E. Like No. 15 in E, this aria features clarinets (in B♭) instead of oboes. The second line, "Fly to my treasure," provides an opportunity for coloratura and Mozart seizes it. The aria is in ternary form, with a middle section that describes Ilia's tears, beginning in tonic minor. Mozart's supreme mastery is everywhere audible, but nowhere more telling than in the unexpected chromatic rise when he varies the closing idea. Ilia is uncertain because of the plan that threw Idamante and Electra together, thus she is apprehensive and confused again at his approach, with which Mozart cuts off the end of her aria. Idamante arrives once again to the chord of B♭, explaining that now he leaves her in order to die. In a beautiful dialogue that eventually becomes obbligato, she makes a breakthrough by confessing her love directly to him and uttering the prophetic words "only I can save you." The following love duet is in A, like most of Mozart's love duets. No. 20a is in two tempos, moving from *Un poco più Andante* in common time to *Allegretto* in 3/8. Its replacement for Vienna in 1786, No. 20b, with a tenor instead of a soprano Idamante, is in common time *Larghetto* throughout, and draws both its musical material and its tempo from the preceding obbligato recitative.[31]

Electra and Idomeneo surprise the lovers, whereupon the music moves immediately to E♭, its destination at the end of the recitative. The tritone trajectory from A to E♭ is emphasized by the reappearance in the strings of a long-held triad on A, before the bass begins its descent, leading to the *quartetto*, No. 21 in E♭. Idamante begins it, saying he will go wandering alone, seeking death. In German this profound ensemble is known as the *Todesquartett*, in English as the Great Quartet. Mozart composed it in such a white heat of inspiration that it is one of the few pieces in the autograph showing compositional decisions being made while the notes were being written down.[32] He was constrained to write as legibly as possible at the same time because the autograph served as the immediate source of the Munich performing score. He had more trouble over this piece with Raaff, who complained that the music gave him no opportunity to spin out his voice. This crisis too was weathered.

Mozart lengthened the obbligato recitative for Arbace preceding his aria, No. 22 in A, at the request of Panzacchi. Like Idomeneo's speech between the choruses at the end of Act II, this recitative approaches the style of melodrama, as Mozart used it in *Zaide*. The orchestral interjections are elaborate, sometimes in imitative counterpoint, and, in the case of the rushing scalar rises in the last one, hark back to the second finale of *Giardiniera*. Arbace's second aria is of much more musical interest than his first one, especially in terms of rhythm, but it too was apparently sacrificed during the course of the first production, as it is crossed out in the Munich performing score. Its loss would work to the detriment of Mozart's tonal planning, in which it emphasizes the tritone conflict with E♭.[33]

The scene changes to a grand square with statues in front of the palace, the façade of which is seen on one side. Mozart provides a suitably pompous fanfare in C, *Maestoso*, for the arrival of the royal party, followed by a measure of rest with fermata. The suitably somber music for the High Priest, a *Largo* in the funereal key of A♭, arrives with no preparation, intoned by the strings in low position doubled by bassoons. If this music sounds familiar, it is because it combines the four afterbeats, marked *portamento*, common to the Idamante motif with the melodic figure at the beginning of Ilia's aria No.

---

[31] For a comparison of the two duets, see Heartz, "Mozart's Tragic Muse." No. 20a was crossed out in the Munich performing score.

[32] See Daniel Heartz, "The Great Quartet in Mozart's *Idomeneo*," *Music Forum* 5 (1980): 233–56.

[33] For an overview of the whole opera, see Daniel Heartz, "Tonality and Motif in *Idomeneo*," *Mozart-Jahrbuch 1973/74*, pp. 140–43, reprinted in *Musical Times* 115 (1974): 382–86.

19 and elsewhere. Mozart's choice of A♭ both here and later in the temple, as Idamante is led in wreathed for the sacrifice, may be a consequence of his love for Georg Benda's *Medea*, in which melodrama the music plunges from D into A♭ when Medea mentions confronting Jason in the temple.

The pantomime music continues with an agitated *Allegro* for the arrival of the populace ("quantità di popolo" in the libretto). Tonally this outburst leads to the grand monologue of the High Priest, which begins with the ominous trills in the violins, echoed in the winds. The trilled figure with descending arpeggio, often open-ended and used to propel modulation, owes much to the threatening monologue of the High Priest in the first act of Gluck's *Alceste*. It produces the intended result. Idomeneo is forced to confess the truth: the victim is Idamante. After a chromatic peroration comparable to that before Electra's first aria, the reaction comes not in the form of an aria, but in the form of a lamenting chorus, No. 24 in c, sung to an *Adagio* in cut time: "Oh voto tremendo! Spettacolo orrendo!" Here Mozart achieved the dramatic breakthrough that his entire century so fervently desired by retrieving the gravity and universality of the ancient Greek chorus, as, for example, in the threnody sung by the people after the truth is learned in *Oedipus Rex*.[34]

The people of Crete dolefully leave the stage, for which action Mozart writes a transition at the end of No. 24 that slowly turns c into C, interpreted at the end as V^7 of F. Meanwhile the stage set changes to a view of the exterior of the magnificent temple of Neptune, surrounded by a vast atrium, through which the seashore is discovered. Lorenzo Quaglio, the scenographer, was no small part of the original production. In fact, the official chronicle mentioned him at the expense of naming the composer and librettist: "Author, composer, and translator are Salzburg born; the decors, among which the view of the port and Neptune's temple stood out, were masterworks by our famous theater architect, court counselor Lorenzo Quaglio, and they drew everyone's admiration." Quaglio's decors are lost. By way of replacement, see J.-D. Dugourc's stage design for the beginning of Gluck's *Iphigénie en Tauride* (Stockholm, 1780) (Figure 9.8).

Mozart's afterthought of a third march, No. 25 in F, for the arrival of the priests may well have been an inspired reaction to the scenery. In any case, the decision gives the audience a chance to savor the new set during the few moments that the solemn strains for orchestra alone sound forth. Idomeneo arrives next and sings his plea to Neptune, "Accogli, oh rè del mar, i nostri voti" (Receive, oh king of the sea, our prayers). The violins play ascending

[34] Daniel Heartz, "Idomeneus Rex," *Mozart-Jahrbuch 1973/74*, pp. 7–20. This "keynote address," delivered at the conference surrounding the first performance of the NMA score at Salzburg, attempted to place the work in the context of neoclassical visions by late eighteenth-century artists.

FIGURE 9.8. J.-D. Dugourc. Stage design for Act I of Gluck's *Iphigénie en Tauride*, Stockholm, 1780.

and descending arpeggios pizzicato, suggesting clouds of incense, perhaps, while the woodwinds become ever more involved, climbing upward in a passage that the first oboe caps by sounding the Idamante motif. The priests have an easy time of it here as they chant the single tone C until falling a fifth to F at the end, which Mozart decorates with a solemn plagal cadence, iv - I.

The third act has already taken nearly fifty minutes up to this point. Yet it is not quite half over, in terms of the complete version of all the music Mozart composed.[35] A third act twice too long flouted the societal purposes of a carnival opera that was allowed roughly three hours altogether. The

[35] When preparing the NMA edition that came out in 1972, I decided to observe cuts made in January 1781 before the premiere, as indicated by Mozart's letters and the second printed libretto (Italian only), which were in agreement. By this token the last three arias, Nos. 27, 29, and 30 for Idamante, Electra, and Idomeneo, respectively, were relegated to the Appendix. In the case of Electra, Mozart composed a fiery obbligato recitative to replace her aria. The cuts Mozart was forced to make did not stop with the loss of three superb arias. They affected the choral numbers as well, and much else according to the Munich performing score.

evening only began with the opera (at 5:30 P.M.); it was followed by supper and a carnival ball in the Redoute. One way to make the opera practical for the stage is to give the audience (and musicians) a respite by dividing Act III into two parts, with a pause after the sacrifice chorus and Idomeneo's prayer (Nos. 25–26). The result is four nearly equal sections.

TABLE 9.6 Act III, Part One, *Idomeneo*

No.:	19	20	21	22	//	23	24	//	25	26
	E	A	E♭	A		A♭	c		F	F

When the action resumes after Idomeneo's prayer, there is a burst of trumpets and drums, to which fanfare in D a chorus hails Idamante for having slain the monster. Idomeneo realizes that this can only increase Neptune's ire. Idamante is led in, dressed in white and garlanded with flowers, surrounded by guards and priests. The orchestra sounds a doleful *Largo* in A♭, after which father and son begin their last farewells. The moment is almost unbearably poignant. Idomeneo vainly tries to summon up strength, rails against fate, and then falls back in a near faint. Mozart's orchestra paints this psychological progression in the minutest detail and with a sense of the real time such an agonized father might take.

Idamante is steadfast and insistent, reminding his father of duty. The tempo returns to *Largo* as he recommends Ilia: "She will not be my bride, but let her be your daughter." At this point the recitative cadence points to the keynote and Idamante's last aria begins, "No, la morte io non pavento" (No, I do not fear death), No. 27a in D. Mozart set the text in ternary form, otherwise characteristic of the older generation (Idomeneo, Arbace)—a telling sign of the hero's new maturity. The music is so finely attuned to the words in this aria that it is no wonder that those who heard it lamented its loss, as Mozart stated in his letter of 18 January 1781. He also said the aria was out of place where it stood, but this may be a rationalization to comfort both himself and his Idamante. There is no question that Idamante's last aria is musically his finest. It is also integrated with the end of the opera because Mozart uses the noble phrase at the words "se alla patria al genitor" as the theme of the instrumental trio in the final chorus, No. 31.

Dal Prato could not have been quite so incompetent a singer as Mozart maintained, for he went on to become a favorite at the Munich court, and highly paid. Perhaps this favor already shone upon him during the run of *Idomeneo*, because the Munich performing score shows evidence that "No, la morte" was restored after having been cut.

Idamante's last aria lends the added advantage of relieving the dramatic intensity of obbligato recitative so that it can claim our full attention again and work its wonders after "No, la morte." Father and son make another attempt to carry out fate's decree. At the *Largo* Mozart pushes all the way to D♭ for the verb "to die" ("mori"), recalling the music with which this key erupted in the *Todesquartett*. Ilia interposes herself between Idamante and the sacrificial knife after a scalar burst in the violins that prevents the threatened cadence in c. The postponement continues as she reasons that the gods could never have wanted a father to kill his heir. Her generous soul prevails. The cadence in c arrives, but it announces a subterranean voice, made awesome by trombones. The heavens relent and pardon Idomeneo, but not as king, in which office Idamante must take his place, with Ilia as his wife.

Much about this short oracular speech is contained in the letters between Mozart and his father. It could scarcely be short enough for the composer, while his father defended Varesco up to a point. Gluck had shown the way as regards oracular pronouncements in his *Alceste*. The trombones, church instruments at that time and thus particularly appropriate to manifestations of the otherworldly, were introduced into the opera house by Gluck (already in *Orfeo*). Mozart had a row with Count Seeau in order to get them and says he succeeded (letter of 10 January), but the Munich performing score betrays a trombone-less *Adagio* for winds. When the strains of whichever of the versions dies out in c transformed into C, a wind ensemble of flutes, oboes, and bassoons takes over, keeping the common tone C and making it into the seventh of a major triad on D. Idomeneo, Idamante, Ilia, and Arbace utter a few words apiece, as if unable to say more. Electra says more. She launches into her greatest obbligato recitative and aria, No. 29a, or, as the case may be, her replacement obbligato recitative, No. 29, which is just as searing but brief, depositing her with a fury of lacerating chords in d, the key of her first aria.

In the old edition of Mozart's complete works Electra's sensational replacement exit was conflated with the recitative and aria it was intended to suppress, with the result that the original recitative was relegated to the limbo of the appendix. Yet the original recitative is a marvel in its own right. Particularly evocative is Electra's summoning of the Eumenides, at which an accented first-beat figure in quick notes is repeated obsessively by the first violins as the winds echo her descending-seventh cry of "Misera." When she says she will follow her brother Orestes to the abyss, the tempo turns to *Andante* and the winds intone falling octaves in long notes and in the key of E♭, traditional ingredients of an *ombra* scene and deployed before she intones "Ombra infelice!" to the same figure. Traetta and Jommelli, the greatest of the Neapolitan composers, made a specialty of such scenes, and their inspiration may be at work here.

The strings lead into Electra's aria with an orgy of descending chromatics reminiscent of the passage just before her first aria, No. 4. The recitative cadence prepares for a piece in f, but this is only a feint, as the orchestra begins the *Allegro assai* in common time, f turns out to be iv, leading with a *crescendo* to V and then the arrival of the tonic, c, given out softly by the whole orchestra, including four horns, two trumpets, and timpani. Her vocal line is not doubled anywhere. The violins are busy with a little rhythmic snap, the seconds doubling the firsts an octave below, while the violas, divided in two, provide a steady stream of parallel thirds in eighth-note motion. Once established, this texture will not let up, like the torment of which Electra sings. Only with the arrival of the relative major is there a respite, as the orchestra takes the lead by announcing a fanfare figure to which she responds. The snaps in the violins creep back soon enough, softly in the first violins as the violas restart their figure. There is another time out from the obsessive figures for the antiphonal calls between voice and winds that make up the closing. The transition back to c is beset with the original texture. When tonic minor arrives, it is with the full orchestra projecting the fanfare figure, or second theme.

Mozart would not again write music with as much dramatic impact as this until the first movement of the Piano Concerto in c, K. 491 of 1786. Electra works over the first-theme material after the second theme, then turns to the antiphonal calls of the closing. She caps them with a rising, offbeat melisma that carries her voice up to high C via a legato chromatic ascent, followed by the descending scale of c, staccato. The effect is bloodcurdling. She repeats the passage. One more chromatic rise up to G in long notes leads to her final cadence and exit.

Electra's last aria, sung by a variety of sopranos in many productions of *Idomeneo* over the past two decades, has consistently brought down the house as has no other number in the opera. It is by far her greatest aria, some would say the greatest in the opera. It builds on her previous music, especially her first aria, where its very key of c was planted as an aberrant reprise. Mozart's one reservation expressed to his father about the aria in his letter of 3 January 1781 was that it seemed silly ("einfältig") that everyone should hurry off the stage just in order to leave Madame Electra alone. The stage in Mozart's day did not have the possibility of blackouts or spot lighting. With modern technology Electra can be cast into her own lonely world in an instant, with the others not visibly present as she goes through her nightmare vision of the torments of hell.

The orchestral postlude after Electra's exit is short but to the point, the winds intoning the falling conjunct fourth (Idamante motif) that has been sounding throughout the opera ever since the beginning of the overture. It will sound again in the following *Adagio* that begins in E♭ and in a new guise, more radiantly beautiful than before, as the falling tritone answered by falling perfect-fifth figure is exchanged among first violins, second violins, and violas (Example 9.15). Dulcet sighs from the clarinets in B♭ soften the precadential area. Before Idomeneo opens his mouth, we know that peace has returned at last to Crete. His renunciation of power in favor of Ilia and Idamante completes the drama.

The negotiations that went on between Raaff, Mozart, his father, and Varesco to produce the final aria for Idomeneo constitute a long saga that is told elsewhere.[36] "Torna la pace" (Peace returns) was the last of several

EXAMPLE 9.15. *Mozart*, Idomeneo, *No. 30*

[36] Daniel Heartz, "Raaff's Last Aria: A Mozartian Idyll in the Spirit of Hasse," *Musical Quarterly* 60 (1974): 517–43.

attempts to arrive at the right text, and with it Mozart created a tuneful masterpiece of a ternary aria, No. 30a in B♭. The middle section in 3/8 evokes an older style of composition in which the great Hasse had especially triumphed, without ceasing for a moment to be purely Mozartian. This aria easily outdoes the king's in Acts I and II because it capitalized on what Raaff did best—spinning out lyrical melodies. How could this aria ever have been sacrificed? There were groans of protest, to be sure. In his last letter on the subject (18 January), Mozart wrote: "The cutting of Raaff's last aria is regretted even more [than that of Idamante's last aria], but one must make a virtue out of necessity."

Mozart had his reservations about both of Idomeneo's previous arias, because the text of the first did not allow enough *cantabile*, and he did not believe the venerable tenor could do justice to the bravura second anymore (letter of 15 November 1780). He was especially critical of the first aria, writing Leopold that if he had composed the piece for the bass Giovanni Battista Zonca (who Mozart at the beginning thought would play the role), it would have suited the text better (letter of 27 December 1780). A bass in the role of Idomeneo was also on Mozart's mind after he settled in Vienna, as we shall see.

"Torna la pace" is about the return of springtime, nature's miracle, in which even old trees become once again verdant. Its choice of the key of B♭, which had belonged to the young and impetuous Idamante throughout the opera, could not be more appropriate. Similarly, an Idamante going to his death (or so he believed) could sing only in the opera's heroic keynote of D. Mozart insisted on these same two keys in the great coronation ballet that ends the opera. Its thrilling musical effect coming directly after the final chorus must be heard to be believed.[37] The tonal schemes of the ballet and Part Two of Act III are similar.

TABLE 9.7 Act III, Part Two, *Idomeneo*						
No.:	27a	28	29a	30a	31	Ballet
	D	c	c	E♭–B♭	D	D–B♭–d–D

We have seen how Mozart tailored *Idomeneo* to the talents at his disposal. Arrived in Vienna once again, he considered a major revision of the opera, to be undertaken by a poet he greatly admired, Johann Baptist Alxinger. Joseph II had commissioned Alxinger to translate Gluck's *Iphigénie en Tauride* into German for the state visit of the Russian crown prince in the fall of 1781. In his letter of 12 September 1781 Mozart confided to his father that he would have retailored the roles of a German-language *Idomeneo* around the best talents in the Burgtheater at the time—the bass Karl Ludwig Fischer (the future Osmin), Antonia Bernasconi (for whom Gluck wrote *Alceste* and Mozart the prima donna role of Aspasia in *Mitridate*), and the tenor Valentin Adamberger (the future Belmonte).

> The man who translated *Iphigénie* into German is a superb poet, and I would have gladly given him my Munich opera to translate. The role of Idomeneo I would have changed entirely, and written it as a bass part for Fischer, making several other changes that would orient the part more along French lines. Bernasconi, Adamberger, and Fischer would have taken the greatest pleasure in singing it. But since they must now learn two other operas [*Iphigénie* and *Alceste* in the original Italian] and such difficult operas ["und so mühsame opern"] I must excuse them, and besides, a third opera would be too much.

Mozart's compliment to the elderly Gluck for his "difficult" operas is sincere. *Idomeneo* as it stands, without being translated into German or reconstituted more along French lines, is unthinkable without the profundity of Gluck's tragedies for Vienna and Paris as inspiration. Mozart carried out at least a part of his revisionary plans for *Idomeneo* in 1786, when he changed the part of Idamante from a soprano to a tenor for a performance in Vienna.

Several national and local strains of music drama flow into *Idomeneo* and contribute to its richness. In terms of Mozart's own music, his grand opera for Munich sums up and surpasses everything he had created since taking his first fledgling steps as a composer. His instrumental works, sacred music, and previous operatic ventures all play their part in the cresting of

---

[37]John Eliot Gardiner's complete recording of 1990 demonstrates this.

this mighty wave. *Idomeneo*, in international terms, lays claim to being nothing less than the greatest lyric tragedy of its century. The effort Mozart put into creating a work of such magnitude and its public success helped precipitate the decisive turning point of his life. Henceforth he could no longer resume the quasi-feudal status of a court musician. Vienna in the spring of 1781 represented for him the beginning of a new voyage.

Conclusion

URING the reign of Maria Theresa an impressive group of musicians, sharing similar training and outlook, came together in Vienna. This group, known as the Viennese School, might well have been called the Austrian-Bohemian School. Many instrumentalists, according to their names, were Czech. Composers of Slavic-Bohemian origin included Gluck, Steffan, and Vanhal. Gassmann was a German Bohemian from the Sudetenland. Although Hungary furnished no comparable influx of composers and performers, it did produce a veritable Maecenas in Prince Nicholas Esterházy, Haydn's generous patron for nearly three decades. And two other major Viennese composers, Michael Haydn and Ditters, worked for a number of years in Hungary.

Devotion to music at the highest level of the monarchy, in the imperial family, had the effect of encouraging its cultivation throughout society. Music became emblematic of the monarchy's unity and special character in that songs and dances of the Austrian and Bohemian countrysides helped shape courtly art music in the metropolis. This process was already apparent in the music of Maria Theresa's first keyboard teacher, Gottlieb Muffat, and it gained strength throughout the century, particularly in the works of Starzer, Ditters, and Haydn. Mozart's music went through a similar process in Salzburg.

During the seventeenth century Italians dominated music and art at the Viennese court. The situation in music began to change slowly with the rise to prominence of Johann Joseph Fux, born around 1660, the son of Styrian

717

peasants. Fux became Kapellmeister to Emperor Charles VI in 1715, thus breaking the Italian hegemony over the imperial court music. Fux was also a crucial forerunner of the Viennese School in another way, as the author of *Gradus ad Parnassum* (1725), a method of strict counterpoint that was studied and taught by all the Viennese masters who came after him.

As a composer, and by authority of his position, Fux held firm against any inroads of the galant style, in which cause he had the support of Charles VI. This attitude changed rapidly after the accession of Maria Theresa in 1740. Her musical idol was Hasse, and she encouraged the newer musical styles streaming north from Italy. Wagenseil quickly became Vienna's leading master of the galant style. He belonged to a generation born around 1710 that also included Reutter, Bonno, Monn, and Gluck. These masters, often demeaned by labels such as "pre-classic," created a body of works in all genres that brought Viennese music to a point increasingly independent of its Italian forebears and models, making possible the further advances of the following generation.

Haydn, born in 1732, eventually came to lead his generation, which included Gassmann, Vanhal, Hofmann, Steffan, and Ditters. Remarks made by Haydn in appreciation of Gluck and Wagenseil only confirm the deep continuities from the older generation to his own evident in the music itself. But as early as 1800 critics began to obliterate this obvious connection and to posit instead a direct succession from north German composers to Haydn and Mozart.[1] Very little subsequent historiography by Germans in the field has escaped the tendency to appropriate Austrian-Bohemian achievements in music. This has led to, among other distortions, playing down the close connections between Italy and the Catholic court of Vienna. These ties became loosened only in a gradual manner, as can be seen by considering the question of musical training.

For the generation of 1710, training in Italy or at the least by Italian hands was still considered indispensable. Bonno was sent with an imperial stipend to study in Naples with Leo. Wagenseil likewise received a court scholarship, but his instruction was at the hands of Fux and Matteo Palotta in Vienna. Gluck managed to reach Italy in the retinue of a Milanese nobleman and is assumed to have studied with Sammartini. Reutter was instructed by Caldara in Vienna; he was also sent to Italy for further study.

With Haydn's generation there was a perceptible shift. Haydn never visited Italy, but his training with Reutter was supplemented by more penetrating lessons imparted by the visiting Neapolitan composer Porpora, as

---

[1] As did three north German historians, all Protestants, cited by Erich Reimer in "Nationalbewußtsein und Musikgeschichtsschreibung in Deutschland, 1800–1850," *Musikforschung* 46 (1993): 17–31.

Haydn stressed in no uncertain terms in his autobiographical letter of 1776. Michael Haydn's training was likewise in Vienna, as was that of Ditters, Hofmann, Vanhal, Albrechtsberger, and presumably Ordonez. Gassmann went to Italy when he was young but under unusual circumstances: he ran away from home. Vanhal, after studying in Vienna, traveled to Italy to put the finishing touches on his musical education. The boy Mozart joined this generation as a composer; he toured Italy not as a student but as a Wunderkind put on display by his father. That he learned much from the experience, even on musical grounds, especially from Italian opera and from Padre Martini, does not change the general picture. To succeed in Vienna, it was no longer necessary for a composer to be trained in Italy or at the hands of Italians.

The loosening grip of Italian music and musicians on Vienna does not apply to opera, but it is obvious from concert programs, which we now possess for the first time in sufficient quantity. Around 1760 the concerts in the Burgtheater become increasingly dominated by local musicians, figuring as soloists as well as composers. Here the role of Ditters and his violin concertos should not be underestimated. In vocal music other than opera—oratorio, for example—Wagenseil, Bonno, and other Viennese composers made a good showing in the Burgtheater's Lenten concerts, and later in the annual concerts of the Tonkünstler Societät. It is thus not surprising to discover that Viennese composers began to feel a sense of parity, and even of superiority, with regard to their Italian competitors. To a certain extent Italian influence was replaced by French, manifest particularly in Gluck's opéras-comiques for the Burgtheater.

"On the Viennese Taste in Music," an article written in 1766 (by Ditters, I argue), forcibly repulses the attacks on Austrian music by north German critics and extols the greatness of Reutter, Hofmann, Wagenseil, Haydn, Ditters, and Gluck, in this order. Not only does the music of these composers excel according to the article, so does the superior way in which it was being performed. Gluck's mastery of the orchestra in the Burgtheater (in which Ditters was a violinist) is singled out for special praise. Compare this with what Ditters has to say in his memoirs about the theater orchestra in Bologna, where he and Gluck repaired in 1763 for the premiere of the latter's *Trionfo di Clelia*.

> At last we heard Gluck's opera, which was a great success, though the performance fell far short of the composer's ideal. We had been told all sorts of things about Italian orchestras, but Gluck was not in the least satisfied with them. There had been seventeen full rehearsals; and in spite of that, we missed the *ensemble* and the precision to which we had become accustomed in Vienna.

On their way back to Vienna Gluck and Ditters traveled by way of Parma. Here they heard a performance of Christian Bach's *Catone in Utica*, of which Ditters wrote: "Some of the airs were quite beautiful, but the main body of the work was written very sketchily, after the Italian style" ("nach italienischer Stil nur so hingeworfen"). Much Italian orchestral writing of the time was indeed thin, and lacking in wind color, in comparison with Viennese orchestration. Gassmann was a worthy follower of Gluck in enriching the palette of the Burgtheater's orchestra.

Haydn rarely had anything bad to say about his fellow composers. An exception occurred when he was told that Mysliveček, upon hearing some quartets by Sammartini, claimed to have discovered the model of Haydn's quartets. Haydn was irritated to the point of calling Sammartini a *Schmierer*, a dauber, or so Griesinger reported. Carpani extended the painterly metaphor by adding that Sammartini "produced here and there the most beautiful bursts of light next to disordered masses of indefinite color." The converse of this analogy in visual terms must be that Haydn kept his colors bright and clear as well as orderly, and easily distinguished. Few would argue with this, although his north German critics claimed that he, like Ditters and the other Viennese, committed the unpardonable sin of placing comic and serious traits side by side in the same work.

Mozart's superiority over the Italians lay partly in his fastidious orchestration. As Leopold Mozart, in his letter of 4 December 1780, wrote his son, who was in Munich finishing the composition of *Idomeneo*, "When your music is performed by a mediocre orchestra, it will always be the loser, because it is composed with so much discernment for the individual instruments and is not insipid as, on the whole, Italian music is" ("nicht so platt, wie die italiän Musik überhaupts geschrieben ist"). Mozart's orchestral wizardry had more to do with Vienna than with Salzburg, where, as he complained, discipline among the performers was lax, and there were no clarinets. In his letter of 5 December 1780 from Munich Mozart requested that Leopold send a trumpet mute "of the kind we had made in Vienna." Even *Idomeneo*, composed for the famed Mannheim orchestra transplanted to Munich, owed many debts to Vienna.

Visitors to Vienna helped confirm what was obvious to local musicians. Burney reached Austria in the late summer of 1772, two years after touring Italy, where he had found, much to his surprise, very little music or music making that met his high expectations. In Vienna he marveled at the richness and depth of the musical life, which he related to an uncommon degree of musicality among the general populace. Specifically, he found the symphonies and the level of orchestral performance in the two imperial theaters superior to what he heard anywhere else. Other visitors, such as Nicolai and Riesbeck, were impressed by the nimbleness and precision of Viennese orchestral playing. Reichardt said that he learned how to perform Haydn's quartets in a "lively and piquant" manner only after hearing them performed by Austrians. This comment throws some additional light on Haydn's claim, in his autobiographical letter of 1776, that Berliners excoriated his music "because they are incapable of performing some of my works, and are too conceited to take the trouble to understand them properly." Viennese music demanded not only the greatest precision in rhythmic interpretation but an unheard-of flexibility in dynamics as well.

Vienna was looked down upon by visitors from Germany and elsewhere because it lacked a well-developed literary culture of its own. True, Metastasio dwelled in the imperial capital for over half a century, but he belonged to all the world of opera and was in fact seldom employed in Vienna once Joseph II turned against opera seria. Joseph's attempt to found an opera in German that was not indebted to Hanswurst and the popular theater failed for lack of good librettos—i.e., for lack of literary, not musical, genius.

The gradual emancipation of Viennese music from Italian hegemony finds a parallel, if not in the literary arts, at least in art and architecture. Great Austrian architects appeared first, perhaps because of the need for so much rebuilding after the siege of Vienna by the Turks was lifted in 1683. The two outstanding figures were Johann Lukas von Hildebrandt, who built the Belvedere Palace, and Johann Bernard Fischer von Erlach, who planned the Karlskirche—both edifices arose outside the old walls, where the devastation was greatest. During the reign of Maria Theresa two superb Austrian painters, Franz Anton Maulbertsch and Johann Christian Brand, outshone all others. Both were trained in Vienna.

Maria Theresa's Vienna was of necessity "multicultural." Calzabigi maintained in his *Riposta* to Arteaga of 1790 that he and Gluck could never have initiated the operatic reform anywhere but Vienna because "Viennese audiences represent the distillation of all nations." Haydn's origin and life in the border area where many diverse peoples came together was a source of strength and, in his music, of infinite variety. More than any other composer Haydn united the Fuxian ideal of the contrapuntal with the *seemingly* popular that made him accessible to all.

Most of the composers contemporary with Haydn had done their best work by the end of the 1770s. After 1780 they seemed to lose spirit, as if there were a collective failure of will or creative energy. Ditters bravely continued to compose symphonies, even string quartets, and in 1786 he scored a triumph with an opera in the Burgtheater. Michael Haydn also persevered. Others faltered, to a greater or lesser degree. That they did so was perhaps a result of realizing how high Haydn was soaring as he pushed his art to still further regions of inventive imagination, and also a result of observing the blinding brilliance of Mozart's last decade. Haydn and Mozart together, reacting to each other's genius and knowing that they were beyond the reach of all other composers—that is a new phenomenon of the 1780s. The subject is sublime. It deserves to be at the center of another volume.

Appendix 1

"The Present State of the Court- and Chamber-Music"

Two reports on Viennese music and musicians date from 1766. Johann Adam Hiller solicited and received from an unnamed source in Vienna "Von dem dermaligen Etat der kaiserl. königl. Hof- und Kammermusik," which he published in the thirteenth *Stück* of his *Wöchentliche Nachrichten und Anmerkungen die Musik betreffend*, dated Leipzig, 23 September 1766. (See the facsimile, Figures 2.4 through 2.7.) A month later in the *Wiener Diarium* dated 18 October 1766, there appeared in the supplementary series called "Gehlehrter Nachrichten" an unsigned article entitled "Von dem wienerischen Geschmack in der Musik." The first essay is retrospective although quite accurate concerning the personnel of the court institutions. The second assesses only the main musicians, but it is forward-looking and almost visionary in predicting great futures for young composers like Carl Ditters and Leopold Hofmann. For this reason the main discussion of this article is relegated to Chapter 6 on Haydn's contemporaries.

A test case revealing the knowledge and attitudes of the authors of the two essays is provided by Gluck. The correspondent of the *Wiener Diarium* is an enthusiast who is aware of Gluck's epochal works of the early 1760s, including *Don Juan* and *Orfeo ed Euridice*. Hiller's correspondent is either unaware of them or unenthusiastic about them to the point of deeming them not worthy of mention. Instead he cites the many *successive* comic operas by

Chevalier Christoph Gluck (who received the Order of the Golden Spur from the pope in 1757). Gluck's successive comic operas stretched from *La fausse esclave* (1758) to *Le cadi dupé* (1761) and included seven such works. Confirming the retrospective view of this correspondent is the repeated mention of Prince Hildburghausen's musical chapel, which was disbanded in 1761.

A friend of music has upon demand written the following report on the actual state of the imperial-royal court and chamber music, as well as providing a short, albeit at the moment incomplete, outline of some other virtuosi and amateurs located in Vienna.

1. Be it known that after the former director, Count Durazzo, left two years ago as ambassador to Venice, the Bohemian count Johann Wenzel Sporck, count of the Holy Roman Empire, acting as general director of spectacles or as quasi *maître des plaisirs,* now has the overall power over the court and chamber music, and at the same time over the theater. He is one of the most knowledgeable nobles, and he is well qualified for his charge, since he is an exacting connoisseur. In instrumental music, especially on the violin, he is held to be very skilled.

2. The famous abbé Pietro Metastasio, sufficiently known to the world for his works, is still our Italian court poet.

3. Present besides the highly famous Kapellmeister Johann Adolph Hasse, formerly court composer of the elector of Saxony, whose presence in person we are fortunate to have, are also Giuseppe Scarlatti, who has written many serious as well as comic operas that have won applause, both here and in Italy, and the chevalier Christoph Gluck, who, in addition to operas known before, has recently composed here a succession of many comic operas with taste. In addition, one can reasonably include a Florian Leopold Gassmann, sent by His Imperial Majesty to Italy for a time, and presently in Venice. He wrote a setting of *Olimpiade* [by Metastasio] at the end of 1764, which was performed with applause here in the carnival of 1765, and his keyboard pieces [?] are very good.

To be noted concerning the court chapel:

COURT KAPELLMEISTER.

Lucas Anton Predieri, a man of service especially in church music, and a composer of operas under the regime of Emperor Charles VI who now lives in retirement.

Georg von Reutter, who is also music director of the cathedral of St. Stephen's, and is likewise known mainly for his church music and motets. Otherwise there is in this kind of composition to be numbered a certain lawyer by the name of [Christoph] Sonnenleitner, who has shown himself most skilled.

CHAMBER COMPOSERS.

Georg Christoph Wagenseil, born in Vienna, and most noted in all genres.

Joseph Bono [Bonno], an Italian. [Hiller corrects this on p. 142, noting that Bonno was "ein geborhner Wiener"].

COURT KEYBOARD MASTERS.

Leopold Hofmann, from Vienna, and Kapellmeister at St. Peter's. He is known for his beautiful symphonies and a host of other things.

Joseph Steffan, a Bohemian, known for his harpsichord concertos, keyboard pieces such as divertimenti and the like, which are engraved in copper for the most part.

FEMALE SINGERS.

Mme. Theresia von Reutter, wife of the court Kapellmeister, but she no longer sings.

Mme. Theresia Pettmann, née Heinisch, a daughter of the famous court trumpeter of the same name.

Mlle. Teuberin [Elizabeth Teyber], at present engaged in the chapel music of Prince Hildburghausen.

SOPRANO.

Joseph Monteriso.

CONTRALTO.

Pietro Rauzzino [Venanzio Rauzzini?] and Pietro Galli.

TENOR.

Cajetan Borghi. In addition we include Leopold Bonscho of Prince Hildburghausen's chapel, who is also an excellent cellist.

BASSES.

Christoph Braun and Carl Herrich.

ORGANIST.

Gottlieb Muffat.

VIOLINISTS.

Carl Joseph Denck, Herr Adam, and his daughter, a great virtuosa.

Franz Thuma [Tuma] from Bohemia, former Kapellmeister of the late prince of Lichtenstein, known for symphonies, concertos, and the like.

Karl Ditters, known for symphonies, concertos, and the like.

Leopold Hofmann, likewise known [corrected on p. 142 to Anton Hofmann].

Carl von Ordonitz [Ordonez], registrar of the rural justice office, known for his symphonies.

Joseph Heyden [Haydn], an Austrian, capellmeister of Prince Esterházy, known for his symphonies and the like.

Ziegler [Joseph], known for symphonies, trios, etc.

Martinus Wisdorffer [imperial court secretary in 1786].

Huber [Pancrazio Huber, music director for the Redoutensaal balls in 1773].

Hoffmann [possibly Joannes Hoffmann, in 1783 violinist of the Minoriten-kirche].

Kreibich [Franz].

Klemm, pupil of Hofmann [possibly Bernard Klemp].

Trani [Giuseppe Trani, the teacher of Ditters].

Aspelmeyer [Franz Asplmayr].

Hasslinger, presently in Pressburg.

Anton Rosetti, chamber musician to Count Althan [he became concertmaster to Althan in 1766, led the Esterházy orchestra from 1776 to 1781, and is not to be confused with the Bohemian composer of the same name].

Johann Schnautz.

Cammermeyer [organist of St. Stephen's].

Mannl.

Curara.

Büschelberger.

OBOES.

Besozzi [Carlo Besozzi], from the electoral court of Saxony.

FLUTES.

Schulz.

ON THE MANDORA.

Molli and Winter.

HARP PLAYERS.

Tretter [Dretter] and Bierfreund.

LUTE PLAYERS.

Kohot [Carl von Kohaut], secretary of the imperial royal court and state chancellery, famous for playing this instrument as well as composing for it.

BASS PLAYERS.

Abbé Koloser; Hofmann [Joseph Nicolas, brother of Leopold?]; Himmelbauer; Ledezki, a Bohemian; Schlosthal, assessor of the city; Franciscello [Francesco Alborea, alias Francischello, and one of the most famous cellists of the century; the appearance of his name here helps confirm suppositions that he lived to be about eighty].

BASSOONIST.

Philipp Friedrich.

TROMBONIST.

Ferdin. Christian, one of the best in church music.

COURT TRUMPETER.

Ernst Beyer, Frantz Kreibich, Andreas Hübler; also Neubold, Koch, and Hofbauer.

The following are famous at the keyboard and in the instruction of same.

Arbesser [Ferdinand], court musician of Prince Schwarzenberg, from Vienna.

Senft, a Viennese, known for *Partien*.

Johann Christoph Mann, known for *Galanteriepartien*, concertos, night music, symphonies, and the like.

Sommer, student of Steffan.

Matthielli [Giovanni Antonio Matielli, student of Wagenseil].

ORGANISTS IN THE SUBURBS.

At the Black Spaniards, Scheibpflug.
At the White Spaniards, Heida.
At the Fourteen Helpers in Distress, Martinides.
At the Karlskirche, Pircher; all known for church style.

To be noted as well are some of our women, whether from the nobility or middle class, who are skilled at the keyboard or in singing, such as:

Mlle. Elizabeth Martínez, raised under the purview of Abbé Metastasio; she composes very skillfully.

Mlle. Countess von Zierotni, in singing.

Mlle. Countess von Wilczec.

A Mlle. Bar: von Gudenus.

A Mlle. von Collenbach.

Mlle. Auenbrugge [Franziska von Auenbrugger].

A Mlle. von Hahn.

Mlle. Plenschütz.
    The wife of Waldstädten, née von Schäfer.
    The wife of Moll, consort of the royal agent, all on the keyboard.

Mme. Hardlin.

Mme. Fraislin, in singing.

Besides other endowed academies, such as for example at Count Collaldo's, at property owner von Rees', and at von Oertel's, weekly concerts take place, at least formerly, at Prince Hildburghausen's under the direction of Joseph Bono.

Vienna, in the month of August, 1766.

Incomplete as this listing admittedly is, it gives a picture of the extent of Viennese music making around 1760 that helps put other accounts into slightly better focus. Unique to this source is the emphasis on amateur musicians and on women. Of greatest disappointment is the minimal knowledge or interest Hiller's correspondent shows concerning wind players. The flowering of the solo concerto for horn and orchestra in Burgtheater concerts of the early 1760s, for instance, such as we learned about from Gumpenhuber's accounts in Chapter 1, finds no confirming evidence here. Indeed, this correspondent does not even include a rubric for the horn, and for his plural rubrics of "Oboists" and "Flautists," he manages only one person apiece.

Appendix 2

An Annotated Translation of Calzabigi's Letter on *Alceste* to Prince Kaunitz.[1]

Vienna, 6 March 1767

Highness!

In transmitting to Your Highness the enclosed letter of Signor Gluck,[2] which I felt obliged to communicate to you, I find it necessary to add some pertinent observations of my own to what he says about my *Alceste*.

When Their Imperial Majesties and Your Highness decide that *Alceste* go on the stage, it is indispensable to choose for it suitable performers, for the parts of Alceste and Admeto cannot be represented by just any singer, given the weaving ["tessitura"] of the new species of dramas, which is founded on the eye of the spectator and in consequence of the action,[3] and given the music suitable to this genus, which revolves more around expression than what the Italians of this century are pleased to call song.

The dramas of Signor Abate Metastasio are on a plan that is dictated by the great lengths corresponding to his large number of verses, and his wish to enhance music's role. They discourage the spectator's attention and deserve the

---

[1] The original letter, in Italian, is printed with a facsimile of the last page by Vladimir Helfert, "Dosud Neznámy dopis Ran. Calsabigiho zr. 1767," *Musikologie* (Prague-Brno, 1938), pp. 114–22. Hans Hammelmann and Michael Rose, "New Light on Calzabigi and Gluck," *Musical Times* 110 (June 1969), pp. 609–11, offer a translation of the letter that is, like the whole article, flawed by inaccuracies.

[2] Gluck's letter is not extant—a great loss in this field of studies.

[3] Here is another description of making operas by means of tableaux, discussed above in connection with *Orfeo*.

privilege of being called *selles à tous chevaux* [saddles for all horses], since in them it has ever been indifferent whether a character in these dramas was represented by Farinello, Caffarello, Guadagni, or Toschi;[4] by Tesi, Gabrielli, or Bianchi.[5] From the singers the public expected and requested no more than a couple of arias and the duet, because before attending the performance, they had abandoned any thought of taking interest in the action, it not being possible to pay attention for five hours to six actors, four of whom are usually so inept that they scarcely know how to enunciate properly, just for the pleasure of becoming passionate about an insipid Clelia, a cold Ersilia, an imaginary Aristea, an impertinent Emira, an indecent Onoria, and a shameless Mandane, who are all in substance no more than Roman or Neapolitan petty courtesans, speaking about love on the stage in a polished and gossipy language.[6] I will say nothing about the heros, who are always unnatural, there existing nowhere in the real world such affected, philosophizing characters as the Metastasian Orazio, Temistocle, Catone, and Romolo.[7]

Interest in the drama being excluded from these works, it was necessary, since they failed to please the soul, to entertain the senses: the eye with live horses against painted scenery, real battles in miniature, and conflagrations of colored paper;[8] the ear with vocal imitations of a violin, and concertos sounded by the voice, whence came that musical gargling that in Naples is called *trocciolette* (because in fact it rather resembles the noise of the wheels passing over the ropes of a pulley) and so many other bizarre musical effects as to resemble the carvings with which Gothic architecture ornamented, or rather deformed its monuments, admired at one time, but now a cause of mirth and nausea to whoever stops to look at them. And to make place for these strange embellishments, the poet applied himself to filling his dramas with comparisons, with winds, tempests, lions, steeds, and nightingales, all of which fit as well in the mouths of impassioned heros, desperate or furious, as beauty spots, rouge, powder, and diamonds fit on the face, head, and neck of an ape.

[4] Farinello leads the parade of castrati not only because he was the most famous singer of the century, but also because he was a close friend and longtime correspondent of Metastasio; see Daniel Heartz, "Farinelli and Metastasio: Rival Twins of Public Favour," *Early Music* 12 (1984): 358–66, and "Farinelli Revisited," *Early Music* 18 (1990): 430–43. Caffarello was almost as famous as Farinello. Gaetano Guadagni created the part of Orfeo in 1762. Giovanni Toschi was rather obscure by comparison; he sang Pilades in Traetta's *Ifigenia* (1763).

[5] Vittoria Tesi was encountered in Chapter 2, and Caterina Gabrielli, mentioned in Chapter 3, sang among other things the title role in Traetta's *Armida*. Marianna Bianchi created the role of Euridice in 1762.

[6] These six prima donna roles are from Metastasio's *Il trionfo di Clelia* (Vienna, 1762), *Romolo ed Ersilia* (Innsbruck, 1765), *Olimpiade* (Vienna, 1733; last heard in Gassmann's setting in Vienna, 1763), *Siroe* (Venice, 1727; heard in Vienna in Wagenseil's setting, 1748), *Ezio* (Venice, 1728; set by Gluck for Prague in 1749 and revived in the Burgtheater in 1763), and *Artaserse* (Rome, 1730; last heard in Vienna in Giuseppe Scarlatti's setting in 1763).

[7] The male roles referred to are from *Il trionfo di Clelia*, *Temistocle* (Vienna, 1736), *Catone in Utica* (Rome, 1728; last heard in Vienna in Gassmann's setting of 1761), and *Romolo ed Ersilia*.

[8] The reference of these three scenic "excesses" is to *Il trionfo di Clelia*.

The matter is in fact different in the new plan of dramas, which if not invented by me, at least was executed for the first time in *Orfeo*, then in *Alceste*, and continued by Signor Coltellini.[9] In the new plan all is nature, all is passion. There are no maxims, no philosophizing, no politics, no comparisons, and none of those descriptions or amplifications that are in fact only a flight from difficulties such as are found in all librettos. The duration is limited to a period that does not tire the mind or disperse concentration. The subjects are simple, not stitched together as in a prose romance; even a listener who is little versed can be apprised of the action, which is always unitary, never complicated, and not duplicated in servile obedience to the mad law of the *secondo uomo* and *seconda donna*, but reduced to the context of Greek tragedy, and having the same privilege of exciting terror and compassion, of acting on the souls of the spectators, as much as would a spoken tragedy. In this plan, as Your Highness can well see, no music enters except to reinforce the expression of the words so that they are not buried by notes, and so that music does not improperly prolong the spectacle, it being ridiculous to hear declarations of love prolonged, for instance to a hundred notes when nature has restricted it to three—in my opinion one note should always be enough for one syllable.[10]

If then this plan, with the addition of pantomime in the choruses and ballets, in imitation of the Greeks, suited the taste of the public, and the pure taste of Her Imperial Majesty, who witnessed fourteen performances of *Orfeo* and signaled her supreme pleasure by making presents to the maestro di cappella [Gluck] and to *il musico* [Guadagni], it is appropriate to adhere to the same and not confound it with that of Metastasio. Ornaments suitable to a beautiful brunette do not suit blondes. In the dramas of the Signor Abate it matters not if the Gabriellis and the Bastardellas and other such creatures exhaust their breath over an aria about the murmuring stream and one hears not one word,[11] but in *Orfeo, Ifigenia,* and *Telemaco,* in *Alceste,* we must have actors who sing what is written by the maestro, not singers who take from their trunk ready-made arias, in which they repeat thirty or forty times "Parto" or "Addio" using their own musical hieroglyphics, of which one could perhaps say, in order to be charitable to them, "Pulchrum est, sed non erat hic locus."

[9] If not invented by Calzabigi, then by whom was the "new plan of dramas" invented? Can this be a reference to the *Armida* (1761) of Durazzo, Migliavacca, and Traetta? More likely it refers to Francesco Algarotti's *Saggio sopra l'opera in musica,* first published in 1755. A year after his letter to Kaunitz, Calzabigi sent another letter defining the new plan to Count Greppi in Milan, dated 6 April 1768. In it he claimed that he had initiated the plan with *Orfeo* eighteen years earlier, i.e., in 1750, "whereas Algarotti proposed his reform subsequently." One way to reconcile the two letters may be this: in 1767 Calzabigi was still willing to allow credit for inventing the new plan to go elsewhere; by 1768 he was yielding no ground to anyone on this issue. It was only a step further then to his absurd claims in the letter of 1784 to the *Mercure de France,* discussed above in connection with *Orfeo.* The letter to Count Greppi of 1768 is printed in its entirety in Carlo Antonio Vianello, *Teatri Spettacoli Musiche a Milano nei secoli scorsi* (Milan, 1941), pp. 238–46; p. 242 contains the reference to Algarotti.

[10] Gluck's music to *Orfeo* and *Alceste* was predominantly of the one-note-to-a-syllable variety, or what in the catalogue of Italian opera styles was known as *parlante,* but so was much of Gluck's earlier music, and especially his opéra-comique settings.

[11] La Bastardella was Lucrezia Aguiari, who was appointed to the court of Parma in 1768.

Putting *Alceste* in the mouths of such warblers and their like would amount to ruining both the music and the poetry, and our aim would not be achieved. On the contrary let the Bastardellas, the Gabriellis and the Apriles be satisfied with an opera by the Arcadian shepherd Artino Corasio [Metastasio], but for *Alceste* let us turn to Mingotti or Francesina, to Manzuoli or Tibaldi.[12] And then we also need a few basses to reinforce the choruses (of which I have already warned Signor Gluck) and for the parts of the High Priest and the oracle, and we need better figurants for the pantomimes. Thus could *Alceste* become a new, majestic, and interesting spectacle, worthy of this court and capital, worthy of the taste of Your Highness, who, to our good fortune, has been willing to intervene. Otherwise it would be better to allow this creation of my poor talent and Signor Gluck's sublimity to be buried, so as not to spoil it, and to await more favorable circumstances. *Orfeo* went well because we came across Guadagni, for whom the part appeared to be made to order, and it would have gone very badly in other hands.[13] Yet *Telemaco,* in spite of its excellent poetry and singularly divine music, went very badly because Madame Tibaldi is no actress, Guadagni misbehaved, and the famous Teuberin was inept in the role of Circe and without sufficient voice to play the part of a magician, or to deliver well a music worthy of an enchantress and an enchantment.[14]

I finish by declaring myself, with the most profound respect,
Your highness'
most humble, devoted, and obedient servant,
De Calzabigi the elder[15]

---

[12] Giuseppe Aprile was a soprano castrato who sang many primo uomo roles for Jommelli in Stuttgart from 1756 on. Calzabigi's candidates for the role of Alceste are surprising. Regina Mingotti was singing in London around 1760 (an added reason for believing that Calzabigi may have visited that capital) and Burney reported that her voice was declining by 1763–64. The French singer Francesina, alias Elizabeth Duparc, was even older. She had been Handel's leading soprano in the late 1730s and 1740s; she appears to have stopped singing in public in the 1750s and died around 1778. The soprano Antonia Bernasconi, who created the part of Alceste in December 1767 and with whom Calzabigi became infatuated, was obviously not being considered for the part when this letter was written the previous spring. Giovanni Manzuoli and Giuseppe Tibaldi were both well known in Vienna. The first was a soprano, the second a tenor. Apparently it mattered little whether Admeto was sung as a treble or a tenor part. For the second production of *Alceste* in Vienna in 1769, Gluck chose the soprano Millico to sing Admeto.

[13] "L'Orfeo andò bene, perche s'incontrò quel Guadagni, per cui pareva fatto a posta, e sarebbe riuscito malissimo in altra mano." I maintain that the role was indeed made for Guadagni, and that Calzabigi suggests otherwise because of his campaign to date the libretto earlier than 1762.

[14] Madame Tibaldi was Rosa Tartaglini, married to Giuseppe Tibaldi; she sang the seconda donna role of Fulvia in Gluck's *Ezio* for Vienna in 1763. Here Calzabigi calls Guadagni "un birbante," meaning a scoundrel or rascal; since he was praised in the previous sentence as Orfeo, it sounds as if this singer willfully did something that contributed to the failure of *Telemaco,* in which he sang the title role. Teuberin is Elizabeth Teyber, a pupil of Hasse and of La Tesi.

[15] Use of this formula may mean that Calzabigi's younger brother, Anton Maria, was also in Vienna at the time and known to Prince Kaunitz.

Appendix 3

"Species facti" Given by Leopold Mozart to Emperor Joseph II on 21 September 1768

AFTER many of the local nobility were convinced of the extraordinary talent of my son, by reports from elsewhere as well as through personal examination and testing, it became one of the events most worthy of admiration of this or any previous time that a boy of twelve years should write an opera and direct it himself. This opinion was strengthened by a learned article from Paris in which, after a detailed description of my son's genius, the author [Melchior von Grimm] asserted that "without doubt, this child will by the age of twelve write an opera for one or another Italian theater." But everyone thought that a German should reserve such a feat only for his fatherland. I was cheered by this unanimous opinion. I acceded to the public's desire. The Dutch minister, Count von Degenfeld, was the first to make the suggestion to Affligio, the theater director, because the boy's ability was already fully known to him in Holland. The singer Carrattoli was the second to propose it to Affligio. The affair was concluded at Dr. Laugier's in the presence of the young Baron van Swieten and the two singers Carrattoli and Caribaldi. Moreover, everyone, but especially the two singers, affirmed in the strongest terms that even a very mediocre music from a boy so young, on account of the extraordinary wonder of it, must draw the whole city to the theater in order to witness this child in the orchestra, directing his work from the harpsichord. I thus allowed my son to write.

As soon as the first act was finished, I invited Carrattoli to hear and judge it, in order for me to be sure. He came, and his astonishment was so great that he appeared the following day at my place and brought Caribaldi with him. Caribaldi, no less astounded, brought Poggi to me a few days later. All of them showed such uncommon approval that upon my repeated questioning, "Do you think it will be good? Do you believe that he should continue?" they took offense at my mistrust and often called out with much excitement "cosa?— come? questo è un portento! questo [sic] opera andera alle stelle! è una meraviglia!— non dubiti, che scrivi avanti!— etc." (How's that? he is a marvel! this opera will excell! it is a miracle! have no doubt that he should proceed! etc.), along with many other expressions. This, namely, Carrattoli told me afterward in his own room.

Assured of the desired success by the approval of the singers, I allowed my son to continue the work and also asked Dr. Laugier to draw up a contract with the impresario concerning payment in my name. It was done, and Affligio promised 100 ducats. In order to shorten my expensive stay in Vienna, I made the provision that the opera be performed before the departure of His Majesty for Hungary; but several revisions that the poet had to make in the text delayed the composition, and Affligio affirmed that he would have it performed at the return of His Majesty.

Now the opera had been completed already for some weeks. The copying began, and the first act was given to the singers and the second act directly afterward. Meanwhile my son had to perform various arias, and yes, even the first-act finale, at the harpsichord for various social occasions of the nobility, who were all astounded, and Affligio himself was aural- and eyewitness at Prince Kaunitz's. Now the rehearsals should have begun.

But—how could I have expected it!—the persecutions of my son also began. It happens rarely that an opera comes out perfectly at the first rehearsal, without changes being made here and there. Exactly for this reason the practice is to begin at the harpsichord alone, and until the singers know their parts, and especially the finales, never to rehearse with all the instruments. Yet here just the opposite happened. The roles were not studied enough, there was no rehearsal of the singers at the harpsichord, the finales were not studied in ensemble, and yet the first act was tried out with all the instruments, in order to give the thing a poor and confused appearance right from the beginning. No one who was present will call that a rehearsal without becoming embarrassed. I will not bring up the loveless behavior of those whose conscience will let them know who they are. May God pardon them this.

After the rehearsal Affligio told me, "It was good; but since here and there the music is too high, changes must be made; I wish only to speak with the singers." And because His Majesty would be here in twelve days, he wished to perform the opera in four or, at the latest, six weeks, so that there would be time to bring everything into good order. I should not be dismayed over this because he was a man of his word and would keep all his promises, he said, and further, revisions were not unusual with other operas and nothing novel, etc. etc.

After this what the singers wanted changed was done, and two new arias were composed for the first act. Meanwhile there was performed in the theater *La Caschina* [by Goldoni and Scolari]. Now the agreed-upon time was up, and I heard that Affligio had distributed the parts to another opera. The talk circulated now that he would not perform our opera, and he let it be rumored that the singers could not sing that which he himself had not only previously pronounced good, but had even praised to the skies. In order to take a firm stand against this gossip, my son had to perform the whole opera at the harpsichord at the young Baron van Swieten's, in the presence of Count Spork, the Duke of Braganza, and other connoisseurs of music. Everyone was amazed to the highest degree over the allegations made by Affligio and the singers. All were very moved and declared unanimously that such an un-Christian, unbelievable, and malicious allegation could not be comprehended. They found this opera preferable to many Italian ones, and yet such a heavenly talent had incited a cabal, which clearly aimed at depriving the innocent boy's path to his earned honor and fortune.

I went to the impresario in order to learn the state of the project. He told me he had never been against performing the opera, but I should not think ill of him if he looked after his own interests. Doubts had been expressed to him that it perhaps would not please. He had rehearsed *La caschina* and wished now to also rehearse *La buona figliuola* [by Goldoni and Piccinni], and then perform the boy's opera. Should it not please as he wished, he would at least be provided with two other operas. I pleaded my already long sojourn and its protraction. He replied, "What difference would eight days, more or less, make? then I'll have it produced." Here matters stood. Carrattoli's arias were altered, and all was settled with Caribaldi, the same with Poggi and Laschi, etc. Everyone assured me often in particular that he had nothing against it, it all depended on Affligio. Meanwhile more than a month had passed. The copyist told me he had received no order to copy the revised arias. At the dress rehearsal of *La buona figliuola* I learned that he planned yet another opera, which I confronted him with in person. Upon this he gave an order to the copyist, in my presence and in the presence of the poet Coltellini, to have everything distributed in two days so that the opera could be rehearsed with the orchestra in fourteen days at the latest.

Yet the enemies of the poor child, whoever they may be, thwarted it once again. On the same day, the order was given to the copyist to stop. A few days later I learned that Affligio had decided not to give the opera in the theater at all. I wanted to be certain about the matter and went to him and received this answer. He had called the singers together, and they admitted that the opera was incomparably composed, but that it was not theatrical, and consequently could not be performed by them. This speech was altogether incomprehensible to me. Should the singers really dare, without shame, to decry what they had previously raised to the stars, what they themselves had encouraged the boy to do, and what Affligio himself had pronounced good? I answered him: "He could not ask that the boy undertook the great effort of writing an opera for nothing." I reminded him of the contract. I gave him to understand that he had led us around for four months, and brought us into debt to the amount of 160 ducats. I reminded him of the wasted time and assured him I would hold him responsible not only for the 100 ducats negotiated by Dr. Laugier but all other expenses as well.

To this, my just demand, he gave me an incomprehensible answer, which betrayed his embarrassment with me, and sought, I know not how, to get free of the whole matter, until finally he lapsed into the most shameful and hostile expressions: "If I wished to prostitute the boy, then he would see to it that the opera was laughed and whistled at." Coltellini heard all this. This was the reward then, that my son received for his great effort in writing an opera, of which the score amounts to 558 pages, for the wasted time and the useless expenses? And where remains finally what matters to me most, the honor and fame of my son? I no longer dared press for a performance, since all means would be taken to see that it was poorly produced. And furthermore the composition was deemed unsingable, or again untheatrical, or again not written according to the text, or again that he was not capable of writing such music. All this contradictory gossip is foolish and can be contradicted by a precise investigation of my child's musical strengths, for which I humbly beg, mainly for his honor and the shame of all those envious and honor-robbing slanderers, whose claims would disappear like smoke. It is all aimed at suppressing and making miserable an innocent creature in the capital of his German fatherland, to whom God has given extraordinary talent, which has been admired and encouraged by other nations.

List of Works Cited

Abert, Hermann. "J. G. Noverre und sein Einfluss auf die dramatische Balletkomposition." *Jahrbuch der Musikbibliothek Peters 1907*: 29–48.

———. "Joseph Haydns Klavierwerke." *Zeitschrift für Musikwissenschaft* 2 (1919–20): 553–73.

———. *W. A. Mozart*, 7th ed., 2 vols. Leipzig, 1956.

Ammerer, Gerhard. "Von Franz Anton von Harrach bis Siegmund Christoph von Schrattenbach—eine Zeit des Niedergangs." In *Geschichte Salzburgs Stadt und Land*, ed. H. Dopsch and H. Spatzenegger, 2: 245–320. Salzburg, 1988.

Arneth, Alfred Ritter von. *Beaumarchais und Sonnenfels*. Vienna, 1868.

Arneth, Alfred Ritter von (ed.). *Briefe der Kaiserin Maria Theresia und ihre Kinder und Freunde*, 4 vols. Vienna, 1881.

Badley, Allan Donald Jeffreys. "A Study and Critical Edition of Three Symphonies by Leopold Hofmann (1738–1793)." M.A. thesis, University of Auckland, 1981.

———. "The Concertos of Leopold Hofmann (1738–1793)," 3 vols. Ph.D. diss., University of Auckland, 1986.

Badura-Skoda, Eva. "Giuseppe Scarlatti und seine Buffa-Opern." In *Musik am Hof Maria Theresias*, ed. Roswitha Vera Karpf, pp. 57–75. Munich and Salzburg, 1984.

———. "Prolegomena to a History of the Viennese Fortepiano." *Israel Studies in Musicology* 2 (1980): 77–99.

———. "Teutsche Comödien-Arien und Joseph Haydn." In *Der junge Haydn*, ed. Vera Schwarz, pp. 59–72. Graz, 1972.

Bartha, Dénes. "Zur Identifikation des 'Strassburger Konzerts' bei Mozart." In *Festschrift Friedrich Blume*, ed. Anna Amalia Abert and Wilhelm Pfannkuch, pp. 30–33. Kassel, 1963.

Baumann, Thomas. *North German Opera in the Age of Goethe*. Cambridge, 1985.

Beales, Derek. *Joseph II*, vol: 1, *In the Shadow of Maria Theresa 1741–1780*. Cambridge, 1987.

Beer, Adolf (ed.). *Joseph II, Leopold II und Kaunitz: Ihr Briefwechsel*. Vienna, 1873.

Bellina, Anna Laura. "I gesti parlanti ovvero il 'recitar danzando,' 'Le festin de pierre,' e 'Sémiramis.' " In *La figura e l'opera di Ranieri de' Calzabigi*, ed. Federico Marri, pp. 107–17. Florence, 1989.

Berlioz, Hector. *A travers chants*. Paris, 1927.

Biba, Otto. "Beispiele für die Besetzungsverhältnisse bei Aufführungen von Haydns Oratorien in Wien zwischen 1784 und 1808." *Haydn-Studien* 4 (1976–80): 94–104.

———. "Grundzüge des Konzertwesens in Wien zu Mozarts Zeit." *Mozart-Jahrbuch 1978/79*, pp. 132–143.

———. "Die kirchenmusikalischen Werke Haydns." In *Joseph Haydn und seine Zeit*, ed. Gerda Mraz, pp. 142–51. Eisenstadt, 1982.

———. "Nachrichten zur Musikpflege in der graflichen Familie Harrach." *Haydn Yearbook* 10 (1978): 36–44.

———. "Die private Musikpflege in der kaiserlichen Familie." In *Musik am Hof Maria Theresias*, ed. Roswitha Vera Karpf, pp. 83–92. Munich and Salzburg, 1984.

———. "Die Wiener Kirchenmusik um 1783." In *Beiträge zur Musikgeschichte des 18. Jahrhunderts*, ed. Friedrich Heller, pp. 7–79. Eisenstadt, 1971.

Biba, Otto (ed.). *"Eben komme ich von Haydn . . .": Georg August Griesingers Korrespondanz mit Joseph Haydns Verleger Breitkopf & Härtel, 1799–1819*. Zurich, 1987.

Bilson, Malcolm."Execution and Expression in the Sonata in E flat, K. 282." *Early Music* 20 (1992): 237–43.

Bourde, André. "Opera seria et scénographie: autour de deux toiles italiennes du XVIIIe siècle." In *L'opéra au XVIIIe siècle*, pp. 229–39. Marseilles and Aix, 1982.

Brago, Michael. "Haydn, Goldoni and *Il Mondo della Luna*." *Eighteenth-Century Studies* 17 (1983–84): 308–32.

Brenner, Clarence D. *The Théâtre Italien: Its Repertory, 1716–1793*. University of California Publications in Modern Philology 63. Berkeley, 1961.

Breunlich, Maria Christine. "Gluck in den Tagebüchern des Grafen Karl von Zinzendorf." *Gluck-Studien* 1 (1989): 62–68.

Brizi, Bruno. "L'impudente provocazione del Paride." In *Paride ed Elena*, ed. Cesare Galla, pp. 57–90. Program Book of the Teatro Olimpico. Vicenza, 1988.

———. "Uno spunto polemico Calzabigiano: 'Ipermestra o Le Danaide.' " In *La figura e l'opera de Ranieri de' Calzabigi*, ed. Federico Marri, pp. 119–45. Florence, 1989.

Brook, Barry S. (ed.). *Breitkopf Thematic Catalogue*, six parts and seventeen supplements, 1762–1787. New York, 1966.

Brown, A. Peter. "The Earliest English Biography of Haydn." *Musical Quarterly* 59 (1973): 339–54.

———. "Haydn and Mozart's 1773 Stay in Vienna: Weeding a Musicological Garden." *Journal of Musicology* 10 (1992): 192–230.

———. "Joseph Haydn and C. P. E. Bach: The Question of Influence." In *Haydn Studies*, ed. Jens Peter Larsen, Howard Serwer, and James Webster, pp. 158–64. New York, 1981.

———. "Joseph Haydn and Leopold Hofmann's 'Street Songs.' " *JAMS* 33 (1980): 356–83.

———. *Joseph Haydn's Keyboard Music: Sources and Style.* Bloomington, Ind., 1986.

———. "Marianna Martines' Autobiography as a New Source for Haydn's Biography During the 1750s." *Haydn-Studien* 6 (1986): 68–70.

———. "The Symphonies of Carlo d'Ordonez: A Contribution to the History of Viennese Instrumental Music During the Second Half of the Eighteenth Century." *Haydn Yearbook* 11 (1981): 5–121.

Brown, Bruce Alan. "Christoph Willibald Gluck and Opéra-Comique in Vienna, 1754–1764." Ph.D. diss., University of California, Berkeley, 1986.

———. "Durazzo, Duni, and the Frontispiece to *Orfeo ed Euridice*." *Studies in Eighteenth-Century Culture* 19 (1989): 71–97.

———. *Gluck and the French Theatre in Vienna.* Oxford, 1991.

———. "Gluck's *Rencontre imprévue* and Its Revisions." *JAMS* 36 (1983): 498–518.

———. "Theatrical Dance in Vienna ca. 1750: New Sources on the Works of Hilverding and Starzer." Paper read at the 50th Annual Meeting of the American Musicological Society, Philadelphia, 1984.

Bryan, Paul. "Haydn's Hornists." *Haydn-Studien* 3 (1973): 52–68.

———. "The Symphonies of Johann Vanhal." Ph.D. diss., University of Michigan, 1955.

Bücken, Ernst. *Musik des Rokokos und der Klassik.* Potsdam, 1929.

Burney, Charles. *The Letters of Dr. Charles Burney*, vol. 1: *1751–1784*, ed. Alvaro Ribeiro. Oxford, 1991.

———. *The Present State of Music in Germany, The Netherlands, and United Provinces*, 2nd ed. London, 1775; reprint 1969.

Buschmeier, Gabriele. "*Ezio* in Prag und Wien: Bemerkungen zu den beiden Fassungen von Gluck's *Ezio*." *Gluck-Studien* 1 (1987): 85–88.

Carpani, Giuseppe. *Le Haydine ovvero Lettere sulla vita e le opere del celebre maestro Giuseppe Haydn.* Milan, 1812.

Casanova, Jacques. *Histoire de ma vie*, 12 vols. Paris and Wiesbaden, 1960.

Chew, Geoffrey. "The Night-Watchman's Song Quoted by Haydn and Its Implications." *Haydn-Studien* 3 (1973): 106–24.

Churgin, Bathia. "Did Sammartini Influence Mozart's Earliest String Quartets?" *Mozart-Jahrbuch 1991*, pp. 529–39.

Corrieri, Susanna. "Marco Coltellini da stampatore a poeta di corte." In *La figura e l'opera di Ranieri de' Calzabigi*, ed. Federico Marri, pp. 203–15. Florence, 1989.

Crankshaw, Edward. *Maria Theresa.* New York, 1970.

Croll, Gerhard. "Ein unbekanntes tragisches Ballet von Gluck." In *Christoph Willibald*

Gluck und die Opernreform, ed. Klaus Hortschansky, pp. 232–35. Darmstadt, 1989.

———. "Eine zweite, fast vergessene Selbstbiographie von Abbé Stadler." *Mozart-Jahrbuch 1964*, pp. 172–84.

———. "Neue Quellen zu Musik und Theater in Wien, 1758–1763." In *Festschrift Walter Senn*, ed. E. Egg and E. Fässler, pp. 8–12. Munich and Salzburg, 1975.

———. "Remarks on a Mozart Quartet Fragment." In *Haydn Studies*, ed. Jens Peter Larsen, Howard Serwer, and James Webster, pp. 405–7. New York, 1981.

Croll, Gerhard and Kurt Vössing. *Johann Michael Haydn: Sein Leben—sein Schaffen—seine Zeit*. Vienna, 1987.

Croll, Gerhard and Monika Woitas (ed.). *Gluck in Wien*. Kongressbericht. Gluck-Studien 1. Kassel, 1989.

Curtis, Alan. "L'opera dei soprani." In *Paride ed Elena*, ed. Cesare Galla, pp. 119–24. Program Book of the Teatro Olimpico. Vicenza, 1988.

Cyr, Mary. "Rameau e Traetta." *Nuova Rivista Musicale Italiana* 12 (1978): 166–82.

Deck, James. "The Dating of Haydn's *Missa Cellensis in honorem Beatissimae Virginis Mariae*: An Interim Discussion." *Haydn Yearbook* 13 (1982): 97–112.

Dent, Edward J. *Alessandro Scarlatti: His Life and Works*. London, 1905.

Deutsch, Otto Erich. "Aus Schiedenhofens Tagebuch." *Mozart-Jahrbuch 1957*, pp. 15–24.

———. "Gluck im Redoutensaal." *Österreichische Musikzeitschrift* 21 (1966): 521–25.

———. "Höfische Theaterbilder aus Schönbrunn." *Österreichische Musikzeitschrift* 22 (1967): 577–84.

Deutsch, Otto Erich (ed.). *Mozart: Die Dokumente seines Lebens*. Kassel, 1961.

Dietrich, Margret. "Theater am Hofe—zwischen Tradition und Wandel." In *Maria Theresia und ihre Zeit*, ed. Walter Koschatzky, pp. 393–403. Vienna, 1979.

Ditters, Karl. *The Autobiography of Karl von Dittersdorf, Dictated to His Son*, transl. A. D. Coleridge. London, 1896; reprint 1970.

Dlabacž, Bohumír Jan. *Allgemeines historisches Künstler-Lexikon*. Prague, 1815.

Donà, Mariangela. "Dagli archivi milanese: Lettere di Ranieri de' Calzabigi e di Antonia Bernasconi." *Analecta Musicologica* 14 (1974): 268–300.

Donath, Gustave. "Florian Leopold Gassmann als Opernkomponist." *Studien zur Musikwissenschaft* 2 (1914): 34–211.

Dreger, Moriz. *Baugeschichte der k. und k. Hofburg in Wien bis zum 19. Jahrhundert*. Österreichische Kunsttopographie 14. Vienna, 1914.

Edge, Dexter. "Mozart's Viennese Orchestras." *Early Music* 20 (1992): 64–88.

Einstein, Alfred. *Gluck*. London, 1936; reprint 1964.

———. *Mozart: His Character, His Work*, Transl. Arthur Mendel and Nathan Broder. Oxford, 1945.

———. "Die Text-Vorlage zu Mozarts 'Zaide.' " *Acta Musicologica* 8 (1936): 30–37.

Eisen, Cliff. "Mozart's Salzburg Orchestras." *Early Music* 20 (1992): 89–100.

———. "The Symphonies of Leopold Mozart and Their Relationship to the Early Symphonies of Wolfgang Amadeus Mozart: A Bibliographical and Stylistic Study." Ph.D. diss., Cornell University, 1986.

Engel, Hans. *Das Instrumentkonzert*. Leipzig, 1932.

Feder, Georg. "Bemerkungen zu Haydns Opern." *Österreichische Musikzeitschrift* 37 (1982): 154–61.

Feldman, Martha. "Staging the Virtuoso: Ritornello Procedure in Mozart, from Aria to Concerto." In *Mozart's Piano Concertos: Text, Context, Interpretation*, ed. Neal Zaslaw. Ann Arbor, Mich., forthcoming.

Fellerer, Karl Gustav. *Die Kirchenmusik W. A. Mozarts*. Laaber, 1985.

Ferrero, Mercedes Viale. *La scenografia del '700 e i fratelli Galliari*. Turin, 1963.

Fillion, Michelle. "The Accompanied Keyboard Divertimenti of Haydn and His Viennese Contemporaries (c. 1750–1780)." Ph.D. diss., Cornell University, 1982.

Finscher, Ludwig. *Studien zur Geschichte des Streichquartetts*, vol. 1: *Die Entstehung des klassischen Streichquartetts: Von den Vorformen zur Grundlegung durch Joseph Haydn*. Kassel, 1974.

Flothius, Marius. "Quintette für Streichinstrumente von Michael Haydn." *Mozart-Jahrbuch 1987/88*, pp. 49–57.

Freeman, Robert Norman. "The Practice of Music at Melk Monastery in the Eighteenth Century." Ph.D. diss., University of California, Los Angeles, 1971.

Fürstenau, Moritz. "Glucks Orpheus in München 1773." *Monatshefte für Musikgeschichte* 4 (1872): 216–24.

Garcins, Laurent. *Traité du Melo-drame*. Paris, 1772.

Geiringer, Karl. "Hector Berlioz und Glucks Wiener Opern." *Gluck-Studien* 1 (1989): 166–70.

Georgiades, Thrasybulos. "Zur Musiksprache der Wiener Klassiker." *Mozart-Jahrbuch 1951*, pp. 51–54.

Gericke, Hannelore. *Der Wiener Musikalienhandel von 1700 bis 1778*. Wiener Musikwissenschaftliche Beiträge 5. Graz and Cologne, 1960.

Ghircoiasiu, Romeo. "Das Musikleben in Grosswardein (Oradea) im 18. Jahrhundert." *Haydn Yearbook* 10 (1978): 45–55.

Goldoni, Carlo. *Tutti le opere di Carlo Goldoni*, ed. Giuseppe Ortalani. Milan, 1935–56.

Gotwals, Vernon (ed. and transl.). *Joseph Haydn: Eighteenth-Century Gentleman and Genius*. Contains the *Biographische Notizen über Joseph Haydn* of G. A. Griesinger (1810) and the *Biographische Nachrichten von Joseph Haydn* of A. C. Dies (1810). Madison, Wis., 1963.

Grave, Margaret G. "First-Movement Form as a Measure of Dittersdorf's Symphonic Development." Ph.D. diss., New York University, 1977.

Green, Robert A. " 'Il distratto' of Regnard and Haydn: A Re-examination." *Haydn Yearbook* 11 (1980): 183–95.

Greisenegger, Wolfgang. "The Italian Opera in Vienna in the XVIIIth Century." In *Venezia e il melodramma nel settecento*, ed. Maria Teresa Muraro, pp. 89–101. Florence, 1978.

Guilcher, Jean-Michel. *La contredanse et les renouvellements de la danse française*. Paris, 1969.

Gumpenhuber, Philipp. "Repertoire de Tous les Spectacles, qui ont été donné au Theatre de la Ville [pres de la Cour] . . ." Harvard Theater Collection MS Thr. 248–248.3; Österreichische Nationalbibliothek, Vienna, Musiksammlung, Mus. Hs.34580a–c. [1758–63].

Haas, Robert. *Aufführungspraxis der Musik*. Potsdam, 1931.

——. *Gluck und Durazzo*. Vienna, 1925.

——. "Die Musik in der Wiener deutschen Stegreifkomödie." *Studien zur Musikwissenschaft* 12 (1925): 3–64.

——. "Von dem wienerischen Geschmack in der Musik." In *Festschrift Johannes Biehle*, ed. E. M. Müller, pp. 59–65. Leipzig, 1930.

——. "Die Wiener Ballet im 18. Jahrhundert und Gluck's *Don Juan*." *Studien zur Musikwissenschaft* 10 (1924): 1–36.

Hadamowsky, Franz. "Barocktheater am Wiener Kaiserhof. Mit ein Spielplan (1625–1740)." *Jahrbuch der Gesellschaft für Wiener Theater-Forschung* (1951–52), pp. 37–39.

——. *Die Familie Galli-Bibiena in Wien*. Leben und Werk für das Theater. Vienna, 1962.

——. *Die josefinische Theaterreform und das Spieljahr 1776–77: Ein Dokumentation*. Quellen zur Theatergeschichte 2. Vienna, 1978.

Harpster, Richard William. "The String Quartets of Johann Georg Albrechstberger: An Historical and Formal Study." Ph.D. diss., University of Southern California, 1976.

Harries, Karstin. *The Bavarian Rococo Church Between Faith and Aestheticism*. New Haven, Conn., 1983.

Haupt, Helga. "Wiener Instrumentenbauer von 1791 bis 1815." *Studien zur Musikwissenschaft* 24 (1960): 120–84.

Hausswald, Günter. "Der Divertimento-Begriff bei Georg Christoph Wagenseil." *Archiv für Musikwissenschaft* 9 (1952): 45–50.

Haydn, Joseph. *The Collected Correspondence and London Notebooks of Joseph Haydn*, ed. H. C. Robbins Landon. London, 1959.

——. *Gesammelte Briefe und Aufzeichnungen*, ed. Dénes Bartha. Kassel, 1965.

Heartz, Daniel. "A Keyboard Concertino by Marie Antoinette?" In *Essays in Musicology: A Tribute to Alvin Johnson*, ed. Lewis Lockwood and Edward Roesner, pp. 201–12. Philadelphia, 1990.

——. "Attacca subito: Lessons from the Autograph Score of *Idomeneo*, Acts I and II." In *Festschrift Wolfgang Rehm zum 60. Geburtstag am 3. September 1989*, ed. Dietrich Berke and Harald Heckmann, pp. 83–92. Kassel, 1989.

——. "The Beginnings of the Operatic Romance: Rousseau, Sedaine and Monsigny." *Eighteenth-Century Studies* 15 (1981–82): 149–78.

——. "Coming of Age in Bohemia: The Musical Apprenticeships of Benda and Gluck." *Journal of Musicology* 6 (1988): 510–27.

——. "The Concert Spirituel in the Tuileries Palace." *Early Music* 21 (1993): 240–48.

——. "The Creation of the Buffo Finale in Italian Opera." *Proceedings of the Royal Musical Association* 104 (1977–78): 67–78.

——. "Ditters, Gluck und der Artikel 'Von dem wienerischen Geschmack in der Musik.'" *Gluck-Studien* 1 (1989): 78–80.

——. "Farinelli and Metastasio: Rival Twins of Public Favour." *Early Music* 12 (1984): 358–66.

———. "Farinelli Revisited." *Early Music* 18 (1990): 430–48.

———. "From Garrick to Gluck: The Reform of Theatre and Opera in the Mid-Eighteenth Century." *Proceedings of the Royal Musical Association* 94 (1967–68): 11–27.

———. "The Genesis of Mozart's 'Idomeneo.' " *Mozart-Jahrbuch 1967*, pp. 150–64.

———. "The Great Quartet in Mozart's *Idomeneo*." *Music Forum* 5 (1980): 233–56.

———. "Hasse, Galuppi, and Metastasio." In *Venezia e il melodramma nel settecento*, ed. Maria Teresa Muraro, pp. 309–39. Florence, 1978.

———. "Haydn und Gluck im Burgtheater um 1760: *Der neue krumme Teufel, Le diable à quatre*, und die Sinfonie 'Le Soir.' " In *Bericht über den internationalen musikwissenschaftlichen Kongress, Bayreuth 1981*, ed. Christoph-Hellmut Mahling and Sigrid Wiesmann, pp. 120–35. Kassel, 1984.

———. "Haydn's 'Acide e Galatea' and the Imperial Wedding Operas of 1760 by Hasse and Gluck." In *Proceedings of the International Joseph Haydn Congress 1982*, ed. Eva Badura-Skoda, pp. 332–40. Munich, 1986.

———. "Idomeneus Rex." *Mozart-Jahrbuch 1973/74*, pp. 7–20.

———. "*Les Lumières:* Voltaire and Metastasio; Goldoni, Favart, and Diderot." In *Report of the Twelfth Congress, Berkeley 1977*, ed. Daniel Heartz and Bonnie Wade, pp. 233–38. Kassel, 1981.

———. "Leutgeb and the 1762 Horn Concertos of Joseph and Johann Michael Haydn." *Mozart-Jahrbuch 1987/88* (Kassel, 1988), pp. 59–64.

———. "Metastasio, 'Maestro dei Maestri di Cappella Drammatici.' " In *Metastasio e il mondo musicale*, ed. Maria Teresa Muraro, pp. 315–38. Florence, 1986.

———. "Mozart, His Father, and 'Idomeneo.' " *Musical Times* 119 (1978): 228-31.

———. *Mozart's Operas*. Edited, with contributing essays, by Thomas Baumann. Berkeley, 1990.

———. "Mozart's Sense for Nature." *19th Century Music* 15 (1991): 107–15.

———. "Nicolas Jadot and the Building of the Burgtheater." *Musical Quarterly* 48 (1982): 1–31.

———. "Operatic Reform at Parma: *Ippolito ed Aricia*." In *Atti del convegno sul settecento parmense nel 2° centenario della morte di C. I. Frugoni*, pp. 271–300. Parma, 1969.

———. "*Orfeo ed Euridice:* Some Criticisms, Revisions, and Stage-Realizations during Gluck's Lifetime." *Chigiana* 29–30 (1975): 383–94.

———. "Portrait of a Court Musician: Gaetano Pugnani of Turin." *Imago Musicae* 1 (1984): 103–19.

———. "Raaff's Last Aria: A Mozartian Idyll in the Spirit of Hasse." *Musical Quarterly* 60 (1974): 517–43.

———. "Terpsichore at the Fair: Old and New Dance Airs in Two Vaudeville Comedies by Lesage." In *Music and Context: Essays for John M. Ward*, ed. Anne D. Shapiro, pp. 278–304. Cambridge, Mass., 1985.

———. "Tonality and Motif in *Idomeneo*." *Mozart-Jahrbuch 1973/74*, pp. 140–43.

———. "Traetta in Vienna: *Armida* (1761) and *Ifigenia in Tauride* (1763)." *Studies in Music from the University of Western Ontario* 7 (1982): 65–88.

———. "The Verona Portrait of Mozart and the *Molto Allegro* in G (KV 72ª)." Forthcoming.

Helfert, Vladimir. "Dosud. Neznám dopis Ran. Calsabigiho zr. 1767." *Musikologie* 1 (1938): 114–22.

———. "Zur Geschichte des Wiener Singspiels." *Zeitschrift für Musikwissenschaft* 5 (1922–23): 194–209.

Hell, Heinrich. *Die neapolitanische Opernsinfonie in der ersten Hälfte des 18. Jahrhunderts.* Tützing, 1971.

Hickman, Roger Charles. "The Nascent Viennese String Quartet." *Musical Quarterly* 67 (1981): 193–212.

———. "Six Bohemian Masters of the String Quartet in the Late Eighteenth Century." Ph.D. diss., University of California, Berkeley, 1979.

Hiller, Johann Adam. *Wöchentliche Nachrichten und Anmerkungen die Musik betreffend.* Leipzig, 1766–70; reprint 1970.

Hintermaier, Ernst. "Das fürsterzbischöflich Hoftheater zu Salzburg (1775–1803)." *Österreichische Musikzeitschrift* 30 (1975): 351–65.

Hoboken, Anthony van. *Joseph Haydn: Thematisch-bibliographisches Werkverzeichnis,* 2 vols. Mainz, 1957–71.

Horányi, Mátyás. *The Magnificence of Esterháza.* London, 1962.

Horsley, Paul J. "Dittersdorf and the Finale in Late Eighteenth-Century German Comic Opera." Ph.D. diss., Cornell University, 1988.

Hortschansky, Klaus. *Parodie und Entlehnung im Schaffen Christoph Willibald Glucks. Analecta Musicologica* 13. Cologne, 1973.

———. "Unbekannte Aufführungsberichte zu Glucks Opern der Jahre 1748–1765." *Jahrbuch des Staatlichen Instituts für Musikforschung Preussischer Kulturbesitz 1969,* pp. 19–39.

Hortschansky, Klaus (ed.). *Christoph Willibald Gluck und die Opernreform.* Darmstadt, 1989.

Howard, Patricia. *C. W. von Gluck: Orfeo.* Cambridge Opera Handbooks. Cambridge, 1981.

Hucke, Helmut. "Pergolesi's *Missa S. Emidia.*" In *Music in the Classic Period: Essays in Honor of Barry S. Brook,* ed. Allan A. Atlas, pp. 99–115. New York, 1985.

Jeffrey, Brian. *Fernando Sor: Composer and Guitarist.* London, 1977.

Joly, Jacques. *Les fêtes théâtrales de Metastasio à la cour de Vienne, 1731–1767.* Clermont-Ferrand, 1978.

Junker, Carl Ludwig. *Zwanzig Componisten: eine Skizze.* Berne, 1776.

Karpf, Roswitha Vera. "Die Beziehungen Maria Theresias zur Musik." In *Musik am Hof Maria Theresias,* ed. Roswitha Vera Karpf, pp. 93–107. Munich and Salzburg, 1984.

Karro, Françoise. "De la Querelle des Bouffons à la réforme de Gluck: Les lettres du Comte Durazzo à Charles-Simon Favart conservées à la Bibliothéque de l'Opéra." *Mitteilungen des österreichischen Staatsarchivs* 38 (1985): 163–96.

Kelly, Michael. *Reminiscences of Michael Kelly.* London, 1826; reprint 1968.

Khevenhüller-Metsch, Johann Joseph. *Aus der Zeit Maria Theresias: Tagebuch des Fürsten Johann Joseph Khevenhüller-Metsch, kaiserlichen Obersthofmeisters 1742–1776,* ed. Rudolf Graf Khevenhüller-Metsch and Hanns Schlitter, 7 vols. Vienna, 1907–25.

Kidd, Ronald R. "The Emergence of Chamber Music with Obbligato Keyboard in England." *Acta Musicologica* 44 (1972): 122–44.

King, A. Hyatt. *Mozart in Retrospect*. Studies in Criticism and Biography. London, 1955.

Kirkendale, Warren. *Fugue and Fugato in Rococo and Classical Chamber Music*. Durham, N. C., 1979.

Kleindienst, Sigrid. "Marginalien zu Giuseppe Bonnos Requiem." In *Musik am Hof Maria Theresias*, ed. Roswitha Vera Karpf, pp. 131–40. Munich and Salzburg, 1984.

Koch, Heinrich Christoph. *Versuch eine Anleitung zur Composition*. Rudolstadt and Leipzig, 1782–93; reprint 1969.

Köchel, Ludwig von. *Chronologisch-thematisches Verzeichnis der Werke W. A. Mozarts*. Leipzig, 1862. 3rd edition [K³] ed. Alfred Einstein, Leipzig, 1937. 6th edition [K⁶] ed. F. Giegling, A. Weinmann, and G. Sievers, Wiesbaden, 1964.

———. *Die kaiserliche Hof-musikkapelle in Wien von 1543–1867*. Vienna, 1869; reprint 1976.

Kramer, Kurt. "Das Libretto zu Mozarts 'Idomeneo': Quellen und Umgestaltung der Fabel." In *Wolfgang Amadeus Mozart: Idomeneo 1781–1981*, ed. Rudolf Angermüller and Robert Münster, pp. 7–43. Munich, 1981.

Krones, Hartmut. "Das 'Hohe Komische' bei Haydn." *Österreichische Musikzeitschrift* 38 (1983): 2–8.

Küchelbecker, Johann Basilii. *Allerneuster Nachricht vom Römisch-Kayserl. Hof*. Hannover, 1730.

Kunz, Harald. "Maria Theresia und das Wiener Theater." *Jahrbuch der Gesellschaft für Wiener Theaterforschung* (1953–54), pp. 3–71.

Kurth, Ernst. "Die Jugendopern Glucks bis *Orfeo*." *Studien zur Musikwissenschaft* 1 (1913): 193–277.

Landon, H. C. Robbins. "A Lost Haydn Autograph Re-discovered." *Haydn Yearbook* 14 (1983): 5–8.

———. *Haydn: Chronicle and Works*, 5 vols. Bloomington, Ind., 1976–80.

———. *Mozart and Vienna*. New York, 1991.

———. "The Operas of Haydn." In *The Age of Enlightenment, 1745–1790*, ed. Egon Wellesz and Frederick Sternfeld, pp. 172–99. London, 1973.

Landon, H. C. Robbins and David Wyn Jones. *Haydn: His Life and Music*. Bloomington, Ind., 1988.

Larsen, Jens Peter. "Haydn's Early Symphonies: The Problem of Dating." In *Music in the Classic Period: Essays in Honor of Barry S. Brook*, ed. Allan A. Atlas, pp. 117–31. New York, 1985.

———. "Wenzel Raimund Birck und Mattäus Schlöger: Zwei Hofmusiker und 'Vorklassiker' aus der Zeit Maria Theresias." In *Musik am Hof Maria Theresias*, ed. Roswitha Vera Karpf, pp. 108–30. Munich and Salzburg, 1984.

———. "Zur Entstehung der österreichischen Symphonietradition (ca. 1750–1775)." *Haydn Yearbook* 10 (1978): 72–80.

LaRue, Jan. "Significant and Coincidental Resemblance Between Classical Themes." *JAMS* 16 (1961): 224–34.

Lattimore, Richard and David Grene (eds.). *The Complete Greek Tragedies, Euripides I.* Chicago, 1955.

Le Huray, Peter. "The Role of Music in Eighteenth- and Early Nineteenth-Century Aesthetics." *Proceedings of the Royal Musical Association* 105 (1978–79): 90–99.

Leblond, G. M. (ed.). *Mémoires pour servir à l'histoire de la révolution operée dans la musique par M. Le Chevalier Gluck.* Paris, 1781; reprint 1967.

Leopold, Silke. "*Le Pescatrici*—Goldoni, Haydn, Gassmann." In *Proceedings of the International Joseph Haydn Congress 1982*, ed. Eva Badura-Skoda, pp. 341–51. Munich, 1986.

———. "Die Metastasianische Oper." In *Neues Handbuch der Musikwissenschaft*, ed. C. Dahlhaus, 5: 73–84. Laaber, 1985.

Leux-Henschen, Irmgard. *Joseph Martin Kraus in seinen Briefen.* Stockholm, 1978.

Levin, Robert D. *Who Wrote the Mozart Four-Wind Concertante?* Stuyvesant, N.Y., 1988.

Libin, Lawrence. "A Rediscovered Portrayal of Rameau and *Castor et Pollux*." *Early Music* 11 (1983): 510–13.

Lippmann, Friedrich. "Haydns 'La fedeltà premiata' und Cimarosas 'L'infedeltà fedele.' " *Haydn-Studien* 5 (1982): 1–15.

———. "Mozart und Paisiello: Zur stilistischen Position des *Lucio Silla*." *Mozart-Jahrbuch 1991*, pp. 580–93.

Löschenkohl, Hieronymus. *Beschreibung der Huldigungsfeyerlichkeiten . . . 1790 . . .* Vienna, 1790.

Lühning, Helga. *Titus-Vertonungen im 18. Jahrhundert: Untersuchungen zur Tradition der Opera Seria von Hasse bis Mozart. Analecta Musicologica* 20. Laaber, 1983.

MacIntyre, Bruce C. *The Viennese Concerted Mass of the Early Classic Period.* Ann Arbor, Mich., 1986.

Mann, Alfred. *Theory and Practice: The Great Composer as Student and Teacher.* New York, 1987.

Marshall, Robert C. *Mozart Speaks.* New York, 1991.

Marx, Adolph Bernhard. *Gluck und die Oper.* Berlin, 1863.

Mattern, Volker. *Das Dramma giocoso 'La finta giardiniera': Ein Vergleich der Vertonungen von Pasquale Anfossi und Wolfgang Amadeus Mozart.* Laaber, 1989.

Maunder, Richard. "Mozart's Keyboard Instruments." *Early Music* 20 (1992): 207–19.

———. "Performing Mozart and Beethoven Concertos." *Early Music* 17 (1989): 139–40.

Metastasio, Pietro. *Memoirs of the Life and Writing of the Abate Metastasio, in which are incorporated Translations of his Principal Letters by Charles Burney*, 3 vols. London, 1796; reprint 1971.

———. *Tutte le opere di Pietro Metastasio*, ed. Bruno Brunelli, 5 vols. Milan, 1943–54.

Michtner, Otto. *Das alte Burgtheater als Opernbühne von der Einführung des deutschen Singspiels (1778) bis zum Tod Kaiser Leopolds (1792). Theatergeschichte Österreichs* III: 1. Vienna, 1970.

Morrow, Mary Sue. *Concert Life in Haydn's Vienna: Aspects of a Developing Musical and Societal Institution.* Stuyvesant, N.Y., 1989.

Mozart, Wolfgang Amadeus. *Mozart: Briefe und Aufzeichnungen. Gesamtausgabe,* ed. Wilhelm A. Bauer, Otto Erich Deutsch, and Joseph Heinz Eibl, 7 vols. Kassel, 1962–75.

Mraz, Gerda and Gottfried. *Maria Theresia: Ihr Leben und ihre Zeit in Bildern und Dokumenten.* Munich, 1979.

Mraz, Gerda and Gottfried, and Gerald Schlag, ed. *Joseph Haydn in seiner Zeit.* Eisenstadt, 1982.

Müller, Johann Heinrich Friedrich. *Genaue Nachrichten von beyden kaiserlich- königlichen Schaubühnen und andern öffentlichen Ergötzlichkeiten in Wien.* Vienna, 1772.

———. *J. H. F. Müllers Abschied von der k. k. Hof und National-Schaubühne.* Vienna, 1802.

Müller, Walther. *Johann Adolph Hasse als Kirchenkomponist: Ein Beitrag zur Geschichte der neapolitanischen Kirchenmusik.* Leipzig, 1910.

Müller von Asow, Erich H. "Ein ungedrucktes Skizzenblatt Mozarts." *Neues Mozart Jahrbuch* 1 (1941): 174–80.

Münster, Robert. "Mozarts Münchener Aufenthalt 1780/81 und die Uraufführung des 'Idomeneo.' " In *Wolfgang Amadeus Mozart: Idomeneo 1781–1981,* ed. Rudolf Angermüller and Robert Münster, pp. 71–105. Munich, 1981.

———. "Neues zum Münchner *Idomeneo* 1781." *Acta Mozartiana* 29 (1982): 10–20.

Muresu, Gabriele. *La ragione dei Buffoni.* Rome, 1977.

Nettl, Paul. "Mozart and the Czechs." *Musical Quarterly* 27 (1941): 329–42.

Nicolai, Friedrich. *Beschreibung einer Reise durch Deutschland und die Schweiz,* 4 vols. Berlin, 1784.

Novello, Vincent and Mary. *A Mozart Pilgrimage: The Travel Diaries of Vincent and Mary Novello in the Year 1829,* ed. Nerina Medici and Rosemary Hughes. London, 1955.

Noverre, J. G. *Letters on Dancing and Ballets,* transl. Cyril Beaumont. London, 1930; reprint New York, 1966.

Olleson, Edward "Haydn in the Diaries of Count Karl von Zinzendorf." *Haydn Yearbook* 2 (1963–64): 45–63.

Panagle, Carl F. "Bilddokumente zu Vivaldis Tod in Wien." *Informazioni e Studi Vivaldiani* 6 (1985): 111–27.

Pauly, Reinhard. "The Reforms of Church Music under Joseph II." *Musical Quarterly* 43 (1957): 372–82.

Pezzl, Johann. *Skizze von Wien: Ein Kultur- und Sittenbild aus der josefinischen Zeit.* Graz, 1923.

Pfannhauser, Karl. "Zu Mozarts Kirchenwerken von 1768." *Mozart-Jahrbuch 1954,* pp. 150–68.

Picton, Howard. *The Life and Works of Joseph Anton Steffan (1726-1797), with Special Reference to His Keyboard Concertos.* Ph.D. diss., University of Hull, 1981. Outstanding Dissertations in Music from British Universities. New York, 1989.

Pincherle, Marc. *Histoire illustrée de la musique.* Paris, 1959.

Plath, Wolfgang. "Zur Datierung der Klaviersonaten KV 279–284." *Acta Mozartiana* 21 (1974): 26–30.

Pohl, Carl Ferdinand. *Denkschrift aus Anlass des hundertjährigen Bestehens der Tonkünstler-Societät.* Vienna, 1871.

———. *Joseph Haydn.* Leipzig, 1875–82.

Pollock, Carla. "Viennese Solo Keyboard Music, 1740–1770: A Study in the Evolution of the Classic Style." Ph.D. diss., Brandeis University, 1984.

Prodinger, Fredericke. "Die Geschichte der Kuenburg-Sammlung." In Fredericke Prodinger and Reinhard R. Heinisch, eds., *Gewand und Stand. Kostüm- und Trachtenbilder der Kuenburg-Sammlung,* pp. 19–22. Salzburg and Vienna, 1983.

Proschwitz, Gunnar and Mavis von. *Beaumarchais et le "Courier de l'Europe": Documents inédits ou peu connus.* Oxford, 1991.

Radant, E. (ed.). *The Diaries of Joseph Carl Rosenbaum, 1770–1829. Haydn Yearbook,* vol. 5. Vienna, 1968.

Radcliffe, Philip. "The Piano Sonatas of Joseph Haydn." *Music Review* 7 (1946): 139–53.

Reichardt, Johann Friedrich. *Briefe eines aufmerksamen Reisenden die Musik betreffend.* Frankfurt and Leipzig, 1774.

Reichart, Sarah Bennet. "The Influence of Eighteenth-Century Social Dance on the Viennese Classical Style." Ph.D. diss., City University of New York, 1984.

Reimer, Erich. "Nationalbewußtsein und Musikgeschichtsschreibung in Deutschland, 1800–1850." *Musikforschung* 46 (1993): 17–31.

Rex, Walter E. "A Propos of the Figure of Music in the Frontispiece of the *Encyclopédie.*" In *Report of the Twelfth Congress Berkeley, 1977,* ed. Daniel Heartz and Bonnie Wade, pp. 214–25. Kassel, 1981.

Rice, John A. "An Early Handel Revival in Florence." *Early Music* 18 (1990): 63–71.

———. "Anton Walter, Instrument Maker to Leopold II." *Journal of the American Musical Instrument Society* 15 (1989): 32–49.

———. "Emperor and Impresario: Leopold II and the Transformation of Viennese Musical Theater, 1790–1792." Ph.D. diss., University of California, Berkeley, 1987.

———. "Vienna under Joseph II and Leopold II." In *Man and Music: The Classical Era,* ed. Neal Zaslaw, pp. 126–65. London, 1989.

Richter, Joseph. *Bildergalerie katholischer Misbräuche.* Frankfurt and Leipzig [Vienna], 1784.

Riedel, Friedrich W. *Kirchenmusik am Hofe Karls VI (1711–1740).* Munich and Salzburg, 1977.

Ripin, Edwin M. "Haydn and the Keyboard Instruments of His Time." In *Haydn Studies,* ed. Jens Peter Larsen, Howard Serwer, and James Webster, pp. 302–8. New York, 1981.

Rosen, Charles. *The Classical Style: Haydn, Mozart, Beethoven.* New York, 1971.

———. *Sonata Forms.* New York, 1980.

Rothschild, Germaine de. *Luigi Boccherini: Sa vie, son oeuvre.* Paris, 1962.

Sadie, Stanley (ed.). *The New Grove Dictionary of Music and Musicians,* 20 vols. London, 1980.

———. *The New Grove Dictionary of Opera*, 4 vols. London, 1992.

Sanders, Samuel Vernon, Jr. "A Stylistic Analysis of Selected Viennese Masses, ca. 1740." M.A. thesis, University of California, Los Angeles, 1972.

Sandgruber, Roman. *Die Anfänge der Konsumgesellschaft*. Konsumgüterverbrauch, Lebenstandard, und Alltagskultur in Österreich im 18. und 19. Jahrhundert. Munich, 1982.

Sauerbrei, Patricia. "The Keyboard Concertos of Georg Christoph Wagenseil (1715–1777)." Ph.D. diss., University of Toronto, 1983.

Schaal, Richard. "Ein angeblich verschollener Brief von Leopold Mozart." *Acta Mozartiana* 26 (1979): 50–51.

Schenk, Johann Baptist. "Autobiography." In *Forgotten Musicians*, ed. and transl. Paul Nettl, pp. 267–68. New York, 1951.

Schering, Arnold. *Geschichte der Musik in Beispielen*. Leipzig, 1931.

Schieb, Wilfried. "Die Entwicklung der Musikberichterstattung im *Wienerischen Diarium* von 1703 bis 1780." Ph.D. diss., University of Vienna, 1985.

Schindler, Otto G. "Das Publikum des Burgtheaters in der josephinischen Ära." In Margret Dietrich, ed., *Das Burgtheater und sein Publikum*, pp. 11–95. Veröffentlichungen des Instituts für Publikumsforschung 3. Vienna, 1976.

Schletterer, Hans Michael. *Joh. Friedrich Reichardt: Sein Leben und seine musikalische Thätigkeit*. Ausburg, 1865.

Schmid, Manfred Hermann. *Mozart und die Salzburger Tradition*. Münchener Veröffentlichung zur Musikgeschichte 24. Tützing, 1976.

Schnerich, Alfred. *Joseph Haydn und seine Sendung*. Zurich, 1926.

Schnoebelen, Anne. *Padre Martini's Collection of Letters in the Civico Museo Bibliografico in Bologna*. New York, 1979.

Schoenbaum, Camillo. "Die böhmischen Musiker in der Musikgeschichte Wiens vom Barock zur Romantik." *Studien zur Musikwissenschaft* 25 (1962): 475–95.

Scholz-Michelitsch, Helga. *Georg Christoph Wagenseil, Hofkomponist und Hofklaviermeister der Kaiserin Maria Theresia*. Vienna, 1980.

Schubart, Christian Friedrich Daniel. *Ideen zur einer Ästhetik der Tonkunst*, ed. Ludwig Schubart. Vienna, 1806.

Schwarz, Ignaz. *Wiener Strassenbilder im Zeitalter des Rokoko*. Die Wiener Ansichten von Schütz, Ziegler, Janscha, 1779–1798. Vienna, 1914.

Sedmayr, Hans. *Johann Bernard Fischer von Erlach*. Vienna and Munich, 1956.

Senn, Walter. *Jakob Stainer, der Geigenmacher zu Absam*. Innsbruck, 1951.

Šetková, Dana. *Klavírní dílo Josefa Antonína Štěpána*. Prague, 1965.

Siegel, Johanna. "Johann Michael Haydn: Kompositionen für Salzburger Bühnen." *Mozart-Jahrbuch 1987/88*, pp. 85–89.

Simon, Edwin J. "Sonatas into Concertos: A Study of Mozart's First Seven Concertos." *Acta Musicologica* 31 (1959): 170–85.

Sisman, Elaine R. *Haydn and the Classical Variation*. Cambridge, Mass., 1993.

———. "Haydn's Theater Symphonies." *JAMS* 43 (1990): 292–352.

———. "Haydn's Variations." Ph.D. diss., Princeton University, 1978.

Smither, Howard E. *A History of the Oratorio*, vol. 3: *The Oratorio in the Classical Era*. Chapel Hill, N.C., 1987.

Somfai, László. "An Introduction to the Study of Haydn's String Quartet Autographs." In *The String Quartets of Haydn, Mozart, and Beethoven*, ed. Christoph Wolff, pp. 5–51. Cambridge, Mass., 1980.

———. *Joseph Haydn: His Life in Contemporary Pictures*. Budapest, 1969.

———. "Mozart's First Thoughts: The Two Versions of the Sonata in D, K. 284." *Early Music* 19 (1991): 601–13.

———. "Vom Barock zur Klassik: Umgestaltung der Proportionen und des Gleichgewichts in zyklischen Werken Joseph Haydns." In *Joseph Haydn und seine Zeit*, ed. Gerda Mraz, pp. 64–88. Jahrbuch für österreichische Kulturgeschichte 2. Eisenstadt, 1972.

Sonnenfels, Joseph von. *Briefe über die wienerische Schaubühne*. Vienna, 1768.

———. *Sonnenfels gesammelte Schriften*. Vienna, 1784.

Stadler, Maximilian. *Materialen zur Geschichte der Musik unter den österreichischen Regenten*, ed. Karl Wagner as *Abbé Maximilian Stadler*. Schriftenreihe der Internationalen Stiftung Mozarteum 6. Kassel, 1974.

Steblin, Rita. *A History of Key Characteristics in the Eighteenth and Early Nineteenth Centuries*. Ann Arbor, Mich., 1983.

Sternfeld, Frederick. "Expression and Revision in Gluck's *Orfeo* and *Alceste*." In *Essays Presented to Egon Wellesz*, ed. Sir Jack Westrup, pp. 114–29. Oxford, 1966.

Stevens, Jane. "An 18th-Century Description of Concerto First-Movement Form." *JAMS* 24 (1971): 85–95.

Stockman, Johann Christoph. *Critischer Entwurf einer auserlesenen Bibliothek für Liebhaber der Philosophie und schönen Wissenschaften. Zum Gebrauch akademischer Vorlesungen, vierte verbesserte und viel vermehrte Auflage*. Berlin, 1771.

Stradner, Gerhard. "Wiener Instrumentenbau zur Zeit Maria Theresias." In *Musik am Hof Maria Theresias*, ed. Roswitha Vera Karpf, pp. 168–78. Munich and Salzburg, 1984.

Strohm, Reinhard. *Die italienische Oper im 18. Jahrhundert*. Wilhelmshaven, 1979.

———. "Zur Metrik in Haydns und Anfossis 'La vera costanza.' " In *Proceedings of the International Joseph Haydn Congress 1982*, ed. Eva Badura-Skoda, pp. 279–95. Munich, 1986.

Strunk, Oliver W. "Haydn's Divertimenti for Baryton, Viola, and Bass (after Manuscripts in the Library of Congress)." *Musical Quarterly* 18 (1932): 216–51.

———. *Source Readings in Music History*. New York, 1950.

Sulzer, Johann Georg. *Allgemeine Theorie der schönen Künste*, 2 vols. Leipzig, 1771–74.

Thayer, Alexander Wheelock. *Life of Beethoven*, rev. and ed. Elliot Forbes as *Thayer's Life of Beethoven*. Princeton, N.J., 1964.

———. *Salieri: Rival of Mozart*, ed. Theodore Allbrecht. Kansas City, 1989.

Thomas, Günter. "Anmerkungen zum Libretto von Haydns Festa teatrale 'Acide.' " *Haydn-Studien* 5 (1982): 118–24.

Tovey, Donald Francis. "Haydn." In *Cobbett's Cyclopedic Survey of Chamber Music*, 2 vols. London, 1962–3.

Tschulik, Norbert. "Musikartikel aus dem *Wienerischen Diarium* von 1766." *Studien zur Musikwissenschaft* 30 (1979): 91–106.

Tyler, Linda L. "*Bastien und Bastienne* and the Viennese Volkskomödie." *Mozart-Jahrbuch 1991*, pp. 576–79.

———. "*Bastien und Bastienne:* The Libretto, Its Derivation, and Mozart's Text-Setting." *Journal of Musicology* 8 (1990): 520–52.

———. "*Zaide* in the Development of Mozart's Operatic Language." *Music and Letters* 72 (1991): 214–35.

Tyrrel, John. *Czech Opera.* Cambridge, 1988.

Tyson, Alan. "The Mozart Fragments." *JAMS* 34 (1981): 471–510.

———. *Mozart: Studies of the Autograph Scores.* Cambridge, Mass., 1987.

Unverricht, Hubert. "Das bekannte und zugleich unbekannte Werk des Carl Ditters von Dittersdorf." In *Carl Ditters von Dittersdorf, 1739–1799: Mozarts Rivale in der Oper,* ed. H. Unverricht and W. Bein, pp. 27–34. Würzburg, 1989.

———. *Geschichte des Streichtrios.* Tützing, 1969.

Verona, Gentili. "Le collezioni Foà e Giordano della Biblioteca Nazionale di Torino." *Vivaldiana* 1 (1969): 2–56.

Vetter, Walther. "Georg Christoph Wagenseil, ein Vorläufer Christoph Willibald Glucks." *Zeitschrift für Musikwissenschaft* 8 (1925–26): 385–402.

Vianello, Carlo Antonio. *Teatri, spettacoli, musiche a Milano nei secoli scorsi.* Milan, 1941.

Viardot-Garcia, Pauline. "Pauline Viardot-Garcia to Julius Rietz (Letters of Friendship)," transl. Theodore Baker. *Musical Quarterly* 2 (1916): 32–60.

Wachernagel, Bettina. *Joseph Haydns frühe Klaviersonaten.* Tützing, 1975.

Wagner, Hans. "Der Höhepunkt des französischen Kultureinflusses in Österreich in der zweiten Hälfte des 18. Jahrhunderts." *Österreich in Geschichte und Literatur* 5 (1961): 507–17.

———. *Salzburg und Österreich: Aufsätze und Vorträge von Hans Wagner.* Salzburg, 1982.

———. "Salzburgs Geschichte im Überblick." *Österreich in Geschichte und Literatur* 7 (1963): 204–16.

Walter, Horst. "On the History of the Composition and the Performance of *La vera costanza.*" In *Haydn Studies,* ed. Jens Peter Larsen, Howard Serwer, and James Webster, pp. 154–57. New York, 1981.

———. "Das Posthornsignal bei Haydn und anderen Komponisten des 18. Jahrhunderts." *Haydn-Studien* 4 (1976–80): 21–34.

———. "Das Tasteninstrument beim jungen Haydn." In *Der junge Haydn,* ed. Vera Schwarz, pp. 237–48. Graz, 1972.

Walterskirchen, Gerhard. "Zur Wiedererichtung der Musikemporen und Orgel in Salzburger Dom: Geschichte—Funktion—Rekonstruktion." *Mozartwoche* (1991), pp. 305–9.

Wangermann, Ernst. *The Austrian Achievement, 1700-1800.* London, 1973.

Weber, Carl Maria von. *Writings on Music,* transl. Martin Cooper, ed. John Warrack. Cambridge, 1981.

Webster, James. "The Chronology of Haydn's String Quartets." *Musical Quarterly* 61 (1975): 1746.

———. *Haydn's "Farewell" Symphony and the Idea of Classical Style: Through-Composition and Cyclic Integration in his Instrumental Music.* Cambridge, 1991.

————. "Remarks on Early Chamber Music." In *Haydn Studies*, ed. Jens Peter Larsen, Howard Serwer, and James Webster, pp. 365–67. New York, 1981.

————. "The Scoring of Haydn's Early String Quartets." In *Haydn Studies*, ed. Jens Peter Larsen, Howard Serwer, and James Webster, pp. 235–38. New York, 1981.

————. "The Scoring of Mozart's Chamber Music for Strings." In *Music in the Classic Period: Essays in Honor of Barry S. Brook*, ed. Allan A. Atlas, pp. 259–96. New York, 1985.

————. "Towards a History of Viennese Chamber Music in the Early Classical Period." *JAMS* 27 (1974): 212–47.

Weimer, Eric. *Opera Seria and the Evolution of Classical Style, 1755–1772*. Ann Arbor, Mich., 1984.

Weiskern, Friedrich. *Beschreibung der k. k. Haupt und Residenzstadt Wien*. Vienna, 1770.

Weiss, Piero. "Venetian Commedia dell'Arte 'Operas' in the Age of Vivaldi." *Musical Quarterly* 70 (1984): 195–217.

Weiss, Piero and Richard Taruskin. *Music in the Western World: A History of Music in Documents*. New York, 1984.

Wellesz, Egon. "Giuseppe Bonno (1710–1788): Sein Leben und seine dramatischen Werke." *SIMG* 11 (1909–10): 395–442.

Wheelock, Gretchen A. *Haydn's Ingenious Jesting with Art: Contexts of Musical Wit and Humor*. New York, 1992.

Winter, Marian Hannah. *The Pre-Romantic Ballet*. London, 1974.

Winter, Robert S. "The Bifocal Close and the Evolution of the Viennese Classical Style." *JAMS* 42 (1989): 275–337.

Winzenberger, Janet B. "The Symphonic Concertante: Mannheim and Paris." M.A. thesis, Eastman School of Music, University of Rochester, 1967.

Wyzewa, Théodore de and Georges de Saint-Foix. *Wolfgang Amadée Mozart: Sa vie musicale et son oeuvre. Essai de biographie*, 3rd ed., 5 vols. Bruges, 1958.

Young, David. "Karl von Ordonez (1734–1786): A Biographical Study." *Research Chronicle* 19 (1983–85): 31–56.

Zaslaw, Neal. "Mozart, Haydn, and the *Sinfonia da Chiesa*." *Journal of Musicology* 1 (1982): 95–124.

————. *Mozart's Symphonies: Context, Performance Practice, Reception*. Oxford, 1989.

Zechmeister, Gustav. *Die Wiener Theater nächst der Burg und nächst dem Kärntnerthor von 1747 bis 1776*. Theatergeschichte Österreichs III: 2. Vienna, 1971.

Zeman, Herbert. "Die österreichische Literatur im Aufbruch—1740 bis 1780." In *Maria Theresia und ihre Zeit*, ed. Walter Koschatzky, pp. 370–78. Salzburg and Vienna, 1979.

Zinzendorf, Charles de. "Journal du Comte Charles de Zinzendorf et Pottendorf." MS in Haus- Hof- und Staatsarchiv, Vienna.

Index

Compiled by Lee Brentlinger